W9-BKY-467

MINNESOTA

TA

TA

IOWA

A

AS

MISSOURI

Mississippi

River

AHOMA

ARKANSAS

LOUISIANA

ATLANTIC

OCEAN

GULF OF

MEXICO

0   150   300 Miles

0   150   300 Km.

Ethel K. Smith Library

Wingate University
Wingate, North Carolina 28174

Encyclopedia

OF THE

AMERICAN WEST

≈ Editorial Board ≈

Editor in Chief
Charles Phillips
ZENDA, INC.

Senior Editor
Alan Axelrod
TURNER PUBLISHING

Associate Editors

Gerald George

Peggy Pascoe
UNIVERSITY OF OREGON

B. Byron Price
NATIONAL COWBOY HALL OF FAME AND WESTERN HERITAGE CENTER

Martin Ridge
HUNTINGTON LIBRARY, ART COLLECTIONS, AND BOTANICAL GARDENS

Hal Rothman
UNIVERSITY OF NEVADA, LAS VEGAS AND
ENVIRONMENTAL HISTORY

Vicki L. Ruiz
ARIZONA STATE UNIVERSITY

Robert M. Utley

Assistant Editors

Patricia Hogan
ZENDA, INC.

Candace Floyd
ZENDA, INC.

Encyclopedia of THE AMERICAN WEST

Charles Phillips
Alan Axelrod

Editors

VOLUME 1

Macmillan Reference USA
Simon & Schuster Macmillan
New York

SIMON & SCHUSTER AND PRENTICE HALL INTERNATIONAL
London • Mexico City • New Delhi • Singapore • Sydney • Toronto

WINGATE UNIVERSITY LIBRARY

Copyright © 1996 by Simon & Schuster

Produced by ZENDA, INC., Nashville, Tennessee
   Design: Gore Studios, Inc.
   Proofreading and Index of Professions: John Reiman
   General Index: Alexa Selph

All rights reserved. No part of this book may be reproduced or transmitted in any form or by any means, electronic or mechanical, including photocopying, recording, or by any information storage and retrieval system, without permission in writing from the Publisher.

Simon & Schuster Macmillan
1633 Broadway, New York, NY 10019

PRINTED IN THE UNITED STATES OF AMERICA

printing number
  2 3 4 5 6 7 8 9 10

LIBRARY OF CONGRESS CATALOGING-IN-PUBLICATION DATA

Encyclopedia of the American West / Charles Phillips and Alan Axelrod, editors
      p   cm.
   Includes bibliographical references (p.   ) and index.
   ISBN 0-02-897495-6
   1. West (U.S.)—Encyclopedias.   I. Phillips, Charles, 1948–
   II. Axelrod, Alan, 1952–
   F591.E485   1996
   978—dc20   96-1685
                                                                      CIP

 Contents

Maps

~ Acknowledgments ~

All books, fiction to philosophy, are—regardless of intention—joint ventures, but encyclopedias are so by design, which means there are even more people to thank for their help and absolve of all blame in the conception, writing, editing, designing, and production of the current work than is usual for authors. First, the *Encyclopedia of the American West* could hardly have come into existence without the vision of Phil Friedman, a publisher of keen taste and good horse sense; the *Encyclopedia* could hardly have been completed without the knowledge, experience, and sheer will of Elly Dickason, whose talents, advice, and direction we more than appreciate—we thank God for Paul Bernabeo, too, who showed a great deal of vision, knowledge, and, importantly for us, patience and equanimity in bringing to fruition nearly five years of our lives. Through thick and thin, these professionals—and their able assistant, Debra Alpern—stuck with us, earning our gratitude and affection.

At Zenda, Inc., the heart and soul of the *Encyclopedia* belong to Patricia Hogan and Candace Floyd. Unlike the folks at Macmillan, they already knew us going into the project, and, even so, they took up the challenge. First among equals has to be Patricia Hogan, who not only oversaw Zenda's text and photograph researchers and a bevy of copyeditors, proofreaders, and indexers, not only worked with some four hundred authors on the substance and style of their writing, not only coordinated the design and production of the completed manuscript—which came to her much too late—but also researched and wrote a substantial number of the entries herself. She and Candace Floyd put in the kind of time few could be expected to devote to any project, and they did so with an affability remarkable under the circumstances. We can only hope pride in the accomplishment compensates in ways other payments cannot. They, too, had able assistants in Candis Hopper and Barbara Harper, and we wish both to know we appreciate the work they did on the project as well. Because Zenda is the sort of firm it is, we—unlike many authors and editors—meet and work with those in the production end of the business, and we know just how much we owe to them. Bruce Gore's design, typically inspired, could not have been more elegant and functional. Jackie Hoskins and Connie Hannah at PrePress worked the design for all it was worth, and we thank them for going the extra distance.

One of the greatest pleasures, and there were many, in putting together the *Encyclopedia* was coming to know the distinguished members of our editorial board. We have mentioned their initial contribution in the Preface, but afterward there remained four more years of work, of reading and responding, of intellectual hand holding and sage advice. Simply working with Peggy Pascoe, Hal Rothman, Martin Ridge, Vicki Ruiz, and Robert Utley was, in many ways, reward enough for the effort the *Encyclopedia* required. Gerald George and Byron Price, with whom we have worked many times in the past, once again proved themselves people you want in the lifeboat with you. Having produced a series of fifty-one books, Jerry had especially useful guidance on how to keep matters in perspective, advice at least one of us much needed to hear. We would also like especially to thank Peggy Pascoe for the time she devoted to a number of authors, two of whom at Zenda, too old to be her students, envy those who are.

Another of the great pleasures of producing the *Encyclopedia of the American West* was the written work generated by scores of authors. Much of what they wrote was a delight to read, and many of them helped make our joint venture enjoyable, indeed. Among them were Henry Fritz, Herbert Hoover, Turrentine Jackson, Elizabeth Jameson, Byron Johnson, Bill O'Neal, James Ronda, Jan Shipps, David Wrobel, and others literally too numerous to mention. A special thanks goes to Patrick Butler for going out of his way (some fourteen hundred miles out of his way, in fact) to help improve the graphic appeal of the *Encyclopedia*. To two of our authors, Bruce Kamerling and Dan Thrapp, we dedicate the *Encyclopedia of the American West*. Those at Zenda who had met Bruce Kamerling described him as a beautiful soul long before he passed away. In the early days of the project, when we were just beginning to feel our way, Dan Thrapp—no stranger to encyclopedic work—took the time to speed the editor-in-chief on what has proven to be a wondrous and rewarding journey.

—*Charles Phillips and Alan Axelrod*

≈ Preface ≈

From at least the time of the French and Indian War, the American West has haunted the imagination of European immigrants to the North American continent. They dreamed of freedom, of cheap land and quick fortunes, of escape and renewal. They moved relentlessly, generation after generation, from the foothills of the Appalachians to the shores of the Pacific, transforming, for better or worse, everything they touched and, in turn, being transformed. The story of this centuries-long migration has frequently been told, often as a series of colorful, violent, and romantic adventures ending in nostalgic, retrospective musings on the disappearance of the old frontier that the settlers had pushed inexorably westward. But this "frontier" was from the start mostly an intellectual construct—an imaginary line on a map beyond which the topography was vague and enticing—turned into a metaphor for organizing Western history.

Since the day a University of Wisconsin historian named Frederick Jackson Turner advanced his "frontier thesis" to a group of academics at the 1893 World's Columbian Exposition in Chicago, writing about the West has itself been a rich vein for exploration by American scholars. Long before Turner, of course, a legion of romanticists—Western publicists, dime novelists, newspapermen, and politicians—had prospected in Western history the way Forty-niners had scratched in the placer fields of California, looking for nuggets, for tales of desperation and derring-do. But with Turner, the "culture industry" had arrived in the West and discovered the motherlode. By mining its history, scholars believed they were striking at the core of the American character, formed on the frontier.

Turner became the most recognized American historian of his generation. His influential thesis came from his reading of the 1890 U.S. Census, which concluded that a "frontier line" could no longer be defined demographically, so at least in this sense the frontier was more than a mere figment of his imagination. And as a metaphor for the migration of Euro-Americans across the North American subcontinent, the frontier proved a very powerful concept indeed, one that dominated

Western history and historiography—and particularly American history textbooks—for half a century or more. True, there were regionalists who insisted on seeing the West as a geographical region first—as a semiarid land with the heart of a desert, to paraphrase Walter Prescott Webb. And here and there, a historian interested in Native Americans might point out that the Indians tended to consider the migration not as an "opening" of "virgin wilderness" but as an occupation of the lands they owned. For the most part, however, the major Western historians paid allegiance to Turner, and the frontier served as the ideological and intellectual underpinning of their work.

By the middle of the twentieth century, however, Turner's thesis was increasingly coming under attack by a number of historians, some of whom saw the frontier as the foundation for an essentially racist ideology that celebrated base greed as a religious calling and social violence as moral regeneration. By the 1960s, a movement had developed that became known as the new Western history. Concentrating on the social aspects of Western history rather than on colorful biographies of great characters or celebratory narratives of national expansion, the new Western historians pointed out that there were many groups of people living in the West (some long before the arrival of Americans of European descent) who did not experience the history of their region as a series of successive frontiers and who did not, in fact, share the American dream spawned by those frontiers, but whose stories and whose contributions were worth recording. The new Western historians also tended to define the West strictly as a region, though one shaped by various cultures and their histories as well as by geography, and a region characterized as much by rapid urbanization as by wide-open spaces. They included in their works the story of groups—Native Americans, Mexican Americans, African Americans, Asian Americans, women—traditionally ignored in the westward sweep of frontier history. They argued that it was more proper to describe such westward movement not as an "expansion" into a "wilderness" but as an "invasion" of other peoples' homelands. And they tended to explore certain of the less flattering constants in the history of the West: the Euro-Americans' belief in their own absolute innocence, the Westerners' treatment of the profit motive as an almost natural passion, the dominant Western social groups' propensity to turn suddenly to violence as an answer to social challenges, Western culture's addiction to racial stereotyping, and the typical Western settler's brutal handling of the environment.

As a result, the West became an ideological battleground and Western history a "hot topic" for the culture industry. And the struggle was more than academic. For the West continued to engage the American imagination, continued to provide the image Americans saw when they looked into their mirrors of cultural myths, traditions, and legacies. We have in mind not just the John Wayne vocabulary Anglo-Americans still use to think of themselves, or at least of their heroes: strong and silent, essentially pure of motive and intolerant of cant, slow to anger but decisive in battle. Anyone who has ever worked with Native Americans will know just how real, how visceral, the (mostly negative) history of the West is to them. And one only has to remember the media images of Japanese Americans recalling their lives in the internment camps of World War II to realize the immediacy of some Western legacies. If nothing else, the perennial life of the popular movie Western testifies to the fascination the American West holds for us. Ever since Edwin S. Porter created *The Great Train Robbery,* a 1903 "flicker" based on the chases and gunfights of the turn-of-the century "Wild West" shows, and turned a vaudeville curiosity into a new popular art form, the Hollywood western has been a Rosetta stone of the American psyche. And just when the pundits had declared the genre dead and the idea of the Old West culturally irrelevant, we are treated to a series of "politically correct" westerns that prove the genre's flexibility for creating narratives that reflect contemporary problems. The "culture wars" of the late twentieth century between the champions of the so-called multicultural history and those of "identity" history had their first clear expression in academe at Western History Association meetings when the traditionalists and the new Western historians took up the tomahawk. And when these culture wars spilled over ivy-covered walls into the arena of public institutions in the spring of 1991, it was an exhibit at the Smithsonian Institution called "The West as America: Reinterpreting Images of the Frontier, 1820–1920" that drew blood. The point is that the interpretation of the American West, more than that of the other regions of the country, still matters—because it still means something—to us.

Of course, an encyclopedia is no place to fight a cultural war. Quite to the contrary, the traditional purpose of an encyclopedia—making knowledge more readily and objectively available to a wider audience—removes it from the arena of the closely argued monograph based on original research in primary sources. On the other hand, one of the more pleasant results of the impact of the new Western history was the explosion of creative new works and the immense growth in the sheer amount of information about the West available to scholars. New books and articles not only expanded scholarly knowledge about the West, not only changed the way in which many viewed the entire history of the West, but were also so well written that they both proved a joy to read and attracted reviews from the general as well as the academic press.

We wanted to capture something of the excitement of the contemporary study of the American West by creating a reference work addressed to a wide range of interested audiences—high-school, college, and graduate-school students; scholars and teachers of Western history; and a broad general readership. To help us do so we assembled a distinguished editorial board whose members could ensure not only that the *Encyclopedia of the American West* would adequately cover the full range of the Western experience but also could achieve a synthesis of scholarly viewpoints that addressed the interests, concerns, and needs of a variety of curricula and bring to them the fresh insights and methods of social history in a language accessible to the high-school student and the general reader.

Certainly the range of viewpoints was evident as our editorial board met for the first time in January 1992 and began to discuss the *Encyclopedia.* Peggy Pascoe made it clear that the *Encyclopedia* would not ignore women, social history, or the recent work done on the American West in the twentieth century. Vicki Ruiz urged that any talk of frontiers had to include all of them, those that moved north and south and west to east, as well as those that moved westward, and that the ethnic richness of American's Western heritage be fully represented. B. Byron Price outlined for us how the material culture of the West was often an area of assimilation for the otherwise disparate peoples of the region, whose lives were formed by their ethnic traditions and community histories, but whose work brought them together doing the same tasks. He also made certain that we did not slight the popular culture of the American West. Martin Ridge insisted that in our concern with social history, the multiethnic nature of the Western population, material culture, and popular culture, we not forget the individuals in Western history. Robert Utley kept us honest by constantly showing us how to balance the traditional with the new and the specific details with the overall picture. And, finally, Gerald George made sure we stayed on track, carefully developing our definition of the topic and setting the goals of the projected work. Later, Hal Rothman kept us up to date on environmental issues central to Western history.

Somewhat to our surprise, within hours of opening our initial discussion the group began to reach a general and genuine consensus on the nature and the scope of the *Encyclopedia*. We would be asking experts—as it turned out, hundreds of them—to sift through the mass of published and, in some cases, unpublished materials available on the West and present to the reader an integrated account of what is generally known and accepted about a given subject. For some readers the *Encyclopedia* would be a stopping point; for others, a doorway to additional reading and study. Either use required not only an authoritative and comprehensive reference work, but one that synthesized the current theories and viewpoints. The only way to achieve such a synthesis was for the editorial board to agree on what the American West represented. Another factor leading our board members to consensus, whether they favored the new Western history or a more traditional approach, was the shared conviction that the American West still mattered.

The *Encyclopedia of the American West* thus covers many of the concerns of traditional Western history within the broader framework of social history. For that purpose, we define the American West as a geographically contained historical space—the area west of the Mississippi and including Alaska, Hawaii, and "spill over" areas in Canada and Mexico—that gave birth to something recognizable as a Western experience. The *Encyclopedia* focuses on the people and peoples of the West, approaching the region as a collection of multiethnic frontiers and as the spawning ground for an array of industries and enterprises that each gave rise to its own culture and carried with it important ecological consequences. The *Encyclopedia* concentrates on the trans-Mississippi West from the early Spanish period through the early twentieth century. However, these geographical and chronological boundaries are crossed freely as adequate coverage of any given topic may demand.

The reader will not, for example, find entries on the nuclear energy or aerospace industries even though both were of tremendous economic importance to the West in the latter half of the twentieth century. They were not, however, unique in that respect to either this region or to the Western experience, and they both clearly developed outside our chronological focus. One will find mention of them elsewhere, for example in the entries on the federal government in the West and on individual Western states and cities, since in the former instance, these industries are part of the story of the West's massive dependence on the United States government throughout its history, and in the latter, they are central to the understanding of the development of the specific state or city. By the same token, the reader will find an entry on the Navajo Stock-Reduction Program, although—because it did not originate until the early 1930s—one might argue it falls outside our temporal focus. A part of the Indian New Deal, the stock-reduction program was directly related to the government's Indian policies and was both unique to the region and necessary to the understanding of the Native Americans' Western experience. Similarly, there are articles on the native peoples of each region of the trans-Mississippi West, including Alaska and Hawaii, who trace their history from the pre-Columbian era to the present day.

The editorial board made a great effort to include a wide range of historical figures who actually inhabited the American West and not just the great politicians, rich businessmen, violent desperadoes, and women of ill repute or aesthetic achievement most frequently covered in Western biography. Thus, the reader will find a comprehensive range of biographies, from the familiar to the obscure, from the legendary Daniel Boone to Ah Quin, a Chinese immigrant who moved to nineteenth-century San Diego and became not merely a prominent local businessman but one of the richest men in California, who as yet has been the subject of no major biography. Except for certain political and cultural figures essential to the history of certain cities and states, the people appearing in the *Encyclopedia*, including historians, are not contemporaries.

The Encyclopedia of the American West also covers extensively the history of twenty-three states, in fact, all the states west of the Mississippi, including Alaska and Hawaii, and excepting Louisiana, which our editors deemed more associated with the history of the American South than with that of the West (although an entry on the Louisiana Purchase is included). Quite aware that such articles would be likely to draw a student into the *Encyclopedia*, we have consciously made an effort to use those histories as windows to further, broader reading within the work.

Few of the historical events, people, and politics east of the Mississippi appearing in traditional histories or textbooks on the American West appear in this *Encyclopedia*. Only when they had a direct bearing on either the understanding or the historical development of our geographically defined historical space did we include them. Therefore, the reader will find the War of 1812, which was fought, in part, to secure the trans-Mississippi West, but not the French and Indian War, whose outcome determined another geographical area—the trans-Appalachian lands—as the American West of its day. Both

Thomas Jefferson and Andrew Jackson are included, because one conceived the policy of removing Indians from their eastern homelands into the recently purchased Louisiana Territory and the other implemented the policy. Neither Georgia nor Alabama, the lands these Indians left behind when they were "removed" to the trans-Mississippi region, are included, since such state histories would be largely irrelevant to the subject.

Readers accustomed to reading histories or textbooks about the American West organized around the steadily advancing American "frontier" may at first be disconcerted by the fact that this *Encyclopedia* does not treat as such the role of the Great Frontier in the establishment of a succession of American Wests. Instead, the frontier is covered in articles dealing with the historical interpretation of the West, such as the "Frontier: Frontier Thesis" and "Turner, Frederick Jackson," or is subsumed in the broader view of a national expansion in phases that is not especially flattering to the westering Americans. As anyone who deals professionally with the American West knows, the very term *frontier* itself is controversial, loaded with political, philosophical, and ideological implications that the general reader may not understand or care about. We advised our authors to use the word judiciously and precisely, if at all; we did recognize that the American meaning of the word—to be on the edge of something: the wilderness; civilization; discovery—is occasionally a useful shorthand. In an attempt to defuse some of its metaphysical significance, we never capitalize the term and sometimes employ *frontier* in its original European meaning to denote an unfortified stretch of land between two, usually armed, hostile entities—the U.S. Army and the Sioux, for example.

With a topic so complex, so rich in primary and secondary sources, so steeped in conflicting interpretations and viewpoints, and so inherently interesting to the general reader, the tools of the encyclopedist's trade are especially helpful. We have made liberal use of the "signpost" entry: by including the title of an umbrella topic, the editors point the reader to related articles throughout the work. For example, we do not include an overall article on the Indian Wars, since Indian conflicts developed sporadically and were experienced as more discrete events, especially by the Indians. Instead, we include "Indian Wars" as a signpost, followed by "See" and a list of the combat actions covered throughout the four volumes of the work: "Apache Wars; Black Hawk's War; Central Plains Indian Wars; Fetterman Massacre; Grattan Massacre; Hancock's Campaign; Little Bighorn, Battle of; Mountain Meadows Massacre; Navajo Wars; Pacific Northwest Indian Wars; Pueblo Revolt; Sand Creek Massacre; Sioux Wars; Texas Frontier Indian Wars; Wounded Knee Massacre; Yuma Revolt." Similarly, we make extensive use of the "blind" entry, which leads the reader to the alternate name for a subject. As an example, one might flip to "American Bison" to find not the article one expected but a blind entry for "American Bison," followed by "See" pointing to the actual entry title under which that article appears, "Buffaloes (American Bisons)." Where appropriate, "See also" listings at the end of articles guide readers to related entries, and within each article relevant cross references are indicated by SMALL CAPITOL LETTERS. Keeping in mind the fascination the American West holds for almost every American, we have provided up-to-date bibliographies for almost every entry. Finally, an index of biographical figures by profession and a thorough index of the entire work appears at the end of Volume 4.

In retrospect, the ease with which our editorial board came to a consensus on a broad definition of the American West seems less startling than it did at first. To begin with, many of the present-day Turnerians are not so much traditionalists as active and creative historians seeking a new synthesis that reinterprets the frontier—or even frontiers—using new methods and information, without throwing away entirely the insights that the notion still proffers and that have proved so powerful for so long. And the new Western historians were not so much tearing down Turner's magnificent edifice as they were trying to free themselves of the ideological incrustations adhering to the notion of the frontier in order to forge their own new synthesis.

Especially now that the culture wars have heated up in the public arena, pitting politicians against academics in a struggle over setting national standards for the teaching of the past, Western historians are longing for the synthesis everyone sees as desirable. Little surprise, then, that Patricia Nelson Limerick, once the *enfant terrible* of the new Western historians, now perhaps their doyenne, in speaking at the 1995 annual meeting of the American Association for State and Local History in Saratoga Springs, New York, called for a truce. Just as the Battle of Saratoga had once proved decisive for American history in the past, she said, let what she called the "Truce of Saratoga" now prove decisive for the history of the American West in the future. What better place to start than a new *Encyclopedia of the American West* that by its very nature needs to be such a synthesis?

Certainly the four hundred writers for this *Encyclopedia* represent a coming together of the practitioners of Western history. A list of contributors and their institutional affiliations and of the more than seventeen hundred entries appear at the beginning of Volume 1. The contributors run the gamut of current historical scholarship. All of them, however, were engaged in the collective enterprise of telling a coherent story about a fascinating subject in a style accessible to those on whose heritage they have expounded.

—*Charles Phillips and Alan Axelrod*

List of Contributors

Abbott, Carl; PORTLAND STATE UNIVERSITY
Bennett, Edward Herbert
Columbia River
Compulsory School Law, Oregon (1922)
Johnson, Edwin Carl ("Big Ed")
Portland, Oregon

Abernethy, F. E.; STEPHEN F. AUSTIN UNIVERSITY
Pecos Bill, Legend of

Ahern, Wilbert H.; UNIVERSITY OF MINNESOTA
Indian Rights Association

Aiken, Katherine G.; UNIVERSITY OF IDAHO
Hutton, May Arkwright

Alexander, Ruth M.; COLORADO STATE UNIVERSITY
Eastman, Elaine Goodale
Lindsey, Benjamin Barr

Alexander, Thomas G.; BRIGHAM YOUNG UNIVERSITY
Grant, Heber J.
Kearns, Thomas
Salt Lake City, Utah
United States v. *Reynolds*
Woodruff, Wilford
Y X Company

Allen, Howard W.; SOUTHERN ILLINOIS UNIVERSITY
Poindexter, Miles

Allen, James B.; BRIGHAM YOUNG UNIVERSITY
Cowdery, Oliver

Allen, John Logan; UNIVERSITY OF CONNECTICUT
Art: Surveys and Expeditions
Cartography

Allen, Michael; UNIVERSITY OF WASHINGTON
Rivermen

Alston, Richard M.; WEBER STATE UNIVERSITY
Forestry
United States Forest Service

Anderson, Douglas Firth; NORTHWESTERN COLLEGE
Christian Socialism
Evangelists
King, Thomas Starr
Protestants

Applegate, Shannon
Lane, Joseph

Argersinger, Peter H.; UNIVERSITY OF MARYLAND,
    BALTIMORE COUNTY
Bland-Allison Act of 1878
Populism
Simpson, Jerry

Arrington, Leonard J.
Danites
Pratt, Orson
Rich, Charles Coulson

August, Jack L., Jr.; UNIVERSITY OF HOUSTON
Hayden, Carl T.

Austin, Judith; IDAHO STATE HISTORICAL SOCIETY
Boone, William Judson
Borah, William E.
California Overland Trails
Fort Hall
Hawley, James Henry
Oregon Trail

Axelrod, Alan; TURNER PUBLISHING
American River
Anderson, "Bronco Billy"
Armadillos
Amour, Philip Danforth

Bailey, Margaret Jewett
Barboncito (Navajo)
Bryant, Sturgis and Company
Buchanan, James
Burlington Northern Railroad
Burnham, Daniel Hudson
Calhoun, John Caldwell
Campbell, Robert
Cattle Breeds and Breeding
Central Pacific Railroad
Cherokee Nation v. *State of Georgia*
Chicago and Northwestern Railroad
Chicago, Milwaukee, St. Paul and Pacific Railroad
Chief Joseph (Nez Percé)
Cíbola, Seven Cities of
Civil War
Clark, Charles ("Badger"), Jr.
Compromise of 1850
Cooper, Sarah Brown Ingersoll
Corn Woman
Cushing, Frank Hamilton
Death Valley
Ferber, Edna
Flynn, Elizabeth Gurley
Ghost Towns
Gibbon, John Oliver
Great American Desert
Great Diamond Hoax
Hall, James
Hancock's Campaign
Harte, Bret
Hetch Hetchy Controversy
Hill, James J.
Hill, Thomas
Hoof-and-Mouth Disease
Hopkins, Mark
Hough, Emerson
Humboldt River and the Great Basin Streams
Humor
Huntington, Collis P.
Jackson, Andrew
Jails and Prisons
Jewish Americans
Judah, Theodore Dehone
Kamiakin (Yakima)
Kearny, Philip
Kino, Eusebio Francisco
Lawyer (Nez Percé)
Little Crow (Sioux)
Looking Glass (Nez Percé)
Manuelito (Navajo)
Marsh, George Perkins
Maybeck, Bernard Ralph
Miller, Alfred Jacob

Miller, Joaquin (Heine [Hiner], Cincinnatus)
Mining: Mining Camps and Towns
Missions: Early Franciscan and Jesuit Missions
Missions: Nineteenth-Century Missions to the
    Indians
Morrill Act of 1862
Natawista (Blood)
Native American Peoples: Peoples Removed from
    the East
Native American Peoples: Pre-Columbian Peoples
Ollokot (Nez Percé)
Olmsted, Frederick Law
Otis, Harrison Gray
Overland Travel
Owens-Adair, Bethenia Angelina
Pacific Northwest Indian Wars
Paul Bunyon, Legend of
Perkins, Charles Elliott
Perouse, Jean de la
Pike's Peak Express Company
Pinchot, Gifford
Plenty Coups (Crow)
Polk, James K.
Powell, John Wesley
Promontory Summit
Provost, Etienne
Pullman, George Mortimer
Railroads
Ripley, Edward Payson
River Transportation
Ruxton, George Frederick
Sand Creek Massacre
Santa Fe and Chihuahua Trail
Scalping
Sequoyah (Mixed Cherokee)
Severance, Caroline Maria Seymour
Sheridan, Philip H.
Sierra Club
Sinclair, Upton
Sod Houses
Southern Pacific Railroad
Stanford, Jane Eliza Lathrop
Stegner, Wallace
Steele, Samuel Benfield
Ten Bears (Comanche)
Territorial Government
Texas and Pacific Railroad
Toohoolhoolzote (Nez Percé)
Tosawi (Comanche)
Trail of Tears
Transcontinental Railroad Surveys
Twain, Mark (Clemens, Samuel Langhorn)
Union Pacific Railroad
United States Indian Policy: Indian Treaties

United States Mail Steamship Company
Utah Expedition
Victor, Frances Fuller
W-Bar Ranch
Webster, Daniel
Western Pacific Railroad
White Bird (Nez Percé)
White Horse (Kiowa)
Worcester v. *State of Georgia*
Wounded Knee Massacre
Wovoka (Paiute)
Yellowstone National Park
Yosemite Act of 1864
Yosemite National Park

Baker, T. Harri; UNIVERSITY OF ARKANSAS AT LITTLE ROCK
Rockefeller, Winthrop

Baker, T. Lindsay; BAYLOR UNIVERSITY
Windmills

Bakken, Gordon Morris; CALIFORNIA STATE UNIVERSITY, FULLERTON
Territorial Law and Courts
Legal System

Balderrama, Francisco E.; CALIFORNIA STATE UNIVERSITY, LOS ANGELES
Mexican Immigration, 1900–1935

Bandurraga, Peter L.; NEVADA HISTORICAL SOCIETY
Mackay, John W.

Barth, Gunther; UNIVERSITY OF CALIFORNIA, BERKELEY
Chinese Wars

Barr, Alwyn; TEXAS TECH UNIVERSITY
National Expansion: Texas and National Expansion

Bartlett, Richard A.; FLORIDA STATE UNIVERSITY (EMERITUS)
Abert, John James
Albright, Horace Marden
Bandelier, Adolph Francis Alphonse
Cabeza de Vaca, Álvar Núñez
Cabrillo, Juan Rodríguez
Corps of Topographical Engineers
Emory, William Hemsley
Hayden, Ferdinand Vandeveer
King, Clarence
United States Geological Survey

Batman, Richard; SAN FRANCISCO STATE UNIVERSITY
Pattie, Sylvester and James

Beecher, Maureen Ursenbach; BRIGHAM YOUNG UNIVERSITY
Relief Society (LDS)
Snow, Eliza Roxcy

Benson, Maxine
Byers, William Newton
Maxwell, Martha Ann Dartt

Berson, Misha; SEATTLE TIMES
Theater: Historical Overview

Bingham, Edwin R.; UNIVERSITY OF OREGON
Bush, Asahel
Oregon Boundary Dispute
Reed, Simeon Gannett

Bitton, Davis; UNIVERSITY OF UTAH
Stereotypes: Stereotypes of Mormons

Blades, John; HENRY FLAGLER MUSEUM
Hearst San Simeon State Historical Monument

Blair, Karen J.; CENTRAL WASHINGTON UNIVERSITY
Women's Clubs and Organizations

Blodgett, Peter J.; THE HUNTINGTON LIBRARY, ART COLLECTIONS, AND BOTANICAL GARDENS
Edge, Rosalie Barrow
Grant Canyon and Grand Canyon National Park
Huntington Library, Art Collections, and Botanical Gardens
Johnson, Robert Underwood
Kent, William
Mather, Stephen Tyng

Bloom, John Porter; HISTORIANS' HAVEN
Elkins, Stephen Benton
Kearny Code
Mexican Cession
St. Vrain, Ceran de Hault de Lassus
Santa Fe Ring

Boessenecker, John; BOESSENECKER & BOESSENECKER, LAW OFFICES
Doolin, William (Bill)
Law and Order
Lillie, Gordon W. ("Pawnee Bill")
Madsen, Christian (Chris)
Middleton, "Doc" (Riley, James M.)
Miller, James B. ("Deacon Jim")

Parker, Isaac Charles
Plummer, William Henry
Starr, Belle
Starr, Henry
Thomas, Henry Andrew ("Heck")
Tilghman, William Matthew, Jr.

Bogue, Allan G.; University of Wisconsin (emeritus)
Malin, James Claude

Borne, Lawrence R.; Northern Kentucky University
Dude Ranching

Bradford, James C.; Texas A&M University
Sloat, John Drake

Bret-Harte, John; Arizona Daily Star
Clum, John Philip

Breun, Ray; Jefferson National Expansion Historical Association
St. Louis, Missouri
St. Louis, Missouri, Fire

Bringhurst, Newell G.; College of the Sequoias
Bernhisel, John Milton
Brooks, Juanita Leavitt
Gates, Susa Amelia Young
Godbe, William S.
Handcart Companies
Jennings, William
Mountain Meadows Massacre
Mormons: Far West Settlement
Smith, Joseph, Jr.
Young, Brigham

Brodhead, Michael J.; National Archives, Central Plains Region
Caribou
Coues, Elliott
Fewkes, Jesse Walter

Brooks, James; University of California, Davis
Ludlow Massacre
Slavery and Indenture in the Spanish Southwest

Brown, Kenny L.; University of Central Oklahoma
Oklahoma

Bunch, Lonnie G., III; National Museum of American History, Smithsonian Institution
African Americans

Burns, Jeffrey M.; Chancery Archives, Archdiocese of San Francisco
Alemany, Joseph Sadoc

Burrows, Jack; San Jose College
Cassidy, Butch (Parker, Robert LeRoy)
Earp Brothers
O. K. Corral, Gunfight at
Ringo, John Peters

Butler, Anne M.; University of Utah
Prostitution

Butler, Patrick H., III; Raven Group
Adams, Charles Francis, Jr.
Alamo
Art: Folk (Ethnic) Art
Banks, Nathaniel Prentiss
Black Legend
Campbellites (Disciples of Christ)
Civil War
Curtis, Samuel Ryan
Dodge, Grenville Mellen
Doheny, Edward Laurence
Donnelly, Ignatius
Durant, Thomas Clark
Dust Bowl
Emigrant Guidebooks
Fannin, James Walker, Jr.
Gadsden Purchase
Galveston, Texas
Garner, John Nance
Greenback Party
Hell on Wheels
Interstate Commerce Act of 1887
Joliet, Louis
Johnson, Lyndon B.
Kansas-Nebraska Act
Kenedy, Mifflin
King, Richard
King Ranch
Know-Nothing Party
Lamar, Mirabeau B.
Marquette, Jacques
Meeker, Nathan Cook
Montoya, Joseph
National Expansion: Slavery and National Expansion
Northwest Passage
Oñate, Juan de
Parker, Cynthia Ann
Pioneer Life: Euro-American Pioneer Life
Pioneer Life: Spanish and Mexican Pioneer Life
Pueblo Revolt

Quanah Parker (Comanche)
Rhodes, Eugene Manlove
Satanta (Kiowa)
Scott, Winfield
Sherman Anti-Trust Act
Sherman Silver Purchase Act of 1890
Spanish Settlement
Steffens, Joseph Lincoln
Teapot Dome
Telegraph
Terry, Alfred Howe
Texas
Trade Catalogs
United States Army: Arms and Equipment
Waggoner, Daniel
War of 1812

Byrkit, James; NORTHERN ARIZONA UNIVERSITY
Lummis, Charles Fletcher

Caffey, David L.; CLOVIS COMMUNITY COLLEGE
Luhan, Mabel Dodge
Taos, New Mexico

Calhoun, Frederick S.; UNITED STATES MARSHALS SERVICE,
DEPARTMENT OF JUSTICE
Federal Marshals and Deputies

Calvert, Robert A.; TEXAS A&M UNIVERSITY
Burnet, David Gouverneur

Campbell, Gregory R.; UNIVERSITY OF MONTANA
Little Wolf (Northern Cheyenne)
Morning Star (Cheyenne)

Campbell, Kenneth E., Jr.; LOS ANGELES COUNTY
MUSEUM OF NATURAL HISTORY
La Brea Tar Pits

Carlson, Paul H.; TEXAS TECH UNIVERSITY
Sheep and Sheep Ranching

Carter, John E.; NEBRASKA STATE HISTORICAL SOCIETY
Butcher, Solomon D.

Chan, Sucheng; UNIVERSITY OF CALIFORNIA,
SANTA BARBARA
Lee, Mary Paik

Chávez, Thomas E.; MUSEUM OF NEW MEXICO
Alvarez, Manuel
Martinez, Antonio José
Museum of New Mexico
Old Spanish Trail

Palace of the Governors (New Mexico Museum)
Santa Fe, New Mexico

Cherny, Robert W.; SAN FRANCISCO STATE UNIVERSITY
Bryan, William Jennings
"Cross of Gold" Speech
Currency and Silver as Western Political Issues
Phelan, James Duval
Rolph, James
Ruef, Abraham (Abe)
San Francisco: Historical Overview
San Francisco: City of Immigrants

Clow, Richmond L.; UNIVERSITY OF MONTANA
Harney, William Selby
Man-Afraid-of-His-Horse (Sioux)
Sully, Alfred
Young-Man-Afraid-of-His-Horse (Sioux)

Coburn, Carol K.; AVILA COLLEGE
Corrigan, Sister Monica

Conard, Rebecca; WICHITA STATE UNIVERSITY
Carey Act of 1894
Lacey, John Fletcher
Lacey Act of 1900

Cooper, Sarah; SOUTHERN CALIFORNIA LIBRARY FOR
SOCIAL STUDIES AND RESEARCH
Bass, Charlotta Spears

Corbett, William P.; NORTHEASTERN STATE UNIVERSITY
Oklahoma Land Rush

Cortés, Carlos E.; UNIVERSITY OF CALIFORNIA, RIVERSIDE
(EMERITUS)
Film: Minority Images in Westerns

Costello, Maurice Law; SAN JOSE CITY COLLEGE
(EMERITUS)
Anderson, William C. ("Bloody Bill")
Guerrillas
Quantrill, William Clarke

Cox, Thomas R.; SAN DIEGO STATE UNIVERSITY
Lumber Industry: Historical Overview
Lumber Industry: Logging Tools and Machinery

Cracroft, Richard H.; BRIGHAM YOUNG UNIVERSITY
Irving, Washington
May, Karl Friedrich

Crum, Annette Reed; UNIVERSITY OF CALIFORNIA, BERKELEY
Indian Shaker Church
Stereotypes: Stereotypes of Native Americans

Crum, Steven J.; UNIVERSITY OF CALIFORNIA, DAVIS
Ghost Dance

Crutchfield, James A.
Beckwourth, James Pierson (Jim)
Bowie, James
Buffalo Soldiers
Columbia Fur Company
Cradlebaugh, John
Crockett, David (Davey)
Studebaker, John Mohler

Cummins, D. Duane; BETHANY COLLEGE
Leigh, William Robinson

Cummins, Light Townsend; AUSTIN COLLEGE
Ferris, Warren Angus
Houston, Sam

Cunningham, Noble E., Jr.; UNIVERSITY OF MISSOURI— COLUMBIA
Jefferson, Thomas

Curry, Catherine Ann; CHANCERY ARCHIVES, ARCHDIOCESE OF SAN FRANCISCO
Parochial Schools

Danbom, David B.; NORTH DAKOTA STATE UNIVERSITY
Colman, Norman J.
North Dakota
Wilson, James

Dary, David; UNIVERSITY OF OKLAHOMA
Carroll, Matthew
Cattle Trails and Trail Driving
Clay, John Henry
Cook, James Henry
Iliff, John Wesley
Nation, Carry Amelia Moore
Trade Routes

Davis, Melissa A.; AUSTIN PEAY STATE UNIVERSITY
Bureau of Indian Affairs
Indian Schools: Indian Schools on the Reservation
Native American Church
Native American Cultures: Demography
Native American Cultures: Disease
Native American Cultures: Spiritual Life
Native American Cultures: Subsistence Patterns

Native American Peoples: Peoples of the Pacific Northwest
Native American Peoples: Peoples of the Southwest
Native American Pottery, Southwestern
Native American Silverwork, Southwestern

Davis, Ronald L.; SOUTHERN METHODIST UNIVERSITY
Opera

de Graaf, Lawrence B.; CALIFORNIA STATE UNIVERSITY, FULLERTON
Immigration Law: Immigration Law before 1900

De León, Arnoldo; ANGELO STATE UNIVERSITY
Rodriguez, Chepita
Rodriguez, In Re
Tejanos

Despain, S. Matthew; BRIGHAM YOUNG UNIVERSITY
Fitzpatrick, Thomas
Hunt, Wilson Price

Dillon, Richard H.; FROMM INSTITUTE, UNIVERSITY OF SAN FRANCISCO
Brannan, Samuel
Canby, Edward Richard Spring
Captain Jack (Modoc)
Farming: Farming in the Imperial Valley and Salton Sea Region
Vallejo, Mariano Guadalupe

Dinges, Bruce J.; ARIZONA HISTORICAL SOCIETY
Big Tree (Kiowa)
Grierson, Benjamin Henry
Howard, Oliver Otis
Kicking Bird (Kiowa)
Lone Wolf (Kiowa)
Navajo Wars

Dippie, Brian W.; UNIVERSITY OF VICTORIA
Art: Western Art
Catlin, George

Dodds, Gordon B.; PORTLAND STATE UNIVERSITY
Adams, William Lysander
Applegate, Jesse
French, Peter
Oregon

Dougan, Michael B.; ARKANSAS STATE UNIVERSITY
Garland, Augustus Hill
Pike, Albert
Robinson, Joseph Taylor

Ducker, James H.; ALASKA HISTORICAL SOCIETY
Atchison, Topeka and Santa Fe Railroad

Dunlay, Thomas William; UNIVERSITY OF NEBRASKA
Lewis and Clark Expedition

Dykstra, Robert R.; STATE UNIVERSITY OF NEW YORK AT
    ALBANY
Abilene, Kansas
Cattle Towns
Dodge City, Kansas

Eddy, Lucinda; SAN DIEGO HISTORICAL SOCIETY
San Diego, California

Edmunds, R. David; INDIANA UNIVERSITY
Montezuma, Carlos

Edwards, G. Thomas; WHITMAN COLLEGE
Fort Vancouver

Eifler, Mark A.; UNIVERSITY OF NEBRASKA AT KEARNEY
Miller, George
Nebraska
Rosewater, Edward

Eldredge, Scott; BRIGHAM YOUNG UNIVERSITY
Ashley, William Henry
Rendezvous

Ellsworth, S. George; UTAH STATE UNIVERSITY (EMERITUS)
Sutherland, George
Thomas, Elbert D.

Emmerich, Lisa E.; CALIFORNIA STATE UNIVERSITY, CHICO
Field Matrons

Emmons, David M.; UNIVERSITY OF MONTANA
Butte, Montana

Engstrand, Iris H. W.; UNIVERSITY OF SAN DIEGO
Anza, Juan Bautista de
Horton, Alonzo Erastus

Erickson, Jon T.
Kachina Carving

Erwin, Sarah; THOMAS GILCREASE INSTITUTE
Cole, Philip Gillette
Thomas Gilcrease Institute

Estrada, Alicia I. Rodriquez
Del Rio, Dolores
Velez, Lupe

Ethington, Philip J.; UNIVERSITY OF SOUTHERN CALIFORNIA
Buckley, Christopher Augustine
Sutro, Adolph

Etter, Patricia A.
Wilbur-Cruce, Eva Antonia

Evans, Gail E. H., IOWA STATE UNIVERSITY
Desert Land Act of 1877
Desert Land Act of 1891

Fabry, Judith
Wallace, Henry Agard
Wallace, Henry Cantwell

Fausold, Martin L.; STATE UNIVERSITY COLLEGE OF
    NEW YORK AT GENESEO
Hoover, Herbert

Fees, Paul; BUFFALO BILL HISTORICAL CENTER
Cody, William F. ("Buffalo Bill")
Wild West Shows: Historical Overview

Fell, James E., Jr.; UNIVERSITY OF COLORADO AT DENVER
Chaffee, Jerome Bonaparte
Douglas Family
Fall, Albert B.
Glass, Hugh
Lead Mining

Fellman, Anita Clair; OLD DOMINION UNIVERSITY
Wilder, Laura Ingalls

Fireman, Janet R., LOS ANGELES COUNTY MUSEUM OF
    NATURAL HISTORY
Hart, William S.
Pico, Pío de Jesus

Fite, Gilbert C.; UNIVERSITY OF GEORGIA (EMERITUS)
Agriculture
Bonanza Farming
Farming: Dryland Farming
Farming: Tools and Machinery
Hogs
Norbeck, Peter

Flanders, Robert; SOUTHWEST MISSOURI STATE UNIVERSITY
Church of Jesus Christ of Latter-Day Saints, Reorga-
    nized
Nauvoo, Illinois

Flores, Dan; UNIVERSITY OF MONTANA
Buffaloes (American Bisons)

Cactus
Horses
Mustang and Horse Trade

Floyd, Candace; ZENDA, INC.
Anaconda Mining Company
Armijo, Manuel
Benton, Thomas Hart
Blount, William
Bradley, Lewis
Bursom, Holm Olaf
Carleton, James H.
Clark, William Andrews
Cortez, Gregorio
Deady, Matthew Paul
Dern, George Henry
Diehl, Charles Sanford
Fair, James Graham
Field, Stephen J.
Glenn-Fowler Expedition
Great Chicago Fire
Gregg, Josiah
Hall, Frank
Harvey, Ford Ferguson
Heinze, Frederick Augustus
Hitchcock, Gilbert Monell
Hoover Dam
Johnson, Hiram Warren
Kearney, Denis
Kelley, Hall Jackson
Larkin, Thomas Oliver
Lee, Jason
Lost Dutchman's Mine
Mason Valley Ranch, Nevada
McCoy, Joseph G.
McKenzie, Alexander ("Big Alex")
McLoughlin, John
Miller, Henry
More, J. Marion
Norris, George W.
Nye, Edgar Wilson (Bill)
Owens, Commodore Perry
Parsons, Elsie Clews
Price, Sterling
Ralston, William Chapman
Robinson, Charles
Stevenson, Matilda Coxe
Stewart, William M.
Thorpe, Thomas Bangs
Townley, Arthur Charles (A. C.)
Vargas, Diego de
Welsh, Herbert Thomas
Wooten, Richens Lacy

Foley, William E.; CENTRAL MISSOURI STATE UNIVERSITY
Chouteau Family

Folsom, J. P.; HUNTINGTON LIBRARY, ART COLLECTIONS, AND BOTANICAL GARDENS
Bessey, Charles Edwin

Foster, Craig L.; FAMILY HISTORY LIBRARY, CHURCH OF JESUS CHRIST OF LATTER-DAY SAINTS
Edmunds Act of 1882
Edmunds Tucker Act of 1887
Mormon Manifesto
Polygamy: Polygamy among Mormons
Smith, Joseph Fielding
Taylor, John

Fowler, Don D.; UNIVERSITY OF NEVADA—RENO
Curtis, Edward Sheriff

Freedman, Estelle B.; STANFORD UNIVERSITY
Van Waters, Miriam

Friedricks, William B.; SIMPSON COLLEGE
Huntington, Henry Edwards

Fritz, Henry E.; ST. OLAF COLLEGE
Brunot, Felix Reville
Dawes, Henry Laurens
Dole, William P.
Grant's Peace Policy
Medill, William
Mitchell, David Dawson
Schurz, Carl
Taylor, Nathaniel G.
United States Indian Policy: Civilization Programs

Fritz, Marie L.
Brunot, Felix Reville
Dawes, Henry Laurens
Dole, William P.
Medill, William
Mitchell, David Dawson
Schurz, Carl
Taylor, Nathaniel G.

García, Juan R., UNIVERSITY OF ARIZONA
Immigration Law: Immigration Law after 1900

Garcia, Richard A.; CALIFORNIA STATE UNIVERSITY, HAYWOOD
San Antonio, Texas

Garcilazo, Jeffrey M.; University of Utah
Segregation: Segregation in Housing and Public
 Facilities

Gaskin, Thomas M.; Everett Community College
Jackson, Henry Martin ("Scoop")

George, Gerald
Jayhawkers
Fetterman Massacre

Gilman, Rhoda R.; Minnesota Historical Society
Olson, Floyd Bjersterne

Goble, Danney; Carl Albert Center, University of
 Oklahoma
Haskell, Charles Nathaniel
Kerr, Robert Samuel
Murray, William ("Alfalfa Bill")

Goodrich, James W.; State Historical Society of
 Missouri
Clark, James Beauchamp ("Champ")

Goodwin, Joanne L.; University of Nevada, Las Vegas
Hoover, Lou Henry
Martin, Anne Henrietta
National Woman's Party
Roche, Josephine Aspinwall

Gould, Lewis L.; University of Texas at Austin
Hogg, James Stephen (Jim)
Roosevelt, Theodore

Gowans, Fred R.; Brigham Young University
Ashely, William Henry
Boone, Daniel
Bridger, James (Jim)
Clyman, James
Fitzpatrick, Thomas
Henry, Andrew
Hunt, Wilson Price
Smith, Jedediah Strong
Rendezvous

Gracy, David B., II; University of Texas at Austin
Austin, Moses
Austin, Stephen Fuller

Graham, Don; University of Texas at Austin
Norris, Benjamin Franklin, Jr. (Frank)

Grandrud, Reba Wells; Arizona State Historic
 Preservation Office
Slaughter, John Horton

Grant, Glen; Grant and Hiuva Consulting
Native American Peopes: Peoples of Hawaii
Volcanoes

Grassham, John; Albuquerque Museum
Beaubien, Carlos

Green, Donald E.; Chadron State College
Ogallala Aquifer
Mead, Elwood

Griswold del Castillo, Richard; San Diego State
 University
Clamor Público, El
Trist, Nicholas

Grossman, James; Newberry Library
Newberry Library

Guice, John D. W.; University of Southern Mississippi
Hallett, Moses

Gullett, Gayle; Arizona State University
Edson, Katherine Philips
Women's Suffrage

Hanley, Mark Y.; Truman State University
Forbes, John Murray

Hanson, Charles E., Jr.; The Museum of the Fur Trade
Fraeb, Henry
Meek, Joseph LaFayette
Trappers
Vasquez, Pierre Louis
Williams, William S. ("Old Bill")
Wyeth, Nathaniel Jarvis
Young, Ewing

Harper, Barbara; Zenda, Inc.
Hale (Smith), Emma
New Madrid Earthquake of 1811

Hartsfield, Larry; Fort Lewis College
Abbey, Edward
Cather, Willa
Garland, Hamlin

Harvey, Mark W. T.; North Dakota State University
Colorado River Storage Project
Echo Park

Hassrisk, Peter H.; Buffalo Bill Historical Center
Buffalo Bill Historical Center

Hata, Donald Teruo, Jr.; California State University, Dominguez Hills
Tanaka, Michiko

Hata, Nadine Ishitani; El Camino Community College
Tanaka, Michiko

Haycox, Stephen; University of Alaska, Anchorage
Alaska
Alaskan Huskies
Brady, John Green
Lathrop, Austin E. ("Cap")
Veniaminov, Ivan (Popov, Ioann)

Haywood, C. Robert; Washburn University (emeritus)
Dodge City War
Rath, Charles

Hedren, Paul L.; Fort Union Trading Post National Historic Site
Black Hills Gold Rush
Denig, Edwin Thompson
Fort Benton
Fort Laramie
Forts
Fort Union
Grattan Massacre
King, Charles
McKenzie, Kenneth

Helms, J. Douglas; United States Natural Resources Conservation Service, Department of Agriculture
Bennett, Hugh Hammond
Soil Conservation Service

Henderson, Arn, FAIA; University of Oklahoma
Architecture: Folk (Ethnic) Architecture

Hibbard, Charles G.
Connor, Patrick E.

Hinckley, Ted C.; Western Washington University
Carter Act
Jackson, Sheldon

Hine, Robert V.; University of California, Irvine
Bartlett, John Russell
Dana, Richard Henry, Jr.
George, Henry
Harriman, Job
Kaweah Cooperative Commonwealth

Llano Del Rio
Royce, Josiah

Hinton, Harwood P.; Texas State Historical Association
Chisum, John Simpson
Goodnight-Loving Trail
Mossman, Burton C.
Poston, Charles Debrille
Wool, John Ellis

Ho, Wendy; University of California, Davis
Stereotypes: Stereotypes of Asians

Hofsommer, Don L.; St. Cloud State University
Kruttschnitt, Julius

Hogan, Patricia; Zenda, Inc.
Ah Quin
American System
Amon Carter Museum
Arizona Historical Society
Asian American Churches
Asiatic Exclusion League
Bailey, Florence Augusta Merriam
Baker, James
Bausman, William
Becknell, William
Bemis, Polly
Bingham, Hiram and Sybil
Bishop, Bernice Pauahi
Bishop, Isabella Bird
Brown, Clara
Browne, John Ross
Burnett, Samuel Burk
Burns, John Anthony
Burns, William J.
Caminetti Act of 1893
Chapman-Barnard Ranch, Oklahoma
Child Rearing: Native American Child Rearing
Child Rearing: Asian American Child Rearing
Chivington, John M.
Chung Sai Yat Po
Chu Pak
Claims Associations
Clay, Henry
Coal Lands Act of 1873
Coal Mining
Collins, Ben
Cook, James
Copper Kings, War of the
Corning Growing
Cortez, California
Crocker, Charles

Winnemucca, Sarah (Paiute)
Women Artists
Women Writers
Woo Yee-Bew

Hoig, Stan; UNIVERSITY OF CENTRAL ARIZONA (EMERITUS)
Black Kettle (Cheyenne)
Central Plains Indian Wars
Chisholm, Jesse

Holsinger, M. Paul; ILLINOIS STATE UNIVERSITY
Van Devanter, Willis

Holt, Marilyn Irvin; KANSAS STATE HISTORICAL SOCIETY
Orphans

Hoover, Carol Goss; HURON UNIVERSITY
American Horse (Elder) (Sioux)
American Horse (Younger) (Sioux)
Black Elk (Sioux)

Hoover, Herbert T.; UNIVERSITY OF SOUTH DAKOTA
American Horse (Elder) (Sioux)
American Horse (Younger) (Sioux)
Big Foot (Spotted Elk) (Sioux)
Black Moon (Sioux)
Forn Horns (Sioux)
Gall (Sioux)
Grass, John (Charging Bear) (Sioux)
Grey Beard (Cheyenne)
Hollow Horn Bear (Sioux)
Little Raven (Arapaho)
Minimic (Cheyenne)
Native American Peoples: Peoples of the Great Plains
Rain in the Face (Sioux)
Sioux Wars
South Dakota
Struck by the Ree (Sioux)
Todd, John Blair Smith

Horton, Loren N.; STATE HISTORICAL SOCIETY OF IOWA
Grimes, James W.
Looking-Glass Prairie
Prairie

Hosley, Edward H.
Native American Peoples: Peoples of Alaska

Hoy, James F.; EMPORIA STATE UNIVERSITY
Dalton Gang

Hudson, W. M.
Adams, Andy

Hunt, David C.; JOSLYN ART MUSEUM
Borein, John Edward
Borglum, Solon Hannibal
Cary, William de la Montagne
Deas, Charles
Johnson, Frank Tenney
Joslyn Art Museum
Kane, Paul
Kern, Edward Meyer
Peale, Titian Ramsay
Proctor, Alexander Phimister (A. P.)
Seymour, Samuel
Stanley, John Mix
Tavernier, Jules
Walker, James

Hurtado, Albert L.; ARIZONA STATE UNIVERSITY
Bolton, Herbert Eugene
Juanita of Downieville
Native American Peoples: Peoples of California
Sutter, John August

Isserman, Maurice; HAMILTON COLLEGE
Whitney, Charlotte Anita

Iverson, Peter; ARIZONA STATE UNIVERSITY
United States Indian Policy: Twentieth-Century
　　Developments

Jackson, W. Turrentine; UNIVERSITY OF CALIFORNIA, DAVIS
Adams Express Company
Butterfield, John
Fargo, William George
Ficklin, Benjamin F.
Holladay, Ben
Ilfeld, Charles
Magoffin, James Wiley
Majors, Alexander
Marcy, Randolph Barnes
Ochoa, Esteban
Overland Mail Company
Pony Express
Roads and Highways
Rocky Mountain Fur Company
Russell, William Hepburn
Russell, Majors and Waddell
Russian-American Company
Waddell, William Bradford
Wells, Henry
Wells, Fargo and Company
Westport Landing, Missouri

Jacobs, Margaret D.
Bidwell, Annie Ellicott Kennedy

Rancho Chico
Women in Wage Work

Jacobsen, Kristen; DE GOLYER LIBRARY,
  SOUTHERN METHODIST UNIVERSITY
DeGolyer Library

Jameson, Elizabeth; UNIVERSITY OF NEW MEXICO
Cripple Creek, Colorado
Cripple Creek Strikes
Working-Class Women

Jeffrey, Julie Roy; GOUCHER COLLEGE
Spaulding, Henry Harmon and Eliza Hart
Whitman, Marcus and Narcissa
Woman's Christian Temperance Union

Jensen, Richard L.; BRIGHAM YOUNG UNIVERSITY
Perpetual Emigrating Fund

Johnson, Byron A.; TEXAS RANGER HALL OF FAME AND
  MUSEUM
Albuquerque, New Mexico
Architecture: Adobe Architecture
Baca, Elfego
Cattle Brands and Branding
Restaurants

Johnson, Susan L.; UNIVERSITY OF MICHIGAN
Bean, Babe
Watson, Ella ("Cattle Kate")

Johnson, William R., Jr.; UNIVERSITY OF ALASKA,
  FAIRBANKS
Dimond, Anthony J. (Tony)
Wickersham, James

Jones, Charles T., Jr.; WILLIAM WOODS COLLEGE
Bonneville, Benjamin Louis Eulalie de
Missouri River

*Kamerling, Bruce
Beardsley, Helen Marston
Theosophical Society

Kanellos, Nicolás; UNIVERSITY OF HOUSTON
Teatro Villalongín (Companía Hernández-
  Villalongín)

Kaufman, Polly Welts; UNIVERSITY OF MASSACHUSETTS AT
  BOSTON
National Popular Education Board
School Life on the Frontier
Teachers on the Frontier
*Deceased

Kemper, Kurt Edward
Ah Toy
Ames, Oakes
Assing, Norman
Broderick, David C.
Butler, Anthony Wayne
Chautauqua
Churchill, Caroline Nichols
Cutting, Bronson
Emma Mine
Farnham, Eliza Wood Burhans
Fletcher, Alice Cunningham
Geary, John White
Gwin, William
Hare, William Hobart
Hollister, William Wells
Kennedy, Kate
Little, Frank
Log Cabins
McBeth, Sue and Kate
Mineral Lands Leasing Act of 1920
Native American Ledger Drawings
Nelson, William Rockhill
Newell, Frederick Haynes
Oregon Steam Navigation Company
Park, Alice
Payne, David L.
San Francisco Building Trades Council
Sheldon, Charles Monroe
Singleton, Benjamin ("Pap")
Texas Fever
Tingley, Clyde
Tuttle, Daniel Sylvester
Tyler, John
Wichita, Kansas
Wheeler, Benjamin Ide
Wheeler, Burton K.
Wilkes, Charles
Wright Irrigation Act of 1887
Young, Ann Eliza Webb

Kessler, Lauren; UNIVERSITY OF OREGON
Duniway, Abigail Scott

Ketner, Joseph D.; WASHINGTON UNIVERSITY
Wimar, Carl (or Charles) F.

Kimball, Stanley B.; SOUTHERN ILLINOIS UNIVERSITY
Kimball, Heber Chase
Mormon Trail

Kirkendall, Richard S.; UNIVERSITY OF WASHINTON
Truman, Harry S

Kitch, Sally L.; OHIO STATE UNIVERSITY
McWhirter, Martha White
Woman's Commonwealth

Kocks, Dorothee E.; UNIVERSITY OF UTAH
Sandoz, Mari

Koestler, Fred L.; TARLETON STATE UNIVERSITY
Bell Ranch, New Mexico
Camino Real, El
Castro, José
Cooke, Philip St. George
Coronado, Francisco Vásquez de
Dallas, Texas
Donner Party
Empesarios
Fredonia Rebellion
Houston, Texas
Muller v. *Oregon*
Navarro, Jose Antonio Baldomero
Northfield Raid
Olive, Ison Prentice ("Print")
Pershing, John James
Rayburn, Samuel Taliaferro (Sam)
Santa Anna, Antonio López de
Snively, Jacob
Stillman, Charles
Vial, Pedro
Zavala, Lorenzo de

Lane, Ann J.; UNIVERSITY OF VIRGINIA
Gilman, Charlotte Perkins

Langellier, John P.; AUTRY MUSEUM OF WESTERN
  HERITAGE
Autry, Gene
Rogers, Roy, and Dale Evans

Langlois, Karen S.; HUNTINGTON LIBRARY, ART
  COLLECTIONS, AND BOTANICAL GARDENS
Austin, Mary Hunter

Langum, David J.; SAMFORD UNIVERSITY
Community Property

Lanford, Kelly L.
Kelly, Fanny
Oatman, Olive

Larsen, Lawrence H.; UNIVERSITY OF MISSOURI—
  KANSAS CITY
Gilpin, William
Kansas City, Missouri

Omaha, Nebraska
Urban West

Larson, Robert W.; UNIVERSITY OF NORTHERN COLORADO
  (EMERITUS)
Gorras Blancas, Las

Lass, William E.; MANKATO STATE UNIVERSITY
Bullwhackers
Minnesota
Overland Freight
Stagecoaches

Lay, Shawn; UNIVERSITY OF GEORGIA
Ku Klux Klan

Layton, Stanford J.; UTAH STATE HISTORICAL SOCIETY
Enlarged Homestead Act of 1909
Homestead Act of 1862
Preemption Act of 1841
Stock Raising Homestead Act of 1916

Lear, Linda J.; SMITHSONIAN INSTITUTION
Carson, Rachel Louise, and *Silent Spring*
Ickes, Harold L.
Leopold, Aldo

Leckie, Shirley A.; UNIVERSITY OF CENTRAL FLORIDA
Custer, Elizabeth

LeCompte, Mary Lou; UNIVERSITY OF TEXAS AT AUSTIN
Pickett, Bill
Rodeo

Lee, R. Alton; UNIVERSITY OF SOUTH DAKOTA
Mundt, Karl E.

Leonard, Karen; UNIVERSITY OF CALIFORNIA, IRVINE
East Indians in the West
Intermarriage: Mariages between Asian Americans
  and Mexicans

Leonard, Kevin Allen; ANTIOCH COLLEGE
Alien Land Laws
Japanese Internment

Leonard, Stephen J.; METROPOLITAN STATE COLLEGE OF
  DENVER
Costigan, Edward Prentiss
Speer, Robert Walter
Waite, David Hanson

LeWarne, Charles P.
Burke, Thomas

Green, Joshua
Home, Washington
Seattle, Washington
Washington

Leyendecker, Liston E.; COLORADO STATE UNIVERSITY
Denver and Rio Grande Railway Company
Mears, Otto
Moffat, David Halliday

Limón, José E.; UNIVERSITY OF TEXAS AT AUSTIN
Corridos

Littlefield, Douglas R.; LITTLEFIELD RESEARCH ASSOCIATES
Central Valley Project

Lothrop, Gloria Ricci; CALIFORNIA STATE UNIVERSITY,
    NORTHRIDGE
Crabtree, Lotta
Hearst, Phoebe Apperson
Italian Americans
Montez, Lola
Tingley, Katherine Augusta

Lowell, Waverly B.; NATIONAL ARCHIVES,
    PACIFIC SIERRA REGION
Brown, Arthur Page
Morgan, Julia
San Andreas Fault

Luckingham, Bradford; ARIZONA STATE UNIVERSITY
Phoenix, Arizona
Tucson, Arizona

Lujan, Roy; NEW MEXICO HIGHLANDS UNIVERSITY
Chavez, Dennis

Lutts, Ralph H.; GODDARD COLLEGE
Boone and Crockett Club
Burroughs, John
Grinnell, George Bird
Nature Fakers

Lyman, Leo; VICTOR VALLEY COLLEGE
Hyde, Orson
People's Party of Utah

Madsen, Carol Cornwall; BRIGHAM YOUNG UNIVERSITY
Ladies' Anti-Polygamy Society
Wells, Emmeline Blanche Woodward

Mangum, Neil C.; NATIONAL PARK SERVICE
Kearny, Stephen Watts

Taylor, Zachary
United States–Mexican War

Mann, Ralph; UNIVERSITY OF COLORADO AT BOULDER
Comstock Lode
Sacramento, California
Virginia City, Nevada

Marín, Christine; ARIZONA STATE UNIVERSITY
Arizona Mining Strikes
Salcido, Abrán

Martel, Carol M.; ARIZONA STATE UNIVERSITY
Gould, Jay

Martínez, Oscar J.; UNIVERSITY OF ARIZONA
Borderlands Theory

Mathes, Valerie Sherer; CITY COLLEGE OF SAN FRANCISCO
Jackson, Helen Maria Fiske Hunt
Women's National Indian Association

Mattes, Merrill J.
Robidoux Brothers

Matthews, Glenna; UNIVERSITY OF CALIFORNIA, BERKELEY
Debo, Angie
San Jose, California

May, Dean L.; UNIVERSITY OF UTAH
Cannon, George Quayle
Deseret, State of
Pioneer Life: Mormon Pioneer Life
Roberts, Brigham Henry
United Order of Enoch

McCarthy, Michael; COMMUNITY COLLEGE OF DENVER
Loggers

McDonald, Archie P.; EAST TEXAS HISTORICAL
    ASSOCIATION
Jones, Anson
Travis, William Barret
Wayne, John

McDonnell, Jeanne Farr
Briones, Juana

McGinnis, Anthony R.
Native American Cultures: Warfare
Native American Cultures: Weapons

McGrath, Roger D.; UNIVERSITY OF CALIFORNIA,
    LOS ANGELES
Coleman, William Tell

San Francisco Committee of Vigilance of 1856
Vigilantism

McKnight, Joseph W.; SOUTHERN METHODIST UNIVERSITY
Spanish Law

McMannon, Timothy J.; UNIVERSITY OF WASHINGTON
Magnuson, Warren Grant

Mercer, Lloyd J.; UNIVERSITY OF CALIFORNIA,
    SANTA BARBARA
Harriman, Edward Henry

Metz, Leon C.
Bean, Roy
Fountain, Albert Jennings
Garrett, Patrick Floyd Jarvis (Pat)
Hardin, John Wesley
Selman, John Henry
Stoudenmire, Dallas

Mighetto, Lisa; HISTORICAL RESEARCH ASSOCIATES
Extinction of Species
Wolves

Mihesuah, Devon A.; NORTHERN ARIZONA UNIVERSITY
Cherokee Male and Female Seminaries

Miller, Darlis A.; NEW MEXICO STATE UNIVERSITY
United States Army: Supply and Logistics

Miller, Jay; NEWBERRY LIBRARY
Mourning Dove

Miller, Sally M.; UNIVERSITY OF THE PACIFIC
O'Hare, Kate Richards

Miranda, Gloria E.; EL CAMINO COMMUNITY COLLEGE
Child-Rearing: Spanish and Mexican Child Rearing
Figueroa, José
Leon, Patricia de
Mexican Settlement

Moehring, Eugene P.; UNIVERSITY OF NEVADA, LAS VEGAS
Las Vegas, Nevada

Moneyhon, Carl H.; UNIVERSITY OF ARKANSAS AT
    LITTLE ROCK
Arkansas

Monroy, Douglas; HULBERT CENTER FOR SOUTHWESTERN
    STUDIES, COLORADO COLLEGE
Vásquez, Tiburcio

Morrison, Ernest J.
Lane, Franklin Knight
McFarland, John Horace
McGee, William John

Moses, L. G.; OKLAHOMA STATE UNIVERSITY
Wild West Shows: Indians in Wild West Shows

Mosser, Duane P.; UNIVERSITY OF NEVADA, LAS VEGAS
Schoolcraft, Henry Rowe

Mothershead, Harmon; NORTHWEST MISSOURI STATE
    UNIVERSITY
Altube, Pedro
Hooker, Henry Clay
Mores, Antonio Marquis de
Swan, Alexander Hamilton (Alec)

Moulton, Gary; UNIVERSITY OF NEBRASKA
Lewis, Meriwether
Ross, John (Cherokee)

Mullin, Michael J.; AUGUSTANA COLLEGE
Parkman, Francis

Murphy, Mary; MONTANA STATE UNIVERSITY
MacLane, Mary
Rankin, Jeannette

Murrah, David J.; SOUTHWEST COLLECTION, TEXAS
    TECH UNIVERSITY
Mackenzie, Murdo
Slaughter, Christopher Columbus
Spur Ranch, Texas

Nall, Garry L.; WEST TEXAS A&M UNIVERSITY
Cotton Farming
Farming: Farming on the Great Plains
Wheat Farming

Naske, Claus-M.; UNIVERSITY OF ALASKA, FAIRBANKS
Juneau, Joe
Gruening, Ernest

Nichols, Roger L.; UNIVERSITY OF ARIZONA
Atkinson, Henry
Dodge, Henry
Leavenworth, Henry
Pike, Zebulon Montgomery

Nilan, Roxanne L.; STANFORD UNIVERSITY
Jordon, David Starr

Noel, Thomas J.; UNIVERSITY OF COLORADO AT DENVER
Denver, Colorado

Nottage, James H.; AUTRY MUSEUM OF WESTERN
    HERITAGE
Autry Museum of Western Heritage

Nunis, Doyce B., Jr.; UNIVERSITY OF SOUTHERN
    CALIFORNIA (EMERITUS)
Bidwell, John
Chapman, William S.
Fort Ross
Horn, Tom
McCulloch, Hartnell and Company
Sublette Brothers

O'Neal, Bill; PANOLA JUNIOR COLLEGE
Arizona Rangers
Black Bart (Boles, Charles E.)
Brooks, William ("Buffalo Bill")
Horrell-Higgins Feud
Horse Theft and Horse Thieves
Leslie, Nashville Franklin (Frank)
Longley, William Preston ("Wild Bill")
Pistol Laws
Sutton-Taylor Feud
Thompson, Benjamin F.
Violence: Historical Overview

O'Neill, Sean; GRAND VALLEY STATE UNIVERSITY
Chatillon, Henri

Oglesby, Richard E.; UNIVERSITY OF CALIFORNIA,
    SANTA BARBARA
Fort Manuel
Greenwood, Caleb
Lisa, Manuel
Missouri Fur Company

Olson, James C.; UNIVERSITY OF MISSOURI—KANSAS CITY
    (EMERITUS)
Bozeman Trail
Morton, J. Sterling
Red Cloud (Sioux)
Spotted Tail (Sioux)

Onuf, Peter S.; UNIVERSITY OF VIRGINIA
Northwest Ordinance

Osburn, Katherine M. B.; AUSTIN PEAY STATE UNIVERSITY
Native American Peoples: Peoples of the Great Basin

Oshio, Kazuto; JAPAN WOMEN'S UNIVERSITY
Boulder Canyon Act of 1928

California Doctrine (of Water Rights)
Colorado Doctrine (of Water Rights)
Lux v. *Haggin*

Owens, Kenneth N.; CALIFORNIA STATE UNIVERSITY,
    SACRAMENTO
Chorpenning, George
Walker, Joseph Reddeford

Pascoe, Peggy; UNIVERSITY OF OREGON
Cable Act of 1922
Cameron, Donaldina McKenzie
Industrial Christian Home for Mormon Women
Intermarriage: Antimiscegenation Laws
Newman, Angie
Ozawa v. *United States*
People v. *Hall*
Picotte, Susan LaFlesche
Schulze, Tye Leung
Tibbles, Susette LaFlesche
Woman's Home Missionary Society (Methodist
    Episcopal)
Wong Kim Ark v. *the United States*
Yick Wo v. *Hopkins*

Pate, J'Nell L.; TARRANT COUNTY JUNIOR COLLEGE
Mackenzie, Ranald Slidell

Paul, R. Eli; NEBRASKA STATE HISTORICAL SOCIETY
Kicking Bear (Sioux)
Short Bull (Sioux)

Paxson, William E., Jr.
Paxson, Edgar Samuel

Peña, Manuel; UNIVERSITY OF TEXAS AT AUSTIN
Conjunto Music

Penick, James; UNIVERSITY OF ALABAMA AT BIRMINGHAM
Ballinger-Pinchot Controversy

Peterson, Charles S.; UTAH STATE UNIVERSITY (EMERITUS)
Bancroft, Hubert Howe
Clarion, Utah
Flake, William J.
Kane, Thomas Leiper
Kimball, J. Golden
Lee, John D.
Utah

Peterson, F. Ross; MOUNTAIN WEST CENTER FOR
    REGIONAL STUDIES, UTAH STATE UNIVERSITY
Church, Frank
Idaho

Smoot, Reed
Steunenberg, Frank
Taylor, Glen Hearst

Phillips, Charles; ZENDA, INC.
Aircraft Industry
Americanization Programs
Architecture: Urban Architecture
Art: Book and Magazine Illustration
Art: Popular Prints and Commercial Art
Astor, John Jacob
Astoria
Atchison, David Rice
Banking
Barrios
Berdache
Billington, Ray Allen
Black Hawk's War
Booms
Bureau of Land Management
Burr Conspiracy
Burros
California
California Ranchos
Catholics
Changing Woman
Chicago, Illinois
Chinatowns
Chinese Americans
City Government
City Planning
Civil War
Climate
Colleges and Universities
Colorado River
Compromise of 1850
Conestoga Wagons
Cooper, James Fenimore
Copper Mining
Crédit Mobilier of America
Crow Dog (Sioux)
Cult of True Womanhood
Diggs, Annie La Porte
Disease
Divorce
Doctors
Domestic Service
Doniphan, Alexander William
Dred Scott Decision
Dubuque, William
El Paso Salt War
El Paso, Texas
Erosion
Exploration: English Expeditions

Exploration: United States Expeditions
Exploration and Science
Federal Government
Film: The Western
Financial Panics
Fire
Fishing Industry
Gambling
German Americans
Giannini, Amadeo Peter
Graham-Tewksbury Feud
Grand Teton National Park
Hawaii
Haywood, William D. ("Big Bill")
Hearst, George
Heney, Francis Joseph
Homesteading
Hudson's Bay Company
Humor
Industrial Workers of the World
Intermarriage: Marriages between Asian Americans and Euro-Americans
Intermarriage: Marriages between Spanish/Mexicans and Native Americans
Intermarriage: Marriages between Euro-Americans and Spanish/Mexicans
Iowa
Irish Americans
Irrigation
Japanese Americans
Jewish Americans
Jones, Mary Harris ("Mother")
Kaiser, Henry J.
Keokuk (Sac and Fox)
Kelley, Oliver H.
Klondike Gold Rush
Labor Movement
Laclède, Pierre
Ladd, Edwin Fremont
Land Policy: Land Companies
Land Policy: Land Ordinance of 1785
Land Policy: Private Land Claims
La Salle, Sieur de (Cavelier, René Robert)
Leadville, Colorado
Literature: Indian Captivity Narratives
Literature: Mexican American Literature
Literature: Native American Literature
Literature: Travel Literature
Lone Wolf v. *Hitchcock*
Los Angeles: Historical Overview
Lynching
Magazines and Newspapers
Manifest Destiny
Maxwell Land Grant Company

Medicine
Métis People
Missions: Early Franciscan and Jesuit Missions
Missions: Nineteenth-Century Missions to the
    Indians
Mississippi River
Montana
Motion-Picture Industry
Mountain Men
National Expansion: Nation Building and Early
    Expansion
National Expansion: The Election of 1844 and
    National Expansion
National Expansion: The Imperial Impulse
Native American Cultures: Ecology
Native American Cultures: Political Organization
Native American Peoples: Pre-Columbian Peoples
Navajo Stock-Reduction Program
Nonpartisan League
Nootka Sound Controversy
North West Mounted Police
Oil and Gas Industry
Owens Valley War
Pacific Mail Steamship
Pentitentes
Pesticides
Phillips, Frank
Photography
Platte River
Posadas, Las
Progressivism
Railroad Land Grants
Railroads
Raynolds Expedition
Riel, Louis David
Reclamation
Rocky Mountains
Santa Fe and Chihuahua Trail
Sacramento River
St. Joseph, Missouri
San Joaquin River
Santa Barbara, California
Segregation: Segregation in Education
Silver Mining
Social Banditry
Socialism
Spanish and Mexican Towns
Stereotypes: Stereotypes of Mexicans
Tariff Policy
Tecumseh (Shawnee)
Temperance and Prohibition
Texas Revolution
Thoreau, Henry David
Union Labor Party, San Francisco

United States Army: Volunteers and Militias
United States Indian Policy: Reform Movement
Violence: Historical Overview
Violence: Myths about Violence in the West
Violence: Racial Violence
Violence: Violence against Women
Walkara (Ute)
Watie, Stand (Cherokee)
Weaver, James Baird
Wilkinson, James
Willamette River
Wilmot Proviso
Whaling
Wolfskill, William
Workingmen's Party of Californa
Yuma Revolt
Zion's Co-operative Mercantile Institution

Pierce, Richard A.; UNIVERSITY OF ALASKA, FAIRBANKS
Bering, Vitus

Pita, Beatrice; UNIVERSITY OF CALIFORNIA, SAN DIEGO
Ruiz de Burton, María Amparo

Pitt, Leonard; CALIFORNIA STATE UNIVERSITY, NORTHRIDGE
    (EMERITUS)
Los Angeles: Commerical and Industrial
    Development
Murieta (or Murietta), Joaquin

Ponce, Merrihelen
Cabeza de Baca, Fabiola

Porter, Joseph C.
Crazy Horse (Sioux)
Crow Dog (Sioux)

Price, B. Byron; NATIONAL COWBOY HALL OF FAME AND
    WESTERN HERITAGE CENTER
Cattle Industry
Cattle Rustling
Chuck Wagons
Cowboy Outfits
Cowboy Tools and Equipment
Fisher, John King
Goodnight, Charles
JA Ranch, Texas
Kinney, Henry Lawrence
Mesquite
Milton, Jeff Davis
National Cowboy Hall of Fame and Western
    Heritage Center
Pierce, Abel Head ("Shanghai")
Prowers, John Wesley

Schrevogel, Charles
Smith, Erwin Evans
Stetson, John Batterson
Strauss, Levi
Tumbleweed
Wyeth, N. C.
XIT Ranch, Texas
Zogbaum, Rufus Fairchild

Pritchard, Linda; UNIVERSITY OF TEXAS AT SAN ANTONIO
American Board of Commissioners for Foreign
    Missions

Procter, Ben; TEXAS CHRISTIAN UNIVERSITY
Hearst, William Randolph
McNelly, Leander H.
Texas Rangers

Quintanilla, Irene
Alamo

Radke, Andrea Gayle; BRIGHAM YOUNG UNIVERSITY
Bridger, James (Jim)
Clyman, James

Raftery, Judith R.; CALIFORNIA STATE UNIVERSITY, CHICO
Public Schools

Rankin, Charles E.; MONTANA HISTORICAL SOCIETY
Villard, Henry

Rattenbury, Richard C.; NATIONAL COWBOY HALL OF
    FAME AND WESTERN HERITAGE CENTER
Barbed Wire
Browning, John Moses
Colt, Samuel
Firearms
Hunting
Loving, Oliver
Matador Ranch

Rawls, James J.; DIABLO VALLEY COLLEGE
San Francisco Earthquake of 1906

Raymond, C. Elizabeth; UNIVERSITY OF NEVADA—RENO
Wingfield, George

Rea, J. E.; UNIVERSITY OF MANITOBA
Odgen, Peter Skene

Reese, Linda; UNIVERSITY OF OKLAHOMA
Barnard, Catherine Ann (Kate)
Robertson, Alice Mary

Reeve, W. Paul; BRIGHAM YOUNG UNIVERSITY
Boone, Daniel

Richmond, Robert W.; RICHMOND GROUP
Kansas
Topeka, Kansas
White, William Allen

Ridge, Martin; HUNTINGTON LIBRARY, ART COLLECTIONS,
    AND BOTANICAL GARDENS
Billington, Ray Allen

Riley, Glenda; BALL STATE UNIVERSITY
Thompson, Era Bell

Rishel, Joseph F.; DUQUESNE UNIVERSITY
Cooke, Jay

Roberts, Phil; UNIVERSITY OF WYOMING
Bradbury, John
Carey, Joseph Maull
Cheyenne, Wyoming
Fort Bridger
Kendrick, John Benjamin
Johnson County War
Nelson, Aven
Warren, Francis E.
Wyoming

Rohrbough, Malcolm J.; UNIVERSITY OF IOWA
California Gold Rush
Colorado Gold and Silver Rushes
Gold Mining
Mining: Mining Engineers

Rolle, Andrew; HUNTINGTON LIBRARY, ART COLLECTIONS,
    AND BOTANICAL GARDENS
Beale, Edward Fitzgerald (Ned)
Camels
Carson, Christopher Houston ("Kit")
Frémont, John Charles
Nicolet, Jean
Pruess, Charles
Stanford, Amasa Leland

Ronda, James P.; UNIVERSITY OF TULSA
American Fur Company
Charbonneau, Jean Baptiste
Clark, William
Colter, John
Dorion, Marie
Exploration: French Expeditions
Exploration: Russian Expeditions
Exploration: Spanish Expeditions

Colorado River Compact
Kansas v. *Colorado*
Mulholland, William
Report on the Lands of Arid Regions
Smythe, William E.
Water

Shipps, Jan; INDIANA UNIVERSITY—PURDUE UNIVERSITY OF
    INDIANAPOLIS
Church of Jesus Christ of Latter-day Saints

Shoemaker, Nancy; TEXAS CHRISTIAN UNIVERSITY
Fertility: Fertility among Native Americans
Polygamy: Polygamy among Native Americans

Stevens, Errol Wayne; LOYOLA MARYMOUNT UNIVERSITY
Los Angeles County Museum of Natural History

Sherwood, Morgan; UNIVERSITY OF CALIFORNIA, DAVIS
Alaskan Exploration
Harriman Expedition

Sims, Robert C.; BOISE STATE UNIVERSITY
Alexander, Moses

Smemo, Kenneth; MOORHEAD STATE UNIVERSITY
Amidon, Charles Fremont

Smith, Dean; ARIZONA STATE UNIVERSITY
Babbit Ranch, Arizona
Goldwater Family

Smith, Duane A.; FORT LEWIS COLLEGE
Colorado
Mining: Historical Overview
Tabor, Horace Austin Warner
Woodruff v. *North Bloomfield et al.*

Smith, Martha, C.S.J.; AVILA COLLEGE
Cabareaux, Sister Mary Catherine
Segale, Sister Blandina

Smith, Sherry L.; UNIVERSITY OF TEXAS AT EL PASO
Crook, George
United States Army: Military Life of the Frontier
United States Army: Women and the Frontier Army

Snell, Joseph W.
Brown, Henry Newton
Brown, John
James Brothers
Landon, Alfred Mossman
Lane, James Henry
Lecompton, Kansas

Mather, Dave
Smith, Thomas James ("Bear River" Tom)
Younger Brothers

Socolofsky, Homer E.; KANSAS STATE UNIVERSITY
Lease, Mary Elizabeth Clyens

Spence, Mary Lee; UNIVERSITY OF ILLINOIS AT URBANA-
    CHAMPAIGN
Harvey Girls

Stanley, Judith M.; CALIFORNIA STATE UNIVERSITY,
    HAYWOOD
Nursing

Steen, Harold K.; FOREST HISTORY SOCIETY
Forest Management Act of 1897
Forest Reserve Act of 1891

Storey, Brit Allan
Bureau of Reclamation
Palmer, William Jackson

Suggs, George G., Jr.; SOUTHEAST MISSOURI STATE
    UNIVERSITY
Western Federation of Miners

Swierenga, Robert P.; KENT STATE UNIVERSITY
Donaldson, Thomas Corwin

Talbot, Vivian Linford; BRIGHAM YOUNG UNIVERSITY
Smith, Jedediah Strong

Tate, Michael L.; UNIVERSITY OF NEBRASKA AT OMAHA
Dundy, Elmer Scipio
Mexican Border Conflicts
Villa, Francisco ("Pancho")

Taylor, Lonn; NATIONAL MUSEUM OF AMERICAN HISTORY,
    SMITHSONIAN INSTITUTION
Baylor, John Robert

Taylor, Quintard; UNIVERSITY OF OREGON
Bush, George Washington
Mason, Biddy
Oakland, California
Pleasant, Mary Ellen ("Mammy")
Walker, Sarah Breedlove

Taylor, Sandra C.; UNIVERSITY OF UTAH
Beeson, Desdemona Stott

Thomas, James H.; WICHITA STATE UNIVERSITY
Miller Brothers 101 Ranch Wild West Show

Thomas, Phillip Drennon; Wichita State University
Alaska Gold Rush
Beavers
Bent Brothers
Bent's Fort, Colorado
Bierstadt, Albert
Bingham, George Caleb
Black Bears
Bodmer, Karl (or Carl)
Condors
Coyotes
Eastman, Seth
Elk
Farny, Henry F.
Grizzly Bears
Jackrabbits
James, Edwin
Long, Stephen Harriman
Moose
Moran, Thomas
Mountain Lions
Prairie Dogs
Pronghorns
Rattlesnakes
Remington, Frederic
Rio Grande
Russell, Charles Marion
Taos School of Artists
Whitetail Deer
Wildlife
Yukon River

Thompson, Gerald; University of Toledo
Gillespie, Archibald H.
Stockton, Robert F.

Thompson, Jerry; Laredo State University
Cortina, Juan Nepomuceno
Sibley, Henry Hopkins

*Thrapp, Dan L.
Apache Kid (Apache)
Apache Wars
Cochise (Apache)
Eskiminzin (Apache)
Geronimo (Apache)
Jeffords, Thomas J.
Juh (Apache)
Mangas Coloradas (Apache)
Naiche (Apache)
Nana (Apache)
United States Army: Scouts
Victorio (Apache)

*Deceased

Topping, Gary; Utah State Historical Society
Buntline, Ned (Judson, Edward Zane Carroll)
Coolbrith, Ina
DeVoto, Bernard
Foote, Mary Hallock
Grey, Zane
Literature: Dime Novels
Literature: The Western
Wister, Owen

Trennert, Robert A.; Arizona State University
Indian Schools: Indian Schools off the Reservation
Pratt, Richard Henry
United States Indian Policy: Reservations

Troccoli, Joan Carpenter; Thomas Gilcrease Institute
King, Charles Bird

Trusky, Tom; Boise State University
Poetry

Tuller, Roger; Texas Christian University
Siringo, Charles Angelo

Tyler, Mary; Southern California Library for Social Studies and Research
Bass, Charlotta Spears

Tyler, Ron; Texas State Historical Association
Audubon, John James
Texas

Unrau, William E.; Wichita State University
Boudinot, Elias (Cherokee)

Utley, Robert M.
"Billy the Kid"
Custer, George Armstrong
Little Bighorn, Battle of
Sherman, William Tecumseh
Sitting Bull (Sioux)

Van Orman, Richard A.
Allison, [Robert] Clay
Bass, Sam
Canton, Frank
Courtright, Jim
Frontier: Comparative Frontier: South Africa
Holliday, John Henry ("Doc")
Hotels
Masterson, Bartholomew (Bat)
Short, Luke

Vigil, Maurilio E.; NEW MEXICO HIGHLANDS UNIVERSITY
Otero, Miguel Antonio, Jr.
Otero, Miguel Antonio, Sr.
Gallegos, José Manuel

Vigil, Ralph H.; UNIVERSITY OF NEBRASKA
Lamy, Jean Baptiste

Voisey, Paul; UNIVERSITY OF ALBERTA
Frontier: Comparative Frontier: Canada

Waiser, W. A.; UNIVERSITY OF SASKATCHEWAN
Thomspon, David
McKenzie, Donald

Walker, Dale L.
Atherton, Gertrude
Bierce, Ambrose Gwinett
Brand, Max (Faust, Frederick Schiller)
London, John Griffith (Jack)
O'Neill, William Owen ("Buckey")

Walker, Ronald W.; BRIGHAM YOUNG UNIVERSITY
Mormons: Historical Overview
Washakie (Shoshone)

Wall, Wendy L.; STANFORD UNIVERSITY
Burke Act
Dawes Act

Walter, David A.; MONTANA HISTORICAL SOCIETY
Broadwater, Charles Arthur
Daly, Marcus
Gibson, Paris
Hauser, Samuel Thomas
Huffman, Laton Alton (L. A.)
Jackson, William Henry
Kohrs, Conrad
Montana Gold Rush
O'Sullivan, Timothy H.
Ryan, John Dennis
Stuart, Granville

Watts, Jill; CALIFORNIA STATE UNIVERSITY, SAN MARCOS
African American Churches
McPherson, Aimee Semple
New Thought

Weber, David J.; SOUTHERN METHODIST UNIVERSITY
Kern, Richard Hovendon
Marcos de Niza, Fray

Weeks, William Earl; SAN DIEGO STATE UNIVERSITY
Adams-Onis Treaty
Lousiana Purchase

Welch, John W.; BRIGHAM YOUNG UNIVERSITY
Book of Mormon

Wessel, Thomas R.; MONTANA STATE UNIVERSITY
The Light (Assiniboin)

West, Elliott; UNIVERSITY OF ARKANSAS
Child Rearing: Euro-American Child Rearing
Saloons
Webb, Walter Prescott

West, John O.; UNIVERSITY OF TEXAS AT EL PASO
Humor

White, Linda; BRIGHAM YOUNG UNIVERSITY
Henry, Andrew

Whitehead, John S.; UNIVERSITY OF ALASKA, FAIRBANKS
Allen, Henry T.
Baranov, Alexsandr
China Trade
Dole, Sanford B.
Missions: Missions in Hawaii
Spreckels, Claus

Williams, Burton J.
Ingalls, John J.

Wilson, John P.
LeFors, Joe
Lincoln County War
Pinkerton National Detective Agency
Reavis, James Adison

Wilson, Raymond; FORT HAYS STATE UNIVERSITY
Eastman, Charles Alexander (Sioux)
Bonnin, Gertrude Simons (Zitkala-Sa) (Sioux)

Wilson, Terry P.; UNIVERSITY OF CALIFORNIA, BERKELEY
Native American Cultures: Acculturation

Winn, Kenneth; Missouri State Archives
Missouri
Missouri Compromise

Wishart, David J.; UNIVERSITY OF NEBRASKA
Chittenden, Hiram Martin

Wong, K. Scott; WILLIAMS COLLEGE
Ng Poon-Chew

Wood-Clark, Sarah; KANSAS STATE HISTORICAL SOCIETY
Oakley, Annie

Woods, Thomas A.; OLD WORLD WISCONSIN
Agrarianism
Daws, S. O.

Woodward, Robert C.;
U'Ren, William Simon

Wooster, Robert; TEXAS A&M UNIVERSITY,
    CORPUS CHISTI
Miles, Nelson Appleton
Texas Frontier Indian Wars
United States Army: Composition
United States Army: Organization
United States Army: Strategy and Tactics

Wrobel, David M.; WIDENER UNIVERSITY
Arid-Lands Thesis
Frontier: Frontier Thesis
Historigraphy, Western

New Western History
Safety-Valve Theory
Turner, Frederick Jackson
West-as-Region School

Yogi, Stan; CALIFORNIA COUNCIL FOR THE HUMANITIES
Literature: Asian American Literature

Yohn, Susan M.; HOFSTRA UNIVERSITY
Blake, Alice
Presbyterian Woman's Board of Home Missions
Protestant Home Missionary Programs

Yoo, David K.; CLAREMONT MCKENNA COLLEGE
Abiko, Kyutaro
Bhagat Singh Thind, In Re

Zall, P. M.
Boeing, William E.
Derby, George Horatio

List of Entries

Malcolm J. Rohrbough

Mining Law of 1872
Patricia Hogan

Minnesota
William E. Lass

Missions
Early Franciscan and Jesuit Missions
Charles Phillips and Alan Axelrod

Nineteenth-Century Missions to the Indians
Charles Phillips and Alan Axelrod

Missions in Hawaii
John S. Whitehead

Mississippi River
Charles Phillips

Missouri
Kenneth H. Winn

Missouri Compromise
Kenneth H. Winn

Missouri Fur Company
Richard E. Oglesby

Missouri River
Charles T. Jones, Jr.

Mitchell, David Dawson
Henry E. Fritz and Marie L. Fritz

Mix, Tom
William W. Savage, Jr.

Moffat, David Halliday
Liston E. Leyendecker

Mojave Desert
Patricia Hogan

Montana
Charles Phillips

Montana Gold Rush
David A. Walter

Montez, Lola
Gloria Ricci Lothrop

Montezuma, Carlos
R. David Edmunds

Montoya, Joseph
Patrick H. Butler, III

Mooney, Thomas Joseph
Patricia Hogan

Moose
Phillip Drennon Thomas

Moran, Thomas
Phillip Drennon Thomas

More, J. Marion
Candace Floyd

Moreno, Luisa
Vicki L. Ruiz

Mores, Antonio Marquis de
Harmon Mothershead

Morgan, Julia
Waverly B. Lowell

Mormon Manifesto
Craig L. Foster

Mormons
Historical Overview
Ronald W. Walker

Far West Settlements
Newell G. Bringhurst

Mormon Trail
Stanley B. Kimball

Morning Star (Northern Cheyenne)
Gregory R. Campbell

Morrill Act of 1862
Alan Axelrod

Morris, Esther Hobart McQuigg Slack
Virginia Scharff

Morton, J. Sterling
James C. Olson

Mosher, Clelia Duel
Patricia Hogan

Mossman, Burton C.
Harwood P. Hinton

Motion-Picture Industry
Charles Phillips

Mountain Lions
Phillip Drennon Thomas

Mountain Meadows Massacre
Newell G. Bringhurst

Mountain Men
Charles Phillips

Mourning Dove
Jay Miller

ABBEY, EDWARD

Author of fiction and nonfiction works Edward Abbey (1927–1989) left an enduring mark on nature writing in the late twentieth century. His work is characterized by an unflinching bluntness and engagement with the politics and culture of his time.

Born in Home, Pennsylvania, Abbey began his career as a novelist but achieved national attention in 1968 with an autobiographical nonfiction work entitled *Desert Solitaire*. Compressing three seasons he spent as a ranger at Arches National Monument in southeastern Utah into a single summer and fall, the work is viewed by most critics as his masterpiece. In *The New West of Edward Abbey*, Ann Ronald writes that the book is made up of "true experiences, far-fetched anecdotes, effusive descriptions, some polemics, and some imprecations" and "presents a composite vision of a modern man struggling to exist in a shrinking natural world."

In addition to *Desert Solitaire*, Abbey produced five other major nonfiction books, works he referred to as "personal histories": *The Journey Home* (1977), *Abbey's Road* (1979), *Down the River* (1982), *Beyond the Wall* (1984), and *One Life at a Time, Please* (1988). In these books, he cogently expressed his opposition to the twentieth-century American addiction to growth and destruction of wild places. "Growth for the sake of growth," he wrote in *One Life at a Time, Please*, "is the ideology of the cancer cell. Cancer has no purpose but growth; but it does have another result—the death of the host."

Abbey also wrote a number of novels; the best known of these is his comic masterpiece *The Monkey Wrench Gang* (1975), which presents the actions of a band of "eco-saboteurs" in defense of the American West. The novel is often credited with being the inspiration behind Earth First!, a radical environmental protection group. Other popular fiction works include *The Brave Cowboy* (1956), *Fire on the Mountain* (1962), *Black Sun* (1971), *Good News* (1980), *The Fool's Progress* (1988), and *Hayduke Lives!* (published posthumously in 1990).

If Abbey's nonfiction provides the most straightforward statement of his ideas, his novels provide the best illustration of his range as a writer. They display his facility with postmodern genre and narration. In them are his experimentations with such formulas as the western, science fiction dystopias, comic adventure novels, and philosophical explorations of anarchism. The "Author's Warning" in Abbey's last novel, *Hayduke Lives!,* illustrates both his awareness of the literary past and his characteristic double-edged wit: "Anyone who takes this book seriously will be shot. Anyone who does not take it seriously will be buried alive by a Mitsubishi bulldozer."

—*Larry Hartsfield*

Suggested reading:

Abbey, Edward. *Abbey's Road*. New York, 1979.
———. *Beyond the Wall*. New York, 1984.
———. *Black Sun*. New York, 1971.
———. *The Brave Cowboy*. New York, 1956.
———. *Desert Solitaire*. New York, 1968.
———. *Down the River*. New York, 1982.
———. *Fire on the Mountain*. New York, 1962.
———. *The Fool's Progress*. New York, 1988.
———. *Good News*. New York, 1980.
———. *Hayduke Lives!* New York, 1990.
———. *Jonathan Troy*. New York, 1954.
———. *The Journey Home*. New York, 1977.
———. *The Monkey Wrench Gang*. New York, 1975.
———. *One Life at a Time, Please*. New York, 1988.
Bishop, James, Jr. *Epitaph for a Desert Anarchist: The Life and Legacy of Edward Abbey*. New York, 1994.
Foreman, Dave. "Edward Abbey, 1927–1989." *Utne Reader* (July-August 1989): 36–37.
Hepworth, James, and Gregory McNamee, eds. *Resist Much, Obey Little: Some Notes on Edward Abbey*. Salt Lake City, 1985.

McCann, Garth. *Edward Abbey*. Boise, Idaho, 1977.

Ronald, Ann. *The New West of Edward Abbey*. Albuquerque, N. Mex., 1982. Reprint. Reno, Nev., 1988.

ABERT, JOHN JAMES

For thirty-two years, Colonel John James Abert (1788–1863) was head of the CORPS OF TOPOGRAPHICAL ENGINEERS in the War Department. His political abilities as well as his professional expertise made him an excellent choice to run the elite bureau.

Abert graduated from West Point in 1811 but resigned from the army and was admitted to the bar in 1813. He volunteered for service during the War of 1812 and two years later rejoined the army with the rank of major in the topographical engineers. Serving as an engineer along the Atlantic Coast until 1829, he worked on harbor improvements, coastal defenses, and canal construction. The topographers reported to the chief of engineers, and the results of their labors were assembled in a topographical office headed by Major Isaac Roberdeau. When Roberdeau died in 1829, Abert succeeded him as head of the Topographical Bureau. In 1831, in part because of his own proselytizing, the Corps of Topographical Engineers was made an independent branch of the War Department. In 1838, the corps became a staff corps of the army, and Abert, as its head, was promoted to the rank of colonel.

Although he was occasionally called to other duties, such as overseeing the removal of Native Americans beyond the Mississippi, most of Abert's duties involved organizing the corps for the enormous task of carrying out topographic and engineering assignments from the Atlantic Coast, across the continent, to the shores of the Pacific. Although the corps was involved in many civil engineering projects and geodetic work along the Great Lakes and inland rivers, its most significant work, as well as its most adventurous, lay in its exploration of the American West. The high point of its history was its contribution to the completion of the Pacific Railroad Surveys from 1853 to 1856. Although most of those involved favored a southern route, four acceptable routes—from near the Canadian border to the Mexican border—were delineated in addition to the route of the Union Pacific–Central Pacific, which was already known to be tenable. The Pacific Railroad Reports are a storehouse of early scientific information about the American West.

Abert retired in 1861, two years before his beloved Corps of Topographical Engineers was merged with the UNITED STATES ARMY CORPS OF ENGINEERS.

—*Richard A. Bartlett*

SEE ALSO: Exploration: United States Exploration; Exploration and Science; Transcontinental Railroad Surveys

SUGGESTED READING:

Goetzmann, William H. *Army Exploration in the American West*. New Haven, Conn., 1959. Reprint. Austin, Tex., 1991.

ABIKO, KYUTARO

Immigrant leader and newspaper publisher Kyutaro Abiko (1865–1936) was born in Niigata prefecture in Japan. He arrived in San Francisco in 1885 and worked his way through school while learning English. After graduating from Boys High School in 1891, he briefly attended classes at the University of California.

After several small business ventures, Abiko became the publisher of the *Nichibei Shimbun (Japanese American News)* in 1899, a Japanese-language, daily newspaper. Under his direction, the *Nichibei* became the leading paper within the Japanese community, branched outside of San Francisco to Los Angeles, and held a readership throughout California. Through the newspaper, he entered into community affairs.

Abiko actively promoted the permanent settlement of Japanese in America. He believed that, given the agricultural background of most immigrants, the foundations for their futures lay in farming. Toward that end, Abiko, in 1906, helped form the American Land and Produce Company, which purchased thirty-two hundred acres of land in Livingston, California, and sold forty-acre tracts to Japanese immigrants. A small group of pioneer farmers moved onto the land in 1907 and formed the Yamato Colony. In 1919, Abiko helped purchase two thousand more acres of farm land in CORTEZ, CALIFORNIA. Abiko and his wife, Yonako, challenged the discriminatory laws and anti-Asian activity that plagued the Japanese community throughout the first decades of Japanese immigration. The passage of the exclusion law in 1924 effectively signaled an end to Japanese migration to the United States, and the Abikos encouraged the second generation, as American citizens, to serve as bridges of cultural understanding between the United States and Japan.

A labor dispute at the *Nichibei* in 1931 over unpaid wages led to a bitter and protracted strike that temporarily crippled the paper's operation and that also seemed to break Abiko's spirit. His health declined soon afterwards, and he died of pneumonia in 1936. He left behind a rich legacy as one of the key leaders in the early history of the Japanese in America.

—*David K. Yoo*

SEE ALSO: Japanese Americans; Magazines and Newspapers

SUGGESTED READING:
Ichioka, Yuji. *The Issei.* New York, 1988.
Matsumoto, Valerie. *Farming the Home Place.* Ithaca, N.Y., 1993.

ABILENE, KANSAS

Founded by a town-site speculator in central Kansas in 1861, Abilene was the first of the famous cattle-trading centers. Because Texas longhorns carried splenic fever, also known as TEXAS FEVER, it was illegal to bring them so far east as Abilene. But with the Kansas governor's informal permission, an Illinois livestock dealer, JOSEPH G. McCOY, established a market there in 1867. For the next four years, herds of Texas cattle followed the Chisholm Trail north to Wichita, then took the Abilene Trail to the new cattle town on the Kansas Pacific Railway. There buyers—dealers or ranchers—purchased the cattle for shipment to Eastern packing houses or for fattening on ranges to the north. In 1867, some 35,000 head reached Abilene; in 1871 the total was about 190,000.

In 1870, Abilene contained perhaps six hundred citizens; its employed citizens were mainly proprietors, craftsmen, and service workers. An estimated fifteen hundred transients provided extraordinary business. A Kansas City bank opened an Abilene branch in 1870 to offer deposit security and large, short-term loans to cattlemen. It handled more than nine hundred thousand dollars during its first two months of operation. Grocers prospered through bulk sales to incoming cattle outfits. Clothier Jacob Karatofsky, a German Jewish immigrant, and Russian-born general merchandiser Mayer Goldsoll catered to the cowboy trade, as did custom boot-maker Thomas C. McInerney.

In 1871, Abilene's Drovers Cottage hotel and stables could accommodate 175 guests, fifty carriages, and one hundred horses. The village also contained eleven saloons, including the elegant Alamo and the Bulls' Head, a cowboy favorite operated by two Texans. Prostitutes came to Abilene its first season. In 1869, the town harbored three brothels and twenty-one whores, and in 1871, Abilene got its first "dance house"—a combination brothel, GAMBLING den, and dance hall.

By 1870, the need for LAW AND ORDER—especially gun control—forced Abilene to establish a municipal government and hire policemen. JAMES BUTLER ("WILD BILL") HICKOK served as "captain of police" in 1871. Since drinking, gambling, and whoring caused most

Top: Abilene flourished as a cattle town from 1867 to 1871. *Courtesy National Cowboy Hall of Fame and Western Heritage Center.*

Bottom: The streets of Abilene in 1892 when the circus came to town. *Courtesy Kansas State Historical Society.*

of the disorder, Abilene instituted a monthly tax on saloonkeepers, gamblers, and prostitutes to pay police salaries, its largest budget item. Only two homicides occurred in 1870; three occurred in 1871.

Abilene's last year as a cattle town was 1871. Local realtors, domestic stock-raisers, and moral reformers successfully lobbied against the return of the cattle trade in 1872. Abilene reverted to its pre-1867 status as a county seat, later notable only as the boyhood home of President Dwight D. Eisenhower.

—*Robert R. Dykstra*

SEE ALSO: Cattle Towns

SUGGESTED READING:
Dykstra, Robert R. *The Cattle Towns.* New York, 1968.

ADAIR, JOHN G. AND CORNELIA

SEE: JA Ranch, Texas

ADAMS, ANDY

Writer of novels and stories about the Great Plains, Andy Adams (1859–1935) was born in Whitley County, Indiana. He ran away from home when he was fifteen years old and eventually drifted to Texas. There, he dealt in horses and cattle. He made several cattle drives to Oklahoma and Kansas. Late in 1893, he was attracted to Colorado by the news of a gold strike. He bought mining stocks, which failed and left him broke in Colorado Springs.

After seeing a popular farce, Adams decided to try his hand at writing a play. He could not find a pro-

Andy Adams's *Log of a Cowboy* provided one of the more realistic accounts of cattle driving. *Courtesy Library of Congress.*

ducer, but he did succeed in placing two short stories in a magazine. He offered twenty-five stories to two publishers, but both refused to publish the manuscript because the work lacked unity. He thought of a plan: he would tell the story of a band of cowboys who, driving a herd of cattle from lower Texas to Montana, met and overcame obstacles along the way. The result was *The Log of a Cowboy*, published by Houghton Mifflin in 1903. Adams's masterpiece, the book has always received high praise because of its fidelity to its subject. It also deserves praise for its language—of both the characters and the narrator. Although *The Log* is fiction, it has often been mistaken for autobiography. It had no resemblance to "Wild West" fiction, which Adams despised.

Adams published six other books and left several full-length manuscripts. *The Log* is now the undisputed classic of the cattle country. Ninety years after publication, it is still available in a reprint edition from the University of Nebraska Press. Adams's mastery of the oral tale is also evident in *Campfire Tales* (stories collected from Adams's other books), available through the same press.

—*W. M. Hudson*

SUGGESTED READING:
Hudson, W. M. *Andy Adams: His Life and Writings.* Dallas, Tex., 1964.

ADAMS, CHARLES FRANCIS, JR.

Author and railroad president Charles Francis Adams, Jr. (1835–1915), was the son of Charles Francis Adams, U.S. ambassador to England during the Civil War, and Abigail Brooks Adams and the grandson of President John Quincy Adams. After graduating from the Boston Latin School and Harvard, Adams studied law but preferred a career as a writer. During the Civil War, he served in the militia, fought at Antietam and Gettysburg, and commanded a black infantry regiment. He was mustered out in June 1865 as a brevet brigadier general and began to write.

Adams decided that RAILROADS were the key to the economic progress of the United States and focused his interest on good regulation and management. He was appointed a member of the Massachusetts Railroad Commission in 1869, became its chair in 1872, and served on the commission until 1879. During this time, he wrote about the railroad war between Cornelius Vanderbilt and JAY GOULD. *A Chapter of Erie* was published in 1871.

At the urging of Secretary of the Interior CARL SCHURZ, Adams became a member, in 1878, of the government-appointed board of the UNION PACIFIC RAILROAD, being reorganized under the terms of the Thurman Act of 1878 in the aftermath of the CRÉDIT MOBILIER OF AMERICA scandal. After a period of management by Gould and during the depression of 1884, Adams served as president of the railroad. Over the next six years, he struggled with the public and private interests that competed for control of the line. He resigned in 1890. Three years later, the line was bankrupt.

—*Patrick H. Butler, III*

SUGGESTED READING:
Adams, Charles Francis. *Charles Francis Adams 1835–1915: An Autobiography.* 1916. Reprint. New York, 1968.
Kirkland, Edward C. *Charles Francis Adams, Jr., 1835–1915: The Patrician at Bay.* Cambridge, Mass., 1965.

ADAMS, JOHN QUINCY

SEE: Adams-Onis Treaty

ADAMS, WILLIAM LYSANDER

Oregon politician, newspaper reporter and publisher, and satirist William Lysander Adams (1821–1906) was born in Painesville, Ohio. Educated at Knox College in Galesburg, Illinois, and at Bethany College in Virginia, he taught school in Illinois and then migrated over the OREGON TRAIL in 1848 (the year Oregon became a federal territory). He continued his career as a schoolteacher—interrupted by a trip to the California gold fields in 1849—until he bought a farm in Yamhill County, Oregon.

Adams soon began to play a role in public affairs in his new territory. In 1852, for the *Portland Oregonian*, he wrote a series of articles that became classics of frontier journalism and a valuable source for early Oregon political history. The articles (published as a pamphlet later in 1852) composed a serialized play entitled *Treason, Stratagems, and Spoils* (the title comes from Shakespeare's *The Merchant of Venice).* While the Democrats were the first of the political parties transplanted to the West with the pioneers, they were soon joined by members of the Whig, American, and Republican parties. Adams was a Whig at the time he wrote his play but later became a Republican. The Democrats, under the skillful leadership of an inner circle labeled by political opponents the "Salem Clique," were the dominant party in Oregon until the presidential election of 1860. *Treason, Stratagems, and Spoils* satirized, through its thirteen characters, the activities of the members of the clique. The play accused them of drunkenness, political partisanship, and favoritism to Mormons (Adams had come to hate the Mormons during his residence in Illinois), among a great many other charges. The play made a sensation and helped Adams's reputation among critics of the Democrats.

Adams left the *Oregonian* and founded the Oregon City *Oregon Argus* in 1855. He took Whig positions in opposing slavery and the expansion of slavery into the West and held the radical view of supporting the prohibition of the sale of alcoholic beverages.

In 1857, Adams broke with the Whigs to become one of the founders of the Oregon Republican party. His services to the party were rewarded with his appointment as collector of customs for the District of Oregon from 1861 to 1867. He secured a medical degree from the Eclectic Medical College of Philadelphia in 1874 and moved from Portland to Hood River, Oregon, in 1877 to farm, practice medicine, and write about a variety of subjects including religion and medical history. Adams was an assiduous writer and speaker about the economic possibilities of his state. His life, like those of his more famous colleagues in Oregon journalism, ABIGAIL SCOTT DUNIWAY and Harvey W. Scott, was a struggle to adapt pioneer values and institutions to industrial and urban conditions of the post–Civil War society.

—*Gordon B. Dodds*

SUGGESTED READING:
Adams, William L. *A Melodrama Entitled "Treason, Stratagems, and Spoils."* Edited by George N. Belknap. New Haven, Conn., 1968.

ADAMS EXPRESS COMPANY

In 1854, several express and steamship companies, with capital of $1 million, consolidated to form the Adams Express Company. Alvin Adams was president, and William Dinsmore was vice-president. Adams, a pioneer in the express business, had founded Adams and Company in 1840 and had opened an office in San Francisco on December 1, 1849, just after the CALIFORNIA GOLD RUSH began. When WELLS, FARGO AND COMPANY entered the express business as a Western ally of Adams's chief rival—the American Express Company—fierce competition in forwarding and banking resulted. The consolidation was formed to combat the new competition. Not included in the consolidation, Adams and Company's California office remained a separate company in which Adams personally retained an interest. The manager of Adams of California, D. H. Haskell, was effective at publicity and promotion but was an incautious businessman. A business depression that started in the East became a panic in California when the banking firm of Page, Bacon and Company failed. On February 23, 1855, the major express and banking houses in California suspended business. Wells, Fargo and Company was found to be solvent and quickly reopened its doors, but Adams and Company (California) did not reopen. Its collapse sent a severe shock through the state's business community. Mobs stormed its offices in hopes of withdrawing funds, but the California company went into receivership. Approximately two hundred business establishments were forced to close, and a serious depression ensued. Wells, Fargo and Company emerged from the crisis as the dominant express company in California.

Former employees of Adams and Company reorganized the business as the Pacific Express Company, a firm that had moderate success for a brief time. Adams Express Company's credit was not destroyed by the failure of its Western affiliate, but Alvin Adams resigned as president.

The Civil War brought prosperity to all express companies. The Adams Express and Southern Express companies provided the only lines of communication between the North and South. With the coming of the railroad era, all express companies sought exclusive and favorable contracts with the railroads to establish regional monopolies and to control strategic terminals. Adams Express Company fought the United States Express Company primarily to control business between New York and Chicago. By 1886, six express companies controlled 90 percent of the nation's business, and Adams Express was one of the more powerful in the group. The company paid the railroads $2 million annually, one-fourth of the amount paid by all the express companies. Adams Express had capital of $12 million, all issued as stock dividends from accumulated earnings.

Prosperity ended during World War I, and Adams was a heavy loser. As a war measure, Adams Express, American Express, Southern Express, and Wells, Fargo and Company were merged into the American Railway Express Company, capitalized at $30 million and supervised by the United States government. Adams Express Company now operates as a closed-in investment company.

—*W. Turrentine Jackson*

SUGGESTED READING:
Harlow, Alvin F. *Old Waybills: The Romance of the Express Companies.* New York, 1934.
Moody, Ralph. *Stagecoach West.* New York, 1967.
Simpson, A. L. *History of the Express Business.* New York, 1881.
Winther, Oscar O. *Express and Stagecoach Days in California.* Stanford, Calif., 1935.

ADAMS-ONIS TREATY

An agreement between the United States and Spain, the Adams-Onis Treaty (1819) acquired Florida and established the first claim of the United States to lands extending to the West Coast. Also known as the Transcontinental Treaty, it proved to be one of the more important treaties in American history.

Signed in 1819 by American Secretary of State John Quincy Adams and Spanish Minister to the United States Don Luis de Onis, the treaty resolved a long-standing territorial dispute between Spain and the United States over the boundaries of the LOUISIANA PURCHASE (1803). Citing a prior agreement with France, Spanish officials first contested the very legitimacy of the sale of Louisiana by France to the United States and then attempted to define the territory's boundaries along the eastern bank of the Mississippi River and excluding the Florida peninsula. The U.S. government, in contrast, claimed that the Louisiana territory extended as far west as the Northwest Coast and as far south as Texas and included the portion of Florida west of the Perdido River. Negotiations between Spain and the United States to resolve the matter were delayed until 1817 by the Napoleonic Wars.

ANDREW JACKSON's invasion of Florida during the First Seminole War from 1817 to 1818 proved decisive in resolving the dispute. Confronted by the prospect of losing Florida to American conquest, the Spanish minister agreed to Adams's proposal, which ceded Florida to the United States and established a transcontinental boundary extending to the Columbia River region. In exchange, the United States gave up its claim to Texas and assumed $5 million worth of claims held by American citizens against the Spanish government for losses on the high seas. Because of opposition in the Spanish court, the treaty was not ratified until 1821.

The Adams-Onis Treaty proved critically important to the NATIONAL EXPANSION westward of the United States. By resolving the long-term dispute with Spain, it finalized the Louisiana Purchase. As a result, Adams and President James Monroe were in a position in December 1823 to declare the Western Hemisphere off limits to further European colonization in a statement of policy later known as the Monroe Doctrine. Through the provisions of the treaty, the United States had access to the first transcontinental river route to the Columbia River region. By relinquishing claims to Texas, the treaty contributed to later agitation for the "reannexation" of Texas, which proslavery expansionists alleged had been wrongly given away. The Western boundary established by the treaty acknowledged California and the Southwest to be Mexican territory, thus setting the stage for the conquest of these lands by the United States in 1848.

—*William Earl Weeks*

SUGGESTED READING:

Bemis, Samuel Flagg. *John Quincy Adams and the Foundations of American Foreign Policy.* New York, 1949.

Brooks, Philip C. *Diplomacy and the Borderlands: The Adams-Onis Treaty of 1819.* Berkeley, Calif., 1939.

Weeks, William Earl. *John Quincy Adams and American Global Empire.* Lexington, Ky., 1992

AEROSPACE INDUSTRY

SEE: Aircraft Industry; Federal Government

AFRICAN AMERICAN CHURCHES

The establishment of African American churches in the West closely followed African American westward migration. Excluded from most white churches and eager for independence anyway, African Americans organized their own congregations. Serving as the foundation of black Western communities, African American churches also functioned as spiritual centers and institutions of political protest.

It was through these churches that the small pre–Civil War population of African Americans in the West pursued civil rights and antislavery activities. After emancipation, more African Americans moved west seeking land and equality. Attempting to replicate the churches they had left behind, African American migrants established branches of mainstream independent black denominations—predominately African Methodist Episcopal, African Methodist Episcopal Zion, Baptist, and Methodist churches. Some organized separate congregations affiliated with white Protestants. Confronted with discrimination in the West, African American churches vigorously fought racism on local and state levels.

While mainstream churches dominated African American religion in the West, other alternatives had surfaced by 1900. As African American migration increased, many new arrivals organized churches in rented homes and storefronts. Some of the new sects had far-reaching influence. One such movement, the Azusa Street Revival, began in Los Angeles in 1906 and was led by William Seymour, an African American minister. During an evening prayer meeting in Seymour's home, members of the congregation began speaking in tongues. Crowds gathered around Seymour's residence, and for three days, Seymour and his followers prayed, sang, and spoke in tongues. While speaking in tongues was not new, it had never occurred on such a large scale. Before long, people of all races from around the country and the world came to participate in what many consider to be the birth of American Pentecostalism.

African American churches in the West also worked to address the community's needs by providing assistance during crises. In the 1930s, for example, disciples of a Northeastern-based African American evangelist, Father Divine, organized branches of his church throughout the West. In California, Washington, and Colorado, followers established rescue missions that fed and clothed the poor during the Great Depression.

African American churches increased in number most dramatically during and after World War II. Lured by jobs in the defense industry, many African Americans moved to the West, where they organized more congregations. Like their sister churches of the South, black churches in the West escalated their drive for equality in the 1950s and 1960s. In California, African American congregations crusaded against restrictive covenants and segregated housing. Western churches also supported civil rights campaigns in the South by sending money and volunteers to fight Southern SEGREGATION.

During the late twentieth century, African American churches in the West continued to mobilize against racism. Many offered social relief, education, and job training to combat poverty and crime. After the Los Angeles riot in 1992, African American churches sponsored community redevelopment, gang summits, and campaigns for justice. Generally, African American churches in the West resembled their counterparts across the United States. Confronting a hostile and segregationist society, African American congregations not only continued the struggle for equality in the West but also supported national campaigns against racism in American society into the 1990s.

—*Jill Watts*

SEE ALSO: Evangelists; Protestants

SUGGESTED READING:

Lincoln, C. Eric, and Lawrence Mamiya. *The Black Church in the African American Experience.* Durham, N.C., 1990.

Murphy, Larry G. "A Balm in Gilead: Black Churches and the Thrust for Civil Rights in California, 1850–1880." In *Religion and Society in the American West.* Edited by Carl Guarneri and David Alvarez. New York, 1987.

Tinney, James S. "William J. Seymour: Father of Modern-Day Pentecostalism." In *Black Apostles: Afro-American Clergy Confront the Twentieth Century.* Edited by Randall Burkett and Richard Newman. Boston, 1978.

Watts, Jill. *God, Harlem U.S.A.: The Father Divine Story.* Berkeley, Calif., 1992.

AFRICAN AMERICANS

"Out here in this matchless Southern California there would seem to be no limits to your opportunities, your possibilities." So wrote the African American scholar W. E. B. DuBois after his first visit to the Far West in 1913. Between 1850 and 1910, thousands of African Americans, lured by the promise of land, opportunity, and most importantly, racial justice, migrated to the trans-Mississippi West. These African Americans influenced the political, economic, and social development of the West and, in turn, found their lives and aspirations shaped by a land that had both significant differences from and disappointing similarities to the regions they left behind.

The black presence in the West predated the nineteenth century. Africans held in bondage by the Spanish toiled as slaves in New Spain during the sixteenth century. As early as 1528, Esteban (or Estevenico), a Spaniard of African ancestry arrived in the Spanish colony of Florida. For more than a decade, he explored the Southwest as a member of numerous Spanish ex-

Many freed slaves found work as cowboys in the latter part of the nineteenth century. As many as one-quarter of the cowboys working cattle trails from Texas to the Midwest were African American. *Courtesy Library of Congress.*

peditions until his death in New Mexico during the Zuni Wars in 1539.

By far, the most significant early black population in the West were the *pobladores,* the initial settlers of the pueblo of Los Angeles in 1781. In 1769, the governor of Alta California decided to create a settlement in the area between the military presidio in Santa Barbara and the mission in San Gabriel in order to prevent the intrusion of other nations into the Spanish colony. Twelve families from the northern Mexico region of Sinaloa, a poor area where one-third of all the residents were descendants of Spanish slaves, agreed to migrate northward. On September 4, 1781, the 44 *pobladores* arrived at the site of the colony. Of the original settlers of Los Angeles, 26 were either black or of mixed African ancestry. These black colonists—including tailor Luis Quintero and his wife Maria Petra Rubio, José Moreno, Antonio Mesa, and Ana Lopez—struggled to create the pueblo. Within a decade, structures were erected, the central plaza was created, and the Zanja Madre, the system of channels that brought water to the colony, was completed. By 1790, Los Angeles was a thriving village with a population of 141. The mixed-race origins of many of the city's founders was often overlooked or underappreciated because the *pobladores* did not fit the traditional pioneer myth of heroic, white frontiersmen.

During the nineteenth and early twentieth centuries, the history of African Americans in the West was marked by a great diversity of individual and communal experiences and by a constant, yet modest, population increase. Before the end of the CIVIL WAR, the black population in the West was quite limited: in 1860 there were 48 blacks residing in Colorado, 627 in Kansas, 128 in Oregon and 4,086 in California. Within twenty years, newly freed African Americans increased their presence in the West significantly: in 1880, 2,435 black residents lived in Colorado, 43,107 lived in Kansas, 487 in Oregon, and 6,018 in California. By the dawn of the twentieth century, the African American populace had more than tripled in California, Colorado, Nebraska, Washington, and Arizona. The bulk of these new Westerners were Southern blacks seeking refuge from the discrimination and hostility of the South. While the ratio of African Americans to whites living in the West was smaller than the ratio in the South, it rivaled that of the North.

The westward migration took many forms. Before the Civil War, some African Americans arrived in the West as slaves accompanying their masters. Others were newly freed men and women searching for a place to make emancipation real. Still others were recruited and relocated into the region to provide labor for agricultural, mining, or railroad interests. A significant num-

Some former slaves, such as the members of this family photographed by Solomon D. Butcher, took a chance at homesteading. *Courtesy Nebraska Historical Society.*

ber of black migrants were part of organized movements like the EXODUSTERS who left the Reconstruction-era South for Kansas. Some were enticed to the West during the early years of the twentieth century by visionaries who created all-black towns such as Allensworth, California. The movement to the West included a diverse array of African American social and economic classes. Laborers, farmers, sharecroppers, cowboys, domestics, shopkeepers, soldiers, dentists, and ministers—who lived in rural enclaves, small communities, and cities from Bush Prairie, Washington, to Boley, Oklahoma, to Los Angeles, California—all were drawn to the West by the hope that in this "new land" old prejudices could be overcome. What they found was an uneven promise, where opportunities were still shaped by race. As the black population increased in the West throughout the nineteenth century so too did the level of discrimination, racial separation, and anti-black sentiment. For every successful black entrepreneur, such as Alexander Leidesdorff, who was considered a leader of both the black community and the white community in antebellum San Francisco, there were numerous African Americans, such as southern Californian James Jefferson, who were unable to school their children and who were relegated to the lowest rungs of the eco-

nomic ladder. Even though Western states were never an oasis free of racial bigotry, they did provide limited opportunities to maintain families, develop occupations, build communities, and nurture dreams to some African Americans.

Central to the lure of the West for African Americans during the nineteenth and early twentieth centuries was economic opportunity. Working as miners, servants, unskilled day laborers, or soldiers, African Americans played an essential role in the region's growth and prosperity. African Americans such as JAMES PIERSON (JIM) BECKWOURTH and Jacob Dodson were part of the community of mountain men who supported the fur trade and whose explorations charted the wilderness and laid the foundation for the settlement of the region. Along the mining frontier from California to Colorado to the Dakotas, African Americans joined in the search for gold and silver. During the California gold rush in 1848 and 1849, nearly three thousand black miners—both slave and free—sought their fortunes. While some, such as Moses Drinks, prospered, many black miners soon looked for other jobs in San Francisco. The opportunity to homestead land after the Civil War also spurred thousands of blacks into the agricultural frontier. African Americans participated in the Oklahoma land rush of 1889, settled on "public" land in Colorado and Montana, and carved farms out of the Kansas prairie.

Several small businesses were created and supported by African Americans in the West. Blacks owned groceries and furniture stores, saloons and barber shops, laundries and hotels, and blacksmith shops and real-estate companies. By 1862, after a decade of providing horses and lumber to the United States Army, Robert Owens had built a successful livery stable in downtown Los Angeles. MARY ELLEN ("MAMMY") PLEASANT became one of the richest and best-known black women in the West through the sale of real estate and the establishment of a first-class hotel in San Francisco. And Millie Ringgold owned a restaurant and hotel in Lewiston, Montana.

The image of the African American in the West is often restricted to colorful cowboys such as "One Horse Charlie" and Nat Love (better known as "Deadwood Dick") and the BUFFALO SOLDIERS. While the black experience is more complex, clearly the role of blacks in the military and in the cattle industry is crucial to understanding the history of the black West. Nearly 25 percent of the more than thirty thousand COWBOYS who worked the cattle frontier were African Americans. Black cowboys performed a wide range of duties and worked at jobs from cooks to trail hands to trail bosses. Usually "treated better on the trail than in town," the black cowboys had skills and experiences that contributed mightily to the success of the cattle industry. Black trail boss Bose Ikard, for example, helped create one of the major cattle drive routes, the Goodnight-Loving Trail.

Blacks played an even more significant role in the U.S. Army. Through a series of laws enacted by Congress in the late 1860s, four black military units, the Twenty-fourth and Twenty-fifth Infantries and the Ninth and Tenth Calvaries, were created for duty in the West. Throughout the nineteenth century, these troops, usually commanded by white officers, provided one-fifth of all the soldiers stationed on the frontier. These soldiers served in forts from New Mexico to California, from Oklahoma to the Dakota Territory. The Buffalo Soldiers fought in the Indian Wars, guarded wagon trains, protected settlers, built roads and telegraph lines, brought law and order to frontier towns, and earned eleven Congressional Medals of Honor—all for thirteen dollars per month. The military provided a rare chance for African Americans to secure employment, economic and educational advancement, and the opportunity and authority to interact with whites as equals.

The goal of obtaining racial justice and equality in the West was rarely achieved. By law and by custom, blacks found limits placed on their lives. Iowa and Oregon, for example, passed exclusionary laws to restrict the number of African Americans in the region. California passed statutes that prevented blacks from testifying in courts against whites and attempted to institute a poll tax in order to decrease the number of black voters. Some communities fought against the integration of schools, businesses, and transportation.

Much like blacks throughout the country, African Americans in the West aggressively confronted discrimination and worked to develop collective and individual strategies to improve their lives. Blacks in Colorado worked against statehood until they were guaranteed the right to vote on an equal basis with whites. Blacks in antebellum California initiated a series of statewide "colored conventions" that sought to articulate African American concerns and develop effective strategies. Black newspapers like *The Mirror of the Times, The Elevator,* and *The Liberator* were created to publicize racial discrimination. While most African Americans in the West struggled to change racial attitudes, others believed that blacks would receive equity and fairness only through the creation of all-black communities. Numerous all-black communities like Nicodemus, Kansas (founded in 1877), and Allensworth, California (founded in 1908), existed in the West. According to the founder of Allensworth, retired army officer Allen Allensworth, these towns would provide an escape from the oppressive burdens of racism. Here blacks could vote, raise families, pursue their careers, revel in African American culture, create a middle-class community, and "enjoy all the rights of citizenship." Ultimately, the location—usually far removed from urban centers—the uneven quality of the land and water, and the continuing hostility of white neighbors limited the success of the all-black ventures.

Central to the African American experience in the West were cities. By the end of the nineteenth century, most blacks in California were what one historian called "pioneering urbanites." Even African Americans who lived in rural environs were influenced by the cultural, political, and social leadership that emanated from Los Angeles, Denver, Topeka, and San Francisco. While the black experience in each Western city differed in style and in substance, there were many commonalities. During the nineteenth century, the black population increased slowly; more dramatic increases occurred during the first decade of the twentieth century. Thus black Los Angeles grew from 12 in 1855 to 102 residents in 1880 to 2,131 in 1900 to 7,599 by 1910. The rapidly expanding cities provided opportunities for black entrepreneurs such as Los Angeles's BIDDY MASON, who amassed a fortune in real estate before her death in 1891. The growing black urban populations founded numerous churches and cultural, educational, and political organizations—such as the Citizens Protective League, the Sojourner Truth Club, and the San Francisco Athenaeum Institute—geared towards mutual assistance, educational improvement, and the development of strategies to ensure racial justice. To the African American, the West was not a Promised Land, but a place of real possibilities. For many, the West provided the opportunities to raise families, develop an economic livelihood, and experience some of the rights of citizenship, especially when compared to the conditions faced by black Southerners throughout the nineteenth and early twentieth centuries.

—*Lonnie G. Bunch, III*

SEE ALSO: Allensworth, Josephine Leavall; Homesteading; Segregation

SUGGESTED READING:

Broussard, Albert. *Black San Francisco: The Struggle for Racial Equality in the West.* Lawrence, Kans., 1993.

Bunch, Lonnie. *Black Angelenos: The Afro American in Los Angeles, 1850–1950.* Los Angeles, 1988.

De Graaf, Lawrence. "Recognition, Racism and Reflections on the Writing of Western Black History." *Pacific Historical Review* 44 (1975): 22–51.

Hamilton, Kenneth. *Black Towns and Profit: Promotion and Development in the Trans-Appalachian West.* Urbana, Ill., 1991.

Lapp, Rudolph. *Blacks in Gold Rush California.* New Haven, Conn., 1977.

Painter, Nell. *Exodusters: Black Migration to Kansas after Reconstruction.* Lawrence, Kans., 1986.

Porter, Kenneth. *The Negro on the American Frontier.* New York, 1971.

Savage, Sherman. *Blacks in the West.* Westport, Conn., 1976.

Taylor, Quintard. *The Forging of a Black Community: A History of Seattle's Central District, 1870 through the Civil Rights Era.* Seattle, 1994.

AGRARIANISM

American agrarianism is rooted in the notion that agriculture has inherent moral qualities and an economic primacy critical to the success and survival of a free and equal American society. Inherited from the European Enlightenment and nourished in the fertile soil of revolutionary America, these ideas were inextricably woven into American culture. According to THOMAS JEFFERSON, the most eloquent spokesman for early agrarian philosophy, landowning, community-oriented farmers were the most reliable American citizens because they were rooted to the land. According to agrarians, monopoly capitalists were selfish, cared little for community, and were eager to capture the economic and social benefits of the farmer's labor for themselves.

In the mid-nineteenth century, farmers found themselves in a changing world. The industrial revolution, growing urban populations, and improved transportation systems had altered the way they farmed and marketed their crops. No longer focused on feeding only their families and a local community, farmers were enmeshed in a complex commercial system. They found themselves dealing with manufacturers, salesmen, buyers, elevator operators, wheat graders, money lenders, and others—middlemen with whom few had had previous experience. Their former independence disappeared.

Throughout the nineteenth and twentieth centuries, agrarian movements emerged, prospered for a while, and then receded. Generally, agrarian groups advocated increased governmental regulation. They believed that a government that fairly represented the common American would and should ensure social justice and preserve economic and political equality. Most agrarian organizations sought to provide protection and relief for themselves through three courses of action: (1) legislation, which usually included government control or intervention, to protect the FARMING class from the economic power of monopoly capitalists; (2) cooperative buying and selling opportunities to reduce the cost of purchased goods and increase the profits on commodities; and (3) a moral purification of the American political and economic system.

The first major agrarian upheaval began just after the Civil War. In 1867, OLIVER H. KELLEY, a farmer from Minnesota, organized the Grange, or Patrons of Husbandry, while working as a clerk in Washington, D.C. The Grange was a fraternal organization for farmers, with secret rituals, educational programs, and social activities, and in its early years, members supported radical antimonopoly parties. Between 1867 and 1875, active Grange organizers advocated a consistent program: farmer cooperatives to eliminate the middleman; competitive water transportation to destroy the railroad monopoly on transporting produce and livestock to market; state laws to regulate railroad rates; a return to a more balanced monetary system; and the elimination of the protective tariff, which raised the cost of manufactured goods farmers needed.

The Grange swept through the Midwest, West, and South in the early 1870s. Farmer cooperatives bought and sold goods, and independent political parties successfully passed "Granger laws" to regulate RAILROADS. As it approached one million members in the mid-1870s, the Grange was beset by conflict between those who advocated political activism and those who preferred a more moderate approach.

The Grange swept through the Midwest in the 1870s. At its peak, it boasted nearly one million members. *Courtesy Library of Congress.*

As the Grange declined, the GREENBACK PARTY emerged in the mid-1870s advocating increased circulation of paper money. With more money in circulation, farmers would have an easier time retiring their debts. The new party reached its peak in the national election of 1880 but quickly disintegrated.

The Farmers' Alliance became the largest and most successful agrarian movement. It emerged in Texas in 1875 and disintegrated amid political bickering in 1879. It reemerged in Texas in 1880 as a nonpartisan group. Borrowing much from the early Grange, the early alliance was a fraternal organization with secret rituals, educational programs, and social activities, but it quickly focused on cooperative activities and then became politically active again. Like the Grange, the alliance negotiated agreements with manufacturers to purchase equipment at reduced costs, and local chapters organized joint-stock stores so members could purchase goods at reduced prices. Cotton and other products were marketed jointly. The alliance soon merged with other regional agrarian groups, like the Agricultural Wheel of Arkansas. In 1892, the alliance, now a na-

tional phenomenon, formed the People's party. The party's supporters, referred to as "Populists," demanded government control of railroads, telegraphs, and the new telephone system; they opposed land ownership by aliens and corporations; and they insisted on a monetary system that was controlled by the government and increased the amount of money in circulation.

Populists joined the Democratic party in endorsing WILLIAM JENNINGS BRYAN as the presidential candidate in 1896. Bryan supported free and unlimited coinage of silver, a popular cause among many agrarians because it would increase the amount of money in circulation. Bryan lost the election to William McKinley, and the People's party soon withered.

The NONPARTISAN LEAGUE emerged in North Dakota in 1915 to demand government control of unfair practices of middlemen in the wheat trade. The NPL captured the North Dakota legislature and governorship and passed significant state legislation, but it failed in its attempt to became a broad-based national party.

The Holiday movement emerged in the Midwest in 1932. The movement demanded government relief programs similar to those proposed by other agrarian organizations. Farmers' Holiday advocates became the most confrontational and militant of agrarian protesters up to that time. Holiday protesters called a national farmers' strike. Supporters dumped milk and shot livestock rather than market them for unfair prices. They created road blocks to prevent others from marketing their produce and disrupted farm foreclosure auctions by bidding five cents per item and intimidating other potential bidders. After the auction, they returned the property to the original owners. These auctions are referred to today as "penny auctions."

The National Farmers Organization spread throughout the West and the Midwest in the 1960s. NFO "holding actions" resembled a farm-holiday strike. To drive market prices up, members tried to reduce commodity supplies. They refused to market their produce and tried to persuade others to withhold their produce from the market too. At times, this led to violent confrontations. Members dumped their milk or shot their hogs in protest.

—*Thomas A. Woods*

SEE ALSO: Booms; Currency and Silver as Western Political Issues; Financial Panics; Land Policy; Populism; Tariff Policy

SUGGESTED READING:

Buck, Solon. *The Agrarian Crusade: A Chronicle of the Farmer in Politics.* New Haven, Conn., 1920.

Goodwyn, Lawrence. *Democratic Promise: The Populist Moment in America.* New York, 1976.

Shover, John L. *Cornbelt Rebellion: The Farmers' Holiday Association.* Urbana, Ill., 1965.

Woods, Thomas A. *Knights of the Plow: Oliver H. Kelley and the Origins of the Grange in Republican Ideology.* Ames, Iowa, 1991.

AGRICULTURE

By the mid-nineteenth century, agriculture in the United States had just about reached the ninety-fifth meridian, and Euro-American farms stretched along a line from Minnesota to Texas. Long before then, others—many of them Hispanic—had taken up farming in small areas of New Mexico and California. Overlanders to Oregon in the early 1840s cleared a few thousand family farms in the Willamette Valley, and by the late 1840s and early 1850s, thousands of Mormons were irrigating farmland in Utah. Some Native Americans, especially members of the Five Civilized Tribes in present-day Oklahoma,

carried on a successful agriculture before the Civil War. For the most part, however, the antebellum American West remained unplowed. But during the war, Congress passed the HOMESTEAD ACT OF 1862, and after Appomattox, the federal government actively promoted Western settlement. By the early twentieth century, nearly every tillable acre in the West had been brought into cultivation.

There were dramatic differences in the geography, CLIMATE, and soils in the American West. The High Plains that stretch from North Dakota to Texas, the desert Southwest, the dry region between the mountain ranges, and the Pacific Coast varied greatly in climate and in the requirements for successful farming. The kind of agricultural development that best suited the different subregions of the West was widely misunderstood by the first settlers who pushed into the area west of Missouri. Initially, many settlers believed they could farm the same way and raise the same crops as farmers did in the more humid Midwest. But this was not the case. The single-most distinguishing feature of the region west of Omaha and Kansas City

Harvesting wheat on the Great Plains. *Courtesy National Cowboy Hall of Fame and Western Heritage Center.*

was the lack of moisture. Annual rainfall in most of the Great Plains was only twelve to sixteen inches, while in much of the region farther west, a mere six to eight inches of rain fell each year. Between the Civil War and World War I, Western farmers gradually developed crop and livestock operations that fit the geography and climate.

In the 1870s and 1880s, a flood of settlers moved into Kansas, Nebraska, and the Dakotas. The first official land rush into the Oklahoma Territory occurred in 1889. Thousands of pioneer farmers took up homesteads of 160 acres under the HOMESTEAD ACT OF 1862 and acquired farms under later land laws. Others purchased land from the RAILROADS, states, and agencies that held large acreages. The Dakotas had only 1,720 farms in 1870, but by 1900, the figure had grown to 97,954. In Kansas, the number of farms increased from 38,202 to 73,098 and, in Nebraska, from 12,301 to 121,525 during the same period.

Elsewhere in the West in the late nineteenth century, the number of farms grew more slowly because farmers had to contend with a different environment. Lack of rainfall in the High Plains and farther west forced farmers to adopt dryland techniques or resort to IRRIGATION. Arizona, southern California, parts of Idaho and Utah, and other subregions in the West received so little rain that farmers had to resort to irrigation. The first settlers in the semiarid and arid parts of the West diverted WATER a short distance from rivers and streams to irrigate a few acres of crops and hay land. Any significant increase in farms in much of the West had to await the construction of large irrigation projects.

Irrigation projects and dryland farming

Groups of farmers and corporations first financed irrigation developments large enough to transport water out of creeks and rivers to the broader tablelands. These efforts generally failed because of the high construction costs and because the projects charged more for the irrigation water than farmers could afford. Many Westerners believed that the federal government should build dams and reservoirs to supply water to farmers at cheaper prices than could be provided by private enterprise. Congress passed the NEWLANDS RECLAMATION ACT OF 1902, which allocated federal funds for the construction of large irrigation projects. The Reclamation Service (later renamed the BUREAU OF RECLAMATION) soon approved projects throughout the West, including those on the Salt River in Arizona, the SNAKE RIVER in Idaho, and the Owens and Salinas rivers in California. The law restricted the amount of land on which water from federal irrigation works could be used to 160 acres per landowner.

The idea was to guarantee water to a large number of family-operated farms. The limitation, however, was generally ignored.

Despite speculative abuses, poor planning, financial difficulties, conflicts over water rights, and other problems, federal RECLAMATION projects did much to enlarge farming opportunities throughout the West. Between 1899 and 1919, the number of irrigated farms in the eleven Far Western states (Arizona, California, Colorado, Idaho, Montana, Nevada, New Mexico, Oregon, Utah, Washington, and Wyoming) rose from 104,328 to 204,042, and the number of irrigated acres rose from 7,263,273 to 17,410,043. Irrigated agriculture became a necessary way of farm life in much of the West. Even ranchers relied on irrigation to grow forage crops for winter livestock feed.

Throughout the West, farms were generally larger than in other parts of the United States. In the Dakotas, Nebraska, Kansas, Oklahoma, and West Texas, the average size farm was not only larger than those found in states farther east, but it also contained more cropland. The average size farm in 1900 was 240 acres in Kansas and 88 acres in Ohio. The average amount of cropland harvested per farm in Kansas in 1900 was 104 acres, compared to only 42 acres in Ohio. Partly because irrigation farming required intensive hand work to control water flows, most irrigated farms had only a small amount of cropland. In 1900, land under cultivation on irrigated farms averaged 52 acres in Idaho, 34 acres in Utah, 26 acres in Arizona, and 88 acres in California. In many cases, the cultivated portion of an irrigated farm was part of a much larger livestock operation. In 1900, the average size farm in Montana was 886 acres, but the average amount of cropland harvested was only 86 acres.

The semiarid, windy, treeless Great Plains of the western Dakotas, Nebraska, Kansas, eastern Montana and Wyoming, eastern New Mexico, and western Texas did not attract many settlers until after 1900. By 1920, however, farmers had settled much of the region and had plowed up range land. The dry climate required farmers outside the irrigated areas of the Great Plains to adopt new farming practices. Tillage that would retain the limited moisture was essential. Agricultural experts advocated using a lister for planting row crops in furrows to reduce wind EROSION. Summer fallowing—leaving part of the land idle each year—and plowing to leave crop stubble on the surface to catch the winter snow were among the methods adopted to preserve moisture and cut wind erosion. Farmers also turned to drought-resistant crops such as some breeds of wheat and maize or kafir corn. But dryland farming techniques had not been perfected sufficiently by the 1920s to save many farmers from failure. There were fewer farmers in Montana in 1925 than in 1920. More successful adjustments came later.

There were some huge farm operations in the West. In the 1870s and 1880s, individuals and corporations bought immense acreages in the Red River valley of North Dakota and Minnesota and began specializing in wheat production. Some operators had more than 5,000 acres. In the Central Valley of California, one wheat ranch covered more than 20,000 acres. Requiring large amounts of capital, these bonanza farms were highly mechanized and used hired labor and professional managers. BONANZA FARMING, an early type of industrialized agriculture, declined in the late 1880s and 1890s, and many of the large farms were sold to family farmers.

While the West had some very large farms and ranches, and many small irrigated farms, the majority of farms in the late nineteenth and early twentieth centuries were family-sized units of 160 to 320 acres. Workers were scarce in much of the West, so farmers had to depend on family members for labor. Moreover, the state of agricultural technology did not permit the average farm family to cultivate much more than about 100 acres, and even less in the irrigated areas. Because most of the farms had a combination of crops and livestock, some acreage was also needed for pasture.

The main crops in the eastern Dakotas, Nebraska, and Kansas were corn, wheat, and oats. Farther west in these states and in Oklahoma and West Texas, wheat was the major grain crop. Another center of wheat production was in California and the Palouse area of eastern Washington, northeastern Oregon, and northwestern Idaho. In the 1870s, German Mennonites settled in the east-central part of Kansas and introduced turkey red winter wheat, which proved to be highly successful. Other new and better varieties were subsequently grown. In Kansas, wheat production rose from 17 million bushels in 1879 to 148 million bushels in 1919. On the Southern Plains, wheat planted in the fall provided cattle pasture during the winter months. By the late 1920s, the Western states produced about 75 percent of the country's wheat crop, and Kansas and North Dakota were the nation's leading wheat producers.

By the 1920s, cotton began to emerge as an important crop. While farmers in Oklahoma and Texas had grown cotton in the late nineteenth century, it was not until early in the twentieth century that the crop spread to the High Plains of West Texas and to Arizona and California. Around Lubbock, Texas, large cotton growers used the latest machinery and irrigated the crop from deep wells. Farmers in Arizona and California relied on deep wells, as well as on established irrigation projects, for water. In 1909, Arizona produced only 59,000 bales of cotton, but by 1939, production had grown to 199,000 bales. In California, the increase was from 46,000 to 435,000 bales in the same period. A decade later, California ranked fourth in production among all cotton states.

Mechanized farming

Western farmers were leaders in mechanizing agricultural production. Bonanza farmers in the 1870s and 1880s used the latest plows, drills, reapers, threshing machines, and steam tractors. When gasoline-powered tractors were introduced in the early twentieth century, Western wheat farmers were among the first to replace horses with mechanical power. In South Dakota, 16 percent of farmers had tractors in 1920; by 1930, the figure had increased to 37 percent. In Kansas, the number rose from 10 to 35 percent, and in California from 10 to 27 percent in the same period. By 1930, 43 percent of North Dakota farmers had tractors, the highest percentage in the nation.

By the 1880s, grain was harvested by first cutting and binding it into sheaves with a reaper pulled by horses. It was then threshed in a threshing machine powered by a steam engine. In the late 1870s, California wheat farmers began experimenting with the combined harvester-thresher, which cut and threshed the grain in a single operation. Some combines were used in the 1880s and later, but it was not until the 1920s that they came into general use in the Great Plains wheat belt, California, and the Palouse region. Early combines were pulled by teams of sixteen to twenty horses, but tractors rapidly replaced horses in the 1920s. Trucks to haul grain also came into widespread use on Western grain farms after World War I.

Cotton farmers on the Southern Plains also mechanized their production by the 1920s. While cotton farmers had used modern plows, planters and cultivators to reduce hand labor, complete mechanization was thwarted by the lack of a successful mechanical picker. In the 1920s, however, farmers in dry western Texas adopted what was known as a "cotton sled." This *V*-shaped machine, pulled along the row to strip off the cotton bolls, saved much hand picking. The cotton harvest was not completely mechanized until the spindle-type picker came into general use in the 1950s.

Specialty crops, fruits, and vegetables

West of the Great Plains where irrigation was generally required, farmers grew a variety of specialty crops. Because hay and forage were important for the many sheep and cattle ranchers, much irrigated acreage was devoted to alfalfa. But Western farmers raised many commercial crops and provided the nation with much of its food supply. By the early twentieth century, sugar beets had become important in Nebraska, Colorado, Utah, and California. Potatoes became a major commercial crop in Colorado, Idaho, and California. Such specialties as pinto beans and chili peppers were grown in increasing quantities in New Mexico.

The Western states were also large fruit producers. By the 1930s, Washington had emerged as the country's premier apple state. Peaches, pears, plums, cherries, apricots, and various kinds of berries also did well in Washington and Oregon.

While most Americans did not view California as a major agricultural state, it had become a leading producer of farm crops by the 1920s and 1930s. Besides wheat and livestock, California farmers raised a variety of products that did well under irrigation in the arid southern part of the state. Vegetables, nuts, and fruits—peaches, pears, grapes, and plums, as well as huge amounts of citrus—were among the major commercial crops. In 1889, California marketed only 1.2 million boxes of oranges, but by 1934, the figure had risen to 47.5 million boxes. Most of the nation's English walnuts, almonds, and hazelnuts were produced in California. Vegetables produced for sale included cauliflower, cantaloupes, lettuce, onions, celery, and tomatoes.

By the 1920s and 1930s, the Western states had become vitally important in the production of fresh fruit and vegetables for the growing urban population. A majority of Americans lived in cities and depended on purchased food. With improved rail and truck transportation, urbanites could be supplied with fresh fruit and vegetables year-round.

Conservation problems

By the early twentieth century, poor agricultural practices had caused serious environmental damage to land in parts of the West. After World War I, farmers plowed up thousands of acres of native grassland in the Great Plains and planted wheat. Much of that land was subject to severe wind erosion. After a period of drought that began in 1930, a large area in southwestern Kansas, southeastern Colorado, northeastern New Mexico, western Texas, and northwestern Oklahoma became the DUST BOWL. Farmers on the northern Great Plains also suffered from extensive wind erosion.

Soil conservation legislation enacted by Congress in 1933 gave farmers advice and financial help to modify their farming practices and protect the soil. Western farmers took advantage of the federal help. By 1940, Kansas had 104 conservation districts, and there were many districts in other Western states. Improved cultivation practices—such as chisel plowing and constructing terraces and dams to prevent water run-off—helped farmers save their soil.

GRAZING lands throughout much of the West also had been overused. In 1934, Congress passed the TAYLOR GRAZING ACT, which gave the secretary of the interior authority to establish grazing districts on 80 million acres of public lands. The secretary could issue permits for grazing, set fees, and regulate the number of livestock allowed on public lands. This was an attempt to improve the range and curb the declining production of grass. Federal policies approved by Congress in the 1930s—and practices by individual farmers—did much to stabilize and conserve the productivity of Western farm and ranch lands.

Ethnic background of Western farmers

Farmers who settled the American West in the late nineteenth and early twentieth centuries represented numerous ethnic groups. Besides Hispanics in the Southwest, tens of thousands of English, Irish, Scandinavians, Germans, Czechs, and others of European ancestry settled the West. By 1920, about one-third of South Dakota's population was of Scandinavian descent. Kansas and Texas drew large numbers of Germans. Oklahoma and Texas had many black farmers, and hundreds of African Americans moved to Kansas from the Southern states in the late 1870s to find land. Native American farmers were most numerous in Oklahoma, and Japanese immigrants became successful truck gardeners in California. Most farmers who settled the West, however, were of European ancestry. Many moved from the East, Midwest, and South, as well as directly from Europe, to that last farming frontier.

By 1940, there were more than 1.5 million farms in seventeen Western states—28 percent of all farms in the United States. Farms in the West produced 46 percent of the value of crops and 44 percent of the value of livestock.

Because much of the region depended heavily on irrigation, the availability of cheap water was a key to successful agriculture. Dryland farmers on the Great Plains had to adopt farming practices that would conserve moisture and grow drought-resistant crops. Farmers gradually adjusted to the semiarid and arid conditions and contributed greatly to the nation's abundant food and fiber supply. Wheat, produced mainly in the West, became one of America's leading exports.
—*Gilbert C. Fite*

SEE ALSO: Cotton Farming; Farming; Federal Government; Fruit and Vegetable Growing; Oklahoma Land Rush; *Report on the Lands of Arid Regions;* Soil Conservation Service; Wheat Farming

SUGGESTED READING:
Ebling, Walter. *The Fruited Plain, The Story of American Agriculture.* Berkeley, Calif., 1979.

Fite, Gilbert C. *The Farmers' Frontier, 1865–1900.* New York, 1966.

Green, Donald E. *Land of the Underground Rain, Irrigation on the Texas High Plains, 1910–1970.* Austin, Tex., 1973.

Haystead, Ladd, and Gilbert C. Fite. *The Agricultural Regions of the United States.* Norman, Okla., 1955.

Hurt, R. Douglas. *The Dust Bowl: An Agricultural and Social History.* Chicago, 1981.

Kraenzel, C. F. *The Great Plains in Transition.* Norman, Okla., 1955.

Lowitt, Richard. *The New Deal and the West.* Bloomington, Ind., 1984.

Malin, James C. *Winter Wheat in the Golden Belt of Kansas.* Lawrence, Kans., 1944.

Shannon, Fred A. *The Farmer's Last Frontier, Agriculture, 1860–1897.* New York, 1945.

AH QUIN

San Diego businessman and labor contractor Ah Quin (1848–1914) received his education in his native Canton from missionaries, who taught him English, the concepts of Christianity, and other subjects. As a young man, he immigrated to the American West Coast and labored for several years as a house servant and cook in San Francisco, Santa Barbara, and Alaska. Employment was not hard to find, as he had a network of relatives in America, could speak English, and had adopted Western manners and dress.

In 1878, Ah Quin visited San Diego and met local businessman George Marston. The two maintained a correspondence, and when the California Southern Railroad began planning a line from San Diego, Marston urged Ah Quin to become a labor contractor for the railroad. He hired hundreds of Chinese laborers, housed them in makeshift camps, and sold them provisions from a store he had opened in San Diego's Chinatown. Construction of the railroad, which extended from National City through desert and solid rock to San Bernardino, was completed in three years, although stretches of the line had to be rebuilt when heavy winter rains in 1884 washed away some thirty miles of lumber and steel.

Ah Quin continued as a labor contractor while he developed interests in ranching, mining, produce farming, and real estate. He became recognized as a spokesman for the Chinese community in San Diego and as the unofficial mayor of the city's Chinatown. When he died after being struck by a motorcycle, he passed on to his twelve children a substantial commercial empire.

—*Patricia Hogan*

SEE ALSO: Chinese Americans

SUGGESTED READING:
Griego, Andrew, ed. "Rebuilding the California Southern Railroad: The Personal Account of a Chinese Labor Contractor, 1884." *Journal of San Diego History* 25 (Fall 1979): 324–337.

AH TOY

San Francisco prostitute and successful business woman Ah Toy (1829–1929) was one of the first Chinese women to immigrate to San Francisco in the early days of the CALIFORNIA GOLD RUSH. The San Francisco she found was overrun with men returning from the mining fields with gold in their pockets, a need for celebration, and, most of all, a desire for female companionship. PROSTITUTION in such a town was big business.

When Ah Toy arrived in San Francisco in 1849 at the age of twenty, she possessed a head for business, uncommon beauty, a wardrobe of jewels and fine clothes, and some command of the English language. Of her life in Hong Kong nothing is known, but she may have been a successful prostitute or madam with a clientele of foreigners. In San Francisco, she became a successful prostitute, commanding an ounce of gold (valued at sixteen dollars) for her services. It was reported that the line of men waiting for her attentions stretched the length of a city block. Within two years, Ah Toy operated her own establishment and traveled to Hong Kong and Canton to recruit women to work in her brothel.

Ah Toy developed her business before prostitution in California became an institution of slavery controlled by Chinese men. She operated as a free agent, and San Francisco court documents record her frequent successes in keeping herself free from domination by her countrymen, such as NORMAN ASSING, who attempted to extort payments from her. She also served a clientele of non-Chinese men, and her customers who were citizens of influence protected her business and employees from San Francisco's efforts to rid its streets of vice.

Ah Toy faded from notice in 1859. The only news of her activities after that year appeared in her obituary in the February 2, 1929, issue of the *San Jose Mercury Herald*. She likely lived in Santa Clara County with her husband and, after his death, with a brother-in-law. She died just months short of the age of one hundred.

—*Kurt Edward Kemper*

SUGGESTED READING:
Hirita, Lucie Cheng. "Chinese Immigrant Women in Nineteenth-Century California." In *Women of America: A History.* Edited by Carol Ruth Berkin and Mary Beth Norton. Boston, 1979.

Yung, Judy. *Chinese Women of America: A Pictorial History.* Seattle and London, 1986.

AH YUP, IN RE

In Re Ah Yup came before the federal Circuit Court for the Northern District of California in 1878. The central question was whether Chinese immigrants could become naturalized citizens of the United States, given the federal statute that limited naturalization to "free white persons" and persons of African nativity or descent. Judge Lorenzo Sawyer held that Chinese could not be naturalized, as they were not "white" within the meaning of the statute. The case had a significant impact on Chinese residents in the United States. It denied them the privileges and rights of citizens. Ironically, however, Chinese born in the United States were American citizens according to a U.S. Supreme Court decision UNITED STATES V. WONG KIM ARK (1898).

—*Lucy E. Salyer*

SEE ALSO: Chinese Americans; Chinese Exclusion; Naturalization Law of 1790

SUGGESTED READING:
In Re Ah Yup, 5 Sawy. 155 (1878)
McClain, Charles J. *In Search of Equality: The Chinese Struggle against Discrimination in Nineteenth-Century America.* Berkeley, Calif., 1994.

AIRCRAFT INDUSTRY

Western aviation began before the Wright brothers made their historic flight along the beaches of Kitty Hawk, North Carolina, in 1903. As early as 1883, a university professor named John Joseph Montgomery was experimenting in Santa Clara with gliders and developed certain designs his heirs would later use to sue the Wright brothers, without success. In 1904, Oakland's Thomas Baldwin built America's first flight-worthy dirigible, the *California Arrow.* After Orville and Wilbur Wright proved that piloted, powered, sustained, and controlled flight was indeed possible, Western entrepreneurs were quick to get into the business of building airplanes. Glenn L. Martin, who later moved to the East, opened an aircraft factory in LOS ANGELES in 1912. Allan and Malcolm Loughead (later changed to Lockheed) built a number of airplanes in Santa Barbara between 1913 and 1921 with the help of John K. Northrop. In Seattle, the lumber king WILLIAM E. BOEING founded the Boeing Airplane Company in 1916. In 1917, in Wichita, Kansas, Clyde Cessna built his first plane. He began regular commercial production two years later and specialized in light private planes. Small-scale, essentially experimental outfits, these businesses formed the nucleus of what in time would become the West's burgeoning aerospace industry, government backed and defense related and an economic key to the prosperity of the entire region.

In 1920, Donald Douglas, a former engineer for Martin, founded Douglas Aircraft Company in Los Angeles for basically the same reason the movie industry had moved to the city: its clear skies, which allowed for both year-round filming and flying. By 1926, Allan Lockheed and John Northrop had relocated, also setting up aircraft-manufacturing shop in Los Angeles. Douglas and Boeing managed to corner most of the market in military planes, with Boeing building fighter planes for the army and Douglas manufacturing observation aircraft. By 1927, the industry had expanded the number of its employees from 2,000 in 1921 to almost 5,500, all working in small factories housing 50 or 60 employees each.

The aircraft industry actually began to make some money in the 1920s. Although the decade's great economic boom in California owed much more to the oil industry and to Hollywood, bull-market investors were quite enthusiastic about the possibilities of aviation, especially after Charles Lindbergh made his celebrated solo flight across the Atlantic in 1927 in a plane—the *Spirit of St. Louis*—built by a San Diego firm owned by T. Claude Ryan. The flying aces of World War I, barnstorming the country after the war, had brought a sense of romance, dash, and daring to aviation that made Lindbergh one of the twentieth century's first major celebrities and helped keep the aircraft industry healthy. Still centered mostly in the East, the industry produced some ambitious merger schemes in the late 1920s before the stock-market crash hit investors hard and the New Deal's Air Mail Act of 1934 forced aviation corporations to split apart their manufacturing and transportation operations. Despite the Great Depression, the industry still managed to employ about 9,000 people in 1933. In the West, only Lockheed had gone into receivership (in 1932) and was quickly bought up by Robert L. Gross's investment syndicate.

Indeed, by the 1930s, Western aircraft companies were fast becoming leaders in aviation. Boeing launched experiments in twin-engine construction in 1932—experiments that ultimately led to the development of all-metal, low-winged monoplanes. Since the federal government had first call on all Boeing products, its competitors turned to Douglas and Lockheed. Douglas came up with the DC series. (Old-timers in aviation still swear the DC-3 was the best plane ever built.) By the close of the decade, Douglas had garnered 95 percent of the country's civil air traffic. Lockheed, too, managed to work its way back into the business by producing a twin-engine transport called the *Electra*. Western aviation was pulling ahead of its competitors in Europe, perhaps even in the East, and new companies began moving to the West Coast. Consolidated Aircraft from Buffalo, New York, relocated to San Diego, hooked up with the Los Angeles–based Vultee Aircraft Corporation, and created the company ultimately known as Convair (and after World War II, General Dynamics). North American, which also located in the West, was a consortium of formerly Eastern companies. And a newcomer sprang up: John Northrop finally went into business for himself. By 1940, almost half the airframe manufacturing capacity of the United States lay along the Pacific Coast, most of it in southern California. Although the industry was small—ranked forty-first among American manufacturing industries—its very concentration made it second only to oil refining in California and gave it a significant impact on the region's economy.

World War II made the New Deal government–private-industry partnerships pioneered by Western entrepreneurs, such as San Francisco banker AMADEO PETER GIANNINI and Oakland construction and ship-building magnate HENRY J. KAISER, standard operating procedure, and perhaps no industry benefited more than aviation. During the war, the top five companies producing military aircraft in terms of airframe weight (60 percent) and five of the top six companies manufacturing aircraft in terms of sheer numbers were Western: Boeing produced the B-17 bomber and B-29 Superfortress; Douglas manufactured most of the U.S. Navy's planes along with troop carriers and military transports such as the DC-3 and the four-engine DC-4; Consolidated-Vultee (Convair) produced the navy's flying boats (the Catalina "PBYs") and a heavy bomber, the B-24 Liberator; North American manufactured the P-51 Mustang fighter plane and the twin-engine B-26 Mitchell bomber; and Lockheed produced two fighter planes, the P-38 Lightning fighter used by the U.S. Army Air Forces and the Hudson bomber favored by the British Royal Air Force. Responding to government fears about concentrated locations, most of the West Coast firms spread their operations inland where they would be safe from enemy attack. Douglas opened plants in Oklahoma City, Tulsa, and Chicago; North American, in Dallas and Kansas City; Convair, in Fort Worth. Boeing expanded

a subsidiary it already owned in Witchita. Only Lockheed, which did expand its main plant in Burbank, California, stood pat on the Pacific. As a result of the wartime expansion, Texas became the fourth Western state, after California, Washington, and Kansas, to be a major player in the industry.

By the middle of the war, Boeing had become Seattle's largest single employer; Los Angeles and San Diego had developed into major industrial centers; and the aircraft industry had hired some 1.3 million people, including 243,000 employees in California, many of them formerly unemployed "Okies" who had first descended on the state during the DUST BOWL days of the Great Depression. But the industry's employees were by no means only men. Urged on by wartime propaganda, women entered the factories en masse—first single women, but by 1943, married women as well. A year later, married women would outnumber the single, and together they would make up 45 percent of the aircraft industry's labor force in Los Angeles, and 47 percent of it in Seattle. By war's end, California had emerged as a major economic power. Los Angeles, the seventh largest manufacturing center in 1939, was second only to Detroit by 1944.

A sharp decline set in following the war, and more than 1 million aircraft workers lost their jobs before the Korean War broke out and employment began to rise again. Between 1949 and 1953, aircraft production accounted for almost 40 percent of the total rise in California's manufacturing employment. By the 1970s, 700,000 people were working in airplane manufacturing, half of them in the West, but the industry itself—fed by federal spending—had branched out to become part of the defense-aerospace complex. The concentration of the aircraft industry in the West put the region in a good position to benefit both from the massive federal investment in defense and aerospace and from industries created by a combination of Cold War fears and a scientific community swelled by wartime research.

During the 1950s, rocket research transformed the aircraft industry, and the West's share of federal spending actually topped World War II levels. In the 1960s, the National Aeronautics and Space Administration spent 50 percent of its funds in California alone. And although California and Washington benefited disproportionately from defense contracts, most Western states did well enough for themselves as the government in general shifted its spending on defense and science from the Northeast to the West and South. Lyndon Johnson, as vice-president of the United States, ensured that Houston got NASA's Spacecraft Center in 1961. Fort Worth's economy continued to be tied to the aircraft industry, centered around military contracts.

By the mid-1950s, Utah employed more people in manufacturing than in agriculture, and defense spending made up more of Utah's total income than it did of any other state in the nation. By the 1960s, Montana had become so dependent on the Defense Department's missile bases and silos that its U.S. senator, Lee Metcalf, described federal spending as the mainstay of the state's economy. Industry in the West had become as addicted to federal spending on defense, "big science," and aerospace as the West's agribusiness had been previously to New Deal–spawned reclamation projects and federally subsidized water.

—Charles Phillips

SEE ALSO: Federal Government

SUGGESTED READING:
Bernard, Richard M., and Bradley H. Rice. *Sun Belt Cities: Politics and Growth since World War II.* Austin, Tex., 1983.
Gluck, Sherna B. *Rosie the Riveter: Women, War, and Social Change.* Boston, 1987.
Gordon, Margaret S. *Employment Expansion and Population Growth: The California Experience.* Berkeley, Calif., 1954.
Grabowicz, Paul. *California, Inc.* New York, 1982.
Hubler, Richard G. *Big Eight.* New York, 1966.
Mansfield, Harold. *Vision: A Saga of the Sky.* New York, 1956.
Morgan, Neil. *Westward Tilt: The American West Today.* New York, 1963.
Nash, Gerald. *World War II and the West: Reshaping the Economy.* Lincoln, Nebr., 1990.
———. *The American West Transformed: Impact of the Second World War.* Bloomington, Ind., 1985.
Rae, John B. *Climb to Greatness: The American Aircraft Industry, 1920–1960.* Cambridge, Mass., 1968.
Simonson, G. R., ed. *The History of the Aircraft Industry.* Cambridge, Mass., 1968.
Wiley, Peter, and Robert Gottlieb. *Empires in the Sun: The Rise of the New American West.* Tucson, Ariz., 1985.

ALAMO

Most famous as the site of the battle fought between Texas soldiers led by JAMES (JIM) BOWIE and WILLIAM BARRETT TRAVIS and the Mexican Army commanded by ANTONIO LÓPEZ DE SANTA ANNA from February 23 to March 6, 1836, the Alamo played an important part in the history of San Antonio for more than a century before the TEXAS REVOLUTION. In the years since the battle, it has been a symbol—both positive and negative—of Texas traditions.

Authorized by the viceroy of Mexico in 1716, the Mission San Antonio de Valero was established in the new city of San Antonio, Texas, by the Franciscan Fray Antonio de Olivares with a company of Indian converts from the Mission San Francisco Solano on the Rio Grande. Named in honor of St. Anthony of Padua and the duke of Valero, viceroy of Mexico, the San Antonio mission was a complex of structures built around a small stone tower and devoted to the agricultural and religious education of the Indians. When the tower collapsed around 1724, the modern site was selected, but a permanent chapel was not erected until about 1744. The stone structure collapsed about 1756, and construction of a second chapel, its floor plan shaped as a cross, was begun. Never completed, it was a part of a four-acre walled complex that included priests' quarters, Indian quarters, a granary, storehouses, and workshops. After epidemics depopulated the San Antonio missions in 1778, the San Antonio de Valero was converted to a parish church in 1793.

Ignored by the church in the early nineteenth century, the structure became barracks for a company of Spanish cavalry, the Segunda Compania Volante de San José y Santiago del Alamo de Parres (Second Flying Company of San José and Santiago of the Alamo of Parras) in the province of Coahuila. The cavalry used the mission from about 1801 to 1812 and gave the structure the name by which it became known to history: the Alamo. Spanish for "cottonwood," the name referred to a landmark cottonwood tree on a ranch near the town of San José y Santiago del Alamo de Parras (today called Viesca) where the cavalry company was organized. The Mexican army occupied the Alamo from 1821 until 1835, when it fell into the hands of rebellious Texans at the outbreak of their war for independence from Mexico.

Mexican General Martin Perfecto Cos used the Alamo as his headquarters before the fall of San Antonio on December 9, 1835, and he had built up the structure as a fortification. In the face of the advance of Santa Anna's army into Texas, a group of about 145 Texans commanded by colonels Travis and Bowie entered the Alamo on February 23, 1836. The thirteen days of siege that followed became the stuff of Texas legend. Despite requests for aid by Travis, only 32 men in a detachment from Goliad, Texas, joined him, breaking into the fort on March 1. Travis had approximately 183 men and at least eighteen pieces of artillery to defend the fort against an estimated 4,000 men. The Alamo's defenders, coming from some eighteen of the United States and several European countries, were, for the most part, relatively new to Texas, although they were joined by a number of native Texans of Hispanic descent.

On the morning of March 6, the Mexican army advanced to end the siege. Thrown back in their first attempt, Santa Anna's men succeeded in entering the fort on their second charge and overwhelmed the defenders. Among the rebels was the former Tennessee Congressman DAVID (DAVEY) CROCKETT. According to some accounts, Crockett and five or six others survived the battle but were executed on Santa Anna's command. Because they were cut off, the defenders of the Alamo did not know that Texas had declared its independence on March 2, 1836. In fact, the flag flown over the Alamo was the Mexican flag with the date "1824" written on it, a date symbolizing the signing of the first constitution of the Mexican Republic after Mexico had won its independence from Spain. It was the Mexican Republic that the Texans claimed to be defending against the tyranny of Santa Anna before declaring their own independence. Nevertheless, the defenders of the Alamo, all of whom were killed, became martyrs to the Texas cause. Santa Anna ordered fifteen noncombatants—women, children, and slaves—released so that they could carry the news of the fate of the Alamo defenders to all Texans in a misguided attempt to strike fear among the rebels. "Remember the Alamo" became a battle cry of the Texas army in its final victory over Santa Anna at San Jacinto on April 21, 1836.

Texas granted the ruined structure to the Roman Catholic church in 1841, but the church did not use the mission. In 1848, after Texas had joined the Union, the Alamo became a supply depot for the U.S. Army. During this period, a scroll was added at the top of the entrance wall while the building was being restored. Gradually, the city grew around the old mission and fort, and developers encroached on the mission grounds. In 1878, after the army relocated to a new supply facility at Fort Sam Houston, the property was purchased by Hugo Grenet, who used the convent as a retail store and the chapel as a warehouse. After Grenet's death in 1882, the convent remained in private hands, and the chapel reverted to the Roman Catholic church, which sold the property to the state of Texas in 1883.

That year, Adina de Zavala, granddaughter of the Mexican-born first vice-president of the Republic of Texas, LORENZO DE ZAVALA, initiated a campaign to raise seventy-five thousand dollars to purchase the convent. After the drive stalled, Clara Driscoll of San Antonio advanced a no-interest loan of twenty-five thousand dollars to hold the convent until the Texas legislature could appropriate the remaining funds, which it did in 1905. The legislature turned the administration and operation of the Alamo complex over to the Daughters of the Republic of Texas, who continue to maintain it. In 1911, after a controversy was settled between Driscoll, who wanted to tear down the convent, and de Zavala, who wanted to save both convent and chapel, the Alamo—including both structures—became a museum and "The Shrine of Texas Liberty."

The Alamo is an icon in the history of Texas and the American West, one that continues to stir strong emotions: for many, it is the cornerstone of Texas's fight for independence and statehood, key to the identity of modern Anglo Texas; for others, it is a symbol of imperial expansion and disestablishment. Although the Alamo remains a point of tension between Mexican American and Anglo populations in San Antonio and Texas, it is also the most visited tourist attraction in the state.

—*Patrick H. Butler, III, and Irene Quintanilla*

SUGGESTED READING:
Brear, Holly Beachley. *Inherit the Alamo: Myth and Ritual at an American Shrine.* Austin, Tex., 1995.
Castaneda, Carlos E., trans. and ed. *The Mexican Side of the Texan Revolution.* 2d ed. Austin, Tex., 1970.
Kingston, Mike, and Mary G. Crawford, eds. *The 1992-93 Texas Almanac.* Dallas, Tex., 1991.
Lord, Walter. *A Time to Stand.* New York, 1961.
Tinkle, Lon. *The Alamo: 13 Days to Glory.* New York, 1958.

ALASKA

Often called the "Last Frontier," Alaska is geographically the largest state in the United States and the least populous. The land that is now Alaska was purchased by the United States from Russia in 1867. The territory became a state in 1959. Situated at the extreme northwestern edge of North America, it is a mountainous land cut by immense rivers. It is bordered on the north by the Arctic Ocean, separated from Siberian Russia on the west by the Bering Sea, and abuts the Gulf of Alaska on the south. Its area, 586,000 square miles, is one-fifth the total land area of the United States. It is nearly eight hundred miles across mainland Alaska from north to south. To the west, the long narrow Alaska Peninsula and Aleutian Islands chain are one thousand miles long. To the southeast, a four-hundred-mile-long strip of islands and adjoining coastal shelf make up the heavily forested Alaska panhandle. Anchorage, Alaska's principal city with one-half the state's five hundred thousand people, lies in the center of the southern coast of mainland Alaska; JUNEAU, the capital, is situated in the panhandle. Across this large land are several different ecological regions, from the rain forest of the panhandle and the sub-arctic boreal forest and huge mountains of the southern and interior mainland to the barren tundra of the Arctic Slope.

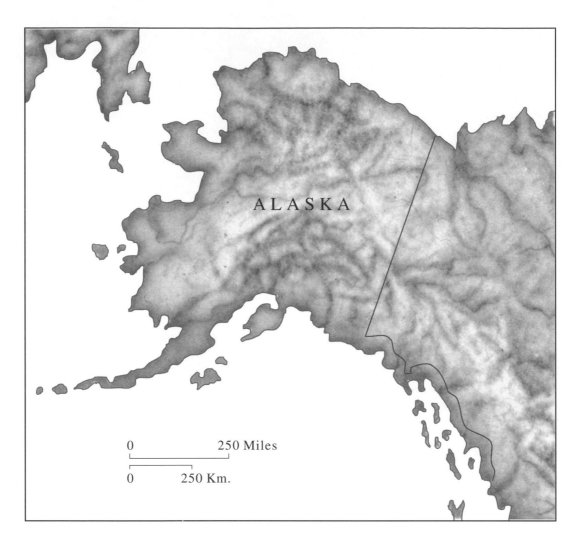

There are several climate zones in Alaska: maritime along the southern coast and in the southeastern panhandle, continental throughout the interior, arctic along the northern coast. Because all of Alaska is in higher latitudes than the continental states, the winter is longer, and the summer shorter. Normal winter temperature in Barrow on the northern coast is -14° F; normal temperature during the intense, three-month summer is 38° F. In Anchorage on the southern mainland coast, where winter lasts from Halloween until Easter, the normal winter temperature is 13° F, and winter snowfall accumulation is normally about four feet; normal temperature in summer is 60° F. The panhandle receives more precipitation than any other area in the United States, annually more than 170 inches in Ketchikan. Above the Arctic Circle, the sun does not set for six weeks in summer and does not rise above the horizon for six weeks in winter. In Anchorage on December 21, there are about five hours of daylight; on June 21, there are nineteen hours of full daylight, with a brightening twilight from 2:00 A.M. to 5:00 A.M. Alaska has more coastline, twenty thousand miles, than all of the continental United States combined. North America's tallest mountain, 20,300-foot-high Mount McKinley, surmounts the Alaska Range, the western- and northernmost spur of the ROCKY MOUNTAINS. The range divides the interior plain of the twenty-three-hundred-mile-long YUKON RIVER from the south-central coast.

Vast in size, Alaska is among the least populated states but includes a rich diversity of people. There are about eighty thousand natives (16 percent of the population)—Eskimo, Aleut, and Athapascan and Pacific Northwest Coast Indians. Most natives live in more than two hundred remote villages. Most nonnative Alaskans live in cities and towns; a majority is Caucasian, with 4 percent African American and 4 percent Asian—principally Japanese, Filipino, and Korean.

Most of the towns are small, but Anchorage is a fully modern city with high-rise office towers, trendy shops and restaurants, and an ocean port. There are few roads in the state, however, and many places are isolated and accessible only by airplane. More than one hundred million acres of the state (28 percent of the total land area) is reserved as national forests, parks, wildlife refuges, and wilderness areas.

Natural resources

Alaska's natural resources have always been the region's link with the rest of the world. The Russians, who first colonized the region, hunted sea otter and other marine mammals for their furs and walrus for their ivory tusks. In the mid-nineteenth century, Americans developed whale fisheries on the Bering Sea and Arctic Coast. By the 1890s, the canned-salmon industry had become a multimillion dollar business and remained so into the 1990s. GOLD MINING began in 1880, achieved spectacular proportions briefly at the time of the KLONDIKE GOLD RUSH in 1898, and continued as a minor industry in the late twentieth century. Copper extraction contributed significantly to investment and development before and after World War I. Pulp timber became important after World War II. The discovery of North America's largest oil field (22 billion barrels) at Prudhoe Bay in 1968 made oil production the most significant economic factor in Alaska's history. In the 1990s, 85 percent of general fund revenue in the state of Alaska was derived from taxation on petroleum development. There is no state income tax; the dividends from a permanent state investment fund, derived from taxation on petroleum production, are distributed equally to all state residents annually (more than $900 per person in 1992 to 1994).

Resource extraction has dictated a boom-and-bust cycle of population increase and stagnation and has kept the region dependent on outside investment. The population has been sparse and somewhat transient, and the costs of developing economic self-sufficiency have proved prohibitive. As a consequence, government support has always played a significant role in Alaska's economic development, both before and after the American purchase.

The Russian period

The first sustained European contact with Alaska was by the Russians in the first half of the eighteenth century. The total aboriginal population at the time may have been as high as two hundred thousand, although estimates are more speculation than science. The Russians, highly dependent on the native population for labor and for the technology of hunting sea mammals, settled only along the coast and did not en-

The first white settlers in Alaska sought the sea-otter pelts hunted by native Aleuts in their kayaks. *Courtesy Special Collections Division, University of Washington Libraries.*

courage permanent colonization. Nonetheless, the effect of diseases, for which the natives did not have natural immunities, coupled with brutalization of the Aleuts by the fur trappers, was devastating, reducing the total native population by perhaps 90 percent, even though the number of Russians in the territory did not exceed 850 at any one time.

The Aleuts, ethnically, culturally, and linguistically distinct inhabitants of the Aleutian Islands, were the first to be affected by Russian contact, and the effect upon them was more pervasive than with Alaska's other natives. Aleut culture was based on fishing and hunting sea-going fur bearers. Their skill with the one- or two-man *baidarka* (called "kayak" by the Eskimos) astonished the Europeans, who also admired the detachable harpoons and *atlatls* used by the hunters.

Individual Russian entrepreneurs were first to exploit the fur resources of the Aleutian Islands. In 1799, however, a government-sponsored monopoly, the RUSSIAN-AMERICAN COMPANY, was created to exploit all discovered resources. The company established a post, Sitka, in the southeastern panhandle region in 1800 but could not subdue the resident Tlingit Indian population.

Sustained white contact with Eskimos began in the 1840s with the development of the WHALING industry. Well adapted to the severe Arctic environment, Eskimos used fur-covered driftwood frames over shallow house pits as their principal habitation and hunted seals and caribou in winter and a variety of fish and ground mammals in summer.

In the southeast, the Pacific Coast Indians managed to remain more independent after European

"Civilization" comes to Alaska. In 1891, the Reverend S. H. King of the Second Presbyterian Church of Juneau stands with some of his worshipers in front of a new church, which until recently had been a miner's cabin. *Courtesy Special Collections Division, University of Washington Libraries.*

contact. English and American maritime fur traders had begun to frequent the coast in 1785, and the Tlingits proved adept at forcing the Europeans to trade principally on the Indians' terms. The highly developed Tlingit culture revolved around the effective use of their abundant resources—salmon, sea and land mammals, and cedar forests. Organized into extended matrilineal clans, the Tlingits' principal habitation was a large cedar longhouse decorated with carved houseposts and freestanding carved and painted totem poles. Daily life revolved around the potlatch, a funerary ritual in which hereditary clan leaders distributed the clan's accumulated wealth in payment for ritual services. A ceremony that proclaimed and maintained social prestige for the Tlingits, potlatching was suppressed by Protestant missionaries and the American government following America's purchase of Alaska.

The interior Athapascan Indians were the last to be affected by European contact, generally after the American purchase. In the 1870s, American and expatriate French-Canadian fur trappers began to penetrate the extended interior river valleys of the Yukon and its tributaries. Because the resources of the interior were more scarce, Athapascans gravitated to the trading posts and villages that grew up along the riverways. The rapid expansion of the nonnative popula-

tion during the gold-rush era strained the resource base considerably and increased native dependence.

Territorial period

Unwilling to invest the resources needed to develop the region's potential, the Russians determined after 1860 to sell Alaska. America's expansionist-minded secretary of state, William Henry Seward, quickly came to terms with the Russian ambassador to the United States and sent the purchase treaty to the Senate in 1867. Although the acquisition seemed foolish to the uninformed and generated such taunts as "Seward's Folly," editorial opinion overwhelmingly supported the Senate's approval of the treaty. Seward's motivation, to use Alaska to support America's eventual Pacific expansion and to hem in British settlement in western Canada, was consistent with American development. But major concerns arose: Alaska was seen as an "icebox," and it shared no borders with the continental United States.

The formal transfer ceremony was held in Sitka on October 18, 1867, now celebrated annually in the state as Alaska Day. Lack of sufficient detailed information about the territory, the absence of an economic base, and uncertainty regarding the character of the native population led Congress to withhold civil governance for the first seventeen years of American possession. In 1880, however, gold was discovered at Juneau and Douglas Island. The discovery led to the establishment of the largest gold stamp mill at the time and to the founding of missions and day schools in native villages across Alaska. These developments encouraged Congress to appoint a governor and judge and provide for rudimentary government in 1884.

Fourteen years later, the Klondike gold rush brought Alaska to national attention and spurred Congress to further action—establishing a telegraph connection to the continental states, passing a homestead act, and providing more civil government. Throughout the region, investors investigated mining prospects. To facilitate development, the government built and operated a railroad, connecting the interior of Alaska to the coast, and provided a territorial legislature in 1912. From 1900 to 1940, the population was between fifty thousand and sixty thousand, evenly divided between natives and nonnatives. Sparse population and prohibitive transportation and labor costs inhibited economic self-sufficiency and kept the territory dependent on extractive industries, most particularly salmon canning and COPPER MINING, which were controlled by absentee investors. At the same time, the government resisted further steps toward self-government on the grounds that the nonnative population was not large enough and was partially transient and that the region's natural resources needed to be preserved. The residents, who prided themselves on their rugged individualism, flexibility, and spirit of adventure, resented both absentee management and government regulation. However, their continuing requests for increased self-government went unheeded.

The collapse of prices during the Great Depression led to the suspension of copper mining in the territory; some gold-mining operations were able to continue due to the government's artificial price support. Civilian Conservation Corps employment, social-security payments, and government construction grants and loans helped the towns through the worst years. A rural rehabilitation agricultural colony in the Matanuska Valley east of Anchorage attracted considerable attention from the national press but did little to develop the territory's agricultural potential or increase population.

Unalaska Island in the Aleutians in 1902. No longer a fur-trading port, the island's Dutch Harbor served as a refueling stop for maritime traffic between Nome and San Francisco. *Courtesy Special Collections Division, University of Washington Libraries.*

Propelling Alaska into the modern world, World War II and its aftermath regenerated the economy, added government infrastructure, revolutionized transportation and communication networks, and brought increased nonnative population. Anticipating war in the Pacific, the U.S. Army began remilitarization in 1940. Not long after the attack on Pearl Harbor, the Japanese invaded and captured several western Aleutian Islands, the first foreign occupation of American soil since 1814. A combined American-Canadian force recaptured the islands in the costly Battle of Attu in May 1943.

Statehood

With new settlement after 1945, residents undertook a campaign for statehood. In 1957, oil discoveries in and adjacent to Cook Inlet south of Anchorage provided a tangible means to finance self-government and drew still more population. Alaska officially became the forty-ninth state on January 3, 1959. The enabling bill conveyed to the new state title to more than one hundred million acres of land (28 percent of the total land area), an area as big as California.

During Alaska's first year as a state, the Tlingit and Haida Indians won a land-claim suit before the U.S. Court of Claims on the basis of their ownership of nearly all of southeastern Alaska. The lawsuit emboldened other native groups to protest on the grounds that much of the land selected to be part of the state's reserves belonged to them. Confusion over land ownership led the secretary of the interior in 1965 to halt all transfers of land to the new state while native claims were investigated. Then, in 1968, America's largest oil field was discovered at Prudhoe Bay. Analysts determined that the oil would need to be transported by means of an overland pipeline crossing hundreds of miles of disputed land.

Lobbied vigorously by the oil industry, Congress passed a native claims settlement act in 1971. It confirmed native title to forty-four million acres (12 percent of the total land) and paid $962.5 million in compensation for the remainder of the natives' claims. The money was used to capitalize economic-development corporations under native control—in thirteen regions and more than one hundred villages. The act also provided for placing one hundred million acres of environmentally sensitive lands under federal protection. Pipeline construction began in 1974 after Congress resolved environmental legal challenges by suspending the Environmental Protection Act.

Many Alaskans felt betrayed by the grant of native land and the commitment to reserve environmentally sensitive lands, both of which took precedence over state selections. The alteration in timing was a result of major changes in national culture regarding the rights of minorities and the importance of the environment. Alaskans had expected statehood to bring less involvement of the federal government in regional affairs; the native settlement act and subsequent reservation of conservation lands in 1980 instead brought greater federal involvement. State leaders were not mollified by the fact that most lands with potential for economic development were included in the state's land selections. Although the rhetoric of ongoing protest is focused on the "lock-up" of Alaska lands, the source of resentment is the continuing large role of the FEDERAL GOVERNMENT in managing Alaska's affairs. The discontent is partially a manifestation of the individualist character of Alaskan culture. The "frontier" mentality holds that, left to themselves, the rugged individuals adventuresome enough to settle in an area so remote and with such a harsh climate have the right to control their own destinies.

While the transient rate is somewhat higher than in other regions, most Alaskans are family-centered, permanent residents living thoroughly modern, urban lives. They have a fierce pride in their state's potential and in their own courage and tenacity in coping with a difficult but spectacularly beautiful and inspiring environment. In the national perception, however, Alaska is no longer the "last frontier," but the "last wilderness."

—*Stephen Haycox*

SEE ALSO: Fishing Industry; Native American Peoples: Peoples of Alaska; Oil and Gas Industry

SUGGESTED READING:
Gruening, Ernest. *The State of Alaska*. New York, 1954.
Hedin, Robert, and Gary Holthaus, eds. *Alaska: Reflections on Land and Spirit*. Tucson, Ariz., 1989.
Kizzia, Tom. *In the Wake of the Unseen Object: Native Cultures of Alaska*. New York, 1991.
McGinniss, Joe. *Going to Extremes*. Boston, 1982.
McPhee, John. *Coming into the Country*. New York, 1977.
Webb, Melody. *The Last Frontier*. Albuquerque, N. Mex., 1985.

ALASKA GOLD RUSH

The history of Alaska, like that of many Western states, has been a chronicle of the sustained commercial exploitation of its natural resources by nonnatives. While furs, salmon, timber, and oil attracted many to this great land, only gold led to the large-scale, ephemeral migrations of poorly prepared, ill-informed, and

Almost overnight the discovery of gold at Cape Nome in 1898 created the city of Nome. In a photograph taken in 1900, supplies just delivered by ship share Nome's beaches with gold-seekers housed in tents. *Courtesy University of Alaska, Fairbanks, Edward Mulligan Collection.*

In 1870, gold was discovered at Sumdum Bay in southeastern Alaska, and in 1872, the Stewart mine was opened in Sitka. While Fred Harris and JOE JUNEAU made the first significant gold strike in 1880 in the Silverbow Basin on Lynn Canal, most gold at Juneau was found in low-grade quartz ore on Douglas Island. Since exploiting the find required substantial resources and the technology of hard-rock mining with deep shafts and stamp mills, no rush of gold-seekers to this site occurred. Yet, before flooding closed its shafts, more than $60 million in gold ore had been extracted from the mine and processed in the world's largest stamp mill.

In the 1870s and 1880s, prospectors began crossing the Coastal Range to search for gold in the vast, unmapped YUKON RIVER basin. In 1875 and 1876, around seventy-five thousand dollars worth of gold was found on the sandbars of the Stewart River. In 1876, Howard Franklin discovered rich placer depos-

underfunded fortune-seekers. The gold rush to Alaska developed over a number of years and at a number of diverse and distant sites. Before the resources were depleted and the energy of the stampedes dissipated, the rush led miners to the Stewart River, Forty Mile, Circle, Nome, Valdez, Dawson, and Fairbanks areas. Gold camps and communities were formed almost overnight, and many areas of Alaska and the Yukon enjoyed, briefly, larger populations than they have ever known. Historically and romantically, this was the world's final global stampede for gold and the last great rush for natural resources by individuals rather than corporations in North America. The international nature of the Alaskan and Klondike gold rushes may be documented by the backgrounds of the individuals who made the most important discoveries. Gold at Juneau was found by an Irishman, German, and Frenchman. Gold on the beach at Nome was discovered initially by Scandinavians. Fairbank's deposits were located by an Italian, and news of this rich find was spread by a Japanese miner. Major strikes along the Klondike in Canada were made by Americans. Nevertheless, for the thousands who dashed north over glaciers, through mosquito-infested bogs and stunted forests, and across roaring rivers to a remote land known only in the broadest details, success came sparingly to just a lucky few.

When the United States purchased Alaska in 1867, sustained attempts to find gold began almost at once.

A Nome prospector at his shanty. *Courtesy Bancroft Library.*

its on a tributary of the Forty Mile River on lands that were on both sides of the American and Canadian border. Although small by later standards, the strike initiated the first stampede to the Yukon. The Pelly, Teslin, Big Salmon, Sixty Mile, Stewart, Forty Mile, Indian, Birch Creek, Rampart, and Klondike tributaries of the majestic Yukon River began to be prospected. By 1896, eight hundred thousand dollars worth of gold had been taken from panning and placer claims along the tributaries on the American side of Forty Mile River. Discoveries in the area led to an increase in the population, and Circle became the first significant mining community along the Yukon.

As fall approached in 1896, gold in quantities never before discovered in the Yukon region was found along the Klondike River. George Washington Carmack filed the first claim on August 17, 1896. Word of his find spread rapidly throughout the Yukon, and by the winter of 1896 to 1897, gold-seekers from throughout the nation made plans to join the stampede to the Klondike to find wealth beyond one's imagination. Seattle became the major port of departure to the Klondike, and the city's Chamber of Commerce aggressively promoted the new gold field through advertisements in hundreds of state newspapers and national publications. Numerous ill-informed guidebooks were published. More than sixty thousand gold-seekers made their way to the Klondike in 1896 and 1897. Skagway and Dyea became the initial destinations for most of those seeking to enter the Yukon through either the Chilkoot Pass or the "Dead Horse Trail" of the White Pass. Having dragged, carried, or pulled their thousand-pound loads over the treacherous passes, the stampeders were still almost six-hundred miles from where claims were being staked.

The discovery of gold by John Brynesen, Erik Lindbloom, and Jafet Lindenberg in the fall of 1898 on Anvil Creek at Cape Nome ignited the largest gold rush in Alaskan history and sparked the almost overnight creation of the city of Nome near the beaches of the Bering Sea. While important gold strikes would be made at other locations in Alaska and the Yukon region, the discoveries along the Klondike and at Nome encouraged the greatest migrations to the north.

—*Phillip Drennon Thomas*

SEE ALSO: Gold Mining; Klondike Gold Rush

SUGGESTED READING:
Hunt, William R. *North of 53°, The Wild Days of the Alaska-Yukon Mining Frontier.* New York, 1974.
Webb, Melody. *The Last Frontier.* Albuquerque, N. Mex., 1985.
Wharton, David. *The Alaska Gold Rush.* Bloomington, Ind., 1972.

ALASKAN EXPLORATION

The first humans to explore ALASKA were Asians who crossed the land bridge in what is now the Bering Sea approximately twenty thousand years ago. These Asians then spread throughout North and South America. They eventually became the Native Americans whom maritime explorers found in the New World during the great age of European discovery from the fifteenth century to the middle of the sixteenth. Alaska was not reached by any of these explorers and remained a blank on world maps.

Maritime exploration

In 1732, Russian navigators anchored off the tip of Seward Peninsula but did not go ashore or report their findings promptly. The expedition that settled the question of Alaska's general location was led by VITUS BERING, a Dane in the service of Peter the Great and Empress Catherine. For years, historians thought Peter was interested mainly in the pursuit of geographical knowledge, but he had geopolitical and economic goals in mind.

Bering, with Alexei Chirikov in another ship, sailed east in 1741 from Kamchatka, Siberia. Chirikov first saw land near Sitka, where two of his longboats were sent ashore and disappeared. The Russians departed without further investigation. Bering's first landfall was Mount St. Elias. A party of Russians went ashore on Kayak Island in the Gulf of Alaska for a few hours. On the way back, both captains sighted some of the Aleutian Islands. Bering died on an island off Kamchatka Peninsula, but Chirikov returned safely. The voyages encouraged Russian maritime fur hunters to trade throughout the Aleutians and established Russia's claim to Alaska, but the Great Northern Expedition did not set foot on the mainland or return with more than sketchy information about Alaska's location. It remained for an Englishman to outline Alaska's profile substantially as we know it today.

Captain JAMES COOK had explored the South Pacific to polar ice, charted New Zealand, and discovered for Europe the Hawaiian Islands before he mapped the Alaskan coast in 1778. That year, he cruised from Sitka to Prince William Sound and Cook Inlet, along the Alaska Peninsula and the Aleutian Islands, some of which had been put on the map by Russian traders. He then sailed through the Bering Strait to the Arctic. Cook hoped to continue his northern explorations in 1779, but he was killed by Hawaiians during the winter.

When the Cook expedition reached Canton, China, on the way home to England, the crew sold northern sea-otter pelts for fabulous sums. Sea-otter fur acquired by Russians in Alaska had been traded only at designated towns on the Chinese-Siberian border. After 1779, especially following the publication of Cook's journals and maps, the Canton trade opened the Pacific Ocean and shores to all maritime commerce, including seal hunting and WHALING, and altered forever the history of the Pacific Basin and its natural environments. Navigators trained aboard Cook's vessels returned to carry on his work. The most important was George Vancouver, who charted the Alaskan coast from Cook Inlet southward from 1793 to 1794.

Cook's explorations stimulated activity by other nations competing for the area. In 1779, Ignacio de Arteaga y Bazán and Juan Francisco de la Bodega y Quadra sailed in two frigates to 60° latitude and claimed Hinchinbrook Island for Spain. Two more ships, one under Estaban José Martínez, went as far as Unalaska Island. Salvador Fidalgo explored Prince William Sound and Cook Inlet in 1790 to reaffirm Spain's claim; there were already two Russian trading posts on the inlet. The Nootka Sound agreements between Spain and England ended Spanish interest in the region in 1794.

The northern probes by Spain and Cook's work encouraged the Russians to resume their voyages of discovery. Joseph Billings, who had been with Cook, and Gavriil Sarychef charted the Aleutian Islands from 1790 to 1792. From 1816 to 1817, Otto von Kotzebue explored Alaska's northwestern coast, a task continued by M. N. Vasil'ev and G. S. Shishmarev from 1819 to 1822. The first two expeditions carried talented scientists whose studies of the biology, ethnology, and geology greatly enhanced the value of the voyages. During the period of coastal exploration, the Russians made almost no attempt to explore the interior systematically, and when inland investigations were undertaken, the results were not always distributed to the contemporary world of science.

Inland exploration

From 1818 to 1819, Petr Korsakovskiy examined southwestern Alaska in the vicinity of Bristol Bay and the Nushagak and Mulchatna rivers. From 1829 to 1830, Ivan Vasilev expanded Korsakovskiy's work to the Kuskokwim River. From 1833 to 1834, Andrei Glazunov explored portions of the Anvik, Yukon, and Stony rivers from the new Russian post of St. Michael. By far the most extensive and scientifically valuable exploration of the region was made by L. A. Zagoskin in the early 1840s.

While the Russians examined the lower YUKON RIVER, the British entered Alaska by way of the upper Yukon under the flag of the HUDSON'S BAY COMPANY. John Bell crossed over from the Peel River to the Porcupine, which he descended in 1842 to the future site

of Fort Yukon, established in 1847 well within Alaska's boundary. ROBERT CAMPBELL, who had explored the Yukon in Canada, reached the fort in 1850.

Systematic exploration of the whole Yukon basin in Alaska was left to an international party sent to mark the trail for an intercontinental telegraph line from the United States through Canada, Alaska, and Siberia to Europe. Robert Ketchum, an American, Michael Lebarge, a French Canadian, and Ivan Lukin, a Russian Creole (who had made the trip secretly once before) left Nulato in May 1866, reached Fort Yukon, and returned. The following summer, Frederick Whymper, an English artist, William Healey Dall, a Yankee scientist, and Kurilla, a native hunter, also made the round trip. Western Union personnel mapped parts of the Seward Peninsula.

When the telegraph was abandoned after the successful completion of the Atlantic Cable, Dall stayed in the country. After the United States bought Alaska from Russia in 1867, Dall continued to make important contributions to knowledge of Alaska as a hydrographic explorer for the United States Coast Survey, as a geologist and paleontologist for the UNITED STATES GEOLOGICAL SURVEY, as an anthropologist for the Bureau of Ethnology, and as an all-around Alaska expert with the Smithsonian Institution.

Edward W. Nelson, an Army Signal Corps weather observer, explored the lower Yukon and Kuskokwim from 1877 to 1881, but it was not until the mid-1880s that important new investigations of the interior were begun. In 1884, George Stoney of the U.S. Navy and John C. Cantwell of the U.S. Revenue Marines (Coast Guard) mounted separate efforts to explore the Kobuk River area in northwestern Alaska. Cantwell beat Stoney into the field, and in 1885, S. B. McLenegan of Cantwell's party completed the pioneer reconnaissance of the Noatak River. Stoney's plans for 1885 to 1886 were more elaborate. He established a winter camp well up the Kobuk and dispatched explorers in several directions. One, W. L. Howard, traced the Colville River to its mouth on the Arctic Ocean.

The most remarkable journey of original geographical discovery by Americans since the LEWIS AND CLARK EXPEDITION was completed by HENRY T. ALLEN in 1885 for the army. With a small party, he ascended the Copper River, took a side trip up the Chitina, crossed over the Alaska Range to the upper Tanana River, and descended it to the Yukon. He then went overland to the headwaters of the Koyukuk River and followed it down to the lower Yukon. In one summer, he investigated and mapped fifteen hundred miles of wilderness.

Other, more limited exploratory work sponsored by government agencies or private parties filled in a few gaps until the Klondike-Alaska gold rushes at the end of the century led to extensive efforts by the army and the Geological Survey. Edwin Glenn of the army was in charge from Cook Inlet north, and William Abercrombie from Prince Edward Sound. Both officers were accompanied by Geological Survey personnel who did most of the important work: W. C. Mendenall (Kenai Peninsula and Matanuska River) with Glenn, and Oscar Rohn (Wrangell Mountains) with Abercrombie. Lieutenant Joseph Herron explored the upper Kuskokwim and got lost; he was rescued by natives. Elsewhere, small Geological Survey parties began systematically to study and fill large blanks on the map. A. H. Brooks and W. J. Peters explored the White River; George Eldridge and Robert Muldrow, the Broad Pass; J. S. Spurr and W. S. Post, the Yentna and lower Kuskokwim river basins; Frank Schrader and T. G. Gerdine, the Chandalar River. By 1903, most of the problems of gross geography had been illuminated, although microgeographical discoveries were made well into the twentieth century.

—*Morgan Sherwood*

SUGGESTED READING:
Brooks, Alfred Hulse. *Blazing Alaska's Trails.* Fairbanks, Alaska, 1953.
Fisher, Raymond H. *Bering's Voyages.* Seattle, Wash., 1977.
Shalkop, Antoinette, ed. *Exploration in Alaska.* Anchorage, Alaska, 1980.
Sherwood, Morgan. *Exploration of Alaska, 1865–1900.* New Haven, Conn., 1965. Reprint. Fairbanks, Alaska, 1992.

ALASKAN HUSKIES

Strong, handsome, wolflike dogs, Alaskan huskies have long been associated with the Arctic and Eskimos and with dog-sled racing. There is not, in fact, a breed called "Alaskan husky," a late nineteenth-century slang word for Eskimo. The traditional Alaskan work and sled dog may be one of three recognized breeds: Alaskan malemute, Siberian husky, and Samoyed. All are hardy, thick-coated, powerful animals well suited to harness work. They are gentle and affectionate, fifty to sixty pounds in weight, and have a remarkable ability to withstand cold. Many mixtures of the three varieties are bred today specifically for dog-sled racing. The dogs love to run and seem to thrive on the training regimen and the challenge of sprint and endurance races.

Sled parts recovered in northwestern Alaska suggest that Eskimos have used dogs to pull sleds for about fifteen hundred years. Modern harnessing methods, however, are not older than three hundred years. After 1900, nonnative Alaskans used dog sleds to deliver mail in winter to isolated communities in the interior.

Alaskan dog-sled racing began in Nome after the turn of the century and grew into a major competitive sport before fading in the 1930s. In recent decades, the sport has once again become popular. The annual one-thousand-mile Iditarod dog-sled race across Alaska has brought huskies to a national audience since 1973.

—*Stephen Haycox*

SUGGESTED READING:
Alaska Geographic Society. *Dogs of the North.* No. 14. Anchorage, Alaska, 1987.
Cellura, Dominique. *Travelers of the Cold: Sled Dogs of the Far North.* Anchorage, Alaska, 1990.
Coppinger, Lorna. *The World of Sled Dogs.* New York, 1977.

ALBRIGHT, HORACE MARDEN

Horace Marden Albright (1890–1987), a leading conservationist of the mid-twentieth century, participated in the creation of the NATIONAL PARK SERVICE in 1916, was superintendent of YELLOWSTONE NATIONAL PARK from 1919 to 1929, and was director of the National Park Service from 1929 to 1933. He then turned to the world of business and became an executive of the American Potash Company.

In 1913, when Albright was twenty-three years old, he joined the staff of the Department of the Interior, then headed by FRANKLIN KNIGHT LANE. In 1915, he was assigned to help STEPHEN TYNG MATHER, a wealthy conservationist brought to the department by Lane to promote the passage of a law creating the National Park Service. After Congress created the service in 1916, Albright became assistant director, and when Mather became ill, Albright was named acting director.

In 1919, he was appointed superintendent of Yellowstone National Park. For ten years, he encouraged TOURISM, defended the park from criticism by nearby residents, and established high standards of management. He assumed leadership in the struggle to establish the GRAND TETON NATIONAL PARK. Strong opposition from ranchers and landowners resulted in the exclusion of Jackson Hole, the natural foreground for observing the mountains, from the park created in 1929. Albright then persuaded John D. Rockefeller to purchase a large tract of land in Jackson Hole for donation to the federal government. In 1949, long after Albright had left the National Park Service, Rockefeller donated the land to the park, and in 1950, an expanded Grand Teton National Park became a reality.

During his four years as director of the National Park Service, Albright was the leading strategist in backroom power struggles over the purchase of huge tracts

of land. He was influential in the creation of the Great Smoky Mountains National Park and Carlsbad Caverns and worked to secure the Grand Teton National Park. After leaving the park service, he remained active in conservation and served on boards of the Grand Teton Lodge Company, Save-the-Redwoods League, Colonial Williamsburg Foundation, and other groups.
—*Richard A. Bartlett*

SUGGESTED READING:
Albright, Horace M., and Robert Cahn. *The Birth of the National Park Service: The Founding Years, 1913–1933.* Salt Lake City, 1985.
Swain, Donald C. *Wilderness Defender: Horace M. Albright and Conservation.* Chicago, 1970.

ALBUQUERQUE, NEW MEXICO

Albuquerque, New Mexico, began as a collection of early seventeenth-century Spanish ranchos (cattle and sheep ranches) and *estancias* (farms and orchards) along the banks of the Rio Grande. Neighboring Pueblo Indians were required to render service under the *encomienda* system, a form of slavery and indenture that was a New World version of the European feudal system. This abuse, coupled with religious intolerance and epidemics of diseases introduced by Europeans, led to the PUEBLO REVOLT of 1680. Colonists left the area and fled south to the vicinity of present-day El Paso, Texas.

After the Spanish reconquest in 1692 and 1693, colonists returned to the Albuquerque area attracted by its rich farmland and pasturage and its prominent location on the Camino Real—the Royal Road from Mexico City to Santa Fe. Spanish officials abolished the *encomienda* system, and Pueblo Indians and colonists lived together in a blending of cultures that persists to this day.

In April 1706, Acting Governor Francisco Cuervo y Valdéz created the settlement of La Villa de San Felipe Neri de Alburquerque as the administrative center for southern New Mexico. Naming the settlement in honor of Saint Philip Neri and of the duke of Alburquerque, who served as viceroy in Mexico City, Cuervo exceeded his authority by calling it a *villa* (the second highest class of Spanish settlement), but in 1712, the Spanish government legalized the designation.

Life was difficult in eighteenth-century Albuquerque (the first *r* was later dropped). Officials described the province as blighted and "remote beyond compare." Fewer than two thousand colonists lived on isolated farms and ranches along the valley. Only a small church and a few "Sunday houses" lined the unfinished plaza because settlers chose to live beside their farms instead of "commuting" from town to their fields.

For more than a century, life in Albuquerque followed predictable cycles based on the Catholic church's calendar and annual plantings and harvests. Social life was centered on holy days, such as Christmas and Easter, and family events such as marriages, christenings, and funerals. Lay Catholic organizations, notably Los Hermanos de Nuestro Padre Jesús (The Brothers of

Albuquerque's Old Town in about 1893. *Courtesy Albuquerque Museum.*

Our Father Jesus, or the PENITENTES) bound the community together with rituals and aid in times of trouble. By the 1730s, relations had stabilized with neighboring Pueblo Indians, who were regarded as respected subjects of Spain. Hispanic settlers and Pueblo Indians intermarried, shared technology, and cooperated in defense.

Contact with the outside world came infrequently through caravans of wagons that brought goods up the Camino Real. Colonists received little help from the government because the province of New Mexico had little strategic or economic value. Bands of as many as four hundred Navajo, Apache, or Comanche warriors made frequent, often devastating raids on Albuquerque. The weather alternated between drought and torrential rains; there were floods and famines; smallpox was endemic; and plagues of moths destroyed the primary exports—wool blankets and serapes.

In 1821, Mexico declared its independence from Spain, and soon afterwards WILLIAM BECKNELL blazed the Santa Fe Trail between Missouri and Mexico. The village of Albuquerque became an important stop along the way. Native families such as the Armijos, Bacas, Oteros, and Chávezes eventually assumed about half the flourishing wagon trade.

In 1846, soon after the outbreak of the UNITED STATES–MEXICAN WAR, the U.S. Army and the Missouri Volunteers annexed New Mexico to the United States. The army established a supply depot and administrative center at Albuquerque and operated them intermittently until 1867. During the CIVIL WAR, the Texan Confederate Army of New Mexico captured the Quartermaster Depot in Albuquerque. Confederate and Union forces fought a minor artillery skirmish around the plaza in April 1862.

After annexation of New Mexico to the United States, the sheep-raising industry expanded rapidly in Albuquerque. California and Colorado miners created a demand for mutton that resulted in great sheep drives during the 1850s and 1860s. The mesas around Albuquerque became home to hundreds of thousands of sheep. Sheepherding and the wool trade continued to be important to Albuquerque's economy until the end of World War II.

In April 1880, a subsidiary of the Atchison, Topeka and Santa Fe Railroad arrived at Albuquerque. Railroad planners selected a site east of the old Spanish plaza for an important repair facility, the largest between Kansas and California. Called "New Albuquerque" or "New Town," it resembled most Western boom towns with dirt streets, dozens of saloons, a horse-drawn streetcar system, and a red-light district.

New Albuquerque became a supply center for southern Colorado, western Texas, eastern Arizona, and northern Mexico. Waves of immigrants accompanied the railroad, and Albuquerque became home to a mix of native Pueblo Indians, Hispanics, Euro-Americans, African Americans, and Chinese. New Town incorporated in 1891 and soon boasted amenities such as a school system, electricity, a waterworks, and telephones. Statehood for New Mexico came only in 1912, because of the small territorial population and its limited political and economic importance.

About 1890, the local Commercial Club began advertising the health benefits of a high, dry climate for people suffering from tuberculosis and other respiratory diseases. Thousands of "lungers" arrived until one-third of the population consisted of consumptives and their relatives. More than a dozen sanitariums offered treatment; the two largest, Southwestern Presbyterian Sanitarium and St. Joseph Sanitarium, survived to become modern regional medical centers.

In the decades that followed, Albuquerque became a transportation and government center. Charles A. Lindbergh selected Albuquerque as a stop on the first transcontinental air routes of the 1920s, and Route 66 brought the first transcontinental motorists through town. In the 1930s, charismatic Governor CLYDE TINGLEY, Senator DENNIS CHÁVEZ, and other Democratic civic leaders secured so many New Deal projects for Albuquerque that Republicans accused them of robbing the national treasury.

The 1940s brought rapid growth with a U.S. Army air field constructed east of town. Kirtland Air Force Base and the Sandia National Laboratories nuclear research facility became the economic foundation for rapid growth. After World War II, the metro population of Albuquerque grew from about fifty thousand to more than five hundred thousand. In the 1990s, the city had a multicultural population retaining its remarkable Pueblo Indian, Spanish colonial, and territorial heritage.

—*Byron A. Johnson*

SEE ALSO: Camino Real, El; Santa Fe and Chihuahua Trail

SUGGESTED READING:

Faulk, Odie B., and Laura Faulk. *Defenders of the Interior Provinces: Presidial Soldiers on the Northern Frontier of New Spain*. Albuquerque, N. Mex., 1988.

Johnson, Byron A. *Old Town, Albuquerque, New Mexico: A Guide to Its History and Architecture*. Albuquerque, N. Mex., 1980.

———, and Robert K. Dauner. *Early Albuquerque: A Photographic History, 1878–1918*. Albuquerque, N. Mex., 1981.

Sanchez, Joseph. *The Rio Abajo Frontier, 1540–1692: A History of Early Colonial New Mexico*. Albuquerque, N. Mex., 1988.

Simmons, Marc. *Albuquerque: A Narrative History*. Albuquerque, N. Mex., 1980.

ALEMANY, JOSEPH SADOC

Joseph Sadoc Alemany, O.P. (1814–1888), first archbishop of San Francisco, was born in Vich, Spain. He began studies to become a Catholic priest at an early age and was ordained in the Dominican Order on March 11, 1837, in Viterbo, Italy. In 1840, Alemany immigrated to the United States to work in the "mission" territories of Ohio, Tennessee, and Kentucky. Ten years later, he was appointed the first bishop of Monterey, and in 1853, he was made archbishop of the newly created Metropolitan See of San Francisco, with a separate Diocese of Monterey and Los Angeles created in southern California.

Alemany faced a complex situation in California. He had to rebuild the basic ecclesiastical institutions, which had been neglected since the mission era and recently overwhelmed by the onslaught of the gold-rush immigrants. He had to be sensitive to the needs of the aging Californio population (Mexican natives of California), while at the same time establishing the church in the new American social order emerging in California.

Alemany's episcopate addressed several pressing concerns. First, he tried to establish the archdiocese on a firm financial basis. To accomplish this, he sought validation of the church's land claims; requested recompense from the government of Mexico, which had confiscated the Pious Fund from the church during the 1840s; and enlisted aid from outside California, particularly from the Society for the Propagation of the Faith in Paris and Lyons, France. Second, Alemany needed to increase the number of clergymen he had. He established his own seminary of St. Thomas and recruited priests from Europe, particularly Ireland. He employed members of various orders to staff the archdiocese's basic educational and charitable work—schools, hospitals, and orphanages. Third, he was charged with tending the needs of an ethnically diverse flock—including people of Irish, Italian, German, French, Spanish, and Native American descent. In some cases, he appointed a priest who spoke their language to care for them; in other cases, he established a "national" parish—French (1856), German (1860), Spanish-speaking (1875), and Italian (1884).

Alemany often visited the vast reaches of his archdiocese by horse or by public stagecoach. Within the city, his humble life style caused one visitor to San Francisco to proclaim, "No man is more poorly lodged in the whole city, and no man preaches the spirit of evangelical poverty" better than Alemany.

On December 28, 1884, Alemany resigned his episcopacy and returned to his native Vich, Spain, where he died and was buried. In 1965, his remains were disinterred and returned for burial in Holy Cross Cemetery near San Francisco.

—*Jeffrey M. Burns*

SEE ALSO: Catholics

SUGGESTED READING:
McGloin, John B., S.J. *California's First Archbishop: The Life of Joseph Sadoc Alemany, 1814–1888.* New York, 1966.

ALEUT INDIANS

SEE: Native American Peoples: Peoples of Alaska

ALEXANDER, MOSES

One of the nation's earliest Jewish governors, Moses Alexander (1853–1932) was born in Obrigheim, Bavaria. He immigrated to the United States in 1867, settled in Chillicothe, Missouri, to work for an uncle in a clothing store, and became a part owner of the store in 1874. He left Missouri in 1891, bound for Alaska, but after stopping in Boise, Idaho, to investigate business opportunities, he decided to stay there. He opened a men's clothing store in Boise and ultimately operated nine stores in the region.

Alexander was a leader in the growing Jewish community in Boise and was instrumental in the construction of the city's first synagogue in 1896. While living in Chillicothe, he had served one term as a member of the city council. He renewed his political interests in Boise and was elected mayor in 1897 and 1901. His involvement in Democratic party politics led to an unsuccessful gubernatorial race in 1908. He tried again in 1914, and, running on a platform that contained a commitment to prohibition, he won. He was reelected for a second two-year term in 1916. During his second term, the state faced some important issues, including opposition to the nation's entry into World War I by the Industrial Workers of the World, whose members were active in Idaho's timber industry. Alexander successfully opposed such groups and proved to be a popular and effective governor. He declined to run for reelection in 1918, but he remained active in the Democratic party for a time and attended several national nominating conventions.

—*Robert C. Sims*

SEE ALSO: Jewish Americans

SUGGESTED READING:
Sims, Robert C., and Hope E. Benedict. *Idaho's Governors: Historical Essays on Their Administrations*. Boise, Idaho, 1992.

ALIEN LAND LAWS

The federal government and many state governments passed laws in the late nineteenth and early twentieth centuries to prevent people who were not U.S. citizens from purchasing land in the West. Although the earliest of these laws took aim at European corporations, most of the laws reflected hostility toward Asian immigrants.

In the wake of the economic crisis of the 1880s, U.S. and territorial officials complained that non-resident aliens were purchasing all of the valuable land in the West. In 1887, Congress passed a law that prohibited aliens who had not declared their intent to become citizens from owning land in federal territories. In 1889, the state of Washington passed a law that prohibited foreign corporations from owning land in the state, and Texas passed a similar law in 1892.

Between 1890 and 1910, seventy thousand Japanese immigrants entered the United States, and Western legislators, newspaper publishers, and labor leaders expressed fears about them. Immigrants from Japan accounted for less than one-tenth of one percent of the U.S. population, but almost all of the Japanese immigrants settled along the Pacific Coast. Many sought to purchase farms. Economic conditions and political turmoil caused anti-Japanese agitation to increase after 1910. In May 1913, the California legislature passed a bill that made it illegal for immigrants who were "ineligible to citizenship"—Asian immigrants—to own land in the state. Governor HIRAM WARREN JOHNSON signed the bill on May 19, 1913.

Although Anglo-Americans celebrated the passage of the 1913 law, it did not seriously inhibit the ability of Japanese immigrants to control land in California. Many immigrants formed corporations that could legally own land, and others transferred land titles to their children born in the United States. Anglo-Americans grew disgruntled because the law had not driven Japanese immigrants from the United States. In the anti-immigrant hysteria of the post–World War I years, California voters passed an initiative designed to close the loopholes in the 1913 law. More than 668,000 people voted for the stronger law in 1920; only 222,000 voted against it. The Alien Land Law of 1920 forced many Japanese immigrants to abandon farming.

California's Alien Land Law inspired legislators in other Western states to pass similar legislation. Arizona enacted a law patterned after the 1913 California statute in 1917. Washington, Nebraska, Louisiana, and Texas passed anti-Asian land laws in 1921; New Mexico in 1922; Oregon, Montana, and Idaho in 1923; and Kansas in 1925. State and federal courts upheld most sections of these laws.

The amount of land owned by Japanese immigrants in Western states declined in the 1920s, but few immigrants were prosecuted in the 1930s. State officials resurrected the alien land laws during World War II, after the federal government had incarcerated Japanese American residents of the Pacific Coast area during World War II. The California legislature amended its alien land law in 1943 and ordered the attorney general to prosecute all violators vigorously. The legislature also placed a proposition designed to strengthen the law on the November 1946 ballot. Japanese Americans campaigned against the measure. The state inadvertently helped their cause by pursuing lawsuits against U.S. citizens of Japanese ancestry, many of whom were decorated war veterans. On election day, the people of California rejected the proposition by a vote of 1,143,780 to 797,067.

The U.S. Supreme Court invalidated a section of the California Alien Land Law on January 19, 1948, when it issued its opinion in the case of *Oyama* v. *California*. The Oregon Supreme Court declared this state's law unconstitutional on March 29, 1949, and the California Supreme Court decreed the state's statute unconstitutional in 1952. That year, Congress rendered the law meaningless by passing the McCarran-Walter Act, which made Asian immigrants eligible for citizenship. California voters repealed the Alien Land Law in 1956.

The alien land laws passed in many states reflected a great fear of Japanese immigrants. The laws stunted the growth of the Japanese American economy and closed options for other Asian immigrants. Civil rights activism on the part of Asian Americans and changing attitudes toward race in U.S. society and culture spelled the demise of the various laws.

—*Kevin Allen Leonard*

SEE ALSO: Japanese Americans

SUGGESTED READING:
Carrott, M. Browning. "Prejudice Goes to Court: The Japanese and the Supreme Court in the 1920s." *California History* 63 (1983): 126–138.
Chuman, Frank F. *The Bamboo People: The Law and Japanese Americans*. Del Mar, Calif., 1976.

Daniels, Roger. *The Politics of Prejudice: The Anti-Japanese Movement in California and the Struggle for Japanese Exclusion.* Berkeley and Los Angeles, 1962.

Leonard, Kevin Allen. "'Is That What We Fought For?' Japanese Americans and Racism in California: The Impact of World War II." *Western Historical Quarterly* 21 (1990): 463–482.

ALLEN, HENRY T.

Henry T. Allen's (1859–1930) fifteen-hundred-mile trip in the summer of 1885 from the Gulf of Alaska to the Bering Sea was the first expedition to chart three major river systems and is considered the most remarkable and extensive exploration of interior Alaska. Born in Sharpsburg, Kentucky, Allen graduated from West Point in 1882 and immediately sought a position in one of the explorations of interior Alaska being organized by the army under General NELSON APPLETON MILES. First stationed in the Washington Territory as Miles's aide in 1882, Lieutenant Allen explored the Copper River in 1885. His expedition followed Lieutenant Frederick Schwatka's successful navigation of the YUKON RIVER in 1883 and William Abercrombie's unsuccessful route to the Copper River in 1884.

Allen organized a party of two enlisted men, two prospectors, and seven Native Americans. A key to his success was his use of local people who had knowledge of the area. The group entered the Copper River region in March 1885 and explored the waterway and one of its tributaries, the Chitina. From the Copper, the group moved down the Tanana River to the Yukon in June. Allen completed the journey by traveling overland to the Koyukuk River and ascending to its headwaters. In August, he descended the Koyukuk to the Yukon and reached Norton Sound on the Bering Sea.

General Miles said that Allen's exploration of the Alaskan interior "excelled all exploration on the American continent since Lewis and Clark." Allen's *Report of an Expedition to the Copper, Tanana, and Koyukuk Rivers in the Territory of Alaska 1885,* published in 1887, was a readable guide that hastened further exploration of interior Alaska. His expedition can also be viewed as evidence of the federal government's early interest in developing Alaska.

Allen left Alaska soon after his 1885 expedition and pursued a career in the army. Promoted to the rank of major general, he served as a military attaché in Russia and Berlin in the 1890s, fought in Cuba and the Philippines, served with General JOHN JOSEPH PERSHING on the Mexican Punitive Expedition, and completed his army career as commander of U.S. occupation forces in Germany after World War I.

—*John S. Whitehead*

SEE ALSO: Alaskan Exploration

SUGGESTED READING:

Allen, Henry T. *Report of an Expedition to the Copper, Tanana, and Koyukuk Rivers in the Territory of Alaska 1885.* Washington, D.C., 1887.

Sherwood, Morgan. *Exploration of Alaska 1865–1900.* New Haven, Conn., 1965.

ALLENSWORTH, JOSEPHINE LEAVELL

Teacher, community leader, and social activist, Josephine Leavell Allensworth (1855–1939) was born to William and Mary Dickerson Leavell in Trenton, Kentucky. An accomplished young pianist, she married the prominent Baptist minister Allen Allensworth (1842–1914) on September 20, 1877, in Bowling Green, Kentucky. After the couple moved to Cincinnati, Ohio, to accept the pastorate of the Union Baptist Church, Josephine Allensworth taught church school, provided musical support, and supervised the women's clubs. In addition to her work with the church, she taught in the Cincinnati schools.

Beginning in 1886, Allensworth accompanied her husband, a commissioned chaplain in the Twenty-fourth Infantry, a black army regiment, to various posts in the West while she taught school, helped with religious services, raised two daughters, entertained families of other black soldiers, and, on occasion, assumed responsibility for the finances of enlisted personnel. Following her husband's retirement in 1906, the couple settled in Los Angeles.

In 1908, she helped her husband and a few supporters establish the California Colony and Home Promotion Association, which provided aid to AFRICAN AMERICANS migrating to California and developed an all-black community in the San Joaquin Valley. The town of Allensworth grew to become a market center for African Americans engaged in farming, dairying, and mercantile activities. Allensworth used her military experiences to help develop the community. An active club woman, she helped establish the Progressive Women's Improvement Association, which created a reading room for the community and then constructed a playground for children. In memory of her mother, she donated land for the Mary Dickinson Memorial Library, which opened on July 4, 1913. (Mary's maiden name was listed as *Dickerson* on her death certificate issued by the state of California, but the memorial library uses the name *Dickinson*, which is probably correct. No birth certificate from Kentucky is available.)

Allensworth continued her efforts for the town after her husband's death in 1914. Although she moved her primary residence to Los Angeles, she spent a portion of each year in Allensworth and maintained an affiliation with the community by serving as president of the school board through at least 1920. She spent her remaining years at her daughter Nella's home in Los Angeles, where she died of influenza. The town did not outlive her. Due to conflicts over water rights, souring soil, and the Great Depression, the town declined. In 1976, it became the Allensworth State Historical Park. A number of reconstructed buildings that housed Allensworth's community programs line the streets as a monument to the efforts of this gentle, refined woman.

—*Dorothy C. Salem*

SUGGESTED READING:
Alexander, Charles. *The Battles and Victories of Allen Allensworth*. Boston, 1914.
Goode, Kenneth G. *California's Black Pioneers: A Brief Historical Survey*. Santa Barbara, Calif., 1973.
Hamilton, Kenneth M. "Allensworth." In *Black Towns and Profit: Promotion and Development in the Trans-Appalachian West*. Urbana, Ill., 1991.

ALLISON, [ROBERT] CLAY

For his first twenty-one years, gunfighter Clay Allison (1840–1887) lived on his family's farm in Tennessee. With the start of the Civil War, he joined the Confederate Army but was released after serving one year because of mental problems. Some months later, he reenlisted and fought until the end of the war as a scout under General Nathan Bedford Forrest.

After the war, Allison moved to Texas with some members of his family and worked as a cowboy for OLIVER LOVING and CHARLES GOODNIGHT. Later, he was a trail boss and ran a ranch near Cimarron, New Mexico.

A quiet, friendly man when sober, Allison became deadly and probably psychotic when drunk. In 1870, for example, he participated in a lynching, after which he cut off the victim's head.

Four years later, in his first documented gunfight, Allison shot and killed Chunk Colbert. Asked why he had had a meal with Colbert before the shooting, Allison replied, "Because I didn't want to send a man to hell on an empty stomach."

After the murder of a Methodist minister who had criticized the Santa Fe Ring, Allison and some friends lynched a Mexican thought to be implicated in the murder. A short time later, two other Mexicans were also killed, probably by Allison. After a New Mexico

newspaper attacked Allison's deeds, he had the press thrown in a river and published his own edition of the paper. He later apologized for these actions.

Allison was thought to be involved in the killing of three black soldiers, as well as in the murder of a deputy sheriff in Colorado, but he was never brought to trial for these killings or others, perhaps because of his deadly reputation.

In the 1880s, Allison settled on the Washita River in Texas where he became known as "the Wild Wolf of the Washita." He had married and had a daughter; a second girl was born after his death.

In July 1887, Allison died of a skull fracture after being thrown from his wagon—an unexciting death for one of the West's most well-known gunfighters.

—*Richard A. Van Orman*

SEE ALSO: Gunfighters

SUGGESTED READING:
Clark, O. S. *Clay Allison of the Washita*. Attica, Ind., 1920.
Schoenberger, Dale T. *The Gunfighters*. Caldwell, Idaho, 1971.
Stanley, F. *Clay Allison*. Denver, 1956.

ALTUBE, PEDRO

Basque cattle and sheep rancher Pedro Altube (1827–1905) was born in Onate in the Spanish Basque province of Guipuzcoa. He immigrated to Buenos Aires in 1845 to join his brother Bernard. Six years later, the brothers moved to the gold fields of Tuolumne County, California. With profits from gold mining, they entered the cattle business in 1860 and, with other Basques, formed Altube and Company to run livestock on Rancho La Laguna in California. In 1870, the Altubes bought cattle in Mexico and drove them to Tuscarora, Nevada, where they also raised sheep. Pedro Altube's practice of paying his sheepherders in sheep and permitting herders to start their own bands earned him the title "father of the Basques in America." His primary interest remained in cattle, and his major land holdings, including the four-hundred-thousand-acre Spanish Ranch, were in California.

—*Harmon Mothershead*

SUGGESTED READING:
Douglas, William A., and Jon Bilbao. *Amerikanuak: Basques in the New World*. Reno, Nev., 1975.

ALVAREZ, MANUEL

Born in Spain and raised in Abelgas in the Spanish Cantabrian Mountains, the Santa Fe trader Manuel

Alvarez (1794–1856) traveled to Mexico in 1818. From there, he traveled through Havana, New York, and St. Louis and then took the newly opened Santa Fe Trail to Santa Fe in 1824.

Living in Santa Fe until his death, Alvarez operated a store on the main plaza, traded over the Santa Fe Trail, trapped for the Rocky Mountain Fur Company (between 1827 and 1833), became the United States's consul and commercial agent in Santa Fe, led the statehood party in New Mexico, and briefly served as lieutenant-governor.

—*Thomas E. Chávez*

SUGGESTED READING:
Chávez, Thomas E. *Conflict and Acculturation: Manuel Alvarez's 1842 Memorial.* Santa Fe., N. Mex., 1989.
———. *Manuel Alvarez (1794–1856): A Southwest Biography.* Niwot, Colo., 1990.

AMERICAN BISON

SEE: Buffaloes

AMERICAN BOARD OF COMMISSIONERS FOR FOREIGN MISSIONS

The American Board of Commissioners for Foreign Missions (ABCFM) was the first American Protestant organization devoted to converting non-Christians in other lands. Organized in 1810, the ABCFM became the first important evangelical reform agency in the West and Hawaii to treat indigenous native populations, Mexicans, Mexican Americans, and Chinese as potential converts. The best-known ABCFM missionaries included Samuel Worcester and Cyrus Kingsbury among the Cherokees, Stephen Riggs among the Dakota Sioux, MARCUS AND NARCISSA WHITMAN among the Cayuse Indians in Oregon, and Melinda Rankin among Mexicans and Tejanos.

ABCFM work with Native Americans became the prototype for missions around the globe. Although missions were not as important on the Anglo frontier as on the Spanish frontier, ABCFM initially sought to Americanize as well as Christianize the native population of new territories. Taking advantage of a federal subsidy to pacify Indians bordering on Anglo settlements, the ABCFM organized its first mission to the Cherokees in 1817. Until the Civil War, the ABCFM supported more Indian missions than any other agency. The organization also participated in the post–Civil War Indian pro-

grams whereby mission boards nominated and supervised superintendents of the BUREAU OF INDIAN AFFAIRS.

Although primarily known for its commitment to assimilation policies, the ABCFM sometimes defended native rights. In the 1820s, Samuel Worcester filed *Worcester* v. *State of Georgia* to help the Cherokees fight removal to the Indian Territory. Jailed for his efforts, he later joined other ABCFM missionaries on the TRAIL OF TEARS. In the 1850s, ABCFM's first secretary, Rufus Anderson, instituted a policy to teach natives how to read and write their own language. By the turn of the century, ABCFM missionaries placed less emphasis on conversion and assimilation and worked to improve the poor living conditions caused by Anglo settlement and to protect indigenous cultures from eradication.

—*Linda Pritchard*

SEE ALSO: Americanization Programs; Missions: Nineteenth-Century Missions to the Indians; United States Indian Policy: Civilization Programs

SUGGESTED READING:
Berkhofer, Robert F. *Salvation and the Savage.* Westport, Conn., 1977.
Hutchison, William R. *Errand to the World.* Chicago, 1987.

AMERICAN FUR COMPANY

Founded by JOHN JACOB ASTOR in April 1808, the American Fur Company was the most powerful and influential FUR TRADE enterprise to operate in that part of the West claimed by the United States. The American Fur Company was part of a group of three companies created by Astor with a single goal in mind. Astor intended his ventures—the American Fur Company, the Pacific Fur Company, and the South West Fur Company—eventually to monopolize the entire American fur business. These plans, including the Fort ASTORIA trading depot at the mouth of the Columbia River, were severely disrupted by the War of 1812. In the years immediately after the war, the American Fur Company did business primarily in the Great Lakes region. Astor relied on Ramsay Crooks as his field manager, while Robert Stuart looked after company affairs from his post at Mackinac.

While the War of 1812 temporarily checked Astor's ambitions, he never gave up on his larger dreams. In 1822, Astor reentered the Western fur business and established the Western Department of the American Fur Company. With headquarters in St. Louis, the Western Department took its day-to-day direction from Ramsay Crooks. The Western Department was a formidable trading concern, but it by no means held a monopoly on the Missouri River. Astor had stiff competition from federally owned trading posts or factories and the aggressive Columbia Fur Company. While the government posts, long the object of Astor's political lobbying, were losing congressional support, the Columbia Fur Company proved to be a worthy opponent. Led by KENNETH MCKENZIE and staffed by many experienced Canadian traders, the company moved quickly to secure commercial agreements with the Crow and Blackfoot Indians. As a fur-trade strategist, Astor sought the security, predictability, and steady profit that came from monopoly. By 1826, it was clear that McKenzie's traders were not going to abandon their Crow and Blackfoot customers. At the same time, McKenzie knew that Astor's financial resources would give the American Fur Company victory in any protracted fur-trade war. Negotiation and merger were in the air as Ramsay Crooks went west to talk. In July 1827, the Columbia Fur Company became the Upper Missouri Outfit of the American Fur Company. The enterprise, directed by McKenzie from Fort Union, was restricted to trading along the Missouri.

For the next six years (from 1828 to 1834), the American Fur Company took on characteristics of a modern corporation with various divisions and field offices. At corporate headquarters in New York City, Astor and his son William made all the essential market decisions. Ramsay Crooks acted as general manager. The Great Lakes trade remained in Robert Stuart's hands. In St. Louis, Pierre Chouteau, Jr., oversaw the Western Department and the Upper Missouri Outfit. Kenneth McKenzie continued as a powerful force, acting as chief factor at Fort Union. Located at the confluence of the Yellowstone and Missouri rivers, Fort Union was the company's most visible presence in the West.

Astor sought monopoly in the trade of beaver, muskrat, and buffalo hides, but even after 1827, there was considerable competition. That competition came from St. Louis traders doing business as part of the Rocky Mountain trapping system. WILLIAM HENRY ASHLEY, William Sublette, and ROBERT CAMPBELL all challenged the power of the Astor establishment. From 1830 until 1834, the American Fur Company waged a fierce trade war, a war it was sure to win given its superior financial backing. In 1834, the year Astor sold the American Fur Company, the Rocky Mountain challengers gave up and joined Astor.

Astor's sale of the American Fur Company at the time that its rivals called off the trade war may seem odd by modern standards. While profits from the Western fur business were still substantial, Astor understood that the entire resource base of the trade was changing. Built on the whims of male fashion and taste in

hats, the fur trade was susceptible to market and biological forces beyond the control of even the most able manager. Changes in fashion and the rise of mass-produced textiles meant a steadily decreasing demand for fur. In the spring of 1834, Astor began to negotiate the sale of the American Fur Company. Ramsay Crooks purchased the Northern Department; the St. Louis-based firm Pratte, Chouteau and Company bought the Western Department, including the Upper Missouri Outfit.

The American Fur Company has often been branded as a frontier villain who sold alcohol and inferior goods to unsuspecting Indians. The relationship between the company and its native customers was always more complex than oppressor and oppressed. Native people proved to be adept bargainers, and the company depended on Indians as trading partners. Selling inferior goods at high prices would surely have destroyed the fragile set of personal relationships. The company's role in the alcohol trade depended on time, place, and circumstance. Traders such as Kenneth McKenzie were willing to use alcohol as a commercial weapon, especially when it might effectively undercut rivals. Independent traders probably brought more alcohol into the fur trade then did Astor's company.

—*James P. Ronda*

SEE ALSO: Chouteau Family; Sublette Brothers

SUGGESTED READING:
Haeger, John D. *John Jacob Astor: Business and Finance in the Early Republic.* Detroit, Mich., 1991.
Sunder, John E. *The Fur Trade on the Upper Missouri, 1840–1865.* Norman, Okla., 1965.
Wishart, David J. *The Fur Trade of the American West, 1807–1840.* Lincoln, Nebr., 1979.

AMERICAN HORSE (ELDER) (SIOUX)

The elder American Horse (1846–1876)—also known as Iron Shield—was an Oglala Lakota. Faint and questionable records indicate that he was the son of Smoke (the Oglala Lakota civilian band "chief" succeeded by Red Leaf). American Horse became the chief or principal spokesman for the band known as "True Oglala." As leader, he defied non-Indian intrusion, seldom if ever appeared at the Red Cloud Agency, but sometimes showed up at the Spotted Tail Agency to claim annuities. He and soldiers from his band evidently participated in battle against GEORGE ARMSTRONG CUSTER in 1876.

Following the defeat of Custer's Seventh Cavalry, the command of General GEORGE CROOK pursued armed Lakotas with a vengeance and learned that in present-day Hardy County, South Dakota, some Oglalas, Brulés, and Cheyennes were assembled. Among them were American Horse and CRAZY HORSE, who shared leadership among Oglalas resisting Euro-American encroachment.

Almost by accident, Colonel Anson Mills, under Crook's command, approached the encampment of American Horse at Slim Buttes. Mills attacked, and the U.S. forces were victorious. When American Horse surrendered to Crook, he had an abdominal wound so severe that he held his own intestines in his hands. At a field hospital, he refused morphine and bit down on a stick to endure the pain while army physicians Bennett Clements and Valentine McGillycuddy worked to close his wound. Soon he died and, like Crazy Horse, left a legacy of resistance at the cost of his life.

—*Herbert T. Hoover and Carol Goss Hoover*

SUGGESTED READING:
National Archives. Record Group 75. Pine Ridge Agency.
Pfaller, Louis L., O.S.B. *James McLaughlin: The Man with an Indian Heart.* New York, 1978.

AMERICAN HORSE (YOUNGER) (SIOUX)

The younger American Horse (ca. 1840–1908) was an Oglala Lakota who was born in the Black Hills. He may have been the nephew of American Horse (Elder) who died of wounds sustained at Slim Buttes or no relation to him at all. The younger American Horse emerged to lead the part of the Oglala tribe that settled on the Medicine Root Creek and other streams at the eastern edge of the Red Cloud Agency jurisdiction and retained close affiliation with the Upper Brulés (Sicangus) who had been led previously by Bull Bear (or Bear Bull). Preferring peaceful negotiation to contention or war, American Horse led and represented this group of Oglalas from 1871 to 1877.

American Horse represented Oglalas in council about the sale of the Black Hills in 1876. At other times, he traveled to Washington, D.C. Also, with SPOTTED TAIL (Sinte Gleska), he went to investigate the Indian Territory (Oklahoma) as a place for relocation. After American Horse, Spotted Tail, and other Lakota spokesmen rejected the idea of removal, federal officials gave it up too and, in 1877, began to plan reservations for the Lakota and Yanktonai (Ihanktuwala)

In 1907, American Horse (Younger) became an American citizen. *Courtesy Denver Public Library.*

peoples west of the Missouri River. Challenging the traditionalist influence of RED CLOUD, the new Pine Ridge agent, Valentine McGillycuddy, courted favor with American Horse as a proponent of accommodation. American Horse supported adaptation to family farming and ranching. In 1884, he presented the five children of his four wives for baptism by an Episcopal missionary (who refused baptism for American Horse because he had more than one wife).

Evidently in 1882 and again in 1888, American Horse opposed any additional surrender of Lakota land. Yet during 1889, when the further reduction of the Great Sioux Reservation seemed inevitable, he did not resist.

Following the WOUNDED KNEE MASSACRE of 1890, American Horse testified in Washington, D.C., and blamed U.S. troops not for their confrontation with Lakota soldiers, but for the escalation of a battle into a massacre of women and children. Nevertheless, in the aftermath of Wounded Knee, he led soldiers from his band to defend Episcopal missionaries, who embraced his family against retaliation by angry Lakotas. In almost every way except perhaps the abandonment of his wives, the younger American Horse gained recognition as a flexible leader who searched for means of intercultural reconciliation without controversy or the loss of life in conflict under arms.

—*Herbert T. Hoover and Carol Goss Hoover*

SUGGESTED READING:
National Archives. Record Group 75. Pine Ridge Agency.
Dykshorn, Jan M. "Leaders of the Sioux Indian Nation." *Dakota Highlights* 3 (1975): 1–8.

AMERICANIZATION PROGRAMS

Historical background

Among Anglo-Americans in the late nineteenth century, nativist fear was rampant. After the Civil War, the rapidly industrializing United States had thrown open its doors to a new wave of immigration. Millions of Italians, Slavs, Jews, and other émigrés from eastern and southern Europe crowded into American cities with the Germans and the Irish, who had been coming in large numbers since at least the 1820s. On the West Coast and in Hawaii, the Japanese swelled the ranks of an Asian immigrant population that traced its origin back to the arrival of the Chinese in California during the gold rush. In the Southwest later in the century, hundreds of thousands of poor Mexicans, rocked by the massive social dislocations caused by the Mexican Revolution, looked for work north of the Rio Grande. Immigration became linked in the minds of Anglo-American Protestants with radical labor, social unrest, and the urban ills of big-city gangs, teeming slums, and violent crime. For Anglo-Americans fed for decades on expansionist rhetoric, it was the MANIFEST DESTINY of the Anglo-Saxon race not only to inhabit the continent but to "civilize" the "lower" races, and American politicians responded to the "influx" of "alien" peoples in the second half of the century (who, at least in the minds of politicians, threatened to overwhelm "white" culture), with calls to cut off immigration altogether. At the same time, American intellectuals began talk of a "melting pot," in which various groups were thrown together, lost their ethnic pasts, and became "pure" Americans. The 1880s saw passage of the first legislation to end the "Yellow Peril," mostly in the West, by excluding the Chinese, and later the Japanese, and by the turn of the century, Americanization programs had become part of a specific social and political movement aimed at coercing immigrants to assimilate into the Anglo-Protestant mainstream of American life.

The term *Americanization* first came into common use during the nativist controversies of the 1850s. It was coined by a Vermont Yankee and a convert to Catholicism named Orestes A. Brownson. In a series of articles beginning in July 1854 in *Brownson's Quarterly Review,* Brownson accused Irish immigrants and Catholic leaders of conflating their religion with their national origin and urged them, for the sake of all Catholics, to conform to American civil ideology instead of openly fighting the anti-Catholicism of the KNOW-NOTHING PARTY, which had risen to great influence in the antebellum United States. By the mid-nineteenth century, Protestant missionaries in the West had so embraced the gospel of manifest destiny that they saw their purpose as not only to "Christianize" but also to "Americanize" those deemed "foreign" but living in the United States—Native Americans, Hispanics, and the Chinese. After the Civil War, the federal government began restricting Indians to reservations with the intent of civilizing the native population. By the time the BUREAU OF INDIAN AFFAIRS assumed responsibility for educating Indian children in the 1890s, the government had mandated a full-fledged Americanization program that, by providing young Indians with an industrial education and direct contact with mainstream society, forced them to work and act like "Americans."

The Americanization movement

During the first two decades of the twentieth century, the Americanization movement went through three phases, the first lasting to about 1914, the second covering the World War I years, and the third springing to life in the immediate postwar years. Before 1914, Americanization was championed by such patriotic groups as the Daughters of the American Revolution and the Boston-based North American Civic League for Immigrants, founded in 1908. Even Chicago-spawned settlement-house workers and other Progressives, who stressed the need for legislation to protect immigrants and who believed immigrant populations had positive contributions to make to American life, sought a more "harmonious" and integrated society. Both groups emphasized the importance of public schools in bringing together the children of diverse ethnic backgrounds and teaching them the responsibilities of U.S. citizenship, and they linked hygiene, domestic "science," and industrial training to Americanization through practical school programs. In a new departure, they also developed adult-education programs for immigrants, with both the settlement houses and the patriotic groups extending special classes. In 1907, for example, the YMCA began offering courses in English and civics, the primary subjects of Americanization.

When the Great War broke out in Europe in 1914, fear of "foreign" elements grew more intense and so did Americanization programs. The hyphen in such compounds as "German-Americans" became a symbol of disloyalty, and in 1918, Iowa's governor William L. Harding, to give just one example, issued a Language Proclamation banning foreign-language newspapers and making it illegal to converse in public or on the telephone in any language other than English. The goal of Americanization programs became "100 percent Americanism." The number of agencies and organizations dedicated to Americanization proliferated and public support for them grew. By 1915 the U.S. Bureau of Education and the Bureau of Naturalization were actively supporting Americanization, and after America entered World War I in 1917, so did the heavy-handed Committee on Public Information. "Standardization" and "preparedness" became the watchwords of government, state and local as well as federal, as numerous private groups, chambers of commerce, and special organizations such as the National Americanization Committee pitched in to ensure that immigrants were loyal, bought war bonds, and learned to speak English. Manufacturers who employed immigrants grafted courses in English and citizenship to existing programs of welfare work or industrial betterment, thus making official the recurrent connection in American immigrant history between assimilation to American culture and the acclimation of "pre-industrial" workers to factory discipline.

Americanization reached a fevered pitch in postwar America, with its great fear of Bolshevik-inspired social revolution. As Woodrow Wilson's Progressive administration launched the Red Scare, patriotic groups stepped up their efforts to inoculate the immigrant mass against contagion from those they believed were the radical few. American businessmen were deeply implicated in these programs, and Americanization became closely identified with business-sponsored "welfare" programs and with antiunionism. Corporate leaders were slightly more moderate than such strongly nativist groups as the National Security League and the American Legion, who called for deporting alien radicals and mounted propagandizing smear campaigns. Various state and local authorities restricted the use of languages other than English in the classroom, required public-school teachers to be American citizens, and—in Oregon—passed a law (ruled unconstitutional in 1925) compelling all elementary-age children to attend public schools. In particular, champions of Americanism targeted foreign-language schools, which, for example, the Daughters of the American Revolution had labeled "subversive to the peace and order of our Nation and the undivided allegiance of our people."

Americanization in the West

The trans-Mississippi West—with its traditions of forced acculturation for Native Americans, racist exclusionary laws for Asians, Anglo-American "frontier" expansion, and cheap, unorganized Hispanic labor—proved especially receptive to the Americanization movement. Working with Chinese prostitutes, orphans, destitute young women, Indian children, and others barred by the color of their skin or economic circumstances from attending public schools, Protestant home missions taught English and vocational skills while preaching about the evils of Romanism, Mormonism, nihilism, communism, and atheism. "White" schoolchildren of immigrant parents from

Germany, Ireland, Italy, and eastern Europe, left foreign-language schools to attend the growing number of public schools. There, they were subjected to civics and history lessons that celebrated Anglo-Saxon NATIONAL EXPANSION. Learning on the one hand the skills and knowledge needed to succeed in American society, they also became to some extent indoctrinated against the traditions and customs of their foreign-born parents.

The treatment of Mexican Americans in the Southwest in particular reveals the mixture of altruism, racism, exploitation, and political opportunism that characterized Americanization programs in the West. From the last two decades of the nineteenth century until the start of the Great Depression, one million Mexican immigrants entered the United States. The West's exclusionary laws in the 1880s reduced the number of Asian agricultural workers and boosted the value of Mexican labor, which proved important when Mexican President Porfirio Díaz's modernization programs pushed poor Mexicans off their lands and the 1910 revolution sent them north in search of jobs. Mexican families became seasonal serfs to the large ranchers and farmers of Texas, New Mexico, Arizona, and California. Unorganized and mostly unskilled but hard working and cheap, the Mexicans formed an indispensable labor pool for the region's railroads, mines, smelters, and urban industries. At the same time, the relationship between economic development and massive immigration increased cultural and racial tensions in the Southwest and led to efforts to Americanize Mexicans in order to make them more efficient and productive.

Civil officials, social reformers, educators, and writers rejected the Mexicans' life style and cultural values as preindustrial and charged that Mexican customs stood in direct contrast to the Southwest's developing urban, industrial culture. They characterized Mexican workers as lazy, drunken, fun-loving, and unclean and set out to change them. EL PASO, for example, passed laws against bathing in the Rio Grande, a traditional habit of the Mexicans who, living in wretched BARRIOS without sanitation and running water, had hardly anywhere else to wash. At the same time, writers such as Pearl I. Ellis, author of *Americanization through Homemaking,* addressed the fears of officials and reformers about the spread of diseases from the barrios to American neighborhoods by reminding readers to take extra care in teaching Mexicans proper hygiene. Employers and reformers looked to the work place as an arena of Americanization, but the major institution for inculcating American values became the public schools. In 1911, J. C. Ross wrote in the *New Mexico Journal of Education* that industrial education for the Spanish-speaking population of New Mexico would provide Mexicans with a trade and teach the "intrinsic value" of all work. Pearl Ellis, too, argued that Americanization programs, besides raising the Mexicans' standard of living and improving their morals, taught skills beneficial to local industries.

As a result, vocational and industrial education became the centerpiece of the curriculum for the so-called Mexican Schools. In El Paso, where most Mexican children left school by the fourth grade, education officials directed their attention in the segregated Mexican schools to manual and domestic education that would help the students find jobs in the city's semi-skilled industries. In Los Angeles, garment manufacturers, the Chamber of Commerce, and the public schools set up a cooperative trade school to meet the city's need for semiskilled workers and emphasized vocational training in the segregated Mexican public schools. San Bernardino, too, responded to its "Mexican problem" by establishing a segregated barrio school emphasizing vocational education. In addition to providing manual training, the schools stressed the need to instruct Mexicans in the ideals and ethics of American society, but they believed the Mexican family and Mexican culture stood in their way. Although not all programs were so blunt, some nevertheless blamed Mexican families for perpetuating ignorance and immorality, and many schools launched attacks on Mexican traditions and the Spanish language. In doing so, they underscored intergenerational conflicts that had developed among the Mexican population and between the Mexican Americans and Mexican immigrants.

Indeed, that may have been part of the point. For although Americanization programs, on the one hand, offered immigrants a doorway into the dominant culture, they were also one of the weapons the ruling American elite used in its attempts to "tame" America's giddy multitudes, check the growing power of labor, and dismantle radical working-class organizations such as the INDUSTRIAL WORKERS OF THE WORLD, all in the name of good government and responsible development.

—*Charles Phillips*

SEE ALSO: Compulsory School Law, Oregon (1922); Houchen Settlement House; Immigration Law; Indian Schools; Language Schools; Protestant Home Missionary Programs; Progressivism; Mexican Immigration, 1900–1935; Native American Culture: Acculturation; Segregation; Stereotypes; United States Indian Policy

SUGGESTED READING:

Derr, Nancy. "The Babel Proclamation." *The Palimpsest* 60 (July-August 1979): 99–115.

Deutsch, Sarah. *No Separate Refuge: Culture, Class, and Gender on an Anglo-Hispanic Frontier in the American Southwest, 1880–1940*. New York, 1987.

Garcia, Mario T. "Americanization and the Mexican Immigrant, 1880–1930." In *From Different Shores: Perspectives on Race and Ethnicity in America*. Edited by Ronald Takaki. New York, 1987.

Gleason, Philip. "American Identity and Americanization." In *Concepts of Ethnicity*. By William Peterson, Michael Novak, and Philip Gleason. Cambridge, Mass., 1982.

Gutman, Herbert. *Work, Culture and Society in Industrializing America*. New York, 1976.

Higham, John. *Strangers in the Land: Patterns of American Nativism*. New York, 1966.

Korman, Gerd. *Industrialization, Immigrants, and Americanization*. Madison, Wis., 1967.

Pascoe, Peggy. *Relations of Rescue*. New York, 1990.

Sánchez, George J. *Becoming Mexican American: Ethnicity, Culture and Identity in Chicano Los Angeles, 1900-1945*. New York, 1993.

AMERICAN PARTY

SEE: Know-Nothing Party

AMERICAN RIVER

An eastern tributary of the SACRAMENTO RIVER, the three-forked American River rises near the crest of the High Sierra of northern California; its waters cascade steeply down six thousand feet in the course of the first fifty of its one-hundred-mile length through forbiddingly narrow canyons. The river, which drains a two-thousand-square-mile basin, flows into Sacramento, where it joins the Sacramento River.

As spectacular as parts of the American River are, it is hardly a great river by the standards of Western topography. However, it figured crucially in the history of the West. At Coloma, along the river's South Fork, JOHN AUGUST SUTTER directed James Wilson Marshall to build a sawmill, and on January 24, 1848, in the mill race of that structure, Marshall discovered gold. Within a year, the great CALIFORNIA GOLD RUSH was under way, forever transforming California and the West. It was to the American River and its environs that the first of the Forty-niners flocked.

The main flow of the American River originates in snow melt from the Sierra Nevada, and the average flow is about three million acre-feet. Run-off, however, is widely variable, and this figure is frequently exceeded. Over the years, a system of levees and floodways has been constructed to manage the flow, and in 1895, the American River became one of the first U.S. waterways to produce hydroelectric power when the

Folsom Dam was completed, generating current for Sacramento. Since 1895, a system of dams has been constructed for the purposes of generating electricity and for control of irrigation.

—*Alan Axelrod*

SUGGESTED READING:
Sanborn, Margaret. *The American River of El Dorado*. New York, 1974.

AMERICAN SYSTEM

HENRY CLAY, a leader in national politics for more than forty years, learned a valuable lesson from the War of 1812. In the years before the war, the United States had traded its raw materials for the manufactured goods of European countries, and this exchange left the young nation at the mercy of foreign powers. Clay devised a program of economic nationalism designed to make the United States less vulnerable to every international crisis.

His plan offered governmental encouragement to economic growth in all sections of the country. It included protection for the country's nascent industries in the form of tariffs on imported goods, a national bank to supply capital for economic growth, and a system of roads and waterways—supported by tariff revenues and land grants—to facilitate the transport of goods between the industrial North and the agricultural South and West.

—*Patricia Hogan*

SEE ALSO: Tariff Policy

SUGGESTED READING:
Baxter, Maurice G. *Henry Clay and the American System*. Lexington, Ky., 1995.

AMES, OAKES

Businessman and Congressman Oakes Ames's (1804–1873) otherwise illustrious career was forever marred by his efforts to secure capital for the construction of the transcontinental railroad. Born in Easton, Massachusetts, Ames entered the family business—a shovel factory—as a laborer after finishing his education. In 1844, he and his brother Oliver took control of the factory. Gold rushes and canals created such a demand for shovels that by the beginning of the Civil War, the brothers had parleyed the company into a $4-million enterprise.

A man of prominence, business acumen, and good contacts, Ames, a Republican, won a seat in the U.S. Congress in 1862. Three years later, President Abraham Lincoln persuaded Ames—with his connections to Eastern capital—to rescue the construction company responsible for the UNION PACIFIC RAILROAD's portion of the transcontinental line, a project Congress had funded with land grants and loans. Ames took over the management of the railroad, placed his brother in the presidency, and raised capital. The construction company, CRÉDIT MOBILIER OF AMERICA, was a good deal for the investors. Run by the directors of the Union Pacific, the company was, basically, paid by the Union Pacific to build the Union Pacific. The scheme, by which the directors made a profit, resulted in padded construction costs and a railroad that was finally completed. On May 10, 1869, the transcontinental railroad connected the East to the West.

In 1872, Ames was still in Congress when accusations of impropriety surfaced in Washington, D.C. In 1867, Ames—concerned that Congress might tighten its regulation of federally backed railroad companies amid rumors of huge profits—had offered to sell to several congressmen stock in Credit Mobilier on favorable terms. The congressional favors went unnoticed until the press revealed the sales in the midst of the 1872 presidential election. The congressmen who had received the stocks weathered the storm and won reelection by turning their backs on Ames.

The subsequent congressional investigations resulted in a February 27, 1873, censure against Ames, who maintained his innocence. He died three months later.

The regulations that Ames had feared came to pass with lasting consequences. Congress ended its land-grant aid to railroads; Union Pacific's stock fell in value; and the panic of 1873, caused in part by the Credit Mobilier revelations, rocked the nation. By the Thurman Act of 1878, Union Pacific was required to tie up its profits in a sinking fund to guarantee payment of the federal bonds that had financed the railroad's transcontinental construction. The Union Pacific never really recovered, and the American public never gave up the notion that it had been swindled by the "robber barons" of the railroads.

—*Kurt Edward Kemper*

SUGGESTED READING:
Ames, Charles Edgar. *Pioneering the Union Pacific: A Reappraisal of the Builders of the Railroad*. New York, 1969.
Martin, Albro. *Railroads Triumphant: The Growth, Rejection, and Rebirth of a Vital American Force*. New York, 1992.

AMIDON, CHARLES FREMONT

Federal judge for the District of North Dakota, Charles Fremont Amidon (1856–1937) was born in Chautauqua County, New York, and was raised in rural poverty. He earned his own way through Hamilton College in Clinton, New York, and after graduating in 1882, he moved to Fargo in the Dakota Territory and worked as the sole teacher in the town's high school. During his teaching career, he read law and was admitted to the bar in 1886. He established himself as an able, successful lawyer and became active in the Democratic party as a reformer in the growing city. He headed the committee that drew up the first law code for the newly admitted state of North Dakota in 1889. He was appointed judge of the federal district by President Grover Cleveland in 1896, a post he held until 1928. He also served on the Eighth Circuit Court of Appeals throughout his long judicial tenure.

An avid supporter of THEODORE ROOSEVELT's brand of PROGRESSIVISM, Amidon corresponded frequently with the former president. The two men visited each other several times, and during the Bull Moose campaign of 1912, Roosevelt often used substantial portions of Amidon's letters to him in speeches and articles. As Roosevelt began leaning toward America's entry into World War I, the two men parted company on the question of what constituted permissible dissent during wartime.

Amidon's judicial district saw more federal prosecutions under the Espionage and Sedition Acts than any other district per capita. He sought to apply the laws narrowly, an interpretation that led to few convictions. Civil libertarians recognized him as being a courageous defender of free speech in wartime, when most federal judges succumbed to the public's demand for suppression of allegedly "disloyal" utterances.

In later years, Amidon upheld the constitutionality of the NONPARTISAN LEAGUE's socialistic industrial program for North Dakota. Because of his advocacy of the rights of labor, the American Civil Liberties Union appointed him chairman of its anti-injunction committee. He was influential in shaping the language of the Norris–La Guardia Anti-Injunction Act of 1932.

Although Amidon lived far from the great centers of American political and intellectual life, he established close and frequently influential relationships with national figures, including Robert M. LaFollette, Jane Addams, Louis Brandeis, Felix Frankfurter, and Max Eastman. He died while wintering in Arizona.

—*Kenneth Smemo*

SUGGESTED READING:

Ratliff, Beulah Amidon. "Charles Fremont Amidon, 1856–1937." *North Dakota History* 7 (1941): 3–20.

Smemo, Kenneth. *Against the Tide: Life and Times of Federal Judge Charles F. Amidon.* New York, 1986.

———. "Judge Charles Amidon's Influence on Theodore Roosevelt's Presidential Campaign of 1912." *North Dakota History* 37 (1970): 5–19.

AMON CARTER MUSEUM

In his lifetime, Amon G. Carter, newspaper publisher and businessman in Fort Worth, Texas, acquired an impressive private collection of CHARLES MARION RUSSELL and FREDERIC REMINGTON paintings and sculpture. In 1945, he established the foundation that bears his name. He left instructions in his will that a museum to house his collection be established in Fort Worth by the foundation under the supervision of his children. In a building designed by Philip Johnson, the international-style museum opened its doors in January 1961. Expansion of the museum's collections and operations required additions, also designed by Philip Johnson, in 1964 and 1977.

Since the museum opened, it has broadened the scope of its collections with outstanding works of nineteenth- and early twentieth-century American art, although its strength remains in its representative examples of Western American artists. Its 350 paintings include works by ALBERT BIERSTADT, GEORGE CALEB BINGHAM, and KARL (OR CARL) BODMER. Works by GEORGIA O'KEEFFE, John Marin, Marsden Hartley, Arthur Dove, and Morris Grave represent twentieth-century art. The museum has more than one hundred sculptures by Remington and Russell in addition to pieces by a number of others. Water colors and drawings include works of early Western artists-explorers such as GEORGE CATLIN, RICHARD HOVENDON KERN, Peter Rindisbacher, and ALBERT JACOB MILLER. The collection of five thousand prints features extensive holdings of city views, Currier and Ives prints, JOHN JAMES AUDUBON birds and quadrupeds, and nineteenth-century Mexican material. The museum boasts one of the foremost collections of American photography, which includes nineteenth-century exploration and pioneer images and twentieth-century works by Ansel Adams, Edward and Brett Weston, Todd Webb, and Pirkle Jones. The library houses thirty thousand volumes, and its extensive collection of nineteenth-century newspapers, periodicals, and rare publications reflects the museum's special interest in Western exploration and photography. The library's facilities are made available to qualified researchers.

Public programs feature rotating exhibitions of the permanent collections, temporary exhibits compiled by the curatorial staff, and traveling exhibits from other institutions. Special tours, workshops, and performances for schoolchildren and adults and an extensive publications program complement the museum's exhibitions.

—*Patricia Hogan*

ANACONDA MINING COMPANY

The Anaconda Mining Company, founded by MARCUS DALY, propelled MONTANA into becoming the leading producer of copper in the United States. In 1875, a Union veteran of the Civil War, Michael Hickey, was prospecting for silver in BUTTE, MONTANA. His claim was a fifteen-hundred-by-six-hundred-foot area called the Anaconda Mine. (The unusual name came from a passage Hickey had read about Ulysses S. Grant's encircling Confederate General Robert E. Lee's forces like an anaconda snake.) After mining only a modest amount of silver, Hickey sold the mine in 1880 for thirty thousand dollars to Marcus Daly, who had gone to Montana in 1876. The following year, Daly's miners stuck a vein of copper three hundred feet below ground. The deposit ran as deep as six hundred feet and, at one point, was one hundred feet wide. While most prospectors in the region disdained copper and concentrated only on silver, Daly decided to build a copper smelter. He also constructed the Butte, Anaconda and Pacific Railway to transport the mineral. Two years after the discovery of copper, the Anaconda Mine was producing one hundred million pounds per year. Much of the copper shipped from Anaconda was used in traditional products—roofing, cooking utensils, hardware, and sheathing for ships. Daly's find, however, came at a time when the growing railroad industry needed copper products. With the discovery of the Anaconda Mine, Montana replaced Michigan as the region with the largest copper deposits. In 1899, Daly sold the mine to H. H. Rogers of Standard Oil. Daly remained president of the company, which became a holding and operating firm of Amalgamated Copper Mining Company, until his death in 1900. Amalgamated was dissolved in 1915.

—*Candace Floyd*

SEE ALSO: Copper Kings, War of; Copper Mining

SUGGESTED READING:
McNelis, Sarah. *Copper King at War.* Missoula, Mont., 1968.

ANDERSON, "BRONCO BILLY"

G[ilbert] M. "Bronco Billy" Anderson (1882–1971) cofounded the Essanay film studio and was the director, producer, and star of two-reel silent westerns. He was born Max Aronson in Little Rock, Arkansas.

After working as a traveling salesman, Anderson went to New York to establish a stage-acting career. While working as a model, he was discovered by the Edison studio, whose principal director, Edwin S. Porter, starred him in a one-reel short, *The Messenger Boy's Mistake* (1902). In 1903, Anderson played several roles in Porter's epoch *The Great Train Robbery.* After appearances in several other Edison pictures, he moved on to Edison's rival, Vitagraph. Next, he joined the Selig Polyscope Company, where he served as the writer and director of several shorts.

In 1907, Anderson formed the Essanay Company with partner George K. Spoor and established studios not in New York City but in the emerging motion picture capital—Los Angeles, California. Essanay produced short comedies and enjoyed particular success with those starring Ben Turpin. Beginning with *The Bandit Makes Good* in 1907, the studio produced nearly four hundred "Bronco Billy" (the original spelling was *Broncho)* western shorts—about one a week. The series, mostly directed and produced by Anderson, starred him as Bronco Billy and made him not only the first cowboy hero on film, but one of the medium's first universally recognized stars.

In 1911, Anderson launched two more series, the "Snakeville Comedies" and "Alkali Ike," and then produced a number of Charlie Chaplin comedies. When Chaplin left Essanay, Anderson sold his interest in the studio to his partner and retired from movie making. He turned to producing Broadway shows but failed. In 1920, Anderson returned to Hollywood, where he directed Stan Laurel (before Laurel teamed up with Oliver Hardy) in a number of comedy shorts for the Metro studio. Anderson's comeback proved short lived. Although he directed and produced sporadically after 1920, he drifted into obscurity. In 1957, the Academy of Motion Picture Arts and Sciences "rediscovered" him with a special Oscar for "contributions to the development of motion pictures as entertainment."

—*Alan Axelrod*

SEE ALSO: Film: The Western; Motion-Picture Industry

SUGGESTED READING:
Fenin, George N., and William K. Everson. *The Western: From Silents to the Seventies.* New York, 1973.

ANDERSON, WILLIAM C. ("BLOODY BILL")

William C. ("Bloody Bill") Anderson. *Courtesy Missouri Historical Society.*

Little is known about Missouri-born William C. Anderson's (1840–1864) life before the outbreak of the CIVIL WAR. After the death of one of his sisters in the collapse of the Kansas City prison for Southern sympathizers, Anderson joined a partisan band from Clay County, Missouri. The band, who later integrated with WILLIAM CLARKE QUANTRILL'S "Raiders," gained a reputation for cold-blooded killing as they harassed Union forces occupying Missouri. Anderson, Cole Younger, and Frank James participated in Quantrill's dawn raid on Union headquarters at Lawrence, Kansas, on August 21, 1863. Quantrill's 450 guerrillas shot every man and boy in sight and then torched the town. In early 1864, Quantrill commissioned Anderson first lieutenant, but soon afterwards, the two men quarreled over the execution of one of Anderson's men. Anderson subsequently formed a renegade band of his own and raided Union strongholds along the Missouri River. By late summer 1864, he was actively engaged in General STERLING PRICE's Confederate cavalry incursion into southern Missouri. Although Union reinforcements halted Price's forces outside St. Louis, the raid sent shock waves through the Union command, who had earlier declared the area pacified.

Anderson's most infamous exploit was his raid on Centralia, Missouri, on September 27, 1864. After pillaging and burning the town, his 225 partisans stopped a train of the Wabash, St. Louis and Pacific Railroad. They murdered the engineer and fireman and then looted an estimated three thousand dollars from the express car. In the coaches, Anderson found twenty-five Union troops on furlough and killed all but one of them while his men murdered several civilians who had tried to hide their valuables. Pursued later that day by 200 Union troops, Anderson's men counterattacked, killing 116. Among the Centralia raiders were two guerrillas later to become notorious postwar outlaws, Frank and Jesse James.

"Bloody Bill" Anderson died in an ambush by a Union militia company in Orrick, Missouri, on October 26, 1864. Union soldiers decapitated him and stuck his severed head on a spiked telegraph pole in Richmond, Missouri.

—*Maurice Law Costello*

SEE ALSO: Guerrillas; James Brothers; Younger Brothers

SUGGESTED READING:
Breihan, Carl W. *Quantrill and His Civil War Guerrillas.* Denver, 1959.
Jones, Virgil Carrington. *Gray Ghosts and Rebel Raiders.* New York, 1956.

ANIAN, STRAIT OF

SEE: Northwest Passage

ANIMALS

SEE: Wildlife

ANK INDIANS

SEE: Native American Peoples: Peoples of the Great Plains

ANTELOPE

SEE: Pronghorn

ANTIQUITIES ACT OF 1906

The Antiquities Act of 1906 is the most important piece of preservation legislation ever enacted by the United States government. Although its title suggests significance in archaeological matters, in practice the law became the cornerstone of preservation in the federal system. By allowing the president unchecked power to preserve historic, prehistoric, and "scientific" features on public land, the law created a mechanism for rapid decision making on the disposition of federal lands. The category of park areas established under its auspices—the national monuments—became the most diverse and varied collection under federal administration. At times, the monument category seemed a storehouse of places with a chance at eventual national park status—places with significant attributes but lacking the qualities associated with national parks—and a collection of curiosities that the political pork barrel made part of the park system.

The passage of the act in 1906 answered an important need in a culture trying to define itself. At the turn of the century, Americans retained a self-induced cultural inferiority that resulted from their short history. Natural wonders and prehistoric ruins testified to a longer past, and many sought to portray that heritage as equal to the castles of Europe. While cultural nationalism was strong, there was no way by law to protect natural and cultural features from depredation and exploitation. The Antiquities Act was created for that purpose.

President THEODORE ROOSEVELT understood the act differently than the Congress that passed it. Supplanting the more narrow intent of Congress, Roosevelt used the act as a primary weapon in the cause of Progressive conservation. It became even more important to him after Congress restricted his executive power to proclaim national forests in 1907. The Antiquities Act contained no restrictions on the size of proclaimed areas, and Roosevelt proclaimed some huge national monuments: the Grand Canyon, established in 1908 as a national monument, was more than eight hundred thousand acres, and Mount Olympus National Monument, now Olympic National Park, was more than six hundred thousand. With that precedent, subsequent presidents had vast leeway.

The Antiquities Act became the initial authorizing legislation for the majority of park areas established before 1933. The monuments included large natural areas, prehistoric ruins, geologic formations, historical sites, and other features of general interest. The law's flexibility remained an asset; as accepted ideas about what constituted an important part of the American past changed, the Antiquities Act remained a malleable tool to fulfill objectives.

Even after its importance declined in the 1940s as a result of controversial uses, the Antiquities Act remained the best way to reserve threatened lands quickly. In 1978, faced with collapsing negotiations on the Alaskan lands to be included in the federal land-reservation system and a deadline after which the process would have to begin again, President Jimmy Carter resorted to the Antiquities Act. He used it to proclaim fifteen new national monuments. In 1980, Carter signed the Alaskan National Interest Lands Conservation Act, which converted these national monuments into more than forty-seven million acres of national parks in Alaska. That kind of use, the first and foremost of the act, remains its legacy.

—*Hal Rothman*

SEE ALSO: Archaeology; National Park Service

SUGGESTED READING:
Rothman, Hal. *Preserving Different Pasts: The American National Monuments.* Urbana, Ill., 1989.

ANTRIM, HENRY

SEE: "Billy the Kid"

ANZA, JUAN BAUTISTA DE

Soldier, explorer, and Governor of Spanish New Mexico Juan Bautista de Anza (1736–1788) was a highly competent and well-respected military officer. He is perhaps best known for his success in opening an overland trail from the presidio of Tubac (Arizona) to California in 1774. He then led a major colonizing expedition to California that resulted in the founding of the presidio and mission of San Francisco.

Born at the presidio of Fronteras, one hundred miles southeast of Tubac, Anza was the son of the presidio captain. Of Basque lineage, he was descended from elite Spanish ranchers in Sonora. He entered military service at Fronteras in 1753 and was promoted to lieutenant two years later. He distinguished himself in a campaign against the Apaches in 1759.

Juan Bautista de Anza. *Courtesy Museum of New Mexico.*

The following year, Anza was named captain of the presidio of Tubac. Already known for his ability, solid disposition, rapport with his soldiers, and skill with weapons, he settled into his military duties: protecting the Jesuit missions and keeping the native populations of Seris, Apaches, and Papagos under control.

When the Franciscans took over Jesuit properties after 1768, Anza met Father Francisco Garcés, who wanted to open a mission at the confluence of the Gila and Colorado rivers. The priest's desire led to Anza's military expedition that opened the route from Tubac to Monterey in 1774 and established friendly relations with the Yuma Indians. In October 1775, Anza led 244 men, women, and children to Monterey and returned to Sonora the following year. He was promoted to colonel and became commandant of arms of the Province of Sonora in 1771. By September 1778, he had become governor of New Mexico, and he began to address the problem of safety from Indian attacks. In 1786, he arranged a lasting peace with the Comanches and entered into an alliance with the Utes and Navajos in an attempt to control the Apaches.

Upon his return to Sonora, Anza continued to pursue peace with the Apaches. He died in Arizpe shortly after his Spanish soldiers had completed a successful campaign against these long-time enemies.

Although the Sonora-California route he had opened was closed after the YUMA REVOLT of 1781, Anza retained a reputation as an exceptional soldier and explorer.

—*Iris H. W. Engstrand*

SUGGESTED READING:
Bolton, Herbert E., ed. *Anza's California Expeditions*. 5 vols. Berkeley, Calif., 1930.
Bowman, J. N., and Robert F. Heizer. *Anza and the Northwest Frontier of New Spain*. Los Angeles, 1967.
Kessell, John L. "Anza Damns the Missions: A Spanish Soldier's Criticism of Indian Policy, 1772." *Journal of Arizona History* 13 (1972): 53–62.
———. "Anza, Indian Fighter: The Spring Campaign of 1766." *Journal of Arizona History* 9 (1968): 155–163.
Thomas, Alfred Barnaby, ed. *Forgotten Frontiers: A Study of the Spanish Indian Policy of Don Juan Bautista de Anza, Governor of New Mexico, 1777–1787*. Norman, Okla., 1932. Reprint. 1969.

APACHE INDIANS

SEE: Native American Peoples: Peoples of the Great Plains

APACHE KID

U.S. Army scout and later outlaw, the Apache Kid (ca. 1860–ca. 1894) was born in southern Arizona. He became first sergeant of Apache scouts as a protégé of AL SIEBER, noted chief of scouts. In 1883, he accompanied General GEORGE CROOK into Mexico's Sierra Madre and served in subsequent operations against GERONIMO. In 1887, he killed an Indian living on a reservation and was sentenced to prison. Following a spectacular escape, the Kid became the most wanted outlaw on the border. His later career was shrouded in myth, and he was accused of numerous crimes, all unproven. After an 1894 shootout, he fades from history, his death date unknown, but his legend imperishable.

—*Dan L. Thrapp*

SEE ALSO: United States Army: Scouts

SUGGESTED READING:
Jess G. Hayes. *Apache Vengeance: The True Story of the Apache Kid*. Albuquerque, N. Mex., 1954.
Williamson, Dan R. "The Apache Kid: Red Renegade of the West." *Arizona Highways* 15 (May 1939): 14–15, 30–31.

APACHE WARS

In the sixteenth and seventeenth centuries, two aggressive peoples—Apaches moving south and Spaniards edging northward from central Mexico—collided in the region now blanketed by southern New Mexico, Arizona, and western Texas and, below the United States–Mexican border, by Chihuahua and Sonora. Warfare was inevitable. It persisted sporadically for two centuries, punctuated by periods of uneasy truce when each faction sought to mollify the other while not surrendering its forward thrust.

The Apaches were a vigorous, though not numerous, people when they contacted the Spanish. The latest arrivals from Alaska, the Apaches were linguistically Athapascan and, upon reaching the Southwest, were grouped into numerous bands and tribal divisions. (The Navajos were considered a distinct tribe, although Apache in language and tradition.) The Apaches encompassed such Eastern or Plains tribes as the Lipans and Kiowa-Apaches. The Western Apaches, with whom the Spanish were primarily concerned, included the Mescaleros east of the Rio Grande; the Mimbres and Mogollons, just west of the river; the Gilenos, primarily Mimbres with perhaps an admixture of Coyoteros or others; and the Chiricahuas.

Frederic Remington's portrayal of the Apache Wars characterizes the guerrilla tactics of much of the two-hundred-year-long conflict. *Courtesy National Cowboy Hall of Fame and Western Heritage Center.*

All were militant, but the most warlike were the Chiricahuas who, when the Spanish encountered them, composed four bands. Together they made up what ethnologists call the Central and Southern Chiricahuas, while the Mimbres constituted the Eastern Chiricahua tribe. The Chiricahuas inhabited southwestern New Mexico, southeastern Arizona, and southward into the Sierra Madre between Chihuahua and Sonora.

The number of Apaches at the time of contact with the Spanish may have totaled 6,000, suggesting a combined warrior strength of around 1,200. Apache belligerence took, in general, two forms: raids and war parties, neither of which included more than several score participants. The Apaches conducted raids for livestock and captives when fighting was avoided; they formed war parties for combat to avenge earlier losses or for other objectives.

Some of the earliest chiefs remembered today include Ojos Colorados, Inclán Tasquienachi, and Vívora—all Mimbres leaders—and Isose, Chiganstege, Juan José Compá, and Pisago Cabezón (perhaps the father of COCHISE, a noted later chief)—all Chiricahua leaders.

The Spanish sought to stabilize the northern domain with a beadwork of presidios, or garrisoned forts. The upper tier of political regions constituted the Provincias Internas. Its officials were generally independent of the viceroy and were subject to the crown. Some of Spain's ablest military officers were prominent in the provincial outposts. Among them were Irish-born Hugo Oconor, a better field commander than administrator; the Marques de Rubí, an innovative, no-nonsense specialist who believed in the extermination of the Apaches; Colonel Jacobo Ugarte y Loyola, practical, humane and just, whose principal struggles were with insensitive superiors; French-born Teodoro de Croix, a highly intelligent, diligent, honest, and capable official; and JUAN BAUTISTA DE ANZA, from Fronteras, Sonora, and perhaps the finest officer to serve Spain north of Old Mexico.

However active the military, the toll exacted by the Indians in Mexico remained enormous. From 1771 to 1776, largely in Chihuahua, 1,674 persons were slain and 154 were captured; 116 haciendas and ranches were abandoned; and 68,256 head of livestock were run off. These figures do not include military person-

U.S. Army troops photographed in 1885 at a telegraph station in the Arizona Territory during the Apache Wars. *Courtesy National Archives.*

nel killed in battle, travelers slain on the roads, or mules and horses stolen from presidios. Nevertheless, by 1800, the Apache-Spanish relationship had approached stability, thanks to Colonel Ugarte.

But then came political upheaval. From 1821 to 1823, Mexico engaged in war to win independence from Spain. A stable military presence and readily available rations for Indians settled near presidios vanished, and assurances to Apaches were no longer meticulously kept. Military organizations were withdrawn for internal scuffling or simply disintegrated. Apache raiders seized upon this tumultuous situation, and their depredations increased. Chihuahua and Sonora began paying for "Apache" scalps, though no one could identify a scalp, once it was taken, as Apache rather than other Indian, or Mexican, in origin. James Kirker and similarly notorious scalp hunters exacerbated the problem. Murder led to murder rather than to either extermination or peace. In 1837, scalp hunter John J. Johnson from Oposura, Sonora, killed Chief Juan José Compá, of the traditionally friendly Chiricahua, and a score of his followers, with long-lasting repercussions.

By 1851, JOHN RUSSELL BARTLETT, engaged in surveying the United States–Mexican boundary, toured northern Mexico, finding "widespread devastation. . . depopulated towns and villages; deserted haciendas and ranches; elegant . . . churches falling into decay. . . . There is scarcely a family . . . but has suffered the loss of one or more of its members or friends. In some instances whole families have been cut off, the father murdered, the mother and children carried into captivity."

From earliest contact, the Apaches had been friendly toward Anglo-Americans. The United States occupied the Southwest in the UNITED STATES–MEXICAN WAR. On October 20, 1846, General STEPHEN WATTS KEARNY met the fearsome Eastern Chiricahua chief MANGAS COLORADAS near the Gila River. Mangas Coloradas invited the officer to join in devastating Mexico; Kearny declined. In February 1852, when Mangas Coloradas and other chiefs met Bartlett's survey party, the encounter again was amicable.

With the Civil War came a disastrous incident that ignited lasting conflict between Americans and Apaches. Early in the war, U.S. forces were withdrawn for service in the East, and as they departed the West, they burned their military installations. The Indians, not understanding the "white men's war," assumed the evacuation was due to Indian pressure. This belief led to increased aggressiveness. Then in February 1861, the notorious Bascom incident launched open warfare between the powerful central Chiricahuas and the Anglos. Led by Second Lieutenant George N. Bascom, operating on a mistaken identification provided by a disreputable and heavy-drinking rancher named John Ward, U.S. troops falsely accused Cochise of kidnapping a white boy and tried to hold the Apache leader hostage until the boy was released. Violence erupted; casualties followed on both sides; and hostilities mounted.

Cochise and Mangas Coloradas joined forces. There were many small skirmishes, in which some 150 whites were killed and a half-dozen stage stations burned. The chiefs laid an ambuscade at Apache Pass to entrap an advance element of the fifteen-hundred-man California Column, en route to the Rio Grande to engage the Confederates and commanded by Brigadier General JAMES H. CARLETON. The Battle of Apache Pass was a minor affair in which ten Apaches and several U.S. soldiers were killed; Mangas Coloradas was wounded. The ambush was abandoned when light artillery routed the besiegers, but enmity remained.

In January 1863, Mangas Coloradas surrendered to a civilian who turned him over to the military. While a prisoner, he was goaded unmercifully, and when he protested, he was shot. An officer reported that he was "killed while trying to escape." His murder is still resented by Apaches.

Inclined toward extermination on principle, Carleton sent Colonel CHRISTOPHER HOUSTON ("KIT") CARSON to Fort Stanton, New Mexico, with five companies under the appalling order that "all Indian men of [the Mescalero] tribe are to be killed whenever and wherever you can find them." Carson believed in obeying orders, but he knew this directive was nonsense and ignored it. Eventually several hundred Mescaleros were dispatched to Carleton's ill-conceived Bosque Redondo Navajo reserve, but they slipped away to their homeland at their earliest convenience.

In postwar Arizona, the U.S. military had to deal with numerous small bands of Indians, thieving to survive, and the absence of any central enemy to fight. Several able military men assigned to the territory failed to pacify it. GEORGE CROOK, then a lieutenant colonel, was promised sufficient resources and authority to confront the problem decisively. He enlisted Apache scouts, "the wilder the better," and several able civilian chiefs of scouts including AL SIEBER, Dan O'Leary, Archie McIntosh, and Ebin Stanley. Crook also sent out numerous single-company columns under junior officers, and within a year or two, he brought the situation under control. For this success, he was promoted to brigadier general. He then turned his attention to the great chiefs of the Apaches following Mangas Coloradas: Cochise, VICTORIO, and JUH.

Angry with Anglos since the Bascom incident although indicating occasionally he was ready to come in, Cochise conferred at length with General OLIVER OTIS HOWARD. Cochise agreed to accept a life on a reservation and abandon warfare. He kept his word until his death, apparently of cancer, in 1874.

Victorio, a Mimbres chief, was among the first victims of the ill-envisioned "concentration policy" by which Indians of various bands and tribes were collected on the San Carlos Reservation in Arizona. Because of traditional feuds and bitter enmities, the huge reserve was awash with turmoil. Continuing to break out of the reservation, Victorio was considered one of the "ablest Indian generals" of record. His warriors regularly bested army elements until October 1880, when he was trapped and killed in the Tres Castillos uplift of Chihuahua by Mexican militia under Lieutenant Colonel Joaquin Terrazas.

In August 1881, an incident that touched off the most sensational series of events in the history of Apache Wars occurred. A medicine man named Noch-ay-del-klinne developed widespread and ominous influence. Colonel Eugene Asa Carr was directed by the San Carlos agent to "capture, or kill—or both" the prophet at Cibecue, northwest of Fort Apache. Through an interpreter's ineptitude, a fight broke out. The medicine man was killed; some Apache scouts mutinied; and an officer and several soldiers were slain. The command regained Fort Apache, which was later attacked. So many soldiers were rushed in that the alarmed Chiricahuas under Juh and GERONIMO bolted for Mexico. Under the military direction of Juh, they blunted an army pursuit and reached the Sierra Madre where they united with others already there. Yet most of the Mimbres and the Eastern Chiricahuas remained at San Carlos. The Chiricahuas in Mexico wished to unite the tribe, and to do so, Juh planned the most stunning operation on Apache record.

With 60 followers, including Geronimo, he swept north in April 1882 through country laced with troops, attacked San Carlos, and at gunpoint herded out a reluctant Chief Loco and several hundred Mimbres and Chiricahua Apaches. Through a region thick with searching military commands, the group withdrew for safety into Mexico. Short of the Sierra Madre, the band ran into the Mexican command of Lieutenant Colonel Lorenzo Garcia; 11 Apache men, about 75 Apache women and children, and 23 Mexican soldiers were killed. But the bulk of the Chiricahuas reached safety in the mountains. In the Sierra Madre, there now was a pool of about 150 warriors, obviously posing the gravest threat in years to Anglo-Americans in the Southwest.

Crook was reassigned to Arizona. Wanting to return the Apaches to San Carlos, he carefully planned an expedition of 196 Apache scouts into the Sierra Madre. The daring 1883 operation succeeded. The general met and talked with important Apaches. He returned with 325 Indians and the pledges that others, too, would return. In February 1884, even Geronimo came in, nearly last. Crook affirmed in his annual report that "for the first time in the history of that fierce people, every member of the Apache tribe is [now] at peace." The Juh campaign and the Crook operation to bring the Apaches back to San Carlos were the climactic events of the Apache Wars.

But in May 1885, the peace once more was broken. The Chiricahuas who had returned to San Carlos staged a prohibited "tizwin drunk," and no immediate reproof followed. (Tizwin, or tiswin, was a mild fermented beer, manufactured and drunk by the Apaches on social occasions. Because these "drunks" caused much tumult on the reservations, they were frequently prohibited by agents.) Fearing a major operation against them was brewing, the Indians, led by Geronimo, broke out of San Carlos. In order to persuade the great subchief, Chihuahua, to join the flight, Geronimo had told him that white officers had been killed and punishment was imminent. Learning later that Geronimo had lied, Chihuahua determined to kill the war leader but was dissuaded. He reluctantly joined Geronimo as his only option. Those leaving the reservation totaled 34 men and 100 women and children.

For fifteen months, U.S. troops and Apache scouts searched for the fugitives. The army caught up with a portion of the group and reached an agreement with them, but Mexican irregulars fired on the troops, mortally wounding Captain Emmet Crawford, and the surrender was aborted.

In March 1886, Geronimo and his party met Crook at Canyon Embudo and agreed to surrender. After Crook left for Fort Bowie, a bootlegger filled many of

The surrender of Geronimo, pictured here with other Apache prisoners being transported by train to exile in Florida, ended two centuries of war. *Courtesy National Archives.*

the Apaches with whiskey and told them tales about the dire fate awaiting those who capitulated. During the night, Geronimo and 19 men and as many non-combatants fled once more for the mountains. The war, although greatly reduced, continued.

Crook was relieved of his command at his own request, and Brigadier General NELSON APPLETON MILES took command with instructions to make prominent use of white troops and forgo Crook's dependence upon Apache scouts. Miles's efforts were futile. He installed a heliograph network, which did not help much. Deep in Mexico, his white troops floundered about with no idea where the Apaches were. Miles grudgingly returned to Crook's methods, sending veteran scout officer Lieutenant Charles B. Gatewood and two trusted Apaches to ferret out Geronimo and persuade him to surrender. The capitulation, in Skeleton Canyon on September 4, 1886, terminated two centuries of Apache warfare.

—*Dan L. Thrapp*

SUGGESTED READING:

Bourke, John Gregory. *On the Border with Crook*. Glorieta, N. Mex., 1969.

Griffen, William B. *Apaches at War and Peace: The Janos Presidio, 1750–1858*. Albuquerque, N. Mex., 1988.

Moorhead, Max L. *The Apache Frontier: Jacobo Ugarte and Spanish-Indian Relations in Northern New Spain, 1769–1791*. Norman, Okla., 1968.

Thomas, Alfred Barnaby. *Teodoro de Croix, and the Northern Frontier of New Spain 1776–1783*. Norman, Okla., 1941. Reprint. 1968.

Thrapp, Dan L. *The Conquest of Apacheria*. Norman, Okla., 1967.

——. *General Crook and the Sierra Madre Adventure*. Norman, Okla., 1972.

APPLEGATE, JESSE

Oregon politician and writer Jesse Applegate (1811–1888) was born in Kentucky and traveled over the Oregon Trail from Missouri in 1843. In Oregon, he became a farmer and entered public life as a surveyor and road builder. Among his many projects were the original survey of Oregon City and the laying out of the Applegate Trail from Fort Hall in Idaho through northern Nevada and California to the Willamette Valley. Applegate helped reorganize Oregon's first government (the Provisional Government), served one term in its legislature, and was a member of the convention that drew up Oregon's constitution in 1857. Originally a Whig, he joined the new Republican party and helped influence Oregonians to vote for Abraham Lincoln in 1860 and to remain loyal to the Union during the Civil War. He also promoted the construction of the Oregon and California Railroad, which was authorized by Congress in 1868 to link Portland with Sacramento.

Applegate's reminiscences, which he dictated for Western historian HUBERT HOWE BANCROFT in 1878, and his classic Oregon Trail essay, "A Day with the Cow Column," which describes the routine of the overland pioneers, are invaluable sources for Oregon history.

—*Gordon B. Dodds*

SUGGESTED READING:

Applegate, Jesse. "A Day with the Cow Column." *Oregon Historical Quarterly* 1 (1900): 371–383.

Applegate, Shannon. *Skookum: An Oregon Family's History and Lore*. New York, 1988.

Schafer, Joseph. "Jesse Applegate: Pioneer, Statesman, and Philosopher." *Washington Historical Quarterly* 7 (1907): 217–233.

ARAPAHO INDIANS

SEE: Native American Peoples: Peoples of the Great Plains

ARCHAEOLOGY

The first widespread interest in the prehistory of the American West grew out of a combination of cultural nationalism, the professionalization of science in the

United States, and the anxiety associated with the pronouncement of the closing of the frontier at the end of the nineteenth century. In the 1890s, Americans still experienced the cultural self-doubt of a former colony; they worried about the worth of their achievements as a nation. Americans and their dollars went overseas to view what they believed were their cultural origins in the castles and museums of Europe, and these travels spurred nationalistic individuals to begin a "See America First" campaign to entice others to view their natural and cultural heritage. At nearly the same time, political and cultural leaders began to emphasize the importance of professional training in fields as disparate as forestry and social work as a counterbalance to the centralization of wealth and power in the industrial elite. The anxiety associated with the urbanization of America and the tension that permeated a rapidly changing industrializing society gave Americans an inherent appreciation for the remains of any world they replaced. In the 1890s and early 1900s, they looked to the professionalizing disciplines of archaeology and anthropology for verification of their success as a people.

Scholars and proto-scholars had been interested in the prehistoric ruins of the American West since they had first been reported in the late eighteenth and early nineteenth centuries. In *Notes on the State of Virginia* (1782), THOMAS JEFFERSON discussed his efforts to excavate "scientifically" a prehistoric Indian mound with an eye toward unlocking its history, but even before him, a Finnish economics professor named Peter Kalm had written in his *Travels in North America* (1772) of the "few marks of antiquity" that led him to speculate the new continent had formerly been inhabited by "civilizations" far in advance of those first discovered by European explorers. The great Indian mounds of Ohio had long aroused European and American curiosity. The Reverend David Jones described the mounds in some detail in the 1770s, and Caleb Atwater (ANDREW JACKSON's commissioner of Indian affairs) carefully surveyed and explicated them in the first volume of the *Transactions of the American Antiquarian Society*

Mesa Verde ruins in southwestern Colorado. *Courtesy Department of Library Services, American Museum of Natural History.*

(1820). EDWIN JAMES, a botanist and geologist on STEPHEN HARRIMAN LONG's expedition, speculated about and carefully measured Indian grave mounds near St. Louis; self-trained archaeologist Ephraim G. Squier and Ohio physician Edwin H. Davis reported on Mississippi Valley mounds in the first volume of the *Smithsonian Contributions to Knowledge* (1848), and in 1858, the *Contributions* carried a 168-page study by S. H. Haven on the "Archeology of the United States," the first attempt to summarize American prehistory. The mid-nineteenth-century surveys in general sparked an interest among amateur scientists in the archaeology of the American West. Accounts of prehistoric communities permeated not only the writings of explorers but also of the military. WILLIAM HENRY JACKSON's photographs of the Mesa Verde region in the 1870s also alerted the literate public to the mysterious remains of a divergent heritage. By the end of the 1870s, it was clear to many American elites that the West held not only an awe-inspiring natural heritage, but an exciting cultural one as well.

Yet archaeology was the exclusive province of enthusiastic amateurs with the resources to enable them to explore. ADOLPH FRANCIS ALPHONSE BANDELIER was among the first to study the prehistory of American West seriously. The lean and craggy scion of a Swiss American banking family, Bandelier trained himself as an anthropologist under the tutelage of Lewis Henry Morgan, the founder of modern anthropology. After becoming, in 1880, the first Anglo-American to see the prehistoric ruins of Frijoles Canyon in northern New Mexico, Bandelier explored widely in the West and Southwest and traveled as far as Casa Grande in northern Mexico. He functioned as a taxonomist, measuring and drawing pictures of ruins and speculating about the nature of prehistoric life. He wrote both scholarly and popular books about his experiences, the best known of which was translated into English as *The Delightmakers,* a fictionalized account of prehistoric life derived from his research.

JOHN WESLEY POWELL's Bureau of Ethnology, founded in 1879, began with an abiding interest in anthropology that quickly spread to archaeology. By the late 1880s, his operatives were inspecting archaeological sites throughout the West as well as the living native peoples of the region and, on occasion, recommending protection of archaeological ruins. But with the many demands on the GENERAL LAND OFFICE, the federal bureau responsible for the public domain, the federal government took little action.

At the turn of the twentieth century, archaeology lacked a systematized scientific methodology. Like many other late nineteenth-century disciplines, it was closely tied to the romantic world view. Archaeologists in both the New World and the Old used evidence to construct broad-based visions that reflected the biases of their cultures. Despite the valuable survey work, many were truer to the way they wanted the world to be than to the evidence they found.

Nor did archaeologists control the places that contained the ruins so crucial to their emergence as a respectable science. American prehistory was at the mercy of anyone who happened along. Farmers smashed prehistoric pots with their plows, traveling parties excavated sites and took away artifacts for private use, and small cottage industries that catered to collectors sprang up in many places. Richard Wetherill, a rancher from Mancos, Colorado, came to symbolize the haphazard management of American prehistory. A cowboy with a sharp intellect and a passionate interest in archaeology, Wetherill became an obsession for American archaeologists. Living in southwestern Colorado, he and his brother-in-law found in 1889 what later became known as Cliff Palace Ruins in Mesa Verde National Park. Fascinated by the prehistoric world, Wetherill excavated Mesa Verde, Chaco Canyon, and numerous other Western archaeological sites, thus earning the enmity of university-based and government-affiliated professionals. A consummate "rugged individualist" of the nineteenth century, Wetherill was in a field increasingly crowded with twentieth-century scientists who had something to prove. Eventually the power and prestige of both the Department of the Interior and the Archaeological Institute of America were allied against him. One result was the ANTIQUITIES ACT OF 1906, which made unauthorized digging on federal land illegal and allowed the government to reserve public-domain lands with historic, scientific, and prehistoric value.

The year 1906 was a banner year for archaeology in the United States. Besides the Antiquities Act, Congress also established Mesa Verde National Park in Colorado. No additional piece of legislation to protect archaeological sites was enacted by Congress between 1906 and the passage of the Archaeological Resources Protection Act of 1979. In 1906, archaeology reflected important cultural themes in American society. Its romantic, story-telling mode helped to assure Americans that the path their society had taken was best.

Following 1906, empirical science gained a foothold in archaeology. Nils C. Nelson helped introduce stratigraphy, the study of the *in situ* layering of prehistoric material, to North American archaeologists. Alfred V. Kidder, who became the preeminent American archaeologist of the first half of the twentieth century, applied the technique to the ruins of Pecos, New Mexico. In 1927, after nearly a decade of study at the site, Kidder convened the Pecos Conference, a meeting of archaeologists during which the Pecos Classification, a system for classifying prehistoric pueblos, was first devised. Kidder's work was a crucial step in developing an empirical, scientific basis for archaeology. It also, in part, brought about the end of archaeology's place in popular literature and culture. Archaeologists stopped telling stories and began comparing pottery shards. As archaeology became an empirical science, its practitioners ceased to speak to the concerns of the broader public.

Dendrochronology, the science of tree-ring dating, was another major scientific advance for archaeology. Developed by Arthur E. Douglass, a University of Arizona astronomer interested in sunspots, dendrochronology offered a better way to date prehistoric sites. In search of historical meteorological data, Douglass used the moisture data accumulated in trees to discern what he could about climate in the past. Evident in sawed timber, tree rings provided a meteorologic chronology of the American Southwest. Assembling information from around the world, Douglass constructed partial historical chronologies that established temporal relationships between different archaeological locations in the American West. A young archaeologist, Emil W. Haury, completed the chronology with a find in eastern Arizona. His half-charred piece of wood linked two independently existing sequences, providing a chronology back to the thirteenth century. Shortly after, links back to 700 A.D. were completed.

Although much of the early work in archaeology was undertaken in the desert Southwest, where tangible remains of prehistory were easily uncovered, since the 1920s, archaeologists have explored all over the West. Modern scientific advances, such as infrared photography, have facilitated much better readings of subsurface archaeological materials. The field has become progressively more specialized and scientific. Although some of the leading archaeologists attempt to write the grand synthesis, the quantity and variety of research defies categorization. Like many other fields, archaeology has been a victim of its own success. Its ability to ask and answer specific questions has made it obscure to a public interested in its broad sweep.

—*Hal Rothman*

SEE ALSO: Casa Grande Ruins Reservation; Native American Peoples: Pre-Columbian Peoples

SUGGESTED READING:
Ceram, C. W. *The First Americans.* New York, 1971.
———. *Gods, Graves, and Scholars: The Story of Archaeology.* New York, 1952.
Fitting, James Edward. *The Development of North American Archaeology.* Garden City, N.J., 1973.
Wiley, Gordon R., and Jeremy A. Sabloff. *The History of American Archaeology.* London, 1973.

ARCHITECTURE

Folk (Ethnic) Architecture
Arn Henderson

Adobe Architecture
Byron A. Johnson

Urban Architecture
Charles Phillips

FOLK (ETHNIC) ARCHITECTURE

One of the most compelling issues related to the material culture of the West is its difference from that of the East. Indeed there is a complex mythology and iconography that identifies the West as a distinct subculture. But why is it different and in what ways do folk and vernacular buildings reveal these differences? There are two opposing explanations that focus on the distinctiveness of the West. One theory—introduced by FREDERICK JACKSON TURNER—holds that the regional culture of the West represents simply a diffusion of earlier traditional Eastern culture. The other theory—most often associated with WALTER PRESCOTT WEBB—explains Western distinctiveness as an effort by pioneers to cope with unique environmental circumstances.

Everyone agreed that settlers moving west faced fundamental challenges to a way of life that was familiar. But how they responded and the particular response they chose was the subject of disagreement. Turner, in his frontier thesis postulated a theory of diffusion. In his view, Western settlers extended and adapted the culture of the archaic East. "Stand at Cumberland Gap," he said, "and watch the procession of civilization, the fur trader and hunter, the cattle-raiser, the pioneer farmer—stand at South Pass in the Rockies a century later, and see the same procession." Similarly, Robert F. Berkhofer, Jr., who later expanded upon this imitation theory, proposed that culture had a primary role in institutional change and the environment was of secondary importance. He believed that a traditional way of doing things and accumulated knowledge were crucial to survival. Moreover, the old ways were known and proven while new notions were risky. And the environment—especially on the Great Plains with harsh wind and dust storms, intense heat in summer and numbing cold in winter—demanded fast response. There was little time for experimentation.

In contrast, Webb proposed an environmental-response theory that reversed the order of influence. It was a theory of innovation, and it held that space rather than culture was the dominant factor in institutional change. Webb noted that when settlers approached the one hundredth meridian, they encountered a treeless, semiarid environment with which they had no experience. The humid forest of the East did not prepare them for life in a harsh and demanding landscape. All of their cultural institutions required a major adaptation to a new environment. New methods of fencing, such as barbed wire, and economical windmills had to be developed to facilitate settlement. The landscape of the West, in large regions, held few traditional building materials, and the climatic extremes offered new problems that required innovative forms of shelter.

Culture's influence on form

Expressions of ethnicity in folk or vernacular architecture are clearly delineated by buildings erected by various immigrant groups. Ethnicity refers to the shared cultural patterns that distinguish one group from others within a society. In their buildings, some immigrants reproduced the forms of memory in familiar patterns that reflected the traditions from their cultural heritage. The expressions of buildings throughout the West, especially in the rural landscape, are diverse, and the distinct differences reveal the ethnic variety of settlers.

French Creoles on the Gulf Coast of Louisiana and Texas built houses of *poteaux-en-terre* (posts-in-earth)

The Bolduc House, built around 1787, represents the *poteaux-en-terre* construction of the French Creoles who settled Sainte Genevieve, Missouri. Photograph by Jack E. Boucher, National Park Service, Historic American Buildings Survey. *Courtesy Missouri State Historic Preservation Office.*

with a traditional hipped roof and continuous *galerie* (porch) on all four sides. African Americans within the same region built "shotgun" houses, one room wide and usually three rooms deep, that reflected a fusion of cultural antecedents of Yoruban houses in Africa and Indian housing in the Caribbean. Immigrant groups from Scandinavia, especially those from Finland, Norway, and Sweden, built finely crafted houses of horizontal log construction that were similar to those of their forested homelands. Italian immigrants who settled in the Great Basin reflected their tradition of stone working by constructing masonry ranch buildings and specialized buildings for the storage and preparation of traditional food. Chinese immigrants, working in railroad construction, mining, and agriculture in the Far West, expressed community identity by constructing traditional benevolent-association buildings and temples. German immigrants who settled in the hill country west of San Antonio, Texas, in the 1840s reflected their culture with buildings of *fachwerk* (half-timber) construction. Dating back to the sixteenth century in Germany, this method of construction incorporated a mortise-and-tenon framework of horizontal and vertical timbers. Builders used diagonal and sometimes curved braces to provide lateral support for the timber frame and filled the spaces between all the structural elements with brick, wattle and daub, or stone to form a continuous wall.

The form of folk housing of early Hispanic settlers in the Southwest reflected the geographic and cultural sphere of both Mexico and Spain. Early Hispanic houses were initially flat-roofed, one-room buildings that were expanded in a linear pattern by adding other rooms. The Spanish, who learned adobe construction from the Arabs, introduced the technique to North America. Adobe bricks were made by combining dirt, water, straw, and sometimes horse hair and placing the mixture into wooden molds. Walls were constructed by laying the brick in horizontal courses with earthen mortar, and the surfaces were stuccoed with earthen plaster.

In the decades following the Civil War, descendants of Germans from Russia, who had settled there a century earlier as farmers at the invitation of Catherine the Great, immigrated to America to escape religious and political oppression. The German Russian settlers homesteaded the Great Plains, a grain-producing environment similar to the steppes of western Russia. Germans who had lived in villages along the Volga River settled primarily in Kansas and Nebraska, while those who had lived around the Black Sea relocated in North and South Dakota. On the American Great Plains, the houses they built—a distinctive amalgam of earlier central European forms combined with vernacular Russian construction technology—featured walls built of puddled clay or rammed earth. Most houses were either a linear continuum of three rooms or arrangements of two rooms wide and two rooms deep with a loft above for grain storage or bedrooms for larger families. A common feature in some houses in the Dakotas was a small centralized room, known as a black kitchen, with a combined bake-oven and furnace. The small room, used exclusively for cooking, was one component of a larger kitchen where food was prepared and served. The term *black kitchen* derived from the appearance of the inside walls, which were blackened from smoke. The centralized location of the walk-in kitchen was critical since the bake-oven, combined with a furnace, heated the house. German Russian builders would frequently extend the walls of the walk-in kitchen into the loft above to provide a large, tapered chimney that could also be used as a smokehouse for curing meat.

Anglo-American log cabins, a product of European building traditions, also influenced the vernacular landscape of the West. Predominant in the East, especially among Scots Irish settlers in Appalachia, the log house spread to the South and West in multiple configurations. As this icon of the American frontier crossed the Mississippi River, it became the dominant house-form in the Missouri Ozarks, Arkansas, western Louisiana, eastern Texas, and the Indian Territory. But the Appalachian log cabin did not dominate the landscape west of the one hundredth meridian because in large parts of the region, there was little timber available. Even in areas with plentiful timber, the building form of Appalachia did not survive the passage west intact. Within the Rocky Mountain region, the Anglo-American log house with a raftered roof and eave entry was not well suited to the environment; melting snow would produce a seasonal quagmire along the drip-line of the eaves. Settlers frequently adopted an archaic Eastern type of Scandinavian origin, appearing initially in the Delaware Valley, for housing in the Western mountains. These houses had a gable entry with a "ridgepole and purlin" roof. This form of shallow-pitched roof featured gable logs that were notched into a center ridgepole with parallel purlins (support beams) extending the length of the cabin.

Environment's influence on form

The physical environment into which settlers immigrated was a powerful determinant of the expression of their architecture. Climate, topography, and available materials in the landscape all influenced the form of buildings, and pioneers adapted to new environments in several ways. In the absence of adequate transportation systems to bring manufactured materi-

The milk and meat cooler from the JA Ranch featured lattice work on the upper section of the walls that allowed air to circulate around meat carcasses stored within. The milk cooler, on the right, contained a water trough in which dairy goods were stored and cooled by evaporation. *Courtesy Ranching Heritage Center, Texas Tech University Museum.*

als to them, they drew from the surrounding landscape for the components of their buildings. They borrowed ideas from other cultural groups within their geographic sphere. And they adapted the building forms they remembered from the past to protect themselves from the unpredictable vagaries of nature—sun, wind, rain, and snow—with considerable ingenuity.

The milk and meat cooler from the JA Ranch, constructed in the 1880s in the Texas Panhandle, was designed to keep large quantities of perishable food. The building consisted of two components butted together, one for meat and the other for dairy products. The meat cooler provided a space for storing and processing beef, deer, elk, and buffalo. The carcasses were wrapped with cloth or canvas to keep flies off the meat and hung from the roof joists. Lattice work on the upper section of the walls allowed air to circulate through the structure. Meat was rarely cured because it was used quickly to feed the fifty employees of the ranch. In the summer, calves were slaughtered, but during winter, when it was cold and the meat would keep longer, larger cattle were killed. The milk cooler, built of thick walls of sandstone laid in mud mortar, had a masonry trough around the inside perimeter that contained flowing water diverted from a nearby stream. (In later years, a windmill provided the source of water.) China and earthenware crocks of milk, butter, and eggs were wrapped in cloth and placed in the trough. The cold water would wick up the cloth and cool the dairy products by evaporation.

A popular form of shelter on the Great Plains was the dugout. Although often built as temporary structures, dugouts continued to be built and lived in even in the years immediately following World War II in some areas of the southern Great Plains. Construction was expedient, fast, and cheap. Dugouts were frequently built into the side of a knoll and enclosed with whatever materials were available. On the open plains, it was common to burrow straight down into the ground with only a slight projection above the surface. The roof would usually be framed with a cottonwood log as the ridgepole with joists of smaller timbers spanning from the ridge to intermediate purlins or exterior walls. Some form of sheathing and tar paper, if available, would then be covered with sod to complete the roof.

The dugout is a house-form associated exclusively with Great Plains settlement. Although its sources are subject to speculation, the dugout was an ingenious adaptation to the environment, and it was an idea that was enormously influential. As people moved onto the landscape, they simply imitated what someone else had done. The idea took hold quickly and became part of the popular culture of the Great Plains for successive waves of immigrants. Thus a concept of environmental adaptation ultimately became transformed to one

of imitation, sometimes with ironic results. One family who homesteaded the High Plains in New Mexico in 1908 illustrates how unquestioning some people were in constructing shelter, even when alternate technology was available:

We decided that if we were to become a nester, we had better get busy and build a house. We hired a man with a team and scraper to dig out 16 x 32 feet. We did not know why, but all were living in dugouts and we thought there was some reason . . . [we] purchased lumber to wall the dugout and for the roof. In fact enough lumber was bought to have built a house [above ground] . . . with seven foot walls.

While local Hispanics derided the Anglos who built dugouts and referred to them as "gopher holes," they also borrowed architectural ideas from the Anglos. In fact, most of the buildings of settlers on the plains of northeastern New Mexico and southeastern Colorado are hybrids—buildings that represent a fusion of ideas derived from both Hispanic and Anglo cultures. With the establishment of saw mills and the arrival of the railroad, Hispanics rapidly accepted the value of the Anglo pitched roof. Houses in Hispanic villages were

The dugout provided housing for settlers on the Great Plains where building materials of any kind were scarce. *Courtesy Western History Collections, University of Oklahoma.*

The adobe style of Santa Fe's Palace of the Governors recalls its years as a Spanish, then Mexican, territorial seat. *Courtesy New Mexico Museum.*

enclosed initially with "board-on-board" roofs and later with corrugated sheet metal, a material still widely used in rural New Mexico. Regardless of the roofing material used, a pitched roof could shed water better than a flat roof, and it became common practice to leave the flat roof in place for insulation. It also provided an *alto* (attic space) for storage accessible by a ladder to an outside opening in the gable.

Anglos also adopted Hispanic techniques and constructed buildings of both adobe and *jacal* (a palisade form of log construction with vertical timbers). The Sumpter Ranch in the Dry Cimarron Valley of New Mexico provides a good example of cultural borrowing. The initial house, an Anglo dugout, later became a root cellar, and it is used today only as a storm cellar. The second house, built of adobe, was later "anglicized" by the addition of bay windows and asphalt siding embossed with a brick pattern. The corral is defined on one side by a linear, flat-roofed continuum of a blacksmith shop, saddle and harness storage, chicken coop, and stable. Those components, all joined together, are a clear expression of Hispanic building traditions.

Vernacular buildings in the initial phases of settlement of the trans-Mississippi West represent architectural hybrids with distinctive regional differences. When settlers first arrived in the West, they were constrained by available resources for construction of their buildings. Although inexpensive, mass-produced tools were available, materials often were not. Regional differences in building materials can thus be attributed to variations of topography, climate, and landscape. But because the various ethnic groups tended to reproduce what they had known in their homelands, the differences also often reflected the origins of the builders. Although their architectural expressions eventually were modified through contact with larger society and changing building technology, there remain even today places that Allen Noble has identified as "ethnic islands." In these communities, there are clear expressions of a cultural heritage. In the southeastern Oklahoma community of Hartshorne, for example, Ukrainian coal miners built Saints Cyril and Methodius Orthodox Church with three onion domes, symbolizing the traditions of their religion; none of the other buildings in this community have any references to Old World culture.

In many regions, the first shelter of pioneers derived its form from materials of the surrounding landscape, but with prosperity, subsequent buildings reflected their cultural origins. For example, an Englishman named John Pratt settled in Studley, Kansas, after the Civil War to raise sheep. The first shelter he built was a two-room sod house. Soon afterwards, he veneered his soddy with limestone, which is plentiful in central Kansas. Later, he added symmetrical wings

Saints Cyril and Methodius Orthodox Church in Hartshorne, Oklahoma. *Courtesy Arn Henderson, FAIA.*

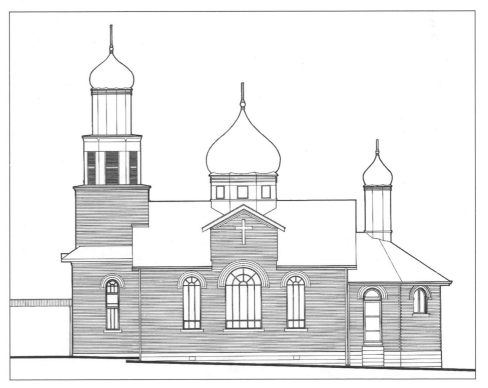

on either side of the original house with pedimented gables, bay windows, and Victorian trim. Over time, a simple sod house—much like the houses of other Kansas settlers—was transformed into an English country house.

Settlers in the West used a variety of strategies in constructing shelter that resulted in architectural hybrids. The physical environment, and the ways they responded to it, both climatically and as a source of materials, was a powerful determinant. The heritage settlers brought with them, with an attendant collective memory, shaped buildings. Cultural borrowing was also an important determinant of the expression of folk buildings. When different groups shared the same space, there was ample opportunity and logical reasons for borrowing ideas for the design of their buildings. But there were other factors that determined the design of shelter such as the economic circumstances of a family or individuals. The kinds of skills a builder had also affected decisions and shaped the product. Thus theories of either cultural imitation or environmental adaptation as exclusive determinants of the expression of folk architecture are not entirely adequate. Both can shape building form. Ultimately, though, there are several variables that can affect the process of design, and the form of vernacular buildings depends on the circumstances of time, place, and the individual builder. It was the interaction of all these variables that produced expressions of both continuity and diversity in the built environment of the American West.

—*Arn Henderson*

SEE ALSO: Frontier: Frontier Thesis; Log Cabins; Sod Houses

SUGGESTED READING:

Berkhofer, Robert F., Jr. "Space, Time and Culture, and the American Frontier." *Agricultural History* 38 (January 1964).

Carter, Thomas. "North European Horizontal Log Construction in the Sanpete-Sevier Valleys." *Utah Historical Quarterly* 52 (Winter 1984).

———. "The Architecture of Immigration: Documenting Italian-American Buildings in Utah and Nevada." In *Old Ties, New Attachments: Italian-American Folklife in the West.* Washington, D.C., 1992.

Henderson, Arn. "Low-Style/High-Style: Oklahoma Architectural Origins and Image Distortion." In *The Culture of Oklahoma.* Edited by H. Stein and R. Hill. Norman, Okla., 1993.

Jordan, Terry G. *Texas Log Buildings: A Folk Architecture.* Austin, Tex., 1978.

———, and Matti Kaups. *The American Backwoods Frontier: An Ethnic and Ecological Interpretation.* Baltimore, 1989.

Kilpinen, Jon T. "Material Folk Culture of the Rocky Mountain High Valleys." *Material Culture* 23 (1991).

Marshall, Howard Wight. "The Pelster Housebarn: Endurance of Germanic Architecture on the Midwestern Frontier." *Material Culture* 18 (1986).

Noble, Allen G., ed. *To Build in a New Land: Ethnic Landscapes in North America.* Baltimore, 1992.

Pratt, Boyd C. "Homesteading the High Plains of New Mexico: An Architectural Perspective." *Panhandle-Plains Historical Review* 63 (1990).

Turner, Frederick Jackson. "The Significance of the Frontier in American History." *Annual Report of the American Historical Association for the Year 1893.*

Upton, Dell, ed. *America's Architectural Roots: Ethnic Groups That Built America.* Washington, D.C., 1986.

———, and John Michael Vlach, eds. *Common Places: Readings in American Vernacular Architecture.* Athens, Ga., 1986.

Webb, Walter Prescott. *The Great Plains.* New York, 1931.

Wilson, Chris, and David Kammer. *La Tierra Amarilla: Its History, Architecture, and Cultural Landscape.* Santa Fe, N. Mex., 1989.

ADOBE ARCHITECTURE

Adobe is an Arabic word referring to a mixture of sand, silt, clay, and a binder. Used as a building material in arid regions of the world, adobe is usually form-molded into sun-baked bricks, also called "adobe." Once considered the most basic of building materials, primarily associated with subsistence cultures, adobe has become fashionable among the affluent of the Southwest as an ecologically sound and rustic building material in recent years. Multimillion-dollar residences are built of adobe in towns such as Santa Fe and Tucson.

Pueblo Indian adobe construction

Pueblo Indians of the Southwest used two types of adobe construction before the arrival of the Spaniards: puddled adobe and turtleback adobe. In puddled adobe, masons formed walls by mixing earth to a plastic consistency and hand forming it into layers twelve to twenty inches thick. The process was very slow because each layer had to dry and shrink before the next was added. Pueblo artisans did not know how to intersect walls at the corners for additional strength. Archaeologists believe that, as a result, structures frequently failed due to the settling of foundations and shearing stress. It did not prevent Indian craftspeople from raising walls as thin as twelve to eighteen inches to several stories in height. The best remaining example of puddled adobe architecture is the massive Casa Grande National Monument south of Phoenix, Arizona.

In turtleback adobe, mud was cupped and shaped by hand into bricks, resembling small turtle shells in cross section. Thousands were mortared together to

The village church of Alamo National Forest, New Mexico Territory typifies the adobe architecture of the Spanish Southwest. Photograph by A. M. Neal *Courtesy National Archives.*

form multistory walls. Significant numbers of turtleback-adobe walls were excavated by Kathryn Sargeant at a site in Alameda, north of Albuquerque, New Mexico, in the 1970s and 1980s.

Introduction of mold-made adobe bricks

Spanish colonists introduced mold-made adobe bricks to the American Southwest in the sixteenth century. The construction technique came to Spain from North Africa and the Middle East, where it had been used for thousands of years by the Mesopotamians, Egyptians, and other cultures.

Most adobe bricks are made in the age-old manner, although machines have been invented to accelerate the mixing and forming process. Sand, silt, clay, and a binder (usually straw) are worked to the proper consistency in a pit. If the proportions are not correct, the bricks will fracture during drying or fail to withstand the load of multiple courses. The mud is then poured in wooden molds (*adoberos*) and leveled into bricks that are placed on the ground to dry in the sun. An unexpected summer rainstorm can ruin many days of production.

Another type of Hispanic adobe is *terrón,* now an almost obsolete construction material. *Terrones* are sod bricks spaded from grassy meadows and allowed to dry in the sun. Vegetable matter in the soil acts as a binder, holding the bricks together. *Terrones* are usu-

ally laid in vertical rows at a forty-five–degree angle, imparting a herringbone appearance to the walls.

Traditional adobe construction

In the seventeenth and eighteenth centuries, Spanish adobe missions were constructed in cruciform shape. Conscripted Indian laborers erected the missions, often of considerable size and height. Construction methods were similar to those used in the most common adobe buildings found in Texas, New Mexico, Arizona, and California—modest single-story dwellings of a few rooms.

Pre-1850 adobe buildings usually were constructed on level earth without stone foundations. Stone-cutting tools were rare in the Spanish borderlands, and agricultural work left little time for such a labor-intensive task. Without stone foundations, adobe walls absorbed ground water through capillary action and eventually weakened. Few adobe buildings were more than one story in height, and without continual maintenance, most disintegrated back to the earth within twenty to thirty years.

Roofs were supported by pine or aspen logs (*vigas*) hauled from the mountains by teams of oxen. Rooms were narrow because it was difficult to transport and install timbers longer than fifteen feet. Carpenters (*carpenteros*) placed limbs (*latias* or *savinos*), rough-adzed boards (*tablas*), split poles (*rajas*), or cedar shakes between the logs at ninety-degree angles. Brush with insect-repellent qualities was placed above the wood, then topped with adobe mud sloped to one side. Water, the worst enemy of adobe, was eliminated through wooden spouts (*canales*) placed at the low side of the roof.

Exterior and interior wall surfaces were often plastered with adobe mud, white gypsum, or colored clays and smoothed with sheepskins. Green, red, and even purple finishes were common; some sparkled because of the use of mica-rich clays. Plaster work usually fell to highly skilled women called *enjaradoras,* who achieved remarkably smooth surfaces.

Interior floors were of earth until sawmills became common after 1850. Some home owners finished the earth floors to a hard consistency with a thin layer of animal blood and clay. They swept the floors repeatedly, and many older adobe buildings had floors below ground level.

Window shutters and exterior doors were made of hand-adzed wood. Window glass was rare until the late nineteenth century. Cone-shaped corner fireplaces (*fogónes*) supplied heat, and the kitchens of larger residences had hooded cooking fireplaces (*fogónes de campana*).

Contrary to popular belief, adobe is a poor insulator. Homes were cool in summer and retained heat in winter only because their walls were usually several feet thick. Maintaining adobe homes was labor intensive because running water eroded walls and rain made roofs leak. Adobe walls were home to colonies of insects that tended to fall from the ceiling during meals.

Improvements in late nineteenth-century adobe homes made them considerably more comfortable. Home owners added glass windows to enclose and light the dim rooms. Steel (tin) roofs eliminated constant roof maintenance. Wood from sawmills and oil cloth were used to cover earthen floors. And stone and later concrete foundations insulated walls from ground water.

—*Byron A. Johnson*

SEE ALSO: Casa Grande Ruins Reservation

SUGGESTED READING:

Bunting, Bainbridge. *Early Architecture of New Mexico.* Albuquerque, N. Mex., 1976.

Sanford, Trent. *Architecture of the Southwest.* New York, 1950.

URBAN ARCHITECTURE

The American West's struggle to find its identity—as a colonial offshoot of the East, as a separate region defined by its distinctive climate and different historical traditions, and ultimately as a mixture of both, an amalgam of East and West—has long been evident in the architecture of its cities and towns. Mid-nineteenth-century mining rushes and the completion of the transcontinental railroads brought surging populations that urbanized Western settlements and transformed the region and its culture. The cultural tension created by the West's settlement spanned the nineteenth and twentieth centuries and resulted in a built environment that blended new and old, wild innovation with slavish imitation. By the last half of nineteenth century, Western architectural styles reflected the new cultural confusion.

Town builders, home owners, and trained architects produced a flood of public buildings for which they imported false-front, wood-frame architecture from Chicago and St. Louis and eventually even the brick and stone structures ubiquitous in the East. Acolytes of the Parisian École des Beaux-Arts proselytized for neoclassical forms that included the Greek revival styles of buildings scattered from the Great Plains to the Pacific Coast. A bit later, Victorian architecture swept westward, as Western moguls—just as their Eastern counterparts had done—sought to announce their wealth and taste in mammoth mansions that dominated their surroundings. In the West, the mansion-building craze was perhaps more nakedly ambitious than in the East because elite Westerners were not only nouveau riche but members of a colonial ruling class as well. They set out to prove their cultural sophistication by outdoing their Eastern models. Gothic monster after Gothic monster mounted San Francisco's Nob Hill as families such as the Hopkinses, Stanfords, and Crockers proclaimed their cultural ambitions. The style reached its zenith in the region's Carson House in Eureka, California. Toward the end of the century, new styles invaded from the East: Queen Anne, Richardson Romanesque, and classical renaissance, only to be replaced themselves by the colonial revival. By the 1890s, Western urban architecture was closely in line with the often changing fashions of the East, and the West of the Gilded Age was as architecturally eclectic as any other region of the country.

In the twentieth century, however, Westerners began to abandon frontier architectural forms that merely illustrated their colonial ties to the East and to experiment with something approaching a regional style. In the trans-Mississippi states of the Midwest, there arose between 1900 and 1920 a school of architects led by Chicago's Louis Sullivan, who had pioneered the steel-frame skyscraper construction for which Chicago was famous (Sullivan actually built his first skyscraper in St. Louis). Called the "prairie style" because its practitioners claimed that the low horizontal lines and projecting eaves of their one- or two-story, sometimes split-level, houses (built with brick or timber covered by stucco) reflected the broad expanses of the prairies. In Sullivan's early examples, homes and public buildings sometimes imitated the functions they served, as in the small Midwestern banks he built shaped like huge jewel boxes. The prairie style was brilliantly developed by Frank Lloyd Wright to meld into the environment, especially the open spaces of the West, although many prairie-school homes were also built on tiny urban lots.

Fin-de-siècle architects who had moved to California, among them BERNARD RALPH MAYBECK in the San Francisco Bay area, Charles Sumner Greene and Henry Mather Greene in Pasadena and Los Angeles, and Irving Gill—a student of Sullivan—in San Diego, adapted earlier styles to West Coast building materials and the grandeur of the landscapes that had perhaps attracted them to the region in the first place. Maybeck, although he executed many of his buildings in Romanesque and Gothic styles, gave his work a Western touch. Between

Charles Sumner Greene and Henry Mather Greene pioneered the California bungalow style. *Courtesy the Archives at Pasadena Historical Museum.*

1901 and 1914 in Berkeley and San Francisco, he designed dozens of spacious homes that blended the Gothic revival style with Bay-region redwood shingle style. The result was a look distinctive enough that historians connect the appearance of these "Maybecks" with the first stirrings of architectural independence for the Far West. And although Irving Gill tended to work in traditional classic and Gothic styles as he rebuilt many of the prominent buildings in San Francisco after the 1906 earthquake and fire, he also helped spark a new vogue for mission architecture in California with his restoration of San Francisco's oldest building, the Mission Dolores.

The true innovators, however, were Pasadena's Greene brothers, who developed a unique Western style: the California bungalow. A simple house designed for outdoor living and well suited to the climate, the bungalow owed something to the floor plans of the nineteenth-century California adobe home; its patio became a form of outdoor living room, and its functional spaciousness reflected the natural Western environment. The Greenes built their first redwood bungalow in 1903, and within a decade, bungalows were popping up everywhere in California and throughout the West, where the brothers found plenty of disciples to copy their style. By World War I, the style had invaded the East, where, in a historical turnabout, Eastern architects began imitating Western forms. But the popular bungalows were themselves soon pushed aside by the mission craze given new life by the Panama-California Exposition in San Diego in 1915.

For the exposition, San Diego's city fathers were determined to illustrate the historical background of their city, and they hired New York architect Bertram Goodhue, who had only recently read a book about Spanish colonial architecture in Mexico. Adopting the dominant seventeenth- and eighteenth-century Spanish and Mexican motifs, Goodhue designed many of the exhibition's buildings with white stucco walls and red tile roofs. This Spanish-colonial or mission-revival style swept California and much of the rest of the West. In New Mexico, Arizona, and Texas, architects and builders modified the mission style using pueblo architecture. Sometimes directly influenced by Goodhue, the pueblo style was in fact a subregional variation developed and championed by John Gaw Meem. Architects and historians have for years argued heatedly over the virtues and shortcomings of the two styles. Clearly they were both adaptations of older, traditional styles and new experiments with forms aimed at developing a distinctive Western look.

Public buildings and homes in Santa Fe, Albuquerque, San Antonio, and elsewhere were marked by the new styles. When WILLIAM RANDOLPH HEARST decided to build a castle, called San Simeon, he hired Goodhue to design its towers. Although, by the mid-1920s, Goodhue himself had begun to experiment with more functional styles, to which his Los Angeles Public Library is a testament, many contractors and builders

Bertram Goodhue's Indian Arts Building, designed for the Panama-California Exposition in 1915 in San Diego, sparked interest in the Spanish-colonial or mission-revival style. *Courtesy San Diego Historical Society.*

The University of New Mexico's Zimmerman Library was designed by John Gaw Meem, champion of the pueblo style. *Courtesy University of New Mexico.*

were adapting Spanish-colonial designs for use in the construction of small homes. Southern California was re-Hispanicized as houses, apartments, flats, commercial stores, post offices and other public buildings, and even gas stations and hotels aped the mission style. After an earthquake struck Santa Barbara in 1925, the entire town was rebuilt in the mission-revival style. The exclusive new Los Angeles suburb, San Clemente, soon followed. By 1925, John Gaw Meem had founded his firm—Meem and McCormick—in New Mexico and was busy turning Southwestern buildings into puebloesque tributes to the region's past. Examples include the University of New Mexico in Albuquerque and the railroad stations of the Santa Fe Railroad and the Southern Pacific.

More broadly, the "new" styles were part of a regional movement affecting the entire country during the late 1920s and the 1930s—a movement that encompassed not merely architecture, but also art, literature, and music. In that sense, Goodhue and Meem were not so different from Pacific Northwestern architects Pietro Bellushi and John Yeon, who were urging their clients to let them make better use of local settings by building the homes they designed with native woods and accommodating their very modern structures to the green expanses along the coasts or the brown stretches in the interior. Certainly, mission-revival and pueblo architecture, as well as the works of Bellushi and Yeon, got a boost from the federal government's attempt to spark an interest in all things local during the 1930s and 1940s through New Deal programs for construction, conservation, and restoration. Well into the late 1930s, adobe-looking, stucco-

walled, red-tile-roofed homes and offices were quite popular. Indeed, both the mission style and the pueblo style profoundly influence California and the Southwest to this day.

But regionalism was not the only movement affecting the urban landscape of the American West in the 1920s and 1930s. The pell-mell settlement of California in the 1920s and especially the growing impact of Los Angeles's "car culture" led to a bewildering, frequently tasteless mixture of Venetian, Norman, old plantation, Italian, Queen Anne, and Elizabethan styles. Folks from Iowa, incredibly rich new movie barons and Hollywood performers, and hundreds of thousands of young people—a high percentage of them women, who were looking for a break in films—moved in and began to search for new identities as well as new homes. By the late 1920s and early 1930s, southern California presaged the look of much of post–World War II America, with its jerry-built tract homes, mushrooming suburbs, and instantly constructed shopping malls. The commuter city was being born in Los Angeles, a line of separate communities connected by a stretch of highway and some high hopes, with no centralized, recognizable downtown. Everyone knows that Gertrude Stein said of Oakland, "There is no there there"; everyone believes she should have been talking about Los Angeles.

Two major architects emerged from the rapid experimentation in urban living that characterized California beginning in the 1920s. Irving Gill, who had experimented mostly with various traditional styles before World War I, began to show more of the influence of his great teacher back at the turn of the century, Chicago architect Louis Sullivan. Producing a new California-modern style well suited to the region's physical environment and its peculiar culture, Gill designed homes that anticipated the ranch-house style by decades. He also pioneered new developments in apartment living by adapting the bungalow court to multiunit dwellings, designed so that each tenant had his or her own entrance, hallway, and garden. In apartment complexes such as Bella Vista Terrace in the Sierra Madre, Gill not only provided outdoor space for the tenants but also designed interiors to capture the exterior light unique to southern California.

Perhaps the most talented and certainly the most innovative of California's early twentieth-century architects was Richard Neutra. Born in Austria, Neutra studied with Adolph Loos in Vienna and became a passionate advocate of the modern international style. Attracted to Chicago by Louis Sullivan and Frank Lloyd Wright, Neutra was later induced into to moving to Los Angeles by another Viennese modernist, R. M. Schindler. (As a resident of California since 1922,

Schindler sang a siren's song of the West's expansive spaces and brilliant light.) Neutra moved to Los Angeles in 1926 and began building strikingly modern homes with the new methods and new materials. Blending interior spaces with the out-of-doors, Neutra used expanses of glass, sliding-glass doors, and self-supporting concrete slabs to lay the foundation for a highly original style deeply rooted in the physical environment. By the mid-1930s, the modern designs of Neutra, Schindler, and their associates Gregory Ain and Harwell Harris were dazzling the architectural profession. Even in the East, new homes appeared that melded exterior and interior spaces by using walls of glass.

In 1936, California's Cliff May first toyed with the notion of adapting the ranch houses of the West's cattle kingdom to suburban living. In Modesto, California, John Funk took a lesson from Neutra and company and applied large glass surfaces to ranch-house design in his Heckendorf House. That set the pattern: soon Neutra and his associates were using the ranch house to realize their glass dreams, and ranch-style homes began their spread across the country. The style became the most distinctive gift of Western architecture to the rest of the nation, and the men who developed it into the 1940s sparked a surge of creative design that would make Western architecture a bellwether for changing architectural styles. The international style found a home in America as Craig Ellwood, A. Quincy Jones, Fred Emmons, Edward Killingsworth, and Wayne R. Williams after World War II joined Neutra, Bellushi, William W. Wurster, Eldridge T. Spencer, Ronald R. Campbell, Donn Emmons, Welton D. Becket, and William L. Pereira in experiments with arc-welded steel skeletons, exposed steel and concrete, aluminum frames and beams, glass walls, picture windows, sliding partitions, fluid room arrangements, and split levels. Even Frank Lloyd Wright went west and designed a few houses and buildings.

In one sense, the West was no different from the rest of the country. A post–World War II housing and building boom led to eclecticism and regional diversity in architectural forms, which ensured that the region was no more architecturally coherent than the South or the North. Ranch-style homes, popular in Far Western suburbs, gained little favor in the Southwest, where pueblo styles continued to flourish. While the sprawling, unplanned growth of the Sunbelt, so typical of Los Angeles, Phoenix, and Houston, equally came to characterize Boise, Billings, and Fargo, the silo and grain-elevator that dominated the horizons of the Midwest remained foreign to the Great Basin and the Pacific Coast, just as the international style associated with California and the Pacific Coast was anathema in the Rocky Mountains and Mormon Salt Lake City.

But in another sense, the West's architecture was all of a piece. From turn-of-the-century Chicago, Louis Sullivan's skyscrapers went to the East, and his prairie homes went to the West. Architecture is all about space, and in the compact settlements of the Atlantic seaboard, the space left for building was vertical, while in the sprawling settlements of the trans-Mississippi West, it spread toward the horizon. The same kind of difference profoundly affected urban planning in the West, for there one could build streets just as wide as one wanted. Colonial America was interested in throwing a civilized facade up against the wilderness, in carving out a space in the woods. The Spanish Southwest was more concerned with cool breezes and open courtyards, in spreading across flat land. For one, inside and outside were clear and defined by the built environment; for the other, structures were more transitional. While the urban West today has its share of tall buildings, the architecture that was distinctive to the West—prairie-school homes, California bungalows, mission-revival beach towns, pueblo-style train stations, California-modern apartments, ranch-style suburbs, international-style office complexes—hugged the horizon or flung themselves open to daylight and the out-of-doors. The sprawl of Western settlement also seems, at least in part, to lie behind more recent developments in the West's urban landscape: the industrial parks, the retirement communities, the theme parks, the neon strips, and the commuter communities, all of them developing first in the urbanized oases of a wide-open dry region.

—*Charles Phillips*

SEE ALSO: City Planning; Urban West

SUGGESTED READING:

Banham, Reyner. *Los Angeles: The Architecture of Four Ecologies.* New York, 1971.

Clark, Robert Judson, and Thomas S. Hines. *Los Angeles Transfer: Architecture in Southern California.* Los Angeles, 1983.

Etulain, Richard. W. "Western Art and Architecture." *Montana: The Magazine of the American West* 40 (August 1990): 2–11.

Gebhard, David, and Robert Winter. *A Guide to Architecture in Southern California.* Los Angeles, 1965.

Markovich, Nicholas C., et al. *Pueblo Style and Regional Architecture.* New York, 1990.

McCoy, Esther. *Five California Architects.* New York, 1960.

Nash, Gerald. *The American West in the Twentieth Century.* Englewood Cliffs, N.J., 1973.

Peisch, Mark L. *The Chicago School of Architecture: Early Followers of Sullivan and Wright.* New York, 1965.

Smith, G. E. Kidder. *The Architecture of the United States: The Plains States and the Far West.* Vol. 3. Garden City, N.Y., 1981.

ARIDITY

SEE: Climate

ARID-LANDS THESIS

In a 1957 article in *Harper's Magazine,* Western historian WALTER PRESCOTT WEBB created a storm of controversy when he highlighted some of the painful realities of the American West. These realities stemmed from a simple, undeniable fact that people refused to face—the West was a desert. Webb's article, "The American West: Perpetual Mirage," declared that Westerners "are a normal people trying to create and maintain a normal civilization in an abnormal land." The land's abnormality, he explained, was a consequence of its aridity. "The heart of the West," he emphasized, "is a desert, unqualified and absolute."

Webb's West included the western and central portions of Texas, Oklahoma, Kansas, Nebraska, and North and South Dakota. These were the six "eastern desert-rim states" that were influenced by aridity and received an average annual rainfall of slightly more than 24 inches. Webb defined the states as "subhumid." Similarly, there were the three subhumid western desert-rim states—California, eastern Oregon, and southeastern Washington—that were also affected by aridity. These states received about 26 ½ inches of precipitation a year. The true western desert—what Webb called "the heart of the West"—consisted of New Mexico, Arizona, Colorado, Utah, Nevada, Wyoming, Idaho, and Montana. The average annual rainfall for the eight "desert states" was only 12 inches per year. Webb labeled them "semiarid." The semiarid and the subhumid area covered more than half of the United States and included all or part of seventeen states.

Webb noted that the more arid portions of the West, the true desert states, were economically impoverished and sparsely populated. The desert-rim states—such as Texas and California—however, were "populous and rich compared to the vast interior." People had tried to conquer the desert, but the desert had repelled them. Quoting the early twentieth-century socialist and sociologist A. M. Simons, Webb noted that every wave of settlers had receded, leaving behind a "mass of human wreckage in the shape of broken fortunes, deserted farms, and ruined homes." Then, in an effort to squeeze life out of the desert, settlers tried new farming techniques, such as dryland farming, but were again beaten back. Next, "[t]he federal government enlisted on the side of the People *vs.* The Desert," building dams to "create tiny islands of water in a sea of aridity." In addition, water was pumped from underground aquifers and diverted from lakes and rivers to supply the needs of city dwellers and farmers. Cities sprang up all over the West, and it became heavily urbanized. The cities were oases with vast, largely empty lands separating them. The great danger, Webb explained, was that the cities of the desert-rim states had "outgrown their water supply" and were in crisis. Los Angeles had built aqueducts to transport water from across the Sierra Nevada and from the Colorado River. El Paso, San Antonio, and Dallas faced similar predicaments and tapped distant water sources to meet their needs. But, Webb warned, these sources were not infinite.

Further deromanticizing the West, Webb noted that the desert was the place to which Mormons and Native Americans had fled. It was the place where atomic testing took place. The West had little history to speak of—few great battles or statesmen, few important historical moments. Nevada, Webb thought, was the worst example of civilization in the desert. With its natural minerals depleted, Nevada survived only by becoming a "haven in the desert" for gambling, divorce, and fornication. "In compensating for what the desert denied it," Webb added, "[Nevada] has created the most bizarre society in the nation." And the absurdity of Nevada was symbolic of the larger absurdity of seeking to establish civilization in a place that is not capable of supporting a large population. To support its growing populace, a fragile desert environment was tampered with, its rivers dammed and redirected. But, Webb suggested at the end of the essay, the environment had more chance of conquering humanity than humans had of conquering the environment: "One generation passeth away, and another generation cometh: but the earth abideth forever."

Webb's arid-lands thesis emphasized the power of environmental forces over human will. He defined the West as a region characterized by the consequences of aridity. This was a serious departure from FREDERICK JACKSON TURNER's famous frontier thesis of 1893, which also emphasized environmental forces—namely the frontier—but found the effects of America's Western environment to be positive. Webb, however, viewed the desert not as a colorful, romantic, positive force, but as a painful, unavoidable reality. Webb's arid-lands thesis was a far cry from Turner's frontier thesis, and Webb's arid lands were actually distant from Turner's frontier. Although Turner acknowledged the semiarid regions of the West, he had focused on the humid lands of the Eastern and Midwestern frontiers, and his thesis applied the same images of natural abundance to the Far West. Webb felt he was setting the record straight. In fact, Webb had first presented his thoughts on Western aridity in his well-known 1931 book, *The Great Plains,* which examined how environmental conditions had affected human behavior. The Dust Bowl of the 1930s, which ravaged the Great Plains and destroyed land and livelihood, brought the reality of Western aridity home to the nation at large. John Steinbeck's famous and controversial novel *The Grapes of Wrath* (1939), which poignantly chronicled the suffering of Dust Bowl refugees, did the same.

Before Webb had developed his arid-lands thesis and before Turner had delivered his frontier thesis, however, others—like Western explorers Zebulon Montgomery Pike and Stephen Harriman Long—labeled regions of the West a great American desert. Later, in 1878, John Wesley Powell presented his controversial Report on the Lands of Arid Regions (1878). A former Civil War major who had lost an arm at the Battle of Shiloh, Powell led expeditions down the Colorado River and through the Grand Canyon in 1869 and 1871. His explorations earned him the directorship of the United States Geological Survey. As early as 1873, he was expressing concern over the West's aridity. A few years later, he presented his report to Congress in an effort to change potentially disastrous land policies. In the humid East and Midwest, 160 acres was sufficient to support a family farm. This was the standard unit of size under the Homestead Act of 1862. But 160 acres, Powell explained, was not an appropriate unit in the lands west of the one hundredth meridian. In irrigated Western lands, half the standard amount—80 acres—would be sufficient to support a family. And for those in the business of grazing livestock, a plot of unirrigated land sixteen times the traditional 160-acre homestead—2,560 acres—would be required to support a family. Powell urged the federal government to abandon the traditional homestead model in favor of models more appropriate to an arid land. Eastern farming techniques were not applicable to the West. If the government did not institute more suitable land policies, Powell warned, disastrous consequences would befall Western settlers. But Powell's vision did not become a reality, in part because too many Americans felt their opportunities for economic gain would be hampered by a policy based on the principle of wise use of limited natural resources. Powell's warnings were not heeded, and settlers, expecting rain to follow their plows, marched defiantly across the Great Plains in the late 1870s and the 1880s, only to retreat eastward in the late 1880s when the drought that Powell had predicted set in.

Drawing on the work of both Webb and Powell, environmental historian Donald Worster has presented the most complete version of the arid-lands thesis. Worster's writings amount to an indictment of federal policies that ignored Powell's warnings and suggestions. In *Dust Bowl* (1979), Worster analyzes the impact of the capitalist system on the Southern Plains, where overuse of the land combined with a prolonged drought created an ecological disaster in the 1930s. In *Rivers of Empire* (1985), Worster argues that the story of the modern West revolves around control of the region's most precious resource—water. He describes the West as a modern-day example of the "hydraulic" social systems that characterized the great river valleys of ancient Mesopotamia, Egypt, India, and China. To meet the needs of growing populations, these societies had to dam rivers and create complex irrigation systems. This process was controlled by elites, including scientists and engineers. But as the elites grew more influential, imperial despots eventually emerged, and the lives of the great mass of ordinary people deteriorated.

The American West, Worster contends, became a hydraulic society when the federal government undertook massive irrigation and reclamation projects. The most elaborate hydraulic society in the world, according to Worster, exists in California where a massive system of reservoirs, dams, canals, pipelines, tunnels, and pumping and power plants has transformed the landscape. But this is not, he warns, an example of humans triumphing over nature. Like Webb, Worster stresses that these massive artificial water systems, constructed to transport water to cities, negatively affect a very fragile environment. While Westerners and tourists enjoy the luxury of a swim in a Beverly Hills pool, sail boats on Lake Mead, or play a round of golf on the well-watered courses around Las Vegas and other Western cities, they should note that the Colorado River, which ensures that their recreational needs are met, now no longer reaches the sea because it is so heavily overused. The massive Hoover Dam, which controls much of the West's water supply, Worster argues, is symbolic of misguided human efforts to conquer nature.

However, Worster explains, nature seems to be taking revenge on human society for misusing its resources. For example, as fields are irrigated by the artificial tributaries of the Colorado River, salinity (salt build up) increases in the river, which increases the water's alkalinity, which in turn destroys the land. The problem of salinity, Worster notes, has "plagued every major irrigation system in history and destroyed many." He urges Americans to realize that "there are more sensible places to put cities than in the desert." Considering, he says, that the Colorado River carved the Grand Canyon, it is naive to think that the Hoover Dam and other similar structures will forever impede its natural goal of reaching the sea.

Another influential and widely read example of the arid-lands thesis is Marc Reisner's *Cadillac Desert* (1986). Reisner's study is a bitter indictment of two federal organizations—the BUREAU OF RECLAMATION and the UNITED STATES ARMY CORPS OF ENGINEERS, which competed for the right to transform the West through the "management" of its water resources. Add to the mix politicians, farmers, and businessmen, all pursuing conflicting agendas, and the end result is a struggle for control of the most precious commodity in an arid land—water. Emphasizing the ultimate futility of attempts to create a garden in an arid land, Reisner states, "Desert, semidesert, call it what you will . . . despite heroic human efforts and many billions of dollars, all we have managed to do is turn a Missouri-sized section green. . . ." Echoing the warnings of Powell, Webb, and Worster, Reisner further notes that throughout history desert civilizations have collapsed, many of them perhaps as a consequence of salt deposits destroying the land.

While the earlier warnings of Powell, and later Webb, were not heeded, the arid-lands thesis was destined to have a growing influence on both the fields of Western history and, more broadly, United States history. The growth of the field of environmental history in the late twentieth century was in large part a response to national concerns over environmental despoliation. Given the strength of these concerns, the writings of Worster, Reisner, and others who stress the aridity and fragility of the Western environment received a warmer response than did Powell in 1878 and Webb in 1957.

—David M. Wrobel

SUGGESTED READING:

Goetzmann, William H. *Exploration and Empire: The Explorer and the Scientist in the Winning of the West.* New York, 1966.

Limerick, Patricia Nelson. *Desert Passages: Encounters with the American Deserts.* Albuquerque, N. Mex., 1985.

Nash, Gerald. *Creating the West: Historical Interpretations, 1890–1900.* Albuquerque, N. Mex., 1991.

Powell, John Wesley. *Report on the Lands of Arid Regions.* Washington, D.C., 1878.

Reisner, Marc. *Cadillac Desert: The American West and Its Disappearing Water.* New York, 1986.

Smith, Henry Nash. *Virgin Land: The American West as Symbol and Myth.* Cambridge, Mass., 1950. Reprint. 1978.

Smythe, William E. *The Conquest of Arid America.* New York, 1899. Reprint. Seattle, Wash., 1969.

Webb, Walter Prescott. "The American West: Perpetual Mirage." *Harper's Magazine* 214 (May 1957): 25–35.

———. *The Great Plains.* New York, 1931.

———. "The West and the Desert." *Montana: The Magazine of Western History* 8 (January 1958): 2–12.

West, Elliott. "Walter Prescott Webb and the Search for the West." In *Writing Western History: Essays on Major Western Historians.* Edited by Richard W. Etulain. Albuquerque, N. Mex., 1991.

Worster, Donald. *Dust Bowl: The Southern Plains in the 1930s.* New York, 1979.

———. *Rivers of Empire: Water, Aridity, and the Growth of the American West.* New York, 1985.

———. *Under Western Skies.* New York, 1992.

———. *An Unsettled Country: Changing Landscapes of the American West.* Albuquerque, N. Mex., 1994.

ARIKARA INDIANS

SEE: Native American Peoples: Peoples of the Great Plains

ARIZONA

Arizona, the "Grand Canyon State," lies between California and New Mexico and shares its southern border with the Mexican state of Sonora. Except for the Colorado River, its western boundary, Arizona's borders are political rather than geographic; they follow imaginary lines on a geometric grid rather than natural land forms. Those borders encompass 113,417 square miles divided into three major physiographic provinces: the Colorado Plateau, which stretches across the northern part of the state; the Central Mountain or Transition Zone, a series of rugged mountain ranges tumbling across the center; and the Basin and Range, which sweep over western and southern Arizona. The Basin and Range are composed of isolated mountain ranges separated by broad alluvial valleys, and much of the Basin and Range falls within the Sonoran Desert, the most botanically diverse of North America's deserts because it receives both summer and winter rains. Despite biseasonal precipitation, however, much of Arizona averages less than sixteen inches of rain a year. The quest for water has therefore been an imperative since prehistoric times.

According to the 1990 census, Arizona had a population of 3,665,228. Hispanics, 89.5 percent of whom are of Mexican origin, compose the largest ethnic minority (18.8 percent), followed by Native Americans (5.5 percent), African Americans (3 percent), and Asian Americans (1.4 percent). And while many people conceive of Arizona as a land of cowboys and Indians, 87.5 percent of its population resides in cities and towns. With 2,122,101 people, PHOENIX and its surrounding satellites—Mesa, Tempe, and Glendale—form the largest metropolitan area between Los Angeles and Dallas–Fort Worth.

Most Arizonans have lived in mining towns or agricultural communities since the eighteenth century, when Tubac (1752) and TUCSON (1775) were founded

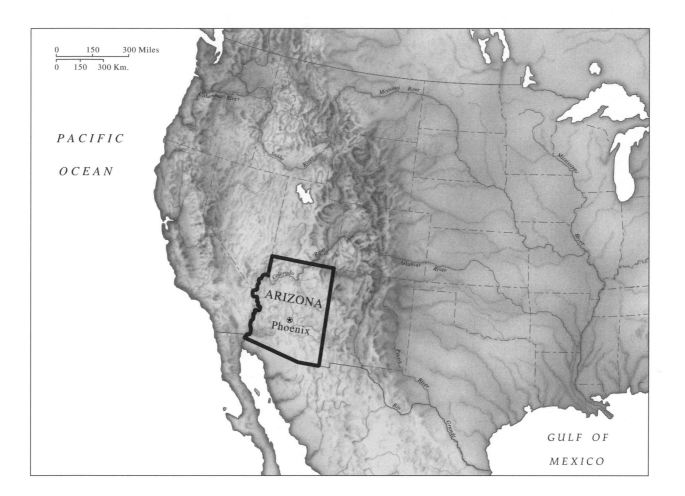

as presidios (military garrisons) of the Spanish province of Sonora. But urban growth exploded during and after World War II, when defense plants and airbases caused the populations of Phoenix and Tucson to rise from 65,414 and 35,752 respectively in 1940 to 983,403 and 405,390 in 1990. During this fifty-year period, Arizona moved from an extractive economy dominated by COPPER MINING, cattle ranching, and COTTON FARMING to an economy driven by light manufacturing, TOURISM, and services. That transformation weakened barriers of race and gender across the state and allowed more women and ethnic minorities access to education, housing, and jobs. Nonetheless, profound economic and political inequality remains a legacy of Arizona's colonial and extractive past as well as its Sunbelt present, which often creates low-paying service jobs.

Native Americans

One of the poorest groups are American Indians, many of whom inhabit twenty-two reservations ranging from the enormous Navajo Nation (nearly sixteen million acres in Arizona, New Mexico, and Utah) to the tiny Tonto Apache Reservation (eighty-five acres in central Arizona). On most reservations, per capita incomes fall below $6,000; the state's average is $13,461. The first reservation to be established was the Gila River Reservation for the Akimel O'odham (Gila Pimas) and Maricopas in 1859. The last was the Pascua Yaqui Reservation southwest of Tucson in 1978. Arizona is a state where the Native American present is as ubiquitous as the Native American past.

This past is at least eleven thousand years old. During late Pleistocene times, small groups of hunters pursued mammoths and other ice-age big game with stone-tipped spears. After these large mammals died out around 8000 B.C. because of growing aridity or "Pleistocene overkill" (their decimation by Paleo-Indian hunters), Native Americans survived by gathering wild plants and hunting small and medium-sized game. This period, known as the Archaic, lasted from about 8000 B.C. to 200 A.D.

By about 1000 B.C., some Archaic peoples began planting primitive varieties of corn in well-watered areas like the Tucson Basin. For the next millennium, agriculture slowly became more important as populations increased and people settled near their fields and began making pottery. These developments led to the florescence of three major prehistoric cultural traditions during the first millennium A.D.: the Anasazi of the Colorado Plateau, who built spectacular cliff dwellings and large multistoried pueblos; the Mogollon of eastern Arizona and western New Mexico, who constructed pueblos oriented around subterranean ceremonial structures known as great kivas; and the Hohokam of south-central Arizona, who created the largest prehistoric system of irrigation canals on the North American continent.

FRAY MARCOS DE NIZA and the expedition of FRANCISCO VÁSQUEZ DE CORONADO passed through Arizona between 1538 and 1542, but their accounts are too fragmentary to reconstruct aboriginal Native American society at contact. By the 1690s, however, Spanish colonists and Jesuit missionaries such as EUSEBIO FRANCISCO KINO were moving into Arizona, and they left a clearer picture. Piman-speaking O'odham (Pimas and Papagos) inhabited the Salt, Gila, San Pedro, and Santa Cruz river valleys and the southwestern desert. Yuma-speaking groups (Quechans and Mojaves) controlled the rich bottomlands of the Colorado River, while Upland Yumans (Walapais, Havasupais, and Yavapais) ranged across western and central Arizona. To the northeast, small groups of Athapascan-speaking ancestors of the Navajos, Western Apaches, and Chiricahua Apaches drifted into Arizona from the eastern foothills of the Rocky Mountains. Meanwhile, the Hopis, a Uto-Aztecan group, built their pueblos on the Hopi Mesas, where they had lived since at least the 1200s. The Hopis are descendants of the Anasazi, but the relationships between other prehistoric and historic groups like the Hohokam and O'odham remain a subject of conjecture and debate.

The arrival of the railroad into the Arizona Territory ended the region's economic isolation from the rest of the country. This image captured the Atlantic and Pacific Railway cars on converging tracks outside of Winslow, Arizona, in 1890. *Courtesy National Archives.*

Spanish colonial period

The arrival of the Spaniards and the Jesuits triggered a cultural and ecological revolution in Arizona. Attempting to convert the native tribes to Roman Catholicism and make them vassals of the Spanish crown, missionaries gave the O'odham gifts of Old World livestock (horses, cattle, goats, and sheep), crops (fruit trees, vegetables, and winter grains like wheat), and tools (iron plows, axes, and wheels). The introduction of these new items, particularly cattle and horses, made the O'odham as well as Spanish settlers targets of Apache raids. And even though many O'odham resented the efforts of the missionaries and rebelled against the Spaniards in 1695 and 1751, Apache pressure forced the O'odham and Spaniards to become allies in a grueling guerrilla war that lasted from the late seventeenth to the late nineteenth century, when the Chiricahua Apaches were finally confined to reservations or deported to Florida and Oklahoma.

Territorial years

Because of Apache hostilities, Spaniards and their Mexican descendants did not establish permanent settlements north of the Tucson Basin. The non-Indian Hispanic population never numbered more than one thousand, and most of them clustered along the Santa Cruz River. Hispanic Arizona became part of the United States under the Treaty of Mesilla (GADSDEN PURCHASE) in 1854, and few Mexican residents resisted the change because they viewed Apaches, not Anglo-Americans, as their real enemies.

In older communities like Tucson, some Mexican families trace their Arizona ancestors back nine generations. Others are more recent immigrants from northern Mexico, particularly Sonora. During the late nineteenth century, Mexican entrepreneurs such as ESTEBAN OCHOA and Leopoldo Carrillo settled in Arizona and founded some of the largest businesses in the Arizona Territory, which was separated from New Mexico in 1863. Because Arizona was not overwhelmed by Anglo immigrants as California was during the gold rush, a small but powerful Mexican middle class established itself in communities like Tucson, Florence, and Yuma. Anglos and Mexicans formed business partnerships, and many Anglo men married Mexican women. Relations between Mexicans and Anglos were often better than in other areas of the Southwest.

Nonetheless, the growth of the Arizona economy ultimately depended on the exploitation of cheap Mexican labor. With the construction of the transcontinental Atlantic and Pacific (later Atchison, Topeka and Santa Fe) and Southern Pacific railroad lines in 1880 and 1881, Arizona's isolation ended, and the territory was incorporated into the national and global economy.

Top: Flagstaff, Arizona, street in 1899. *Courtesy National Archives.*

Bottom: The Roosevelt Dam brought water to Phoenix. In this photograph, Theodore Roosevelt speaks at the dedication ceremonies on March 18, 1911. *Courtesy National Archives.*

Early statehood

These extractive industries dominated Arizona politics and society between 1880 and 1940. In the early 1900s, an alliance between Progressive small businessmen and unionized mine workers shaped Arizona's new constitution when it became the forty-eighth state in 1912. But this alliance was destroyed during World War I when business leaders such as Walter Douglas, president of Phelps Dodge Corporation and later chairman of the board of the Southern Pacific, broke the power of organized labor in Arizona. That counteroffensive culminated in the Bisbee deportation of 1917, when 1,186 striking miners were herded into boxcars and dumped in the southern New Mexican desert. The U.S. Justice Department indicted Douglas and twenty others on charges of conspiracy and kidnapping, but the case was turned over to state courts, and the defendants were acquitted. The next successful strike did not occur until 1946, when Mexican veterans of World War II won wage increases from Phelps Dodge in the copper towns of Clifton-Morenci.

By then, Arizona's economy was being transformed by forces unleashed by World War II. The FEDERAL GOVERNMENT had played a major role in Arizona since the 1860s, when U.S. military posts and Indian reservations provided the largest markets for Arizona livestock and produce. During the early 1900s, the newly created U.S. Reclamation Service built Roosevelt Dam and enabled the Salt River Project to turn Phoenix into the center of the largest irrigated agricultural oasis in the Southwest. National parks, monuments, and forests stimulated the tourist industry, and New Deal projects like the Civilian Conservation Corps and the Public Works Administration built roads, schools, and the enormous HOOVER DAM on the Colorado River. World War II and the Cold War made Arizona a magnet for military training and the defense industry, with airbases like Luke and Davis-Monthan and companies like Goodyear, AiResearch, Motorola, and Hughes swelling the work forces and payrolls.

Arizona is a collection of contradictions. In a state that prides itself on its political conservatism, 70 percent of the land belongs to or is held in trust by the federal government (27 percent Indian reservations, 17 percent Bureau of Land Management, 16 percent

Railroads allowed the development of large-scale livestock raising and copper mining—industries that extracted Arizona natural resources and shipped them outside the territory to be turned into finished products. The railroads also brought more Anglos and Anglo capital into Arizona. With few exceptions, Mexicans did not have the financial resources to compete. After Anglo and Mexican workers drove Chinese laborers imported by the Southern Pacific off the railroad and out of the mines, Mexicans provided much of the labor that maintained tracks, dug copper, ran cattle, and picked cotton in Arizona.

national forests, 5 percent Department of Defense, 5 percent national parks or monuments), while much of the economy depends on federal cotton subsidies, grazing leases, water projects, and defense spending. Most of Arizona is arid or semiarid, yet farmers and cities like Tucson continue to pump far more ground water from subsurface aquifers than is replaced by rain or snow. The massive CENTRAL ARIZONA PROJECT, which transports water from the Colorado River to Phoenix and Tucson, is designed to supply water for the state's explosive growth. But the river may already be overallocated, and the water it does provide may prove to be too expensive for the farmers it was originally supposed to serve. Despite the antiquity of human habitation, modern Arizona is a transient society where, in 1990, only 37 percent of its inhabitants had been born in the state and only 43 percent had lived in the same house since 1985. With an often boom-and-bust economy—gold, silver and copper mining; cotton farming; defense industries; real-estate speculation—many people come to Arizona and then move away.

—*Thomas E. Sheridan*

SEE ALSO: Apache Wars; Douglas Family; Native American Peoples: Peoples of the Southwest; Sheep Ranching

SUGGESTED READING:
Bowden, Charles. *Killing the Hidden Waters*. Austin, Tex., 1977.
———. *Blue Desert*. Tucson, Ariz., 1986.
Byrkit, James W. *Forging the Copper Collar: Arizona's Labor-Management War, 1901–1921*. Tucson, Ariz., 1982.
Luckingham, Bradford. *Phoenix: The History of a Southwestern Metropolis*. Tucson, Ariz., 1989.
Miller, Tom, ed. *Arizona: The Land and the People*. Tucson, Ariz., 1986.
Officer, James. *Hispanic Arizona, 1536–1856*. Tucson, Ariz., 1987.
Sheridan, Thomas E. *Los Tucsonenses: The Mexican Community in Tucson, 1854–1941*. Tucson, Ariz., 1986.
———. *Arizona: A History*. Tucson, Ariz., 1995.
Sonnichsen, C. L. *Tucson: The Life and Times of an American City*. Norman, Okla., 1982.

ARIZONA HISTORICAL SOCIETY

Founded in 1884 as the Society of Arizona Pioneers, the Arizona Historical Society administers a statewide network of museums, historic sites, and archival repositories. The society's operations include regional facilities in Flagstaff, Tempe, and Yuma, and headquarters in Tucson. Organized to preserve, interpret, and disseminate the history of Arizona and the Southwest, the society's collections reflect the Spanish and Mexican heritage of the region as well as the history of Anglo-American settlers. Tucson's museum holdings are extensive: twenty-five thousand artifacts from the cultures of Native Americans and Spanish and Mexican colonists; military weapons, ranching and mining equipment; household furnishings; and clothing. In addition, the Tucson facility manages more than one million historical photographs and a forty-thousand-volume library, which is opened to the public. Public programs feature permanent exhibits on transportation and mining, temporary exhibits on a variety of subjects, guided tours, festivals, concerts, and lectures, and day-camps and outreach programs for schoolchildren. Its publications department produces a quarterly journal, *The Journal of Arizona History*, and occasional books and catalogues. In Yuma, the society maintains the Yuma Century House Museum and Gardens and in Flagstaff, the Arizona Historical Society Pioneer Museum.

—*Patricia Hogan*

SUGGESTED READING:
Sonnichsen, C. L. *Pioneer History: The First Century of the Arizona Historical Society*. Tucson, Ariz., 1984.

ARIZONA MINING STRIKES

Anglo-American entrepreneurs and investors brought capital and technical knowledge to the mining regions of Arizona and displaced the independent Mexican placer miners, who used simpler and less sophisticated means to extract ore from the hard rock. Investors sought ways to mine copper at a cheaper and faster rate by employing laborers from Mexico and paying them low wages. Mexicans became the backbone of the copper industry's rise to economic power in the Southwest. Mine owners and managers used a double-standard wage scale that paid them less than Anglo-American workers. When Mexican miners demanded fair wages, Anglo-American unions viewed them as wage competitors and refused to welcome them into their organizations. Mexicans then organized to demand equal pay and to stage strikes.

The causes for the strikes varied. In mining communities such as Globe, Ray, Clifton, Morenci, Metcalf, and Bisbee, Mexican workers were central figures in labor conflicts from 1885 to World War II. By 1893, the WESTERN FEDERATION OF MINERS (WFM) represented Anglo-American miners in wage negotiations in copper camps in the West. Arizona's first WFM local was organized in Globe in 1896 when a new mine superintendent of the Old Dominion Mine hired Mexican miners to replace the Anglo-American miners who had demanded higher wages. The Mexicans were being paid $2.50 a day, at least fifty cents less than the Anglo-Americans. When the company lowered the Anglo-American miners' pay to $2.25 per shift, a reduction that again was blamed on the Mexicans, the WFM demanded that the Anglo-Americans' pay be reinstated to the previous $3 wage. The union also demanded that mine officials release the Mexican workers, whom they believed were responsible for the mine's financial troubles and for their own reduction in wages. In response, the company closed the mine for thirty days. The two sides reached agreement in the dispute when the company restored wages to $3.

By 1903, labor relations between Mexican workers and Anglo-American mine officials in the Clifton, Morenci, and Metcalf regions in eastern Arizona were headed toward a breakdown. The catalyst was the Eight-Hour Law, which prohibited more than eight hours of underground work in mines employing Mexican workers. Anglo-Americans saw the underground miner as a threat to their WFM pay scale of $3 per ten-hour day. The Arizona Copper Company and the Detroit Company had no intention of paying the Mexicans the WFM scale and offered instead to pay them an hourly rate for fewer hours. As calculated on a daily pay scale, the Mexicans faced a 10 percent pay cut. The Mexicans refused. The striking workers, 90 percent of whom were Mexican and 10 percent of whom were Italian, had other grievances: they wanted to end both the *boleta* system of pay and the arbitrary increases in prices of goods sold in the company store.

Mexican underground workers were paid in *boletas,* a form of scrip or promissory notes, redeemable at the company store. The prices of goods such as beans, flour, coffee, and sugar often rose on payday. *Boletas* were equal to about 66 to 80 percent of their American face value. Scrip not used in the store could be exchanged for cash at the end of the month, but at a 25 percent reduction in face value. On June 9, 1903, at least 2,000 workers conducted a one-hour parade through the Morenci streets in a pouring rain. The governor called out six companies of the state militia and the Arizona Rangers to end the strike. Five companies of federal troops joined them. A violent flood brought an end to the labor dispute. The governor placed the town of Morenci under martial law and arranged for the arrest of all the strike leaders. The WFM began to organize Anglo-American workers in the Clifton-Morenci region after the 1903

The Globe, Arizona, copper mines, pictured here along with the reduction works, were the scene of many clashes between workers and management during the Arizona mining strikes. *Courtesy National Archives.*

strike. The Arizona Federation of Labor (AFL) also organized miners.

By 1915, other strikes broke out in some Arizona copper districts as a result of increases in the cost of living, low wages, and poor living conditions. Rumblings of discontent among Mexican miners were again heard. Miners in the Clifton-Morenci region paid high prices for food and other essentials at the company stores and were forced to bribe some mining officials to keep their jobs. Anglo-American miners received $2.89 per day, while Mexican miners earned $2.39 for the same number of hours. Both the Anglo-Americans and Mexicans wanted $3 a day. The Mexicans called an organizer from the WFM to the Clifton camp. Mine officials called a meeting with the Mexican workers to discourage them from affiliating with the WFM and to discredit the union. When a WFM organizer appeared at the meeting to speak for the Mexicans and the Anglo-Americans, company officials refused to meet with him and his delegation. In an attempt to intimidate the workers, company officials discharged miners who expressed an interest in the WFM or who had joined the union. On September 11, at least 5,000 Mexican workers went on strike. On September 27, they presented their demands to company officials: higher wage scales, an eight-hour workday, free hospital boarding, assurances that no discrimination would be imposed on strike leaders, and the reinstatement of miners who had been previously discharged for union activity. Company officials refused all the demands.

The Mexican-led strike lasted five months. No outbreak of violence of any kind occurred. The miners won a pay raise to $2.50 per day for surface workers and $3 for underground workers. The miners were forced to reject the WFM for the Arizona State Federation of Labor, an affiliate of the AFL. The 1915 victory did not end the grievances of the Mexican miners in the Clifton-Morenci region, however. Throughout the decade, they continued to struggle for union recognition and to end to the dual-wage system.

One of the more controversial and explosive confrontations between union and management occurred in Bisbee in the summer of 1917. The INDUSTRIAL WORKERS OF THE WORLD (IWW), or "Wobblies," called for a strike against the Bisbee mines to protest unsafe working conditions underground. Mine owners accused the IWW membership of being radical German sympathizers intent on stopping copper production for the war effort in Europe and charged that some Wobblies had strong political ties to the German government. With the country at war, the demand for copper rose, and so did its price. While mining companies reported huge increases in net profit, the workers saw no increase in pay. On June 27, 1917, at least 4,000 Bisbee workers demanded higher wages and an end to the dual-wage system. Walter Douglas, president of Phelps Dodge Corporation, had no patience for the demands. On the morning of July 12, armed vigilantes acting on orders from Douglas, raided the homes of IWW supporters and arrested 2,000 strikers. At gunpoint, the strikers were marched into Bisbee's downtown plaza. While those who pledged loyalty to Phelps Dodge and to the United States were released, 1,186 prisoners were marched to the edge of town and loaded onto cattle cars of the El Paso and Southwestern Railroad, owned by Phelps Dodge. At least 33 percent of the miners were Mexicans. Packed 50 to a car, they were taken two hundred miles to Columbus, New Mexico. There, they were dumped in the desert with no food or water and were threatened with death if they returned to Bisbee. President Woodrow Wilson appointed the Mediation Commission in 1917 to investigate the legality of the deportation of the miners. The committee found the Bisbee deportation a deplorable violation of fundamental constitutional rights. The commission also learned that Phelps Dodge and Calumet-Arizona mining officials were responsible for the deportations.

Mexican miners continued to work toward an end to the dual-wage system. They sought union recognition and opportunities for equal advancement in various positions.
—*Christine Marín*

SEE ALSO: Copper Mining; Labor Movement

SUGGESTED READING:

Byrkit, James R. *Forging the Copper Collar: Arizona's Labor Management War of 1901–1921.* Tucson, Ariz., 1982.

Gómez-Quiñones, Juan. "The First Steps: Chicano Labor Conflict and Organizing, 1900–1920." *Aztlán: Chicano Journal of the Social Sciences and the Arts* 3 (1973): 13–49.

Johnson, Vernon H. *Heritage of Conflict: Labor Relations in the Non-Ferrous Metals Industry.* Ithaca, N.Y., 1950.

Kluger, James R. *The Clifton-Morenci Strike: Labor Difficulty in Arizona.* Tucson, Ariz., 1970.

Mellinger, Philip. "'The Men Have Become Organizers': Labor Conflicts and Unionization in the Mexican Mining Communities of Arizona, 1900–1915." *Western Historical Quarterly* 22 (1992): 323–347.

ARIZONA RANGERS

The Arizona Rangers were established on March 13, 1901, by Republican Governor Nathan Murphy and the territorial legislature. Criminal activity was rampant in the Arizona Territory at the turn of the century, and prominent citizens demanded a law-enforcement company similar to the TEXAS RANGERS. Captain of the rangers, BURTON C. MOSSMAN (a rancher who had helped write the enabling legislation) was paid $120 per month, his sergeant received $75 per month, and 12 privates, many of them former cowboys who knew the habits of livestock rustlers, earned a monthly wage of $55. The rangers possessed no uniforms and often did not openly display their badges so they could pose as cowboys. Most rangers carried a Colt single-action .45 handgun; the model 1895 .30-40 Winchester, the first lever-action repeater to use a box magazine, was the official rifle.

Private Carlos Tafolla was the only ranger ever slain in the line of duty; he was killed on October 8, 1901, during a wilderness fight with rustlers. Mossman tracked down Arizona's most wanted felon, the vicious killer Augustín Chacón, and the rangers hounded other desperadoes. Mossman resigned after one year by prior arrangement and was succeeded by THOMAS H. RYNNING, a gifted administrator who recruited only unmarried men and initiated careful training procedures.

In 1903, the legislature expanded the ranger force to 26 men and increased salaries. The enlarged force pressured so many criminals out of Arizona that a crime epidemic began in New Mexico. To respond to this crime wave, the New Mexico Rangers were formed in 1905.

Rynning resigned in 1907 to become superintendent of Yuma Territorial Prison, and Lieutenant Harry Wheeler was promoted to fill the vacancy. A former cavalryman, Wheeler had enlisted as a ranger private in 1903 and was the only man to hold every rank in the company. Although a conscientious administrator, Wheeler loved field duty and was an expert marksman who outdueled several antagonists.

Over the years, 107 men served as rangers, including relentless and deadly officers such as Sergeants

Frank Wheeler (no relation to the captain) and Jeff Kidder (fatally wounded during a controversial fight in which he shot three Mexican officers). By 1909, the rangers had subdued outlawry to the point that many taxpayers regarded the company as a waste of public funds. Critics of the rangers were led by local sheriffs and Democratic politicians. On February 15, 1909, the Democratic-controlled legislature abolished the rangers, although in contemporary times, several companies of Arizona Rangers carry on the traditions of their hard-riding forbears as auxiliary law officers.

—*Bill O'Neal*

SUGGESTED READING:
Miller, Joseph. *The Arizona Rangers.* New York, 1972.
O'Neal, Bill. *The Arizona Rangers.* Austin, Tex., 1987.

ARIZONA V. CALIFORNIA

In *Arizona* v. *California* (1963), the U.S. Supreme Court ruled that the state of Arizona could draw 3.8 million acre-feet of WATER from the COLORADO RIVER, a decision that threatened the source of water for much of southern California.

World War II and the following years brought huge population growth and water demands to Phoenix and Tucson, Arizona. By the early 1950s, Arizonans had made full use of the Salt and Gila river sheds and had depleted ground-water reserves in several areas. As a result, irrigators encountered cutbacks in water supplies and the failure of productive farmlands. Dwindling water reserves threatened the future growth of Phoenix and Tucson, something city planners and businesspeople hoped desperately to avoid.

Beginning in 1947, Arizonans, led by the persistent prodding of Senator CARL T. HAYDEN, asked Congress to fund the Central Arizona Project (CAP) to bring Colorado River water to the state. Congress, however, refused because of Arizona's dispute with California over the water allocations stipulated in the COLORADO RIVER COMPACT of 1922 and the BOULDER CANYON ACT OF 1928. Because California was taking 5.2 million acre-feet of water as opposed to the 4.4 million acre-feet recommended in the Boulder Canyon Act, California congressmen were especially vigilant in guarding against congressional legislation that would threaten California's water supply. The proposed Central Arizona Program would certainly mean a curtailment of water diversions into thirsty southern California.

In 1952, Arizonans took their case to the United States Supreme Court. The litigation, like so many other modern water cases, involved hydrologists, economists, and lawyers who presented complex and contradictory data. The court had selected a special master, Simon Rifkind, to sort through the testimony and exhibits and to present the facts before the justices. Eleven years, more than 340 witnesses, and almost fifty lawyers took a terrible toll on Rifkind, who suffered from exhaustion and a heart attack halfway through the case. Attorney Northcutt Ely masterfully prolonged the case for Californians as they continued to divert water from the Colorado River.

In 1963, most knowledgeable Westerners anticipated a court ruling favoring California. The justices, however, surprised nearly everyone by ruling that the Boulder Canyon Act had constituted a congressional division of the Colorado River, rather than basis for a future interstate river compacts between California and Arizona. The justices gave Arizona altogether 3.8 million acre-feet from the lower Colorado River basin. With water available for the Central Arizona Project, Arizona congressmen successfully secured its inclusion in the Colorado River Basin Project Act, which passed in 1968. In addition, the justices protected any water rights to the Colorado River predating the Colorado River Compact of 1922. This part of the decision gave several Indian tribes the right to more than 900,000 acre-feet of water. The Navajo and Tohono O'odham tribes made agreements with Arizona for water deliveries, but some critics believed the tribes did not receive their fair share of water.

The decision amounted to a bitter defeat for California. The Metropolitan Water District, representing the large urban centers of southern California, scurried to locate alternative sources of water to replace what had to be given to Arizona. The water shortages resulting from the Supreme Court ruling increased conflict between urban dwellers and farmers over the use of water in southern and central California and spurred the construction of intrastate water projects.

—*James E. Sherow*

SUGGESTED READING:
Hundley, Norris, Jr. "Clio Nods: *Arizona* v. *California* and the Boulder Canyon Act: A Reassessment." *Western Historical Quarterly* 3 (1972): 17–51.
———. *The Great Thirst: Californians and Water, 1770s–1990s.* Berkeley, Calif., 1992.

ARKANSAS

Known as the "Bear State," the "Wonder State," or the "Land of Opportunity," Arkansas is bound on the east by the states of Tennessee and Mississippi, on the south by Louisiana and Texas, on the west by Oklahoma, and on the north by Missouri. The state con-

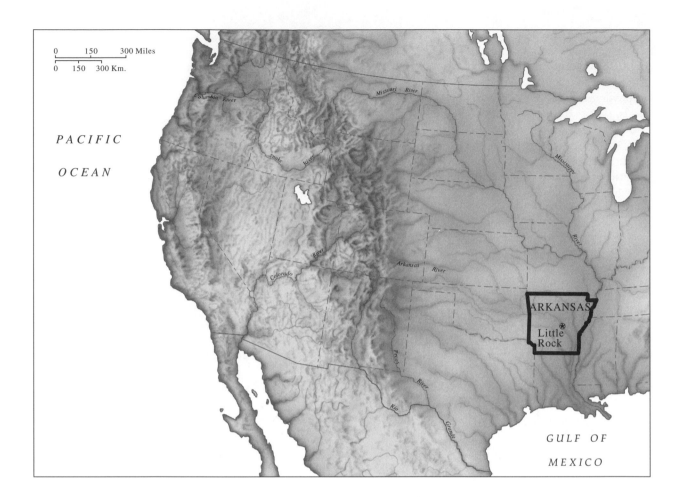

tains 53,187 square miles of land. The 1990 population was 2,350,725 of which 82.7 percent was white, 15.9 percent black, and 0.8 percent Hispanic. The capital city is Little Rock, with a population in 1990 of 175,795.

Geographical features

The state consists of two distinctive geographical areas, a lowland and an upland, composed of five different natural regions. The lowland area occupies roughly the southeastern two-thirds of the state and contains the Mississippi River Alluvial Plain, the West Gulf Coastal Plain, and the Arkansas River valley. These regions possess the state's richest lands, including fine silt and clay alluvium and sandy loams. The upland area contains the Ouachita Mountains and the Ozark Plateau in the northwestern third of the state and Crowley's Ridge, which penetrates the eastern part of the state along a roughly north-south line to the west of the St. Francis River. The Ouachita and Ozark regions have shale, sandstone, and limestone soils. Crowley's Ridge is composed of wind-deposited loess.

The climate of the entire state is humid subtropical, with long, hot summers and short, mild winters. Statewide temperatures average 39.5° F in January and 81°

F in July. The average annual precipitation is forty-eight inches. The mild temperatures produce a growing season of from 180 to 230 days, and the abundance of rainfall contributes to the continued importance of agriculture in the economy of the state.

The state possesses numerous natural resources in addition to its rich soils. Its forests, composed of hardwood trees in the north and east and pines in the south, were among the first forests in the country exploited commercially. The state's most important mineral resources have been barite, bauxite, gemstones, sand, gravel, and vanadium. Of modern economic significance are coal and lignite, natural gas, and petroleum.

Native American life

As early as 8000 B.C., Paleo-Indian communities were present at major sites along the upper White and Ouachita rivers. Prehistoric agricultural communities emerged about 1000 B.C. throughout the state, but particularly along the White and St. Francis river valleys in northeastern Arkansas. By 1000 A.D., large villages of peoples associated with the Mississippian culture had developed. The villages were fortified with moats and palisades and included mound structures within their boundaries. In the sixteenth and seventeenth centuries, Europeans located at least five culturally distinctive Native American groups in Arkansas—the Caddos along the Ouachita River, the Tunicas in the southeast along the Mississippi River, the Michgameas in the northeast, the Osages located in the northwest, and along the lower Arkansas River, the people from whom the state derived its name, the Arkansas or Quapaws, the "Downstream People."

European exploration

Europeans entered Arkansas in 1541 during the expedition of the Spanish explorer Hernando de Soto. The French made the next contact in 1673, when Father JACQUES MARQUETTE and LOUIS JOLIET explored the Mississippi River. Subsequent travels across Arkansas were made by Robert Cavelier, SIEUR DE LA SALLE, in 1682; Henri de Tonti in 1686; Henri Joutel, leading the remnants of La Salle's ill-fated Texas expedition, in 1687; and Benard de La Harpe in 1722.

In 1686, Henri de Tonti made the first attempt to establish a permanent European settlement at Arkansas Post. His effort was unsuccessful, and the next venture came in 1721 when colonists moved into the same area under a charter given to John Law, a Scottish financier, by the French government. Law's Western Company went bankrupt before his plan was carried out, but a few settlers remained in the area. In the Treaty of Paris of 1763, the French government ceded to Spain its territory that included Arkansas. In order to encourage settlement as a barrier to U.S. expansion, the Spanish government made several land grants along the Arkansas and White rivers, but it was the Americans who took advantage of the Spanish land policy. In 1798, Elisha Winter and Joseph Stillwell, the first Anglo-American settlers, established farms near Arkansas Post.

Territory to state

Arkansas became a part of the United States in 1803 as a result of the LOUISIANA PURCHASE. First administered as part of the Missouri Territory in 1812, the region was separated as the Arkansas Territory in 1819. During the territorial years, the national government removed Native Americans from Arkansas, and white settlers arrived in increasing numbers. By 1830, the territory had 30,388 inhabitants scattered throughout the region but primarily located along the river valleys that provided the main transportation routes. The territory became a state on June 15, 1836.

The new state's economy boomed as the cotton frontier advanced. Farmers in the lowland areas quickly took up cotton cultivation, and by 1860, the state was the sixth largest producer in the United States with 367,393 bales harvested annually. Expansion of the cotton kingdom led to the importation of large numbers of black slaves in the 1840s and 1850s; by 1860, the black population had reached 111,259, about one-fourth of the total 435,450 people in the state. The population of the uplands, to a great extent cut off from markets by natural barriers and with less fertile soils, grew slower; there the economy was centered largely on wheat farming, livestock herding, or subsistence agriculture.

Before the CIVIL WAR, regional economic diversity and factional rivalries provided the basis for political conflict within the state. A group of politicians known as the "Family" or the "Dynasty," because many were related to the politically prominent Conway and Sevier families, dominated state government. While personal and economic rivalries often splintered the group, its policies of low taxes and limited state services generally favored the interests of the lowland planters at the expense of those of the upland small farmers.

Civil War and Reconstruction

Conflicting regional needs produced disagreements among Arkansans in the secession crisis of 1861. In the northwestern part of the state, Arkansans were concerned with frontier protection and the loss of federal support for various internal improvements. Most of the state's political leaders, however, identified Arkansas's interests with those of the rest of the South, and when war finally broke out, they took the state out of the Union on May 6, 1861.

While Arkansas itself played only a small role in Confederate strategy, several battles in the state helped determine the war's outcome. Major battles at Pea Ridge on March 2, 1862, and Prairie Grove on December 7, 1862, forced the Confederates to abandon northern Arkansas and ensured Union control of Missouri during the rest of the war. These battles set the scene for the Union army's successful campaigns on the Mississippi River. The Union capture of Arkansas Post on January 11, 1863, was a part of the effort to reopen the Mississippi River. Major battles took place at Helena on July 4, 1863, and during the Red River campaign in April 1864, but they were of less strategic consequence.

Reconstruction began in Arkansas after the Union army captured Little Rock on September 10, 1863. A Union government was established under Governor Isaac Murphy the following spring. Murphy's government continued after the war, but it was never recognized by Congress. The end of the state's reconstruction occurred when Arkansas was readmitted to the Union with a constitution embracing black suffrage on June 22, 1868.

Late nineteenth-century changes

In the postwar years, the state faced serious economic problems caused by the cost of the war and the collapse of the cotton market. Many farmers went broke. The freed African Americans and landless whites were quickly integrated into a system of farm tenancy. The new conditions left the vast majority of Arkansans impoverished and challenged the state's political leaders to produce any form of economic growth and development.

For six years after 1868, the Republican party controlled the state. The party carried out a program of economic development with legislation supporting railroad and levee construction, funding the state debt, creating an immigration bureau, establishing public schools and the state university, creating a state school for the deaf, and reestablishing law and order and suppressing the KU KLUX KLAN. Because of the high cost of the Republican program, the Democratic party was successful in regaining control of state politics in 1874 with the election of AUGUSTUS HILL GARLAND as governor.

The Democrats, in order to cut taxes, reversed many of the programs initiated by the Republicans, repudiated the state debt in 1884, and initiated severe retrenchment of state services. While the program relieved taxpayers, it immobilized the poor and doomed most to lives as agricultural workers. While desiring economic growth, Democratic administrations promoted economic change primarily by offering new industries tax breaks and the promise of a low-wage work force.

After the 1870s, the one major change promoted successfully by both Reconstruction Republicans and Democrats was the spread of railroads through the state. The railroads improved transportation and led to modest economic diversification, primarily the introduction of industries exploiting the state's natural resources. By the 1880s, railroad construction made the state's forests accessible to the timber industry. COAL MINING also became a major economic activity. The mining of bauxite began around 1900. In 1921, the first producing oil well was opened in Ouachita County.

Expanding economic opportunities caused some social changes, including at least some European immigration between 1870 and 1900. The state's population had been dominated by white and black settlers from the older Southern states. After 1870, several small communities of Germans and Italians located in the state.

Such changes, while important, did not displace agriculture, particularly cotton production, as the dominant factor in the state's economy. Farm problems remained a drag on the overall economy. In the 1880s and 1890s, Arkansas became a center of agrarian protest as the home of the Brothers of Freedom and the Agricultural Wheel, and its people maintained a tradition of agrarian radicalism into the twentieth century.

Twentieth-century developments

Technological innovation, changing markets, improved transportation facilities, and government programs ultimately revolutionized the economy of modern Arkansas, beginning in the 1930s and 1940s. The introduction of mechanical cotton pickers, the increased use of agricultural chemicals, and New Deal agricultural policies ended tenancy. World demand for rice, soybeans, and chickens offered the state's farmers alternatives to cotton as a cash product. War orders promoted the emergence of the aluminum industry within the state. Improved transportation contributed to the increasing importance of Arkansas as a center for distribution of retail goods and for retail operations. Beginning in the 1950s, the state's economy shifted from agriculture to manufacturing and national retailing. Industry was dominated by consumer-goods industries such as food products, electrical equipment, petroleum and coal products, paper products, and chemicals. The state's retail importance was established with the location of major trucking firms within its boundaries as well as corporate headquarters for important retail businesses.

Economic shifts after 1950 generated major social adjustments. Rural counties lost population, while urban communities grew. In 1980, the census showed for the first time that the state's urban population was larger than the rural. By 1990, two of the state's metropolitan areas had populations of more than 100,000: Little Rock with 513,117 residents and Fort Smith with 175,911. Another change was a decline in the black population, through out-migration that accompanied the transformation taking place in agriculture. Between 1940 and 1970, the black population declined in absolute numbers and as a percentage of the total population, a trend not reversed until the 1980s.

Arkansas remained relatively poor in the midst of the economic shifts between 1950 and 1990, but it exerted an increasingly important role in the modern nation, especially through the work of dynamic entrepreneurs. Major trucking firms, such as J. B. Hunt, and retail operations, such as Dillard's department stores and Wal-Mart discount stores, spread beyond the state to have an impact across the country. Food processors and manufacturers, such as Tyson's poultry, exercised a major role in the nation's food industries. Further indicating the state's ability to assert a greater role within the nation despite its relative poverty was the successful campaign by former Governor Bill Clinton for the Democratic nomination for the presidency and his victory in the election of 1992. Such success in the face of historical patterns of adversity gave credence to at least one of the state's nicknames, "the Land of Opportunity."

—*Carl H. Moneyhon*

SEE ALSO: Lumber Industry; Oil and Gas Industry

SUGGESTED READING:

Ashmore, Harry S. *Arkansas: A History.* New York, 1984.

Hanson, Gerald T., and Carl H. Moneyhon. *Historical Atlas of Arkansas.* Norman, Okla., 1989.

Tucker, David M. *Arkansas: A People and Their Reputation.* Memphis, Tenn., 1985.

Williams, C. Fred, et al., eds. *A Documentary History of Arkansas.* Fayetteville, Ark., 1984.

ARKANSAS RIVER

Flowing south from headwaters near Leadville, Colorado, the Arkansas River—a large tributary of the Mississippi—drops more than 6,600 feet in less than 150 miles as it cuts a 60-mile swath through the Sawatch Range of the Rocky Mountains, bends east near Salida, Colorado, and rushes and tumbles through the 1,100-foot Royal Gorge it has gouged in the eastern Rockies to reach the edge of the Great Plains near Pueblo, Colorado. There, clear waters flow through a narrow canyon, and the Arkansas becomes a muddy, unpredictable stream. By the time the Arkansas reaches Wichita, Kansas, it is only 1,300 feet above sea level; when it hits Tulsa, Oklahoma, it has dropped to 698 feet. In the Ouachita Mountains, its waters once again briefly clear as the river flows past Fort Smith, Arkansas, then Little Rock at 233 feet, and at last into the Mississippi at an elevation of around 100 feet.

The 1,460-mile Arkansas and its major tributaries—the Purgatoire, Salt Fork, Canadian, Verdigris, Grand, and Cimarron rivers—drain an area of some 161,000 square miles. The region ranges from semiarid mountain slopes to fast-eroding plains to easily flooded bottomlands. Melting mountain snows gush into the river during spring, but in summer, the weather

Arkansas River.

turns dry, and the river's flow slackens precipitously, unless thunderstorms strike the right spots; if summer rains come frequently, the river floods. The varied terrain and the changeling water flow created a need to store and supplement the Arkansas's water and to guard against sudden floods, thus leading Colorado and Kansas to form a river compact dividing the flow of the river.

Named after the area's Arkansas Indians, the river was explored early by FRANCISCO VÁSQUEZ DE CORONADO near present-day Dodge City but was first recorded and identified by LOUIS JOLIET in 1673. Hardly navigable except on occasion near its mouth, the Arkansas appeared to the French missionaries and *coureurs de bois* an impediment, although Henri de Tonti—one of La Salle's lieutenants—did establish near the river's mouth the Poste aux Arkansas, or Arkansas Post, in 1686, the first French settlement west of the Mississippi. Various traders, British and French, trapped the area. After Pierre and Paul Mallet made contact with the Spanish Southwest settlements in 1739, it appeared as if trade between the French and the Spanish might develop over the route from St. Louis to the Arkansas Post and then down to the Rio Grande. Not until the United States bought Louisiana, however, and Mexico won its independence from Spain in the following century would such a Santa Fe trade flourish.

The Arkansas—including its upper reaches—had been part of the reconnaissance conducted by ZEBULON MONTGOMERY PIKE for the United States in 1806. Although a group of Alsatians and their slaves attempted briefly to settle along the Arkansas in 1820 before moving downriver to New Orleans, the first American settlement grew out of the fur trade: BENT'S FORT was built in 1833 where the Arkansas and the Purgatoire meet. By the 1840s, the beaver were trapped out, fur hats were no longer fashionable, and Bent's Fort had become a way station of the northern branch of the Santa Fe Trail. The Arkansas River was the southern boundary of the United States until General STEPHEN WATTS KEARNY and his troops followed the waterway to Bent's Fort heading south for New Mexico, California, and glory in the United States–Mexican War from 1846 to 1848. Forty-niners taking the southern route to the California gold fields passed the same way. After the Civil War, the railroads fostered settlement in the Arkansas basin, and cattle ranchers watered their herds at the river. But the region was considered too dry for crops—without irrigation—until dryland farming developed just before World War I. Travel along the river reached its peak between 1840 and 1870, with steamboats plying the Arkansas as far north as Little Rock, but the completion of the railroads killed the river traffic. Beginning in 1874, Colorado farmers diverted water from the Arkansas to irrigate the agricultural oases at Rocky Ford.

Farming only accelerated the river's high potential for erosion, and the turn-of-the century wheat boom on the Southern Plains ultimately resulted in the DUST BOWL, which severely depopulated the Arkansas Basin. Beginning with the New Deal, the notion of damming the Arkansas into a useful river took hold. Water-control projects abounded, ensuring that the river fed Pueblo, Colorado; Wichita, Kansas; Tulsa, Oklahoma; and Fort Smith and Little Rock, Arkansas. Today dams stretch from the foot of the Rockies to the river's mouth, turning the once turbulent Arkansas into a series of long, lazy lakes filled with the flat-bottom barges of profit-hungry businesses and the buzzing speed boats of leisure-loving vacationers.

—*Charles Phillips*

SUGGESTED READING:
Ashmore, Harry S. *Arkansas: A History.* New York, 1984.
Fletcher, John Gould. *Arkansas.* 1947. Reprint. Fayetteville, Ark., 1989.

ARMADILLOS

Armadillos, nocturnal, burrowing mammals, belong to the family *Dasypodidae,* order *Edentata.* There are nine genera and some twenty species of armadillos. The earliest Spanish explorers gave the animal its name, roughly meaning "small armored one" and referring to the armadillo's unique natural armor of bony plates covering its upper and side surfaces as well as parts of its legs and undersides. This armor, which is highly patterned and ranges in color (on different animals) from brown to pink, provides formidable passive protection. When attacked, the animal retracts its feet and nose into its hornlike armor. Some species roll into an armored ball, and the nine-banded armadillo possesses extensive air passages and a highly efficient circulatory system that allow it to hold its breath for up to six minutes, so that it appears inert.

The nine-banded armadillo, *Dasypus novemcinctus,* is the only species found in the United States and is especially prevalent in eastern Texas. It also ranges down through Central and South America. The animal is about sixteen inches long, including its head and body, with its tail typically adding another fourteen inches. It weighs up to eighteen pounds.

The armadillo is a night feeder, living on frogs, snakes, insects, and carrion. While many Texans have adopted the distinctive animal as a kind of informal state mascot, it is also easy prey for target shooters—for the slow-moving, unaggressive animal is more properly called a target than game—and is the frequent victim of nighttime road kills on Texas highways. All other species of armadillos live in Central and South America.

—*Alan Axelrod*

SUGGESTED READING:
Talmage, Roy Van Neste. *The Armadillo* (Dasypus Novemcinctus): *A Review of Its Natural History, Ecology, Anatomy, Reproduction, and Physiology.* Houston, Tex., 1954.

ARMIJO, MANUEL

Mexican Governor of New Mexico (from 1827 to 1829, from 1837 to 1844, and from 1845 to 1846), Manuel Armijo (1792?–1853) was born near Albuquerque. He amassed a fortune, according to tradition, by stealing livestock from ranchers in the area. While his first term as governor of New Mexico was uneventful, his second began with the rebellion of 1837. During the conflict, José Gonzalez seized power from Governor Albino Perez, but Gonzalez and his fellow rebels were defeated by Armijo's troops at La Canada. Armijo then claimed the office of governor for himself and executed Gonzalez. During this second term, he directed his troops against the Texas–Santa Fe expedition led by General Hugh McLeod, whose goal was to annex New Mexico to the Republic of Texas. Including fifty merchants and teamsters plus 270 armed volunteers, the expedition left Texas on June 18, 1841. The group planned to distribute leaflets encouraging the New Mexicans to revolt from Mexico and join with the Texans in establishing a new nation. Along the way, the expedition got lost, changing the already arduous six-hundred-mile trip into one much longer. Toward the end of the journey, the group split in two. Armijo's troops intercepted the Texans at the Peeks River and arrested and disarmed them. Armijo ordered Captain Dames Salazar to march the Texans, in shackles, back to El Paso. Many people died on the march, and Salazar kept count by threading the ears of the dead onto a piece of rawhide. The Mexican government decorated Armijo for his role in the campaign.

Armijo became active in Santa Fe trade during his terms as governor. Using his political office, he gained trade for his supporters and attempted to wipe out all competition from the Anglo-Americans. He also granted to his friends large tracts of land in which he retained an interest.

In 1846, when American troops under STEPHEN WATTS KEARNY marched on Santa Fe during the

Manuel Armijo. *Courtesy Museum of New Mexico.*

United States–Mexican War, Armijo met with Captain Philip St. George and JAMES WILEY MAGOFFIN, who persuaded the governor that resistance was hopeless. Armijo called Santa Fe citizens to arms, erected defenses at Apache Canyon, and then fled south with his troops without ever firing a shot. Charged with treason by the Mexican government, he was tried and acquitted in Mexico City. He later returned to New Mexico and lived the rest of his life as a businessman and rancher. He died at Lemitar, south of Albuquerque.

—*Candace Floyd*

SUGGESTED READING:
Weber, David J. *The Mexican Frontier, 1821–1846: The American Southwest under Mexico.* Albuquerque, N. Mex., 1982.

ARMOUR, PHILIP DANFORTH

Born in Stockbridge, New York, Philip Danforth Armour (1836–1901) was the meat-packer principally responsible for developing the Chicago stockyards. Armour's first vocation was as a miner, from which he moved into farming and then the wholesale-grocery business. By the late 1860s, a primitive form of refrigerated railroad car became available, and Armour, seeing an opportunity, went into the meat-packing business in 1870. Since Chicago had already developed into the rail hub at which Eastern lines met Western and Southwestern routes, it was the logical place for a meat-packing industry. Armour pioneered the shipping of hogs to Chicago, where they were slaughtered, canned, and shipped both nationally and internationally. He also purchased his own fleet of refrigerator cars to ship fresh meat to the East Coast.

Armour made a fortune and greatly expanded the market for Western beef producers, but he also became the target of censure—in the East as well as the West—for his strong-arm antilabor tactics and monopolistic practices. Like other captains of industry of his day, he did have a philanthropic side; he established the Armour Institute, which subsequently became the prestigious Illinois Institute of Technology.

Late in his life, Armour was among those in the packing industry charged with purveying what the Muckraking press called "embalmed beef"—inferior canned meat, treated with toxic chemicals—to the armed forces during the Spanish-American War of 1898. The tainted meat was responsible for numerous cases of food poisoning, including fatalities, among soldiers. The scandal helped spark a reform movement that culminated in such Progressive legislation as the Pure Food and Drug Act of June 30, 1906.

Despite antitrust actions and the "embalmed-beef" scandal, Philip D. Armour's son, J. Ogden Armour, continued to build Armour and Company and made it the world's largest meat-packing firm.

—*Alan Axelrod*

SUGGESTED READING:
Leech, Harper, and John C. Carroll. *Philip D. Armour and His Times.* 1938. Reprint. New York and London, 1979.

ARMY

SEE: United States Army

ARMY CORPS OF ENGINEERS

SEE: United States Army Corps of Engineers

ART

Western Art
  Brian W. Dippie

Surveys and Expeditions
  John Logan Allen

Book and Magazine Illustration
  Charles Phillips

Popular Prints and Commercial Art
  Charles Phillips

Folk (Ethnic) Art
  Patrick H. Butler, III

WESTERN ART

Western American art can be understood as both *description* and *interpretation*. Traditionally, it was appreciated for what it revealed about nineteenth-century Western life and was praised for its accuracy. At its best, Western art was thought to mirror Western reality. It showed remote landscapes and the colorful types that peopled them. It is now recognized, however, that Western art expresses cultural assumptions and values as well. It is a reliable reflector not only of what was but also of what the artists and their patrons wanted the West to be.

While Western art can be traced back to the earliest European images of the New World, it assumed its typically American form in the nineteenth century when the United States acquired the Louisiana Territory from France in 1803. Under President THOMAS JEFFERSON, the federal government undertook the exploration of the tributaries of the Mississippi—to the remotest western borders of the territory. Exploration began with the LEWIS AND CLARK EXPEDITION (from 1804 to 1806) and was subsequently advanced by those of ZEBULON MONTGOMERY PIKE (from 1806 to 1807) and STEPHEN HARRIMAN LONG (from 1819 to 1820). Draftsmen and, after the invention of the camera, photographers accompanied most expeditions over the next seventy years. SAMUEL SEYMOUR, TITIAN RAMSAY PEALE, JOHN MIX STANLEY, RICHARD HOVENDON KERN, EDWARD MEYER KERN, and others made the exotic familiar to Americans curious about what lay "out there" beyond the borders of civil society. Most of these artists depicted the native tribes and recorded features, costumes, habitats, and customs. The Indian exerted a strong romantic appeal as the incarnation of natural man, uncorrupted and noble in his simple way. And there was something else. The Indians were doomed by a higher law ordaining civilized progress. Their forests and prairies and the animals they hunted would vanish with the advance of a white population destined to overspread the continent. There was not room for trees *and* farms, for wilderness *and* cities, for shady glades *and* factories. The Indians were a vanishing race.

GEORGE CATLIN was the best-known painter of the American Indian in the nineteenth century. A Pennsylvanian trained in the law, he opted for art as his profession and established an acceptable reputation as a portraitist in Philadelphia and New York in the 1820s. But he yearned for more. He wanted an animating purpose in his art, and he found it in 1828 when a visiting delegation of Indians fixed his resolve to become their pictorial historian. They were, he thought, "noble and dignified-looking," worthy subjects for a lifetime's work. Speed was of the essence, for they could not long survive in their uncorrupted state. Civilization was even then invading their remotest hunting grounds, changing and destroying the Indians in the process. Catlin subsequently made four trips into Indian country and painted some five hundred portraits and scenes of Indian life in the 1830s. He was an avid collector; Blackfoot, Crow, Lakota, Assiniboin, Wichita, Comanche, Kiowa, Ojibwa, and Dakota Indians, all made their way into his "Indian Gallery." Others had created collections of Indian portraits before Catlin—notably CHARLES BIRD KING, who became painter-in-residence specializing in Indian visitors to Washington, D.C., on commission from the Indian Office of the War Department, and James Otto Lewis, who anticipated Catlin in publishing a portfolio of the portraits he made as an observer at treaty councils in the Old Northwest in the mid-1820s. Peter Rindisbacher had actually lived in the West while establishing a reputation during his short career as a painter of Indian life along the upper Mississippi.

But none of the other Indian painters had Catlin's vision. He wanted to create a comprehensive record of the natives of the Western Hemisphere—a record that would endure long after their cultures had disappeared. A self-promoter with a vision, he was the prototypical Indian painter; and although he was unsuccessful in selling his collection, it was widely seen on tour in America and Europe and through reproduction.

Some artists who viewed his paintings were inspired to surpass him. KARL (OR CARL) BODMER, the Swiss artist who accompanied Prince Maximilian of Wied-Neuwied up the Missouri River, thought Catlin's work too romantic; Rudolph Friederich Kurz, who made the same journey in the 1850s, thought it too unrefined, even grotesque. But Catlin's example inspired them all: PAUL KANE, the Canadian artist who traveled to the West Coast and back in the 1840s, creating a gallery of his own; CHARLES DEAS, the St. Louis-based artist who aspired to rival Catlin in the 1850s; the soldier-artist SETH EASTMAN, who painted Indian life while he was stationed on the Mississippi, in Florida, and in Texas from the 1820s to the 1850s; and especially John Mix Stanley, who created a collection of 154 paintings based on his travels in the Indian Territory, the Southwest, California, the Oregon Territory,

Karl Bodmer, *Assiniboin Medicine Sign,* 1833. *Courtesy Joslyn Art Museum.*

Alfred Jacob Miller. *Trappers Crossing the River.*
Courtesy National Cowboy Hall of Fame and Western
Heritage Center.

and across the Northern Plains. Stanley's gallery, the only real American rival to Catlin's, was exhibited at the Smithsonian Institution through the 1850s before fire destroyed it in 1865.

Western art is defined by its content *and* its Euro-American perspective. It narrates a culturally specific version of events, one in which the Indian may play the noble savage in the past, or the bloodthirsty savage in the present, but can have no role in the future. To the white American pioneer—mountain man, prospector, farmer, soldier, cowboy—belongs the future. While a sunbonneted pioneer mother may also make an appearance, Western art is essentially a masculine art, dominated by images of heroic men testing themselves against the wilderness, their enemies, and (in gunfights, for example) one another. ALFRED JACOB MILLER is best known for recording white pioneer experience. A Baltimore native, he accompanied his Scottish patron Sir William Drummond Stewart to the 1837 fur-trade rendezvous on the Green River and created a unique record of MOUNTAIN MEN at work and play. Amity prevails; Indians and trappers alike, frolicking in an unspoiled paradise, race their horses across an uncluttered land and exult in a freedom without limits. While painters recorded the clash of cultures and made battles between white pioneers and Indians warriors a staple subject that eventually evolved into the full-blown turn-of-the-century celebration of the conquest of the West by Uncle Sam's heroic boys in blue, there would always be a tinge of bittersweet regret in Western art—a sense that progress was closing in on something wonderful. The mundane was about to overtake the romantic; mountain men and hard-riding COWBOYS were about to yield their place to the sober adulthood of

dryland farming and town planning—and dull reality. The West before it was tamed—the Wild West—was what fascinated writers, artists, showmen, and a vast public that could not seem to get enough of pioneering derring-do.

CHARLES (OR CARL) F. WIMAR, a St. Louis painter trained in his native Germany, was a transitional figure in Western art. The Indian as Indian might satisfy some, but "pictures of pure savage life, like those of Mr. Catlin, cannot excite our sympathies as strongly as do the representations of beings who belong to our own race," a New York journal observed in 1845. Wimar made two trips up the Missouri River into Indian country in 1858 and 1859 and painted serene landscapes populated by BUFFALOES and the native peoples he had seen on his travels. But before actually going West, he had created imaginary scenes of Indian-white conflict—white women being carried off into captivity, dragoons charging fleeing warriors, and wagon trains under attack. Captivity narratives, with their heart-tugging appeals to sentiment, and pulp fiction about brutal Indian raids had served as Wimar's original inspiration, and even after seeing

Albert Bierstadt, *Jim Bridger. Courtesy National Cowboy*
Hall of Fame and Western Heritage Center.

Charles Marion Russell, *Cinch Ring. Courtesy National Cowboy Hall of Fame and Western Heritage Center.*

Western life for himself, he still let imagination dictate to personal observation.

Wimar's subjects anticipated the illustrated papers and magazines from the 1860s through the 1890s. Even as successive Western tribes made their last, futile resistances and yielded to confinement on reservations, artists concentrated on showing white sacrifice. GEORGE ARMSTRONG CUSTER's "last stand," fought in the nation's centennial year, fit the formula perfectly. Pictures showing trappers, cowboys, settlers, and soldiers bravely resisting their savage foes fascinated the American public. They confirmed the cost of civilized progress by shifting its burden from the soon-to-be-dispossessed Indians circling in the distance to the stalwart band of white men standing tall in the foreground. Such pictures pointed the way to the future in Western art. An elegiac undercurrent remained, but it would surface infrequently in an art devoted to establishing the white hero's credentials and justifying the displacement of native peoples. The obvious exception was landscape painting.

The Western landscape had always fascinated artists, as *terra incognita* and as a properly exotic setting for heroics. The expeditionary artists were expected to work in a descriptive mode—to render what they saw with the scientific precision of topographical draftsmen. Inevitably, the artists added their own perceptions to the mix, and in their renderings, mountains rose a little higher, canyons plunged a little deeper, and strange rock formations became even stranger. Thus interpretation augmented description—a process already evident in the landscapes of Catlin, Bodmer, and Miller, but especially in the work of the major landscape painters of the nineteenth century: ALBERT BIERSTADT, who made the Sierra Nevada his special theme, and THOMAS MORAN, who transformed Yellowstone National Park and the Grand Canyon into geological spectacles with soft contours, swirling mists, and rainbow hues.

Such a romantic Western landscape was tailor-made for larger-than-life deeds. Montana's CHARLES MARION RUSSELL caught the essence of the match-up. "The mountains and plains seemed to stimulate man's imagination," he wrote. "A man in the States might have been a liar in a small way, but when he comes west he soon takes lessons from the prairies, where ranges a hundred miles away seem within touchin' distance, streams run uphill and Nature appears to lie some herself."

The conquest of the West was the master theme of FREDERIC REMINGTON and the legion of artists who followed his lead in the 1880s and 1890s when he was at the height of his fame as a prolific magazine illustrator and all-around expert on the American West. Indeed, Remington was unavoidable: to think of the West was to think of Remington's lean, muscular cowboys and troopers and his fierce Indians racing pell-mell across a barren expanse of desert and plain. Remington often relied on photographs, and some of his illustrations were static; but he was known for his ability to portray horses and riders in motion. Many of his images—in pen and ink, paint, and beginning in the mid-1890s, in bronze—have planted themselves in the collective memory. He gave shape to the West by creating "types"—instantly recognizable "men with the bark on." His prospectors and cowboys were the leathery personifications of self-reliance; his bushy-bearded mountain men, burly and bearlike in their buckskins, were a match for the rugged terrain that nurtured them. Remington is controversial today for what made him popular in his own time: the vivid and unblushing celebration of white civilization's conquest of the West.

Remington ranged widely in his subjects. The body of his work serves as a catalogue of the themes that have dominated Western American art and, for that matter, Western literature, movies, and television in the twentieth century. He showed gunfights in saloons and in the streets of ramshackle Western towns; bucking broncos and cattle stampedes; explorers topping the rise to gaze upon a new land; mountain men at work and play; buffalo hunts and cavalry patrols in deserts shimmering with heat; running fights with Indians and desperate stands; wagon trains and stagecoaches under attack; range wars; and lone riders silhouetted against sunset skies. It is hard to think of a Western cliché that Remington did not invent, or at least, perpetuate. His influence, in his time and since, has been enormous. One of his contemporaries, the New Jersey artist CHARLES SCHREYVOGEL, who specialized in painting Indian fights filled with plunging horses, blazing guns, flashing sabers, and bodies crashing to the ground, was compared to Remington, to Remington's considerable annoyance. Other Western artists—Maynard Dixon, Edwin Willard Deming, and Carl Rungius—turned to Remington for encouragement and received it, perhaps because their work did not directly rival his own. Dixon rendered the Southwest with a poet's appreciation for land and sky and a modernist's vision; Deming focused on the mystical side of native life and was, as Dixon was, best known for his murals, a decorative form foreign to Remington; Rungius specialized in Western wildlife.

Charles Russell was another matter. He was Remington's direct contemporary, and his subjects superficially resembled Remington's. Both men went West

at the beginning of the 1880s—Remington as an upstate New Yorker fresh from a year at Yale's art school; Russell as a restless St. Louis teenager, his imagination already overheated by dime-novel derring-do, cheap prints, the paintings of Carl Wimar, and the legendary deeds of frontiersman-showman WILLIAM F. ("BUFFALO BILL") CODY. Remington, with the exception of one year's residence in Kansas, would never live in the West; Russell never lived anywhere else after 1880. Montana became his home, and though he traveled widely, he was still living in Great Falls, Montana, when he died in 1926. Remington, as an artist-correspondent on assignment for Eastern journals, gained a broad exposure to the entire Western region; the frontier army was his specialty. Russell was a working cowboy from 1882 to 1893; he painted on the side and garnered national attention in 1887 for a crude water-color sketch of a starving steer surrounded by wolves. Known as *Waiting for a Chinook,* it became a Western icon. But Russell's reputation was mainly local; he was Montana's "cowboy artist." In the same period, Remington's graphic renderings of Western life were regularly appearing in such periodicals as *Harper's Weekly* and *Century Magazine,* ensuring a huge audience for his work. Interestingly, Remington's very success imprisoned him in a role he found increasingly uncongenial. He wanted recognition as an artist rather than as an

Frederic Remington, *An Arizona Cowboy. Courtesy National Cowboy Hall of Fame and Western Heritage Center.*

Top: Charles Schreyvogel, *My Bunkie. Courtesy National Cowboy Hall of Fame and Western Heritage Center.*

Bottom: William R. Leigh, *Buffalo Hunt. Courtesy National Cowboy Hall of Fame and Western Heritage Center.*

on the doors of publishers and galleries. Only then did Russell occupy the same stage as Remington. The two men might be the "titans of Western art," but they left the titanic struggle over relative merit to their respective champions.

To this day, Remington and Russell are often seen as the flip side of the same coin. But there are important differences in their work. One is subject matter. Both showed cowboys and Indians, but soldiers never interested Russell, nor did the story to which they were central, the winning of the West. And this suggests a second, fundamental distinction in their views of the West. Remington was given to celebrating progress, while Russell consistently lamented change. His work, in paint, clay, pen and ink, and prose, constitutes a sustained elegy. While he portrayed many violent scenes, his standard subjects were cowboys at work, buffalo hunts, and parties of Indians riding across an open land. It was not the bloody clash of natives and settlers but the puzzled encounter between two different ways of life that interested him. The land and the wild creatures that roamed it were part of his art. He was an instinctive conservationist: he liked things as they were before the farmer came along and plowed under romance.

In rejecting the imperative of conquest, Russell paralleled the artists who late in the nineteenth century began making New Mexico their home and achieved national prominence in the first three decades of the twentieth century as the TAOS SCHOOL OF ARTISTS. Painters such as Ernest L. Blumenshein, Oscar E. Berninghaus, Eanger Irving Couse, Bert G. Phillips, Walter Ufer, and Russell's friends W. Herbert Dunton and Joseph Henry Sharp shared Russell's romanticism. But their master theme was permanence, not loss. The violent clash of contesting cultures never interested them as much as the blending over time of diverse, vital traditions—native, Hispanic, and Anglo. They painted the unchanging land, ancient pueblos, and Indians whose cultures were old before Columbus touched shore in the New World. The Taos artists did not entirely abandon the sentimental notion of the

illustrator, and after 1900, he made such recognition his top priority. He earned critical acclaim in his last years for his painterly, even impressionistic canvases. Russell was always an artist, struggling to make a living from his work in isolation from the Eastern markets. In 1903, he traveled to New York and knocked "vanishing Indian," but acculturation rather than cultural extinction was their usual message. In the Southwest, the old had found a future in the new. Fittingly, then, it was there that modernism established a toehold in the 1920s in the work of painters such as Marsden Hartley, John Marin, and especially GEORGIA O'KEEFFE, whose images of adobe structures, crosses, animal skulls, and the desert landscape over time have become, like those of Remington and Russell, icons of Western art.

But the legacy of Remington and Russell continues to loom largest in Western art. Technically sophisticated painters such as FRANK TENNEY JOHNSON and WILLIAM ROBINSON LEIGH extended the legacy deep into the twentieth century, and a still-thriving tradition has never lost sight of its nineteenth-century roots. Contemporary Western artists turn to their predecessors for information and inspiration. Their mode is consciously unfashionable; their style, rigorously representational; their detail, precise. Apart from an interest in magic realism and camouflage art, experimentation is essentially limited to a Remingtonesque flirtation with impressionism. Subjects still matter to these artists, who adhere to old values. Their vision of the West is one Russell would have found congenial. They portray a pristine world unscarred by highways, litter, and pickup trucks full of urban reality.

Those who would know the Western art tradition must visit the West, not only to understand the tradition in context, but also to see representative collections. New York state offers two honorable exceptions—the Rockwell Museum in Corning and, for an important collection by one of the defining figures, the Frederic Remington Art Museum in Ogdensburg. In Montana, Charles Russell is strongly represented at the Montana Historical Society in Helena and at the C. M. Russell Museum in Great Falls. In Wyoming, one can visit the BUFFALO BILL HISTORICAL CENTER in Cody. In Colorado, the Museum of Western Art in Denver offers a representative sampling. In Oklahoma, the NATIONAL COWBOY HALL OF FAME AND WESTERN HERITAGE CENTER in Oklahoma City, the Woolaroc Museum near Bartlesville, and the THOMAS GILCREASE INSTITUTE in Tulsa have collections of Western art. In Texas, the AMON CARTER MUSEUM and the Sid W. Richardson Collection in Fort Worth, the Stark Museum in Orange, and the Harry Ranson Humanities Center at the University of Texas in Austin all have choice collections of Western art. The R. W. Norton Art Gallery in Shreveport, Louisiana, the Eiteljorg Museum in Indianapolis, and the AUTRY MUSEUM OF WESTERN HERITAGE in Los Angeles offer representative collections. Other museums hold significant Southwestern collections—the Desert Caballeros Museum in Wickenburg, Arizona, and the Palm Springs Desert Museum in California, for example.

—*Brian W. Dippie*

SUGGESTED READING:

Axelrod, Alan. *Art of the Golden West.* New York, 1990.
Broder, Patricia Janis. *The American West: The Modern Vision.* Boston, 1984.
Bruce, Chris, et al. *Myth of the West.* Seattle, Wash., and New York, 1990.
Dippie, Brian W. *Catlin and His Contemporaries: The Politics of Patronage.* Lincoln, Nebr., 1990.
———. *Charles M. Russell, Word Painter: Letters, 1887–1926.* Fort Worth, Tex., 1993.
———. *Looking at Russell.* Fort Worth, Tex., 1987.
Eldredge, Charles C., et al. *Art in New Mexico, 1900–1945: Paths to Taos and Santa Fe.* New York, 1986.
Hassrick, Peter H. *The Way West: Art of Frontier America.* New York, 1977.

SURVEYS AND EXPEDITIONS

Seeking to understand the West, the American government, in the nineteenth century, dispatched exploratory and surveying expeditions on lengthy reconnaissances. Some of these survey expeditions merely sought information about unknown lands. Others looked for feasible routes for transcontinental transportation systems, particularly railroads. Still others were involved in scientific inquiry and in the determination of the proper uses for the public lands of the West. Artists—whose role it was to convey accurate impressions of landscapes, peoples, and natural phenomena—accompanied most of the government surveys. In the early years of the nineteenth century, the survey artists worked in water color and pen and ink; by the end of the century, they had changed their medium to photography, which allowed some measure of individual artistic expression but imparted visions of the West that were more accurate than the graphic arts of earlier years. While few survey artists can be listed among the most famous Western masters, their works often were of greater importance in translating the results of government surveys into public perceptions of the Western landscape. Whether reproduced directly in widely available government publications such as *The Pacific Railroad Reports* or copied and lithographed for newspapers and other periodicals, the works of the nearly anonymous survey artists were seen by many more people than ever viewed paintings by ALFRED JACOB MILLER or ALBERT BIERSTADT. Indeed, it was not until the late nineteenth and early twentieth centuries, when the works of Western artists such as FREDERIC REMINGTON graced the pages of *Harper's Weekly,* that independent artists, unassociated with government surveys, became more important as shapers of the American view of the West.

William Henry Jackson's view of the Grand Canyon on an expedition in 1875. *Courtesy National Archives.*

JOHN MIX STANLEY, EDWARD MEYER KERN, RICHARD HOVENDON KERN, Heinrich B. Möllhausen, Gustave Sohon, F. W. von Egloffstein, A. H. Campbell, A. B. Gray, J. C. Tidball, and Arthur Schott created thousands of images of Western landscapes, native inhabitants, and wildlife. Whether these artists accompanied field expeditions searching for geographical knowledge (such as those of JOHN CHARLES FRÉMONT), determining the best routes for a proposed transcontinental railroad, or locating the United States–Mexican boundary, their work was widely available to the public. The government published most accounts of military explorers, and many of the reports were enormously popular among an American public hungry for information about the West. Some of the army artists were American-trained; others had been educated in Europe. Some were professionals who accompanied expeditions for the specific purpose of creating visual records; others were amateurs (often army officers) who added informal sketching to their other duties. But whatever their background or level of artistic skill, nearly all the artists of the military surveys produced works that enhanced the romantic image of the West. They offered Americans their first glimpse of the American Southwest and Great Basin regions and greatly augmented earlier works on the Rocky Mountains.

The Civil War interrupted Western exploration. Resumed in the postwar years, exploration took on a new emphasis: scientific investigation. Artists whose work was both more precise and more artistic than that of the earlier generations accompanied the government-sponsored scientific surveys of JOHN WESLEY POWELL, FERDINAND VANDEVEER HAYDEN, CLARENCE KING, and others. Because of their work on such surveys, William Holmes and THOMAS MORAN became famous, the former for his precisely detailed, panoramic illustrations and the latter for his romantic oil and watercolor paintings of the West's natural wonders. Less well known but also important were Sanford R. Gifford, Gilbert Munger, Henry Elliot, and Henry Newton.

The era of scientific exploration, which lasted nearly through the end of the nineteenth century, produced the first artists whose medium was the photographic

Thus, as little known as many of them are today, the survey artists had a lasting impression on American images.

Neither of the first two major government-sponsored expeditions—the LEWIS AND CLARK EXPEDITION from 1804 to 1806 and the expedition of ZEBULON MONTGOMERY PIKE in 1807—included field artists. By the time of STEPHEN HARRIMAN LONG's 1820 expedition to the central Rocky Mountain region, however, the need for visual as well as verbal record keeping was acknowledged, and two Philadelphia artists, SAMUEL SEYMOUR and TITIAN RAMSAY PEALE, accompanied Long. In the official capacity as "naturalist," Peale produced pencil, pen-and-ink, and water-color sketches of flora and fauna. Seymour was charged with portraying landscapes and the native peoples of the region. As the first artists producing images of the West, Seymour and Peale shared responsibility for planting in the public's mind the notion of the West as an exotic region. Their illustrations, appearing in the official publication of Long's report, set the tone for a later generation of artists—those accompanying the U.S. Army expeditions between 1842 and the Civil War.

During the heyday of the U.S. Army CORPS OF TOPOGRAPHICAL ENGINEERS, while the army explorers engaged in a massive reconnaissance of the entire region between the Mississippi and the Pacific, artists such as plate rather than canvas or sketch pad. The most noted of the early photographers was WILLIAM HENRY JACKSON, who provided the first photographs of the Colorado Rockies and the Yellowstone region. But also important were photographers TIMOTHY H. O'SULLIVAN, C. E. Watkins, John K. Hillers, and William Bell.

The addition of the camera to the brush and pen did little to change the nature of the recorded images. Whether painting or photograph, the Western scenes captured by survey artists were exotic, romantic, and filled with wonder. They contributed enormously to the emerging conservation movement and shaped the impressions of the West that led to the creation of the first national parks. Even more important, the survey artists of the nineteenth century shaped American attitudes toward the West.

—*John Logan Allen*

SEE ALSO: Exploration and Science

SUGGESTED READING:

Ewers, John C. *Artists of the Old West.* Garden City, N.Y., 1973.

Goetzmann, William H. *Army Exploration in the American West, 1803–1863.* New Haven, Conn., 1959.

———. *Exploration and Empire: The Explorer and the Scientist in the Winning of the American West.* New York, 1967.

———, and William N. Goetzmann. *The West of the Imagination.* New York, 1986.

Prown, Jules David, et al. *Discovered Lands, Invented Pasts: Transforming Visions of the American West.* New Haven, Conn., 1992.

Trenton, Patricia, and Peter H. Hassrick. *The Rocky Mountains: A Vision for Artists in the Nineteenth Century.* Norman, Okla., 1983.

Truettner, William H., ed. *The West as America: Reinterpreting Images of the Frontier, 1820–1920.* Washington, D.C., 1991.

Tyler, Ron C. *American Frontier Life: Early Western Painting and Prints.* New York, 1987.

———. *Visions of America: Pioneer Artists in a New Land.* New York, 1983.

Viola, Herman. *Exploring the West.* Washington, D.C., 1987.

BOOK AND MAGAZINE ILLUSTRATION
Books

In the wake of Alexander von Humboldt's monumental geographical explorations of South and Central America and GEORGE CATLIN's massive documentation of the "vanishing life" of the American Indian, a whole generation of German explorers, children of continental Europe's romantic movement, traveled to the New World to visit the American wilderness where they believed they would find a natural world both exotic and pristine. Amateur scientists and titled and elegant tourists, men such as Frederick Paul Wilhelm, duke of Württemburg, and his friend Prince Maximilian of Wied-Neuwied, kept for later publication meticulous journals of what they saw. Many of them illustrated their journals (or hired artists to illustrate them) with sketches and paintings of outposts and towns, scenic sites, exotic flora and fauna, and, especially, Native American life. They then used these illustrations to produce magnificent engravings for what at bottom were brilliantly illustrated travel books, the most celebrated being Maximilian's *Travels in the Interior of North America in the Years 1832 to 1834.*

After the mid-nineteenth century, book illustration, notions about nature, and the popular image of the American West all grew cruder: romantic concepts of nature as the book of God gave way to social-Darwinian views of the wilderness as "raw in tooth and claw"; the trans-Mississippi region was no longer thought of as a distant and safe haven for Indians, but as the Wild West where rugged individuals were establishing a continental empire. The delicate and detailed, hand-tinted lithographs produced by engraved metal were often replaced in books by primitive woodcuts similar to those found in the immensely popular dime novels. Not only books, but also tabloid newspapers, temperance tracts, and illustrated rags such as the *California Police Gazette* carried images in keeping with the melodramatic and lusty tone and the mediocre tastes of dime-novel hacks. Historical accuracy hardly entered the picture, although perhaps something of the spirit of gold-rush and cattle-boom times was captured in the woodcuts illustrating Deadwood Dick's endless adventures or the thick bold lines of *Police Gazette* pictures with such titles as *Panic in a Brothel during the San Francisco Earthquake.*

Some book illustrators rose above the common herd. Two who were also well known for their engraved prints achieved a measure of fame: Felix Octavius Darley and Charles Nahl. Born in 1822 in Philadelphia, the son of an English comedian, Darley showed artistic promise at an early age, although he never received formal training. As a young man, he took up a business career but executed woodcuts on the side for an illustrated journal in the Western travel book tradition, *Scenes of Indian Life* (1843). He did not become a professional book illustrator, however, until he moved to New York in 1848 to accept a commission illustrating the novels of WASHINGTON IRVING and JAMES FENIMORE COOPER. The job took two years and earned him a reputation for skilled and original work. For several years thereafter, he produced illustrations for standard editions of English and American authors and a popular series of historical lithographs, many with frontier themes. Nahl, on the other hand, was a trained artist. Born in 1818 in Kessel, Germany,

The images in publications such as *Harper's Weekly* supplied many Americans with their only impressions of the West. The top image, *A Drove of Texas Cattle Crossing a Stream*, sketched by A. R. Ward, appeared in an October 1867 issue of *Harper's Weekly. Indian War—Indians Attacking a Wagon-Train* adorned a September 1868 issue. *Courtesy Patrick H. Butler, III.*

into a family of artists, he studied art in Paris before immigrating in 1849 with his brother, Hugo, first to New York, then to gold-rush California. Failing to strike it rich in the gold fields, the brothers took up art again in San Francisco. Working as commercial photographers and illustrators, they executed serious paintings in off moments until 1867, when Charles attracted a patron. For Judge E. B. Crocker, Nahl painted large canvases that became locally popular and earned for him, by the time of his death in 1878, a reputation as one of the leading painters of California's pioneer days. Darley and Nahl had similar, almost academic styles, characterized by smooth, clean, elegant draftsmanship that, while charming, might well strike someone who actually knew what the American West was like as too tidy. One could hardly imagine Darley's Indians—highly polished studies of the male nude—scalping anyone or Nahl's attractive well-shaven prospectors jumping a claim.

Magazines

In the late nineteenth century, a new generation of illustrators gave the reading public images of the American West more tastefully conceived and better drawn than dime-novel-style woodcuts and less genteel than Darley's and Nahl's book illustrations. Illustrated magazines had been around for decades before the industry, spurred by new technology in printing and reproduction, experienced a boom in the 1890s. Already popular in Nahl's and Darley's days, the *Illustrated London News, Harper's Weekly,* and *Frank Leslie's Illustrated Newspaper* were full of wood engravings of excellent quality. A growing love of pictorial journalism among their readers led the illustrated weeklies to send professional artists, such as FREDERIC REMINGTON, to the scene of Western events to provide drawings for upcoming issues. The drawings were copied or pasted onto fruitwood or end-grain boxwood and turned over to engravers for cutting. Frank Leslie developed the breakthrough of dividing engravings into sections, then putting wood blocks together so that the seams fit, thus allowing him to speed up production by using teams of engravers. So great was the demand for magazine illustrations that a number of craftsmen made lifelong careers of wood engraving. They translated the fine work of others—Winslow Homer's Civil War drawings, for example, or Frank Church's Western landscapes—into prints worthy of respect on their own merit. Not infrequently, they ruined their eyesight, since eye fatigue and even blindness were occupational hazards of working with thousands of fine lines late into the night by gaslight.

Improvements in printing presses and lithography helped publishers meet the apparently insatiable de-

Frederic Remington supplied *Garza Revolutionsts in the Texas Chaparral* for a January 1892 issue of *Harper's Weekly. Courtesy Patrick H. Butler, III.*

mand for illustrations of the American West—and everything else, for that matter. Between 1890 and 1940, more than ten thousand new magazines appeared on the American market. The illustrated weeklies were joined by such publications as *Collier's, Cosmopolitan, Ladies Home Journal, Red Book,* and the *Saturday Evening Post,* all of them depending on a dozen or so Western illustrators for the images that accompanied their articles, short stories, and novellas about the American West. Their illustrations may have been more accurate than the old dime-novel woodcuts (although not always), but—pandering to a readership for whom the "Wild West" was a given—the illustrators were certainly no less romantic than the European travel-literature artists. Many of the illustrators, in fact, felt they were preserving a "vanishing frontier," much as Catlin thought he was capturing for history a disappearing "race," although they were making a better living at it than he did. Remington led the pack and influenced those who came after him: N. C. WYETH, William H. D. Koerner, Frank Schoonover, among others.

Koerner, for example, produced some twenty-five hundred illustrations during his career, more than six hundred of them set in the West. He illustrated the works of any number of Western writers, among them BERNARD DEVOTO, Oliver La Farge, and ZANE GREY. Between 1930 and 1935, at least forty stories in the *Saturday Evening Post* boasted Koerner illustrations, although he became best known for his 1922 portrait of a pioneer women whose head is haloed by the arch of the Conestoga wagon behind her. *Madonna of the Prairie,* although itself a book-jacket cover, captured the tenor of turn-of-the-century magazine illustration of the West. The artists produced appealing images of frontier life and presented rugged individuals of character, integrity, and even a certain refinement. Generally portraying a positive attitude about the West, they provided readers, lambasted by change, mechanization, and industrialization, a nostalgic look back at what was fast becoming an imaginary golden age. Some chafed under the commercial constraints of deadlines and ideologically defined style and tried to break away from the popular-magazine stereotypes. Maynard Dixon, for example, disappeared on extended field trips into the Southwest during the early decades of the century. He returned fascinated by aridity, and his illustrations of parched landscapes, wracked by foul weather and oppressed by a harsh nature, ran completely contrary to the lush horizons of many of his fellow illustrators. Since at least the days when the railroads paid artists to produce promotional Western landscapes, illustrators had been idealizing a desert. For the most part, as the twentieth century marched resolutely forward through World War I, the Roaring Twenties, the Great Depression, and World War II, magazine illustrators kept before the public the idea of a wild and beautiful national frontier that had made America great, which was intended precisely to reinforce the stories they illustrated, uplifting tales of frontier struggle and ultimate triumph.

—*Charles Phillips*

SEE ALSO: Magazines and Newspapers

SUGGESTED READING:
Ballinger, James K., and Susan P. Gordon. "The Popular West." *American West* 19 (July-August 1982): 36–45.
Ewers, John C. *Artists of the Old West.* Garden City, N.Y., 1965.
Gambee, Budd L. *Frank Leslie and His Illustrated Newspaper, 1855–1860.* New York, 1964.
Hamilton, Sinclair. *Early American Book Illustration and Engravings, 1670–1870.* Princeton, N.J., 1958. Reprint. 1968.
Hamlin, Edith. "Maynard Dixon: Painter of the West." *American West* 19 (November-December 1982): 50–59.
Hutchinson, W. H. "The Western Legacy of W. H. D. Koerner." *American West* 16 (September-October 1979): 32–44.
Hyde, Anne Farrar. *An American Vision: Far Western Landscape and National Culture, 1820–1920.* New York, 1990.
Phillips, Charles. "Maximilian's Missouri, 1833–34." *The Palimpsest* 60 (November-December 1979): 178–183.
Taft, Robert. *Artists and Illustrators of the Old West, 1850–1900.* New York, 1953.

POPULAR PRINTS AND COMMERCIAL ART

Before the invention and widespread use of photography, popular prints provided Americans with images of the American West. At first made from wood engravings, these often idealized and romantic prints were more frequently—as the nineteenth century progressed—lithographs. Produced from engravings etched on metal, lithography depended on heavy stones and special presses, which discouraged the kind of itinerant work that could be accomplished with woodcuts. The substantial commercial success of Currier and Ives in the East and the growing popularity of lithographs resulted in a burgeoning of lithographic firms in America, which, in turn, fed the boom in weekly magazines that characterized late nineteenth-century publishing.

The federal government played a major role in the development of both lithography and the printing industry. Indeed, many Western printers, who were often Western newspapermen as well, depended on government contracts for their very existence, while U.S. military surveys and expeditions frequently employed lithographic artists. The United States–Mexican War proved a boon for print-makers as those on the home front eagerly awaited the idealized popular prints of battles and engagements. Built in part on this audi-

William H. D. Koerner's *Madonna of the Prairie* was painted in 1921 as an illustration for an Emerson Hough novel. *Courtesy Buffalo Bill Historical Center.*

A hand-colored lithograph of Burlington, Iowa, from the mid-1850s. *Courtesy Iowa State Historical Society.*

like the 1848 lithograph *The Great Mormon Temple at Nauvoo,* have true historical interest. Most are perhaps more significant for what they say about contemporary notions of the West they portray. Artists such as Herman J. Meyer, John Casper Wild, Rufus Wright, William Bourne, W. J. Gilbert, J. M. Peck, L. C. Turner, Phillipe Ronde, Seth Eastman, Lucinda Farnham, and George Simons produced lithographs that sold separately *à la* Currier and Ives or circulated nationally in such periodicals as *Ballou's Pictorial Drawing Room Companion* and *Frank Leslie's Illustrated Newspaper.*

ence, certainly after the 1850s, lithographic illustrations proliferated in papers, journals, advertising, and posters—especially Wild West show posters, which, along with circus posters, represented the apotheosis of chromolithography.

Even before the 1850s, however, decidedly commercial artists were plying the Mississippi and producing popular lithographs of panoramic views of such areas as Iowa, Missouri, and Wisconsin. Entrepreneurs mounted exhibits consisting of a series of pictures portraying entire regions of the country on enormous canvases that could be dramatically unrolled before an audience. An English-born carpenter who moved to St. Louis in 1829, Henry Lewis conceived the idea for a gigantic panorama of the Mississippi, which he then painted along with several assistants and unveiled in St. Louis in 1849. The section portraying the upper Mississippi valley was 825 yards long and 12 feet wide while the section devoted to the lower valley was a mere 500 yards long. Held in the city's Concert Hall, the premier lasted two hours, cost fifty cents, and played to packed houses for more than a fortnight, after which Lewis took the show on the road, first to cities in the East and then to Europe.

By the 1850s, Lewis was turning his panoramas into hand-colored lithographic prints, serene images of wooded valleys and peaceful villages; a number of them appeared among the seventy-eight color plates in *Das illustre Mississippithal* (1858) published in Dusseldorf. Panoramic views became the rage. Some,

After the Civil War, the serenity of wooded hills overlooking sleepy villages on a lazy river that were typical of panoramic prints gave way to bird's-eye views of bustling towns with smoke billowing up from every conceivable source. Compilers of state and county atlases, commercial cartographic and lithographic firms, and wide-circulation periodicals all hired artists who fanned out over the United States to draw pictures of towns, farmsteads, individual buildings, and landscapes. Madison and Milwaukee, Wisconsin, and Chicago, Illinois, were the major publishing centers for the bird's-eye views of American progress. Their emphasis on urban growth distinguished them from more traditional late nineteenth-century images of the West as a land of cowboys, Indians, and rustic frontiers, which may have been why they were much more popular in the East than in the West and South.

Other images of the American West also began to appear among popular prints of the kind made so appealing by Currier and Ives. The California gold rush was amply depicted in popular prints by Britton and Ray, frequently called the Currier and Ives of San Francisco. Among the avalanche of prints illustrating prospecting, gambling, vigilante violence, and public hangings, the company also produced a number that showed daily life in the mining camps in some detail. Two Cuban artists, José Baturone and August Ferrán, produced comic and entertaining lithographs, which they included in their *Album Californio,* printed in Havana in 1840; the book offered a veritable rogues' gallery of dirty, disheveled, hairy, and drunken "California types," as Baturone and Ferrán called them.

As national magazines began to promote the notion of the "Wild West," then the "Old West," to boost circulation, lithographs first of action and adventure and then of a nostalgic vanishing way of life became popular with subscribers and other readers. The railroads, too, moving West, hired commercial artists to make wide-horizon prints of a land ideal for settlement: wooded, watered, and fecund. These breathtaking landscapes were clearly aimed at spurring migration to unsettled areas of the interior, much of which the railroads owned. The work of commercial illustrators (many of them—such as FREDERIC REMINGTON—artists of some merit) whether in the form of a weekly magazine illustration or of a hand-colored lithograph suitable for framing and hanging on a parlor wall, made its way into the homes and the daily lives of Americans. Properly inspired by idealized popular prints, Easterners could always dream of escape to a West where, to quote a New York songwriter enamored by the kind of West popular prints in general portrayed, the buffalo roamed and the skies were not cloudy all day.

—*Charles Phillips*

SUGGESTED READING:

Horton, Loren. "Through the Eyes of Artists: Iowa Towns in the 19th Century." *The Palimpsest* 59 (September-October 1978): 133-147.

McDermott, John Francis. *The Lost Panoramas of the Mississippi*. Chicago, 1958.

Peters, Harry. *America on Stone*. New York, 1931.

Tyler, Ron, et al. *American Frontier Life: Early Western Painting and Prints*. New York, 1987.

———. *Prints of the West*. Golden, Colo., 1994.

Truettner, William H., et al. *The West as America: Reinterpreting Images of the Frontier, 1820–1920*. Washington, D.C., 1991.

FOLK (ETHNIC) ART

The tradition of creating art objects in the West began with the first settlers who entered the region. The earliest European settlers of New Mexico created art objects that were used in domestic, religious, and political settings. When the French went upriver from New Orleans and established the new city of St. Louis, they brought their own traditions to the settlement. As other ethnic groups, including Germans, Czechs, Scandinavians, Chinese, and Poles entered the trans-Mississippi West, either directly from European or Asian homelands or from communities in the East or on the West Coast, their traditions came with them.

The first, and, to many, the definitive Western ethnic tradition is associated with the Spanish settlements in the Southwest. The earliest products of New Mexico artisans have almost disappeared, lost in the PUEBLO REVOLT and over time, although a few fragments of woodwork and architecture remain to suggest continuities with Spanish-baroque traditions. After the return of the Spanish to New Mexico in a campaign lasting from 1692 to 1696, the Pueblo and Spanish populations blended and created their own, unique material culture. Isolated by distance from the center of the Spanish empire in Mexico and by both distance and law from other European communities in the East, Southwestern material culture took on a character of its own—a character shaped by Indian and Spanish visual traditions and by the sparse countryside with limited materials.

Although some historians of Southwestern culture have suggested that the artistic forms were a barbaric regression from both Hispanic and Indian achievements, in recent years, scholars have argued that the material culture, particularly the architecture and furniture, of eighteenth- and early nineteenth-century New Mexico, was a sophisticated statement. Clearly, evidence of obedience to formal Spanish craft traditions, found in accounts of settlement as well as in the objects themselves, suggests that the arts were of a high quality although shaped by their environment.

Formal fine art production in the Hispanic culture of the eighteenth and early nineteenth centuries focused on religious art. Using local woods and gesso for the surface and homemade mineral pigments, local artists in New Mexico produced paintings of the saints, called *santos*, for the devout households of New Mexico. Statues, called *bultos*, of religious figures were produced for domestic and ecclesiastical use. The religious art was emotional and effective, serving to reinforce the values of the Christian tradition. In the twentieth century, the Hispanic tradition in the fine arts continued to flourish. Modern artists, whether in Los Angeles, San Antonio, or other centers of Hispanic life, documented the Hispanic experience in North America through public projects, such as expressionistic murals. Some artists, including Mel Casa, Luis Jimenez, and others, used irony and satire to communicate their vision of the West.

The decorative arts of the Spanish Southwest in the seventeenth, eighteenth, and nineteenth centuries were also influenced by limits on available materials, particularly metals, and by the relative isolation of the settlements. Yet the decorative arts, particularly textiles, furniture, and ceramics, all demonstrate a complex vision. When the Spanish imported sheep into New Mexico, they brought with them the weaving techniques of Spain and introduced them to the Indian cultures. Hispanic and Indian textiles are sophisticated statements of the mix of techniques, iconography, and material.

Furniture in New Mexico reflected the impact of the Spanish craft tradition brought to the New World. While homes were sparsely furnished, particularly in

A pine chest made in the early 1800s in northern New Mexico. *Courtesy Museum of New Mexico.*

Ethnic traditions of the Germans, Poles, and the many other ethnic groups who migrated to the West shaped the folk arts and decorative arts of the West as well. Craftsmen and artists with varying levels of training moved to the West from the 1830s on. Genre paintings of homesteads and portraits of settlers by a variety of artists were important in the experience of the settlers. Similarly, until the impact of the mass production and distribution of the decorative arts was felt in the last third of the nineteenth century, much of the furniture for the immigrant communities was produced locally by artisans who remembered the designs of Europe but used iconographic devices and materials from America.

Reflecting continuing and growing interest in the cultural traditions of all ethnic groups within the various states and communities of the West, hundreds of museums exhibit collections of local materials. Some communities, such as Santa Fe and San Antonio, are museums in and of themselves; they document all the ethnic traditions of their region, and a walk down the streets of such cities is the best way to become acquainted with the architecture. Among the many museums with substantial collections reflecting the ethnic

the eighteenth century, a variety of forms was used, and as the colony prospered in the early nineteenth century, there is evidence of an increasing amount of furniture. Chests, used for many types of storage, were the most popular form, followed by the chair. Ornamentation, usually a low-relief carving, was popular and reflected the influence of proportional systems of measure based on the *vara,* which equaled eighty-four centimeters. Until the early nineteenth century, furniture design and production was conservative, and furniture was imported from Michoacan as well as produced locally. After 1820, production was influenced by the United States, as contact between New Mexico and the United States increased. While local production continued, there was a rapid expansion of the importation of furniture and decorative arts from the United States. After the Civil War, locally produced pieces, particularly in northern New Mexico, demonstrated the mix of influences at work in the culture. In the twentieth century, the image became more complex, particularly during the 1930s, as craftsmen mixed old and new, creating a Spanish-colonial revival.

The architecture of the Southwest was based on locally available mud bricks and timber, coated with a stucco finish. The great churches of New Mexico, Arizona, Texas, and the California coast reflected a continuity with Native American structures in terms of material, but the interiors, particularly those of churches, reflected the impact of European decorative traditions combined with local influences.

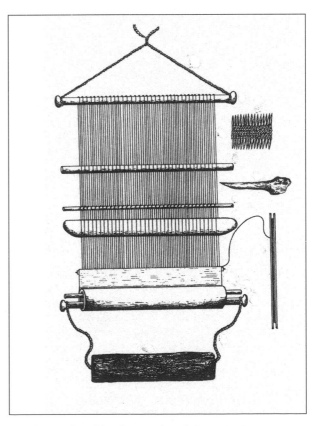

Textiles produced by the peoples of New Mexico on looms such as this one are a sophisticated mix of techniques, iconography, and materials. *Editors collection.*

influences in the West are the New Mexico Museum of Fine Arts, the PALACE OF THE GOVERNORS History Museum, and the International Museum of Folk Art in Santa Fe; the Albuquerque Museum; the ARIZONA HISTORICAL SOCIETY in Tucson; the Pioneer Memorial Museum in Fredericksburg, Texas; and the Witte Museum in San Antonio.

—*Patrick H. Butler, III*

SUGGESTED READING:

Bunting, Bainbridge. *Early Architecture in New Mexico.* Albuquerque, N. Mex., 1976.

Fairbanks, Jonathan, et al. *Frontier America: The Far West.* Boston, 1975.

Goetzmann, William H., and William N. Goetzmann. *The West of the Imagination.* New York, 1986.

Kennedy, Roger, ed. *The Smithsonian Guide to Historic America.* 12 vols. Washington, D.C., 1981–1989.

Steinfeldt, Cecilia. *Art for History's Sake: The Texas Collection of the Witte Museum.* Austin, Tex., 1993.

———. *Texas Folk Art: One Hundred and Fifty Years of the Southwestern Tradition.* Austin, Tex., 1981.

Taylor, Lonn, and Dessa Bokides. *New Mexican Furniture, 1660–1940.* Santa Fe, N. Mex., 1987.

Weigle, Marta, Claudia Larcombe, and Samuel Larcombe, eds. *Hispanic Arts and Ethnohistory in the Southwest: New Papers Inspired by the Work of E. Boyd.* Santa Fe, N. Mex., 1983.

ASHLEY, WILLIAM HENRY

William Henry Ashley (1778?–1838) was lieutenant-governor of the state of Missouri, congressman, soldier, land speculator, and fur trader. As a partner in the Henry-Ashley Fur Company, he played a key role in opening the Rocky Mountains to the FUR TRADE and developing the RENDEZVOUS system employed from 1825 to 1840 in the region.

Born in Chesterfield County, Virginia, Ashley migrated as a young man to what later became Missouri, where he lived until his death. Following his arrival in Missouri around 1802, he engaged in land speculation and mining. Active in the territorial militia, he reached the rank of lieutenant colonel during the War of 1812. He was elected lieutenant-governor of the new state of Missouri in 1820, later became a brigadier general of militia, and thereafter maintained the title of general.

Ashley advanced the American fur trade into the northern and central Rockies and revolutionized the business. While free trappers under his direction established the rendezvous system, Ashley himself attended only the first two rendezvous and kept a diary of a portion of his travels.

After making considerable profits in the fur trade, Ashley sold his interest in the Henry-Ashley Fur Company in 1826 and returned his focus to politics. Nevertheless, he retained a certain amount of power in the fur trade as he handled financial arrangements, from 1826 to 1830, for the Smith, Jackson, Sublette Company, who bought out his company and, after 1830, for the company's successor, the ROCKY MOUNTAIN FUR COMPANY. His impact on the fur trade continued to be felt over the next fifteen years, as his successors carried on the rendezvous tradition he established.

Elected to the U.S. House of Representatives in 1831, Ashley served three consecutive terms. As a congressman, he was a spokesman for Western expansion and fur-trade interests. The discoveries of his men, particularly the existence of South Pass through the Rocky Mountains, influenced the debate on the future of the Oregon Country, yet Ashley never involved himself in the expansionist movement regarding the region. More interested in the Great Plains and Rocky Mountain regions, he pushed for the formation of a mounted military force to serve as escort for wagon trains. He made two unsuccessful bids for the governorship and was planning to run for Congress again when he died of pneumonia.

—*Scott Eldredge and Fred R. Gowans*

SUGGESTED READING:

Ashley, William H. *The West of William Ashley.* Edited by Dale L. Morgan. Denver, 1964.

Carter, Harvey L. "William H. Ashley." In *The Mountain Men and the Fur Trade of the Far West.* Vol. 7. Edited by LeRoy R. Hafen. Glendale, Calif., 1969.

Clokey, Richard M. *William H. Ashley: Enterprise and Politics in the Trans-Mississippi West.* Norman, Okla., 1980.

Morgan, Dale L. *Jedediah Smith and the Opening of the West.* Indianapolis, Ind., 1953.

ASIAN AMERICAN CHURCHES

Asians immigrating to the American West in the nineteenth and early twentieth centuries found a host society whose elite welcomed their labor but whose average citizens barely tolerated their presence, and only then so long as they kept in their place at the bottom of the social ladder. Without an expansive panoply of private, social, and religious organizations and clubs, pioneers from China and Japan would have found it difficult indeed to survive, much less thrive in their new world. Parochial villagers traveling great distances to a strange land initially felt at ease only among those who resembled themselves, and while few of them had been joiners back in their homelands, where kinship frequently formed the basis for most aspects of their daily social lives, they found themselves out of necessity forming and becoming members of a vast array of civic organizations, social clubs, and religious congregations in America. The churches or missions that served Asian immigrants were seldom strictly houses of worship but more often educational, political, and social organizations as well—and frequently, especially in the case of Christian churches, vehicles of indoctrination and acculturation.

For the Chinese, who were the first Asians to arrive during the California gold rush, there was hardly a distinction between political and social organizations and spiritual ones. Because the popular religion of the Chinese was a blend of ancient Confucian, Taoist, Buddhist, and animist beliefs, it was fairly simple for family and district associations to satisfy their religious needs, which required little more of the Chinese than that they go to temples or pray in front of altars as the spirit called or as special occasions demanded. Each district or family association that owned a building simply set aside a room with one or more altars for use by members who desired to meditate or pray. The Chinese placed a high value on ancestral ties, which meant that those in America—far from their native soil and family roots—became especially concerned about rites of passage. Since, in the early years especially, there were few marriages and not many births, they focused their attention mostly on funerals, which the family associations and the district clubs helped to conduct with care and much ceremony.

Some Chinese and a large percentage of Japanese, who arrived later in the nineteenth century, were Buddhists, and five of the more than forty divisions within Japanese Buddhism were represented in the United States. But the first Japanese immigrants in America were a group of student converts to Christianity who organized the Gospel Society. Established in San Francisco on October 6, 1877, with the goals of providing space for the study of scripture and of spreading the gospel among Japanese immigrants, the society was made up primarily of Japanese Methodists and Congregationalists. Meeting every Saturday for Bible study at the Chinese Methodist Episcopal Mission, whose adjoining room became a bunkhouse for members, the Gospel Society engaged in activities such as hosting a reception for a Japanese warship visiting San Francisco and helping establish a Japanese cemetery in the city. Between 1882 and 1883, the Congregationalists split from the Chinese mission, perhaps in response to the growing anti-Chinese sentiment in San Francisco, and formed close ties with a Presbyterian group, with whom they founded the First Japanese Presbyterian Church

of San Francisco and, later, the Japanese YMCA. Meanwhile, the Gospel Society became an official Methodist mission. In 1891, KYUTARO ABIKO became president of the society, and over the years, it dropped its association with Christianity entirely and became a self-help organization that provided cheap room and board for Japanese immigrants, served as a job clearinghouse, and gave English lessons. Playing a major role in indoctrinating many Japanese to American life, the society worked with white community leaders, many of whom were among the few to defend the Japanese when exclusionary sentiments began to sweep the city.

The first Japanese Buddhist missions were founded not on the mainland, but in Hawaii, after Japanese plantation workers requested religious help from the homeland in the summer of 1887. Over the course of a decade, the Buddhists sent a few priests but established no permanent mission until 1897, when the contract workers complained that impostors had been collecting funds to build temples and then absconding with the money. A veteran missionary who had served Japanese emigrants in Russia and Taiwan arrived in Hawaii and established the Honpa Hangwangi. He was succeeded in 1899 by the popular Yemyo Imamura, an energetic and dedicated priest, who organized a Young Men's Buddhist Association (YMBA). After learning that the Christian language school routinely mocked his religion, he also started a Buddhist language school to teach English to workers at night and published a Japanese newsletter. He fought with Christian arch-rival Taki Okumura for influence over Hawaii's Japanese population and was able to demonstrate to white islanders the importance of Buddhism to Japanese life in 1904, when striking plantation workers would speak with no one but Imamura. In the same year Imamura arrived in Hawaii, the Nishi Hongwanji (Jodo Shinshu) sect also sent two missionaries from its Kyoto headquarters to San Francisco. They returned to Japan to request more missionaries, and within a few years, there were twenty-five Buddhist churches and branches spread across the West. In 1914, they established the North American Buddhists Mission (NABM), which in time became known as the Buddhist Churches of America, the largest Japanese American Buddhist organization. The use of the word *church* became significant, because it was one of several ways—including the installation of pews and the use of hymn books—in which Japanese Buddhism adapted itself to America.

Protestant denominations competed with the Chinese and Japanese religious institutions for the souls of Asian Americans. They began their proselytizing among the Asians in California in 1851, when the Presbyterians started to hold Bible classes for the Chinese in San Francisco. William Speer, who had been a missionary in China and spoke Cantonese, opened a mission in 1852 but made few converts before he left San Francisco in ill health. The Presbytery closed the mission in 1857 but reopened it two years later when Augustus Loomis, another former missionary to China, arrived to stay until his death in 1891. The Baptists, Methodists, and Congregationalists also worked actively to convert Asian immigrants and succeeded best when they hired mainland Chinese or Asian Christians from Hawaii to assist them. Although the Christian missions both on the mainland and in Hawaii never won large numbers of Chinese or Japanese adherents, those they did convert played a role significant far beyond their numbers. As the most acculturated members of their communities, they often served as bridges between two cultures, and the fact that Euro-Americans preferred to deal with them rather than those belonging to "native sects" placed a mantle of legitimacy on their shoulders they might not otherwise have enjoyed within the immigrant communities.

There were also other Asian immigrants in the American West—Koreans, Asian Indians, and Filipinos, but before the 1930s, their numbers were quite small compared to the Chinese and Japanese. Most of the thousand or so Koreans living along the Pacific Coast during the first two decades of the twentieth century had already converted to Christianity before they left their homeland, and their churches in America served social and political needs, since they too became isolated from the mainstream of American society because of the color of their skin. The eight hundred or so Muslim, Buddhists, and Hindus from India living in the West were generally dismissed by the Euro-Americans as "Hindoos" and were left to themselves to practice their faiths as best they could. Asian Indians of three faiths established the Hindustani Welfare Reform Society in 1918 in the Imperial Valley, where many of them farmed. Most of the Filipinos were Catholic, although their Catholicism developed some unique features in the American West. Unwelcome in Euro-American churches, the Filipino Catholics established two parishes on the mainland: Our Lady Queen of Martyrs Church in Seattle, staffed by Maryknoll fathers with Filipino assistants, and St. Columban's Church in Los Angeles, founded by the Columban fathers. In Stockton, California, perhaps the most important center of Filipino immigrant life, three Protestant institutions—the Lighthouse Mission, the Filipino Christian Fellowship, and the House of Friendship—threw open their doors to the small numbers of Protestant Filipino migrant workers who passed seasonally through the town.

Asian American churches of whatever religion became quite important as immigration exclusion cut immigrants off from their homelands, thereby isolating even further the already isolated Asian populations of the West. The churches, along with the social clubs and political organizations they so much resembled or, in many cases, were indistinguishable from, not only assimilated the Asians to America, but helped them forge a larger ethnic identity with which to fight back against the prejudice and the hatred visited on them by the dominant Euro-American culture.

—*Patricia Hogan*

SEE ALSO: East Indians; Chinese Americans; Japanese Americans

SUGGESTED READING:
Ichioka, Yugi. *The Issei: The World of the First Generation Japanese Immigrants, 1885–1924.* New York, 1988.
Chan, Sucheng. *Asian Americans: An Interpretive History.* Boston, 1991.
Kashima, Tetsuden. *Buddhism in America: The Social Organization of Ethnic Religious Institutions.* Westport, Conn., 1977.

ASIATIC EXCLUSION LEAGUE

Founded in San Francisco on May 14, 1905, by delegates representing sixty-seven organizations, the Asiatic Exclusion League incited the anti-Japanese movement on the West Coast. Most of the delegates attending the first meeting represented labor unions in the Bay Area, and their concern that Japanese immigrants would take away jobs from white Americans barely disguised the racism behind the league's mission. "No community of foreigners, so cocky, with such distinct racial, social, and religious prejudices, can abide long in this country without serious friction," its manifesto proclaimed.

The league's first leaders included Andrew Furuseth and Walter MacArthur of the Sailor's Union and Patrick Henry McCarthy of the powerful SAN FRANCISCO BUILDING TRADES COUNCIL. McCarthy's underling, Olaf Tveitmoe, ascended to the presidency. The league's leaders, themselves immigrants, albeit from Europe, presided over a Japanese-exclusion movement composed of little more than vituperative rhetoric and paper. Although claiming at times two hundred thousand members, the league operated on an annual budget of about five thousand dollars, most of it likely supplied from McCarthy's union and a few others.

The league promoted its mission through propaganda, boycott, and beatings. Not one of its specific proposals to stop Japanese immigration or to curb Japanese commerce on the West Coast ever became law, but in 1905, California congressmen used league arguments to introduce Japanese-exclusion legislation in the House of Representatives. Unsuccessful in swaying legislating, the league attempted to sway public opinion by organizing boycotts of Japanese businesses and inciting violence against their owners. One league-organized boycott of Japanese restaurants lasted for three weeks in October 1906. Meanwhile, other San Francisco institutions, notably the board of education, proved more effective in curtailing Japanese immigration, when it forced the U.S. government to negotiate the GENTLEMEN'S AGREEMENT with Japan.

By 1911, the Asiatic Exclusion League had all but faded from public consciousness. That year, President Tveitmoe announced that the league did not support the anti-Japanese alien land law then being considered in the California state legislature. The surprising turnabout resulted from a compromise, engineered by the Mayor Patrick Henry McCarthy, to support San Francisco's bid to host the PANAMA-PACIFIC INTERNATIONAL EXPOSITION.

—*Patricia Hogan*

SEE ALSO: Alien Land Laws; Chinese Americans; Chinese Exclusion; Japanese Americans

SUGGESTED READING:
Daniels, Roger. *The Politics of Prejudice: The Anti-Japanese Movement in California and the Struggle for Japanese Exclusion.* Berkeley and Los Angeles, 1962. Reprint. New York, 1972.

ASPEN, COLORADO

SEE: Colorado Gold and Silver Rushes; Mining: Mining Camps and Towns

ASSING, NORMAN

Little is recorded of businessman and Chinese leader Norman Assing beyond the newspaper accounts and court documents regarding his activities in San Francisco between 1850 and 1855. He called himself a "naturalized citizen of Charleston, South Carolina," and "a Christian too." His mixing of American and Chinese ways contributed to his prominence in San Francisco society. His successful restaurant evidenced

his entrepreneurial skills, and his correspondence to city fathers and politicians demonstrated his adeptness at communicating in his adopted culture. At the city's public celebrations, he led delegations of invited Chinese guests.

But there was another side to Assing. He headed one of the several merchant organizations that controlled the lives of other Chinese immigrants in San Francisco. Such organizations often supplied much needed housing and services to immigrants in an unfamiliar world, but Assing also ruled the businesses and daily activities of the Chinese immigrants under his "protection" through threats, extortion, and violence.

Contemporary observers labeled Assing "the recognized chief of the Chinese," and the city directory of 1854 listed him as the Chinese representative, even though China did not send an official consul to San Francisco until 1879. Assing faded from public notice around 1855.

—*Kurt Edward Kemper*

SUGGESTED READINGS:
Barth, Gunther. *Bitter Strength: A History of the Chinese in America, 1850–1870.* San Francisco, 1964.

ASSINIBOIN INDIANS

SEE: Native American Peoples: Peoples of the Great Plains

ASTOR, JOHN JACOB

When it came to audacity of vision and stockpiling of profits, few in North America could match John Jacob Astor (1763–1848). One of twelve children born to a poor butcher in Waldorf, Germany, Astor followed his brother Henry's lead and set sail for United States after its War for Independence. In 1784, he arrived in New York penniless but determined to make a fortune and became a clerk for a fur trader, whose business he soon mastered. Astor's employer entrusted him with increasing responsibilities, including the purchase of upstate furs for resale in London. Soon operating on his own, Astor prospered enough to invest seven thousand dollars in Manhattan real estate between 1789 and 1791. In 1803, he paid twenty-five thousand dollars for seventy acres north of downtown at the city's far limit. Today the area is called Times Square.

Hoping to increase his fortunes in the lucrative Chinese markets, Astor had entered the CHINA TRADE in 1800. Selling furs to mandarins, he made huge profits, sometimes as much as fifty thousand dollars off a single voyage. By 1808, having decided to branch out into the production side of the fur trade, he planned to exploit the evacuation of the Old Northwest by the British in 1796 and to expand into the newly acquired Louisiana Purchase and into the Pacific Northwest. In 1810, he founded the Pacific Fur Company and, under its auspices, built a trading post the following year at the mouth of the Columbia River, which he called "Astoria." The enterprise collapsed when he lost a ship at sea and the War of 1812 cost him the loyalty of his Canadian partners and their contacts north of the border. It was his one great failure.

He managed to recoup his losses on the West Coast—and then some—when he made the federal government, strapped for cash because of the War of 1812, a large loan by paying forty cents on the dollar in exchange for government bonds. Although Astor considered himself a patriot, this was business, and he drove the hardest bargain he could. After the war, Astor shifted his attention back to the Old Northwest, where, in 1811, he had helped found the South West Company (southwest of Montreal, headquarters of the great British fur monopolies), and to the fast-growing fur trade in the Rocky Mountains. By 1817, he controlled the South West Company and dominated the fur trade below the Great Lakes to the Ohio River valley. From this base, he moved onto the Great Plains and into the Rockies and established, in 1823, the Western Department of the AMERICAN FUR COMPANY, which soon ran many of the region's small, formerly independent operations out of business. Old hands in the Western trade, headquartered in St. Louis, remained hostile to Astor, so he bought them out, adding Bernard Platte's company to his holdings in 1826. Ruthless competition had by then nearly trapped out the beaver in the Upper Missouri and Rocky Mountain regions, and Astor—astute as always—sold out and retired in 1834 to his home in New York City, where he pursued his extensive real-estate dealings.

New York investments, war-loan returns, and fur-trade profits had made Astor the richest man in America. He died leaving an estate of some $40 million, mostly to his son, although he did set aside $400,000 to establish the Astor Public Library—one of three that later merged to become the New York Public Library. When asked shortly before he died if he would have done anything differently, Astor replied—or so some accounts claim—that he only regretted not having bought all of Manhattan.

—*Charles Phillips*

SEE ALSO: Fur Trade; Mountain Men

SUGGESTED READING:
Haeger, John D. *John Jacob Astor: Business and Finance in the Early Republic.* Detroit, Mich., 1991.
Sinclair, David. *Dynasty: The Astors and Their Times.* New York, 1984.

ASTORIA

By the time John Jacob Astor founded the AMERICAN FUR COMPANY in 1808, he was already dreaming of empire and fortune in the American Far West. In 1810, he organized the Pacific Fur Company. His idea was to beat the Canadian monopolies to the vast raw supply of pelts in the Pacific Northwest. In a plan heartily approved by President THOMAS JEFFERSON himself, Astor hoped to establish a fur-trading outpost on the Columbia River discovered two decades before by the America sea captain John Gray. Some historians have claimed that Astor was inspired by the LEWIS AND CLARK EXPEDITION, although others have pointed out more recently that his plans were already far advanced by the time that MERIWETHER LEWIS and WILLIAM CLARK headed west, and his enterprise was launched before an edited version of their secret report was published. More likely, Astor was inspired to create a Western fur-trading empire by the Canadian explorers of the North West Company, with whom he had been keeping company for years since his business frequently took him to Montreal.

Astor knew he would be competing directly with the great British monopolies, not only the Nor'westers, but also HUDSON'S BAY COMPANY, and he reasoned he would need seasoned professionals to do so. He hired a number of North West Company employees—Alexander McKay, who had accompanied Alexander Mackenzie on his two Canadian transcontinental expeditions, Duncan McDougal, DONALD MCKENZIE, David Stuart, and Robert Stuart, all of whom Astor gave shares in the enterprise. He also employed New Jersey-born St. Louis storekeeper named WILSON PRICE HUNT and some French Canadian and American freelance trappers. The group would form two parties: one to travel by land, the other by sea, to the far side of the continent to found Fort Astoria. From there, the Pacific Fur Company would carry on commerce not only with Europe, where fashion demanded beaver hats, but also engage in the incredibly lucrative CHINA TRADE.

Astor's parties left in 1810. Thirty-three men traveled aboard the brig *Tonquin* out of New York and around Cape Horn to the Oregon coast; sixty-four left St. Louis and headed across the Rocky Mountains to a rendezvous at the mouth of the Columbia River. The ship reached the spot first on March 22, 1811, and lost several men to the seas during a hasty landing. Half of the group remained behind to build the fort as the *Tonquin* sailed upriver to trade with Indians. The bargaining did not go well; the *Tonquin's* arrogant and abrasive captain slapped a Salish chief, and the Indians retaliated by butchering all but five aboard the ship a few days later. Four of the survivors escaped by boat under the cover of darkness, but one—gravely wounded—crawled into the hold to die. When the Indians returned the next morning, he touched off the brig's store of gunpowder, killing hundreds of Indians and reducing the ship to 290 pounds of splinters.

Seven months later, the overland crew began straggling into Fort Astoria with few furs but with many tales from what had been an epic of suffering. Led by Hunt, who knew nothing about the wilderness, the party had started in a race against MANUEL LISA's employees for the then beleaguered Fort Lisa, only to break off and head across country for fear of the Blackfoot Indians. All went surprisingly well until they broached the Rockies and reached the Snake River. They tried to maneuver the river in canoes, and soon found themselves swirling beneath sheer, mile-high walls. Those who did not drown managed to scale the icy walls of Hell's Canyon and faced a winter march through barren land devoid of game. Forty-five of them made it, some in early 1812, others not until the spring, and seven as late as January 1813.

A supply ship, the *Beaver,* arrived in May. Finally the Astorians began trapping and buying furs by the thousands. Robert Stuart headed off overland to tell Astor that at last it seemed his project might work. Stuart trekked south and found easier routes than had Lewis and Clark—routes that would become the Oregon Trail, the major highway of Far West migration. Gratified by Stuart's report, Astor declared, "I have hit the nail on the head." He was soon to discover, however, that he had shot himself in the foot. In the East, the United States and Britain were at war. Fearing attack by British warships, the Astorians—led by former Canadian fur company employees, many of them British subjects—sold their furs to their Canadian competitors at much reduced prices and turned the fort over to the first ship they saw flying the Union Jack. The United States got the post back under the Treaty of Ghent, which ended the War of 1812, but Astor was finished with the place by then. He had lost sixty-one men, and more to the point as far as he was concerned, he had not seen a single penny of profit. In fact, he was out some four hundred thousand dollars, which in 1813 was enough of a fortune to give pause even to a man with pockets as deep as the founder of the American Fur Company.

—*Charles Phillips*

SEE ALSO: Exploration: English Expeditions, United States Expeditions; Fur Trade

SUGGESTED READING:

Haeger, John D. *John Jacob Astor: Business and Finance in the Early Republic.* Detroit, Mich., 1991.
Goetzmann, William H. *Exploration and Science: The Explorer and the Scientist in the Winning of the American West.* New York, 1966.
Ronda, James P. *Astoria and Empire.* Lincoln, Nebr., 1990.
Wishart, David J. *The Fur Trade of the American West, 1807–1840.* Lincoln, Nebr., 1979.

ATCHISON, DAVID RICE

U.S. Senator from Missouri David Rice Atchison (1807–1886) was a staunch advocate for Western expansion and the man in no small measure responsible for the bloodshed along the Missouri-Kansas border following passage of the KANSAS-NEBRASKA ACT in 1854. Born in Frogtown, Kentucky, Atchison graduated from Transylvania College in Lexington. He first practiced law in Kentucky before moving west and hanging out his shingle in Liberty, Missouri. Appointed to the U.S. Senate in 1843 following the death of Lewis L. Linn, Atchison followed in his predecessor's footsteps and urged the government to extend its protection of American settlements to Oregon, becoming thereby one of the leading spokesmen in the failed "54° 40' or Fight" movement. An advocate of fair treatment for the Native Americans in his early years in the Senate, Atchison later fell under the influence of states' rights proponent JOHN CALDWELL CALHOUN, who, by the 1840s, was the major defender of black slavery in the Congress.

When Calhoun died, Atchison became the leader of the ultraconservative proslavery faction and ultimately broke with his Missouri colleague, THOMAS HART BENTON, over the issue of extending slavery into the Western territories. Following the bitter debate over the Kansas-Nebraska Act, Atchison—having played a major role in repealing the MISSOURI COMPROMISE so despised by slaveholders—took charge of the proslavery movement in Missouri and led the fight to make Kansas a new slave state under the rubric of "popular sovereignty." Forming posses of men Horace Greeley soon called "border ruffians," Atchison encouraged direct attacks on Free-Soil enclaves in Kansas. During the Civil War, he backed Missouri's Southern-sympathizing governor, Claiborne Jackson. After the Union victory at the Battle of Pea Ridge, Atchison retired (along with Missouri's government in exile) to Texas. In 1867, he returned to Missouri and lived out the rest of his days far from public life on his Clinton County farm.

—*Charles Phillips*

SUGGESTED READING:

McCandless, Perry. *A History of Missouri.* Vol. 2. Columbia, Mo., 1972.

Parrish, William E. *David Rice Atchison of Missouri: Border Politician.* Columbia, Mo., 1961.

Phillips, Charles. *Missouri: Mother of the American West.* Northridge, Calif., 1988.

ATCHISON, TOPEKA AND SANTA FE RAILROAD

The Atchison, Topeka and Santa Fe Railroad was the dominant railroad from Kansas to the Southwest and southern California. Cyrus K. Holliday came west to Kansas in 1854 to increase his small fortune of twenty thousand dollars by building a railroad across Kansas into the Southwest. Soon after reaching Kansas, he joined other speculators in founding and buying land in the town of Topeka, which became the capital of the new state in 1861. Holliday was a strong supporter of the Republican party, and when the party took over

Atchison, Topeka and Santa Fe Railroad courses over Canyon Diablo in this 1900 image. *Courtesy California Museum of Photography, Keystone-Mast Collection, University of California, Riverside.*

power in Washington, D.C., in 1861, its support proved crucial to Holliday's plans.

The Atchison and Topeka Railroad (Santa Fe was added in 1863) began on paper in January 1859 when Holliday wrote its articles of incorporation and secured the support of other Kansas businessmen. But these investors did not have the capital to buy rails or locomotives. Holliday's Republican friends lobbied Congress for land and for approval of a treaty by which the company purchased Native American lands near Topeka at cut-rate prices. Meanwhile, Holliday cajoled Shawnee County residents and those of three other Kansas counties to authorize the sale of bonds to finance the railroad. With land assets—potential and actual—and local bonds in hand, Holliday enticed Easterners, particularly Bostonians, to invest in his railroad.

T. J. Peter, a gruff, brilliant, and determined contractor, began laying track south from Topeka in the fall of 1868. In order to obtain its land grant from Congress, the railroad had to reach Colorado by March 1873. By late 1872, Peter's crews regularly laid two or three miles of track a day over frozen ground and won the race to the border just before Christmas.

After resting a few years from its frenzied push across Kansas, the AT&SF, particularly under the leadership of William B. Strong in the 1880s, became the dominant line between the Midwest and the Southwest. The railroad bought lines, or built its own, to gain routes through the mountains, tap new markets, and defend its own territory and invade that of competitors. A competing line got control of a route to Salt Lake City via Royal Gorge, but the AT&SF succeeded in building a route through Raton Pass, the gateway from eastern Colorado to New Mexico. The railroad extended track to Albuquerque in 1880 and across Arizona to Needles, California, in 1883. To prevent companies building west from Chicago from capturing all the traffic between Kansas and the nation's railroad center on Lake Michigan, the AT&SF built its own line to Chicago by 1888.

The AT&SF bought other important segments of its line. In 1872, it paid for a railroad that T. J. Peter and local investors constructed from Wichita to Santa Fe and gained business by serving Wichita's booming cattle trade. In the early and mid-1880s, it purchased southern California roads and linked them to its system, thus obtaining entrance to San Diego and Los Angeles. Similarly, to enter the Midwest-Texas market, Strong acquired the Gulf, Colorado and Santa Fe Railroad, which connected Galveston to the AT&SF's track in Oklahoma in 1886.

Expansion and rate wars in the late 1880s undermined the AT&SF's finances, and when the country headed into depression in 1893, the railroad could not pay its debts and entered receivership. It emerged two years later with a new president, Edward P. Ripley, who guided the railroad for a quarter of a century. Carefully positioning the AT&SF to take advantage of the growing economy of the Southwest, he extended track in Oklahoma and captured traffic from new oil discoveries. He expanded into eastern Texas and carried out huge quantities of lumber. Farther west in Texas, he laid rails that tapped the area's booming sheep industry. And he built or bought lines that shortened the AT&SF's haul to California from both Chicago and Texas—important improvements as the Golden State's economy and population surged in the twentieth century. Ripley's successors, William B. Storey in the 1920s and Samuel T. Bledsoe through most of the 1930s, continued his judicious expansion to gain better markets and better connections. Storey added lines in Kansas, Oklahoma, Texas, and New Mexico to funneled oil and agricultural traffic along the AT&SF. Bledsoe, hampered early in the 1930s by the Great Depression, kept the railroad solvent and took advantage of cheap prices to build or buy routes, some of which improved the company's Texas-Denver and Texas-California schedules.

Ripley also improved the Santa Fe's passenger and tourist service. Beginning in the late 1870s, the line attracted travelers by featuring "Meals by Fred Harvey." Harvey's palatable food, served by HARVEY GIRLS, set a standard far above the usual fare in Western RESTAURANTS. Ripley placed still more emphasis on the AT&SF's passenger offerings. He promoted the *California Limited,* a train that raced passengers between Chicago and Los Angeles in seventy-two hours and fed them Harvey's food in dining cars. He and Harvey's firm established a string of hotels featuring a Southwest motif along the AT&SF line. Ripley built a spur to the rim of the Grand Canyon, where he erected two massive lodges. The AT&SF did much to promote the canyon and Carlsbad Caverns as well as the allure of the Spanish and Indian cultures of the Southwest in order to attract tourist traffic.

Freight, not passengers, was the railroad's main business. In the 1920s, Storey's programs of building or encouraging others to locate manufacturing plants, warehouses, and markets along the AT&SF line helped the railroad maintain a healthy freight traffic despite the introduction of truck competition. In 1935, Bledsoe began buying truck companies to funnel freight to the railroad. During World War II, the AT&SF, which had the most direct connection between the Midwest and southern California industrial centers, ran at peak capacity hauling war goods. After the war, the AT&SF adopted innovations, such as piggyback trailers, container services, and computerized switching, in a battle for freight in the face of a trucking industry aided by an expanding interstate-highway system.

In its search for profits, the company increasingly placed emphasis on its nonrailroad assets—land, oil, timber, and trucking. The railroad itself became part of a larger holding company, Santa Fe Industries, in 1968. In the 1980s, an effort to consolidate with the SOUTHERN PACIFIC RAILROAD partially succeeded; the Interstate Commerce Commission did not approve joining the rail operations, but the new Santa Fe Pacific combined Santa Fe Industries with the Southern Pacific's nonrail holdings. In 1988, the company thwarted a hostile takeover, but to handle the resulting debt, it trimmed assets including more than a quarter of its track.

—*James H. Ducker*

SEE ALSO: Railroads; Tourism

SUGGESTED READING:

Bryant, Keith L., Jr. *History of the Atchison, Topeka and Santa Fe Railway.* New York, 1974.

Ducker, James H. *Men of the Steel Rails: Workers on the Atchison, Topeka and Santa Fe Railroad, 1869–1900.* Lincoln, Nebr., 1983.

Marshall, James. *Santa Fe: The Railroad That Built an Empire.* New York, 1945.

Waters, L. L. *Steel Trails to Santa Fe.* Lawrence, Kans., 1950.

ATHAPASCAN INDIANS

SEE: Native American Peoples: Peoples of Alaska

ATHERTON, GERTRUDE

Novelist Gertrude Atherton (1857–1948) was born Gertrude Horn in San Francisco and grew up on her grandfather's ranch outside the city. She was educated in private schools in California and Kentucky. After the family's financial security disappeared in the failure of the Bank of California, her hopes of a social debut were dashed. Unhappy with her life on the family ranch, she sought to remedy her boredom by stealing her mother's suitor. She married George Bowen Atherton, the wealthy son of a San Francisco merchant in 1876 and confessed later (in *Adventures of a Novelist,* published in 1932) that the marriage was disappointing and oppressive. It did produce, however, a son and daughter. After her husband died at sea in 1887, Atherton spent the next fifty years traveling in California, New York, and Europe and writing dozens of novels, stories, memoirs, biographies, and magazine articles. In all, she published fifty books and was still writing at the time of her death at the age of ninety-one.

Her eighteen novels, written between 1890 and 1942, were mostly set in California and were known for their unsentimental heroines with rebellious spirits, daringly free in their sexuality, careers, and marriages—a prototype of the "new American woman." Her novels and many of her shorter works portray the social history of California from Spanish-colonial times to the 1930s. Atherton found her first critical acclaim in Europe. Only after her success among Europeans was she accepted by America's critics. Her novels, however, were always popular in America, and most sold well.

Atherton's biographer, Charlotte McClure, states that the author strove to have her heroines stand for "the evolution of a western woman from dependence on an aristocratic birth as the basis for self-identity to an independent, self-knowing confidence that allows her to contribute responsibly to civilization."

Atherton's California novels include *Los Cerritos: A Romance of the Modern Times* (1890), *Patience Sparhawk and Her Times* (1897), *The Californians* (1898), *Ancestors* (1907), *Sleeping Fires* (1922), and *The Horn of Life* (1942). She also wrote popular nonfiction books about her native state, including *California: An Intimate History* (1914), *Golden Gate Country* (1945), and *My San Francisco: A Wayward Biography* (1946).

—*Dale L. Walker*

SUGGESTED READING:
Atherton, Gertrude. *Adventures of a Novelist.* New York, 1932.
Jackson, Joseph H. *Gertrude Atherton.* New York, 1940.
McClure, Charlotte. *Gertrude Atherton.* New York 1979.

ATKINSON, HENRY

Born in North Carolina, the son of a tobacco grower, Henry Atkinson (1782–1842) served as an army officer from 1808 until his death and led expeditions to the Yellowstone region.

From 1808 to 1813, as a captain in the Third Infantry, Atkinson served along the coast of the Gulf of Mexico. In April 1813, he became a staff officer and was transferred to the New York–Canada border region. Two years later, he was promoted to the rank of colonel in the Sixth Infantry, and he remained with the unit for the rest of his career.

Assigned to the 1819 Yellowstone Expedition, Atkinson was given the task of moving troops northwest to the mouth of the Yellowstone in eastern Montana. When the steamboats carrying men and supplies broke down, the troops halted north of present-day Omaha, Nebraska, where the soldiers built Fort Atkinson. On May 13, 1820, Atkinson became a brigadier general, but he lost the rank the next year because of army reductions. In 1825, he and Indian agent Benjamin O'Fallon led a 475-man expedition up the Missouri to the Yellowstone. This time they reached their objective, and they negotiated treaties of peace with fifteen tribes along the way.

Atkinson next supervised the construction and operation of the infantry school at Jefferson Barracks just south of St. Louis. In 1827, he helped prevent a war between miners and angry Winnebagos in Wisconsin. He commanded the troops in 1832 in BLACK HAWK'S WAR in Illinois and Wisconsin. Then for the next decade, he supervised the removal of Indian tribes west beyond the Mississippi River. He died suddenly at age sixty while at home at Jefferson Barracks.

During his army career, Atkinson helped secure American military power in the Upper Mississippi and Missouri river valleys. While his work fostered peace, it also damaged the societies and cultures of tribal people in that region.

—*Roger L. Nichols*

SUGGESTED READING:
Nichols, Roger L. *General Henry Atkinson: A Western Military Career.* Norman, Okla., 1965.

ATLANTIC AND PACIFIC RAILROAD

SEE: Atchison, Topeka and Santa Fe Railroad

ATOMIC ENERGY

SEE: Federal Government

AUBURN, CALIFORNIA

SEE: Ghost Towns

AUDUBON, JOHN JAMES

Naturalist and American wildlife painter John James Audubon (1785–1851) was born in Les Cayes, Santo Domingo (Haiti), the illegitimate son of Jean Audubon,

John James Audubon. Engraving by Alonzo Chappel. *Editors' collection.*

a French ship captain, and Jeanne Rabin (or Rabine), a French servant girl who died soon after her son's birth. Audubon showed an early interest in drawing wildlife but received naval training at Rochefort-sur-Mer from 1796 to 1800. He later claimed to have studied with artist Jacques Louis David of the Napoleonic court.

Audubon moved to America in 1803 to manage the Mill Grove, Pennsylvania, estate his father had purchased. He married neighbor Lucy Bakewell in 1808. The young couple moved to Kentucky, where Audubon attempted several businesses but failed in the economic crisis of 1819 and declared bankruptcy. He moved to Cincinnati, where he worked as taxidermist, portraitist, and art teacher at the Western Museum.

In 1820, Audubon set out to fulfill his dream of documenting all the birds of North America. With his young assistant Joseph Mason, he floated down the Ohio and Mississippi rivers, searched the forests of the Great Lakes area and Louisiana, and produced brilliant paintings of birds. Mason painted the handsome plants that provided the habitats for the birds.

Failing to find support in Philadelphia or New York for the publication he envisioned, Audubon sailed for Great Britain in 1826. He was welcomed into society and found support for his "great work," *The Birds of*

John James Audubon's *White headed Eagle. Courtesy National Cowboy Hall of Fame and Western Heritage Center.*

America (published between 1827 and 1838), which contains 435 hand-colored aquatint engravings of 1,065 individual birds in life size. Audubon financed the huge book by selling subscriptions for approximately one thousand dollars each and made several trips back to America to visit Florida, Labrador, and Texas in search of additional birds and subscribers. He used his extensive field notes to produce simultaneously five volumes of text, *The Ornithological Biography,* to accompany the plates.

When Audubon returned to the United States for the final time in 1839, he announced a new work, *The Viviparous Quadrupeds of North America,* in which he hoped to document mammals in the same way that he had birds. He also began publication of an octavo edition of *The Birds of America,* which ultimately sold more than one thousand subscriptions at a retail price of one hundred dollars per set. He finally visited the trans-Mississippi West in 1843, steaming up the Missouri River to Fort Union. *The Quadrupeds,* published between 1845 and 1848, contains 150 hand-colored lithographs, approximately one-half of which are the work of Audubon's son, John Woodhouse Audubon.

Audubon was one of the foremost romantic artists in America. He anthropomorphically depicted his birds in a heroic manner. His birds composed a revolution in natural history art. Many contemporaries criticized his birds for awkward and animated poses, but his intense observation and knowledge of birds has been confirmed in most instances, and he usually selected the poses to show certain aspects of the species. The habitats and landscapes in the backgrounds of the paintings—such as the *Greater Prairie Chicken* (published in 1824 and in the collection of the New-York Historical Society)—produced by Audubon, Mason, George Lehman, and perhaps others, are a virtual catalogue of American landscapes. He died at his home on the Hudson River on January 27, 1851.

—*Ron Tyler*

SUGGESTED READING:

Blaugrund, Annette, and Theodore E. Stebbins, Jr., eds. *John James Audubon: The Watercolors for* The Birds of America. New York, 1993.

Ford, Alice. *John James Audubon: A Biography.* New York, 1988.

Tyler, Ron. *Audubon's Great National Work: The Royal Octavo Edition of* The Birds of America. Austin, Tex., 1993.

AURORA, NEVADA

SEE: Ghost Towns

AUSTIN, MARY HUNTER

A Western writer, known for her evocative descriptions of the desert landscape and its inhabitants, Mary Hunter Austin (1868–1934) was born in Carlinville, Illinois. She graduated from Blackburn College in 1888 and migrated that year to southern California to homestead in the desert high country. She married Wallace Stafford Austin in 1891, relocated to Owens Valley, and gave birth to her only child. She lived for fifteen years in Owens Valley and then moved to Carmel, California, and New York. In 1924, she settled permanently in Santa Fe, New Mexico. In each locale, her sense of place contributed greatly to her writing.

Austin wrote more than thirty books, including five collections of short fiction, which often appeared first in Eastern magazines such as *The Atlantic Monthly* and *The Century.* Although her early short stories, such as "The Shepherd of the Sierras" (1900), were frequently of the picturesque, sentimental, local-color variety, her style matured over the years. In *The Land of Little Rain* (1903), her signature work, she established herself as an astute and sympathetic interpreter of desert life. Her first literary efforts, and arguably her finest achievements, explore the arid terrain and the native cultures of California. *The Basket Woman* (1904), *The Flock* (1906), and *Lost Borders* (1909) are significant for their poetic nature writing, Indian tales, and mining and sheepherding lore. Four of Austin's novels are set in California, including the historical *Isidro* (1905) and the contemporary *Ford* (1917). *Starry Adventure* (1931) takes place in New Mexico. Her Paiute Indian drama, *The Arrow Maker,* was produced on Broadway in 1911. Austin's regional work also includes two books of poetry, a volume of Indian tales entitled *One Smoke Stories* (1934), and the Southwest desert classic *Land of Journeys' Ending* (1924). Her spare, ironic, ambiguous short stories, exemplified by "The Walking Woman" (1909), are significant contributions to Western literary realism. In 1932, she published her autobiography, *Earth Horizon,* an absorbing account of her struggle for acceptance and achievement as a Western woman writer.

Austin died in 1934 in Santa Fe. During her life, she enjoyed a national reputation as a mystic, a feminist, a primitivist, an antimodernist, and a nature writer in the tradition of HENRY DAVID THOREAU. In her last years, she was celebrated as a champion of the American literary tradition, the Western landscape, and indigenous American culture. Her writing is an imaginative blend of observation, experience, legend, myth, and fact. Although her work was neglected for nearly a half-century after her death, it experienced a revival of interest in the 1980s because of its feminist, multicultural, and environmental themes.

—*Karen S. Langlois*

SEE ALSO: Women Writers

SUGGESTED READING:
Stineman, Esther Lanigan. *Mary Austin: Song of a Maverick*. New Haven, Conn., 1989.

AUSTIN, MOSES

Moses Austin (1761–1821), founder of the American lead industry, obtained initial permission to establish an American colony in Spanish Texas. Born in Durham, Connecticut, and orphaned at the age of fifteen, Austin engaged in the dry-goods merchandising business with family members in Middletown, Connecticut, and later in Philadelphia, Pennsylvania. An entrepreneur, he extended the business to Richmond, Virginia, where, in 1789, he gained control of Virginia's richest lead deposit, established Austinville (Wythe County) in 1792, brought experienced miners and smelterers from England, and created the American lead industry.

In 1797, he obtained a grant to part of the richest lead deposit in Spanish Upper Louisiana (at present-day Potosi, Missouri), where he established the first Anglo settlement west of the Mississippi River in Missouri. Using the efficient reverberatory furnace, he gained control of nearly all smelting in the region and amassed a wealth of $190,000. The second period in the history of the American lead industry is known as the "Moses Austin period," and Austin's contributions influenced the lead industry until heavy machinery revolutionized mining and smelting after the Civil War.

With sales lost because of the Aaron BURR CONSPIRACY, the War of 1812, and subsequent depressed economic conditions, Austin joined others seeking to increase the money supply in circulation by founding the Bank of St. Louis, the first bank west of the Mississippi River. In 1816, he relinquished the Potosi mine to his son, Stephen Fuller Austin, moved to Herculaneum, Missouri, a town he established in 1808 as a river shipping point for his lead, and returned to merchandising.

Unsuccessful in escaping debt through traditional business pursuits, Austin developed a plan for settling an American colony in Spanish Texas in 1819. After the ADAMS-ONIS TREATY clarified ownership of Texas, he traveled to San Antonio (1820) to seek permission for his colony. Spurned by the governor, he happened to meet the Baron de Bastrop, a resident of San Antonio, who returned with him to the governor's office to request the permission. He subsequently received permission, but he died on June 10, 1821, of the effects of exposure during his trip.

Stephen Austin accepted his father's deathbed request to carry out "the Texas Adventure."

—*David B. Gracy, II*

SUGGESTED READING:
Gracy, David B., II. *Moses Austin: His Life*. San Antonio, Tex., 1987.

AUSTIN, STEPHEN FULLER

Stephen Fuller Austin (1793–1836), the "father" of Texas for whom the state capital is named, was born in Austinville, Virginia, and grew up on the frontier in Virginia and Spanish Upper Louisiana (at modern Potosi, Missouri) where his father, Moses Austin, operated lead mines. Stephen attended school in Connecticut and Kentucky from 1804 to 1810 before beginning work in his father's mercantile and lead businesses in Potosi.

Stephen Fuller Austin. *Courtesy Patrick H. Butler, III.*

Austin began to shoulder significant responsibility for business affairs in 1812 when he took a load of lead to New Orleans. He served in Missouri's territorial militia from 1813 to 1816 and the territorial legislature from 1815 to 1816 and led the work to revise the civil and criminal codes and to pass banking legislation.

Because of a depression in the lead industry and his father's unwise business commitments, the financial stability of the formerly well-to-do family deteriorated through the 1810s. In 1816, Austin took over the family's lead-mining operation but demonstrated no special aptitude for business.

In 1819, after his father proposed establishing an American colony in Spanish Texas, Austin moved to Arkansas to develop a resting point on an overland route. He served as a circuit judge in 1820, but dissatisfied with economic opportunities, he abandoned Arkansas and the "Texas Adventure" for an editorial appointment and law studies in New Orleans.

In 1821, Austin accepted his father's deathbed request to carry out the plan to colonize Texas. Diplomatic where his father was irascible, but equally determined in pursuit of goals, Austin assumed his final and successful role as a colonizer and community leader.

When the government of newly independent Mexico refused to approve Moses Austin's old Spanish land grant, Stephen Austin traveled to Mexico City, where he spent a year learning Spanish and threading Mexican political upheavals until he had drafted the Imperial Colonization Law under which he then received an empresario contract. He received or participated in five empresario contracts, under which he settled more than fifteen hundred settlers. His first contract, for three hundred families, was the only empresario contract fulfilled nearly to the letter.

Throughout his Texas years, Austin felt a responsibility to and for the settlers. Until 1828, he presided over the civil and military affairs of the Anglo settlements, an authority he exercised with patience and tact that minimized friction between the culturally disparate Anglo settlers and Mexican authorities.

Austin presided over the conventions of 1832 and 1833, which drafted petitions opposing the restriction of immigration from the United States (through the Law of April 6, 1830) and called for separate statehood. He carried the petitions of the convention of 1833 to Mexico City, where he obtained repeal of the Law of April 6, 1830, and other reforms. Returning home, he was arrested in 1834 on suspicion of inciting insurrection and was held in Mexico City for eighteen months (six in solitary confinement, which damaged his health). Back in Texas after twenty-eight months'

absence, he openly opposed the Mexican central government under Antonio López de Santa Anna. When revolution erupted in 1835, Austin briefly headed the revolutionary government and commanded Texan forces. More valuable as a diplomat, he served as a commissioner to the United States from 1835 to 1836.

Defeated in his bid for the office of president of the Republic of Texas, he accepted appointment as secretary of state but died in office.

—*David B. Gracy, II*

SEE ALSO: Empresarios

SUGGESTED READING:
Eugene C. Barker. *The Life of Stephen F. Austin: Founder of Texas, 1793–1836.* Reprint. Austin, Tex., 1990.

AUTRY, GENE

Singing cowboy in movies and television programs, Orvon Gene Autry (1907–) was born in Tioga, Texas. At an early age, he moved with his family to Oklahoma. It was there, as a member of his grandfather's church choir, that his lifelong interest in music began. He bought a mail-order guitar, and in the 1920s, he landed a recording contract. In 1933, for his single, "That Silver Haired Daddy of Mine," he received the first gold record ever presented by the recording industry.

Gene Autry. *Courtesy National Cowboy Hall of Fame and Western Heritage Center.*

In 1934, Autry provided two songs for the Ken Maynard film entitled *In Old Santa Fe.* This work launched him into yet another area, the movies. In his first feature film, *Tumbling Tumbleweeds,* Autry played the lead role. In the early 1950s, Autry became a television pioneer by bringing his family-oriented shows into the living rooms of America, just as he had done on his "Melody Ranch" radio shows, which ran from 1939 through 1956. His more than ninety films and as many episodes on television programs helped shape the singing-cowboy genre.

In addition to his entertainment accomplishments, Autry was a successful businessman. He entered into a wide range of interests, including the ownership of a major league baseball team, the California Angels. After World War II, he began collecting materials to serve as the basis for an educational and cultural institution, and in 1988, the Gene Autry Western Heritage Museum (now the Autry Museum of Western Heritage) in Los Angeles opened its doors to the public.

—*John P. Langellier*

SUGGESTED READING:

Autry, Gene, with Mickey Herskowitz. *Back in the Saddle Again.* Garden City, N.Y., 1978.

AUTRY MUSEUM OF WESTERN HERITAGE

In 1961, fire destroyed the Western art and artifacts collected by singing cowboy and business executive Gene Autry and thus apparently ended his lifelong dream of creating a Western museum. In 1984, however, the idea was revived, and with the leadership of Autry, his wife Jackie Autry, and friends Joanne and Monte Hale, the Autry Museum of Western Heritage was established.

The museum opened in the Griffith Park area of Los Angeles in the fall of 1988. It clearly expresses its institutional mission: to collect and preserve the cultural, artistic, and other evidence of the West from prehistoric cultures to the present. Interpreting this material is a corollary purpose to the museum's overall mission to educate the public about the past.

The museum presents materials ranging from prehistoric pottery to Spanish armor; from objects of the fur trade to stagecoaches and Native American cultural materials. A balanced view of the Western experience is provided by a focus on cultural and ethnic diversity with special sections on Asian, Mexican, African American, European, and Canadian immigration and settlement. The collection of cowboy gear, 1700s to the present, ranks with the best in the world. Notable sections of the collections show how art, advertising, Wild West shows, film, literature, radio, and television have affected perceptions of the region. Significant works of art by THOMAS MORAN, ALBERT BIERSTADT, FREDERIC REMINGTON, A. F. Tait, GEORGE CATLIN, JOHN MIX STANLEY, SETH EASTMAN, Maynard Dixon, FRANK TENNEY JOHNSON, and many others are featured. In the film section, of course, Gene Autry is placed in historical perspective. The museum also houses a remarkable collection of historical firearms.

More than a half-million visitors each year experience exhibits, use an exceptional research facility, and enjoy a wide variety of programs.

—*James H. Nottage*

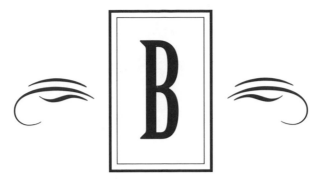

BABBITT RANCH, ARIZONA

David and William Babbitt, two of five brothers from Cincinnati, Ohio, went to Flagstaff in the Arizona Territory in 1886 and bought a ranch, which they renamed the CO-Bar. Their other three brothers, Charles, George, and Edward, soon joined them, and all but Edward stayed on and became prominent Arizonans.

The Babbitts acquired many additional ranch properties and cattle and sheep. Early in the twentieth century, their Arizona holdings extended from near the Grand Canyon almost to the New Mexico border. Counting their ranches in Kansas and California, the y pastured livestock on one hundred thousand square miles of grassland. Among the many brands they acquired were the A-1, the OG-Rail, and the famed Hashknife. In addition, the Babbitt mercantile and Indian trading-post empire extended over much of northern Arizona. Many of their holdings have been sold in recent years, but the family is still a major force in northern Arizona affairs. One of Charles Babbitt's grandsons, Bruce Babbitt, became governor of Arizona and secretary of the interior in President Bill Clinton's cabinet.

—*Dean Smith*

SUGGESTED READING:
Smith, Dean. *Brothers Five: The Babbits of Arizona*. Tempe, Ariz., 1989.

BABY DOE

SEE: Tabor, Horace Austin Warner

BACA, ELFEGO

Elfego Baca (1865–1945) was one of the best-known Hispanic figures of the West. While some of his legendary escapades are factual, many are spurious, and Baca himself greatly embellished others during his many campaigns for public office. His larger-than-life adventures interested Walt Disney Productions, which produced a short-lived television series called "The Rousing Life of Elfego Baca."

Born in Socorro, New Mexico, Baca moved to Topeka, Kansas, with his family, who worked in the wagon-freighting business over the Santa Fe Trail. Legend holds that Indians kidnapped the one-year-old Baca en route to Topeka, found him to be too much to handle, and returned him to his family four days later. When Baca's mother died in 1872, his father sent him to live with relatives in southern New Mexico, where he worked as a cowboy. His father joined him soon afterwards, when the Atchison, Topeka and Santa Fe Railroad ended the wagon-freighting business.

Around 1878, the elder Baca served as sheriff of Los Lunas, a rough-and-tumble cattle and railroad town south of Albuquerque. Violence was commonplace, and Sheriff Baca shot two popular cowboys during an altercation in a saloon. When the Anglo establishment placed him on trial, his teenaged son was incensed. He engineered a jail break from the Socorro County Courthouse and hid his father at the Indian pueblo of Isleta for seven years.

The most celebrated event in Baca's life occurred in 1884 when, as a nineteen-year-old deputy sheriff, he arrested a cowboy for assault in Frisco, New Mexico. About eighty cowboys forced Baca to take refuge in a jacal. During the ensuing thirty-six-hour gunfight, Baca killed two men, and his assailants allegedly fired more than four hundred rounds into the brush structure. He survived because the dirt floor of the shed was below ground level, and the bullets passed overhead. A passing sheriff negotiated a cease fire and took Baca to Albuquerque, where a court of inquiry exonerated him.

In subsequent years, Baca passed the bar and became county clerk, mayor, school superintendent, and district attorney in Socorro County. After leaving public office, he engaged in legal and illegal trade across the Mexican border. He befriended bandit and revolutionary FRANCISCO ("PANCHO") VILLA; the friendship soon soured, however, and Villa placed a thirty-thousand-dollar price on Baca's head.

During the Mexican Revolution, Baca served as legal counsel to General José Inez Salazar, who was jailed in Albuquerque for border violations. Baca could not arrange Salazar's release, so he engineered a jail break that returned Salazar safely to Mexico. Although Baca had remained in a neighboring saloon during the escape, the general yelled a thankful good-bye from his speeding getaway car, and newspaper accounts claimed Baca was involved in the incident.

After other escapades as a sheriff, border lawyer, influence peddler, and newspaper publisher, Baca died in Albuquerque at the age of eighty.

—*Byron A. Johnson*

SEE ALSO: Law and Order

SUGGESTED READING:
Crichton, Kyle. *Law and Order Limited*. Albuquerque, N. Mex., 1928.

BAILEY, FLORENCE AUGUSTA MERRIAM

Ornithologist and nature writer Florence Augusta Merriam (1863–1948) developed an abiding passion for natural history while growing up on her family's country estate in Locust Grove, New York. At Smith College in the mid-1880s, she led groups of students on bird-watching expeditions and began submitting articles to *Audubon Magazine*—articles that were later published as *Birds through an Opera Glass* (1889). Her studies in natural history were interrupted briefly by a bout of tuberculosis, but she used a curative trip to the American West to gather material for two works, *My Summer in a Mormon Village* (1894) and *A-Birding on a Bronco* (1896).

Returning to the East, she moved to Washington, D.C., where she met and married Vernon Bailey, a naturalist with the U.S. Biological Survey. Their marriage in 1899 began a long collaboration on the study of Western WILDLIFE. Vernon's works documented mammals, reptiles, and plants; Florence reported on bird life. Over the years, the Baileys worked in Texas, New Mexico, California, Arizona, and the Pacific Northwest.

Florence Bailey's *Handbook of Birds of the Western United States* (1902) went through several editions and complemented Frank M. Chapman's *Handbook of Birds of Eastern North America* (1895). Her other works included *Birds of New Mexico* (1928) and *Among the Birds in the Grand Canyon National Park* (1939), in addition to numerous articles for *Bird-lore* and other magazines. Her skill in field observation, combined with a talent for writing, produced works that advanced scientific knowledge of Western bird life and popularized bird watching as a pastime.

—*Patricia Hogan*

BAILEY, MARGARET JEWETT

An early Oregon settler, Margaret Jewett Bailey (ca. 1812–1882) wrote the first novel to be printed on the Pacific Slope. She was born Margaret Jewett Smith in Saugus, Massachusetts. Most of the particulars of Bailey's life are surmised from her autobiographical novel entitled *Grains, or Passages in the Life of Ruth Rover with Occasional Pictures of Oregon, Natural and Moral* (1854).

In 1837, after breaking an engagement with a Bostonian, Margaret Smith joined a party organized to augment JASON LEE's Methodist mission in Oregon. En route, she quarreled with the group's leader, the Reverend David Leslie, and accused him of moral lapses. After arriving in Oregon, she took her case to Lee, who sided with Leslie and effectively demoted her among the missionaries—although she did teach for a period at the missionary school.

In 1838, Smith became engaged to William H. Willson, a layman attached to the mission, but severed the engagement when she learned that Willson was engaged to a woman in Boston. Apparently in retaliation, Willson confessed to Leslie that he and Smith had had sexual relations. Smith denied the charges but yielded to pressure from Leslie and signed a secret confession. Leslie and Willson revealed the confession to Dr. William J. Bailey when he became engaged to Smith. Dr. Bailey was apparently convinced of his bride's innocence, and the two were married in 1839.

Margaret Bailey was not active as a writer until after the launching of the *Oregon Spectator,* first newspaper on the Pacific Coast, in February 1846. She contributed poetry and prose to the paper, even as her marriage deteriorated—her "confession" having festered in her husband's mind for some years. At last, in 1854, she divorced Dr. Bailey and published the first part of *Ruth Rover,* which embodied much of her anguish and bitterness. The novel was greeted by a single, scathing review in the *Portland Oregonian*. The second part of the novel met with an even harsher response; the reviewer called for Bailey's prosecution under territorial obscenity laws.

In truth, the novel is no worse, stylistically, than most popular fiction of its day. As a portrait of domestic life in the Far West and as a feminist document, *Ruth Rover* is significant. It was, however, so obscure that only a single complete copy is now known to exist (in the Coe Collection at Yale University), and Bailey apparently quit writing after its publication. She married and divorced twice again and died, alone and penniless, in Seattle.

—*Alan Axelrod*

SEE ALSO: Women Writers

SUGGESTED READING:
Nelson, Herbert B. "Ruth Rover's Cup of Sorrow." *Pacific Northwest Quarterly* (July 1959).

BAKER, JAMES

Mountain man and guide James Baker (1818–1898) left his Belleville, Illinois, home around the age of twenty to begin a life in the wilderness as a fur trapper for the AMERICAN FUR COMPANY. He continued in the FUR TRADE for twenty years, working with such legendary TRAPPERS such as THOMAS FITZPATRICK and JAMES (JIM) BRIDGER. Like many MOUNTAIN MEN, Baker seemed most comfortable in unsettled regions of the country. When the fur trade in the Rocky Mountains declined, he served as a guide and interpreter to pioneers and military expeditions in the mountains. As part of the UTAH EXPEDITION in 1857, he guided a detachment of federal troops to Utah. During the Colorado gold rush, he managed a store in Denver. He then operated a toll bridge and took a turn at ranching. In 1865, he became a guide to the Ute Indian agency. Baker's recollections of his life in the wilderness made for good reading in magazines and newspapers and nurtured the popular image of the rugged mountain man. He retired to the wilds of Wyoming, not far from the Colorado border, where he died at the age of eighty.

—*Patricia Hogan*

SUGGESTED READING:
Mumey, Nolie. *The Life of Jim Baker, 1818–1898: Trapper, Scout, and Indian Fighter.* New York, 1931.

BALLINGER-PINCHOT CONTROVERSY

Contributing to the bad feeling that developed between William Howard Taft and THEODORE ROOSEVELT, the

James Baker. *Courtesy Huntington Library.*

Ballinger-Pinchot controversy split the Republican party in 1912 and made possible the election of the Democratic presidential candidate, Woodrow Wilson. Although the controversy occurred during President Taft's term in office, its origins lay in the Roosevelt presidency.

Richard Achilles Ballinger served as commissioner of the GENERAL LAND OFFICE under Roosevelt from 1907 to 1908. During his tenure, he clashed repeatedly with GIFFORD PINCHOT, the head of the UNITED STATES FOREST SERVICE. Pinchot was far from pleased, therefore, when Ballinger returned to public life in 1909 as Taft's choice to head the Department of the Interior. A Seattle resident who had lived in the Puget Sound region since 1890, Ballinger had a Westerner's view of conservation as a set of policies that favored large established economic interests while placing the small entrepreneur at a disadvantage.

In September 1909, Louis Glavis, a young field agent of the General Land Office, provided President

Taft with a document that made serious charges against the secretary of the interior. Glavis gained direct access to the president because he was armed with a letter of introduction from Pinchot. The document charged that Ballinger, while commissioner of the General Land Office and later as secretary of the interior, had assisted a group of thirty-three people, known as the Cunningham claimants, in acquiring coal lands in Alaska, despite evidence they had agreed to join illegally with the Morgan-Guggenheim Syndicate, a notorious trust. After a month's deliberation, Taft exonerated Ballinger of wrongdoing and dismissed Glavis. When Glavis made his charges public in an article published by *Collier's Weekly* in November, Taft imposed an order of silence on government officials in an effort to dampen criticism.

There were soon calls for a congressional investigation, and in January 1910, an incensed Ballinger demanded that any investigation embrace the activities of the Forest Service and the chief forester. That was a tactical mistake that gave Pinchot the means to bypass the presidential gag order. It became clear that the original charges against Ballinger, and the article that appeared in *Collier's Weekly,* were prepared by officials in the Forest Service with the knowledge and approval of Pinchot. When Pinchot defended his subordinates and criticized the president in a letter to the chairman of the Senate's agriculture committee—a letter deliberately made public—Taft dismissed Pinchot. A joint committee of Congress investigated the matter that spring and exonerated Ballinger. Among the public, however, his reputation was tarnished, and within a year, he returned to Seattle. Great harm was done also to the Taft administration, especially by Glavis's lawyer, Louis Brandeis, who succeeded in creating the impression that Taft had allowed Ballinger to write his own exoneration.

Pinchot considered Ballinger a threat to the work of the Forest Service. An opponent of the effort to change the system whereby natural resources were disposed of by outright sale, Ballinger rejected the multiple-use doctrine with ownership and the regulatory power retained by the government. He also moved to end the informal agreements negotiated between bureaus within and across department lines, thus striking at another vital aspect of the conservation policies. He even canceled an agreement with the BUREAU OF INDIAN AFFAIRS that gave Pinchot control over the forests on Indian reservations.

Until Taft exonerated Ballinger, the issue for Pinchot was who would have the presidential ear. Pinchot had pioneered many of the policies of Roosevelt's conservation program and had enjoyed unparalleled influence as a bureau chief, functioning as a virtual secretary of conservation in the shadowy "tennis cabinet." Sending Glavis as an instrument to discredit Ballinger in the eyes of Taft was Pinchot's last attempt to perpetuate his influence. Recognizing his defeat within the administration, Pinchot forced his own dismissal and took his case to the public, at the cost of wrecking the Taft administration. His actions during the controversy were also the first steps toward restoring his influence by working for the restoration of Roosevelt—unsuccessfully as it turned out.

—*James Penick*

SUGGESTED READING:

McGeary, M. Nelson. *Gifford Pinchot: Forester Politician.* Princeton, N.J., 1960.

Penick, James. *Progressive Politics and Conservation: The Ballinger-Pinchot Affair.* Chicago, 1968.

Pinchot, Gifford. *Breaking New Ground.* New York, 1947.

BANCROFT, HUBERT HOWE

Historian, collector, and businessman, Hubert Howe Bancroft (1832–1918) was born in Granville, Ohio, to a family of Puritan background. He attended Granville's public schools, spent several years in Missouri, returned to Ohio, and worked in a relative's bookstore in Buffalo, New York. Joining the California gold rush in 1852, he soon established a profitable paper supply and publishing business in San Francisco—a business that served much of the Pacific Slope.

Bancroft was convinced that California presented an almost sublime consummation in the progress of mankind. He began collecting California history in the early 1860s. He first searched local records, and then recognizing regional and Hispanic influences, he "rifled" the rare-book shops of the East Coast and Europe. Making huge purchases through auctions, he aggressively collected public and private papers and newspapers.

In the 1870s, Bancroft turned to the production of history. He constructed a succession of libraries, and over the years, he employed some six hundred archivists, reductionists, and copyists. Bancroft and a select, but unknown, group of historians wrote prodigiously. Starting with series on Native Americans, Central America, and Mexico, *Bancroft's Works* took form. By 1890, it numbered thirty-nine volumes and included books on the Pacific Slope, the Southwest, and California. Issued on a production-line schedule, each volume was released under Bancroft's own byline. Most of the volumes were published by The History Pub-

Hubert Howe Bancroft. *Courtesy Oakland Museum of California.*

SUGGESTED READING:
Bancroft, Hubert Howe. *Literary Industries.* Vol. 29 of *The Works of Hubert Howe Bancroft.* San Francisco, 1890.
Caughey, John W. *Hubert Howe Bancroft: Historian of the West.* Berkeley, Calif., 1946.
Clark, Harry. *A Venture in History: The Production, Publication, and Sale of the Works of Hubert Howe Bancroft.* Berkeley, Calif., 1973.
Peterson, Charles S. "Hubert Howe Bancroft: First Western Regionalist." In *Writing Western History: Essays on Major Western Historians.* Edited by Richard W. Etulain. Albuquerque, N. Mex., 1991.

BANDELIER, ADOLPH FRANCIS ALPHONSE

Pioneer anthropologist, ethnologist, and ethnohistorian of the American Southwest, Adolph Francis Alphonse Bandelier was born into a prominent family in Berne, Switzerland. He immigrated to the United States with his family and in 1848 settled in Highland, Illinois, a village populated by Swiss immigrants. His father was a banker and raised his son to enter that profession, but young Bandelier was fascinated not by the world of finance but by the world of science—especially of ancient peoples.

In 1873, Bandelier met Lewis Henry Morgan, sometimes called "the father of modern anthropology." Morgan took an interest in Bandelier and encouraged him. Morgan's forte was the Iroquois Indians; Bandelier's became the Indians of the Southwest, Mexico, and western South America. A brilliant scholar who already knew English, French, and German, Bandelier taught himself Spanish and set out to read about the peoples in Spanish and Mexican archives and then to conduct field work to substantiate the written record.

First, however, he had to establish his reputation. Conducting research at the St. Louis library and any other sources he could find, he wrote monographs on the native peoples of Mexico and had them published by the prestigious Peabody Museum of American Archaeology and Ethnology. When his health broke down, he was offered work out of Santa Fe under the auspices of the Archaeological Institute of America. After 1880, he was constantly on the move: to the pueblos around Santa Fe; to Arizona and El Paso, Texas; into Mexico; and finally into Peru and Bolivia. Widowed while in Bolivia, he then married Fanny Ritter, a Swiss whom he had met in La Paz. A talented woman, gifted in languages, she greatly enhanced his productivity. In 1911, he was appointed research assistant for the Carnegie Institution.

lishing Company, his own firm, and were sold by salesmen who appealed to the vanity of potential purchasers in selling full sets. The books were profusely annotated, fact-laden, narrative history that defined the West in terms of a Pacific regionalism and established approximate proportions that have influenced all subsequent study of the West. Some readers saw *Bancroft's Works* as only partially digested data. Others held, with Bancroft, that the first step was to make a factual rendering of his vast sources.

In the 1890s, fire, business reverses, and discord took a toll on his enterprise. Several of his writer-historians rebelled against his failure to attribute their work by name. Bancroft moved on to a series aimed even more directly at vanity buyers. In 1907, he sold his collection to the University of California, a sale that had long-lasting benefits for researchers and writers of frontier and borderlands history. After a long twilight that included published works on American expansionism, Bancroft's life ended in 1918 after a streetcar accident.

—*Charles S. Peterson*

Bandelier's writings are voluminous; he wrote seventy-one books and articles. His contributions did not receive just praise until long after his death. His fourteen-hundred-page manuscript written for Pope Leo XIII's Gold Jubilee, *A History of the Southwest,* was not published in English until 1969.

—*Richard A. Bartlett*

SEE ALSO: Exploration and Science

SUGGESTED READING:

Fontana, Bernard L. "A Dedication to the Memory of Adolph F. A. Bandelier, 1840–1914." *Arizona and the West* 2 (Spring 1960): 1–5.

Rodack, Madeleine Turrell. "Adolph Francis Alphonse Bandelier." In *Adolph F. Bandelier's The Discovery of New Mexico by the Franciscan Monk, Friar Marcos de Niza in 1530.* Translated and edited by Madeleine Turrell Rodack. Tucson, Ariz., 1981.

BANKING

Though the attitudes of individual Westerners toward banks and banking varied depending on social class and economic circumstances, a traditional hostility—especially among the entrepreneurial and the impoverished—based on historical experiences as well as financial needs developed as something of a regional trait. Those who went west to make a fortune or to start over, those already living in the West who suddenly found themselves caught up in the market of an expanding capitalist nation, and those dispossessed by the rapid BOOMS and even more sudden busts of a developing industrial economy frequently fell into debt and, not surprisingly, grew disenchanted with the rich who seemed to control their destinies—often from afar—through the financial mechanism of banking.

Historical background

Western hostility to banking had its historical roots in the early years of the American republic. When the twenty-one-year charter of the First Bank of the United States, which Alexander Hamilton had persuaded Congress to establish in 1791, ran out in 1811, a number of powerful politicians, mostly from the South and the trans-Appalachian West, opposed rechartering the institution on the grounds that Congress did not have the authority under the Constitution to create national banks. The controversy revealed early the diverging economic interests of different sections of the country. Meanwhile, the WAR OF 1812—pursued (despite objections from New England) by "War Hawks," again, mostly from the South and the West—proved difficult to finance without a strong central bank. Although the inconclusive war, hailed as a national victory, boosted the prestige of the federal government, fostered a new patriotism, and forged a sense of common identity, it also battered the economy and saddled the government with heavy war debts. A high tariff passed in 1816 to protect the United States's flagging industry, wild speculation in the Western lands "opened" by the war, overextended investments in manufacturing, and the collapse of foreign markets for American goods set off the financially devastating panic of 1819.

When the war had broken out, state banks, which proliferated before the war and dispensed credit recklessly, suspended specie payment (the practice of converting upon demand paper bank notes into gold or silver). The value of paper money dropped precipitously, and in 1816, Congress finally chartered the Second Bank of the United States to help stabilize currency. Largely mismanaged, the bank—acting on orders from Congress—resumed specie payment, a move that strained the resources of state banks, in many cases past the point of failure. Amid the bank failures and financial crisis, investors and debtors alike suffered. The Second Bank managed to regain a sound footing only by curtailing credit and maintaining a hard line on existing debt payments, thus preserving the creditworthiness of the nation as a whole. But, as one economist at the time wrote: "The Bank was saved, and the people were ruined."

Especially hard hit were the Southern and Western states and territories. Some of them were forced to enact constitutionally controversial legislation for the relief of debtors. While the nation ultimately weathered the panic of 1819, the crisis brought about a lasting resentment against the Bank of the United States in the South and West, where Missouri's U.S. Senator THOMAS HART BENTON had begun to call it "The Monster." That resentment reached its apotheosis during the presidency of ANDREW JACKSON, who seemed almost obsessed by a desire to destroy the bank.

Run by Nicholas Biddle, an aristocratic and cultivated Philadelphian, the bank had become a reasonably responsible, if quite powerful, business enterprise by the time Jackson was elected in 1828. A reliable depository for government funds and an important source of credit for the business community, the bank issued sound paper currency, sold government bonds, and acted as a check on state banks by forcing them to back their bank notes (paper money) with gold and silver. Controlling a fifth of the country's paper money and a third of both its bank deposits and silver and gold reserves, Biddle had an immense influence over the national economy and over prominent politicians, many of whom were personally indebted to the bank for loans. A talented banker but an inept politician, Biddle wielded his authority tactlessly and made enemies of both the "soft-money" men and "hard-money" advocates.

The issues were not by their nature necessarily sectional. Soft-money men, their interests best served by abundant paper currency, called for more notes from state banks. Many a Westerner could be found among their ranks, which included state bankers, land speculators, and small-business owners. On the other hand, hard-money advocates, who considered any currency other than gold and silver dishonest, consisted not merely of Southern and Western agrarians, but also of Eastern working men who resented being paid wages in paper of uncertain value. In general, however, the regional resentments growing from the bank's seemingly selfish behavior in the panic of 1819 fit comfortably with hard-money hostility to banks of any kind, state or federal, that issued paper. Both the West's common men and the South's wealthy planters tended to see banking as a parasitic activity.

Andrew Jackson, a Democrat sprung from common stock, came to the White House as their champion, the first president to be hailed by Americans as a "Westerner." The battle between Biddle and Jackson consumed much of the latter's presidency and nearly wrecked the American economy. From his first day in office, Jackson promised to veto any bill to recharter the bank. Biddle, encouraged by U.S. Senators DANIEL WEBSTER and HENRY CLAY, applied for a new charter before the old one had expired in order to make Jackson's veto an issue in his reelection. The recharter bill sailed through Congress in 1832; quickly exercising his veto, Jackson declared the bank a dangerous monopoly that profited the wealthy few. Webster and Clay made sure the bank charter became a central issue in that year's presidential election. They accused Jackson of seeking "to inflame the poor against the rich." The only trouble was that Jackson better understood the ordinary voters, their numbers swelled by the new states from the trans-Appalachian West. Reelected by a wide margin, he pressed his war against the bank, that "Hydra of corruption" as he called it, all the harder.

Now Jackson was the one who refused to wait for the bank to be rechartered, fearing that, given time, Biddle might simply buy a veto-proof majority in Congress. Shortly after the election, Jackson decided to deprive the bank of federal support by ceasing to use it as a depository for federal funds. He distributed money from federal revenues to numerous state institutions, which his critics called "pet banks." Biddle responded by calling in the bank's loans and contracting credit, both to protect himself and to create deliberately the kind of economic distress that would force the government to return deposits and renew the charter. State banks rushed in to fill the credit void and, especially in the West where they were all but unregulated, indulged in "wildcat financiering"—making risky loans without securing adequate collateral and issuing paper money backed by insufficient silver and gold reserves. By 1836, Biddle's bank was operating under a state charter, and the economy was seriously overheated. When Great Britain, hit by hard times, stopped buying American cotton just as cotton production from the newly developed Western lands greatly increased supply, the United States plunged into one of the worst depressions in its history.

Coming only two months after Jackson left office, the panic of 1837 only hardened Jacksonian Democrats in their hatred of banks. Despite the fact that the depression dragged on into the mid-1840s, hard-line Jacksonians refused to recharter a central bank. Indeed, most Westerners attributed the crisis to "overbanking" and "overtrading." Banks remained firmly in the hands of the states, and a few Western states abolished banking altogether. Throughout the South and West, Jacksonians established "free-banking" systems that allowed promoters to secure a bank charter without a special act of the legislature. In the banking chaos that followed, many Westerners became firmly convinced that no bank was trustworthy. And, indeed, few were, until the Civil War came along, and united against the South, the North and West passed the National Banking Act of 1863 in order to sell bonds to support the war effort.

Banking in the trans-Mississippi West

In large part, banking in the trans-Mississippi West developed after the National Banking Act, which cleared up much of the confusion and irregularity in the hodgepodge system of state banks, set up chartered banks that maintained reserves with the Treasury Department, rationalized the issuing of bank notes as legal tender, and subjected chartered banks to regular federal inspection. Thus, a number of Western states and territories never really had the chance to charter "wildcat" banks that freely floated their own bank notes. It was simply no longer possible to form local banks for the sole purpose of generating credit by issuing paper money. Indeed, most states in the West chartered banks to provide only basic financial services.

From the earliest days of the fur trade, trans-Mississippi communities, at least initially, needed currency more than they needed credit. In the mining camps, gold, gold dust, and even raw silver might serve as a temporary form of currency, but it was a difficult currency to use in transactions and a dangerous one to transfer. Middlemen sprang up—gold brokerage firms, stagecoach lines, even merchants—who accepted deposits of the precious metals and issued certificates in receipt. Such certificates of deposit operated as a medium of exchange, and hence those issuing them became de facto bankers. One firm in Denver actually minted coins and put them in circulation before a local bank opened to ease the currency problem. Still, these were only stopgap measures and did not prevent critical shortages. In San Francisco, for example, gold flowed in abundance from the mines, but there was no currency to exchange for dust or bullion, much to the chagrin of local merchants, who stood to make fortunes off supplying the miners and who needed to pay cash for goods from the East. Not surprisingly, banks began appearing in rapid order.

A Miners Bank opened in California in 1848. Seattle had a bank even though its population scarcely topped four hundred and transportation consisted of a single steamer that arrived once a week. Given the absence of incorporation laws, most Western banks were partnerships, and any merchant with a safe might launch a banking enterprise with his own capital and that of a group of partners. Seldom did the early local bankers turn to the East for capital, though they would not infrequently establish close connections with Eastern banks that could serve as conduits for currency. Bankers in Western towns knew their depositors by name. They belonged to the same civic organizations and churches as their customers and sent their children to the same local schools the children of their clients attended. Bankers such as WILLIAM CHAPMAN RALSTON, who cofounded the most significant house in SAN FRANCISCO, the Bank of California, in 1864, were typical. He launched first a small bank with friends and then built a reputation as a civic leader and sound businessman as he expanded his enterprise through friendships, community connections, and sheer energy. The community nature of local banking in the West helped to deflect some of the traditional distrust and hostility Westerners felt toward banks. In general, Westerners understood that the region's economy had to be based on more than bartering in trade goods and that they needed banks and bankers if they were to grow and prosper. What all of them—miners, farmers, merchants, builders, promoters, real-estate agents— wanted were sound banks and bankers they could respect since, lacking state or territorially chartered banks, a banker they could trust was the only hope depositors had in a freewheeling economy.

Even as the regional banking system expanded at an extraordinary pace after the Civil War, the trans-

Mississippi West as a whole was experiencing a rapid industrialization that began with the coming of the RAILROADS. Precisely because they were so expensive to build, the railroads became the first enterprises beyond the Mississippi to require extensive capital from outside the region. Even before the Civil War, the source of such capital was New York City, which had outstripped both Boston and Philadelphia as the center of American finance by the 1850s. Private investment firms, such as the House of Morgan, emerged to link American companies looking for funds with investors in the East and in Europe. Western railroads were mortgaged to New York financiers, and their stockholders and bondholders overwhelmingly resided outside the West. As the railroads developed a usable infrastructure, "foreign" capital flowed into the West's massive extractive industries—mining, lumber, wheat, and later oil—and created a boom-and-bust economy that was, if anything, more volatile than the economy originally tied to Western land speculation. And as the FINANCIAL PANICS struck and depressions followed with their bank collapses and mortgage foreclosures, historical resentments against central banks and Eastern capital resurfaced as a dislike of foreign investors and the "monied interests."

Some of the resentment took root locally as well. In many Western towns, bankers and merchants formed both the financial and social elite. Not a few were the sons, sons-in-law, or nephews of Eastern bankers or merchants sent West to open branches and oversee local investments. German immigrants made up an unusually large proportion of the merchant and banking class, and some of them were German Jews. Boasting European connections and sporting lines of credit from continental banking houses, these recent arrivals enjoyed the same access to capital and high social status that the other bankers and merchants did. Miners, farmers, ranchers, and professionals frequently resented the merchant and banking class as a whole and the "foreigners" in particular. Since the elite often controlled transportation, consumers blamed high prices on class collusion rather than on the relatively high cost of doing business in the West.

Strains became evident especially after the depressions of 1873 and 1893 led farmers and many others to join the mining interests in calling for "free silver," the creation of currency inflation and lower interest rates by freeing silver coinage from a set ratio of value to gold. Western bankers were placed in a dilemma. Ideologically committed, like the national banking community, to the gold standard, they could not satisfy the credit demands of their customers without becoming little more than suppliers of currency. By the late 1880s at least, regional banks had become a major source of credit. And, as banking houses with connections in the East and abroad were created, not only San Francisco, but PORTLAND, HOUSTON, AND SALT LAKE CITY grew as centers of Western finance.

Still, little of POPULISM's venom was directed at local banks, except for a certain amount of racial scapegoating that betrayed the "nativist" strain in the radical movement. Mostly the antibanking rhetoric was aimed at the monied interests in the East and only underscored the West's ambivalent attitude toward banking and speculation. The West experimented with usury laws and the suspension of payments on public debts—even its outright repudiation—since such debts were usually held by concerns in the East or on the continent. Yet, outside capital was often welcomed, even sought out, if it went into the financing of internal improvements and the building of towns and cities. And although Western states and territories generally favored government aid for building railroads, they also sought to regulate those lines and lower their rates.

Some regional bankers were able to play on those ambivalent attitudes and on Western industry's naked reliance on Eastern banking and finance to build up their own houses. Regional financial leaders, such as Jesse Jones of Houston, Marriner Eccles of Utah, and perhaps most importantly AMADEO PETER GIANNINI, chafed under what they considered the West's colonial status, created by its subservience to Eastern finance. Giannini built his Bank of Italy into a branch empire that by 1929 controlled 40 percent of California's bank capital. Renamed the Bank of America in 1930, the bank itself might well be viewed as an instrument of California's colonizing of much of the West. With the coming of the Great Depression in the 1930s, many of these bankers were able to use the antibanking sentiment typical of the West to begin, with help from the FEDERAL GOVERNMENT, to free themselves entirely of Eastern financial dominance.

—*Charles Phillips*

SEE ALSO: Agrarianism; Booms; Currency and Silver as Western Political Issues

SUGGESTED READING:

Buenger, Walter L., and Joseph A. Pratt. *But Also Good Business: Texas Commerce Banks and the Financing of Houston Texas, 1886–1986.* College Station, Tex., 1986.

Doti, Lynne Pierson, and Larry Schweikart. *Banking in the American West: From the Gold Rush to Deregulation.* Norman, Okla., 1991.

Schweikart, Larry. *A History of Banking in Arizona.* Tucson, Ariz., 1982.

Woods, L. Nilton. *Sometimes the Books Froze: Wyoming's Economy and Its Bankers.* Boulder, Colo., 1985.

BANK OF AMERICA (CALIFORNIA)

SEE: Giannini, Amadeo Peter

BANKS, NATHANIEL PRENTISS

Politician and Civil War General Nathaniel P. Banks (1816–1894) was born in Waltham, Massachusetts. An unsuccessful candidate for the Massachusetts legislature in seven campaigns, he was finally elected in 1849 and then served one term in the U.S. Congress before winning election as Massachusetts governor in 1858.

An important Republican ally of President Abraham Lincoln, Banks received a commission in the Union Army as a major general at the outbreak of the CIVIL WAR. He faced Stonewall Jackson in the Shenandoah Campaign of 1862 and lost battles to him at Front Royal, Winchester, and Cedar Mountain. In the fall of 1862, Banks was made commander of the Department of the Gulf, based in New Orleans. His principal mission was to disable Confederate traffic on the Mississippi River, although a campaign to capture Texas occupied his first months in the West. His maneuvers to capture the Texas Gulf Coast failed, but he successfully captured Port Hudson on July 9, 1863. His 1864 Red River Campaign was not successful, however, and he was replaced by EDWARD RICHARD SPRING CANBY.

After military service, Banks returned to the U.S. Congress and was reelected each term, except one, until 1877. A final term in Congress, from 1889 to 1891 ended his career in public life.

—*Patrick H. Butler, III*

SUGGESTED READING:

Josephy, Alvin M., Jr. *The Civil War in the American West.* New York, 1991.

BANNOCK INDIANS

SEE: Native American Peoples: Peoples of the Great Basin

BAPTISTS

SEE: Protestants

BARANOV, ALEKSANDR

Russian fur trader and first chief manager of the RUSSIAN-AMERICAN COMPANY (RAC) Aleksandr Baranov (1746–1819) was born in Kargopol, Russia. He was an established fur trader in Siberia by the late 1780s. In 1790, he agreed to manage the Shelikhov-Golikov fur company in Russian America (Alaska) and sailed for Kodiak Island. With firm discipline and by improving relations with natives, he extended the Shelikhov trading territory to Prince William Sound, to Yakutat Bay, and in 1799, to Sitka, a fortified settlement burned by the Tlingit Indians in 1802. That year, he learned that the Shelikhov interests had secured a trade monopoly in Russian America, had been chartered as the RAC in 1799, and had named him chief manager. With the help of the Russian warship *Neva*, Baranov recaptured Sitka in 1804 and made it the capital of the RAC.

Constantly in search of ways to feed and supply the colony, Baranov made agreements with American fur traders plying North Pacific waters. He loaned Aleut hunters to American ship captain Joe O'Cain and also depended on American ships to carry RAC furs to Canton, where the Chinese forbade direct trade with Russia. He tried unsuccessfully to secure a supply contract with the Astoria colony but did establish the Fort Ross settlement in northern California as an agricultural outpost in 1812.

After years of declining health, Baranov was relieved of his duties as chief manager in 1818. En route to Russia, he became ill and died at sea in April 1819.

—*John S. Whitehead*

SEE ALSO: Alaskan Exploration; Exploration: Russian Expeditions; Fur Trade

SUGGESTED READING:

Chevigny, Hector. *Russian America: The Great Alaskan Adventure*. New York, 1965.

Pierce, Richard A. *Russian America: A Biographical Dictionary*. Fairbanks, Alaska, 1990.

BARBED WIRE

An innovative fencing element, barbed wire was both an agent of change and a symbol of change in the West. It played an important technological role in altering the environment and transformed the CATTLE INDUSTRY from open-range practices to enclosed husbandry methods, thus contributing to the predominance of the twentieth-century stock farmer.

For thousands of years, people erected walls and fences of natural materials to mark property lines, protect crops, or contain livestock. In New England, farmers built walls of stone pulled from the fields, while those in the forested South and Midwest used cleared trees to make split-rail fences. On the prairies and plains of the West, however, such natural materials were unavailable, and settlers were forced to devise new means of enclosing land.

During the 1850s and 1860s, Nebraska farmers tried "ditching and embanking," a process that created earthen barriers some three feet high. Impractical on a large scale, such "fencing" consumed too much labor to build and maintain. More widespread was hedge-row fencing, the use of thorny trees like honey locust, mesquite, and Osage orange. Such "live fencing" made practical boundaries, fended off stray livestock, and served as a windbreak when mature. Although hedges consumed tillable land and were susceptible to prairie fires, they were used fairly extensively on the eastern Great Plains and in the Southwest.

During the 1840s and 1850s, farmers stretched smooth, drawn wire between posts to protect crops in the East and Midwest but with little success. Single-strand wire sagged in summer heat, broke in winter cold, and made little impression on roving cattle or hogs. Practical experience with thorny hedges probably

Aleksandr Baranov. *Courtesy Library of Congress.*

inspired the creation of "armored fencing," which appeared in the late 1860s and early 1870s. The first attempts incorporated wooden slats fixed with sharp metal points or nails that attached to the horizontal elements of the fence.

The best-known armored fence attachment was patented by Henry Rose of DeKalb County, Illinois, in 1873. While impractical, it inspired two inventive DeKalb men to perfect the concept using separate, shaped wire barbs fixed on lengths of drawn wire stretched between vertical posts—the barbed wire fence. Lumberman Jacob Haish received the first patent for practical barbed wire early in 1874. Farmer Joseph Glidden, considered "the father of barbed wire," developed a better design using shaped barbs fixed on a twisted, double-strand wire. He received patent rights later in 1874 and was joined by hardware manufacturer and entrepreneur Isaac Ellwood in forming the Barb Fence Company of DeKalb.

The practical applications of barbed-wire fencing were obvious, particularly for the West, and many inventor-entrepreneurs sought a share of the market through exclusive patent designs. Some of the most prolific were T. V. Allis, Jacob and Warren Brinkerhoff, E. M. Crandal, Jacob Haish, Hiram Scutt, and A. J. Upham, who among them registered 69 patents covering 148 variations. More than 350 unique patents were awarded in the United States between 1875 and 1890 covering vicious, obvious, and modified wires. Comparatively few designs proved successful. Certainly the most practical was Joseph Glidden's basic Winner wire, which was manufactured in more than 30 variations and remained a standard pattern.

Competition among barbed-wire inventors and manufacturers fostered prolonged legal battles. Isaac Ellwood of DeKalb and wire magnate Charles Washburn of Washburn and Moen Manufacturing Company in Worcester, Massachusetts, teamed up in 1876—with control of Glidden's basic patent—to monopolize the barbed-wire market. Through control of prior-use patents and licensing arrangements with small manufacturers, they succeeded in eliminating most "moonshine" wire production and "bootleg" sales by 1880. Yet, litigation remained constant until 1892, when the U.S. Supreme Court ruled in favor of the design preeminence of Glidden's Winner wire and its farsighted patent holders.

Although barbed wire appeared at the right time and place, it met with early resistance in the West, its greatest potential marketplace. Some felt the product was inhumane to livestock. Cattlemen, in particular, feared that livestock cut by barbs would be infected with screwworms, although cattle in fact quickly acclimated and avoided the wire. More crucial, ranchers

and drovers rightly believed that enclosure of free grass and WATER on public lands would end the open-range cattle culture and promote an influx of small farmers. Others simply resented the potential obstruction of travel or the influence of "Yankee inventions."

Actually, more pervasive forces in the West—the coming of the RAILROADS, the resulting increase of farm settlement, the damaging effects of overgrazing, and the rapid capitalization of ranching—already were ensuring the ultimate ascendancy of barbed wire. Between ranchers and farmers, the issue was control—free land versus enclosure—and both parties used barbed wire as an "improvement" for exclusion. Controversy and conflict were inevitable.

Texas first attempted unsuccessfully to exclude the wire as inhumane and obstructive. In the early 1880s, the state's free-grass element initiated a series of fence-cutting wars that resulted in VIOLENCE, property destruction, and legislative acts making fence cutting a felony. On federally owned public lands, in contrast, fencing was outlawed in 1885 and range improvements by cattlemen, such as those erected in the Indian Territory, were ordered removed.

Despite these conflicts, the market for barbed wire boomed. While Midwestern farmers bought quantities of wire, the bulk of production went to ranchers, railroads, and grangers in the trans-Mississippi West. During the mid-1880s, the three-million-acre XIT RANCH in Texas was enclosed and partitioned with fifteen hundred miles of four-strand fencing amounting to six thousand miles of barbed wire. Railroads were among the largest consumers in the 1880s and 1890s, enclosing thousands of miles of right-of-way across the West. While in 1875 some three hundred tons of barbed wire were sold, by 1880 the figure exceeded forty thousand tons. By 1890, consumption was measured in miles and rail-car loads instead of tons.

A crucial technology in the settling of the Great Plains, barbed wire was a catalyst for new laws affecting travel, property, and water rights. Its influence helped transform the West.

—*Richard C. Rattenbury*

SUGGESTED READING:

Campbell, Robert O., and Vernon L. Allison. *Barriers: An Encyclopedia of United States Barbed Fence Patents*. Denver, 1986.

Clifton, Robert T. *Barbs, Prongs, Points, Prickers, & Stickers*. Norman, Okla., 1970.

McCallum, Henry D., and Frances T. McCallum. *The Wire That Fenced the West*. Norman, Okla., 1965.

McClure, C. Boone. "History of the Manufacture of Barbed Wire." *Panhandle-Plains Historical Review* 31 (1958): 1–113.

Webb, Walter Prescott. *The Great Plains*. Boston, 1931.

BARBONCITO (NAVAJO)

A Navajo ceremonial singer, Barboncito (ca. 1820–1871) was a war chief during the Navajo War of 1863 to 1866. He was born at Canyon de Chelly (in present-day Arizona). Barboncito's brother, Delgadito, was also a leader in the Navajo War.

Barboncito was inclined to cooperate with the whites and signed a treaty of friendship with Colonel ALEXANDER WILLIAM DONIPHAN during the UNITED STATES–MEXICAN WAR. Relative peace endured until April 1860, when soldiers killed some Navajo horses during a dispute over grazing rights in the vicinity of Fort Defiance, Arizona. Barboncito participated with MANUELITO in an attack on the fort, but by 1862, Barboncito and Delgadito had become leaders of the Navajo faction favoring peace. The following year, however, General JAMES H. CARLETON set as a condition of peace the removal of the Navajos to the desolate and much-hated Bosque Redondo Reservation. With Delgadito, Barboncito joined Manuelito in renewed rebellion, only to be captured in September 1864 by Colonel CHRISTOPHER HOUSTON ("KIT") CARSON.

Forced to retire to the reservation, Barboncito led some five hundred followers in a June 1865 escape, rejoined Manuelito, resumed fighting, and surrendered a second time in November 1866. Two years later, Barboncito, Manuelito, and other chiefs traveled to Washington, D.C., where they met with President Andrew Johnson to describe the intolerable conditions at the Bosque Redondo. The meeting resulted in the formation of a peace commission, whose members visited the Bosque and confirmed the "absolute poverty and despair" of the place. Accordingly, a new reservation was created in the Chuska Mountains. Barboncito was among the chiefs who signed a June 1, 1868, treaty and agreed to retire to the reservation. He died there three years later.

—*Alan Axelrod*

SEE ALSO: Navajo Wars

SUGGESTED READING:
Axelrod, Alan. *Chronicle of the Indian Wars: From Colonial Times to Wounded Knee.* New York, 1993.

BARNARD, CATHERINE ANN (KATE)

Reformer and politician Catherine Ann (Kate) Barnard (1875–1930) was born to Irish immigrant parents in Geneva, Nebraska. After her mother's death, her father moved her to an isolated homestead near Newalla, in the Oklahoma Territory, in 1889. Living alone in a frame shanty in fierce poverty, she held down the claim while her father practiced law in Oklahoma City. When her father secured the claim, he moved Kate to Oklahoma City, where she attended St. Joseph's Academy.

In 1904, Barnard represented the Oklahoma Territory at the St. Louis World's Fair. Inspired by the speeches of leading exponents of PROGRESSIVISM, she returned to Oklahoma determined to correct the deteriorating conditions in her own city. She assumed leadership of the struggling Provident Association of Oklahoma City and made her home a distribution center for food and clothing for needy families. Using the organization as a base of operations, Barnard organized and led labor unions for women and unskilled workers and formed chapters of the Child Labor League across the territory.

In 1906, Barnard caught the attention of major Democratic party leaders at the Shawnee Convention meeting, which hammered out a list of twenty-four demands to be incorporated into the new state constitution. Her compulsory-education and child-labor planks were included with other progressive reforms such as the secret ballot, eight-hour workday, and mining controls. At the state constitutional convention, Barnard's supporters created the position of commissioner of charities and corrections specifically for her leadership. She won that office in 1907, polling more votes than any other candidate. While she became the first woman elected to statewide office, she did not support women's suffrage.

As commissioner of charities and corrections, Barnard inspected the jails, asylums, and orphanages of the new state and publicized the filth, inefficiency, and brutality she found there. She initiated legislation and crusaded for increased appropriations to create modern, humane facilities. In 1909, she received national attention for her exposure of conditions in the Kansas prison system that housed Oklahoma inmates. Other states soon sought her advice on penal reform.

Barnard's efforts on behalf of Indian orphans alienated her political supporters and led to her forced retirement from public life. After she used her office to prosecute cases involving the flagrant theft of Indian lands from orphans who had been sent to live with unscrupulous guardians by Oklahoma probate courts, the legislature cut her appropriations and investigated her affairs. Broken in health and spirit, she made only a brief fight for her office through a People's lobby; after 1915, she became a virtual recluse.

While living in an Oklahoma City hotel and writing a history of the state, Barnard died, embittered and alone. Her accomplishments in an all-male electorate qualify her as one of the most important figures in early Oklahoma politics and the driving force behind the social-justice reform of Oklahoma progressivism.

—*Linda Reese*

SUGGESTED READING:

Bryant, Keith L., Jr. "Kate Barnard, Organized Labor, and Social Justice in Oklahoma during the Progressive Era." *The Journal of Southern History* 35 (1969): 148–151.

Goble, Danney. *Progressive Oklahoma, The Making of a New Kind of State.* Norman, Okla., 1980.

BARRIOS

The notion of the barrio is an old one, born of a marriage between Spanish and pre-Columbian cultures. The Aztecs lived in communal clans and called a group of extended families who were related to each other by blood or marriage a *calpulli*. When Spanish conqueror Hernán Cortés arrived at the Aztec capital of Tenochtitlán in 1519, the city was made up of more than sixty *calpullis,* and the Spaniards dubbed these family neighborhoods "barrios" since they resembled certain urban neighborhoods called that back in Spain. During the course of the Spanish colonization of Mexico, *barrio* came loosely to designate a section of a city or pueblo, usually in which the working class lived. In New Spain's northern reaches, the frontier regions of upper Mexico and Alta California that would eventually become part of the United States, Spanish-speaking pioneers often used the word to mean the areas where the Indians lived. Many of the pueblos in New Mexico and Northern Mexico had Indian barrios. In Santa Fe, for example, the Nahua-speaking Indians who had accompanied JUAN DE OÑATE's 1598 expedition lived in a barrio, and in the California pueblo of LOS ANGELES, the nearby village of the Yangna Indians may have been considered a barrio.

After the United States–Mexican War in the late 1840s, the term *barrio* north of the new border came to signify that part of town where the residents spoke only Spanish. Before the Anglo conquest, the Mexican

Los Angeles's early barrio, Sonora Town about 1870. Photograph by William Godfrey. *Courtesy Los Angeles County Museum of Natural History.*

elite in the North American provinces—the Californios and the *ricos* of New Mexico—tended to hold themselves aloof from their government centered in far away Mexico City. They engaged in a growing trade with the United States and intermarried with Anglo merchants and adventurers, who took up residence in their pueblos and often adopted their religion and their social habits. After the Norte Americanos annexed the Southwest and California lands, however, many residents began to look toward Mexico as a homeland and, in step with the mass of poorer Mexicans living in the United States, to develop a sense of ethnicity. Economically, the Mexican Americans suffered sharp declines in property holding and were more and more excluded from the growth of the urban American West. The new American arrivals broke down the traditional rancho economy by smothering it with new laws, extortionate legal fees, excessive taxes, and a racist-inspired violence. Fewer and fewer Mexican Americans found the new American West a place in which they could live comfortably and raise their families, and large numbers of them left to "return" to a homeland in which many of them had not been born.

Still, so long as the Mexican American populations of the Southwest and California significantly outnumbered the Anglos, segregation was primarily social, not geographic. As late as 1860, for example, Pueblo Los Angeles was divided into rich and poor areas rather than into Spanish-speaking and English-speaking districts. Wealthy Californios owned town houses around the pueblo's plaza while the working class, the poor, and recent Mexican immigrants lived in a barrio north of First Street. The area was called by the Anglos "Sonora Town" because so many of its early transient inhabitants had come from the Mexican province of Sonora during the gold-rush days. By the mid-1860s, the Californios had largely abandoned the plaza as the barrio expanded along with the American economy and its economic dislocations. The plaza was now a slum that included a Chinese ghetto the Americans called "Nigger Alley," where saloons and brothels—by official decree limited to Sonora Town—abounded. Mexican American ranchers and ranch hands, cheated of their land or (later) ruined by an economic bust, moved into the barrio, as did Mexican and Mexican American railroad workers building the Southern Pacific and Los Angeles Independent Railroad.

How much of the trend toward concentration and segregation was forced and how much of it was self-imposed is unclear. Probably it was a mixture of both, a complex matter of economic exclusion, racial segregation, poverty, transience, cultural distress, pride, language, a close-knit family life, and ethnic solidarity. Spanish-speaking immigrants from rural areas of California, the Southwest, and Mexico poured into the urban American barrios. Unaccustomed to urban life and speaking little if any English, they depended heavily on already established Mexican Americans and were convinced that it was easier—and safer—to look for jobs, find places to live, and make friends in the barrio. In that sense at least, the creation of the barrio was a positive accomplishment for the Mexican Americans; the barrio provided the dispossessed and the poor with a geographic identity, a sense of tradition, and some security from the social and economic turmoil of rapidly industrializing post–Civil War America. On the other hand, the growth of barrios all but ensured an even more rapid isolation from the political, cultural, spiritual, and economic opportunities America offered its Anglo citizenry. Thus, while the barrio provided family warmth and brotherhood, it was also a center of poverty, crime, illness, exploitation, and despair.

Within the barrio itself, Hispanic traditions and culture soon began to change. Extended families gave way to more fluid arrangements as young Mexican American women lived in common-law marriages or intermarried with Anglos. Others married later and had fewer children. As the "nuclear" family came to dominate the domestic life of Spanish-speaking people, the traditional family and the Catholic church ceased to be the main institutions of socialization. Many sent their children to public schools where they learned to speak English, and more Mexican Americans learned to read and write. Spanish-language newspapers appeared to serve the new ethnically concentrated readership, and Mexican American political and social clubs sprang up. Both the newspapers and the clubs provided the barrio with an internal life that was separate from Anglo-American society and which gave meaning to communities wracked by "anti-Mexican" violence and discrimination. In the barrios' cantinas, on their street corners, and around their plazas, citizens organized celebrations of patriotic Mexican holidays while Chicano youths sang heart-rending songs about the legendary deeds of quasi-revolutionary *banditos*. And even as the Spanish-speaking in the barrios turned their eyes nostalgically toward Mexico, they began more to resemble their Anglo neighbors in dress and manner than their Mexican cousins. The wealthy few among them built Victorian mansions and joined literary clubs; the toiling masses wore work denims and took the streetcar. Many anglicized their names, and most spoke a dialect of Spanish laced with Anglo words and phrases.

By the 1880s, America's Spanish-speaking population by and large lived in ethnic enclaves built of adobe and surrounded by Anglo-American suburbs built of brick and wood. The Anglos found the barrios quaint—

sleepy little Mexican villages squat in the middle of their frontier cities and towns. Although many barrio residents were eager to participate in the larger society, Anglos tended to see them not as Americans but as Mexicans, "foreigners" doomed to disappear as had the Indians. Anglos justified the poverty and the segregation of the Mexican Americans by pointing to their refusal to speak or act like "Americans." Anglos closed their eyes to the fact that barrio residents, isolated by Anglo economic and social prejudice, could hardly afford to live anywhere else or act much differently. A few succeeded in "escaping," in meeting the Anglo requirements for and definitions of success, but the masses, labeled a people of color, remained aliens in their own country. The barrios also became a destination for newly arrived Mexican immigrants, especially after the Mexican Revolution in 1910, when hundreds of thousands, lured by promises of jobs and a better life, moved to the United States. They arrived in the old barrios and expanded their borders, and they have been coming ever since to settle, if only for a short time, as they take up menial jobs, move into cheap houses, and make fleeting friendships, before moving on to another barrio.

U.S. barrios grew as a response to forces unleashed by the Anglo conquest and the BOOMS and busts of capitalist America's market economy. Faced with accelerating commercial and technological change, the Spanish-speaking people turned to the culture and traditions they had developed in pre-conquest times—Indian, Spanish, and Mexican traditions that they used to direct them in a new era. But those old ways proved in the long run unreliable for dealing with the new social order, and during some fifty years of confused grappling with Anglo-American rule, the older "Hispanic" culture of the Southwest and California lost its ability to infuse meaning into everyday life. In its place grew a new ethnic culture, one that fit better the changed world. The barrio was the spawning ground of this culture and would remain so for much of the twentieth century.

—*Charles Phillips*

SEE ALSO: Mexican Settlement; Santa Barbara, California

SUGGESTED READING:

Camarillo, Albert. *Chicanos in a Changing Society: From Mexican Pueblos to American Barrios, 1848–1930.* Cambridge, Mass., 1979.

Griswold del Castillo, Richard. *The Los Angeles Barrio, 1850–1890.* Berkeley, Calif., 1979.

———. "Tucsonenses and Angelenos: A Socio Economic Study of Two Mexican American Barrios." *Journal of the West* 18 (July 1979) 58–66.

BARTLETT, JOHN RUSSELL

Artist and ethnologist John Russell Bartlett (1805–1886) served as commissioner of the Mexican Boundary Survey after the UNITED STATES–MEXICAN WAR. Born in Providence, Rhode Island, he was part owner of a New York City bookstore beginning in 1836. During his time at the store, he sharpened his interests in ethnology and languages and published *The Progress of Ethnology* (1847) and *Dictionary of Americanisms* (1848). When for health and financial reasons he sought other work, well-placed friends advanced his name for the commissionership of the Mexican Boundary Survey.

The Treaty of Guadalupe Hidalgo at the end of the United States–Mexican War called for a joint Mexican-American commission to draw the exact boundary between the two countries. Realizing the job on the commission would allow him to pursue his scholarly interests, Bartlett accepted the sensitive political position on June 19, 1850, and the field survey began the following spring. Bartlett and Mexican Commissioner García Conde determined the initial point of the boundary on the Rio Grande and the subsequent westward line at 32° 22'. Their decision led to much controversy since that line gave Mexico the Mesilla Valley, particularly desirable for the southern route of a transcontinental railroad. Bartlett's critics contended that he had surrendered a sizable chunk of territory, roughly 50 by 190 miles. The matter festered until the United States bought the parcel of land in the GADSDEN PURCHASE of 1853.

In the field, Bartlett exercised his artistic skills in a remarkable series of drawings and water colors. He collected specimens of plants and animals, studied the languages and cultures of Native American tribes, and took some of the earliest measurements of Southwestern archaeological ruins. The route surveyed for the boundary lay up the Rio Grande to Dona Ana, then to the Gila, and down that waterway to its confluence with the Colorado.

Anti-Bartlett factions rose both among the survey party and in Washington. Southern Democrats accused Bartlett, a Northern Whig, of selling short the Southern cause, and Bartlett was removed shortly after the Democrats took control of the government under Franklin Pierce. WILLIAM HEMSLEY EMORY of the Corps of Topographical Engineers, a Southerner who had served under and disagreed with Bartlett, was placed in charge of the survey and on its completion was granted most of the credit for the work. Without government assistance, Bartlett published his own *Personal Narrative*, a vivid, literate account.

—*Robert V. Hine*

SEE ALSO: Transcontinental Railroad Surveys

SUGGESTED READING:
Bartlett, John R. *Personal Narrative of Explorations and Incidents... Connected with the United States and Mexican Boundary Commission. . . .* 2 vols. New York, 1854. Reprint. Chicago, 1965.
Hine, Robert V. *Bartlett's West: Drawing the Mexican Boundary.* New Haven, Conn., 1968.

BASCOM AFFAIR

SEE: Apache Wars

BASQUE RANCHERS

SEE: Sheep Ranching

BASS, CHARLOTTA SPEARS

Charlotta Spears Bass (1879–1969) was the crusading editor and publisher of the Los Angeles–based *California Eagle,* the West Coast's oldest African American newspaper. She was also the first African American woman to run for the office of U.S. vice-president. As editor of the *Eagle* from 1912 to 1951, Bass led campaigns against SEGREGATION and discrimination in Los Angeles voting procedures, employment practices, and housing.

Born in Sumter, South Carolina, Charlotta Spears moved to Providence, Rhode Island, to be with her brother. She attended public schools and went to Pembroke College for a short time. She also took classes from the University of Los Angeles and correspondence courses from Columbia University. She began working for the *Eagle* shortly after moving to Los Angeles in September 1910. In 1912, when John J. Neimore, founder of the *Eagle,* died, Captain G. W. Hawkins bought the newspaper and turned it over to her.

Soon afterwards, she married Joseph Blackburn Bass, a founder of the *Topeka Plaindealer.* He became editor of the *Eagle,* and she became managing editor. When her husband died in the early 1930s, she continued to manage the paper on her own.

Long affiliated with the Republic party, Bass served as Western regional director of Wendell Willkie's 1940 presidential campaign. In 1948, however, she became a supporter of HENRY AGARD WALLACE and the Progressive party. In 1952, she was the Progressive party's candidate for U.S. vice-president on the ticket with Vincent Hallinan.

In 1960, Bass published *Forty Years: Memoirs from the Pages of a Newspaper.* The book describes the relationship between the *California Eagle* and the community it served and is incidentally an autobiography.

In the last years of her life, Bass settled in Elsinore, California. The *California Eagle* ceased operations in 1965.

—*Mary Tyler and Sarah Cooper*

SEE ALSO: African Americans

SUGGESTED READING:
Bass, Charlotta Spears. *Forty Years: Memoirs from the Pages of a Newspaper.* 1960.

BASS, SAM

Before starting his career as a bank and train robber, Sam Bass (1851–1878) was a farmer, teamster, gambler, and saloon owner. Born near Mitchell, Indiana, he was raised by his uncle after his parents died. In 1869, he left home, and after a brief stay in Missouri, he moved to Mississippi and worked in a sawmill.

By 1870, Bass had arrived in Denton, Texas, where he worked as a teamster and hired hand for Sheriff W. F. Egan. He was a good worker, made friends easily, and seemed to save his money.

But his life changed in 1874 after Bass purchased a race horse, known as "the Denton mare." Upon winning a number of races, Bass left his jobs. He then joined up with Joel Collins, a small-time crook. In 1876, the two men drove some cattle to Deadwood in the Dakota Territory. For a short period, they ran a freight business, but they soon grew tired of the work and sold the business to open a gambling saloon.

Sam Bass, standing at left, poses with J. E. Gardner, also standing, and Joe Collins and his gun-toting brother, Joel. *Courtesy Western History Collections, University of Oklahoma Library.*

After losing most of their money in a mining venture, Bass and Collins organized a band of robbers. Within a short time, they held up seven stages in the Black Hills region. On the night of September 18, 1877, near Big Springs, Nebraska, the gang robbed a Union Pacific train and took more than sixty thousand dollars. Shortly thereafter, three members of the gang, including Collins, were killed by posses.

Returning to Texas, Bass organized another gang of outlaws and started to hold up trains around Dallas, but his luck began to run out. Texas was filled with stories about Bass, as the press exhibited an inordinate interest in his exploits. The Texas Rangers launched a manhunt for Bass. Suffering losses in his gang, he was joined by outlaw Jim Murphy, who had agreed to work undercover for the rangers in exchange for dropping criminal charges against him. In July 1878, Bass planned to rob the Round Rock, Texas, bank. Murphy revealed the plan to the authorities, and as the gang rode into town, a gunfight erupted. Bass was shot but escaped. He was later found mortally wounded. Two days later, this good-natured badman died on July 21, 1878, his twenty-seventh birthday.

—*Richard A. Van Orman*

SEE ALSO: Social Banditry; Violence

SUGGESTED READING:
Gard, Wayne. *Sam Bass*. Boston, 1936.
Smith, Helena Huntington. "Sam Bass and the Myth Machine." *American West* (January 1970): 31–35.
Webb, Walter Prescott. *The Texas Rangers*. Boston, 1935.

BAUSMAN, WILLIAM

Journalist and frontiersman William Bausman (1820–1893) was born in Allegheny County, Pennsylvania, and received his education at William and Mary College in Virginia. At the age of thirty, he ventured west, spending two years with JOHN RUSSELL BARTLETT on a survey to determine the border between the United States and Mexico. Arriving in Sacramento after the expedition, Bausman tried his luck at gold mining but lasted only a few months. In 1855, he settled in San Francisco and became editor of the *Daily Sun*. In subsequent years, he served as the editor of a variety of newspapers in the Bay Area: the *Maryville Appeal, San Francisco Transcript,* and the *San Francisco Call.* He was credited with having written *The Idle and Industrious Miner* (1854) and a five-act play, *Early California,* which closed in San Francisco after only sixteen performances.

—*Patricia Hogan*

John Robert Baylor in 1858. *Courtesy Western History Collections, University of Oklahoma Library.*

BAYLOR, JOHN ROBERT

Texas Indian fighter and Confederate officer John Robert Baylor (1822–1894) was born in Paris, Kentucky. He attended school in Cincinnati and moved to Fayette County, Texas, in 1840. In 1844, he married Emily Hanna, and the couple had ten children.

While living in Texas, Baylor was elected to the state legislature in 1851 and was admitted to the bar in 1853. In 1855, he was appointed U.S. Indian agent at the Clear Fork Comanche Reservation in northwestern Texas. After a conflict with his supervisor, he left the Indian Service in 1857. He then took up ranching near the reservation. His experiences as an agent embittered him to the Comanches, and he became a leader in the movement to expel them from Texas. In 1859, he led an attack on the reservation, and after it was moved to Fort Sill, Oklahoma, he used his newspaper, *The White Man,* published at Weatherford, Texas, to encourage hostility by Euro-Americans toward all Native Americans.

When Texas seceded from the Union, Baylor became a lieutenant colonel in the Second Regiment of the Texas Mounted Volunteers. He and his troops occupied federal posts between San Antonio and El Paso. He launched a successful attack on the Union post at Fort Fillmore, New Mexico, and by August 1861, when he proclaimed all of New Mexico south of the thirty-fourth parallel to be the Confederate Territory of Arizona under his governorship, he had cleared that vast region of federal troops. He envisioned a Confederate conquest of California and northwestern Mexico, but in November 1862, Confederate President Jefferson Davis stripped him of his rank and office because he had ordered Confederate troops in Arizona to exterminate or enslave Apaches. He returned to Texas and in 1863 was elected to the Confederate Congress, in which he remained an advocate of Western military action.

After the CIVIL WAR, Baylor moved to San Antonio. He pursued the Democratic party's nomination for governor in 1873 but was unsuccessful. In 1878, he moved to a ranch at Montell in Uvalde County and lived there until his death.

—*Lonn Taylor*

SUGGESTED READING:

Baylor, George Wythe. *John Robert Baylor.* Tucson, Ariz., 1966.

Thompson, Jerry Don. *Colonel John Robert Baylor: Texas Indian Fighter and Confederate Soldier.* Hillsboro, Tex., 1971.

BEALE, EDWARD FITZGERALD (NED)

Naval officer, frontiersman, surveyor general of Western lands, Indian agent, and diplomat Edward Fitzgerald (Ned) Beale (1822–1893) was born in the District of Columbia. He attended Georgetown College for a few years and in 1836 entered the United States Navy at the age of fourteen as an "acting midshipman." After visiting several ports, he was assigned to the equivalent of today's Annapolis, from which he graduated in 1842.

Posted to California in 1846, he joined the command of Commodore ROBERT F. STOCKTON on the eve of the UNITED STATES–MEXICAN WAR. In perhaps the best-known aspect of his life, Beale served with United

Edward Fitzgerald Beale. *Courtesy Decatur House Museum, a property of the National Trust for Historic Preservation.*

States land forces in California. After the besieged Brigadier General STEPHEN WATTS KEARNY suffered a defeat at the Battle of San Pasqual on December 8 and 9, 1846, Beale slipped through the Mexican lines with the frontier scout CHRISTOPHER HOUSTON ("KIT") CARSON and a Delaware Indian. Risking his life, Beale reported Kearny's dilemma to Stockton, who sent a relief force to the general from San Diego.

After the conquest of California, Beale became a dispatch-bearer to Washington and made six coast-to-coast journeys. In mid-1848, he brought back East the first news of the discovery of gold in the Sierra Nevada foothills. He resigned from the navy in 1851 and became the manager of Aspinwall transport and mercantile interests as well as a land agent for Stockton, now a civilian. In subsequent years, he speculated in real estate with JOHN CHARLES FRÉMONT, one of the principals in California's conquest.

By 1852, President Millard Fillmore appointed Beale the first superintendent of Indian affairs for California and Nevada. Office work did not appeal to him, and at the behest of Missouri Senator THOMAS HART BENTON, Beale undertook an unofficial railroad survey that ran from Westport Landing on the Missouri River to Los Angeles. In 1856, after he resigned his Indian post, he was named brigadier general of California's state militia. He also helped organize a camel corps in the arid Southwest under Secretary of War Jefferson Davis.

Less well known are Beale's activities as surveyor general of both California and Nevada. Appointed in 1861 by President Abraham Lincoln, Beale remained in that office during the Civil War. Afterwards, he settled on the huge Tejon Ranch near present-day Bakersfield and surveyed thousands of acres of land thrown open for settlement by the federal government.

Beale's last official assignment was in 1876 and 1877 as minister to Austria in the administration of President Ulysses S. Grant. In the 1880s, he cofounded the Maritime Canal Company of Nicaragua. He died at Decatur House, near the White House in Washington, D. C.

Although sometimes awkward in personal relations, emotional, and blunt, Beale tackled a variety of jobs in times of great stress. His varied career paralleled the transition of the Far West from wilderness to American empire.

—*Andrew Rolle*

SEE ALSO: Camels; Transcontinental Railroad Surveys

SUGGESTED READING:

Briggs, Carl, and Clyde Trudell. *Quarterdeck and Saddlehorn: The Story of Edward F. Beale.* Glendale, Calif., 1983.

Thompson, Gerald. *Edward F. Beale and the American West.* Albuquerque, N. Mex., 1983.

BEAN, BABE

Cross-dresser, reporter, and nurse Babe Bean (1869–1936), sometimes known as "Jack Bean" or "Jack Garland," was probably born Elvira Virginia Mugarrieta in San Francisco, California. Her father was the former Mexican consul in San Francisco, José Marcos Mugarrieta, who had been ousted from the consulate several years earlier. Her mother was Eliza Alice Denny Garland Mugarrieta, daughter of a U.S. congressman and judge from Louisiana. In later years, Eliza Mugarrieta wrote of her daughter Elvira, "She was always a most peculiar, original child, and a regular tomboy, never caring anything at all for the many trifles which usually interest and delight youthful femininity." Elvira's father died when she was about sixteen years old, and what became of her in the years immediately following is unclear. She may have entered a convent for a time and may have been married briefly. But by the late 1890s, Elvira reemerged as "Babe Bean," a woman who passed (although not always successfully) as a man in Stockton, California. There, Babe, sometimes known as "Jack," lived on an ark on McLeod's Lake, wrote newspaper articles, and captured the attention of townspeople, who debated Bean's identify and habits in the press.

When the Spanish-American War broke out in 1898, Bean wrote, "A newspaper woman and the daughter of an army officer, all my ambition and interest and inclination naturally gave me the fever to go to Manila." Dressed in men's clothing, Bean gained entry as a cabin boy on an army transport destined for the Philippines. Although discovered and arrested by military police there, Bean escaped prosecution and went on to report on the war. Bean returned to San Francisco in 1900, where she continued to pass as a man. Around that time, she abandoned the last name of Bean and adopted her mother's maiden name, Garland.

During the aftermath of the San Francisco earthquake of 1906, Garland served as a male nurse for the Red Cross. In the late 1920s, Garland lived in Berkeley, California, for a time and wrote for the local newspaper. She then returned to San Francisco. On the evening of September 18, 1936, Garland collapsed at the corner of Post and Franklin streets. An autopsy at the municipal mortuary revealed the female body that was clad in a blue suit and men's shoes. Although Babe Bean–Jack Garland was the subject of numerous newspaper articles and local color accounts during her lifetime and at the time of her death, she was lost to historical scholarship until Allan Berube of the San Francisco Lesbian and Gay History Project recovered the story in the late 1970s. As of the late twentieth century, historians had not yet explored the range of meanings Elvira Virginia Mugarrieta–Babe Bean–Jack Garland may hold for the study of ethnic, gender, and Western history.

—*Susan Lee Johnson*

SEE ALSO: Passing Women

SUGGESTED READING:

Mugarrieta, José Marcos. Correspondence and Papers. Bancroft Library, University of California, Berkeley.

San Francisco Lesbian and Gay History Project. "'She Even Chewed Tobacco': A Pictorial Narrative of Passing Women in America." In *Hidden from History: Reclaiming the Gay and Lesbian Past.* Edited by Martin Duberman, Martha Vicinus, and George Chauncey, Jr. San Francisco, Calif., 1989.

Sullivan, Louis. *From Female to Male: The Life of Jack Bee Garland.* Boston, 1990.

Judge Roy Bean, the "Law West of the Pecos." *Courtesy National Archives.*

BEAN, ROY

Frontiersman, saloonkeeper, and justice of the peace Roy Bean (1825?–1903) was born in Mason County, Kentucky, the son of Francis and Anna Bean. After the United States–Mexican War, he and his older brother Sam headed down the Santa Fe Trail to Chihuahua City, Mexico. There, Roy Bean allegedly killed a man and then fled to California. After a duel in San Diego and a dispute over a girl in Los Angeles, he went to Mesilla, New Mexico, and attached himself as a spy and scout to the Confederacy. Bean joined the Confederate retreat from New Mexico to San Antonio, Texas. On October 28, 1866, he married Virginia Chavez, but spent his time carousing, smuggling arms into Mexico, and arguing lawsuits in court. After sixteen years, he left his wife and four children and opened a series of tent saloons along the Southern Pacific rail lines.

Near Eagle's Nest, Texas, the Southern Pacific had a tiny settlement twenty miles from the Pecos River. Bean christened the village "Langtry," after the actress Lily Langtry. The Pecos County commissioners court appointed him the justice of the peace on August 2, 1882. At the age of fifty-seven, he anointed himself "judge" and built a frame structure—a combination saloon, sleeping quarters, and center for gambling and social gatherings. The legend of "Judge Roy Bean, the Law West of the Pecos" was born.

Despite colorful anecdotes to the contrary, Bean never shot anyone in Langtry and never sentenced anyone to hang. Most of his decisions were based on common sense and involved such crimes as brawling, stealing, drunkenness, wife beating, burglary, and minor theft. He used law books as fuel to heat his building in winter. He performed marriages, and explaining he was "correcting earlier mistakes," he often divorced the same parties. During the inquest of a dead man with a bullet between his eyes, Bean noted he was "killed by a damn good shot."

When state authorities banned the Peter Maher and Bob Fitzsimmons championship fight scheduled to take place in El Paso, Texas, Bean took it to Langtry. On February 21, 1896, the fight took place across the Rio Grande in Coahuila, Mexico. The big fight was Bean's last hurrah. Due to a bad heart and an equally bad liver, his health deteriorated, and he died in the Jersey Lilly Saloon. He is buried in Del Rio, Texas.

Bean worshiped Lily Langtry, but he never met her. She visited Langtry ten months after his death.

—*Leon C. Metz*

SUGGESTED READING:
Sonnichsen, C. L. *The Story of Judge Roy Bean: Law West of the Pecos.* New York, 1943.

BEARDSLEY, HELEN MARSTON

One of California's most dedicated activists for peace and human rights, Helen Marston Beardsley (1892–1982) was the youngest of five children of prominent San Diego merchant and civic leader George Marston. She decided to devote her life to peace and public service after seeing the effects of World War I during a trip to Europe with her family in 1914. After graduating from Wellesley College in 1917, she joined the Women's International League for Peace and Freedom (WILPF) and attended the organization's 1921 Congress in Vienna. Serving on the national board of the WILPF and as vice-president of the organization for one term, she then helped organize the California branch and became president of the San Diego chapter. In the early 1930s, she devoted much time to the San Diego Disarmament Conference Committee.

As a founder of the San Diego chapter of the American Civil Liberties Union, she served as its first president. In 1934, she and several other WILPF and ACLU members made six trips to Imperial Valley, California, to help striking farm workers hold public meetings under a federal injunction secured by the ACLU to prohibit police interference. In 1935, she married Superior Court Judge John Beardsley and continued her activities in Los Angeles. Her husband died in 1946, and she remained in Los Angeles until 1960. Returning to San Diego, she reorganized the local chapter of the WILPF and became its president. In 1973, she was amused to learn during the Watergate hearings that her name was on the "enemies list" maintained by the Nixon White House.

—*Bruce Kamerling*

BEAR FLAG REBELLION

SEE: United States–Mexican War

BEAUBIEN, CARLOS

New Mexican merchant, community leader, and politician Carlos Beaubien (1800–1864), a native of Trois-Rivières, Canada, participated in a fur-trade expedition to New Mexico and settled in Taos in 1823. He distinguished himself as a successful fur trader, merchant, and political leader. His marriage in 1829 to María Pabla Lovato y Chávez, a member of a prominent Taos family, facilitated his entry into New Mexican society. In 1841, along with Guadalupe Miranda, he received a Mexican land grant known as the Beaubien-Miranda Land Grant (later called the MAXWELL LAND GRANT) from Governor MANUEL ARMIJO. After acquiring another grant, the Sangre de Cristo, Beaubien owned nearly three million acres of land. In August 1846, Beaubien was appointed a judge in both the territorial supreme court and the district court.

—*John W. Grassham*

SUGGESTED READING:

Grassham, John W. "Charles H. Beaubien, 1800–1864." M.A. thesis, New Mexico State University, Las Cruces, 1983.

Keleher, William A. *The Maxwell Land Grant*. Santa Fe, N. Mex., 1975.

Pearson, Jim Berry. *The Maxwell Land Grant*. Norman, Okla., 1961.

BEAVERS

The beaver *(Castor canadensis)* was the first animal of the American West to be systematically exploited by Euro-American society. Semiaquatic animals, beavers are marvelously adapted for the habitat in which they live. They played a significant role in the ecosystem of Western rivers and creeks. Beavers are the only members of the family *Castoridae*. As with other members of the order *Rodentia,* beavers have incisors (gnawing teeth) that become sharper the more they are used. Beavers, as vegetarians, prefer the bark of aspen, willow, cottonwood, alder, and birch trees, although they will also eat grasses, berries, mushrooms, and sedges. To obtain the bark of their favorite trees, beavers have felled trees up to three and a half feet in diameter. They rarely eat the bark of conifers.

North America's largest rodent and the second largest rodent in the world, beavers may reach a weight of 110 pounds. Their average weight is between 40 and 60 pounds. Including their sixteen- to seventeen-inch tail, their average overall length is about forty-eight inches. Their wide, thick tails are unique features. Beyond its base, the tail becomes six to seven inches wide and three-quarters of an inch thick. The thick portion of the tail is covered with scales and short, coarse hair. The tail helps the animal establish direction while swimming and diving, alert other beavers, and stabilize itself while felling trees.

Much more agile in the water than on land, the beaver can remain under water for up to fifteen minutes and can swim a half mile under water at speeds up to five miles an hour. When diving, the beaver's nose and ears are closed by valves. Transparent eyelids allow the beaver to see easily under water, and folds of skin shut behind its front incisors allowing it to gnaw wood while under water. Propulsion in the water comes not from the tail but from the webbed toes on the rear feet, which are also used for grooming.

In water, beavers enjoy a security that is denied them on land. They excel as dam builders and will work incessantly and with diverse materials (rocks, mud, coal, railroad ties, grasses, and heavy stones) to dam a stream in order to maintain the depth of water they desire. Beavers have been known to construct dams up to four thousand feet long, eighteen feet high, and thirty feet wide. Behind the dams, they build lodges where they live throughout the year. Beaver dams also create a fertile habitat for numerous other birds, fish, insects, and animals. The dams are also substantial checks on flooding and erosion. After becoming silted in and being abandoned by beaver, the dams are often the first stage in the creation of a fertile mountain meadow.

The color of the beaver's coat varies from deep sable, to light brown, to tan, and even occasionally to cream. The beaver's body is protected by an outer coat of guard hairs and a dense undercoat of shorter hairs. Beneath the fur is a thick layer of subcutaneous fat, which also insulates the animal. The guard hairs are long, silky, and easily oiled with castoreum from the castors, the perineal scent glands.

In the eighteenth century, the English church permitted the eating of the beaver's tail on meatless fast days because the scales on its tail made it fish rather than meat. Neither Indians nor Euro-American settlers, however, found the beaver's body desirable as meat. It was the coat of the beaver and its castoreum that made it an object of such value in the first half of the nineteenth century. The search for new populations of beavers to be trapped led MOUNTAIN MEN to explore many of the tributaries and drainage of Western mountains and rivers. The pursuit of the beaver prompted exploration, stimulated settlement, and encouraged the establishment of the FUR TRADE companies including the HUDSON'S BAY COMPANY, the AMERICAN FUR COMPANY, the Pacific Fur Company, the Rocky Mountain Fur Company, the St. Louis, MISSOURI FUR COMPANY, and Bent, St. Vrain and Company. From 1853 to 1877, the Hudson's Bay Company, alone, traded for more than three million beaver pelts. In untrapped mountain valleys, TRAPPERS often took three beavers a day. In the latter half of the nineteenth century, beaver pelts brought from four dollars to eight dollars each. The beaver's fur was used primarily to make men's top hats. The pelt would be carefully worked with a special comb to remove the dense under hairs, which would then be soaked in a vat and, after they began to mat together, worked into a felt. Sheared beaver fur was also used for stoles and for fur collars on coats. The price for beaver pelts dropped dramatically after 1840 when silk top hats became popular.

Castoreum was frequently used in medicines for pleurisy, arthritis, colic, fevers, and rheumatism. The thick, rich, yellow, oily liquid is produced by the four- to five-inch castor glands found on each side of the cloaca. Castoreum is also an ideal fixative for perfumes. When mixed with a base fragrance, it assumes and fixes that scent and then releases it as the human body warms. Castoreum is also used in trapping, for it attracts not only beavers but many other animals as well.

Because beavers were so easily trapped, their populations in state after state were decimated. By 1900, their future as a wild animal in the West was bleak. In the last decade of the nineteenth century, some states took steps to protect the species through legislation. Since the 1940s, a decline in predators and new trapping restrictions have allowed beavers to reoccupy most of their former range. Because of their high rate of productivity and their ability to alter water courses, beavers are a significant wildlife management problem for most Western states.

—*Phillip Drennon Thomas*

SEE ALSO: Wildlife

SUGGESTED READING:

Bailey, Vernon. *Beaver Habits and Experiments in Beaver Culture.* Technical Bulletin 31. United States Department of Agriculture. Washington, D.C., 1927.

Chittenden, Hiram Martin. *American Fur Trade of the Far West.* 3 vols. New York, 1902.

Mills, Enos A. *In a Beaver World.* Boston and New York, 1913.

Rue, Leonard Lee, III. *The World of the Beaver.* New York, 1964.

BECKNELL, WILLIAM

Trader and explorer William Becknell (ca. 1790–1865) established the trade link between American settlements in Missouri and farther east with Mexican settlements in New Mexico and farther south. The route he forged became known as the Santa Fe Trail.

Likely born in Kentucky, Becknell spent his early adult years as a merchant in Franklin, Missouri. In 1821, when the United States was in a financial depression, Becknell experienced business troubles of his own. In the summer of 1821, he assembled an expedition to the southern Rocky Mountains to capture horses, mules, and "wild animals of every description." Leading pack horses from Franklin, Becknell and some twenty traders traveled westward to trade with Native Americans in present-day Colorado and New Mexico. The party encountered Mexican soldiers, who told the traders about Mexico's independence from Spain and encouraged them to head southward to Santa Fe. Becknell led his expedition to the city and quickly sold his small cache of goods for a healthy profit.

Becknell's success in Santa Fe was a new turn of events for American traders. Before Mexico won its independence in 1821, Spanish officials barred foreigners from their territory. Luckless American trappers and traders caught on Spanish land were imprisoned. Robert McKnight, a trapper from Missouri, for example, spent nine years in a Chihuahua prison after he was apprehended in Santa Fe in the fall of 1812.

By January 1822, Becknell returned to Franklin and amassed a caravan of more goods for sale. This time, he struck westward across present-day Kansas and dipped southward to follow the Cimarron River through the southeastern corner of Kansas and the northeastern deserts of New Mexico. Taking the "Cimarron Cutoff," as his route was called, Becknell avoided the treacherous southeastern Colorado mountain passes that he had encountered on his first expedition and which his wagons could not traverse.

Becknell's route to Santa Fe opened trade in both directions between the United States and northern Mexico, made huge profits for Becknell and the traders who followed him, and proved that wagon travel across the arid lands of the West was possible, thus encouraging the migration to and settlement of the region.

Becknell continued in the Santa Fe trade for several years, but by 1828, he was operating a ferry on the Missouri River. He ran for a seat in the 1828 Missouri General Assembly and served two terms. Later moving to Texas, he joined the fight for independence from Mexico. He settled in Clarksville and remained there until his death.

—*Patricia Hogan*

SEE ALSO: National Expansion; Santa Fe and Chihuahua Trail

SUGGESTED READING:

Goetzmann, William H. *Exploration and Science: The Explorer and the Scientist in the Winning of the American West.* New York, 1966.

Weber, D. J. *The Taos Trappers: The Fur Trade in the Far Southwest, 1540–1896.* Norman, Okla., 1971.

BECKWOURTH, JAMES PIERSON (JIM)

Fur trapper, mountain man, and U.S. Army scout James Pierson Beckwourth (1798–1866), sometimes called "Jim Beckwith," was born a slave in Fredericksburg, Virginia, to a Revolutionary War major and a mulatto slave woman. After moving in 1810 to St. Louis, where his father manumitted him, Beckwourth worked as a blacksmith and lead miner and at other odd jobs until he joined General WILLIAM HENRY ASHLEY's fur-trapping expedition to the Rocky Mountains in 1824.

Over the next four years, Beckwourth proved to be an expert trapper and mountain man. Befriended by Crow Indians, he was welcomed as a member of the tribe, married several Crow women, and assumed a position of importance among his adopted people.

Beckwourth lived a varied life. He worked at times for the AMERICAN FUR COMPANY, served in the Second Seminole War in Florida with General ZACHARY TAYLOR, rustled horses from Mexican ranchos in California, participated in the suppression of the Taos Revolt in 1847, became one of the first settlers of present-day Pueblo, Colorado, and served the U.S. Army as a scout. He died among his Crow people in 1866.

—*James A. Crutchfield*

SEE ALSO: Fur Trade; Mountain Men; United States Army: Scouts

SUGGESTED READING:

Bonner, T. D. *The Life and Adventures of James P. Beckwourth, Mountaineer, Scout, and Pioneer, and Chief of the Crow Nation of Indians.* New York, 1856.

BEESON, DESDEMONA STOTT

Born in Eureka, Utah, and educated at the University of Utah and Stanford, Desdemona Stott Beeson (1897–1976) is known as a pioneer woman mining engineer and geologist. In 1919 in Bingham, Utah, she and her husband, Joe Beeson, began a partnership that took them to a mining prospects in Utah, California, and Nevada. Her expertise and tough-mindedness as a business manager and accountant brought her respect, despite the fact that she worked underground, something the male mining world had long informally prohibited women from doing.

After World War II, the Beesons continued mining but Desdemona suffered several accidents, including one in which her neck was broken. The Beesons culminated their career at the Cardiff mine near Alta. Desdemona, wearing a brace and using crutches, and Joe attempted to drain the water-filled mine and excavate ore beneath the tunnel level. But the venture barely broke even, and the building of the Snowbird ski resort forced them out. They retired to Salt Lake City, where she died of cancer in 1976.

Desdemona Beeson was a trail-blazer; she combined marriage, motherhood, and a mining career and opened the way for other women in geology and mining engineering.

—*Sandra C. Taylor*

SEE ALSO: Mining: Mining Engineers

SUGGESTED READING:

James, Laurence P., and Sandra C. Taylor. "Strong Minded Women: Desdemona Stott Beeson and Other Hard Rock Mining Entrepreneurs." *Utah Historical Quarterly* 46 (1978): 136–150.

BELL RANCH, NEW MEXICO

The Bell Ranch of New Mexico began as part of two Mexican land grants—the Baca Location Number Two and the Pablo Montoya Grant of 1824. Located in the northeast corner of New Mexico, the ranch began operations in 1824 and was sold in 1947.

The ranch was named by Wilson Waddingham, who registered the Bell brand for his cattle on March 15, 1875. E. G. Stoddard, founder of the Red River Valley Company, bought the ranch in 1898. Stoddard and his successor, Julius G. Day, transformed the ranch into a large (750,000 acres) and prosperous business operation by hiring excellent managers—Arthur J. Tisdall (manager from 1893 to 1898), Charles M. O'Donel (1898 to 1933), and Albert K. Mitchell (1933 to 1947). They established agricultural research stations, used internal fencing to increase grass production, developed water resources, balanced land and grass with the size of the herd, and managed herd production and sale by transporting cattle by railroad. The Bell Ranch became one of the most advanced centers of production of Hereford, Aberdeen Angus, and Santa Gertrudis cattle and Durham, Morgan, Quarter, Americo-Arab, Langley, and Old Sorrel horses. The ranch also developed sophisticated techniques in cattle breeding and animal husbandry.

—*Fred L. Koestler*

SEE ALSO: Cattle Breeds and Breeding; Cattle Industry; Horse and Mule Trade

SUGGESTED READING:
Remley, David. *Bell Ranch: Cattle Ranching in the Southwest, 1824–1947.* Albuquerque, N. Mex., 1993.

BELLA COOLA INDIANS

SEE: Native American Peoples: Peoples of the Pacific Northwest

BEMIS, POLLY

Born Lulu Nathoy in Mongolia, Polly Bemis (1852–1933) became a Western legend as a prostitute who gained her freedom and survived the harsh frontier to become a beloved member of her community. In 1871, she was sold into PROSTITUTION and slavery, smuggled into San Francisco, and sent to her Chinese master, a tong leader or saloonkeeper in the mining town of Warren, Idaho. Soon after her arrival, her master lost her in a poker game to Charlie Bemis, a miner and avid gambler. Some time later, Bemis was shot in a game of faro, and Lulu Nathoy extracted bullet fragments from his cheek with a crochet hook. Upon recovering from his injuries, Bemis and Nathoy moved to the backwoods at the juncture of the Salmon River and Cripple Creek. They established a small ranch, and "Polly," as she became known, worked a vegetable garden and sold produce to local miners. The couple, known for their generosity and hospitality, eventually married. The Bemises became something of a legend in Idaho, and Polly, especially, was renowned for her nursing skills. Charlie Bemis died in 1920. Polly Bemis continued to work her little ranch and tended to sick

Polly Bemis. *Courtesy Idaho State Historical Society.*

miners and settlers. Upon her death at the age of eighty-one, the title to her land and herd, as stipulated in her will, passed to the two ranchers who had looked after her in her last years. Members of the Grangeville City Council honored Bemis by serving as pall bearers at her funeral and naming the stream on her property Polly Creek.

—*Patricia Hogan*

SEE ALSO: Chinese Americans

SUGGESTED READING:
McCunn, Ruthanne Lum. *Thousand Pieces of Gold.* San Francisco, 1981.

BENNETT, EDWARD HERBERT

A leading practitioner and proponent of CITY PLANNING in the first decades of the twentieth century, Edward Herbert Bennett (1874–1954) had a major influence on the development of SAN FRANCISCO, PORTLAND, DENVER, and Pasadena among other Western cities.

Born in Cheltenham, England, Bennett was educated as a architect. He moved to the United States in 1890, worked briefly in San Francisco, and then returned to Europe to receive a diploma from the École des Beaux-Arts in Paris in 1902. After a year and a half with the leading New York architectural firm of George B. Post and Sons, he worked with Chicago architect and planner DANIEL BURNHAM in the preparation of plans for the city of San Francisco. Working from 1904 to 1905 in an office on the city's Twin Peaks, Bennett directed the draftsmen and assistants who sketched a grand plan for restructuring San Francisco around new boulevards and public spaces. For the city of CHICAGO, he and Burnham then prepared an even more ambitious plan, completed and presented to the Commercial Club of Chicago in 1909. The plans for San Francisco and Chicago are usually considered the climax of the "city-beautiful" approach to American city planning.

From 1910 to 1911, Bennett was the chief designer of the Greater Portland Plan. Like the San Francisco and Chicago documents, the Portland plan proposed a substantial rebuilding of the city. It called for constructing new diagonal boulevards, relocating the docks and port activities downstream on the Willamette River, and creating three centers of civic activity focused on government buildings, museums, and transportation terminals. Voters and the city council enthusiastically endorsed the plan, but an economic recession blocked implementation.

Bennett then received commissions from Ottawa-Hull, Minneapolis, Denver, Pasadena, and other cities. From 1916 to 1918, he worked with Denver Mayor ROBERT WALTER SPEER to salvage flawed designs for the Denver Civic Center. In the early 1920s, he consulted on the planning of a civic center for Pasadena.

Bennett's work in the late 1910s and 1920s helped establish the basis for a distinct city-planning profession. He was a charter member of the American City Planning Institute in 1917 and worked from 1919 until his retirement in 1935 as a consultant on comprehensive plans and zoning ordinances for cities, the Regional Plan for New York, the design of Grant Park in Chicago, and the Century of Progress exposition in Chicago in 1933. He died in Tryon, North Carolina.

—Carl Abbott

SEE ALSO: Architecture: Urban; Urban West

BENNETT, HUGH HAMMOND

Known as the "father of soil conservation," Hugh Hammond Bennett (1881–1960) was born near Wadesboro in Anson County, North Carolina. Following his graduation from the University of North Carolina at Chapel Hill in 1903, he joined the Bureau of Soils of the U.S. Department of Agriculture in Washington, D.C. During his early years with the bureau, he traveled throughout the South to make soil surveys and later supervised the field work of soil surveyors. The experience persuaded him that soil EROSION posed a threat to the nation's future ability to produce food. He resolved to alert the nation and became a prolific writer on the subject; he wrote not only for professional journals but also for the popular press. Perhaps his best-known and most influential publication was a USDA bulletin, *Soil Erosion: A National Menace.*

In 1929, through Bennett's influence, Congress authorized soil-erosion experiment stations. Bennett selected the locations and directed the research activities of stations. Meanwhile, the Great Depression started, and Bennett successfully argued that some of the funds for emergency employment should be made available for work with farmers to demonstrate the value of soil-conservation methods. Bennett served as director of the temporary Soil Erosion Service from September 1933 to April 1935 and then as chief of the service's successor, the SOIL CONSERVATION SERVICE, from April 1935 to November 1951.

Despite his considerable skills in scientific and technical work, Bennett is best remembered for the zeal and urgency he brought to his speeches and writing in the cause of soil conservation. His efforts earned him a place among that small group of career civil servants who undertake a cause, successfully argue for legislation, lead their agency in its formative years, and remain an icon for a movement.

—J. Douglas Helms

SUGGESTED READING:
Brink, Wellington. *Big Hugh, The Father of Soil Conservation.* New York, 1951.

BENT BROTHERS

The four Bent brothers played a substantial role in the development of overland commerce and the FUR TRADE in the American Southwest. Their parents, Silas Bent and Martha (Kerr) Bent, were part of a generation of Americans who were constantly moving west. The family ultimately included seven sons and four daughters. Silas Bent's father, after studying law and serving as a judge, became in 1806 the deputy surveyor for the Louisiana Territory and settled in St. Louis, Missouri. Silas Bent himself later served as a justice of the Supreme Court of Missouri from 1813 to 1821.

Born in Charleston, Virginia (now West Virginia), Charles Bent (1799–1847) was the eldest child and grew to maturity in the thriving community of St. Louis. While many of the details of his early career are sketchy, it is clear that by 1822 he was a member of Joshua Pilcher's MISSOURI FUR COMPANY and that by 1825 he was a partner in the company. With the decline of the company's fortunes as a result of competition with the AMERICAN FUR COMPANY, Charles turned his attention to the Southern Plains and the growing trade with Santa Fe. In 1829, he captained a trading caravan of thirty-eight wagons on the 775-mile journey from St. Louis to Santa Fe. Despite an attack by a large force of Kiowa Indians, the trip demonstrated that the profits from the trade compensated for the dangers encountered. While in Santa Fe in 1830, Charles formed a partnership with CERAN DE HAULT DE LASSUS ST. VRAIN. Always the dominant partner in the firm, Charles Bent transformed Bent, St. Vrain and Company into the most aggressive, successful, and diverse mercantile and fur-trading company in the Southwest. Three trading centers were established by the company: BENT'S FORT on the ARKANSAS RIVER, Fort St. Vrain on the South Platte, and a trading post on the Canadian River. By 1832, Charles had made TAOS, NEW MEXICO, his home, and three years later, he married Maria Ignacia Jaramillo. Involved in the politics of the region, he became an ally of Governor MANUEL ARMIJO and a political foe of the powerful Martinez family of northern New Mexico. His role in awarding large land grants alienated many of the Spanish families in the region. At the outbreak of the UNITED STATES–MEXICAN WAR in 1846, he was named governor of New Mexico. A prominent and successful Anglo-American politician and businessman, he was killed in the Taos Revolt of January 19, 1847.

The fortunes of the company were left to the stewardship of William Bent (1809–1869). Born in St. Louis, William had trapped on the upper Arkansas in 1824 and then had become a partner with his brother Charles and St. Vrain. He directed the construction of the fort they built on the Arkansas River and became its first manager. Developing great empathy with the Indians with whom he traded, he gained their confidence and respect. His three wives were Indian. In 1846, he guided General STEPHEN WATTS KEARNY's forces from Bent's Fort to Santa Fe. Widely admired for his integrity, he supervised the complex field operations of the company, and with the retirement of St. Vrain near the end of 1848, he became its sole owner. When the U.S. government refused to pay the modest price he requested for Bent's Fort, he blew it up with gunpowder and built a new trading center thirty-eight miles downstream. The influx of settlers, the gold rush of 1859, and increasing conflicts between Native Americans and Euro-Americans on the plains limited opportunities for the type of trade he had developed. The community he established at the mouth of the Purgatoire River became the first Anglo-American settlement in Colorado.

Two other Bent brothers, George (1814–1847) and Robert (1816–1841), also played a role in history of Bent's Fort and the Santa Fe Trail. While never providing the leadership that Charles and William did, they were nevertheless important in the development of trade and commerce in the region. George was born in St. Louis and joined his brothers as a trapper and trader

in 1832. He probably aided in the construction of Bent's Fort. In 1837, he supervised the construction of the company's fort on the South Platte River, and by that date, he was a full partner in Bent, St. Vrain and Company. Often wintering in Taos, he supervised the operations of Bent's Fort when William was absent. He died of a fever at the fort on October 23, 1847.

Robert Bent was the youngest of the four Bent brothers. He was born in St. Louis, and in the tradition of his brothers, he became a trader. His precise relationship to the company his brothers founded is unclear, however. He lived off and on at Bent's Fort from 1832 until his death at the hands of Comanches in 1841 while buffalo hunting.

—*Phillip Drennon Thomas*

SEE ALSO: Mountain Men; Santa Fe and Chihuahua Trail

SUGGESTED READING:

Arnold, Samuel P. "William Bent." In *The Mountain Men and the Fur Trade of the Far West*. Edited by LeRoy R. Hafen. Vol. 6. Glendale, Calif., 1968.

Carter, Harvey L. "George Bent." In *The Mountain Men and the Fur Trade of the Far West*. Edited by LeRoy R. Hafen. Vol. 4. Glendale, Calif., 1966.

———. "Robert Bent." In *The Mountain Men and the Fur Trade of the Far West*. Edited by LeRoy R. Hafen. Vol. 4. Glendale, Calif., 1966.

Dunham, Harold H. "Charles Bent." In *The Mountain Men and the Fur Trade of the Far West*. Edited by LeRoy R. Hafen. Vol. 2. Glendale, Calif., 1965.

Lavender, David. *Bent's Fort*. Lincoln, Nebr., 1954.

BENT'S FORT, COLORADO

Located in southeastern Colorado, on the north bank of the ARKANSAS RIVER, twelve miles west of the mouth of the Purgatoire River, Bent's Fort was established as a private trading post through the entrepreneurial energies of CERAN DE HAULT DE LASSUS ST. VRAIN and the brothers Charles and William Bent. While Charles provided much of the impetus and design for the structure, William supervised its construction. Completed around 1833, the massive adobe compound, near the present-day city of La Junta, Colorado, was located near the hunting grounds of the Cheyenne, Arapaho, Ute, Comanche, and Kiowa Indians and adjacent to the Mountain Branch of the Santa Fe Trail on the river that was the boundary between the United States and Mexico. From this location, the Bent brothers engaged in trade for buffalo hides and robes and beaver and bear pelts and participated in the overland commerce that was evolving between St. Louis and Taos and Santa

Bent's Fort. *Courtesy National Cowboy Hall of Fame and Western Heritage Center.*

Fe. Bent's Fort, or as it was known to its builders, Fort William, functioned as a trading center for less than sixteen years. In 1849, William Bent offered to sell the fort to the U.S. government at a reasonable price, and when the government refused, he blew up the fort with gunpowder, moved downstream some thirty-eight miles, and established a new trading center.

Bent's Fort was not only the largest trading center in the mountain plains region, it was also the site of the first ditch constructed for irrigation in Colorado and the home of the first registered cattle brand in that region. In 1963, the National Park Service began reconstructing the fort as it stood in 1845 and 1846; the reconstruction was completed in 1976.

—*Phillip Drennon Thomas*

SEE ALSO: Fur Trade; Santa Fe and Chihuahua Trail

SUGGESTED READING:
Lavender, David. *Bent's Fort.* New York, 1954.
Thompson, Enid. "Life in an Adobe Castle, 1833–1849."
In *Bent's Old Fort.* Colorado Springs, Colo., 1979.

BENT, ST. VRAIN AND CO.

SEE: Bent Brothers; St. Vrain, Ceran de Hault de Lassus

BENTON, THOMAS HART

From 1821 to 1851, Missouri politician Thomas Hart Benton (1782–1858) served in the U.S. Senate, where he promoted Western settlement and cheap land for settlers. Born in the Piedmont region of North Carolina, Benton, at the age of sixteen, enrolled at the University of North Carolina. Only a few months later, however, he was expelled for petty theft and returned home in disgrace. His mother then decided to move her family to Tennessee. In July 1806, Benton was admitted to the bar, and three years later, he was elected state senator. During the War of 1812, he quarreled with his friend and mentor General ANDREW JACKSON. The dispute ended in a brawl in a Nashville hotel during which Benton's brother Jesse wounded Jackson. Once again, Benton moved to escape further embarrassment. He settled in ST. LOUIS, MISSOURI, in 1815.

Benton resumed his law career in St. Louis and became editor of the *St. Louis Enquirer,* a newspaper he used to promote a system of national roads and canals, the sale of federal lead-mine resources, the acquisition of Cuba, the independence of Mexico, the occupation of Oregon, and the development of trade routes along the Missouri and Columbia rivers. He became a U.S. senator in 1821. Over the next thirty years, he gained a reputation as an advocate for Western settlers. Al-

Thomas Hart Benton. *Courtesy Library of Congress.*

though his views on westward expansion were influenced by his son-in-law, the well-known explorer JOHN CHARLES FRÉMONT, Benton had always had his eye on the West. Earlier, in the Tennessee legislature, he had espoused a preemption law that would allow settlers to purchase the land on which they had settled. In 1841, the PRE-EMPTION ACT became a national law. In 1862, four years after his death, Benton's views on Western expansion became the basis of the federal HOMESTEAD ACT OF 1862. He promoted the establishment of a commission on LAND POLICY to settle land claims derived from Spanish and French land grants, and a commission was formed in 1829. He also promoted fur trade in the Rocky Mountains by calling for an end to the governmental factory system and for a new commitment by the FEDERAL GOVERNMENT to protect fur traders in the West. In addition, he promoted the construction of a toll-free road to Oregon for use by settlers.

Benton called for gradually decreasing prices of public land until they reached twenty-five cents an acre. The Graduation Act became law in 1854. As chairman of the Committee on Indian Affairs, he obtained the cession of Creek lands in Georgia and started the removal of Indian tribes from the East.

Although a slave-holding aristocrat, Benton tried to remain outside the sectional dispute over slavery. He opposed the annexation of Texas because of the slavery question and later because of the threat of war with Mexico. His refusal to allow the slavery question

to influence his views on Western expansion eventually brought him the disfavor of his constituents. He was defeated in his bid for reelection in 1851.

Benton then ran for the House of Representatives and served from 1852 to 1854. In 1856, he ran for governor of Missouri and was defeated. He spent the remainder of his life writing a two-volume history of the national government, a sixteen-volume abridgment of congressional debates, and a legal refutation of the *DRED SCOTT* DECISION.

—*Candace Floyd*

SEE ALSO: National Expansion

SUGGESTED READING:
Chambers, William Nisbet. *Old Bullion Benton: Senator from the New West.* Boston, 1956.
Smith, Elbert B. *Magnificent Missourian: The Life of Thomas Hart Benton.* Philadelphia, 1958.

BERDACHE

The term *berdache* generally refers to men in some American Indian tribes who adopt the dress and social role of women. Frequently studied by anthropologists, berdaches are often considered the equivalent of male homosexuals and transvestites, and the word has also been employed to denote Native American lesbians. Originally an Arabic word for a boy sex-slave or a male child used sexually by adults, *berdache* was the euphemism of choice—much like the present-day *gay*—for the English-speaking in the nineteenth century, when a number of Euro-Americans and Europeans began serious study of the Native American cultures they sometimes seemed intent on destroying. For example, the painter GEORGE CATLIN attempted to chronicle what he considered the "vanishing" Indian way of life and was once invited to attend a feast in honor of certain Sac (Sauk) and Fox (Mesquakie) males he described as berdaches. Most observers, those inclined to "scientific" study as well as to journalism, found much about the Native Americans—from food ways to child rearing to gender classification—repugnant, as Catlin did in his visit among the "berdache." "This," he wrote, "is one of the most unaccountable and disgusting customs that I have ever met in Indian country." He refused to describe it further and expressed the hope that "it might be extinguished before it [was] more fully recorded."

Catlin's attitude was typical of the traditionally male-dominated and homophobic Christian cultures of Western Europe and their North American offshoot. From the beginning, European colonizers reacted adversely—and often violently—to female-centered Indian cultures, the homoerotic aspects of some Native American rituals, and the gender-crossing freedom allowed by many native societies. In California in 1513, the conquistador Vasco Núñez de Balboa set wild dogs loose on the Chumashes' "gay" medicine men, whom the Santa Barbara Indians called by a term the Spanish translated as *Joya* (the Jewels). Not surprisingly, Native Americans developed a sharp reluctance to talk to Europeans about such matters, and many Indians—as they became Christianized—rejected gender crossing altogether. Beyond fear of reprisal and assimilated moral attitudes, Native Americans also may have found it impossible to make Europeans understand those the latter called "berdaches." Homosexuality is a social construct of Western cultures that fits poorly the widely varying gender-related activities and notions of diverse tribes who, for the most part, had a strong tradition of respect for persons and their individual autonomy, regardless of what we would call "sexual orientation." This made it difficult for scholars and historians later to judge just how widespread such practices were among the native peoples of America.

Clearly, most native societies strictly segregated rights and duties by sex. Tribes carefully defined the roles of both men and women and expected their people to adapt to those roles and perform the duties called for efficiently and effectively. In spiritual matters and in ceremonial rituals, too, Indians designated gender roles and followed them fastidiously. Indian children, both male and female, were carefully indoctrinated to gender roles through informal education and by adult example. Just as clearly, however, not all individuals followed gender patterns, nor did they assume the roles expected of them, and many tribes exhibited a certain flexibility in responding to cross-gender behavior. Some native societies institutionalized gender crossing. In fact, in many cases gender roles seemed to have taken precedence over the sex of the individual fulfilling the duties connected with them. In other words, for many Indian tribes, there were clear divisions between "women's work" and "men's work," but some individuals took up that work based more on proclivity, inclination, and temperament than on their biological sex. Men we might call "gay," the Indians would simply describe as women, and women we consider lesbians (perhaps the pejorative term *dykes* is closer), tribal cultures might define as men.

Among the tribes of the Southwest, for example, men often developed considerable skill at pottery making, weaving, and other domestic arts. Most famous among those individuals perhaps was We'wha, the so-called Zuni man-woman, who was esteemed among his Pueblo people and who moved freely in the high society of Washington, D.C. Some recent scholars have elevated his role in Zuni culture to one of sacredness. If a family of Kaska Indians in Canada produced only daughters, one of them would frequently be "turned" into a boy: when she was at about five years old, her parents would tie a pouch of dried bear ovaries to her belt; she would began dressing in men's clothing; and for the rest of her life, she would function as a male. She hunted and fished and was free of sexual advances from males, who would be punished for attempting the kind of sexual intimacy that might ruin her luck during the hunt. Mojave *hwames*—gender-crossing women—assumed male names and took up masculine roles, officially marrying other females who were themselves not considered *hwames* but simply women. Among the Plains Indians' cultures, which historians frequently describe as male-dominated warrior societies, women also had gender options. A woman occasionally went with the tribe to war, usually to avenge the death of a male family member. There were also the "manly-hearted women"—especially among the Piegan Blackfoot Indians—who were economically self-sufficient and sexually aggressive. Especially during the days of the fur trade on the plains, they used domestic skills such as tanning hides to establish their independence.

The Quinaults, the Apaches, the Ojibwas (Chippewas), and the Eskimos accepted lesbians, and the Navajos considered them an asset. Scholars have identified some eighty-eight tribes, in every part of North America, who not only allowed homosexuality but also made positive reference to it in the historical record, including the Apache, Navajo, Winnebago, Cheyenne, Pima, Crow, Shoshone, Paiute, Osage, Acoma, Zuni, Sioux, Pawnee, Choctaw, Creek, Seminole, Illinois, Mojave, Shasta, Aleut, Sac and Fox, Iowa, Kansa, Yuma, Tlingit, Ponca, Klamath, and Quinault. Still, when dealing with Native Americans and the many and wide variations among tribes, one should keep in mind that modern categories do not always adequately cover traditional Native American life.

The Sioux term *winkte,* for example, which many scholars translate as "like a woman," meant simply a man who assumed some aspects of a woman's traditional role, nurturing children, say, or learning skills the Sioux considered "feminine"; it might, but did not have to, involve homosexuality. In fact, in the Lakota-Dakota language from which the terms derives, one of its connotations could be translated as "kills women," which comes closer perhaps to the Sioux notion—men who displace women by assuming their roles in tribal life. Similarly, one scholar has asserted that *koskalaka* is the Lakota word for "dyke," when in fact it means "male youth" or "prepubescent male"; Lakota has a matching term for the opposite gender, *wikoskalaka,* meaning "maiden" or "young woman." It does, however, seem apparent that North America's aboriginal peoples were often more tolerant of sex and gender variation than many other cultures, especially those of modern Europe and the United States.

—*Charles Phillips*

SUGGESTED READING:
Allen, Paula Gunn. *The Sacred Hoop.* Boston, 1992.
Medicine, Beatrice. "Warrior Women: Sex Role Alternatives for Plains Indian Women." In *The Hidden Half: Studies of Plains Indian Women.* Edited by Patricia Albers and Beatrice Medicine. Langam, Md., 1983.
Roscoe, Will. *The Zuni Man-Woman.* Albuquerque, N. Mex., 1991.
Williams, Walter L. *The Spirit and the Flesh: Sexual Diversity in American Indian Culture.* Boston, 1992.

BERING, VITUS

The Danish navigator Vitus Bering (1681–1741) joined the Russian navy as a sub-lieutenant in 1703. He rose steadily in rank, and in 1725, Peter the Great appointed him, as captain of first rank, to lead an expedition to settle the old question of whether Asia and North America were joined and to find and claim presumed lands to the east of Siberia. In 1728, with a crew of forty-four, Bering sailed north in *Sv. Gavriil (St. Gabriel)* as far as 67° 18' north latitude and then turned back because of the lateness of the season. Bering discovered St. Lawrence Island and one of the Diomede Islands but because of bad weather did not sight the east side of the strait that has since borne his name. Critics thought the voyage inconclusive, but an appeal by Bering to the Empress Anna gained him promotion to captain-commander and appointment to head a six-hundred-man Great Northern expedition to explore first the entire north coast of Siberia and then, again, the still-unknown shores opposite Kamchatka. On June 5, 1740, the vessels *Sv. Petr (St. Peter)* under Bering and *Sv. Pavel (St. Paul)* under Captain Alexei Chirikov left Petropavlovsk. After wasting time seeking a mythical "Juan de Gama Land," the two vessels lost contact. Bering sighted some of the Aleutian Islands and Mount St. Elias on the Alaskan mainland, landed briefly on Kayak Island, and then turned back. Near Kamchatka on November 6, 1741, the *Sv. Petr* was wrecked on an unknown island, later named for Bering. En route, twelve men had died of scurvy, and during the winter, nineteen more died, including Bering on December 6, 1741. The survivors built a smaller vessel from the wreckage of the *Sv. Petr* and reached Kamchatka in the spring of 1742. Sea-otter furs they brought back sparked a "fur rush" by Russian private companies along the Aleutian chain, culminating in 1783 with the establishment of a permanent outpost on Kodiak Island, followed by others on the mainland. Chirikov, with the *Sv. Pavel,* got as far south as 55° 36' (the southern tip of the Alaska Peninsula). The expedition gave Russia a firm claim to what became known as Russian America, sold to the United States in 1867. In 1990, a joint Russian-Danish expedition discovered on Bering Island the campsite of Bering's party and his grave.

—*Richard A. Pierce*

SEE ALSO: Alaskan Exploration; Exploration: Russian Expeditions; Fur Trade

SUGGESTED READING:
Fisher, Raymond H. *Bering's Voyages, Whither and Why.* Seattle, Wash., 1977.
Steller, Georg Wilhelm. *Journal of a Voyage with Bering, 1741–1742.* Edited and with an introduction by O. W. Frost. Trans. by Margritt A. Engel and O. W. Frost. Stanford, Calif., 1988.
Waxell, Sven. *The American Expedition.* With introduction and notes by M. A. Michael. Trans. London, 1952.

BERNHISEL, JOHN MILTON

An early Mormon leader and Utah's first territorial delegate to Congress, John Milton Bernhisel (1799–1881) was born in Tyrone, Pennsylvania. Trained as a physician, he graduated from the University of Pennsylvania and practiced medicine first in Philadelphia and then in New York City. He converted to Mormonism (the CHURCH OF JESUS CHRIST OF LATTER-DAY SAINTS) in 1837 and was ordained a Mormon bishop in 1841. Two years later, he migrated to the Mormon Church headquarters in NAUVOO, ILLINOIS.

Bernhisel developed a close relationship with both JOSEPH SMITH, JR., and his wife EMMA HALE and lived with the Smith family in Nauvoo. Bernhisel advised Smith on political matters and served as the family's physician. He assumed the role of political advisor to BRIGHAM YOUNG after Smith's death in 1844.

Following the Mormon migration to Utah, Bernhisel was assigned to travel to Washington, D.C., to lobby the United States Congress for Utah statehood on behalf of the Mormon-dominated region. Although this effort failed and Utah MORMONS were forced to accept territorial status, Bernhisel so impressed Young that he was appointed the region's first territorial delegate to Congress in early 1851. He held that position for the next eight years. Dignified, calm, and conciliatory, Bernhisel mediated on behalf of the Mormon church in its often difficult relationship with a suspicious and sometimes hostile federal government. Although Bernhisel served the Mormons well, he was eager to retire. He left Congress in 1859, but the following year, Young coaxed Bernhisel into serving once more as Utah territorial delegate. Finally in 1863, at the age of sixty-four, he retired permanently from Congress. He returned to the full-time practice of medicine in Salt Lake City. As a devout Mormon, he accepted the Mormon principle of polygamy, albeit with some reluctance, marrying a total of seven wives. He died in Salt Lake City.

—*Newell G. Bringhurst*

Suggested reading:

Berrett, Gwynn W. "John M. Bernhisel: Mormon Elder in Congress." *Utah Historical Quarterly* 68 (Spring 1968): 143–167.

Blance, Rose. "Early Utah Medical Practice." *Utah Historical Quarterly* 10 (1942): 18–19.

Campbell, Eugene E. *Establishing Zion: The Mormon Church in the American West, 1847–1869.* Salt Lake City, 1988.

Furness, Norman F. *The Mormon Conflict, 1850–1859.* New Haven, Conn., 1960.

BERNINGHAUS, O. E.

See: Taos School of Artists

BESSEY, CHARLES EDWIN

Charles Edwin Bessey. *Editors' collection.*

One of the most influential botanists of the nineteenth century, Charles Edwin Bessey (1845–1915) was born in Milton, Ohio, the son of a teacher. He attended Michigan Agricultural College, received his Ph.D. from the University of Iowa, and pursued academic careers at Iowa Agricultural College (Iowa State) and the University of Nebraska. A complete scientist and educator, Bessey was a dedicated professor and contributor to the Hatch Act and other programs to improve agricul-

ture. A researcher and author, he wrote numerous reports, many of which involved microscopy, and botanical textbooks, which became the standard at the end of the nineteenth century. He also served as editor of the *American Naturalist* and *Science* and as president of the Iowa Academy of Sciences, the Nebraska Academy of Sciences, the Botanical Society of America, the American Association for the Advancement of Science, and the National Educational Association.

His most recognized accomplishment was the formulation of his "dicta," ground rules for interpreting the evolutionary history of flowering plants (phylogenetics). Until the late twentieth century, Bessey's dicta formed part of the basic training of botanists. A genius for synthesis and communication allowed him to compile his own experience and research with the important contributions of others to advance concepts and learning.

—*J. P. Folsom*

Suggested reading:

Isely, D. *One Hundred and One Botanists.* Ames, Iowa, 1994.

Overfield, R. A. *Science with Practice: Charles E. Bessey and the Maturing of American Botany.* Ames, Iowa, 1993.

BHAGAT SINGH THIND, IN RE

In Re Bhagat Singh Thind delivered a U.S. Supreme Court decision (1923) written by Justice George Sutherland upholding the U.S. Circuit Court of Appeals, Ninth District, which had stripped Thind of his U.S. citizenship. Although the court admitted that Thind belonged to the "Caucasian race," it ruled that he was not "white" as commonly understood and as stipulated in the Naturalization Law of 1790, which extended the right to become a naturalized citizen only to "free, white persons."

Thind, who had resided in America since 1913, served in the U.S. military during World War I and received his American citizenship from the U.S. district court in Oregon in 1920. Because of Thind's support for India's independence, federal immigration officials sought to deport him and took him to court to revoke his citizenship. Along with Ozawa v. United States (1922), the *Thind* case represented the ongoing efforts of the United States to deny citizenship to immigrants from Asia. Federal officials used the *Thind* decision to revoke the citizenship of several dozen other Asian Indians.

—*David K. Yoo*

See also: Chinese Exclusion; East Indians; Gentleman's Agreement; Immigration Law

Suggested reading:
Jensen, Joan. *Passage from India*. New Haven, Conn., 1988.
Kim, Hyung-chan, ed. *Dictionary of Asian American History*. Westport, Conn., 1986.

BIDWELL, ANNIE ELLICOTT KENNEDY

Born in Washington, D.C., to a prominent middle-class family, Annie Ellicott Kennedy Bidwell (1839–1918) became a devoted Indian reformer, a member of the National Woman Suffrage Association, and a follower of the Women's Christian Temperance Union. In 1868, she married General John Bidwell, an early settler in northern California and a U.S. congressman from 1864 to 1868.

Joining her husband in 1868 on Rancho Chico, in present-day Chico, California, Annie Bidwell became fascinated with the Native Americans, mostly Maidu Indians, who, in exchange for working for the general, lived in a village on his land. Known as "Bahapki" by its residents, the village became a refuge for dispossessed northern California Native Americans fleeing from Euro-American violence.

As other women reformers of the late nineteenth century had done, Annie Bidwell decided to convert the Bahapki residents to Christianity and to promote their adoption of Euro-American clothes, homes, and values. She established a school for Native American women and children in 1875 and built a Presbyterian church for the Bahapki residents in 1882. In the 1890s, she served as vice-president of the Women's National Indian Association, a reform organization of middle-class white women who worked to assimilate Native Americans into mainstream Euro-American society. In her efforts to promote Christianity and Euro-American life styles, Bidwell also discouraged Bahapki burial practices and ceremonial dances. Despite her efforts to stifle them, however, the Native Americans at Bahapki secretly maintained many of their own traditions. Some historians view Bidwell as a humanitarian while others criticize her for pressuring Native Americans to abandon their culture.

—*Margaret D. Jacobs*

See also: United States Indian Policy: Reform Movement

John Bidwell. *Courtesy Washington State Historical Society.* Annie Ellicott Kennedy Bidwell. *Courtesy Bancroft Library.*

SUGGESTED READING:

Azbill, Henry. "Bahapki." *Indian Historian* 4 (Spring 1971): 57.

Hill, Dorothy J. *The Indians of Chico Rancheria.* Sacramento, Calif., 1978.

Jacobs, Margaret D. "'Resistance to Rescue': The Indians at Bahapki and Mrs. Annie E. K. Bidwell." In *Writing the Range: Race, Class, and Culture in the Women's West.* Edited by Elizabeth Jameson and Susan Armitage. Norman, Okla., 1996.

Mathes, Valerie Sherer. "Indian Philanthropy in California: Annie Bidwell and the Mechoopda Indians." *Arizona and the West* 25 (Summer 1983): 153–166.

BIDWELL, JOHN

A leading California citizen and member of the state's constitutional conventional, John Bidwell (1819–1900) was born in Ripley, New York. He grew up in Ohio and was well educated. Splitting his time between teaching and farming, he worked his way west to Missouri. Captivated by glowing accounts of Mexican California, he helped organize the Western Emigrant Society, which planned the first overland migration to Alta California. After twenty-four grueling weeks of travel, the thirty-four pioneers of the 1841 Bidwell-Bartleson party finally reached the Central Valley. Bidwell clerked for JOHN AUGUST SUTTER at his Sacramento fort for some years, became a Mexican citizen, and settled on land along Chico Creek in present-day Butte County. In 1844, he was a staunch supporter of the embattled Mexican governor, Manuel Micheltorena. That attachment, however, did not deter him from drawing up a declaration of independence from Mexico in 1846 and enlisting as a lieutenant in JOHN CHARLES FRÉMONT'S California Battalion.

On the eve of the UNITED STATES–MEXICAN WAR, Bidwell became interested in the welfare of the local Indians, an interest shared by his wife, ANNIE ELLICOTT KENNEDY BIDWELL. At the same time, the discovery of gold in 1848 accelerated the prospect of statehood for California. Bidwell was elected a delegate to attend what evolved into a state constitutional convention. He took advantage of the gold discovery and profited not only from mining but also from operating a trading post in the northern mines.

His new wealth made possible the acquisition of RANCHO CHICO, a splendid property that he added to his other holdings in the vicinity. His twenty-two-thousand-acre ranch became the prototype of modern agricultural development.

After California's statehood, Bidwell continued to be politically active. He was appointed brigadier general in the state militia in 1861, a title he used consistently thereafter. He served as a state senator and as a U.S. congressman for one term. He ran for governor of California un-

successfully three times and for the presidency of the United States on the Prohibition ticket in 1892.

—*Doyce B. Nunis, Jr.*

SUGGESTED READING:

Hunt, Rockwell D. *John Bidwell: Prince of California Pioneers.* Caldwell, Idaho, 1942.

Royce, C(harles) C., comp. *Addresses, Reminiscences, etc. of General Bidwell.* Chico, Calif., 1907.

———. *John Bidwell, Pioneer Statesman, Philanthropist, a Biographical Sketch.* Chico, Calif., 1906.

BIERCE, AMBROSE GWINETT

Journalist and author Ambrose Gwinett Bierce (1842–1914?) was born in Meigs County, Ohio, the tenth of thirteen children in an impoverished farm family. At the age of nineteen, he joined the Ninth Indiana Infantry and fought in such Civil War battles as Shiloh, Chickamauga, Murfreesboro, Franklin, and Nashville.

A brevet major in the Union Army at the end of the war, Bierce moved to San Francisco. His contributions of verse, satire, and iconoclastic humor to local newspapers and magazines and his subsequent editorship of the *San Francisco News Letter* put him in touch with such literary figures as BRET HARTE, MARK TWAIN, INA COOLBRITH, and Charles Warren Stoddard.

Bierce married in 1871, and from 1872 to 1875, he traveled in England, where he published three books of satirical writings. He returned to San Francisco in 1876 and resumed his newspaper work. For more than twenty years, he wrote columns and stories for WILLIAM RANDOLPH HEARST'S newspapers in San Francisco, New York, and Washington, D.C.

His *Tales of Soldiers and Civilians,* a collection of Civil War stories, was published in 1891; *The Devil's Dictionary* (containing such aphorisms as "Marriage: a master, a mistress and two slaves, making in all two") appeared in 1911.

Bierce retired in 1909 to edit his twelve-volume *Collected Works* (published between 1909 and 1912). In September 1913, he visited the Civil War battlefields of his youth, and in November of that year, he crossed the Rio Grande into revolution-torn Mexico. His last message was sent from Ciudad Chihuahua on December 26, 1913.

Many theories have been advanced on Bierce's fate; one states he was killed on orders from revolutionary general FRANCISCO ("PANCHO") VILLA. But no real evidence exists to support that conclusion or any other. The most likely guess is that, in his seventies and ill with asthma, he died of natural causes and was buried in a hasty and unmarked grave.

—*Dale L. Walker*

SEE ALSO: Magazines and Newspapers

SUGGESTED READING:
Bierce, Ambrose. *Collected Works.* 12 vols. New York, 1909–1912.
Fatout, Paul. *Ambrose Bierce, the Devil's Lexicographer.* Norman, Okla., 1951.
O'Connor, Richard. *Ambrose Bierce: A Biography.* Boston, 1967.

BIERSTADT, ALBERT

Born in Solingen, Germany, Albert Bierstadt (1830–1902) became the first landscape artist to interpret in a number of paintings the majestic topography of the American West. He created an enduring romantic vision of the Rocky Mountains, Wind River valley, Sierra Nevada, and Yosemite. His paintings contributed to the manner in which the nation thought about those lands beyond the Mississippi River and visually demonstrated the monumental dimensions of life in the West.

Bierstadt grew up in New Bedford, Massachusetts, in which his parents had moved when he was two years old. He received informal training in art in Düsseldorf, Germany, from 1853 to 1857. There, he became part of the artistic community, met many young artists, and acquired the techniques of composition and color that he would later use successfully in his Western landscapes.

Bierstadt first journeyed to the American West in 1859 when he accompanied the Lander expedition through the South Pass of the Rocky Mountains. Intrigued by the beauty of the mountains, he sought to capture their grandeur on canvas when he returned to his studio in New York. Twenty-eight paintings resulted from this initial incursion into the West, including *The Rocky Mountains; The Rocky Mountains, Lander's Peak;* and *Wasatch Mountains, Wind River Country, Wyoming.* In the spring of 1863, Bierstadt once more traveled west passing through Kansas, Nebraska, Colorado, and Utah on his way to California and Oregon. That was an important trip for Bierstadt, for he made sketches and photographs on which he based several of his significant paintings: *The Last of the Buffalo, Emigrants Crossing the Plains, Storm in the Rocky Mountains, Domes of Yosemite, In the Yosemite Valley,* and *Merced River.* By the end of 1864, he had completed two large paintings, *The Rocky Mountains* (six feet by ten feet) and *Storm in the Rocky Mountains* (seven feet by twelve

feet), and public praise for these massive works was immediate. For the next decade, Bierstadt was one of the more popular and financially successful painters in America. Given to self-promotion, Bierstadt believed that he had found the key to success—prepare large paintings of expansive landscapes enduring the wrath of nature's storms in regions that lay beyond the experience of most of his viewers. When he completed *Domes of Yosemite* (nine feet, eight inches by fifteen feet), however, art critics began to assail him for the size of his works.

In the 1880s, new vogues in art reduced his popularity, and in 1889, his striking *Last of the Buffalo* was rejected by the American jury selecting pieces for the Exposition at Paris. His portrayals of towering peaks, storm-nourished clouds, majestic homes of the Indian, haunts of the mountain man, and habitats of the buffalo and elk nourished the nineteenth century's perception of the nation's sublime Western wilderness.

—*Phillip Drennon Thomas*

SEE ALSO: Art: Western Art

Albert Bierstadt around 1870. Photograph by Napoleon Sarony. *Courtesy National Portrait Gallery, Smithsonian Institution.*

Emigrants Crossing the Plains by Albert Bierstadt. *Courtesy National Cowboy Hall of Fame and Western Heritage Center.*

SUGGESTED READING:
Anderson, Nancy K. *Albert Bierstadt: Art and Enterprise.* New York, 1990.
Baigell, Matthew. *Albert Bierstadt.* New York, 1981.
Hendricks, Gordon. *Albert Bierstadt, Painter of the American West.* New York, 1975.
Trump, Richard Shafer. "Life and Works of Albert Bierstadt." Ph.D. diss., Ohio State University, 1963.

BIG FOOT (SPOTTED ELK) (SIOUX)

The Minneconjou (Mnikowozu) Lakota leader Big Foot (Si Tanka, ?–1890)—also called Spotted Elk— was best known after his death at the WOUNDED KNEE MASSACRE on December 29, 1890, as the subject of a photograph that depicted his frozen body. In life, he was best known for diplomatic efforts to resolve differences among divergent forces within the Lakota tribes and to prevent war between Native Americans and non-Indians.

Next to SITTING BULL, Big Foot was most feared by federal officials in the upper Missouri River valley and most courted by U.S. Army leaders charged with keeping the peace in the Cheyenne River Agency. Big Foot's father, Long Horn, was the undisputed primary leader of Minneconjous, and Big Foot succeeded his father in that role.

Big Foot earned a reputation as a diplomat after the Fort Bennett Agency was established in 1869 to accommodate four Lakota tribal groups—the Minneconjou, Two Kettle (Oohe Numpa), Sans Arc (Itazipcola), and Blackfoot (Siha Sapa) Lakota. Some eighty miles up the Cheyenne River, Big Foot assembled his group to build a cluster of cabins, while he watched non-Indians filter in around them. In concert with Hump and the GHOST DANCE leader KICKING BEAR, Big Foot advised nonmilitary resistance.

Members of Big Foot's camp participated in the Ghost Dance until Hump withdrew to accept a new residence close to the agency. Big Foot nurtured his large following at a suitable location below the fork of the Cheyenne River. Personally, he soon withdrew from the dance, but at the encouragement of Yellow Bird, many of his followers participated. Because of their participation, federal officials remained suspicious of Big Foot. Indeed General NELSON APPLETON MILES considered Big Foot and Sitting Bull to be the principal leaders of resistance to federal policies; Miles planned to have both of them placed under arrest.

After the death of Sitting Bull on December 15, 1890, Colonel EDWIN V. SUMNER and two hundred men under his command were ordered to watch Big Foot from an encampment along the Cheyenne and to protect settlers along the Cheyenne and Belle Fourche river valleys from possible attack. After Sumner and Big Foot talked, the colonel reported the Minneconjou leader to be disposed toward peace and cooperation.

During their deliberations, Sumner offered to give Big Foot one hundred ponies if he would use his diplomatic skills among the sixteen "chiefs" of the tribes under the jurisdiction of the Pine Ridge Agency. Evidently, Big Foot delayed making a decision until after the next date for annuity payments at the Fort Bennett Agency, but news of Sitting Bull's death brought a change in plans. Two days later came orders from Fort Meade for the arrest of Big Foot. At the same time, Hunkpapas in Sitting Bull's former camp descended from the Standing Rock Agency jurisdiction.

Sumner at first hesitated and then sent a column toward Big Foot's camp to prevent a merger of Hunkpapas with Minneconjous. By December 19, however, Big Foot had offered sanctuary to Standing Rock refugees. Some of them followed Hump into surrender and relocation at Fort Sully on the Missouri River. Sumner and Big Foot evidently reached an agreement whereby the other Hunkpapas could remain with Minneconjou relatives at their tribal village along the Cheyenne River.

Big Foot came under increasing pressure from the Lakota people to help settle intertribal differences at the Pine Ridge Agency, while General Miles urged Sumner to incarcerate Big Foot at Fort Bennett or Fort Meade. Again Sumner waffled, giving Big Foot an opportunity to escape toward Pine Ridge. Understandably, federal observers were alarmed by the prospect of a merger of bands near Pine Ridge. Such a merger would comprise three groups of the martyred Sitting Bull's allies: a group of Cheyennes, one of Minneconjous, and many Oglalas—all under the influence of the powerful orator and diplomat Big Foot. If the Indians did not talk of war, according to tribal memory, they certainly discussed a massive movement onto the Missouri River plateau near the Wyoming-Montana border.

En route to Pine Ridge, Big Foot fell ill with pneumonia; near death, he rode into Wounded Knee Creek

Big Foot. *Courtesy National Archives.*

valley on a wagon. There, he discovered that he had led his Minneconjou-Hunkpapa party on a collision course with federal troops, including the reconstructed Seventh Cavalry. After shooting began, he tried to raise himself to speak, and an army officer shot him in the head. He died instantly.

The following day, a photographer captured the image of the frozen corpse of Big Foot, an image that became a symbol of the tragedy at Wounded Knee. Making good their vow to avenge the death of members of GEORGE ARMSTRONG CUSTER's unit, soldiers in the Seventh Cavalry not only prevented intertribal resistance to Lakota confinement but also placed in the historical annals the unbending determination of Lakota people, the martyrdom of Big Foot, and the memory of a Minneconjou leader long committed to an honorable search for freedom through diplomacy as the alternative to war.

—*Herbert T. Hoover*

SUGGESTED READING:
National Archives. Record Group 75. Cheyenne River Agency and Pine Ridge Agency.
Utley, Robert M. *The Last Days of the Sioux Nation.* New Haven, Conn., 1963.

BIG TREE (KIOWA)

As a young subchief with a reputation for reckless bravery, Big Tree (Addo-etta or Adocette, ca. 1850–1929) played a prominent role in the Warren Wagon Train Raid near Fort Richardson, Texas, on May 18, 1871. He was arrested along with SATANTA and SATANK at Fort Sill in present-day Oklahoma. Satank was killed trying to escape. Big Tree and Satanta were tried in Jacksboro, Texas, and sentenced to be hanged. The prosecuting attorney described Big Tree as a "mighty warrior athlete, with the speed of the deer and the eye of the eagle" and as a "tiger-demon who is swift as every species of ferocity." Bowing to pressure from humanitarian groups, President Ulysses S. Grant instructed Texas Governor E. J. Davis to commute the sentences to life imprisonment at the Huntsville Penitentiary. At the request of Secretary of the Interior Columbus Delano, Davis paroled the two chiefs on October 8, 1873.

During the 1874 Red River War, Big Tree and Satanta were among the Kiowas who bolted from the reservation following the fight between Lieutenant Colonel John W. Davidson and Comanches at the Anadarko Agency. The pair surrendered in October, and Satanta was returned to Huntsville, where he jumped to his death on October 11, 1878. Big Tree, however, remained on the Fort Sill Reservation and, following Satanta's death, assumed leadership of the

Big Tree, on the left, with fellow militant White Bear. *Courtesy Archives Division, Texas State Library.*

tribe. In 1900, he unsuccessfully opposed opening the Indian Territory to white settlement. Big Tree ridiculed the GHOST DANCE religion when it appeared among the Kiowas in the late 1880s, and he eventually embraced Christianity and became a deacon of the Rainy Mountain Indian Baptist Church. Occasionally, he traveled to the East to raise funds for the mission.

—*Bruce J. Dinges*

SEE ALSO: Central Plains Indian Wars

SUGGESTED READING:
Hamilton, Allen Lee. *Sentinel of the Southern Plains: Fort Richardson and the Northwest Texas Frontier.* Fort Worth, Tex., 1988.
Nye, Wilbur S. *Carbine and Lance: The Story of Old Fort Sill.* Norman, Okla., 1974.

BILLINGTON, RAY ALLEN

A distinguished historian, Ray Allen Billington (1903–1981) followed and amplified FREDERICK JACKSON TURNER's theory that an advancing Western frontier historically shaped American life. In the course of a long and productive career, Billington became one of the leading proponents of American "exceptionalism," the notion that the United States and its immigrant peoples developed in ways unique to the North American continent and outside the general sweep of European history. Born in Bay City, Michigan, and reared in Detroit, Billington attended the University of Wisconsin for his Ph.B. and the University of Michigan for his M.A. (in American history) with the intention of becoming a journalist. Before he left Michigan (1927), however, he had decided to pursue his academic studies and was accepted into the doctoral program at Harvard, where he met Frederick Merk (the leading Turnerian of the day), Samuel Eliot Morison, William Langer, and Arthur M. Schlesinger, Sr. Before receiving his degree, Billington accepted a position at Clark University where he launched a teaching career that spanned three decades. He received his Ph.D. in 1933. He taught at Smith College (from 1938 to 1944) and ultimately at Northwestern University, with stints at Harvard and Oxford. In 1963, he resigned from Northwestern to join Allen Nevins as a senior research associate at the Huntington Library, where he took up the life of a scholar and remained until his death.

Billington's first scholarly work was of a decidedly non-Turnerian cast. Although he had participated in Merk's seminar on Western history, Billington wrote his dissertation under Arthur Schlesinger on the "Social Backgrounds of the KNOW NOTHING PARTY," which he expanded and published in 1938 as *The Protestant Crusade*. A book squarely in the Schlesinger tradition of social and intellectual history, it mentioned the frontier only once and then only to play down its significance in favor of the persistence of European influence on American life, especially on its nativism and anti-Catholicism. Billington did not turn to frontier history until Brown University's James Hedges suggested to him that the two coauthor a book based on Harvard's Western history course, first developed by Frederick Jackson Turner. Early on, Hedges dropped out of the project, and Billington wrote *Western Expansion* (1949). A magisterial work tracing the westward movement from Spanish, French, and English explorers through some nine-hundred pages to the closing of the frontier and its heritage, *Westward Expansion,* which went through five revisions, was Billington's most successful book outside, perhaps, the seminal biography of Turner he wrote toward the end of his career.

Hailed by many as the book Turner himself should have written, *Western Expansion* rescued the frontier thesis from the attacks it had suffered at the hands of New Deal social historians and placed Billington among the leaders in Western history. He became a founder and the first president of the Western History Association as well as president of the American Studies Association and the Organization of American Historians. And he continued to write about the frontier and in defense of Turner. Recruited to author a volume in the "New American Nation" series, he produced *The Far Western Frontier, 1830–1860* in 1956 and then initiated a multivolume series in the 1960s on the "Frontier in American History" with *America's Frontier Heritage,* in which he said he "hoped not only to enlighten, but to convert." By the early 1970s, Billington was at work on the biography of Turner, a summary of almost thirty years of thought and research. First, however, he came out in 1971 with *The Genesis of the Frontier Thesis: A Study in Historical Creativity,* which covered the sources and evolution of Turner's thought. *Frederick Jackson Turner, Historian, Scholar, Teacher* was published in 1973 and won the coveted Bancroft Prize in American History. Billington's last work of Western history, *Land of Savages, Land of Promise: The European Image of the American Frontier in the Nineteenth Century* appeared in 1981, the year he died.

—*Charles Phillips and Martin Ridge*

SEE ALSO: Huntington Library, Art Collections, and Botanical Gardens; Frontier: Frontier Thesis

SUGGESTED READING:

Billington, Ray Allen. *Westward Expansion: A History of the American Frontier.* 1st ed. New York, 1949. Later eds., 1960, 1967, 1974, with James Blaine Hedges, and 1982, with Martin Ridge.

Ridge, Martin. "Ray Allen Billington (1903–1981)." *Western Historical Quarterly* 12:3 (July 1981): 244–250.

———. "Ray Allen Billington, Western History, and American Exceptionalism." *Pacific Historical Review* 56:2 (May 1987): 494–511.

"BILLY THE KID"

Premier Western outlaw of history and legend "Billy the Kid" (1859?–1881) was born Henry McCarty in New York City's Irish ghetto. His life, however, is identified with New Mexico, where his mother remarried in 1873 and where young Henry took his stepfather's name, Antrim. Known as Henry Antrim and later by the alias of William H. Bonney, he was most often simply called "Kid"—because he was one. Only six months before his death at the age of twenty-one did he become known as "Billy the Kid."

The Kid began his short life of crime and violence at the age of fifteen in Silver City, New Mexico, where he was jailed for a petty theft. After escaping to Arizona, on August 17, 1877, he shot and killed "Windy" Cahill, an older and bigger man who had bullied him in a saloon fight. The Kid fled back to New Mexico.

Taking refuge in the sparsely settled southeastern corner of the territory, the seventeen-year-old youth, now also calling himself Billy Bonney, arrived on the eve of the LINCOLN COUNTY WAR of 1878 to 1879. In that conflict between rivals for commercial monopoly and government contracts, Billy signed on with the Tunstall-McSween "Regulators." In a series of gunfights with the Murphy-Dolan forces, he showed himself to be a fearless fighter and a crack shot. In the final battle in the blazing McSween House in Lincoln on July 19, 1878, he took charge and led the breakout by which some of the defenders escaped.

One of six Regulators who on April 1, 1878, had gunned down Sheriff William Brady, the Kid was wanted for murder. In March 1879, however, he struck a bargain with Territorial Governor Lew Wallace. In return for testimony against other murderers, the governor would drop the charges against Billy. The Kid lived up to his promise. The governor did not.

In fact, the Kid did not give Wallace a chance. Based at old Fort Sumner on the Pecos River east of Lincoln, he and a handful of comrades rustled the cattle of Texas stockmen. He intended to go straight but never quite got around to it. Wallace put a price on the Kid's head, and in December 1880, following a shootout at Stinking Springs, Sheriff PATRICK FLOYD JARVIS (PAT) GARRETT and other lawmen took him into custody.

Convicted of murder and sentenced to be hanged, the Kid was held under guard in the old Murphy-Dolan store, which had been converted into the Lincoln County Courthouse. On April 28, 1881, he over-

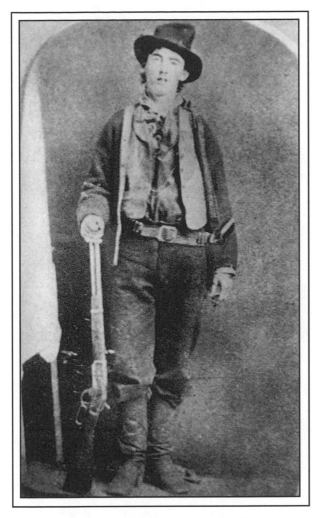

Billy the Kid. *Courtesy Museum of New Mexico.*

inventions. It gave rise to the mighty legend of Billy the Kid that still dominates his image in American folklore.

The legend vastly inflated the boy's actual criminal career. He did not kill the twenty-one men credited to him, but four by his gun alone and several more with the participation of others. He rustled cattle and stole horses on a minor scale but never robbed a bank or store or stagecoach or engaged in any other serious criminal activity. He was not, as the newspapers charged, the captain of an outlaw gang. Nor was he a homicidal maniac. Instead, he was an intelligent, cheerful, and well-liked youth with a deadly temper—a young man who was capable of rationalizing his killings as well as any other behavior that got him in trouble.

Regardless of the reality, however, Billy the Kid has become a legend cherished not only by Americans but by people all over the world.

—*Robert M. Utley*

SEE ALSO: Literature: Dime Novels; Social Banditry; Violence

SUGGESTED READING:
Mullin, Robert N., ed. *Maurice G. Fulton's History of the Lincoln County War.* Tucson, Ariz., 1968.
Nolan, Frederick. *The Lincoln County War: A Documentary History.* Norman, Okla., 1992.
Utley, Robert M. *Billy the Kid: A Short and Violent Life.* Lincoln, Nebr., 1989.

BINGHAM, GEORGE CALEB

A perceptive observer of life in the West, George Caleb Bingham (1811–1879) chronicled in his art the unique and distinctive life of settlers on the Missouri and Mississippi rivers. He poignantly portrayed the men and women of the emerging towns and cities, the squatters, the boatmen, and politicians. Born in the Blue Ridge Mountains of Virginia, Bingham moved at the age of eight with his family to Franklin, Missouri; for the balance of his life, that state and that region would be central to his life, career, and art.

By 1834, Bingham had become a portrait painter in Columbia, Missouri; by 1838, he had produced his first genre painting, *Western Boatmen Ashore.* Captivated by the drama of human activities along the great rivers of the West, Bingham began to make life on the Missouri and Mississippi rivers important subjects for his art. These themes were colorful, immediate, and dramatic. He first gained substantial public notice with his enigmatic 1845 painting *Fur Traders Descending the Missouri,* which was distributed in the thousands by the American Art Union as an engraving. Bingham's

powered and killed his guard, fatally shot another deputy, and escaped from Lincoln. Already the newspapers had falsely branded him New Mexico's foremost outlaw and dubbed him "Billy the Kid." The breakout from Lincoln seemed to confirm the portrait and made him the Southwest's most notorious criminal.

Sheriff Garrett and his deputies again tracked Billy to old Fort Sumner. There on the night of July 14, 1881, Garrett accidentally confronted his quarry in the darkened bedroom of one of the old military houses. Billy's famous query, *"Quien es? Quien es?"* ("Who is it? Who is it?"), prompted the sheriff to draw his pistol and fire twice. The first bullet struck Billy in the chest and killed him instantly. He was buried the next day in the Fort Sumner cemetery.

Criticized for not giving Billy a chance to defend himself, Garrett wrote a defense in *The Authentic Life of Billy the Kid,* published less than a year later. Most of the book was ghostwritten and filled with imaginative

The Trappers Return by George Caleb Bingham. *Courtesy Detroit Institute of Arts.*

interest in politics led him both to run as a Whig candidate for the state legislature in 1846 and to prepare a series of unique paintings that chronicled Western political life—*In Canvassing for a Vote* (1852), *County Election* (1851–1852), and *Verdict of the People* (1854–1855). With the outbreak of the Civil War, his paintings became less imaginative and vital and more polemical. He found it difficult to support himself as an artist. In 1862, he became state treasurer of Missouri; in 1877, he became the first professor of art at the University of Missouri.

Bingham's art usually emphasized the life of the common Western man engaged in the mundane tasks of frontier existence. His genre paintings emphasize their daily struggles and, with the exception of *Daniel Boone Escorting Settlers through the Cumberland Gap* (1851), avoided heroic figures. Curiously, while men and boys are drawn and painted from all angles and in all manners of clothes, women are generally absent from his paintings.

Although essentially self-taught as an artist, Bingham developed pronounced technical skills as an artist working with oils. His body of work includes portraits, a genre series of river and political life, landscapes, and historical paintings. His paintings are characterized not only by their painterly qualities but also by irony, humor, and close observation.

—*Phillip Drennon Thomas*

SEE ALSO: Art: Western Art

SUGGESTED READING:

Constant, Alberta Wilson. *Paintbox on the Frontier: The Life and Times of George Caleb Bingham.* New York, 1974.

McDermott, John Francis. *George Caleb Bingham, River Portraitist.* Norman, Okla., 1959.

Rash, Nancy. *The Paintings and Politics of George Caleb Bingham.* New Haven, Conn., 1991.

BINGHAM, HIRAM AND SYBIL MOSELEY

Missionaries in HAWAII for twenty years, Hiram Bingham (1789–1869) and his wife Sybil Moseley

Bingham (1792–1848) converted Hawaiian peoples to Christianity and, in the process, radically changed Hawaiian culture and community.

Born in Bennington, Vermont, Hiram Bingham received his education at Middlebury College and Andover Theological Seminary. By the time of his ordination in September 1819, he had offered himself to the AMERICAN BOARD OF COMMISSIONERS FOR FOREIGN MISSIONS for service in the Hawaiian Islands. Because the board did not allow unmarried men to serve in foreign missions, Bingham hastily married Sybil Moseley of Westfield, Massachusetts, whom he had met at his ordination ceremony and who was answering her own calling to missionary work. In Boston, the Binghams joined other missionaries and New England-educated Hawaiian natives aboard the brig *Thaddeus* on October 23, 1819. They sailed eighteen thousand miles around Cape Horn to Hawaii, studied the Hawaiian language on board ship, and arrived at the islands five months later.

Their reception was mixed. Nothing in their New England background prepared the missionaries for the cultural differences they faced on the islands, and the Hawaiian natives were suspicious of foreigners whose very presence had already changed their way of life. Bingham saw in the Hawaiian people "destitution, degradation, and barbarism, among the chattering, and almost naked savages. . . ." Hawaii's ruler King Liholiho made the missionaries remain on their ship while he decided whether to grant them permission to settle on his islands. After several days of deliberation, Liholiho informed the Christians that they could stay for a probationary period of one year.

The Binghams settled in Honolulu on Oahu and set about the task of converting the native peoples. They intended to convert Hawaiians not just to Christianity but also to adopting American customs and values. While Hiram devised a Hawaiian alphabet and instructed Hawaiians to study his translations of the Bible, Sybil and the other missionary wives operated schools and taught domestic skills. Lay missionaries printed the first works in the Hawaiian language and taught farming techniques. In addition to managing their own households and serving as schoolteachers, Sybil and the other wives sewed European-style clothing on demand for high-ranking Hawaiian men and women.

By 1821, the Binghams gave up their native hut for a frame house, dismantled and shipped from America. In August of that year, the missionaries constructed a church. Soon churches and schools dotted the landscape. Encouraged by the conversion in 1825 of Kaahumanu (widow of the ruler Kamehameha I), converts attended church services and school classes in great numbers. Kaahumanu's conversion came about when Sybil Bingham nursed her back to health after a serious illness.

With the missions established and accepted among the Hawaiian people and their rulers, Bingham's influence in governmental matters increased, but membership in his church did not. After seventeen years, although thousands of Hawaiians practiced Bingham's teachings, only thirteen hundred Hawaiians had been admitted to membership in the church. Bingham received orders from the American Board in Boston to expand his criteria and open the church's membership rolls. By the late 1830s, however, it became clear that Bingham's authoritarian ways were more hindrance than help to the mission's cause. In 1840, the American Board recalled the Binghams, ostensibly because of Sybil's failing health.

After the Binghams returned to New England, Hiram wrote memoirs of his missionary experiences. *A Residence of Twenty-One Years in the Sandwich Islands* was published in 1847. Sybil died the next year. Hiram continued to write and preach and served for a time as the pastor of an African American church in New Haven, Connecticut. In 1854, he married Maomi Emma Morse. He died shortly after his eightieth birthday.

—Patricia Hogan

SEE ALSO: Missions: Missions in Hawaii

SUGGESTED READING:

Bingham, Hiram. *A Residence of Twenty-One Years in the Sandwich Islands, or the Civil, Religious, and Political History of Those Islands.* Rutland, Vt., 1987.
Grimshaw, Patricia. *Paths of Duty: American Missionary Wives in Nineteenth-Century Hawaii.* Honolulu, Hawaii, 1989.

BISHOP, BERNICE PAUAHI

A direct descendant of Hawaii's ruler, Kamehameha I, Bernice Pauahi Bishop (1831–1884) was a philanthropist and a champion of Hawaiian peoples and culture at a time when both were challenged by American and European attempts to gain control over the islands. Born in Honolulu, she was adopted at birth by the high chieftess Kinau, and, following island custom, lived with her foster mother for seven years. After a year with her own parents, she entered a boarding school for Hawaiian royalty.

She remained at the Royal School until her marriage in 1850 to Charles Reed Bishop, an American-born customs collector, whom she had chosen over Prince Lot. The prince, the choice of her parents, later became native ruler of Hawaii as Kamehameha V.

Her husband's successful business ventures enabled the couple to enjoy extensive travel and philanthropic works benefiting native Hawaiians. Bishop's strong sense of civic duty drew her into prominent charitable organizations such as the Stranger's Friend Society, and her social rank and poise made her a link between the Hawaiian and American communities.

An only child, Bishop had inherited her parents' land when they died, and upon the death of her cousin in 1883, she added to her holdings the immense lands of the Kamehameha royal estates. When Bishop died, her will stipulated that the lands be used to establish the Kamehameha Schools for the education of native Hawaiian children. Charles Bishop served as a trustee of the schools and established in her memory the Bernice Pauahi Bishop Museum, a repository of Hawaiian and Polynesian cultures in Honolulu.

—*Patricia Hogan*

BISHOP, ISABELLA BIRD

Author and adventurer Isabella Bird Bishop (1831–1904) flouted nineteenth-century notions of womanly conduct, roamed the earth in a most unconventional manner, and told the world about it in her engaging travel books. Bishop's book about the American West, *A Lady's Life in the Rocky Mountains,* proved to be among her most popular.

Born in Yorkshire, England, Bishop spent most of her years living the virtuous life of the minister's daughter that she was. She was seldom in good health (a chronic back ailment gave her almost constant pain), and she suffered episodes of depression. In 1854, her doctor suggested travel as a cure. With one hundred pounds in her pocket, she set off, by herself, for Canada and the United States. Traveling more than two thousand miles on the continent, she became resourceful and energetic. She bounced along rough roads in the wilds of Canada and aboard ship decks on Lake Ontario, dined on pork and onions in Chicago, and endured traffic jams in New York City. Her ailments disappeared, and the result was her first book, the deceptively titled *Englishman in America* (1856), in which her writing talents and her perceptive observations of the people she met were apparent.

Returning to England, she remained for a time, but a recurrence of her ailments and the death of her father set her to traveling again. In 1872, unmarried and at the age of forty, she began an eighteen-month trip around the world—a trip that ended with a stay in the Sandwich Islands (Hawaii), where she climbed to the top of a volcano and camped. She next traveled to

Colorado, where she lived in a log cabin for three months in Estes Park, rode horses comfortably in Turkish trousers, drove cattle, climbed mountains, and fell in love with "Rocky Mountain Jim," part trapper, part gentleman, part scoundrel, and part windbag. All of her adventures she recorded in descriptive letters to her sister back in Edinburgh. These letters became the substance of her *Six Months in the Sandwich Islands* (1875) and *Lady's Life in the Rocky Mountains* (1879).

In 1881, Isabella Bird married John Bishop, a doctor ten years her junior. Neither her marriage nor her husband's death in 1886 interfered much with her travels, which she duly recorded in books about Japan, (1880), Persia (1891), Korea (1898), and China (1894 and 1899). In time, however, her ailments overcame her, and she spent her last years confined to a bed.

—*Patricia Hogan*

Suggested reading:
Barr, Pat. *A Curious Life for a Lady: The Story of Isabella Bird, a Remarkable Victorian Traveller.* London, 1970.

BISONS

See: Buffaloes

"BLACK BART" (BOLES, CHARLES E.)

A stagecoach robber from Jefferson County, New York, Charles E. Boles (ca. 1830–1917) apparently moved to California about 1850 during the gold rush. He claimed to have served as a Union officer during the Civil War, although his commission cannot be documented. Certainly he was back in California after the war, because on July 26, 1875, he robbed a Wells, Fargo and Company stagecoach of three hundred dollars. Wearing a linen duster and a derby hat perched atop a flour sack with eye holes, he intercepted the stage near Copperopolis and indicated a band of concealed confederates, whose gun barrels were pointing through nearby bushes. When the strongbox was dropped to the ground, he produced a small axe, extracted the gold coins, and then disappeared on foot. When the driver retrieved the strongbox, he discovered that the gang's guns were sticks tied to bushes.

Encouraged by his success, the solitary bandit who became known as "Black Bart" executed at least twenty-eight stage holdups during the next several years. He always robbed Wells Fargo vehicles; he always wore a duster, flour-sack mask, and derby; and held onto the gold he had pilfered but dropped several personal articles before hiking into the wilderness. Hume found a laundry mark on a dropped handkerchief, and a painstaking search revealed a San Francisco laundryman who identified Charles "Bolton" as the owner of the handkerchief. Bolton matched the physical description of Black Bart—five feet, eight inches tall; broad shoulders; blue eyes; a large gray mustache—and soon he was arrested. After pleading guilty in a San Andreas court in November 1883, he was sentenced to six years in San Quentin. Pardoned after four years and two months, he was rumored to have moved to Harrisburg, Pennsylvania, to marry a childhood sweetheart. Other rumors persisted that Wells Fargo paid him not to resume his career of robbery.

—*Bill O'Neal*

SUGGESTED READING:
Dillon, Richard H. *Wells Fargo Detective*. New York, 1969.

BLACK BEARS

A member of the family *Ursidae,* the black bear *(Ursus americanus)* is the most numerous of the three bears found in North America and the only bear found east of the Mississippi River. Black bears range from Alaska to Mexico and the Atlantic to Pacific oceans. Smaller than GRIZZLY BEARS and polar bears, mature male black bears normally weigh between 250 and 350 pounds, although bears weighing up to 750 pounds have been found. Females are smaller and seldom exceed 180 pounds. Mature black bears may be four to six feet long and stand three and a half to four feet high. Their five-inch ears are longer than the ears of other North American bears. Their tails seldom exceed five inches in length.

Unlike most other large animals, bears frequently stand on their hind feet. In gross anatomy and skeleton, skinned bears have a superficial resemblance to the human body. Beneath their thick fur, there is an extensive layer of fat, which provides nourishment during their hibernation. Black bears are not always black; some are brown or cinnamon, and in the Glacier Bay region of southeastern Alaska, some are steel-blue gray. In rare instances, they have light tannish-cream coats. They can run and climb trees faster than a human. Indeed, for short distances they can run more than thirty miles an hour. Maturing between three and four years of age, they give birth after a seven month gestation period to two to three cubs. While black bears are omnivorous, most of their diet is vegetarian. In the spring, carrion also becomes a major part of their diet.

Black Bart. *Courtesy Wells Fargo Bank.*

he always was on foot. A horse could be tracked, and he proved to be a swift and tireless hiker. But his schedule was unpredictable: sometimes he waited months between holdups, then he robbed stages on successive days thirty miles apart. Occasionally he left behind short, lighthearted verses, which he signed "Black Bart, the Po-8."

Wells Fargo's chief of detectives, James B. Hume, carefully investigated Black Bart's modus operandi, but little progress was made until the robber was slightly wounded during an 1882 holdup at Copperopolis. He

The bear was regarded more highly than any other animal by many Indian tribes, and the power of the bear and bear spirit were invoked through elaborate Bear Dances. Indians believed that the bear was a powerful force for healing illnesses. Medicine men, as the paintings of GEORGE CATLIN and other contemporary sources reveal, often adorned themselves with accouterments from the bear—paws, claws, teeth, and hide. Since bears were deemed to be healthy and since they were often seen in clearings eating a variety of plants, medicine men believed that dreaming of a bear brought knowledge of what herbs and botanicals should be used to bring relief from a particular illness. The skin of a bear conveyed the same honor as a human scalp. Most of the bear was used when killed by Native Americans. The pelt was worked into thick bear robes that could be used as blankets or made into diverse items of clothing. Claws and teeth were made into ceremonial necklaces and fetishes. Roasted, stewed, or "jerked," bear meat was a favorite food of many tribes.

Both Indian and Euro-American society esteemed not only the meat of the bear but also bear oil, which came from the thick layer of fat beneath the skin. Careful processing produced from ten to fifteen gallons of oil from the average black bear. Bear oil was the principal cooking oil used by settlers and Native Americans in the first half of the nineteenth century. It was also used to flavor other foods, such as wild greens. Bear oil was used in a variety of medicines and cosmetics and was praised as a hair oil, baby oil, and lineament. Special glass bottles were manufactured to hold bear oil, and the belief in its efficacy as a hair restorer was maintained until the beginning of the twentieth century. Bearskin robes were also important commercial commodities and, at times, equaled beaver pelts in value. Market hunters also pursued the black bear, and, at holiday seasons, bear hams were much desired as food.

Euro-American settlement led to the decline and fragmentation of the black bear's habitat through logging and clearing forests for agriculture. Farmers, ranchers, and state and federal agents hunted and trapped bears as predators. Bounty systems placed sustained pressure on black bears. Direct hunting pressure was reduced between 1900 and 1950 when various Western states began to designate black bears as game animals with special and closed seasons dependent on regional populations. Bears that were destructive to property were selectively hunted. States that experienced the greatest reduction in forests also experienced the greatest reduction in bear populations. In the last decade of the twentieth century, Alaska and Idaho had the largest populations of black bears in the United States although significant populations were also found in Washington, Oregon, California, Montana, Wyoming, and Colorado.

—*Phillip Drennon Thomas*

SEE ALSO: Wildlife

SUGGESTED READING:

Burk, Dale, ed. *The Black Bear in Modern America.* Clinton, N.J., 1979.

Ford, Barbara. *Black Bear, The Spirit of the Wilderness.* Boston, 1981.

BLACK ELK (SIOUX)

Lakota Oglala holy man (Nicholas) Black Elk (1863–1950) was probably born in Wyoming. His family belonged to the Lakota Oglala (Sioux) tribe, which also included CRAZY HORSE and RED CLOUD. Black Elk is best known for the publication of *Black Elk Speaks,* an artistic biography written by Nebraska poet John Neihardt and released in 1932.

Black Elk's early years were spent in flight and fear. Following the demise of GEORGE ARMSTRONG CUSTER at the Little Bighorn in 1876, the U.S. Army actively pursued the Lakota people. With SITTING BULL, Black Elk's followers fled to Canada and remained there until 1880, when they filtered back to the United States and joined their relatives around the Pine Ridge Agency in southwestern Dakota Territory. During the years, Black Elk had the great vision that haunted him for the rest of his life, a vision that Neihardt devoted so much attention to in *Black Elk Speaks.* Black Elk was never able to interpret or act upon his vision as the traditional way required because pressure from missionaries committed to Christian conversion interfered with traditional ceremonies. By the end of the century, he retired his sacred objects, no doubt because he feared their desecration by well-meaning Christians. His conversations with Neihardt indicate that Black Elk never abandoned his traditional beliefs in spite of actions that would indicate otherwise.

From 1886 to 1889, Black Elk performed in WILLIAM F. ("BUFFALO BILL") CODY's Wild West show, which traveled through the Eastern states and to England. Black Elk became separated from the group and traveled through France and Italy. He returned to Pine Ridge in 1889 as federal officials reduced the remaining acreage in the Great Sioux Reservation to six smaller reservations. He also witnessed the phenomenon of the GHOST DANCE, which had spread throughout western Sioux country and provided hope that traditionalism would prevail over the intruding Euro-Americans. After federal officials suppressed the Ghost Dance, Black Elk converted to Roman Catholicism. He was given the baptismal name "Nicholas" by missionary Jesuits in 1904; by 1907, he was traveling regionally as a missionary to Indian people.

Neihardt met Black Elk in 1930 at Manderson, an isolated community of the Pine Ridge Reservation. Devoutly Catholic yet haunted by his youthful vision, Black Elk permitted Neihardt to conduct a series of interviews. The resulting *Black Elk Speaks* provides a picture of a medicine man tortured by unfulfilled potential, unrequited spirituality, and covert traditionalism. Black Elk is revered as a spokesperson for the Lakota traditions he preserved, as well as for his capacity to display quiet leadership in cross-cultural understanding. The book itself is considered a classic, both for its style and substance.

As an old man and in the company of Neihardt, Black Elk visited the sacred Black Hills (Paha Sapa), where he issued a plea to the Great Spirit (Wakantanka Tunkasila) for which he is best known: "Hear me, not for myself, but for my people; I am old. Hear me that they may once more go back into the sacred hoop and find the good red road, the shielding tree!" Black Elk died not knowing that, through his inspiration, Lakota people soon would expose to public view the traditions he represented and stand their ground against congressional, judicial, social, and religious forces that worked to the contrary.

—*Carol Goss Hoover*

Black Hawk. *Courtesy Library of Congress.*

SEE ALSO: Literature: Native American Literature; Sioux Wars; Wild West Shows: Indians in Wild West Shows

SUGGESTED READING:

Brown, Joseph Epes. *The Sacred Pipe.* Norman, Okla., 1953.

DeMallie, Raymond J., ed. *The Sixth Grandfather: Black Elk's Teachings Given to John Neihardt.* Lincoln, Nebr., 1984.

Neihardt, John. *Black Elk Speaks.* New York, 1932. Reprint. Lincoln, Nebr., 1961.

Rice, Julian. *Black Elk's Story: Distinguishing Its Lakota Purpose.* Albuquerque, N. Mex., 1991.

Steltenkamp, Michael F. *Black Elk: Holy Man of the Oglala.* Norman, Okla., 1993.

BLACKFOOT INDIANS

SEE: Native American Peoples: Peoples of the Great Plains

BLACK HAWK'S WAR

Black Hawk's War represents one of the last and best known major resistances by Indians living east of the Mississippi to being "removed" to the trans-Mississippi West. Black Hawk was a war chief of the Sac (Sauk) and Fox (Mesquakie), two closely related tribes chased by the fur-trading French and their Indian allies in centuries past into the Mississippi Valley, where they occupied parts of western Illinois and eastern Wisconsin and Iowa and became implacable foes of the Americans and quite friendly with the British. Black Hawk's band fought with the British-backed TECUMSEH during his 1811 uprising that in part led to the War of 1812. In 1831, after ANDREW JACKSON had begun forcing the Indians of the Old Northwest as well as those of the Southeast beyond the borders of the United States, Black Hawk returned with his warriors from the winter hunt west of the Mississippi to discover Saukenuk—the tribe's main village at the mouth of the Rock River near Rock Island, Illinois—overrun by American squatters; he threatened war.

A spurious treaty signed a quarter century before and either never understood or never recognized by Black Hawk had ceded all the Sac and Fox lands in Illinois to the United States. As a matter of expediency, Territorial Governor William Henry Harrison had allowed the tribe to remain on those lands until the area was needed for settlement. Around 1830, a rush of miners to the Galena lead fields had brought "illegal" farmers—squatters—in its wake, and they destroyed or appropriated the Indians' homes, harvested for themselves the Indians' corn, ripped down fences, trampled unused crops, and beat those Sac and Fox in the village who protested. Quick action in 1831 by government officials helped avert violence that summer and fall, and Black Hawk reluctantly returned to Iowa for the winter hunt, which went badly. In April 1832, he led his starving, homeless "British band"—some four hundred warriors and their families, two thousand in all—back across the Mississippi to look for food. Territorial authorities panicked, marched troops off to engage the Indians, and called to arms an excessive number of militia.

Black Hawk won the first encounter, the result more or less of the Americans' blundering into conflict, but his victory only incensed the settlers along the frontier. In the long run, he was betrayed by his allies, the British and the Winnebago Indians, both of whom had promised aid and shelter but failed to deliver. He was also betrayed by a member of his own tribe, an ambitious young chief named KEOKUK, who urged a substantial number of Sac and Fox Indians to do nothing, thus establishing himself with the Americans as a "peaceful" tribal leader. The Indians were relentlessly hunted down as they fled north along the Rock River into Wisconsin; many were killed when they tried to recross the Mississippi into Iowa. Black Hawk survived to face arrest, trial, and conviction, after which his execution was stayed as the U.S. government, putting him on display, packed him off on a tour of the United States. Greeted in some towns and cities with hatred, treated in others as a celebrity, Black Hawk also served as an example to those Indians still fighting removal to the trans-Mississippi West of the hopelessness of armed resistance. Black Hawk died of natural causes in 1838.

—*Charles Phillips*

SEE ALSO: Native American Peoples: Peoples Removed from the East

SUGGESTED READING:
Axelrod, Alan. *Chronicle of the Indian Wars: From Colonial Times to Wounded Knee.* New York, 1993.
Hagan, William T. *The Sac and the Fox Indians.* Norman, Okla., 1958.

BLACK HILLS GOLD RUSH

An 1874 surveying expedition, commanded by Lieutenant Colonel GEORGE ARMSTRONG CUSTER, and an 1875 scientific expedition, headed by Walter P. Jenney

of the Columbia School of Mines, confirmed reports of gold in the Black Hills of present-day South Dakota. News from both parties spurred a rush to the Black Hills, and a gold-mining enterprise was founded and flourishes to this day.

The Black Hills lay squarely within the Great Sioux Reservation that had been set aside by the Fort Laramie Treaty of 1868. That meant little, however, to the hordes of civilian miners lured there by the prospect of riches. The Sioux Indians vehemently opposed opening the hills to white settlement, resisted repeated political maneuvering, and ultimately engaged in the Great Sioux War from 1876 to 1877 to protect their lands. The federal government prevailed, however, and the hills were formally opened by war's end.

Access to the Black Hills gold fields was largely via the UNION PACIFIC RAILROAD and trails originating in Sidney, Nebraska, and Cheyenne, Wyoming. Soldiers stationed at military posts like Camp Robinson and FORT LARAMIE safeguarded traffic along the route.

The first miners in the region prospected placer gold deposits around French Creek, the boom town of Custer, Whitewood Creek, and the city of Deadwood. While the placer deposits were profitable, they proved much less durable than those in California, Montana, and Idaho. The lack of water to work the placer claims was a nagging problem that often necessitated the construction of expensive and lengthy flumes. By the spring of 1877, placer mining had climaxed, and attention shifted to hard-rock mining.

Hard-rock prospects dotted the Black Hills and were most prevalent around Deadwood and the neighboring towns of Gayville, Central City, and Lead. The underground mines in those areas tapped a rich, broad belt of ore. Dozens of stamp mills pulsed night and day from the mines and towns as production soared.

The greatest and most enduring of hundreds of Black Hills gold mines was the HOMESTAKE MINE at Lead. In the spring of 1876, four prospectors discovered the deposit, which they believed was the source of all Black Hills gold. GEORGE HEARST and his partners purchased the claim in 1877 and incorporated it as the Homestake Mining Company. Acquiring and consolidating adjacent mines and expanding Homestake's milling capacities, Hearst intended to profit on the moderate- to low-grade ores that would surely outlast the rich ore. The Homestake Mine remains the largest, continuously operating gold mine in the United States.

Gold remains a potent force in the region's economy. Beyond Black Hills gold jewelry, MINING museums, actual and recreated mining towns, and abandoned mine sites, tailings, and foundations, no greater reminder of the gold industry exists than the

Homestake Mine itself. Its payroll, hoisting works, and mill overshadow Lead, Deadwood, and virtually all the Black Hills.

—*Paul L. Hedren*

SEE ALSO: Booms; Gold Mining; Sioux Wars

SUGGESTED READING:

Greever, William S. *The Bonanza West: The Story of the Western Mining Rushes, 1848–1900.* Norman, Okla., 1963.

Hedren, Paul L., ed. *The Great Sioux War 1876–77.* Helena, Mont., 1991.

Marks, Paula Mitchell. *Precious Dust: The American Gold Rush Era: 1848–1900.* New York, 1994.

Parker, Watson. *Gold in the Black Hills.* Norman, Okla., 1966.

BLACK KETTLE (CHEYENNE)

A principal chief of the Cheyenne Indians, Black Kettle (Mo-ta-vato, 1804?–1868) was a proponent of peaceful relations with the United States. Born near the Black Hills of present-day South Dakota, Black Kettle rose to tribal prominence in wars with the Utes, Pawnees, Comanches, and other enemies of his tribe. He first came to the attention of the U.S. government as the leading Cheyenne signatory of the Treaty of Fort Wise, Colorado Territory, in 1860. When war broke out on the Great Plains during the spring of 1864, Black Kettle tried to stop the fighting. After using his own horses to purchase and return white captives, the Cheyenne chief bravely traveled to Denver to talk peace.

A "boom town" in the Black Hills during the gold rush. *Courtesy National Archives.*

While Black Kettle was there, Colonel JOHN M. CHIVINGTON promised safety for him and his people if they would turn themselves over to the military at Fort Lyon. When Black Kettle did so, Major Scott Anthony instructed him to camp forty miles north of the post at Sand Creek. There at dawn on November 29, 1864, Chivington made a surprise attack from which Black Kettle and his wife barely escaped. Many other Cheyennes were killed in what has become known as the SAND CREEK MASSACRE.

The notorious Cheyenne Dog Soldiers, members of a militant warrior society, then renewed their attacks against wagon trains. Black Kettle, however, took his band south of the Arkansas River in an effort to remain peaceful. Despite dire threats from the Dog Soldiers, he participated in the Little Arkansas Treaty of 1865 and the MEDICINE LODGE TREATY OF 1867.

In the fall of 1868, Black Kettle followed the instructions of General PHILIP H. SHERIDAN for all peaceful Indians to go to Fort Cobb in the Indian Territory. When he arrived there, General William B. Hazen refused to accept his band. Although Hazen offered to give Black Kettle sanctuary, the Cheyenne peacemaker would not leave his people. He returned to his village, located on the west end of a long series of Plains Indian encampments along the Washita River.

There on the morning of November 27, 1868, Lieutenant Colonel GEORGE ARMSTRONG CUSTER and the Seventh Cavalry made another surprise attack on Black Kettle's camp. This time Black Kettle and his wife were among the many Cheyennes killed.

—*Stan Hoig*

SEE ALSO: Central Plains Indian Wars

SUGGESTED READING:
Berthrong, Donald J. *The Southern Cheyennes.* Norman, Okla., 1963.

George Armstrong Custer's attack at the Washita River led to the death of Black Kettle. *Courtesy Library of Congress.*

Grinnell, George Bird. *The Fighting Cheyennes.* Norman, Okla., 1915.
Hoig, Stan. *The Battle of the Washita.* New York, 1976.
———. *The Peace Chiefs of the Cheyennes.* Norman, Okla., 1980.
———. *The Sand Creek Massacre.* Norman, Okla., 1961.

BLACK LEGEND

The term *Black Legend* refers both to the early view of Spain as a brutal exploiter of the Indians of the New World and to the body of Hispanophobic reaction and thought that shaped many elements of the contact between Hispanic settlers and Anglo-Americans moving into Texas, New Mexico, and California in the nineteenth century. The origins of the distrust and dislike between Hispanics and the English are to be found in the rivalry for empire in the fifteenth and sixteenth centuries—a rivalry strengthened by the antipathy that grew up in the sixteenth century during the struggle between Protestant England and Catholic Spain. Spanish critics of the policies of the conquistadors contributed to the formation of the legend. Father Bartolme de Las Casas, one of a number of priests who disapproved of the policies, provided the earliest publication of the vision of the Black Legend in his 1542 book, *The Destruction of the Indies,* describing how the Spanish exploited and brutalized the Indian population in Peru.

Religious difference, combined with the centuries of economic and political rivalry for empire, carried over into the relationship between the United States and the nations, particularly Mexico, that grew out of the old Spanish empire. The mixed Indian-Hispanic or mestizo people, whom the Anglo-Americans found in the Spanish settlements of the Southwest, violated the concept of racial purity that shaped much of the value system in the United States—whether North or South—and contributed to the distaste for the Spanish legacy. Finally, just as the rivalry between Britain and Spain on economic, political, and religious levels had shaped the hostility between the two European imperial powers, the rivalry between the United States and Mexico for control of the American Southwest gave impetus to the distaste for Mexico among many U.S. citizens.

While rivalry had existed in the Southeast, with the remnants of the Spanish empire in Florida and Louisiana, the occupation of these territories in the early nineteenth century mitigated these feelings. In Texas, however, the struggle between the Anglo-American settlers and the Mexican government for control in 1835 and 1836 was, from the Anglo side, colored by rhetoric from STEPHEN FULLER AUSTIN, among others, who portrayed the TEXAS REVOLUTION as a struggle between mongrel, despotic barbarism—represented by Mexicans—and civilization—represented by Texans, despite the presence of Hispanics among the Texas revolutionaries. This strain of thought, which degraded the Hispanic contribution to Texas history, was used to control Hispanics in Texas for generations. Among the elements of the tradition was the emphasis on the barbarism of the Catholic church in its control of Indians, in the Inquisition, and in the brutality of the conquistadors.

The coming of the UNITED STATES–MEXICAN WAR—which added the Republic of Texas, as well as the Southwest border territories of New Mexico, Arizona, and California to the United States—intensified the rhetoric that had been generated by the Texans and their supporters in the United States.

Later in the nineteenth century, a reaction began to take shape against the extreme vision of the Black Legend. In part, the reaction reflected a more generous view of Spanish history associated with WASHINGTON IRVING and other popular authors and historians. From HUBERT HOWE BANCROFT on, historians of California portrayed the Spanish period of that region's history in a simplified, racist, and yet sentimental style. Popular authors, including BRET HARTE, romanticized the Hispanic era by giving it a quiet dreamlike quality it never had. This view was reinforced by the mission style of architecture, which crept into the national consciousness by the late nineteenth century.

In New Mexico, the same changing romantic vision of the Hispanic period also appeared. Both in California and in New Mexico, the commercial impetus of tourism encouraged the growth of that view, as did the arrival of an artistic community—particularly in Santa Fe and Taos—and the work of authors of fiction, including WILLA CATHER.

In the twentieth century, historians reevaluated the Spanish traditions. Led, in the first generation, by HERBERT EUGENE BOLTON at the University of California at Berkeley, a group of historians pressed a larger vision of the Hispanic role in the Southwest borderlands. Texas historians, particularly WALTER PRESCOTT WEBB, acknowledged the impact of the Spanish but modified their position by claiming that the Spanish, as they mixed with the Indians, lost the drive that led them to imperial greatness. In the 1960s, as a new generation of historians, influenced by changes in the historical communities of Spain and Mexico, challenged the vision of Bolton and his followers as romantic excess. The trend was also influenced by Chicano historians, who emphasized the place of the Indian cultures, rather than Hispanic culture, in the Southwest. Even in the late twentieth century, the image of the Black Legend is found in some circles, but its importance is

Harsh Spanish treatment of Native Americans gave rise to the "Black Legend." Here, in an engraving dating from 1594, Indians struggle like beasts of burden driven by Spanish soldiers. *Courtesy New York Public Library, Rare Book and Manuscript Collection.*

in understanding how it shaped the attitudes of Anglo-Americans as they created their own continental empire in the first half of the nineteenth century at the expense of the Spanish, Indians, and mestizo cultures already in place.

—*Patrick H. Butler, III*

SEE ALSO: Borderlands Theory; National Expansion; Stereotypes: Stereotypes of Mexicans

SUGGESTED READING:

De Leon, Arnoldo. *They Called Them Greasers: Anglo Attitudes towards Mexicans in Texas, 1821–1900.* Austin, Tex., 1983.

Powell, Philip Wayne. *Tree of Hate: Propaganda and Prejudices Affecting United States Relations with the Hispanic World.* New York, 1971.

Weber, David J. *The Spanish Frontier in North America.* New Haven, Conn., 1992.

BLACK MOON (SIOUX)

The Hunkpapa Lakota Black Moon (1814–1888) was a "cousin" of SITTING BULL and a spokesman for more than fifty lodges (three hundred to four hundred people). Although never a "shirt wearer" (intertribal leader), he was an influential field commander as well as a medicine man from 1864 to 1876.

He appeared as one of RED CLOUD's war leaders at the FETTERMAN MASSACRE in 1866. So prominent was Black Moon that some considered the Oglala CRAZY HORSE and the Northern Cheyenne Roman Nose to be among his lieutenants.

During the 1860s and 1870s, Black Moon traveled with Sitting Bull and openly supported him above others for elevation to central leadership among all Lakotas. He accompanied Sitting Bull to a guarded, informal meeting with a federal spokesman about the Fort Laramie Treaty. Subsequently, Black Moon evidently was among the medicine men who put Sitting Bull up on the hill to fast and to fill his pipe, for it was Black Moon who announced Sitting Bull's Sun Dance vision about resistance.

So visible was Black Moon that for a time federal officials dealt with him as the "recognized leader of the Missouri River Indians"—meaning that he served a role in diplomacy through contacts with officials and merchants who appeared at the mouth of Grand River. Black Moon was a stern supporter of resistance to any intrusion on the traditional way of life or on the territory of Lakota people. He appeared at the beginning of the Battle of Little Bighorn in June 1876 as the man in charge of the Hunkpapa war camp. After he was injured in battle, GALL replaced him as a leader of Lakota military forces.

Black Moon and Sitting Bull led 154 lodges (more than 1,000 people) into exile in Canada. Black Moon guided approximately one-third of them and became a central leader of the exiles at Wood Mountain. He slipped away from Sitting Bull in 1879, however, and accompanied the group of 1,149 who surrendered at Fort Yates in May 1881. With him and his lodges also came Gall, Crow King, Low Dog, and Fools Heart with their lodges.

Evidently Black Moon supported Sitting Bull's opposition to the surrender of land on the Great Sioux Reservation through the 1880s. Nowhere on a Standing Rock Agency list of nearly fifty band "chiefs and headmen" did his name appear. Never in the 1880s did he emerge as a principal spokesman in opposition to the sale of land, and he died the year before the Agreement of March 2, 1889, which reduced the 21.7 million acres remaining to the Sioux after 1877 by yet another 9 million acres.

—*Herbert T. Hoover*

SEE ALSO: Little Bighorn, Battle of; Sioux Wars

SUGGESTED READING:
National Archives. Record Group 75. Standing Rock Agency.

BLAKE, ALICE

A Presbyterian missionary stationed in New Mexico for more than forty years, Alice Blake (1867–1950) exemplified the range of social services performed by Protestant women assigned to missions in the West. Born in Iowa, Blake lived with her family in Kansas and Texas before her father, a "health-seeker," moved his family to New Mexico. After attending Bethany College in Topeka, she returned to New Mexico in 1888, joined the PRESBYTERIAN WOMAN'S BOARD OF HOME MISSIONS in 1889, and served in Rociada, Buena Vista, and El Aguila before opening a school in 1902 in Trementina, where she remained until 1931. Rather than limit her work to teaching and spreading the gospel, Blake organized the digging of a community well, helped establish a post office, campaigned for better sanitation and hygiene, and argued for expanded medical services. She also earned a certificate in public health, helped inoculate residents, and volunteered with the U.S. Children's Bureau to weigh and measure children in the community. The secular tendency in Blake's work was reflected in her changing attitudes towards Hispanic clients. Discarding her initial preoccupation with religious convictions, during which she condemned clients as living in "Sodom and Gomorrah," she came to recognize the impact of poverty and to place greater emphasis on reforming material conditions.

—*Susan M. Yohn*

SUGGESTED READING:
Blake, Alice. "Memoirs of Alice Blake: Interviews with Missionaries, Teachers and Others in Northern New Mexico." Unpublished manuscript, Menaul Library of the Southwest, Albuquerque, N. Mex.

Foote, Cheryl. "Alice Blake of Trementina: Mission Teacher of the Southwest." *Journal of Presbyterian History* 60 (Fall 1982): 228–242.

BLAND-ALLISON ACT OF 1878

The Bland-Allison Act of 1878 was a compromise measure in the national currency disputes of the late nineteenth century. Introduced by Missouri's Democratic Representative Richard Parks ("Silver Dick") Bland, the bill, passed by the House, provided for the free and unlimited coinage of silver as a means of creating inflation to lessen the burden of debt by the manipulation of the money system. The Senate weakened the bill by adopting an amendment introduced by Iowa's Republican Senator William B. Allison. The amendment limited the proposed coinage of silver to no more than $4 million (nor less than $2 million) per month. President Rutherford B. Hayes, an orthodox gold supporter, vetoed the bill, but an awkward coalition of congressmen—those disappointed by the bill's failure to provide for free silver and those fearful that the alternative would be free silver—enacted it over his veto. The act thus remonetized silver but within strict limits. It pleased few people and deferred rather than resolved the silver issue.

—*Peter H. Argersinger*

SEE ALSO: Currency and Silver as Western Political

Issues

SUGGESTED READING:
Unger, Irwin. *The Greenback Era: A Social and Political History of American Finance, 1865–1879.* Princeton, N.J., 1964.

BLEEDING KANSAS

SEE: Atchison, David Rice; Brown, John; Kansas; Kansas-Nebraska Act

BLOUNT, WILLIAM

North Carolina and Tennessee politician William Blount (1749–1800) was born in Bertie County, North Carolina. During the Revolutionary War, he served on the Committee of Safety, as paymaster with the Third North Carolina Battalion of Continental Troops, and as commissary to General Horatio Gates.

In 1781, Blount was elected to the North Carolina legislature. He was a witness to the Hopewell treaties with the Cherokee and Choctaw Indians in South Carolina in 1784 and 1785. In 1787, he served as a delegate to the Constitutional Convention.

Blount was extremely interested in land speculation, especially in the area of the Tennessee River at Muscle Shoals. Using his political office, he encouraged legislation favorable to land speculators, and he and his brothers, along with John Sevier, secured claims to hundreds of thousands of acres in the region.

Blount and others, including JAMES WILKINSON, Harry Innis, George Muter, John Sevier, and James Robertson, were involved in the Spanish conspiracy in the late 1780s. Had they been successful, settlers of

William Blount. *Courtesy Tennessee State Library and Archives.*

Kentucky and North Carolina lands west of the Appalachians would have withdrawn their holdings from the United States and ceded them with Spanish territories in the West. The settlers were inclined to do so because hostilities among Great Britain, France, and Spain had decreased free access to the Mississippi River, because they felt that the Spanish would protect them against the Native Americans in the area, and because they felt the Spanish would provide them with great opportunities for land speculation.

Blount survived the minor scandal surrounding his involvement in the conspiracy and was named governor of the Southwest Territory on June 8, 1790. When Tennessee was admitted as a state in 1796, he became U.S. senator. He did not hold that position for long, however. Because of his involvement in the Chisholm and Romayne affair, the Senate expelled him in 1797. In this international incident, Blount and others encouraged the British to attack Spain in an attempt to keep Florida and Louisiana from falling into French hands.

—*Candace Floyd*

SUGGESTED READING:
Masterson, William. *William Blount.* Baton Rouge, La., 1954.

BLUMENSCHEIN, ERNEST LEONARD

SEE: Taos School of Artists

BODMER, KARL (OR CARL)

Karl Bodmer (1809–1893) became one of the more meticulous and accurate graphic delineators of the tribes of the Upper Missouri when in 1833 he began to chronicle in water colors and drawings the tribes he encountered during an expedition to the region. His eighty-one aquatints and thirty-three vignettes, published in Prince Maximilian's *Reise in das Innere Nord-America in den Jahren 1832 bis 1834,* were the most artistically stunning and ethnographically correct representations of the Indians of the American West to appear in the nineteenth century. The images were borrowed, copied, and modified by numerous European and American illustrators who had never seen an Indian.

Born in Zurich, Switzerland, Bodmer received training in drawing, painting, and engraving from his maternal uncle Johann Jakob Meyer and engaged in additional studies at Paris under Cornu. In 1832, he agreed to accompany Alexander Philipp Maximilian of Wied on a journey up the MISSOURI RIVER. Bodmer was to aid in the collection of natural-history specimens and to prepare drawings and water colors of the peoples, places, and objects encountered on the expedition. The next decade of Bodmer's life was devoted to traveling to the United States, exploring the Upper Missouri, preparing the water colors and sketches, and supervising the creation of the copper plates for the illustrations in Prince Maximilian's great work.

Bodmer was an exceptionally accurate draftsman with a distinct ability to portray the details of an individual, ceremony, or setting without overpowering the viewer with extraneous materials. While his portraits are remarkably detailed, he nevertheless was able to convey a strong sense of the kinetic energy. His genre scenes and portraits are exceedingly valuable in reconstituting the life of the Indians of the Upper Missouri. With the subsequent decline of the Mandan Indians to disease, his paintings join those of GEORGE CATLIN's in presenting an important visual and ethnographical record of those people.

—*Phillip Drennon Thomas*

SEE ALSO: Art

SUGGESTED READING:

Axelrod, Alan. *Art of the Golden West.* New York, 1990.

Bodmer, Karl (introduction by William H. Goetzman, annotations by David C. Hunt and Marsha V. Gallagher, artist's biography by William J. Orr). *Karl Bodmer's America.* Lincoln, Nebr., 1984.

Ewers, John C. *Views of a Vanishing Frontier.* Lincoln, Nebr., 1984.

Phillips, Charles. "Maximilian's Missouri, 1833–34." *The Palimpsest* 60 (November-December 1979): 178–183.

Thomas, David, and Ronnefeldt Thomas. *People of the First Man.* New York, 1976.

An engraving after Karl Bodmer's portrait of Massika (Sac or Sauk) on the left and Wakusasse (Fox or Mesquakie) on the right. *Courtesy Joslyn Art Museum, gift of the Enron Art Foundation.*

BOEING, WILLIAM E.

A pioneer in aircraft manufacture and transport, William E. Boeing (1881–1956) was born to a wealthy family engaged in the lumber business in Detroit. He attended Yale University for two years and learned to fly from Glenn L. Martin. He competed with Martin during World War I in supplying military aircraft to the government, and after the war, he founded the Pacific Aero Products Company. Aided by Phil Johnson and Claire Egtvedt, young engineering professors from the University of Washington, Boeing built a flying boat for the first private airmail service (in July 1920), flying between Seattle, Washington, and Vancouver, British Columbia. In March 1927, his Seattle-based Boeing Air Transport won the first contract for private airmail west of Chicago. The contract led to a merger with Pratt and Whitney and later with National Airlines. Then named United Aircraft and Transport, Boeing's company offered coast-to-coast passenger flights in 28 hours. Three years later, in 1933, the flight time was cut to 19.75 hours, thanks to the Boeing 247 Monomail, the first all-metal, stress-skinned monoplane structure. Other firsts for Boeing included night flights for passengers over long distances and two-way radio communications. He won the coveted Guggenheim Medal in May 1934 for "successful pioneering and achievement."

Boeing retired as president of United Aircraft in mid-1933, but he remained chairman of the board. During that time, the company split into United Airlines, United Aircraft, and Boeing Airplane Company. Boeing remained in constant touch from his farm while his company constructed flying boats for international transport, bombers for World War II, jet transports of the 707 series, and Bomarc and Minuteman missiles. He died at the age of seventy-four on his yacht in Puget Sound.

—*P. M. Zall*

See also: Aircraft Industry

Suggested reading:
Boyne, Walter J. *Boeing B-52: A Documentary History.* Washington, D.C., 1981.
Mansfield, Harold. *Vision.* New York, 1956.

BOLES, CHARLES E.

See: "Black Bart"

BOLTON, HERBERT EUGENE

Herbert Eugene Bolton (1870–1953), professor at the University of California at Berkeley and founder of the Spanish borderlands school of history, was born near Tomah, Wisconsin. Bolton worked as a rural schoolmaster before enrolling, in 1893, at the University of Wisconsin, where he studied with Frederick Jackson Turner. When the University of Pennsylvania offered Bolton a fellowship, he went to the East to study with John Bach McMaster, one of the leading American historians of the day. Bolton wrote his dissertation on freedmen in the South before the Civil War and completed his doctorate in 1899.

After a teaching stint at the Wisconsin State Normal School, Bolton took a position in medieval and European history at the University of Texas in 1901.

There he began to explore the Mexican archives for sources of Texas's Spanish colonial history. He found a vast trove of important documents that opened a field of investigation not only for Texas but also for the United States from Georgia to California—the Spanish borderlands. He shrewdly established his credentials as the leading authority on Spain in North America through articles in scholarly journals and personal correspondence with leading historians.

In 1909, Bolton moved to Stanford University, but his sojourn there was brief; in 1910, he accepted an offer to become professor of history and director of the Bancroft Library at the University of California at Berkeley. He taught at Berkeley until he retired in 1940 and then returned to the faculty for two years during World War II.

Bolton compiled a record of publication and teaching at Berkeley that is nearly without parallel in the annals of American scholarship. His publications included dozens of books and scores of articles concerned mainly with Spain's military and religious explorers. He gave these men heroic treatment with multivolume editions of their translated writings and biographies. Because he thought it was important to retrace their steps, he traveled extensively throughout the West and northern Mexico. The results of his travels may be found in the detailed maps that accompany his books. During his career, he received more than the ordinary number of honors, awards, and accolades, including the presidency of the American Historical Association, honorary degrees, and knighthoods from Spain, Italy, and the Vatican.

Bolton and the borderlands school were once dominant forces in Western and Latin American history, but their importance later waned. Nevertheless, Bolton's contribution to our knowledge of Spain in the American West remains significant. He is rightly remembered with Turner and Walter Prescott Webb as a founder of modern Western historical studies.

—*Albert L. Hurtado*

See also: Borderlands Theory

Suggested reading:
Bannon, John Francis. *Herbert Eugene Bolton: The Historian and the Man.* Tucson, Ariz., 1978.
Caughey, John W. "Herbert Eugene Bolton." In *Turner, Bolton, and Webb: Three Historians of the American Frontier.* By Wilbur R. Jacobs, John W. Caughey, and Joe B. Frantz. Seattle, Wash., 1965.
Worcester, Donald E. "Herbert Eugene Bolton: The Making of a Western Historian." In *Writing Western History: Essays on Major Western Historians.* Edited by Richard W. Etulain. Albuquerque, N. Mex., 1991.

BONANZA FARMING

Large-scale, specialized agricultural operations, known as bonanza farms, were found in some parts of the West between 1870 and 1900. The best examples of bonanza farming were in the Red River valley of North Dakota and in Central Valley in California. In the Red River valley, investors obtained thousands of acres of land from the Northern Pacific Railroad at very cheap prices and organized large, specialized wheat farms. Units of five thousand to ten thousand acres were common. Some of the largest wheat ranches in California were more than twenty thousand acres.

The huge farms required large amounts of capital to purchase land and machinery and to hire labor. Professional managers rather than owners, who were often absentee corporations, usually operated the farms.

Bonanza farms were highly mechanized. Hired workers, using the latest innovations in farm machinery, did the plowing, harvesting, and threshing. In California, some horse-drawn combines, which cut and threshed wheat in one operation, were used. Steam-driven tractors furnished power for threshing machines and plowing. With scores of workers and the latest equipment, one California wheat ranch produced 1.14 million bushels of wheat in 1872.

Bonanza farming reached its height in the 1880s. Poor crops, declining commodity prices, the cost of capital, and labor and management problems caused most of the large operators to fail or to sell out to family farmers. Bonanza farming succeeded for a time, but it could not compete with diversified family farms. Bonanza farming reflected the size, spirit, and even the flamboyance of the American West.

—*Gilbert C. Fite*

SEE ALSO: Agriculture; Booms; Farming: Farming on the Great Plains, Farming in the Imperial Valley and Salton Sea Region, Tools and Machinery; Homesteading

SUGGESTED READING:
Drache, Hiram M. *The Day of the Bonanza.* Fargo, N. Dak., 1964.

BONNEVILLE, BENJAMIN LOUIS EULALIE DE

U.S. Army officer, fur trader, explorer of the Far West, and subject of WASHINGTON IRVING'S last book in his trilogy on the early nineteenth-century American West, Benjamin Louis Eulalie de Bonneville (1796–1878) was born near Paris, France. He fled to America with his family, who had fallen in disfavor with the Emperor

Benjamin Louis Eulalie de Bonneville. *Courtesy Denver Public Library, Western History Department.*

Napoleon, and settled in New York in 1803. Appointed in 1813 to the recently established U.S. Military Academy at West Point, he graduated in 1815 and was assigned to duties in the East. During the 1820s, he served at posts in Arkansas, Texas, and the Indian Country. He developed an intense interest in the Rocky Mountain FUR TRADE and wanted to work in that business. By 1830, Bonneville had formulated a plan for an expedition to explore the region west of the Continental Divide for the government and to engage in the fur trade. After securing funds from private sources, he hired 110 men, loaded twenty wagons with provisions, and, with a two-year leave of absence from the army, set out from Fort Osage, Missouri, on May 1, 1832. The expedition headed for the Green River that flows through the Wind River Range of the Rockies in western Wyoming. For three years, Bonneville and his men trapped and traded furs, competed with veterans of the ROCKY MOUNTAIN FUR COMPANY, AMERICAN FUR COMPANY, and HUDSON'S BAY COMPANY, and endured the rigors of life in the wilderness and threats by the Indians. Bonneville explored the region west of the Rockies, drew maps, lived among the Nez Percé Indians, and made two journeys into the territory along the Columbia River to scout the activities of the British fur traders. He kept a detailed record of his time in the West. In 1835, bankruptcy forced him to return home, where he found he had been discharged from the army for overstaying his leave.

After President ANDREW JACKSON restored his commission in 1836, Bonneville met Washington Irving, who paid him one thousand dollars for the narrative account of his fur-trading experiences. Irving rewrote the account and titled it *The Adventures of Captain Bonneville* (1837). Detractors of the book claim Irving's heroic portrait of Bonneville is overdone, while defenders maintain it is a valuable contribution to the early history of the Rocky Mountain fur trade.

Bonneville remained in the army and fought in the United States–Mexican War. Although he retired in 1861, he served the military in various capacities until the end of the Civil War. In 1865, breveted brigadier general for "long and meritorious service," he retired to Fort Smith, Arkansas, where he died.

Named in his honor, the Bonneville Dam on the Columbia River near Portland, Oregon, is an important source of hydroelectric power for the region.

—*Charles T. Jones, Jr.*

SEE ALSO: Exploration: United States Expeditions; Literature: Travel Literature

SUGGESTED READING:

Chittenden, Hiram M. *The American Fur Trade of the Far West.* New York, 1935.
DeVoto, Bernard. *Across the Wide Missouri.* Boston, 1947.
Irving, Washington. *The Adventures of Captain Bonneville U.S.A. in the Rocky Mountains and the Far West.* Edited by Edgeley W. Todd. Norman, Okla., 1961.

BONNEY, WILLIAM H.

SEE: "Billy the Kid"

BONNIN, GERTRUDE SIMMONS (ZITKALA-SA) (SIOUX)

Gertrude Simmons Bonnin (1876–1938), whose Indian name was Zitkala-Sa, was a well-known Indian reformer, writer, and musician. Through her writings and lectures, she demanded better treatment of Indians and supported giving Indians more control over decisions that affected their lives.

Zitkala-Sa was born at the Yankton Sioux Reservation in South Dakota. At the age of eight, she left the reservation to attend a Quaker missionary school in Indiana. From 1895 to 1897, she attended Earlham College (Indiana), where she excelled in oratory. In 1899, she studied violin at the Boston Conservatory of Music, and in late 1900, she performed at the Paris Exposition and toured Europe.

Returning to the United States, she embarked on a literary career. Her articles were published in the *Atlantic Monthly* and *Harper's Monthly* and in two books, *Old Indian Legends* (1901) and *American Indian Stories* (1921). Her writings dealt with needed Indian reforms, Indian stories, and her experiences.

She taught at the Carlisle Indian School in Pennsylvania from 1897 to 1899. In 1902, she served as issue clerk at Standing Rock Reservation in North Dakota, where she married Raymond Bonnin, another Sioux employee. She then worked as a teacher, issue clerk, and band organizer at the Uintah and Ouray Reservation in Utah from 1902 to 1916. In 1916, Bonnin moved to Washington, D.C., to become secretary of the Society of American Indians, a pan-Indian organization, and to assume the editorship of its journal, the *American Indian Magazine*. She called for educational and social reforms on reservations and denounced the use of peyote by Indians.

During the 1920s, Bonnin accomplished some of her most effective work through the General Federation of Women's Clubs, an organization that had as one of its main interests the improvement of Indian conditions. She called for better educational opportunities and improved health care for Indians and worked with a research team to investigate corruption and graft in Oklahoma against the Five Civilized Tribes. In 1926, Bonnin and her husband established the National Council of American Indians, an organization that lobbied for Indian reform legislation in Washington, D.C. She headed the council until its demise in the mid-1930s.

—*Raymond Wilson*

SEE ALSO: Literature: Native American Literature

SUGGESTED READING:

Bonnin, Gertrude Simmons (Zitkala-Sa). *American Indian Stories.* 1921. Reprint, Glorieta, N. Mex., 1976.
———. *Old Indian Legends.* Boston, 1901.
———. Charles A. Fabens, and Matthew K. Sniffen. *Oklahoma's Poor Rich Indians.* Philadelphia, 1924.
Johnson, David L., and Raymond Wilson. "Gertrude Simmons Bonnin, 1876–1938." *American Indian Quarterly* 12 (1988): 27–40.
Willard, William. "Gertrude Bonnin and Indian Policy Reform, 1911–1938." In *Indian Leadership.* Edited by Walter Williams. Manhattan, Kans., 1984.

BOOK OF MORMON

Published in 1830 in western New York, the *Book of Mormon* claims to be a translation of ancient religious records written mainly by two groups of people (the Nephites and the Jaredites) who inhabited the Americas centuries ago. Accepted as Christian revelation by members of the CHURCH OF JESUS CHRIST OF LATTER-DAY SAINTS (MORMONS), the scripture was influential in the settlement of the West, and it remains a significant American religious text.

The volume contains fifteen books. Most detailed are three sections that cover the prophet Lehi's migration by sea from Jerusalem to the New World (ca. 600 B.C.), the 150 years leading up to and including appearances of the resurrected Jesus Christ among the Nephites (34 A.D.), and writings from the time of their demise (385 A.D.). One of the final books gives an account of the earlier history of the Jardites, who arrived from the ancient Near East and eventually perished in battle (ca. 200 B.C.). Other groups, notably the Lamanites, figure in the account; Mormons believe that the descendants of the Lamanites may be found among the Indians of North and South America. The volume states that it was abridged by Mormon and his son Moroni, the last two Nephite prophets. The record contains prophetic and sacred teachings about Christ, accounts of spiritual experiences, and admonitions regarding religious practices and moral behavior.

With many eighteenth- and early nineteenth-century works, the *Book of Mormon* shares an interest in Indian origins. The *Book of Mormon* offers theological explanations for the arrival, separation, rise, and fall of ancient populations in the Western Hemisphere. JOSEPH SMITH, JR., asserted that he translated the book from gold plates by divine power. Testimonies of witnesses and some circumstantial evidence support Smith's claims, but those assertions ultimately remain in the domain of faith and revelation.

Smith dictated the text to OLIVER COWDERY in 1829. In 1830, five thousand copies were printed in Palmyra, New York; with minor changes, three thousand or five thousand were published in Kirtland, Ohio, in 1837, and two thousand in Cincinnati in 1840 (Nauvoo, Illinois, edition). Most were sold or given away by Mormon missionaries traveling through these regions and abroad. Mormons introduced the book to Indian tribes in Missouri and elsewhere as early as 1831. Addressed on the title page "to the Lamanites, who are a remnant of the House of Israel," as well as to the Jew and Gentile, the book became a touchstone of belief among Latter-day Saints. It showed that God speaks to all people, remembers and delights in his covenant peoples, and holds America as a promised land. The *Book of Mormon*'s millennial vision of Indian destiny fueled political sentiments against the Mormons in Missouri, gave Christianizing purpose to the westward movements of Mormon pioneers, shaped practical policies such as BRIGHAM YOUNG's openness to Indian affairs, and encouraged ongoing LDS efforts to convert and nurture Indians. Several Mormon settlements bear *Book of Mormon* names (such as Nephi, Bountiful, Manti, Lamoni).

—*John W. Welch*

SUGGESTED READING:
"Book of Mormon." In *Encyclopedia of Mormonism*. 5 vols. New York, 1992.
Walker, Ronald W. "Seeking the 'Remnant': The Native American during the Joseph Smith Period." *Journal of Mormon History* 19 (1993): 1–33.

BOOMERS

SEE: Oklahoma Land Rush

BOOMS

"Such opportunities for making money," wrote Pittsburgh's Judge Thomas Mellon in 1863 of the American economy emerging out of the Civil War, "had never existed before in all my former experience." But the war had done more than open up opportunities for fortune-builders. It had eliminated the Southern planter as a rival of the capitalists for control over Washington, while fostering new conditions favorable to the rise of large-scale industry. The United States now outstripped all other nations with industrialized economies. The United States, coddling business even as it erected high protective-tariff walls around its new markets, threw open its doors to European immigrants who flooded its cities after the Civil War in unprecedented numbers. An economy already expanding before the war exploded into massive growth in the decades after Appomattox. The United States had become the greatest market-dominated economy in the world, and America's industrial entrepreneurs and financial wizards had become lords of all they surveyed.

And what they surveyed with most pleasure was their built-in empire, the trans-Mississippi American West, from whence came the raw materials, the minerals, the beef, the wheat, and the oil that had made them rich. More than any inevitable march of pioneers westward, the sudden expansions of the American market in a series of dramatic economic booms (and busts) in the last half of the nineteenth century had conquered the West and determined its character.

The changes after the Civil War were more a matter of degree than kind. The U.S. economy had always been addicted to booms, and the booms had always affected the American West, particularly booms in cotton and real estate. And, since the late eighteenth century, Westerners had relied heavily on the FEDERAL GOVERNMENT to provide them with inexpensive land, transportation, and protection. In fact, federal largess had long been one of the West's major resources. The tendency to look to Washington for help in underwriting the region's economy was one Western habit that would live on long into the twentieth century, with its giant freeway projects, huge defense installations, and massive reclamation programs.

The coming of the railroad, itself a boom in construction, made all the other Western booms possible. A train awaits the arrival of Eastern capitalists, newspaper reporters, and prominent officials while Union Pacific Railroad directors pose for posterity. Photograph by John Carbutt. *Courtesy National Archives.*

Booms were not restricted to mineral extraction. Ranching, too, made investors wealthy in the 1880s until a drought and a blizzard created a bust. During more sober and less freewheeling times, cowhands on the Sherman Ranch in Genesee, Kansas, keep watch on the herd. *Courtesy National Archives.*

The oil boom produced so much wealth that even the Indians benefited. In Cleveland, Oklahoma Territory, oil derricks dominate the scenery a year after the discovery of oil in 1904. Oklahoma's Osage Indians became the richest ethnic group in the world at the time. Photograph by Dick Man. *Courtesy National Archives.*

Gold Hill, Nevada, was one of the mining towns that boomed in the late 1860s. Photograph by Timothy H. O'Sullivan. *Courtesy National Archives.*

First and last, real-estate booms underlay the economy of the West. Depicted here are the first train and wagons arriving in 1893 at one of the bigger land grabs in the region's history. *Courtesy National Archives.*

None of the post–Civil War Western booms would have been possible without the initial boom in railroad construction. As Judge Mellon's comment made clear, in the aftermath of the war, America's prominent capitalists recognized that the American West offered huge vistas of untapped wealth. Out West, there were silver, and gold, and copper, and timber; back East, the industrial machines to mine it or cut it lay at hand. Out West, there was room to grow enough beef and wheat to feed the millions of new factory workers back East who made those machines. Clearly, all one had to do was connect "out West" with "back East" to make a fortune. What the West desperately needed were markets for its raw materials, and the RAILROADS seemed the best way to reach them. That meant building railroads, which meant finding the land to lay the tracks across, hiring men desperate enough to take on

the backbreaking labor of construction, producing enough steel to make the tracks, and coming up with the money to pay for it all.

The federal government was willing to provide the land; the West Coast was filled with much-maligned and ostracized Chinese immigrants for whom railroading offered at least a chance to keep from starving in the mine fields; in the East, millions of Irishmen were languishing in the hellish slums of the major cities, eager for work of any kind; Eastern industrialists had plenty of steel; and Eastern financiers knew where to find the necessary funds. "Railroad through" soon became the ubiquitous cry of capitalists, politicians, laborers, and fast-talking boosters, as everywhere from the Mississippi to the Pacific, cowcatchers and smokestacks chugged into view and dominated the imagination, the politics, and the livelihood of the postwar generation. As financial enterprises, railroads may have been as rickety and jerry-built as their rail lines, but they did open the West to new industries. Across the TELEGRAPH lines built along their tracks went the information needed to coordinate the Eastern financial markets with Western production sites, and along the rails traveled the raw materials for manufacturers in the East. The big American industrialists, who had already introduced large-scale, specialized production, could now practice "vertical integration," controlling not merely the manufacture and sale of a final product but also the raw resources the product required. The financiers among the Eastern capitalists set up large trusts and provided loans to the industrialists to use out West. For these men, scarcity was anathema, and they were not interested, except in a sentimental and ideological way, in the West's "pristine" landscape and its wide open spaces: they were after the stuff underneath that arid land.

The MINING industry set the pace. Modern mining had been born in the played-out placer fields of the CALIFORNIA GOLD RUSH and was fed by fresh finds along Cripple Creek in Colorado and near the junction of the Klondike and the Yukon rivers in Alaska. With the coming of electricity and its copper wiring, the profits from GOLD MINING found a new field for investment. Armed with new equipment, especially the steam shovel, a group of Cripple Creek entrepreneurs began to exploit vast, low-grade copper deposits in Bingham Canyon south of the Great Salt Lake and, within thirty years, had extracted some six billion pounds. The techniques developed in Utah spread to Arizona and Montana. By 1903, mining interests were so powerful that they could blackmail state legislatures into passing any law simply by closing mines, smelters, lumber camps, and mills and threatening to leave twenty thousand men out of work in the dead of winter. Inevitably, the mines played out, production dropped off, and the bust that accompanied every boom left the Rocky Mountain West dotted with GHOST TOWNS.

Lumber, too, had a venerable pedigree in the gold rush. In the early 1840s, the huge forests of the Pacific Coast had been hardly touched. Scattered along the sea from California to Washington, a few sawmills produced enough lumber for local settlement, with a little left over for export. But with the coming of the Forty-niners, San Francisco and the boom towns needed much more lumber than the two-man teams, working with an eight-foot whipsaw off a pit and a platform, could produce. At first, the lumber for Western city building was imported by ship from Maine, but soon entrepreneurs were staking out vast tracks along the coast up to Puget Sound and bringing in well-organized teams with steam-powered circular saws and the beasts they needed for transport. Lumber ships the world over crowded into harbors such as Port Blakely and Port Gamble to pick up the sea of timber floating in Puget Sound. By the turn of the century, railroads began replacing the ships as the transport of choice, and with their arrival came the Great Lakes timber barons, eager to exploit the seemingly endless stretch of Douglas fir. Highly industrialized, those companies used the railroads to bring Western timber to Eastern markets, markets that had already consumed the great American forests written about with such awe by the first East Coast settlers. Soon, too, the Western forests were thinned by the lumber boom, and the LUMBER INDUSTRY began to cast hungry eyes at the beautiful trees abounding in national parks and reserves.

By the turn of the century, the boom-and-bust cycle—created in large measure by the excessive dependence on extractive industries—had become part of the very essence of the American West. The Southwest's oil boom is a classic example. By 1900, inventors had discovered that oil, once used mostly for producing kerosene and for lubricating machines, could, in one of its distillations—gasoline—propelled the motors of the new, strange-looking horseless carriages. Some eight thousand vehicles pinged and banged their way along America's dusty highways in the year a bullheaded Texan named Pittillo Higgens conjured a tower of thick, dark liquid to spew heavenward from a rise of sand just outside a hick town in South Texas. The great 1901 Spindletop gusher, near Beaumont, made oil the "black gold" not only of Texas, but of Oklahoma, southern California, and even Wyoming. The twentieth-century prospectors who arrived in the Western oil fields came not with picks and shovels on a covered wagon, but by railroad, armed with drills and pipe. To towns like Batson, Texas, and Cushing Field, Oklahoma, and even Los Angeles, California, they came—a horde of would-be millionaires (plus some confidence men, thugs, whores, and gamblers). Within a few months of the first discovery at Spindletop, some forty thousand people descended on little Beaumont, Texas. The stakes were more astronomical than any of the gold rushes. In 1919, within forty miles of Ranger, Texas, wildcat mines pumped oil worth nine times all the gold mined in California in 1849. The boom towns were as raucous and dangerous as any in the Rockies, with saloons, dance halls, and whorehouses sweeping into every oil town on the torrent of money that followed a strike, while the amenities of normal life—beds and food and water and laundries—seemed to vanish under the flood.

There was so much money that even the Indians benefited. The Osage Indians had been forced out of Kansas in the 1870s onto barren land in Oklahoma, where they lived in grinding poverty until someone found oil. As whites began competitive bidding for oil leases on Indian land, the Osages became—courtesy of Messieurs Frank Phillips and Henry Sinclair—the richest ethnic group per capita in the world. With an average annual family income of sixty-five thousand dollars, a fortune for the time, the Osages went on a spending binge, buying, among other goods, Cadillacs and Pierce Arrows, which they drove until the cars gave out, then abandoned for new ones. Schemes to separate the Osages from their money abounded, and although swindle and murder occurred with frightening frequency, the regular checks kept coming.

A reckless oil boom in East Texas in the 1930s finally led to overproduction. The price plummeted in a single year from $1.30 to 5¢ a barrel, and for every barrel shipped, ten more oozed into the Texas dirt.

Geologists warned of depleting oil reserves; Texas imposed limits on production; and the other states followed suit. It took the Texas National Guard to enforce compliance with the new rules, but soon wildcatters grew choosier about picking sites, and roustabouts drifted to steadier jobs, while oil wells were tapped for a few barrels a day, a few days a month.

But the booms were not limited to minerals. As the railroads pushed westward, cattlemen had a means of selling their beef to someone other than the U.S. Army. In the boom years of the 1880s, the monarchs of the cattle kingdom grew drunk with the vastness of their domains and the immense riches they represented. They had weathered the severe depression of the 1870s; they had helped destroy the once massive buffalo herds; they had, in part, caused the Native American peoples to be driven off the plains and onto reservations; they had grabbed former hunting grounds to feed their cows; and beef prices were soaring. Little wonder the cattle "king" felt so powerful, so potent, so positive. His optimism had spread around the world, and investors with money so hot in their pockets that it affected their brains rushed from every corner of the globe to the plains to seek their fortunes. In Cheyenne, Wyoming, the cattlemen's club served caviar and rare wine. A local journalist described the scene:

> Sixteenth Street is a young Wall street. Millions are talked of as lightly as nickels and all kinds of people are dabbling in steers. The chief justice of the Supreme Court has recently succumbed to the contagion and gone out to purchase a $40,000 herd. . . . A Cheyenne man who don't pretend to know a maverick from a mandamus has made a neat little margin of $15,000 this summer in small transactions and hasn't seen a cow yet that he has bought and sold.

The cattle kings were seduced by the West's vast, seemingly "free" spaces and its apparently unending supply of virgin grassland. They ran their herds onto it, exposed them to weather hazards, and ensured that they could not provide adequate care to the animals and could only with difficulty improve the breeds. They handled their cows roughly and wastefully, confident they could get more, as they always had. They resorted to land fraud, to monopoly, to ruthless violence and costly range wars. And in their greed, they overcapitalized their industry, overstocked their herds, and overgrazed the range. When reality hit in 1885 and beef prices started to tumble, it took only one severe winter and a summer drought to toll the death knell of the great beef bonanza. Larger corporations and many individu-

als were ruined, and the heart went out of the enterprise. By 1888, the range industry lay in ruins, and the reckless confidence and arrogance of the cattle kings vanished as quickly as did investors. Those cattlemen who survived to pick up the pieces of their shattered empires would have to husband the animals with more discipline and care, breed heartier stock, and fence what was left of the open range. There were still trail drives, but they covered much shorter distances to railheads located closer to the principal ranching regions. The trade in cattle had become a sober business instead of a high-riding, freewheeling adventure.

As the railroads developed and sold their excess lands, they created booms in farming that far more resembled the cattle boom than they did the legendary westward movement of small landholders. After the panic of 1873, for example, the Northern Pacific Railroad put on a demonstration of how to make a 100 percent profit in wheat growing, which sparked a land rush that covered three hundred miles of the Red River valley with "bonanza farms" that were a far cry from the "democratic" small farms promoted by the HOME-STEAD ACT OF 1862. By 1880, WHEAT FARMING had filled out Kansas and Nebraska to the edge of the semiarid plains. Farther north, three successive "Dakota Booms" followed three successive gold rushes. And as the railroads rushed passed the mining ghost towns and the declining cow towns to supply the new breed of farmer and take his cash crop to market, they also brought regular mail service and dry goods. Mail service meant that the new mail-order houses—Sears, Roebuck and Company, Montgomery Ward, the Chicago Mail Order House, Spiegel—could spread the products of the post–Civil War's revolution in farm machinery. Farther west, new equipment spawned a boom in California BONANZA FARMING, though it paled beside the oceans of wheat the industrial inventions of the East had made possible on the Great Plains by the mid-1880s. As with the mining, lumber, oil, and cattle industries, wheat and bonanza farmers would suffer severe setbacks in the inevitable bust that followed the boom, and by the 1890s, farmers everywhere in the West were not merely desperate, they were in an angry revolt against the entire market economy.

The economic transformation that followed the Civil War established the basic boom mentality of a Western economy that in many ways persists to this day. The American economy had transformed a land of Indian villages and Hispanic towns into a new West whose inhabitants did not usually consume what they produced, nor did they produce what they consumed. It was a West where heedless exploitation had been established by rapid market expansions, where rich, on-the-make Westerners, having persuaded themselves

they had found their Eden, continually fell victims to their own illusions, their own dreams of inexhaustible resources, and their own beliefs in unlimited markets.
—*Charles Phillips*

SEE ALSO: Banking; Cattle Industry; Cattle Trails and Trail Driving; Copper Mining; Crédit Mobilier of America; Farming: Farming on the Great Plains, Farming in the Imperial Valley and Salton Sea Region; Financial Panics; Mining: Mining Camps and Towns; Oil and Gas Industry; Oklahoma Land Rush; Silver Mining

SUGGESTED READING:

Cox, Thomas. *Mills and Markets: A History of the Pacific Coast Lumber Industry to 1900.* Cambridge, Mass., 1974.

Fahey, John. *The Inland Empire: Unfolding Years, 1879–1929.* Seattle, Wash., 1986.

Fite, Gilbert. *The Farmer's Frontier, 1865–1900.* New York, 1966.

Gressley, Gene M. *Bankers and Cattlemen.* New York, 1966.

Harley, C. Knick. "Western Settlement and the Price of Wheat, 1872–1913." *Journal of Economic History* 38 (December 1978): 865–878.

Perloff, Harvey S., et al. *Regions, Resources, and Economic Growth.* Baltimore, 1961.

Peterson, Richard. *The Bonanza Kings: The Social Origins and Business Behavior of Western Mining Entrepreneurs, 1870–1900.* Berkeley, Calif., 1970.

BOOM TOWNS

SEE: Cattle Towns; Gambling; Mining: Mining Camps and Towns; Prostitution; Saloons; Urban West

BOONE, DANIEL

With a lust for the wilderness and an adventurous spirit, Daniel Boone (1734–1820) epitomizes the American

Daniel Boone as depicted by William T. Ramey. *Courtesy National Cowboy Hall of Fame and Western Heritage Center.*

frontiersman. In 1775, he spearheaded the opening of the Wilderness Road leading to Kentucky and there established Boonesborough, the principal Euro-American settlement in the region; in 1799, pushing farther west, he led settlers into what is now Missouri.

Born in Berks County, Pennsylvania, Boone began exploring the backwoods surrounding his home as a young man. At the age of sixteen, he moved with his family to the Yadkin Valley of North Carolina. Four years later, he volunteered as a wagoner during the French and Indian War. During that service, Boone heard stories from his companion John Findley (or Finley) of abundant game and virgin lands in Kentucky. Boone put his zeal for exploration on hold and returned to the Yadkin Valley to marry Rebecca Bryan on August 14, 1756. Over the next twelve or thirteen years, he concerned himself with providing for his growing family.

In 1768, Findley asked Boone to head an expedition through a gap in the Cumberland Mountains and locate an Indian trail known as the Warrior's Path leading into Kentucky. On May 1, 1769, Boone, Findley, and four others began their journey. Almost without incident the group arrived in Kentucky, which Boone found to be everything he had expected. Soon the explorers had a bounteous load of furs and skins for trade; twice, however, a band of Shawnee Indians stole Boone's skins and supplies. After two years in Kentucky, he returned to his family deeper in debt than when he departed.

In 1773, Boone decided to explore Kentucky again and establish a settlement there. He recruited relatives and neighbors to join his venture. Following an attack by Indians, who killed some of the group including Boone's eldest son, James, the settlers returned home.

Richard Henderson, a lawyer and land speculator, spurred Boone's next attempt at settling Kentucky. Henderson had formed the Transylvania Company and planned to cash in on the West's abundant land after establishing a new American colony in Kentucky. Under Henderson's supervision, Boone negotiated the purchase of a huge tract of land from the Cherokee Indians in 1775 and soon thereafter began cutting a trail from Virginia to Kentucky. The resulting path, known as the Wilderness Road, led settlers to the banks of the Kentucky River where Boone established Fort Boonesborough.

Indian assaults continually plagued Boonesborough. One of the attacks resulted in the capture of Boone's daughter, Jamima, and her two friends. During Boone's surprise attack against the Indian captors, he retrieved the girls unharmed but was himself seized later by Chief Blackfish's Shawnee tribe. In order to free himself, Boone skillfully found favor with the Indian chief, and the tribe adopted him. He soon learned of Blackfish's plan to attack Boonesborough, however, and after more than four months of acting as a loyal Shawnee brave, Boone escaped to warn the settlers. Shortly after his return to Fort Boonesborough, the Indians attacked; Boone and the settlers repelled the onslaught. On other occasions, however, the Indians had greater success.

Despite those troubles, settlers continued to pour into Kentucky. Boone became heavily involved in selling portions of his land, yet problems with overlapping claims and his failure to secure proper legal titles led to numerous lawsuits. When he began to feel the crunch of too many people in Kentucky, he led a group of settlers into Missouri, in 1799, where the Spanish government issued him 850 acres of land. Following the Louisiana Purchase in 1803, however, his land transferred from Spanish to American hands and his claim was invalidated. In 1814, the U.S. Congress reissued his original 850 acres as a reward for his effort in opening the West, but Boone's deep indebtedness forced him to sell the land. Despite his unfortunate financial circumstances, Boone continued to hunt, trap, and enjoy the wilderness, which he had been so instrumental in exploring and opening for America's westward push.

—*W. Paul Reeve and Fred R. Gowans*

SUGGESTED READING:

Bakeless, John E. *Master of the Wilderness: Daniel Boone.* New York, 1939.

Elliott, Lawrence. *The Long Hunter: A New Life of Daniel Boone.* New York, 1976.

Faragher, John Mack. *Daniel Boone: The Life and Legend of an American Pioneer.* New York, 1992.

Lofaro, Michael A. *The Life and Adventures of Daniel Boone.* Lexington, Ky., 1978.

BOONE, WILLIAM JUDSON

Idaho minister and educator William Judson Boone (1860–1936) was born in Lawrenceville, Pennsylvania. In 1887, he accepted the pastorate of a new Presbyterian church in the young town of Caldwell, Idaho. In 1891, he began the College of Idaho, the state's first institution of higher education, and a year later, he resigned his church position to head the college full-time—a post he held for the rest of his life.

Boone's prodigious energy resulted in the development of a lively college with particular strength in the biological sciences—a field in which he had great interest and considerable knowledge. He conducted a botanical survey of southwestern Idaho before grazing and irrigation displaced natural flora.

Many smaller churches in the region owe their beginnings to Boone's determination, and he was a significant force in Caldwell's development. A skilled amateur photographer, Boone recorded the development of both the college and the community.

—*Judith Austin*

SUGGESTED READING:
Hayman, H. H. *That Man Boone: Frontiersman of Idaho.* Caldwell, Idaho, 1948.

BOONE AND CROCKETT CLUB

An elite group of influential hunters dedicated to the preservation of big-game animals in North America, the Boone and Crockett Club was devised by THEODORE ROOSEVELT after discussions with GEORGE BIRD GRINNELL, editor of the *Forest and Stream* magazine. The club was organized in December 1887. Roosevelt was elected its first president in January 1888, and he held the position for six years. The club was a small organization with regular membership limited to one hundred sportsmen. Each must have shot three American big-game species with a rifle to qualify for membership. Early members included Grinnell, writer OWEN WISTER, artist ALBERT BIERSTADT, historian FRANCIS PARKMAN, Senator Henry Cabot Lodge, and General WILLIAM TECUMSEH SHERMAN.

The influence of its membership and the support of Grinnell's *Forest and Stream* made the Boone and Crockett Club a powerful advocate for game protection. Its members worked to preserve YELLOWSTONE NATIONAL PARK from commercial exploitation. Their efforts, especially Grinnell's, led to the passage of legislation protecting the park in 1894. The club also supported legislation establishing the first forest reserves in the United States, the National Zoo, and the New York Zoological Park (Bronx Zoo). It also supported laws regulating unsportsmanlike HUNTING practices. Roosevelt and Grinnell coedited a series of Boone and Crockett Club books on hunting themes.

While the club is best known for its early contributions to wildlife protection during the birth of the conservation movement, it has continued to promote wildlife management and habitat protection through the twentieth century. It maintains hunting-trophy statistics that are a standard reference for big-game records.

—*Ralph H. Lutts*

SUGGESTED READING:
Cutright, Paul Russell. *Theodore Roosevelt: The Making of a Conservationist.* Urbana, Ill., 1985.

Reiger, John F. *American Sportsmen and the Origins of Conservation.* Rev. ed. Norman, Okla., 1986.
Trefethen, James B. *An American Crusade for Wildlife.* New York, 1975.

BOOTS

SEE: Cowboy Outfits

BORAH, WILLIAM E.

Idaho lawyer and politician William E. Borah (1865–1940) was born in Fairfield, Illinois. He read law in Kansas and moved to the new state of Idaho in 1890. Borah was a successful attorney who supported labor unions as well as corporations. He was a prosecutor in WILLIAM D. ("BIG BILL") HAYWOOD's trial for conspiracy in the murder of FRANK STEUNENBERG in 1906. More progressive than the state Republican party, Borah ran for Congress unsuccessfully twice (once as a Silver Republican) before his first election to the U.S. Senate in 1907.

As a senator, Borah brought RECLAMATION money to Idaho and believed that control—and development—of public lands should be given to the states. He focused most of his attention on national and international issues. He was the chief sponsor of two constitutional amendments: allowing the graduated income tax and providing for direct election of U.S. senators. He strongly supported child-labor laws and was a major force behind the creation of the U.S. Department of Labor.

From 1924 to 1932, Borah chaired the Senate Committee on Foreign Relations. He is remembered as a diehard isolationist. While he opposed the Versailles Treaty and the League of Nations, he did advocate diplomatic recognition of the Soviet Union and the Washington Disarmament Conference in 1921. Ultimately, however, he opposed the conference's results. Borah advocated neutrality in advance of World War II.

His independent political outlook became a hallmark of his career in the Senate. Above all else, Borah was known as an orator, whose verbal powers of persuasion were unequaled in the Senate, and as a man of strong moral force who believed that war should be outlawed. He supported presidents and colleagues of both parties on the basis of their views rather than on their political affiliations.

—*Judith Austin*

SUGGESTED READING:
Maddox, Robert James. *William E. Borah and American Foreign Policy.* Baton Rouge, La., 1969.
McKenna, Marian C. *Borah.* Ann Arbor, Mich., 1961.

BORDER CONFLICT

SEE: Mexican Border Conflicts

BORDERLANDS THEORY

Awareness of the United States–Mexico border region as a distinct area deserving serious attention from scholars began in the 1920s when HERBERT EUGENE BOLTON promoted the teaching and research of the history of the "Spanish Borderlands" as an essential part of the history of the United States. Bolton pioneered numerous studies that focused on Spanish exploration and colonization of the region. Continuing this tradition, his students built an impressive body of historical literature. Since Bolton's time, other scholars from both nations have done considerable work on binational borderlands history and have emphasized in particular events of the nineteenth and early twentieth centuries, when Mexico and the United States clashed repeatedly over numerous boundary-related issues. Most of the research examines the borderlands in the context of the relations between the two countries.

Both traditional studies and the more recent literature on the history of the American West have devoted relatively little attention to the impact that the binational borderlands have had on regional evolution. For example, studies that focused in decades past on the "colonial" nature of the Western economy ignored the pronounced colonialism clearly evident along the border. With few exceptions, "NEW WESTERN HISTORY" studies fail to integrate the transborder processes with the larger story. The habit of viewing the West and Southwest as regions that stop abruptly at the Mexican boundary is reflected even in some of the literature on Chicanos.

In the 1950s and 1960s, social scientists from various disciplines became interested in a host of issues associated with rapid population growth and economic development in the border communities. Studies on such topics as demographic trends, migration, poverty, urbanization, industrialization, transboundary relations, and environmental concerns began to appear with regularity. By the 1970s, there were enough American and Mexican scholars engaged in borderlands research to merit the creation of a professional association, which became known as the Association for Borderlands Scholars. The ABS began publishing the *Journal of Borderlands Studies* in 1986.

There is general agreement among scholars and other observers that northern Mexico and the American Southwest constitute a distinct geographic and cultural unit, but interpretations vary regarding its geographic limits. Many think of the borderlands simply as the border states of both the United States and Mexico. Some point out that the various corridors into the interiors of the United States and Mexico—corridors through which influence of the border travels—need to be taken into account. For example, using the flow of migration from Mexico as a prime indicator of border reach, the borderlands would run along some U.S. interstate highways and air routes into such cities as Denver and Chicago. Going the opposite way and following American forms of influence (for example, tourism), the border would extend all the way to Mexico City and Acapulco. A more restricted definition visualizes the borderlands as consisting of the forty-nine U.S. border counties and the thirty-six Mexican border *municipios* plus population centers within 200 to 250 miles of the boundary.

The dual nationality of the area is well established historically, and innumerable relationships spanning across the border continue to this day. The interdependence of the Mexican and American sides of the border is most evident in the economies of cities like Ciudad Juárez and EL PASO, but such interdependence extends also into interior centers such as Monterey and San Antonio. In the borderlands, industrial exchanges, trade, tourism, migration, and cultural interaction take place daily on a grand scale.

Border zones are distinct within nation-states because of their location, which in many cases is far from heartland areas, and because of the international climate produced by their proximity to another country. The unique forces, processes, and characteristics that set borderlands apart from interior zones include transnational interaction, international conflict and accommodation, ethnic conflict and accommodation, otherness, and separateness. In their totality, those elements constitute what might be called the "borderlands milieu."

Transnational interaction

Their location at the edges of nation-states places borderlanders in international environments that have wide-ranging implications. Where extensive cross-border movement exists, as in the case of the United States–Mexico borderlands, cross-border interaction makes it possible for border Mexicans and Americans to be active participants in transnational economic and social systems that foster substantive trade, tourism, migration, information flow, cultural and educational exchanges, and sundry personal relationships. The same holds true for the United States–Canadian boundary.

The relatively open international environment exposes borderlanders to foreign values, ideas, customs, traditions, institutions, tastes, and behavior. Residents of borderlands find it easy to see how people from each nation make their living, how they cope with daily life, how they acquire their education, and how they exercise their responsibilities as citizens. Consumers are able to purchase desired foreign products; business-people find it possible to expand their clientele beyond the boundary; and employers with a need for labor have access to foreign workers.

The North American Free Trade Agreement (NAFTA) exemplifies the pronounced economic inter-action on the United States–Mexican border and, on a grander scale, throughout the North American region as far north as Canada. By the mid-1990s, binational trade was at an all-time high from Matamoros-Brownsville to Tijuana–San Diego, and greater surges were expected in the future. Yet many years before NAFTA, border towns already had highly interdependent econo-mies. For example, Mexican cities, such as Cuidad Juárez and Tijuana, had relied heavily on earnings from transborder commuter workers, foreign-oriented tour-ism, and externally financed *maquiladoras* (assembly plants). Historical links with the United States were also revealed in the migration of Mexicans, who had long used the Mexican border communities as strate-gic way stations on their northward journey and on their return to the homeland.

International conflict and accommodation

Border-related strife emanates from international dis-putes and border instability. Residents of borderlands face special challenges innate to the boundary itself, while in-terior populations are shielded from such stresses.

As troubled borders achieve some stability through accommodation, the dangerous climate to which resi-dents of borderlands are exposed diminishes, but con-flict still remains a constant feature. Americans and Mexicans living in the borderlands, for example, have had to overcome historical alienation and to confront new challenges posed by changing border conditions. Having progressed to the stage of interdependence, they faced frictions associated with international trade, smuggling, undocumented migration, heavy cross-border traffic, and international pollution. Thus while increased interaction diminished strife related to border-location, it has not eliminated other forms of conflict. For example, new disputes have arisen out of efforts to maintain border restrictions while the economies and societies of both sides have drawn closer together. Along the United States–Canadian border, similar pat-terns are evident.

Ethnic conflict and accommodation

In contrast to populations in the heartlands of nation-states, where cultural homogeneity is the norm,

Herbert Eugene Bolton and other historians urged an examination of the unique experiences of those living in the borderlands. Here the border runs through the middle of 1890's Nogales, Arizona, with "Americans" living on one side and "Mexicans" on the other without much but national labels to distinguish them. Photograph by W. J. Neumann. *Courtesy National Archives.*

people of border regions are more likely to live in heterogeneous environments. Immigration from con-tiguous countries and cultural diversity inevitably pro-duce interethnic frictions, especially if the groups represented have a history of adversity. The greater the divergences in race, religion, customs, values, and level of economic development, the more pronounced the intergroup tensions.

Ethnic tension often begins with forceful attempts of mainstream societies to assimilate all groups within the nation-states. Such efforts precipitate strong resis-tance among peoples determined to preserve their dif-ferent identities and life styles. Opposition is found especially in cases where a group is more strongly tied to people of the same ethnic background who reside across the boundary than it is to the dominant society in its own country. For the nation-state concerned with national integration, interethnic friction poses particu-larly troublesome problems. For border minorities caught up in cultural tugs-of-war, the perplexities are equally pronounced.

In the United States borderlands, ethnic conflict has been commonplace from Texas to California. Major events in Chicano history—such as the TEXAS REVOLU-TION in 1836, the UNITED STATES–MEXICAN WAR from 1846 to 1848, the raids by JUAN NEPOMUCENO CORTINA from 1859 to 1860, the EL PASO SALT WAR in 1877, the raids associated with the Plan of San Diego from 1915 to 1916, and countless other dramatic clashes—can be traced partly to ethnic and cultural antipathies that flourished in the border region. On the other hand, substantial accommodation and cooperation are also evident in the relationship between English-speaking whites and people of Mexican descent, especially in the interdependent border communities in the latter half of the twentieth century.

Otherness

Aware of the unique environment that shapes their lives, residents of borderlands think of themselves as different from the people living in interior zones, and outsiders perceive them that way as well. One distinction entails relationships with citizens from the adjoining nation. Because of their remoteness from the heartland and their sustained external interaction, nationalism among many residents of borderlands is diluted, and they are more tolerant of ethnic and cultural differences. On the United States–Mexico border, large numbers of people live and function in several different worlds: the world of their national culture, the world of the border environment, the world of their ethnic group if they are members of a minority population, and the world of the foreign culture on the other side of the boundary. Considerable versatility, including the ability to be multilingual and multicultural, is required to be an active participant in each of these universes. By contrast, in the interior zones in the United States and Mexico, individuals who live in homogeneous environments have little need to develop such multifaceted proficiencies or to be knowledgeable and sensitive to the perspectives of other peoples. Thus geographic location, economic interaction with foreigners, and cultural diversity make the lives of borderland residents stand out from their respective national norms.

Separateness

By virtue of their distance and isolation from the core of the nation-state and their unique ethnic and economic characteristics, residents of borderlands frequently develop economic and political interests that clash with those of the central government or the mainstream culture. Consequently, a sense of separateness and even alienation from the heartland is not uncommon. Borderland residents clamor for authorities to recognize their special needs and often insist that some national laws that have detrimental regional effects should be changed or enforced differently in border zones.

Americans in the borderlands, for example, have developed a strong sense of independence. National authorities view the border as a barrier and a safeguard to national sovereignty, but borderland residents, especially those deeply involved in transnational in-

teraction, see the boundary as a nuisance whose injurious effects must be neutralized for the sake of maintaining the welfare of their binational region. Consequently, over time many confrontations between agencies, such as the U.S. Immigration and Naturalization Service and the U.S. Customs Service, and border politicians and businesspeople have occurred.

—*Oscar J. Martínez*

SEE ALSO: Mexican Settlement; Spanish and Mexican Towns, Spanish Settlement; Women on the Spanish-Mexican Frontier

SUGGESTED READING:

Bannon, John F. *The Spanish Borderlands Frontier, 1513–1821.* Albuquerque, N. Mex., 1974.

Bolton, Herbert E. *The Spanish Borderlands: A Chronicle of Old Florida and the Southwest.* New Haven, Conn., 1921.

Fernández, Raúl A. *The Mexican-American Border Region: Issues and Trends.* Notre Dame, Ind., 1989.

———. *The United States Mexico Border: A Politico-Economic Profile.* Notre Dame, Ind., 1977.

House, John W. *Frontier on the Rio Grande: A Political Geography of Development and Social Deprivation.* New York, 1982.

Martínez, Oscar J. *Border People: Life and Society in the U.S.–Mexico Borderlands.* Tucson, Ariz., 1994.

———. *Troublesome Border.* Tucson, Ariz., 1988.

Martínez, Oscar J., ed. *Across Boundaries: Transborder Interaction in Comparative Perspective.* El Paso, Tex., 1986.

McWilliams, Carey. *North from Mexico: The Spanish-Speaking People of the United States.* Edition updated by Matt S. Meier. New York, 1990.

Weber, David J. *The Mexican Frontier, 1821–1846: The American Southwest under Mexico.* Albuquerque, N. Mex., 1982.

———. *The Spanish Frontier in North America.* New Haven, Conn., 1992.

BOREIN, JOHN EDWARD

Illustrator and print-maker John Edward Borein (1872–1945) was one of the few artists of the American West actually to have lived for much of his life in the region. He was born in San Leandro, California, and later moved with his family to neighboring Oakland. At the age of seventeen, he quit school. He found work as a cowhand and became well acquainted with Southwestern ranch life. Showing a talent for art, he sold his first drawing in 1894 to a local newspaper. Around 1902, he opened a studio in Oakland and attempted to make a living as an illustrator.

Detail from *Blackfoot Women Moving Camp, No. 2,* by John Edward Borein. *Courtesy Buffalo Bill Historical Center. Gift of Corliss C. and Audrienne H. Mosley.*

In 1907, Borein moved to New York City, where he studied at the Art Students League under Childe Hassam and Ernest Roth. During this period, he became interested in metal-plate engraving. After working for several years in New York as a commercial artist, he returned to his native California and opened a studio in Santa Barbara. During the 1920s, he taught drawing and print-making at the Santa Barbara School of Arts.

Borein was acquainted with such Western celebrities as WILLIAM F. ("BUFFALO BILL") CODY and CHARLES MARION RUSSELL. Over the years, his studio in Santa Barbara became a popular meeting place for other artists, writers, and film stars of the period. Reportedly advised by Russell to "leave oil painting to others," Borein concentrated on drawing and etching. He is represented today in collections throughout the United States, chiefly by his etchings, of which he issued more than three hundred in various editions.

—*David C. Hunt*

SEE ALSO: Art: Western Art

SUGGESTED READING:
Axelrod, Alan. *Art of the Golden West.* New York, 1990.
Rossi, Paul A., and David C. Hunt. *The Art of the Old West.* 1971. 4th ed. New York, 1989.
Davidson, Harold G. *Edward Borein, Cowboy Artist: The Life and Works of John Edward Borein, 1871–1945.* Garden City, N.Y., 1974.

BORGLUM, SOLON HANNIBAL

Sculptor Solon Hannibal Borglum (1868–1922) was born in Ogden, Utah. He moved as a child to Fremont, Nebraska, where he attended public schools. He later enrolled briefly at Creighton University in Omaha. While working on his father's ranch, he developed a keen interest in animals, anatomy, and drawing. His ability attracted the attention of his elder brother Gutzon, who encouraged Solon to pursue a career in art. In 1893, he joined Gutzon in Santa Ana, California, rented studio space, and made his first mature studies of the human figure.

In 1895, Borglum enrolled in the Cincinnati Academy of Art, where his clay figures of horses received high praise from Louis Rebisso, head of the sculpture department. Borglum subsequently studied in Paris at the Academie Julien with fellow-sculptor ALEXANDER PHIMISTER (A. P.) PROCTOR. Borglum married in Paris in 1898 and continued to execute sculptures of horses and Western subjects. In 1899, he returned to the United States to gather material for a commission from the Paris Exposition of 1900. In 1907, he and his wife settled in Silvermine, Connecticut, where Borglum established a permanent studio.

Although his reputation as a sculptor was eventually overshadowed by that of his brother, Solon Borglum created numerous life-size works for expositions and civic monuments expressive of the character and spirit of pioneer life in the American West. In New York City, he organized the School of American Sculpture and served as its director until his death. He is widely represented today in both public and private collections.

—*David C. Hunt*

SUGGESTED READING:

Broder, Patricia Janis. *Bronzes of the American West.* New York, 1973.
Davies, A. Mervyn. *Solon H. Borglum.* Chester, Conn., 1974.
Kovinick, Phil. "South Dakota's 'Other' Borglum." *South Dakota State Historical Quarterly* 1 (1971).

BOUDINOT, ELIAS (CHEROKEE)

Editor of the *Cherokee Phoenix* and leader of the Cherokee faction that favored relocation to the Indian Country (Oklahoma), Elias Boudinot (1803–1839) was born in Oothcaloga just south of New Echota in the Cherokee Nation (later Cass County, Georgia). His father, Oowatie, was a full-blooded Cherokee; his mother, Susanna Reese, was of mixed-blood birth. Named Kilakeena (The Buck) at birth, he adopted, sometime after 1818, the name of Elias Boudinot, a New Jersey philanthropist and benefactor of the AMERICAN BOARD OF COMMISSIONERS FOR FOREIGN MISSIONS School in Cornwall, Connecticut.

Boudinot attended the Moravian Mission Schools in Springplace, Cherokee Nation, and Brainard, Tennessee. At these schools, he received English instruction in oratory, spelling, reading, grammar, accounting, and the fundamentals of the Moravian faith. After graduating from the school in Cornwall, he married Harriet Gold, daughter of Benjamin Gold, despite local hostility regarding interracial marriages. Returning with his new bride to Cherokee country, which by the mid-1820s was seething over the question of removal to the Indian Country in the distant West, he was eager to use his intellectual talents to sustain Cherokee nationality and cultural integrity.

In Cherokee country, mixed-blood George Guess (Sikwaji, or SEQUOYAH) had in the meantime developed a rudimentary Cherokee syllabary that was used in publication of the *Cherokee Phoenix,* a weekly newspaper sponsored by the Cherokee National Council. In 1824, Boudinot became editor of the paper, and with the assistance of medical missionary Samuel A. Worcester, penned numerous articles highly critical of white encroachments on Cherokee land. Boudinot and Worcester translated several books of the New Testament into Cherokee. Following CHEROKEE NATION V. STATE OF GEORGIA (1831), he toured the Northern states with his cousin JOHN RIDGE in an attempt to rally support for the Cherokee cause against white domination and dispossession.

In 1831, JOHN ROSS, an intractable opponent of Cherokee removal, was elected principal chief. His election exacerbated the conflict between the nonremoval faction led by Ross and the Ridge–Boudinot–Stand Watie group that favored relocation to the Indian Country as the only means of preserving Cherokee sovereignty. In February 1835, Georgia officials suppressed publication of the *Cherokee Phoenix,* and urged on by federal negotiators, Boudinot and other members of the removal faction signed the two New Echota treaties on December 29. The result was the forced relocation (sometimes called the TRAIL OF TEARS) of a majority of the Cherokees to the Indian Country and a bitter schism that was to plague the tribe for years. In an act of revenge for Boudinot's role in the removal, unidentified Ross partisans brutally murdered him near the Worcester Mission in Indian Country on June 22, 1839.

—*William E. Unrau*

SEE ALSO: Native American Peoples: People Removed from the East

SUGGESTED READING:

Dale, Edward Everett, and Gaston Litton. *Cherokee Cavaliers: Forty Years of Cherokee History as Told in the Correspondence of the Ridge-Watie-Boudinot Family.* Norman, Okla., 1940.

Franks, Kenny A. *Stand Watie and the Agony of the Cherokee Nation.* Memphis, Tenn., 1979.

Gabriel, Ralph Henry. *Elias Boudinot: Cherokee and American.* Norman, Okla., 1941.

BOULDER CANYON ACT OF 1928

The Boulder Canyon Act of 1928 gave congressional approval to the COLORADO RIVER COMPACT and authorized the construction of the All-American Canal and HOOVER DAM and the generation and sale of hydroelectricity. The legislation was first introduced in 1922 by Congressman Phil Swing and Senator HIRAM WARREN JOHNSON. The Colorado River upper basin states—Colorado, New Mexico, Utah, and Wyoming—opposed the legislation because California was growing so rapidly that they would lose their water by default. Another group opposed the "public" power to be generated by the proposed dam. Congress approved the bill in December 1928, and in June 1929, President Herbert Hoover signed it into law. With the passage of the law, the federal government became a major player in making policy on Western WATER.

—*Kazuto Oshio*

SEE ALSO: Climate; Colorado River

SUGGESTED READING:

Hundley, Norris, Jr. *Water and the West: The Colorado River Compact and the Politics of Water in the American West.* Berkeley, Calif., 1975.

———. *The Great Thirst: Californians and Water, 1770s–1990s.* Berkeley, Calif., 1992.

BOULDER DAM

SEE: Hoover Dam

BOWIE, JAMES

Texas Ranger and commander of the ALAMO James Bowie (1795 or 1796–1836) was born in Sumner County, Tennessee. He moved to Louisiana with his family around 1802. With his brother, Reason (sometimes spelled "Rezin"), Bowie operated a sawmill. The brothers achieved financial success and became the owners of a large sugar plantation, the first in Louisiana to use steam power to grind sugar cane.

James Bowie. *Courtesy Library of Congress.*

Although James Bowie is generally credited with the invention, it was Reason who made the first "Bowie" knife. Reason, himself, wrote in 1838 that:

> the first Bowie knife was made by myself. . . .
> The length of the blade is 9 ¼", its width 1 ½",
> single edged and blade not curved.

Since the time that James successfully used the knife in a fight in Louisiana, the legendary weapon has been associated with him, not his brother.

Bowie moved to Bexar (San Antonio), Texas, in 1828, was baptized in the Catholic church, and married the daughter of the vice-governor. In 1833, Bowie's two children and wife, along with many members of her family, died of cholera. Devastated by the loss, he immersed himself in his work as a colonel in the Texas Rangers.

In 1835, when it became clear that Texas would seek its independence from Mexico, Bowie—who was a Mexican citizen and had close ties with the Mexican government through his marriage—declared that his fate lay with Texas. In early 1836, he commanded a small army of volunteers at the Alamo in San Antonio, but when WILLIAM BARRET TRAVIS arrived in late February with a contingent of the Texas army, the two men decided to share the command of the mission. On February 24, Bowie contracted typhoid pneumonia and was incapacitated during the siege of the Alamo by the

Mexican army. When Mexican troops finally overran the defenders on March 6, Bowie, according to some accounts, killed several enemy soldiers from his sickbed with his knife before he, himself, was killed. According to his sister-in-law, the Mexicans "tossed Bowie's body on their bayonets until his blood covered their clothes and dyed them red."

Texas historian Joe B. Frantz has written that Bowie "was the stuff of which heroes are made, a man of huge passions and appetites, a 'big dealer' who liked to plunge against long odds, and a natural candidate for folklore." Unlike other American heroes, however, Bowie has passed down not one, but two traditions that have made him legendary: the famous "Bowie" knife and his final hours at the Alamo.

—*James A. Crutchfield*

SEE ALSO: National Expansion: Texas and National Expansion; Texas Revolution

SUGGESTED READING:
Douglas, Claude L. *James Bowie: The Life of a Bravo.* Dallas, Tex., 1944.

BOZEMAN TRAIL

Known variously as the Bozeman Road, the Montana Road, and the Powder River Trail, the Bozeman Trail ran northwest from Deer Creek Crossing on the North Platte River (now Glenrock, Wyoming), between the Black Hills and the Bighorn Mountains. It crossed the Powder, Tongue, and Bighorn rivers to the gold fields along the Yellowstone River and ended at the town of Bozeman, Montana, established in 1864.

The trail was "discovered" by John M. Bozeman (1835–1867) from Pickens County, Georgia. In 1860, Bozeman left his wife and two small children to seek his fortune in the gold fields of Colorado. Two years later, he joined a party of prospectors bound for the newly discovered gold fields of Montana. The existing routes to Montana—by way of South Pass and Fort Hall or from the head of navigation at Fort Benton on the Missouri River—were long and difficult. In 1863, in an effort to find a shorter route, Bozeman and John M. Jacobs, a veteran mountain man, explored what would later become the Bozeman Trail. They took a party of emigrants over the trail in 1864, and others followed. Almost from the beginning, the trail was contested by the Indians, particularly the Sioux. Bozeman was killed by Indians on April 18, 1867, while traveling from the Yellowstone River to Fort C. F. Smith.

In 1866, in an effort to protect the trail, the U.S. Army established Forts Fetterman, Reno, Philip Kearny, and C. F. Smith. The forts were under almost constant attack by the Sioux under Chief RED CLOUD, and the Bozeman Trail became unusable. In 1868, as part of the effort to induce Red Cloud to participate in the Fort Laramie negotiations, the army abandoned all of the Powder River forts except Fetterman, and the Bozeman Trail ceased to be a factor in Western migration.

—*James C. Olson*

SEE ALSO: Fetterman Massacre; Montana Gold Rush; Mountain Men; Sioux Wars

SUGGESTED READING:
Burlingame, Merrill G. "John M. Bozeman, Montana Trailmaker." *Mississippi Valley Historical Review* 27 (March 1941): 541–568; also published as *John M. Bozeman, Montana Trailmaker.* Bozeman, Mont., 1941.
Hebard, Grace R., and E. A. Brininstool. *The Bozeman Trail.* 2 vols. Cleveland, Ohio, 1922.
Johnson, Dorothy M. *The Bloody Bozeman.* New York, 1971.
Olson, James C. *Red Cloud and the Sioux Problem.* Lincoln, Nebr., 1965. Reprint. 1975.

BRADBURY, JOHN

Naturalist and author John Bradbury (1768–1823) was born in Scotland and studied botany in England. The Botanical Society of Liverpool sent him to the United States in 1809 to investigate flora in the American West. Soon after his arrival, he met THOMAS JEFFERSON, who advised Bradbury to make St. Louis his exploration headquarters. From there, he made several trips into the surrounding area. In 1811, he traveled with a fur-trading expedition to the Upper Missouri River and kept detailed journals of his observations. He planned to return to England, but the War of 1812 prevented his doing so. He spent the next four years traveling widely, again recording much of what he observed. In 1815, he finally returned to England where his journals were published as *Travels in the Interior of America.* The book remained an important source about the American West for generations of Europeans. Bradbury returned to St. Louis in his later years and died there in 1823.

—*Phil Roberts*

SUGGESTED READING:
Thwaites, Reuben Gold, ed. *Bradbury's Travels in the Interior of America, 1809–1811.* Reprint. Cleveland, Ohio, 1904.

BRADLEY, LEWIS R.

The second governor of Nevada, rancher Lewis R. Bradley (1806–1879) was born in Virginia. Between 1844 and 1852, he raised stock in Missouri. After driving a herd of cattle to California in 1852, he decided to enter the trail-driving business. Ten years later, however, he settled in Nevada, started a ranch to supply beef to miners of the COMSTOCK LODE, and began his political career. He served as county commissioner and treasurer in Elko County and as governor for two terms beginning in 1870. As governor, he oversaw the founding of the state university and pushed through the state legislature a bill that lessened the favored tax position of mining companies. After the bill passed in 1875, the Bonanza mining firm began a fight against the new tax rates. When Bradley vetoed a compromise bill designed to reduce the firm's tax liability, mining interests put forth John Kinkead as a candidate for governor, and Bradley lost to him in 1878.

—*Candace Floyd*

SUGGESTED READING:
Elliott, Russell R. *History of Nevada.* 2d ed., rev. Lincoln, Nebr., 1987.

BRADY, JOHN GREEN

An Alaskan missionary, businessman, and, during the KLONDIKE GOLD RUSH, territorial governor, John Green Brady (1847–1918) was noted for his enlightened attitude toward natives.

Born in New York City, Brady ran away from home at the age of eight. The Children's Aid Society found him living on the street and sent him to a foster family in Indiana in 1859. There he attended the local school while farming, and by the age of twenty, he had acquired seven acres of his own. He taught school before entering a private academy and then going to Yale College in 1870. Upon graduation, he attended Union Theological Seminary in New York and was ordained a Presbyterian minister in 1878. After meeting the church's dynamic Alaska advocate, Dr. SHELDON JACKSON, Brady accepted an assignment as a mission teacher at Sitka.

A new community with numerous business opportunities, Sitka was the principal nonnative settlement in Alaska. Brady taught school there for two years and then married and left the ministry to open a general mercantile business, the Sitka Trading Company. He soon added a sawmill and a freight steamer to his company holdings. He maintained good relations with the mission and the government and became a leading citizen in the community. In 1885, he passed the Alaska bar and was appointed U.S. commissioner, the chief magistrate for the town.

As commissioner, Brady administered justice with a fair hand. He campaigned for more efficient and effective government. He used his office and influence to clarify and protect fishing and property rights of natives. Active in territorial politics, he was appointed Alaska's territorial governor in 1897, when the Klondike rush was beginning.

Alaska's nonnative population increased from five thousand to forty thousand during the gold rush, and the ensuing challenges outstripped the government's capacity to respond and perhaps Brady's administrative abilities. His attempts to protect the natives were laudable but largely ineffective, as were his efforts at policing the raucous new communities. When he unwittingly allowed himself to be manipulated by an unscrupulous promoter, the government demanded his resignation in 1906.

Brady retired to Sitka and developed trading contacts in China. In 1914, he opened a vocational training school in Canton. He returned to Sitka in 1916 where he died two years later.

—*Stephen Haycox*

SEE ALSO: Alaska Gold Rush

SUGGESTED READING:
Gruening, Ernest. *The State of Alaska.* New York, 1954.
Hinckley, Ted C. *Alaskan John G. Brady: Missionary, Businessman, Judge, and Governor, 1878–1918.* Miami, Ohio, 1982.

BRAND, MAX (FAUST, FREDERICK SCHILLER)

A prolific writer of fiction, Frederick Schiller Faust (1892–1944) was better known by his pen name "Max Brand." Born in Seattle, Washington, Faust was educated in public schools in California and at the University of California at Berkeley. In 1915, eager to get to France for the war, he enlisted in the Canadian Expeditionary Forces but deserted and subsequently joined the United States Army Corps of Engineers. He fell ill during training and was discharged.

In 1917, Faust married Dorothy Schillig and began his professional career in earnest. He wrote stories and poems for such magazines as *Century, All-Story Weekly,* and *Argosy.* Munsey editor Bob Davis is credited with launching Faust into writing westerns by giving him a copy of ZANE GREY's *Riders of the Purple*

Sage (1912), which Faust read and admired. Soon afterwards, he wrote a western himself, entitled *The Untamed,* and saw it published by Munsey's *All-Story Weekly* on December 7, 1918, under the pen name "Max Brand."

By the late 1920s, Faust was earning four cents a word in the pulp magazines and was the highest-paid pulp writer of his time. His literary agent Carl Brandt estimated that Faust was writing up to two million published words a year. His markets included not only the pulp magazines, but also the full market of "slick" magazines such as *Harper's, American, Collier's, Esquire, Liberty,* and *Saturday Evening Post.*

Faust moved into a twenty-two–room villa near Florence, Italy, in 1926 and was among the highest paid writers in the world, with a writing income exceeding one hundred thousand dollars a year in 1930. Called "Heinie" by his friends, he was a cultured man who wrote serious poetry and loved good wines, Bach, and classical literature, especially Chaucer, Dante, and Shakespeare.

His output is astonishing: more than three hundred book-length westerns plus hundreds of other novels, stories, and poems. Only his verse was under his given name; the other works appeared under more than a dozen pen names. Among his most memorable creations are "Whistling Dan" Barry of *The Untamed* and several sequels, *Destry Rides Again* (1930), and the "Dr. Kildare" stories, first published in *Cosmopolitan* magazine in 1936. More than eighty films have been made from his works.

Faust was killed in action in Italy on May 12, 1944, while serving as a war correspondent for *Harper's.*

—*Dale L. Walker*

See also: Literature: The Western Novel

Suggested reading:

Easton, Robert. *Max Brand: The Big "Westerner."* Norman, Okla., 1970.

Richardson, Darrell C. *Max Brand: The Man and His Work.* Los Angeles, 1952.

BRANDS

See: Cattle Brands and Branding

BRANNAN, SAMUEL

An "empire builder" in early San Francisco, Mormon leader, and initiator of the California gold rush, Samuel Brannan (1819–1889) was born in Maine to parents of Irish descent. He left home in 1833, fleeing a drunken and abusive father, and moved to Ohio to live with his sister and her husband. There, the young man became an apprentice printer.

In 1843, Brannan converted to the new religion, the Church of Jesus Christ of Latter-day Saints. In part to escape an unhappy marriage, he plunged into the work of the church, remarried, and moved to New York to publish a sectarian journal entitled *The Prophet.*

Although he was closer to Prophet Joseph Smith, Jr., than to Smith's successor, Brigham Young, the latter chose him to lead a colony of 238 Saints to Mexican California at about the same time as the 1846 Mormon trek overland to the Great Salt Lake. From the deck of his chartered *Brooklyn,* Brannan saw the American flag flying over Yerba Buena (later San Francisco), just captured in the United States–Mexican War. Because of the persecution of Mormons in the United States, Brannan was said to have exclaimed either "there's that damned *flag,* again!" or "there's that damned *rag,* again!"

The dynamic young Mormon quickly made his peace with the citizens of San Francisco. He was the first since Francis Drake's Chaplain Fletcher (1579) and the Orthodox priests at Fort Ross (1812 to 1841) to preach a non-Catholic sermon in California. He built the second or third flour mill on the West Coast. He also set up a job printing press and published one of the state's first two newspapers, the *California Star.*

Brannan then made the arduous and dangerous crossing of the Sierra Nevada and the Utah desert to try to persuade Brigham Young to shift his Zion to the San Francisco area from Salt Lake City. Back in San Francisco, his religious ardor began to cool, and his business opportunism turned into a new faith: materialism and even hedonism. Accusations of misuse of Mormon tithes eventually led to his excommunication, but he was already drifting into apostasy.

While running a prosperous general store at Sutter's Fort (later Sacramento), Brannan ignited the explosive California gold rush. Parading through the streets of San Francisco in May 1848, he flaunted a vial of "dust" and shouted "Gold! Gold from the American River!" But Brannan, himself, made his money as a storekeeper and real-estate speculator, not in the drudgery of placer mining.

Brannan diversified his business interests. He owned office buildings, a bank, a lumber mill, a bookstore, a biscuit factory, a cattle ranch, and even a vineyard, distillery, and posh resort, Hot Springs, in Napa Valley's Calistoga. He made the latter into the Saratoga of the Pacific. It was said that, at one time, he owned a fifth of San Francisco. He was probably the state's first millionaire in 1856.

Samuel Brannan. *Courtesy Bancroft Library.*

repeat the process. As a vigilante, Brannan revealed flaws in his character, such as a penchant for reckless meddling and violence. He was always the first to haul away a criminal suspect on a hangman's rope. In 1851, he dabbled in a filibustering fiasco in Hawaii. From 1864 to 1865, he sent arms and mercenaries to Mexico to help Benito Juárez fight Maximilian. In 1868, he was badly wounded at Calistoga when his hot temper got him into a shooting incident.

After a costly divorce in 1870, the spendthrift and overextended Brannan lost his Midas touch. As he acquired notoriety as a hard drinker and a womanizer, the remnants of his fortune slipped through his fingers. He faded into obscurity.

During his last years, he was virtually forgotten. After he died in Escondido, California, his body lay in an undertaker's vault for sixteen months until a nephew paid the embalming bill and arranged for burial in San Diego.

—*Richard H. Dillon*

SEE ALSO: Vigilantism

SUGGESTED READING:
Bailey, Paul. *Sam Brannan and the California Mormons.* Los Angeles, 1943.
Stellman, Louis J. *Sam Brannan, Builder of San Francisco.* New York, 1953.

BRIDGER, JAMES (JIM)

James (Jim) Bridger (1804–1881) lived an illustrious life as a mountain man, guide, and founder of an overland emigrant fort. Born in Richmond, Virginia, Bridger was orphaned at age fourteen after his family had moved to Missouri. With no formal education, Bridger instead learned from life experiences, which provided him with the necessary qualities to endure frontier hardships. He willingly responded to WILLIAM HENRY ASHLEY's call for "one hundred enterprising young men" to enter the FUR TRADE and worked as a mountain man trapping and exploring in the Central and Northern Rocky Mountains.

Some historians believe that Bridger was one of two trappers selected by ANDREW HENRY to bury HUGH GLASS, who was thought, wrongly, to have died from wounds received in an attack by a grizzly bear. Instead of burying him, the two trappers abandoned him and took his gun. Glass somehow survived and vowed to seek revenge against his companions. Upon finding Bridger, however, Glass forgave him.

Bridger's adventures in the mountains ranged from the headwaters of the Missouri River to the Spanish

Brannan was also a civic leader. He founded the prestigious Society of California Pioneers and organized an informal vigilante movement in 1849 to rid the city of a predatory gang of criminals. He was named president of the First Vigilance Committee (1851) to

Jim Bridger. *Courtesy Kansas State Historical Society.*

He also provided services for big-game hunters, mail delivery, and the U.S. military.

Bridger achieved acclaim as the founder of FORT BRIDGER on Black's Fork of the Green River in present-day Wyoming. The post supplied the Oregon and California trails throughout the 1840s and 1850s. BRIGHAM YOUNG, governor of the Utah Territory, suspected Bridger of instigating Indian hostilities and forced him to abandon his fort in 1853. The Mormons legitimately purchased the fort in 1855; Bridger nonetheless claimed that the transaction was illegal. The United States Army took control of the fort during the UTAH EXPEDITION, and Bridger spent the rest of his life trying to persuade the government to compensate him for his losses. After his death, his widow finally secured partial payment for the fort.

Several towns and sites in the West bear Bridger's name: Bridger, Wyoming; Bridger, Montana; Bridger-Teton National Forest; Bridger Pass; and Bridger Lake.

—*Andrea Gayle Radke and Fred R. Gowans*

SEE ALSO: California Overland Trails; Mountain Men; Oregon Trail

SUGGESTED READING:

Alter, J. Cecil. *James Bridger.* Salt Lake City, 1925.

Gowans, Fred R. *Fort Bridger: Island in the Wilderness.* Provo, Utah, 1975.

Ismert, Cornelius M. "James Bridger." In *The Mountain Men and the Fur Trade of the Far West.* Vol. 6. Edited by LeRoy R. Hafen. Glendale, Calif., 1968.

BRIGHAM YOUNG EXPRESS AND CARRYING COMPANY

SEE: Y X Company

BRIONES, JUANA

Juana Briones (1802–1889) was a first-generation Californian who amassed a personal fortune by ranching in the San Francisco area. Her parents, Marcos Briones and Isidora Tapia, were born in Mexico. Her mother arrived in California as a child with the JUAN BAUTISTA DE ANZA colonizing expedition of 1775 to 1776. Her father, a soldier at Monterey, accompanied the expedition to San Francisco. During the late eighteenth century, Spain discouraged commerce to avoid foreign influence in California. Without markets, settlers grew and produced little more than they themselves required. Mexico lifted these trade restrictions

Southwest. During his career, he participated in thirteen RENDEZVOUS, witnessed the smallpox epidemic of 1837, saw the wonders of what one day would become YELLOWSTONE NATIONAL PARK, and engaged in numerous conflicts with Native Americans. In 1824, Bridger followed the Bear River to its outlet into the Great Salt Lake. Upon tasting the salty water, he expressed amazement at being on the Pacific Ocean! Subsequent research has shown that others encountered the lake prior to Bridger's sighting. Nevertheless, the story of his "discovery" endures in Western legends.

Using his knowledge of wilderness life and Western geography, Bridger began work as a guide. From 1844 to 1850, he guided emigrant trains west, and in 1850, he outlined a trail for the CORPS OF TOPOGRAPHICAL ENGINEERS, a trail that later became part of the routes for the Overland Stage and UNION PACIFIC RAILROAD.

after achieving independence from Spain in 1821. A seigniorial style of living evolved as the government provided settlers with lands from the vast mission holdings and in an atmosphere that encouraged trade, many rancheros, including Briones's family, prospered.

Juana Briones married and took on the duties of a young wife and mother during this period of transition. Briones was an industrious and hospitable woman, who cared for orphaned children and the sick. Exceptionally skilled in healing, she educated her nephew, Pablo Briones, who was for fifty years the respected doctor of Bolinas, a community north of San Francisco.

Juana Briones's most remarkable achievement was the prosperity that she maintained throughout her life despite overwhelming disadvantage. Through persistence, careful management, and good judgment, she reached and sustained a position of honor and affluence. The American occupation in 1846 and the acquisition of statehood in 1850 greatly diminished the status of the Hispanic people and drove many of them to destitution or to marginal employment. Furthermore, even under the relatively equitable property and business laws of Spanish and Mexican California, the status of women was far from equal. Women received only 13 percent of the land grants, and property was usually registered under the name of husbands. After the death of her own husband in 1847, Briones pursued her claim to the property at the foot of Lyon Street hill along the present-day boundary of the San Francisco Presidio. It took her fifteen years to validate the title and her claim to it for herself and her children.

She moved in 1835 to land at the foot of Alta Loma, now Telegraph Hill, to increase her farm-land holdings and to live closer to the ships that were her market for fresh food. She was one of the first inhabitants of the newly founded pueblo of Yerba Buena (later San Francisco). She built a brush fence to provide a corral, garden, and orchard—a rectangular plot that today is Washington Square Park. Her ranch buildings angled across the land that is now the corner of Filbert and Powell streets. One early map identifies the nearby cove as Juana Briones Beach.

In 1844, Briones took three steps to strengthen her position as the sole supporter of her eight children. She applied to religious authorities for a separation from her second husband; she petitioned the local authorities for the third time for title to the property she had farmed since 1835 in Yerba Buena; and she purchased from Indians a forty-four-hundred-acre ranch thirty-five miles to the south, where Los Altos Hills and Palo Alto now draw their political boundaries.

Part of the house she constructed on the Purisima ranch still stands in present-day Palo Alto and is occasionally opened to the public as a historic site. Chester Lyman, a visitor in 1847, wrote that he had arranged for his comfortable stay at Briones's home, meaning probably that he paid for his accommodations. He noted that Briones was caring for two sick people and that there was considerable coming and going of guests and members of the bustling household.

Available evidence suggests that Juana Briones never left the San Francisco Bay area, yet her name and accomplishments remain a California legacy.

—*Jeanne Farr McDonnell*

SEE ALSO: California Ranchos; Women on the Spanish-Mexican Frontier

SUGGESTED READING:
Bowman, J. N. "Juana Briones de Miranda." *Historical Society of Southern California Quarterly* (September 1957): 227–241.
Lothrop, Gloria Ricci. "Rancheras and the Land: Women and Property Rights in Hispanic California." *Southern California Quarterly* (Spring 1994): 59–84.
Lyman, Chester S. *Around the Horn*. New Haven, Conn., 1924.
Monroy, Douglas. *Thrown among Strangers: The Making of Mexican Culture in Frontier California*. Berkeley, Calif., 1990.
Thomas, William H. *On Land and Sea*. Boston, 1884.

BROADWATER, CHARLES ARTHUR

Montana entrepreneur and capitalist Charles Arthur Broadwater (1840–1892) was born in St. Charles, Missouri. As a child, he worked in St. Louis, Missouri, business houses. In 1861, he moved to Colorado and, in 1862, to the booming gold camp of Bannack in what would become the Montana Territory. Broadwater helped plat the town site of Deer Lodge and, by 1863, had settled in Virginia City. The young, aggressive entrepreneur managed the dominant Diamond R Freighting Company until 1869 and remained a partner in that lucrative business until 1879. At the same time, he invested in open-range cattle, quartz mining, federal supply contracts for forts and Indian agencies, timber cutting, and dry-goods retail operations.

In 1882, Broadwater organized the Montana National Bank in Helena and thereafter served as its president. He also became president of the Montana Central Railroad Company, which was aligned with JAMES J. HILL's Great Northern Railway and constructed lines to link Butte with Helena and Great Falls from 1886 to 1887. From 1888 to 1889, he also constructed an elegant, Victorian, hot-springs natatorium-hotel complex west of Helena, known simply as The Broadwater.

Never an officeholder himself, Charles Broadwater became—with Marcus Daly, William Andrews Clark, and Samuel Thomas Hauser—one of the Democratic party's "Big Four" in Montana. This quartet wielded great behind-the-scenes political influence during the 1880s and benefited on many levels from their power.

—*David A. Walter*

Suggested reading:

"Charles A. Broadwater." In *Progressive Men of the State of Montana*. Chicago, ca. 1902.

Lang, William L. "Charles A. Broadwater and the Main Chance in Montana." *Montana: The Magazine of Western History* 39 (Summer 1989): 30–36.

———. "Corporate Point Men and the Creation of the Montana Central Railroad, 1882–1887." *Great Plains Quarterly* 10 (Summer 1990): 152–166.

Miller, Robert E. "Montana's Enterprising 'Colonel' Broadwater." *Montana Magazine* 11 (May-June 1981): 18–23.

BROCIUS, "CURLY" BILL

Cattle rustler "Curly" Bill Brocius (ca. 1857–1882? 1890s?), whose real name seems to have been William Graham, went to Arizona from his native Texas in 1878 with a herd of cattle for the San Carlos Apache reservation. He soon turned up in the Tombstone area, where he worked for the McLaury brothers—Tom and Frank. He was suspected of being involved in CATTLE RUSTLING with members of the Clanton Clan—Ike, Billy, Finn (or Phinn), and their father N. H. "Old Man" Clanton—but was never arrested for any of those alleged activities. As a member of Tombstone's so-called cowboy element, he became an enemy of the EARP BROTHERS—Wyatt, Virgil, and Morgan—and was involved in the ongoing Earp-Clanton feud. In October 1880, he engaged in an altercation that resulted in the accidental shooting of Tombstone city Marshal Fred White. Legend has it that Wyatt Earp pistol-whipped Brocius after the shooting and took him to jail, but many historians think it is more likely that Virgil Earp arrested Brocius. In May 1881, Brocius was wounded in the neck in a gunfight in Galeyville, Arizona. Wyatt Earp claimed to have killed Brocius in the spring of 1882 at Iron Springs in the Whetstone Mountains, but others who knew Brocius said he had left Arizona

months earlier, after the Galeyville incident, and that he lived to an old age in Texas, Montana, or Wyoming.

—*Charlie Seemann*

See also: O. K. Corral, Gunfight at

Suggested reading:

Horan, James D. *The Authentic Wild West: The Lawmen*. New York, 1980.

Waters, Frank. *The Earps of Tombstone*. New York, 1960.

BRODERICK, DAVID C.

Deified as the "Pacific Coast Lincoln," David C. Broderick (1820–1859) was a prominent California politician who came to advocate the Free-Soil position against the spread of slavery into new states of the American republic. Born in Washington, D.C., Broderick moved to New York City and took his first lessons in the rough-and-tumble world of politics as a street tough for Tammany Hall. While operating a profitable saloon in New York, Broderick served as a ward boss for the radical Locofoco faction of the Democratic party. In 1846, he ran unsuccessfully as the Tammany nominee for the Fifth Congressional District.

Heading west with the Forty-niners, Broderick relocated to San Francisco and became a partner in a lucrative assayer's office. He again became involved in politics and secured a seat on California's constitutional convention shortly after his arrival. Some months later, Broderick was elected to fill a vacancy in the California senate. When the state's lieutenant-governor ascended to the governor's office in January 1851, Broderick became president of the senate. Using methods learned during his Tammany Hall days, Broderick ruled the California Democratic party with an iron fist for the next three years.

By 1854, Broderick aspired to a seat in the United States Senate. Because California's senators were elected by the state legislature, winning the seat was a matter of making deals with rivals and securing favors from supporters. Broderick struck a bargain with his rival, William Gwin, who sought reelection to the U.S. Senate when his term expired in March 1855. Broderick agreed to support Gwin's reelection in exchange for Gwin's support of both Broderick's campaign for the second Senate seat and of Broderick's claim to control federal patronage in California. Gwin and Broderick made a deal, but U.S. President James Buchanan continued to funnel his patronage through Gwin. Although he had not previously been opposed to slavery,

Broderick retaliated by jumping to the lead of the state's Free-Soil party and decrying Buchanan's position favoring slavery in Kansas. In a vitriolic personal attack, Broderick questioned the honesty of proslavery advocate California Chief Justice David S. Terry. The judge, in response, resigned from the bench and challenged Broderick to a duel. The two met on September 13, 1859, and Broderick was killed. Broderick became a martyr to the cause of antislavery, in part because HUBERT HOWE BANCROFT's *History of California* reported that Broderick's last words were: "They killed me because I was opposed to the extension of slavery." In the West, Broderick became a symbol of the coming violence over the nation's sectional differences.

—*Kurt Edward Kemper*

SUGGESTED READING:

Quinn, Arthur. *The Rivals: William Gwin, David Broderick, and the Birth of California.* New York, 1994.

Williams, David A. *David C. Broderick: A Political Portrait.* San Marino, Calif., 1969.

BROOKS, JUANITA LEAVITT

Historian and compiler of early Mormon documents, Juanita Leavitt Brooks (1898–1989) was born in Bunkerville, Nevada. A descendant of Mormon pioneers, she was educated in local schools, including the "normal school," which provided training for teachers. She married Leonard Ernest Pulsipher in 1919. Pulsipher died within two years, just after the birth of their only child.

A mother widowed at the age of twenty-two, she returned to school and graduated with a bachelor's degree in English from Brigham Young University and a master's degree from Columbia University. She settled in St. George, Utah, where she taught school and became dean of women at Dixie College. In 1933, she married Will Brooks, a widower with three children. The couple then had four children of their own.

Despite her extensive responsibilities as a wife and mother to eight children, Brooks found time to write, publishing twelve books in all, focused on varied aspects of local Mormon history. Her most famous work, *The Mountain Meadows Massacre,* provided an account of one of the most tragic and controversial events in Utah Mormon history. Brooks also collected and preserved hundreds of Mormon pioneer diaries, most of which she deposited in the Huntington Library, Art Collections, and Botanical Gardens in San Marino, California. The diaries are invaluable sources of primary information on Mormon history.

Despite her fascination with the controversial aspects of early Utah Mormon history, Brooks steadfastly affirmed her religious faith as a practicing Latter-day Saint. She died in St. George, Utah. Because of her outstanding contributions as a writer and archivist, she is acknowledged as "the dean of Utah historians."

—*Newell G. Bringhurst*

SEE ALSO: Mormons; Mountain Meadows Massacre

SUGGESTED READING:

Bitton, Davis, and Leonard J. Arrington. *Mormons and Their Historians.* Salt Lake City, 1988.

Bringhurst, Newell G. "Juanita Brooks and Fawn Brodie—Sisters in Mormon Dissent." *Dialogue: A Journal of Mormon Thought* 27 (Summer 1994).

Peterson, Levi S. *Juanita Brooks: Mormon Woman Historian.* Salt Lake City, 1988.

BROOKS, WILLIAM L. ("BUFFALO BILL")

Born in Willington, Kansas, William L. "Buffalo Bill" (or "Bully") Brooks (ca. 1849–1874) was a buffalo hunter and stagecoach driver. Affecting the shoulder-length hair of the plainsman and always toting a Winchester, Brooks drove a stage on the Newton-Wichita route. When Newton was organized as a third-class city in 1872, Brooks was elected the first city marshal. As marshal, he suffered three wounds in a duel with roistering cowboys. Later in 1872, he pinned on the badge of an Ellsworth police officer. Soon afterward, he turned up in DODGE CITY, where he engaged in three gunfights and killed two men. Brooks and his wife moved to Caldwell, Kansas, where he joined a gang of horse and mule thieves organized by a stage line to drive a rival company out of business. Finally apprehended and incarcerated at Wellington, Brooks and two confederates were lynched on July 29, 1874.

—*Bill O'Neal*

SUGGESTED READING:

Miller, Nyle H., and Joseph W. Snell. *Great Gunfights of the Kansas Cowtowns.* Lincoln, Nebr., 1963.

BROTHERHOOD OF PENITENTS

SEE: Penitentes

BROWN, ARTHUR PAGE

Renowned San Francisco architect Arthur Page Brown (1859–1896) was born in Adams, New York. Although he attended Cornell University's architecture school in 1878, he left after one year to work in the office of New York architects McKim, Mead and White as a student draftsman. It was there and during an extensive European tour that he acquired his professional education and developed his architectural skills.

Brown opened his own practice in New York in 1884. His firm, which included architects Willis Polk and Albert Schweinfurth, designed the Museum of Historic Art at Princeton University (1887 to 1892). In 1889, Brown went to San Francisco with a commission to design a mausoleum for railroad magnate CHARLES CROCKER.

Brown made a remarkable contribution to San Francisco's architectural landscape. His firm employed as draftsmen and designers some of San Francisco most famous architects including Albert Schweinfurth, BERNARD RALPH MAYBECK, and Willis Polk. A proponent of the "city-beautiful" movement, Brown designed the Ferry Building and Southern Pacific Depot, his most enduring legacy. Begun in 1895, the project was completed by colleague Edward Swain in 1903.

Brown brought a new look, new styles, and new ideas to the architecture of San Francisco. His Crocker Old People's Home was an early example of the Bay Area shingle style, and his ten-story Crocker Office Building on Market Street was one of San Francisco's first skyscrapers. For the Chicago 1893 Columbian World Exposition, his office designed the California building, often identified as the beginning of a national interest in the mission-revival style. The success of that project resulted in commissions to design several buildings for the city's 1894 Midwinter Exposition.

In 1896, when Brown was just thirty-five years old, he died in Burlingame, California, from injuries he suffered during a carriage accident.

Although many of his projects were lost in the SAN FRANCISCO EARTHQUAKE OF 1906, his remaining landmarks include the Swedenborgian Church of the New Jerusalem (with interior paintings by William Keith) and the Children's merry-go-round and rustic bridge in Golden Gate Park.

—*Waverly B. Lowell*

SEE ALSO: Architecture: Urban Architecture ; City Planning

SUGGESTED READING:
Longstreth, Richard W. *On the Edge of the World: Four Architects in San Francisco at the Turn of the Century.* New York, 1983.

Clara Brown. *Courtesy Denver Public Library, Western History Department.*

BROWN, CLARA

Born a slave in Virginia, Clara Brown (1803–1885) moved to Colorado in search of her family, settled down and, through her charitable deeds and generosity, earned the sobriquet "Angel of the Rockies." When she was three years old, she and her mother were sold to an owner who moved to Kentucky. By 1835, Brown had married and had had three children. In this year, her owner died, and Brown, distraught, watched as her family members were auctioned off to several slave owners. Reuniting her family became her life's goal.

To this end, she determined to save her money and to purchase her own freedom, which she accomplished twenty years later in 1857. On a rumor that her daughter had been taken west, she went to St. Louis in search of her. Two years later, she joined a caravan of gold prospectors to Colorado and, once settled in Denver, became a cook.

Later, she moved to Central City and operated a laundry, worked as a nurse and a midwife, invested in prospectors' claims, and became one of the first

African American women to own land. By the mid-1860s, her gold mines had produced about ten thousand dollars.

Wise with her money, Brown was also very generous, especially to churches. She supported a Sunday school in Denver and, after moving to Central City, organized the Methodist Episcopal church and the city's first Sunday school. Her charity extended to newly arrived pioneers. Those who were hungry or destitute found in Brown's home a safe haven, a meal at the table, and money if they needed it, until they got on their feet.

Well established by 1866, Brown began her search for her husband and children. In the course of her quest, she financed the relocation of thirty-four relatives and friends from back East. With their help, Brown located her daughter, Eliza Jane, in Council Bluffs, Iowa. Brown and her daughter were reunited in 1882, but she never found the rest of her family.

Brown returned to Denver in 1880, and when she died in 1885, she was remembered as a "kind old friend whose heart always responded to the cry of distress."

—*Patricia Hogan*

SUGGESTED READING:
Bruyn, Kathleen. *Aunt Clara Brown: Story of a Black Pioneer.* Boulder, Colo., 1970.

BROWN, HENRY NEWTON

Henry Newton Brown (1857–1884), cowboy, buffalo hunter, outlaw, and peace officer, was born near Rolla, Missouri. At the age of seventeen, Brown headed west and worked as a cowboy and buffalo hunter. He then rode with "BILLY THE KID" in the LINCOLN COUNTY WAR. For some time, he drifted back and forth between New Mexico and Texas. In the summer of 1882, he was appointed assistant marshal of Caldwell, Kansas. Six months later, he became marshal, killed two people in the line of duty, and won the respect of townspeople, who gave him a gold-mounted Winchester in appreciation. A month later, Brown received permission from the mayor to take his assistant into the Indian Territory to track a murderer. Instead, with two cowboys, he tried to rob a bank in Medicine Lodge. The three men were captured and lynched by a mob.

—*Joseph W. Snell*

SUGGESTED READING:
Miller, Nyle H., and Joseph W. Snell. *Why the West Was Wild.* Topeka, Kans., 1963.
O'Neal, Bill. *Henry Brown, the Outlaw-Marshal.* College Station, Tex., 1980.

BROWN, JOHN

Tanner, surveyor, sheepherder, farmer, wool merchant, and land speculator, John Brown (1800–1859) was best known as a preacher and abolitionist who led the Pottawatomie Creek Massacre and the raid on Harper's Ferry. Born in Torrington, Connecticut, the son of an ardent abolitionist, Brown spent most of his adult life speaking and acting against slavery in America. Although he has often been described as a failure in business, he was sometimes quite successful, particularly in the tanning and wool businesses, but he tended to move into other areas of endeavor whenever an operation of his collapsed.

The father of twenty children (only twelve of whom reached maturity) by two wives, he lived in Ohio, Pennsylvania, Massachusetts, and New York and traveled to England and the European continent.

While he shelved his desire to become a minister after developing eye problems, religion remained the driving force behind his political feelings. He detested slavery from his earliest years and was an active participant in the antislavery movement beginning in the 1850s.

Henry Newton Brown. *Courtesy Kansas State Historical Society.*

With the creation of the Kansas Territory, the doctrine of popular sovereignty went into effect. As a result, that region became a jousting field between proslave and abolitionist forces, each determined to secure Kansas as a state. As settlers from both philosophies poured into the region, five of Brown's sons pioneered near Osawatomie as "free-staters." In October 1855, their father joined them.

Confrontations between proslavers and free-staters accelerated in late 1854 and culminated in the bloodless Wakarusa War, which ended in December 1855 with the dispersal of armed forces at the order of the territorial governor. At the time, Brown, as captain of a militia company, proposed continued armed resistance rather than cooperation.

Tensions increased in early 1856. In retaliation for the partial destruction of Lawrence, Kansas, by a proslave "posse" on May 21, Brown and a small band of men, including four of his sons, killed five proslavery men on Pottawatomie Creek in Franklin County three days later. The first serious reprisal against proslave violence, the killings were later hailed by abolitionists as the single-most important act to make Kansas a free state.

During the ensuing months, Brown defeated proslave forces at the Battle of Black Jack, three miles east of Baldwin; helped defend Osawatomie when it was sacked on August 29; and wrote numerous letters to newspapers and individuals condemning slavery. His fanaticism and acts of violence brought him national recognition.

In 1857, the armed clashes between proslavers and free-staters moved to east-central Kansas. Eventually, free-staters assumed the ascendancy, and the fight in Kansas turned from violence to politics with proslavers and free-staters calling themselves Democrats and Republicans. It had become obvious that Kansas would ultimately be admitted to the Union as a free state. Brown continued to battle against slavery in the West, however. In December 1858, he led a raid from Kansas into Missouri, where he destroyed considerable property, killed a slave holder, and freed nearly a dozen slaves whom he took northward. He never returned to Kansas.

Years before the fight in Kansas, Brown had determined to invade the South to free the slaves. After years of self-admitted procrastination, he finally developed a plan that he hoped would cause slaves to rise up in revolt. To accomplish his plan, he needed arms and a daring coup to rouse public sentiment and the slaves' cooperation.

The act was the attack on the United States arsenal at Harper's Ferry. As early as 1857, he had begun training troops in Iowa, but when his intentions leaked out, he shelved the plan for two years. In June 1859, he was ready to start over; he rented a farm near Harper's Ferry and began gathering supporters.

On Sunday evening, October 16, 1859, he and a small force, including two of his sons, attacked and took possession of the arsenal. A group of marines, under the command of U.S. Army Colonel Robert E. Lee, arrived from Washington, D.C., the next evening and trapped Brown and his band in the engine house. After his sons were killed, Brown surrendered to the federal authorities.

Two weeks later, he was tried for treason and found guilty. He was hanged on December 2, 1859.

—*Joseph W. Snell*

SEE ALSO: Kansas-Nebraska Act; National Expansion: Slavery and National Expansion

SUGGESTED READING:
Oates, Stephen B. *To Purge This Land with Blood: A Biography of John Brown.* Boston, 1984.

BROWNE, JOHN ROSS

Author and artist John Ross Browne (1821–1875) immigrated to America from his native Dublin, Ireland, and grew up near Cincinnati, Ohio. A popular author in his time, he produced essays, official reports

John Ross Browne. *Courtesy Oakland Museum of California.*

for the U.S. government, and travel books often illustrated with his own sketches. In 1841, Browne and his father worked as journalists covering the U.S. Congress, but in a pattern that was to shape his life, he grew restless and ventured onto the high seas. He wrote of the experience in *Etchings of a Whaling Cruise with Notes of a Sojourn on the Island of Zanzibar* (1846). Always something of a crusader, Browne revealed in his travelogue the ill-treatment seamen endured on whaling voyages. Through his government connections, he took on jobs investigating irregularities in federal agencies and surveying U.S. natural resources. He produced several reports on mining, for example. He served for a time as the United States minister to China and later settled in Oakland, California.

Literary scholars credit Browne's works with having influenced Herman Melville's *Moby-Dick* and several of MARK TWAIN's works. Browne's works include *Crusoe's Island . . . with Sketches of Adventures in California* (1864) and *Adventures in Apache Country* (1869), among others.

—*Patricia Hogan*

SUGGESTED READING:
Brown, Lina Fergusson, ed. *J. Ross Browne, His Letters, Journals, and Writings.* Albuquerque, N. Mex., 1969.

BROWNING, JOHN MOSES

Recognized as "the greatest firearms inventor the world has ever known," John Moses Browning (1855–1926) was among the foremost contributors to America's national defense in the twentieth century.

Browning was born in Ogden in the Utah Territory. His talent for FIREARMS design was fostered by his father, a frontier gunsmith who supplied arms to BRIGHAM YOUNG's Mormon immigrants. As a young man, Browning augmented his limited education with the rudiments of gunsmithing at his father's shop, but his genius in arms design was innate and self-taught.

Browning designed his first practical gun, a single-shot, breech-loading rifle, in 1878 for the commercial market. With brothers Matthew, Edward, Samuel, and George, and gunsmith Frank Rushton, he established the Browning Brothers Factory in 1880 to manufacture the new rifle and service the Western trade.

In 1883, the Winchester Repeating Arms Company purchased manufacturing rights to the single-shot rifle and inaugurated a twenty-year relationship in which Browning sold the firm all his designs for sporting longarms. The famed Winchester repeating rifles, Models 1886, 1892, 1894, and 1895, were all Browning creations.

During the 1890s, Browning designed semiautomatic and automatic actions for pistols and machine guns and worked with Colt's Patent Fire Arms Manufacturing Company. He also developed the first semiautomatic shotgun, manufactured by Fabrique Nationale of Belgium and later by Remington Arms Company. He received little public acclaim for his inventiveness because all his sporting arms were produced by others under their marque.

Browning's genius finally was manifested during two world wars and in later American conflicts. His military contributions included the regulation Model 1911 Colt Automatic Pistol, the Browning Automatic Rifle (BAR), and all the light and heavy machine guns used by U.S. forces in the field or mounted on tanks, ships, or planes.

In all, Browning received 128 patents for eighty distinct firearm mechanisms. By 1980, more than twenty-four million Browning arms of sporting and military design had been manufactured; many patterns remain in production.

—*Richard C. Rattenbury*

SEE ALSO: Colt, Samuel

SUGGESTED READING:
Browning, John, and Curt Gentry. *John M. Browning, American Gunmaker.* Garden City, N.Y., 1964.
Chinn, Lt. Col. George M. *The Machine Gun: History, Evolution, and Development of Manual, Automatic, and Airborne Repeating Weapons.* Vol. 1. Washington, D.C., 1951.

BRUNOT, FELIX REVILLE

Felix Reville Brunot (1820–1898) is remembered for his service on the Board of Indian Commissioners, which was created by Congress on April 10, 1869, and for his opposition to the "treaty system" as well as to the transfer of the Indian Office to the War Department. The board, consisting of ten prominent businessmen, church leaders, and philanthropists, was given the task of making recommendations on how to deal with Native Americans during the crisis in Indian-white relations, a crisis that had resulted from the rapid expansion of white settlement on the Great Plains following the Civil War. The board was also expected to work toward the elimination of fraud and corruption, for which the Indian service had a notorious reputation.

Born in Newport, Kentucky, Brunot attended Jefferson College in Cannonsburg, Pennsylvania, and embarked on a career as a civil engineer helping to build locks and dams on the Monongahela River near Pittsburgh. As a result of hard times following the panic of 1837, young Brunot changed professions in 1842 and became a flour miller in Rock Island, Illinois. This career change demonstrated his business sagacity; the 1840s was the decade of the Irish famine, which drove up bread prices. With profits from the mill venture, Brunot returned to Pittsburgh in 1847 and purchased an interest in a steel mill. His reputation as an industrialist was established by 1851 when he promoted the building of a railway up the Allegheny Valley, thus facilitating the development of northwestern Pennsylvania through the exchange of lumber, coal, iron, and steel, while making Pittsburgh the commercial center of these industries.

With his fortune secured during his twenties, Brunot turned his energies to philanthropic activities. He helped establish the Young Men's Mercantile Library Association in 1848 and served as the organization's president for many years. During the Civil War, he took charge of a voluntary corps of physicians and nurses who attended the needs of the sick and wounded. His service was particularly notable at Libby Prison in Richmond and after the battles of Shiloh and Antietam in 1862. But his great achievement was the 1864 Pittsburgh Sanitary Fair, which raised $320,000 for the benefit of sick and wounded soldiers, $80,000 of which was used at the end of the war to build a soldier's home. A prominent member of the Protestant Episcopal church, Brunot devoted much energy to the reconciliation and reunification of the church and the nation.

His reputation for philanthropy and service to unfortunate humanity made him an excellent candidate for appointment to the first Board of Indian Commissioners from 1869 to 1874. The board was originally made up of Protestant churchmen including William Welsh, a businessman and Episcopalian from Philadelphia. Serving first as secretary of the board, Brunot became chairman in November 1869 after Welsh resigned, having failed to obtain joint control of Indian administration with the commissioner of Indian affairs. The role of the board was to give advice on making Indian policy and to combat fraud in supplying Native Americans with goods furnished by contractors. In that role, Brunot contributed to the making of GRANT'S PEACE POLICY. The policy was designed to pacify hostile tribes by using the army to drive them onto reservations where they came under the influence of church-appointed agents, who supervised education in the mechanical arts as well as in basic academic subjects. As was true of all members of the board, Brunot visited Western tribes during five successive summers to make certain they were receiving the quality and quantity of commodities contractors had agreed to

supply and to gather information on which to base recommendations to eliminate corrupt practices and generally to improve the administration of Native American affairs. During these years, the board annually advocated the allotment of reservation land in individually held parcels and the encouragement of farming as a means of self-support, thus preparing the way for the General Allotment or DAWES ACT of 1887. The board also called for the fulfillment of treaty obligations and the adoption of a system of wardship toward "uncivilized" Indians. The use of missionary teachers to inculcate Christian ideals among the young, education in the academic and industrial arts, and ultimately citizenship for Native Americans were central points in the reform proposals of the board while Brunot was chairman.

In his later years, Brunot was a strong supporter of the Young Men's Christian Association of which he became a trustee in 1881. Within that organization, he worked for temperance reform and for municipal laws making Sunday a day of rest.

—*Henry E. Fritz and Marie L. Fritz*

SEE ALSO: Temperance and Prohibition; United States Indian Policy

SUGGESTED READING:

Mardock, Robert W. *The Reformers and the American Indian.* Columbia, Mo., 1971.

Prucha, Francis Paul. *American Indian Policy in Crisis: Christian Reformers and the Indian, 1865–1900.* Norman, Okla., 1976.

Slattery, Charles L. *Felix Reville Brunot, 1820–1898.* New York, 1901.

BRYAN, WILLIAM JENNINGS

Democratic party leader William Jennings Bryan (1860–1925) was born in Salem, Illinois, the son of a judge. He graduated from Illinois College in 1881 and Union Law School (Chicago) in 1883, began to practice law, married Mary Baird, and moved to Nebraska. Blessed with a commanding voice and an engaging smile, he won election to the House of Representatives in 1890 after a campaign in which he endorsed some Populist party proposals, including direct election of U.S. senators and silver coinage. He received enough Populist votes in 1892 to give him a narrow victory in his bid for reelection. In Nebraska, he worked closely with the Populists, helping them to capture a U.S. Senate seat in 1893 and the governorship in 1894. In Congress, Bryan won national attention with speeches supporting the income tax and silver coinage. He decided not to seek a third term in 1894 and hoped instead to be elected to the U.S. Senate, but the Republican-controlled legislature of Nebraska did not select him.

By 1894, Bryan had emerged as a national leader in the silver movement, and he traveled the country promoting silver and reform. Silver coinage was only the most prominent among his list of proposed reforms. In 1896, Bryan—only thirty-six years old—captured the Democratic presidential nomination with his "CROSS OF GOLD" SPEECH. Prominent Western Republicans organized the Silver Republican party and enthusiastically endorsed Bryan. Populists named a separate vice-presidential candidate but also nominated Bryan. Traveling eighteen thousand miles and delivering six hundred speeches, he appealed directly to the voters. During his campaign travels, he earned the nickname "the Great Commoner" for his unassuming ways; he continued to emphasize silver but did not ignore other reforms. William McKinley, the Republican candidate, defended the gold standard and the protective tariff. He won by carrying urban and industrial areas and the prosperous farming regions of the northeastern quarter of the nation; his victory marked a significant, long-term voter shift toward the Republicans. Bryan took nearly all the West and South.

In 1900, Bryan again won the presidential nominations of the Democrats, Silver Republicans, and one faction of the now-divided Populists. His campaign condemned the imperialism that followed the Spanish-American War, attacked big business, and reaffirmed support for silver. Carrying most Western states, McKinley, the Republican candidate, was elected by a larger margin than in 1896.

Despite his two defeats, Bryan remained the Democrats' most significant leader. His books and weekly newspaper, *The Commoner*, reached thousands of homes, and he traveled extensively to speak in hundreds of cities and towns every year. Devoted to equality and self-government, Bryan nonetheless accepted arguments by Southern Democrats that African Americans should not participate in Southern politics. With this exception, he championed an increased popular role in politics. Equally importantly, he and his allies fused the antimonopolism of ANDREW JACKSON to proposals for strong federal action on behalf of "the people" and against powerful economic interests. A pivotal figure in the transformation of the Democratic party, Bryan led the party to abandon much of the commitment to minimal government that had characterized the group from the time of Jackson through the presidency of Grover Cleveland.

Changing economic conditions—and, perhaps, the experience of losing twice—led Bryan to abandon the silver issue before his next presidential campaign. In his third campaign, in 1908, he declared the major issue to be "Shall the people rule?" and emphasized a range of progressive issues, including corporate regulation, tariff reform, an income tax, and a bank deposit insurance fund. His Republican opponent was William Howard Taft, but Bryan had to run as well against the legacy of the popular incumbent, THEODORE ROOSEVELT, who also claimed strong progressive credentials. Roosevelt had become president when McKinley was assassinated and was elected in his own right in 1904. The 1908 election brought a third presidential defeat to Bryan and victory to Taft.

Bryan served as secretary of state from 1913 to 1915 in the administration of Woodrow Wilson. He also took a strong interest in domestic economic policy making; when Congress was drafting the Federal Reserve system, Bryan urged significant federal control over banking. He promoted bilateral "cooling off" treaties to maintain peace. When Europe plunged into war in 1914, Bryan thought that staying out of war took precedence over all other considerations; he resigned when Wilson made decisions that he feared would bring war with Germany. Nonetheless, in 1916, Bryan worked for Wilson's reelection, especially in the West, and was pleased that the West gave Wilson his margin of victory.

After 1915, Bryan campaigned for WOMEN'S SUFFRAGE and prohibition; many credited him with doing more than any other person to bring about national prohibition. During his final years, Bryan focused on the concept of evolution, which he considered dangerous because it undermined religious faith. In 1925, he assisted in the prosecution of John Scopes, a biology teacher who violated a Tennessee law forbidding the teaching of evolution. Clarence Darrow, the nation's most prominent trial lawyer, defended Scopes. Darrow humiliated Bryan by revealing his woeful ignorance of science and archaeology. Bryan died in his sleep a few days later.

—*Robert W. Cherny*

SEE ALSO: Banking; Currency and Silver as Western Political Issues; Populism; Temperance and Prohibition

SUGGESTED READING:

Ashby, Leroy. *William Jennings Bryan: Champion of Democracy.* Boston, 1987.

Bryan, William Jennings. *Memoirs.* Philadelphia, 1925.

Cherny, Robert W. *A Righteous Cause: The Life of William Jennings Bryan.* Boston, 1985. Reprint. Norman, Okla., 1994.

Clements, Kendrick A. *William Jennings Bryan: Missionary Isolationist.* Knoxville, Tenn., 1982.

Coletta, Paolo E. *William Jennings Bryan.* 3 vols. Lincoln, Nebr., 1964–1969.

Glad, Paul W. *The Trumpet Soundeth: William Jennings Bryan and His Democracy, 1896–1912.* Lincoln, Nebr., 1960.

Koenig, Louis W. *Bryan: A Political Biography.* New York, 1971.

Levine, Lawrence W. *Defender of the Faith: William Jennings Bryan, The Last Decade, 1915–1925.* New York, 1965.

BRYANT, STURGIS AND COMPANY

Based in Boston, Bryant, Sturgis and Company was a major force in the Western hide trade, exchanging New England manufactured goods for cowhides. The commerce began in 1822 with the arrival of the company's agent William A. Gale in Monterey, California, aboard the ship *Sachem.* The hide trade formed the first substantial connection between the East Coast and the West; indeed, among the residents of Mexican California, "Boston" and the "United States" became synonymous. Knowledge of California spread to the East as well, especially after the publication of RICHARD HENRY DANA's classic memoir *Two Years before the Mast,* published in 1840 and recounting his service from 1834 to 1836 aboard Bryant, Sturgis and Company vessels plying the hide trade.

—*Alan Axelrod*

BUCHANAN, JAMES

Fifteenth president of the United States (from 1857 to 1861), James Buchanan (1791–1868) served during the beginning of the secession crisis leading to the Civil War and supported the controversial proslavery LeCompton Constitution for the Kansas Territory.

Born to Scots-Irish parents in Cove Gap, near Mercersburg, Pennsylvania, Buchanan graduated from Dickinson College in Carlisle, Pennsylvania, in 1809, studied law in Lancaster, and opened a practice there in 1813. After serving as a volunteer in the defense of Baltimore during the War of 1812, he was elected to the Pennsylvania House of Representatives. In 1820, Buchanan was elected to the U.S. House of Representatives and supported ANDREW JACKSON in his first bid for the presidency. Retiring from Congress in 1831, Buchanan was appointed Jackson's minister to Russia (from 1832 to 1834). Upon his return to the United States, he was elected to the Senate and served from 1834 to 1845, when he became secretary of state under President JAMES K. POLK. As secretary of state,

Buchanan was instrumental in consummating the annexation of Texas in 1845 and in the settlement of the OREGON BOUNDARY DISPUTE. He was a strong supporter of the United States–Mexican War.

Franklin Pierce, who had defeated Buchanan in the 1852 race for the Democratic presidential nomination, named Buchanan minister to Great Britain (from 1853 to 1856). His absence from the United States during the bitter controversy over the KANSAS-NEBRASKA ACT (1854) enhanced his viability as a presidential candidate, and he won the Democratic nomination and the presidential race in 1856.

Immediately after Buchanan's inauguration, the Supreme Court handed down the DRED SCOTT DECISION, ruling that Congress had no power over slavery in the territories. Buchanan welcomed what he thought was an end to the controversy at the federal level over organizing the Kansas Territory, and he urged Congress to accept the territory's proslavery LeCompton Constitution, even though it had been drafted by an unrepresentative convention that had refused to submit it for popular approval. Fellow Democrat STEPHEN A. DOUGLAS broke with the president over this issue as a violation of the doctrine of popular sovereignty. Kansans ultimately rejected the LeCompton document.

The secession crisis became most acute during the last two years of Buchanan's presidency. When seven Southern states formed the Confederacy after Lincoln's election but before his inauguration, Buchanan branded the action illegal yet refused to act because he believed that the executive branch of government had no authority to coerce a state. After leaving office, Buchanan generally supported Lincoln's conduct of the war and felt compelled to publish a defense of his own administration, *Mr. Buchanan's Administration on the Eve of the Rebellion,* in 1866.

—*Alan Axelrod*

SUGGESTED READING:

Binder, Frederick M. *James Buchanan and the American Empire.* Cranbury, N.J., 1994.

Reisman, David A. *The Political Economy of James Buchanan.* College Station, Tex., 1990.

BUCKLEY, CHRISTOPHER AUGUSTINE

Democratic party leader and business entrepreneur Christopher Augustine Buckley (1845–1922) briefly enjoyed the dubious title of "the Blind Boss" of San Francisco. The son of an Irish immigrant stone mason, Buckley was born in New York City and moved with his family to California when he was seventeen years old. By working as a bartender for theater impresario Tom Maguire, Buckley gained a political education from Democratic party notables. Eventually, Buckley acquired his own saloons. Since many political deals took place in the back rooms of saloons, Buckley's success gave him a position of influence, and he rose within the party. He suddenly lost his sight in 1873 for reasons that remain unclear. Undaunted, he continued his rise until, reaching the height of his power from 1882 to 1891, he became an arbiter of the party slate-making process. During these years, Democratic party nominations in the city usually needed his approval. Although colorful images of urban "bosses" such as Buckley typically include lore about their alleged support for poor immigrant masses, Buckley was not democratic and rarely spent money on anything but himself and other politicians. He presided over a circular system of party "contributions" from the SOUTHERN PACIFIC RAILROAD and other large concerns and the dispensing of favors to those interests. Buckley never had formal control over city politics; he had to compete with other party manipulators, such as the Republicans Martin Kelly and Phil Crimmins. A coalition of labor and business leaders organized the overthrow of his informal regime in 1891 by winning the adoption of the Australian, or secret, ballot. That year, Buckley, facing a grand-jury indictment, fled to Canada. Although he managed to return and live a prosperous life, his political career was finished. He died in 1922 in his Clay Street home of a "severe attack of indigestion."

—*Philip J. Ethington*

SUGGESTED READING:
Bullough, William A. *The Blind Boss and His City: Christopher Augustine Buckley and Nineteenth-Century San Francisco.* Berkeley, Calif., 1979.
Ethington, Philip J. *The Public City: The Political Construction of Urban Life in San Francisco, 1850–1900.* New York, 1994.

BUFFALO BILL

SEE: Cody, William F. ("Buffalo Bill")

BUFFALO BILL HISTORICAL CENTER

Founded in 1917 as the Buffalo Bill Memorial Association, the center preserves and promotes the history of the West and the memory of one of its leading citizens, WILLIAM F. ("BUFFALO BILL") CODY. The first building, erected in 1927, was known as the Buffalo Bill Museum. The first object in the collection had actually been commissioned and put in place three years earlier: a heroic-sized equestrian statue of "Buffalo Bill" entitled *The Scout*. The work of American artist and philanthropist Gertrude Vanderbilt Whitney, the statue was situated directly west of the museum.

In 1959, a large wing—the Whitney Gallery of Western Art—was constructed. In 1969, that structure was expanded to hold the Buffalo Bill Museum and a newly added Plains Indian Museum. In 1976, the Winchester Firearms Collection came to the museum complex as the Winchester Museum. New facilities to house the various collections were added in subsequent years—the Plains Indians Museum in 1979 and the Cody Firearms Museum in 1991.

The Buffalo Bill Historical Center is today one of the largest museums of history and art in the United States. In contains collections related to the history, art, ethnology, and technology of the American West with particular focus on the region of the Northern Plains and Rocky Mountains. Nearly three hundred thousand visitors come to the museum annually. Aside from its permanent installations in the four museums, the center carries on an active program of seminars, workshops, classes, and outreach programs in order to extend its educational mission beyond the walls of the institution itself.

—*Peter H. Hassrick*

BUFFALO BILL'S WILD WEST SHOW

SEE: Cody, William F. ("Buffalo Bill"); Wild West Shows

BUFFALOES (AMERICAN BISONS)

The North American buffalo, a recently evolved member of the genus *Bison*, was the most important large mammal in the American West until its near extinction in the 1880s. For one hundred centuries, it and its larger ancestors, *Bison latifrons* and *Bison antiquus*, were cornerstones of Western Indian lifeways and economies. In the years after 1820, bison robes—hides softly tanned with the hair on—were important items of trade between Indians and the Euro-American fur companies. Briefly, in the 1870s and 1880s, buffalo were hunted by Euro-American hunters, armed with

Karl Bodmer's *Buffalo and Elk on the Upper Missouri* hints at the majesty of the powerful animals that roamed the American West. *Courtesy Joslyn Art Museum. Gift of the Enron Art Foundation.*

.45 and .50 caliber rifles, as sources of cheap leather. At a point when fewer than two thousand buffalo were left in the United States and Canada, they were placed under strict protection. At the end of the twentieth century, buffalo in government refuges such as Wood Buffalo Park in Canada and Yellowstone National Park in the United States and on a growing number of private ranches across the West have once again become important, iconic animals of the modern American West. Groups such as the Intertribal Bison Cooperative in Rapid City, South Dakota, have made the buffalo cornerstones for rebuilding traditional Indian cultures. And the growing herds have become a commercial source of lean, healthy beef.

The buffalo's ancestors were Eurasian, having migrated across the Bering land bridge into North America during the Wisconsinan Ice Ages. From its evolutionary beginnings, the historical bison was intertwined with the Indian population of America. One of the few survivors of a great extinction crash that swept the Americas ten thousand years ago, the genus *Bison* underwent a dwarfing in the centuries following that is believed to have been related to hunting pressures of humans. The new, modern buffalo filled the void left by the extinction of most of its grazing competitors—like HORSES—by growing into so many millions of animals that to Indian hunters the herds joined the stars and winds as supernatural in origin. While their main range was always the Great Plains, the vast sweep of semiarid grasslands between the

Mississippi and the Rocky Mountains, buffalo were adaptive enough to range from sea level up to ten thousand feet in places like South Park, Colorado.

As the populations of both Indians and bison increased in America, Indian management strategies, such as burning and forest clearing, expanded the available range for the bison at the same time that intensive hunting and climate swings on the Great Plains pushed the herds eastward and westward. Despite fanciful estimates of seventy-five million to one hundred million buffalo, by the time of European contact, the average carrying capacity of the Great Plains grasslands was actually about twenty-four million to twenty-eight million. Even herds of that size were in part the result of the climate anomaly called the "Little Ice Age," which produced bumper crops of bison on the Great Plains for three centuries after 1450. And the increase in buffalo population combined with a dramatic decline in Indian population from Old World diseases brought by Europeans to send another five to six million animals west into the valleys of the Rocky Mountain West and east almost to the Atlantic by the seventeenth century. Those periphery herds were the first animals to disappear in the great bison contraction of the seventeenth through the nineteenth centuries.

The contraction and demise of the American bison had its origins in the contact between Europeans and native Western tribes. While favorable climate and a much diminished Indian population allowed the bison herds to balloon in the first two centuries after contact, those same surging herds attracted many more

Buffalo carcasses litter the frozen plain after a hunt in 1872. Unlike the Indians, Euro-Americans slaughtered the buffalo mainly for profit and sport. *Courtesy National Archives.*

tribes to the Great Plains than had ever hunted there before. Drawn into the global market economy by the fur companies and the attraction of manufactured goods, a fluctuating population of nearly one hundred thousand horse-mounted Indian hunters flocked to the plains after the Pueblo Revolt of 1680 diffused horses across the West. The Plains tribes hunted not only for subsistence but for the market.

The real watershed for the North American bison came in the 1840s and represented a convergence of forces that not only were unique, but were sufficient to shift a nine-thousand-year-old ecological system to a new and unstable condition. Returned to America by the Europeans, horses not only facilitated hunting by the Indians, they also increasingly became competitors with bison for grass and water. Emigrant travel on the overland trails disrupted the herds and apparently served as the vanguard to a succession of exotic bovine diseases—anthrax, tuberculosis, and burcellosis—that may have seriously depleted wild buffalo. President ANDREW JACKSON's Indian removal program, which sent an additional eighty-seven thousand Indians to the West, brought mounting hunting pressures. That was compounded by the end of the Little Ice Age and the onset of drought that stands as one of the most severe on record on the Great Plains. Now unable to migrate away from the searing dryness because of the encircling human population, buffalo were hit hard by the drought. By the 1860s, a badly stressed remnant of fewer than eight million animals was left.

What played out in the 1870s and 1880s, then, was an end game that only served to take out the last few million bison more suddenly and dramatically than would have otherwise been the case. After the Civil War, technological changes, like the advance of RAILROADS and the invention of new tanning techniques, converted bison hides into an economic resource. Since the animals were available to all, an orgy of free-market greed ensued that sent as many as twenty thousand hide hunters to the Great Plains. It took only a decade and a half to very nearly eradicate the remaining buffalo population.

At the end of the twentieth century, the North American buffalo population was estimated at more than 120,000 animals.

—*Dan Flores*

SEE ALSO: Fire; Native American Cultures: Subsistence Patterns; Native American Peoples: Peoples of the Great Plains; Wildlife

SUGGESTED READING:
Flores, Dan. "Bison Ecology and Bison Diplomacy: The Southern Plains from 1800 to 1850." *Journal of American History* 78 (September 1991): 465–485.

Roe, Frank G. *The North American Buffalo: A Critical Study of the Species in Its Wild State.* Toronto, Ontario, 1970.

BUFFALO GRASS

SEE: Prairie

BUFFALO SOLDIERS

Four black regiments of U.S. Cavalry and U.S. Infantry sent to the Indian Wars, the Buffalo Soldiers were active from the end of the Civil War until the full integration of the army during the Korean War. African American soldiers in the United States first saw action as members of organized units in the Civil War. Five regiments of black soldiers were active and were reorganized into the Thirty-third, Seventy-third, Seventy-fourth, Seventy-fifth, and Seventy-ninth Regiments of U.S. Colored Troops. Before the war was over, fourteen states had raised black troops, who eventually became part of the U.S. Colored Troops. Nearly 190,000 black soldiers and sailors served their country by the time the war ended in 1865.

With peace finally established between the Union and the former Confederacy, a large army was no longer necessary, and U.S. forces were reduced to ten cavalry and twenty-five infantry regiments, about thirty thousand men in all. Although several of those regiments remained in the South to enforce Reconstruction, the vast majority of men were sent to the West to patrol the mountains and plains against attacks by Indians.

In 1866, Congress authorized the formation of the Ninth and Tenth Cavalries and the Twenty-fourth and Twenty-fifth Infantry Regiments. All four units were composed totally of black enlisted men, mostly former slaves. Although white officers traditionally held command of the African American units, in time, several black officers—including Lieutenant Henry O. Flipper and Lieutenant Charles Young of the Tenth Cavalry and Lieutenant John H. Alexander of the Ninth Cavalry—stepped into leadership positions.

The four black regiments were sent to the trans-Mississippi West, and for the next twenty-five years, they saw some of the bloodiest, most vicious fighting in the annals of the U.S. Army. African American soldiers of the Ninth, Tenth, Twenty-fourth, and Twenty-fifth Regiments won several Congressional Medals of Honor for their bravery and valor during the Indian Wars of the late 1800s.

The Indians called the black troopers "Buffalo Soldiers," either out of the respect they had for both the

Buffalo Soldiers, 1894. Photograph by A. B. Coe. *Courtesy Montana Historical Society.*

soldiers and the buffalo, or because the blacks' hair reminded them of the thick mane that covered the buffalo's shoulders. Either way, the men of the four regiments took the name as a compliment.

The Buffalo Soldiers saw much of their action against the Apache Indians of Arizona and New Mexico, but the troopers were also involved in skirmishes with the Utes, Comanches, Cheyennes, Kiowas, and Sioux as well. The army's campaign against the Apache chiefs VICTORIO and NANA was conducted almost entirely by Buffalo Soldiers and their white officers. And, on more than one occasion, the African American regiments came to the rescue of their white counterparts, most notably the Tenth Cavalry's rescue of Major George A. Forsyth's command at the Battle of Beecher Island in northeastern Colorado in 1868 and Ninth Cavalry's action to relieve besieged soldiers at the Battle of Milk Creek near the Ute Agency in western Colorado in 1879.

Intricately woven into the story of the Buffalo Soldiers is the moving saga of Lieutenant Henry Flipper. In 1877, Flipper became the first black man to graduate from the U.S. Military Academy. Upon leaving West Point, the young Georgian was offered the position of commander of the Liberian Army, but he refused in order to accept a role as an officer in the Buffalo Soldiers. Four years later, Flipper was court-martialed and driven from the army he loved over false charges trumped up by jealous white officers. Until his death in 1940, Flipper tried to exonerate himself from the spurious conviction. In 1976, ninety-four years after his dismissal from the army, his case was reconsidered by a military review board, and he was issued an honorable discharge.

Colonel BENJAMIN HENRY GRIERSON, the white commander of the Tenth Cavalry, summed up the prevailing attitude that most career army officers had of the Buffalo Soldiers: "The officers and enlisted men have cheerfully endured many hardships and privations, and in the midst of great dangers steadfastly maintained a most gallant and zealous devotion to duty . . . and they may well be proud of the record made, and rest assured that the hard work undergone in the accomplishment of such . . . valuable service to their country cannot fail, sooner or later, to meet with due recognition and reward."

During the Spanish-American War, Buffalo Soldiers assisted THEODORE ROOSEVELT with his charge up San Juan Hill. They served in the Philippines, and in 1916, they rode with one of their old officers, General JOHN JOSEPH PERSHING (whose nickname "Black Jack" derived from his former duty with the all-black Tenth Cavalry) into Mexico in pursuit of FRANCISCO ("PANCHO") VILLA. During the Korean conflict, the Buffalo Soldier units were integrated into the rest of the army.

—*James A. Crutchfield*

SEE ALSO: African Americans; United States Army: Composition

SUGGESTED READING:

Fowler, A. L. *The Black Infantry in the West, 1869–1891.* Westport, N.Y., 1971.

Leckie, W. H. *The Buffalo Soldiers: A Narrative of the Negro Cavalry in the West.* Norman, Okla., 1967.

BUILDING TRADES COUNCIL, SAN FRANCISCO

SEE: San Francisco Building Trades Council

BULLWHACKERS

The word *bullwhacker,* meaning a driver of ox-drawn freight wagons on overland trails, was derived from *bullwhack,* a word Louisianans and Texans used for the short-handled, long-lashed whip to motivate animals. Bullwhackers are best known for their long drives from Missouri River settlements to destinations on the SANTA FE AND CHIHUAHUA TRAIL and the Platte River Road. Usually, they were young, robust men who were experienced in farming and who could control oxen and readily adapt to arduous trail life. Female bullwhackers were exceedingly rare. Ingeborg Botne Knutson drove oxen during the Black Hills gold rush, and the notorious CALAMITY JANE (Martha Cannary Burk) claimed to have bullwhacked for a short time.

—*William E. Lass*

SEE ALSO: Overland Freight

Bullwhacker "Arizona Mary" drives her eight yoke of oxen. Most bullwhackers were men. *Courtesy California Historical Society, Los Angeles Title Insurance.*

SUGGESTED READING:

Lass, William E. *From the Missouri to the Great Salt Lake: An Account of Overland Freighting.* Lincoln, Nebr., 1972.

BUNTLINE, NED (JUDSON, EDWARD ZANE CARROLL)

Born in Stamford, New York, Ned Buntline (1823–1886) was a sailor, soldier, gunfighter, drunken temperance lecturer, and womanizer who did not always wait for the benefit of divorce before marrying his next wife. He is best known as a publisher and writer of both serious and popular fiction, often based on his embellishments of his own or others' actual experiences.

Buntline ran away to sea as a teenager and sailed extensively both on commercial vessels and, in the late 1830s, as a member of the U.S. Navy during the Second Seminole War. During the 1840s, he began publishing a serious literary magazine in Cincinnati, the *Western Literary Journal* (later *South-western Literary Journal*), which included the best Western writers he could find and attacked lurid popular books of the type later known as dime novels. Eventually, though, he realized the tremendous sales potential of such popular stories and began writing them himself.

Appalled at the massive Irish immigration during the 1840s, Buntline became one of the major organizers of the antiforeign, anti-Catholic political party called the "Know-Nothings," a name he himself popularized. He enlisted as a sergeant in the Union Army during the Civil War but saw no action and was reduced in rank to private for overstaying a furlough to visit his wife. (He later claimed to have been a colonel and posed for photographs in a colonel's uniform.) Impressed by the massive sales of the Beadle Company's dime novels, which arrived in huge bales at his military post, Buntline began writing similar novels for the Street and Smith publishing company, and later for Beadle as well.

Returning from an unsuccessful lecture tour of California in 1869, Buntline stopped in Nebraska to research a recent Indian battle for a possible dime novel and was referred to a scout named WILLIAM F. ("BUFFALO BILL") CODY. Impressed with Cody's handsome appearance and bearing, he turned him into a character he called "Buffalo Bill" and featured him in several novels and plays in which Cody himself played the lead role. From that show-business beginning, Cody developed his famous Wild West show. Buntline became so associated with the West in the popular mind that one of SAMUEL COLT's revolvers was universally called the "Buntline Special."

Buntline was a prolific writer who claimed to be able to produce a six-hundred–page novel in sixty

Ned Buntline. *Courtesy Buffalo Bill Historical Center.*

hours. His output included not only dozens of dime novels westerns, but many magazine articles on fly fishing and social-reform topics as well. He was a major contributor to the popular Western literary tradition based on factual incidents and characters, but greatly exaggerated and distorted to fit the fantasies of a vast audience.

—*Gary Topping*

See also: Know-Nothing Party; Literature in the West: Dime Novels, the Western Novel; Wild West Shows

Suggested reading:
Monaghan, Jay. *The Great Rascal: The Exploits of the Amazing Ned Buntline.* New York, 1951.

BUNYAN, PAUL

See: Paul Bunyan, Legend of

BUREAU OF INDIAN AFFAIRS

The Bureau of Indian Affairs (BIA) was created by Secretary of War John Caldwell Calhoun on March 11, 1824; he appointed Thomas L. McKenney to oversee its activities. The BIA was launched in response to the growing problems caused by the westward expansion of the United States into territories mainly inhabited by the Indians. Since 1789, the country's dealings with Native Americans had been under the control of the office of the secretary of war. In 1824, Congress was considering granting bureau status to the organization then known as the Indian Department, but Calhoun acted before Congress had a chance to approve the creation of the BIA; therefore, McKenney had no legal standing. He might work out the details of financial transactions with the Indians, but his actions required Calhoun's direct approval. It was not until July 9, 1832, that Congress established the post of commissioner of Indian affairs, with the position going to Elbert Herring. Two years later—on June 30, 1834—Congress finally authorized the BIA.

The 1834 act gave Congress the sole power to make organizational changes within the bureau, and it did so immediately, starting by cutting nearly in half the number of administrators living among the Indians. The BIA emerged that summer as a three-tiered bureaucracy. Those at the top of the agency, including the commissioner, lived in Washington, D.C. Throughout Indian-occupied lands, superintendents manned territorial-level agencies, which, in turn, deployed agents and subagents among the various tribes, and they were joined in the field by interpreters, who were also considered part of the bureau's administration.

Apache Indians deliver hay to Fort Apache, Arizona, in 1893, the result of the BIA's attempt to transform Indian nomads into Euro-American farmers. *Courtesy National Archives.*

The BIA remained within the War Department for fifteen years until March 3, 1849, when Congress created a cabinet-level position, secretary of the interior, and transferred—on paper at least—the Indian agency to the Department of the Interior. But for the next two decades, Indian affairs were in turmoil. The U.S. military was home to enough of the nation's Indian policy-makers to prevent the transfer of genuine authority to the Interior Department. While the military demanded to be present on reservations to guard against rebellions, civilian administrators objected that the presence of soldiers was unnecessary and incendiary. The feud between American military leaders (who wanted to abandon Indians to the vicissitudes of conquest) and civilian policy-makers (who deplored the unofficial genocide that accompanied military policy) was not resolved until 1870, when Congress prohibited the appointment of military personnel to agency positions, all but eliminating their presence on reservations.

The BIA's initial mandate was to assist the U.S. government in the acquisition of Indian land. In keeping with such purpose, the bureau focused on confining Indians to specific geographical territories—that is, reservations—and promoting their acculturation to Euro-American society. The BIA was born of the same long-term political movement that produced the Indian Removal Act of 1830 and that led some thirty years later to the creation of the Indian Territory. Both acts helped the bureau carry out its mandate. The Indian Removal Act gave President ANDREW JACKSON the authority he needed to force Indians off their lands in the Southeast in exchange for land west of the Mississippi, at that time an area that most policy-makers considered an uninhabited wilderness more suited to the native "savages" than their homelands near the cotton plantations of the South and the farms of the Old Northwest. By 1866, however, the wilderness itself had been settled by Euro-Americans, and Congress created the Indian Territory (in present-day Oklahoma) to further limit lands on which Native Americans could reside. During the three intervening decades, the BIA concentrated on Indian removal and relocation.

Although treaties—and the concept of Indian tribes as nations—had been part of American diplomacy since 1776, the so-called close of the American frontier coincided with a new definition of the relationship between Indians and the federal government, a relationship overseen by the BIA. Having by conquest, legal chicanery, and direct purchase secured most of the present-day United States from the Indians, the Americans now, through Commissioner of Indian Affairs Ely S. Parker, declared Indians to be wards of the government and called for the abandonment of treaties as an instrument of Indian policy. In 1871, Congress made

The BIA used rations to control Indian behavior. Here Indians form a line while officers and Indian agents dole out flour at Camp Supply, Indian Territory, now Oklahoma, in 1871. *Courtesy National Archives.*

it official, passing an act legitimizing the government-Indian ward relationship.

Even the reservations were not safe from federal encroachment. On February 8, 1887, Congress passed the General Allotment Act (DAWES ACT), designed to force on Indians the concept of individual ownership by dividing the reservations into tracts and allotting one to each Indian. The BIA was responsible for executing the Dawes Act, which entailed sales, leasing, and determination of heirs. The tracts were to be held in trust for twenty-five years, by which time it was assumed that the Indians would have become so assimilated and productive that they could be entrusted with U.S. citizenship. In the meantime, the act called for instructing the Native Americans in the techniques of Euro-American agriculture, for guiding them in the purchase of the proper equipment needed to turn allotments into farms, and for directing them in the effective use of irrigation to water crops in a semiarid land not much suited for traditional European husbandry. Of course, "excess" land—that is, those vast tracts of territory still belonging to the reservations at the time of the Dawes Act but that were "left over" after the government assigned individual allotments—was purchased at bargain rates by the government for non-Indian use. The relatively paltry proceeds from the sale of such lands became tribal funds.

The BIA embraced as policy the destruction of the Indians' social and political systems in an effort to "Americanize" the natives. The General Allotment Act basically created powerful Indian agents while attacking tribal unity and undermining traditional leaders, helping, in the process, to decimate what was left of Indian life. Forcing the Indians to abandon hunting and become farmers, the BIA rationed food during the transition. The rations became weapons used by the agency to starve into submission those Indians who refused to crop their hair short, who continued to paint their faces, or who persisted in engaging in traditional religious ceremonies and rituals—in other words, Indians who acted in any way not consistent with what BIA agents considered civilized behavior. Overall, BIA apportions were not adequate even to maintain the Indians who took up farming in accordance with governmental policy, so the agency administered annuities of money or goods to the Indians as payment for the lands they had relinquished. Agents set out to stop the cash annuities by claiming that Indians were mismanaging their money. Eventually, the government and the bureau ceased to regard the annuities as land payments altogether, and Congress passed legislation requiring work from the Indians before they received payment. Shortly after 1900, the bureau discontinued rations altogether. By the time the changes spawned by the Dawes Act had run their course, the Indians had lost 67 percent of their reservation land.

In the meantime, the bureau had also assumed responsibility for the formal education of Indians. Indian education included schools both on and off of the reservation. The policy of the BIA regarding formal education was to provide young Indians with the knowledge and skills necessary to fit into Euro-American society and to understand the changing situation in which they were embroiled. Low attendance, truancy, and poorly trained teachers contributed to the failure of early Indian schools, whose quality always lagged behind mainstream public schools. Boarding schools off the reservation attracted particular criticism from those who argued that shipping youngsters off the reservation merely stripped them of tradition and culture, while failing to provide real opportunities elsewhere. After twenty years of futile, if widespread, attempts to assimilate Indian children to the dominant culture by removing them at a tender age from their parents, the boarding schools, particularly those in the East, were closed down. By the 1920s, only eighteen of twenty-five remained open.

From the beginning, the BIA was plagued by allegations of abuse, mismanagement, and corruption, particularly after Congress transferred control of the agency from the War Department to the Department of the Interior, where BIA appointments became political plums. In 1865, the government set up a nonpolitical board of inspectors to mediate the constant disputes between military leaders and civilian agents and to serve as a watchdog on corruption. The board reported yearly to Congress on the five area agencies, but since Congress lacked the authority to review specific appointments, the BIA remained part of the almost inherently corrupt political spoils system. By 1869, observers were claiming that bureau adminis-

trators managed to retire wealthy after five years at the BIA, despite the fact that no agency annual salary ever exceeded two thousand dollars. Not until appointees became subject to the Civil Service Act in 1891 could natives truly hope for honesty and decency in the agency's handling of Indian affairs.

It took Franklin D. Roosevelt's New Deal government, which reversed the policy of assimilation that dated back to the origins of the American republic, to change the basically hostile attitude of the BIA toward Indian life. By the mid-1930s, the government was willing to admit that the Dawes Act had failed to benefit the Indians. Those reservations still owned and operated communally, on the other hand, had thrived. John Collier, whom Roosevelt appointed commissioner of Indian affairs, called the General Allotment Act more than a "huge white land grab; it was a blow, meant to be fatal, at Indian tribal existence." With the passage of the Indian Reorganization Act of 1934, the allotment of Indian land came to a halt. Under Collier, the BIA claimed to admire the "sense of community" among the Indians. Asserting that the role of government was to help, but not coerce, tribal efforts, Collier's BIA sought not to absorb Native Americans into the American mainstream, but to help them maintain their cultures on their communally owned lands. The 1934 act turned the management of reservations over to the tribes, and it included provisions for self-government and economic rehabilitation. Reservation schools were free to teach traditional Indian culture and languages in the classroom.

Not all tribes subscribed to the Indian New Deal, under which the federal government—however liberal—still had authority to meddle in Indian affairs, and the BIA proved on occasion that it could be as insensitive and paternalistic as ever. In 1934 and 1935, for example, the BIA pressured the Navajos to reduce their stock of sheep under the NAVAJO STOCK-REDUCTION PROGRAM—with disastrous results. But in general, the BIA's attempt to give back to the Indians some control over their own destinies allowed the Native Americans to edge toward cultural and tribal revitalization.

After the Indian New Deal, it was more difficult for a Bureau of Indian Affairs—historically rooted in the notion of the Indian as a "problem" and fueled by ethnocentric and often violent beliefs about how best to deal with the Indians—to do with the natives as it saw fit. Politically, the ensuing decades witnessed a relatively stronger Native American population and a relatively weaker BIA, which laid the groundwork for more radical movements among Indian traditionalists and for the success many native tribes came to enjoy in pressing various claims in the U.S. courts.

—*Melissa A. Davis*

SEE ALSO: Burke Act; Grant's Peace Policy; Indian Schools; United States Indian Policy

SUGGESTED READING:
Hill, Edward E. *The Office of Indian Affairs, 1824–1880: Historical Sketches*. New York, 1974.
Jackson, Curtis E., and Marcia J. Galli. *A History of the Bureau of Indian Affairs and Its Activities among Indians*. San Francisco, 1977.
Taylor, Theodore W. *The Bureau of Indian Affairs*. Boulder, Colo., 1984.

BUREAU OF LAND MANAGEMENT

At the urging of GIFFORD PINCHOT, a conservation-minded President THEODORE ROOSEVELT transferred in 1905 the vast tracts of public lands he had just declared national forests from the control of the GENERAL LAND OFFICE into the safe haven of the UNITED STATES FOREST SERVICE. It was a first step toward ending the era when the express goal of the federal government was to sell public land cheaply to private owners. That era was not truly brought to a close, however, until 1934 when the TAYLOR GRAZING ACT removed 142 million acres of Western land and reserved them for grazing under federal control. Oversight of the reserves would rest with the newly established Grazing Service, housed within the U.S. Department of the Interior. In 1946, the Grazing Service and the old General Land Office were merged into yet a new agency, the Bureau of Land Management.

As one of the federal management agencies administering publicly owned Western land, the bureau—along with the Forest Service and the NATIONAL PARK SERVICE—touched every corner of Western life. As the FEDERAL GOVERNMENT's policies of collecting fees from users, providing allotments of public timber for clear-cutting by lumber companies, and generally assisting in some "development" of public land grew more and more controversial over the years, the bureau was frequently criticized for being captive to local advisory boards. The critics charged that the boards, operating as tools of the big stock growers, gave them preferred access and public grass rather than practicing sound conservation as custodians of a common heritage. The West's public lands became a battleground between Western ranchers and businessmen who wanted to exploit and develop the natural resources of the national forests and militant and dedicated environmentalists who demanded strict conservation practices, preservation, and limited use.

When the "green" groups began to exercise a growing influence over the federal agencies after 1960, Western developers and promoters grew to resent the federal bureaucrats as much as or more than the environmentalists. Western developers voiced a complaint not uncommon in the history of the American West: that the federal government should subsidize the Westerners' economic activities in the name of natural economic growth but should stay out of their private affairs. By the 1990s, Western discontent with a purportedly too-powerful bureaucracy led to the "sagebrush rebellion," headed by conservative Western Republicans, against increased regulation and grazing fees on public land.

—*Charles Phillips*

BUREAU OF RECLAMATION

In 1902, Congress passed the Reclamation Act, which created the U.S. Reclamation Service as an office in the United States Geological Survey in the Department of the Interior. In effect in all states west of the one hundredth meridian (except Texas, which became a reclamation state in 1905), the act authorized the construction of IRRIGATION projects studied by the Geological Survey. FREDERICK HAYNES NEWELL became its first director.

The service was created to solve the need for irrigation in the West. The fertile and arid lands challenged all agricultural cultures—prehistoric and historic Indian, Hispanic, and Anglo—that sought to use them. Complex laws were developed in the West to govern the ways in which settlers used WATER. During the high flows of spring and early summer, settlers wanted to store water in reservoirs for later use on crops. Small private and state irrigation projects were often successful, but major projects failed because they lacked capitalization, sophisticated engineering, intricate canal systems, and the ability to handle legalities. By the 1890s, both the UNITED STATES GEOLOGICAL SURVEY and the UNITED STATES ARMY CORPS OF ENGINEERS were studying irrigation projects in the West. Settlers actively promoted the intervention of the FEDERAL GOVERNMENT, and the Reclamation Service was created.

Among the earliest projects of the service were the Minidoka (Idaho), Salt River (Arizona), Uncompahgre (Colorado), North Platte (Wyoming and Nebraska), Milk River (Montana), Truckee-Carson (Nevada), Shoshone (Wyoming), Yuma (Arizona), Lower Yellowstone (Montana and Wyoming), Rio Grande (New Mexico), and Klamath (California and Oregon). The original intent of the Reclamation Act was to create new family farms in the West. Settlers on new farms were optimistically expected to repay costs of construction in ten years.

In its early years, the Reclamation Service faced numerous problems. Settlers often disputed repayment terms, and the service overestimated the amount of land its projects could serve. Mistakes were made in the design and location of dams and canals, and seepage often made some farm land unusable. Water supplies were sometimes erratic, and land speculation occurred. Frugal farmers sometimes continued dry farming in the area of a RECLAMATION project rather than pay for water. It was only during the depths of the drought in the 1930s that settlement on some reclamation projects solidified. Other settlers on project land fought over whether or not to fund expensive drainage systems.

The Reclamation Service addressed engineering problems with numerous laboratories around the West. These technical and experimental laboratories eventually consolidated into the Denver Office in charge of design and construction oversight. Testing facilities were also established at each construction location. In 1944, regional offices were established, and some functions of the Denver Office went to those regions.

In 1907, the Reclamation Service became independent of the Geological Survey, and in 1923, the agency was renamed the Bureau of Reclamation. During the 1930s and 1940s, the bureau undertook many of its major projects. Funding sources changed, and hydroelectric revenues supplemented the repayments by settlers. Larger projects were then possible.

HOOVER DAM, the Columbia Basin Project with Grand Coulee Dam as its centerpiece, the CENTRAL VALLEY PROJECT, and the Colorado–Big Thompson Project were products of the late 1920s and the 1930s Great Depression and its vast public works programs. During that time, ELWOOD MEAD and his successor John C. Page were the commissioners of the agency. During World War II, Congress authorized the massive Pick-Sloan Missouri Basin Program of Reclamation and established the Corps of Engineers. Other large projects soon followed.

In the bureau's early years, its programs were well accepted for forwarding a national mandate to develop the West. As early as the late 1930s, however, the bureau found itself embroiled with environmental groups interested in preserving Grand Lake, Colorado, from the Colorado–Big Thompson Project. After World War II, the public's concerns for protection of natural and scenic wonders and for budgetary constraints curtailed bureau programs. Projects were canceled, and by the 1970s, large new dam and irrigation construction projects were becoming politically, economically,

and environmentally infeasible. New social, political, and economic issues decisively altered the direction of the bureau. The Bureau of Reclamation currently directs its efforts to the operation and maintenance of its existing facilities. Water conservation, environmental enhancement, and water management are emerging as major concerns of the agency. Few large new construction projects are expected. Reclamation projects currently provide agricultural, household, and industrial water to about one-third of the population of the American West.

—*Brit Allan Storey*

SEE ALSO: Dust Bowl; Farming: Dryland Farming; Owens Valley War; Reclamation Act of 1902

SUGGESTED READING:

Dunar, Andrew J., and Dennis McBride. *Building Hoover Dam: An Oral History of the Great Depression.* New York, 1993.

Kluger, James R. *Turning on Water with a Shovel: The Career of Elwood Mead.* Albuquerque, N. Mex., 1992

Smith, Karen L. *The Magnificent Experiment: Building the Salt River Reclamation Project, 1890–1917.* Tucson, Ariz., 1986.

Stevens, Joseph E. *Hoover Dam: An American Adventure.* Norman, Okla., 1988.

Warne, William E. *The Bureau of Reclamation.* Boulder, Colo., 1985.

BURK, MARTHA CANNARY

SEE: "Calamity Jane"

BURKE, THOMAS

Thomas Burke (1849–1925) was a Seattle business and civic leader. Born in Chateaugay, New York, Burke moved in 1875 to Seattle, a town of approximately three thousand people, and plunged into the practice of law; short terms as a probate judge and territorial chief justice brought him the title of "judge," which he cherished all his life.

Burke's career was entangled with the promise of rail connections with Eastern states and resulting economic activity. He speculated heavily in real estate, mineral and industrial production, and locally financed rail lines tapping nearby coal fields and eastern Washington. He was an active Democrat in territorial politics and a chief spokesman for business groups who supported Chinese laborers during a time when the public agitated for their expulsion.

Closely identified with JAMES J. HILL and his Great Northern Railroad, which reached Puget Sound in 1893, Burke helped secure the concessions that made Seattle the Great Northern terminus. He remained Hill's Western consul and chief advocate. Accepting outside investments to supplement local capital, Burke participated in most of the business and civic ventures that marked Seattle's transition from a sawmill village to a burgeoning metropolitan center.

—*Charles P. LeWarne*

SUGGESTED READING:
Nesbit, Robert C. *"He Built Seattle": A Biography of Judge Thomas Burke.* Seattle, Wash., 1961.

BURKE ACT

Passed by Congress on May 8, 1906, the Burke Act amended the DAWES ACT, the 1887 law that provided for the division of tribal lands and the granting of plots or "allotments" to individual Indians. To prevent Indians from immediately selling their plots, the Dawes Act stipulated that title to the property would be held in trust by the FEDERAL GOVERNMENT for twenty-five years. The Burke Act waived the trust period and gave the secretary of the interior the right to issue fee-simple titles to allotments whenever he deemed the Indian owners capable of managing their own affairs. Under the Dawes Act, Indians became U.S. citizens as soon as they received allotments. The Burke Act delayed citizenship until Indians received title to their land. The Burke Act was supported both by Westerners who hoped to pry more land out of Indian hands and by reformers who hoped to extend the trusteeship period. Some reformers opposed the act, however, on the grounds that delaying citizenship would hurt efforts to "civilize" American Indians. Ultimately, the act did little to stanch the loss of Indian lands.

—*Wendy L. Wall*

SEE ALSO: Bureau of Indian Affairs; United States Indian Policy

BURLINGTON NORTHERN RAILROAD

The longest railroad in North America, the Burlington Northern operates a network of twenty-six thousand miles of track centered on Chicago and Minneapolis–St. Paul and radiating across the West, to the Gulf of Mexico, to Denver, and throughout the Pacific Northwest. It was created on March 3, 1970, after the U.S. Supreme Court upheld the Interstate Commerce Commission's approval of the controversial merger of the Chicago, Burlington and Quincy; the Northern Pacific; the Great Northern; the Spokane, Portland and Seattle; and the Colorado and Southern.

Of the merged lines that made up the Burlington Northern, the most venerable was the Chicago, Burlington and Quincy, which was chartered in 1849 as the Aurora (Illinois) Branch Railroad, connecting Aurora and other communities southwest of Chicago with the Galena and Chicago Union Railroad (the forerunner of the CHICAGO AND NORTHWESTERN RAILROAD). Only twelve miles long when it began operations on September 2, 1850, the Aurora Branch was an immediate financial success and soon attracted the interest of James F. Joy, a Detroit lawyer who arranged financing from a bloc of Eastern investors headed by JOHN MURRAY FORBES of Boston. The group acquired the Northern Cross, Central Military Tract, and Peoria and Oquawka railroads, joined them to the Aurora, and formed a major through line from Chicago to the Mississippi at Burlington, Iowa, and Quincy, Illinois. Connecting with other Midwestern railroads, the CB&Q became the most powerful line in the Midwest, and it progressed beyond the Mississippi through a connection with its subsidiary, the Burlington and Missouri River Railroad. By 1872, CB&Q joined the UNION PACIFIC RAILROAD at Kearney, Nebraska, forming a connection to the West Coast.

Despite economic depression during the 1870s, the CB&Q prospered under the direction of Forbes (Joy had been ousted over a conflict of interest created by his having acted as a railroad officer and a construction contractor for the railroad). Extended to Denver and to Minneapolis–St. Paul in the 1880s, the line provided a link between Chicago and the Northern Pacific and Great Northern railroads. The link was strengthened during the 1890s when the CB&Q expanded to Billings, Montana. By the beginning of the twentieth century, it acquired the Colorado and Southern Railroad and the Fort Worth and Denver City Railroad and forged a direct link between the Northwest and the Southwest. Forbes and, after him, CHARLES ELLIOTT PERKINS had made the CB&Q the strongest and most profitable railroad in the Midwest. When Perkins retired in 1901, J. P. Morgan and JAMES J. HILL acquired a controlling interest in the railroad and effectively operated the vast line in concert with the Great Northern and Northern Pacific.

The Northern Pacific, chartered in 1864, foundered in its early years under the direction of JAY COOKE and as a result of the depression of the 1870s. Even then, it had a significant impact on life in Minnesota and North Dakota, since it was forced to sell large portions of its fifty-million-acre government land grant, giving rise to BONANZA FARMING in the region. In 1883, HENRY VILLARD made the Northern Pacific a transcontinental route by joining its track to that of his Oregon Railway and Navigation Company. But the depression of the 1890s sent the line once again into receivership, and it was taken over by Hill and Morgan in 1898.

The Great Northern was the creation of James J. Hill, who formed a syndicate to purchase the ailing St. Paul and Pacific from the equally ailing Northern Pacific in 1878. Hill built the railroad into a link between Winnipeg and St. Paul and into the northern Great Lakes region at Duluth, Minnesota. Throughout the 1880s, Hill extended his main and branch lines in a successful effort to outperform and undersell the Northern Pacific. He christened his creation the Great Northern in 1889 and expanded his lines from Montana through to the Pacific Coast, which it reached in 1893.

By the turn of the century, then, Morgan and Hill controlled the Great Northern, Northern Pacific, and the CB&Q. However, EDWARD HENRY HARRIMAN, head of the Union Pacific, began acquiring Northern Pacific stock, through which he could control the CB&Q. While Harriman came to hold a majority of the preferred stock, Hill and Morgan held the bulk of the common stock, thereby creating a standoff. Worse, the price of the stock had been bid beyond a thousand dollars a share, bringing Wall Street to the brink of a panic. In response, Hill and Harriman agreed to pool all of their Northern Pacific and Great Northern stock (and, with it, that of the CB&Q) into a holding company. The giant Northern Securities Company was dissolved, however, as a violation of the SHERMAN ANTI-TRUST ACT, but this action had no real effect on what had become a commonality of interest among Morgan, Hill, and Harriman.

Through the 1920s, the CB&Q, Northern Pacific, and Great Northern grew into the most prosperous, strongest, and most efficiently run of the nation's Western railroads. Unlike some of the Southwestern roads, most notably the SOUTHERN PACIFIC RAILROAD, the rising profits did not come at the expense of agricultural and other shippers. The Hill-controlled roads actually lowered freight rates dramatically. After successfully weathering the Great Depression, the railroads enjoyed even greater growth during World War II. A full-scale merger among the three railroads, first envisioned as early as the 1920s, was actively sought during the 1960s. While the ICC supported the proposal, the Department of Justice opposed it, and litigation consumed much of the decade.

—*Alan Axelrod*

SEE ALSO: Financial Panics; Railroads; Railroad Land Grants

SUGGESTED READING:
Hedges, J. B. *Henry Villard and the Railways of the Northwest.* New Haven, Conn., 1930.
Martin, Albro. *Railroads Triumphant: The Growth, Rejection and Rebirth of a Vital American Force.* New York, 1992.
Overton, Richard C. *Burlington Route: A History of the Burlington Lines.* New York, 1965.

BURNET, DAVID GOUVERNEUR

Vice-president of the Republic of Texas from 1838 to 1841 and president for a few months in 1841, David Gouverneur Burnet (1788–1870) was born in Newark, New Jersey. He volunteered for Francisco de Miranda's Venezuela expedition against Spain. Burnet supported the Mexican Revolution from 1806 to 1813. He then established a trading post in Natchitoches, Louisiana, and when that venture failed, he went to the upper–Colorado River region, where he lived with Native Americans. From 1819 to 1825, he practiced law and engaged in business ventures in Ohio, Louisiana, and Texas. He moved to Texas in 1806 and participated in the events leading to the TEXAS REVOLUTION. He served in the Convention of 1833, as judge of the Department of the Brazos in 1834, and in the Consultation of 1835. The Convention of 1836 elected him president of the interim government. He served until SAM HOUSTON won the first election in 1836 for the presidency of the Republic of Texas. Burnet hated Houston, and although Burnet was always important, his political star dimmed as Houston's shined. Burnet did serve, however, as vice-president of the republic from 1838 to 1841 and as president upon MIRIBEAU B. LAMAR's resignation in December 1841. Burnet opposed Texas's secession during the CIVIL WAR. Nevertheless, when he was elected to the U.S. Senate in 1866, he was denied his seat because Texas was still an "unReconstructed" former slave state. He retired to Galveston and died four years later.

—*Robert A. Calvert*

BURNETT, SAMUEL BURK

Texas rancher Samuel Burk Burnett (1849–1922) grew up on a ranch in Denton, Texas. He was only twenty-five years old when he purchased his first herd of cattle.

By 1876, he had established the Burnett Ranch in Wichita County, Texas, where he began a lifelong concern for rationalizing livestock marketing practices.

In the mid-1880s when Texas cattlemen had a consuming and constant need for grazing lands, Burnett negotiated leases for the use of one million acres of pasture land in the Indian Territory for himself and other Texas cattlemen. Using Indian lands meant that the Texas ranchers could avoid the hazards of trailing their herds long distances to the grazing lands on the Northern Plains. Burnett and other ranchers used the Indian Territory lands profitably until the opening of the region for settlement.

—*Patricia Hogan*

SEE ALSO: Cattle Industry

BURNHAM, DANIEL HUDSON

In 1872, Daniel Hudson Burnham (1846–1912), architect and urban planner known for his visionary city designs, joined a CHICAGO firm whose head draftsman was John Wellborn Root, soon to become his partner in the firm of Burnham and Root. The city of Chicago, then an emerging commercial metropolis that served as a gateway for the growing of East-West commerce, had recently been devastated by the great fire of 1871. Its rebuilding presented great opportunities—and great challenges—to architects. Land rents were so high that architects were forced to find vertical rather than horizontal building solutions. Fortunately, new technological developments—including the electric light and electric elevator—made tall buildings feasible. Taking advantage of this potential, Burnham and Root presided over Chicago's transition from all-masonry construction to steel-cage construction. Their earliest Chicago skyscrapers, including the Calumet Building (constructed from 1882 to 1884), the Rookery (1885 to 1888), the Monadnock Building (1889 to 1892), and the Reliance Building (1890 to 1894), all had exterior walls of masonry. The Monadnock Building took all-masonry construction to its practical limit. At sixteen stories, it was the tallest masonry building ever built and featured load-bearing walls that sloped up smoothly from a fourteen-foot thickness at the base to six feet at the top. In contrast, the nine-story Rand-McNally Building, of 1890, did not require the impressive—but extraordinarily expensive—thick load-bearing walls because it used an all-steel frame. The twenty-story Masonic Temple Building, completed

in 1891, was the tallest building in the world; it employed an all-steel, lateral bracing system developed by Burnham and Root's structural engineer, E. C. Shankland.

During 1891, Burnham and Root was commissioned to oversee the design of some 150 temporary white-plaster-facaded buildings for the World's Columbian Exposition of 1893. Root died shortly after the commission was received, and Burnham invited leading Eastern architects to assist him. The task rapidly evolved into a grand and comprehensive vision of the new American city. Collaborating chiefly with landscape architect FREDERICK LAW OLMSTED as well as Richard Morris Hunt; McKim, Mead, and White; Van Brunt and Howe; George Post; and Peabody and Stearns, Burnham used the World's Columbian Exposition to formulate the first new all-encompassing urban plan since Paris and Vienna had been redesigned earlier in the century. The exposition not only introduced the Beaux-Arts Style (so called because most of the Eastern architects with whom Burnham had worked were trained at the École des Beaux-Arts in Paris) to the Midwest and West but also established the Greco-Roman columnar architecture as *the* style of choice for public buildings in America for the next two decades.

In his later years, Burnham created extensive urban plans for Washington, D.C. (1901 to 1902), Cleveland (1902 to 1903), and SAN FRANCISCO (1905 to 1906). Between 1906 and 1909, at the behest of the Commercial Club of Chicago, Burnham developed his most ambitious plan—nothing less than the redesign of Chicago—the first truly comprehensive plan of regional scope ever created for an American city. While Burnham's sweeping plan was never fully adopted, it left its mark on the city, especially its lake front and harbor, and it inspired efforts at integrated, rational CITY PLANNING elsewhere.

—*Alan Axelrod*

SEE ALSO: Architecture: Urban; Great Chicago Fire

SUGGESTED READING:
Hines, Thomas S. *Burnham of Chicago*. New York, 1974.
Moore, Charles. *Daniel H. Burnham*. Boston, 1921.

BURNS, JOHN ANTHONY

Leader of HAWAII's push for statehood and its second state governor, John Anthony Burns (1909–1975) moved to Hawaii in 1913 when his father, an army sergeant, was stationed at Fort Shafter in Honolulu.

After his father deserted Burns, his mother, brother, and sisters, the family remained as one of the few mainland American families on the islands not of the ruling planter class. It may have been Burns's early socializing with the native Hawaiians, Chinese, and Portuguese that lead him to champion the cause of a more democratic and inclusive Hawaii later in life.

After attending the University of Hawaii, Burns worked at several odd jobs and then joined the Honolulu police force in 1934. By 1940, he was captain, and during World War II, he served as Espionage Bureau Chief. After the war, Burns spearheaded a group of activist Democrats who agitated for statehood as a means to wrest control of the islands from the landowners' oligarchy.

Burns entered politics with little initial success. He lost a 1946 election for a seat on the Honolulu Board of Supervisors and lost bids in 1948 and 1954 to become Hawaii's territorial delegate to Congress. When he was elected to Congress in 1956, he began pushing for Hawaii's statehood, which was accomplished in 1959.

Burns served three terms as governor of Hawaii, from 1962 to 1974. His administration oversaw improvements in consumer and environmental protection and land-use laws; an expansion of the public education system; development of new housing, office space, government buildings, and tourist facilities; and construction of the state capitol building.

Before his third term ended, Burns was diagnosed with cancer and died only three months after stepping down from the governor's seat.

—*Patricia Hogan*

SUGGESTED READING:
Amalu, Samuel C. *Jack Burns: A Portrait in Transition.* Honolulu, Hawaii, 1974.

BURNS, TOM

SEE: Rivermen

BURNS, WILLIAM J.

In a life spent in law enforcement, William J. Burns (1861–1932) rooted out corruption in federal, state, and city governments, founded the William J. Burns Detective Agency, and served a stint as the director of the Bureau of Investigation, forerunner of the Federal Bureau of Investigation. Born in Baltimore, Maryland, Burns, at the age of twenty-four, moved to Columbus, Ohio, and uncovered the culprits behind the state's fraudulent 1885 election. Working for the United States Secret Service from 1889 to 1903, he investigated counterfeiters and, at one time, went undercover in Indiana to expose the vigilantes responsible for five lynchings.

In 1903, Burns joined the Department of the Interior as an investigator and turned his attention to scandals involving the sale of public lands for private profit. His investigation led to the indictments of several public officials, including Oregon's Senator John Mitchell. From Oregon, Burns went to San Francisco with federal prosecutor FRANCIS JOSEPH HENEY to investigate the corrupt city administration of ABRAHAM (ABE) RUEF. It took four years, but Burns and Heney eventually put Ruef in prison.

Leaving government service, Burns established the William J. Burns Detective Agency, which quickly became second in prestige and case load only to the much older PINKERTON NATIONAL DETECTIVE AGENCY. Like the Pinkerton Agency, the Burns organization often operated as a private police force for the interests of big business against organized labor. In a widely publicized case, the Burns agency investigated the 1910 bombing of the headquarters of the *Los Angeles Times,* long a vehement enemy of unionism. Burns successfully implicated John J. McNamara and his brother James, militant members of the American Federation of Labor.

With his detective agency firmly established, Burns returned to government employment in 1921 to head the Bureau of Investigation. His tenure was not successful. The administration of President Warren G. Harding was corrupt, and the corruption spilled into several federal agencies including the Department of Justice. Burns's bureau was slow to investigate high-level scandals, including the notorious TEAPOT DOME affair. Unable to overcome the taint of scandal, Burns resigned as director of the bureau in 1924 and retired from public life.

—*Patricia Hogan*

BURR CONSPIRACY

Shortly after the LOUISIANA PURCHASE, two prominent politicians—Aaron Burr, vice-president of the United States, and JAMES WILKINSON, territorial governor of Upper Louisiana—hatched a plot to take over the trans-Mississippi West and sever it from the United States. Known at the time as the "Western conspiracy," it came later to be called the "Burr conspiracy," since it proved to be Burr's final hour on the stage of American politics and brought down the curtain on one of the more checkered political careers in the nation's history. Although details about the plot and all those involved were and have remained murky, the sheer fact that it existed says much about the unsettled quality of the new territory, the country's still quite tenuous hold on its Western lands, and the difficult time even the West's best citizens had with questions of loyalty, not to mention legality, before the WAR OF 1812 inextricably bound the region to the young democracy east of the Mississippi. Also, in an exaggerated way, both Burr and Wilkinson were classic "Westerners," men who looked to the West as a land of second chances and new opportunities, men with less than spotless pasts who thrived in a crude country where there were few rules and even fewer who followed them.

Everyone in the Mississippi River valley knew that Wilkinson was deeply involved with Burr in some sort of scheme. Burr spent two weeks in the fall of 1805 consulting long into the night with Wilkinson. The lawless conditions in the territory, created in large measure by the wide-open speculation resulting from disputed Spanish land grants and the burgeoning mining business, made Upper Louisiana a perfect spot for such plots—and for the likes of Aaron Burr.

Like Wilkinson's, Burr's star rose in the American Revolution. A young graduate of the College of New Jersey, he along with Wilkinson survived Benedict Arnold's disastrous Canadian campaign. Burr joined General Washington's staff but was dismissed when he antagonized his commander. Admitted to the bar after the war, he was elected to the New York Assembly in 1784, became attorney general of New York in 1789, and a United States senator two years later. When he was defeated for reelection, he served another two-year term in the New York Assembly but had garnered sufficient national prominence to run for president in 1800.

Under the procedures then prevailing, the electoral college cast its votes for THOMAS JEFFERSON and Burr, without indicating which should be president and which vice-president. The contest went to the House of Representatives for a decision. Burr's adamantine political foe, Alexander Hamilton, lobbied against him, and the House elected Jefferson. Burr became the nation's third vice-president. Toward the end of his term, in 1804, he ran for governor of New York. Burr, a Republican, struck a secret deal with a group of rabid Federalists who promised to support his candidacy if he would swing New York into a secessionist "Northern Confederacy of New England and New York." Hamilton, a more orthodox Federalist, caught wind

of the apparent conspiracy and advised his Federalist friends to vote against Burr, who was, indeed, defeated.

Subsequently, newspapers reported that Hamilton had called Burr "a dangerous man, and one who ought not to be trusted with the reins of government." Burr demanded a printed retraction of the slur; Hamilton refused; Burr challenged him to a duel. They met on a hill in Weehawken, New Jersey. Hamilton fired first, apparently discharging his pistol into the air; Burr leveled his piece and shot Hamilton in the chest. He died some thirty hours later. That Aaron Burr was vice-president of the United States and presiding over the Senate did not prevent his being indicted in New Jersey and New York for murder. While he was never actually tried, his political career was ruined. But he was not entirely an outcast. He had friends in the West; many considered him a hero for having slain a dangerous Federalist; some even suggested that he run for Congress from Tennessee.

The vice-president of the United States had other ideas. Desperate to start over, Burr began conspiring with any number of malcontents. He courted an 1804 delegation of French residents protesting the government Jefferson had instituted in their city of New Orleans; he consulted with the British diplomats on how he might facilitate the separation of the West from the United States; and he sold information about American designs on Florida and Texas to the Spanish minister to the United States. It was not that he was loyal to Spain; in fact, it was the Spanish Southwest that spurred his Napoleonic hopes.

In April 1805, little more than a month after his vice-presidential term had ended, Burr rode west. He had been in constant communication with his old friend and companion of the Benedict Arnold campaign, James Wilkinson. The two passed back and forth what in time would become incriminating correspondence, often in code. They planned, apparently, to fan the boundary disputes with Spain over the territories along the Sabine River in Texas into a full-scale war. The two would not be content, however, with simply gaining Florida and Texas for the United States, as they led many of their supporters to assume. They would invade Mexico and establish an independent government in the Southwest; that done, they would encourage the West to break with the Union and form a new empire with their new government in Mexico—all administered from a capital to be established in New Orleans.

Canvassing the West, Burr made himself known and gathered support. In New Orleans, he solidified his relations with that city's discontented French residents. All of these contacts encouraged Burr in his plans, and luring backers with promises of power and wealth, he returned to the East. To the Spanish, he proposed a scheme to seize Washington, D.C., and exploit the confusion that was bound to result in order to appropriate navy ships, sail to New Orleans, capture that city (with the aid of the city's ethnic French), and thus effect the secession of the entire West and its defection to the Spanish camp. Except for the fees from the Spanish, Burr was unable to raise money for his plan from foreign governments. However, a wealthy Irish immigrant, Harmon Blennerhasset, who lived in a manor house on an island in the Ohio River near Marietta, was sufficiently impressed with Burr to advance him five thousand dollars as a down payment on a four-hundred-thousand-acre tract on the Ouachita River in Kentucky. Burr recruited men ostensibly to settle the tract, but actually to fight a war with Spain.

Burr's activities did not escape the notice of the press, and Thomas Ritchie—among others—published an account of them in the Richmond, Virginia, *Enquirer*. Public disclosure made Burr a marked man, and even the ever-opportunistic Wilkinson began to cool toward him and their plans. When Burr returned to the West in August 1806, communities along the Ohio were buzzing with rumors, and Federalist Joseph Hamilton Daveiss, United States district attorney, hauled Burr into court and before a Kentucky grand jury on a charge of preparing to make "war upon the subjects of the King of Spain." The jury was dissolved for lack of witnesses, whereupon Daveiss petitioned for a second grand jury, which again refused to indict Burr. The fact was, as Burr well knew, many Westerners *wanted* war with Spain, and Burr was so evasive about his objectives that most people never suspected his ultimate aims.

Burr was once again free to press down the Mississippi to link up with James Wilkinson and take the city of New Orleans. Wilkinson—who had moved to Natchez and New Orleans to negotiate for the United States a treaty with Spain pertaining to the territory along the Sabine River—led his old friend to believe that he was ready to proceed. But on October 21, 1806, even before Burr had been arraigned in Kentucky, Wilkinson revealed the entire scheme in an urgent dispatch to President Jefferson. The president issued a proclamation denouncing Burr, and such was Jefferson's prestige that Burr's Western supporters turned against him. Among them was Tennessee's ANDREW JACKSON. (Although Jackson admired Burr and approved of what he thought was Burr's intention to annex the Spanish Southwest to the United States, Jackson was no traitor. He always blamed Wilkinson, not Burr, for betraying a perfectly good plan in order to carve out a personal empire that included Tennessee and Kentucky.) A militia party seized many of the boats Burr had gathered and even raided

Blennerhasset's island. Burr himself was already on his way to New Orleans.

Wilkinson now spread the alarm in the city. Burr, he said, was about to invade with a vast army. William Claiborne, the territorial governor of Lower Louisiana, declared martial law, began the construction of fortifications, and raised a military force of his own. Burr's "army"—sixty men in thirteen boats—was taken by Natchez militiamen, and Burr, believing that he would be tried in a territorial—a Western—court, surrendered to civilian authorities. While, indeed, a grand jury in Natchez declined to indict Burr and even denounced Wilkinson and Claiborne for inciting public hysteria, authorities continued to hold him prisoner while a trial in the states—back East—was being arranged. The former vice-president of the United States put on some worn-out clothes and a floppy white hat and made a run for it.

Headed for Spanish-held East Florida and Pensacola, Burr stopped at the house of Nicholas Perkins in lower Alabama Territory to ask directions to a plantation where he planned to spend the night. A backwoods lawyer, Perkins had never seen Aaron Burr, yet he somehow felt certain that the stranger who had asked directions was Burr. Perkins called on the sheriff, who refused to intervene, whereupon Perkins rode to Fort Stoddard and persuaded its commander to arrest the conspirator. Once Burr was in custody, Perkins volunteered to deliver him to federal officials in Virginia, where he would collect more than three thousand dollars in reward money, along with the thanks of the president.

Aaron Burr was tried for high treason, despite the efforts of Supreme Court Chief Justice John Marshall, brought to Richmond to preside, to reduce the charge to a misdemeanor. During the trial, Marshall ruled the prosecution's principal evidence inadmissible. All the government could offer was evidence that Burr *intended* to commit treason, he said, since Burr's plan to attack the United States was thwarted before he could commit any overt act. Marshall then ruled that Burr could not be convicted for his intentions, and the jury had no alternative but to find him not guilty.

A free man yet again, Burr left for Europe, where he tried to interest Napoleon Bonaparte in a scheme to conquer Florida. After four impoverished years abroad, Burr returned to New York in 1812 and practiced law for almost a quarter century. He died in 1836. As for Wilkinson, Burr's trial provided enough evidence to implicate him as well, and a sensationalized book entitled *Proofs of the Corruption of General James Wilkinson* by Daniel Clark, one of the plot's co-conspirators, further compromised Wilkinson's position. He had finally overplayed his hand, and his conspiratorial penchant and double-crossing ways created so much bitter opposition to him in St. Louis that Jefferson removed him from office on March 3, 1807.

—*Charles Phillips*

SUGGESTED READING:
Abernathy, Thomas Perkins. *The Burr Conspiracy.* New York, 1954.

BURROS

Burros, small donkeys brought to the Western Hemisphere by Spanish conquistadors, became the standard beasts of burden for the poor, mostly mestizo peasants and the penny-pinching desert prospectors for gold and other precious metals in the American Southwest. Descended from the African wild ass *(Equus asinus),* donkeys have been used as work animals since at least 4000 B.C. The average donkey stands some forty inches at the shoulder, although the sizes of different breeds vary greatly, ranging from the small Sicilian donkey to the large ass of Majorca. Brought to Iberia during the Moorish conquest, donkeys were called in Spanish *burros,* and the words are often used interchangeably outside the Southwestern United States, where *burro* refers specifically to a small donkey.

Varying in color from white to gray to black, often with a dark stripe running from mane to tail and crosswise on the shoulders, the burro has very long, dark-tipped ears and a tail more cowlike than equine. Slower moving than HORSES, they were valued by Spanish explorers for their sure-footedness and ability to carry heavy loads over the rough terrains of the strange new world the conquistadors had penetrated, the very qualities that recommended them to Mexican villagers and Death Valley fortune hunters. To improve their speed—or to enhance the agility and ruggedness of the relatively fragile horse—burros were cross-bred with horses to produce the hybrid mule, which became the backbone of Hispanic trade in the Southwest. Merchants and traders preferred the mule and Indian warriors the horse, while the poor were left with their reliable, manageable, and inexpensive cousin, the burro.

Desert prospectors often abandoned their cheap beasts of burden when their search for precious metals proved futile, and the animals became wild. Along with donkeys, mules, and HORSES escaped from domestic service, they roamed the deserts of the Southwest. Descended from these released and escaped animals, wild burros flourished, building up a population of some eight to ten thousand concentrated in and around Death Valley, California, and on both sides of the Colorado River in Arizona and California. Competing for limited forage in an arid land, the wild burros may have driven the desert bighorn sheep to extinction and, some claim, threaten the existence of other species and domestic livestock. Many, however, consider burros a significant emblem of the history of desert exploration and argue they do not deserve their destructive reputation, a position given support in some environmental studies. When burros became target animals in California, the public reaction was so intense that very restrictive legislation was passed, culminating in the Wild Horse and Burro Act, which provides both animals—who share much the same wilderness areas—the protection of the federal government.

—*Charles Phillips*

SEE ALSO: Mules and Mule Trade; Mustangs and Horse Trade

BURROUGHS, JOHN

A renowned nature essayist, John Burroughs (1837–1921) became one of America's best-known and respected proponents of nature and the simple life in the late nineteenth and early twentieth centuries. Raised on a farm in Roxbury, New York, Burroughs first worked as a school teacher. In 1863, he moved to Washington, D.C., and worked at the Treasury Department. He became a lifelong friend and proponent of Walt Whitman. Burroughs's first book, *Notes on Walt Whitman as a Poet and Person* (1867), was also the first book written about the poet. His next books, *Wake Robin* (1871) and *Winter Sunshine* (1876) established his reputation as a literary naturalist. In 1873, he moved to New York's Hudson River valley, where he made his living as a bank examiner, farmer, and writer. He eventually published more than two dozen volumes of natural history, geology, travel, literary, and philosophical essays.

His writing helped initiate and then rode the flood of public interest in nature study. His pleasant and accessible studies of birds and other wildlife of woodland and farm helped Americans appreciate nature close to home. Textbook editions of his essays were widely used in public schools. John Burroughs Society nature clubs, promoted by his publisher, appeared

John Burroughs. *Editors' collection.*

in schools throughout the nation. In his later years, he was idolized by many people who discovered his essays in their youth, including THEODORE ROOSEVELT and Henry Ford.

Although his roots were in the East and he suffered from homesickness when away from familiar ground, Burroughs occasionally ventured into the West. In 1899, he joined JOHN MUIR and other notables on the HARRIMAN EXPEDITION to Alaska, a trip he described in *Far and Near* (1904). He also traveled with Roosevelt to Yellowstone in 1903 and then wrote *Camping & Tramping with Roosevelt* (1907). Essays in *Time and Change* (1912) were based on a 1909 trip to the Grand Canyon and Yosemite with Muir and to Hawaii.

Burroughs played an important role in establishing standards and a definitive form for the nature essay. He believed that literary naturalists should blend the perceptions of both artist and scientist. Writers, he argued, must be scientifically accurate while reporting their emotional responses to nature. In 1903, he accused Ernest Thompson Seton, JOHN GRIFFITH (JACK) LONDON, and other prominent writers of deceiving their readers with "sham natural history." This launched the NATURE FAKERS controversy, which was debated in the popular press until Roosevelt publicly defended Burroughs's position four years later.

—*Ralph H. Lutts*

SUGGESTED READING:
Barrus, Clara. *The Life and Letters of John Burroughs*. 2 vols. Boston, 1925.
Westbrook, Perry D. *John Burroughs*. New York, 1974

BURSOM, HOLM OLAF

A successful New Mexico rancher, Holm Olaf Bursom (1869–1953) entered politics in 1894. Among his many posts were sheriff of Socorro County, member of the territorial senate, and superintendent of prisons. As chair of the Republican territorial central committee from 1905 to 1911 and as a delegate to the Republican national conventions in 1904, 1908, 1912, and 1928, he undertook his most important political work—promoting statehood for New Mexico. During the 1908 convention, he persuaded the national committee to insert in the party platform a plank calling for the immediate admission of New Mexico and Arizona as separate states. He was a delegate to the New Mexico constitutional convention in 1910. While he was defeated in his bid for the governor's seat in 1911, he remained active in politics and served as a U.S. senator from 1921 to 1925.

—*Candace Floyd*

SUGGESTED READING:
Larson, Robert W. *New Mexico's Quest for Statehood, 1846–1912*. Albuquerque, N. Mex., 1968.

BUSH, ASAHEL

An Oregon newspaper editor, Asahel Bush (1824–1913) was active in the "Salem clique," which controlled Democratic party politics in the territory. Born in Westfield, Massachusetts, Bush apprenticed as a printer in New York, studied law, and was admitted to the Massachusetts bar. In 1850, "Oregon Fever" propelled him to Portland. As editor of the *Oregon Statesman* in Salem, Bush led the "Salem clique," including, among others, James Nesmith and MATTHEW PAUL DEADY. The clique controlled territorial Democratic politics until the slavery issue split the party with Bush and the *Statesman* squarely behind the Union wing. He practiced a libelous brand of journalism called the "Oregon style." For example, he claimed the editor of the Whig *Oregonian* seldom told the truth "even by mistake." In 1868, Bush joined William S. Ladd to found a Portland banking firm in which Bush was active until his death.

—*Edwin R. Bingham*

SEE ALSO: Magazines and Newspapers

BUSH, GEORGE WASHINGTON

An African American agriculturalist who led the first settlers into present-day Washington, George Washington Bush (1790–1863) became one of the region's most successful farmers. Born in Pennsylvania, Bush lived in Missouri before migrating to the Oregon Country in 1844. After a two-thousand-mile, eight-month journey, Bush, his wife, and their six children reached the north bank of the Columbia River. Unlike most of Oregon's settlers who homesteaded south of the Columbia in the Willamette Valley, Bush moved north to the Puget Sound, beyond the enforcement of the territory's black exclusion law. Near present-day Olympia, the family claimed land that became known as Bush Prairie.

The Bush homestead prospered. One observer noted in 1851 that the farm was the best north of the Columbia River. In 1856, Bush introduced the first mechanical mower and reaper into the Washington Territory and shared the new implements with his neighbors.

Those neighbors challenged the racial restrictions that threatened the Bush family's land claim. In 1854, fifty-five citizens of the Puget Sound region successfully petitioned Congress to grant a special exemption validating Bush's claim. Ten years after Bush arrived in the region, the U.S. government officially recognized his claim at Bush Prairie. In 1876, wheat from his field won prizes at the Centennial Fair in Philadelphia.

—*Quintard Taylor*

SUGGESTED READING:
Taylor, Quintard. "A History of Blacks in the Pacific Northwest, 1788–1970." Ph.D. diss., University of Minnesota, 1977.

BUSINESS

SEE: American System; Banking; Bonanza Farming; Booms; Cattle Industry; Coal Mining; Copper Mining; Cotton Farming; Currency and Silver as Western Political Issues; Farming; Federal Government; Financial Panics; Fishing Industry; Fur Trade; Gold Mining; Land Policy; Lumber Industry; Mining; Motion-Picture Industry; Mustangs and Horse Trade; Oil and Gas Industry; Overland Freight; Railroads; Rendezvous; Restaurants; Sheep Ranching; Silver Mining; Tariff Policy; Tourism

BUTCHER, SOLOMON D.

A Nebraska photographer who compiled an impressive collection of photographs of pioneers living on the prairies in the nineteenth century, Solomon D. Butcher (1856–1927) was born in Burton, Virginia (later West Virginia). He moved as a young child with his family to Winona, Illinois. In 1874, he was apprenticed to a local tintypist.

In 1880, Butcher accompanied his father to the prairies of Nebraska and homesteaded. He abandoned his sod house and moved to Minneapolis in 1881 to pursue medicine. Two years later, he returned to Nebraska, without a medical degree but with a wife. By teaching school, he earned enough money to buy photographic equipment and build an adobe studio. For several years, he photographed whenever he could, but mostly he helped his father farm.

In 1886, Butcher decided to compile a photographic history of pioneering. He borrowed money to outfit a wagon as a darkroom and began traveling around the county to photograph its inhabitants. Over the next fifteen years, he photographed nearly half the settlers in the county, more than fifteen hundred in all. His work is considered to be the best visual document of settlement on the American plains.

Solomon D. Butcher captured the life of the sodbuster. *Courtesy Nebraska State Historical Society.*

His *Pioneer History of Custer County and Short Sketches of Early Days in Nebraska* was published in 1901 and was a great success. Always the dreamer, Butcher spent the remainder of his life engaged in get-rich-quick schemes that included dowsing for oil, hawking patent medicine, and speculating on land. Nothing Butcher did ever made much money; he died in Greeley, Colorado, thinking himself a total failure. The Nebraska Historical Society houses a large collection of Butcher images.

—*John E. Carter*

SUGGESTED READING:
Carter, John. *Solomon D. Butcher: Photographing the American Dream.* Lincoln, Nebr., 1985.

BUTLER, ANTHONY WAYNE

United States minister to Mexico under President ANDREW JACKSON, Anthony Butler (1790–1849) attempted to negotiate America's purchase of Texas in the years preceding the TEXAS REVOLUTION. Born in South Carolina, Butler moved with his family to Kentucky. After Butler's father died in 1805, Andrew Jackson, a family acquaintance, became legal guardian of the Butler sons.

Anthony Butler served in the infantry during the War of 1812 and eventually attained the rank of colonel. He participated in Jackson's victory at the Battle of New Orleans. After the war, Butler moved to Texas and began a lucrative career in land speculation. When Jackson became president of the United States, Butler appeared in Washington, D.C., to seek a federal appointment from his former guardian and to attempt to influence Jackson on a course of action regarding Texas favorable to Butler and the many other Americans who had settled in the Mexican territory.

In December 1829, Butler arrived in Mexico City with the charge from Jackson to negotiate the purchase of Texas. Jackson and Butler were unaware that Mexican officials, suspicious of the United States's interest in Texas, feared an acquisition of Texas was only the first of series of transactions through which the United States intended to gobble up Mexican lands. Butler, a diplomat neither by training nor by temperament, attempted to bully Mexican officials into the sale, and when that failed, he suggested that five hundred thousand dollars in bribes to Mexican officials would secure the purchase. In the five years Butler served as minister, he failed in his mission. Mexico's resolve to retain Texas became more absolute, and American settlers in Texas raised their guns in armed rebellion against Mexico in September 1835. While he served under General Zachary Taylor throughout the war, Butler's role in American diplomacy was at an end. He died on April 19, 1849, trying to save fellow passengers on a burning Mississippi River steamboat.

—*Kurt Edward Kemper*

SUGGESTED READING:

Lamar, Quinton Curtis. "A Diplomatic Disaster: The Mexican Mission of Anthony Butler, 1829–1834." *The Americas* 15 (July 1988): 1–17.

BUTTE, MONTANA

Home of the ANACONDA MINING COMPANY and the richest deposits of copper in the United States, by any reckoning, Butte, Montana, is one of the most fascinating and important towns in America. Butte never exceeded one hundred thousand in population, and its historical significance is wildly disproportionate to its size. Put simply, it produced more history than its domestic market could absorb.

The place had its origins in the distant geological past. A series of geological shudders gathered up uncounted megatons of minerals and dumped them just west of the Continental Divide in what is now southwestern Montana. Gold, silver, copper, zinc, and other trace metals piled on top of one another on Big Butte, which came to be known as the "Richest Hill on Earth." Butte was built on and around the hill. For the last 130 years, its people have made their living by forcing the hill to yield its riches to them.

They began with gold. Placer and quartz miners were active in the mid-1860s, and the place began to take on some of the appearances of a town. But Western gold camps were notoriously evanescent, and Butte was no exception. By 1870, the placer mines had played out; the men had moved on. It was then that the Big Butte began to reveal exactly what "Richest Hill" meant. WILLIAM ANDREWS CLARK arrived in 1872 and immediately began exploring for copper. Two years later, William Farlin constructed a roasting mill for silver. By the time MARCUS DALY got to town in 1876, Butte had recovered from the hard times of the late 1860s.

Daly deserves the credit for transforming the still-struggling silver camp into the world's greatest mining town. An experienced hard-rock miner, the Irish-born Daly invested his and others' money in a massive industrial complex of copper mines in Butte, smelters in Anaconda and Great Falls, and lumber operations near Missoula. The Anaconda Mining Company was born in 1880; Thomas Edison electrified New York in 1882, creating a demand for copper wire; the Northern Pacific Railroad arrived in Butte in 1883; the Anaconda smelter was first fired up in 1884. And Butte boomed.

Predictably, corporate warfare accompanied the boom. Butte's "Copper Kings"—Clark, Daly, and Clark's sometimes ally, FREDERICK AUGUSTUS HEINZE—fought for control not just of Butte's mines, but also of the ethnic composition of the town's work force, the location of the state's capital, and, in Clark's case, the Senate seat from Montana. From 1888 until Daly's death in 1900, the three slugged it out in courtroom and legislative chamber; a round to Daly, the next to Clark or Heinze. After Daly's death, the struggle was less personal but scarcely more gentlemanly. It ended in 1910 with the consolidation of Butte's mines by Anaconda (for a time, Amalgamated) Copper.

But capitalists were not the only ones drawn to Butte. Thousands of hard-rock miners, men with less grandiose dreams, also made their way to the place—Cornish, Irish, and American at first; Finn, Italian, and Serbian followed. They worked underground in mines that reached depths of more than four thousand feet, never closed, and produced wealth of storybook proportions. They made the highest wages in industrial America; indeed, by 1905, in proportion to population, Butte had the largest payroll in the world. It also had what might have been the largest local union standing guard over those wages, the Butte Miners' Union. Pragmatic rather than ideological, the BMU played on both ethnic and corporate rivalries to maintain the wage structure, secure the eight-hour day, and ensure the closed shop.

The relationship between labor and management was satisfactory only until 1912. From then to 1920, ethnic and class tensions—exacerbated by World War I, the presence of the INDUSTRIAL WORKERS OF THE WORLD, and the open-shop drive of Anaconda—destroyed the BMU and changed the social and economic calculus that had defined the town. It remained wide open, as raucous and fun-loving as ever, but the miners were without union protection until 1934, and the always unstable balance of social classes was permanently upset.

More fundamental changes followed World War II. Underground mining gave way to the open-pit variety; Anaconda expanded its operations to Chile—with disastrous consequences when the Chilean government nationalized the company's properties there in 1971. By 1977, Anaconda had sold out to Atlantic Richfield, which then closed the Butte operations. The town was still on the "Richest Hill on Earth," but the frantic pursuit of a share of the riches had slowed to a walk.

During its prime, however, Butte was everything the West was not supposed to be: intensely urban, massively industrialized, overwhelmingly immigrant— and Catholic. In the final analysis, its role as antidote to the historical myth of a Protestant and rural West may prove more important than the hundreds of millions of dollars in ore taken out of its mines.

—*David M. Emmons*

SEE ALSO: Booms; Copper Kings, War of the; Copper Mining; Mining

SUGGESTED READING:

Emmons, David M. *The Butte Irish: Class and Ethnicity in an American Mining Town, 1875–1925.* Urbana, Ill., 1989.

Malone, Michael. *The Battle for Butte: Mining and Politics on the Northern Frontier, 1864–1906.* Seattle, Wash., 1981.

Work Projects Administration. *Copper Camp: Stories of the World's Greatest Mining Town, Butte, Montana.* New York, 1943.

BUTTERFIELD, JOHN

Expressman, businessman, and financier John Butterfield (1801–1869) was born on a farm at Berne, near Albany, New York. More interested in horses and transportation than in farming, at the age of nineteen he obtained his first job as a stagecoach driver in Albany and later in Utica. He soon bought a small stable and went into the livery business, which he expanded to include a boarding house after his marriage to Melinda

John Butterfield. *Courtesy The Bettmann Archive.*

Harriet Baker in 1822. As his business interests prospered, Butterfield obtained a controlling interest in most of the stage lines carrying mail and passengers in northern and western New York. He invested in packet boats on the Erie Canal, steamers on Lake Ontario, and post roads. In 1849, he formed the express company of Butterfield, Wasson and Company and, the following year, merged his interests with Wells and Company and Livingston, Fargo and Company to form the American Express Company. At the same time, he was interested in telegraphic communication, and with HENRY WELLS and Crawford Livingston, he established the New York, Albany and Buffalo Telegraph Company. He took great pride in his home town of Utica and invested his growing fortune in real estate there. In 1856, he was elected mayor of Utica as a Republican.

The greatest achievement of Butterfield's career was his role in founding and organizing the OVERLAND MAIL COMPANY to undertake a federal-government contract in 1857 to deliver the mails on a transcontinental route twenty-eight hundred miles long from St. Louis through Texas and the Southwest to San Francisco. A highly competitive man of great energy and determination, he planned to establish a daily, rather than a semiweekly, mail service and proposed to establish a pony-express service to compete with that on the central route. His partners were unwilling to expand further, and Butterfield was relieved from the presidency of the Overland Mail Company in 1860.

Already past the customary age of retirement, Butterfield remained in seclusion for more than two years. He then engaged in business activities in New York City until October 1867 when he suffered a stroke. He died at his home in Utica two years later.

—*W. Turrentine Jackson*

See also: Pony Express; Stagecoaches; Telegraph

SUGGESTED READING:
Conkling, Roscoe P., and Margaret B. Conkling. *The Butterfield Overland Mail, 1857–1869*. Glendale, Calif., 1947.
Jackson, W. Turrentine. "A New Look at Wells Fargo, Stagecoaches, and the Pony Express." *California Historical Society Quarterly* 45 (1966): 291–324.

BYERS, WILLIAM NEWTON

Editor and publisher William Newton Byers (1831–1903) was born in Madison County, Ohio. He moved to Iowa with his parents in 1850. He worked as a surveyor in Iowa and in the Pacific Northwest before settling in Nebraska, where he helped plat Omaha and was elected to the first territorial assembly in 1854. Hearing reports of gold discoveries in 1858, Byers set out for the Pikes Peak region in the spring of 1859. There on April 23, he and several associates issued the first newspaper, the *Rocky Mountain News,* in Auraria, which merged with nearby Denver City in 1860.

Byers continued as editor and publisher until 1878, and both during and after his tenure, he tirelessly promoted the development of Colorado and Denver. Certain that agriculture was as important economically as mining, he spearheaded the founding of the Colorado Agricultural Society in 1863. He headed the territorial Board of Immigration and was general manager for Colorado for the National Land Company, which sold railroad lands to the colonists who founded Greeley in 1870 and Longmont in 1871. In the mountains, Byers acquired and surveyed the town site of Hot Sulphur Springs, which he promoted as a fashionable spa and resort.

In addition, Byers helped organize the Denver Pacific and other railroads, the Denver Tramway Company, and the telegraph firm that built a line from Denver into New Mexico. He was president of the Denver Chamber of Commerce, the Colorado State Forestry Association, The Society of Colorado Pioneers, and the State Historical and Natural History Society. He

William Newton Byers and his wife, Elizabeth. *Courtesy Denver Public Library, Western History Department.*

also served two terms as Denver postmaster (from 1864 to 1866 and from 1879 to 1883).

As a Republican, Byers participated in statehood movements in 1859 and 1864 that preceded Colorado's admission into the Union in 1876. His political career ended, however, after a romantic entanglement with milliner Hattie Sancomb, who, in 1876, fired her pistol at him in full view of his wife Elizabeth (she missed).

Today, Byers's name in Colorado is perpetuated by the town of Byers and by Byers Peak, which the pioneer editor climbed in 1901. More than thirty years earlier, in 1868, Byers and a party that included JOHN WESLEY POWELL made the first recorded ascent of 14,255-foot Longs Peak in present-day Rocky Mountain National Park. In Denver, Byers's *Rocky Mountain News* is still published. His stained-glass portrait is one of sixteen in the Hall of Fame in the Colorado State Capitol.

—*Maxine Benson*

SUGGESTED READING:
Perkin, Robert L. *The First Hundred Years: An Informal History of Denver and the* Rocky Mountain News. Garden City, N.Y., 1959.

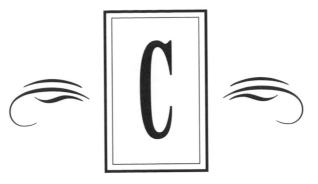

CABAREAUX, SISTER MARY CATHERINE

A Catholic nun who worked with Native Americans of the West, Mary Teresa Cabareaux (1813–1903) was born in Nismes, Belgium. In 1832, she entered the Sisters of Notre Dame de Namur (SSND) and received the name Sister Mary Catherine. She and six other SSNDs went to Oregon in 1843 to work with the Chinook Indians. During the 1850s and 1860s, she founded schools in San Jose and San Francisco and was extremely active in establishing the Sisters of Notre Dame in California.

Cabareaux wrote a memoir detailing the considerable hardships of her early work at the Oregon mission. The memoir provides compelling evidence of the extreme privation and backbreaking labor that Catholic sisters shared with other women in the West. She learned both English and Chinook while teaching Native American children. The sisters were dependent on their own resources, and they grew and harvested most of their food and kept cows and chickens. They took in destitute Native American children as boarders. A series of disasters—including a fire and an epidemic that killed eleven children—led to the sisters' decision to close the mission and direct their efforts to California.

—*Martha Smith, C.S.J.*

SEE ALSO: Catholics; Missions: Nineteenth-Century Missions to the Indians

SUGGESTED READING:
Cabareaux, Sister Mary Catherine. "Memoirs." Archives of Sisters of Notre Dame de Namur, Belmont, California.
Luchetti, Cathy, and Carol Olwell. *Women of the West.* St. George, Utah, 1982.

CABEZA DE BACA, FABIOLA

Fabiola Cabeza de Baca (1894–1991), a Hispanic New Mexican writer, was born in La Liendre, New Mexico, and from the age of five, when her mother died, she lived on her grandparents' hacienda. She attended Loretto Academy in Las Cruces and graduated from New Mexico Normal School with a teaching certificate in 1912. She taught school in El Rito and Santa Rosa for twelve years. She obtained a B.A. in pedagogy from New Mexico Highlands University in 1921 and a B.S. in domestic sciences from New Mexico State University in 1929. The first Hispanic woman hired by the New Mexico Agricultural Extension Service, she worked with rural women for more than thirty years. In 1929, she married Carlos Gilbert. The marriage ended in divorce, and soon afterwards, she lost her left leg in an automobile accident.

In 1950, Cabeza de Baca was "loaned" by the extension service to the United Nations to establish a home-economics program in Mexico. She retired in 1959 and, in her later years, wrote for the *Santa Fe Scene* and *New Mexico Magazine.*

Her writing career began with the publication *Los Alimentos y su Preparacion* (1933), a pamphlet on nutrition for the New Mexico Agricultural Extension Service. Other works include *Historic Cookery* (1939), a compilation of Hispanic New Mexican food recipes, and *The Good Life* (1954), a series of vignettes combining folklore and foods. *We Fed Them Cactus* (1954), her best-known work, combined her own memoir with the first definitive description of Indo-Hispanic cooking.

—*Merrihelen Ponce*

SUGGESTED READING:
Cabeza de Baca, Fabiola. *We Fed Them Cactus.* Albuquerque, N. Mex., 1954.

Jensen, Joan M. "'I've Worked, I'm not Afraid to Work': Farm Women in New Mexico." In *New Mexico Women: Intercultural Perspectives.* Edited by Joan M. Jensen and Darlis A. Miller. Albuquerque, N. Mex., 1986.

CABEZA DE VACA, ÁLVAR NÚÑEZ

Álvar Núñez Cabeza de Vaca (ca. 1490–1557) received the royal appointment of second in command of the expedition of PÁNFILO DE NARVÁEZ to Florida in 1527. The disastrous foray ended in a shipwreck on the Texas coast. Within three or four years, all but four of the eight survivors of the wreck had died.

The four men—Cabeza de Vaca, Dorantes, Castillo, and Esteban (a black slave)—spent seven and a half years wandering across the American Southwest. Cabeza de Vaca first traveled as a trader, penetrating the mainland of present-day eastern Texas as far north as the Red River. He then joined the other three and began a long odyssey across Texas, southern New Mexico, Arizona, and south into Mexico. They were finally rescued in 1536 in the province of Sinaloa.

Six years after his rescue, Cabeza de Vaca published *La Relación,* later published as *Los Naufragios.* This work, along with an "Official Report" written by the three Spaniards upon their arrival in Mexico City, greatly enhanced knowledge of the American Southwest. The publications inspired the expeditions of Hernando de Soto and FRANCISCO VÁSQUEZ DE CORONADO and remain a source of information about the native tribes of the Gulf Coast.

—*Richard A. Bartlett*

SEE ALSO: Exploration: Spanish Expeditions

SUGGESTED READING:
Covey, Cyclone, ed. *Cabeza de Vaca's Adventures in the Unknown Interior of America.* Albuquerque, N. Mex., 1961.

CABLE ACT OF 1922

The Cable Act, passed in 1922, was intended to make the citizenship status of wives independent of their husbands. Supported by a coalition of women's groups, the law expressed widespread concern for American women who had automatically lost their U.S. citizenship when they married noncitizen men. Although the act allowed most American-born women to retain their citizenship after marriage, it created a number of new problems. In severing citizenship from marital status, the Cable Act made it more difficult for foreign-born wives of U.S. citizens to become citizens themselves, and it meant that American women who married men "ineligible for citizenship" (a legal code phrase for the Chinese) would lose their U.S. citizenship for the duration of the marriage.

—*Peggy Pascoe*

SEE ALSO: Immigration Law

CABRILLO, JUAN RODRÍGUEZ

Spanish conquistador Juan Rodríguez Cabrillo (?–1543) earned his niche in history by leading one of the first voyages of exploration up the coast of Alta California.

The background of Cabrillo's voyage is steeped in the politics of Spanish exploration. Álvar Núñez Cabeza de Vaca's narrative had spurred the explorations of Hernando de Soto in the American Southeast and FRANCISCO VÁSQUEZ DE CORONADO in the Southwest, but what lay up the West Coast of North America remained a mystery. The Spanish believed the North American continent curved northwestward and nearly touched the Asian mainland. Antonio de Mendoza, the viceroy of Mexico, and Pedro de Alvarado, the conqueror of Guatemala, envisioned two explorations. One, led by López de Villalobos, was to sail west to the Moluccas Islands. The other, led by Cabrillo, was to sail up the coast of Mar del Sur (South Sea, as the Spanish called the Pacific) and, veering westward along the coast, advance eventually to the Far East, taking possession of the lands observed along the way.

Sailing in a vessel he owned, stocked, and manned, Cabrillo set sail from the Mexican port of Navidad on June 27, 1542. His flotilla consisted of three vessels: his own *San Salvador* (also called the *Juan Rodríguez*). *La Victoria,* and a launch probably called the *San Miguel.* The expedition lasted nine months.

Although the expedition was beset with adverse weather, Cabrillo and his chief pilot, Bartolomé Ferrer, probably reached the vicinity of the Russian River, about forty miles north of San Francisco Bay, which they missed. The expedition then turned south to winter at Santa Catalina Island. There Cabrillo died. Ferrer then headed north again, this time advancing to the vicinity of the present-day border between California and Oregon. Beset by storms, the expedition turned back and arrived in Navidad on April 14, 1543.

To their credit, the members of the Cabrillo expedition explored San Diego Bay, most of the islands lying close to the California coast, Santa Monica Bay, and Monterey Bay. Although complete records of the expedition are missing, it is clear that its achievements were considerable—exploring a broken coastline in tiny ships facing variable winds, fog, and treacherous currents.

In later years, Spain promoted voyages of the Manila galleons, ships sailing from West Mexican ports for the riches obtainable in the Philippine Islands. Although the trip west took but a month, the return voyage lasted three months; crews were decimated by scurvy. Then the Spanish conceived the idea of sailing in a great circle north and east and touching the California coast where crews took on fresh water and fruits and vegetables, obtained from the Indians. Mendoza's and Alvarado's ideas about trade across the Pacific had not been entirely wrong.

—*Richard A. Bartlett*

SEE ALSO: Exploration: Spanish Expeditions

SUGGESTED READING:
Kelsey, Harry. *Juan Rodríguez Cabrillo*. San Marino, Calif., 1986.
Wagner, Henry Raup. *Juan Rodríguez Cabrillo, Discoverer of the Coast of California*. San Francisco, 1941.

CACTUS

The cactus, like the tumbleweed, is known worldwide as a natural icon of the American West. However, unlike the tumbleweed, which is an exotic plant that was introduced to the West from Eurasia in the nineteenth century, cacti are indigenous to the Americas. Evolving in South America twenty thousand years ago, the cactus family has spread across mainland North America all the way to the Arctic Circle. Although members of the genus *Euphorbia*, particularly some of its species in Africa, superficially resemble cacti, true cacti occur naturally nowhere in the world except the Americas.

Along with members of the lily family—yuccas, sotols, and the agaves (known as century plants)—cacti are succulents, or water-storing plants, an adaptation to life in arid and semiarid environments. Most cactus species have thick, waxy outer skins and fleshy green stems, pads, and arms that perform the function of leaves. Nearly everything about cactus design is intended to reduce water loss. Cacti are particularly notable for a variety of prickly hairs and spines, which not only serve as a deterrent to predators but also act as shade from the sun, gutters for rainfall, and, in some species called "chollas," even provide a means of propagation. With the help of insects, most cacti propagate

sexually, however. When conditions are right (intense heat following spring rains), Western deserts like the Sonoran and Chihuahuan are briefly spangled with the colors of flowering cactus. Cactus fruits, known as tunas in some species, follow later in the year. They are not poisonous and are often sweet and edible. Western Indian tribes relied on cactus fruit as a major source of food.

Like all other forms of life, cacti as a family have responded variously to human history. The Sonoran Desert's characteristic species is the impressive saguaro, a cactus that has not fared well with human sprawl. On the other hand, species of the genus *Opuntia,* the prickly pears and chollas, have spread rapidly with overgrazing by domestic cattle and sheep.

—*Dan Flores*

SUGGESTED READING:
Weniger, Del. *Cacti of Texas and Neighboring States.* Austin, Tex., 1984.

CAHIULLA INDIANS

SEE: Native American Peoples: Peoples of California

"CALAMITY JANE" (BURK, MARTHA CANNARY)

Celebrated Western heroine Calamity Jane (1852?– 1903) was born Martha Cannary probably on a farm near Princeton, Missouri. At an early age, she demonstrated skill at riding and shooting. In 1865, her family moved to the gold-mining town of Virginia City, Montana. She recalled that, on the trip, she spent her time hunting "with the men when there was excitement and adventures to be had." Her father died in 1866, and her mother a year later.

Forced to rely on her own resources, the teen-ager survived by cultivating talents that Western society considered more appropriate to men than to women. In a cultural milieu that often identified mobility as masculine and settlement as feminine, Martha Cannary was a woman out of place. She worked the roads and trails of Montana, Wyoming, and the Dakotas as a stage driver, bullwhacker, tracker, hunter, and scout and traveled with railroad crews, hunting expeditions, and, on at least one occasion, the U.S. Cavalry. Given the physical demands of her way of life, it is not surprising that in numerous photographs she is dressed in men's clothing rather than in the constricting female fashions of

"Calamity Jane," also known as Martha Cannary Burk. *Courtesy National Cowboy Hall of Fame and Western Heritage Center.*

the day. Between stints on the road, she reportedly worked as a prostitute and gained the admiration of the citizens of Deadwood, South Dakota, for her tireless work nursing the sick during a smallpox epidemic. Unlike many other such working women, however, she insisted loudly that she could drink, cuss, and work as the equal of any man.

The origin of her nickname is unclear, but by 1876, one of General GEORGE CROOK's soldiers reported in his diary that "Calamity Jane is hear going up with the troops." By 1877, Erastus Beadle regularly featured "Deadwood Dick," the Robin Hood of the Dakotas, and his dashing female partner "Calamity Jane" in his dime novels. Cannary herself fostered much of the legend surrounding her life and stated in an 1896 autobiography that she had ridden with the PONY EXPRESS, seen combat in the Indian Wars, and prospected for gold. She toured the East briefly with a Wild West show. She also claimed an 1885 marriage to Clinton Burk and a love affair with JAMES BUTLER ("WILD BILL") HICKOK. The latter contention was repeated in 1941 by a woman claiming to be Calamity Jane and Hickok's daughter. She died in Deadwood and is buried next to Hickok.

—*Virginia Scharff*

SUGGESTED READING:
Faber, Doris. *Calamity Jane: Her Life and Legend*. Boston, 1992.
Mueller, Ellen C., Jean R. James, and Bob Kirkpatrick, eds. *Calamity Jane*. Amarillo, Tex., 1981.

CALDWELL, KANSAS

SEE: Cattle Towns

CALHOUN, JOHN CALDWELL

John Caldwell Calhoun (1782–1850), leading proponent of the doctrine of states' rights, apologist for slavery, and champion of the Southern cause, engineered the annexation of Texas (as secretary of state under President JOHN TYLER) and opposed the COMPROMISE OF 1850.

Born near Abbeville, South Carolina, Calhoun was the son of a slave-holding farmer. He was educated at Moses Waddell's Log College in Georgia and at Yale University and then studied law with Tapping Reeve at Litchfield, Connecticut. After gaining admission to the South Carolina bar in 1807, Calhoun served in the state legislature from 1809 to 1811 and was elected to the U.S. Congress in 1811. He was prominent among congressional War Hawks, who advocated war with England in 1812. President James Monroe appointed Calhoun secretary of war in 1817. He became an eloquent advocate of the AMERICAN SYSTEM, a policy calling for the vigorous exercise of federal power to nurture American industry and commerce by passing a protective tariff, establishing a federally chartered Bank of the United States, and providing federal funds for a system of roads, canals, and ports.

Calhoun had presidential ambitions. He hoped to succeed Monroe in 1824 but bowed to ANDREW JACKSON when Pennsylvania threw its support to the candidate from Tennessee. Instead, Calhoun secured the endorsement of Southern and Western Jacksonians—as well as Northeastern followers of John Quincy Adams—in a bid for the vice-presidency. Calhoun was elected in 1824 and served with President Adams.

As vice-president, Calhoun took his first steps toward states' rights, although he was not yet an advocate of the doctrine, which was identified with a body of conservative Southern politicians. He did recognize that the interests of the slave-holding, cotton-cultivating South would not be served by a strong federal government aggressively fostering commerce and industry.

Accordingly, Calhoun repudiated the American System he had helped create and, over this issue, broke with the Adams administration. During the next four years, Calhoun increasingly became an advocate of states' rights. In 1828, after Congress passed the protective tariff reviled in the South as the "tariff of abominations," Calhoun secretly authored the "South Carolina Exposition and Protest," holding that a state had the power of "nullification" of any federal law it deemed unconstitutional.

Partly in the hope that Andrew Jackson would support states' rights, Calhoun ran for the vice-presidency in 1828 and was elected with Jackson. Jackson steadfastly refused to endorse Calhoun's position, and in 1832, Jackson forced a showdown with South Carolina during the nullification crisis, in which South Carolina sought to exercise what it held as its right to nullify another protective tariff. Calhoun resigned from the vice-presidency.

Elected senator from South Carolina, Calhoun served from 1842 to 1843 and from 1845 until his death in 1850. In the Senate, he was an intractable and powerful spokesman-apologist for slavery and for Southern interests. He left the Senate briefly during 1844 and 1845 to serve as secretary of state under President John Tyler. In this position, he engineered the annexation of Texas, which had long been stalled over the issue of slavery in the republic.

After returning to the Senate, Calhoun devoted the rest of his career to promoting the right of Americans to expand slavery into federal territories, and he was eloquently vocal in predicting civil war if this right were "trampled upon." Aged and ailing, he bitterly opposed the Compromise of 1850—which staved off civil war for a decade—because he held that it failed to recognize Americans' right to own slaves in the territories.

—*Alan Axelrod*

SEE ALSO: National Expansion: Slavery and National Expansion

SUGGESTED READING:
Ames, Herman. *John C. Calhoun and the Secession Movement of 1850*. North Stratford, Conn., 1977.
Brown, Warren. *John C. Calhoun*. New York, 1993.
Calhoun, John C. *The Papers of John C. Calhoun*. 15 vols. Edited by Robert L. Meriwether and C. N. Wilson. Columbia, S.C., 1959–1983.
Coit, Margaret L. *John C. Calhoun*. Englewood Cliffs, N.J., 1950. Reprint. Atlanta, Ga., 1977.
Niven, John. *John C. Calhoun and the Price of Union*. Boston, 1988.
Peterson, Merrill D. *The Great Triumvirate: Webster, Clay, and Calhoun*. New York, 1988.
Van Holst, Herman E., and Clyde N. Wilson. *John C. Calhoun*. American Statesmen Series. New York, 1980.

CALIFORNIA

California, the "Golden State," lies along the Pacific Ocean north of Mexico, west of Arizona and Nevada, and south of Oregon. The most populous state in the nation, California—with 158,706 square miles—is larger than all the other states except Alaska and Texas. The most urban of states with 91 percent of its population living in metropolitan areas, California also boasts the highest personal income per capita. In 1990 three-fourths of California's 29,760,021 people lived near the coast, packed into greater Los Angeles, San Francisco, and San Diego. The state capital Sacramento—whose first burst of growth came during the gold rush—was home to more than one million people and several companies related to the defense and space industries.

California's landscape is wondrously varied. The highest peak south of Alaska, Mount Whitney at 14,494 feet, rises a mere sixty miles from the lowest point in the Western Hemisphere—DEATH VALLEY at 282 feet below sea level. At a weather station called Bagdad in the MOJAVE DESERT two years have elapsed without a drop of rain, while Honeydew, along the northern coast, once recorded 190 inches in a single year. Thick forests, bleached deserts, snow-capped mountains, and fecund valleys house a people—often under threat from earthquakes and a cycle of wind, fire, floods, and mud slides—whose resilient social, economic, and political lives have made the state something of a legal and historical laboratory for the rest of the country.

Predominantly white, California's population also includes a pronounced mixture of ethnic groups. Of all fifty states, it has the largest number of Spanish-speaking, Native American, Chinese, Filipino, Japanese, Korean, and Vietnamese inhabitants and the second largest number of AFRICAN AMERICANS and EAST INDIANS. More than one-third of the nation's Mexican Americans live in California. Although the state's early Spanish heritage remains evident in its architecture and place names, the Spanish surnames of many of its people reflect a twentieth-century immigration from Mexico, beginning with the Mexican Revolution in 1910. By 1987, hundreds of thousands of Mexicans had entered the state illegally, and when the federal government offered amnesty in 1988, half of the 1.7 million Hispanics who received temporary-resident status under the new laws were found in California.

The first settlers who journeyed from the United States to Spanish and Mexican California were Midwestern Anglo-Saxon farmers, but the 1849 gold rush lured a more cosmopolitan crowd, most of them males in their twenties, who made up more than half the

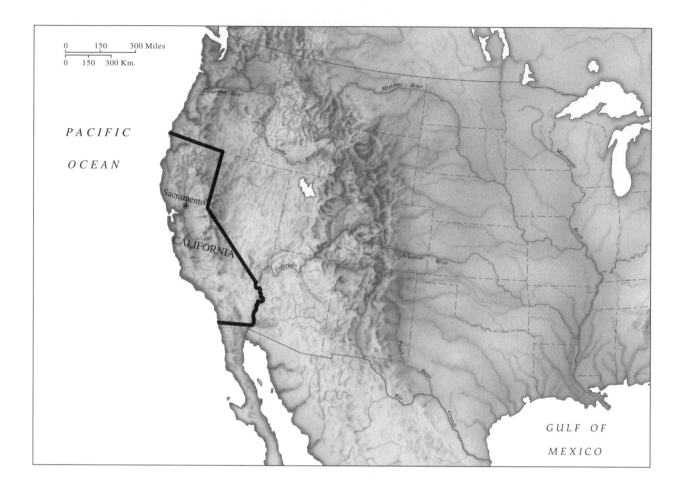

population in 1850. The gold rush also attracted immigrants from China, and by 1852, one in ten Californians was Chinese, usually performing menial labor. By the twentieth century, SAN FRANCISCO's Chinatown had become—and would remain—the country's largest Chinese settlement. Irish workers followed the railroad boom to California in the 1860s, and the majority settled along with French and Italian immigrants in San Francisco. Los Angeles's early spurts of growth in the late nineteenth century attracted Mexicans and Russians but even more Anglo-Saxons from the Midwest. The Japanese, encouraged to immigrate after the Chinese Exclusion Act of 1882, also settled in southern California, many of them taking up farming. By 1920, LOS ANGELES had become the center of the nation's Japanese community, and the Japanese, who made up 2 percent of California's population, controlled ten percent of its farm land.

Around 1940, African Americans for the first time began to arrive in large numbers in California mostly from the South; many of them settled in Los Angeles and OAKLAND. Metropolitan San Francisco's black population, for example, rose from 5,000 in 1940 to more than 86,000 in 1980 and Los Angeles's from

64,000 to more than 900,000 during the same period. Also around mid-century, California's Native American population, which had declined drastically during the days of the Spanish missions, again began to increase to around the current number of 200,000, some 6 percent of whom continue to live on reservations. During the 1970s and 1980s, Asian immigration also surged again, with Filipinos, Vietnamese, and South Koreans numbered among the newcomers. By 1987, Asians made up 6 percent of California's population.

They came for the climate, the freedom, the jobs, the "life style," a dream of easy living in beautiful surroundings frequently promoted by real-estate hucksters, often glamorized by the Hollywood MOTION-PICTURE INDUSTRY, and typically supported by government subsidies. Much of the twentieth-century growth in particular was sparked by workers who streamed into defense industries during World War II and who stayed behind when the war was over to be joined by hundreds of thousands of others who had first visited the state on tours of duty as U.S. military personnel. Seventy-five percent of the population crowded into the quarter of the state that lies below the Tehachapi Mountains just north of Los Angeles, mostly along the coast but also in artificial paradises, which once were desert. Sprawling suburbs, expansive highways, and speeding automobiles came to characterize one of the most "engineered" societies in history, what Donald Worster has called a "hydraulic civilization," one that seeks to support massive urban growth in an essentially waterless land.

Natural California

Scholars debate the origin of the state's name, but many of them support the notion that it may have derived from a Spanish novel written around 1500 by García Ordóñez de Montalvo, which described an island that was called California and was inhabited by Amazons and rich in gold—"on the right hand of the Indies" and "very near to terrestrial paradise." Probably first applied to Baja (Lower) California, which the early Spanish explorers mistook for an island, the name California indeed came to signify for many an earthly paradise, remarkable not the least for its natural splendor.

Northern California's rugged, mountainous coastline stretches north from present-day San Francisco. South along the coast, rolling fogs engulf Big Sur's cliffs, some rising eight hundred feet above ocean breakers. Creeks and rivers flow down the coastal mountains, which extend inland for thirty or forty miles. Just inland lie the mountains' damp, dark forests, including those of the majestic fifteen- to thirty-feet-wide RED-WOODS that soar two hundred to three hundred feet high and live from four hundred to four thousand years. Once, conservationists estimate, the redwoods covered 1.5 million acres along the north coast. Today, homes of the rich perch on Big Sur's bluffs, Humboldt County's chief cash crop is marijuana, Eureka's superb natural harbor opens out from the world's largest redwood mills, and most of the giant trees have been cut except for those on 109,000 acres protected in state and national parks, including Redwood National Park.

Ranging south from Mount Lassen for some 430 miles to the fringes of Los Angeles are the Sierra Nevada. Fifty to eighty miles wide, with ten peaks higher than 14,000 feet, the 27,000 square miles of the Sierra form a granite block separating California from the rest of the continent. On the east, the Sierra's sheer wall drops ten thousand feet in ten miles around Owens Lake onto a sparse desert. To the west, the range slopes by gradual foothills into the Central Valley. Few passes exist through the Sierra Nevada, and those that do are high, some above 9,000 feet. Hundreds of lakes lie among the mountains; the largest is the eleventh deepest lake in the world, Lake Tahoe, 193 miles square, 1,200 feet deep at the shoreline, 400 feet deeper in the middle. Straddling the border between California and

Nevada, Lake Tahoe is a battlefield between the environmentalists on the west and the gamblers on the east, the former trying to keep "their" side fairly pure, the later allowing casinos and industries to pollute the water. The Sierra also contain Mount Whitney and three national parks: Kings Canyon, Sequoia, and Yosemite, the latter thought by many to be the most beautiful valley in North America. Rising from the purple foothills where Californians first discovered gold through valleys carved by Pleistocene ice melting into the Merced and Tuolumne rivers, Yosemite is home to great sequoia groves (where there are trees that began growing fifteen hundred years before the birth of Christ), to alpine meadows, to vast stretches of pine, to rushing streams, and to waterfalls dropping dramatically from granite domes. While much of the region remains accessible only by foot or on horseback, the first road was built into Yosemite in 1920; sixty-one years later 2.6 million tourists motored into the valley in 935,821 cars. Today, a tram runs up to Mariposa Grove, a shuttle bus system serves the campers and travelers, and plans exist—unimplemented—to eliminate automobile traffic altogether.

California's Central Valley—rugged and sparsely populated in the north, heavily timbered and wet along the coast, dry and barren in the east—runs 450 miles through the middle of the state. Lying between the coastal ranges to the west and the Sierra Nevada on the east, the valley is a huge trough, one big enough to hold the Appalachian mountain range. The Central Valley is California's agricultural heartland, sealed off on the northeast by the Cascades, on the northwest by the Klamath Mountains, and on the south by the Tehachapi Mountains (the traditional dividing line between northern California and what Californians call the "Southland.") Covering a sixth of California's land area, the Central Valley actually consists of two river valleys—the San Joaquin and the Sacramento—and its only natural access to the outside world is the delta through which those rivers drain into San Francisco Bay. Both the Sacramento and San Joaquin river valleys depend on water flowing down the Sierra Nevada through one of the more elaborate IRRIGATION systems ever built, a labyrinth of dams, pumping stations, and canals financed by the federal government through the CENTRAL VALLEY PROJECT, which transfers water from the upper reaches of the Sacramento to the low, dry stretches of the San Joaquin Valley. There the combination of plentiful water and high natural temperatures produce the longest growing season in America: nine, sometimes ten, months per year.

Much of California is a desert. Covering nearly a quarter of California's entire land surface, the harsh California deserts of treeless mountains, baked flat lands, and expansive rock and sand have, as many have remarked, a beauty all their own. High desert dominates the state's northeast corner, a jumbled land of barren plains, bleak mountains, and blackish lava, sparsely populated, sustaining little life and a bit of open-range ranching. California's east central region, butting up against the walls of the Sierra Nevada, consists of trans-Sierra desert ranging from 2,000 feet to 7,400 feet above sea level, part of a large, multistate Great Basin. Its largest towns lie in the Owens Valley, once a fertile farmland before Los Angeles diverted (Owens Valley residents used the word *stole)* its ground water through a gigantic series of conduits built between 1908 and 1913. To the southeast sits the Mojave Desert, where temperatures compare with those in Africa's Sahara. Covering 25,000 square miles, the Mojave is bigger than any number of Eastern states put together and makes an ideal testing site for aviation and for ordnance; Edwards Air Force Base, the landing site of the space shuttle, lies in the Mojave, whose sparse population lives in small towns and military barracks on its southwestern edge. The otherworldly Death Valley is a massive 140-mile ditch in the Mojave where ground temperatures in July 1958 reached 190° F; Death Valley attracts some 650,000 visitors a year. Farther south, the lower Colorado Desert begins in the Coachella Valley, where desert Palm Springs has spawned a string of resorts. The Colorado wasteland descends to the Imperial Valley, the pride of California's hydraulic civilization just north of the Mexican border. Known for its winter crops, the Imperial Valley—4,000 miles square—sits below sea level,

fed by water from the COLORADO RIVER. The valley's siphoning of the river, which began in 1901, caused the Colorado to break out of its channel between 1905 and 1907 and form the 300-square-mile Salton Sea, today an immense, salt-filled, shallow lake with no natural outlet.

Most of coastal California is sunny and balmy; the average mean temperature in both summer and winter falls quite close to the annual mean temperature. Although the climate grows less remarkably pleasant inland, everywhere but in the mountains California's winters are mild, and its summer heat is made more agreeable by its dry air, which quickly absorbs moisture. Unlike Baja California to the south and Oregon to the north, California experiences two seasons, one dry, one wet. Fourteen inches of rain fall on an average each year in Los Angeles (where the average annual temperature is 65° F), twenty-one inches in San Francisco (at 57° F).

The deserts, of course, are dry and hellishly hot, and the mountain tops of the Sierra are wet and as cold as the Arctic, but in general it was California's truly salubrious climate that first led Los Angeles boosters such as WILLIAM MULHOLLAND to promote the city nationwide as a haven for carefree living under the sun in the early 1900s. Those who heeded the call came to realize there was a price to pay for the perfect weather: over the low hills near the ocean grows chaparral, a squat, parched brush, which the slightest spark can set ablaze. The conflagrations begin in the long dry summers when ocean winds change and the crackling, powerful Santa Anas blow in from the desert; the fires rage along the chaparral and into the pine forests on inland hills. When torrential winter rains later pound the hills denuded by fire, huge mud slides trundle down to the ocean and take with them everything—automobiles, telephone poles, houses—in their path.

Not only the climate, but the geography of California holds a cruel joke: paradise exists on a fault. The longest and most exposed crack anywhere in the earth's crust, the SAN ANDREAS FAULT runs, for all practical purposes, the entire length of the state. For sixty-five million years, it has been in motion, its two sides slipping a couple of inches a year, its abutting edges—near San Francisco to the north, Los Angeles to the south—frozen together, building up tremendous pressure. Dozens of severe earthquakes have hit California since the Spanish arrived in the sixteenth century. In 1857, a quake in the Tehachapis split the earth by a thirty-foot jump in the San Andreas' western edge. The SAN FRANCISCO EARTHQUAKE OF 1906, and the fires that came in its wake, all but destroyed the city and killed nearly seven hundred people. A quake of similar force struck the area in 1989; while the damage was mas-

The mining town of Placerville, California, as it appeared in the early 1850s. *Courtesy Wells Fargo Bank.*

sive and costly, the quake did not level the town but did remind Californians of the potential for such destruction, as did the devastating Los Angeles quake along the San Gabriel fault (part of the San Andreas network) in 1992. As geologists watch carefully the Palmdale bulge, more than 150 miles long and at points ten inches high, and talk about the destructive potential of the "big one," a super earthquake they predict will be many times more powerful than any yet experienced, Californians live uneasily with the notion that their state may one day simply slide into the Pacific Ocean like some contemporary Atlantis.

Early settlement and statehood

The earliest inhabitants of California were Indians who most likely migrated from Asia fifteen thousand or so years ago. The peoples of California had even less centralized unity than other Native Americans in North America; instead, each group had its own territorial and political structures, perhaps because—with the Pacific Ocean on the west and the vast stretches of mountain and desert to the east—they were, in effect, isolated from the rest of native North America. For thousands of years, they lived in basically static societies at the level of what is popularly called the Stone Age, which means they mainly relied on California's natural bounty—its kind climate and rich supply of food. So bounteous were these resources in fact that, before the coming of the Spanish in the sixteenth century, nearly a third of all the Indians living north of Mexico could be found in California. Even after the Spanish navigator JUAN RODRÍGUEZ CABRILLO discovered and partially explored the coast of what came to be called Alta (Upper) California in 1542, thus proving that Baja California was not an island, the Europeans gave the region scant attention for more than three centuries because of its extreme geographic isolation.

In 1602 and 1603, Sebastián Vizcaíno chartered much of the California coast and proposed a port of call at the Bay of Monterey, which he had just named, but prevailing winds and sea currents made it so hard for ships to sail north from Mexico that his projected settlement was all but forgotten for another century and a half. In the middle of the eighteenth century José de Galvéz became New Spain's visitor-general. Galvéz used Russian encroachments on Alta California as an excuse to launch a "defensive" expedition that, he hoped, would make his New Spain appear not only to be flourishing, but also expanding. Sent by Galvéz, Franciscan friar JUNÍPERO SERRA established a Spanish mission in Alta California in 1769, the first in a long chain of twenty-one Franciscan missions from SAN DIEGO to Sonoma. While individual missions were fairly effective as agricultural centers based on the forced labor of the Indians, the padres considered their official goal—to create self-governing, Christian Indian communities—impractical and seldom seriously attempted to secularize the system; instead they managed so to debilitate their native "neophytes" through deliberate abuse and the unintentional introduction of exotic diseases that California's mission-based Indian population fell from hundreds of thousands to a mere thirty thousand in the course of half a century.

In 1821, Mexico won independence from Spain, and the mission system fell apart as California sank into political chaos under a series of weak, generally corrupt Mexican administrators. In 1833, Mexico confiscated mission properties and parceled them out to the government's political favorites. As California politics degenerated, according to Richard White, into maneuvers by coalitions of ranchero families to obtain the huge government land grants, enterprising traders out of Boston and Rocky Mountain trappers moved into Mexican California, married into elite Mexican families, and took up business based on the ranching economy created by the missions. By the time the first wagon train left Missouri for California in 1841, the American merchants had infiltrated the rancheros to such an extent that some among the Californio elite questioned the value of Mexican rule in favor of a closer relationship with the United States. The seven thousand or so Californios, however, grew resentful and suspicious as more and more Americans traveling the CALIFORNIA OVERLAND TRAILS arrived in the area and acted, in general, as if Alta California belonged to them.

In 1846, the Pacific Northwest became part of the United States, and settlers at Sonoma declared an independent California republic. In May, the United States went to war with Mexico, and in July the U.S. flag was hoisted at Monterey. A few minor skirmishes, including daring attacks by seasoned vaqueros on horseback, only delayed the ultimate Californio surrender to troops led by JOHN CHARLES FRÉMONT in January 1847. On February 2, 1848, Mexico turned California over to the United States under the Treaty of Guadalupe Hidalgo; a little more than a week earlier, James Wilson Marshall had discovered gold near JOHN AUGUST SUTTER's mill at Coloma on the south fork of the American River.

The CALIFORNIA GOLD RUSH made few of the Forty-niners rich, but it did ensure that the sparsely populated former Mexican frontier province filled up within a year with the sixty thousand souls required for an American territory to become one of the United States. In part because of the quick settlement and in part because the national squabble over how the West should be settled, as a free or slave-owning region, California never went through the formal territorial

"Bankers and Railroad Men's Party on Blue Grass Lawn at Calexico," about 1904. The California Development Company entertained potential investors in the hope that they would finance Imperial Valley development. *Courtesy National Archives.*

phase of development. Instead, it became embroiled in the sectional wrangle that resulted in the national COMPROMISE OF 1850, which made California the thirty-first state on September 9. The state constitution, submitted to Congress by California after bitter debate, rejected the Indian civil rights championed by Hugo Reid, on the one hand, and slavery on the other, chiefly because its framers—whose constituents were gold miners—feared slaves would be used to compete with white miners at the diggings. The question of slavery, however, was hardly settled by statehood. California Democrats split over the issue, with U.S. Senator WILLIAM GWIN leading the proslavery faction, which sought to divide California into two states and promoted a slave-holding Pacific Coast republic. The Free-Soilers, led by DAVID C. BRODERICK, held sway, however, and California sided with the North when the Civil War broke out.

Even before the Civil War, the last of the placer fields had played out, and big-capital mining concerns had moved to California and opened hard-rock and hydraulic mining operations. Inflated prices and bitterly disappointed young men made for a violent and disorderly society in San Francisco and led to the outbreak of VIGILANTISM. As white immigrants looked for someone to blame for their misfortunes, Indians, Mexicans, and the Chinese increasingly became scapegoats. Around the mines in the purple foothills of the western Sierra Nevada, Anglos hunted Indians for sport and drove Mexicans from the region with threats of indiscriminate murder. Both Mexicans and the Chinese were subjected to a steep foreign miners' tax. From statehood forward, the legacy of intolerance, however hard for Californians—and Americans—to admit,

would continue to color California history from the CHINESE EXCLUSION movement in the 1880s, to the 1913 Webb Alien Land Law aimed at preventing the Japanese from owning property, to the anti-Hispanic Zoot Suit riots by American sailors and the JAPANESE INTERNMENT of World War II, to the all-but-official police abuse of inner-city African Americans in the second half of the twentieth century and the subsequent riots in Watts and South Central Los Angeles, to the "backlash" immigration laws of the 1990s. Even the nascent labor movement born in the unsettled early days of statehood would—during the decade of depression and social turmoil that California author GERTRUDE ATHERTON called "the terrible [eighteen] seventies"—become only vaguely anticapitalist but explicitly anti-Chinese under labor leader DENIS KEARNEY.

Economic growth

Although today mining is of little consequence and the foundation of California's wealth lies in agriculture, in the days of early statehood, the reverse was true. The discovery of the COMSTOCK LODE's huge silver deposits in western Nevada in 1859 revived the flagging industry throughout the region and allowed San Francisco to flourish as a financial center, while agriculture was severely hampered by the long, expensive legal wranglings over Mexican land grants during which Anglos generally used the courts to dispossess the old Californio rancheros. Wheat fields in the Sacramento and San Joaquin valleys and vineyards in the coastal valleys of northern California had, however, become abundant by the time the CENTRAL PACIFIC RAILROAD completed its transcontinental line in 1869, and the decade following would witness the phenomenal growth of southern California's citrus industry.

A remarkable accomplishment made possible by huge federal loans and land grants, the transcontinental railroad would also secure the fortunes of four small-time Sacramento businessmen: AMASA LELAND STANFORD, COLLIS P. HUNTINGTON, MARK HOPKINS, and CHARLES CROCKER. The Big Four used the windfall profits reaped from their small initial investment in what became the SOUTHERN PACIFIC RAILROAD to gain control of California's river and steamboat transportation as well as its railways. Prospering from a nearly complete monopoly on transportation, they built huge mansions on San Francisco's Nob Hill and dominated not only the state's economy but also its government and its politics.

The biggest boom since the gold rush in both California's economy and population, however, came at the turn of the twentieth century with the discovery of oil and the birth of the motion-picture industry. Often called "California's other mineral," oil became the state's "black" gold after EDWARD LAURENCE DOHENY ran across rich deposits in Los Angeles between 1892 and 1895. New strikes were soon made in the San Joaquin Valley after 1900 and still larger strikes in the Los Angeles Basin during the 1920s: at Huntington Beach, at Santa Fe Springs south of Whittier, and at Signal Hill in Long Beach. Between 1900 and 1936, California led all states in petroleum production; in 1937 another vast deposit of oil was discovered at Wilmington. The timing was perfect: California's oil became available at precisely the point when—and in precisely the region where—automobile use was growing faster than anywhere else in the world. Greater Los Angeles, originally a string of whistle stops along an urban railway line, sprouted highways and suburbs and a budding new "car culture" of drive-ins and take-outs. By 1970, much of the West resembled sprawling Los Angeles, and California was producing one-sixth of the nation's oil.

The movies, too, attracted people to southern California. "Pioneering" film moguls, many of them Jewish, a number of them from New York, found southern California, with its cloud-free skies, mild climate, varied terrain, cheap real estate, good labor market, and fluid social structures, congenial to their temperaments and well suited to their needs. The first narrative film produced in California was the *Count of Monte Cristo,* begun in Chicago by William N. Selig in 1907, stalled by the onset of winter, and then finished in Los Angeles by Francis Boggs in 1908. Two years later, the Nestor Film Company set up shop in a nearby backwater suburb called Hollywood, and California's movie "colony" was born.

Hollywood's "independents" were all—in the eyes of the law—crooks, violating the camera patents held by Thomas Alva Edison's hated New York–based Motion Picture Patents Company, which its enemies called the "trust." The brash independents loved the Hollywood area because it was close to the Mexican border, across which they could escape when the trust's strong-arm men, process servers, and lawyers showed up to close down a production. San Francisco's far-sighted banker AMADEO PETER GIANNINI financed Hollywood film productions, and soon men such as William Fox and Carl Laemmle were not only making fortunes but challenging the trust's stranglehold on the industry. When the trust was dissolved under the SHERMAN ANTI-TRUST ACT in 1915, Hollywood became the center of a movie industry with a worldwide market, and southern California forever afterward would be associated with entertainment, sex scandals, and a freewheeling style of living and doing business.

The booming economy created by the oil industry and the dream factory also sparked a real-estate boom:

in 1920, Los Angeles surpassed San Francisco as the state's largest urban area. Statewide, California's fast-paced urban growth put a tremendous strain on its limited water supply. San Francisco turned for its water to the gorgeous Hetch Hetchy Valley in YOSEMITE NATIONAL PARK only to run up against the stubborn opposition of SIERRA CLUB founder JOHN MUIR, who led the bitter fight against the Hetch Hetchy dam from 1908 to 1913 and delayed its construction for years. When Los Angeles struck out imperially to build a huge aqueduct from the Owens River between 1908 and 1913, valley residents put up a fight and even dynamited the construction. But residents lost the OWENS VALLEY WAR, and Los Angeles drained the eastern Sierra community dry before turning its thirsty eyes to the Colorado River. Southern Californians built earthen dams that made the Imperial Valley bloom and the Colorado River jump its course in 1905. The state spent millions of dollars and employed Southern Pacific Railroad crews to return the rampaging Colorado to its normal course. Despite this and other problems, such as bursting dams, irrigation and RECLAMATION became the religion of California development. The state enthusiastically backed the great Central Valley Project, built by the BUREAU OF RECLAMATION, and begun in the 1930s with the construction of the massive HOOVER DAM. The only trouble was that the NEWLANDS RECLAMATION ACT OF 1902 limited the amount of land for which a single owner could purchase federal water for irrigation to 160 acres. Initially the U.S. Supreme Court upheld the constitutionality of the limit when California's big agribusinesses challenged it, so the state itself undertook its own vast projects.

An expanse of California wheat fields with ranch buildings and windmill in the background, about 1903. Photograph by C. Hart Merriam. *Courtesy National Archives.*

Champagne corking at the Buena Vista Vineyard in Sonoma, California, in the early 1870s. *Courtesy National Archives.*

The Great Depression of the 1930s at first struck California hard. Not only did the real-estate boom collapse, but hundreds of thousands of displaced Midwestern farmers—some of them "Okies"—poured into the state looking for work in a farming industry that was based on luxury crops such as oranges, the first items chopped from poor families' budgets. By 1934, 25 percent of those living in California were on the public dole. Soon, however, the coalition between Western business and federal funding that men such as Peter Giannini and HENRY J. KAISER had been putting together began to pay dividends, and in the long run, the depression was not as devastating in California as it was elsewhere in the country. The huge New Deal construction projects disproportionately benefited California, and by World War II, the federal government would be spending nearly a tenth of its $400 billion budget in California alone, the money going mainly to the burgeoning aircraft industry and for wartime shipbuilding. Such massive federal pay-outs not only revived California's economy but launched it on a period of sustained growth that lasted for much of the century.

By 1947, it was clear that California had reached an economic turning point. This was the year farm output in California first exceeded that of any other state. Eventually the oil began to run out, and the state had to import fuel and natural gas as well as water. Motion pictures, too, suffered a blow from television, which the industry was ill prepared to face, and studios lost much of their power, hawked their backlog of films to corporate raiders, and sold off their facilities to television networks. But California's big farmers never looked back.

Counseled by the agricultural wizards at the University of California at Davis, California came to lead America in the value of farm products (in the tens of billions of dollars) and produced most species of temperate and subtropical fruits, vegetables, and field crops—except tobacco—known to humankind. The state ranked second only to Florida in citrus and only to Texas in cotton and outstripped most other states in beef and dairy cattle. The state's great vineyards in the Napa, Sonoma, and Salinas valleys produced 90 percent of all wine made in the United States and gross annually in excess of five billion dollars. From the earliest days of SPANISH SETTLEMENT, California farms have been huge operations; in the twentieth century, they became highly mechanized operations belonging to absentee owners. They owed their impressive productivity to an army of MIGRANT WORKERS, but their powerful owners so consistently ignored even the basic needs of the migrants that labor strife became endemic.

By the 1960s, California had surpassed New York as the country's most populous state. Housing nearly a tenth of the people in the entire nation, California's annual production and income ranked sixth among the nations of the world, behind the United States, Russia, West Germany, Britain, and France, and slightly ahead of Japan by 1965. California's mid-century prosperity owed much to federal spending in aerospace, electronics, and "big science": California laboratories and factories produced the immensely expensive equipment demanded by the Defense Department and the National Aeronautics and Space Administration.

In the 1970s, California's powerful agricultural interests once again launched an attack on the federally funded Central Valley Project's acreage limitations, and thirteen years later, the U.S. Supreme Court finally caved in, ruling that the Imperial Valley was somehow exempted from the 1902 Newlands Act by a 1933 Interior Department decision. California's hydraulic civilization had triumphed, and both federal and state tax dollars fed its needs. Today the All-American Canal—a 200-foot-wide concrete-lined river carrying two billion gallons of water a day—links the Colorado River with the Imperial Valley, whose big owners tap irrigation water through feeder canals at a minuscule percentage of the true costs and soak up twice as much moisture each day as consumed by all 119 southern California cities serviced by the Colorado River Aqueduct, which moves water from the river near the Arizona border across southern California's desert and mountains to greater Los Angeles. In addition, the California State Water Project, one of the larger water-transfer systems in the world, is designed to deliver water daily from the Feather River in the north to communities as far south as the Mexican border.

Northern Californians protest that the export of water threatens growth in their own region and severely harms the environment, but most of California is a similarly engineered society. Profits from northern California's electronics and computer industries depend on the delicate balance of public funds and private enterprise just as the Southland does for cheap water. And, without question, the benefits of California's public-private economy have been immense. California's public schools, including the elaborate state-funded university system, have been the envy of the world; its museums, both publicly and privately funded institutions such as the Getty Museum, the Los Angeles County Museum of Art, and the OAKLAND MUSEUM OF CALIFORNIA, are internationally renowned for their collections, exhibits, and public programs; the state's social-service organizations and welfare system have long been considered among the most generous and humane in the country. Tourists by the millions visit California each year to marvel at the spectacle and the true beauty of much of California's public space, and perhaps there is no better metaphor for California's engineered wonderland than the highly sanitized and doggedly positive version of history and life offered them by the incredibly popular Disneyland, which opened its doors in Anaheim in 1955.

Yet, as with natural California, social California, too, is plagued by increasingly volatile fault lines. In the 1960s, long-abused farm workers—all low-income, many of them migrants crossing the Mexican border in harvest seasons—struck back under the leadership of Cesar Chávez against economic and social inequities. Chávez launched local strikes and a nationwide boycott of California produce that at last brought the powerful agribusinessmen briefly to the bargaining table before his United Farm Workers Union was undercut by employer-backed Teamster organizing drives. In the 1980s, California's middle class revolted, passing antitax legislation in a popular initiative called Proposition 13. As state public funds dried up and services Californians had long taken for granted were cut back, the federal government too began to retrench, closing military bases and defense establishments. By the 1990s, a white backlash developed that laid much of the blame for California's woes at the feet of the low-paid immigrant laborers. Calling the migrants illegal aliens, Californians threatened to cut off completely the social safety nets that had long underwritten its cheap labor pool. In the mid-1990s, Orange County—one of the country's richest areas per capita—announced that it was bankrupt, owing to poor investments by the county's chief financial officer. By century's end, not only did the long wave of prosperity that had sustained the state seem to be coming to a close, but the very social fabric of its engineered society was threatening to unravel.

Politics

After the Civil War, the California governor's office passed back and forth between Democrats and Republicans until the end of the century. Regardless of who was in office, the state was controlled by the Southern Pacific Railroad's political machine. Exercising more control over the government than the state exercised over the railroad, the company installed its chief counsel, William F. Herrin, as head of its "political department." For two decades, beginning in 1893, Herrin personally selected governors, congressmen, and judges with the help of local political bosses. Anthony Caminetti, a gadfly opposed to the railroads, sparked a statewide rebellion against the corrupt political system with his prosecution of San Francisco's political boss, ABRAHAM (ABE) RUEF, for graft in 1906. In 1907, the progressive leaders of the Los Angeles "good government" movement joined Caminetti in calling for the ouster of the cynical leader of the UNION LABOR PARTY. U.S. President THEODORE ROOSEVELT intervened directly by sending federal prosecutor FRANCIS JOSEPH HENEY and the head of the Bureau of Investigation (later the Federal Bureau of Investigation), WILLIAM J. BURNS, to help in the cleanup. But even here, Californians split north and south: the San Franciscans wanted to name their reform organization after Roosevelt; the more conservative Los Angelinos argued for Abraham Lincoln. In 1910, the Lincoln-Roosevelt Republican League nominated HIRAM WARREN JOHNSON for governor, and he carried the banner of PROGRESSIVISM to victory.

Johnson fulfilled his campaign promise to "kick the Southern Pacific Railroad out of politics" and bulldozed through the legislature a remarkable body of reforms in 1911, many of them based on the radical proposals of late-nineteenth-century POPULISM. Johnson's reforms regulated the railroads and public utilities, introduced a state-budget system, and initiated a workingman's compensation act. Johnson also proposed a number of measures aimed at removing control from party bosses and giving it directly to the people. By 1913, direct primaries, voter initiatives, public referendums, and recall votes gave Californians the power to pass and repeal laws independently of the legislature and immediate control over elected officials. Cross-filing, which allowed a candidate to run for the nomination of more than one party, was a direct attack on party machines. All of these measures weakened the power of political parties, but it was the Democrats who suffered most, since Progressives tended to be Republicans. Progressives held such sway in the early decades of the twentieth century that California became virtually a one-party state.

The Progressive reforms also, however, established a legacy of citizen participation in California's politics—a legacy that frequently has had surprising effects, as for example in the social-welfare schemes that arose during the Great Depression. One such scheme, End Poverty in California (EPIC), served as the platform on which Socialist author UPTON SINCLAIR ran for governor in 1934. Sinclair's candidacy was so radical—and viable enough—that it frightened many mainstream Democrats into supporting the conservative Republican candidate, Frank F. Merriam. In general, despite temporary Democratic gains late in the New Deal, Republicans dominated the statehouse until the end of the 1950s. Riding a national Democratic trend

in 1958, Edmund ("Pat") Brown took office in Sacramento as both U.S. Senate seats went to the Democrats and, for the first time in the twentieth century, the Democrats controlled both houses of the California legislature; they promptly repealed the hated crossfiling system that seemed to favor the Republicans.

U.S. Supreme Court Chief Justice Earl Warren was in many ways a typical product of California politics, a former welfare-bashing Republican governor who came to head the most liberal high court in the nation's history. Typical, too, of California politics were the Berkeley Free Speech movement (so-called because it "erupted" on the Berkeley campus of the University of California) and the anti-Vietnam War student radicalism of the 1960s, as was the reaction that put ultraconservative Ronald Reagan in the governor's mansion in 1967, a way station on Reagan's road to the presidency in 1981. Like Richard Nixon before him, Reagan was the product of conservative southern California, where local wags joked that directions to Orange County should read "head into the desert and turn right." Northern California, on the other hand, remained a bastion of liberal, even radical, political sentiment.

In the traditional struggle between northern and southern California, the Southland seemed increasingly destined to influence California's political fortunes. During the 1970s, 1980s, and even into the 1990s, shifting demographics resulted in the marked growth of new urban centers and smaller California cities. Although for a century San Francisco had served as a financial and corporate center, by the late 1980s, most of California's major corporations had relocated their headquarters to the more populous Southland. San Diego's metropolitan population topped 2 million and included among its number the highest proportion of college graduates of America's ten most populated cities; many of those graduates were conservative engineers who suddenly became radicalized in the 1990s when the aerospace industry laid them off. The rate of population growth in general, however, had been slowly declining since the 1960s, and in the 1990s, the bottom dropped out of San Diego's real-estate market as federal retrenchments began to hurt the economy.

Southern California's political dilemma seemed especially acute as the twentieth century drew to a close. Conservative Republicans, dominating the Southland's political life, called for a downsizing of the federal government. But the consequent loss of federal funds exacerbated the region's growing social ills because its economy was based on a partnership between government and private industry. The partnership had long been dedicated to sustaining the development of a basically artificial community in a land that traditionally flowered—and flowered magnificently—only when watered by government funds. Hoping to cut funds spent on social services for the poor, Californians at least ran the risk of shutting off the spigot from which flowed their own prosperity.

—*Charles Phillips*

SEE ALSO: Alien Land Laws; Architecture; Banking; Barrios; Bonanza Farming; California Ranchos; Caminetti Act; Chinatowns; Chinese Americans; Echo Park; Farming: Farming in the Imperial Valley and Salton Sea Region; Foreign Miners' Tax of 1850; Fruit and Vegetable Growing; Gentlemen's Agreement; Hetch Hetchy Controversy; Humboldt River and the Great Basin Streams; Immigration Laws; Irish Americans; Japanese Americans; Jewish Americans; Mexican Immigration; Mexican Settlement; Mining: Mining Camps and Towns; Missions: Early Jesuit and Franciscan Missions; National Expansion; Native American Peoples: Peoples of California; Oil and Gas Industry; Oxnard Agricultural Strike; *Ozawa* v. *United States;* Rancho Chico; Spanish and Mexican Towns; United States–Mexican War; Warner's Rancho; Water; Workingmen's Party of California

SUGGESTED READING:
Cook, Warren L. *Flood Tide of Empire: Spain and the Pacific Northwest, 1543–1819.* New Haven, Conn., 1973.
Daniel, Cletus F. *Bitter Harvest: A History of California Farmworkers, 1870–1941.* Ithaca, N.Y., 1981.
Grabowicz, Paul. *California, Inc.* New York, 1982.
Gregory, James N. *American Exodus: The Dust Bowl Migration and Okie Culture in California.* New York, 1989.
Hofsommer, Don L. *The Southern Pacific, 1901–1985.* College Station, Tex., 1986.
Hundley, Norris, Jr. *The Great Thirst: Californians and Water, 1770s–1990s.* Berkeley, Calif., 1992.
Lotchin, Roger. *Fortress California, 1910–1961: From Warfare to Welfare.* New York, 1992.
Lowitt, Richard. *The New Deal and the West.* Bloomington, Ind., 1984.
McWilliams, Carey. *California: The Great Exception.* New York, 1949.
———. *Southern California: An Island on the Land.* New York, 1946. Reprint. Salt Lake City, 1986.
Mowry, George E. *The California Progressives.* Berkeley, Calif., 1951.
Pisani, Donald J. *From the Family Farm to Agribusiness: The Irrigation Crusade in California and the West.* Berkeley, Calif., 1984.
Pitt, Leonard. *The Decline of the Californios: A Social History of the Spanish-Speaking Californians, 1846–1890.* Berkeley, Calif., 1970.
Pomeroy, Earl. *The Pacific Slope: A History of California, Oregon, Washington, Idaho, Utah, and Nevada.* New York, 1965.
Putnam, Jackson K. *Modern California Politics, 1917–1980.* San Francisco, 1980.
Reisner, Marc. *Cadillac Desert: The American West and Its Disappearing Water.* New York, 1986.
Rogin, Michael R., and John L. Shover. *Political Change in California: Critical Elections and Social Movements, 1890–1966.* Westport, Conn., 1970.
Ruiz, Vicki L. *Cannery Women, Cannery Lives: Mexican Women, Unionization, and the California Food Processing Industry, 1930–1950.* Albuquerque, N. Mex., 1987.
Selvin, David F. *A Place in the Sun: A History of California Labor.* San Francisco, 1981.
Starr, Kevin. *Americans and the California Dream, 1850–1915.* New York, 1973.
———. *Inventing the Dream: California through the Progressive Era.* New York, 1985.
———. *Material Dreams: Southern California through the 1920s.* New York, 1990.
Worster, Donald. *Rivers of Empire: Water, Growth, and Aridity in the American West.* New York, 1985.

CALIFORNIA DOCTRINE (OF WATER RIGHTS)

A dual system of WATER rights, the California Doctrine encompasses both riparian rights and appropriation rights. Riparian rights are primarily determined by the legal possession of land bordering the stream; appropriation rights are primarily determined by the priority of actually using water. In 1886, the California State Supreme Court heard the case of LUX V. HAGGIN (69 Cal. 225). Henry Miller and Charles Lux sued James Haggin and Lloyd Tevis for diverting the flow of the Kern River. Citing as evidence the first California legislature's adoption of the common law in 1850, Justice E. W. McKinstry ruled that the riparian doctrine governed property rights in water on private lands but that the appropriation doctrine would prevail under certain conditions. An appropriator would possess a superior right to that of a riparian owner if the former had begun using water from a stream before the latter acquired the property. The California Doctrine eventually spread to eight Western states: Kansas, Nebraska, North and South Dakota, Oklahoma, Oregon, Texas, and Washington. There was, however, a wide range of variation in implementing the doctrine. While California courts strongly enforced riparian rights, in all the other states except Texas, the courts and the legislatures have whittled away at riparian rights until there is not much left.

—*Kazuto Oshio*

SEE ALSO: Colorado Doctrine (of Water Rights)

SUGGESTED READING:

Dunbar, Robert G. *Forging New Rights in Western Waters.* Lincoln, Nebr., 1983.

Hundley, Norris, Jr. *The Great Thirst: Californians and Water, 1770s–1990s.* Berkeley, Calif., 1992.

CALIFORNIA GOLD RUSH

The "CALIFORNIA gold rush" is the term used to describe the surge of immigration into California and the development of mining that followed James W. Marshall's discovery of gold in JOHN AUGUST SUTTER's mill race on January 24, 1848, and the many economic, social, political, and environmental consequences of the discovery. The California gold rush was the first of a series of MINING rushes that spread across the West in the next half century. In its economic, social, political, and environmental consequences, the California gold rush was the most significant national event between the Louisiana Purchase and the Civil War.

News of the gold discoveries generated a series of large immigrations. California's population jumped from 14,000 in 1848 to about 100,000 at the close of 1849 and then to 250,000 by the end of 1852. Within the first decade, more than 500,000 so-called Forty-niners came to California in search of the many economic opportunities created by the gold discoveries. The immigration included Americans from every state and territory; representatives of every occupation, social class, and ethnic group; African Americans, both slave and free; and eventually foreign-born immigrants from Europe, Latin America, and after 1852, Asia.

Mining was concentrated along the Mother Lode on the western slope of the Sierra Nevada, a belt about 120 miles long and 2 miles wide, from Coloma in the north to central Mariposa County in the south. The belt later extended to include gold strikes in and around Shasta and other northern counties. Of the gold-producing areas, Nevada County was the richest. Historians have divided the gold country into the northern and southern mines, with the dividing line at the Mokulmne River. Among the major mineral strikes were those at Feather River, Coloma, and in the Columbia diggings.

Across the expanded mining region, the Forty-niners harvested $10 million in 1848, $41 million in 1850, and $81 million in 1852. The total returns from the gold fields exceeded $300 million in the first six years. Production slowly declined thereafter to about $20 million annually by 1865 and remained at that level for the rest of the century. The economic impact of the gold harvest spread from the scores of mining camps to major towns such as Sacramento, Stockton, and San Francisco and eventually across the nation to the East Coast and even to the financial capitals of Europe. The United States became a major gold-producing nation for the first time.

The number of miners in the gold diggings rose from 5,000 in 1848 to 40,000 at the close of 1849 (the first great immigration), to 50,000 a year later, and peaked at 100,000 in 1852, where it remained for the rest of the decade. The returns for individual miners reflected the rising numbers: from $20 a day in 1848 and $16 in 1849, the yield gradually fell to $5 in 1853, held at that level until the late 1850s, and then sank to $3 a day. Miners had to pay inflated prices for food, tools, transportation, and access to water. They also spent many days idle when claims played out, when water was insufficient, or when winter rains shut down mining and forced them to winter over or leave the mountains for the towns and cities, where they sought employment.

Mining began with a pick, pan, and shovel in the placers. The rocker (or cradle) and long tom had become standard equipment by 1849, followed soon by the sluice. Miners also began using mercury to amalgamate with gold dust. By late 1849 and early 1850, miners had organized into larger companies for damming rivers and hydraulic mining; by 1851, vein or lode mining using stamp mills was established. Opportunities for individuals in washing gravel had ended by the mid-1850s, as the exhausted waterways had been dug over many times.

The California gold rush, especially in its early years, was primarily a placer experience, well suited to limited skills, primitive equipment, minimal capital, and lack of patience. Success in quartz mining came only late in the 1850s. The California gold rush served as a laboratory for mining technology (the most immediate practical application was in Nevada in conjunction with the COMSTOCK LODE).

The California gold rush produced societies that were predominantly male in composition and beliefs, and the more so as one moved farther into the mines. Miners dressed alike, pursued similar strategies in work and recreation, and maintained a powerful sense of loyalty to their own small mining company. Miners asked few questions and guarded their privacy. Living conditions were generally temporary, and the Forty-niners often took turns at domestic chores. At informal meetings in the camps and bars, miners drew up regulations for registering claims, adjudicating disputes, and ensuring the preservation of order. Those charged with violations were tried by juries of their peers, and sentences were carried out immediately. It was a society largely without formal institutions, such as law and courts, churches, and schools.

The tens of thousands of miners in the diggings generated the need for a wide range of goods and services. Many people came to California, not to work in the mines, but to meet miners' needs: large numbers of merchants who sold food, clothing, and whiskey and exchanged gold dust; workers and owners of transportation facilities including freight services, stagecoaches, and, later, express companies; professionals from doctors and lawyers to newspaper publishers; skilled tradesmen, especially carpenters, builders, and sawmill operators; and, soon, individuals engaged in the entertainment industry, including saloonkeepers, gamblers, and prostitutes. While these groups were as temporary as the mining communities they served, they often ended up with most of the gold.

The consequences of the California gold rush were dramatic and far-reaching—for the miners, their families, their communities, and the nation. Because the gold rush was open to everyone regardless of education, family name, or social standing, it fired the hopes of thousands to improve their economic conditions and to short-cut the lifetime of work that seemed to be the lot of most Americans at mid-century. The prolonged absences of the Forty-niners from their families demanded new arrangements for supporting families and involved new roles for women. The California gold rush also introduced the nation to California; the contradictory images of wealth, opportunity, and physical beauty juxtaposed against hardship, impersonality, and failure would help shape popular attitudes toward California for generations. The consequences for the environment were lasting, for the impact of the miners on the landscape was devastating, particularly in the water courses, where the digging and damming were succeeded by dredging.

—*Malcolm J. Rohrbough*

See also: Gold Mining

Suggested reading:
Bancroft, Hubert Howe. *History of California*. Vol. 6. San Francisco, 1889.
Holiday, James S. *The World Rushed In: The California Gold Rush Experience*. New York, 1981.
Paul, Rodman W. *California Gold: The Beginning of Mining in the Far West*. Cambridge, Mass., 1947.
———. *The California Gold Discoveries: Sources, Documents, Accounts, and Memoirs Relating to the Discovery of Gold at Sutter's Mill*. Georgetown, Calif., 1966.

CALIFORNIA INDIANS

See: Native American Peoples: Peoples of California

CALIFORNIA MISSIONS

See: Missions: Early Franciscan and Jesuit Missions

CALIFORNIA OVERLAND TRAILS

While the California Trail may be best known for the Donner Party's disaster in the Sierra Nevada in the winter of 1846 to 1847 and for the gold-seekers of 1849, it carried hundreds of thousands of emigrants from the Missouri River to California between 1841 and 1860. Some, particularly from 1849 to the early 1850s, sought their fortunes; but most intended to make California their home.

Only Jedediah Strong Smith, in 1827, and Joseph Reddeford Walker, in 1833 and 1834, had led groups (but not emigrants) across the Sierra. The first years' emigrants relied on the reports of trappers and explorers for information about routes across the continent. The first true emigrant group was the Bidwell-Bartleson Party in 1841, which was accompanied part of the way by Catholic missionaries returning to the Northwest. The party included thirty-one men, one woman, her baby, and nine wagons, which were abandoned in the

Travelers to California could not avoid passage through the Sierra Nevada nor, in some months of the year, its heavy snows. An 1866 photograph captured freight teams passing through the mountains. *Courtesy Library of Congress.*

Nevada desert as the party swung far south of the best routes. The next year, no party headed for California, but the first part of the route there was improved by travelers to OREGON. In 1843, only a single party made the trip. This group was led by Joseph Chiles, who had been with the Bidwell-Bartleson party, and was guided by Joe Walker with the assistance part of the way of missionary doctor Marcus Whitman, who, in 1836, had taken wagons farther west than anyone had before. Again, no good crossing of the Sierra was found, and wagons had to be abandoned, this time in the Owens Valley of California.

Not until 1844 did a party get wagons all the way to its destination. It had made its way as far as possible following Joe Walker's tracks from the previous year and then had the good sense to go westward rather than southward over the Sierra on the advice of Truckee, a Paiute Indian after whom the emigrants named the river they followed. Most of the emigrants crossed the Sierra—at what is now Donner Pass—in late November; all in the party made it eventually, some by alternate routes and some a full year after they left Missouri. By 1846, the wagon count grew to fifty-two, but conditions crossing the Sierra were still very bad, even with the Truckee route known and used.

The first emigrants on the two-thousand-mile trek used the "jumping-off places" familiar to fur traders and to freighters on the route to Santa Fe. These original towns were Independence and WESTPORT LANDING on the Missouri side of the MISSOURI RIVER. Many emigrants started their travel on river boats from St. Louis up the Missouri.

Gradually, the "jumping-off places" moved west as settlement increased along the Missouri and more routes across the Sierra were opened. The Truckee route, used by the Donner Party and known best by their name, included a narrow canyon, many crossings of a rock-bedded river, and a sheer steep ascent; it is the most familiar route to modern travelers, since it is visible from present-day Interstate 80. A better used route, more gradual in ascent and along a broader canyon, lay along the Carson River to the south. It was originally developed eastward by MORMONS returning to the Salt Lake Valley and then followed westward by Joseph Chiles's 1848 party. It served as the major entry into California for many years. Also in 1848, Peter Lassen led a party via the Applegate Trail (which ran to Oregon) and then south to his ranch one hundred miles north of Sacramento; this difficult and lengthy alternate route was little used after 1849. By the 1850s, settlement in the gold country had increased, and rivalry between various communities and camps resulted in construction of roads eastward across the Sierra to encourage emigrant settlement.

The area from South Pass in Wyoming (the gentle crossing of the Continental Divide) to the Humboldt River in Nevada also had, by the later 1840s, a variety of options: Sublette's Cutoff, which avoided FORT BRIDGER; Hudspeth's Cutoff, which avoided FORT HALL; the route through Salt Lake City, which avoided Hudspeth; and two branches westward from that city—one back up to the California Trail at City of Rocks and the other south of the Great Salt Lake and entering California on the Humboldt. This last route, known as Hastings' Cutoff, was the route taken by the Donner Party.

For the first twelve hundred miles, the California Trail followed the same route as the OREGON TRAIL: up the Platte and North Platte rivers to the supply post of FORT LARAMIE in Wyoming, then westward up the Sweetwater to South Pass, on to the Soda Springs and Fort Hall in Idaho, and southwest to Raft River. There the routes divided. California-bound emigrants who did not detour via Salt Lake City struck southwestward along the Humboldt River to its disappearance in the desert of Nevada and then crossed a desert stretch to water at the foot of the Sierra. This route was—depending on the Sierra crossing—some eight hundred miles, for a total of about two thousand miles.

There were other routes than those across the middle of the country. It was possible to go to Santa Fe on the well-used freighting road and then strike southwest and west across the desert into southern California. The route was much longer and, while more "civilized" in its first half, offered fewer resources of water and forage in its second half.

Of the roughly 2,735 people who crossed from 1840 to 1848, 1,500 traveled in 1846 alone. With the gold rush, there was a fifty-fold increase in travel from 1848 to 1849—and a temporary population shift from potential settlers to individual gold-seekers. From 1849 to 1860, almost 200,000 emigrants crossed the country to California, a quarter of them in 1852. New developments occurred steadily, many prompted by entrepreneurial interests. Even after the transcontinental railroad was completed in 1869—and into the twentieth century—many families chose to move to the West by wagon along a route that could by then legitimately be called a set of roads.

—*Judith Austin*

SEE ALSO: Platte River; Overland Travel; Whitman, Marcus and Narcissa

SUGGESTED READING:
Paden, Irene D. *The Wake of the Prairie Schooner.* New York, 1943.
Read, Georgia Willis, and Ruth Gaines, eds. *Gold Rush: The Journals, Drawings, and Other Papers of J. Goldsborough Bruff.* 2 vols. New York, 1944.

Stewart, George R. *The California Trail.* New York, 1962. Reprint. Lincoln, Nebr., 1983.

Unruh, John D., Jr. *The Plains Across: The Overland Emigrants and the Trans-Mississippi West, 1840–60.* Urbana, Ill., 1979.

CALIFORNIA RANCHOS

California ranchos originally developed as adjuncts to Spanish missions, and they flourished briefly after Mexico declared independence from Spain in 1821 until the American conquest of Alta (or Upper) California in 1848. Father JUNÍPERO SERRA established the first of the missions at San Diego in 1769. He was accompanied in his expedition by Captain Gasper de Portolá. As other missions spread northward, they too would be protected by Spanish troops and accompanied by mostly mestizo settlers, the former who occasionally established nearby presidios and the latter who sometimes lived in pueblos alongside the missions.

While the mission system did not succeed in its (in truth, halfhearted) goal of transforming the Indians into CATHOLICS and the missions into secularized and self-governing native communities, the missions did frequently function as effective agricultural enterprises based on the forced labor of the Indians. Indeed, with Indian labor, the padres created a rough economy. The Indian neophytes built irrigation systems for the vast mission ranchos and served as the working backbone of a small trade in hides, tallow, wine, brandy, olive oil, grain, and leather work. Not surprisingly, soldiers and settlers living in the nearby presidios and pueblos engaged in this economy, and a few built up ranchos of their own. Rancher-merchants depended on the presidios for protection and on the missions for their labor supply and for some products, and by the mid-nineteenth century, they had begun to exchange agricultural goods for various manufactured items brought by Boston Yankees around Cape Horn.

For a while, it seemed, almost any *español* (a Mexican, theoretically, of pure Spanish descent) might become a rancher; provided he ranked high enough in the military or caste system, he might borrow a few seed cows and the odd bull from the missions or from an already established rancher, set them free on the readily available range land, and wait for his enterprise to thrive sufficiently to pay back his debts. As the commerce with the U.S. merchants increased, however, and traders and trappers married into elite Spanish families, local rancheros found they needed more land to maintain their generous life styles and expanding trade. Ultimately, they grew covetous of mission real estate, livestock, and Indian labor. As Mexico fell into the turmoil that led to its first revolution, they joined Mexican liberals in pushing for secularization of the mission system, although for different reasons.

In 1833, the liberal-dominated, anticlerical Mexican government confiscated the land belonging to California's mission under the rubric of secularization and freed the Indians from the missions. The mission system fell apart. The liberals did bequeath the Mission Indians some land, but once freed, many of them showed little interest in taking up farming. Large numbers headed inland to find the remnants of their own or related tribes still living the traditional Native American life. Liberated in a single stroke, the departing neophytes looted the missions and slaughtered vast numbers of mission cattle—thirty thousand at the San Gabriel Mission, for example.

Those Indians who decided to stay and tried to become independent farmers on small land holdings quickly discovered that the Californios had not the slightest intention of allowing them what the territory's governor called "a legal equality [that] would unhinge society." The potential windfall was immense. California was by far the richest of the borderlands. Its chain of missions—twenty-one of them, fourteen leagues apart (one day's journey), stretching from San Diego to Sonoma—had harbored thirty thousand Indians in 1830, all "converted" to Christianity and all engaged in massive farming and stock operations. When they were secularized, the missions held 400,000 cattle, 60,000 horses, and 300,000 sheep and swine. At the San Gabriel Mission alone, the Indian neophytes had tended 150,000 cattle, 20,000 horses, and 40,000 sheep. As with other sudden land and property bonanzas in the West, greed and anarchy triumphed as speculators grabbed everything in sight.

For the most part, mission lands and their extensive herds fell under the control of majordomos chosen by liberal officials from the ranks of Californios. The majordomos in turn sold the land cheaply and in huge proportions to their cronies among the elite. A few poor settlers, most of them descended from the more modestly ranked soldiers, secured from the government big grants of former mission land, acquired cattle, gained access to Indian labor, and grew rich, but in general it was the already well-off who benefited from the breakup of the missions. For all the liberals' pieties about saving the Indians, their reforms merely delivered mission wealth into the hands of the rich Californios, and by secularizing the missions, they ushered in the heyday of the huge California ranchos.

When the smoke cleared from the sudden secularization, California's Mexican elite owned immense tracts of land, ranging from 4,428 to 48,708 acres. A few hundred of these large ranches dominated the entire coastal landscape. California politics, says Richard White, became, in large measure, a question of wealthy ranchero families combining to gain control of more land. By the late 1830s, such Boston firms as BRYANT, STURGIS AND COMPANY and McCULLOCH, HARTNELL AND COMPANY, who had pioneered the export of tallow and hides, were operating thriving commercial enterprises. In the years following the revolution up to 1845, Mexico issued some eight hundred additional land grants, and ranchos ultimately accounted for nearly 14 million acres of California land, stretching along the Pacific Coast from San Diego to Sonoma and scattered within the Sacramento Valley. The ranchos of PÍO DE JESUS PICO and Andres Pico, for example, in San Diego County totaled 100,000 acres. The Nieto family owned twice as much land and built Rancho Los Cerritos in 1844. The Cabrillos operated all of Santa Rosa Island as a sheep ranch. While the large ranchos were owned by some 3 percent of the population, most of the settlers in Mexican California remained small farmers.

To Anglo observers, the rancheros seemed to preside over small kingdoms; their ample tiled-roof adobe homes were simplified imitations of the great country houses of Spain; their huge families and vast numbers of servants were a New World mirror of Spanish nobility. Many seemed addicted to horse racing, lassoing bears, bullfighting, staging fights between bulls and bears, cock fighting, all accompanied by incessant betting, and they called themselves the *gente de razon,* the "people of reason," and bragged to the Americans that they were the true "pioneers of the Pacific coast." For them, Ronald Takaki suggests, wealth was less important for the accumulation of capital and investment than as a means to support their genteel life of "splendid idleness," as one of them called it. Along the coast, life in what the Californios would later romanticize as California's "Golden Age" did indeed seem to American observers one of indolence and ease.

Except, of course, for the Indians. Many Indians, having been turned loose from the missions, now labored in exchange for food and shelter on the ranchos that had mushroomed out of former mission lands. "Throughout all California," wrote JOHN MARSH in 1836, "the Indians are the principal laborers; without them the business of the country could hardly be carried on." Another visitor observed that the Indians herding the cattle were kept "poor" and "in debt," being paid "two or three bullocks per month or six dollars in goods." It worked like this: The rancheros advanced erstwhile Mission Indians some goods, a bit of money, a spot of liquor, and—by offering essential provisions—in effect enticed them into peonage. Once sunk into debts they were unable to pay, the Indians were required by Mexican law to give their creditors a year's worth of work to clear the books, with new debts, of course, requiring further such service. The Native Americans, technically and legally free, were in fact at the least indentured servants, and they included among their number some of the celebrated vaqueros, the first COWBOYS.

Twice a year, the ranchers sent the hard-riding vaqueros to round up their herds, once in the spring for branding and once in late summer or fall for *matazana,* or "slaughter." Horses too roamed free in California, and the wild herds had multiplied over the years until they at least equaled the number of cattle. The vaqueros culled the best of the herds and broke them for their Californio employers, whose lives seemed to be conducted on horseback. In the early years, ranchers slaughtered beef mostly for home use—for food, eaten fresh or dried for storing; for making shoes and lariats and clothes; for fat for cooking and tallow for candles and soap. The vaqueros took only the few hundred pounds the ranchers needed and left the rest to rot. Coyotes and vultures picked the bones clean. Occasionally, a rancher would gather up bones to make a corral, topped with horned skulls, but for the most part, they stayed where they fell. The expanse of California's free range lay littered with bare white bones bleaching in the sun. As the American trade developed, many of the ranchos came to resemble factories, with Indian laborers tanning hides and cooking tallow for export.

As in Mexico, California's *español* elites lived in great luxury, even perhaps with more Spanish punctilio than the Mexican grandees south of the Rio Grande. Long after the people of the Mexican republic were calling themselves *ciudadano,* "citizens," the stiff and formal *españols,* living in a society consisting of elite wealthy ranchers, a large group of mestizo settlers—farmers, artisans, and vaqueros—and an underclass of Indian peons, expected to be addressed as *Don* and *Doña.* Some historians have recently argued that the relations between the Hispanic elite and the Indian servant class was one of *noblesse oblige* and reciprocity, and that is indeed how the elite described matters—"their" Indians were like family to them; for the Indians, the historical record is more silent.

Increasingly, the Californios drew closer to their American trading partners, the Yankee merchants plying the coastal harbors and overland traders. More and more, as family members and local land owners themselves, the Americans urged the rancheros to expand their cattle production beyond their own needs to deliver hides in exchange for American commodities and amenities. As word of California's abundance spread by merchant ship and fur trappers returning east, Anglos—beginning with the first wagon train out of Missouri in 1841—trekked to the region, attracted by the same fertile pastures that had brought Spanish and Mexican settlers. They brought their families and saw themselves as Americans, not as future Mexicans. They also brought their dreams—generated by feverish pamphleteers and authors like RICHARD HENRY DANA, JR., who observed in *Two Years before the Mast* (1840): "In the hands of an enterprising people, what a country [California] might become."

The Anglos seemed determined to transform the territories into their own image, a fact not lost on the Californios. Intensely political, many Californios—including the ranchero elite—had backed the republican revolt against Spain and felt California to be a semi-independent province of Mexico. They worried about the growing American influence. The earlier American emigrants, bemoaned Juan Alvarado, "settled among us and contributed with their intelligence and industry to the progress of my beloved country. Would that the foreigners that came to settle after 1841 had been of the same quality as those who preceded them!" And if the newly arrived Americans thought the Mexicans lazy, the Mexicans found them holier-than-thou and dangerously arrogant. "The idea these gentlemen have formed for themselves is, that God made the world and them also, therefore what there is in the world belongs to them as sons of God," complained one Mexican. Another, not immune to irony, observed: "These Americans are so contriving that some day they will build ladders to touch the sky, and once in the heavens they will change the whole face of the universe and even the color of the skies." By 1846 California's governor, a nervous PIO DE JESUS PICO, was noting: "We find ourselves threatened by hordes of Yankee immigrants who have already begun to flock into our country and whose progress we cannot arrest."

When the UNITED STATES–MEXICAN WAR broke out in 1846, there were Anglos in sufficient number to effect quickly the surrender of the seven thousand or so Californios to U.S. forces led by JOHN CHARLES FRÉMONT. After the Treaty of Guadalupe Hidalgo in 1848 under which Mexico formally turned California over to the United States, Congress established a land commission to review rancho land claims. Californios had to defend their Spanish and Mexican land grants in processes that dragged on frequently for years and often required huge legal fees. A number mortgaged or sold off portions of their land to pay Anglo lawyers, so that many of those who managed to defend their claims in court lost their lands in fact. Other rancheros lost additional land when floods, disease, and an extended drought in the 1860s wiped out their herds of cattle. When the end of the Civil War brought thousands of immigrants to California, a number of the remaining ranchos diversified their operations or sold off acreage to small farmers and new towns, sometimes to both. A few remained prominent in California society, especially those who intermarried with wealthy Anglos; some returned to a Mexican "homeland" in which they had not been born and frequently had never visited; some joined other impoverished Hispanics and new Mexican immigrants in the growing BARRIOS of the American towns and cities.

—*Charles Phillips*

SEE ALSO: Intermarriage: Marriages between Spanish/Mexicans and Euro-Americans; Mexican Settlement; Missions: Early Jesuit and Franciscan Missions; Rancho Chico; Spanish Settlement; Warner's Rancho; Women on the Spanish and Mexican Frontier

SUGGESTED READING:

Almaguer, Tomáas. *Racial Fault Lines: The Historical Origins of White Supremacy in California.* Berkeley, Calif., 1994.

Camarillo, Albert. *Chicanos in a Changing Society: From Mexican Pueblos to American Barrios in Santa Barbara and Southern California, 1848–1930.* Cambridge, Mass., 1979.

Gerhard, Peter. *The North Frontier of New Spain.* Princeton, N.J., 1982.

Monroy, Douglas. *Thrown among Strangers: The Making of Mexican Culture in Frontier California.* Berkeley, Calif., 1990.

Pitt, Leonard. *The Decline of the Californios: A Social History of the Spanish-Speaking Californians, 1846–1890.* Berkeley, Calif., 1970.

Takaki, Ronald. *A Different Mirror: A History of Multicultural America.* Boston, 1993.

Time-Life Books. *The Spanish West.* Alexandria, Va., 1976.

Weber, David J. *The Mexican Frontier, 1821–1846: The American Southwest under Mexico.* Albuquerque, N. Mex., 1982.

———. *The Spanish Frontier in North America.* New Haven, Conn., 1992.

CAMELS

Pack animals native to the Middle East, camels were used for a brief time by the U.S. Army in the American Southwest. In 1857, the United States War Department ordered EDWARD FITZGERALD (NED) BEALE to test the use of camels in the deserts during a wagon-road survey. Imported from the Middle East, seventy-five camels joined Beale's overland party at Camp Verde near Bandera, Texas. Packing the camel loads proved to be complicated, and the strange beasts scared both horses and mules. Only two drivers—"Greek George" Caralambo and Hadji Ali, or "Hi Jolly," a Syrian—proved adept at handling the stubborn animals. The camels were left unshod and preferred mesquite and other desert plants to grass or hay.

Beale's party moved through western Texas to El Paso, then up the Rio Grande to Albuquerque, and on

The U.S. Army briefly experimented with the use of camels as pack animals in the American West. *Courtesy Denver Public Library, Western History Department.*

to the Colorado River (which the camels swam across) and California via Fort Defiance. But the use of camels in the West was a short-lived experiment. When Secretary of War Jefferson Davis left office in 1857, the army's interest in the camels declined. Beale, however, kept some of them at Fort Tejon, California.

During the Civil War, Confederates captured some of the animals in Texas. At the end of the war, sixty-six camels remained at Camp Verde. Some were sold to traveling circuses; others were used by miners and loggers until the last of them died in the late 1880s. General Douglas MacArthur remembered seeing some of the exotic animals as a boy when his father commanded cavalry troops in Texas.

—*Andrew Rolle*

SUGGESTED READING:
Fowler, Harlan. *Camels to California.* Stanford, Calif., 1950.
Greenly, Albert H. *Camels in America.* New York, 1952.
Lewis, Lesley B., ed. *Uncle Sam's Camels.* Glorieta, N. Mex., 1929. Reprint. 1970.

CAMERON, DONALDINA MACKENZIE

Superintendent of the Presbyterian Mission Home for Chinese women in San Francisco, Donaldina Mackenzie Cameron (1869–1968) was born in New Zealand to Scottish sheep ranchers, who took their six daughters and one son to California in 1871. After her mother died in 1874, Cameron was raised by her older sisters while her father worked as a manager on several California ranches. She attended grade school in San Jose and high schools in Oakland and in southern California. After her father's death brought an abrupt end to her teacher-training course, she went into missionary work at the suggestion of a friend.

Once started as a missionary, Cameron proved to be unstoppable. In 1895, she took a position as a helper at the Presbyterian Mission Home at 920 Sacramento Street in San Francisco; by 1900, she was its superintendent, a post she held for thirty-four years. The Mission Home served as a refuge for a wide variety of female Chinese immigrants, including children seeking educations, teenagers sent by the juvenile court, and wives who complained about harsh treatment from their husbands. Its most dramatic work—and Cameron's specialty—was in "rescuing" prostitutes from brothels operated by Chinese vice rings. Highly effective at attacking the so-called slave trade in women, Cameron was also willing to intervene with police, immigration, and juvenile-court authorities on behalf of Chinese immigrant women. Seeing herself as a motherly figure, Cameron helped several home residents obtain higher educations and arranged for dozens of others to marry Chinese Christian men. She earned the devoted admiration of many of the hundreds of Chinese women and girls who passed through the Mission Home.

Cameron left the Mission Home (which was later renamed Donaldina Cameron House) when she reached the mandatory retirement age of sixty-five. During her later years, she cared for her older sisters in Palo Alto, where she died at the age of ninety-eight.

—*Peggy Pascoe*

SUGGESTED READING:
Martin, Mildred Crowl. *Chinatown's Angry Angel: The Story of Donaldina Cameron.* Palo Alto, Calif., 1977.
Pascoe, Peggy. *Relations of Rescue: The Search for Female Moral Authority in the American West, 1874–1939.* New York, 1990.

CAMINETTI ACT OF 1893

Passed by the U.S. Congress, the Caminetti Act attempted to control environmental damage to California rivers while permitting the practice of hydraulic MINING. The act was proposed by Congressman Anthony Caminetti of California after the case of *Woodruff* v. *North Bloomfield et al.* in 1884 led to a court injunction against hydraulic mining. The law required mining companies to clean up the debris produced by hydraulic mining of rivers and established the SACRAMENTO

RIVER Commission with the authority to devise a means of flood control on California's waterways.

Hydraulic mining was doomed by the restrictions placed on it and soon ceased to be an important factor in California's economy. The commission built a series of river levees and dug a network of by-passes or auxiliary riverbeds to handle floodwaters, but its work was only marginally successful. The system of levees and auxiliary river beds did not prevent crop destruction when the Sacramento River flooded in 1904. Only when California joined with local and federal governments and private enterprise to establish the Sacramento Flood Control Plan in 1911 were the waters of the Sacramento adequately contained and were the farm lands of the Sacramento Valley cultivated and irrigated to their phenomenally productive potential.

—*Patricia Hogan*

SEE ALSO: Agriculture; Irrigation; Water

SUGGESTED READING:
Kelley, Robert L. *Gold vs. Grain: The Hydraulic Mining Controversy in California's Sacramento Valley.* Glendale, Calif., 1959.

CAMINO REAL, EL

In the United States, there are two Camino Reales (royal roads)—one in Texas and the other in California. El Camino Real in Texas was the first road mapped and built in the Western part of the United States. It was used by the governments of Spain, France, Mexico, the Republic of Texas, and the United States. When built, the road linked Mexico City, Monclova, Presidio Bautista on the Rio Grande, San Antonio, Nacogdoches, and Natchitoches. First used on May 16, 1691, during an expedition headed by Domingo Teran de Los Rios, Father Damian Massanet, and Captain Alonso de Leon, the road allowed Catholic missionaries to establish several missions in East Texas and facilitated the transportation of troops and material needed to build several Spanish settlements and military posts. The highway provided for the beginning of the town known today as San Antonio. In Texas, El Camino Real is now called O.S.R., the Old San Antonio Road.

In 1769, General José de Galvéz began constructing El Camino Real de California, which ran from Mexico City through Baja California, San Diego, and San Luis Obispo to San Francisco and Sonoma. El Camino Real de California is now called U.S. 101.

—*Fred L. Koestler*

SUGGESTED READING:
Corle, Edwin. *The Royal Highway.* Boston, 1949.

CAMPBELL, ALEXANDER

SEE: Campbellites

CAMPBELL, ROBERT

A partner of William Sublette, Robert Campbell (1804–1879) was a mountain man who amassed a fortune from the FUR TRADE and became a successful St. Louis merchant. Born in Tyrone County, Ireland, he immigrated to the United States in 1824 and settled in St. Louis.

Campbell, who suffered from weak lungs, joined General WILLIAM HENRY ASHLEY's 1825 Far Western fur-trading expedition on the advice of his physician. Campbell soon proved so capable that Ashley appointed him a brigade leader, and he earned the respect and friendship of such legendary MOUNTAIN MEN as JAMES (JIM) BRIDGER, THOMAS FITZPATRICK, and JEDEDIAH STRONG SMITH. He became especially close to William Sublette, whose life he saved in the 1832 Battle of Pierre's Hole against the Blackfoot Indians. In December 1832, Sublette and Campbell became partners in a fur-trading enterprise and challenged the formidable AMERICAN FUR COMPANY by building, in the spring of 1833, Fort William on the upper Missouri River just four miles from the American Fur Company's FORT UNION.

Campbell successfully ran the outpost in 1833 and 1834 and then sold out to the American Fur Company. On the Laramie River in southeastern Wyoming, the partners next built FORT LARAMIE (at first also called Fort William), which they also eventually sold to their much larger rival. Campbell sold his interest in the fur business to Sublette in 1842 (the two remained devoted friends thereafter) and set himself up as a merchant in St. Louis. He became president of two major banks—the State Bank of Missouri and the Merchants' National Bank—and the owner of a grand hotel. He was appointed commissioner to the Laramie peace conference of 1851, and President Ulysses S. Grant appointed him commissioner to the treaty-making commission of 1869.

—*Alan Axelrod*

SEE ALSO: Sublette Brothers

SUGGESTED READING:
Chittenden, Hiram M. *The History of the American Fur Trade in the Far West.* 3 vols., New York, 1902.

CAMPBELL, THOMAS

SEE: Campbellites

CAMPBELLITES (DISCIPLES OF CHRIST)

The Disciples of Christ, more popularly called the "Campbellites," were a product of the revival spirit of the trans-Appalachian West initiated at the Cane Ridge Revival of 1801. Led by three former Presbyterians—Barton W. Stone, Thomas Campbell, and his son Alexander Campbell—the denomination combined Methodist doctrine, Baptist polity and practice, and Presbyterian heritage in a church that emphasized primitive New Testament–based Christianity over creed. Eventually, three denominations—The Churches of Christ, The Christian church (Disciples of Christ), and the Undenominational Fellowship of Christian churches and Churches of Christ—grew out of the movement, which began along the borders of western Virginia, Ohio, and Kentucky in the early nineteenth century.

The first of the Campbellite ministers to separate from the more traditional religions was Barton W. Stone, whose participation in the Cane Ridge Revival made him critical of Presbyterian emphasis on creed rather than on simple, primitive Christian faith. Separating from the Presbyterian Synod of Kentucky in 1803, Stone formed the Springfield Presbytery with four others but ended that Presbytery a year later and announced that the group would accept only the name "Christian." Stone's democratically structured church, which practiced baptism by total immersion, grew rapidly in Kentucky, Tennessee, and Ohio. By 1830, it had established a newspaper, the *Christian Messenger*. Stone would soon find himself comfortable with the Arminian theology (the doctrine that Christ died for all men, not merely the elect), developed by Thomas and Alexander Campbell; he allied himself and his followers with them in 1832.

Meanwhile, Thomas Campbell, a Northern Ireland Presbyterian, settled in western Pennsylvania to improve his health. He and his son, Alexander, had been a part of a group of Scottish Presbyterians who disapproved of the exclusiveness of their church. Thomas Campbell was disturbed by the emphasis on creed among churches. In 1809, he founded the Christian Association of Washington (Pennsylvania), which endorsed the maxim "Where the Scriptures Speak, we speak; where the Scriptures are silent, we are silent" and advocated a return to a more primitive Christianity.

In 1809, Alexander Campbell joined his father and, within three years, assumed the leadership of the movement. Accepting baptism by immersion in 1812, the Campbells became uneasy Baptists in an association that lasted until the 1830s. *The Christian Baptist,* Alexander Campbell's first newspaper, was established in 1823 and attracted a large number of new followers. Campbell believed in the importance of democracy and in the ability of the laity to understand scripture. By 1832, his friendship with Barton Stone led to a loosely unified "Christian" church structure. Stone and the Campbells believed that all Christians should live together in love without concern for creed.

Although the Campbells were critical of learned ministers who were unable to speak to the people, they were nonetheless concerned enough with education to capture control of Transylvania University during the 1830s and establish Bethany College in 1841 and Hiram College in 1850. Alexander Campbell served as Bethany's president until his death. He summarized his theology in *The Christian System,* published in 1835. He emphasized historical precedent in the Bible, particularly in the New Testament, rather than mystical experience and repudiated miracles in the Calvinist tradition. He became a prominent evangelical intellectual, but when called to take a stand on the issue of slavery, he expressed the view that it was a matter of opinion.

Although Alexander Campbell attacked the newly formed CHURCH OF JESUS CHRIST OF LATTER-DAY SAINTS in his writings, the MORMONS were deeply influenced by the Disciples of Christ, perhaps because an ex-Campbellite minister, SIDNEY RIGDON, who had once challenged Alexander Campbell for leadership of his church, became an important early convert to Mormonism. Rationalism, communitarianism, opposition to priest craft, plain doctrine, and the doctrine of baptism "unto remission of sins" were ideas associated with Campbell that found their way into Mormon thought.

Unlike many other denominations, the Disciples of Christ were not split by the Civil War. Instead, doctrinal differences over organization, missionary activities, the use of musical instruments, and ecumenical activities led to a split into three different faiths: the Christian church, the Churches of Christ, and the Disciples of Christ. By 1906, the Christian church identified itself as a separate denomination and established churches in the West, particularly in Arkansas, Texas, Oklahoma, and southern California. After the split, the Churches of Christ emphasized a strict construction of scripture and eschewed instrumental music, central organization, and ecumenical activities, while the Disciples of Christ were more flexible in their

interpretation. In the twentieth century, reformers among the Disciples of Christ advocated pragmatic tradition, while conservatives remained committed to strict interpretation. In the 1960s, the Disciples were restructured to reflect an overall denominational organization, while the Churches of Christ and the Christian church remained based in independent congregations.
—*Patrick H. Butler, III*

SEE ALSO: Protestants

SUGGESTED READING:
McAllister, Lester G. *Thomas Campbell: Man of the Book.* St. Louis, Mo., 1954.
————, and William Tucker. *Journey in Faith: A History of the Christian Church.* St. Louis, Mo., 1975.
West, Robert Frederick. *Alexander Campbell and Natural Religion.* New Haven, Conn., 1954.

CANADIAN FRONTIER

SEE: Frontier: Comparative Frontiers: Canada

CANBY, EDWARD RICHARD SPRING

Commander of Union forces in the Southwest during the CIVIL WAR and later commander of the Pacific Division, Edward Richard Spring Canby (1817–1873) was murdered by the Modoc Indian CAPTAIN JACK. Called the "prudent general" by his biographer, Canby earned a reputation for caution and dependability rather than for military brilliance during his long army career. His one imprudent act cost him his life in the Modoc War. He was the only regular army general to

The 1873 shooting of Edward Richard Spring Canby by Captain Jack of the Modocs as depicted in the nineteenth-century press. *Courtesy Library of Congress.*

be killed in an Indian war. (GEORGE ARMSTRONG CUSTER was a lieutenant colonel, holding the brevet rank of general, at the Battle of Little Bighorn.)

Born in Boone County, Kentucky, Canby graduated next-to-last in his class at West Point in 1839. He performed well, however, in the Seminole War and in the removal of the Civilized Tribes from the East to the Indian Territory. In the United States–Mexican War, he won brevets of major and lieutenant colonel while serving as chief of staff of a brigade.

Canby organized the Union's defense of the Southwest after its initial collapse during the Civil War. Although he lost to Confederate General HENRY HOPKINS SIBLEY at the Battle of Valverde, his continued resistance, coupled with the arrival of the California Column and Colorado Volunteers, forced the Confederates to retreat to Texas.

After staff duties in the East and command of New York during the draft riots of 1863, Canby reorganized the Union forces retreating from General NATHANIEL PRENTISS BANKS's botched Red River campaign. He then cooperated with the navy to capture Mobile, an act for which he received the personal thanks of President Abraham Lincoln. In May, he accepted the surrender of Confederate Generals Richard Taylor and Edmund Kirby-Smith.

In 1866, Canby was promoted to brigadier general in the regular army and in 1870 was given command of the Department of the Columbia. Three years later, he became commander of the Division of the Pacific.

As head of a peace commission to end the Modoc War, Canby abandoned prudence—and forfeited his life. He stubbornly ignored warnings of Modoc perfidy and depended on "carrot-and-stick" Indian diplomacy. His last message to Captain Jack before meeting him was, "If you will come in and surrender to us, we will . . . allow you a voice in selecting your future home. If you do not comply . . . , we will resign and leave the matter with the military, and you will have no choice in the selection of your future home."

At the peace tent pitched in the Lava Beds, Captain Jack shot Canby in the face, and two other warriors finished him off on April 11, 1873.

Captain Jack's murder of Canby not only sealed his own fate—to be hanged as a murderer—it also reversed the sympathetic attitudes of much of the press and public. General of the Army WILLIAM TECUMSEH SHERMAN echoed the rage and grief of the nation at Canby's murder when he urged "utter extermination" of the Modocs.

—*Richard H. Dillon*

SEE ALSO: Pacific Northwest Indian Wars

SUGGESTED READING:
Heyman, Max L., Jr. *Prudent Soldier: A Biography of Major General E. R. S. Canby.* Glendale, Calif., 1951.

CANNARY, MARTHA

SEE: "Calamity Jane"

CANNON, GEORGE QUAYLE

George Quayle Cannon (1827–1901) became a chief advisor to BRIGHAM YOUNG, a key negotiator between the MORMONS and the U.S. government during UTAH's bid for statehood, and counselor to JOHN TAYLOR, WILFORD WOODRUFF, and Lorenzo Snow, the three Mormon prophets who succeeded Brigham Young. Husband of four plural wives and father of twenty-eight children, Cannon was the founder of a notable dynasty still important in the Great Basin.

Cannon's parents were British converts to the CHURCH OF JESUS CHRIST OF LATTER-DAY SAINTS in 1840. After his parents died, he was taken into the household of his father's sister, Leonora, and her husband, John Taylor. Cannon learned printing from Taylor and helped him publish two Mormon journals, the *Times and Seasons* and the *Nauvoo Neighbor.* Cannon migrated with other Mormons to the Salt Lake Valley in 1847. From 1850 to 1854, he filled a church mission to the Hawaiian Islands where he translated the BOOK OF MORMON into the Hawaiian language.

In 1855, he moved to San Francisco, where he published the *Western Standard* from early 1856 until it was abandoned late in 1857 because of the UTAH EXPEDITION. Shortly after returning to Utah, he was assigned to publish the church-owned *Deseret News* out of Fillmore in a remote central Utah valley.

In September 1858, Cannon was assigned to undertake the duties of lobbyist and diplomat for the church in Washington, D.C. He was recalled to be ordained an apostle on August 26, 1860, and six weeks later, he departed for his native Liverpool where he helped preside over the LDS European mission and publish the church-owned *Millennial Star.* He returned briefly to Washington in 1862 to lobby in vain for Utah's admission to the Union and then returned to his duties in Liverpool, where he remained until 1864.

Back in Salt Lake City in 1866, Cannon founded the *Juvenile Instructor* and the next year again became editor of the *Deseret News.* He returned to Washington in 1871 to smooth the way for another bid at statehood and served a full decade as territorial delegate, until Congress refused to seat him under the Edmunds antipolygamy bill of 1882. He was principal executor of Brigham Young's highly complicated and controversial estate and became first counselor to Young's successor, his uncle, John Taylor in 1880.

Cannon was himself imprisoned in 1888 and 1889 under antipolygamy laws. He returned to the East to negotiate terms that would lead ultimately to the demise of the Mormon practice of polygamy and to Utah statehood in 1896.

—*Dean L. May*

SEE ALSO: Edmunds Act of 1882; Polygamy: Polygamy among Mormons

SUGGESTED READING:
Alexander, Thomas G. *Mormonism in Transition: A History of the Latter-Day Saints, 1890–1930.* Urbana, Ill., 1986.
Larson, Gustive O. *The "Americanization" of Utah for Utah for Statehood.* San Marino, Calif., 1971.
Lyman, Edward Leo. *Political Deliverance: The Mormon Quest for Utah Statehood.* Urbana, Ill., 1986.

CANTON, FRANK

A Western lawman and range detective, Frank Canton (Joe Horner, 1849–1927) was born near Richmond, Virginia, and moved with his family to Denton, Texas, after the Civil War. At about the age of nineteen, he became a cowboy. The years between 1871 and 1878 are a question mark in his life. It was probably because of illegal activities that he changed his name from Joe Horner to Frank Canton.

In 1878, he moved a herd of cows from Texas to Nebraska. Thereafter he was a detective for the Wyoming Stock Growers' Association. In 1880, he settled in Johnson County, Wyoming, and was elected sheriff for two terms.

In the early 1890s, Canton played a leading role in the JOHNSON COUNTY WAR as a range detective for the association. He harassed small ranchers and was part of an expedition of gunmen sent to kill cattle rustlers in 1892. Later implicated in the murder of John A. Tisdale, a small rancher accused of rustling, Canton moved to Nebraska to run a packing plant. Next, he went to Oklahoma where he became a lawman—first a deputy U.S. marshal and then, in 1900, a deputy sheriff.

In 1897, Canton moved to Alaska and became a deputy U.S. marshal; he returned to Oklahoma three years later, still a lawman. When the territory became a state in 1907, he was selected adjutant general of the Oklahoma National Guard.

—*Richard A. Van Orman*

Frank Canton. *Courtesy Western History Collections, University of Oklahoma Library.*

SEE ALSO: Cattle Rustling; Law and Order; Violence

SUGGESTED READING:
Canton, Frank. *Frontier Trails: The Autobiography of Frank Canton.* Norman, Okla., 1966.
Smith, Helena Huntington. *The War on Powder River.* Lincoln, Nebr., 1967.

CAPITOL (FREEHOLD) SYNDICATE RANCH

SEE: XIT Ranch

CAPTAIN JACK (MODOC)

A warrior subchief of the Modoc tribe of northeastern California, Captain Jack (1837?–1873) was a leader in the Modoc War from 1872 to 1873. Called "Captain Jack" by settlers on the remote Oregon border in the 1850s because of his fondness for U.S. Army uniforms, the Modoc warrior was named Kientpoos, or

Captain Jack (Modoc). *Courtesy National Archives.*

Kintpuash. He led about fifty warriors in the Modoc War and seized the imagination of the American press and public until his story was eclipsed by GEORGE ARMSTRONG CUSTER's 1876 debacle at the Battle of Little Bighorn.

After a massacre of emigrants and a counter-massacre by Indian fighter Ben Wright, the Modocs settled down to coexist with local ranchers and farmers. They sometimes worked as cowboys or farm hands, adopted Western clothing and names, and picked up a smattering of English. In short, they tried to adapt to the impact of Euro-American settlement on their culture.

The adaptation was in vain. Settlers confiscated Modoc land north of Tule Lake, and the federal government exacerbated a deteriorating situation by bureaucratic bungling. The government forced the Modocs onto the Klamath Reservation instead of giving them the small reservation they desired. The Klamaths harassed the strangers, whom they saw as interlopers. The Modoc tribe split, and Captain Jack led one band back to his Lost River, Oregon, birthplace. There, on November 29, 1872, he began the Modoc War by defeating a cavalry force sent to take him back to the Klamath Reservation. Unfortunately, Captain Jack was also blamed for a subsequent massacre of civilians by a rival warrior, Hooker Jim.

Captain Jack withdrew into the Modoc Lava Beds, a *malpais,* or "badland," on the south edge of Tule Lake. The maze of volcanic caves and fissure-trenches was an ideal fortress. In January 1873, the army sent four hundred regulars and volunteers to sweep Captain Jack's stronghold. He drove them back with no casualties.

The government then tried diplomacy by sending a peace commission headed by General EDWARD RICHARD SPRING CANBY. Some Modocs urged taking advantage of the flag of truce to murder the commissioners. Preferring peace to war, Captain Jack protested. The war party clapped a woman's bonnet on his head, placed a shawl around his shoulders, and taunted him as a coward and a squaw. He was thus shamed into killing Canby.

Despite a stunning victory by Captain Jack's loyal lieutenant Scarfaced Charley, an all-out attack by some 750 troops in April drove away the Indians' ponies and cut them off from their source of water. Most of the Modocs surrendered, and the army enlisted Hooker Jim as a scout to find Captain Jack. He surrendered on June 1, 1873, complaining that his legs just gave out.

Hooker Jim was granted immunity for testifying against Captain Jack, who, with three others, was hanged at Fort Klamath, Oregon, on October 3, 1873, for violating the rules of war in murdering men protected by a flag of truce.

—Richard H. Dillon

SEE ALSO: Pacific Northwest Indian Wars

SUGGESTED READING:
Dillon, Richard H. *Burnt-Out Fires: California's Modoc Indian War.* Englewood Cliffs, N.J., 1973.

CAPTIVITY NARRATIVES

SEE: Literature: Indian Captivity Narratives

CAREY, JOSEPH MAULL

Joseph Maull Carey (1845–1924), U.S. senator, governor of WYOMING, and cattle rancher, was born in Milton, Delaware, and educated at the University of Pennsylvania law school. He moved to the Wyoming Territory in 1869 following his appointment as territorial attorney. He served in various capacities during territorial days, including five years on the territorial Supreme Court and a term as mayor of Cheyenne. He was elected territorial delegate in 1884, and over the next six years, he worked for Wyoming statehood. When Wyoming became a state in 1890, Carey (called "the father of Wyoming statehood" for his efforts) was chosen by the legislature to serve as a U.S. senator. A supporter of agricultural development in the West, he authored the Carey Act of 1894, pioneering legislation that provided public funds for RECLAMATION.

In 1894, Carey was defeated for reelection, largely through the efforts of fellow Republican FRANCIS E. WARREN, who had once been Carey's political ally and business associate. Carey returned to ranching and reclamation development. His CY cattle company was one of the state's largest, and he served as an officer in the powerful Wyoming Stock Growers' Association.

The feud with Warren continued. In 1910, Carey sought the Republican nomination for governor, but Warren allies chose another nominee. Carey accepted the nomination by the Democrats and won the general election. His term as governor was marked by Progressive measures.

Carey remained a conservative Republican by philosophy, but in 1912, he supported THEODORE ROOSEVELT's presidential bid in the Bull Moose party. Carey did not seek reelection in 1914 but supported the eventual winner, Democrat and fellow cattleman JOHN B. KENDRICK. Carey's feud with Warren finally came to an end in 1918 when his son Robert Carey gained Warren's support and the governorship.

—*Phil Roberts*

SUGGESTED READING:
Erwin, Marie. *Wyoming Historical Blue Book*. Cheyenne, Wyo., 1943.
Paulson, George W. "The Congressional Career of Joseph Maull Carey." M.A. thesis, University of Wyoming, 1962.

CAREY ACT OF 1894

The Carey Act of 1894 represented a new approach to the disposal of public desert land by recognizing that RECLAMATION was too large an undertaking for individual settlers. During the 1880s, Western states and territories pressed Congress for legislation to develop arid lands through IRRIGATION. By 1892, Western political interests had aligned to support a bill introduced by Senator Joseph Maull Carey, a Republican from Wyoming and chairman of the Senate Public Lands Committee. Carey proposed to cede arid lands to the states in exchange for their pledge to reclaim the lands. Bolstering support for the bill was a report of the House

Committee on Irrigation of Arid Lands, which concluded that the federal government was unlikely to undertake the task of reclaiming arid lands. Congress did not pass the 1892 bill, but two years later, it passed a compromise measure attached to the 1894 Sundry Civil Appropriations Bill. The amendment authorized the federal government to donate up to one million acres to each of ten arid states, provided that they cause the lands to be reclaimed, settled, and cultivated.

Although Western states supported the Carey Act, few of them had the financial resources to take advantage of it. HENRY AGARD WALLACE, secretary of agriculture from 1933 to 1940 and later vice-president under Franklin D. Roosevelt, called the Carey Act "one of the greatest land acts ever passed," but its effects were limited. By 1900, only one state, Wyoming, had developed agricultural lands under the provisions of the law, a circumstance that lent support to calls for the federal government to take responsibility for reclamation. Ultimately, states were granted a total of about 4 million acres under the act, but as of 1930, Census Bureau data showed that only 1.17 million acres had been patented by private individuals.

—*Rebecca Conard*

SUGGESTED READING:
Hibbard, Benjamin Horace. *A History of the Public Land Policies*. Madison, Wis., 1965.
Wallace, Henry A. "The Twin Falls Project of Southern Idaho." In *Henry A. Wallace's Irrigation Frontier*. Edited by Richard Lowitt and Judith Fabry. Norman, Okla., 1991.

CARIBOU

Members of the deer family, caribou once ranged over most of Canada, Alaska, and the northernmost portions of the United States. Except for a small band in northern Idaho and neighboring areas in Washington and British Columbia, caribou have disappeared from the contiguous forty-eight states.

It is generally agreed that American caribou (*Rangifer tarandus*) are related to the reindeer of Eurasia. Most scientists recognize six North American subspecies. The principal division of the twenty-five to thirty herds is into the barren-ground and woodland groups. The former's range is the tundra and nearby taiga (subarctic evergreen forests) of Canada and Alaska. The latter is found in the northern boreal forests and some alpine habitats. Both groups are migratory. The movements of woodland caribou are within relatively restricted areas; barren-ground caribou's seasonal migrations are much more extensive.

Caribou feed on lichen, fungi, evergreen leaves, and twigs. *Rangifer* is the only genus of the deer family in which both sexes have antlers.

Caribou were central to the existence and culture of the Inuits and the Indians of the central tundra. The animals' hide and sinew were used for clothing, foot gear, tents, sleeping bags, boat covers, mattresses, insulation, blankets, and thread. Hides, sinews, antlers, and bones from caribou provided material for tools and weapons. Their fat was burned for light. Caribou continue to be a major source of meat for the native peoples of the Far North.

The drastic decline of barren-ground caribou populations in the twentieth century is generally ascribed to overhunting after the native peoples acquired firearms, while the decline of woodland caribou populations is due to the destruction of forests. Some scientists argue, however, that long-range fluctuations in caribou numbers have occurred in which humans were not a factor.

—*Michael J. Brodhead*

SEE ALSO: Wildlife

SUGGESTED READING:
Burch, Ernest S., Jr. "The Caribou/Wild Reindeer as a Human Resource." *American Antiquity* 37 (1972): 339–368.
Hall, E. Raymond. *The Mammals of North America.* 2d ed. 2 vols. New York, 1981.
Miller, Frank L. "Caribou." In *Wild Mammals of North America: Biology, Management, and Economics.* Edited by Joseph A. Chapman and George A. Feldhamer. Baltimore, 1982.

CARLETON, JAMES H.

James H. Carleton (1814–1873) was the departmental commander in New Mexico during the CIVIL WAR. Waging a deadly war with the Navajos and the Mescalero Apaches, he pursued a policy that called for killing all adult male members of the tribes and for forcing surviving tribal members to live on a reservation at Bosque Redondo near Fort Sumner on the Pecos River.

Born in Maine, Carleton joined the Maine militia and saw his first action during the 1838 boundary dispute, known as the Aroostock War, between Maine and Canada. The following year, he joined the regular army as a second lieutenant with the First Regiment of United States Dragoons. Patrolling the mountain frontier and the Oregon Trail, he wrote two accounts of the Dragoons' expeditions—accounts that were published in *The Spirit of the Times* from November 9, 1844, to April 12, 1845, and from December 27, 1845,

James H. Carleton. *Courtesy Museum of New Mexico.*

to May 30, 1846. At the beginning of the United States–Mexican War, he became the aide-de-camp for General JOHN ELLIS WOOL.

At the beginning of the Civil War, Carleton was named brigadier general in the California Volunteers. In command of the California Column, he succeeded General EDWARD RICHARD SPRING CANBY as departmental commander of New Mexico in 1862. In March of that year, Carleton set out from Los Angeles with two thousand men to reopen the southern mail route to the region. The route had been closed by Confederates, who had captured Fort Fillmore and Tucson. Carleton's troops spent ten months traveling to Tucson, where they found no evidence of Confederates, and then pushed on to Santa Fe. The slow progress brought out the sarcastic voices in New Mexico newspapers, whose editors pointed out that Carleton's forces had traveled at a rate of three miles a day.

The Native American problem then occupied Carleton's attention. He dispatched CHRISTOPHER HOUSTON ("KIT") CARSON and other Indian fighters to battle the Mescalero Apaches and Navajos. Prohibiting further negotiations with the tribes, Carleton ordered the killing of all Apache and Navajo males. More than six hundred Apaches, including one hundred warriors, fled to Fort Stanton and surrendered to Carson. Rather than carry out Carleton's death policy, Carson sent the Apaches to the reservation at Bosque Redondo. Carleton's troops then invaded Navajo lands at Canyon de Chelly in northeastern Arizona, destroyed their crops and fruit trees, and ultimately forced the tribe to surrender. Thousands of Navajos were then forcibly marched to Bosque Redondo. Known as the Long Walk, the march followed a three-hundred-mile route from Fort Defiance in Arizona to Fort Sumner in New Mexico. Carleton's attempts to Christianize and "civilize" the tribes failed. While the Mescalero Apaches fled the reservation, the Navajos remained there, but at great cost to the government.

Because of his arbitrary and tyrannical policies, Carleton soon fell out of favor among New Mexico politicians. Not only did they begin to question his treatment of the Mescalero Apaches and the Navajos, they also balked at his establishment of martial law in the territory.

After the Civil War, Carleton remained in the army and was headquartered in Texas.

—*Candace Floyd*

SEE ALSO: Apache Wars; Navajo Wars

SUGGESTED READING:
Axelrod, Alan. *Chronicle of the Indian Wars: From Colonial Times to Wounded Knee.* New York, 1993.
Carleton, James Henry. *The Prairie Logbooks: Dragoon Campaigns to the Pawnee Villages in 1844, and to the Rocky Mountains in 1845.* Lincoln, Nebr., 1983.

CARLISLE INDIAN SCHOOL

SEE: Indian Schools

CARROLL, MATTHEW

Wagon freighter and trader Matthew Carroll (1837–1909) came to America from his native Ireland in 1857. He became a trader at FORT BENTON, Montana. In 1868, Carroll, E. G. Maclay, and George Steele bought the Diamond R, the largest and best-known overland wagon-freighting line in the Northwest. Carroll directed the freight line's operations when it provided transport for the U.S. Cavalry during the Sioux War of 1876. He helped bury dead soldiers from the Battle of Little Bighorn. In 1879, he left the freight line to work as an independent trader.

—*David Dary*

SEE ALSO: Overland Freight

SUGGESTED READING:
Henry P. Walker, *The Wagonmasters.* Norman, Okla., 1966.

CARSON, CHRISTOPHER HOUSTON ("KIT")

Born in Kentucky, Christopher Houston ("Kit") Carson (1809–1868) became a famous frontier scout, trapper and mountain man, Indian agent, and soldier. In 1826, he ran away from an apprenticeship with a saddlemaker in Missouri and joined a wagon train to Santa Fe, New Mexico. From those beginnings as a teamster, Carson would achieve an almost mythical reputation as a Western hero—a reputation promoted by the explorer and politician JOHN CHARLES FRÉMONT and his ambitious wife, JESSIE BENTON FRÉMONT. The friendship between Carson and Frémont was born of the adversities they experienced together during Frémont's government expeditions of the mid-1840s. Carson not

Christopher Houston ("Kit") Carson. *Courtesy Museum of New Mexico.*

only acted as Frémont's scout into the Rockies, Great Basin, Oregon, and California, but he also provided essential trail-blazing services and developed valuable Indian contacts for other explorers, hunters, and trappers.

One of those trappers was EWING YOUNG, who employed Carson from 1828 to 1831 on beaver hunts in the American Southwest and California. In 1836, Carson also worked briefly for the HUDSON'S BAY COMPANY. From 1841 to 1842, he operated out of BENT'S FORT (in present-day Colorado) on the Arkansas River. While accompanying Frémont's third expedition to California in 1845 and 1846, Carson participated in the UNITED STATES–MEXICAN WAR. As a member of Frémont's Battalion of Mounted Riflemen, Carson was indirectly enmeshed in the Bear Flag Revolt at Sonoma. He later undertook courier duties and guided General STEPHEN WATTS KEARNY's forces into California from New Mexico.

After 1849, Carson settled with his wife Josefa on a ranch near Taos, New Mexico, where he raised sheep. Following a final trapping foray in 1852, he joined Lucien Maxwell in driving sheep to new markets in California. He next became an Indian agent in New Mexico until 1861.

During the Civil War, Carson rose to the rank of brigadier general in the Union army after taking part in the Battle of Valverde. Carson was the only general in the army who could not read or write. His duties included hemming in the hostile Mescalero Apache, Kiowa, and Navajo tribes. Although successful in controlling the Indians, Carson displayed ambivalence toward them. At times, he was sympathetic, having been married, though unsuccessfully, to two Indian women early in life. At other times, he could be ruthless, as seen in his attempts to herd about three thousand Southwestern natives onto government reservations. The center of his command was Fort Garland in southern Colorado.

Late in life, Carson dictated his autobiography, which has been embellished by others. After the Carsons moved to Boggsville, Colorado (near present-day Las Animas), Josefa died. Within a month, Carson, too, died at Fort Lyon, Colorado.

—Andrew Rolle

SEE ALSO: Mountain Men; Navajo Wars; United States Army: Scouts

SUGGESTED READING:

Carson, Christopher. *Kit Carson's Autobiography.* Edited by Milo Milton Quaife. Chicago, 1935.

Carter, Harvey L. *Dear Old Kit: The Historical Christopher Carson.* Norman, Okla., 1968.

Estergreen, Marion. *Kit Carson, A Portrait in Courage.* Norman, Okla., 1962.

Guild, Thelma, and Harvey L. Carter. *Kit Carson: A Pattern for Heroes.* Lincoln, Nebr., 1984.

Kelly, Lawrence C. *Navajo Roundup: Selected Correspondence of Kit Carson's Expedition against the Navajo, 1863–1865.* Boulder, Colo., 1970.

CARSON, RACHEL LOUISE, AND *SILENT SPRING*

Internationally famous as a scientist and nature writer for her trilogy on the sea, Rachel Louise Carson (1907–1964) began the research for *Silent Spring* in 1958. As a government biologist in the Fish and Wildlife Service from 1936 to 1952, she had followed the controversy over the widespread use of synthetic PESTICIDES, especially DDT, after their development in World War II. Concerned about humankind's increasing arrogance toward the living world, she saw in the careless use of chemical pesticides, which she called "biocides," the same potential for the destruction of the living world as the unknown effects of atomic radiation.

Assisted by scientists from all over the world who recognized her unique ability to present complex material in accurate but understandable terms, she published *Silent Spring* in the fall of 1962 after it had been serialized in *The New Yorker.* Carson indicted the government, the powerful agri-chemical industry, and the scientific establishment for acting irresponsibly. Although her enemies tried to undermine her conclusions and attacked her as an alarmist and a poor scientist, she illustrated, as no one else had, that humankind was part of the earth's ecosystem and that by destroying any part of nature, all life was at risk. The book had such an enormous public impact that the federal government conducted its own investigation of pesticide pollution and later banned the domestic use of DDT. *Silent Spring* was a book that changed the course of history.

Although Carson died of cancer at the age of fifty-six, she lived long enough to see her conclusions validated and to inspire a public movement to protect the environment from technologies whose effects were uncertain. Her vision of the interconnectedness of all life placed the nature of industrial order on the environmental agenda. For many, *Silent Spring* marks the beginning of the contemporary environmental movement. Carson was honored by the public and by awards from science and arts organizations and was awarded the Presidential Medal of Freedom, posthumously, in 1980.

—Linda J. Lear

SUGGESTED READING:

Brooks, Paul. *The House of Life: Rachel Carson at Work.* Boston, 1972.

Lear, Linda J. "Rachel Carson's Silent Spring." *Environmental History Review* 17 (1993): 23–48.

Hinckley, Ted C. *Alaskan John G. Brady, Missionary, Businessman, Judge, and Governor, 1878–1918.* Columbus, Ohio, 1982.

CARTER ACT

The Carter Act was legislation passed by Congress to establish in the ALASKA Territory a criminal code, a code of criminal procedure, a political code, a code of civil procedure, and a civil code. By the late 1890s, the KLONDIKE GOLD RUSH, Alaska's technically illegal courts, and the need for "colonial legislation" following the Spanish-American War mandated an authentic code of laws.

Senator Thomas H. Carter, who annotated *The Laws of Alaska . . .*, was one of the leaders in securing what is known as the Carter Code. Born in Ohio, Carter typified the westward moving Americans of his generation. In 1882, having passed the Iowa bar, he moved to Helena, Montana. When that territory achieved statehood in 1889, Carter was elected to the House of Representatives on the Republican ticket. Although defeated for reelection in 1890, he remained active in party affairs. From 1895 to 1901 and again from 1905 to 1911, he served as a U.S. senator.

Two acts by Congress constitute the Carter Code. The first was approved on March 3, 1899; the second on June 6, 1900. The code, although modified, reflected the Revised Statutes of the United States and the Oregon and California codes.

Among its many provisions, the Carter Code clarified business taxes. With slight changes, it persisted for more than fifty years. Henceforth Alaska had legal juries. The code attempted to resolve the controversy over liquor prohibition in Alaska by allowing local-option licenses; that action, however, only briefly resolved the vexing issue of prohibition. District courts were established at St. Michael and Eagle City to deal with expanding mining activities. The laws did not provide for a domestic police force, and, most grievously, the laws failed to eliminate the fee system frequently exploited by lower-court judges, or commissioners. Although the transfer of Alaska's capital would have to wait for supplemental legislation, the move from historic Sitka to bustling Juneau was set in motion by the Carter Code.

—*Ted C. Hinckley*

SUGGESTED READING:

Gruening, Ernest. *The State of Alaska.* New York, 1954.

CARTOGRAPHY

From the time of the earliest Spanish explorations, down through the American scientific surveys of the late nineteenth century, Western expeditions included individuals whose job was to map or make cartographic representations of the region. The first maps of the West were crude affairs, drawn with charcoal or ink on parchment and preserved only in manuscript form. Rarely were they reproduced in atlases or otherwise made available for public viewing. Over time, maps became increasingly elaborate until, by the post–Civil War years, they reached the level of artistic works, worthy of exhibition alongside other graphic representations of the West. Reproduced as part of published exploratory accounts, in atlases, or as single sheets, the later maps were readily accessible to the public. But whether they were rarely viewed manuscripts or broadly disseminated printed works, the maps of the American West were often critical elements in shaping beliefs about the nature and content of the lands between the Mississippi and the Pacific. Cartographers attempted to answer questions about the most basic elements of North American geography: How wide was the North American continent, and what was its shape? What was the nature of the drainage system, and was it possible to travel by water—via either sea-level straits or river and lake systems—from Atlantic to Pacific? Did great interior bodies of water exist, and, if so, did they connect with either the eastern or western oceans? What was the nature and location of mountain ranges in the interior; would they provide barriers to transcontinental travel, or would they permit access from East to West? Many of these questions were not answered until the nineteenth century, as mapping of the West by American explorers supplanted the earlier and less accurate productions of the Spanish, French, and English during the colonial period.

Spanish cartography

The history of Western cartography began early in the sixteenth century with the first penetration of the trans-Mississippi region by the Spanish. Early Spanish maps depicting the great *entradas* of Hernando de Soto and FRANCISCO VÁSQUEZ DE CORONADO consisted of simple line drawings, primitive in form and containing relatively little significant geographical information. Spanish navigators, such as JUAN RODRÍGUEZ

CABRILLO and Sebastian Vizcaíno, began probing northward into the Gulf of California and even along the outer Pacific Coast of Baja and Alta California as early as 1540 and continued their explorations of the Pacific regions for the next two and a half centuries. The cartography produced during these explorations, however, provided relatively little detailed information. Nor was further Spanish penetration of the interior in the eighteenth century valuable in cartographic terms. Spanish mapping of the sixteenth and seventeenth centuries was closely guarded, and the Spanish became increasingly protective of their territories in New Spain. By the eighteenth century, sketches from field exploration were sent to draftsmen in Mexico City for compilation, and the completed maps were forwarded to the archives in Seville where they lay for nearly two centuries—and are only now being investigated by scholars. The detailed maps were not available to the non-Spanish world; those maps that *were* made available can best described as minimal, showing only a hint of the region's complex geography or Spain's understanding of it. At the time of the American Revolution, Spanish explorers had traveled the Pacific Coast as far north as the fifty-fifth parallel, penetrated into the Great Plains region as far as central Kansas, probed the interior Great Basin region, and established connections between Mexico and California. Published maps based on Spanish geographical accounts were still filled with error and guesswork. California was variously shown as an island or part of the mainland. There was no clear recognition of the courses of interior rivers such as the Missouri, Platte, or Arkansas, all of which Spanish explorers had seen, or even of the Rio Grande north of the New Mexican colony. Indeed, the prevailing Spanish cartographic image on available maps showed the source of the Missouri very near the headwaters of the Rio Grande. In spite of Spaniards' considerable experience in the southern Rockies and Great Basin, the great interior mountain range and the region between the mountain ranges to the west was poorly delineated in public cartography. Mythical rivers, such as the Rio San Buenaventura, were shown flowing west from the Rockies and entering the Pacific near San Francisco Bay. And the Strait of Anian, a mythical sea-level connection between the Atlantic and the Pacific near the fiftieth parallel, still appeared in Spanish maps.

French cartography

The French penetrated the continental interior relatively early in the period of exploration. By 1700, the French had traveled from the St. Lawrence to the mouth of the Mississippi, to the western Great Lakes. A few decades later, French explorers (the Vérendryes) reached as far west as either the Black Hills or the Bighorn Mountains of central Wyoming. During the period of French control of the Louisiana Territory, the explorer Jean Truteau and others traveled up the Missouri toward the Mandan villages, and the Mallet brothers crossed the Great Plains to New Mexico. French cartography, much of it produced by draftsmen accompanying the expeditions and then translated into beautifully colored maps by French cartographers (particularly those of Dieppe school), was somewhat more accurate than that of the Spanish, but it was not without its significant flaws. The prime incentive for French exploration was the fur trade, which placed a high value on water travel. From the very first French maps of the continent (based on Giovanni da Verrazzano's exploration of the Atlantic Coast in the 1520s), French cartography was fixed on the presence of great interior bodies of water that would provide easy passage from the St. Lawrence and Mississippi, through a "Great Sea of the West," and down equally mythical great rivers to the Pacific. In spite of the failure of French explorers to locate such geographical features, late eighteenth-century maps of the Western interior still depicted inland seas and "heights-of-land" (rather than interior mountain ranges) similar to the drainage divides of the Laurentian Shield area north of the St. Lawrence.

British cartography

The British also produced maps of the Western interior before the American Revolution. The British explorers in the American West were associated with the FUR TRADE and sought the location of water routes between the Atlantic and the Pacific. British exploration and cartography, however, was more systematic than that of either the Spanish or the French. Hence, it was technically more precise and contained few, if any, geographic elements of myth or fancy. The standard practice was for the "corporate" explorers of the HUDSON'S BAY COMPANY or the North West Company to provide raw data to English cartographic houses in London. There, some of the most accurate and elegant maps of the West before the nineteenth century were produced. With the exception of the Pacific Coast explorations of JAMES COOK and George Vancouver (explorations that yielded extremely accurate maps of the Pacific Northwest), the British were late-comers in the American West. Not until DAVID THOMPSON of the North West Company reached the Mandan villages of central North Dakota in the late 1700s did British explorers penetrate the trans-Mississippi region. Nevertheless, based on British explorations in western Canada and a more scientific approach to map making, cartographers such as Aaron Arrowsmith extrapolated from British contacts with the Rocky Mountains to the mountains below the fiftieth parallel. Therein lay the basic inaccuracy of British cartography of the West. One of the greatest British explorers, Alexander Mackenzie, had crossed the Canadian Rockies from Hudson's Bay to Pacific drainage via a portage of approximately a half mile. If such a portage existed between the upper Peace River and the upper Fraser (mistakenly assumed to be the Columbia by nearly all British cartographers), such a portage must also exist in a core drainage region farther south—where the upper Missouri, the southern headwaters of the Columbia, and the headwaters of other major Western streams like the Arkansas, Platte, Rio Grande, and Colorado all converged. Arrowsmith postulated such a core drainage area on his early nineteenth-century maps of North America, and it was on that concept that the first American exploring and mapping expedition into the West was based.

American cartography

Early in 1802, THOMAS JEFFERSON acquired both a copy of Alexander Mackenzie's *Travels from Montreal . . . to the Pacific Ocean* and an 1802 Arrowsmith map of North America. These materials, along with Jefferson's interest in a commercially viable transcontinental water route, propelled him to sponsor the exploration and cartographic expedition of MERIWETHER LEWIS and WILLIAM CLARK. Their expedition from 1804 to 1806 to the Pacific and back produced the first American maps of the West based on actual field experiences. Clark, a skilled cartographer, and Lewis painstakingly surveyed the land. On his 1810 manuscript map, Clark used not only those surveys but also the cartographic information he received from fur TRAPPERS in the upper Missouri basin. The result of Clark's mapping was the elegant 1814 map, engraved by Samuel Lewis from Clark's manuscript and published with the official account of the expedition. Much subsequent cartography of the West would be based on that map. For the areas actually covered by the expedition—the Missouri and Yellowstone system and the southern portions of the Columbia drainage—Clark's map was remarkably accurate. Away from the expedition's line of travel, however, Clark used speculation and the geography of hope. Unsuccessful at finding a short portage between the upper Missouri and the upper Columbia, Clark positioned the core drainage region farther south on his map and showed the headwaters of the Missouri, Yellowstone, Platte, Arkansas, Rio Grande, Colorado, Snake, and the purely mythical Multnomah within an area of approximately four hundred square miles. That error would persist in Western cartography until near the middle of the century.

Between the LEWIS AND CLARK EXPEDITION and the beginning of mapping in the West by the U.S. Army CORPS OF TOPOGRAPHICAL ENGINEERS in the early 1840s, Western cartography was a mixture of scientifically derived maps from the field surveys of government explorers such as ZEBULON MONTGOMERY PIKE and STEPHEN HARRIMAN LONG and the informal sketch mapping of Rocky Mountain fur traders. Although neither Pike nor Long was skilled in cartography, the maps derived from their field notes and engraved by artisans in Washington and Philadelphia provided reasonably accurate depictions of the Great Plains region. Long even contributed to a myth about the Plains by inserting the words "GREAT AMERICAN DESERT" across the southern region portrayed on his map. And Pike substantiated the core drainage thesis of the British and of William Clark by representing in the Colorado Rockies an area of "perpetual snows and fountains," an area that provided the source waters for nearly all major Western rivers.

Members of the Rocky Mountain fur trade also contributed to American mapping efforts, although in a much less formal way than the official government explorers. Trappers' maps were crude affairs, much like Native American maps, sketched in the dirt or drawn on elk hides to illustrate the essential points of Western geography. Few published maps came out of the Rocky Mountain fur trade before 1840. Those that did, however, were significant. Published in WASHINGTON IRVING's *Scenes and Adventures in the Rocky Mountains* (1837) were maps prepared by Captain BENJAMIN LOUIS EULALIE DE BONNEVILLE, an American army officer involved in the fur trade of the late 1830s. His maps, like those produced by David Burr, the geographer to the House of Representatives, presented trappers' most current and up-to-date information on the Rockies and the region farther west. While still containing some inaccuracies and retaining some fictions of earlier maps (such as the mythical Rio San Buenaventura that drained the country between the central Rockies and the Pacific), the maps omitted most of speculative geography derived from lore of fur trappers.

Truly scientific Western cartography, based on accurate astronomical observations and careful field surveys, began with the first explorations of the Corps of Topographical Engineers in the early 1840s and continued through the Pacific Railroad Surveys of the 1850s and the scientific explorations between the end of the Civil War and the turn of the century. The first, and in many ways the most prominent, of the topographical engineers was JOHN CHARLES FRÉMONT, who explored, surveyed, and mapped the country between the Mississippi and the Pacific from 1842 to 1848.

Frémont was the first to recognize the existence of the Great Basin. His meticulous maps, prepared by his topographer CHARLES PREUSS and then engraved in the printing houses of Washington, D.C., for publication, were the first truly accurate cartographical representations of the West. The details not provided by Frémont's surveys were filled in by other army explorers or topographers engaged in surveying potential routes for a transcontinental railway or in delineating the United States–Mexico boundary following the war between those countries. Standard practice among the topographical engineers was to coordinate the surveying and mapping activities of a team of skilled draftsmen who prepared maps in the field. Those field maps—often elegant productions in their own right—were then carefully engraved on metal plates for printing. Virtually all of the reports and accompanying maps of the government explorations were published and widely available for sale; the *Pacific Railroad Reports* alone ran to twelve volumes. The capstone of military mapping was the publication, in 1857, of Lieutenant Gouverneur Kemble Warren's "General Map of the Territory of the United States from the Mississippi to the Pacific Ocean." Warren consolidated data from expeditions of the Corps of Topographical Engineers in producing his map.

After the Civil War, other government explorers engaged in nonmilitary, scientific reconnaissances took over Western mapping from the army. Operating under such fledgling government agencies as the U.S. Geographical and Geological Survey of the Territories, explorer-scientists, such as JOHN WESLEY POWELL, FERDINAND VANDEVEER HAYDEN, CLARENCE KING, Grove Karl Gilbert, and George Wheeler, completed the cartographic tasks begun more than three centuries earlier by the first Spanish explorers of the Western interior. The maps produced in the 1870s and 1880s by those first scientific geologists and geographers were often elaborate works of art: shaded relief representations and three-dimensional topographic drawings of the more prominent and scientifically interesting features of Western topography. Dramatic and striking from a purely visual standpoint, these scientific cartographic depictions of the West also served utilitarian purposes. Long a sparsely populated region, the West was beginning to fill with Americans determined to exploit the region's resources. Miners, farmers, ranchers, loggers, and railroad and town builders demanded accurate, detailed information on natural resources, mineral deposits, geologic structures, and land classification in addition to topographical representation. Their demands were met by the scientist-explorers. As the century drew to a close, the American West was understood not only in a scientific sense but also in a practical sense. The cartographic consequences of that understanding—the finely detailed small-scale maps that were the forerunners of today's UNITED STATES GEOLOGICAL SURVEY topographical quadrangle maps—were a far cry from the first primitive mapping attempts of European explorers in a new and strange land.

—*John Logan Allen*

SEE ALSO: Exploration: English Expeditions, French Expeditions, Spanish Expeditions, United States Expeditions; Exploration and Science; Transcontinental Railroad Surveys

SUGGESTED READING:

Allen, John Logan. *Passage Through the Garden.* Urbana, Ill., 1975.
———. "Maps of the Mountains: The Cartography of the Rocky Mountain Fur Trade." In *The Intermountain West.* Edited by Lary Dilsaver and William Wycoff. Lincoln, Nebr., 1994.
Bartlett, Richard A. *The Great Surveys of the American West.* Norman, Okla., 1962.
Goetzmann, William H. *Army Exploration in the American West, 1803–1863.* New Haven, Conn., 1959.
———. *Exploration and Empire: The Explorer and the Scientist in the Winning of the American West.* New York, 1967.
Klemp, Egon. *America in Maps Dating from 1500 to 1856.* New York, 1976.
Luebke, Frederick C., et al. *Mapping the North American Plains: Essays in the History of Cartography.* Norman, Okla., 1987.
Ristow, Walter W. *Maps for an Emerging Nation: Commercial Cartography in Nineteenth Century America.* Washington, D.C., 1977.
Wheat, Carl Irving. *Mapping the Trans-Mississippi West, 1540–1861.* 5 vols. San Francisco, 1954.

CARY, WILLIAM DE LA MONTAGNE

Painter and illustrator William de la Montagne Cary (1840–1922) was born in Tappan, New York, and grew up in New York City. At the age of fourteen, he was apprenticed to a commercial engraver. Before his twentieth year, he was contributing illustrations to *Aldine's* and other magazines of the period. Although his family urged him to go abroad to study art, he decided instead to travel in the American West; he was inspired to do so, he later recalled, by reading the tales of JAMES FENIMORE COOPER and the published journals of the LEWIS AND CLARK EXPEDITION.

In 1861, he set out with two companions from St. Louis on an American Fur Company steamboat bound for the upper Missouri River country. The young travelers left the river at Fort Benton, Montana, and continued overland to Fort Walla Walla, Washington. From there, they made their way to San Francisco and booked passage on a ship bound for New York via the Isthmus of Panama. An account of their adventure later appeared in *Recreation Magazine.*

Cary again traveled in the West in 1867 and visited U.S. military posts in Kansas. In 1874, he ascended the Missouri River a second time when he accompanied an official survey sponsored by the U.S. Northern Boundary Commission. Cary's Western views were regularly featured throughout the 1870s in *Harper's Weekly* and *Frank Leslie's Illustrated Newspaper.* During that period, he maintained a studio in New York on West 55th Street, where he was associated with ALBERT BIERSTADT, George Inness, and other notable artists of the day.

Cary exhibited his paintings of Western life in New York City and Washington, D.C., as well as abroad in London and Berlin. One of the last exhibits of his work in New York was held at the American Museum of Natural History. By that time, he had moved his studio to West 14th Street, where, surrounded by the souvenirs of his earlier travels in the West, he was said to be active as late as 1921. The largest collection of his work is found today at the THOMAS GILCREASE INSTITUTE in Tulsa, Oklahoma.

—*David C. Hunt*

SEE ALSO: Art: Book and Magazine Illustration, Western Art

SUGGESTED READING:
Ladner, Mildred D. *William de la Montagne Cary: Artist of the Missouri River.* Norman and Tulsa, Okla., 1984.
Rossi, Paul A., and David Hunt. *The Art of the Old West.* 1971. Reprint. New York, 1989.
Taft, Robert. *Artists and Illustrators of the Old West, 1850–1900.* New York, 1953.

CASA GRANDE RUINS RESERVATION

Located in central Arizona, the Casa Grande Ruins Reservation was the first archaeological ruin preserved by the FEDERAL GOVERNMENT. In 1889, Congress authorized the president to reserve lands containing the ruins; the reservation came into existence in 1892, when President Benjamin Harrison designated it a "national reservation" and appropriated funds for its upkeep. In 1918, in an effort to standardize administration and nomenclature, the area became a national monument and was placed under the jurisdiction of the NATIONAL PARK SERVICE.

The first and only national reservation, Casa Grande was established to protect the ruins of a four-story, coursed caliche-earth construction building of the fourteenth century. Atypical of Hohokam structures, Casa Grande more resembles prehistoric ruins in Mexico than others in the Southwest. Europeans first saw the structure in 1694 when Father EUSEBIO FRANCISCO KINO gave it its modern name.

The preservation of Casa Grande was an extremely early example of the forces that later drove the conservation and preservation movements of the early 1900s. Growing anxiety about the transformation of American society inspired interest in the fate of the nation's natural and cultural resources. Most of those concerned were affluent Northeasterners, many of whom had never been to the Southwest. Influential people closely tied to the power structure of the nation, they initiated a process that came to reflect the basic tenets of the Progressive movement. Not everyone was thrilled by the reservation of Western land, and the ideas behind the establishment of the Casa Grande Ruins Reservation became the source of friction between the federal government and citizens and government in the West.

—*Hal Rothman*

SEE ALSO: Archaeology

SUGGESTED READING:
Clemensen, A. Berle. *Casa Granda Ruins National Monument, Arizona; A Centennial History of the First Prehistoric Preserve, 1892–1992.* Denver, 1992.
Rothman, Hal. *Preserving Different Pasts: The American Natinal Monuments.* Urbana, Ill., 1989

CASSIDY, BUTCH (PARKER, ROBERT LEROY)

Outlaw and member of the Wild Bunch, Robert LeRoy Parker (1866–1937?) was born in Beaver, Utah, the oldest of thirteen children. He moved with his family to Circleville, Utah, and settled on a small ranch in 1878. His sister, Lula Parker Betenson, told the story of how ranch hand Mike Cassidy, an outlaw, taught young LeRoy, or Bob, the fundamentals of rustling and shooting. Sometime after leaving home in 1884, young Parker assumed Cassidy's name. "Butch" was reputedly added to his name after he worked briefly in a butcher shop in Rock Springs, Wyoming.

Butch Cassidy began his outlaw career as a cowboy-cum-rustler. By 1889, he had graduated from petty rustling to bank and train robbery. On June 24 of that year, Cassidy and two well-known outlaws, Matt Warner and Tom McCarty, robbed the San Miguel County Bank in Telluride, Colorado. Their "take" was $10,500. About the time of the Telluride robbery, or shortly after, Cassidy, William Ellsworth "Elza" Lay, Harry Lonabaugh (the "Sundance Kid"), Harvey Logan ("Kid Curry"), Ben Kilpatrick (the "Tall Texan"), and Will Carver formed the gang that came to be known as the Wild Bunch.

Unquestionably, the Wild Bunch was the West's best organized gang. Operating out of such exotically named hideouts as Hole-in-the-Wall in Wyoming's Bighorn Mountains, Robbers Roost near the San Rafael Swell in Utah, and Brown's Hole in Colorado, the gang covered incredible distances. On September 19, 1900, Cassidy, Lonabaugh, and Carver robbed the bank in Winnemucca, Nevada. On July 3, 1901, they robbed the Great Northern Railroad in Wagner in northern Montana. They robbed the Union Pacific Railroad in Wilcox and Tipton, Wyoming. For its time, the Wild Bunch's modus operandi was both sophisticated and successful. The gang carefully cased banks, often days before the robberies. They staged railroad holdups in remote areas where lawmen had difficulty gathering posses. They kept fresh horse relays a hard ride from the scene of each robbery. Cassidy, however, had not always been so resourceful. He was convicted of horse theft in Lander, Wyoming, in 1894 and was sent to the state penitentiary. Pardoned in January of 1896, he promised to "go straight." He did: straight back to the Wild Bunch in Brown's Hole.

Weary of constant pursuit, the Wild Bunch disbanded by 1900. Cassidy and Sundance, along with the latter's *inamorata* Etta Place, fled to Argentina in late 1901 or early 1902. Their exploits in South America were epochal. They robbed banks and trains in Argentina, Chile, and Bolivia. Cassidy and Sundance were presumed to have been killed in San Vicente, Bolivia, in 1909. (In the 1969 movie *Butch Cassidy and the Sundance Kid,* both were killed in the San Vicente shootout.) Recent scholarship holds that both men, along with Etta Place, returned to the United States. Lula Betenson wrote that Cassidy came home in 1925. He died in 1937 and was buried under the alias of Roberts somewhere in Washington state.

—*Jack Burrows*

SUGGESTED READING:
Betenson, Lula Parker. *Butch Cassidy, My Brother.* Provo, Utah, 1975.
Cunningham, Eugene. *Triggernometry: A Gallery of Gunfighters.* Caldwell, Idaho, 1947.
Holbrook, Stuart H. *The Story of the American Railroads.* New York, 1947.
Horan, James D. *The Wild Bunch.* New York, 1958.
Howard, Robert West, ed. *This Is the West.* Chicago, 1957.
Kirby, Edward M. *The Rise and Fall of the Sundance Kid.* Iola, Wis., 1983.

CASTRO, JOSÉ

Mexican governor of Alta California from 1835 to 1836, José Castro (1810–1860) served as *commandante general,* or military commandant, between 1838 and 1842. Born in Mexico, Castro, at the age of eighteen, worked as a secretary in the municipal government of Monterrey. He then joined the Mexican army and began his career in Alta California. As an independent province of Mexico, California had twelve governors between 1822 and 1835; some ruled for as long as six years; others for as few as twenty days.

Castro was appointed governor of Alta California in 1835, a crucial year in the history of Mexican California. He succeeded governor JOSÉ FIGUEROA, who had actively participated in the secularization of the Spanish missions of California. Not readily accepted by some of the most influential of the seven thousand Californios (descendants of the Spanish-Mexican colonists who had settled in California in the 1760s), Castro resigned his office in January 1836, allowing Nicolás Gutiérrez to assume gubernatorial responsibilities.

In 1836, Juan Bautista Alvarado began recruiting a force to overthrow the centralist government of Governor Gutiérrez. Castro joined the movement immediately and was appointed military chief. On November 7, 1836, Alvarado's troops defeated the forces of the new governor, PÍO DE JESUS PICO, occupied the governor's mansion, and declared California independent. Most Californios, however, were against independence, and Pico was restored to power.

The peace and stability of the region continued to suffer as a result of internal disorder. In the 1840s, a new governor, General Manuel Micheltorena, commanded an army of exconvicts who exacerbated the need for order and security in Alta California. A revolt broke out against Micheltorena in November 1844. After several weeks of fighting, the governor was forced to sign an agreement to send his disorderly army back to Mexico. When the terms of the agreement were not followed, Castro renewed the revolt against Micheltorena and defeated him in February 1845. Pico was restored to power, and Castro was reappointed the military commander of California.

During a dispute between Pico and Castro over financial matters and the location of the capital, JOHN CHARLES FRÉMONT and his "Bear Flag Forces" began asserting their power and forced Castro to retreat to Mexico. He returned to California as a private citizen in 1848.

—*Fred L. Koestler*

SUGGESTED READING:
Chapman, Charles E. *A History of California: The Spanish Period*. New York, 1939.

CATAMOUNTS

SEE: Mountain Lions

CATHER, WILLA

A major American writer best known for her novels of the Nebraska prairie and the American Southwest, her lyrical prose, her theory of the unfurnished novel, and her condemnation of American materialism in the years after World War I, Willa Cather (1873–1947) was born in Gore, Virginia. She moved at the age of nine to western Nebraska where she lived on a prairie farm for a year and a half before moving to the small town of Red Cloud. She finished high school in Red Cloud and then attended the University of Nebraska. After graduation, she settled in Pittsburgh where she worked in journalism and taught high-school English. In 1906, she moved to New York City to work as an editor for *McClure's Magazine*, the preeminent magazine of the muckraking era. She left *McClure's* in 1911 to devote herself completely to her writing.

Cather first garnered attention with her novels of the American prairie; the most important of these are *O Pioneers!* (1913) and *My Ántonia* (1918). In *O Pioneers!* the character of Alexandra Bergson, the daughter of a Swedish immigrant, tells the story of immigrant women and the harsh life on the frontier prairie. *My Ántonia* recounts the life of Ántonia Shimerda, a young Bohemian girl who grows from a child to a beloved matriarch. Cather's experiments with literary point of view and her glowing prose are notable aspects of the novel, which is told through the eyes of Jim Burden, a male friend of Ántonia.

Cather's second major interest, the American Southwest, provided the setting of the central episode of *The Professor's House* (1925) as well as *Death Comes for the Archbishop* (1927)—the novel Cather called her favorite. *The Professor's House* best reflects Cather's disillusionment following World War I and her despair over materialism in American life. The novel, in which Cather furthered her experiments in narrative structure, point of view, and symbolism, is one of the high points of American literary modernism. *Death Comes for the Archbishop*—which tells the story of Bishop JEAN BAPTISTE LAMY of Santa Fe—foreshadowed her later turn to historical fiction, which dominated the last fifteen years of her career.

Cather has always been celebrated as a Western writer and as a literary modernist, but in recent years, her work has attracted considerable interest from feminist scholars and critics who focus on the novels from her middle and late period such as *A Lost Lady*, *My Mortal Enemy*, *Lucy Gayheart*, and *Sapphira and the Slave Girl*. She has also received attention for her literary theory, especially for her use of the organic principle and for her theory of the unfurnished novel, a theory which she set forth in an essay entitled "The Novel Démeublé" (1922). In that essay, she argued that the artistic process was one of simplification and wrote, "If the novel is a form of imaginative art, it cannot be at the same time a vivid and brilliant form of journalism. Out of the teeming, gleaming stream of the present it must select the eternal material of art."

—*Larry Hartsfield*

SEE ALSO: Literature; Women Writers

SUGGESTED READING:
Bennett, Mildred R. *The World of Willa Cather*. New York, 1951.
Brown, E. K., and Leon Edel. *Willa Cather: A Critical Biography*. New York, 1953.
Cather, Willa. *Death Comes for the Archbishop*. New York, 1927.
———. *A Lost Lady*. New York, 1923.
———. *Lucy Gayheart*. New York, 1935.
———. *My Ántonia*. Boston, 1918.
———. *My Mortal Enemy*. New York, 1926.
———. *Not Under Forty* (essays). New York, 1936.
———. *One of Ours*. New York, 1922.
———. *O Pioneers!* Boston, 1913.
———. *The Professor's House*. New York, 1925.
———. *Sapphira and the Slave Girl*. New York, 1940.
———. *Shadows on the Rock*. New York, 1931.
———. *The Song of the Lark*. Boston, 1915.
Woodress, James. *Willa Cather: A Literary Life*. Lincoln, Nebr., 1989.

CATHOLICS

Roman Catholicism played as intricate and complex a role in the history of the trans-Mississippi West as Puritanism did in the history of New England, and like the Puritan church in New England, the Catholic church in the West was not only a religious institution, but also a social and political force that helped determine the development of the region. Rivaling the Spanish crown as an agency of colonization during most of the Spanish era, the Catholic church—while still wealthy and important—had fallen into political decline by the time Mexico won its independence in 1821. The present-day American Southwest and California were then remote ecclesiastical outposts that threatened to be overwhelmed by a surge of evangelical PROTESTANTS from the East, who saw their manifest destiny in many ways as a moral injunction, in Richard White's words, "to save the West from Mormons and Catholics." By the time Protestants began arriving in great numbers in the 1840s, Roman Catholicism was not only the major religion of the West but also the largest individual denomination in the United States, a distinction it still maintains today. That its nineteenth-century growth had been fueled largely by Irish and German immigration did little to change its image as a "foreign" faith in predominately Anglo-Protestant America. It was the interplay between American Catholicism's Hispanic heritage, its multiethnic congregation, and its "ghetto" status in mainstream American culture that shaped the spiritual lives of Catholics in the West.

Missionary background

From the beginnings of the European invasion in the sixteenth century, Catholic missionaries—mostly Franciscans and Jesuits, but also Recollets and Capuchins—accompanied expeditions to the Western Hemisphere in search of Native American souls to save. Imperial Spain—and later, France—were in fact more interested in the mercantile and geopolitical potential of the Americas, but since at least 1492 when Christian soldiers finally managed to drive the Muslim Moors from Iberia, the glory of conquest and the spread of the gospel had gone hand in hand for the Spaniards. In fact, Spain's conquistadors came to believe they owned the "New World," mapped that year by Columbus, largely because the Spanish Pope, Alexander VI, gave it to the Crown of Castile in the papal donations of 1493. Occasionally, the religious impulse behind New World conquest triumphed over greed. When JUAN DE OÑATE (and his king) grew disillusioned with the potential of the colonial outposts Oñate had established in the 1590s in New Mexico and prepared to abandon them, the Franciscan friars among Oñate's colonizers persuaded Felipe III that they had baptized sufficient numbers of Pueblo Indians to be allowed to stay. Isolated eight hundred miles north of New Spain's already remote mining districts, New Mexico attracted few immigrants and, for most of the seventeenth century, endured primarily as a missionary frontier.

For eight decades, the Franciscans who occupied the Southwest were persuaded that they were converting Tanoan- and Keresan-speaking Pueblos and Zunis to Catholicism. For the most part, however, Pueblo Indians simply added Jesus, Mary, and Christian saints such as Santiago (Saint James) to their native pantheons and accepted the friars into their communities as new shamans. But the very presence of the Franciscans undermined native culture through exotic diseases, new tools, different crops and domestic animals, and a growing shift from hunting to agriculture that, while increasing their prosperity, also made the Pueblo Indians more attractive targets for nomadic raiders. As the terms of exchange shifted, Catholicism lost some of its luster. Violent native reactions, which the friars called rebellions, erupted occasionally, and in 1680 the Pueblo Indians drove the Catholics out entirely, only to be reconquered in 1692 by Don DIEGO DE VARGAS.

Meanwhile, France had launched its own colonial enterprise, also accompanied by Catholic missionaries. Recollet friars first arrived in Quebec in 1615, but they had little success in Canada and were displaced by the Jesuits beginning in 1625. The Jesuits soon discovered that neither the European civility of the Recollets nor the "reduction" of native populations to fixed missions (called *reducciones*, from the Spanish, *reducir*, "to bring together") practiced by the Jesuits in South America and Spanish Franciscans in the American Southwest worked very well in the north country. Long before Father LOUIS JOLIET joined JACQUES MARQUETTE to travel down the Mississippi in 1673, the Black Robes (as the Indians called the Jesuits) had displayed a marked ability to adapt to local circumstances in order to bring souls to Christ. The Jesuits traveled with Indian bands and took up residence in distant Indian villages and not a few became "martyrs" to the cause. They spread the influence of Catholicism—and of France—into the Ohio and Mississippi river valleys. In the course of doing so, they alarmed both the British imperialists east of the Mississippi and the Spanish to the west and south.

By the end of the seventeenth century, Spain was suffering the effects of an overextended empire and had become a nearly bankrupt nation unable to defend its North American holdings against Indian raiders or other European colonizers. In 1699, when the French established their first enduring colony in Louisiana near present-day St. Louis, the Spanish colonial government in Mexico City decided that it could no longer depend on Madrid and, on its own authority, gave the Jesuits permission to build a series of mis-

The Mission of San Juan, near San Antonio, Texas, as pictured in *Gleason's Pictorial Drawing-Room Companion* of the nineteenth century. *Courtesy Patrick H. Butler, III.*

helped produce a distinctive style of Catholicism whose heritage is still evident. The Native Americans whom the various Hispanic Catholic missionaries encountered enjoyed a diversity of indigenous beliefs, but as Oñate's friars first discovered—ultimately to their chagrin—American Indians had long engaged in "religious borrowing and synthesis," as anthropologist Robert Brightman has noted. When Indians grafted European Catholicism onto their own faiths, writes Brightman, this was "simply one more instance of a traditional receptivity to religious innovation." The rich blending of native ceremony with Christian beliefs was not unique to Indian-Hispanic religious interaction; the American West would soon see Sioux-Episcopal and Pima-Presbyterian amalgamations, for example, as well as Pueblo–Roman Catholic blends. But combined with the sparsity of priests (at their peak, the California Franciscans numbered thirty-eight friars) and the relative neglect of the frontier missions by the church, Indian blending of beliefs helped promote a lay Catholicism, closely associated with the poor and marked by local religious holidays and celebrations, that was unique to the American West.

Folk Catholicism

When Napoleon invaded Spain in 1808, he sparked a revolt by Spanish liberals in the Cortes (Spain's hitherto weak parliament) that spread throughout the Spanish empire and resulted in liberation movements in Latin America and in Mexico. Well before Mexico began agitating for independence from Spain around 1810, a century of attacks from Spanish liberals had sent the Roman Catholic church into political decline and had decimated its Southwestern missions pretty much everywhere but California. Missions had always been questionable operations in Texas, where the Indian neophytes languished and died or resisted and ran away in the face of the almost constant warfare with nomadic tribes, who stole or destroyed the mission herds. But even in New Mexico and Arizona, where the Franciscans took over after liberals expelled the Jesuits, the friars had difficulty maintaining their neophyte populations, and the number of padres be-

sions in present-day New Mexico, Arizona, and Texas. Here, unlike farther north, the Jesuits practiced the reduction techniques pioneered in the region by the Franciscans. Best known among the Jesuits was Father EUSEBIO FRANCISCO KINO, who traveled some twenty thousand miles and founded twenty-four missions. Although Kino himself seemed much beloved, few of the New World Jesuits were as beneficent as he. In fact, they were harsh task masters, which Spanish liberals found less objectionable than their tendency to arrogate authority to themselves. The era was dominated by a bitter church-state rivalry, and in 1717, Spanish liberals achieved a significant victory by forcing the Spanish crown to expel all Jesuits from New Spain. The expulsion caused missions in many parts of the empire to fall into rapid decay. In the American Southwest, however, the Franciscans again quickly stepped in to the fill the vacuum left by the departure of the Jesuits. Half a century later, Father JUNÍPERO SERRA established the first of twenty-one missions in present-day San Diego. The Catholic mission system would reach its apotheosis in eighteenth-century Alta California where highly motivated Franciscans forced native groups into Christian enclaves stretching as far north as Sonoma.

Although the mission system ravished the native populations and threatened the native cultures, it also gan to dwindle in the waning hours of the empire. The decline spawned a power struggle between Mexican bishops and the Catholic religious orders, with the bishops trying to "secularize" the missions so that the mission priests would come directly under their control instead of remaining independent Franciscans or Capuchins. In practice, such partial "secularizing" meant placing the missions in the hands of a military answering to the bishops, as happened in Texas—the Alamo mission being one example—and in New Mexico. Under the circumstances, it was hardly surprising to find padres such as Miguel Hidalgo and José María Morelos, priests with an extensive following of impoverished Indians and mestizos, deeply involved in the early revolutionary upheavals.

The Mexican Revolution shattered a church already cracked by such internal struggles. It forced Spanish priests out of the country and further crippled the missions. They became easy prey for Mexican liberals who wanted truly to secularize them and turn them into parishes. Partly the liberals wished to free the Indians from the clutches of the padres, whose treatment of their crypto-slaves was often onerous, although the church and Mexican conservatives argued that it was precisely these friars and their missions that offered the best hope of controlling the Indians. Although many Californios and Mexicans, including some liberals, longed for access to the missions' vast wealth and Indian labor even more than they wished to see the Native Americans free at last, conservative military officials in California—where levies on the wealthy and powerful missions paid for both administrative sala-

Catholics of Santa Fe, New Mexico, partake in a street festival in the late nineteenth or twentieth century. *Courtesy National Cowboy Hall of Fame and Western Heritage Center.*

ries and Mexican garrisons—offered enough resistance to force the revolutionary government to move carefully, at least at first.

When ANTONIO LÓPEZ DE SANTA ANNA became president of Mexico with liberal backing in 1832, he retired to his estate at Jalapa and put his vice-president, Valentin Gomez Farias, in charge of the Mexican government. A diehard liberal called by his enemies Gomez "Furioso," Farias abruptly secularized the Catholic missions in 1833. In Texas, as Richard White notes, this amounted "to the dismembering of a corpse," but its effect on the other borderlands was more profound. Not only did Farias eliminate the missions, he also lifted the compulsory annual 10 percent tithe the church collected on crops and livestock. In this one stroke, Rome lost both the title to its vast borderland estates and its income. Not only the missions, but much of the Roman Catholic church as an institution vanished in the American Southwest under the onslaught of liberal Mexican reform. Even as the wily Santa Anna distanced himself from Farias and began to court the conservative Mexican centralists, Farias's full frontal assault put to the lie the liberal goal of turning the missions into parishes. Few priests were attracted to the northern provinces and the region's now impoverished church, and Mexico found it could not replace the padres it had chased back to Spain. Only eight secular priests served all of New Mexico in 1829; there were two priests in Texas in 1830; in 1846, five churchmen ministered to California, and no priests at all graced present-day Arizona.

As a result of the paucity of clergy in an American Southwest where all residents were officially Catholic, Hispanic settlers in southern Texas, Arizona, California, and especially New Mexico, influenced by Indian and mestizo religious blends, developed a folk Catholicism all their own. Characteristic of Southwestern folk Catholicism were an immense respect for local patron saints (who were frequently credited with performing miracles), an especially strong "Mariolatry" (evident in the region's devotion to the Virgin of Guadalupe), and the frequent celebration of religious holidays—including the feast of San Antonio (January 17); San Juan's Day (June 24); the feast of Corpus Christi (the seventh week after Easter); All Saints' Day (November 1); All Souls' Day (November 2). The holidays climaxed in a month of celebration— December—with a medieval Spanish miracle play, *Los Pastores,* and a reenactment of the nine days Mary and Joseph wandered about Bethlehem in search of shelter before finding the manger in which Jesus was born.

One example of the extreme piety to which folk Catholicism might lead was a lay brotherhood named the Brothers of Our Father Jesus, but popularly known as the PENITENTES. The Penitentes developed their own liturgy and ceremonies, and, like all religious orders, worshiped together guided by those canons. The church did not recognize them as a bone fide order, but they conducted charitable works in its name nevertheless, helping the sick and the poor, burying the dead, and functioning as something resembling a mutual-aid society. Obsessed with the shortness and brutality of human life, its fragility, and its ubiquitous suffering, they punished themselves with extreme penances, whipping each other during Lent to achieve mystical union with the suffering Christ and in some years hanging one of their members on a cross on Good Friday until he passed out from pain and exhaustion. In addition to the Penitentes, there were such folk Catholic groups as the *curranderas,* who practiced faith healing, and from the early nineteenth century, the small chapel at Chimayo, New Mexico, drew those seeking to be healed by faith and became known as "The Lourdes of the Southwest." The Santos, the bultos, and the retablos, all produced folk carvings based on cultural beliefs developed among Hispanic Catholics.

While this pervasive folk Catholicism, which Arnoldo De Leon has described as "an attitude more consonant with life experience than theology," was tolerant of the influx of Anglo-Protestants to the trans-Mississippi West, the reverse did not prove true. Anglo-Americans associated the version of Catholicism practiced in New Mexico and the other borderlands with Hispanic Catholics in general, especially with poor Mexican Americans and Mexican immigrants. The official Catholic church also viewed the beliefs and practices of folk Catholicism with displeasure, and as a result, Mexican American Catholicism developed differently from that practiced by other Catholics who migrated to the West with increasing frequency after the 1830s. After the Anglo conquests of the TEXAS REVOLUTION and the UNITED STATES–MEXICAN WAR, Hispanic Catholics—more and more marginalized economically and socially by the dominant Anglo-Protestants and the more mainstream Euro-American Catholics—turned to the lay practices of folk and pastoral Catholicism, with their mysticism, special Saints, focus on the Virgin Mary, and numerous holidays and celebrations, as a fount of common identity and a source of social mediation among the Spanish-speaking, who were by then often confined to BARRIOS in the center of Anglo frontier towns. Such an identification would only be reinforced as the Mexican Revolution of 1910 sent huge numbers of Mexican immigrants northward into Texas, New Mexico, Arizona, and California looking for jobs and a better life, and bringing with them the syncretized lay Catholicism of the common folk of the Mexican homeland.

Immigrant Catholicism

For centuries, Catholicism had been the official state religion of the Spanish empire in America, and it remained so for Mexican North America. Both Spanish and Mexican authorities had required Anglo immigrants taking up residence in the trans-Mississippi West to convert to the Roman Catholic church in order to hold title to the lands the government granted them often in generous proportions. Although these Anglo settlers, attracted to French and Spanish lands by cheap prices and low taxes, consciously abandoned their nationality and their religion, they did not cease to be what they called "Americans," and they shied away from French and Spanish village life. Compulsive doers, used to local political talk, jury duty, and local elections of all kinds, they looked on the Catholics not as charming and relaxed, but as supercilious and lazy, and regardless of their oaths, they rejected Catholic values and institutions and continued to practice their more emotionally intense and internalized brand of Christianity. Whereas Catholics saw no reason for harsh distinctions between religious and social life and treated Sundays not only as a day of worship but also as one of celebration, the Anglo-Protestants held the Sabbath inviolate and frowned upon mixing piety and parties. The Catholics' church holidays, which featured music and dancing, where everyone—old, young, rich, poor, free, and slave—joined in the festivities, struck the Anglos as sinful and idolatrous. As Anglo populations increased in the trans-Mississippi West, Protestant denominations sent missionaries to minister to Native Americans and to keep their own congregations from straying from the fold.

From the mid-nineteenth century on, Euro-American and European Catholics, at first Germans and Irish, but later Italians and other groups, migrated to the West in ever greater numbers. The Catholic church continued to consider the West a mission region and organized new territories through the American Catholic church: Louisiana in 1803, Texas in 1845, the Oregon Country in 1846, and California and the Southwest in 1848. There developed a competition between the American Protestants and the American Catholics for the souls of Native Americans, Hispanics already living in the region, and the new immigrants from Europe. When groups of Native Americans from the Pacific Northwest, for example, arrived in St. Louis in 1833 and 1836 to appeal for a representative of "white religion" to come minister to their tribes, Catholic journals broadcast the Indians' pilgrimage as a call for "Black Robes" who said "Great Prayers," that is, the Mass, while Protestant literature described the Indians' request as one for the "white man's book of heaven." The result was that both Protestant and

Catholic missionaries, sometimes traveling on the same wagon trains, headed for the Pacific Northwest looking to save Indian souls. Jesuit PIERRE JEAN DE SMET's journey from St. Louis to the homeland of the Flatheads and Pend d'Oreilles beginning in June 1840 was the first step in what the Jesuits would call "the grandest missionary work of the nineteenth century. While the Protestant missionaries in many ways used their religious communities as a springboard for further Anglo-American settlement in the region, the Jesuits established mission communities based on the "holy experiment" in the Central Highlands of South America and the Spanish missions of the Southwest; they sought to reduce the Indian populations to agricultural communities. Although De Smet himself proved a skilful negotiator whose peace-keeping efforts on the Northern Plains saved hundreds of lives, the string of Jesuit missions never fulfilled their founders' hopes. The region's harsh climate was unsuitable for extensive farming, the Native Americans preferred their traditional hunting, fishing, and gathering ways to settled mission life, and this time the padres had no Spanish troops to help impose their wills.

The American Catholic church also ministered to European immigrants in the West. Texas, for example, in the first half of the nineteenth century was a post-mission region with only a handful of priests to serve the mostly Hispanic Texas Catholic community. But after Texas declared itself independent and established, at least on paper, freedom of religion, Jean Marie Odin, the first bishop of Galveston, oversaw the new growth in Texas Catholicism engendered by the arrival of the Europeans. German Catholics occupied the Texas Hill Country in the mid-1840s; in 1856, the Polish Franciscan Leopold Moczygemba led a group of Silesian Poles to Panna Maria. Texas Catholics, both Mexican American and Euro-American were, however, put in the minority in the 1850s by a vast influx of Baptists, Methodists, and CAMPBELLITES, whose evangelical styles played a major role in Texas history and continue to influence the state today. While Texas Catholics did suffer from the same kind of Know-Nothing anti-Catholicism that characterized the American Catholic experience in the East, on the whole Western Catholicism enjoyed a more tolerant social atmosphere, and, indeed, in the early years of trans-Mississippi migration, immigrant Catholics came to dominate for a while some Western communities such as BUTTE, MONTANA, and, most importantly, SAN FRANCISCO both politically and socially. The fact that California's first territorial governor, for example, was a convert to Catholicism did not prevent his political rise. And San Francisco's major banker in the late nineteenth century, AMADEO PETER GIANNINI, who contrib-

uted vast sums of money to Catholic causes, was widely respected in the state. But even in cosmopolitan San Francisco, Protestant resistance to the "foreign" religion was sometimes quite evident. Many historians view the VIGILANTISM that sprang up there more as an attack against Irish Catholic dominance of the city's political life than as the crusade against corruption and lawlessness it claimed to be. And in San Francisco, as throughout the West, Protestant and Catholic missionaries competed for "alien" souls, although there those souls were Asian—Chinese and Japanese—rather than Native American.

Ethnic rivalries also developed within the Catholic communities of the West between Irish and German Catholics and the more demonstrative Italians, all of whom disdained to worship with Mexican Americans. In fact, the Catholic hierarchy faced a dilemma unique among Western churches because of its multiethnic membership. Although Mass was conducted in Latin, regardless of the national origins of the celebrants, European immigrants pressured the church to provide their parishes with priests who spoke their native tongues. In Texas, for example, Bishop Odin labored mightily to match priests to his Belgian, Irish, German, Polish, Swiss, Czech, Alsatian, and Mexican American congregations. The Bohemians of Tabor, Nebraska, celebrated wildly when, after years of requesting a German-speaking priest, the bishop of St. Paul finally sent them a Bohemian father. In larger urban areas, like Denver and San Francisco, Irish, Italian, and French congregations frequently threatened "secession" when sent priests whose ethnic identities were different from their own.

Particularly troublesome for the Catholic hierarchy were the Hispanic Catholics, the church's oldest ethnic group in America, and the one toward which the hierarchy in general was least tolerant. While, despite their ethnic differences, most of the recent European immigrants shared the same basic assumptions about their faith, the religious folk culture developed by the Mexican Americans and Mexican immigrants over generations of isolation and poverty set them apart. The Hispanics were likely to be the least influential ethnic group in any given Catholic parish, with perhaps the best example being the contrast between the immense prominence and power enjoyed by the San Francisco immigrant Catholics throughout the city and the marginalized, impoverished existence common to Los Angeles' Spanish-speaking Catholics concentrated in the barrio of the original pueblo at the city's center.

In 1850, the Catholic church split the California diocese apart, assigning San Francisco to the United States under JOSEPH SADOC ALEMANY as bishop of the

Californias and archbishop of San Francisco, and placing Los Angeles under Mexico with Thaddeus Amat, Bishop of Monterey, taking up residence in the city. Alemany, a native of Spain with some sympathy for the Mexican Americans, allowed Spanish-speaking Catholics to be married by Spanish priests and eventually built a national church for Hispanics in San Francisco in 1875, but Amat attacked the Hispanic practice of selling burial shrouds, suspended some Mexican Franciscans for what he labeled as "fomenting superstition," and built a large cathedral for the California elite in direct competition with the old Mexican Our Lady, Queen of the Angels Church on the plaza in the barrio called Sonora Town (because so many of its newer and poorer residents had immigrated from the Mexican province of Sonora). Rejected by their church, poorer Mexican Americans stopped attending, except for baptisms, marriages, and funerals, and practiced their faith in adobe homes where they created little shrines consistent with their folk Catholicism.

Nowhere was the clash between Euro-American Catholicism and Hispanic folk religion more evident than in New Mexico. There the French archbishop of Santa Fe JEAN BAPTISTE LAMY made his scorn for the popular pastoral church quite evident. Dismissing Hispanic folk art as primitive, Lamy replaced it with French paintings. Little appreciating the strength of the Penitentes, he moved to suppress the brotherhood. Disdainful of the local belief in miracles and healing, he pushed for shutting down the shrine at Chimayo. Novelist WILLA CATHER glamorized Lamy as "Bishop Latour," a cleric deeply interested in bringing Hispanic Catholicism into the Catholic mainstream in *Death Comes for the Archbishop* (1927), but in truth, Lamy's treatment, like that of the church's in general, of Mexican American Catholicism was based on Euro-centric prejudice.

Ironically, even as the church attacked folk Catholicism in the Southwest, the region in general began to rediscover the Roman Catholic mission heritage that gave birth to the folk-religious culture. A former Massachusetts Yankee named CHARLES FLETCHER LUMMIS spent his adult life persuading California's Midwestern Protestant majority that Spanish missions were as essential to the identity of their new home as the Puritan churches of Massachusetts had been to New England. In 1919, Lummis wrote: "The old missions are worth more money, are greater assets to Southern California than our oil, our oranges, or even our climate." Around the same time, the Catholic bishop at Tucson restored the Mission San Xavier del Bac. Out of such efforts grew what Ferenc M. and Margaret Connell Szasz have called "a romantic, mildly nondenominational saga of Catholic missions and missionaries," a tale of Old California that fed the region's tourist industry and revived the reputation of Father Junípero Serra, whose statue Californians placed in the rotunda of the Capitol in Washington, D.C. While the statue serves as an image of the West's Catholic heritage, protests against Serra's canonization by some California Native Americans in the 1980s revealed just how troubled that heritage could be.

—*Charles Phillips*

SEE ALSO: California Ranchos; Missions: Early Jesuit and Franciscan Missions; Pueblo Revolt

SUGGESTED READING:

Bowden, Henry Warner. *American Indians and Christian Missions: Studies in Cultural Conflict*. Chicago, 1981.

Burns, Robert Ignatius. *The Jesuits and the Indian Wars of the Northwest*. New Haven, Conn., 1966.

Cinel, Dino. *From Italy to San Francisco*. Stanford, Calif., 1982.

Dolan, Jay P. *The American Catholic Experience*. Garden City, N.Y., 1985.

———. *The American Catholic Parish: A History from 1850 to the Present*. Vol 2. New York, 1987.

Engh, Michael. *Frontier Faiths*. Albuquerque, N. Mex., 1992.

Frankiel, Sandra Sizer. *California's Spiritual Frontiers: Religious Alternatives to Anglo-Protestantism, 1850–1910*. Berkeley, Calif., 1988.

Guarneri, Carl and David Alvarez, eds. *Religion and Society in the American West: Historical Essays*. Lanham, Md., 1987.

Horgan, Paul. *Lamy of Santa Fe: His Life and Times*. New York, 1975.

Moore, James Talmadge. *Through Fire and Flood: The Catholic Church in Frontier Texas*. College Station, Tex., 1992.

Schoenberg, Wilfred P. *A History of the Catholic Church in the Pacific Northwest*. Washington, D.C., 1987.

Szasz, Ferenc M., ed. *Religion in the American West*. Manhattan, Kans., 1984.

Weber, Donald J. *The Mexican Frontier, 1821–1826: The American Southwest under Mexico*. Albuquerque, N. Mex., 1982.

———. *The Spanish Frontier in North America*. New Haven, Conn., 1992.

CATLIN, GEORGE

The best-known artist who painted the Western Indian tribes before the Civil War, George Catlin (1796–1872) was a dreamer and a schemer—heartfelt and exploitative in his causes, loving and egocentric in his domestic relations, loyal and unreliable in his friend-

George Catlin produced hundreds of paintings of the Native Americans he observed on his Western sojourns. This lithograph, after a Catlin painting, demonstrates an Indian snowshoe dance. *Courtesy Library of Congress.*

ships, possessed of zeal, energy, drive, ambition, and vision. He was one of the first American artists to travel to the West. From 1832 to 1836, he made four trips into Indian Country and created a collection—the "Indian Gallery"—of some five hundred paintings. More than three hundred of them were individual portraits; the remainder were landscapes and group scenes. The scope of Catlin's enterprise was exceptional. He wanted to record the likeness of all the native peoples of North America and, at his most ambitious, of the entire Western Hemisphere. He fell somewhat short of that goal, but in the 1850s, after a mixed career as a showman promoting his "Gallery" at home and abroad, he made a series of visits to South and Central America and, if he is to be believed, the West Coast of North America. On these voyages, he rounded out his original collection of Indian paintings and secured his reputation as the nineteenth century's premier painter of Native Americans.

Born in Wilkes-Barre, Pennsylvania, Catlin studied law, beginning in July 1817, in Litchfield, Connecticut. Admitted to the bar the following year, he practiced for only a brief time. In 1821, he moved to Philadelphia where he planned to make a living as a portrait painter. He specialized in miniatures and was sufficiently adept that the Pennsylvania Academy of Fine Arts and the National Academy of Design elected him a member. In 1827, yearning to work on a larger scale, he moved to New York City and again established himself as a portraitist.

Catlin had a few weaknesses as an artist. He was often unsure of anatomy and had difficulty keeping standing figures in proportion. But he was generally successful at capturing the likeness of his sitters, and at his best, he created powerful portraits notable for their strong modeling and their empathy. He was good at faces, if not at anatomy.

A career as a portraitist was an unfulfilling one for Catlin, who aspired to the lofty title of "history painter." While faced with increased family responsibilities after his marriage in 1828, he devised an escape route from the ordinary. According to his published accounts, he spied a delegation of Indians during a visit to Philadelphia in 1828. There before him was a subject worthy of "a whole lifetime of enthusiasm." Individuals, learned societies, and the government would rush to support his efforts, he was convinced, and in the spring of 1830, he headed to St. Louis to begin his career as an Indian painter.

After honing his artistic skills by painting visiting tribesmen, Catlin boarded a steamboat on March 26, 1832, for the eighteen-hundred-mile trip up the Missouri River to Fort Union, deep in the heart of Indian Country. He painted Blackfoot and Crow Indians and all the river tribes, notably the Mandan, who would be devastated by smallpox five years later. Subsequently he toured the Southwest (1834), the Mississippi and the Great Lakes region (1835), and the sacred red pipestone quarry on the Coteau des Prairies (1836). He described his travels for the newspapers (his letters were collected in 1841 and published as *Letters and Notes on the Manners, Customs, and Conditions of the North American Indians,* a vastly influential book) and exhibited his growing collection between trips.

Catlin often boasted that he created his "Gallery" without direct patronage or assistance. Help from the federal government, however, was his main hope. He first approached Congress in May 1838, and periodically thereafter, to present his case for the government to purchase his "Gallery."

Disappointed in his hopes at home and certain he would find a ready audience for things Indian in Europe, he moved to England in November 1839. He entered the London show scene and exhibited his "Gallery" throughout Great Britain before moving to Paris in April 1845. After his wife and only son died in Paris, he was forced to flee, in the face of revolution, to London and eke out an existence with his three daughters. He had mortgaged his "Gallery" and accumulated debts along the way. His pitch to Congress in 1852 was a desperate one. "We have come to this old acquaintance of ours, who has been here longer than I have been," an exasperated senator snapped. "We have heard every session of 'Mr. Catlin and his Indian portraits,' 'Mr. Catlin and his Indian portraits.'" The senator's tone told the story: the resolution to buy the "Gallery" went down to defeat yet again, and Catlin's work was lost to his creditors.

Catlin himself entered a period of obscurity and frequent despair, punctuated by three astonishing expeditions to South America in the 1850s and feverish activity as he lived by his wits. He sold pencil outlines of his original portraits traced from copies he had retained—"albums unique," he called them—and painted a new collection on pasteboard panels of uniform size, his "Cartoon Collection." He finished it in 1870, exhibited it in Brussels, and the next year crated it up and returned to America after an absence of thirty-two years. The final disposition of both Indian collections preoccupied him. He exhibited his "Cartoon Collection" in New York and at the Smithsonian Institution in Washington, D.C., in February 1872. That May, he again petitioned Congress to buy his original gallery. Congress had taken no action on the matter before adjourning in June; when it reconvened in December, Catlin was two weeks from death.

Among Catlin's last words was a plaintive question: "What will become of my gallery?" He need not have worried. In 1879, the widow of his Philadelphia creditor willed the "Indian Gallery" to the U.S. National Museum, and in 1912, the "Cartoon Collection" passed from his heirs to the American Museum of Natural History and then, in the 1960s, much of it to the National Gallery of Art. Today, the federal government, which had never seen fit to buy a Catlin painting while he was alive, owns both of his Indian collections. They have taken their place among the nation's—and Western art's—greatest treasures.

—*Brian W. Dippie*

SEE ALSO: Art: Western Art

SUGGESTED READING:

Catlin, George. *Letters and Notes on the Manners, Customs, and Conditions of the North American Indians.* London, 1841.

Dippie, Brian W. *Catlin and His Contemporaries: The Politics of Patronage.* Lincoln, Nebr., 1990.

Troccoli, Joan Carpenter. *First Artist of the West: George Catlin Paintings and Watercolors.* Tulsa, Okla., 1993.

Truettner, William H. *The Natural Man Observed: A Study of Catlin's Indian Gallery.* Washington, D. C., 1979.

CATTLE ASSOCIATIONS

SEE: Cattle Raisers' Associations

CATTLE BRANDS AND BRANDING

Branding is the custom of claiming livestock by burning marks into the cattle's hides. It probably originated in the ancient Middle East and was introduced to the Americas in the sixteenth century by the Spaniards. Branding was necessary on the American free range because animals owned by different ranches mingled with each other. Cattlemen still brand to protect cattle from modern rustlers and to claim animals grazing on land leased from the government.

Roundup activities included branding new cattle, as these cowboys are doing in an image from the Arizona Territory in the late 1890s. *Courtesy National Archives.*

Most branding took place during spring roundups. Drovers gathered their herds and then roped and dragged calves and unbranded cattle (mavericks) to a branding fire. Two cowboys threw each animal on its side, while another, using a hot iron, burned the brand on the animal's hide, usually on the left hip. Some cattlemen burned brands into the flanks (called "trail" or "road" brands) or the jaw for easier identification.

Blacksmiths forged branding irons in lengths of about thirty-six to forty-five inches so that the grips would remain cool when cowboys heated the ends red hot. Spanish and Mexican branding irons were shorter than American irons because they had wooden handles mounted in sockets. Some brands were little more than straight pokers; others featured complex symbols and numbers.

When cattle changed hands, the new owner obtained a bill of sale, marked a slash over the old brand with a straight venting iron, and added his own brand. Cattle thieves carried running irons, which were short irons that allowed them to alter brands. Running irons were illegal in most places, and a man caught with one was lucky to escape with his life.

—*Byron A. Johnson*

SEE ALSO: Cattle Industry; Cattle Rustling

SUGGESTED READING:

Dale, Edward E. *The Range Cattle Industry: Ranching on the Great Plains from 1865 to 1925.* Norman, Okla., 1969.

Myers, Sandra. *The Ranch in Spanish Texas.* El Paso, Tex., 1969.

Rouse, John E. *The Criollo: Spanish Cattle in the Americas.* Norman, Okla., 1977.

Taylor, Lonn, and Ingrid Marr. *The American Cowboy.* Washington, D.C., 1983.

CATTLE BREEDS AND BREEDING

In 1493, Christopher Columbus imported cattle to the West Indies on his second voyage to the New World. Conquistador Hernán Cortés introduced the offspring of that original herd into Mexico. The remnant population of present-day Texas longhorns are the descendants of those early cattle.

The next great wave of cattle importation came in the early seventeenth century, when English colonists brought their English shorthorns to the East Coast. These were ideal animals for life in a new country, since they served multiple purposes, including the production of meat, milk, tallow, and hides. Westering settlers took their English shorthorns with them, and the cattle interbred with wild herds of Spanish origin.

By the outbreak of the Civil War, the CATTLE INDUSTRY of the Corn Belt states was highly developed, but that of the Great Plains and the mountain states did not get into full swing until the beginning of the 1880s. Shorthorns, introduced to upgrade the herds, were soon replaced by Herefords and Aberdeen Angus imports from Great Britain.

By the end of the nineteenth century, the longhorn population had been largely displaced in the West by Herefords and other breeds. Then, beginning in the 1960s, the longhorn made a partial resurgence; it is still very much in evidence on Western ranges and ranches. The Hereford has been described as the matriarch of the modern cow business. It was often interbred with the Angus to produce a black baldy calf, which combined the good mothering instincts and foraging traits of the Hereford with the fattening ability and disease-resistance of the Angus. Second-cross cattle—the product of hybrids rather than of two different pure breeds—tend to lack the vigor of first-cross hybrids, and, today, Herefords, Anguses, and black baldys compose the majority of standard Western range herds. The Santa Gertrudis breed, developed on the King Ranch in Texas in the early twentieth century by crossing Brahman bulls with shorthorn cows, is the heaviest of the beef breeds.

Dual-purpose cattle breeds, raised for milk production as well as for beef, have become increasingly important in the Western cattle industry. The more prevalent dual-purpose breeds include the British Red Poll and milking shorthorn, and the continental European breeds: the Charolais, Simmental, Chianina, and Limousin. Yet another important dual-purpose breed in the West is the Brahman, originally developed in India. The Brahman is more suited to hot, humid regions than to more arid areas.

As in other regions of the country, a number of breeds are raised strictly as dairy cattle. The Holstein, Jersey, Guernsey, and Ayrshire breeds produce three to four times as much milk as the beef cow. Male calves and cows that are culled from the dairy herds after they are no longer productive contribute about 20 percent of the U.S. beef supply and much of the meat destined to be sold as ground beef.

Over the years, enthusiastic partisans have touted the virtues of one breed over another, and a variety of breed associations have played an important role in establishing breed standards and promoting healthy production. The sudden demise of the range-cattle industry after the disastrous winter of 1886 to 1887 resulted in the widespread use of barbed-wire fencing to contain individual herds and thereby reduced indiscriminate crossbreeding. By the early twentieth century, scientifically controlled breeding practices were increasingly common. Today, artificial insemination of cattle is common, particularly in dairy herds. The practice allows carefully selected, genetically superior bulls to sire thousands of calves a year. By the 1970s, embryo-transfer techniques were also being employed to improve herds. A common but increasingly controversial aspect of such artificial breeding techniques is the injection of hormones to stimulate multiple ovulation. The eggs produced are then artificially insemi-nated. The resulting embryos are withdrawn from the cow, and each is implanted in the uterus of another cow.

—*Alan Axelrod*

SUGGESTED READING:

Dobie, J. Frank. *The Longhorns*. Boston, 1941.

Jordan, Terry. *North American Cattle Ranching Frontiers: Origins, Diffusion, and Differentiation*. Albuquerque, N. Mex., 1993.

Rouse, John E. *The Criollo Spanish Cattle in the Americas*. Norman, Okla., 1977.

CATTLE INDUSTRY

The Western range cattle industry of the late nineteenth and early twentieth centuries was the hybrid product of European and African ancestry and more than three centuries of adaption and innovation. The Andalucía and Extremadura regions in Spain, the highlands of Great Britain, and tropical West Africa all contributed distinctive traits to the mix.

The Spanish introduced cattle and HORSES into the Caribbean in 1494 and New Spain in 1521. Later implantations occurred in Florida, Mississippi, and Louisiana. By the 1760s, Hispanic colonists and their cattle had spread northward from central Mexico to Texas and California. Herds, tended by Indian and mixed-blood vaqueros, developed on large private estates and around Catholic missions.

Cowboys were the laborers of the cattle industry. Here cowboys on the Texas-Oklahoma Panhandle pause at mealtime beside a chuck wagon. *Courtesy Western History Collections, University of Oklahoma Library.*

Under favorable environmental conditions, cattle multiplied rapidly and, in the absence of fences and regular supervision, became wild. Over time, their European characteristics gave way to the distinctive attributes associated with longhorn cattle.

Government regulation and taxation, conflicts with Indians, and the absence of strong commercial markets, restricted cattle raising to a subsistence enterprise in Spanish colonial North America. Nevertheless, the Spaniards bequeathed rich and lasting traditions of horsemanship, roping, roundups, equipment, and vocabulary to future ranching generations.

British cattle breeds and herding methods, meanwhile, had arrived in South Carolina from the highlands of Scotland, England, and Ireland by way of the British West Indies in the late seventeenth century. Over the next 150 years, the descendants of these early British cattle-raisers spread westward through the pine barrens and uplands of the South into Texas. By the mid-nineteenth century, distinct herding cultures had developed in Texas and California.

Before the rise of significant commercial markets for Western beef, ranching remained part of the local subsistence economy. The lean, tough cattle that inhabited the ranges of the Southwest were valued more for their hides and tallow than for their meat. Their carcasses yielded an astonishing array of by-products—leather, soap, candles, fertilizer, combs, buttons, and glue.

By the 1850s, however, increased demand for beef among rapidly growing urban populations in the North and East, coupled with the availability of a free range and the requirement of only a minimal capital invest-

ment, enabled many stock-raisers in Texas and elsewhere to abandon other agricultural pursuits. Louisiana provided the largest and most consistent market for Texas cattlemen during the antebellum era. Cheap longhorn beef fed slaves on many cotton and sugar plantations. Other cattle, driven overland to New Orleans or shipped there by river boats from Shreveport or Alexandria, supplied local consumers and exporters. New Orleans commission merchants also regularly handled seaborne consignments of cattle, hides, bones, and horns from the Texas Gulf Coast.

The vast Western overland migrations of the 1840s and 1850s offered cattle-raisers in Texas and the Indian Territory lucrative markets for both beef and work cattle. Drovers found an even larger market among Midwestern farmers, who bought young cattle to winter on corn before selling them to Eastern and Northern packing houses. Even so, Texas longhorns could not compete in the marketplace with the heavier animals of British ancestry that inhabited farms in the Midwest.

The discovery of gold in California in 1848 stimulated the growth of West Coast ranching. Between 1849 and 1856, the mining regions of the new state offered an especially profitable beef market. American cattlemen, eager to supply the demand, arrived in huge numbers, filling the valleys of the central and southern regions of the state and displacing many Hispanic ranchers in the process.

The Civil War severely restricted the Texas cattle trade by closing its Northern markets and sapping its manpower. At least some cattle were delivered to Confederate troops east of the Mississippi before Union forces closed the river to commerce. Others reached buyers in Mexico. Many Texas ranchers obtained exemptions from military service and, although short-handed, managed to conduct their business as beef contractors while serving as members of state militia and ranger units.

Cattle thieves operating from Mexico and the frontier regions of Texas took full advantage of unsettled conditions to pillage herds for profit. A general and prolonged drought further decimated herds throughout the Southwest. The adverse weather reduced bovine numbers in California by 50 percent and drove countless ranchers out of business. Many of those who survived migrated to other regions and established foundation herds in parts of Nevada, Idaho, Utah, the Pacific Northwest, and even British Columbia.

Following the war, demand for beef in the industrial North and East, coupled with an abundance of Texas cattle, precipitated a two-decade-long boom in the Western cattle industry. Long drives to traditional markets like New Orleans, Kansas City, St. Louis, and

"Driving Cattle into a Corral in the Far West," an illustration from a nineteenth-century magazine suggests the Spanish-Mexican origins of the American West's cattle industry. *Courtesy Patrick H. Butler, III.*

WAITING FOR A CHINOOK

The Last of 5000

Artist Charles Marion Russell spent his early years in the West working as a ranch hand. Mr. Kaufman of Kaufman and Stadler inquired after the well-being of the five thousand cattle in Russell's care during the disastrous winter of 1886 to 1887. Russell sent in reply a water-color painting of an emaciated steer in deep snow surrounded by several wolves—a work he had entitled *Waiting for a Chinook: The Last of 5,000* (a chinook was the dry wind off the mountains that would bring relief from the bitterly cold winter). In 1903, Russell produced a larger version of the 1886 water color pictured here. *Courtesy Buffalo Bill Historical Center.*

Chicago resumed in 1865. Although drovers, many of them recently returned Confederate veterans, found beef prices profitable, they also encountered hostile Missouri and Kansas farmers and stockmen, who were concerned about deadly outbreaks of TEXAS FEVER, a disease borne by tick-infested longhorns. Vigilance committees confiscated some herds, turned others back, and threatened violence to all who attempted to run the blockade. Legislatures in the affected states, meanwhile, established quarantines and enacted statutes prohibiting the introduction of cattle from Texas during much of the year.

By 1867, drovers had abandoned the Shawnee Trail and other traditional routes to Missouri and Illinois for the Chisholm Trail, an old Indian trace terminat-ing at ABILENE, Kansas, on the Kansas Pacific Railroad. Over the following decade, extensions of the railroad south and west allowed drovers to keep west of the line of farm settlement. This period also brought brief and sometimes bloody notoriety to cow towns like WICHITA, Ellsworth, Newton, Caldwell, and DODGE CITY, Kansas.

Beginning in the mid-1860s, another group of intrepid Texas drovers contracted with the government to supply forts and Indian reservations in New Mexico over a dry and dangerous route known as the GOODNIGHT-LOVING TRAIL. This trail was eventually extended northward to furnish meat and stock cattle to consumers and ranchers in Colorado, Wyoming, and Montana.

Professional trail crews hired by droving contractors delivered three-fourths of all cattle driven to market for fees that ranged between $1.00 and $1.50 per head. Ten or eleven drovers managed an average herd of twenty-five hundred to three thousand head for a wage of $25 to $30 per month.

An estimated ten million head of cattle were driven north from Texas breeding grounds between 1865 and the early 1890s. Relatively few of these animals were shipped directly to slaughter. A much larger number supplied the Midwestern feeder market or filled government contracts to sustain soldiers and Indians. After about 1875, large numbers of yearlings and two-year-olds were conveyed to finishing ranges on the Northern Plains. Many Texas ranches also maintained acreage in Montana, Wyoming, and the Dakotas for this purpose.

By 1880, the wholesale slaughter of BUFFALOES and the removal of Plains tribes to reservations opened an immense grassland stretching from Montana to Texas to large-scale occupation by ranchers. Strong demand, firm prices, easy credit, and substantial profits fueled the expansion and attracted substantial Eastern and foreign investment, especially from Great Britain. Between 1882 and 1884 alone, Texas chartered more than one hundred new cattle corporations. The small-scale, individually owned ranch, long the staple of the cattle country, gave way to huge operations owned by individuals, partnerships, corporations, and syndicates. The largest of these behemoths, the Capitol (Freehold) Syndicate Ranch (or the XIT RANCH), acquired more than three million acres. Unlike the typical open-range outfit, these highly capitalized operations invested heavily in land, cattle, horses, and improvements.

Absentee owners often were not well informed about their investments, and many bought vastly inflated or even nonexistent herds and property. Some corporate ranches hired experienced local managers, while others imported expertise.

Ranchers depended on a seasonal, nomadic work force of COWBOYS to conduct roundups each spring and fall. A typical gathering held in northern New Mexico in 1887 involved some twenty-two CHUCK WAGONS, 250 cowboys, and three thousand horses. During such periods of heavy activity, roundup crews spent weeks and even months at a time living in the field, often in adverse weather and rugged terrain. They separated herds that had become mixed on the open range, branded their increase, and selected steers for market. After the fall gathering, managers laid off most of their cowboys and retained only a few line or fence riders in isolated camps to look after stock during the winter.

Many ranchers instituted rules banning firearms, gambling, and drinking among employees. During the late nineteenth century, the Western cattle industry experienced relatively little of the labor unrest that characterized other sectors of the American economy. Although labor organizers made little headway among the fiercely independent herdsmen, discord between ranch hands and owners occasionally manifested itself in individual or collective actions. One of the most famous of these labor confrontations occurred in 1883, when cowboys in the Texas Panhandle briefly struck their employers for higher wages.

In the absence of formal and effective legal institutions, the earliest arrivals to a region usually established their claim to grass and water by range custom, buying or leasing only what land was absolutely necessary. Capital investment and corporate involvement forced cattlemen to purchase more land in order to protect their ranges from interlopers. As the range became more crowded, however, competition and disputes intensified. Local and state CATTLE RAISERS' ASSOCIATIONS, the lineal descendants of the Spanish *mesta* and mid-nineteenth-century American agricultural societies, helped settle such disagreements. These organizations adopted rules governing roundups and brand ownership, engaged in political lobbying, promoted breed improvement, hired range detectives, and stationed brand inspectors at shipping and marketing points.

The Cherokee Strip Live Stock Association one of the strongest and most renowned of cattlemen's groups, negotiated a controversial multiyear lease of Cherokee tribal lands on which its members grazed as many as three hundred thousand head of cattle. Other enterprising cattlemen obtained grazing rights on Indian reservations throughout the West. Several tribes developed significant cattle herds of their own, used mostly for subsistence. At least a few Native American cattle-raisers, however, became commercially successful.

In the fall of 1884, beef prices began to weaken. Within a year, they had collapsed altogether, thanks largely to overproduction. By 1887, beef cattle commanded less than a quarter of their price of four years earlier; cows, even less. After years of unsound speculation, many overextended cattle companies, some of whose investors had enjoyed several successive years of handsome dividends, struggled to meet their debts. Tight credit, in turn, forced cattlemen to market their animals at lower prices in order to pay operating expenses and meet loan obligations. Fooled by a series of abnormally wet years between 1882 and 1885, cattlemen had also severely misjudged the carrying capacities of their ranges. They were ill prepared for the siege of severe weather that battered the Great Plains from 1885 to 1887. Extended drought and brutal cold destroyed cattle by the thousands and forced cattlemen to market others prematurely. Few ranches possessed the prudent management and sufficient reserve funds needed to endure such hardship. Financial and environmental reverses bankrupted an estimated half of Texas cattlemen between 1883 and 1887.

The effects of glutted markets, overstocked ranges, quarantines, and persistent farmers lingered even longer. Labor strikes and a generally depressed national economy in the early 1890s also contributed to the havoc, as did escalating railroad freight rates, which made shipping cattle to market more expensive.

The mid-1880s marked the collapse of the old open-range system of cattle ranching. It was replaced by a diversified, capital- and labor-intensive model. Barbed-wire fencing, improvements in transportation and communication, and scientific advances in the treatment of livestock diseases helped foster the new system.

Although a diehard "free grass" element resisted diversification and opposed the relentless advance of new settlement through political lobbying, intimidation, and occasional violence, most of the traditional ranchers either anticipated the inevitability of change and planned accordingly or gradually accepted the new innovations. Those ranchers who would not or could not adapt to the new realities moved their herds to regions less conducive to growing crops.

Some ranchers actively encouraged settlement by purchasing local farm produce and engaging in colonizing activities. Several forward-thinking types established experimental farms to demonstrate the fertility of their land to potential settlers. Others raised or bought hay, drought-resistant sorghums, and other forage crops to supplement their own grass.

By the 1890s, overgrazing had left erosion and undesirable vegetation in its wake throughout the West and had reduced the carrying capacity of some ranges by 50 percent. As nutritious plant species gave way to weeds and brush, herds failed to fatten properly, and ranchers experienced greater losses of cattle during periods of adverse weather. In time, however, at least a few ranchers adopted range conservation programs that included pasture rotation, reseeding, irrigation, and brush control through grubbing and burning.

Droughts and the scarcity of surface water also forced prudent ranchers to develop additional water resources. They erected windmills to tap underground aquifers, created earthen reservoirs to capture rainwater, laid pipelines to deliver water to dry pastures, and even engaged in rain-making experiments.

Barbed-wire fences had made their first appearance on the range in the 1870s. Their advantages were soon evident, and many ranchers began to enclose their pastures. The XIT Ranch, for example, required more than six thousand miles of the barbed ribbon.

Some cattlemen erected illegal barriers on the public domain to protect leases and discourage settlers. Legal and political battles ensued, and the offending enclosures were invariably removed. In some regions, law-enforcement agencies also dealt with gangs of fence cutters.

At first, BARBED WIRE simply defined property lines, separated neighboring herds, or limited the annual winter drift of stock. In time, however, cross-fencing and the erection of pens and corrals at strategic points on the range enabled ranchers to trim their labor costs and improve their herds by restricting the movement and breeding of stock. Smaller pastures also allowed cattle-raisers to address the problem of overgrazing by resting and rotating pastures.

By the mid-1890s, the proliferation of barbed wire helped to force Southern Plains cattlemen to abandon long drives to shipping points and finishing ranges on the Northern Plains. In 1886, a two-year effort by the Texas Livestock Association and its allies had failed to secure congressional legislation establishing a National Cattle Trail.

Of even greater significance were expanded state and federal quarantines instituted against tick-infested cattle. In 1889, the Bureau of Animal Industry finally linked ticks to the transmission of Texas fever. A national quarantine law soon followed, dictating and restricting the movement of infected cattle. Trial and error eventually produced a satisfactory method of dipping stock to rid them of the pest, and in 1898, quarantines were relaxed on treated animals.

A rapidly expanding railroad network eased the transition from droving, although it was still considerably cheaper to trail livestock than to ship them by rail. And while railroads simplified ranch supply, they also facilitated the migration of farmers.

The dissolution of many large corporate operations during the debacle of the mid-1880s, coupled with the arrival of large numbers of farmers in ranch country, signaled a fundamental shift to smaller, more diversified operations, many of which required little labor beyond that of the owner's family and willing neighbors. These stock farmers accounted for the vast majority of Western beef production.

After a decade of depression, land and livestock prices slowly began to recover. The demand for beef quickened with the growth of urban populations and income levels. Consumers, however, demanded a better quality of beef. Although a few visionaries in Texas had attempted to improve their longhorn herds with imported breeding stock before the Civil War, tick fever had thwarted most of their efforts. Ranchers on the Northern Plains, meanwhile, were reluctant to invest in the expensive animals, in the erroneous belief that they could not withstand the rigors of winter without shelter and fodder. Nevertheless, by the late 1870s, high-grade Durham, shorthorn, Polled-Angus, and Hereford cattle, mostly from the Midwest, had gained footholds on Western ranges. Brahman cattle were successfully introduced in South Texas after the turn of the century. Thanks to vigorous advertising and promotion, Herefords gradually attained the predominate position among breeders, some of whom developed and maintained purebred herds.

Proponents of breeding stock founded breed organizations and organized livestock fairs to promote their products. By the 1890s, cities like Fort Worth, Denver, Kansas City, and San Francisco began sponsoring annual "fat-stock" shows, which both publicized the various breeds and educated raisers on the latest scientific advances in husbandry. The thorough upgrading of Western herds, however, required decades, lasting into the 1930s in some areas.

Costly blooded cattle, fencing, water systems, and other improvements required cattle-raisers to have access to reliable sources of credit. When the foreign sources that had largely fueled the boom of the 1880s disappeared, ranchers turned to cattle loan companies, commission firms, and so-called stockyard banks, for operating capital.

Advances in communication, science, and veterinary medicine, the ongoing trend toward mechanization, and the vagaries of weather and the global market all had an impact on the industry in the twentieth century. By 1900, telephones, their wires running along barbed-wire fences, already linked at least some ranches with the outside world, thus mitigating the isolation of ranch life. Within a few short years, motorized vehicles began to replace animal-powered chuck and freight wagons. Although horses continued to be a mainstay in the handling of cattle at roundup time, most ranches required cowboys to grease windmills and operate farm machinery as well as rope and ride.

Cattlemen of the new century also sought help from state and federal governments in controlling predators and treating livestock maladies such as blackleg, foot-and-mouth disease, and screw worms. They also demanded government intervention in long-standing disputes with railroads over freight rates and meat packers over price fixing. By the advent of World War I, the cattle industry of the West had been transformed from a freewheeling, speculative open-range enterprise into a diversified, scientific, and businesslike economic institution.

—*B. Byron Price.*

See also: Cattle Brands and Branding; Cattle Breeds and Breeding; Cattle Rustling; Cattle Towns

Suggested reading:
Dale, Edward Everett. *The Range Cattle Industry: Ranching on the Great Plains from 1865–1925.* Norman, Okla., 1960.
Dary, David. *Cowboy Culture: A Saga of Five Centuries.* New York, 1981.
Jordan, Terry G. *North American Cattle Ranching Frontiers: Origins, Diffusion, and Differentiation.* Albuquerque, N. Mex., 1993.
Schlebecker, John T. *Cattle Raising on the Great Plains, 1900–1961.* Lincoln, Nebr., 1963.

"CATTLE KATE"

See: Watson, Ella

CATTLE RAISERS' ASSOCIATIONS

Roughly comparable to Eastern trade associations developed by manufacturers in the mid-nineteenth century, associations of cattlemen flourished in the trans-Mississippi West in 1870s and 1880s. Usually organized in response to some immediate problem, such as cattle rustling, the associations ultimately formalized range-land practices known collectively as cow custom. Associations kept records of members' brands and ranges, organized and supervised roundups, employed stock detectives, maintained brand inspectors at principal shipping points, and were generally involved with advancing the profitability of the cattle industry. By representing the interests of owners and often ignoring the requirements of labor, associations heightened the economic distinctions between cattlemen and COWBOYS that led to occasional attempts to organize cowboys into labor unions.

Cattlemen with similar concerns formed associations or joined existing ones without reference to state or territorial boundaries. Dakota ranchers, for example, joined either the Montana Stock Growers' Association or the Wyoming Stock Growers' Association, depending on the proximity of their ranges. An association formed in Idaho in 1883 included cattlemen from adjacent areas in Oregon and Nevada. Some large state organizations resulted from the consolidation of several smaller district associations, while others created their own member groups. Whereas one association might prefer to regulate the activities of member groups on the occasion of a roundup, another might leave the details to those smaller units.

Among the largest of the cattlemen's organizations was the Cherokee Strip Live Stock Association, incorporated in Kansas in 1883 to lease the six-million-acre Cherokee Outlet in northwestern Indian Territory. It functioned until the federal government evicted cattlemen from the Outlet in 1890. The Wyoming Stock Growers' Association, with antecedents in the early 1870s, virtually owned the territorial legislature during the 1880s and was politically the most powerful of the nineteenth-century organizations. In the twentieth century, the New Mexico Cattle Growers Association became a force in local politics; its members controlled, at one time, nearly half of the seats in the state senate. The Northwest Texas Cattle Raisers' Association, formed in 1877, grew to become the Cattle Raisers' Association of Texas in 1893; it changed its name in 1921 to the Texas and Southwestern Cattle Raisers' Association to reflect an expanded regional membership.

—*William W. Savage, Jr.*

Suggested reading:

Jackson, W. Turrentine. "The Wyoming Stock Growers' Association: Political Power in Wyoming Territory, 1873–1890." *Mississippi Valley Historical Review* 33 (1947): 571–594.

Savage, William W., Jr. *The Cherokee Strip Live Stock Association: Federal Regulation and the Cattleman's Last Frontier.* Norman, Okla., 1990.

———. "Stockmen's Associations and the Western Range Cattle Industry." *Journal of the West* 14 (1975): 52–59.

CATTLE RUSTLING

One of the most celebrated crimes against property in the American West, cattle theft flourished on the open range. Difficult to apprehend, rustlers proved even harder to prosecute and convict.

Rising beef prices in the wake of the Civil War accelerated cattle stealing, especially in the vast breeding grounds of Texas. Large gangs of cattle thieves operated with impunity on both sides of the Rio Grande, while farther north, the lucrative Comanchero trade between Texas and New Mexico encouraged Indian bands, usually more apt to take horses than cattle, to traffic in stolen beef. By the late 1870s, however, the Texas Rangers and the United States Army had largely suppressed such wholesale larceny; still engaged in rustling, however, were out-of-work cowboys operating individually or in small groups.

Busiest during the winter months when only a few scattered line riders looked after the herds, experienced thieves sought large, unbranded calves that had been overlooked during the summer and fall roundups. If necessary, they altered brands with the help of a running iron. When expertly applied, modified brands were difficult to detect until hides were removed.

The advent of widespread corporate investment in ranching curtailed loose range practices that encouraged thievery. Similarly, the coming of barbed-wire fences not only impeded the mobility of rustlers but also helped clarify herd ownership.

Corporate ranchers and cattlemen's associations fought stock thieves by employing range detectives and brand inspectors. Sometimes, they resorted to the sort of vigilante justice dispensed by Montana rancher Granville Stuart's band of "stranglers" during the early 1880s. Cattle barons also used acts of cattle theft, real and imagined, as pretexts for forcing small operators from their range. Such incidents sometimes precipitated range wars, such as the Johnson County War in Wyoming in 1892.

—*B. Byron Price*

See also: Cattle Brands and Branding; Cattle Industry

Suggested reading:

Haley, J. Evetts. *The XIT Ranch of Texas and the Early Days of the Llano Estacado.* Chicago, 1929.

Rollins, Philip Ashton. *The Cowboy.* Rev. ed. New York, 1936.

CATTLE TOWNS

Cattle towns included countless cities, villages, and hamlets with railway connections that served as reception and shipping points for livestock in the frontier West. According to both the historical literature and the popular imagination, a bona fide cattle town (or cow town—a less honorific derivative) was not merely a market facility located in ranch country; it was a community sited on a major cattle trail. With its hinterlands bare of settlers, a cattle town was suited for holding large herds awaiting purchase and was the place where thousands of "through" Texas cattle exchanged hands each summer. Nearly all aspects of local life in a cattle town accommodated, in one way or another, the cattle trade. Cattle towns were located from New Mexico to Montana—wherever Texas drovers regularly took their herds for sale.

Economics governed the fate of the cattle towns: the westward movement of railroads gave them life; the westward movement of agriculture killed them. A cattle town and conventional farming could not occupy the same ground for two reasons. First, Texas cattle carried splenic fever (also known as Texas

Top: A Dodge City dance hall of the cattle-town era. *Courtesy Kansas State Historical Society.*

Bottom: Wichita, Kansas, in the days it served as a cattle town, as illustrated in *Harper's Weekly. Courtesy Patrick H. Butler, III.*

FEVER), which proved lethal to herds bred in northern regions. Second, incoming pioneer farmers, by purchase or homesteading, overran the government lands previously devoted to trails and holding grounds.

The most famous cattle towns were those of post–Civil War Kansas, especially ABILENE, Ellsworth, WICHITA, DODGE CITY, and Caldwell. In 1867, a wealthy Midwestern cattle dealer established a market facility in Abilene, despite the state's splenic-fever quarantine line forbidding him to do so, and for the next few years the business provided by hundreds of transients overcame all local objections. Eventually a coalition of cattle-trade critics and rural settlers, who choked off the northern extension of the Chisholm Trail, proved fatal to the cattle trade in Abilene. Ellsworth and Wichita then assumed roles as major cattle towns, and from 1872 through 1875, these two communities, urged on by railroads, competed for the Chisholm Trail traffic. Ultimately, rural settlement ended their careers as cattle towns.

Served by two Texas trails, Dodge City became a cattle town in 1876. A severe drought from 1878 to 1881, which temporarily halted the westward advance of farmers, prolonged Dodge City's cattle trade until 1885. That year, in fear of splenic fever, the state closed its borders to Texas cattle, and in 1886, western Kansas finally surrendered to farmers. Caldwell, located on the south line of the state, flourished as a cattle town from 1880 through 1885. Its agricultural enemies were those pressuring the government to open the adjacent Indian Territory to settlement, but the end of the cattle trade in Caldwell came when ranchers in northern Texas fenced off the Chisholm Trail.

A cattle town's largely male business community tended to dominate its civic life. The most common political lines were drawn, understandably, between outlying farmers and the cattle-oriented local establishment. Townsmen habitually closed ranks against rural criticism. They also cooperated in attracting railroads, in winning and holding their cattle trade against rival towns, and in responding to the problem of VIOLENCE. But the geopolitics of urban growth—that is, the intended locus of downtown development—tended to factionalize them and led to fights over the placement of courthouses, post offices, and city halls.

In every cattle town, entrepreneurial conflict eventually gave way to the quite different politics of reform. Most townsmen viewed "immoral" entertainments—drinking, gambling, and whoring—as necessary attributes of the Texas cattle trade. Others called for their eradication. Three reform positions emerged. Traditionalists fond of the lingering frontier ambiance of saloons, dance houses, and brothels resisted change. Moderates, mainly business and professional men, favored ameliorative measures: strong law enforcement to ensure that good order accompanied commercial sin; tax assessments on saloonkeepers, gamblers, and whores to finance police supervision; segregation of brothels and dance houses from the business district; and removal of displays that were shocking to middle-class visitors—street prostitutes, front-room gambling, and SALOONS open on Sundays. Finally there were the radical reformers—mostly evangelically inspired men and women—who became increasingly active after Kansas adopted liquor prohibition in 1880. With the saloons of Dodge City and Caldwell now wholly illegal, opponents of all forms of social immorality rallied under the antiliquor "temperance" banner. "The backbone of the temperance element of [Dodge] are the ladies," reported a state official, ". . . and I found their views to be much more practical and sensible than those of many of the men." Indeed, the mysterious lynching of a Caldwell bootlegger and the twice-attempted arson of downtown Dodge City in order to rid it of saloons and whorehouses were apparently the work of male zealots.

The legendary street violence in cattle towns turns out to have been much overdrawn. Between 1870 and 1885, only forty-five people died violently in the Kansas cattle towns—an average of one and one-half per cattle-trading year. That figure is also the average for the town held by tradition to be the most violent of them all: Dodge City. Only in Ellsworth in 1873 and in Dodge City in 1878 did violent deaths total as many as five. During several cattle-trading seasons no homicides occurred at all.

Two of the cattle towns' forty-five violent fatalities were women—one a victim of spouse abuse; the other a theatrical entertainer. Another fatality was a Pawnee Indian whom a city marshal deemed a nuisance. Four deaths were caused by accidental shootings. Although gunshots proved to have been the principal means of death, nobody died in a "traditional" quick-draw street duel. Less than a third of the victims returned fire; a number of them were apparently not even armed. Such gunfighting residents or sojourners as CLAY ALLISON, JOHN HENRY ("DOC") HOLLIDAY, BARTHOLOMEW (BAT) MASTERSON, and BENJAMIN F. THOMPSON killed no one. In Abilene, JOHN WESLEY HARDIN fatally shot a man who was snoring too loudly in an adjoining hotel room; Wyatt Earp and another Dodge City policeman shot a celebrating cowboy, but that was Earp's only possible homicide; JAMES BUTLER ("WILD BILL") HICKOK, Abilene's marshal, killed only two men—a hostile saloonkeeper and, by mistake, a security guard rushing to his aid.

The low homicide rate was no accident. It resulted from the business community's fear of violence and, in consequence, a program to suppress it. No lone peace officer bore sole responsibility for law enforcement in a cattle town. A police force typically consisted of five individuals—a marshal, an assistant marshal, and three policemen. Since their comparatively high salaries composed the largest single budget item, city fathers responded to business-community pressure, as noted earlier, by instituting a sin tax to pay them.

The foundation of every antiviolence program was gun control. COWBOYS and cattlemen entering Wichita in 1872 had to check their six-shooters with deputized toll-keepers on the Chisholm Trail bridge; in 1873, signboards ordered them to "Leave your revolvers at police headquarters, and get a check." A well-placed sign in downtown Dodge City warned visitors that the carrying of firearms was "Strictly Prohibited." In a novel by ANDY ADAMS, who had been a cowboy on the trail, a character alerts some cowhands about to visit Dodge City for the first time. "I want to warn you to behave yourselves," he says. "You can wear your six-shooters into town, but you'd better leave them at the first place you stop, hotel, livery, or business house. And when you leave town . . . don't ride out shooting." This would have been good advice: Dodge City's policemen twice killed cowboys firing their weapons on the way out of town.

Potential violence always presented something of an entrepreneurial quandary. Cattle-town leaders felt it necessary to suppress the disorder to which drunken visitors became prone, but to do so without causing the ethnocentric Texas drovers to take their business elsewhere. Only the end of the cattle trade resolved the dilemma.

—*Robert R. Dykstra*

SEE ALSO: Cattle Industry; Earp Brothers; Gambling; Law and Order

SUGGESTED READING:
Adams, Andy. *The Log of a Cowboy.* Cambridge, Mass., 1903.
Dykstra, Robert R. *The Cattle Towns.* New York, 1968.
Miner, Craig. *Wichita: The Early Years, 1865–1880.* Lincoln, Nebr., 1982.

CATTLE TRAILS AND TRAIL DRIVING

Although the practice of driving cattle overland is ages old, it was not romanticized until after the Civil War when Texans on horseback drove cattle long distances to seek markets. Those armed men, wearing large-brimmed hats and using working tools with foreign-

"A Long, Long Trail A-Winding" shows a herd of fifteen hundred cattle trailing across a blizzard-swept range. Photograph by Charles Belden. *Courtesy Buffalo Bill Historical Center, Charles Belden Collection.*

sounding names, became known as COWBOYS, and they appealed to the fancies of Easterners.

As early as 1834, Texans were driving herds of wiry longhorns to Shreveport and New Orleans, and some accounts suggest a few herds were driven to Missouri by the early 1840s. Some longhorns were driven from Texas to California after the gold rush created a demand for beef there. In 1854, an estimated fifty thousand Texas cattle were driven north to Chicago; thousands more made the journey in 1855. Most Texans followed the Shawnee Trail from Preston in northern Texas across the Indian Territory into Missouri. But late in 1855, the Missouri state legislature made it illegal for Texas cattle to be driven through the state. Missourians thought longhorns transmitted a disease known as TEXAS FEVER that killed other cattle. It was not until 1889 that Texas fever was traced to a tick carried by longhorns, which were immune to the disease.

To avoid Missouri, Texans drove their cattle north along the eastern border of the Kansas Territory to the growing Kansas City market. Kansas stock-raisers soon complained about cattle losses due to Texas fever, and early in 1859, the Kansas territorial legislature passed a measure similar to Missouri's prohibiting longhorns from eastern areas of the territory.

The Civil War stopped Texas drives to the north, but more than one hundred thousand longhorns were driven east from Texas as far as Mississippi and perhaps beyond to feed the Confederacy. Such drives were halted in the summer of 1863 when Union forces gained control of the Mississippi River.

After the Civil War, cattle were so plentiful in Texas that their hides were worth more than their meat. Texas rancher CHARLES GOODNIGHT laid out a trail from the Cross Timbers region of Texas to Fort Sumner in the New Mexico Territory and sold longhorns to the military. But the greatest demand for beef was in the North and East, and Texans resumed driving herds northward in search of markets. The arrival of the railroad in Kansas and the establishment of the first railhead market in ABILENE, Kansas, in 1867 gave Texans a needed link to Eastern markets. Herds of longhorns were trailed north from Texas and followed the Chisholm Trail, which ran from Red River Station in northern Texas to Abilene. The year 1867 marked the beginning of the boom for Texas cattle, a boom that lasted into the 1880s.

The boom made trail driving a full-fledged business in the West. Although some Texas ranchers accompanied their herds north on trail drives, many ranchers entrusted their cattle to professional drovers who made contracts with buyers in Kansas for specific numbers of cattle by age, sex, condition, and type. The drovers would then contact ranchers and either buy their cattle or take the animals on consignment.

Most herds driven north from Texas averaged twenty-five hundred longhorns, and the techniques used to drive them over long distances were standardized. Before leaving Texas, the drover hired about a dozen cowboys for twenty-five to thirty dollars a month. The trail-drive boss or captain, who was paid about ninety dollars a month, served as field manager of the stock, equipment, and men. In addition, the drover acquired a camp-wagon, two teams of mules or oxen, cooking utensils, and other necessities. The drover also hired a cook, who drove the camp-wagon. After the cattle were road-branded, the first herds took to the trail from Texas in early spring. A trail drive averaged twelve to fifteen miles a day. A trail boss usually rode ahead of the herd. The chuck wagon came next. Off to one side were the horse wrangler and the remuda, or remounts. Behind the camp-wagon came the point riders, whose job was to lead the cattle. Many drives used a lead steer that had made the drive before. Next, where the cattle began to swell, came the swing riders, and farther back, the flank riders. Where the remaining cattle bunched together toward the end were three or more drag riders, usually young men new to cowboying. They ate dust in dry weather and kept the cattle moving. A trail drive from central Texas to a Kansas railhead usually took two to three months depending on the weather.

The railroad that transported cattle to the East also brought settlers West. As farmers and stock-raisers settled in the region, Texas fever again became a political issue. The quarantined areas of Kansas were expanded six times by the legislature between 1867 and 1883. Each time the quarantine was extended westward, new railhead CATTLE TOWNS were established. After Abilene, the major Kansas cattle towns were Newton, Ellsworth, WICHITA, Caldwell, and DODGE CITY, a cattle town reached by the Western Trail, which began at Doan's Store near the Red River in northern Texas. Beyond Dodge City, the trail was known as the Jones and Plummer Trail and ran north to Ogallala, Nebraska, through what is now South Dakota to Fort Buford in the northwestern part of present-day North Dakota. Between 1867 and 1885, nearly ten million longhorns were driven from Texas, many to populate new ranches established on the Northern Plains. The year 1885, however, was the last year Texas cattle were driven overland into or through Kansas. In this year, the Kansas legislature quarantined the whole state.

Trail drivers then skirted the western border of Kansas, many using the GOODNIGHT-LOVING TRAIL from Fort Sumner, New Mexico, north to Pueblo, Colorado. The trail had been laid out years earlier by Charles Goodnight and his partner OLIVER LOVING. Another branch of the trail led north to Cheyenne and later stretched into southern Canada. Longhorns were driven north to Wyoming, Montana, Idaho, and the Dakota territories over this route. Still others were driven over a portion of the OREGON TRAIL west from Fort Laramie into central Wyoming and Idaho. Another route used for a time was the BOZEMAN TRAIL, which ran from eastern Wyoming northwest into Montana. Many other cattle were also driven eastward from Oregon and Washington over the Bozeman Trail and some over Mullin Road, which ran from Oregon City eastward to Walla Walla, Washington, across northern Idaho to Helena and Great Falls, Montana, to Fort Buford in present-day North Dakota.

The arrival of railroads in ranching country eliminated the need for long trail drives. By the 1890s, the trail-driving era and many of the cattle trails were fading into history.

—*David Dary*

SEE ALSO: Cattle Industry

SUGGESTED READING:
Brown, Dee, and Martin F. Schmitt. *Trail Driving Days: The Golden Days of the Old Trail Driving Cattlemen.* New York and London, 1952.
Dary, David. *Cowboy Culture.* New York, 1981.
Hunter, J. Marvin, ed. *The Trail Drivers of Texas.* Nashville, Tenn., 1925.

CAYUSE INDIANS

SEE: Native American Peoples: Peoples of the Pacific Northwest

CENTRAL CITY, COLORADO

SEE: Ghost Towns

CENTRAL OVERLAND CALIFORNIA AND PIKE'S PEAK EXPRESS

SEE: Pike's Peak Express

CENTRAL PACIFIC RAILROAD

The Central Pacific, the western portion of the nation's first transcontinental railroad, was built eastward from Sacramento, California, across the Sierra Nevada, to PROMONTORY SUMMIT, Utah, where it joined the UNION PACIFIC RAILROAD on May 10, 1869.

The origins of the Central Pacific may be traced to 1832 when Dr. Harwell Carter of Rochester, New York, proposed the construction of a transcontinental railroad in a series of articles published in the *New York Courier & Enquirer*. Then, in 1848, Missouri Senator THOMAS HART BENTON persuaded his congressional colleagues to send his son-in-law, JOHN CHARLES FRÉMONT, on an expedition to survey a possible transcontinental rail route. The results were inconclusive, and Secretary of War Jefferson Davis obtained authorization from Congress in 1853 to fund a series of more detailed surveys. A combination of greed, pre–Civil War sectionalism, and inadequate information delayed action on the project. But, in 1854, Colonel Charles Wilson, president of the Sacramento Valley Railroad, hired THEODORE DEHONE JUDAH, a brilliant young engineer from Bridgeport, Connecticut, to survey a right of way for a railroad to link the gold-mining town of Fulsom with Sacramento. Concluding his survey, Judah reported to Wilson that the route could well serve as the Pacific end of a transcontinental railroad.

Perhaps Judah would have succeeded in moving Wilson to action, but the gold petered out in Fulsom, and the Sacramento Valley Railroad progressed no far-

A campsite and train mark the progress of Central Pacific Railroad construction near the Humboldt River canyon in Nevada in 1869. *Courtesy National Archives.*

ther than twenty-two miles. Yet Judah had seen the light and published a pamphlet entitled *A Practical Plan for Building the Pacific Railroad*. He became a vigorous lobbyist in Washington, D.C., and alternated his work there with ongoing survey expeditions in the West. At last, in 1860, after searching the region north of Lake Tahoe for a pass across the mountains, he received a letter from Daniel ("Doc") Strong, a pharmacist and amateur surveyor. Strong had read Judah's pamphlet, and he told the engineer that, years earlier, he had charted a relatively easy wagon corridor through the Sierra Nevada to Dutch Flat, the mining town in which he lived. Judah investigated and immediately concluded with Strong an agreement to incorporate a Pacific railroad association.

Armed with his route through the formidable Sierra Nevada, Judah gathered seven backers, including a core who would become known as California's "Big Four": COLLIS P. HUNTINGTON and MARK HOPKINS, partners in a hardware store; AMASA LELAND STANFORD, a wholesale grocer; and CHARLES CROCKER, a dry-goods merchant. Construction inched toward the California-Nevada line. In the meantime, Judah returned to Washington, D.C., where he successfully lobbied for the passage of the Pacific Railway Act of 1862, which authorized the Central Pacific and Union Pacific to begin constructing a transcontinental railroad and granted huge tracts of land not only for the right of way but to finance its construction. With the authorization and funding in place, Judah returned to California only to find that his Big Four had decided to halt construction at the Nevada line at least until settlement caught up with the end of track. Disgusted by his backers' failure of vision, Judah set off again for the nation's capital to find new financing. He traveled by way of the Isthmus of Panama, where he contracted yellow fever, fell desperately ill, and subsequently died at the age of thirty-seven.

Spurred by the benefits of government subsidies and land grants tied to mileage of track completed, the Big Four resumed work on the line after Judah's death. Crocker directed construction and pushed the railroad through the mountains during harsh winter weather and heavy snows. He imported Chinese laborers, who, despite the abuse and mistreatment heaped upon them, proved to be remarkably energetic and efficient workers, outperforming the Irish, who had been the mainstay of railroad labor in the West.

Both the Central Pacific and the Union Pacific were built by construction companies organized by the backers of the railroad. Construction was financed by the sale of bonds received from the railroad company, and the construction companies took their profits in railroad stock—essentially worthless until the railroad was completed, operational, and making money. Although the railroad and the scheme by which it was built offered the prospect of enormous profit, the undertaking was extremely risky.

The heyday of the Central Pacific was brief. Less than a decade after it connected with the Union Pacific, the Thurman Act of 1878, enacted to ensure that the Central and Union Pacific railroads would pay their debts when they were due, halted further development of both roads for a time. The Big Four then turned to developing the SOUTHERN PACIFIC RAILROAD instead, which took control of the Central Pacific. In 1895, the Central Pacific could not pay the money due on its government-subsidy bonds. In desperation, Huntington used the credit of the Southern Pacific to back a refunding plan. By this means, the Central Pacific became free of its government obligations.

The Central Pacific, although functionally the western extension of the Union Pacific, operated independently of that railroad until 1900, when EDWARD HENRY HARRIMAN gained control of the Union Pacific and the Southern Pacific—and, through it, the Central Pacific. Government antitrust forces compelled the Union Pacific to relinquish control of the Southern Pacific and the Central Pacific in 1913. However, in terms of function, the Union Pacific and the Central Pacific have continued to operate as a single, nation-spanning route.

—*Alan Axelrod*

SEE ALSO: Financial Panics; Railroads; Transcontinental Railroad Surveys

SUGGESTED READING:
Lewis, Oscar. *The Big Four.* New York, 1938.
Martin, Albro. *Railroads Triumphant: The Growth, Rejection and Rebirth of a Vital American Force.* New York, 1992.

CENTRAL PLAINS INDIAN WARS

During the mid-nineteenth century, the Indian tribes of the Central Plains—the region between the Platte and Red rivers—fought to maintain control of their homelands. To the Southern Cheyennes and Arapahos, who dominated western Kansas and eastern Colorado, and to the Comanches, Kiowas, and Plains Apaches, who held western Oklahoma and the Texas Panhandle, the flood of Euro-American settlers moving across the region constituted an invasion of their territory and hunting grounds.

To the United States, the Plains tribes presented a barrier to migration and commerce. When conflicts

To readers in the East, *Frank Leslie's Illustrated Newspaper* delivered reports of the great council of the Plains Indians at Medicine Lodge Creek in October 1867. The council did not provide a lasting peace. *Courtesy Library of Congress.*

erupted along the Oregon and Santa Fe trails, the government sought to protect its interests through treaties with the various tribes. The pacts only increased travel across the plains and brought strings of army posts, U.S. troops, and government surveyors.

Trouble erupted between the Cheyennes and troops in April 1856 when soldiers killed a warrior they were trying to arrest on the charge of horse stealing. Cheyenne war parties began harassing travelers along the Platte Trail in Kansas and Nebraska. After troops attacked a Cheyenne camp and killed and wounded several of its occupants, the Cheyennes responded with forays on emigrant wagon trains.

Cheyenne leaders attempted to make peace, but army officers were determined to punish the tribe. In the spring of 1857, Colonel EDWIN V. SUMNER organized a military expedition for this purpose. He divided his command into two segments that united on the South Platte. From there, he drove eastward to the headwaters of the Solomon River in western Kansas. Forewarned by William Bent of BENT'S FORT, a trading post on the Arkansas River, the Cheyennes knew of Sumner's plan to attack. Preparing the warriors for the coming battle, Cheyenne medicine men persuaded the warriors that if they dipped their hands in a certain lake, they could hold up their hands, and the soldiers' bullets would fall harmlessly to the ground. But when Sumner unexpectedly ordered a saber charge, the disconcerted Cheyennes were easily routed.

Following this defeat, elderly chief Yellow Wolf indicated that his people were ready to take up the planting and raising of crops. In 1858, however, gold was discovered on Colorado's Cherry Creek, and the Cheyenne-Arapaho lands were invaded by hordes of gold-seekers.

During that same year, a force of TEXAS RANGERS, reacting to Kiowa and Comanche raids into Texas, conducted the first invasion of the western region of the Indian Territory. Marching northward along the one hundredth meridian with a unit composed of rangers and Brazos Reserve Indians, Captain John S. Ford located a Comanche village on Little Robe Creek, a tributary of the Canadian River just north of the Antelope Hills. During the attack on the encampment, Ford's troops killed some seventy villagers.

Under orders from General David Twiggs, commanding the Texas U.S. military department, Major Earl Van Dorn established Camp Radziminski in the far southwestern corner of the Indian Territory. In September 1858, Van Dorn learned of a large cavalcade of Comanches who were visiting with the Wichita Indians on Rush Creek. Van Dorn was unaware that the Comanches were on their way to Fort Arbuckle, where they had been invited by the post commander for peace talks. After a long, overnight march, Van Dorn launched a surprise dawn attack on the Comanches and killed more than fifty of the party. He also burned their lodges and captured their horses.

Van Dorn followed the attack with another foray to the north during the spring of 1859. There, in the Battle of Crooked Creek, he assaulted a Comanche camp just across the Kansas border. The outbreak of the Civil War in the spring of 1861, however, brought a suspension of both army and Texas Ranger action against the Plains tribes of the Indian Territory.

That was not the case in the newly founded Colorado Territory and in Kansas. Although the Indians had not resisted the gold-rush invasion onto their domain, isolated conflicts between whites and Indians occurred. Assuming the Indians were to blame, Colonel JOHN M. CHIVINGTON, commanding the Colorado military district, ordered troops of the Colorado First Regiment to retaliate. In one severe attack, a Denver-based unit marched into western Kansas in the spring of 1864. Coming onto a Cheyenne buffalo hunt, the troops shot and killed Chief Lean Bear as he was riding up to meet them.

Lean Bear's murder touched off the powder keg of Cheyenne resentment and anger. During the summer of 1864, Cheyenne warriors ravaged the roads leading to Colorado along the Platte, Smoky Hill, and Arkansas rivers. In August, BLACK KETTLE, principal chief of the Cheyennes, made peace overtures that resulted in a council at Denver with Governor JOHN EVANS.

Chivington indicated then that if the Indians turned themselves over to the military, they would be safe. Black Kettle did so, bringing his band to camp near Fort Lyon. Betraying his promise, Chivington attacked the Cheyenne village in southeastern Colorado on the morning of November 29, 1864. In the SAND CREEK MASSACRE, many Cheyenne men, women, and children were killed, although Black Kettle escaped.

Infuriated by Chivington's act, the Cheyenne warriors struck back from their Republican River stronghold in an assault on Julesburg and Fort Rankin, Colorado, in January 1865. The U.S. government attempted to make peace with the Cheyennes and other Central Plains tribes and to remove them from Kansas with the Little Arkansas Treaty of 1865 and the MEDICINE LODGE TREATY OF 1867. Neither treaty, however, pacified the Cheyenne war societies, who were further antagonized by advancing settlements in Kansas and the building of the Kansas-Pacific Railroad across their hunting grounds.

In 1866, General Winfield S. Hancock and Lieutenant Colonel GEORGE ARMSTRONG CUSTER conducted a fruitless campaign in western Kansas in an effort to intimidate the Cheyennes. When General PHILIP H. SHERIDAN was assigned to replaced Hancock, the fiery Civil War hero tried more of the same. By his authority, Major George Forsyth rode into the Cheyennes' stronghold with fifty civilian scouts and barely escaped complete annihilation at Beecher's Island in eastern Colorado. At the same time, General ALFRED SULLY conducted an inept military foray into northwestern Indian Territory.

Sheridan then decided on a three-pronged winter's invasion of the Indian Country. His main force marched into northwestern Indian Territory and established Camp Supply. From there, Custer led his Seventh Cavalry south down Wolf Creek during a heavy snowstorm. At the Antelope Hills, he picked up an Indian trail that led to an encampment on the Washita River. At dawn on November 27, 1868, Custer launched a surprise attack against the sleeping Indian village. The victims would prove to be Cheyennes, and among the dead was Chief Black Kettle, who only a few days before had attempted to turn himself and his band over to authorities at Fort Cobb.

On December 25, the command of Major A. W. Evans from Fort Bascom, New Mexico, destroyed a Comanche village west of the Wichita Mountains. Shortly after the attack, Sheridan established Fort Sill at the eastern base of the mountains.

Eventually even the most determined Cheyenne leaders were forced to capitulate; their people were so starved that they were eating their horses. Tall Bull, leader of the Cheyenne Dog Soldiers, headed north with 165 lodges only to be severely mauled by U.S. troops at Summit Springs near the Platte River the following August.

Early in 1869, the government's Indian affairs were turned over to the Quakers. A reservation area and an agency were established for the Southern Cheyennes and Arapahos, and for a time, the region was relatively quiet. In December 1872, however, Cheyenne warriors, stimulated by the wares of white whiskey dealers, massacred a surveying party. On June 27, 1874, the Cheyennes joined with Kiowas and others in an unproductive attack on a buffalo-hunter settlement at Adobe Walls in the Texas Panhandle. More Cheyenne strikes followed, including the massacre of Pat Hennessey and three teamsters; the killing of surveyor O. F. Short and his crew; and the capture of four young girls of a German family, following the murder of their parents.

During this time, Comanche and Kiowa war parties were regularly raiding settlements and trade routes in northern Texas. The arrest and imprisonment of Kiowa leaders SATANTA and BIG TREE brought only a temporary respite in the depredations.

During the final months of 1874, the U.S. Army launched a punitive campaign. Military units took to the field from five locations surrounding the Plains Indian range in western Indian Territory and the Texas Panhandle. In the Red River War, forces under Colonel NELSON APPLETON MILES and other officers fell upon village after village. The most severe loss to the Indians was Colonel RANALD SLIDELL MACKENZIE's destruction of a large consolidated encampment in the bottom of the Palo Duro Canyon.

Great losses in lodges, horses, and food supplies had left the tribes completely unable to withstand the rigors of winter on the open prairies. Band after band straggled into Forts Sill, Supply, and Reno to accept their fate as wards of the U.S. government. Some of the war leaders of the tribes were placed in chains and sent off to imprisonment at Fort Marion, Florida.

—*Stan Hoig*

SEE ALSO: Native American Peoples: Peoples of the Great Plains; Texas Frontier Indian Wars

SUGGESTED READING:
Berthrong, Donald J. *The Southern Cheyennes.* Norman, Okla., 1963.
Hoig, Stan. *The Battle of the Washito.* New York, 1976.
———. *The Sand Creek Massacre.* Norman, Okla., 1961.
———. *Tribal Wars of the Southern Plains.* Norman, Okla., 1993.
Nye, W. S. *Carbine and Lance.* Norman, Okla., 1937.

CENTRAL VALLEY PROJECT

The Central Valley Project (CVP) is a major WATER storage and distribution system in California's San Joaquin and Sacramento valleys, collectively known as the Central Valley. Although the system was built by the U.S. BUREAU OF RECLAMATION beginning in the 1930s, its antecedents can be traced to California's own efforts in the late nineteenth and early twentieth centuries to develop a well-coordinated plan for the state's water resources. Studies by various California agencies eventually led State Engineer Edward Hyatt to propose the State Water Plan in 1931. He called for controlled releases of stored flood waters from a major reservoir on the upper SACRAMENTO RIVER to improve navigability downstream, control salt-water intrusion into the Sacramento–San Joaquin Delta, provide new freshwater supplies for San Francisco Bay Area cities, deliver IRRIGATION water via an interconnected system of canals and reservoirs to dry lands in the San Joaquin Valley, and develop hydroelectric power to repay construction costs.

California was unable to fund the State Water Plan during the Great Depression, and in 1937, the U.S. government took responsibility for building what had become known as the Central Valley Project. The first CVP irrigation water was delivered to the San Joaquin Valley in 1951.

When the FEDERAL GOVERNMENT took over construction, the Bureau of Reclamation imposed a 160-acre limitation for CVP water recipients—a restriction that was largely ignored for many years and was broadened to 960 acres in 1982. In 1992, Congress further changed CVP regulations by establishing fish and wildlife protection as an additional purpose for the system, and this modification limited some water deliveries to farms. The same legislation also permitted CVP farmers to sell their water supplies to parties outside the project's service area, including to towns and cities. While such changes were aimed at making the CVP more efficient and responsive to the needs of California as a whole, they also encouraged state officials to consider purchasing the CVP from the U.S. government to prevent further federal modifications.

—*Douglas R. Littlefield*

SEE ALSO: San Joaquin River

SUGGESTED READING:
Hundley, Norris, Jr. *The Great Thirst: Californians and Water, 1770s–1990s.* Berkeley, Calif., 1992.
Pisani, Donald J. *From the Family Farm to Agribusiness: The Irrigation Crusade in California and the West, 1850–1931.* Berkeley, Calif., 1984.

CHAFFEE, JEROME BONAPARTE

Banker, miner, and politician Jerome Bonaparte Chaffee (1825–1885) was born in Niagara County, New York. He obtained a modest education fairly typical of the period. Then he moved West, first to Michigan, then to Missouri, where he engaged in banking, and then to Kansas, where he engaged in town building. When news of the Pikes Peak gold rush flooded the headlines, Chaffee decided to make his fortune in the booming mines of the Rocky Mountains. In 1860, he set his sights on the Central City–Black Hawk area of Gilpin County, Colorado, the heart of the region's MINING country until the late 1870s.

With capital to invest in development, Chaffee quickly became one of Colorado's foremost mine owners. He invested heavily in gold mines near Central City and Black Hawk, silver mines in Caribou in western Boulder County, and a host of other mines. When the great LEADVILLE boom eclipsed that of the Central City–Black Hawk area in the late 1870s, Chaffee got in on the ground floor. While he himself did not engage in mining, he put the management in the hands of Eben Smith and other professionals and directed operations from afar.

Chaffee developed his mining interests in tandem with his other great business interest—BANKING. In 1865, he helped organize and became the first president of the First National Bank of Denver. Many of his mining associates were prominent in the bank's development and used it to enhance their mining investments.

Chaffee's political career paralleled his work in mining and banking. A Republican, Chaffee served in the territorial legislature and became the Colorado Territory's delegate to Congress. He was a leader of the statehood movement, and once Colorado entered the Union in 1876, he became one of its first two senators. But his term was for only two years, and with his health in decline, he did not run for election to a full term in 1879. After leaving office, he moved to New York, where he spent his final years.

Although little-known today, Chaffee's impact on Colorado's early development was large. As a mine owner, banker, and politician, he helped guide Colorado's development in the formative period. His mines produced huge tonnage of ore; the First National Bank of Denver remained the state's largest bank until the 1980s; and his political acumen helped establish the Republican party as the predominant political element in the state.

—*James E. Fell, Jr.*

SEE ALSO: Colorado Gold and Silver Rushes

SUGGESTED READING:
Adams, Eugene H., Lyle W. Dorsett, and Robert H. Pulcipher. *The Pioneer Western Bank: First of Denver, 1860–1890.* Denver, 1984.

CHAMPION, NATE

SEE: Johnson County War

CHANDLER, ALEXANDER J.

IRRIGATION pioneer Alexander J. Chandler (1859–1950) was born in Coaticook, Canada, and moved to Arizona to work as an animal inspector during a drought in August 1887. While treating malnourished animals, Chandler became interested in irrigation. In 1890, he formed a company to build Mesa Canal and then led the company's participation in the Salt River Project, one of the first built by the U.S. Reclamation Service. In 1911, he founded the city of Chandler, which Frank Lloyd Wright designed. He completed the San Marcos Hotel, an early Arizona resort, in 1913.

—*James E. Sherow*

SEE ALSO: Bureau of Reclamation; Water

SUGGESTED READING:
"Death Claims A. J. Chandler, Town Founder" *The (Phoenix) Arizona Republic,* 9 May 1950: 1–2.

CHANGING WOMAN

According to the Navajos, Changing Woman—a central figure in the Navajo cosmos—created the Navajo people by rolling old skin from her body into balls and using her mountain-soil bundle (a medicine bag consisting of four pieces of unwounded buckskin brought by her father from the underworld) to create out of the balls four couples, the ancestors of the four original Navajo clans. Changing Woman was the daughter of Long Life Boy and Happiness Girl, a handsome young man and beautiful young woman who represent the means by which all life passes through time. Changing Woman was raised by First Man and First Woman, the first pair to exist in the world, who—

some Navajos believe—were transformed from two primordial ears of corn and who directed the emergence of the Navajo people in a journey from four lower worlds. Taking her name from her many changes of dress, her spiritual correspondence to the change of seasons, and the repetitions of the life cycle that she experiences, Changing Woman is associated with a young Navajo woman's change at puberty and with the four-day rite, *kinaalda*, accompanying the change. Celebrated in the Blessingway, a night-long Navajo song and prayer ceremony aimed at bringing good fortune and long life, Changing Woman is synonymous with life and creative power and is the foundation and the measure of Navajo time. She matures and ages only to repeat the process endlessly. She is the mother of twins—Monster Slayer and Born for Water—whose father is the sun and who, in tests of their manhood and to establish their paternity, acquire weapons, prayers, and songs, slay monsters, and in general prepare the way for human beings. Changing Woman also appears in Navajo ceremonial blessings such as the Beadway, Eagleway, Monsterway, and Shootingway. Given the Navajos' love for duality and pairing, Changing Woman is sometimes coupled with an evil twin. Also known as Whiteshell Woman (who in some accounts is her sister), Turquoise Woman, Abalone Woman, and Jet Woman, Changing Woman has a counterpart among the Apaches (White Painted Woman), the Keresans (Iatiku), and the Pawnees (Moon Woman).

—*Charles Phillips*

SEE ALSO: Native American Cultures: Spiritual Life

SUGGESTED READING:
Gill, Sam D., and Irene F. Sullivan. *Dictionary of Native American Mythology.* Santa Barbara, Calif., 1992.

CHAPMAN, WILLIAM S.

California land speculator, real-estate developer, and innovative farmer William S. Chapman (1828–1906) was born in Ohio. He came to California in 1864 and threw himself into a frenzy of land-related activities. He built immense real-estate holdings by buying undeveloped land from the federal and state governments for a pittance and then developing and selling it for huge profits. He was among the first to raise alfalfa as a food crop for beef in Merced County in the late 1860s. In association with Isaac Friedlander, he purchased large undeveloped tracts in Fresno County for cultivation of wheat, much of which was exported to Liverpool, England. To enhance and sustain crop production, Chapman and Friedlander established the Fresno Canal and Irrigation Company in early 1871. Chapman pioneered innovative farming techniques, including IRRIGATION, the planting of various fruit trees, and the importation of thousands of muscatel grape cuttings from Spain to launch the state's raisin industry. To promote land use and sales, he created subdivisions by bringing a ready supply of water to the land and then laying out planned farming communities in 1875 with the founding of the Central California Colony in Fresno County. He reputedly amassed one million acres of land before overextending himself. As a result, archrivals HENRY MILLER and Charles Lux, among others, acquired much of his holdings. HUBERT HOWE BANCROFT in his *Chronicles of the Builders* observed that Chapman "was a man of unusual ability of shrewdness, widely known on the Pacific Coast as a speculator in land and as a litigant in cases of disputed land questions."

—*Doyce B. Nunis, Jr.*

SUGGESTED READING:
Elliott, Wallace W. *History of Fresno County, California.* San Francisco, 1882.
Thickens, Virginia E. "Pioneer Agricultural Colonies of Fresno County." *California Historical Society Quarterly* 25 (March 1946): 17–38.
Winchell, Lilbourne A. *History of Fresno County and the San Joaquin Valley.* Fresno, Calif., 1933.

CHAPMAN-BARNARD RANCH, OKLAHOMA

Located in Osage County, Oklahoma, the Chapman-Barnard Ranch began operations in 1915 when oil men J. A. Chapman and his partner H. G. Barnard acquired their first fifteen thousand acres. By the 1940s, the ranch was among the largest in Oklahoma and boasted some eighty-five thousand acres of deeded and leased tallgrass pasture land. Chapman and Barnard raised their own Herefords and contracted to fatten Texas steers for market. Every spring from the 1920s to the 1950s, the Midland Valley Railroad delivered carloads of cattle to the nearby Blackland shipping pens; ranch hands on horseback then drove the cattle to the Chapman-Barnard pastures. At the end of summer, the cattle were shipped to stockyards in Kansas City, St. Louis, and Oklahoma City. The ranch continued operations for nearly seventy-five years. The old ranch house later became headquarters for the Tallgrass Prairie Preserve in Osage County.

—*Patricia Hogan*

SUGGESTED READING:
Rhonda, Jeanne, and Richard W. Slatta. "Cowboying at the Chapman-Barnard Ranch." *Persimmon Hill* (Spring 1993): 36–40.

CHAPS

SEE: Cowboy Outfits

CHARBONNEAU, JEAN BAPTISTE

The son of the Shoshone woman SACAGAWEA and French-Canadian trader Toussaint Charbonneau, Jean Baptiste Charbonneau (1805–1866) was born at the LEWIS AND CLARK EXPEDITION's Fort Mandan along the Missouri River in present-day North Dakota. The youngest member of the American expedition, Jean Baptiste was taken along with his parents from the Missouri River to the Pacific Ocean. Captain WILLIAM CLARK called him "my little dancing boy" and named a prominent rock pillar on the south bank of the Yellowstone River Pompy's Tower after the boy he sometimes called "Pomp." After Sacagawea's death in 1812, Clark became legal guardian for Jean Baptiste Charbonneau and his sister Lisette. Both children received some formal education.

By the 1820s, Charbonneau was living in an Indian village at the mouth of the Kansas River. There he caught the eye of Prince Paul Wilhelm of Württemberg, an aristocratic traveler and naturalist. In 1823, Charbonneau joined the prince's entourage and eventually returned with him to Europe. Unconfirmed legend has it that Charbonneau accompanied Prince Paul throughout Western Europe and Africa on journeys of scientific exploration. Charbonneau returned to North America in 1829 and immediately became engaged in the FUR TRADE, both as a free trapper and as an employee for various fur companies. By the 1840s, with the decline of the Rocky Mountain fur trade, Charbonneau switched from trapping to guiding. He served as a guide for the Scottish adventurer and sportsman Sir William Drummond Stewart and signed on as a scout for the Mormon Battalion bound for California in 1846 and 1847. Once in California, he became alcalde (chief magistrate) at San Luis Rey mission. During the 1850s, he pursued mining in the CALIFORNIA GOLD RUSH. Wealth eluded him, and the year 1861 found him working as a hotel clerk in Auburn, California. News of gold lured him towards Montana, and he died on the way to the gold fields in 1866.

—*James P. Ronda*

SUGGESTED READING:
Anderson, Irving R. *A Charbonneau Family Portrait*. Fort Clatsop, Oreg., 1988.

CHASTA-COSTA INDIANS

SEE: Native American Peoples: Peoples of the Pacific Northwest

CHATILLON, HENRI

Few would remember Henri Chatillon (1808 or 1816–1873) if he had not led historian FRANCIS PARKMAN and his party on a tour of the eastern prairies in the summer of 1846. According to Parkman, Chatillon was born about 1816, but if the *Missouri Republican* account of his death on August 8, 1873, is accurate, he was born in 1808 in Carondelet, a town his grandfather had founded in 1767 and now a part of St. Louis.

Little is known of his life before 1846. Parkman wrote that Chatillon began hunting in the Rocky Mountains at the age of fifteen and that he was married to Bear Robe, the daughter of an important Oglala Sioux leader. When Parkman returned to the East, Chatillon, known as "Yellow Whiteman," resumed hunting for the AMERICAN FUR COMPANY. After marrying his second wife, Odile Delor Lux, in the St. Louis Cathedral in 1848, Chatillon became an urban developer, building and selling houses.

It was a noble Henri Chatillon whom Parkman portrayed in *The Oregon Trail*. In the 1849 and 1852 editions, Parkman added a note about his guide on the last page: "If sincerity and honor, a boundless generosity of spirit, a delicate regard to the feelings of others, and a nice perception of what was due to them, are the essential characteristics of a gentleman, then Henri Chatillon deserves the title." Parkman portrayed Chatillon as a living example of a JAMES FENIMORE COOPER hero. He was "gracefully moulded . . . had a natural refinement and delicacy of mind. . . . His manly face was a mirror of uprightness, simplicity, and kindness of heart." Parkman wrote that as a hunter Chatillon had but one rival, and that the only men braver were soon dead. Chatillon was a respectful hunter, though; he did not waste animals as Parkman and his cousin Quincy Adams Shaw did. He was "human and merciful . . . gentle as a woman, though braver than a lion."

Chatillon was an important influence on Parkman's development as a historian. Chatillon not only brought the often-ill Boston Brahmin back from his summer adventures alive, but because of his relation to Sioux Chief Bull Bear, Chatillon was able to place Parkman in the Oglala village where he made personal observations of Native American life—observations he later used in his histories.

—*Sean O'Neill*

SUGGESTED READING:
Jacobs, Wilbur. *Francis Parkman, Historian as Hero: The Formative Years.* Austin, Tex., 1991.
———. "Henry Chatillon." In *Mountain Men and the Fur Trade.* Edited by LeRoy R. Hafen. Glendale, Calif., 1965.
O'Leary, Mrs. James L. "Henry Chatillon." *Missouri Historical Society Bulletin* (January 1966): 123–142.
Parkman, Francis. *The Oregon Trail.* Boston, 1892.

CHAUTAUQUA

One of the largest and most successful community education programs in the nation, the Chautauqua movement attempted to expose families to a cultural education. Founded on the shore of Lake Chautauqua, New York, in August 1874 by John H. Vincent, a Methodist clergyman and later bishop, and Lewis Miller, the program was initially intended to be an extension of Sunday-school education and a forum for other intellectual pursuits not necessarily related to religion. Visitors went to the lake for a family church-camp atmosphere, which quickly developed into a summer colony; by 1878, the program was extended to two months. As the program grew, it relied less on religion and more on simply exposing people to new thoughts and innovative ideas. The initial New York site eventually accommodated twenty-five thousand visitors and offered instruction in mathematics, science, library science, domestic science, music, arts and crafts, and even agriculture. One particular strength of the program was that, although it was founded as an instrument of the Methodist church, it was not identified solely with this church; instead, it offered programs for families of many Christian denominations.

The success of the New York program spread. The Chautauqua Literary and Scientific Circle (CLSC) offered collegiate instruction in the liberal arts from some of the more renowned scholars of the late nineteenth and early twentieth centuries. Equal to the success of the CLSC was the summer-school program initiated by William Rainey Harper. It was Harper who began the Chautauqua correspondence courses. After founding the University of Chicago, Harper used his Chautauqua experience to develop an extension program at the university. As a backhanded tribute to its usefulness, the program was soon obsolete as almost every major university in the country offered similar correspondence courses.

The programs, like those offered at Chicago, enjoyed success, but few of them reached the thousands of people scattered throughout the Far West. In an attempt to reach sparsely populated regions, "tent Chautauqua" was developed by Keith Vawter. Tent Chautauqua was actually more akin to the lyceum movement that traveled from town to town and offered musical symposiums and lectures. Tent Chautauqua had less emphasis on continuing education.

A tent Chautauqua, or "little Chautauqua," advertised itself for weeks before it hit a town. Pasteboard advertisements proclaimed, "You don't have to go to Omaha to hear something good. Come to Chautauqua!" Preachers mentioned it from the pulpit, and all around town, tickets were for sale. The typical engagement lasted seven to ten days in a community and was held in a large tent with makeshift seating. Each day offered a different program, and daytime programs were usually geared toward women and children, while men were at work. Programming included lectures on any number of subjects, various musical performances, and exhibitions of art and sculpture.

The Chautauqua movement proved an ideal platform for another phenomenon then sweeping the county: social reform and muckraking. Social reformers flocked to the Chautauqua tents and found audiences eager to embrace the cause of social change. Thomas Mott Osborne preached prison reform; Marcus Kavanaugh lectured on the need for court reform; and Jacob Riis debuted his book of photographs, *How the Other Half Lives,* about urban poverty. In some form or another, WOMEN'S SUFFRAGE, the graduated income tax, school-lunch programs, pure food and drug acts, juvenile courts, and many other social ideas were brought to the masses via Chautauqua. Along with social reform, the movement provided a forum for differing political views as well and featured debates between Senators Albert Beveridge, George Norris, Robert La Follette, labor leaders Lincoln Steffens and Eugene V. Debs, and many others.

Initially, tent Chautauqua did not include drama of any kind. Gradually, however, Chautauqua began to include short dramatic performances that changed the public perception of the art. Tent Chautauqua included performances of Dickens and Shakespeare, either individual soliloquies or short one-act selections. Eventually, full-fledged dramatic presentations took up a good portion of an evening's program.

Most Chautauqua troupes traveled by train, although the movement truly became a rural phenomenon after the invention of the Model T Ford in the 1920s. Typically, Chautauqua troupes lived nomadic lives similar to those of circus performers. Troupes traveled a prearranged circuit for a short time, although each act was not necessarily tied to the others. For instance, the New York City Marine Band toured Montana, Idaho, Oregon, Washington, and California in 1914. The band played the circuit sometimes with the same acts, sometimes with others, as several circuits were operating simultaneously. A drama troupe might leave the Marine Band in Idaho only to meet up with it again in northern California.

The Chautauqua movement, which appealed mostly to white working-class Americans, achieved its heyday in 1924, when there were hundreds of troupes touring the country to bring Christian morality and entertainment to an estimated one-third of the population of the United States. However, from there, the Western movement crashed. The very vehicle that helped its growth also sped its demise. The automobile came into wider use and allowed people to spend a day simply driving or visiting relatives out of town. Also, with the advent of radio and its family-oriented programming, people had access to similar entertainment without ever leaving home. The end of the Western Chautauqua movement came with motion-picture houses and eventually television. Chautauqua became obsolete, although the initial program at Lake Chautauqua continued its original summer activities and a number of cultural agencies and museums have revived the medium in the 1990s. The legacy of the Western movement continues in the present in the form of continuing education programs, correspondence schools, and community reading clubs.

—*Kurt Edward Kemper*

Suggested reading:
Case, Robert Ormond, and Victoria Case. *We Called It Culture: The Story of Chautauqua.* Freeport, N.Y., 1949.
Gould, Joseph E. *The Chautauqua Movement: An Episode in the Continuing American Revolution.* Albany, N.Y., 1961.
Morrison, Theodore. *Chautauqua: A Center for Education, Religion, and the Arts in America.* Chicago, 1974.
Vincent, John H. *The Chautauqua Movement.* New York, 1929.

CHÁVEZ, CESAR (ESTRADA)

See: California

CHAVEZ, DENNIS

U.S. senator from New Mexico, Dennis Chavez (1888–1962) was born in Los Chavez, New Mexico. He was admitted to Georgetown University Law School, despite his lack of formal education, and graduated in 1920. A lifelong Democrat, he was elected to the New Mexico State House of Representatives in 1922. In 1930, he was elected to the U.S. House of Representatives, where he served two terms. He did not seek reelection in 1934 but ran for the U.S. Senate and was defeated. Upon the death of Senator Bronson Cutting, Chavez was appointed to the Senate on May 11, 1935, and was elected in his own right on November 3, 1936. He served in the Senate until his death.

While in public office, Chavez sponsored and supported legislation for the benefit of his constituents and the state of New Mexico. In the state legislature, he sponsored a bill providing free textbooks for public schoolchildren. As a member of Congress, he personified the New Deal and its reforms in an effort to cope with the Great Depression. During World War II, he remained in contact with families of soldiers, and he sponsored legislation benefiting American GIs. An advocate of civil rights, he introduced the Fair Employment Practices Commission Bill in 1944 to prohibit discrimination in employment on the basis on race, creed, color, national origin, or ancestry. Although the bill was defeated, Chavez played a pioneering role in advancing civil rights.

Chavez was the first Hispanic born in the United States to serve in the Senate. By the end of his legislative career, he was outranked in seniority by only three senators.

—*Roy Lujan*

Suggested reading:
Lujan, Roy. "Dennis Chavez and the Roosevelt Era, 1933–1945." Ph.D. diss., University of New Mexico, 1987.
———. "Dennis Chavez and National Legislation: 1933–1946." *National Social Science Journal* 3 (1990–1991): 3.

CHEHALIS INDIANS

See: Native American Peoples: Peoples of the Pacific Northwest

CHEMEHUEVI INDIANS

See: Native American Peoples: Peoples of California

CHEROKEE INDIANS

SEE: Native American Peoples: Peoples Removed from the East

CHEROKEE MALE AND FEMALE SEMINARIES

Nondenominational boarding schools, the Cherokee Male and Female Seminaries were established and financed by the Cherokee Nation in 1851 in Tahlequah, Indian Territory (now Oklahoma). The curriculum of the seminaries was designed to teach Cherokee children the ways of white society and to educate the future leaders and teachers of the Cherokee Nation. Housed in large three-story brick buildings, Cherokee children from grades one through twelve studied rigorous curricula patterned after those of Mount Holyoke Female Seminary and Yale University. The first seminary teachers were non-Indian graduates of prominent Eastern schools. After the 1870s, former seminary students returned to teach at their alma maters.

Because the seminaries educated and influenced thousands of Cherokee children of all socio-economic and cultural backgrounds, the schools had a tremendous impact on the tribe. Almost three thousand Cherokees studied at the Male Seminary before it burned in 1910, and at least this many studied at the Female Seminary before the building was sold to the state of Oklahoma in 1909. Many of the men and women who studied at the seminaries later earned degrees from universities and colleges across the country. Graduates later became Cherokee chiefs, attorneys general, lawyers, physicians, social workers, and educators; some have been inducted into the Oklahoma Memorial Hall of Fame.

The seminaries were major instruments of Cherokee acculturation and of the loss of traditional tribal culture. Because not all Cherokees believed that tribal monies should have been spent on the schools, they were major causes of intertribal strife.

The Female Seminary building, known today as Seminary Hall, survives on the campus of Northeastern State University in Tahlequah.

—*Devon A. Mihesuah*

SEE ALSO: Indian Schools

SUGGESTED READING:
Mihesuah, Devon A. *Cultivating the Rose Buds: The Education of Women at the Cherokee Female Seminary, 1851–1909.* Urbana, Ill., 1993.

Top: Students of the Cherokee Male Seminary. *Courtesy Western History Collections, University of Oklahoma Library, Ballenger Collection.*

Bottom: A group of students pose in front of the Cherokee Female Seminary at Tahlequah in the Indian Territory. *Courtesy Western History Collections, University of Oklahoma Library, Ballenger Collection.*

———. "Out of the Graves of the Polluted Debauches: The Boys of the Cherokee Male Seminary." *American Indian Culture and Research Journal* 15 (1991): 503–521.

CHEROKEE NATION V. STATE OF GEORGIA

In the case of the *Cherokee Nation* v. *State of Georgia* (1831), the U.S. Supreme Court ruled that Indian tribes were not to be regarded as independent nations but as "dependent domestic nations."

The case arose when the state of Georgia tried to void both a tribal constitution and a set of laws written by Cherokee Indians. In response, the Cherokee Nation appealed to the Supreme Court. Chief Justice John Marshall dismissed the appeal and ruled that because Indian tribes were "dependent domestic nations" rather than independent foreign nations, they could not seek relief from the Supreme Court.

The decision had two profound effects on relations between Euro-Americans and Native Americans. Most immediately, it allowed Georgia to strip the tribe of its governmental forms. Over the long run, it transformed the relationship of the federal government to the Indians. Before the decision, the United States treated Indian tribes as if they were sovereign foreign powers. After 1831, however, treaties with Indians became mere formalities, their terms generally dictated by the government. In part because the treaties were such hollow documents, they were frequently violated by acts of Congress and by local jurisdictions and individuals, thereby provoking much of the violence between Euro-Americans and Native Americans in the latter two-thirds of the nineteenth century. In 1871, Congress ended the use of treaties altogether, and Indian affairs were henceforward governed by congressional legislation, executive orders, or executive agreements.

—*Alan Axelrod*

SEE ALSO: Native America Peoples: Peoples Removed from the East; United States Indian Policy: Treaties; *Worcester* v. *State of Georgia*

CHEYENNE INDIANS

SEE: Native American Peoples: Peoples of the Great Plains

CHEYENNE, WYOMING

Cheyenne, Wyoming, was founded in July 1867 by General GRENVILLE M. DODGE, leader of a railroad survey crew. Dodge chose the site along the Crow Creek as a division point for the transcontinental railroad and named it for the Cheyenne Indian tribe. After the transcontinental railroad reached Cheyenne in November 1867, the town remained economically robust. While track layers built over the Laramie Range to the west and bridge builders erected a trestle over a deep ravine, the army established Fort D. A. Russell to protect railroad workers from possible Indian attacks, although none directly threatened the town.

When Wyoming became a territory in 1869, Cheyenne was made its capital. Over the next two decades, cattle barons built expensive homes, and the Cheyenne Club was the headquarters for European and Eastern cattlemen who ran stock on the open ranges to the north.

Sixteenth Street in Cheyenne, Wyoming, as it appeared in 1886. *Courtesy American Heritage Center, University of Wyoming.*

Although stockmen exercised considerable influence, the railroad remained the chief economic base. The railroad's presence brought ethnic groups of many nationalities, including Mexican Americans and Eastern and Southern Europeans, into Cheyenne. The African American population has been significant but never large. In 1879, Cheyenne barber W. J. Hardin became the first African American elected to the Wyoming legislature, and at various times, all-black army units were stationed at nearby Fort Russell. The fort, renamed Fort Warren in 1929, became an air-force base after World War II. Since the 1950s, it has been successively an Atlas, Minuteman, and MX missile command center. JOHN JOSEPH PERSHING, Mark Clark, and Sammy Davis, Jr., were among the thousands of troops stationed at the post.

With a 1990 population of just over fifty thousand, Cheyenne has been Wyoming's largest city except for brief periods in the 1920s and 1980s when Casper held this distinction. Cheyenne is the seat of Laramie County, the state's oldest county, established before statehood. At statehood in 1890, when the population was nearly twelve thousand, Cheyenne was designated the temporary capital. When the election for a permanent site was finally held in 1904, Cheyenne gained the most votes but not the majority required by the state's constitution. Technically, it remains the temporary capital. Prominent residents have included the nation's first woman governor Nellie Tayloe Ross, Broadway producer George Abbott, and sports announcer Curt Gowdy.

—*Phil Roberts*

SUGGESTED READING:
Centennial Historical Commission. *The Magic City of the Plains, 1867–1967.* Cheyenne, Wyo., 1967.

Jones, Gladys Powelson. *Cheyenne, Cheyenne: Our Blue-Collar Heritage*. Cheyenne, Wyo., 1983.

Laramie County Chapter, Wyoming Historical Society. *Cheyenne Landmarks*. Cheyenne, Wyo., 1976.

———. *Early Cheyenne Homes, 1880–1890*. Cheyenne, Wyo., 1962. Reprint. 1982.

CHICAGO, ILLINOIS

With the opening of the Union Stock Yard on Christmas Day, 1865, Chicago, Illinois, became the de facto capital of the trans-Mississippi West. Already an important point of transshipment for Western wheat and lumber before the Civil War, Chicago benefited from the war's shutdown of Southern trade routes for pork and the rerouting of the North-South railroad infrastructure along an East-West course to replace Cincinnati as America's "Porkopolis" and ST. LOUIS as its "gateway to the West." Innovations in refrigerated railroad cars, developed initially to transport vegetables and citrus from the Far West, and the establishment of a string of ice-house stations, fed by frozen rivers and lakes in Wisconsin and other states rimming the Great Lakes, allowed Chicago's slaughterhouse merchants to corner the market in dressed meat, accumulate immense capital, and breakdown the RAILROADS' insistence on shipping only live beef to the East. A wild, wide-open town with streets filled by cows and pigs driven to slaughter and black smoke belching from its factory chimneys, Chicago was at once the world's biggest cow town and a harbinger of the urban life to come.

By the late nineteenth century, Chicago had grown from a frontier outpost on the western shores of Lake Michigan where the United States government in 1804 established Fort Dearborn to strengthen its position against the British and their Indian allies in the Northwest Territory to the major metropolitan entrepôt of the West. In America's rapid economic expansion after the Civil War, which had spawned—according to a frequently cited magazine article of 1892—some four thousand millionaires, two hundred (or 5 percent) of them, newly rich benefactors of the extractive industries of the West, had settled in Chicago. Here lived the "Lords of Packingtown"—PHILIP DANFORTH ARMOUR, Gustavus Swift, Nelson Morris, John and Patrick Cudahy—and the dry goods magnates: Potter Palmer, Marshall Field, and Montgomery Ward. Cyrus Hall McCormick and his offspring made Chicago their home, as did GEORGE MORTIMER PULLMAN and Charles T. Yerkes, both of whom made their money in transportation. Local real estate, too, had produced fortunes, like that of Marshall Field's sometimes partner, Levi Leiter.

Philip Armour, a Quaker native of upstate New York, had accumulated his vast $48 million fortune from government contracts during the Civil War and certain stock "speculations," including an incredible $2 million profit he somehow managed to turn in pork futures during a three-month period. Now the "Croesus of Packingtown" slaughtered almost three million cows, pigs, and sheep a year, employed (some said "exploited") nearly eight thousand workers, and prided himself in living near his smelly operations; he made a moral point of arriving at work early, and he posted more than $65 million in annual sales.

Charles T. Yerkes, a coarse, candid, and notorious womanizer and—like so many Chicago plutocrats—a transplanted Easterner, had once done a stint in a Philadelphia jail for market hanky-panky during the panic of 1873 before he obtained a pardon, moved his wife and half-dozen children West, and gained control of two vital Chicago street railways. Accused of bilking the city's citizens of millions with his excessive fares, he nevertheless operated a transportation fiefdom of some five hundred miles of tracks that a contemporary called "one of the best street railways systems in the world." Novelist Theodore Dreiser was fascinated with this titan, who would become the model for the protagonist of Dreiser's Frank Cowperwood trilogy.

The richest of the Chicago nouveau-riche entrepreneurs, Marshall Field was a rags-to-riches merchant with a reputation for being public-spirited and with a private life that was anything but stolid. Field's wife left him and Chicago for Paris, while he continued to amass a personal estate, which by the early 1890s was measured at $200 million.

George Pullman was as well known for the "model" city he built for his employees as he was for his $10 million enterprise in railroad cars. But he so itched to control every aspect of his workers' lives that one critic noted "[t]he autocrat of all the Russias could not more absolutely disbelieve in government by the people, for the people, through the people" than George Pullman.

These were men who had grown rich off the West, and Philip Armour perfectly captured the ethos of their world when he confessed that he had no other interest in life than his business. As novelist Henry B. Fuller observed of the town they had built: "[Chicago] is the only great city in the world to which all its citizens have come for the one common, avowed object of making money."

In the late nineteenth century, Chicago was a phoenix, a new city risen from the ashes of the GREAT CHICAGO FIRE of 1871, which had destroyed the old Western entrepôt much to the delight of the citizens of St. Louis, who had long been in competition with Chicago to hold on to their claim that St. Louis was the true gateway west. But the fire only allowed Chicago to become more itself. From the beginning, the American West had been dedicated to the notion of the "new"—new beginnings, new lands, new industry, new wealth, a new Eden. The two commercial enterprises in Chicago that had achieved world prominence, the McCormick Harvesting Machine Company and the PULLMAN PALACE CAR COMPANY, were based on innovations that created superior products in a highly specialized field. Chicago's Gustavus Swift also refined both the refrigerated car and the way meat was cut and sold and used his innovations to open new world markets for the city's famed stockyards. And Potter Palmer, like Philip Armour, had been a retailing innovator as well, shocking competitors and customers alike when he extended credit and the right to return merchandise to his shoppers. While making fools of those who scoffed at the "bargain" sales he held in the bowels of his emporium, he became a rich young man before he nearly ruined his health and sold out to Marshall Field. Finally, there was Montgomery Ward and his mail-order business (launched in 1871), also something different under the sun in dry goods. A former telegraph operator named Richard Sears and his partner, Alvah Roebuck, adopted Ward's idea and also set up their catalogue business in Chicago in 1889 as Sears, Roebuck and Company.

It was major technological breakthroughs as well—such as the invention (by Elisha Graves Otis) of the elevator, indoor plumbing, central-heating systems, and finally steel-frame construction—that allowed Chicago to symbolize for the world the very essence of the "new" in "modern" America. By early 1889, the *Chicago Tribune* was referring to the many recently constructed tall buildings as "skyscrapers." The Chicago architectural firms of William Le Baron Jenney and Holabird and Roche pioneered the steel skeletons that would support the loads of these very tall buildings, and Jenney's Home Insurance Company Building was the first in the United States to use steel beams in 1884. But the Masonic Temple, designed by John Wellborn Root and built on the corner of Randolph and State streets in 1891, soared twenty-three stories high and remained for years the tallest commercial building in the world. Contemporary observers defined the skyscraper as "a very tall building such as are now being built in Chicago." Chicago was the hometown of one of the country's outstanding architects, Louis Sullivan, and one of the first cities caught up in the contemporary "city beautiful" movement. Courtesy of the Great Fire, Chicago was emerging as the leading center of modernism in architecture, and—as Ross Miller noted in *American Apocalypse*—"the testing ground for its own and imported ideas."

Towering upward from the "City of Big Ideas," as some promoters called Chicago, the skyscraper was the perfect expression of the manly sentiments of its captains of industry, who—preoccupied with success—erected gaudy Gilded Age mansions along Michigan Avenue ("Millionaires Row"), Lake Shore Drive, and Prairie Avenue, lived in ostentatious luxury, and prided themselves on their city's dynamic vitality and openness to change while dismissing those who pointed out its rawness, its crudity, and its lack of established "society." Sojourner Paul de Rousiers noted in 1890 that Europeans thought New York was America, but that instead it was this city on the prairie that was the quintessential American city of its time. Chicago displayed "the marvelous energy of the Western settlers, their true sense of their dignity and independence, and that superb self-confidence, which makes them undertake such astonishing projects."

The immense wealth of its entrepreneurs and the skyscraper were not all that was new about Chicago. By 1890, the city counted among its citizenry an enormous number of the foreign-born, just under one-half million in a population of just over one million. Faced with a housing shortage in a city whose business-district real estate had skyrocketed in less than a decade from $130,000 an acre to $900,000, 167,000 Germans, 73,000 Scandinavians, 70,000 Irish, 14,000 Chinese and significant numbers of Italians, Jews, Poles, Dutch, Bohemians, Lithuanians, Croats, Slovaks, and Greeks pressed together in crowded tenements and ramshackle houses in frequently squalid conditions that gave the city an estimated slum population of 160,000, second only to New York. Down in the slums, among the teeming masses of humanity, another of Chicago's big ideas was born, sprung from the heads of two dedicated women and close friends, Jane Addams and Ellen Gates Starr, founders of Hull House.

Located on South Halstead in the heart of the city's worst West Side slum, the first settlement house quickly demonstrated how a concerned middle class could do something more than wring its hands at the collective problems and prospects of the poor. There, amid great promise, PROGRESSIVISM was born in the fall of 1889. Addams's and Starr's dedicated and pioneering social work made them what today would be called role models for young men and women around the country and soon attracted the likes of John Dewey and George Herbert Mead, who developed a pragmatic philosophy based on that work to solve the problems of democracy. A new breed of journalists, derisively labeled "muckrakers," not only subscribed to the philosophy but also, by publicizing the social problems it addressed, helped create a network of social workers, intellectuals, and reporters that could be loosely called a "movement." The movement captured the imagination of two charismatic young men—New York's THEODORE ROOSEVELT and Wisconsin's Robert La Follette—and its political fortunes were made.

Hull House intellectuals had much to reform in Gilded Age Chicago. If Chicago's CITY GOVERNMENT was not the worst and the most corrupt west of New York—muckraker JOSEPH LINCOLN STEFFENS twice made a case for St. Louis in the pages of *Harper's Weekly*—it was close. Locally, folks called Chicago's forty aldermen "the forty thieves." They made up for the low pay the city gave them, three dollars a week, by taking—sometimes extorting—bribes from Chicago's entrepreneurs, to whom they felt grateful and for whom they ran the place. John Powers, the "Prince of Boodlers," controlled the Nineteenth Ward where Hull House was located and where Jane Addams fought a constant but losing battle against Johnny de Pow's "bossism." But it was Powers who had helped Charles T. Yerkes obtain municipal transportation franchises, and hence Powers was pretty much reform-proof. And some considered Powers's two major political rivals much worse. One was "Bathhouse" John Coughlin, who ran the city's Turkish baths and wore very strange clothes—crimson ties, lavender vests, fawn-colored trousers; "probably," said one wit, "the best free entertainment in the city." The other was the subdued, highly intelligent "Hinky Dink" Mike Kenna. Together they epitomized corruption in Chicago; together they controlled Chicago's notorious First Ward. The First Ward housed the city's business district and most of its wealth, plus a goodly percentage of Chicago's seven thousand saloons and several hundred of its one thousand whorehouses. Perhaps not surprisingly, the district played a key role in city politics.

At the heart of the First Ward was the Levee, an area stretching from Twelfth to Van Buren streets and from State Street to Pacific Avenue, where "Bathhouse" John and "Hinky Dink" offered a mecca of unlimited GAMBLING and PROSTITUTION. The area was home to much of the city's urban demimonde: dips (pickpockets), boosters (shoplifters), ponces (pimps), yeggs (safecrackers), plug-uglies (urban toughs), drug dealers, and murderers. Here one could find the Lone Star Saloon and Palm Garden owned by Mickey Finn, famous for the potent mix of drugs and alcohol he served in his drinks to the unwary and the uninformed customers he called "marks." Here, too, were the cheap House of All Nations and the posh Everleigh Club. The latter, run by two Kentucky-born sisters, Ada and Minna Everleigh, catered to a wide variety of expensive tastes. Chicago was a town that, far from hiding its vices, paraded them, and the Levee was only one of many downtown districts rich in sin and violence. Just as much trouble could be had, just as much money lost, just as much life wasted in areas like the Black Hole, the Bad Lands, and Dead Man's Alley, where the establishments were run by any number of Irish, Jewish, or Chinese "mobsters." The Italian areas had their problems, too; their communities were plagued by seventy or eighty extortion gangs calling themselves the Black Hand and claiming lineage from the Sicilian Mafia or the Neapolitan Camorra. Satan's Mile, Little Cheyenne, and Hell's Half Acre were so vicious that even the police refused to enter them except in pairs. The police themselves were underpaid and overwhelmed by the criminal activity in a town where one of eleven citizens could expect to be arrested each year, and the cops, too, were easily corrupted.

Realizing that vice could not thrive without the support of the police, who, in turn, needed corrupt aldermen such as John Coughlin, Mike Kenna, John Powers, and their fellow "grey wolves" (as Chicagoans sometimes referred to their civic leaders), reformers hoped to change things by electing a sympathetic mayor. Instead, for five terms from 1879 to 1895, they got real-estate maven Carter Henry Harrison, whom the "Bath," "Hinky Dink," and the "Prince of Boodlers" called "Our Carter." The political machines that ran the town stayed in power because they provided a necessary service. To the poor immigrant, they offered a place to turn: jobs, charity, legal aid, protection from the authorities. Carter, for example, had refused to order the police to break up the Haymarket rally on May 4, 1886, only allowing policemen on the scene after the crowd had begun to disperse under heavy rains late in the afternoon; after the gathering degenerated into the Haymarket riot and the police opened fire on the crowd, the wealthy Carter, a Yale graduate, spent many a Sunday kissing babies and refurbishing his image as a "man of the people" in the slums of the foreign-born. All a boss and his designated politicians wanted in return was for those they helped to remember them come election time. To their rich overlords, the city political mechanics promised to keep taxes and real-estate assessments on their businesses and mansions low and to keep the teeming mass of the working poor and the unemployed under control.

For Chicago's growing number of labor radicals, if not for its middle-class reformers, it seemed clear that the city was dangerous and vice-ridden not because Coughlin and Kenna had cloven hooves, nor because the Jewish, Irish, and Italian mobsters were genetically criminal, but because the laissez-faire benefactors of the Western economy did not want to pay the price to make the city safe for anyone other than themselves and their families, any more than they wanted to pay for clean water or paved sidewalks outside the "better" neighborhoods in which they lived. Consequently, UPTON SINCLAIR singled out the "Lords of Packingtown" as the real villains in his novel *The Jungle* (1906), which depicted the new metropolis on the prairie as a place drunk with the excess profits of Western industry, discolored by rampant corruption, reeking of the slaughterhouse, and straddling a river so thick with grease that its surface "seemed a liquid rainbow." Since the 1880s, the federal government had been investigating the meatpackers. Responding to charges of monopoly and price fixing, one congressional committee found Chicago's slaughterhouse kings guilty of creating an "artificial and abnormal centralization of markets" and that "for all practical purposes the market at that city dominates absolutely the price of beef cattle in the whole country." Sinclair's book now sent the entire country spinning into an era of reform. Six months later, Congress passed the Pure Food and Drug Act regulating the industry.

As William Cronon has pointed out, what looked artificial and abnormal at the end of the nineteenth century would look conventional in the twentieth, when integrated markets based on new technologies and vertically integrated corporations became commonplace. The final irony for Chicago was that the meatpackers were moving their operations out of Chicago even as the city bloomed from the profits they had produced. In 1888, Swift replicated his Chicago operation in KANSAS CITY. Two years later, he built a new plant in OMAHA, NEBRASKA. By the end of the century, Omaha was butchering one-third as many steers as Chicago, and Kansas City packed about one-half of Chicago's volume. By the 1930s, Chicago's stockyards were in steady decline, and by 1960, all the major packers had closed down their Chicago factories. Chicago continued to thrive, of course, in part as a financial center for the trans-Mississippi West, but it was no longer a destination for the raw wealth—on the hoof, as it were—of the region to its West.

—*Charles Phillips*

SEE ALSO: City Planning

SUGGESTED READING:

Cronon, William. *Nature's Metropolis: Chicago and the Great West.* New York, 1991.

Miller, Ross. *American Apocalypse: The Great Fire and the Myth of Chicago.* Chicago, 1990.

Muccigrosso, Robert. *Celebrating the New World: Chicago's Columbia Exposition of 1893.* Chicago, 1993.

Wendt, Lloyd, and Herman Kogan. *Bosses in Lusty Chicago: The Story of Bathhouse John and Hinky Dink.* Bloomington, Ind., 1967.

CHICAGO, BURLINGTON AND QUINCY RAILROAD

SEE: Burlington Northern Railroad

"CHICAGO JOE"

SEE: Hensley, Josephine

CHICAGO, MILWAUKEE, ST. PAUL AND PACIFIC RAILROAD

"The Milwaukee Road" was the last major railroad to be extended to the Pacific Coast. Begun in 1906, the line was completed in 1909. Through much of the nineteenth century, the railroad served the West as a vital link between the major lines of the East and the UNION PACIFIC RAILROAD.

The Milwaukee and Waukesha Railroad was incorporated in Wisconsin in 1847. Lines did not reach the Mississippi River until 1857. Ten years later, the railroad was renamed the Milwaukee and St. Paul. By 1874, lines to Chicago were established, and the company became the Chicago, Milwaukee and St. Paul. The period of greatest westward expansion came after the Civil War. The line reached Chamberlain, South Dakota, in 1881; Omaha, Nebraska, in 1882; Fargo, North Dakota in 1884; and Kansas City, Missouri, in 1887.

Byron Kilbourn, the first president of the Milwaukee Road, envisioned a company financed by the farmers it served. He encouraged investment among them by arguing that ownership by farmers would break the railroads' dependency on Eastern investment capital. Unfortunately, his vision failed, and the Milwaukee Road went into receivership in 1860, but investment funds from the accursed Easterners saved the line later that year. In other respects, however, vision and innovation paid off. Although the Milwaukee Road was the last of the great lines to cross the continent, it was among the first to cross the Mississippi—via an innovative pontoon bridge at Prairie du Chien, Wisconsin. The railroad also pioneered the refrigerator car, thereby revolutionizing the transportation not only of produce but of livestock and meat as well. Seeking independence from outside suppliers wherever possible, the Milwaukee Road ran its own sleeping cars and even manufactured its own locomotives and rolling stock.

The railroad prospered, even through the FINANCIAL PANICS and depression of the 1890s, but by the end of the nineteenth century, lines that had Pacific Coast connections, particularly in the Northwest where the demand for freight service had grown prodigiously, outclassed the Milwaukee Road. At last, in 1906, construction of a line to Seattle began at Evarts, South Dakota. The extension was ambitious and, as usual for the railroad, innovative, including 650 miles of electrified track in Montana, Idaho, and Washington. Yet, at $234 million, construction costs had greatly exceeded the $60 million budgeted, and the railroad again went into the hands of the receivers during the 1920s. Reorganized as the Chicago, Milwaukee, St. Paul and Pacific in 1927, the company revived, only to return to receivership during the Great Depression. The company was reorganized again in 1945.

—*Alan Axelrod*

SEE ALSO: Railroads

SUGGESTED READING:
Derleth, August W. *The Milwaukee Road: Its First 100 Years.* New York, 1948.

CHICAGO AND NORTHWESTERN RAILROAD

A major Midwestern link between the Western trunk lines and the UNION PACIFIC RAILROAD, the Chicago and Northwestern Railroad originated in 1836 as the Galena and Chicago Union Railroad. Its founder, CHICAGO Mayor William Butler Ogden, wanted to create a direct and economical line between the lead mines of Galena and the refineries of Chicago, 165 miles to the southeast. Financing proceeded very slowly, and it was not until 1848 that the first locomotive pulled out of Chicago to what was then the end of track at the present-day Chicago suburb of Oak Park. From Oak Park, a lone farmer shipped a single load of wheat on the railroad's only freight car, thereby becoming the first person to ship wheat into Chicago by rail. Despite its modest beginning, the Illinois Central Railroad beat the Galena and Chicago Union to Galena. Its managers were determined to build due west to the Mississippi. In 1850, the line reached Elgin; Rockford came next in 1852; and Fulton, on the Mississippi, became the terminus in 1855.

By the 1860s, Galena was bustling, and a number of rail lines served it. One of those, the Chicago and Northwestern, merged with the Galena and Chicago

Union, and the combined lines became known as the Chicago and Northwestern. In 1866, the railroad acquired a line to Milwaukee, and in 1867, the railroad had pushed westward to Council Bluffs, Iowa. By the 1880s, the line had reached Pierre, South Dakota, and Minneapolis–St. Paul, Minnesota.

The great era of development for the Northwestern began in 1872 when Marvin Hughitt left his post as general manager of the PULLMAN PALACE SLEEPING CAR COMPANY to become general superintendent of the railroad. He became president ten years later and served until 1917. Under Hughitt's leadership, the railroad became one of the more efficient and profitable lines in the nation. It was ably financed by the Vanderbilts, who used it as a Western feeder for their New York Central System.

The Northwestern was badly hit by the Great Depression and went into the hands of the receivers in 1935. In 1944, the Northwestern was reorganized and prospered into the 1950s. After weathering financial crises during the 1960s, the railroad continued as a major freight operator and as a commuter link to Chicago's northern lake-side suburbs.

—*Alan Axelrod*

SEE ALSO: Railroads

SUGGESTED READING:
Casey, Robert J., and W. A. S. Douglas. *Pioneer Railroad: The Story of the Chicago and Northwestern System.* New York, 1948.

CHIEF JOSEPH (NEZ PERCÉ)

Chief Joseph (ca. 1840–1904) is best remembered for his leadership during the Nez Percé War of 1877 and for his eloquent surrender speech, which seemed to summarize the tragic history of conflict between Euro-Americans and Native Americans. Chief Joseph, also known as Young Joseph to distinguish him from his father, Joseph the Elder or Old Joseph, was born in the Wallowa Valley of Oregon. His Nez Percé name, variously transliterated as Heinmot Tooyalaket, In-mut-too-yah-lat-lat, Hin-mah-too-yah-lat-kekt, and Hinmaton-yalatkit, means "thunder coming from water over land." (Old Joseph, who had been Christianized, baptized his son Ephraim.)

Old Joseph was among the Nez Percé leaders who, in 1855, signed a treaty with Isaac Stevens, Washington's territorial governor. The treaty ceded much of Nez Percé land to the federal government in return for the guarantee of a large reservation in Oregon and

Chief Joseph (Nez Percé).
Courtesy National Archives.

Idaho. Stevens almost immediately violated the treaty by pushing settlement into the reservation, provoking the Yakima War of 1855 to 1856. Old Joseph managed to keep the Nez Percés out of the conflict until 1861, when gold prospectors encroached on the Wallowa Valley. Demanding a revision of the 1855 treaty, government negotiators at the Lapwai Council called for a great reduction in the size of reservation in 1863. For the most part, those Nez Percés whose homes remained undisturbed by the proposed revision signed the new treaty and agreed to sell the old lands, while those—such as Chief Joseph the Elder—whose homes lay outside the new boundary resisted and refused to sign. Those so-called nontreaty Nez Percés nevertheless lived in relative peace because Euro-American settlement was slow to invade the Wallowa Valley, and there was no attempt to move the nontreaty bands by force.

In 1871, Chief Joseph the Elder died, and Young Joseph continued his father's policy of passive refusal to move. Shortly after the death of Chief Joseph the Elder, homesteaders began pushing into the Wallowa Valley, and Young Joseph gained prestige by successfully protesting the incursion to the Indian Bureau. The result, in 1873, was a proclamation by President Ulysses S. Grant establishing the Wallowa Valley as a reservation.

Chief Joseph's triumph was short lived. Settlers ignored the reservation boundaries, established homesteads at will, and soon became a political constituency powerful enough to prompt Grant in 1875 to reverse his decision. Although a number of other Nez Percé chiefs, older and more established, outranked Chief Joseph, he was recognized by U.S. authorities as the most influential of the Indian leaders, and it was with him that General OLIVER OTIS HOWARD decided to negotiate. He met with Chief Joseph and another leader, TOOHOOLHOOLZOTE, at Fort Lapwai on November 13 and 15, 1876. Chief Joseph succeeded in winning Howard's sympathy as well as his acknowledgment that Old Joseph had never sold the Wallowa Valley, yet the general persisted in his mission and gave the Indians one month to move to a reservation or be driven off by force.

Chief Joseph demonstrated great restraint in resisting tribal pressure (especially from his own brother,

OLLOKOT) to fight because he realized that war against the far more numerous settlers would be fruitless. However, on June 13 and 14, 1876, a number of young disheartened and drunk warriors, led by Wahlitits, murdered four whites who were implicated in the death of Wahlitits's father. Despite Chief Joseph's protests to authorities that the killings had not been sanctioned by the tribal council, Howard dispatched one hundred cavalrymen to pursue the nontreaty Nez Percés, who had begun to move south toward the Salmon River. The killing of fifteen more settlers increased the urgency of the mission, yet the Indians consistently eluded the pursuers. It was at Chief Joseph's insistence that a delegation of Nez Percés met with Captain David Perry on June 17. The first to encounter the Indian party were undisciplined civilian volunteers, who opened fire, thereby igniting general warfare between the Nez Percés and the U.S. Army.

The first battle went to the Indians, and a series of Nez Percé victories followed, always against superior numbers, as Chief Joseph led his band of eight hundred over seventeen hundred miles of the most forbidding terrain the West had to offer. At each turn, Chief Joseph eluded the pursuing army, and when an engagement took place, it was the army that took the greater punishment.

Yet the pursuit steadily took its toll on the Nez Percés. Chief Joseph sought haven for his people among the Crows, but when he discovered that Crow scouts had been working for Howard, he determined to press on to Canada. He hoped that the great Hunkpapa leader SITTING BULL, self-exiled there, would welcome the Nez Percés as his brothers. On September 30, 1877, Chief Joseph and his followers were encamped on the northern edge of the Bear Paw Mountains, a mere forty miles south of the Canadian border. Three hundred fifty to four hundred troopers commanded by NELSON APPLETON MILES attacked in a bitter, snow-whipped battle that developed into a six-day siege. Realizing that the situation was hopeless, Chief Joseph counseled surrender but was resisted by two other leaders, LOOKING GLASS and WHITE BIRD, who wanted to fight to the end. When Looking Glass was struck in the head and killed by a stray bullet on October 5, Chief Joseph at last spoke to Miles in speech of extraordinary sorrow and dignity:

> I am tired of fighting. Our chiefs are killed. Looking Glass is dead. Toohoolhoolzote is dead. The old men are all dead. It is the young men who say yes or no. He who led on the young men [that is, Olikut] is dead. It is cold and we have no blankets. The little children are freezing to death. My people, some of them,

have run away to the hills, and have no blankets, no food; no one knows where they are—perhaps freezing to death. I want to have time to look for my children and see how many of them I can find. Maybe I shall find them among the dead. Hear me, my chiefs! I am tired; my heart is sick and sad. From where the sun now stands I will fight no more forever.

Consigned with his followers to a reservation, Chief Joseph spent many years petitioning the government for permission to return to the Wallowa Valley. In these efforts, he was aided by the military adversaries whose respect and admiration he had won: Generals O. O. Howard and Nelson Miles. The petitions nevertheless proved fruitless, and Chief Joseph died on the Colville Reservation in the state of Washington.

—*Alan Axelrod*

SEE ALSO: Pacific Northwest Indians Wars

SUGGESTED READING:
Axelrod, Alan. *Chronicle of the Indian Wars: From Colonial Times to Wounded Knee.* New York, 1993.
Beal, Merrill D. *"I Will Fight No More Forever": Chief Joseph and the Nez Percé War.* Seattle, Wash., 1963.
Josephy, Alvin M., Jr. *The Nez Percé Indians and the Opening of the Northwest.* New Haven, Conn., 1965.

CHICKASAW INDIANS

SEE: Native American Peoples: Peoples Removed from the East

CHIHUAHUA TRAIL

SEE: Santa Fe and Chihuahua Trail

CHILD REARING

Asian American Child Rearing
  Patricia Hogan

Euro-American Child Rearing
  Elliott West

Native American Child Rearing
  Patricia Hogan

Spanish and Mexican Child Rearing
  Gloria E. Miranda

ASIAN AMERICAN CHILD REARING

The words *child rearing* and *Asian American* in one sentence have little meaning for the nineteenth-century American West, for the truth of the matter was that fifty years after the appearance of the first Chinese immigrants on the West Coast, there were very few children of Chinese immigrants and very few children with parents from any Asian country.

United States laws in the late nineteenth and early twentieth centuries restricted the immigration of first the Chinese, then the Japanese, and later Koreans, Filipinos, and EAST INDIANS. Such restrictions, as well as Asian traditions limiting women's mobility, created an immense imbalance in the number of Asian American women in the United States relative to the number of men from Asia. With few women to marry, few Asian men could begin families. For example, in 1870, there were about five hundred American-born children of Chinese parents in the United States; in 1900, nine thousand. Not until 1940, did Chinese American children outnumber their parents, making up about 52 percent of the Chinese American population. In 1910, there were about forty-five hundred second-generation (Nisei) JAPANESE AMERICANS in the country. By 1920, the number had increased to thirty thousand. By the beginning of the 1930s, children of Japanese ancestry made up 49 percent of the Japanese American population. In 1910, Koreans in America numbered about a thousand; twenty-nine of them were children. Figures for Filipinos and Asian Indians are smaller still.

The experiences of native born CHINESE AMERICANS, Japanese Americans, and Korean Americans have much in common. Children born of Asian Indian fathers and Mexican American mothers frequently learned Spanish

The Quon Mane family of San Diego, California.
Courtesy San Diego Historical Society.

A Chinese youth group gathers in San Diego, California, in the 1930s. *Courtesy San Diego Historical Society.*

and English but seldom spoke the language of their fathers.

The arrival of a newborn child was a joyous event among Asian people whose culture was based in large measure on family ties and ancestral devotion. Children, especially sons, were welcomed in the western United States, not only by their parents, but by members of the community who looked upon babies "with a kind of awe" for being so rare.

The children's indoctrination into the ways of the homeland began early. Boys and girls were taught to respect and honor their parents and to pledge unswerving obedience to them. Instruction in the native language began at home, along with lessons in literature, history, and geography. New Year's celebrations with traditional foods and events, rituals honoring ancestors, games, community gatherings for native ceremonies, festivals, and other activities helped Asian children learn the ways of their parents' homeland. Children received further instruction in LANGUAGE SCHOOLS, which they attended each day after public school and on Saturdays.

If Asian parents treasured their children and took pains to inculcate them in the ways of their ancestors, they were also practical about the importance of child labor to the family's economic well-being. Often forced into low-paying, labor-intensive work, Asian fathers and mothers quickly brought their children into the family businesses of laundering, farming, restauranting, seamstressing, and store keeping. Eight-year-olds ran laundry presses, peeled shrimp, chopped vegetables, learned to operate sewing machines, and worked beside their parents in the fields, tending to and harvesting crops.

Even as Asian parents worked long hours and required their children to work beside them, they were determined that their children have a better life than they had themselves. Children were counseled to make the most of the public education that was available to them, to apply themselves and make good grades, and perhaps, most importantly, to shrug off the ridicule and racist slurs from their Anglo-American contemporaries.

Most native-born Asian children learned their lessons well. The American ways they learned in school clashed with their parents' attitudes in customs, dress, demeanor, and independence. Many sought to be thoroughly Americanized, including the freedom to choose their own spouses, a choice traditionally made by Asian parents. For young Asian women, the conflict between the way parents expected them to behave according to Asian tradition and the freedom to marry or not, go to college or not, or pursue a career or not was particularly intense.

Native-born children of Chinese, Japanese, and Korean parents often faced a confusion in cultural identity. Although trained in the language and culture of their parents, most second-generation Asians had no firsthand experience with their parents' homeland. Many resented the customs that set them apart from other Americans and the language of their parents that served only as a barrier to life outside their homes. On the other hand, although born in the United States and therefore American citizens, some second-generation Asians resented the discrimination they faced in social situations and employment opportunities. Children of both Asian culture and American culture, they felt comfortable in neither.

—*Patricia Hogan*

SUGGESTED READING:

Chan, Sucheng. *Asian Americans: An Interpretive History.* Boston, 1991.

Leonard, Karen. *Making Ethnic Choices: California's Punjabi Mexican Americans.* Philadelphia, 1992.

Takaki, Ronald. *Strangers from a Different Shore: A History of Asian Americans.* New York, 1989.

Yung, Judy. *Unbound Feet: A Social History of Chinese Women in San Francisco.* Berkeley, Calif., 1995.

EURO-AMERICAN CHILD REARING

Children were important and valued members of all Euro-American societies established in the West during the nineteenth and twentieth centuries. The proportion of children to adults varied considerably from place to place. Early in the development of areas dominated by industrial labor, such as mining towns and lumber camps, young people under the age of fifteen might compose 5 percent or less of the population. Farming regions, by contrast, had some of the highest birth rates in the nation, and in the homesteading country of Nebraska or Kansas, up to 60 percent of the population might be children.

Wherever they lived, boys and girls played crucial roles in helping their parents meet the many challenges facing them. On homesteads and ranches, they took a hand in the many domestic tasks and in preparing fields, planting, and harvesting. They were often mainly responsible for herding and caring for the growing crops, and many provided much of the family's daily food by hunting and by gathering wild plants. In towns, where families were caught between uncertain wages and high prices, children contributed income by working at a variety of jobs, including hawking newspapers, running errands, selling pies baked by their mothers, tending animals, and doing chores around mines and other enterprises. The children of urban families were some of the West's most useful and versatile workers.

Conditions in the West were working counter to developments elsewhere in the nation. Especially in the middle class of more settled regions, young people played less of a role in their families' economic lives, and the work they did was increasingly divided according to sex. Because of the labor demands in areas newly opened to Euro-American settlement, however, children had to work and contribute more, not less, and girls in particular were expected to take part in many types of "men's work," such as herding, field labor, and hunting. It was one of several ways in which growing up and rearing children in the West were distinctively regional experiences.

In this image, young Mary Zimmerman of a Kansas homestead helps her family tend to the farm chores. *Courtesy Kansas State Historical Society.*

Children at play in a Kansas settlement. *Courtesy Kansas State Historical Society.*

Children were crucial to the development of the frontier in other ways. A significant part of a community's earliest political life centered on one of the primary goals of early settlers—establishing public education. Territorial laws required that schools be provided, but typically families themselves took the lead, banding together informally to raise money, hire a teacher, and build or rent a building for classes. Some of the first community entertainment, at least its more respectable variety, came in the form of performances by schoolchildren and benefits to raise funds for education.

This collective concern was an outward expression of the private determination of parents, especially mothers, to educate their daughters and sons and, in a broader sense, to pass on to their children the heritage of the parents' past. The process of settlement, then, involved much more than transforming the land and building a new economic life. Just as important were the hundreds of hours spent by a mother and father teaching the basics of reading, mathematics, and grammar at the end of long, exhausting days. Many domestic details of a pioneer household, from books and pieces of porcelain to embroidered tablecloths and chromo prints on the wall, were intended as visual and tactile reminders to children of their familial roots and the culture they were expected to perpetuate in their new homes.

In all these ways, children were an integral part of frontier history. They did much of its labor and carried much of their families' responsibilities. They stood close to the center of both their parents' concerns and the social life of emerging communities.

But children have always had their own history, on the American frontier as everywhere else. Their story was also a part of the human experience in the pioneer West. One of the rich and revealing aspects of child life, for instance, was play. For all the work they did, most children also found time to amuse themselves. Having carried and transplanted their own traditions to the West, they passed time with dozens of games and sports, many of them part of a folk culture of childhood. Some, like "Ring-a-rosie," variations of tag, and "How Many Miles to Miley Bright," were hundreds of years old. In other play, boys and girls acted out what they saw among the adults around them, including the conflicts and tragedies. In this form of play, children were not perpetuating tradition but learning to cope with the unique aspects of life in the frontier West.

On the grimmer side of life, children faced their own peculiar dangers. Contrary to their common fears, they had little to fear from wild animals and Indians. More threatening were accidents, from falling under moving wagons to being injured by whirling blades of farm machinery. The greatest threat came from diseases the pioneers brought with them—diphtheria, cholera, pneumonia, measles, scarlet fever, whooping cough, influenza, and others, all of them spread efficiently under the often primitive living conditions in the developing West.

The experience of frontier children was also fundamentally different from their parents' experiences because the basic perceptions and values of those young pioneers were still being shaped. This process—the formation of their characters—was accomplished partly through the children's exploration of and interaction with the world around them. The result was that young people grew up intimately connected to their Western homes in ways never possible for their elders born and reared in other places. The girls and boys who grew into women and men on the frontier were in may ways the first genuinely Western generation produced by the Euro-American westward movement. The study of the lives of children holds important keys to understanding the more recent history of the post-frontier West.

—*Elliott West*

SUGGESTED READING:
Hamptsen, Elizabeth. *Settlers' Children*. Norman, Okla., 1991.
Werner, Emily E. *Pioneer Children on the Journey West*. Boulder, Colo., 1995.
West, Elliott. *Growing Up with the Country*. Albuquerque, N. Mex., 1989.

NATIVE AMERICAN CHILD REARING

It is difficult to generalize about child-rearing practices among native peoples, given the hundreds of Native American tribes in the trans-Mississippi West. In essence, however, the purpose of tribal child-rearing techniques was to prepare young boys and girls for their adult roles in a culture of interdependent individuals and groups. Each child who learned his or her role by imitating elders developed a lifelong sense of responsibility and self-reliance and assured the tribe of one more productive member.

Children were much valued by native peoples, an attitude reflected in child-rearing practices. Corporal punishment was seldom used on children; shame and ridicule accomplished much the same ends. Parents guided their children to maturity in manners that were gentle, affectionate, relaxed, and, some observers noted, permissive. The care of young children was the responsibility of the mothers, who nursed their offspring until the age of eighteen months or three years. Frequently, the Indian equivalent of toilet training was accom-

A family of Potawatomi Indians. *Courtesy Kansas State Historical Society.*

Young Cheyenne women. *Courtesy Kansas State Historical Society.*

plished by the age of three. Some tribes made use of cradle boards, devices for transporting young children and for confining them while their mothers attended to chores. In some Northern Plains cultures, the cradle board also served to shape a child's forehead or the back of the head. When children were old enough to walk and talk, the socialization process began.

Children, for the most part, were raised within the nuclear family—a women, her husband, and their children. In many tribes, children learned, too, from their grandparents, aunts and uncles, and cousins.

Young girls were taught women's roles—tending crops, gathering wild foods, preparing and preserving foodstuffs, tanning hides and making clothes, and learning to care for their younger sisters and brothers. Boys, on the other hand, learned the skills needed for hunting and making war from their fathers. At a young age, boys undertook the challenges that would toughen them for their future roles. A youngster might be required to prove himself by feats of strength and bravery, including jumping into the icy waters of a river, running long distances in the hot sun with a mouthful of water and instructions not to swallow it, and stinging himself with bees and ants.

Even the games and leisure-time activities that Indian children played prepared them for their future responsibilities. The universally popular game hide-and-seek developed skills in stalking and avoiding capture. Another common game, the mud and willow-stick fight, taught warrior skills as well. Boys armed with mud balls flung them from the end of a willow stick at their opponents, and even though the assault might sting, boys were admonished not to cry out or cower. Other rough games and sports such as wrestling also steeled youngsters for their roles as warriors.

All children received a good portion of their socialization through storytelling. Most stories described a prank or a trick, often involving animals with human characteristics, and, like the fairy tales common to Euro-American childhood, contained a moral or a lesson. Grandparents and tribal elders were usually excellent storytellers.

Puberty rites varied considerably among Native American tribes. Among some cultures, girls were isolated in a separate lodge at the onset of menstruation. Frequently, they went without food, water, or light for the three or four days of their confinement. Other rituals involved tattoos, body-piercing ceremonies, or knocking out teeth. Boys of the Plains tribes often undertook the vision quest, a few days of isolation during which a young man ventured into the wilderness to commune with the spirits. In many tribes, puberty signaled the age of marriage. At such a coming of age, parents would seek a mate for their child, and the cycle of family life would begin anew.

Much tribal socialization of the young came to an abrupt halt among the Native Americans in the West when the United States government began confining them to reservations after the Civil War. Indeed, assimilation became the explicit goal of U.S. Indian policy, the achievement of which required agents to undercut as much as possible the social lessons Native American parents so carefully taught their children. On the reservations, Indians were forced to give up their culture and adopt the ways of white Americans. Indian children of the reservation era were also forced to attend government schools, often sent hundreds of miles from their families in order to remove them from the tribal environment and indoctrinate them in Christianity, the English language, and the "American way of life." Not only were Indian children Americanized, but their family life was often shattered, which further fractured Indian cultures already under assault in numerous ways.

—*Patricia Hogan*

See also: Indian Schools; Native American Cultures: Family Life, Kinship, and Gender; United States Indian Policy

Suggested reading:
Allen, Paula Gunn. *The Sacred Hoop: Recovering the Feminine in American Indian Traditions.* Boston, 1986.
White, John Manchip. *Everyday Life of the North American Indian.* New York, 1979.

SPANISH AND MEXICAN CHILD REARING

Before 1848, frontier society from Texas to California assigned responsibility to the family for socializing future generations of community residents to the culture, customs, and religious values of the Hispano-Mexican way of life. Because frontier society remained quite provincial and isolated from the rest of the country, only minor alterations in child-rearing practices along class lines took place in Spanish colonial and Mexican times. Families in the north were patriarchal, but in each province or territory, heads of households included widowed or single women. Class distinctions influenced the education and the material degree of socialization children experienced in New Mexico, California, and Texas. Family sizes varied in each northern outpost, but in the late eighteenth century, families averaged from one to four children.

Letters and diaries of frontier residents illustrate the significance of children to married life. Fathers-to-be prepared for the birth of their children by constructing toys and furniture for newborn infants. Many grandparents celebrated with congratulatory letters to their children, while new parents recorded neonatal growth and sent their relatives clipped locks of their infants' hair as mementos.

Cultural rites of passage guided the upbringing of Hispano-Mexican children through their formative years. Families focused on teaching religious values, proper etiquette, good manners, and social graces along with a domestic apprenticeship program aimed at preparing children for productive adult roles. Beginning at birth, children generally received religious first names, such as Maria and José, which were popular among Californians. Children named for favorite saints celebrated their birth dates twice yearly; the *día de santo* was as significant an event as an individual's own birthday.

Another important infant rite of passage, baptism, introduced children to the custom of *compadrazgo* (godparenthood) and celebrated the spiritual dimension of new life. Parents selected godparents for their moral character, but in California, influential public figures assumed the role of spiritual sponsors for purposes of cementing ties among influential clans. *Compadrazgo* took on greater significance if the biological parents died prematurely, because tradition dictated that baptismal sponsors would provide financial and religious support for their orphaned godchildren.

By the time children had reached the age of seven, they had received a moral education designed to nurture the ideal of respect for parents and elders and instruction in proper social etiquette and the family's own religious customs and traditions. Recalcitrant youths received verbal admonitions or corporal punishment, which served as an extreme parental measure to correct behavior.

Much of a child's life in colonial and Mexican times revolved around a pastoral existence on ranchos or adjacent towns and military garrisons. In California, even before children learned to walk, they received riding lessons. A boy's apprenticeship, regardless of social class, included the development of skills in the use of a lasso. Boys practiced the skill by using twine to rope chickens or kittens as a prelude to later ensnaring bulls and bears as adults. As boys grew older, they competed in bull and bear fights, bullfighting, and the roping of cattle and colts and gained recognition for their skills. Girls in cattle-ranching communities throughout Texas and California also became accomplished in riding skills and occasionally gained fame as bullfighters. At family social gatherings—called "fandangos"—music, song, and dance served as settings for interaction and courtship among adolescents.

By early adolescence, Hispano-Mexican female socialization included traditional domestic role-playing to develop skills in barbering, soap making, embroidery, and sewing; young men worked as apprentice carpenters or leather-makers. Because of limited formal educational institutions, frontier literacy rates across class lines were affected. Wealthy families provided tutors for their sons and daughters, and books of Greek and Roman classics and Enlightenment-age writings enriched their education. After the United States–Mexican War, new socio-economic patterns in the West gradually disrupted the pastoral nucleus of Hispano-Mexican socialization, but the cultural emphasis of child rearing continued into this century.
—*Gloria E. Miranda*

SUGGESTED READING:

Miranda, Gloria E. "Hispano-Mexican Childrearing Practices in Pre-American Santa Barbara." *Historical Society of Southern California Quarterly* 65 (Winter 1983): 307–320.

CHILKAT INDIANS

SEE: Native American Peoples: Peoples of the Pacific Northwest

CHINATOWNS

When Chinese immigrants reached the trans-Mississippi West around the middle of the nineteenth century, they were not accepted into the established communities, and like many immigrant groups, they created their own neighborhoods. The ghettos became known as Chinatowns, and old and new immigrants moved there to find housing, employment, and social and educational services and to make contact and carry on commerce and intercourse with other Chinese. The first Chinatown—in San Francisco—developed almost simultaneously with the arrival of Chinese immigrants. It grew rapidly after the discovery of gold in 1848 sparked

a rush to the area from China as it did from many parts of the globe. As the Chinese moved to other areas of the country looking for work and seeking new opportunities, Chinatowns, too, spread to different American towns and cities—to mining communities in the West, such as Sacramento, California, and Butte, Montana, and to large metropolitan areas across the country, such as Chicago and New York.

In the 1850s and 1860s, San Franciscans called the local Chinese quarters by various names such as "Little Canton" and "Little China." As early as 1853, they were also being called "Chinatown" in some newspapers, but the Chinese residents referred to Sacramento Street, where they had first set up canvas houses in 1849 between Kearny and Dupont streets, as the Tiang Gai, t'ang-jen chieh—the Street of the Men of T'ang, Chinese (Cantonese) Street. Not all of the Chinese in San Francisco lived there. But while the early Chinese occupied scattered locales throughout the town, over time they did indeed come to be concentrated in the strictly defined area encircled by California, Stockton, Broadway, and Kearny streets, and the area became known quasi-officially as Chinatown. This was the area that San Francisco's Special Committee of the Board of Trade would cover in its "Official Map of Chinatown in San Francisco," published in July 1885, and this was the area that long before 1885 had become the prototype of Chinatowns throughout the country. Especially after the passage of the Chinese Exclusion Act in the late nineteenth century, these Chinatowns grew in size.

Shortly after mid-century, certainly, San Francisco's Chinatown was a vibrant and bustling Chinese colony taking up six blocks of the city and, as Ronald Takaki has described it, boasting thirty-three general stores, fifteen drugstores, five restaurants, five herb shops, three boarding houses, five butcher shops, and three tailor shops, all with beautiful, even poetic, names painted on the signs above their doors. Chinese warehouses, for example, were called "everlasting harmony, producing wealth," "unitedly prospering," "the flowery fountain," or "ten thousand profits." Chinese apothecaries promised their customers that their wares were safe by using such names as "the hall of approved medicines of every province and of every land." The scrolls on the walls of general stores generally advertised the owner's success: "Ten thousand customers constantly arriving. Let rich customers continually come." Chinese restaurants touted their culinary and olfactory delights with such phrases as "chamber of the odors of distant lands" or "fragrant tea chamber" or "fragrant almond chamber." Chinese GAMBLING dens—fan-tan saloons—lured the reckless with promises of an instant fortune, the dream of all immigrants to the San Francisco of the era: "Get rich, please come in" and "riches ever flowing." For those who fared poorly, there was always the solace of the opium stalls, which described their goods matter-of-factly: "Opium dipped up in fractional quantities, Foreign smoke in broken parcels, No. 2 Opium to be sold at all times."

The language was lost on the growing number of Chinatown visitors who did not speak Chinese. What they saw were brilliantly colored and lettered boards, several yards of red ribbon streaming from their bottoms, suspended over doors attached to buildings mostly built in the "Chinese" style—frequently nothing more than American structures outfitted with elaborate balconies, paper or bronze lanterns, and rows of porcelain pots. All the doors were open, and the stores behind them were stocked with ham, tea, dried fish, dried ducks, copper pots and kettles, fans, shawls, chessmen, and curiosities of all sorts. The goods and groceries spilled over onto sidewalks that lined streets, thronged with Chinese men, talking loudly and moving from store to store. The crowds roamed the streets of Chinatown all day and long into the night, for most of the Chinese were either bachelors or married men who had left their families behind in China, who stayed out late talking to other bachelors and married men without families. Peddlers, shopkeepers, dealers, laborers home from work, they strolled about in what observers called their "loose pajamalike" clothes, with the crowns of their heads shaven, and wearing neatly braided queues trailing down their backs.

They talked, visited, traded, laughed, shouted, and gathered in groups at street corners to watch passersby. When they tired of that, they might head for a Chinese theater to watch members of the Hong Fook Tong perform, or if it was late, gamble a little. They played mahjong, fan-tan, a game something like keno they called *baakgapbiu,* and poker, a game they had learned after coming to America. Occasionally, they might visit one of the high-toned Chinatown brothels, where Chinese prostitutes—dressed in silk and satin and wearing glimmering jewels—sat in front of big picture windows as men came by, looked them over, and made their picks for the night. (Not all Chinese brothels were so well appointed, of course; some consisted of crude and miserable cribs.) But more frequently, the Chinese men spent much of their free time in the back rooms of their stores, writing and reading letters to and from China, discussing family life and local events, and complaining about their isolation and their loneliness.

The American Chinatowns abounded in organizations. *Fongs,* composed of family members and fellow villagers, and clans, made up of larger groups of village associations, maintained establishments that operated as both residences and social clubs. The *fongs,* or neighborhood associations, and the clans, or kinship associations, also set up temples, handled the mail to and from villages back in China, and arranged for shipping home the remains of those who died in America. There were also district associations, which ran the credit-ticket system and checked to make sure that any Chinese returning to China had paid all debts, especially those loaned to them for the passage over. Chinatown, too, was home to the *tongs. Tongs* were fraternal organizations with their roots in the homeland. Having begun back in China as underground antigovernment movements, the *tongs* were mutual protection leagues, but they expanded to take control of Chinatown's opium trade, gambling, and PROSTITUTION. Also in San Francisco's Chinatown, there was a group of merchants who represented the Chinese in the white business community and maintained connections with local politicians by creating the Chinese Six Companies. The Six Companies controlled Chinatown much the way political "machines" controlled many of the big cities in the late nineteenth century and the first half of the twentieth century: they distributed patronage, settled community conflicts, offered educational opportunities, and provided health services.

Gunther Barth has suggested that these associations represented an "invisible control system," based on old district loyalties, filial piety, and fear that reinforced the basic allegiances of Chinese traders, miners, field hands, laundrymen, domestics, cooks, and day laborers and that formed sentiments more confining than the strongest of visible walls or even chains. As a result, Barth argues, Chinatowns merely needed to symbolize the presence of such control without duplicating the whole system. Chinatowns also permitted an emotional release from tempers checked by restraint and fear; they worked as the "safety values" of the control system. Thus, in Chinatown, islands of freedom and license—all within reach of the lowest and poorest Chinese—lay next to centers of authority and oppression. In a rude mixing of order and chaos, says Barth, the headquarters of district associations and the *tongs* bordered the neighborhood theaters and gambling dens. In the latter, the visions of leisure that had prompted the Chinese to leave home and risk years of hardship could be recaptured in a few hours of escape from the alien and monotonous world of work mediated for them by those running the organizations next door.

If the associations and the night life determined the psychological borders of Chinatown for the Chinese, the colorful celebrations of traditional holidays perhaps best captured the flavor of Chinatown's life in the minds of those outside the community. For the Chinese, observing the traditional holidays interrupted their routine and provided regular outlets from the rigid controls of the work world. They momentarily linked the Chinese émigrés in Chinatown with familiar scenes from the homeland, many of them associated with the Pearl River Delta from which large numbers of the Chinese had immigrated. Although set in San Francisco or in one of the California mining-camp communities, the Chinatown ceremonies formed part of the popular cycle of the three festivals of the living and the three festivals of the dead and reminded them of life back in the villages and towns along the waters of the Chui Kiang. Among the six traditional holidays, the Dragon-boat festival never truly took hold, but from the start the Chinese New Year's celebration assumed ascendancy as the largest and loudest annual occasion. The first Chinese New Year's celebration, on February 1, 1851, was a private party thrown by NORMAN ASSING to enhance his image. Assing entertained a number of policemen, "many ladies," and some "China boys," and the affair only incidentally served as a community celebration. Within two years, however, the celebration had lost its private associations and had become a "grand holiday," and by the 1860s, the Chinese New Year's holiday was a Chinatown ritual. For six days, noise raged and smoke billowed as workers crowded the roofs of brick stores and set off packets of firecrackers or tossed ceremonial smoke bombs into crowded streets and alleys. Chinatown's aristocracy donned their finest furs, silks, and satins and made their rounds of New Year's calls. A haze hung over Chinatown's freshly cleaned streets during the few "quiet hours" negotiated by the chief of police and the district leaders, and then the din started over again. The celebration reached its climax in the wild colors and twisting contortions of the lion dance, which frightened away evil spirits and welcomed fresh beginnings.

With their color, charm, noise, and crowds, both the Chinese New Year's celebrations and Chinatowns themselves soon began to attract tourists, who—fascinated by the sights and sounds of an "alien" culture in their midst—in turn helped perpetuate stereotypes about the Chinese among other Americans. Certainly to the Anglo-Protestant majority, the early Chinatowns were exotic places with their preponderance of oddly dressed males, opium dens, houses of prostitution, secret associations, and occasional—and highly publicized—*tong* wars. But the celebrations and the sin were deceptive, for the vast majority of the Chinese hardly ever shook off the shackles of work for longer than it took to celebrate New Year's, visit the theater, or waste a night playing fan-tan. For a few hours, Chinatown may have eased their homesickness

and their work-weary bones, but their world the next day was one considerably less exotic and colorful, an ordinary world of labor and, for many, debt bondage. At base, Chinatown—though perhaps more clearly confined, more harshly controlled, and more closed in—served much the same purposes as any other urban ethnic enclave in the United States: as a network of community organizations and services; as a retreat for worship, socializing, and cultural renewal; as a center in which to carry on business and purchase necessary goods; and as a setting for political bosses to exercise influence and control. In other words, Chinatowns were both havens of safety for the Chinese and zones of isolation from the mainstream culture that rejected them.

—*Charles Phillips*

SEE ALSO: Chinese Americans; Chinese Wars

SUGGESTED READING:
Barth, Gunther. *Bitter Strength: A History of the Chinese in America.* Cambridge, Mass., 1964.
Chan, Sucheng. *Asian Americans: An Interpretive History.* Boston, 1991.
Takaki, Ronald. *A Different Mirror: A History of Multicultural America.* Boston, 1993.
———. *Strangers from a Different Shore: A History of Asian Americans.* New York, 1989.

CHINA TRADE

American entry into the China trade began in 1784 with the arrival of the Boston ship *Empress of China* in Canton, the only port open to foreigners. The ship had sailed eastward via the Cape of Good Hope with a cargo of ginseng. In colonial times, American ships had been excluded from Canton because of the monopoly of the British East India Company. The American Revolution ended that exclusion and stimulated an interest in Asia because of the disruption of colonial trade with England and the West Indies.

A perennial problem was finding a product acceptable to exchange for silks, teas, and porcelain in Canton, particularly as Americans had little specie. Accounts of Captain JAMES COOK's third voyage, published in the mid-1780s, alerted Yankee traders to potential trade markets with the Hawaiian islands in the mid-Pacific and with Canton, where there was a profitable market for sea-otter pelts obtained in Pacific Northwest, particularly at Nootka Sound on Vancouver Island. In 1787, two Boston ships, the *Columbia* and the *Lady Washington,* sailed for the Pacific Northwest Coast. When the *Columbia* returned to Boston in 1790 with a cargo of Chinese goods, the voyage heralded the economic success of the western route to China. By 1800, Americans dominated the Pacific FUR TRADE with China. English activity virtually ceased during the Napoleonic Wars. Hawaii became the principal way station for the approximately twenty Boston-registered ships that plied the route annually. In 1810, American merchants received a monopoly on the Hawaiian sandalwood trade from King Kamehameha I, thus adding an important product to their China-bound cargoes. From 1800 to 1820, the annual value of furs and sandalwood routed through Hawaii to China averaged between $300,000 and $1 million.

The search for furs stimulated American exploration of the Pacific Coast and drew Americans north to Russian America (Alaska) as well as south into California waters. By 1830, the Northwest fur supply was nearly exhausted. American merchants searched the Pacific for new trade products including *bêche de mer* (sea cucumber) and edible birds' nests. Although traders found moderate success with those products, contempt of the Chinese for Western goods led to the dominance of opium as a trade medium in the 1830s by American as well as British merchants. When Chinese government officials attempted to ban opium, the English navy crushed the opposition in the Opium War (from 1839 to 1842). In the treaty of Nanking (1842), which ended the war, the Chinese ceded Hong Kong to Britain and opened five new ports to foreign trade. Americans, who had stayed out of the hostilities, gained equal trade status with the Treaty of Wanghia (1844), which also allowed trade along interior Chinese rivers where American manufactured goods were in demand.

The expanded trade in the 1840s coincided with the development of the American clipper ship, the fastest sailing vessel in the world. In the 1850s, clipper ships gave Americans a dominance in the tea-carrying trade for English as well as American merchants. The value of Yankee imports to China reached $10 million annually.

The China trade diminished after the Civil War. American clipper ships lost their marine dominance to English steam-powered vessels. Northeastern merchants who had made fortunes in China turned their attention to investments in domestic manufacturing, railroads, and mining.

—*John S. Whitehead*

SUGGESTED READING:
Battistini, Lawrence. *The Rise of American Influence in Asia.* East Lansing, Mich., 1960.
Gibson, Arrell M. *Yankees in Paradise: The Pacific Basin Frontier.* Albuquerque, N. Mex., 1993.
Morison, Samuel E. *The Maritime History of Massachusetts.* Boston, 1921.

CHINESE AMERICANS

In the middle of the nineteenth century, pressed by poverty at home and attracted by job opportunities in America, thousands of Chinese, mostly from the southern province of Guangdong (Kwang-tung), immigrated to the United States. They planned to put in a few years of hard work on Gam Saan, or "Gold Mountain," as they referred to America, then return home wealthy and respected, but they instead found themselves working in mines, clearing forests, building RAILROADS, tunneling through mountains, fishing along the Pacific Coast, gathering wheat and cash crops in the Far West and Southwest, and, in general, helping to "open" the trans-Mississippi West for settlement. Some, from Fujian as well as Guangdong, went first to Hawaii to work as contract laborers on the islands' sugar plantations before heading home or on to the mainland of the United States after their work contracts had expired, but most traveled directly to California. Especially after 1848, the year gold was discovered near San Francisco, the Chinese began to arrive in significant numbers on the coast and then headed inland to the gold fields and other destinations. Their numbers reached perhaps a total of one-half million before the immigration was abruptly halted by the legal fiat of CHINESE EXCLUSION in 1882.

Historical background

Although Chinese emigration had begun centuries before Europeans and Americans became involved with China, many of those in this latest exodus left for reasons that were related to recent turmoil created by Western opium smuggling. In the Opium Wars of 1839 to 1842, the British and other Europeans forced the Chinese government to allow the hitherto illegal traffic in the drug and pried open additional Chinese ports. American merchants, anxious to keep a toehold in the China trade, pressured the U.S. government to move quickly and intervene in their behalf. Negotiations surrounding the Treaty of Wanghia in 1844 gave the United States access to the ports opened to the Europeans, the same "rights" in China enjoyed by the Europeans, and any future concessions granted the Europeans. The huge postwar indemnities demanded by the Western powers caused China considerable problems. To pay them, the Manchu (Qing) government imposed high taxes on peasant farmers, who were unable to meet the levies and consequently lost their

Chinese American laborers built much of the system of railroads in the American West. The workers pictured here are constructing rail lines in southern California in the early 1880s. *Courtesy San Diego Historical Society.*

lands. Then beginning around 1847, a series of floods caused the rice crop to fail, and starvation stalked much of rural China. The chaos in the countryside led to rebellions by the now landless peasants, whom the Chinese government described as bandits, and a civil war broke out in the river deltas of South China. "Ever since the disturbances caused by the Red Turban bandits and the Keija bandits," a Chinese government report from the period read, "dealings with foreigners have increased greatly. The able-bodied go abroad."

By then, stories about America's gold-rich hills were floating around China as they were most of the world. Ronald Takaki has described how, after mid-century, U.S. labor brokers circulated fliers in the port cities of China announcing: "Americans are very rich people. They want Chinamen to come and make him very welcome. There you will have great pay, large houses, and food and clothing of the finest description." America was "a nice country, without mandarins or soldiers" where "[m]oney [was] in great plenty and to spare. . . ." In addition, the Chinese who had already returned to their villages from Hawaii or America were local legends for the money they had made, the "palaces" they had built, and the land they had bought. The young, the impatient, the daring, and the desper-

ate reasoned that they, too, could find fortunes on Gold Mountain. Some immigrants were lured by labor recruiters, but most Chinese left of their own free will. Others paid their own way, but many borrowed the funds for the trip under the credit-ticket system, in which they took money from a broker to cover passage and paid off the loans, plus interest, from their earnings in America. Many of them were illiterate or had little schooling, but they were not coolies, "shanghaied" and forced into foreign labor as myth would have it. In 1849, 325 Chinese came looking for gold on the AMERICAN RIVER. The next year, 450 Chinese arrived; in 1851, 2,718; in 1852, 20,026. By 1870, there were 63,000 Chinese in the United States, three-fourths of them living in California. The 1880 U.S. Census counted 105,465 Chinese on the mainland and around 10,000 living in Hawaii. Between 1880 and 1882, 57,271 Chinese arrived in the United States, and 26,788 returned to China, leaving a net increase of 30,483.

Chinese workers in the American West

When the Chinese first began to arrive in any numbers in America, as Takaki notes, there were signs that they were welcomed. The *Daily Alta California* reported, for example: "Quite a large number of the

Immigrants from China faced discrimination, hatred, and out-and-out violence in the American West. An illustration from *Harper's Weekly* magazine records an anti-Chinese riot in Seattle, Washington, which occurred on February 8, 1886. *Courtesy Special Collections Division, University of Washington Libraries.*

Celestials have arrived among us of late, enticed thither by the golden romance that has filled the world. Scarcely a ship arrives that does not bring an increase to this worthy integer of our population." One Chinese merchant in San Francisco observed: "The people of the Flowery land [China] were received like guests [and] greeted with favor. Each treated the other with politeness. From far and near we came and were pleased." Such treatment did not last. Not all of the Chinese headed for the gold fields or stayed long if they did. Many, chased from claims or treated violently in the mining regions, returned to the city of their disembarkation. Bigotry and racial hatred denied them full access to the San Francisco job market and forced a number of them into self-employment. They opened stores, RESTAURANTS, and, especially, laundries.

The Chinese laundryman was an American phenomenon. In China, men did not do laundry, and there were no wash houses. The Chinese considered washing to be women's work, and a Chinese man would have lost social standing if he had taken up such an occupation. But in America, a laundry, like a Chinese restaurant, could be launched with very little capital. A few hundred dollars, even as little as seventy-five dollars, would buy a stove, a trough, a dry-room, an apartment to sleep in, and a sign to hang over the door, which was all the Chinese immigrant needed. Laundrymen did not have to speak English, except perhaps to say "yes" or "no." By the 1850s and 1860s, Chinese laundries were common sights in San Francisco and in rural towns whose Chinese business communities catered to the needs of Chinese miners and farmers—Sacramento, Marysville, Stockton. By the end of the century, one in every four Chinese workers in the United States was a laundryman, and the Chinese made up more than 70 percent of all laundry workers. Other jobs also traditionally associated with women became the province of Chinese men in the West, especially in San Francisco, including work in DOMESTIC SERVICE. As cooks, the Chinese found another profession that, like laundering, would become one of the four "pioneer" occupations—as they were called by historian Sucheng Chan. All were jobs that enabled the Chinese to move eastward across the country.

Restaurants enabled the Chinese to thrive in communities where few of their fellows lived because restaurants attracted a clientele that was not exclusively Chinese. Gold-rush California, rampant with young men in their twenties but boasting precious few women of any age, was the perfect setting for launching such a venture. Men of any nationality who learned to cook could earn an easy living. Quick to realize that the food typically served in the West was, in a word, awful and that here lay the opportunity for a steady income, the Chinese took positions as cooks in private homes, on ranches, and in hotels. Soon, they opened their own restaurants and, in the late nineteenth century, moved to other parts of the country to launch new enterprises as well. In the bigger towns and cities, Chinese restaurant owners served nothing but Chinese food and employed only the Chinese as cooks, waiters, and bus boys. But in smaller communities, they tried their hand at more traditional American dishes and hired local women to work as waitresses. Chinese restaurants frequently shared a feature with other Chinese businesses: a large group of those who worked in the restaurants owned small pieces of the operations. Such employee participation helped ameliorate conflicts between management and labor and enhanced their ability to get along in close quarters, a crucial ethnic survival skill.

According to Chan, the four pioneer occupations of the Chinese also included MINING and railroading. By the 1860s, two-thirds of the Chinese in America, some 24,000 people, were working in California mines. Most were independent prospectors, although some organized into small groups and formed companies of twenty or thirty. According to one newspaperman, they were "inhabiting close cabins, so small that one . . . would not be of sufficient size to allow a couple of Americans to breathe in it. Chinamen, tools, tables, cooking utensils, bunks, etc., all huddled together in indiscriminate confusion, and enwreathed with dense smoke, presented a spectacle." Chinese miners became a common sight in their blue cotton shirts, baggy pants, wooden shoes, and wide-brimmed hats with queues trailing down their backs. They played penny-ante poker; they took opium rather than alcohol; they seemed frugal and industrious. Isolated by culture, language, and even work habits, they tended to keep to themselves as they worked mainly placer claims in the California foothills, especially along the Yuba River.

Despite their industriousness, they soon became scapegoats for frustrated fortune-hunters and targets of American nativist movements. As early as 1850, when the infant California legislature passed a foreign miners' tax aimed primarily at the Chinese, the cry from the Sierra Nevada gold fields was: "California for Americans." Every foreign miner who did not desire to become a citizen was required to make a monthly payment of three dollars. Chinese men could not become American citizens under the 1790 immigration law that reserved naturalized citizenship for "white" people, so even those men who had no plans to return to China were required to pay the monthly fee. The tax remained in force until voided by the 1870 Civil Rights Act, by which time California had collected $5 million from the Chinese, an amount tantamount to between 25 and 50 percent of all state revenues. In the mining camps themselves, racial antagonism was more direct. Allowed to work only abandoned claims and placer finds others considered unworthy of effort, the Chinese were soon scorned by white Forty-niners who described poor-yielding claims as those that "even the Chinese passed by." The Californians called for every Chinese man to cut his queue, which they called his "pigtail," before qualifying for residence in the state, and the miners often took the matter in their own hands and cut off the braids themselves. Some drove off Chinese who turned up promising prospects and

worked the claim themselves. One story making the rounds of the camps claimed that a miner had hung up six Chinese by their queues and cut their throats. Although some Chinese abandoned hope and returned to San Francisco, many continued to scratch out an existence in mining despite the drawbacks, and eventually mining drew the Chinese to the Pacific Northwest and to the northern Rocky Mountains and Great Plains.

Large numbers of the Chinese immigrants to the American West went to work on the railroad after the Civil War, when the fever for a transcontinental line gripped the country. Hired as an experiment to do grading for the CENTRAL PACIFIC RAILROAD in 1865, the Chinese soon became the mainstay of railroad construction despite sneers about their size and physical strength. By the end of the year, three thousand Chinese were working for the Central Pacific. They formed the bulk of unskilled labor for the road and did more than their share of the demanding—and dangerous—work, such as hanging from the sides of cliffs to place the dynamite charges needed to blast through Western mountains. In the winters, they worked underground in snow tunnels, which occasionally collapsed. A good many died, although the railroad did not keep count. The Chinese were indispensable to the Central Pacific's race east against the UNION PACIFIC RAILROAD building westward not only because they did the hard and dan-

Many Chinese American families managed to prosper in the West. A 1922 image captures members of the Quon Mane family inside their San Diego establishment. *Courtesy San Diego Historical Society.*

gerous work, but also because they were paid considerably less than the wages demanded by similarly skilled Euro-American workers. Thus they allowed the Central Pacific to overcome the two disadvantages it suffered at the beginning of its rivalry with the Union Pacific: the more difficult terrain it had to traverse and the fact that California boasted the highest wages in the nation. Other Westerners resented the Chinese railroad crews not simply because they worked cheaply. Many reasoned that cheap Chinese labor also allowed the railroads to keep the price of the land granted it by the federal government artificially high rather than selling it off, as had been anticipated, to settlers at affordable rates in order to finance construction. The railroads first introduced the Chinese to Utah, Nevada, Arizona, New Mexico, and Texas, but upon completion, the railroads also stranded them there. The companies kept several hundred men for maintenance work and fired the rest, some 10,000 Chinese in all. Denied free passage back to California along rails they had built, the Chinese trekked westward on foot in small groups. Some found work along the way as common laborers and migrant farm workers. Those who straggled back to California found that the railroad was bringing in ever more Euro-Americans, who disliked the fact that they had to compete against the Chinese for local jobs.

Chinese society in the American West

In the American West, the Chinese, like most others, lived in a society full of young males. But while other communities experienced increases in the number of women, the Chinese community remained predominantly a world of bachelors and married men far from their families. Hence, as some scholars have pointed out, the Chinese immigrants could not create replicas of traditional Chinese society in miniature. Given the scarcity of women, the Chinese population remained rootless, which only fueled the racial agitations against them and helped give rise to anti-Chinese outrages. This, in turn, led the Chinese to band together in Chinese quarters for protection. The small, often crowded CHINATOWNS in San Francisco, Sacramento, Honolulu, and other urban communities were national enclaves, not unlike those of other immigrants, where many residents clung to their traditions even as they created new social institutions. In Chinatown, the residents built temples and public halls, established businesses and set up shops, opened restaurants and ran laundries, and formed clan associations, regional organizations, and secret societies for their safety and welfare. These organizations functioned as instruments of social control over the mass of Chinese immigrants and as "legitimizers" of the status of immigrant leaders,

who operated as power brokers between their compatriots and the outside world.

The most important associations in the American Chinatowns were those made up of people from the same districts in China. Called *huiguan,* the first of these district associations were the Sam Yup Association (Sanyai Huiguan, sometimes called in English the Canton Company) and the Sze Yup Association (Siyi Huiguan), both established in San Francisco in 1851. The more cosmopolitan Sam Yup, who went both to Hawaii and to the U.S. mainland, became merchants, grocers, butchers, tailors, and entrepreneurs; the poorer Sze Yup, who flocked to California, got their start as laborers and miners. Other district associations also formed after 1851, and members of those groups took to tenant farming in the Central Valley delta or set up as nurserymen around Santa Clara. Another key to Chinese immigrant life was its family or clan structure. In China, those with the same surnames assumed they were related, and in America each such clan, when large enough, established an association of its own; the smaller clans formed coalition family associations. Both types of associations provided mutual aid. They met ships with new arrivals; offered short-term lodging; outfitted aspiring miners, workers, and farmers; transmitted mail and money back to China; offered health-care services; maintained cemeteries; built altars and temples; handled funerals; and set up rotating credit operations that allowed both individuals and groups to start businesses.

To mediate disputes among members of the various associations, the leaders of the six *huiguans* located in California in 1862 created a loose confederacy composed of representatives from each association. They called the federation a *gongsuo* (or public hall), but the Euro-Americans dubbed it the "Six Chinese Companies." After the Chinese Exclusion Act of 1882 was passed, the Chinese leaders established a formal organization named the Zhonghua Huiguan, or the Chinese Consolidated Benevolent Association, and it too, soon became known by a variation of the English nickname, the Chinese Six Companies. Dominated by merchants, who in traditional China had been at the bottom of Chinese society, the Chinese Six Companies claimed that one of its principal functions was to fight anti-Chinese legislation, and it hired a series of talented Euro-American lawyers to carry on the fight. But the Six Companies also exercised great control over Chinese immigrant life, a control some scholars have described as despotic. Because the organization regulated the issuing of "exit permits" to any Chinese who wished to return to China, it exerted immense influence within the community. No Chinese could acquire a permit unless either the Chinese Six Companies itself or one

Balboa Park in San Diego hosted a parade of Chinese Americans during a mid-1930's Chinese Day celebration. *Courtesy San Diego Historical Society.*

of its constituent associations had cleared him (and more rarely, her) of all debt. Steamship companies would not sell tickets to those without permits. The Chinese Six Companies, without question, functioned also as a charitable and benevolent organization. In 1884, for example, it opened the first Chinese language school for the children of Chinese immigrants. Some have compared the Chinese Six Companies to Gilded-Age America's big-city machines, which operated by providing patronage, mutual aid, and social services in return for ethnic loyalty and the power to act on the entire community's behalf. Certainly as Chinese Consolidated Benevolent Associations spread to New York, Honolulu, Vancouver (Canada), Lima (Peru), Portland, and Seattle from 1883 to the end of the decade, they all looked to the San Francisco Chinese Six Companies for leadership. Even after the Chinese Communist Revolution of 1949, China's mainland government continued to attempt to use the organization to influence American Chinatowns.

Chinese immigrants also formed groups based on common interests such as trade guilds, political parties, and "secret" or "sworn" brotherhoods. Craft guilds and labor unions had existed for centuries in China, where they trained apprentices, established work standards, set prices, and protected territorial

and professional prerogatives. The Chinese in America followed suit, setting up guilds for laundrymen, shoemakers, tobacconists, and the like, which established uniform prices for different merchandise, divided up neighborhoods among members to decrease competition and, thus, help ensure survival, and collected dues to pay lawyers to fight anti-Chinese ordinances against the guild's specialities. More notorious than either the various associations or the guilds, however, were the *tongs* (or *tangs*), which cut across common geographic origins and kinship ties. Although in Chinese *tong* meant simply "hall," in the American West of the nineteenth century, the word came to mean a fraternal organization whose members were bound by secret initiations and brotherhood oaths. Among the Chinese, the best-known *tong* was the Chee Kung Tong, or Zhigongtang, whose roots lay in secret Chinese societies formed to overthrow the Manchu dynasty and restore the Ming (Han) dynasty. Most Chinese scholars call these secret mainland Chinese revolutionary groups Triads, a number of which participated in the Taiping Rebellion before the Manchus suppressed it in 1864. Many Triad members escaped to Southeast Asia, Hawaii, and the Pacific Coast. By the 1870s, there were dozens of *tongs* in different parts of the United States, including some in Hawaii, and the former Triads attracted especially the declassé among the immigrant population with the beliefs, rituals, and antiestablishment organizations they had brought from China. Soon the groups were being called "fighting *tongs*" by American newspapers. Using "hatchetmen" to murder their rivals, the *tongs* battled for control over the profits to be made in Chinatowns from GAMBLING, opium dealing, smuggling (after Chinese exclusion), and PROSTITUTION. Enough money was to be had that not a few formerly respectable merchants joined the *tongs*.

Tong control was especially onerous for the Chinese women, who, in the early years, formed a small proportion of immigrants. During the early decades, most of them had come to the United States alone. Many of them were prostitutes, forcibly transported from China by white slavers and the Chinese *tongs* or by their parents who sold them into the trade. Some went into debt peonage to cover their passage to America and became prostitutes under contracts that stipulated the house of ill repute where they would work, the number of years—usually around five—they would be required to stay, the amount of the advance—usually around five hundred dollars—they would be given, and other conditions and considerations. It was a hard life, whether the young women wound up in the high-class Chinatown brothels of San Francisco, Marysville, and Sacramento or worked in the run-down houses or four-by-six-foot barred-window cribs of mining outposts, railroad camps, and small farming towns. A good number of them became opium addicts and not a few committed suicide by taking an overdose of drugs or throwing themselves into San Francisco Bay. Some prostitutes did escape the life and forgot their past in happier and safer times. Many paid their debts and went free. Some fled to the Presbyterian Mission in San Francisco's Chinatown. A number of them found husbands among the lonely bachelors of Gam Saan, who bought their freedom and brought them into Chinese society, where they lived full and productive lives. In the 1870 census, 61 percent of the 3,536 Chinese women in California listed their occupation as prostitute.

The fact that so many Chinese women were prostitutes adversely affected the lives of the slowly growing number of Chinese women who were not. The latter seldom appeared on the streets of Chinatown alone for fear that they would themselves be kidnapped and forced into slavery or that local Chinese men would assume they were prostitutes and press unwanted attentions. This legacy of exploitation combined with white prejudice to last for decades. The United States attempted to bar Chinese women from the very beginning, and San Francisco officials tried again and again to close brothels staffed by Chinese women. Both the California legislature and the U.S. Congress passed laws against female immigration on the assumption that most, if not all of them, would take up prostitution. The PAGE LAW OF 1875, prohibiting the entry of Asian contract laborers, felons, and prostitutes, was used primarily to keep Chinese women out of America. Chinese women arriving in Western ports were detained and subjected to humiliating searches and brutal treatment regardless of their reasons for coming to America. Women who left the country to visit their families in China were required to prove they were married to Chinese men on the mainland or the daughters of Chinese families born in the country during lengthy and draconian questionings, and then they were frequently denied entry anyway on the smallest of pretexts. When the Chinese fought up to the U.S. Supreme Court on behalf of twenty-two women denied entry by the California immigration commissioner, they were rudely rebuffed by the judges in *Chy Lung* v. *Freeman* (1876). Only some 1,340 Chinese women entered the United States legally between 1875 and 1882. When a Chinese exclusion law seemed imminent in 1880, 50,000 Chinese rushed into the country over the next two years, but there were only 219 women among their number. By 1890 there were twenty-seven Chinese men for every Chinese woman on the mainland, and the number of Chinese children, which was around 500 in 1870, reached a mere 9,000 in 1900, fifty years after the Chinese had first begun immigrating to the United States. Only in 1940, after almost a century of settlement, would the American-born people of Chinese ancestry outnumber the foreign-born.

Those Chinese who remained in the country after exclusion continued to live mostly in the West and primarily in Chinatowns. While millions of European immigrants found jobs in the growing industries of the East and Midwest, the Chinese (and other Asian Americans) worked in the fields, orchards, private homes, laundries, and restaurants of the trans-Mississippi West. Their experience separated them from the European immigrants and resembled in many ways that of all the West's "peoples of color"—African Americans, Native Americans, Mexicans Americans. Although recent scholarship on Chinese Americans is beginning to fill in the picture of the neglected years between World War I and World War II, most historians still believe that, with exceptions, the majority of the Chinese were limited to noncompetitive jobs and—once the waves of anti-Chinese violence had passed—basically ignored by whites except as domestics and ethnic curiosities in narrative fiction and movies. Certainly, the Chinese were isolated from and rejected by the culture surrounding them until at least World War II, when China became an ally of the United States. During the war, the perceptions of many mainstream Americans toward China changed, and the United States repealed all anti-Chinese exclusion laws. This in turn allowed Chinese Americans to make important political, legal, and social gains and begin to find acceptance—even frequent admiration and recognition—in a country that once seemed so adamantly opposed to their very presence.

—*Charles Phillips*

SEE ALSO: Chinese Wars; Foreign Miners' Tax of 1850; Stereotypes: Stereotypes of Asian Americans; Violence: Racial Violence

SUGGESTED READING:
Asian Women United of California, eds. *Making Waves: An Anthology of Writings about Asian American Women.* Boston, 1989.
Barth, Gunther. *Bitter Strength: A History of the Chinese in America.* Cambridge, Mass., 1964.
Chan, Sucheng. *Asian Americans: An Interpretive History.* Boston, 1991.
Cheng, Lucie, and Edna Bonacich, eds. *Labor Immigration under Capitalism: Asian Workers in the United States before World War II.* New York, 1993.
Daniels, Roger. *Asian America: Chinese and Japanese in the United States since 1850.* Seattle, Wash., 1988.
———. *The Politics of Prejudice.* Berkeley, Calif., 1962.
Okihiro, Gary. *Margins and Mainstream: Asian Americans in History and Culture.* Seattle, Wash., 1994.
Takaki, Ronald. *A Different Mirror: A History of Multicultural America.* Boston, 1993.
———. *Strangers from a Different Shore: A History of Asian Americans.* New York, 1989.
Yung, Judy. *Chinese Women of America: A Pictorial History.* Seattle, Wash., 1986.
———. *Unbound Feet: A Social History of Chinese Women in San Francisco.* Berkeley, Calif., 1995.

CHINESE EXCLUSION

On May 6, 1882, Congress forbade the further immigration of Chinese laborers under the Chinese Exclusion Act. The law marked the end of the "open-door" era and introduced into America's immigration policy discriminatory distinctions based on race and national origin. The Chinese exclusion policy remained in effect until 1943, when the United States and China became allies during World War II.

In 1880, 105,465 Chinese lived in America and constituted only 1.5 percent of the foreign-born in the country and .2 percent of the total population. However, the vast majority of Chinese lived in the West,

and 71 percent of their population resided in California. Early histories of exclusion by Mary Coolidge and Elmer Sandmeyer emphasized the movement's origins in California, especially among the state's working class. Combining racial and economic arguments, the WORKINGMEN'S PARTY OF CALIFORNIA led by DENIS KEARNEY and other organizations argued that white workers could not compete with "cheap" Chinese laborers who, by their willingness to work long hours at low pay, threatened to lower the living standards of all workers and to increase the power of corporate employers. Historian Alexander Saxton argued that labor leaders embraced the anti-Chinese movement because it proved to be a powerful unifying issue for the fledgling labor movement in California rather than because of any significant economic threat. Responding to anti-Chinese furor in 1870, the California legislature limited Chinese immigration, but its efforts were held unconstitutional. Exclusionists then turned to the federal government.

To obtain national legislation, the Chinese exclusion movement had to move beyond its regional origins. Sandmeyer argued that the ongoing struggle for dominance between the major political parties in an era of close elections made the Pacific Coast states a valued "swing vote" and allowed those states to place exclusion on the national agenda. Broad national support of exclusion reflected, in Sandmeyer's opinion, bipartisan efforts to court the voters of the West rather than genuine concern about Chinese immigration.

Other historians have emphasized instead the cultural and racial motives behind exclusion. Long before the first Chinese immigrants arrived, accounts of missionaries and traders spread images of Chinese as deceitful and sexually and morally perverse. These stereotypes, reinforced by racialist theories regarding the evolution of civilization, predisposed Americans to view Chinese immigrants as aliens impervious to assimilation. Cultural misconceptions of Chinese as "coolie" laborers contributed further to exclusionist fervor as Americans compared Chinese to African Americans and rejected the prospect of a new system of slavery. In focusing attention on racial arguments for exclusion, historians Stuart Creighton Miller, Gunther Barth, and Shih-Shan Henry Tsai drew attention to the significant middle-class as well as working-class support for the Chinese exclusion policy.

Chinese exclusion was not accomplished by the passage of a single law; it took almost thirty years to secure. Exclusionists met opposition from large-scale employers, missionaries, and traders, as well as from Chinese immigrants themselves. The first step towards exclusion came with the PAGE LAW OF 1875, which forbade the immigration of Asian laborers brought to the United States involuntarily and of women for the purposes of prostitution (a provision aimed primarily at Chinese prostitutes). At the urging of Californians, a joint congressional committee investigated Chinese immigration in 1876 and issued a report, written by California Senator Aaron Augustus Sargent, calling for restriction. In 1879, Congress responded by passing the Fifteen Passenger Act, which limited the number of Chinese passengers on any steamship sailing to America to fifteen. Arguing that the law violated the Burlingame Treaty of 1868 between China and the United States—a treaty that explicitly provided for the free migration of Chinese to America—President Rutherford B. Hayes vetoed the law.

Chinese exclusion became possible only after the United States negotiated a new agreement, Angell's Treaty of 1880, in which the Chinese government conceded to the United States the right to regulate or suspend, but not to prohibit absolutely, future immigration of Chinese laborers. The treaty explicitly guaranteed the right of other Chinese ("whether . . . teachers, students, merchants") and of Chinese laborers already residing in the United States to continue "to go and come of their own free will." Soon after ratification of the treaty, Senator John F. Miller of California proposed a law forbidding the immigration of Chinese laborers for twenty years. The law passed Congress but was vetoed by President Chester A. Arthur. With broad majorities, Congress quickly passed a new bill, which the president did sign. The Chinese Exclusion Act of 1882 suspended the immigration of Chinese laborers for ten years. Chinese laborers already in the United States and those arriving within ninety days of the act's passage remained exempt from the law, as did Chinese who were not laborers. The law also forbade the naturalization of Chinese.

Passage of the 1882 act did not end the struggle over exclusion. Chinese actively resisted the policy through evasion, political negotiation, and litigation, which, in turn, prompted a series of amendments designed to strengthen exclusion and close loopholes in the laws. In 1884, Congress tightened the requirements for documentation of exempt Chinese, and the Scott Act of 1888 prohibited the return of any Chinese laborer who left the United States. While acknowledging that the Scott Act violated Angell's Treaty, the Supreme Court upheld the law in *Chae Chan Ping* v. *United States* (1889).

Similarly, the court upheld another severe measure, the GEARY ACT OF 1892, which extended Chinese exclusion another ten years and required Chinese laborers in the United States, upon threat of deportation, to obtain within one year certificates of registration prov-

ing legal residence. After the court's decision to uphold the law in *Fong Yue Ting* v. *United States,* Congress allowed Chinese another six months to register but also placed greater evidentiary requirements on Chinese merchants applying for entry. The Gresham-Yang Treaty of 1894 modified the exclusion policy by providing that Chinese laborers having wives, children, or parents living in the United States or property or debts owed them of at least one thousand dollars in value could return to the United States if they left for a visit.

By 1902, exclusion and registration had been applied to all U.S. territories. The final piece of exclusion legislation came in 1904 when China, responding to complaints at home about the discriminatory exclusionary policy, denounced the treaty of 1894. Congress then passed a law extending exclusion without a time limit. Congress did not legislate again on Chinese exclusion until 1943, when, as a result of America's wartime alliance with China, it repealed the law and subjected the Chinese to the general immigration laws.

After the passage of the Chinese Exclusion Act of 1882, U.S. courts eventually held that the status of Chinese women followed that of their husbands. Thus, Chinese wives of laborers were excluded while the wives of merchants and other exempt Chinese were admitted. Beginning with the Page Law of 1875, restrictive legislation slowed the growth of families in Chinese communities in America.

The most obvious effect of the Chinese exclusion policy was a dramatic reduction in the number of Chinese in the United States. The Chinese population in the United States fell from 105,465 in 1880 to 89,863 in 1890 and then to 61,639 in 1920. For the Chinese who remained in the United States, exclusion undoubtedly had other effects difficult to quantify. For example, the exclusion policy shaped the socio-economic characteristics of the Chinese American community by allowing the domination of the exempt merchant class. Those laborers who continued to come to the United States became illegal immigrants, living under a cloud of secrecy and fear. The exclusion policy stratified Chinese communities and set a precedent for a series of future restrictive immigration laws based on race.

—*Lucy E. Salyer*

SEE ALSO: Immigration Law

SUGGESTED READING:

Chan, Sucheng, ed. *Entry Denied: Exclusion and the Chinese Community in America, 1882–1943.* Philadelphia, 1991.

Miller, Stuart Creighton. *The Unwelcome Immigrant: The American Image of the Chinese, 1785–1882.* Berkeley, Calif., 1969.

Salyer, Lucy E. *Laws Harsh as Tigers: Chinese Immigrants and the Shaping of Modern Immigration Law.* Chapel Hill, N.C., 1995.

Sandmeyer, Elmer C. *The Anti-Chinese Movement in California.* Urbana, Ill., 1939.

Saxton, Alexander P. *Indispensable Enemy: Labor and the Anti-Chinese Movement in California.* Berkeley, Calif., 1971.

Tsai, Shih-Shan Henry. *China and the Overseas Chinese in the United States, 1868–1911.* Fayetteville, Ark., 1983.

CHINESE WARS

In the mid-1850s, California newspapers coined the phrase *Chinese wars* for the pitched battles of the Chinese district companies fighting for control of Chinese immigrants. The companies consisted of merchants who paid for the immigrants' passage from China and acted as controlling benevolent institutions once the immigrants arrived in America. They provided some of the structure of home in a hostile, foreign setting and regimented the immigrant-debtors to ensure they worked for their merchant-creditors.

In any work camp of the mining regions, the overseer of a district company faced hostility from white miners and fierce rivalry from competing district companies for the placers vacated by white miners. When compromises failed, battles erupted. At times, those fights continued as traditional clan and village rivalries. Few white outsiders understood the hostilities; some regarded them as extensions of the campaigns between Taiping rebels and Imperial armies.

Various lengthy preparations usually preceded the battles in the gold fields. Most Trinity County blacksmiths spent the summer of 1854 forging weapons for the first war at Weaverville. In other skirmishes, rifles, revolvers, and knives substituted for traditional armament. Campaigns of intimidation raised the martial spirit and morale of competing district companies.

In the mining areas, armies consisted of about two hundred men, but in May 1854, a proposed battle at Jackson in Calaveras County attracted two thousand Chinese before the sheriff arrested the leaders and prevented bloodshed. Near Kentucky Ranch in Tuolumne County in October 1856, twenty-five hundred fighters of competing district companies clashed. Skirmishes in Nevada City, Sacramento, and San Francisco seldom involved more than two hundred participants, with the exception of a great melee on Sacramento's I Street in September 1854, which involved six hundred fighters.

No account listed more than twenty-one killed in any of the Chinese wars. After the first war at Weaverville in July 1854, one newspaper reported ten dead and twelve severely wounded; another counted twenty-one dead. In the second war in Weaverville in April 1857, eight died; in the third in April 1858, one died. At the beginning of the 1860s, a coordinating council that dealt with the general affairs of the district companies gained prominence. Administered by the headmen of each company, the organization became known to Americans as the Chinese Six Companies. Until the 1960s, the company controlled to a considerable degree life and labor in the CHINATOWNS of the United States.

—Gunther Barth

SEE ALSO: Chinese Americans

SUGGESTED READING:

Barth, Gunther. *Bitter Strength: A History of the Chinese in the United States, 1850–1870.* Cambridge, Mass., 1964.

CHINOOK INDIANS

SEE: Native Americans Peoples: Peoples of the Pacific Northwest

CHIPPEWA INDIANS

SEE: Native American Peoples: Peoples of the Pacific Northwest

CHISHOLM, JESSE

Jesse Chisholm (1805 or 1806–1868) was a trader, scout, interpreter, and government emissary among the Plains Indians of present-day Texas and Oklahoma. The famous Chisholm Trail used by cattle drovers was named for him.

Born in Tennessee to a Scottish father and a Cherokee mother, Chisholm went to Arkansas with the Cherokees in 1810. As a trader at Fort Gibson in the Indian Territory, he accompanied the Leavenworth Expedition to the Comanche and Wichita Indians as a scout and guide in 1834. He then established a trading post on the Canadian River of present-day Oklahoma and made long excursions to trade with the Plains tribes as far south as San Antonio, Texas.

While engaged in trade, he won the close friendship of many tribal chiefs and learned to speak a large number of Indian dialects. By virtue of those accomplishments and his great knowledge of the Great Plains,

Chisholm became extremely valuable to the governments of both the United States and the Republic of Texas as a scout, emissary, and interpreter. He often rode miles and miles into hostile territory to persuade chiefs to attend peace councils. He also helped to rescue Anglo-American children held captive by the warring Plains tribes.

Chisholm served his Cherokee Nation in similar ways. In 1845, he traveled to Mexico to locate the famous SEQUOYAH, inventor of the Cherokee alphabet, who had gone there and died. In 1846, following the Treaty of Comanche Peak in Texas, Chisholm accompanied a delegation of Plains Indians to Washington, D.C. While there, he interpreted for President JAMES K. POLK in the White House.

During the CALIFORNIA GOLD RUSH, Chisholm worked to restrain the prairie tribes from attacking wagon trains. He later lent his expertise to aid U.S. exploring expeditions such as the 1853 survey of a transcontinental railroad route under Amiel Weeks Whipple and EDWARD FITZGERALD (NED) BEALE's wagon-road survey of 1858.

During the Civil War, Chisholm settled at the site of present-day Wichita, Kansas, and made numerous trips into the Indian Country in the service of Indian agent Jesse Leavenworth to bring chiefs in for peace talks. After the war, he returned to his trading-post site at Council Grove in present-day West Oklahoma City. He was trading among a large gathering of the Plains tribes near present-day Canton, Oklahoma, in April 1868 when he ate tainted bear grease and died.

—*Stan Hoig*

SEE ALSO: United States Army: Scouts

SUGGESTED READING:
Gard, Wayne. *The Chisholm Trail.* Norman, Okla., 1954.
Hoig, Stan. *Jesse Chisholm, Ambassador of the Plains.* Niwot, Colo., 1991.
Taylor, T. U. *Jesse Chisholm.* Bandera, Tex., 1939.

CHISHOLM TRAIL

SEE: Cattle Trails and Trail Driving

CHISUM, JOHN SIMPSON

Southwestern cattle king, John Simpson Chisum (1824–1884) was born near Bolivar, Tennessee. He attended schools in Tennessee and then moved to Lamar County, Texas, in 1837. He clerked in and ran several small grocery stores and served as county clerk

John Simpson Chisum. *Courtesy Western History Collections, University of Oklahoma Library.*

from 1852 to 1854. Chisum joined Stephen Fowler, a New Orleans businessman, in a cattle operation in Denton County, and by 1860, he was a major cattle dealer with five thousand head valued at twenty-five thousand dollars. At first, he supplied cattle to the Confederate army, but as he became more and more disenchanted with the Confederacy, he joined other cattlemen who, in 1863, began moving their herds to West Texas. He then broke ties with Fowler and adopted the distinctive jinglebob earmark and long-rail brand of his own business. Selling cattle to Union contractors beginning in 1864, he supplied beef to eight thousand Navajos living on a reservation on the Pecos River near Fort Sumner, New Mexico.

Chisum himself delivered cattle from 1867 to 1872 to buyers on the Pecos. He then left Texas and established his headquarters near Roswell, New Mexico, in 1874. He ran large herds there and on the Eureka Springs Ranch in Arizona. In November 1875, he sold his operation to Hunter and Evans, a St. Louis commission firm, which assumed his debts of more than three hundred thousand dollars.

Working as an agent for Hunter and Evans, Chisum faced increasing stock losses in Lincoln County and sought legal assistance from Alexander McSween, a local attorney. In the struggle to break the hold on the county by the mercantile interests of James J. Murphy and Lawrence G. Dolan, McSween and his associate John Tunstall were killed. As lawlessness spread, Hunter and Evans cleared its herds from the Pecos in 1878, and Chisum moved his remnant herd to the Texas Panhandle for more than a year. He then returned to Roswell, where he and his brothers James and Pitser operated a small-scale ranch.

Chisum was a sterling example of the open-range entrepreneur who built a flimsy empire on partnership cattle, credit, and free grass.

—*Harwood P. Hinton*

SEE ALSO: Cattle Industry; Lincoln County War

SUGGESTED READING:

Clarke, Mary Whatley. *John Chisum, Jinglebob King of the Pecos.* Austin, Tex., 1984.

Hinton, Harwood P., Jr. "John Simpson Chisum, 1877–84." *New Mexico Historical Review* 31–32 (July, October 1956; January 1957): 177–205, 310–337, 53–65.

CHITTENDEN, HIRAM MARTIN

Hiram Martin Chittenden (1858–1917), army engineer and historian, was born in Yorkshire Town, Cattaraugus County, New York, to a farming couple. At an early age and with his parents' encouragement, Chittenden developed a lifelong zeal for learning, a zeal that propelled him to a distinguished career as an engineer and an equally illustrious avocation as a historian.

After a brief but stimulating period at Cornell University in 1879, Chittenden pursued a rigorous technical training at the United States Military Academy at West Point. He graduated with high honors on June 15, 1884, and was assigned as a second lieutenant to the UNITED STATES ARMY CORPS OF ENGINEERS. On December 30, 1884, he married Nettie M. Parker of Arcade, New York, and together they raised three children. The couple spent the next three years at Willets Point, New York, where Chittenden completed his formal training in civil and military engineering.

After serving as an engineer officer in the Department of the Platte and on the Missouri River Commission in 1887 and 1888, Chittenden was assigned to YELLOWSTONE NATIONAL PARK where his duties were to build roads for tourists. Based on his work there, he wrote his first book, *The Yellowstone National Park: Historical and Descriptive,* published in 1895. From this point, his scientific and literary interests proceeded in tandem.

Chittenden's next military assignment led him to undertake navigational improvements on the Ohio River–Lake Erie canals from 1894 to 1896 and in the Missouri River watershed in 1897 and 1898. He returned to his Yellowstone road-building assignment in 1899 and worked there seasonally until 1906. Historian John Ise would later credit Chittenden for the high quality of roads in Yellowstone Park. Chittenden also served as chief engineer in the Fourth Army Corps in the Spanish-American War. His other achievements included constructing the Lake Washington Canal that linked Puget Sound to lakes in the Seattle area; laying out the road to the top of Rubidoux Mountain in Riverside, California; and devising major theories on the relationship among forests, run-off, and flood control. Success in his military assignments brought promotions—to major in 1904, lieutenant colonel in 1908, and, on retirement, brigadier general in 1910.

Chittenden wrote a number of highly respected books that, arguably, are an even greater legacy than his engineering feats. In addition to the Yellowstone park book, his works include *The American Fur Trade of the Far West,* a three-volume work published in 1902; *History of Navigation on the Missouri River,* a two-volume work published in 1903; *Life and Letters of Father De Smet,* a four-volume work written with A. T. Richardson and published in 1905; and *War or Peace,* published in 1911. Of these, the massive study of the fur trade stands out as a classic; it has since been updated and expanded, but it still endures. Dale L. Morgan, the next generation's leading historian of the fur trade, claimed that Chittenden's influence on the development of the historiography of the West was equal to that of FREDERICK JACKSON TURNER and WALTER PRESCOTT WEBB.

Chittenden died in Seattle, Washington, on October 9, 1917, two months after he had witnessed the formal opening of the Lake Washington Canal. His biographer, Gordon B. Dodds, characterized him as a multifaceted man, whose personal ambition was fused with a passion for social service, a scientist and historian who also devoted much time to his family, a progressive and innovative thinker who accomplished much in his fifty-eight years of life.

—*David J. Wishart*

SUGGESTED READING:

Dodds, Gordon B. *Hiram Martin Chittenden: His Public Career.* Lexington, Ky., 1973.

Ise, John. *Our National Park Policy: A Critical History.* Baltimore, 1961.

Morgan, Dale L. "The Fur Trade and Its Historians." *The American West* 3 (1966): 28–31, 35, 92–93.

CHIVINGTON, JOHN M.

A man of God and war, John M. Chivington (1821–1894) was born in Warren, Ohio, and spent the first years of his adulthood as a Methodist minister in his native state. He took his ministry ever westward, first to Illinois and then Missouri, Kansas, and Nebraska. By 1861, he had arrived in Denver, Colorado, where he served with the First Methodist Episcopal Church and preached to the inhabitants of the region's mining towns.

During the Civil War, Chivington took a commission with Colorado's Union volunteers. He led Colorado's First Regiment south to join with New Mexico's Union forces to defeat Confederate troops at Glorieta Pass in the spring of 1862. Chivington emerged from this campaign as a military hero.

Having quelled the Confederate threat, Chivington turned his attentions to the Cheyenne and Arapaho Indians, whose hunting grounds white prospectors and settlers coveted. Authorized by territorial governor JOHN EVANS to raise a militia against Indian raids on white settlers and transportation routes, in the summer of 1864, Chivington organized the Third Colorado Cavalry, a group of one-hundred-day volunteers, most of whom came from the rough mining camps of the region.

Frustrated by a summer of inaction, Chivington, on November 29, 1864, led about one thousand troops in a brutal assault against a Cheyenne camp on Sand Creek, near Fort Lyon. BLACK KETTLE, the Cheyennes' leader, had led his people to this site believing that in so doing he and his people were under military protection.

The cavalry's dawn attack on the village of about five hundred Cheyennes prompted Black Kettle to raise a U.S. flag and a white flag of surrender near his lodge. The assault continued, however, leaving about two hundred Indians dead and mutilated; many were women and children.

At first, Chivington was praised for his actions by Coloradans, who for many months lived in fear of Indian attacks. But as eyewitness accounts of the SAND CREEK MASSACRE became public, Chivington's actions were assessed in a different light. In the following year, three investigative bodies gathered testimony and condemned Chivington and the attack by his "Bloody Thirdsters" as nothing but wanton slaughter. The former preacher faced the threat of a court-martial. His resignation from the army ended the proceedings but not the damnation that plagued him for the rest of his life and on into history.

—*Patricia Hogan*

SEE ALSO: Central Plains Indian Wars

SUGGESTED READING:

Craig, Reginald. *The Fighting Parson.* New York, 1959.

Hoig, Stan. *The Sand Creek Massacre.* Norman, Okla., 1961.

John M. Chivington was known as "The Fighting Parson." *Courtesy Colorado State Historical Society.*

CHOCTAW INDIANS

SEE: Native American Peoples: PeoplesRemoved from the East

CHORPENNING, GEORGE

Western transportation pioneer George Chorpenning (1820–1894) cofounded the first regular mail service linking California with Salt Lake City and the Eastern states. Born in eastern Pennsylvania, Chorpenning joined the California gold rush in 1849. Two years later, he and Absalom Woodward won a federal contract to carry mail between Sacramento and Salt Lake City, where their service made connections with another line that ran to Independence, Missouri. The two men agreed to make monthly deliveries over the established overland trail route, a distance of about 910 miles, for $14,000 a year.

Service began on May 1, 1851, when Chorpenning left Sacramento with several employees. Deep snow in the Sierra Nevada and the Goose Creek Mountains of southern Idaho, cold weather, and hostile encounters with Native Americans hindered the enterprise. After Woodward was killed by Indians in northern Utah late in 1851, Chorpenning adopted a southern route for the winter months; he sent the mail from northern California by boat to Los Angeles, then overland by way of Cajon Pass and the MORMON TRAIL to Salt Lake City.

In 1854, Chorpenning opened mail service between San Diego and Salt Lake City over the Old Spanish Trail–Mormon Trail route, but he returned to the original route in 1858 and provided service between San Francisco and Salt Lake City every sixteen days for $130,000 a year. To support this line across the Sierra Nevada and the Great Basin, he purchased ten STAGE-COACHES and other equipment, built stations, improved the route, and hired men who maintained a remarkably reliable schedule.

Because of charges of corruption (later proved false), the postmaster abruptly canceled Chorpenning's contract in May 1860, and a rival firm headed by WILLIAM HEPBURN RUSSELL took over the entire operation, including all the company's stations and supplies. Feeling wronged and cheated, Chorpenning sought repayment from Congress until his death.

—*Kenneth N. Owens*

SUGGESTED READING:
Hafen, LeRoy R. *The Overland Mail, 1849–1869: Promoter of Settlement, Precursor of Railroads.* Cleveland, Ohio, 1926.

CHOUTEAU FAMILY

The Chouteau name occupies a prominent place in the annals of the American West. Members of the influential St. Louis family created a powerful commercial dynasty that helped make their city the hub of an international trade network and a major center for Western economic development. The ubiquitous Chouteaus assumed active and vital roles in founding new settlements, in developing the Western FUR TRADE, in establishing commercial relations with key Missouri and Mississippi river Indian tribes, and in initiating a variety of business and financial enterprises.

Auguste Chouteau became the leading merchant of St. Louis, Missouri, and built a family dynasty from trading with the Osage Indians. *Courtesy Library of Congress.*

The dynasty's founder and matriarch, Marie Therese Bourgeois, was born in New Orleans in 1733. In 1748, she married René Chouteau, a local tavern-keeper, and the following year, their son Auguste was born in New Orleans. René Chouteau subsequently abandoned his wife and young child and returned to his native France. The indomitable "Widow" Chouteau, as she called herself, defied convention to make a new life for herself and her son. She lived with Pierre Laclede, a New Orleans merchant, and they had four children. Jean Pierre Chouteau, who was born in New Orleans in 1758 and preferred to be called Pierre, was in fact Laclede's son. He and his three younger sisters, all of whom later married prominent traders, took Chouteau as their family name to escape the stigma of illegitimacy.

In 1764, Laclede founded St. Louis as a trading headquarters with Auguste Chouteau's assistance. Madame Chouteau, who joined Laclede in St. Louis later that year, became a successful businesswoman in her own right. She foiled the legal maneuvering by her long-estranged husband who sought to reassert his marital rights after his return to New Orleans. When Madame Chouteau died in 1814, she was revered as the matriarch of St. Louis and of Upper Louisiana.

Auguste Chouteau became the leading merchant in St. Louis. He gained the confidence of Spanish officials, who awarded his family a monopoly of the profitable Osage trade. Chouteau reciprocated by using his considerable influence to assist the Spanish in conducting Indian diplomacy with the Osages and other Western tribes. Following the LOUISIANA PURCHASE, Auguste transferred his allegiance to the incoming American authorities, who frequently solicited his advice and enlisted his service. He retired from active involvement in the fur trade following the War of 1812 and died in St. Louis in 1829.

Pierre Chouteau first gained public recognition while serving as the family's resident agent in the Indian Country. His familiarity with Native American customs and his ascendancy among the Western tribes materially advanced the Chouteau trading interests. In 1804, President THOMAS JEFFERSON appointed Pierre Chouteau the first U.S. Indian agent for the tribes west of the Mississippi. On two occasions, he escorted Native American delegations to Washington, D.C., for conferences with the president and other U.S. officials. In 1809, he joined forces with MANUEL LISA and other prominent traders to form the St. Louis Missouri Fur Company. Pierre Chouteau withdrew from active participation in the fur business in the 1820s, but he kept a watchful eye on the activities of his sons and sons-in-law, whom he had groomed to carry forward the family's business operations. He died in St. Louis in 1849.

Pierre Chouteau's progeny dominated the second-generation of the family's trading operations. His eldest son, Auguste Pierre, known as A. P., was born in St. Louis in 1786. A graduate of the U.S. Military Academy at West Point, he resigned from the army to engage in the fur business. A. P. joined his father as a partner in the St. Louis Missouri Fur Company in 1809, and in 1815, he and Jules DeMun headed a disastrous trading expedition that landed them in a Santa Fe prison under charges of trading illegally in Spanish territory. The Spanish officials confiscated their trade goods, and A. P., having lost everything, returned to St. Louis. His debts mounted further when a store that he operated in partnership with DeMun and John B. Sarpy failed in 1821. The firm of Berthold and Chouteau, in which his brother Pierre Chouteau, Jr., was a partner, had to cover A. P.'s substantial losses. The following year, A. P. moved to present-day Oklahoma where he carried on trade with the Osages in association with numerous members of the Chouteau family, including several of his younger brothers and cousins. After leaving his wife and children in St. Louis, A. P. established a new life for himself, his Osage wife, and his mixed-blood children by several Indian women. He died in 1838 at Fort Gibson, still mired in debt. Although he lacked the legendary Chouteau propensity for business, he was much admired by traders and Indians alike.

Pierre Chouteau, Jr., born in St. Louis in 1789, provided a stark contrast with his older brother and his profligate ways. Pierre Chouteau, Jr., also known as "Cadet," elevated the family's fortunes to new heights and became the most renowned of all the Chouteaus. Following an apprenticeship in his Uncle Auguste's office, he accompanied his father on trading expeditions in the Indian Country. Pierre, Jr., served a brief stint overseeing Chouteau lead-mining operations near present-day Dubuque, Iowa, before returning to St. Louis where he opened a store in partnership with his brother-in-law Bartholomew Berthold in 1813. The firm, part of a complex network of family business partnerships, reorganized frequently and operated under several names before settling on Pierre Chouteau Jr. and Company. The enterprise struggled to hold its own in the highly competitive fur business increasingly dominated by outsiders. When JOHN JACOB ASTOR entered the St. Louis market, Pierre Chouteau, Jr., cautiously moved to link his operations to Astor's AMERICAN FUR COMPANY. The arrangement proved mutually profitable, and in 1826, Pierre, Jr., and Astor entered an agreement making Chouteau's firm the exclusive Western agent for the American Fur Company. Pierre, Jr., introduced steamboats on the Upper Missouri, and when Astor retired in 1834, Pierre, Jr., purchased the company's Western Department. He subsequently acquired control of the firm's Minnesota trade. Pierre, Jr., had become the dominant figure in the Western fur trade. In later years as the traffic in furs declined, he diversified his holdings with investments in railroads, ironworks, and real estate. By the time Pierre, Jr., died in St. Louis in 1865, the family had sold its Western interests and dissolved its long-standing ties with the fur business.

—*William E. Foley*

SUGGESTED READING:
Foley, William E., and C. David Rice. *The First Chouteaus: River Barons of Early St. Louis.* Urbana, Ill., 1983.
LeCompte, Janet. "Auguste Pierre Chouteau" and "Pierre Chouteau, Junior." In *Mountain Men and the Fur Trade of the Far West.* Vol. 9. Edited by LeRoy R. Hafen. Glendale, Calif., 1965–1972.

CHRISTIAN SOCIALISM

Christian socialism in the United States was an ideology and movement born of nineteenth-century European influences, especially British Christian socialism and Fabianism. The movement was modified by American political and religious traditions, industrialization, and Edward Bellamy's utopian novel *Looking Backward* (1888). During the heyday of political SOCIALISM and the American social-gospel movement, from about 1890 to 1920, Christian socialism was espoused most prominently by individuals associated with institutions. Christian socialists differed over how partisanly "socialist" to be and over their theological orthodoxy and formal ties to Protestant churches. They held in common, however, the conviction that a socialist "cooperative commonwealth"—a society in which economic, political, and other public institutions were owned and operated in the interests of all—was the best expression of the social principles of Jesus and the Hebrew prophets. Eastern and Midwestern leaders—such as W. D. P. Bliss (Episcopalian), George D. Herron (Congregationalist), and Walter Rauschenbusch (Northern Baptist)—and national organizations—such as the Christian Socialist Fellowship (CSF, a nondenominational organization founded in 1906) and the Church Socialist League (founded in 1911 by the Episcopalians)—helped weave an explicitly religious thread into the more radical side of progressive thought and activity.

Critical of the impact of the economy and social modernization on the region in the 1890s, many Westerners turned to Christian socialism. In California, Bellamy's "nationalism" stirred widespread interest, and Bliss's and Herron's tours of California helped awaken such Christian socialists as J. E. Scott, a Presbyterian clergyman and editor of a series of Christian socialist periodicals in San Francisco in the 1890s, and John Randolph Haynes, an Episcopalian medical doctor and wealthy backer of direct legislation in southern California.

The formation of the Socialist Party of America (SPA) in 1901 under the leadership of Eugene V. Debs provided Christian socialists with an indigenous social-democratic party that deemphasized Marx and was not hostile to religion. Texas and Oklahoma, in particular, provided the SPA with its strongest electoral support in the nation from 1904 to 1914. Spokesmen such as Thomas A. Hickey, editor of the *Rebel* in Hallettsville, Texas; the Reverend M. A. Smith (Methodist); and W. S. Nobel (Church of Christ) promoted "Bible socialism." Summer socialist encampments deliberately borrowed the structure and tone of Protestant camp meetings to create a popular and effective tool for solidifying socialism on the Southern Plains.

During the first two decades of the twentieth century, many clergymen in the West represented, directly or indirectly, the influence of Christian socialism. In Butte, Montana, Unitarian clergyman Louis J. Duncan won election as the SPA candidate for mayor in 1911. J. Stitt Wilson, a former Methodist minister who moved to California after 1901, became a nationally recognized speaker for the SPA and CSF. In 1910, Wilson polled more than 12 percent of the vote as the Socialist candidate in the governor's race, and a year later, he won the mayor's office in Berkeley. He was a close associate of JOB HARRIMAN, another California Socialist. A former Disciples of Christ minister, Harriman ran an impressive but unsuccessful campaign for mayor

of Los Angeles in 1910. Four years later, he founded LLANO DEL RIO, a socialist agricultural colony in the Mojave desert. The colony was more secular—and more successful—than Altruria, an explicitly Christian socialist community founded by Berkeley Unitarian pastor Edward Biron Payne. Other prominent Christian socialists in the West included Robert Whitaker, pastor of Los Gatos, California, Baptist Church and editor of the *Insurgent;* the Reverend Thomas Woodrow (Unitarian), editor of *Woodrow's Monthly* in Oklahoma; Franklin S. Spalding, Episcopal bishop of Utah and a leader of the Christian Socialist Fellowship; and George Washington Woodbey, an African American Baptist pastor in Omaha and San Diego and member of the SPA and the CSF.

World War I and Bolshevism brought internal division to the SPA, and public interest in socialism of any sort waned. Although the New Deal Democratic coalition effectively co-opted what remained of Christian socialism in the 1930s, echoes of the older movement appeared in UPTON SINCLAIR's End Poverty in California (EPIC) campaign for the governorship of California in 1934. Morally grounded in his Methodist-Episcopalian upbringing, Sinclair gained fame as the author of the socialist novel *The Jungle* (1906). In 1934, he toned down his moralistic socialism and registered as a Democratic candidate; he won the Democratic party primary but lost the election. Traditional Christian socialism has not revived; perhaps, though, in the 1990s, liberation theologies and the religious character of the work of Cesar Chávez to organize farm labor might best be seen as more contemporary forms of the radical social Christianity represented by Christian socialism.

—*Douglas Firth Anderson*

SUGGESTED READING:

Anderson, Douglas Firth. "Presbyterians and the Golden Rule: The Christian Socialism of J. E. Scott." *American Presbyterians* 67 (1989): 231–243.

———. "The Reverend J. Stitt Wilson and Christian Socialism in California." In *Religion and Society in the American West: Historical Essays.* Edited by Carl Guarneri and David Alvarez. Lanham, Md., 1987.

Foner, Philip S., ed. *Black Socialist Preacher: The Teachings of Reverend George Washington Woodbey and His Disciple Reverend George W. Slater, Jr.* San Francisco, 1983.

Green, James R. *Grass-Roots Socialism: Radical Movements in the Southwest, 1895–1943.* Baton Rouge, La., 1978.

Handy, Robert T. "Christianity and Socialism in America, 1900–1920." *Church History* 21 (1952): 39–52.

Hine, Robert V. *California's Utopian Colonies.* New York, 1973.

Sitton, Tom. *John Randolph Haynes: California Progressive.* Stanford, Calif., 1992.

CHUCK WAGONS

Mobile kitchens known as "chuck wagons" fed nomadic cowboys in isolated regions of the American West. After the Civil War, ranchers began fitting heavy-duty freight wagons with homemade wooden cupboards, the covers of which folded down into worktables supported by wooden legs.

A honeycomb of shelves and drawers inside this chuck box held condiments, tableware, medicine, and personal items of the crew. Cast-iron cookware occupied a boot underneath the chuck box or joined bedrolls and bulk staples like coffee, flour, beans, dried fruit, and canned goods inside the wagon. Some cooks suspended a hide known as a *cuña* (cradle) or coonie between the axles to carry extra fuel for cook fires. A barrel supplied water for cooking and drinking.

Mule-drawn chuck wagons began to disappear with the advent of motor vehicles in the early twentieth century.

—*B. Byron Price*

On the worktable of a chuck wagon, a cook prepares biscuits for cowboys working the range. Placed in a Dutch oven, the biscuits—like most chuck-wagon food—are cooked over an open fire. *Courtesy National Cowboy Hall of Fame and Western Heritage Center.*

CHUMASH INDIANS

SEE: Native American Peoples: Peoples of California

CHUNG SAI YAT PO

The most successful and long lasting of the Chinese-language newspapers of the early twentieth century, *Chung Sai Yat Po* was founded by a Presbyterian minister, NG POON-CHEW, in 1900 and enjoyed wide circulation until its demise in the 1930s. The newspaper played an important role in advocating and reporting on reform in China and equal rights for CHINESE AMERICANS, including rights for women. Existing at a time when Chinese people in America were excluded from participation in American society, the newspaper was more oriented to events in China than to those in the United States. It called for the modernization of China as a means of staving off foreign domination and as a way of securing for Chinese Americans a strong international ally in their attempt to overcome the racial prejudices and restrictive laws that constricted their lives in their adopted land.

One measure of modernization *Chung Sai Yat Po* sought was an elevation in the status of Chinese women, including an end to foot binding, polygamy, slavery, arranged marriages and other practices degrading to women; education for women; women's rights; and women's participation in China's reform movements of the early twentieth century.

—*Patricia Hogan*

SEE ALSO: Magazines and Newspapers

SUGGESTED READING:
Yung, Judy. "The Social Awakening of Chinese American Women as Reported in Chung Sai Yat Po, 1900–1911." In *Unequal Sisters: A Multicultural Reader in U.S. Women's History.* Edited by Ellen Carol DuBois and Vicki L. Ruiz. New York, 1990.

CHU PAK

Arriving in California in 1850 at the age of fifty-three, Chu Pak (1797–1866) was "Chief Director, Master, and Trustee" of the Sze Yup Huiguan, one of the district companies, or organizations of Chinese natives from the Pearl River Delta in China that controlled the lives of Chinese immigrants in San Francisco in the mid-nineteenth century. Information about Chu Pak is scarce, but he was involved in a murder trial in 1862. To clear Chu Pak's name, the heads of the five other district companies at the time offered an address to the public in defense of the "Venerable Old Man," as he was respectfully called by his contemporaries.

—*Patricia Hogan*

SEE ALSO: Chinese Americans, Chinese Wars

SUGGESTED READING:
Barth, Gunther. *Bitter Strength: A History of the Chinese in the United States, 1850–1870.* Cambridge, Mass., 1964.

CHURCH, FRANK

Frank Church (1924–1984), a native of Boise, Idaho, served in the U.S. Senate from 1957 through 1981. He attended Stanford University, served in the Burma theater during World War II, and received a law degree from Stanford after the war. He practiced law for a short time and then won election to the Senate in 1956 at the age of thirty-two. He became a protégé of LYNDON B. JOHNSON.

Church is known for his numerous environmental legislative victories. The National Recreation Areas concept, Wild and Scenic River Bill, and "wilderness" designation for remote regions made him a champion for preservation. A severe critic of the Vietnam War, Church diligently sought an end to the conflict. He later served as chairman of the Foreign Relations Committee and the select Committee on Intelligence in the aftermath of Watergate. Defeated in the 1980 Reagan landslide, Church remained in Washington, D.C., with his wife, Bethine. He died of pancreatic cancer on April 7, 1984.

—*F. Ross Peterson*

SUGGESTED READING:
Church, F. Forester. *Father and Son.* New York, 1975.
Peterson, F. Ross. *Idaho.* New York, 1976.
Pierce, Neal R. *The Mountain States of America.* New York, 1972.

CHURCHILL, CAROLINE NICHOLS

Caroline Nichols Churchill (1833–1926), editor and publisher, was born in Canada and immigrated to the United States at the age of thirteen. After a brief marriage that ended with the death of her husband in 1862, Churchill came down with a strain of tuberculosis and was forced to seek a drier climate. In 1869, she moved to California, where the warm dry air soon banished her cough and restored her health. While in California, she helped defeat a "social evil" bill that would have regulated and controlled "immoral women." Angered by the attempt to hold women accountable for something men were not, Churchill published a farcical bill that would do the same for men.

In the late 1870s, Churchill settled in Denver, Colorado. An advocate of WOMEN'S SUFFRAGE, she was unhappy with how little support the cause received in Colorado. To promote greater interest, in 1879, she began publishing the monthly *Colorado Antelope,* its masthead heralding "The Interests of Humanity, Woman's Political Equality and Individuality." The paper covered everything from local history to social oppression but was mainly dedicated to women. Churchill used the *Antelope* to champion prohibition, and when the local women's temperance movement elected a male president for the sake of respectability, she denounced that, too. Within three years, the paper had gained enough fame, or notoriety, for Churchill to make it a weekly. Renamed the *Queen Bee,* the paper continued to publish Churchill's attacks on drinking and male privilege, which she considered "the arch enemy of the race." She argued for equal education and training for women and pensions for mothers with dependent children. Churchill's efforts bore fruit in 1893 when women were given the vote in Colorado.

—*Kurt Edward Kemper*

SEE ALSO: Temperance and Prohibition

SUGGESTED READING:

Dichamp, Christiane Fischer. *Let Them Speak for Themselves: Women in the American West, 1849–1900.* Hamden, Conn., 1977.

Stefano, Carolyn. "Networking on the Frontier: The Colorado Women's Suffrage Movement, 1876–1893." In *The Women's West.* Edited by Susan H. Armitage and Elizabeth Jameson. Norman, Okla., 1987.

CHURCH OF JESUS CHRIST OF LATTER-DAY SAINTS

The Church of Jesus Christ of Latter-day Saints is the institutional embodiment of Mormonism, a religious movement that started in western New York during the mid-1820s and is now headquartered in Salt Lake City, Utah. Initially controversial, the movement was launched by a small band of millennialists expecting an imminent return of the Messiah and Christian primitivists searching for a church from which the barnacles of tradition and cultural accommodation had been shorn away. Led by the Prophet JOSEPH SMITH, JR., an impoverished young farmer, the group included many of Smith's relatives.

The production of the *BOOK OF MORMON* by Smith involved translation "by the gift and power of God" of a record engraved in hieroglyphics on a set of golden plates to which Smith had been directed by an angel. Because the resulting work appeared to be such a mystery, because the prophet had once been a secular seer, and because the Smith family had Masonic connections, several historians have suggested that the Mormon movement was particularly attractive to people interested in hermeticism and magic. But when the new Mormon "Church of Jesus Christ" was founded in April 1830, it was formulated on principles that would have been more familiar to the primitivist and millennialist wings of traditional Christianity than to those conversant with the occult. Organized along primitivist lines with leaders and followers whose privileges and responsibilities were clearly specified, with baptism by immersion following repentance, and with signs (that is, spiritual gifts such as healing and speaking in tongues) following belief, the members of the new church were confident that, as revelation promised, the "great and dreadful day of the Lord" was at hand.

In the early years of the church, the *Book of Mormon* seems to have been most important as a "new witness for Christ" and a signal of the nearness of Christ's Second Coming. At the time of its founding, the institution's most singular claims were that it was led by a living prophet, that it possessed the only legitimate priesthood, and that it was a restoration of the original Christian church, which had been removed from the earth at the end of the Apostolic age. (Since members of that ancient church were called "Saints," members of this new organization called themselves "Latter-day Saints," a designation often shortened to "LDS.") Soon after the organization of the church, the prophet announced a revelation calling for a gathering of the Saints by creating Mormon cultural enclaves, a departure from the usual religious pattern in the United States in which members of churches gather for worship and return afterwards to homes dispersed across community and countryside.

Smith moved with his family to Kirtland, Ohio, in 1831. As Saints from New York and converts from Canada, New England, and all across the Midwest gathered to create the first LDS enclave, Mormonism took on other distinctive characteristics. New revelation and subsequent institutional elaboration sharpened Mormon singularity by adding a powerful Hebraic dimension to Mormonism's primitivist and millennialist rendering of Christianity. The prophet's father was called to be patriarch to the church and charged with giving Saints patriarchal blessings that, among much else, informed them of their Hebrew tribal heritage. This made the Saints symbolically peculiar, a chosen people, and consigned non-Mormons to Gentile status, an attitude that would set the MORMONS apart much as the Jews had historically been set apart. Other Hebraic elements included introduction of temples into Mormonism and a temple ceremony known as the Endowment (an ordinance said to be of ancient origin); inauguration of a communally based economic system called the "Order of Enoch" (subsequently replaced with the tithing principle); and clarification of differences between the nature of and responsibilities connected with the lower and higher priesthoods of Aaron and Melchizedek (Hebraic offices the Saints believed restored to them by prophetic proclamation). Taken together, these expanded the concept of restoration from a return of the true church to a Hebraic as well as Christian restoration.

As significant as these new elements were, it was the Mormons' gathering in one place and creating a culture that vested both secular and religious authority in prophetic and ecclesiastical leadership that first generated external opposition to Mormonism's atypical form of Christianity. As long as Joseph Smith resided there, Kirtland was Mormonism's center place. But soon after his arrival in Ohio, the prophet had made a trip to the West where he identified a portion of Jackson County, Missouri, as the "Land of Zion" and dedicated a temple site. A community of Saints subsequently settled in Independence, thus becoming a second "stake in the tent of Zion."

C. C. A. Christensen's *Crossing the Mississippi on Ice* (ca. 1879) depicts pioneer Mormons on the way to Utah. *Courtesy Museum of Art, Brigham Young University.*

Populated mainly by Mormons sent out from Kirtland and Midwestern converts who had been encouraged to gather to Zion, this enclave appeared to prosper only to be destroyed by the area's original settlers. The precipitating factor seems to have been the Saints' invitation to free blacks to join them. But the anger of those responsible for the violence was clearly exacerbated by the Saints who, understanding that they were God's chosen people living in His promised land, did not hide their confidence that Jackson County would be given to them as an inheritance.

For the next dozen years, Mormons experienced a tragic variation of the Western boom-and-bust phenomenon. Driven from one area, they settled in another where hard work led to prosperity, which was followed by persecution and another expulsion. Just this type of prosperity-persecution-driving paradigm occurred when the Saints, after being driven from Jackson County, settled in nearby Clay County, only to experience renewed persecution when they started to prosper. This time, however, the prophet tried to interrupt the cycle by leading an expedition from Kirtland to their rescue.

Known as Zion's Camp, the expedition failed miserably in accomplishing its mission. But from the perspective of the history of the church, the expedition was vitally important since Saints who proved their loyalty to the prophet and the faith during this terrible cholera-ridden journey became Mormonism's future leaders. Organized into a potent institutional entity known as the Council of the Twelve, veterans of Zion's Camp formed the bulk of the church's "traveling high council," which would one day stand at the head of the church beside the First Presidency (the prophet, who was—and is—president of the church and his two counselors). By tradition, when a prophet-president dies, the Apostle with the longest tenure in the Council of the Twelve becomes president.

Contentious relations between Gentiles and Saints in Clay County caused the state to set a virtually uninhabited county aside for the Mormons. Most of the Missouri Saints moved there, but the rapidity of Mormon settlement in western Missouri is explained by a dramatic deterioration in Kirtland of the Mormons' economic situation that forced Joseph Smith and many Ohio Mormons to flee. In Far West, Missouri, and its environs, a prosperous community again took shape only to be destroyed by violence. But this time the Saints' response was vehement enough to cause the Missouri governor to call out the militia and order the Saints "exterminated or driven from the state." In the ensuing melee, Mormons were massacred, the prophet and other LDS leaders were imprisoned, and the main body of Saints was driven away. Destitute and weary, yet still committed to the LDS gospel, they streamed back across the state. Recrossing the Mississippi under the leadership of Apostle BRIGHAM YOUNG, they poured into western Illinois.

Settling in and around a town renamed NAUVOO, the Mormon community experienced a period of peace that lasted long enough for them to build a "kingdom on the Mississippi." As converts from throughout the nation and from England joined them, the town and the Mormons prospered, so much so that, for a time, Nauvoo was the largest town in the state. Without relinquishing his prophetic role, Smith, who had escaped from prison with the connivance of his guards, assumed leadership of the economy (he was land merchant and storekeeper), the civil government (eventually he become mayor), and the military (he commanded the well-appointed militia, which became known as the Nauvoo Legion).

In Nauvoo, all distinction between church and culture disappeared. Citizen Saints lived in wards that both divided the town politically and served as religious divisions; the preaching they heard dealt with civic and religious matters indiscriminately; and they watched the mayor, who was prophet and church president, command militia assemblies. At the same time, new revelation obliterated distinctions between past, present, and future by setting forth visions of Saints, their progeny, "and their dead" united as families stretching backward to Father Abraham and forward through many generations. Distinctions between humanity and divinity were also blurred when revelation presented a vision of God as an exalted man and provided a plan that allowed Saints to take steps in the here and now that would permit progress toward Godhood in the eternities.

The most crucial Nauvoo revelation (now Section 132 in the *Doctrine and Covenants* of the church) made "celestial marriage" the centerpiece of this plan. Given to the Saints because they were of the seed of Abraham, this conjugal state, attained through sacramental bonding of a man and a woman in a Mormon temple under proper priesthood authority, made eternal continuation of the family unit possible. The new revelation on celestial marriage also extended to worthy male Saints the privilege of having more than one wife, a common practice among those the Saints regarded as their Old Testament forefathers. Added to the patriarchy, the temple, and the ancient priesthoods, this "new and everlasting covenant" of marriage that made eternal progression possible was the culmination of the restoration to the Saints "of all things."

As critically important to Mormonism's future as this 1842 revelation was, it was not immediately made public. While Joseph Smith and the Mormon leaders closest to him contracted plural marriages in Nauvoo, the plural-marriage *principle* was revealed selectively, creating within Nauvoo an almost gnostic separation between those who had certain knowledge of this esoteric thing and those who only suspected or were totally uninformed about its existence. This potentially divisive situation was accompanied by opposition on the part of some Saints to theocratic control of all aspects of Nauvoo life. The gravity of this internal situation was aggravated by outside suspicion about polygamy and Gentile anxiety about the political, economic, and military features of the Mormon kingdom.

In 1844, Joseph Smith was murdered by renegade members of the state militia, and a ground swell of violence against the Mormons drove most of them from Nauvoo by 1847. Many outsiders expected the prophet's death to lead to the movement's demise. It did not. But the murder initiated a leadership struggle whose most significant outcome was that the Saints to whom restoration of the New Testament church was the defining element of Mormonism were eventually separated from those who believed that gospel "fullness" lay in "the restoration of all things."

Most of those in the former category abandoned the enclave pattern, stayed in the Midwest, and reconvened under the leadership of the prophet's eldest son in 1860 to create the Reorganized Church of Jesus Christ of Latter Day Saints. The Mormons in the latter group remained in Nauvoo long enough to complete the temple—designed by the prophet and begun during his lifetime—and receive their Endowments. Then, appropriating "Camp of Israel" rhetoric, they escaped from the land that had become Babylon to them and departed for a new Promised Land. Saints in both groups (and those in a multitude of other small, usually ephemeral, bodies) continued to believe that the *Book of Mormon* was a new testament of Jesus Christ and that Joseph Smith had been a prophet. But from this point in Mormon history forward, the Church of Jesus Christ of Latter-day Saints would be the institutional embodiment of the part of the Mormon movement that Apostle Brigham Young took to the West.

Young, whose claim to lead was based on his position at the head of the Council of the Twelve, did not assume the role of president of the church until his leadership abilities had been tested during a remark-

In the late 1840s, Brigham Young, the "American Moses," led Mormon followers to new settlements in the Great Salt Lake region. *Courtesy Library of Congress.*

able trek that carried the Saints across Iowa, the Great Plains, and the Rocky Mountains to the valley of the Great Salt Lake. When he became president, Young also became—as all church presidents do—the church's "prophet, seer, and revelator." Rather than announcing new revelations, however, Young harnessed his authority to the task of realizing the prophet Joseph Smith's vision of a new heaven and a new earth.

His chief biographer called Young an "American Moses." Certainly he was that. But he was also an "American Solomon" who presided over the "kingdom in the tops of the mountains" built under his direction and guidance. While many Gentiles also settled in the Great Salt Lake region, this was an LDS realm that sought statehood as a means of maintaining its independence. Turned instead into the Utah Territory, which made it a creature of the federal government, the Mormon theocratic kingdom continued to exist, almost as a separate governmental body. In the economic arena, the church bureaucracy initially controlled the means of production, parceled out land and water rights, and, in making critical decisions about material and financial matters, maintained control of where and how Saints would make their livings. Of

even greater consequence, even more than in Nauvoo, virtually all distinction between church and culture was eradicated during the remainder of Young's life.

Membership in the LDS ecclesia came to signify brother- and sisterhood in an extended family of peculiar people, an ethnic body whose structures of belief and behavior were unique. Recognizing the rigors of migration as a mechanism for creating Mormon ethnicity, Young said that the trail was for "making Saints." This acculturation process was carried forward as those who arrived, physically separated from the rest of the world by the mountains surrounding the Great Basin, adjusted to and lived in a culture with unconventional economic and political arrangements and extraordinary marriage practices. Equally important in the Saint-making process was the concept of "believing blood," which, for a time, overshadowed the Christian notion of "adoption into Israel." While patriarchal blessings identifying bloodline were, finally, symbolic attributions, Joseph Smith and Brigham Young both believed that most of those who responded positively to the LDS gospel message already had the blood of Abraham flowing in their veins. If Gentiles believed, repented, and were baptized, a blood exchange occurring during that ritual made them Mormon. Thus were converts as well as birthright Saints fashioned into peculiar people.

That people outside the community failed to recognize what was happening in the Great Basin kingdom is evident in the nature of the protracted struggle between the Mormons and non-Mormons that lasted for more than fifty years. Failing to recognize the presence of the restoration of the New Testament church in the Mormon belief and worship mix, Protestant home missionaries and Catholic fathers alike believed that an opportunity to hear the Christian gospel was all that this "deluded" and "heathen" people needed. Naturally they were perplexed when Saints with several wives responded that they were already in possession of the Gospel and that theirs was the only true Christian church. Comparably baffled were the nation's secular leaders who, convinced that Mormonism was un-American, were unable to comprehend the Saints' expressions of loyalty to the nation and their declaration that the U.S. Constitution was divinely inspired. Small wonder that the nation first used its military and then its politico-legal system to force national political, economic, and social patterns onto this "wayward" society.

While many Gentiles seemed concerned about Mormonism's "un-American" theocratic system, plural marriage was the universal irritant that led church and state to cooperate in forcing change. Often at the behest of Protestant church leaders and their members,

The Church of Jesus Christ of Latter-day Saints complex in Salt Lake City, with the Temple in the foreground and the church's modern offices behind. *Courtesy Church of Jesus Christ of Latter-day Saints.*

a series of federal antipolygamy measures was passed, each law harsher than the one it replaced. In 1887, the government finally made a concerted effort to bring plural marriage to an end not simply by threatening polygamists with prison, but also by using the escheating process to place the very existence of the church in jeopardy. An invasion of the Utah Territory by U.S. marshals sent LDS leaders underground and led to what many have termed Mormon surrender.

In reality, while it forced the dissolution of the kingdom and an end to the legal practice of plural marriage, the essential point of the agreement that concluded this extended struggle was that as long as Latter-day Saints behaved as other U.S. citizens did, their beliefs would be left alone. On the Mormon side, hallmarks sealing this accord were the church president's 1890 Mormon Manifesto announcing suspension of church-sanctioned plural marriage and disbanding the LDS political party the following year. Non-Mormon emblems of the pact were presidential amnesty and pardon to polygamists in 1893 and, in 1894, passage of the Enabling Act that would allow Utah to become a state.

If these events in the 1890s laid the groundwork for profound modification in the relationship between the Mormons and the nation and, in time, fundamental alterations in the church and in the very nature of what being Mormon means, change did not occur immediately. The extended length of transition reflects the complicated nature of a process that integrated Utah and Mormonism into the nation's political culture and American life generally, that transformed the LDS Church from a regional and idiosyncratic faith into a universal church, and that saw being Mormon change from peoplehood to church membership.

The simultaneous demise of the kingdom and plural marriage precipitated separation of church and state in the new Mormon commonwealth, at least as far as church and state are likely to remain separated whenever a majority of voters belongs to the same ecclesiastical institution. It also cleared the way for development within the Mormon community of a capitalist economy and a political culture surprisingly like the economy and political culture of the rest of the nation. In addition, release from the necessity of pledging primary loyalty to the LDS kingdom allowed the Mormons' patriotic emotions to surface, especially in LDS participation in the wars and military actions of the past century, but also through participation in local, state, and national politics.

Yet the disappearance of the kingdom and the Saints' peculiar marriage system did not separate the church from the culture. However much the situation had changed, much about it stayed the same. Still living in ethnic communities, Saints dealt with the new order by "following their file leaders" and orienting their lives around ward (parish) and stake (diocese) activities. Managing the transition from kingdom to state effectively, if not always smoothly, the church hierarchy anticipated the future by recognizing that Mormonism would not forever remain a regional enterprise. The church prophet-president separated the faith from the land by declaring that wherever the people of God are, there Zion is. Making tithing and keeping the "Word of Wisdom," which forbade the use of tobacco and consumption of coffee, tea, and alcohol, central to the Mormon message, church leaders also stressed the importance of being married (monogamously, of course) in the temple. Without plural marriage—which had functioned as the preeminent mark of Mormon identity—church activity, tithing, temple marriage, and keeping the "Word of Wisdom" became the new marks of being a Latter-day Saint. But Mormons still placed great emphasis on patriarchal blessings, and being born Mormon was still analogous to being born Jewish. Yet the developments that occurred around the turn of the century laid the groundwork for a shift from peoplehood to church membership.

The Second World War proved to be the turning point that would lead to this change. Although what happened might well have occurred in any event, educational and economic opportunities in the postwar period led to swift dispersion of Saints all across the United States. At the same time, acceleration of the church's traditional missionary activity started to bring converts into the church at such an unprecedented rate that by 1960 convert baptism would be a larger factor in yearly church growth than natural increase. In the next half-century, membership would increase from around nine hundred thousand to nine million. While before the war, the membership was concentrated in the region between the Rocky Mountains and the Sierra Nevada and in southern California (the land mass Mormons once claimed as the State of Deseret), after the war, areas all across the nation (and eventually the world) were organized into branches, wards, and stakes. Initially both peopled and led by Saints whose parentage and background made them ethnic Mormons, this scattering of the gathering provided an institutional structure that allowed for integration of massive numbers of new Saints into the church.

Significantly, LDS experience outside traditional Mormon areas has rarely involved living in exclusively LDS communities. Although such enclaves continue to exist in what geographers call the "Mormon culture region," being a Latter-day Saint is now different even there because the church has, since 1980, been fashioning a faith that makes clear distinctions between the religious and the secular.

When the church relinquished the practice of plural marriage and dismantled the Mormon kingdom, what was revealed was a community of Saints disposed, by underlying capitalistic practice and patriotic sensibility, to enter the American cultural mainstream. Ready to be in the world but not of it, they replaced what was lost with church activity, tithing, new signs of Mormon identity, and attention to temple work. In like manner, the disappearance or attenuation of LDS enclave culture and the diminution of the sense of Mormon ethnicity has decreased the visibility of Mormon peculiarity to such an extent that Mormonism's public face is much closer to what it was at the time of the founding of the church than to what it became after the Saints entered the Great Basin. What was once tangible and therefore transitory now abides in the church and in temple ordinances that seal women and men together for time and eternity.

The Church of Jesus Christ has not and likely will never become some idiosyncratic form of Protestant-ism. As embodied in the Church of Jesus Christ of Latter-day Saints, Mormon Christianity retains its peculiarity, its distinctiveness. Many Saints tithe and most keep the "Word of Wisdom" (most of the time), but that is not sufficient explanation. What finally makes Mormon Christians peculiar is that they possess—and read and try to live by—the Bible *and* the *Book of Mormon,* an additional testament of Jesus Christ, and that they are a temple-going people.

With Mormons living and building temples in every corner of the world, the American West recedes in importance in Mormonism. Although the church is headquartered in Utah and will likely remain there, although church conferences (and concerts of the Mormon Tabernacle Choir) will continue for the foreseeable future to be conducted in and broadcast from Mormonism's historic tabernacle, and although the administrative and bureaucratic machinery that supports the church is located in downtown Salt Lake City, the LDS church is rapidly becoming a church universal whose circumference is everywhere and whose center is a Mormon temple, wherever that structure happens to be. Temple Square—once the center of the Mormon kingdom and location of the temple in which the First Presidency and the Council of the Twelve still hold their weekly meetings—is one of the preeminent pilgrimage places in the Western Hemisphere. "This is the place," said Brigham Young when he first saw the Great Salt Lake valley. It truly is the place from which the Mormonism represented by the Church of Jesus Christ of Latter-day Saints started to move outward to the ends of the earth.

—Jan Shipps

SEE ALSO: Catholics; Edmunds Act of 1882, Edmunds-Tucker Act of 1887; Evangelists; Protestants; Polygamy: Polygamy among Mormons; United Order of Enoch; Utah Expedition; Zion's Co-operative Mercantile Institution

SUGGESTED READING:

Alexander, Thomas. *Mormonism in Transition: A History of the Latter-Day Saints, 1890–1930.* Urbana, Ill., 1986.

Allen, James B., and Glen M. Leonard. *The Story of the Latter-day Saints.* Salt Lake City, 1976.

Arrington, Leonard J. *Brigham Young: American Moses.* New York, 1985.

———, and Davis Bitton. *The Mormon Experience: A History of the Latter-Day Saints.* New York, 1979.

Bushman, Richard. *Joseph Smith and the Beginnings of Mormonism.* Urbana, Ill., 1984.

Mauss, Armand L. *The Angel and the Beehive: The Mormon Struggle with Assimilation.* Urbana, Ill., 1994.

Shipps, Jan. *Mormonism: The Story of a New Religious Tradition.* Urbana, Ill., 1985.

CHURCH OF JESUS CHRIST OF LATTER DAY SAINTS, REORGANIZED (RLDS)

The largest of the churches of the Mormon "dispersion," the RLDS Church (the common acronym for the Reorganized Church of Jesus Christ of Latter Day Saints) is characterized by a presidency of direct male descendants of JOSEPH SMITH, JR., the prophet-founder of Mormonism, and by a historical mix of religious elements drawn from Mormonism and Protestantism. The world headquarters is in Independence, Missouri, the location designated in 1831 by Smith to be "the Center Place of Zion." The 1990 membership was about 240,000.

The RLDS Church originated among MORMONS who rejected BRIGHAM YOUNG's claims to the prophet's mantle after Smith's assassination in 1844. A central principle of Mormonism, modeled and personified by Joseph Smith himself, was a dominant prophet-president above a priestly hierarchy of lay leaders. First in that hierarchy was the Council of the Twelve Apostles, of whom Brigham Young was president. Young's claim to succeed Smith was therefore easily understood. He was the successful de facto claimant in NAUVOO, ILLINOIS, and, supported by most of the Apostles, he led the majority of the Nauvoo population to the Great Basin from 1846 to 1848. But Smith had not anticipated his own demise, and he had not made firm institutional arrangements for it. Indeed, he had suggested a variety of succession paths. Other claimants in addition to Young made plausible cases. A turbulent succession struggle was virtually ensured.

For many Mormons who did not go West, including those of several "branches," or congregations, in Illinois and Wisconsin, the question of the "True Prophet" successor remained open. In 1851, Jason Briggs, presiding elder at Beloit, Wisconsin, had a spiritual insight—a "revelation" in Mormon terminology. He wrote it down, printed it in pamphlet form, and distributed it to other nearby branches. The pamphlet included four tenets: denounce all present claimants to Mormon leadership; preach against "false doctrines," (especially polygamy); teach the "original law" as found in the Bible, BOOK OF MORMON, and *Doctrine and Covenants* (the latter containing many, but not all, of Smith's revelations); and promise that a "True Prophet" would come from among the lineage of Joseph Smith, Jr.

Those instructions were to define the course—and spirit—of the RLDS Church for at least a century. Briggs's pamphlet proposed a course of opposition to and denunciation of "Utah Mormons" or "Brighamites."

It also set forth a negative self-definition: adherents to Briggs's tenets claimed they were "not Mormon." A conservative, even reactionary, course of theological development was pursued. The church was devoted to doctrinal replication of both the primitive Christian church and the primitive (or "original") Mormon church, despite its belief in continuous revelation through a living prophet. Finally, the RLDS evangel emphasized the necessity that "the seed of the Prophet Joseph" must occupy the church presidency—a doctrine interesting primarily to other Mormons.

Briggs and an associate, Zenas Gurley, began to call periodic meetings, or "conferences," of the "Scattered Saints," as they called themselves. The conferences anticipated Joseph Smith, III, the martyred prophet's eldest son (who was as yet unaware of their activities) to be the promised new prophet. The 1856 conference decided to send a delegation and an invitation to Nauvoo, where young Smith still lived.

Joseph Smith, Jr., had suggested as many as eight possible modes of prophetic succession; one was that Joseph Smith, III, would follow him. Only twelve years of age at his father's death, "Young Joseph," as he came to be known, was held aloof from the turmoil of Nauvoo's final years by his mother, EMMA HALE (SMITH), who had refused to go West. She remained in Nauvoo with her children, remarried, and lived there until her death in 1879. Young Joseph grew up working in the boardinghouse operated by his mother and stepfather. When the 1856 delegation arrived with its extraordinary invitation, Smith, then twenty-four years old, firmly (some reports say angrily) rejected both invitation and delegation.

But over the next four years, Smith changed his mind. He and his mother went to the 1860 conference at Amboy, Illinois, and asked to be received into fellowship. His new conviction, he testified, grew out of personal prophetic experiences. He was at once ordained president of the Reorganized Church of Jesus Christ of Latter Day Saints, an office he was to hold until his death fifty-four years later.

Joseph Smith, III, was succeeded in turn by three of his sons, Frederick Madison, Israel Alexander, and William Wallace, and by a grandson, Wallace B. Each successor served an apprenticeship as an apostle or president's counselor. The first three served as president until their deaths, after which the successor's name was revealed in a kind of last will and testament. William Wallace Smith changed the pattern when in 1976 he named his ophthalmologist son, Dr. Wallace B. Smith, as "president designate." Two years later, the son succeeded the retiring seventy-eight-year-old father.

Joseph Smith, III, exercised great influence during his long tenure. He melded together the disparate and often conflicting "Scattered Saints." His missionary program, spearheaded by his brothers, picked up disaffected "Utah Mormons." He edited and published a periodical, *The True Latter Day Saints' Herald*, which has continued to the present as the official church organ.

The doctrine of scripture shaped during the administration of Joseph Smith, III, remains an RLDS hallmark. The RLDS Bible is distinctive: entitled *The Inspired Version*, it is based on the King James version and contains changes in particular passages made by Joseph Smith, Jr. The *Doctrine and Covenants* omitted some—but not all—teachings of Joseph Smith, Jr. Pronouncements subsequently made by Joseph Smith, III, and his successors as official, divine guidance to the church (usually procedural and personnel matters) and so received by the General Conferences, became part of a growing *Doctrine and Covenants* and are regarded as scripture. The *Book of Mormon* is essentially the same as that of the Utah Mormons.

Joseph Smith, III, while embracing most Mormon scripture and embodying the RLDS doctrine of a Smith-line presidency, was cool to much of Mormonism. He rejected polygamy not only as immoral and false doctrine, but also on the grounds that his father had had nothing to do with it. Brigham Young, he believed, was its probable author. His position became the official RLDS church position. By a similar historical-doctrinal process, the church dealt with many issues arising from its claim to be the "true" successor to early Mormonism. A combination of denial and rejection became a marker by which the RLDS people differentiated themselves from the LDS. (New historical accounts of early Mormon history appearing in the 1960s and thereafter began to persuade the RLDS leadership and many members of the error of denying Joseph Smith, Jr.'s, authorship and practice of the celestial-marriage doctrine.)

Among other Mormon beliefs and practices rejected by Joseph Smith, III, were the Adam-as-God and plurality-of-gods doctrines, the exclusion of blacks from priesthood, a political-territorial kingdom of God governed by an absolute theocracy, and a corollary policy of gathering all converts to that territory. Smith was ambivalent about secret temples and some of the rites performed in them, including baptism for the dead. His policy was to await divine guidance. Abstinence from alcohol, tobacco, coffee, and tea was not made an RLDS doctrine as it was in Utah; however, probably the majority of RLDS members have abstained.

What remained was a mix of Mormon-derived organization, devotion to the memory of the miraculous Mormon church founding, an idealized portrayal of the Prophet Joseph, and an understanding that the RLDS was a "righteous remnant" destined to "redeem the waste places of Zion," finally defined as Independence, Missouri. A last-days millennialism was shared with other restoration churches, notably the Churches of Christ (CAMPBELLITES), against whose elders the RLDS zealously contended. Congregational leadership was by local, spirit-directed lay elders, educated for their calling by personal experience within the sect. Sabbath worship was much like that of many small evangelical Protestant sects of the nineteenth-century American Midwest. A Pentecostal tendency developed in the church and emphasized the gifts of prophecy and healing.

Despite attempts by Joseph Smith, III, to discourage the Mormon practice of "gathering," or congregating in a center place or places, the RLDS members were not easily dissuaded. "Where is Zion to be?" and "When shall we go there?" were persistent questions. A few unbidden communal enterprises began, including one in Iowa centered at a town named "Lamoni," after a *Book of Mormon* king. Joseph Smith, III, moved to Lamoni in 1881 and established the church headquarters and publishing operations there. In 1895, the church founded Graceland College in Lamoni.

Frederick Madison Smith, president from 1914 to 1946, attempted to make many changes in the church. A well-educated intellectual, he moved church headquarters to Independence, Missouri, in 1920, where thousands of RLDS members had already gathered. In so doing, they braved the residual hatred Missourians had for Mormons, a hatred dating back to the Mormon War of the 1830s. But the RLDS were "not Mormon" and were determined to live the hatred down. The new president began to emphasize Independence as the "Center Place of Zionic witness." The church bought land and established communal farming operations. A large headquarters and conference building, the Auditorium was begun, as was a hospital. Training programs for the lay ministry were planned. The missionary program was expanded. Church administration was centralized. The president intended to modernize a church that was in many ways old-fashioned, rustic, fractious, and rooted in a naive, rural folk culture.

Trouble lay ahead. A faction of prominent elders and apostles objected to Fred M. Smith's use of presidential power, declared him a false prophet, and withdrew from the church in 1925. A few years later, the Great Depression struck. Income dropped, and most employees, including the missionary force, were let go. Through fiscal austerity, the church retired a two million dollar debt in 1942. Despite difficulties, membership grew from 74,000 at the time of Fred M. Smith's anointing to 133,000 at his death.

Recovery and prosperity were apparent during the tenure of Israel Alexander Smith, president from 1946 to 1958. A well-respected attorney, he was seventy-one years of age at his anointing. His style was courtly and mild-tempered. He established "diplomatic relations" with the LDS church presidency after a century of hostility. The Auditorium moved toward completion (it was finished in 1962), financial reserves were built, and health- and social-service institutions were expanded. Israel A. Smith presided over a post–World War II generation of church members who were better educated, more affluent, more cosmopolitan, and more critical-minded than their elders.

William Wallace Smith, president from 1958 to 1978, presided over revolutionary changes. He planted the church in more than twenty countries in Africa, Asia, and Latin America. Some converts were polygamous, a practice abhorrent to the RLDS. Painful accommodation to that and similar issues posed by the fellowship of non-Western peoples changed the church, especially its self-definition. New theological winds blew through the church.

In the administrations of all the presidents except perhaps Frederick M. Smith, presidential policies did not diverge widely from a mainstream of member opinion. The traditional conservatism was tested in the administration of Wallace B. Smith, who in 1986 promulgated the ordination of women to the priesthood. The male RLDS priesthood was profoundly patriarchal. Controversy erupted, the most serious since 1925, and numerous small schisms ensued, often of whole branches. However, the church survived the schisms and was invigorated by the controversy.

Equally dramatic was Wallace B. Smith's revelation to build a temple in Independence, as prophesied by Joseph Smith, Jr., in 1831. Unlike Mormon temples, it is open to visitors. The church's multinational character is emphasized. "Temple ministries" include peace and reconciliation, "wholeness of body, mind, and spirit," and Christian education. In the words of the revelation, the temple expresses the "essential meaning of the church as healing and redeeming agent, inspired by the life and witness of the Redeemer of the World."

The RLDS Church approached the twenty-first century with a gender-inclusive lay priesthood and an open temple committed to peace and reconciliation. Could the denomination successfully trade its historic "truth ethic" for a "peace ethic"? The church historian, Richard P. Howard, wrote, "The RLDS Church seems intent on shedding many of the vestiges of its sectarian background of early Mormonism. To what extent it can discard these while retaining its identity as a recognizable part of Latter Day Saintism remains to be seen."

—*Robert Flanders*

SEE ALSO: Polygamy: Polygamy among Mormons

SUGGESTED READING:

Blair, Alma R. "The Tradition of Dissent—Jason W. Briggs." In *Restoration Studies I*. Independence, Mo., 1980.

Hidgon, Barbara. "The Reorganization in the Twentieth Century." *Dialogue: A Journal of Mormon Thought* 7 (Spring 1972): 94–100.

Howard, Richard P. *The Church through the Years, Volume II, The Reorganization Comes of Age*. Independence, Mo., 1993.

———. "Reorganized Church of Jesus Christ of Latter Day Saints (RLDS Church)." In *Encyclopedia of Mormonism*. Edited by Daniel H. Ludlow. New York, 1992.

Launius, Roger D. *Joseph Smith III: Pragmatic Prophet*. Chicago, 1988.

McMurray, W. Grant. "True Son of a True Father: Joseph Smith III and the Succession Question." In *Restoration Studies I*. Independence, Mo., 1980.

Newell, Linda King, and Valeen Tippets Avery. *Mormon Enigma: Emma Hale Smith: Prophet's Wife, "Elect Lady," Polygamy's Foe, 1804–1879*. New York, 1984.

Vlahos, Clare D. "Images of Orthodoxy: Self-Identity in Early Reorganization Apologetics." In *Restoration Studies I*. Independence, Mo., 1980.

CÍBOLA, SEVEN CITIES OF

The Seven Cities of Cíbola—also called the Seven Cities of Gold—had basis in fact, rumor, imagination, and greed. Early sixteenth-century Spanish conquistadors heard, cultivated, and embellished rumors that Zuni Indian villages in present-day New Mexico possessed great wealth. ÁLVAR NÚÑEZ CABEZA DE VACA, who had survived the calamitous 1520 expedition of PÁNFILO DE NARVÁEZ, brought back tales of rich pueblos—though he never claimed actually to have visited them in the course of his eight-year sojourn in the Southwest. Another survivor of the Narváez expedition, a black slave called Esteban, was part of FRAY MARCOS DE NIZA's 1539 expedition to locate the Seven Cities. Zunis killed the unfortunate Esteban at Hawikuh pueblo, but Marcos returned to Mexico City and gave a vivid account of the pueblo and its treasures—although he had failed to gain entry into Hawikuh. FRANCISCO VÁSQUEZ DE CORONADO mounted a bigger expedition to Hawikuh in 1540 and captured the pueblo only to find that neither it nor the other Zuni villages he entered contained treasure, gold, or jewels.

—*Alan Axelrod*

SEE ALSO: Exploration: Spanish Expeditions

SUGGESTED READING:
Clissold, Stephen. *The Seven Cities of Cíbola.* New York, 1961.

CITIES

SEE: Urban West

CITY GOVERNMENT

In the second half of the nineteenth century, the United States experienced a massive growth in its cities. The trans-Mississippi West, while it contained many fewer large cities than the East, also saw its urban areas expand rapidly as the region was industrialized. The combination of new wealth and new people left the towns and cities of the West as open to chaos and corruption as any Eastern metropolis. There were political bosses in SAN FRANCISCO before the Civil War, just as there were in New York. After the Civil War, with the expansion of the railroad and the growth of major extractive enterprises, increasingly widespread corruption and a rise in machine politics struck ST. LOUIS and KANSAS CITY and DENVER just as they did Boston and New York and Philadelphia.

If anything, the municipal governments in the West were weaker than those in the East since Western cities were often hastily platted and promoted without much thought to their charters or civic functions, and they were frequently subject to interference from territorial or state legislatures and even the FEDERAL GOVERNMENT. Already accustomed to wide-open atmospheres, where GAMBLING, drinking, and PROSTITUTION were commonplace, Western cities made good breeding grounds for the corrupt combination of business owners and politicians that accompanied the growing demand for expanded utilities—water, gas, transportation, electricity—and construction of public buildings, sewage systems, docks, streets, and sidewalks. The opportunities for boodle from new contracts, franchises, monopolies, subsidies, and privileges to be granted by municipalities were obvious in a region whose growth rested on the coming of the railroad and the private incorporation of huge tracts of public land and vast natural resources. Only it was the city "machines," not the federal or state governments, that now let these contracts, awarded these franchises, allowed these monopolies, made these subsidies, and granted these privileges.

Political bosses ran the city machines that, for a vote come election time, offered the cities' urban poor, ethnic immigrants, and working men and families food when they were hungry, rent and clothing when they were down and out, legal help when they were in trouble, entertainment to cheer them up, cold beer to help them forget their troubles, and, now and then, a job to get them on their feet. As a result, the machines controlled enough votes to keep their candidates in office, and thus they could provide businessmen with the lucrative city contracts they desired and, on occasion, could prevent the labor strife they feared. In St. Louis in the late nineteenth century, it was "Colonel" Edward Butler, a blacksmith become political mechanic, who put together an outfit called the Combine. In Kansas City, JAMES PENDERGAST, a lucky Irish saloon-keeper, built a machine that he turned over to his brother THOMAS J. PENDERGAST, who would run the town into the 1930s. In San Francisco, there were a succession of Irish bosses, beginning with DAVID C. BRODERICK, but by the end of the century, the machine would be controlled by ABRAHAM (ABE) RUEF.

The Anglo-Protestant, tax-paying middle class viewed with suspicion the rise of these political organizations and their bosses who sought votes from apparently uneducated and ill-bred foreigners and padded city payrolls with newcomers from Europe. The middle class was alarmed by the rising taxes and growing municipal debt, which went to pay private companies who bribed city officials to award franchises for operating trollies, providing water, or producing electricity, only to cut costs and offer inferior service once the franchise was in hand. The middle class was disturbed by the way city business was run and political deals were struck in SALOONS and political clubs and the back rooms of gambling dens. By the 1890s, a "good government" movement had broken out in the West, spearheaded by middle- and upper-class reformers who called for municipal ownership of utilities, changes in the structure of city government to limit the influence of political bosses, and the shutting down of saloons, gambling dens, and houses of prostitution. The "good government" movement was the first wave of Progressive reform to sweep through the West, and largely because of its successes at the municipal level, PROGRESSIVISM would go on to reshape national politics and introduce nationwide Prohibition.

In San Francisco, Progressive reformer JAMES DUVAL PHELAN was elected the Democratic mayor after putting together a coalition of merchants, middle-class residents, and unionized workers with promises of the benefits they would all receive from expanding the public sector. In 1900, after GALVESTON, TEXAS, was ravaged by a hurricane and tidal wave that killed some six thousand people, the city introduced the "city commission" form of government, and soon the idea spread around the country as cities dumped mayors and their councils in exchange for small boards of commissioners, each elected at large, each responsible for a different area of city government. The at-large elections undercut the influence of the neighborhood politicians controlled by the urban political machines and made officeholders who failed to do their jobs easy to identify. If the sewers backed up, voters knew to blame the public-works commissioner, and when the city treasury suddenly became mysteriously short of funds, they looked to the public-finance commissioner for explanations. The accountability of the system, however, came at the cost of overall direction and coordinated action. In response, some reformers advocated a city-manager scheme under which an elected council appointed a professional manager to run the city's day-to-day operations while council members set general policies. In both cases, advocates of good government sought first and foremost businesslike efficiency in city government.

As the century turned, the pace of reform increased, and Progressives began to rack up victories across the West. In 1902, JOSEPH LINCOLN STEFFENS attacked St. Louis as the one of the country's most corrupt cities in *McClure's Magazine* and made a hero of the city's young lawyer, Joseph W. Folk, who, as circuit attorney, launched an investigation that led to the downfall of Boss Butler and collapse of the Combine. St. Louis went on to become the star of Lincoln Steffens's book, *Shame of the Cities,* and Folk, Missouri's first Progressive governor. In Seattle, advocates of good government, led by R. H. Thomson and GEORGE COTTERILL, managed to secure a municipal water system in 1900 and, after a long battle with Seattle Electric, its first municipal power plant in 1902. After Cotterill's attack on the franchise system finally landed him the mayor's job in 1912, Thomson—as the city's engineer—ultimately succeeded in creating a municipal power system. In San Francisco, an alliance including journalist Fremont Older and millionaire Rudolph Spreckels (with help from Los Angeles's "good government" movement and from THEODORE ROOSEVELT's federal government) deposed a corrupt mayor, Eugene Schmitz, and sent machine boss Abe Ruef to prison in 1906.

Not all the Progressive campaigns for good city government succeeded in the West. Some ended in compromise, some in outright defeat, and some in new abuses of power. Denver's aggressive reform coalition, including wealthy activist JOSEPHINE ASPINWALL ROCHE and two men who later became nationally prominent, Judge BENJAMIN BARR LINDSEY and George Creel, proposed a new city charter that called for municipal ownership of utilities, restricted saloons, banned gambling, and included the police and fire departments under the civil-service system. They were defeated by another coalition aimed at stopping the new charter and led by ROBERT WALTER SPEER, who—although he expanded the sewer and street system and even brought in a city planner to create new boulevards and parks—sought to regulate rather than take over utilities.

Denver and WICHITA, KANSAS, spearheaded the compromise that encouraged cities to consolidate smaller companies and transform the franchise system into one of regulated public utilities with such names as Denver Gas and Electric and Kansas Gas and Electric Company. Soon such municipalities as DALLAS, Oklahoma City, and LOS ANGELES had followed suit. Such consolidations, however, could create monsters far more powerful than the old franchise-holders, such as San Francisco's gigantic Pacific Gas and Electric Company (PG & E), which became the largest utility on the West Coast. In other Western cities, private corporations consolidated utilities but held on to these critical pieces of the urban infrastructure, and they made fortunes. Men such as Los Angeles's HENRY EDWARDS HUNTINGTON (nephew of the Southern Pacific's COLLIS P. HUNTINGTON), who controlled the city's trolley lines under a franchise, used consolidation to combine his railway company with utilities and land purchases and created a transportation and real-estate empire. The Los Angeles interurban, which Huntington controlled and—as a typical franchise owner—kept in poor repair, connected his land holdings in Venice, San Marino, and Huntington Beach to the city. He then developed this real estate, and once the new communities were part of the spreading Los Angeles complex, his utility companies supplied them with gas and light.

By the 1920s, the "good government" movement had spent much of its initial energy. One of the country's best known advocates of city reform was the owner of the *Kansas City Star,* WILLIAM ROCKHILL NELSON, who for decades had fought the growing influence of the Pendergast machine. In 1925, the city introduced a reform charter establishing the city-manager system, which, much to the reformers' surprise, Tom Pendergast had supported. But Pendergast managed to control enough council-seat elections to have his own man, Henry F. McElroy, appointed city manager, and McElroy, in turn, hired a very agreeable police chief. Pendergast took over the entire city council, and the town stayed wide-open, much to the delight of the chamber of commerce, hotel owners, and many small businessmen. National magazines and Eastern newspapers ran features on Pendergast and Kansas City's Prohibition-era night life, which went on around the clock in gangster-owned nightspots like the Sunset Club, the Reno Club, and the Subway Club, all protected by the police for a cut of the action. At election time, a few never-say-die reformers complained about the corruption and the illicit goings on, but the chamber of commerce merely pointed to the U.S. Department of Justice's statistics, which gave Kansas City the lowest crime rate in any city of its class. Comparing his city to Al Capone's Chicago, Tom Pendergast boasted: "Ours is a fine, clean, well-ordered town."

Thus, despite some successes in the West, the "good government" movement never managed to dislodge the machines entirely or to do away with urban corruption. Partly this had to do with demographics and the city's immigrant populations, partly with the fact that by imposing national Prohibition the Progressives had overplayed their hand and alienated some of their middle- and upper-class support while providing machines with a whole new source of income from illicit liquor sales. On the other hand, municipal ownership of utilities had become widespread, and the notion that it was a function of city government to provide decent basic services efficiently and at reasonable rates had taken root. Voters generally had a new benchmark by which to judge city governments regardless of who controlled their politics.

—*Charles Phillips*

SEE ALSO: Cattle Towns; Temperance and Prohibition; Urban West

SUGGESTED READING:

Ethington, Philip J. *The Public City: The Political Construction of Urban Life in San Francisco, 1850–1900.* New York, 1994.

Hughes, Thomas. *Networks of Power: Electrification in Western Society, 1880–1930.* Baltimore, 1983.

McDonald, Terrence J. *The Parameters of Urban Fiscal Policy: Socioeconomic Changes and Political Culture in San Francisco, 1860–1906.* Berkeley, Calif., 1986.

Teagarden, Jon C. *Unheralded Triumph: City Government in America, 1870–1900.* New York, 1984.

Wade, Richard C. *The Urban Frontier: The Rise of the Western City, 1790–1830.* Cambridge, Mass., 1959.

CITY PLANNING

In a sense, all the cities in the trans-Mississippi West were planned. Contemporaries made decisions to establish towns at given spots and made provisions to use the land in certain ways and to distribute it to owners and residents. Certainly, these cities did not come about, as FREDERICK JACKSON TURNER once held, by the arrival first of trail-blazing frontiersmen, then of pioneering farmers, and finally of merchants, lawyers, and tradesmen; in most cases the establishment

A deserted railroad town in Kansas. *Editors' collection.*

of Western cities came before outlying settlement of any size developed or at least occurred simultaneously with such settlement. The early Southwestern cities, for example, grew from carefully planned communities, Spanish missions, villages, or forts intended to secure and protect the far reaches of Spain's North American empire. Anglo-American cities were, from the start, the domain of boosters and speculators, who drew up town plans, filed them in county courthouses, and envisioned great cities that would attract large populations, push up property values, and make them lots of money. Their reasons for planning a city in one spot as opposed to another varied, but all of them recognized that cities came first and outlying settlement later when it could be supported by urban growth. City founders invariably laid out their towns on the characteristic American gridiron pattern of streets crisscrossing at right angles interrupted occasionally by an open square. Cities so planned became, as American cities had always been, primarily containers for business and served as centers for the conduct of economic activities. They were never imagined as beautiful places to inhabit, and few Westerners ever considered the possibility that a city might enrich the lives of its denizens in any but a commercial sense.

City founders located Western towns at a given place because gold (or silver, or copper, or lead) had been discovered nearby, or because an already existing Spanish or Mexican town had grown as a center of trade, or because the railroad had designated the spot for a while as the end of its line, or because the federal government had just thrown cheap land in the area open for settlement. Merchants, boosters, and real-estate agents cooperated with local political leaders—

A view of F Street in Denver, Colorado, in 1867. *Editors' collection.*

frequently they were the local political leaders—to plan how they would attract people to the newly platted land they had divided among themselves and how to do so against rival groups who had established similar towns. None of them, however, planned how to manage the growth they solicited, which, when it came at all, frequently came quite quickly indeed. Sometimes when the reason for planning the city disappeared—when the gold or silver ran out or the railroad moved on—this lack of planning caused the city to fall into rapid decline or disappear altogether, but more often, the typical result was cities whose streets were too narrow and unpaved, whose public services were few and poorly managed, and whose buildings were ramshackle and fire hazards.

CHEYENNE, Laramie, and Benton, Wyoming; RENO, NEVADA; and North Platte, Nebraska, all got rude starts as makeshift terminal depots on the transcontinental railroad. DENVER, even as late 1900, had eight hundred miles of roads, but only some twenty-four miles of paved surface. ST. LOUIS, SAN FRANCISCO, and SEATTLE were crammed between steep hills and expanses of water, and fire was a constant worry; the first two burned to the ground more than once in the nineteenth century. Most Western cities lacked the open spaces,

water, sewers, transportation, and health facilities they needed for the future growth they so desperately wanted. Unable to absorb the growth they did attract, they constantly feared being left behind by those they perceived as rivals. By 1890, both St. Louis and CHICAGO claimed to be the "gateway to the West," and St. Louis's civic hatred of Chicago at times seemed pathological. Around the same time, PORTLAND, a rare and well-built beauty of a Western city, fretted that Seattle, thriving as the supply depot of the ALASKA GOLD RUSH, would take its place as the "queen of the Pacific Northwest." By then, too, San Francisco was already casting nervous glances southward toward LOS ANGELES. Besieged by rapid population growth, by growing evidence of urban problems, and by intense competition, cities began, late in the nineteenth century, to flirt with more careful planning.

The "city beautiful" movement, tied to Progressive reforms and to the development of new professions in sanitation, public health, landscape architecture, and city planning, was a nationwide movement advocating attractive cities that were enjoyable to live in and which functioned well by integrating people, traffic, and goods. Such plans commissioned by Western cities usually came from Eastern city planners and landscape architects such as DANIEL HUDSON BURNHAM, EDWARD HERBERT BENNETT, and FREDERICK LAW OLMSTED. Olmsted drew a boulevard and park system up for Seattle in 1903. For San Francisco in 1905, Burnham drew up a plan that included a comprehensive system of parks and bold new streets aimed at moving traffic quickly, dividing the town into coherent districts, and creating beautiful public spaces. Bennett produced a similar plan for Portland in 1911. For the most part, however, such plans never made the transition from paper to reality. Western cities found that, although they could imagine beautiful new cities, they could not afford them. Even after the SAN FRANCISCO EARTHQUAKE OF 1906 destroyed the city on April 18 and seemed to offer the perfect opportunity to use Burnham's plans for its rebuilding, city leaders and residents built a new San Francisco resembling as closely as possible the old San Francisco and took pride in the accomplishment.

In the long run, Western cities continued to develop on the standard gridiron patterns of their founding, growing out in space rather than upward as Eastern cities did. In time, such development became something of an ideal, with city officials arguing that the wide-open spaces afforded to cities in the West allowed low-density growth that avoided the congestion of London or New York. Los Angeles, with its urban sprawl first along railway then along highway lines, became the quintessential model for the West's modern cities, and it was copied by such Southwestern cities as PHOENIX, SAN DIEGO, ALBUQUERQUE, and HOUSTON, which continued to annex outlying tracts in order to grow overland. Such low-density, lateral expansion also characterized many of the new types of planned communities that the West pioneered in modern-day America: the first industrial park was developed as an environment of the future by Stanford University for an exhibit at the 1958 Brussels World's Fair; Sun City, Arizona, produced a comprehensive retirement community, yoking together words that to earlier generations would have been an oxymoron: *active retirement.* Disneyland gave America the world's original theme park in 1955, where culture, history, and entertainment were as carefully planned as the built environment in which they were presented. The Las Vegas Strip, too, which at first blush would seem the antithesis of planning, owed its creation to the Western city's desire to "spread widely rather than reach high," a plan for controlled chaos that postmodern architects such as Robert Venturi, Denise Scott Brown, and Steven Izenour have praised as "vital" in contrast to "the deadness . . . of present-day modern architecture" with its "too great a preoccupation with tastefulness and total design." In many ways, the Las Vegas Strip is the perfect grandchild of Western cities, a stretch of land that

is completely dedicated to commercial ventures, is planned for endless growth, and allows virtually no room for permanent residency.

—*Charles Phillips*

SEE ALSO: Architecture: Urban Architecture; Progressivism; Spanish and Mexican Towns; Urban West

SUGGESTED READING:
Abbott, Carl. *The Metropolitan Frontier: Cities in the Modern American West.* Tuscon, Ariz., 1993.
Banham, Ryener. *Los Angeles: The Architecture of Four Ecologies.* Middlesex, England, 1971.
Barth, Gunther. *Instant Cities: Urbanization and the Rise of San Francisco and Denver.* New York, 1965.
Jackson, Kenneth T. *Crabgrass Frontier: The Suburbanization of the United States.* New York, 1986.
Reps, John W. *Cities of the American West: A History of Frontier Urban Planning.* Princeton, N.J., 1969
———. *The Forgotten Frontier: Urban Planning in the American West before 1890.* Columbia, Mo., 1981.

CIVIL WAR

The Civil War in the American West was not the same epic struggle that raged east of the Mississippi. No great cities were lost or won, and no decisive strategic ends were achieved. Men fought and men died—a great many of them Indians. In some places, most notably the Far Southwest, withdrawal of federal troops to other battlegrounds gave Indians license to raid; but in many other areas, residents took advantage of unsettled local conditions to settle old scores or to launch new attacks on Indians. These skirmishes led to NAVAJO WARS and APACHE WARS that distracted Union forces in the West. Arkansas and Texas would join the Confederacy, but the rest of the trans-Mississippi West remained in the Union. Kansas and Missouri had experienced a prelude to the war following the passage of the KANSAS-NEBRASKA ACT and the violence that broke out in what became known as "Bleeding Kansas." For the most part, the warfare along the Kansas-Missouri border had abated by 1860. But on both sides of the line there were those who had not forgotten the destruction of the late 1850s, those who longed for revenge, and those who sought, in the new outbreak of hostilities, an excuse to resume the midnight raids, the bushwhacking, and the reign of terror. Because Missouri never seceded from the Union, it escaped the harshest aspects of the military occupation visited on the South after the war during Reconstruction. But because of its lawless past and the deep-seated hatreds of its divided population, it spent most of the war under martial law and witnessed within its own borders a struggle harsher than Reconstruction ever could have been. For that reason, the Civil War was more destructive in loyal Missouri than in most of the states—except Virginia and Tennessee—that actually joined the rebellion, and the scars were long in healing.

Missouri

After South Carolina fired on Fort Sumter in 1861, Missouri's pro-Southern governor, Claiborne Fox Jackson, called a convention to debate the possibility of secession. Owing mainly to the efforts of a conservative St. Louis attorney and former Missouri Supreme Court justice named Hamilton R. Gamble, the convention refused to pass a resolution to secede, and two armed camps quickly appeared in St. Louis. Street fighting broke out and resulted in twenty-eight deaths. The Unionists, supported by the state's large German population, lined up behind Francis Blair, a close friend and confidant of Abraham Lincoln, who had been authorized by the president to go to St. Louis and organize a pro-Union Home Guard, and Captain Nathaniel Lyon, a little fiery-headed former New Englander and veteran of the 1850's border war, who trusted almost no one in Missouri but Blair. Southern sympathizers organized military forces—the Missouri Guard—that Governor Jackson placed under the direction of STERLING PRICE, a veteran of the United States–Mexican War and himself a former Missouri governor. Bowing to the "Western" thinking of Missouri's moderates, who still hoped to avoid conflict, Lyon and Blair met with Jackson and Price at the Planter's House in St. Louis on June 11, 1861, to discuss the growing tension in the state. The meeting degenerated into an exchange of threats as both sides held firm and vowed to take up arms. Afterward, Jackson and Price fled St. Louis by rail to Jefferson City, Missouri's capital, literally burning their bridges—those across the Gasconde and Osage rivers—behind them. Once there, Jackson called out fifty thousand state troops to "repel the invasion" of Union forces under Lyon and abandoned the capital. Before the day had passed, Lyon was in hot pursuit. Against the will of the vast majority of the voters, hostilities were under way in earnest. Nine months, a few significant skirmishes, and a couple of major engagements later, the Civil War was over—strategically—in the American West.

Finding Jefferson City deserted, Lyon struck northwest and caught up with Jackson's State Guard a few days later on June 17, 1861, at Boonville. Price was ill, so Jackson took command of the ill-trained Rebel troops himself. Their field commander, understanding the predicament, refused to lead them into battle, but Jackson ordered them into a reckless headlong charge, which Lyon easily routed. Jackson ran, Lyon became an instant hero, and Hamilton Gamble was appointed the new governor of Missouri. But the little general's glory was short-lived. Sterling Price's plan had been to lead the militia toward the Arkansas border, where he could join forces with the regular Confederate Army, raising volunteers as he went. From Jefferson City, Lyon detached the Home Guards under Colonel Franz Siegal to cut off the retreating Confederate irregulars. By the time Siegal came face to face with Price at Carthage, Missouri, on July 7, he was outnumbered four to one. When he charged anyway, Price brushed him aside and continued on his way. Meanwhile, Lyon was facing political problems, and President Lincoln placed him under a new commander, JOHN CHARLES FRÉMONT, the Western adventurer familiar to Missourians as the son-in-law of the great, now deceased, former U.S. senator, THOMAS HART BENTON.

While Frémont dallied in St. Louis, Lyon in the field had to deal with Sterling Price, who was determined to gain control of the Missouri River and free the state from federal captivity. Price's confidence soared when he defeated Lyon at Wilson's Creek near Springfield on August 10, 1861. Lyon had desperately urged Frémont to send reinforcements, but Frémont instead ordered him to avoid the fight. With little love lost between the two Union officers, Lyon chose to ignore Frémont's orders, lost the battle, and died in the effort. Frémont, like many Northern commanders at the time, had been busy politicking, wrangling with Gamble, angering Missourians, and irritating the president. Declaring martial law, Frémont also proclaimed the emancipation of Missouri's slaves (something Lincoln would avoid for another three years) and began confiscating property of Southern sympathizers—actions that only encouraged the growing guerrilla warfare between Missourians. As a result, by the time Frémont finally decided to engage the enemy, Price was ready. Price's subsequent victory at Lexington on September 13 cost the blustering and militarily inept Frémont his perhaps undeserved reputation, and he was transferred from his short-lived command in the West to a short-lived command in West Virginia.

But radicals such as Blair and Lyon, on one side, and Jackson and Price on the other, had always been at least a jump ahead of most Missourians, and when Jackson followed his victories with a general call to arms, few recruits appeared to rally to his cause. The call came after the pro-Southern members of the legislature had met in October in Neosho and, in the absence of a quorum, finally passed an act of secession. Although Missouri was immediately accepted into the Confederacy, Jefferson Davis was suspicious of Price because of his former relationship with the Yankee

General WILLIAM SELBY HARNEY and possibly because of reservations conveyed to him via Claiborne Jackson. Davis was reluctant to commit troops to help. Meanwhile, Union General Henry Halleck, who had replaced Frémont, ordered Brigadier Samuel R. Curtis to drive the Confederates out of the state. When Curtis launched his offensive in February 1862, Price—without CSA support—had no choice but to move south into Arkansas where his forces were soundly defeated at the Battle of Pea Ridge on March 7 and 8, 1862.

Price was transferred east of the Mississippi, and Jackson's rump government went into exile, first in Arkansas and then in Texas, by which time Jackson had died and been replaced by his lieutenant-governor. After Pea Ridge, the Civil War in Missouri degenerated into the vengeful marauding of red-legged JAYHAWKERS and irregular GUERRILLAS. But it was no less bloody and brutal for that. The first attacks had come in the summer of 1861. JOHN BROWN was dead, but his spirit lived on in the crew of Kansas irregulars led by such men as James Montgomery, JAMES HENRY LANE, and Dr. Charles Jennison. Acting loosely as an advance guard of the Union army, a band under "Doc" Jennison sacked Harrisonville in July. Since there were no Confederate troops anywhere near the town, western Missourians understood the terror of the 1850s had returned. At the outbreak of war, Jennison's Independent Mounted Kansas Jayhawkers were commissioned as the Seventh Kansas Cavalry, and in the fall of 1861, they invaded Jackson County. The troops occupied the county seat and then sacked and looted at will. They murdered all those they suspected of being Southern sympathizers and anyone else who dared to protest their actions or disobey their orders. On September 23, Sterling Price chased Lane back into Kansas, but the Jayhawkers returned the minute Price moved his major forces to Lexington. Red Legs swept into the wealthy port of Osceola, stole some $1 million worth of goods, and burned the city to the ground. Next they ravished Butler and then Parkville.

Perhaps not surprisingly, when a handsome, twenty-four-year-old named WILLIAM CLARKE QUANTRILL gathered around him a few Missouri boys and struck back, he was seen at first as a savior not just by the state's slave owners and Southern sympathizers, but by the entire sullen, silent, and abused population. Quantrill's slight build, his boyish wavy hair, and his heavy-lidded pale eyes belied his ruthlessness. The son of a schoolmaster, and a former schoolmaster himself, Quantrill had moved to Lawrence, Kansas, at the height of the border war, joined in several raids on Missouri, and even freed a few slaves. Now, he changed sides and led his band against Doc Jennison's raiders in mid-December as they looted a farm house in Jackson

County. Soon Quantrill was Missouri's most notorious bushwhacker, for which he received a commission as a captain in the Confederate Army. Quantrill was recruited by Major General Thomas C. Hindman, commanding the CSA's District of Arkansas, under the Confederate Partisan Ranger Act of April 21, 1862. In addition to Quantrill, Hindman commissioned at least a dozen other Missouri officers early that summer to return to their respective areas and recruit both Confederate regulars and guerrillas who could be left behind.

Men such as WILLIAM C. ("BLOODY BILL") ANDERSON, George Todd, and Cole Younger joined Quantrill to wreak havoc on the Kansas border patrols and Missouri's Union militia. In March of that year, Quantrill's Raiders sacked Aubrey, Kansas, and in October, they hit Olathe. Shooting settlers "like so many hogs," Quantrill and his men proved to be enemies entirely worthy of Jim Lane or Doc Jennison. It was under Quantrill's tutelage that the JAMES BROTHERS and the YOUNGER BROTHERS learned the art of ambush and of handling the Colt revolvers that were the Raiders' weapons of choice. They also learned a code of killing that knew no moral boundaries, as Quantrill stopped at nothing to accomplish his objective, including wearing captured federal uniforms to surprise the enemy. At Baxter Springs, Kansas, sixty-five of a troop of one hundred federals were slain when Quantrill and his men approached them in Union blue. (Quantrill himself would be killed on May 10, 1865, by Union guerrillas as he traveled through Kentucky, reportedly on his way to Washington, D. C., where he planned to assassinate President Lincoln.)

As the deprivations mounted on both sides, Union General John Schofield, replacing Henry Halleck and charged with pacifying the Missouri countryside, mulled over a plan by his subordinate, General Thomas Ewing. Ewing's job was to guard the long boundary between Kansas and Missouri, and he had grown to distrust entirely the citizens he was bound to protect. He proposed to Schofield that they try to control the guerrillas by mass evacuation, removing everyone known to have aided or abetted the guerilla cause. Although reluctant, Schofield approved the plan on August 14, 1862, with the provision that the evacuation be limited to the smallest number of people possible. Ewing had already rounded up the wives, mothers, and sisters of suspected guerrillas and jailed them in a decrepit three-story brick building in Kansas City. The same day Schofield approved his evacuation plan, the makeshift prison collapsed from overloading. Several of the women were severely injured, and five were killed, among them the sister of "Bloody Bill" Anderson, one of Quantrill's most effective guerrilla leaders. Immediately, the rumor spread that Ewing had engineered the outrage from the start.

With 450 men, Quantrill took his revenge on Lawrence, Kansas. Riding all night, the raiders hit the town at dawn with Quantrill's order to "kill every man big enough to carry a gun" ringing in their ears. They did. Moving from house to house, they murdered 150 men, often deliberately in front of their wives and children. Eighty widows and 250 orphans fled into the streets as Quantrill's men set more than 185 buildings ablaze. While $2 million worth of property burned to the ground, Quantrill sat in the dining room of a Lawrence hotel, enjoying his breakfast and complaining that Jim Lane had escaped a Missouri hanging when he sprang from his bed in a nightshirt and hightailed off into the nearby cornfields. As suddenly as they had appeared, the guerrillas vanished. They lost only one man, a drunk who had lingered long enough to be gunned down by an Indian. A bereaved mob dragged his dead body into the street and tore it to pieces—which is what everybody in Kansas—and, shortly thereafter, in the rest of the nation—wanted to do with Quantrill once the news had spread. Since Quantrill was unavailable, Jim Lane turned on those who were. He blamed Schofield. He blamed Governor Gamble. He blamed the people of Missouri. They were too lax, or too softhearted, or too treasonous, he said. Soon the radical press picked up Lane's complaint and lay the responsibility at the feet of Governor Gamble. The *Missouri Democrat* even charged him with personally supporting Quantrill.

Schofield rushed to the border to take charge of the situation, but he was too late. Without waiting for his commander, Ewing instituted a general evacuation policy, one much harsher than Schofield had authorized. Vindictively placing Lane in command of the evacuation, Ewing proclaimed General Order Number 11, perhaps the most controversial of the war. The edict ordered everyone in Jackson, Cass, Bates, and the northern half of Vernon counties, who lived one mile's distance from a Union military post, to leave their homes within fifteen days. Those who could prove their loyalty might remain in a post in the area. All other people would be forced to move completely out of the military district. The order also required them to take all grain and hay from their farms to the nearest military post. Their other crops and perishable goods would be destroyed.

Doc Jennison and his hated Kansas cavalry went to work enforcing the order. Ruthlessly driving farmers off their homesteads, Jennison forced many to leave without adequate clothing or transportation. The Kansas troops stole whatever furniture, household goods, and livestock the farmers left behind. Everything else

the troops put to the torch. For one hundred miles around, the wind swept the fires across the prairie and left in their wake only smoke-stained chimneys, blackened stumps, and the scorched earth. Within two weeks, much of the border area lay in ruins. For decades afterward, it was referred to acidly as the "Burnt District." By mid-September, five thousand refugees a week were crossing the Missouri River at Lexington. Of the ten thousand people who lived in Cass County when the war began, only six hundred remained. Bates County was hit even harder.

Union generals, whether battling Price's forces early in the war or hunting down guerrillas thereafter, were notoriously lax with their men, often allowing them unlicensed and indiscriminate raiding and pillaging. Like Major General JOHN POPE, who patrolled northern Missouri, they would move into an area, set up committees of public safety in each county, and fully expect them to call out their citizenry as militia when trouble started. When the communities failed to respond, the Union commander automatically assumed the failure was due to Rebel sympathies. The county would be occupied by federal troops, and countywide levies would be placed on local resources to sustain them. If county officials could not meet the levies, the general simply ordered his troops to take what they needed, regardless of the owners' political leanings.

While he was still alive, Governor Gamble protested the abuses visited on Missouri civilians, and when he was still in command, General Halleck acknowledged the justness of Gamble's protest. Schofield, too, had made a real effort to curb excesses, but the truth was that maintaining order in a bitterly divided society during the middle of a civil war was no easy task. Honest differences of opinion, which might have once caused little more than a heated debate, now led almost inevitably to bloodshed. For example, even after the Union Army began relying more heavily on the state militia, commanders found that militiamen often used their new power to settle old grudges, political or otherwise. And sensitivity to the rights of citizens is not the long suit of military men facing a hostile civilian population under conditions of civil war and martial law.

In the countryside, the abuses grew increasingly worse. Now a guerrilla, now a militiaman, now an army regular might show up at a farm with varying demands. None of them considered property sacrosanct any longer, and to say life was cheap would be an understatement. As pillage and assassination became commonplace, Missouri's refugee problem assumed major proportions. Because it was big and safe and well located, St. Louis turned into a mecca for the state's homeless masses. The first wave came in the winter of 1861 to 1862 from the southwest. Many died on the way in the bitter cold. Those who made it had often been robbed by various vigilante groups of the few possessions they managed to cart from the homes burning behind them. To care for these victims of the war, the women of St. Louis formed the Ladies Union Aid Society to establish a number of refuge homes supported by voluntary contributions and compulsory assessments on Southern sympathizers. When Lincoln suspended the latter because of the corruption associated with them, the federal government underwrote the costs of the homes. By then, houses like those in St. Louis had sprung up in Pilot Knob, Rolla, Springfield, and Cape Girardeau. Agents of the Western Sanitary Commission supervised them all. But by 1863, in the darkest of the war years, a vast number of Missourians had simply decided to pull up stakes and head farther West. By the thousands, they joined wagon trains leaving for California and points in between—anywhere, just out of Missouri.

In January 1864, Sterling Price, now something of a hero in the state, led one last invasion of Missouri. Accompanied by a colorful fellow Missourian, General Joseph O. Shelby, a cavalry leader who rode a Missouri mule, Price had sent orders to guerrilla leaders to attack north of the Missouri River in order to draw troops from St. Louis and the South. Once again the terror raged. "Bloody Bill" Anderson led the most effective of the bands, dashing here and there through central Missouri a step ahead of pursuing Union troops and militia. On September 27, Anderson and thirty of his men rode into Centralia on the North Missouri Railroad. As they bullied and tortured Centralia's citizens, robbed its homes, and looted its stores, the Columbia stage rolled into town. On board was Missouri Congressman James S. Rollins. They pulled him from the stage, stuck a gun under his nose, and then let him go after he pledged his love of the rebellion. Hiding in a nearby attic, Rollins could hear the noon whistle of a train coming from the east.

The raiders blocked the tracks with railroad ties and then hid from view till the train had stopped. They jerked helpless citizens from the cars and relieved them of their valuables. And then they came across twenty-five unarmed Union soldiers headed home to Iowa on furlough. Anderson lined them up on the station platform, demanded they strip off their uniforms, and asked any officers to please step forward. One, a Sergeant Thomas Goodman of the Missouri Engineers, defiantly did so. "Bloody Bill" Anderson laughed and ordered him to move aside. Then he turned to Little Archie Clemens, his second in command, whose pathological grin played permanently on his lips. "Muster out the troops," Anderson told him. The shots came at point-blank range, Clemens firing with a pistol in each hand, the others blasting away at will, murdering twenty-four Union soldiers. Guerrilla leader Cole Younger's fifteen-year-old cousin, Jesse James, already an icy-blooded killer, watched as Anderson told Goodman he was free to go on home and enjoy his furlough.

Price and Shelby reached Jackson County before they were defeated at Westport on October 23 in a three-day decisive battle, a kind of engagement rare in West's war history. The Centralia Massacre was much more typical, and therefore a more fitting end—a futile and senseless slaughter in a theater of the war that had not counted strategically to North or South for nearly three years. After Price recognized he was beaten and scurried south across the Arkansas border, the irregular Confederate bands began to break up. But robbery and murder had become a way of life for them, the only vocation a goodly number would ever know. Many of them teenagers when the war started, they had lost their innocence in the 1,162 battles or skirmishes fought on Missouri soil, 11 percent of all the engagements in the Civil War, the third highest number in the entire nation—a savage passage to manhood.

Texas and the Southwest

At the start, Texas, too, was a major problem for the North. Pro-Union governor SAM HOUSTON was forced out of office when the state seceded in February 1861, and General David E. Twiggs, federal commander of the army's Department of Texas, soon surrendered all property and supplies to the Confederates. Union forces enjoyed a temporary victory in October 1862 when a seaborne squadron captured Galveston. The town, a crucial Confederate supply point, was occupied by federal troops in December, but quickly retaken by Confederates aboard river boats that had been converted to gunboats. By 1863, the Union threw a blockade around Galveston, which reduced but did not stop the flow of Confederate supplies. Combined with Admiral David G. Farragut's capture of New Orleans in April 1862, however, the blockade ultimately helped sever Texas and the rest of the Confederate West from the Confederate states east of the Mississippi.

The outbreak of the Civil War wreaked havoc on the Union Army, especially its officer corps. In the West, 313 officers, one-third of the army's officer corps, left Western commands to take up arms for the Confederacy. "We were practically an army without officers," one Union soldier complained. Unionists in the West feared that the Confederates would actively cajole or purchase Indian allies in the struggle. In fact, the Confederacy did find some recruits among the Caddos, Wichitas, Osages, Shawnees, Delawares, Senecas, and

Harper's Weekly's January 31, 1863, issue reported on the *Rebel Attack upon the Forty-Third Massachusetts Volunteers at Galveston, Texas. Courtesy Patrick H. Butler, III.*

Quapaws. Both the North and the South recruited some troops from tribes who had been removed to the Indian Territory, including the Cherokees, Chickasaws, Choctaws, Creeks, and Seminoles. The Cherokee leader Stand Watie became a Confederate general of considerable tenacity; his command was the last Rebel unit to lay down arms, fully a month after Appomattox. It is also true that, for a time, the Confederates armed the Comanches and Kiowas on the Southern Plains. For the most part, however, Indian-white conflict during the period of 1861 to 1865 had little to do directly with the white man's war against himself, except that in the Far Southwest, the withdrawal of federal troops to fight elsewhere unleashed a torrent of Indian raids, and in many other places, the massed presence of troops provided sufficient excuse for local settlers to bring the war to the Indians. Many soldiers and settlers believed—or convinced themselves—that the Indians had sided with the Confederacy.

Early on in the Southwest, Confederate Lieutenant Colonel JOHN ROBERT BAYLOR took advantage of the Union's weakened position to sweep up from the Rio Grande into southern New Mexico Territory. Fort Bliss in El Paso fell to him in July 1861, and he marched into the Mesilla Valley of New Mexico and took Fort

Fillmore and Fort Stanton, whereupon Baylor grandiosely proclaimed the Confederate Territory of Arizona (which, in theory, included all of present-day Arizona and New Mexico south of the thirty-fourth parallel) and named himself governor.

Santa Fe was the headquarters of Union Colonel EDWARD RICHARD SPRING CANBY, commander of the Department of New Mexico. As the Texas invaders threatened, Canby had his hands full with Navajo raids in New Mexico and unauthorized, highly provocative New Mexican counterraids. Indeed, the very people he was trying to protect, the citizens of New Mexico, repeatedly provoked the Navajos by raiding and taking captives, who were subsequently sold as slaves. In retaliation, the Navajos (as well as Mescalero Apaches, Utes, Comanches, and Kiowas, for their own reasons) ravaged the countryside. Learning that the majority of New Mexicans were loyal to the Union, Canby hastily sought to organize them as the First and Second Regiments of New Mexican Volunteers. This gesture, however, failed to bring the volunteers under Canby's control.

One episode suggests something of the tenor of white-Indian relations during the war. Lieutenant Colonel Manuel Chaves, second in command of the Second Regiment, was placed in charge of Fort Lyon at Ojo del Oso on August 9 with a detachment of 210 officers and men. As the Canby Treaty of February 1861 had promised, Chaves's men began distributing rations, including liquor, to the Navajos in August and September. Along with the liquor, came gambling. A series of horse races were run, the featured event being a contest between Chief MANUELITO on a Navajo pony and an army lieutenant on a quarter horse. Many bets were laid. Early in the race it was apparent that Manuelito had lost control of his mount, which soon ran off the track. The horse's rein and bridle, the Indians claimed, had been slashed with a knife. Despite Indian protests, the "judges"—all soldiers of the Second New Mexican Regiment—declared the quarter horse the winner. The soldiers formed a victory parade into the fort, as the angered Navajos stormed after them, only to have the gates shut in their faces. One Navajo tried to force his way into the fort. A sentinel shot and killed him. Then Colonel Chaves turned his troops on the five hundred or so Navajos gathered outside the fort and opened fire. Thirty or forty Navajos were killed. The rest fled and began a campaign of raiding.

After relieving Chaves and arresting him, Canby ordered John Ward, the Indian agent, to attempt to persuade the Indians to gather at Cubero, where they could be given the "protection" of the government during the impending Confederate invasion. Canby's primary aim, of course, was to concentrate the Indians where they could be watched and kept from alliances with Rebel forces. Canby dispatched the celebrated CHRISTOPHER HOUSTON ("KIT") CARSON, commander of the First Regiment of New Mexican Volunteers, to move vigorously against any Navajos who persisted in raiding. He was ordered to take no prisoners.

On the Confederate side, Baylor was having his own problems with the Indians. While his troops were suffering through an epidemic of smallpox, Chiricahua and Mimbres Apaches, convinced that the Union soldiers had permanently withdrawn from the region, intensified their raids in the new Confederate territory. Blue-clad or gray, the white men who had invaded their country were all fair game. Confederate authorities organized a company of Arizona Rangers to punish the Indians. This unit was soon augmented by a volunteer group calling itself the Arizona Guards. Neither was very effective at halting the raids.

If soldiers ostensibly under Canby's command had created an outrage at Fort Lyon, Baylor soon proved that the Confederates could be equally vicious. An-

Bivouac of Confederate Troops on the Las Moras, Texas, with Stolen U.S. Wagons, etc. from the June 15, 1861, edition of *Harper's Weekly. Courtesy Patrick H. Butler, III.*

gered by the poor showing of the Arizona Guards, Baylor sent their commander a letter announcing that "the Congress of the Confederate States has passed a law declaring extermination of all hostile Indians. You will therefore use all means to persuade the Apaches or any tribe to come in for the purpose of making peace, and when you get them together, kill all the grown Indians and take the children prisoners and sell them to defray the expense of killing the Indians." The ghastly worded document soon reached the public, caused great embarrassment to the Confederacy, and, of course, set back Southern efforts to win allies among the tribes.

Baylor's efforts were followed during the winter of 1861 to 1862 by a larger Confederate invasion led by General HENRY HOPKINS SIBLEY and aimed at seizing the Colorado gold mines (and, eventually, the capture in fact as well as theory of all New Mexico). Once again, Indian troubles figured into the mix. Tucson, Arizona, which had come into existence in the decade before the Civil War as a mining boom town, lay deep in the heart of Apache country and depended for its survival on a garrison of federal troops. When these men were withdrawn at the outbreak of the war, the town and its strongly pro-Confederate miners were virtually besieged by raiding Apache bands. Late in January 1862, Sibley sent a small detachment of fifty-four men to Tucson, whose citizens greeted the troops as saviors.

Sibley, in the meantime, turned his principal attention not to the Indians, but to Colonel Canby, engaging his forces at Valverde, New Mexico, on February 21, 1862. Victorious here, Sibley next took Santa Fe and pressed on toward Fort Union, the best-provisioned Union post in the Southwest. En route, at La Glorieta Pass, the Confederates encountered a Union force under the command of Colonel John Slough. In a battle sometimes called "the Gettysburg of the West," from March 26 to 28, Slough's regulars, reinforced by Colorado volunteers, defeated the Texans. Major JOHN M. CHIVINGTON—soon to become infamous for his unbridled policy of Indian extermination—led a flanking party that destroyed the Confederates' supply train. Sibley's invaders, who had seemed unstoppable, were forced to retreat from New Mexico.

Simultaneously with the victories of Slough and Chivington, JAMES H. CARLETON was sweeping through the Southwest. Carleton commanded a volunteer outfit, the First California Regiment of Infantry, which, when mustered into the federal army, became known as the "California Column." A colonel when he raised his regiment in California, Carleton was promoted brigadier before he reached New Mexico Territory. With the California Column newly authorized by the War Department as Union regulars, General Carleton now pushed the Confederates out of present-day Ari-

zona—fighting the westernmost battle of the Civil War, at Picacho Peak on April 15, 1862—and southern New Mexico. By the end of 1862, the short-lived Confederate Territory of Arizona was no more, and both Arizona and New Mexico were securely in Union hands.

Back in Texas, the Gulf Squadron had been unable to check Rebel blockade runners and, in January 1863, had seen two Union Navy vessels overpowered by Confederate river boats at Sabine Pass, Texas. Finally, the squadron managed to take control of the Mississippi River late in 1863 and cut Texas off from the South. West of the river, the job of Union troops became to keep Confederate forces in Arkansas and western Louisiana from reinforcing their beleaguered compatriots to the east. President Lincoln, who had long believed cotton vital to the Union war effort, grew frustrated when the unofficial and limited trade he had permitted with Southern cotton planters degenerated into scandalous abuse by speculators in the cotton trade, and he turned General NATHANIEL P. BANKS's Red River campaign, from March to May 1864, into a long cotton raid. Designed to take Shreveport and gain control over East Texas, the expedition became a farce. A joint U.S. Army-Navy action floundered in the tricky river waters, Confederate General Edmund Kirby Smith's troops escaped defeat, and Rebels burned their cotton rather than see it fall into the hands of the Yankee soldiers weighing down Banks's clumsy boats. The Confederates routed Banks's troops at both Sabine Cross Roads and Pleasant Hill, and the troop-heavy Union armada was lucky to avoid running aground in a fast-falling river.

Smith managed to keep his soldiers fighting with money from the sale of Southern cotton to Northern traders. He also used the money to purchase supplies from throughout Mexico, all under the winking eyes of the 10-percent governments (so-called because 90 percent of the populations the Union puppet regimes supposedly governed remained in rebellion) Lincoln had set up in Louisiana and Arkansas. When General Canby took over from Banks in May 1864, he complained mightily about both the trade policy and the rump rule, but his complaints fell on deaf ears. Smith finally surrendered to Canby on May 26, 1865, about a month after Appomattox, and Galveston formally capitulated a few weeks later in June. The war in the West, finished years before strategically, finally came to an end.

There was bitterness. Between 1862 and 1864, when the Confederacy was trying to check Kansas bushwhackers, it had also intrigued with the natives in the Indian Territory. Chicasaws, Choctaws, Creeks, Seminoles and—more reluctantly—Cherokees, many of them slave owners, had contributed a brigade of warriors to the cause. Now the victorious Union penalized them in familiar fashion, forcing new land concessions from the Five Civilized Tribes. In Missouri, those who had suffered at the hands of the Confederate guerrillas made it clear that former rebels, no matter how penitent, were not welcome. In Jackson County, Radical Republican-leaning juries indicted former guerrillas for war crimes even after President Andrew Johnson had granted them amnesty. Not a few of the accused took to the bush, and before long, word of a robbery here, a murder there, began to appear in the newspapers. As the political agitation continued throughout the fall and winter months of 1865 and 1866, a lawlessness very much like that which had plagued the state during the war broke out again. In one among many such incidents, a group of armed men held up the Clay County Savings Association for sixty thousand dollars in February 1866. They were led by a former guerrilla named Jesse James. Jesse, and his brother Frank, had launched their civilian careers. Lawless men, robbing, looting, and killing without conscience, they hid behind a facade of romantic terrorism that would become associated with the state's attempt to escape the influence of the Radical Republicans, which in turn would lead to a long-standing tradition of SOCIAL BANDITRY in the area called the Missouri "breaks." The return of the Democratic party, which would dominate Missouri for a century to come, was one legacy of the Civil War, born of a lingering resentment and bitterness toward the federal government. There was another: in the backwoods hollows and the seedier city saloons, Jesse James was becoming a folk hero. An early death by treacherous murder and a few dime novels would turn the local folk hero into one of the West's legendary outlaws.

—*Alan Axelrod, Patrick H. Butler, III,*
and Charles Phillips

SEE ALSO: Central Plains Indian Wars; Sioux Wars; Texas Frontier Indian Wars

SUGGESTED READING:

Austerman, Wayne R. *Sharps Rifles and Spanish Mules.* College Station, Tex., 1985.

Axelrod, Alan. *Chronicle of the Indian Wars: From Colonial Times to Wounded Knee.* New York, 1993.

Buenger, Walter L. *Secession and the Union in Texas.* Austin, Tex., 1984.

Castel, Albert. *A Frontier State at War: Kansas, 1861–1865.* Ithaca, N.Y., 1968.

———. *General Sterling Price and the Civil War in the West.* Baton Rouge, La., 1968.

Colton, Ray C. *The Civil War in the Western Territories.* Norman, Okla., 1959.

Johnson, Ludwell N. *Red River Campaign: Politics and Cotton in the Civil War.* Baltimore, 1958.

Josephy, Alvin J. *The Civil War in the American West.* New York, 1991.

Kerby, Robert Lee. *The Confederate Invasion of New Mexico and Arizona, 1861–1862.* Los Angeles, 1958.

MacPherson, James M. *Battle Cry of Freedom: The Civil War Era.* New York, 1988.

Parish, William E. *A History of Missouri: Volume II, 1860 to 1875.* Columbia, Mo. 1973.

Phillips, Charles. *Missouri: Mother of the American West.* Northridge, Calif., 1988.

Utley, Robert M. *Frontiersmen in Blue: The United States Army and the Indian, 1848–1865.* New York, 1967. Reprint. Lincoln, Nebr., 1967.

CLAIMS ASSOCIATIONS

In the nineteenth-century westward migration of settlers across the American continent, squatter pioneers and farmers often claimed and improved lands before the federal government had a chance to survey the acreage and sell it. To protect their hold on lands they did not own, settlers established claims associations and squatters clubs. These extralegal organizations recorded member claims for a nominal fee, mediated claim disputes, protected members from outsiders "jumping a claim," and, in the absence of law officers, served as local law enforcement until such institutions could be established.

Claims associations were often the first democratic institutions in the Western wilderness. The members called a meeting, elected officers, and drew up the governing rules. Disputes over land were presented to a five-member board of review or jury. A member dissatisfied with a decision of the board could appeal the ruling to the entire membership. An association occasionally resorted to violence in settling disputes; claim jumpers were beaten, and their property was destroyed after other measures failed to remove them from the land in dispute.

After the PREEMPTION ACT OF 1841 guaranteed a settler's claim to a maximum of 160 acres of federal land he or she had improved, the claims clubs also protected squatters' claims in excess of the federally guaranteed acreage. Farmers often sold off the excess acreage to pay for the purchase of the remaining lands and thus, by speculation on a small scale, secured title to their 160-acre farms.

—*Patricia Hogan*

SUGGESTED READING:

Opie, John. *The Law of the Land: 200 Years of American Farmland Policy.* Lincoln, Nebr., 1987.

Rohrbough, Malcolm J. *The Land Office Business: The Settlement and Administration of American Public Lands.* New York, 1968.

CLAMOR PÚBLICO, EL

A Los Angeles newspaper for Spanish-speaking native Californians, *El Clamor Público* was published between December 13, 1856, and December 31, 1859. Following the UNITED STATES–MEXICAN WAR from 1846 to 1848, southern California underwent a series of rapid social and economic changes that displaced the Spanish-speaking, native Californians (Californios). Among the important champions of the Californios' way of life was *El Clamor Público*. Its founding editor, Francisco P. Ramírez, was a young Mexican immigrant. His writings protested the economic and political discrimination the Mexican Americans experienced.

El Clamor Público was a weekly written in Spanish. Occasional articles appeared in French and English. Ramírez, a Republican who supported JOHN CHARLES FRÉMONT for president in 1856, stood for the principles of "law and order" and "moral and material progress." He believed the Declaration of Independence and the Constitution of the United States promised liberty for Mexicans in California. *El Clamor Público* championed the cause of prison reform and opposed slavery, the death penalty, and antiforeign sentiment found in the Know-Nothing party and the idea of MANIFEST DESTINY. Ramírez believed in education and used his newspaper to teach the Spanish-speaking community about the need for improved civil rights. Advocating the need for Mexicans to learn to read, write, and speak English, he published an English-language section. He also constantly inveighed against the unequal system of justice the Californios faced.

The articles appearing in *El Clamor Público* ranged from poetry to editorial invective. Anyone who would write was invited to publish his or her thoughts. The paper also published news of events in Mexico. The editor occasionally advocated that Mexican Americans should return to Mexico; yet he also criticized the Mexican government's intolerance toward religious freedom. *El Clamor Público* first reported that Mexicans had, in fact, discovered gold (in 1842 at San Francisquito canyon) before John Marshall and that Mexicans were being persecuted in the gold fields.

Ultimately, *El Clamor Público* failed because of the liberal and even radical ideas of its editor. Los Angeles in the 1850s was a pro-Southern, Democratic town whose Anglo population considered the Californios obstacles to commercial development. Ramírez left Los Angeles and became a state printer for the government of Sonora. He returned to Los Angeles in 1862 and became postmaster and later an official state translator. In 1872, he briefly edited *La Cronica*, another Spanish-language newspaper in Los Angeles.

—*Richard Griswold del Castillo*

SUGGESTED READING:

Griswold del Castillo, Richard. *The Los Angeles Barrio: A Social History, 1850–1890*. Berkeley and Los Angeles, 1980.

Pitt, Leonard. *The Decline of the Californios: A Social History of the Spanish Speaking Californios, 1846–1890*. Berkeley and Los Angeles, 1966.

Dawson, Muir. "Southern California Newspapers, 1851–1876: A Short History and Census." *Historical Society of Southern California Quarterly* 32 (March and June 1950): 23.

Newmark, Harris. *Sixty Years in Southern California, 1853–1913 . . . the Reminiscences of Harris Newmark*. New York, 1916.

CLANTON CLAN

See: O. K. Corral, Gunfight at

CLAPPE, LOUISE (SMITH, AMELIAN KNAPP)

SEE: "Dame Shirley"

CLARION, UTAH

Few Western settlements reflected more clearly the complexity of converging local and global forces than did Clarion, a Jewish colony that survived from 1911 to 1916 in central Utah. Among the era's millions of Jewish immigrants were a few who saw the back-to-the-land and country-life movements then underway as a means of escaping harsh urban conditions and of giving expression to yearnings inherent in their own traditions. Led by a persuasive but naive immigrant with the unlikely name of Ben Brown, Philadelphia and New York Jews of Russian background organized the Jewish Agricultural and Colonial Association. In April 1911, Brown headed to the West to locate a suitable site for a colony.

The West Brown saw was itself deeply influenced by agrarian impulses. Reclamation projects were booming, land speculation was rife, and homesteading and land projects flourished. In Utah, Indian reservations were opened, railroads promoted projects through the CAREY ACT OF 1894, and the state government developed reservoirs, canal systems, and state lands. Encouraged by a prospering Jewish community in Salt

Lake City, Brown committed his followers to a desert tract at the end of an extended state canal in Sanpete County.

First came a pioneer party of twelve men, who, during the winter of 1911, lived in tents, struggled to outfit themselves, and laid out farms, ditches, and homes. In 1912, the first of eighty-one families arrived. They soon took up their lands individually, an arrangement that compromised the colony's idealistic hope of generating back-to-the-soil sentiments and divided the colonists in their ideological and economic interests. Unfortunately, few of them knew anything about farming, and none had experience with irrigation. Even worse for that first year of settlement, the state failed to deliver adequate water to the colony.

Crisis followed crisis. Key members of the community died, and weather conditions worsened. Brown failed to meet the leadership demands placed upon him. State concessions on payments and funds from Salt Lake City Jews and Eastern supporters were inadequate and were extended more as charity than as an investment. For a time, new colonists took the place of those who gave up in defeat, but all but a few successful farmers had abandoned the colony by 1916. Gradually, even those few found conditions in rural Utah to be oppressive.

Clarion did have some lasting effects: the Intermountain Farmers Association, which grew out of a poultry products cooperative Brown helped to found, and the mercantile empire of Maurice Warshaw. Clarion, the Jewish community, is defunct as are the state's land promotions and early twentieth-century AGRARIANISM.

—*Charles S. Peterson*

SUGGESTED READING:
Cooley, Everet L. "Clarion, Utah, Jewish Colony in 'Zion.'" *Utah Historical Quarterly* 36 (Spring 1968): 113–131.
Goldberg, Robert Alan. *Back to the Soil: The Jewish Farmers of Clarion, Utah, and Their World.* Salt Lake City, 1968.
Warshaw, Maurice. *Life More Sweet Than Bitter.* Salt Lake City, 1975.

CLARK, CHARLES ("BADGER"), JR.

Cowboy poet, the poet laureate of South Dakota, and author of the well-known and widely reprinted "Cowboy's Prayer," Badger Clark (1883–1957) was born in Iowa. He was an infant when his clergyman father moved the family from Iowa to the Dakota Territory. Clark attended Dakota Wesleyan University for one year before joining a group of would-be colonists-farmers bound for Cuba. Financial problems ended the project, but Clark remained in Cuba, only to get caught in the middle of a feud between two Spanish families. He was arrested and brought to trial on charges of carrying a gun and stealing coconuts. After his acquittal, he returned to South Dakota, where he took a job as reporter for the *Lead Daily Call*. A bout of tuberculosis sent him to the dry heat of Arizona, where he became a range rider for the Cross I Quarter Circle Ranch near Tombstone.

Clark wrote letters in verse to his family and described the pleasures and pains of cowboy life. His stepmother sent one of the letters to *Pacific Monthly* magazine, which published the verse and paid Clark ten dollars. From that moment on, Clark called himself a poet and earned a living by writing, lecturing, and giving poetry readings.

His first—and best—poetry collection was published in 1915 as *Sun and Saddle Leather* and has been reprinted many times. In 1925, he wrote a well-received novel, *Spike,* based on the exploits of the Cross I Quarter Circle's foreman Robert ("Spike") Axtel.

Clark, a lifelong bachelor, lived in a log cabin, dubbed "The Badger Hole," near Custer, South Dakota. It is now maintained as a state historical site.

—*Alan Axelrod*

CLARK, JAMES BEAUCHAMP ("CHAMP")

James Beauchamp ("Champ") Clark (1850–1921) served as a congressman from Missouri for twenty-six years (from 1893 to 1895 and from 1897 to 1921) and held the position of Speaker of the House from 1911 to 1919. Before he won election to Congress, he had been a teacher, college president, lawyer, and newspaperman.

A noted orator, Clark played a significant role in limiting the powers of the Speaker from 1910 to 1911. He lost the 1912 Democratic presidential nomination to Woodrow Wilson on the eighty-fourth ballot. Considered a moderate Progressive during his congressional career, Clark supported tariff reforms, isolationism, and a voluntary army.

—*James W. Goodrich*

SUGGESTED READING:
March, David D. *The History of Missouri.* 4 vols. New York, 1967.

CLARK, WALTER VAN TILBURG

SEE: Literature: The Western Novel

CLARK, WILLIAM

William Clark (1770–1838) is inevitably associated with the epic journey he made to the Pacific in the company of MERIWETHER LEWIS and the Corps of Discovery from 1804 to 1806. But Clark's life was much more than the events of one journey. His long Western adventure took him from Virginia and Kentucky to the northern Great Plains and the Pacific Northwest.

Born on the eastern edge of the Allegheny Mountains in Virginia's Caroline County, Clark grew up in a world shaped by the values of order, authority, honor, and ambition. The struggles of the American Revolution were the common talk of the family and the region. Five Clark family sons served in the Revolution. Two of them—Jonathan and George Rogers—gained special distinction for courage and dedication to the Revolutionary cause. George Rogers Clark's daring drive into British-occupied Illinois captured Eastern attention and did much to aim the Clark family westward. At the close of the Revolution in 1784, the Clarks moved to Kentucky, and it was there that young William expanded his own knowledge of frontier ways.

The years after the American Revolution were marked by steadily increasing violence between Euro-American settlers and native people. Indians saw the greater Ohio Valley invaded by land-hungry squatters; white Americans saw that country as their rightful prize for winning the war against England. Coming of age

Captain Clark and His Men Shooting Bears illustrated the *Journal of Voyages and Travel of the Corps of Discovery,* by Patrick Gass, published in 1811. *Courtesy Library of Congress.*

in a culture that celebrated the military professions, William Clark soon found his place in the company of soldiers. First as a member of a local militia detachment and later as an infantry officer in the army led by General Anthony Wayne, Clark earned distinction for leadership and courage under fire. To his obvious military skills, Clark added abilities as a diplomat.

While military service shaped Clark's entire public life, the obligations he owed to family were perhaps even more influential. By the mid-1790s, George Rogers Clark's descent into debt and alcohol seriously endangered family landholdings in Kentucky and Indiana. Duty to family pulled William Clark away from the army, and he resigned his captain's commission in 1796. For the next eight years, he struggled to preserve and then expand the family estate. By the first years of the nineteenth century, he was a man rich in land and slaves—the real measure of Virginia culture transplanted to the Ohio country.

Like so many other Virginians, Clark valued sociability. While his close friends were few, he had a wide circle of acquaintances. In that circle was fellow Virginian and brother officer Meriwether Lewis. Both had served in the Ohio campaigns, and Clark had been for a brief time Lewis's commanding officer. They had never been close friends, but they had stayed in touch after Clark left the army. In June 1803, while THOMAS JEFFERSON was busy completing instructions for the proposed expedition to the Pacific, Lewis wrote Clark to invite him to join the Corps of Discovery as a coleader. While there would be considerable official confusion about Clark's military rank on the journey, Lewis and Jefferson always viewed him as part of a joint command.

On their way up the Missouri, across the mountains, and down the Columbia to the sea, Lewis and Clark worked out a predictable pattern of duties and responsibilities. First and foremost, Clark was the expedition's cartographer. By training and temperament, Clark had the uncanny ability to comprehend complex land forms, rivers, and mountains and then reduce the three-dimensional world to the paper and ink of a two-dimensional map. He also proved to be an able negotiator in councils with native leaders. Because Clark's daily journal entries have survived and most of Lewis's have not, modern readers see and understand the journey through his eyes.

Clark never romanticized his two-and-a-half-year voyage to the Pacific. He saw the trip as just one more part of his long tour of duty as a soldier. The rest of his life (from 1806 until his death in 1838) was a continuation of that Virginia military code of conduct. In 1807, Clark assumed duties in St. Louis as federal Indian agent for the Western tribes. Clark believed, as did Jefferson, that commerce, especially the FUR TRADE, was the key to establishing peaceful relations between native nations and the young United States. Clark was especially concerned that heavy-handed American traders and scheming Canadian merchants would incite violence in the West. To stop such trouble, Clark supported strict federal regulation of the fur business. But while Clark urged such regulation, he saw no reason to avoid personal participation in the lucrative fur trade. In 1809, he joined other prominent St. Louis citizens in forming the MISSOURI FUR COMPANY. Led by MANUEL LISA, the company engaged in some of the earliest American fur ventures up the Missouri and into present-day Montana.

Clark's greatest test as an Indian agent came in the WAR OF 1812 and its aftermath. In the West, the war came a full year before the beginning of its Atlantic phase. William Henry Harrison's attack on TECUMSEH's camp at Tippecanoe Creek in 1811 was the signal for a wider war between Indians and Americans. While many Americans urged war, some thoughtful Western officials knew that area defenses were thin and poorly organized. As chief Indian agent, Clark did what he could to gather reliable information and strengthen alliances with friendly bands and tribes. Clark's military responsibilities increased when he was appointed Missouri territorial governor in June 1813. Many in the territory urged him to attack British posts on the upper Mississippi, especially Prairie du Chien, a key British establishment. In the spring of 1814, Clark organized a massive assault force of gunboats and infantry for the Prairie du Chien campaign. The British post fell easily, prompting Clark to withdraw most of his force back to St. Louis. A large British and Indian army returned to Prairie du Chien in July 1814 and successfully reclaimed the post. As Clark discovered to his dismay, the Prairie du Chien fiasco had consequences long after the official end of the War of 1812.

In July 1815, Clark moved to repair the damage done to Indian relations caused by the war in general and the Prairie du Chien disaster in particular. At a series of treaty councils held at Portage des Sioux, Clark concluded agreements with more than a dozen tribes. The treaties all followed a common pattern. Each reasserted American sovereignty, emphasized friendly commerce between American traders and Indians, and made arrangements for handling problems of law and criminal justice. The treaties also offered the blessings of American civilization—schools, churches, plow agriculture, and private ownership of land. Clark was convinced that such institutional arrangements would preserve peace between Euro-Americans and Native Americans. If Clark's trust in rational negotiation and formalized institutions was misplaced, his commitment

to peace was genuine. Indians who came to talk with him in St. Louis affectionately called him "the red-head chief."

William Clark's last years were marked by a steady decline in his diplomatic and political leadership. When Missouri became a state in 1819, Clark ran for governor and was soundly defeated. In BLACK HAWK's WAR crisis, he proved to be an ineffective negotiator. As a patron for artists and explorers heading West, he had greater success. Artists such as GEORGE CATLIN and KARL (OR CARL) BODMER and explorers and travelers such as WILSON PRICE HUNT, Prince Maximilian of Wied-Neuwied, and WASHINGTON IRVING all stopped to consult with the man one adventurer called "the patriarch of the West."

—*James P. Ronda*

SEE ALSO: Cartography; Lewis and Clark Expedition

SUGGESTED READING:

Loos, John. "A Biography of William Clark, 1770–1813." Ph.D. diss., Washington University (St. Louis), 1953.

Ronda, James P. *Lewis and Clark among the Indians.* Lincoln, Nebr., 1984.

Steffen, Jerome O. *William Clark: Jeffersonian Man on the Frontier.* Norman, Okla., 1977.

CLARK, WILLIAM ANDREWS

Mining magnate and politician William Andrews Clark (1839–1925) took part in the "War of the Copper Kings," which threw MONTANA politics into turmoil in the late nineteenth and early twentieth centuries. Born in Pennsylvania, Clark grew up in Iowa and in 1863 moved to Bannack, Montana, where he engaged in freighting, contracting mail routes, wholesale trading, and banking. Mining soon captured his interest, and he attended Columbia University's School of Mines for a year. In Butte, he invested in the first smelter for silver and copper and the town's first water system and electric plant.

In 1884 and 1889, Clark served as president of the Montana constitutional convention. He was a candidate for election as Montana's territorial delegate to Congress but was defeated, largely due to the opposition of MARCUS DALY, another of the Copper Kings. The two men started the "War of the Copper Kings" when the Montana legislature divided along party lines over the selection of U.S. senators. The Democrats selected two men to serve as did the Republicans. Clark was one of the men chosen by the Democrats, but when he and the other three men traveled to Washington, the Republican-controlled Senate seated Clark's political rivals and sent the Democratic candidates back to Montana. In 1893, he ran again for the Senate, but was again denied a seat. The legislature finally selected him on January 28, 1899, after he was cleared on charges of campaign misconduct. After Clark traveled to the nation's capital, Daly stirred up trouble again by petitioning the Senate to investigate Clark's campaign activities. The Committee on Privileges and Elections recommended that the Senate refuse to seat Clark, but before the Senate voted on the matter, Clark resigned. Still determined to serve in the Senate, Clark persuaded Lieutenant Governor A. E. Spriggs, in charge while Governor Robert B. Smith was out of the state, to appoint him to fill the Senate seat he had just vacated. Governor Smith revoked the appointment, however, and named PARIS GIBSON to the post. In 1900, Clark's political aspirations finally came true. He won a Senate seat and served in Washington from 1901 to 1907.

Clark gave the city of Butte the Columbia Gardens, a recreational park that closed in the 1970s. He also donated his library to the University of California at Los Angeles and gave $1 million to the University of Virginia for its law school.

—*Candace Floyd*

SEE ALSO: Copper Kings, War of

SUGGESTED READING:
Malone, Michael P., Richard B. Roeder, and William Lang. *Montana: A History of Two Centuries*. Rev. ed. Seattle, Wash., 1976.

CLAY, HENRY

Statesman Henry Clay (1777–1851) devoted his political career to the development of a politically integrated and economically interdependent United States. Born in Hanover County, Virginia, Clay studied law and passed the bar before traveling west at the age of twenty to the young state of Kentucky. Settling in Lexington, he developed a prosperous law practice, became a Jeffersonian Republican, and was elected to the state legislature in 1803. His election to the U.S. Senate in 1810 launched a forty-year career in national politics.

He supported war against Great Britain as the means of maintaining foreign markets for American products and, as Speaker of the U.S. House of Representatives in 1812, was a prominent War Hawk. Following the WAR OF 1812, which Clay caused to conclude

Henry Clay, senator from Kentucky, argues for the Compromise of 1850 in the U.S. Congress. *Courtesy Library of Congress.*

as a member of the U.S. peace commission that negotiated the Treaty of Ghent, Clay returned to the office of the Speaker of the House in late 1815.

There, Clay, a resolute nationalist, began formulating his AMERICAN SYSTEM, an integrated economic plan based on tariffs to protect American goods from foreign competition, a system of transportation networks built by the FEDERAL GOVERNMENT to encourage the easy exchange of raw materials and manufactured goods among the sections of the country, and a national bank that supplied uniform currency and regulated credit. The pieces of Clay's program were never fully implemented, in part because the very sectional interests his plan attempted to overcome intensified as the country expanded throughout the first half of the nineteenth century.

Clay's vision of a unified nation was severely tested when MISSOURI petitioned Congress for admission to the Union as a slave state. Clay, a slave owner himself but an advocate of gradual abolition, played a major role in engineering the MISSOURI COMPROMISE (or the Compromise of 1820), which balanced Missouri's slave-state status with the admission of Maine as a free state. The immediate crisis was averted through the efforts of "the Great Compromiser," but the slavery issue shaded the deliberations of Congress and the politics of the nation for the next forty years.

The tariff issue of the 1820s and 1830s challenged Clay's skills at making peace among the nation's sections again. A North of industry and manufacture benefited from high tariffs on goods imported from foreign countries. The cotton-producing South was required to pay higher prices for imported goods at a time when the price of cotton was falling. Displeased with tariffs passed in 1828 and 1832, South Carolina declared the taxes null and void and threatened to secede from the Union. President ANDREW JACKSON stood poised to squelch South Carolina's assertion of states' rights, but Clay proposed the Compromise Tariff of 1833. South Carolina accepted; Jackson backed down; and, once again, Clay engineered an abatement of sectional rivalries.

For all of his skill and devotion to conciliation, however, Clay did not shy away from political opponents. It was his own ambitions to become president that set him on a collision course with Andrew Jackson, popular hero of the Battle of New Orleans and symbol to the American people of the frontier's possibilities. Clay clashed with Jackson over a number of issues, most spectacularly the national bank. Clay was instrumental in forming the Whig party in reaction to Jackson's policies.

In the 1840s, Clay opposed the annexation of Texas and saw it as a trap for drawing the United States into war with Mexico. When the Congress attempted to resolve the issue of slavery in the lands the United States acquired as a result of the UNITED STATES–MEXICAN WAR, Clay outlined a series of provisions that had something for everyone but pleased no one. The passage of the COMPROMISE OF 1850 was largely the work of STEPHEN A. DOUGLAS, but Clay's proposals averted war for another decade. Clay himself was spared the vision of a nation split in two; he died of tuberculosis in 1852.

A persuasive man of charm, passion, and decision, Henry Clay was the most influential member of Congress in the difficult years preceding the Civil War. A man who counseled moderation when the interests of the South were at odds with those of the North or West, he had the misfortune of living in a time when another Westerner, Andrew Jackson, epitomized the common man in a land of limitless opportunity. Although Clay was frustrated in four attempts to win the presidency, his leadership in Congress prevented bloodshed and preserved the Union for several decades.

—*Patricia Hogan*

SEE ALSO: Banking; National Expansion; Tariff Policy

SUGGESTED READING:

Eaton, Clement. *Henry Clay and the Art of American Politics.* New York, 1957.

Mayo, Bernard. *Henry Clay: Spokesman of the New West.* Boston, 1937.

Peterson, Merrill D. *The Great Triumvirate: Webster, Clay, and Calhoun.* New York, 1987.

Van Deusen, Glyndon G. *The Life of Henry Clay.* 1937. Reprint. Westport, Conn., 1979.

CLAY, JOHN HENRY

Cattleman John Henry Clay (1851–1934) was a prime example of the link between Eastern and foreign investors and the economic growth of the American West. A native of Scotland, Clay received a university education in Edinburgh and spent five years managing Scottish farms before traveling to the United States and Canada in 1874. He soon was managing a stock-breeding farm near Brantford, Ontario, and serving as a representative of a royal commission to survey the American livestock industry. Clay moved to Chicago in 1882 and represented Scottish companies with cattle investments in the West. Four years later, he established his own commission office in Chicago and became very successful. Between 1888 and 1896, he managed the financially troubled Swan Land and Cattle Company in Wyoming. He may also have helped organize and finance the vigilante expedition against settlers in northern Wyoming that resulted in the JOHNSON COUNTY WAR of 1892. Later, he owned the Stock Growers National Bank in Cheyenne while also operating the John Clay Commission Company. His autobiography is a thoughtful memoir detailing the financial side of cattle ranching during the late nineteenth century.

—*David Dary*

SEE ALSO: Cattle Industry

SUGGESTED READING:

Clay, John. *My Life on the Range.* Chicago, 1924.

CLEMENS, SAMUEL L.

SEE: Twain, Mark

CLIMATE

Some Western historians argue that what makes the American West a coherent region with a history distinct from the rest of the country is not necessarily its politics, its industries, or its population, but its aridity— that is to say, its climate. Certainly today when people talk about the American West, they usually have in mind the dry areas of the country. These areas cover an immense portion of the continental United States sprawling from Mexico to Canada across the Great Plains and the Rocky Mountains to the Sierra Nevada. Beyond the sweep of moist sea air, the fierce, sometimes dangerous, dry West gripped the national imagi-

Cattle Blizzard on the Plains, by Charles Graham from a sketch by H. Horrall. *Courtesy Patrick H. Butler, III.*

nation in the nineteenth century when the region became the last to be settled by Euro-Americans.

Variations in a dry region

Water is the key to the arid and semiarid West, and even though temperatures vary dramatically throughout the region, the degree of aridity is what defines the important regional differences: extremely dry weather produces desert; small amounts of rainfall result in what the Eastern Hemisphere would call "steppes." Mistaken notions about climate in the early nineteenth century created the myth of the GREAT AMERICAN DESERT, which most Americans of the period assumed to occupy some one-third of the entire subcontinent, when in reality only the American Southwest, for the most part, houses true desert lands. A few patches of desert lie outside the Southwest, all of them in the lowland rain shadows of mountain ranges, but most of the West is a semiarid region, where scanty rains barely support a thin layer of bunchgrass or scrub brush.

Even the deserts vary: in some areas, mostly salt flats and sand dunes, nothing grows at all—a rare event anywhere in the world. In other areas, a low cover, consisting of widely scattered woody shrubs and short-lived annuals, springs into bloom whenever it rains. Some parts of the desert are home to a bare pavement of broken rock carved by strong winds that have blown away the sand, while in others, the thin, light soils are extraordinary rich in mineral salts. The semiarid lands, too, can change dramatically depending on the amount of rain they receive. Some, like the desert, have mineral soils, made up calcium and other soluble material. With just a bit more rain, however, the West produces land rich with humus from decayed grass roots, and this dark brown soil of the steppes, when carefully managed, proves extremely fertile.

As in all dry regions, the weather in the American West is extreme, violent, and predictably unreliable. Rainfall on the plains is notorious for its local variety in any given year, in effect creating an almost infinite number of microclimates. The less it rains, the more extreme and volatile the climate. Complicating its changeable nature, Western weather falls prey to alternating cycles, sometimes lasting for years, of relatively wet periods and savage droughts. Temperatures stray all over the scale, dropping and rising convulsively, and strong winds rage throughout the region, changing within minutes entire weather patterns. East of the Rockies, the weather in general changes slowly, subtly, almost imperceptibly across a huge transitional region in which arid and humid conditions alternate without warning from year to year.

Stretching from Texas to North Dakota between the ninety-fifth and the one hundredth meridian, this giant, vaguely defined band of change is unique not only for its size and its hardly noticeable shift from too little to too much rain, but also for its strange combinations of soils and plant and animal life. Apparently in its native state, the band was prairie, an ocean of well-rooted, high grass, that today has been replaced with plowed and planted seas of wheat and other grains. In the north, the soil was produced by piles of loess deposited by melting glaciers, and it includes the immensely productive black earth that scientists call "chernozem." To the south, the dirt is red but hardly less fertile. Everywhere on the prairie, the winters are bitterly cold and the summers always scorchers. At the prairie's western edge occurs the slow gradation to High Plains caused by slowly diminishing overall rainfalls. On its eastern boundary lies a rare disjuncture between weather and earth, climate and biology. There, a great swath of grassland cuts across humid Illinois and Indiana, a strange situation many scholars think is artificial, something created by the FIRE of Indians who constantly burned prairie grass at the edge of the forests to expand the range of such game as the buffalo.

The dry West is also home to ranges of mountains that make up the Rocky Mountain chain and the Sierra Nevada, with stretches of highlands between the ranges. These ranges shatter the general weather patterns of the West and create numerous tiny climates, which change drastically depending on how high or how close to sea level they occur. So varied are these mini-climates that scientists despair of including them in the grand scheme of Western weather and call them collectively a "mountain climate." The lowland valleys are typically dry, but the highlands are colder and wetter and, if the winds are right, sometimes quite wet indeed. Mountain soils vary widely, but mountain plant life is fairly predictable. Desert or steppe valleys rise to open savannas, which give way increasingly to humid, then boreal forests, which, if the mountains are high enough, turn to tall timber and Arctic tundra. Although the tallest mountains are snow-capped, only in the Pacific Northwest does the cool, wet climate produce permanent glaciers.

In fact, the Pacific Coast has a humid climate different from the rest of the trans-Mississippi West but also different from the humid climates of the East. Stuffed into a tiny belt of land between the Sierra-Cascade ranges and the Pacific Ocean, the region is dominated by mild Pacific breezes and is chopped up into a number of various subclimates. Different parts of the coast get varying amounts of rain, mostly in the winter. Summer droughts are standard, but they are much shorter around Seattle (two months, usually) than they are around San Diego (nearly five months). As in Europe, winters in Washington, Orgeon, and northern California hit the coast raw, cloudy, and wet, and huge amounts of snow drop on the mountains during subfreezing weather creating alpine glaciers. Come summer, cloudless skies, cool temperatures, and foggy beaches prevail, while inland the weather is warmer. In all, it is a perfect climate for evergreen forests, and it is no accident that the Pacific Northwest furnishes the country with most of its lumber. Farther south in California, the weather turns Mediterranean, although there are endless local environments. Scant rains never compensate for the summer droughts, and the land is distinctly arid, plagued by dry hot Santa Ana winds from the desert that regularly turn brush fires into infernos. Sudden downpours pound the stripped earth and produce immense mud slides, which roll down to the sea.

Climate and the history of the West

Native Americans, adjusting their lives and their cultures to the demands of climate, long lived in the arid and semiarid American West, and a few Spanish friars, soldiers, and pioneers took up residence there when the region composed the northern reaches of a Spanish New World empire, but for Anglo-Americans eager to conquer a continent, the region proved bedeviling, in large part because of its weather. Throughout their history, the descendants of English and European colonizers had called other regions the American West, in particular the Ohio Valley west of the Appalachians and that part of the country historians refer to as the Old Northwest. This new American West was different from the rest of the country not merely by virtue of being the area on the map not yet defined as part of the body politic, as this or that state, but also because of its geography and climate—it was a region as well as a political construct. To paraphrase historian WALTER PRESCOTT WEBB, this American West was an actual place, a place that could be marked off on a map, traveled to, and seen, a place that everyone knew when they got there.

That so few got there before the end of the Civil War had much to do precisely with the region's climate and terrain. Since the 1840s, except for a few fur traders and a number of Texans, most of the American pioneers heading into the trans-Missouri West skipped right over the forbidding new environment.

Dry, nearly treeless, pretty much flat, the plains, semi-arid lands, and deserts had their own bizarre soil, odd weather, weird plant life, peculiar animals, and Indians especially ferocious when it came to protecting their hunting grounds. So hard and lonely did the region seem to early westering Euro-Americans that they wrote it off as a vast wasteland, and up until 1860, most maps still called it "The Great American Desert," the label given to the region by American explorers. After the Civil War, however, a rapidly industrializing United States, seeking expanded markets and new sources of raw materials, began to encourage settlement of the region by offering generous land policies and, in effect, financing the construction of a massive network of RAILROADS. A semiofficial myth held that "rain followed the plow" and encouraged farmers to move ever farther onto the Great Plains. A huge new demand for beef, the destruction of the once massive buffalo herds, and the "pacification" of native tribes encouraged the rise of the CATTLE INDUSTRY, which made use of the region's expansive grasslands. Discoveries of gold, silver, copper, and lead produced a thriving mining industry. Depletion of the Great Lakes forests led big lumber companies to turn to the stretches of virgin timber in the Pacific Northwest. In the saga of this new "taming" of the West, its volatile climate loomed large.

First, there were the mountains, largely impassable except for a few gaps discovered by TRAPPERS and explorers. The history of the DONNER PARTY, pioneers who after becoming lost in a Rocky Mountain winter turned to cannibalism to survive, quickly spread, in part, as a cautionary tale about the dangers of the Western climate. Indeed, it seemed at time as if the weather was at war with the Western settlements.

During the severe winter of 1885 and 1886, large numbers of cattle on the Southern Plains either starved or froze to death. A bad drought followed that summer, scorching the grass. By then the cattlemen were beginning to worry. They believed that even the autumn after the bad winter of 1885 and the summer drought of 1886 had, in bringing heavy rains, "soaked the strength out of the grass." There were just too many animals and not enough good grass to go around. As a consequence, the stock was not healthy as another winter approached. But no one could have predicted the now legendary destructiveness of the winter of 1886 and 1887. That winter, nature took a cruel grip on the Great Plains, driving humans and beasts to panic as the climate visited upon the weakened cattle and the foolish cattlemen a series of blizzards unlike any either had ever seen. When the thaw finally came, the emaciated corpses of huge numbers of cattle lay stacked against fences or piled deep in ditches, while a few ghastly survivors staggered about on legs frozen stiff.

A single, terrible season had destroyed perhaps as much as 90 percent of the range animals. The disaster tolled the death of the West's beef bonanza. Large corporations and many individuals were ruined, and the heart went out of the enterprise. By 1888, the cattle industry lay in ruins, and the reckless confidence and arrogance of the cattle kings had vanished with the snow.

Western farmers, too, frequently seemed under attack by the weather. During the first great rush onto the Great Plains, the West was undergoing one of its wet cycles, which in turned encouraged more settlement. When the years of drought followed, many families lost their farms. By the 1870s, consolidations, new FARMING techniques, and better weather again began to produce bonanzas, much of it in wheat, booms that also collapsed with foul weather and a financial panic. The cycle continued with farmers plowing under ever more prairie, especially when World War I produced huge demands for wheat in foreign markets. In what became known as the "Great Plow Up," suitcase farmers (absentee investors) plowed under millions of acres. Combined with a long cycle of drought in the 1930s, the "Great Plow Up" turned much of the West's farmland in a ecological disaster known as the DUST BOWL. John Steinbeck's novel, *The Grapes of Wrath,* became a classic description of farmers enticed to the Oklahoma farming frontier only to be driven out by insensitive capitalists because of problems that, in the end, were caused by a savage drought.

The New Deal response to the Great Depression in many ways resembled a military counterattack on nature during which an army of RECLAMATION set out to subdue the West's dry climate with modern technology. One school of historians has come to see this century-long battle to turn a semiarid land with the heart of a desert into an economic Eden as sheer hubris, but without doubt, the effort has produced what Donald Worster calls one of the greatest hydraulic civilizations the world as ever seen. Certainly, the very climate that has attracted much of the country's population to southern California and the American Southwest remains the biggest challenge to the continued prosperity of the region, since no matter how many dams, irrigation canals, aqueducts, and pumping stations Westerners build, the West's generally dry climate continues to produce too little water to replenish that used each year by its residents, farmers, and industries.

—*Charles Phillips*

SUGGESTED READING:

Bonnifield, Paul. *The Dust Bowl: Men, Dirt, and Depression.* Albuquerque, N. Mex., 1979.

Cooke, Ronald U., and R. W. Reeves. *Arroyos and Environmental Change in the American Southwest.* New York, 1976.

Limerick, Patricia Nelson. *Desert Passages: Encounters with the American Deserts.* Albuquerque, N. Mex., 1995.

Reisner, Marc. *Cadillac Desert: The American West and Its Disappearing Water.* New York, 1986.

Smith, Henry Nash. *Virgin Land: The American West as Symbol and Myth.* Cambridge, Mass., 1950. Reprint. 1978.

Webb, Walter Prescott. "The American West: Perpetual Mirage." *Harper's Magazine* 214 (May 1957): 25–35.

———. *The Great Plains.* New York, 1931.

Worster, Donald. *Dust Bowl: The Southern Plains in the 1930s.* New York, 1979.

———. *Rivers of Empire: Water, Aridity, and the Growth of the American West.* New York, 1985.

———. *Under Western Skies.* New York, 1992.

———. *An Unsettled Country: Changing Landscapes of the American West.* Albuquerque, N. Mex., 1994.

Young, James A., and B. Abbot Sparks. *Cattle in the Cold Desert.* Logan, Utah, 1985.

John Philip Clum (standing, center) at San Carlos Indian Reservation. *Courtesy Arizona Historical Society.*

CLUM, JOHN PHILIP

An agent at the San Carlos Indian reservation in the Arizona Territory from 1874 to 1877, John Philip Clum (1851–1932) was one of the most important Indian service officers of his time. He was the first North American Indian agent to use successfully a native police force and the first in Arizona to establish an Indian court that fused native custom with Anglo-American law. During his administration, he championed and led the concentration of nearly all the Apaches in Arizona on a single reservation. Clum, himself, claimed to have been the only white man to whom the famous Chiricahua Apache renegade GERONIMO ever surrendered.

In the 1870s and 1880s, the army struggled with civilian managers over control of Indian reservations. Army officers generally believed that civilian agents were weak and corrupt; backers of civilian control protested that the army was brutal and could teach only war to the Indians. As a civilian, Clum eagerly championed the civilian side of the argument, and from the beginning of his administration, he sought to end any military authority over the Apaches. General August V. Kautz, military commander in the Arizona Territory, distrusted Clum and thought him incapable of keeping peace at San Carlos. Clum repeatedly denounced Kautz and offered to take over all the army's duties with two companies of Apache policemen.

Clum made it his business to be on good terms with nearly all of the territory's officialdom, its prominent merchants, and the editor of its most important newspaper. These influential men supported his administration at San Carlos and took his side in the ongoing contest with the military. At the same time, the peace at San Carlos during his tenure won him the support of the settlers around the reservation. The charge by his enemies that he conspired with the infamous "Tucson Ring" to cheat the government with fraudulent contracts was almost certainly untrue.

—*John Bret-Harte*

SUGGESTED READING:

Bret-Harte, John. "The San Carlos Indian Reservation, 1872–1886: An Administrative History." Ph.D. diss., University of Arizona, 1972.

Clum, Woodworth. *Apache Agent.* New York, 1936. Reprint. Lincoln, Nebr., 1978.

Ogle, Ralph H. *Federal Control of the Western Apaches, 1848–1886.* Albuquerque, N. Mex., 1970.

CLYMAN, JAMES

Farmer, hunter, Indian fighter, and fur trapper James Clyman (1792–1881) was born in Faquier County, Virginia. As a young man, he moved with his family to Ohio, where he helped protect frontier settlements from hostile Indians during the War of 1812. After failing at farming and surveying in the Midwest, Clyman moved to St. Louis in 1823. That year, he joined WILLIAM HENRY ASHLEY's fur company as a clerk on an expedition to the Upper Missouri River. The Ashley expedition encountered immediate tragedy in the Arikara War of 1823, when fifteen men died at the hands of "Ree" warriors. Clyman narrowly escaped death by jumping into the river and fleeing onto the prairie.

In a last-ditch attempt to save his floundering company, Ashley ordered Clyman and JEDEDIAH STRONG SMITH to proceed overland and establish a trade alliance with the Crow Indians. During the expedition, a grizzly bear attacked Smith and mangled his scalp and ear. Clyman, using a needle and thread, reattached Smith's ear, and the men continued their journey. In 1824, they reached South Pass. As they crossed the Continental Divide, they found a wealth of BEAVERS in the Green River Valley. This ushered in the period of the fur-trade RENDEZVOUS, in which Clyman actively participated until 1827.

During his few years in the mountains, Clyman participated in first rendezvous in 1825, the first circumnavigation of the Great Salt Lake, and, in 1826, the first documented experiences in the region that later became Yellowstone National Park. Clyman returned to the Midwest in 1827, where he fought in BLACK HAWK'S WAR with, among others, a young Abraham Lincoln. Following the war, Clyman settled in Wisconsin (from 1834 to 1843).

In 1844, Clyman joined an immigrant train to Oregon, where he spent the winter before moving south into California. A year later, he met LANSFORD WARREN HASTINGS, who persuaded him to return East via the dangerous Hastings Cutoff. Clyman recognized the disadvantages of the trail and attempted to discourage overland parties from taking the route. He failed to dissuade the DONNER PARTY, whose members used the cutoff and came to a tragic demise in the Sierra Nevada.

Clyman ultimately satisfied his wanderlust and returned to California in 1848. He and his wife, Hannah McCombs, settled on a ranch in Napa, California, and raised one daughter.

—Andrea Gayle Radke and Fred R. Gowans

SEE ALSO: Fur Trade; Mountain Men

SUGGESTED READING:
Camp, Charles L. "James Clyman." In The Mountain Men and the Fur Trade of the Far West. Vol. 1. Edited by LeRoy R. Hafen. Glendale, Calif., 1965.
Clyman, James. James Clyman, Frontiersman. Edited by Charles L. Camp. Portland, Oreg., 1960.
———. Journal of a Mountain Man. Edited by Linda M. Hasselstrom. Missoula, Mont., 1984.

COAL LANDS ACT OF 1873

Passed by the U.S. Congress, the Coal Lands Act of 1873 governed the sale of public lands to be used for extracting coal. Requiring a minimum price of ten dollars per acre, the law limited the number of acres that could be purchased by one individual or group.

The restrictions did not stop railroads and coal companies who filed coal-lands claims in the name of dummy entries to obtain more land than they were entitled to by law. By the early 1900s, railroad companies had all but monopolized the coal-mining industry; having grabbed huge tracts of coal lands, they then drove competitors out of business by charging exorbitant freight rates for transporting the fuel to markets. Subsidiaries of the DENVER AND RIO GRANDE RAILWAY Company, for example, owned nearly all of the operating coal mines in Utah. In Wyoming, coal mining was dominated by the UNION PACIFIC RAILROAD.

President THEODORE ROOSEVELT attempted to tighten control of purchases of federal coal lands in 1906. When Congress moved slowly on a bill to lease rather than sell coal lands, he withdrew from entry sixty-six million acres of coal lands in six Western states and the territories of New Mexico and Alaska. Mining interests protested Roosevelt's move and delayed passage of a leasing law until the MINERAL LANDS LEASING ACT OF 1920.

—Patricia Hogan

SUGGESTED READING:
Wyant, William K. Westward in Eden: The Public Lands and the Conservation Movement. Berkeley, Calif., 1982.

COAL MINING

In the popular imagination, coal MINING in the United States is perhaps most closely associated with the East, particularly with the coal fields of Appalachia. But after the Civil War, when a rapidly industrializing United States opened up the trans-Mississippi West to several extractive industries, coal mining became a part of the West's economic order. The engine of the postwar industrialization was the railroad, providing the critical transportation link between coal field and market. By the late nineteenth century, the railroad itself consumed prodigious amounts of coal to fuel its evergrowing fleet of steam engines. Thus coal mining, an industry highly destructive of local environments, joined other kinds of mining, the LUMBER INDUSTRY, and the CATTLE INDUSTRY in the degradation of the West's fragile ecology and in the exploitation of immigrant labor, all the while boosting the West's economy.

Coal mining hardly existed in the West before 1870, but within about twenty years, coal mines dotted the landscape of nearly every state and territory, as the nation increasingly used coal rather than wood to power the steam engines of its trains, river boats, and factory machinery. The markets for Western coal were mostly local; the cost of transporting the bulky fuel long distances to Eastern consumers was prohibitive. Railroads became a major coal consumer, and in the vertical integration of the railroad industry, many rail companies established subsidiaries to operate their own coal mines. Railways eliminated competing coal companies by charging high freight rates to transport the fuel while subsidizing their own mines. The development of such monopolies explains, in part, why Western coal lands, which contain half of the nation's recoverable coal (located chiefly in Montana, Wyoming, North Dakota, Colorado, New Mexico, and Utah), never produced more than 25 percent of the nation's total supply.

As the demand for coal increased in the late nineteenth and twentieth centuries, engineers developed sophisticated methods of mining. In the least expensive means of extraction, surface mining, laborers simply broke off pieces of exposed coal with pick axes and loaded them on wagons to be hauled to a transportation center. Coal veins located hundreds of feet beneath the earth's surface required shaft and drift mining, in which miners burrowed vertical and horizontal tunnels deep into the earth. Shaft mining was labor intensive and dangerous. The use of dynamite to blast out tunnels produced frequent cave-ins and deadly coal dust that miners inhaled. Later, open-pit mining, using huge shovels to scoop out vast quantities from veins located near the earth's surface, eliminated the need for a large labor force. Strip mining was first used in the United States in 1866 near Danville, Illinois. Horse-drawn plows removed the overburden (top soil and clays lying above the coal), which workers hauled away in wheel barrows and carts. Steam-powered shovels appeared in 1911. In strip mining, a particularly destructive form of surface mining, huge trenches of coal were extracted from one end of the vein to the other. The entire vein was harvested in successive, parallel gashes.

The widespread use of strip mining in the twentieth century—accounting for about one-half of the surface mining accomplished in the United States—severely altered the Western environment. The large abandoned trenches exacerbated erosion and inhibited the growth of vegetation. In the 1970s, Western states, such as Montana, led the nation in enacting laws that required mining companies to restore the lands after stripping. Companies were required to back-fill the trenches and cover them with a layer of limestone and top soil sufficiently rich to support the rapid growth of vegetation. Piles of overburden had to be graded to a gentle contour and planted with grasses and trees to prevent erosion.

Inside an Oklahoma coal mine. *Courtesy Western History Collections, University of Oklahoma Library.*

The use of coal as fuel diminished as railroads converted their operations to diesel-powered engines in the 1930s and as home owners increasingly switched from coal to oil and natural gas to heat their homes. The coal-mining industry in the West enjoyed a resurgence in the 1970s when the United States attempted to cushion itself from OPEC manipulations in world fuel prices.

—*Patricia Hogan*

SUGGESTED READING:
Long, Priscilla. *Where the Sun Never Shines: The Bloody Coal Industry.* New York, 1989.

COCHISE
(APACHE)

One of the more famous Apache chiefs, Cochise (ca. 1810–1874) was born, perhaps in southeastern Arizona, probably the son of chief Pisago Cabezón. While his people were temporarily at peace with Mexico at the time of his birth, the Apaches soon turned to war with the Spanish and Mexicans, and hostilities, with scant, short-lived truces, lasted for most of Cochise's life.

Early in life, he had become prominent in war. Possibly his first fight was in May 1832 on the Gila River; by 1835, he was raiding deep into Sonora. Intervals of uneasy truce with the Mexicans alternated with outright hostility, particularly from 1847 onward. By 1856, Cochise was a Chiricahua band leader, sometimes operating with MANGAS COLORADAS, another great Apache chief.

Cochise kept his people at peace with Anglo-Americans until 1861, when he was falsely accused of kidnapping a white boy and stealing cattle. An army officer, Lieutenant George Bascom, sought to detain Cochise until the boy was returned. The boy had been stolen by another Apache faction not under Cochise's control. Fighting erupted, and captives on both sides were executed. The incident launched twenty-five years of sporadic Apache-white conflict in which Cochise was prominently involved for a decade.

Within sixty days of the Bascom affair, 150 whites were killed, five stage stations were destroyed, and numerous fiery engagements on a small scale had occurred between Indians and whites. Soon afterwards, however, U.S. troops were removed from the Southwest for service in the Civil War. The Indians interpreted the withdrawal as a response to Apache pressure, which therefore increased.

Cochise and Mangas Coloradas combined forces to ambush an advance element of the California Column bound for the Rio Grande to fight Confederates. The resulting Battle of Apache Pass was a minor affair but was symbolic of the interracial enmity.

Cochise remained at war with the Anglo-Americans for years after the Civil War, although now and then he met briefly with military personnel for inconclusive talks. In 1872, General OLIVER OTIS HOWARD was assigned to negotiate an end to the "Cochise War," if he could. He persuaded THOMAS J. JEFFORDS, Cochise's one white friend and confidant, to take him to the Apaches' Dragoon Mountains stronghold. At a ten-day conference, Cochise agreed to accept life on a southeastern Arizona reservation, maintain peace with the United States, if not with Mexico, and refrain from depredations, provided that Jeffords was named reservation agent. The chief kept his word until his death, apparently from cancer, two years later.

Cochise had become a semimythic figure of national prominence. His friendship with Jeffords was depicted in *Blood Brother*, a novel by Elliott Arnold later made into the popular movie *Broken Arrow*. The movie starred the blue-eyed Jeff Chandler as the black-eyed Cochise and James Stewart as Jeffords.

—*Dan L. Thrapp*

SEE ALSO: Apache Wars

SUGGESTED READING:
Sweeney, Edwin R. *Cochise: Chiricahua Apache Chief.* Norman, Okla., 1991.

CODY, WILLIAM F. ("BUFFALO BILL")

William Frederick Cody (1846–1917), who would become known as "Buffalo Bill," was born in a log

William F. Cody, known to millions as "Buffalo Bill," about 1910. *Courtesy Buffalo Bill Historical Center.*

cabin near LeClaire in the Iowa Territory. His father, Isaac, worked variously as a trader, a surveyor, and an overseer for an absentee landowner.

Isaac Cody himself was a product of westering pioneers. The first Codys in America were Huguenots, who fled France for the Isle of Jersey to escape religious persecution. By 1698, the family owned land in Massachusetts. Isaac was born in Ontario in 1811 and grew up in Ohio. Twice widowed, he married schoolteacher Mary Bonsell Laycock in 1840 at Cincinnati. She was a descendant of Pennsylvania Quaker pioneers. With Martha, Isaac's five-year-old daughter from his first marriage, the couple moved to Scott County, Iowa, where six of their seven children were born: Samuel, Julia, William, Helen, May.

A prolonged illness kept Isaac from striking out for California during the gold rush. After the accidental death of Samuel in 1853, the Codys headed west, settling briefly in Missouri and then in Kansas where Isaac supplied hay and wood to Fort Leavenworth and traded with the Kickapoo Indians. Another son, Charles, was born in 1855. Isaac, a man of principle and an active civic leader, was stabbed in 1854 while making a speech against slavery. The attack did not deter him from his economic or political activities, but its lingering effects led to his death in 1857.

Bill (known as Willie to his family) and Julia supported and cared for the younger children and their ailing mother. Bill took a job as a herder and mounted messenger with RUSSELL, MAJORS, AND WADDELL, the Leavenworth freighting firm and organizers of the PONY EXPRESS. A year later, he accompanied a wagon train to distant and exotic Fort Laramie.

During the next two years, young Cody trapped beaver, trekked to the gold fields of Colorado, and found time for several months of schooling. He also joined ("to my shame," he admitted) in some of the "border war" mischief committed by antislavery gangs of JAYHAWKERS.

It has been generally assumed, not without controversy, that Cody rode for the Pony Express at age fourteen or fifteen. Because of internal contradictions in his autobiography, scholars have made a good argument for denying his participation. However, most of his actions in 1860 and 1861 cannot be independently verified. The crucial role he and his Wild West show later played in commemorating the Pony Express, and his friendship with men central to the enterprise, both cloud the issue and in some ways make the debate irrelevant. In the absence of other records, the most it may be possible to say is that as a skilled horseman, an adventurous youth, and an erstwhile employee of the company, Bill was in the right place at the right time.

Mary Cody died on November 22, 1863. Bill mourned deeply. Early in 1864, he enlisted in the Seventh Kansas Cavalry, a volunteer Union regiment, which included many of his Jayhawking comrades. In St. Louis, he met Louisa Frederici, and the two were married in 1866. They moved to Kansas to be with his family. Bill and Louisa had four children: Arta Lucille, Kit Carson, Orra Maude, and Irma Louise.

Bill seldom stayed long at home. After a stint as a stagecoach driver and a halfhearted effort at innkeeping near Leavenworth, he set out to make a living on the plains. His talents and physical gifts, combined with an apparent fearlessness, made him successful at contract jobs for the army and the railroads. Supplying 4,280 buffaloes to feed railway construction workers during eight months in 1867 and 1868 earned him his nickname, "Buffalo Bill." General PHILIP H. SHERIDAN considered him a modest and well-spoken natural leader and made him chief scout for the Fifth Cavalry in 1868. During his years as scout (1868 to 1872; 1874; 1876), he fought in nineteen battles and skirmishes, was wounded once, was cited and rewarded for valor and "extraordinarily good services," won the Medal of Honor for gallantry, and a month after GEORGE ARMSTRONG CUSTER's defeat, he killed a Cheyenne warrior in hand-to-hand combat.

Sheridan assigned Cody in 1872 to guide the Grand Duke Alexis of Russia on one of the century's most celebrated hunts. The resulting publicity helped launch Cody's acting career when, later that year, he and "Texas Jack" Omohundro opened in Chicago in "Scouts of the Prairie" written by dime-novelist NED BUNTLINE. The "flavor of realism and nationality" that one perceptive critic found in the melodrama defined not only Cody's stage plays for the next dozen years but also his great arena show, Buffalo Bill's Wild West (active from 1883 to 1913). Better than any other medium of its day, the Wild West tied America's development to "the winning of the West" and presented the story in a clear narrative format to millions of people in the United States and abroad. In Europe, Buffalo Bill is still one of the most recognizable of Americans.

Cody invested his earnings in the modern West—mining in Arizona, ranching in Nebraska, town building in Wyoming, film making, and tourism. Most of his ventures did not return profits in his lifetime. When his Wild West show failed in 1913, his indebtedness forced him to tour through 1916 as an attraction with other shows. His death in Denver on January 10, 1917, led the press to lament "the passing of the Great West." He was accorded a state funeral, still perhaps the largest in Colorado history.

In his person, Cody reconciled for Americans the seemingly contradictory values of individualism and wilderness on the one hand with those of civilization and progress on the other. A Chicago newspaper editor summed up: "He has been more than picturesque; he has been worthwhile."

—*Paul Fees*

SEE ALSO: Wild West Shows

SUGGESTED READING:
Hedren, Paul. *First Scalp for Custer.* Lincoln, Nebr., 1987.
Hutton, Paul Andrew, ed. *Ten Days on the Plains.* Dallas, Tex., 1985.
Rosa, Joseph, and Robin May. *Buffalo Bill and His Wild West.* Lawrence, Kans., 1989.
Russell, Don. *The Lives and Legends of Buffalo Bill.* Norman, Okla., 1960.

COEUR D'ALENE INDIANS

SEE: Native Americans Peoples: Peoples of the Pacific Northwest

COFFEYVILLE RAID

SEE: Dalton Gang

COLE, PHILIP GILLETT

Philip Gillett Cole (1883–1941) amassed an extensive collection of Western art and books on Western history. Soon after Cole's birth in Illinois, his family moved to the Montana Territory. He graduated from Princeton University in 1906 and, in 1910, completed a medical degree. His medical practice in Helena, Montana, was interrupted by military service during World War I.

Following the war, Cole joined his father's thriving manufacturing firm in New York. Seemingly in response to his life in the East, Cole began to purchase Western art. His collection grew to include the work of CHARLES MARION RUSSELL, FREDERIC REMINGTON, Joseph Henry Sharp, and Olaf C. Seltzer. A Danish-born Montanan, Seltzer met Cole in 1926, and Cole's patronage secured Seltzer's artistic career. Cole eventually acquired almost two hundred of Seltzer's paintings. Following Cole's death, Thomas Gilcrease purchased his collection, which remains at the THOMAS GILCREASE INSTITUTE in Tulsa.

—*Sarah Erwin*

SUGGESTED READING:
Ladner, Mildred D. *O. C. Seltzer, Painter of the Old West.* Norman, Okla., 1979.
"The Old West Revisited, The Private World of Doctor Philip Cole." *American Scene Magazine* 4:4 (1967).

COLEMAN, WILLIAM TELL

Prominent merchant William Tell Coleman (1824–1893) was president of the SAN FRANCISCO COMMITTEE OF VIGILANCE OF 1856 and organizer of the "Pick-Handle Brigade." Born in Kentucky, the son of lawyer and state legislator Napoleon Bonaparte Coleman, William Tell Coleman arrived in California during the gold rush of 1849 and first settled in Sacramento. After some success in construction, he established the mercantile firm of William T. Coleman and Company in San Francisco in 1850. A number of profitable deals with ship captains gave the tall and handsome Coleman a good reputation as a businessman. In 1852, Coleman married Carrie Page, the daughter of Daniel Page, founder of the banking firm of Page, Bacon and Company of St. Louis. They had two sons, Carlton and Robert.

Coleman played a leading role in the Committee of Vigilance in 1851, and when the committee was revived in 1856, he was elected its president. Robert Louis Stevenson called him the "lion of the vigilantes."

After living in New York for fourteen years (from 1856 to 1870), Coleman returned to San Francisco and built a mansion on Nob Hill. In 1877, he organized the Committee of Public Safety, commonly known as the "Pick-Handle Brigade," to disperse mobs of men who had gathered at San Francisco's wharves to protest the importation of Chinese laborers. Coleman's business interests eventually included real-estate development, sugar refining, fruit canning, and borax production. The last activity, conducted in California's DEATH VALLEY, forced his company into bankruptcy in 1888, but by liquidating his property, he ultimately paid his creditors in full.

—*Roger D. McGrath*

SEE ALSO: Vigilantism

SUGGESTED READING:
Bancroft, Hubert Howe. *Popular Tribunals.* San Francisco, 1887.
Nunis, Doyce B., Jr., ed. *The San Francisco Vigilance Committee of 1856: Three Views.* Los Angeles, 1971.
Scherer, James A. B. *The Lion of the Vigilantes: William T. Coleman and the Life of Old San Francisco.* Indianapolis, Ind., 1939.
Senkewicz, Robert M. *Vigilantes in Gold Rush San Francisco.* Stanford, Calif., 1985.

COLFAX COUNTY WAR

SEE: Maxwell Land Grant Company

COLLEGES AND UNIVERSITIES

Before the American Civil War, as historian Robert V. Hine has noted, religious denominational colleges played almost as large a role in the westward migration of Anglo-Americans as did the covered wagon. But with the passage of the MORRILL ACT OF 1862 the trans-Mississippi West became, in general, the province of the state-funded college and university. Prior to this act, state funds for higher education had usually gone to what would later be termed "private" institutions, and schools such as the University of Ohio, created by the state and receiving state funds but not controlled directly by the state, would take their place beside the 182 colleges founded in America before 1861 by Baptists, Campbellites, Catholics, Congregationalists, Methodists, Presbyterians and others. Both religious schools and private colleges could, of course, also be found west of the Mississippi. Grinnell College in Iowa and Stanford University in California, the former a respected small liberal-arts college, the latter a world-class research university, are both examples of such private institutions, but, by and large, higher education developed in the region as public education dedicated to the pursuit of practical knowledge and the inculcation of patriotic virtues.

Before 1862, the United States senator from Vermont Justin Smith Morrill had for years drafted bill after bill that he hoped would turn some of the public lands the FEDERAL GOVERNMENT was giving away in the American West to a use better than wild speculation. The Morrill Act, which like the HOMESTEAD ACT OF 1862 hoped to change the pattern of Western land development, gave each state thirty thousand acres for every member it had in Congress, those acres to be dedicated to the founding of colleges offering training in agriculture and the mechanical arts. Called "land-grant colleges," they were to teach what a dean at the University of Missouri would characterize as "the science of higher production," a fit description of the function a rapidly industrializing nation might demand of schools in the economic colony for extractive enterprises it was creating in the West. Private academies opposed the new schools because, with some justification, they believed land-grant colleges posed a threat to their own sources of support. And, indeed, states did withdraw funds from obviously sectarian schools, reasserted their control over the existing universities—Michigan and Iowa, for example—they had already funded, and created new state institutions: Kansas in 1865; California in 1868; Nebraska in 1869.

Private schools in the West increasingly turned to the region's business elite, self-made men arrogant enough to want to produce other competitive souls like themselves and fearing nothing so much as the rise of SOCIALISM. Private schools promoted themselves as training grounds for rugged individualists forged by the white hot light of Cicero and Virgil, and although they achieved much success, not a few of the region's rugged individuals were themselves attracted to the practical alternative offered by state education. AMASA LELAND STANFORD only gave up his original hope to make a large bequest to the University of California in 1882 when the state senate, controlled by Democrats, refused to confirm the Republican Stanford's nomination as a regent. And even when he did fund a private institution to carry on the family name, Stanford

University's first president was the dynamic DAVID STARR JORDAN, a former president of Indiana University who had often expressed the belief that the future of education in the United States lay with state schools. At any rate, the social agenda of private schools, producing strong-minded individuals and right-thinking leaders, was distinct from that of the public institutions, where the watchword was *utility*.

"All true education," intoned the University of Michigan's president in the 1850s, "is practical." State schools did not so much ignore as neglect the classics, or as Frederick Rudolph would have it, "enthrone the practical and ignore the traditional." The long-term effect of such an early emphasis on the mechanical arts was to push the scientist and the engineer to the forefront of Western education. Somewhat surprisingly, the study of agriculture did not at first flourish in these schools, which themselves blossomed, according to Rudolph, because of the westward migration of farmers. One reason was that young men did not go to college in order to return to the farm, but instead to escape the oppressive atmosphere of small-town, mainstreet culture for the excitement and freedom of the cosmopolitan East. They did not wish to be "fancy farmers," and enrollment in the agriculture courses that promised to make them such lagged well behind others until their admissions standards were substantially lowered. The Hatch Act of 1887 remedied the situation by offering federal funds for new scientific studies in agriculture and, more importantly, by creating agricultural extension services, which allowed the practical results of such studies to be conveyed directly to farmers. By the turn of the century, not only had agriculture studies expanded dramatically but schools like the State University of Iowa and the University of California were developing hybrid strains, fertilizers, PESTICIDES, and new methods of plowing and irrigating that worked miracles for Iowa corn production, Central Valley citrus, and Sonoma wine.

State-funded higher education also affected lower schools. On the one hand, secondary public education grew more slowly in the West than in the East, especially during the Progressive era, largely because the tax base of Western communities and states, struggling to build more diverse economies, was limited. Although the West spent more per capita on education than any other region between 1880 and 1920 and California's willingness to tax for education—many believe—produced the best nineteenth-century school system in the nation, even California was unable to require compulsory education as late as 1874 and could not provide free textbooks until 1912. At the turn of the century, California had fewer than forty high schools, and other states lagged far behind it in providing textbooks and high-school training. Many Western towns had trouble getting good teachers since the best Eastern educators wished to avoid the colonial "provinces," especially their more remote areas, and looked askance at the region's emphasis on the practical. On the other hand, the state institutions pretty much dictated how secondary students should be prepared to enter college, and while in the East, private academies tutored wealthy scions for private colleges, in the West, which was short on academies, public schools took up the burden. Western universities accepted more subjects for admission than those in the East, and by 1900, when Progressive reform was afoot in the East, California already recognized thirty electives while the liberal Yale, often touted for its innovation in elective subjects, accepted only thirteen.

Innovation and *experimentation* became bywords of higher education in the West. For example, the West's state universities accepted women early on, and the state universities became women's best avenue to equal education. The Universities of Minnesota, Iowa, and Kansas all admitted women from the day they opened their doors in 1851, 1855, and 1861 respectively. By 1870, five others had followed suit—Wisconsin, Indiana, Missouri, Michigan, and California. True, the schools subjected the women to special regulations (Missouri required a guard to escort females to class), and there were only three hundred women attending all eight colleges at a time when thousands of women were attending high schools in the region, but it was a start. California especially became known for its educational experiments, particularly for its attempts to make higher education available to all citizens at low costs. Toward that end, in the 1910s and 1920s, California began turning state teacher's colleges into four-year institutions in Los Angeles, San Francisco, and San Jose, eventually creating a state-university system that reached every region of the state. More startling, however, was the state's authorizing in 1907 of two-year junior colleges under the auspices of various municipalities and counties. Fresno became the first community to establish a junior college three years later, and by 1929, there were thirty such schools in California. The junior-college idea quickly spread throughout the country, and even in the late twentieth century, community colleges, many of them now also four-year institutions, still composed the fastest growing segment of higher education.

Richard White has argued that industrializing California paid such attention to its universities in order to free itself from dependence on Eastern universities as quickly as it tried to escape the "thrall of Eastern factories." Certainly throughout the West during the first and second decades of the century, Western colleges

and universities developed a regional consciousness, perhaps even something approaching a movement. The University of Iowa's widely respected Writers' Workshop began as a self-consciously regional program, and, indeed, some of the greatest Western regional writers were associated with state universities: BENJAMIN FRANKLIN (FRANK) NORRIS, JR., and JOHN GRIFFITH (JACK) LONDON with California; WILLA CATHER with Nebraska; JOHN MUIR with Wisconsin. WALLACE STEGNER helped found the writing program at Stanford, after Iowa probably the most respected in the nation. And it was no accident that FREDERICK JACKSON TURNER, who not only formulated the famous frontier thesis but founded a school of regionalism in Western history, was a product of the University of Wisconsin.

Still, practicality and utility remained the keynotes of these institutions, and as a result, they became a bastion of "big science" in the twentieth century. In the late nineteenth century, E. W. Scripps made a substantial donation to the University of California for the establishment of the Scripps Institute of Oceanography at LaJolla, which, by World War I, had became the leading research center of its kind. The Lick Observatory had been built by the University of California in 1874, and by the 1920s, the school was one of the more distinguished centers for research in astronomy in the nation. Nobel Prize winners in the natural sciences were attracted to the Berkeley campus because of the freedom it offered to experiment and because of its climate and location. After the world's largest telescope was installed at the Mount Wilson Observatory in 1917, nearby Throop College of Technology (soon renamed California Institute of Technology) became a leading scientific center, particularly strong in physics, biology, and genetics. In Flagstaff, Arizona, the Lowell Observatory, run by Harvard University, developed as a major facility for planetary research. California schools were home to many of the scientists who planned the atomic bomb, including the director of the Manhattan Project, J. Robert Oppenheimer, and they were leaders in the development of the aerospace industry.

By 1960, California alone was spending more than one billion dollars a year on education, a figure that irked many taxpayers when the campus at Berkeley became the birthplace of the "free speech" movement, a forerunner to the radical student protests against the War in Vietnam that made California schools a hotbed of unrest. Still, the state built a school a day; it was possible, until recently, for any Californian to enjoy a free public education through graduate school; and the state, until the 1980s, continued to boast one of the best educational systems in the world. Throughout the West, higher education remained overwhelming public, and—with a few exceptions in the Southwest—high on the agenda for public funding, especially in Midwestern states like Wisconsin and Iowa. Despite such private institutions as Stanford and Caltech, only in one Western state, Utah, did private colleges enroll a substantial proportion of college students.

—*Charles Phillips*

SUGGESTED READING:

Cremin, Lawrence A. *American Education: The National Experience, 1783–1876.* New York, 1980.

Hine, Robert V. *The American West: An Interpretive History.* Boston, 1984.

Veysey, Laurence. *Emergence of the American University.* Chicago, 1965.

COLLINS, BEN

The first Native American to serve as a deputy U.S. marshal, Ben Collins (?–1906) began his career as a police officer in the Indian Territory. Little is known about Collins's life prior to his accepting the position of deputy U.S. marshal for Emet, Oklahoma, a position he took quite seriously. His dedication often led to friction with some of the area's prominent citizens. In 1905, Collins attempted to arrest Port Pruitt, one of Emet's wealthiest residents. Pruitt resisted, and in the ensuing confrontation, each man drew his gun. Collins wounded Pruitt, who was initially charged with attempted murder. Even though the charges were dropped, Pruitt, in revenge, offered a five-hundred-dollar bounty to anyone who would kill Collins. Pruitt paid the bounty to "Killin' Jim" Miller who murdered Collins on August 1, 1906.

—*Patricia Hogan*

SEE ALSO: Federal Marshals and Deputies; Law and Order

COLMAN, NORMAN J.

An agricultural editor and public official, Norman J. Colman (1827–1911) was born in Otsego County, New York. He edited the *Valley Farmer* (entitled *Colman's Rural World* after 1865) in St. Louis beginning in 1855. He served in the state legislature and as lieutenant-governor of Missouri and then was named United States commissioner of agriculture by President Grover Cleveland in 1885. Colman became the first secretary of agriculture in 1889 when the post was added to the president's cabinet. He transformed the U.S. Department of Agriculture into a reputable scientific agency and facilitated and championed the Hatch Act (1887), which created the federally funded system of agricultural experiment stations.

—*David B. Danbom*

SUGGESTED READING:

Lemmer, George F. *Norman J. Colman and* Colman's Rural World: *A Study in Agricultural Leadership.* Columbia, Mo., 1953.

COLOMA, CALIFORNIA

SEE: Ghost Towns

COLORADO

Colorado, the thirty-eighth state, joined the union in 1876: its nickname is the Centennial State. The Spanish word Colorado, meaning "red," recalls the region's vermilion landscapes. The eighth largest state, Colorado comprises sixty-three counties. It is nearly a perfect rectangle; at its widest, it is 387 miles east to west and 276 miles north to south. Its southwest corner, known as the Four Corners, is the only place in the country where four states—Utah, New Mexico, Arizona, and Colorado—meet at one point. Mount Elbert, at 14,431 feet, is the highest point in the state; the lowest point, at 3,350 feet, is near Holly. Colorado has fifty-four peaks higher than 14,000 feet. Five major rivers—the Colorado, Rio Grande, South Platte, Arkansas, and North Platte—have their headwaters within the mountains. Only about half of Colorado's 104,091 square miles is in the ROCKY MOUNTAINS.

Geography

Colorado's splendor and diversity were immortalized in the lyrics of "America the Beautiful." College professor Katherine Lee Bates wrote the words after returning from a trip to the summit of Pikes Peak in the summer of 1893. The natural landscape ranges from the High Plains in the east through the Colorado Piedmont to the mountain ranges and plateaus of the Rocky Mountains in the west. While generally thought of as a mountain state, Colorado actually has several geographic sections. The Eastern Plains, part of Great Plains, extend west as far as the foothills. This region is underlain by layered rocks, sandstone, shales, and limestone. Over these rocks grows short grasses, in which prairie dogs, jackrabbits, coyotes, rattlesnakes, antelopes, and various birds thrive. This farming and

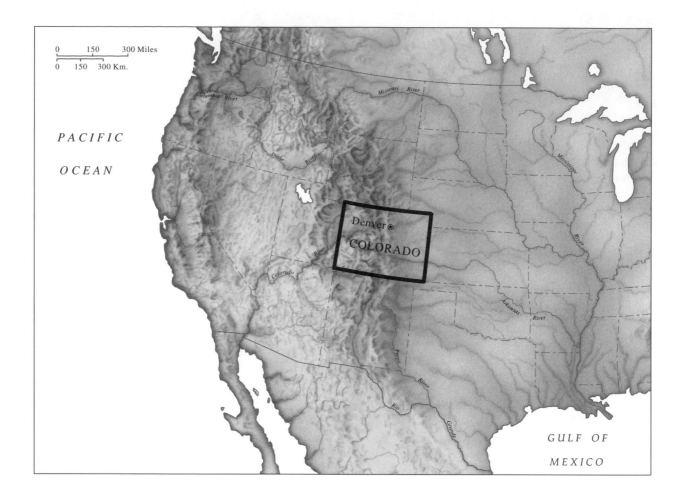

ranching region is higher than many hilly or mountainous regions elsewhere in the United States. The soil is fertile but lacks moisture.

The Colorado Piedmont, measuring about 50 miles wide and 275 miles long, is a hilly to mountainous region between the plains and the Rocky Mountains. The state's major cities are located in the piedmont region, and fourth-fifths of the state's population resides there. Natural attractions in the region include the Garden of the Gods, a multicolored agglomeration of sandstones northwest of Colorado Springs, and Red Rocks Park, an outdoor amphitheater southwest of Denver.

The western part of Colorado includes the mountains that gave Colorado the nineteenth-century name "the crest of the continent." The Continental Divide cuts across the state north to south. The arid to semiarid western portion includes plateaus, mesas, rich river valleys, and deserts.

Colorado's climate varies tremendously from region to region. Temperature extremes range from below zero to over 100° F. Annual precipitation averages about fifteen inches where most Coloradans live, but some areas receive fewer than ten inches and others as much as forty inches per year. Snowfall, one of Colorado's significant natural resources, averages eight inches at Karval and more than 350 inches on Wolf Creek Pass. Snowfall supports irrigated agriculture (Colorado ranks fifth nationally in irrigated acres) where otherwise only dryland farming would be possible. Snow provides a multimillion-dollar winter tourist attraction—skiing. Finally, Colorado's high country serves as the watershed for much of the West; melting snow provides water for six states plus parts of Mexico.

Native Americans

The earliest people to live in Colorado were hunters and food gatherers known as Paleo-Indians. They arrived on the Eastern Plains at least fifteen thousand years ago. The best-known Indian group, because of their spectacular village sites in the southwestern corner of the state, is the Anasazi (ancient ones). They migrated into the Four Corners region more than two thousand years ago and developed a farming and village culture. Excellent weavers, potters, and stone masons, they traded for goods from the West Coast to the Mississippi Valley. For hundreds of years, the Anasazi people farmed the river valleys and mesa tops and then, in the late thirteenth century, migrated out of the region.

They left behind the cliff dwellings that are the core of Mesa Verde National Park, thousands of other archaeological sites, and enduring mysteries. Why did some of them abandon the valleys to move into the cliff caves? Why did they leave the land they had lived for generations? Perhaps the answer to the latter provides a warning to Coloradans today. Increased population pressure, worn-out land, decreased natural resources, and changing weather patterns may have prompted the Anasazi people to move from the area.

The Utes moved into the Western Slope, the area west of the Continental Divide, a century or so after the Anasazi left. Various migrating tribes, including the Apaches and Comanches, hunted over the Eastern Plains before the Cheyennes and Arapahos arrived in the eighteenth century.

The lives of all of these peoples changed with the coming of the Spanish into the Rio Grande Valley. From the Spanish, the Native Americans eventually secured the horse (which influenced almost every aspect of their culture), the gun, trade goods, and other European materials. Spanish expeditions, mining efforts, and trading ventures marked the land with names and legends.

United States control

Spain's hold on the region remained nominal at best, and after a series of diplomatic maneuvers, the United States acquired the eastern section of Colorado with the LOUISIANA PURCHASE in 1803. The remainder of the territory came under United States control with the 1848 treaty ending the United States–Mexican War. American exploration, starting with ZEBULON MONTGOMERY PIKE's expedition in 1806 and 1807, made the region better known. STEPHEN HARRIMAN LONG, who explored the region in 1820, described the Eastern Plains as part of the "Great American Desert." JOHN CHARLES FRÉMONT's five expeditions from 1842 to 1853 and his journals added a strong dash of romance, adventure, and economic potential to the evolving picture of the central Rockies.

The first significant economic exploitation of Colorado's natural resources came with development of the fur trade in the 1820s and 1830s. Controlled and financed by outside individuals, the fur trappers and traders explored the region in their quest for beaver and other animals. BENT'S FORT on the ARKANSAS RIVER, Colorado's first "urban hub," was strategically located to tap commerce along the Santa Fe Trail, the

fur business, and the Indian trade. However a changing international market and a decline in the number of beaver doomed the fur trade by the 1840s. In the 1850s, only a few small Hispanic settlements had taken hold in the San Luis Valley and farther east. The rest of Colorado remained unsettled and undeveloped.

A decade after the discovery of gold in California in 1848, two separate parties went to Colorado to search for gold in the Pikes Peak region. The small amount discovered in present-day Denver laid the basis for the second largest gold rush in American history. More than 100,000 people started west in 1859, although the majority turned around upon hearing that the discovery was a "humbug." It was not, and the gold deposits found in Clear Creek, Gilpin, and Boulder counties made the Pikes Peak rush a success.

Out of this 1859 rush, Colorado would eventually be born, the child of the American dream of getting rich without working. The next two generations of Coloradans would continue to scramble for the elusive bonanzas. The placer, or free gold, era proved very brief, and by the end of 1860, hard-rock mining had come to the forefront. In the urban frontier of mining, little settlements sprang up throughout the mountains as the prospectors searched for gold. Denver and, to a lesser degree, Boulder and Canon City emerged as gateway towns and supply points. Attracted by the potential profit, farmers settled along the streams, planted their crops, and shipped their harvest into the mountains.

When the heated slavery debate prevented Colorado from gaining territorial status, politicians organized their own Territory of Jefferson (1860 to 1861). After the South seceded, however, Northern states dominated Congress and created the new Colorado

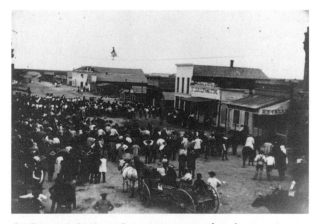

On Denver's Larimer Street two years after the town's founding, citizens watch Mademoiselle Carolista dancing a highwire. *Courtesy Colorado Historical Society.*

Thousands of individuals headed to Colorado hoping to get rich on gold and silver. The circumstance of the Colorado miner pictured here, however, was a far more common experience. *Courtesy Colorado Historical Society.*

Territory in 1861. The Republican party selected the first territorial officials and for thirty years dominated the political scene.

No Civil War battles were fought in the Colorado Territory, but its troops played a major role in repelling the one serious Confederate invasion threat at the battles of La Glorieta Pass and Apache Canyon, New Mexico, in March 1862. The war affected the territory in many ways including withdrawal of federal troops and increased tensions with Plains Indians. These tensions culminated in the infamous attack by whites on a Cheyenne and Arapaho village at Sand Creek, November 29, 1864, an attack that only intensified the Indian Wars. The long-term result was the removal of the Cheyennes and Arapahos from the Eastern Plains.

During 1863 and 1864, Colorado mining attracted capital from Eastern financiers, who had money to invest and who believed mines to be a golden opportunity. Coloradans, even those who owned gold mines, had little specie. The result—a frenzy of buying and selling—ended in economic collapse in April 1864, and

for the next decade, investors avoided pumping their money into Colorado.

The decade after the war was difficult for the territory. The transcontinental railroad bypassed Colorado and Denver, and only the determined efforts of Denverites secured a railroad connection in 1870. Mining problems, however, particularly ore refining and lack of finances, continued to bedevil Coloradans. Brown University chemistry professor Nathaniel Hill and his smelter solved many refining problems and helped place Colorado on a much more scientific metallurgical basis. However, investors still went elsewhere, Colorado's population growth stagnated, and new Rocky Mountain mining rivals seized the headlines.

Statehood

Statehood in 1876 brightened the scene, and then the discovery of Leadville's bonanza silver deposits ushered in a new age. As author MARY HALLOCK FOOTE, a New Yorker who accompanied her mining engineer husband to Colorado, wrote, "All roads lead to

Leadville." Colorado soon became the premier mining state in the nation. For the next decade and a half, the state prospered, and stories about men such as Horace Austin Warner Tabor caught the public's fancy. Tabor, an investor in Colorado mines, was worth seven million dollars, and he constructed lavish opera houses in Leadville and Denver during the 1880s before his empire collapsed. Leadville silver built Denver into the "Queen of the Mountains and Plains" with an 1890 population of 106,000—nearly triple what it had been ten years earlier.

The 1870s and 1880s witnessed a railroad boom into the mountains and over the plains. The Denver and Rio Grande Railway Company built south and then west, establishing such towns as Colorado Springs and Durango and opening the Western Slope to settlement. It and other railroads tapped the major mining districts of Central City, Aspen, Silverton, Georgetown, and Telluride and opened coal fields in Boulder, Huerfano, and Las Animas counties. Under the railroads' guidance, tourism flourished and healthseekers came to find cures in the dry, crisp, "ozone filled" air or in the many mineral and hot springs. Agriculture expanded. With the outstanding success of the Union Colony at Greeley, which organized Colorado's initial major irrigation district, other colonies blossomed with less success. Colorado's 1890 population doubled to 412,000. Pressure on water resources forced Colorado to pioneer water laws. The new laws abandoned the principle of riparian rights, determined by legal possession of land bordering a stream, and instead adopted prior appropriation rights, determined by the priority of actually using water.

The 1890s proved a bittersweet decade. The decline in the price of silver, lower grade ore, and increased mining costs placed the industry on the defensive. The coup de grace came with the crash of 1893 and depression. Colorado took nearly a decade to recover. Politically the "silver issue" became the touchstone. Members of the Greenback party called for the remonetization of silver and the issuance of silver dollars, which had been dropped from Congress's list of approved coins in 1873. The issue was popular in silver-mining regions such as Colorado because the metal would become more valuable if coined. When the Populist and then the Democratic parties embraced the issue, Colorado switched political allegiance. Congress passed the Sherman Silver Purchase Act of 1890, a measure that increased the number of silver dollars but maintained some limits. In 1893, however, the nation plunged into a depression, and blaming the Sherman Silver Purchase Act for the country's economic hard times, President Grover Cleveland persuaded Congress to repeal the law. Fortunately for the state, Cripple Creek's great gold deposits opened during the 1890s and softened the depression's impact.

Twentieth-century developments

Cripple Creek also foreshadowed twenty years of labor violence as the Western Federation of Miners and the United Mine Workers fought to unionize the coal and hard-rock fields. The resulting turmoil gave Colorado a reactionary image as the unions were eventually crushed amid death, destruction of lives and property, and high costs. The political scene proved no better, and in 1905 amid charges of graft and corruption, Coloradans had three governors in twenty-four hours.

Meanwhile, the United States moved into the Progressive era, and Colorado, after a slow start, jumped on the reform bandwagon. John Shafroth, who served as governor from 1909 to 1913, brought the state into the twentieth century with a series of Progressive reforms (including initiative, referendum, and recall) and returned power to the people. The reform era died by the 1920s, and a reactionary cloud settled over the land. As a result, the Ku Klux Klan captured the Republican party, elected a governor and senator, and won support for its "America first" notions from 1921 to 1925.

Mining had declined since its earlier heyday, and agriculture slumped after World War I. The crash of 1929 and the Great Depression only increased the state's economic woes. President Franklin D. Roosevelt's federal New Deal brought renewed vigor and in many ways conquered Colorado. Colorado ranked tenth among the forty-eight states in per capita receipt

Coaches and buckboards travel down the carriage road of Colorado's Pikes Peak in this 1911 photograph. *Courtesy National Archives.*

of New Deal agency expenditures during the years between 1933 and 1939. The state recovered economically, and government involvement increased from military bases to private industry. With the demands of World War II, mining and agriculture prospered. Tourism thrived, and the population soared, thanks to the many veterans who had fallen in love with Colorado during their stateside service there.

Denver dominated the state economically, politically, and commercially. Other Front Range urban centers also benefited, while the rest of the state trailed. The growth of the skiing industry provided Colorado with a needed winter attraction to balance summer outdoor activities. Meanwhile, the Western Slope was involved with a uranium excitement that lasted from the late 1940s into the early 1960s. An oil-shale boom a decade and a half later died quickly, however. The boom-and-bust cycle of earlier years reappeared with familiar results. Agriculture dwindled during these years, the number of farms declined, the rural areas lost population and political power and found themselves overrun by urban and tourism interests.

Denver, the capital city and the largest community in the state, had a 1990 population of 467,619. The Front Range urban corridor running from Fort Collins to Pueblo contains more than 80 percent of the state's population and the major industrial, commercial, and banking centers. The 1990 census counted 3,294,394 Coloradans, more than half living in Denver and its immediate surrounding counties. Slightly more than 50 percent of the state's population was women; 4 percent of the population was foreign-born. While the Colorado's average population density is 31.8 people per square mile, Denver has 3,050.3. Hinsdale County at .4 and Mineral County .6 people per square mile are the least populated regions.

Colorado in the 1980s and 1990s again emerged as highly urbanized as it had been a century before. The state had become, like most of its Western sisters, concerned about growth, urban crime, environment, water, pollution, taxes, and its role with respect to the federal government.

—*Duane A. Smith*

SEE ALSO: Colorado Gold and Silver Rushes; Colorado River Compact; Cripple Creek Strikes; Currency and Silver as Western Political Issues; Gold Mining; Mining; Silver Mining; Sand Creek Massacre

SUGGESTED READING:
Abbott, Carl, Stephen J. Leonard, and David McComb. *Colorado: A History of the Centennial State*. Rev. ed. Boulder, Colo., 1982.
Sprague, Marshal. *Colorado: A Bicentennial State History*. States and the Nation. New York and Nashville, Tenn., 1984.
Ubbelohde, Carl, Maxine Benson, and Duane A. Smith. *A Colorado History*. 6th ed. Boulder, Colo., 1988.

COLORADO DOCTRINE (OF WATER RIGHTS)

The Colorado Doctrine is a system of WATER rights first instituted in 1882. That year, the Colorado State Supreme Court, in *Coffin* v. *Left Hand Ditch Company* (6 Colo. 443), abolished the riparian right in surface waters and established prior appropriation as the exclusive water right of the state. Riparian rights are primarily determined by the legal possession of land bordering a stream; prior appropriation rights are primarily determined by the priority of actually using water. Jurists in the state had assumed that when Colorado entered the Union it did so with full control over all water within its borders; therefore, it had the authority to invalidate riparian rights at will and did so. Since Colorado was the first state to take such action, the legal system became known as the Colorado Doctrine. Eventually Alaska, Arizona, Idaho, Montana, Nevada, New Mexico, Utah, and Wyoming adopted the doctrine. Although details vary from state to state, the doctrine's elements dealing with beneficial use and water conservation play important roles, because in these states, water is scarce. Under the system, waste, nonuse, and nonbeneficial uses can be discouraged.

—*Kazuto Oshio*

SEE ALSO: California Doctrine (or Water Rights)

SUGGESTED READING:
Dunbar, Robert G. *Forging New Rights in Western Waters*. Lincoln, Nebr., 1983.
Hundley, Norris, Jr. *Water and the West: The Colorado River Compact and the Politics of Water in the American West*. Berkeley, Calif., 1975.

COLORADO GOLD AND SILVER RUSHES

Gold was discovered in July 1858 near the present-day site of Denver, and by the spring of the following year, more than fifty thousand people flocked to the Pikes Peak gold rush, making it second only to the 1849 CALIFORNIA GOLD RUSH in terms of numbers of participants. The settlements the gold miners created

Top: "Camp of the Miners of the North Star and Mountaineer Lodes, on King Solomon Mountain, about Cunningham Gulch." Photographed by William Henry Jackson in San Juan County, Colorado Territory, 1875. *Courtesy National Archives.*

Dolly Varden Mine on Saxon Mountains, Georgetown, Colorado, about 1890. *Courtesy Museum of New Mexico.*

were not permanent, and many miners returned home—mostly to the East—the same year. Annual immigrations to the gold fields continued up to the mid-1860s. The important towns that emerged included Georgetown, Idaho Springs, Silver Plume, and Central City. The most significant mining was concentrated in Gilpin County. Mining quickly progressed from panning to ore reduction, but the boom collapsed in the middle of the 1860s because of technical difficulties in extracting the ore and the continuing need for capital.

The second major period of Colorado mining was associated with silver and the largely deserted mining camp of LEADVILLE. Prospectors had panned for gold near Leadville as early as 1860, but the results were small. The great silver strikes in 1877, however, made Leadville the most active mining town in the world; its population grew to an estimated forty thousand in 1880, the year the DENVER AND RIO GRANDE RAILWAY

COMPANY reached the city. While the climate and physical isolation of Leadville, located at ten thousand feet above sea level, posed special problems for miners, the silver mines turned out to be among the richest in the world, producing $700 million in metals (mostly silver and lead). Leadville's silver production made Colorado a center of smelting operations. The city's boom years were from 1877 to 1885, when it took on the characteristics associated with mining communities: numerous saloons, beer gardens, gambling halls, and houses of prostitution all overlaid with a growing respectability that included churches, schools, banks, and daily newspapers. The city was also home to some of Colorado's most important mining personalities, such as HORACE AUSTIN WARNER TABOR. As a result of high altitudes, labor troubles, and the failure of long-range development, Leadville declined as a mining center in the late 1880s.

In 1890, Leadville was overtaken as the leading silver producer by Aspen, a mining city on the Roaring Fork River. Founded in 1879, Aspen grew slowly in size and ore production until the arrival of the railroad in 1887, when output increased tenfold and the town changed to a city. Aspen and Leadville and other silver-mining centers were all but closed down by a law in 1893 that repealed the SHERMAN SILVER PURCHASE ACT OF 1840. Forced through Congress by President Grover Cleveland as a response to the depression of 1893, the repeal law effectively marked the end of the great silver-mining period in Colorado.

The third and final stage in Colorado's gold and silver mining rushes was centered in the town of CRIPPLE CREEK, located on a high plateau some fifty miles west of Colorado Springs. Geologists and large investors developed the gold deposits, and by 1892, Cripple Creek's population had reached five thousand. It became the popular reincarnation of gold mania as people flocked there to take advantage of the economic opportunities associated with the great gold discoveries. Cripple Creek's appeal was enhanced by the depression of 1893 and the decline of the price of silver that closed the silver mines in Colorado. Mining people from towns all over the West flocked to the new gold bonanzas that seemed to promise relief from hard times. The mines were immensely rich, and they required modern mining techniques and a large labor force. Under the leadership of the WESTERN FEDERATION OF MINERS, the miners went out on strike in 1894 against increased hours at the same wage and in 1904 to increase union membership. Both strikes failed, and in 1904, company forces drove the union leadership from the town and reopened the mines with nonunion labor. The defeat marked the end of the Western Federation of Miners' influence in Colorado. Gold production in Cripple Creek peaked in 1901, but advances in technology kept the mines in operation until the end of World War II.

Colorado mining, after the early years of placer diggings near Denver, was associated with rich mines, the most modern mining techniques, and large mining work forces that sometimes led to labor violence. Perhaps no where else was the contrast between the wealth of the owners and the hard-living conditions of the miners so clear. The collapse of silver mining in Colorado in 1893 elevated the so-called silver question to the status of a national political issue. "Free silver" became the rallying cry of WILLIAM JENNINGS BRYAN and the Democratic party. Bryan and other Democratic candidates ran strongly in Western states and poorly in the East. At the close of the silver- and gold-mining rushes, the mining regions in Colorado had been devastated, especially by the clear-cutting of forests and the residue of the chemicals that had come quickly into widespread use.

—*Malcolm J. Rohrbough*

SEE ALSO: Cripple Creek Strikes; Gold Mining; Mining; Silver Mining

SUGGESTED READING:

Dorset, Phyllis. *The New Eldorado.* New York, 1970.

Griswold, Jean H. *The Carbonate Camp Called Leadville.* Denver, 1951.

Paul, Rodman W. *Mining Frontiers of the Far West, 1849–1880.* New York, 1963.

Rohrbough, Malcolm M. *Aspen.* New York, 1986.

Smith, Duane A. *Rocky Mountain Mining Camps.* Bloomington, Ind., 1967.

COLORADO RIVER

Named by Spanish explorers in the eighteenth century for its reddish water, the Colorado River begins 8,369 feet high at Grand Lake on the western slopes of the Rocky Mountains and runs for 1,450 miles. Dropping 14,000 feet to the sea in the Gulf of California, the Colorado has been grinding away for some thirteen million years at sandstone and shale, cutting through massive rocks downward for hundreds of miles, and carving the most spectacular canyons found anywhere in the world. As the river swirls and winds to the southwest, it drains a basin 246,000 miles square, much of it arid and semiarid lands composing parts of seven states: Wyoming, Colorado, Utah, New Mexico, Nevada, Arizona, and California. Containing some of the more colorful and dramatically angled landscapes in

Colorado River.

the country, the Colorado Basin is also home to 17 miles of international border between Arizona and Mexico. Always the region's major river, the Colorado, in the twentieth century, fell prey to intense development, and—dammed from tip to toe—became the life line of the urban and arid Southwest.

Flowing across Colorado from its source, the river was long called at that point the Grand, a name sometimes still used by the locals. Cutting steeply and swiftly through the mountains, the Colorado plunges nearly 400 feet in 5 miles around Gore Canyon, located 80 miles north of Glenwood Springs. Fed by tributaries—the Gunnison, Dolores, San Juan, and Little Colorado from the east and the Green, Dirty Devil, Escalante, Paria, Kanab, and Virgin from the west—that only sporadically flow to the river and contribute little or no run-off, the upper Colorado has produced a labyrinth of deep gorges, the largest and most spectacular being the Grand Canyon, which extends from the mouth of the Paria to the Grand Wash Stream. Where the Colorado meets the Green River in southeastern Utah lies another of the massive trenches, today known as Canyonlands National Park. Flanked by two great deserts, California's Mojave to the west, Arizona's and Mexico's Sonoran to the east, the lower Colorado flows through a broad flood plain to reach its delta in Baja California. Along the way, two other tributaries join the Colorado, the Bill Williams and Gila rivers, which drain much of western New Mexico and central Arizona.

In the northern reaches, the Colorado Basin houses grassy mountain meadows and evergreen forests of pine, fur, spruce, and aspen; on the lower slopes and higher, humid plateaus, chaparral and juniper forests

Distant view of Ancient Ruins in lower part of Canon de Chelle. . . . Showing their position in the walls and elevation above bed of canon. A member of the Wheeler expedition in the foreground sketches the ruins. Photograph by Timothy H. O'Sullivan. *Courtesy National Archives.*

abound; down in the desert grow clump grass, woody shrubs, yucca, cactus, and—in some areas—nothing at all. Rugged, isolated, thinly populated, the basin supports wildlife in an abundance seldom seen elsewhere in the country. Once home to grizzly bears and gray wolves, the area still boasts numerous large mammals such as elks, mountain sheep, pronghorns, mule deer, mountain lions, bobcats, and coyotes, as well as smaller creatures like beavers, muskrats, gophers, and rabbits. Birds, too, including the bald eagle, favor the streams of the Colorado system, which are lined with willows, cottonwoods, and tamarisk.

Despite its sparse human population, the basin suffered major disruptions to its species and habitats from modern river development. Introduced by accident in the nineteenth century, the thirsty tamarisk shrub, for example, spread rapidly along the river, drinking down large quantities of water. Local ranchers, driven by ranching's relentless economy, systematically killed off large predators like the grizzly and the wolf. Once flourishing in the lower Colorado, river otters have vanished from the scene. In the mid-twentieth century, some

people began intentionally to eradicate four native fishes—humpback chubs, bonytail chubs, Colorado squawfish, razorback suckers—only to have others later place them on a list of animals to be protected, at great expense, under the Endangered Species Act.

The waters of the Colorado are fed mostly by winter rains and snow, both of which fall frequently on the upper basin. From the middle of the river to the ocean, the area is relatively dry, though sometimes subject to flash floods from summer thunderstorms sweeping up from the Gulf of Mexico or the Pacific Ocean off Mexico's west coast. Otherwise, the summer rains quickly evaporate, and only about 10 percent of the basin's precipitation ever sees its way into the river. When the winter snows pack high, the spring thaws cause the Colorado to rage in torrents that spill over its banks. In dry years, when the river is fed only by far away melting snow, the torrents become trickles by summer. Before the Colorado was dammed, it flooded huge areas in the south and sometimes spilled into the Salton Basin to create temporary lakes and seas, and today, the annual fluctuations in the flow of the river are exaggerated by the amount of water diverted for agricultural and domestic use.

For centuries, Native Americans—Utes and Southern Paiutes—hunted and gathered along the plateaus and in the canyons of the upper basin while, amid the lower reaches of the basin along the Gila and Salt rivers, the Hohokam built the largest prehistoric system of IRRIGATION canals in the American West. Indian pueblos dot the drainage basin of the San Juan and other tributaries in the area where the corners of Utah, Colorado, Arizona, and New Mexico meet on today's maps. In the flood plain of the Colorado, where the river was too wild for canals, the Yumas were practicing a more expansive pattern of farming and hunting than these agriculturalists who diverted streams, grew crops, and built villages hundreds of years before the arrival of Europeans. Most of the villages had been abandoned by the time Athapascan-speaking raiders arrived in the region late in the thirteenth century, first the Apaches, then shortly thereafter the Navajos. Those Hopi, Zuni, and Rio Grande pueblos that continued to function were probably the source of the rumors about seven cities of gold called CÍBOLA that first attracted the Spaniards north from Mexico where they found rude adobes housing poor Indians, who scratched out a living in the desert by tapping the Colorado.

After exploring the area and discovering the Grand Canyon but no gold and silver, disappointed conquistadors left the basin to a few determined missionaries, the hapless soldiers sent to guard them, and a sprinkling of settlers, who clustered along the northern reaches of Spain's new world empire at Tubac and

Tucson, where they irrigated their crops with water from the Santa Cruz River. During much of the Spanish and Mexican occupation of the region, the Colorado was more obstacle than life line, cutting off New Spain from California. The one attempt the Spanish made to establish a toehold at the Yuma crossing led to the YUMA REVOLT. After 1820, fur-trapping MOUNTAIN MEN explored the Colorado basin in search of beavers. The descriptions produced by early government explorations discouraged settlement in the rugged mountains and the GREAT AMERICAN DESERT drained by the river until JOHN CHARLES FRÉMONT challenged such descriptions in the 1840s. Following the United States–Mexican War, most of the intermediate areas and lower stretches of the Colorado basin became part of the United States under the Treaty of Guadalupe Hidalgo in 1848 and the GADSDEN PURCHASE in 1853. In 1851, steamboats began carrying military supplies upriver from Fort Yuma, established near the spot where the Indians had destroyed Spanish missions and settlements and, in the years following, ran their own ferrying operation for Anglo-Americans traveling west. By 1858, inland-shipping entrepreneurs such as Joseph Christmas Ives were investigating the Colorado's navigability. In the 1870s, the federal government sponsored major scientific surveys of the region, the most celebrated being that of JOHN WESLEY POWELL, who was the first to concentrate directly on the river itself and the first to discuss the full implication of its use in the region's future development in his landmark REPORT OF THE LANDS OF ARID REGIONS.

The discovery of rich mineral deposits in the upper Colorado prompted MINING ventures in the region, and railroads—some of them narrow-gauge—built to service the mining camps and towns also encouraged farming settlements. Farming required irrigation, and Thomas Blythe was the first to make a filing on Colorado River WATER in California in 1877. By 1883, the Grand Valley Canal tapped the Colorado at its juncture with the Gunnison to irrigate valley farms in western Colorado, and around the turn of century, the California Development Company began diverting the river to water the Imperial Valley. Faulty engineering and heavy spring rains caused the Colorado to jump the canal, flood into the valley, and create the Salton Sea. The SOUTHERN PACIFIC RAILROAD, whose tracks ran through the valley, fought to return the Colorado to its proper course between 1905 and 1907. Although the effort was successful, the disaster itself, coming at a moment when the nation was engaged in a debate on the West's water, sparked interest in controlling the Colorado. In 1922, seven states signed the COLORADO RIVER COMPACT dividing the river among themselves and "opening" it for development. The "lower compact" states

were Arizona, Nevada, and California, the "upper compact" states, Wyoming, Utah, Colorado, and New Mexico. Jointly, they introduced the doctrine of multiple use, making the Colorado Basin the first such region subject to planned development, irrigation, recreation, flood control, and navigation. Congress passed the BOULDER CANYON ACT OF 1928 authorizing the construction of the first of twenty dams that would control—and claimed some environmentalists, kill—the river. An engineering marvel, Boulder Dam, now known as HOOVER DAM, and the artificial Lake Mead created by the water the dam "impounded" became major tourists attractions after they were completed in 1936. There followed, to name only the more notable, GLEN CANYON DAM, impounding Lake Powell, and Parker Dam, impounding Havasu Lake, which supplies water to southern California. Other water projects, many initiated during the New Deal under the auspices of the BUREAU OF RECLAMATION, diverted Colorado River water through tunnels and aqueducts to irrigate crops in northern Colorado and to supply Southwestern cities with tap water.

So much water was diverted that both Mexico and the Native Americans voiced concerns. A treaty with Mexico in 1946 had guaranteed the country 1.5 million acre-feet of water annually, but no mention was made in the document about the quality of water. When the growth of irrigated agriculture along the river produced increasing salt run-off, the water reaching Mexico not only was unfit for use but also began to pile up huge saline deposits that eventually blocked the flow of the river to the sea. In 1963, the federal government stepped into a growing controversy between the Native Americans and the river-compact states to clarify the amount of water apportioned to the lower basin states and the amounts that had been implicitly reserved for the Indians. That decision paved the way for the Central Arizona Project, which would divert huge amounts of water to the booming Sun Belt cities of Phoenix and Tucson. In 1972, a international agreement with Mexico led to desalinization experiments in the lower basin and attempts to manage irrigation more closely in the upper basin in order to dispose of saline water.

Today, in some seasons, the Colorado River no longer reaches the Gulf of California. On the Mexico-Arizona border the Morelos diversion dam sends virtually every drop of Colorado River water that reaches Mexico to irrigation canals in the Mexicali Valley and to the border towns of Mexicali and Tijuana. And still tensions run deep among the compact states themselves, between them and the Indians, and between the United States and Mexico, because in truth there is not enough water to go around in an arid region where more water from the Colorado is used each year than rains or melting snow can replenish.

—*Charles Phillips*

SEE ALSO: Farming: Farming in the Imperial Valley and Salton Sea Region; Mojave Desert; Multiple-Use Doctrine; Reclamation;

SUGGESTED READING:

Hundley, Norris, Jr. *Water and the West: The Colorado River Compact and the Politics of Water in the American West.* Berkeley, Calif., 1975.

Pisani, Donald J. *To Reclaim a Divided West: Water, Law, and Public Policy, 1848–1902.* Albuquerque, N. Mex., 1992.

Reisner, Marc. *Cadillac Desert: The American West and Its Disappearing Water.* New York, 1986.

Stevens, Joseph E. *Hoover Dam: An American Adventure.* Norman, Okla., 1988.

Worster, Donald. *Rivers of Empire: Water, Aridity, and the Growth of the American West.* New York, 1985.

COLORADO RIVER COMPACT

The Colorado River Compact of 1922, the first agreement between states over the use of WATER, had its origins in Charles Rockwood's vision for the Valley of the Dead, a bone-dry basin in southern California. In 1892, Rockwood renamed the place Imperial Valley and began building and promoting an extensive IRRIGATION project. Agricultural production proved magnificent, but problems mounted in taming and diverting the Colorado River. The Imperial Valley irrigators needed a huge dam on the Colorado River to regulate stream flows. In April 1922, Congress began pondering the Swing-Johnson (or Boulder Canyon) Bill, that would authorize the building of an immense dam on the Colorado near the southern tip of Nevada to protect the Imperial Valley.

A project of such magnitude, however, would surely affect the flow of the Colorado all along its main stem and along its tributaries. These potentially adverse effects drew the attention of water users in six Western states. Believing that Californians would drain their watersheds, people in the upriver states and their congressional representatives took great exception to the prospect of California benefiting at their expense. Before all of these people lay the pressing questions of how to divide the economic returns of such a mammoth project and how to protect their own present and future interests in Colorado River flows without costly interstate litigation.

In 1904, FREDERICK HAYNES NEWELL, the first director of the Reclamation Service, suggested interstate compacts, essentially treaties between states approved by Congress, as an alternative to litigation. Delph Carpenter, a savvy Colorado water lawyer who had written several articles championing interstate compacts, suggested a compact for resolving the congressional stalemate over the passage of the Boulder Canyon Bill. He brought representatives from the seven Colorado River basin states to a resort near Santa Fe, New Mexico, in the fall of 1922. HERBERT HOOVER, then secretary of commerce, represented the federal government and presided over the negotiations.

The delegates devised fairly straightforward and simple provisions. Engineers for the Reclamation Service had already estimated the annual flow of the Colorado River at 17.5 million acre-feet a year. With that figure in mind, the delegates divided the basin and its water at Lee's Ferry, Arizona, just below the Utah line: the upper part of the basin (Colorado, New Mexico, Utah, and Wyoming) would have rights to 7.5 million acre-feet a year; the lower-basin region (Arizona, California, and Nevada) would have rights to the same quantity of river flow. The division allowed the upper-basin states to protect "their" water until such time that they had developed the means to use it. The delegates set aside an additional 1.5 million acre-feet eventually destined for Mexico, and another 1 million acre-feet for the lower basin states from their own tributaries, mainly those in Arizona. In November 1922, the delegates signed the compact and returned to their respective states to sell their fellow citizens on the virtues of their handiwork.

The Colorado River Compact paved the way for future interstate water compacts affecting every Western state. Many Westerners, such as Carpenter, wanted the water "experts" to devise rational terms for dividing interstate flows. By extension, negotiations could sidestep costly litigation and politics. Consequently, a relatively small group of water bureaucrats, hydraulic engineers, and water lawyers negotiated and perfected compacts on nearly every interstate stream with any flow. The compacts have determined who gets water and how much. In the arid West, this has meant whose economy grows and whose withers.

In the case of the Colorado River Compact, the lower-basin states seemed to have gained more than their upper-basin counterparts. The eventual construction of Boulder Dam, now called HOOVER DAM, brought regulated flows to the Imperial Valley and cheap hydroelectric power and water to sustain urban population growth in southern California and Nevada. With the conclusion of *ARIZONA V. CALIFORNIA* in 1963 and the building of the Central Arizona Project to bring water to Phoenix and Tucson, Arizona has emerged as the state that may have gained the most through the compact.

The Reclamation Service, however, miscalculated the average flow of the Colorado River. By 1945, California had projects in place to divert 5.6 million acre-feet of water a year, and its citizens built cities and farms fully anticipating using that amount of water and more. While the upper states faced the prospects of only 4.3 million acre-feet at their disposal if the river flow continued at the averages computed between 1931 and 1940, Californians continued their uses unabated. Arizona, naturally, objected to California's taking the lion's share of the lower-basin allocation of 7.5 million acre-feet. In 1963, the U.S. Supreme Court subtracted water from California's portion to augment Arizona's, and Californians had to scramble to compensate for the water lost to Arizona.

With the compact in place, the river itself suffered when the BUREAU OF RECLAMATION constructed dams along the main stem and several diversion systems across the mountains. The projects affected national monuments like Rainbow Bridge, threatened Dinosaur National Monument and the Grand Canyon, and raised a public backlash. The regulated flows of the river altered water temperatures, which destroyed native fish populations and raised the salinity level in the river flow.

Overall, the compact has acted as a doubled-edged sword. The compact negotiators achieved their initial goals regarding the Imperial Valley, and setting water allocations for the affected states made possible the phenomenal growth of Los Angeles, Las Vegas, Phoenix, Tucson, Albuquerque, and Denver. But the compact, with its attendant dam-building, has led to serious environmental problems throughout the entire basin. Moreover, the erroneous average-flow assumptions incorporated into the compact have spawned decades of interstate litigation, the very thing Delph Carpenter hoped to avoid in using compacts to settle interstate water disputes in the West.

—*James E. Sherow*

SEE ALSO: Boulder Canyon Act of 1928; Reclamation

SUGGESTED READING:

Fradkin, Philip L. *A River No More: The Colorado River and the West*. Tucson, Ariz., 1968.

Hundley, Norris, Jr. *Water and the West: The Colorado River Compact and the Politics of Water in the American West*. Berkeley, Calif., 1975.

Reisner, Marc. *Cadillac Desert: The American West and Its Disappearing Water*. New York, 1987.

COLORADO RIVER STORAGE PROJECT

Comprising a number of large storage dams, power plants, and IRRIGATION works along the upper COLORADO RIVER and its tributaries in Arizona, Utah, Colorado, New Mexico, and Wyoming, the Colorado River Storage Project was designed and undertaken by the BUREAU OF RECLAMATION. The project arose out of the region's economic and population surges sparked by World War II. Legislation to authorize the project reached Congress in the early 1950s. Once there, the proposed ECHO PARK Dam in Dinosaur National Monument delayed its passage until pressure from conservationists forced the removal of the dam from the bill. After Congress passed the bill, President Dwight Eisenhower signed the Colorado River Storage Project Act into law in April 1956.

In the following two decades, the Bureau of Reclamation constructed GLEN CANYON DAM on the main stem of the Colorado River in northern Arizona, Flaming Gorge Dam on the Green River in northern Utah, Navajo Dam on the San Juan River in northwestern New Mexico, and Blue Mesa, Morrow Point, and Crystal dams on the Gunnison River in western Colorado. These large storage dams regulate the flow of the river and fulfill the terms of the Colorado River Compacts of 1922 and 1948 as well as other legal obligations. Hydropower generated at the dams funded initial construction costs and subsidized so-called participating projects, which irrigated 1,017,689 acres in 1990. In addition, Lake Powell, Navajo Lake, and Blue Mesa and Flaming Gorge reservoirs attracted thousands of visitors annually for boating, fishing, and various water sports and remain major recreational sites in the West.

Some parts of the project created environmental controversy. During the construction of Glen Canyon Dam in the early 1960s, conservationists feared that Lake Powell would intrude into Rainbow Bridge National Monument and became distressed when Congress refused to appropriate funds for a protective dam. The filling of Lake Powell was a sorrowful event for those who considered Glen Canyon a splendidly scenic part of the Colorado Plateau. Inundation of the canyon inspired the SIERRA CLUB to publish *The Place No One Knew*, a work that symbolized the vigilance of environmental organizations toward the Colorado River in the 1960s.

In the 1970s and 1980s, environmentalists expressed concerns over the Central Utah Project. Dubious about its many canals, power plants, dams, and reservoirs, environmentalists lamented the loss of wildlife habitat and charged the Bureau of Reclamation with disregarding the ecological value of free-flowing rivers.

Construction of the Colorado River Storage Project resulted in a highly regulated river and an altered ecology. Completion of Glen Canyon Dam ended annual flooding of the Colorado River downstream in the Grand Canyon and fostered the growth of plants such as tamarisk, arrowweed, and various willows. The once heavily silted river began to run clear and cold below the dam and led to the demise of native fish such as the humpback and bony chubs, while helping rainbow trout to flourish.

The Bureau of Reclamation and the Western Area Power Administration manage the dam for power customers across the Southwest. Releasing water at regular intervals allows "peaking power" demands to be met but with harmful results for sandbars and beaches in the Grand Canyon. Congress established new regulations on the releases in the Grand Canyon Protection Act of 1992.

—*Mark W. T. Harvey*

SEE ALSO: Reclamation

SUGGESTED READING:

Carothers, Steven W., and Bryan T. Brown. *The Colorado River through Grand Canyon: Natural History and Human Change.* Tucson, Ariz., 1991.

Harvey, Mark W. T. *A Symbol of Wilderness: Echo Park and the American Conservation Movement.* Albuquerque, N. Mex., 1994.

COLT, SAMUEL

Founder of an industrial empire based on revolving cylinder, repeating FIREARMS that played an instrumental role in Western settlement, Samuel Colt (1814–1862) was born near Hartford, Connecticut. During a sea voyage from 1830 to 1831, the mechanically minded young man carved a wooden pistol with a multichambered, revolving cylinder that rotated to fire successive charges. Back in the United States, he hired gunsmith John Pearson to perfect working models and raised money for the endeavor by conducting demonstrations of nitrous oxide (laughing gas) as the "Celebrated Dr. Coulte of New York, London, and Calcutta."

Colt received a patent for his invention in February 1836, and the Patent Arms Manufacturing Company of Paterson, New Jersey, was incorporated with Pliny Lawton as superintendent. Colt moved from inventor to salesman-promoter and persuaded the government of the Republic of Texas to buy his arms. In the hands of the TEXAS RANGERS, his No. 5 Belt Revolver clearly demonstrated its superior firepower in mounted combat with Comanche Indians during the 1840s.

Although Colt's Paterson enterprise failed, his early revolvers won the devotion of frontiersmen. During the UNITED STATES–MEXICAN WAR, former Texas Ranger Samuel H. Walker collaborated with Colt in creating the Colt-Walker revolver, an improved design adopted by the military. The new revolver helped ensure Colt's success with a new firm, Colt's Patent Fire Arms Manufacturing Company of Hartford.

During the California gold rush and the subsequent period of increased westward immigration, the innovative arms maker introduced a series of improved weapons—notably the .36 caliber, Model 1851 Navy Revolver—to an appreciative market. With foreman Elisha Root, he opened the largest, most advanced private armory in the world in Hartford in 1855, a facility using the machinery and mass-production principles of the "American System of Manufacturing." Although Colt died in 1862, his enterprise was secure, in part, because of a growing Western market.

Colt's inventive and entrepreneurial genius helped advance and protect the Western frontier for several decades. Historian WALTER PRESCOTT WEBB has cited the Colt revolver (in company with BARBED WIRE and WINDMILLS) as a decisive technological factor in the settlement of the Great Plains. Colt firearms—in particular the famed Single Action Army Revolver, or "Peacemaker"—were so popular and ubiquitous that they ultimately became icons of America's frontier myth.

—*Richard C. Rattenbury*

SUGGESTED READING:

Keating, Ben. *The Flamboyant Mr. Colt and His Deadly Six-Shooter.* Garden City, N.Y., 1978.

Webb, Walter Prescott. *The Great Plains.* Boston, 1931.

Wilson, R. L. *Colt: An American Legend.* New York, 1985.

COLTER, JOHN

Few explorers of the American West packed more discovery and adventure into a few short years than John Colter (ca. 1775–1812). Between 1804 and 1810, Colter traveled through much of the mountain West, first as a member of the LEWIS AND CLARK EXPEDITION and later as an employee of MANUEL LISA'S MISSOURI FUR COMPANY.

Born in Virginia, Colter later moved with his family to present-day Maysville, Kentucky. It was there on October 15, 1803, that MERIWETHER LEWIS recruited

Colter as a hunter in the Corps of Discovery. Expedition records reveal that Colter found military discipline hard to accept. During the winter of 1803 to 1804, when the expedition was at Camp Dubois outside St. Louis, Colter was anything but a model soldier. Sometimes insubordinate and often rowdy, he was more than once reprimanded by superior officers. Despite this inauspicious beginning, Colter proved to be a valuable member of the expedition. His skills as a hunter were important to the success of the expedition, and the journey gave him a broad view of Western geography.

The second phase of Colter's career began in early August 1806 as the Lewis and Clark Expedition headed down the Missouri towards St. Louis. Meeting with Forest Hancock and Joseph Dixon, two fur hunters headed for the Yellowstone country, Colter asked Lewis and Clark for an early discharge. After receiving permission from the expedition leaders, Colter joined his new partners. The partnership did not last long, and Colter then joined Manuel Lisa's trading expedition bound for the Yellowstone in July 1807. From Lisa's Fort Manuel, Colter made an epic journey of exploration through the Bighorn Basin from 1807 to 1808. That journey and a second one from 1809 to 1810 expanded the geographic reach of the FUR TRADE. The vital information he gained on his travels was recorded on the great master map of the West that William Clark kept in his St. Louis office. Colter left the Western fur trade in 1810 and died in 1812.

—James P. Ronda

SEE ALSO: Exploration: United States Expeditions

SUGGESTED READING:

Goetzmann, William H. *Exploration and Empire: The Explorer and the Scientist in the Winning of the American West.* New York, 1966.

Harris, Burton. *John Colter: His Years in the Rockies.* New York, 1952.

COLT REVOLVER

SEE: Colt, Samuel; Firearms

COLUMBIA FUR COMPANY

The Columbia Fur Company was organized around 1822, when Joseph Renville, a British trader and veteran of the War of 1812, invited two former HUDSON'S BAY COMPANY employees, KENNETH MCKENZIE and William Laidlaw, to join him in the business. Since United States law prevented foreigners from engaging in the American FUR TRADE, Renville added a U.S. citizen, Daniel Lamont, to the list of the company's owners.

The company's initial area of influence was the upper Mississippi River valley and the western Great Lakes region. Important posts were also located along the middle stretch of the Missouri River, where the company competed directly with JOHN JACOB ASTOR's powerful AMERICAN FUR COMPANY. In 1827, the Columbia and American Fur companies merged, and Lamont, Laidlaw, and McKenzie became partners in a newly formed department of the American Fur Company named the Upper Missouri Outfit.

At the time of the merger, McKenzie was president of the Columbia Fur Company. He later became one of the more important influences in the Western fur trade and an indispensable manager of the American Fur Company, where he was universally known as the "king" of the Upper Missouri Outfit.

—James A. Crutchfield

SUGGESTED READING:

Chittenden, Hiram M. *The American Fur Trade of the Far West.* New York, 1902.

COLUMBIA RIVER

Rising on the western slopes of the ROCKY MOUNTAINS in British Columbia and Montana, the Columbia River flows through the state of Washington and turns west between Washington and Oregon to reach the Pacific Ocean. The river stretches 1,214 miles and discharges 180 million acre-feet of water in an average year, making it the fourth largest river in North America as measured by flow. Its drainage basin covers 219,000 square miles in the United States and 40,000 square miles in Canada. Major tributaries include the Clark Fork-Pend Oreille (rising in Montana), Okanogan (British Columbia), Kootenay (British Columbia), Snake (Idaho and Wyoming), Yakima (Washington), and Willamette (Oregon). The river and its tributaries link three contrasting environments—the forested and mineral-rich valleys of the northern Rocky Mountains; the wide bunchgrass and sagebrush steppes of eastern Washington, eastern Oregon, northern Nevada, and southern Idaho; and the moist slopes of the Cascade Mountains.

The Columbia has been an artery of trade and travel for many centuries. It was a trading corridor that linked

Columbia River.

the Native Americans of the Northwest Coast with those of the Great Basin. Celilo Falls (near the present-day city of The Dalles) marked a point of commerce where Chinook-speaking Indians from the lower Columbia could exchange coastal products for the hides and furs of the Shoshones, Paiutes, and Nez Percés.

The Columbia was also a broad avenue for English and American fur traders and explorers. The English-speaking discoverer of the river was the American trader Robert Gray, who entered the mouth of the river in May 1792. Later that year, Lieutenant James Broughton of the British navy was the first European to explore the lower Columbia. MERIWETHER LEWIS and WILLIAM CLARK followed the lower Columbia to and from the Pacific Ocean in 1805 and 1806. JOHN JACOB ASTOR's Pacific Fur Company attempted to develop a trading network from a post at ASTORIA near the mouth

of the river in 1811. The HUDSON'S BAY COMPANY coordinated a more successful fur-trading business from FORT VANCOUVER from 1825 to 1845. Interior trading posts and forts at such places as Walla Walla and Spokane dotted the river and tributaries. During the same years, epidemic diseases brought by the Europeans wiped out the overwhelming majority of the native people of the lower river.

As the United States looked westward after the LOUISIANA PURCHASE, Missouri's Senator THOMAS HART BENTON described the Columbia as the "North American road to India." After the acquisition of the bulk of the Oregon Country by the United States, the Columbia River emerged in fact as the major corridor of access. River steamboats and railroads connected Portland to the upstream mining and farming regions of the Columbia River basin and made fortunes for Portland merchants after the discovery of gold in Idaho in 1860. Ocean-going ships connected Portland to world markets for Columbia Basin timber, wool, grain, and other agricultural products. The federal government began channel improvements in 1877. A canal and lock system opened navigation to Lewiston, Idaho, on the SNAKE RIVER in the 1910s. The first railroad along the south side of the Columbia Gorge was completed in 1882, followed by a north bank line in 1908. In the 1990s, the river offered an updated version of the transportation system of the 1890s. The Columbia-Snake system had undergone repeated improvements and carried substantial barge traffic as far inland as Lewiston. Two trunk railroads and an interstate highway paralleled the river through the Cascades and fanned out across its interior drainage basin to Spokane, Boise, and other points to the east. Portland-Vancouver remained a major international port.

The twentieth century brought new uses for the river in the form of IRRIGATION and hydroelectric power. The Columbia's two great dams are Bonneville (completed in 1938) and Grand Coulee (completed in 1941). The first was built to generate electricity and assist navigation; the second, for electricity and to irrigate tens of thousands of acres of dry land. The Columbia is now crossed by more than a dozen dams in the United States and Canada, most built since 1950. Dozens of smaller dams block its tributaries, particularly for irrigation in the Yakima and Snake valleys.

The river in the late twentieth century became caught among conflicting uses and demands. It was in danger of contamination by radioactive wastes from the atomic energy facilities at Hanford, Washington, which were located adjacent to the Columbia in World War II because of its abundant supply of water for cooling. The dams improved navigation and assisted agriculture but have also seriously damaged the salmon runs that once choked the river, fed Native Americans, and supported an Anglo-American fishing and canning industry in the late nineteenth and early twentieth centuries. Hydroelectric capacity amounting to more than one-third of the total capacity in the United States facilitated the growth of cities like Spokane and Portland. In turn, urban residents placed new demands for recreational use on stretches of the river such as the Gorge through the Cascades, designated a national scenic area in 1986.

—*Carl Abbott*

SUGGESTED READING:
Lyman, William Denison. *The Columbia River: Its Myths, Its Scenery, Its Commerce.* New York, 1909.
Meinig, D. W. *The Great Columbia Plain: A Historical Geography, 1805–1910.* Seattle, Wash., 1968.

COMANCHE INDIANS

SEE: Native American Peoples: Peoples of the Great Plains

COMMUNITY PROPERTY

Community property, a system of ownership that treats the possessions of married people as legally belonging to both husband and wife, came to North America through the colonizing of the Spanish and, to a lesser extent, of the French. East of the Mississippi River, the Anglo-Americans imposed a system based on British common law, but out West, even states without a significant Hispanic history adopted laws modeled on those first introduced by Spain into the Southwest borderlands that became Louisiana, Texas, New Mexico, Arizona, and California.

Originally under English common law, wives were legal extensions of their husbands and were not allowed to own property. Common law considered husband and wife to be mystically united into one legal personality. In practice (as a classic joke told by lawyers would state), if husband and wife were one, the husband was the one. He had the absolute right to manage not only his property, but also all property acquired during the marriage. He could also, if he chose, sell or give away all personal property owed by his wife before the marriage, and he had managerial control over her real property. Even after a husband died, all a wife could hope for legally was to hold on to one-third of her husband's real property during her lifetime.

In contrast, the community-property system began with the idea that marriage was a partnership and treated all the property acquired by either spouse during a marriage much like the assets of a business. The notion of community property seems to have originated among the German tribes of central Europe. In ancient Rome, wives generally had few property rights, and whatever was theirs became their husbands' upon marriage. By the Middle Ages, the Goths and Franks had spread the community-property concept throughout the Iberian Peninsula, and Spain, France, Germany, and Holland all had a form of marital property held in common. The French and the Spanish carried these practices to the Americas where they became entrenched in American law through Spain's control of Louisiana and the Southwest.

Under the original Hispanic law—and in America until the mid-twentieth century—the husband managed the community property acquired during the marriage. But because the property belonged to both, he was charged with the responsibility of managing it with their mutual interests in mind and was expected not to squander the property. If one spouse earned an income or bought land, it was automatically assumed to belong equally to both. On the other hand, property that a husband or wife owned before the marriage remained his or her private property, as did any property a spouse might receive after marriage either as a gift or through an inheritance. If a spouse earned money from rent or dividends on property he or she owned separately, that income, too, originally became community property, but in most community-property states is now separate. Otherwise, everything was considered joint property, half of which belonged to the husband, half to the wife. When one spouse died, half of the community property went to the other, regardless of whose name lay on the deed. And, since a husband or wife owned only one-half of their community property, he or she could only dispose of one-half—through a will, for example—upon his or her death.

In the late nineteenth century, various statutes in both England and the United States drastically revised common-law practice. Married women as well as men came to "own" and manage the income they earned, and married women gained the right to hold title to and control real and personal property. Still, although each might own his or her property, neither had a claim to the property of a spouse other than a limited right, as determined by a court, to take a portion (usually one-third) if he or she were dissatisfied with the terms of a will. In the American Southwest, however, a full-fledged community-property system continued to hold sway. The Texas constitution of 1845 provided a skeletal framework for community property that was copied by California in 1849. Both states later adopted more detailed descriptions of the system that matched the later explicit laws of Louisiana, New Mexico, and Arizona. Three Western states with little or no Hispanic background also adopted community property—Nevada, Washington, and Idaho.

Beginning around the middle of the twentieth century, the eight community property states expanded the power of a wife to manage her property. In all of them by the end of the century, she controlled her own earnings, and in some—California, for example—both husband and wife had equal management powers over all community property. California, New Mexico, and Louisiana applied the logic of the system to DIVORCE as well and required an equal division of community property upon the dissolution of a marriage. The others permitted the courts to make an "equitable division" of community property.

The community-property system worked well and was generally popular in the states that adopted it, in part because it comported with the "modern" understanding of marriage as a partnership. A heritage of the Spanish traditions of the Southwest, community property was resisted by the remainder of the states, mainly by lawyers and legislators who did not study the system in law school and who did not understand it. In the last decades of the twentieth century, a model uniform act on marital property, essentially community property without using the name, was developed and proposed to states nationwide for adoption, but by 1995, only Wisconsin had written it into law.

—*David J. Langum*

SUGGESTED READING:

de Funiak, William Q., and Michael J. Vaughn. *Principles of Community Property*. 2d ed. Tucson, Ariz., 1971.

Langum, David J. *Law and Community on the Mexican California Frontier: Anglo-American Expatriates and the Clash of Legal Traditions, 1821–1846*. Norman, Okla., 1987.

McClanahan, W. S. *Community Property Law in the United States*. Rochester, N.Y., 1982.

Reppy, William, Jr., and Cynthia A. Samuel. *Community Property in the United States*. 2d ed. Charlottesville, Va., 1982.

COMOX INDIANS

SEE: Native American Peoples: Peoples of the Pacific Northwest

COMPANY TOWNS

SEE: Mining Camps and Towns

COMPROMISE OF 1820

SEE: Missouri Compromise

COMPROMISE OF 1850

Threatened by mounting regional tensions over whether new territories in the trans-Mississippi West should be admitted into the Union with or without slavery, the United States Congress in 1850 hammered out a compromise that staved off civil war for more than a decade but that allowed Westerners, clamoring for recognition, to become full-fledged citizens of the

United States. It had been the discovery of gold in California in 1848 that brought to a boil the long-simmering sectional differences over slavery. More than eighty thousand people from the East and the Midwest had flooded into California during 1849 alone, making the establishment of territorial government an urgent necessity in an area that already met the population requirement for statehood.

The question of whether territories and new states would be slave holding or free had been settled—many national leaders thought—by the MISSOURI COMPROMISE of 1820, which prohibited slavery in all parts of the Louisiana Purchase north of the latitude of 36° 30', except in Missouri itself. Then, in 1846, David Wilmot, congressman from Pennsylvania, introduced an amendment to a bill appropriating two million dollars to facilitate negotiations with Mexico for "territorial adjustments" as a way of bringing an end to the United States–Mexican War. His amendment—the Wilmot Proviso, as it came to be called—would have prohibited slavery in any land acquired by the United States as a result of war. In opposition to the proviso, during February 1847, South Carolina's Senator JOHN CALDWELL CALHOUN proposed four resolutions that articulated the South's position with regard to slavery. Calhoun proposed that the new Western territories were the common and joint property of the states; that Congress, as an agent for the states, had no right to make laws discriminating between the states and depriving any state of its full and equal right in any territory acquired by the United States; that the enactment of any national law pertaining to slavery would be in violation of the Constitution and states' rights; and that the people had the right to form their state governments as they chose, the Constitution imposing no conditions for the admission of a state except that its government should be republican. Calhoun warned that failure to maintain a balance between the interests of the South and those of the North would result in "political revolution, anarchy, civil war, and widespread disaster" and that, "if trampled upon," the South would resist.

During the next three years, various compromises on the issue of slavery in the new Western territories and would-be states were proposed, including an extension of the line drawn by the Missouri Compromise across the full breadth of the continent. But the atmosphere in Congress itself had changed since 1820, when the Missouri Compromise had been reached. Most Northerners were no longer willing to allow slavery to extend into any territory, no matter whether it lay above or below the compromise line. Faced with a widening gulf of irreconcilable positions, Senator Lewis Cass of Michigan proposed that territories should be organized without mention of slavery. Then, when the territory wrote its own constitution in preparation for admission to statehood, the citizens of the territory would decide for themselves whether they wished to live in a free or slave-holding state. Called "popular sovereignty," the concept held great appeal for President ZACHARY TAYLOR, who was faced with the decision of what to do about California. He proposed that popular sovereignty be allowed to run its course and that California should be admitted directly as a state. The controversy over whether slavery would be allowed in California would be avoided, he reasoned, since no territorial government would be set up and since the state of California would determine the issue for itself.

Southern states were horrified by Taylor's proposal. They calculated that since not only California but also New Mexico and perhaps Mormon-dominated Utah would doubtless organize as free states, the balance of slave versus free states as represented in the Senate would be destroyed. Some compensation was required, and the venerable HENRY CLAY, who had been among the framers of the Missouri Compromise, worked with Senator DANIEL WEBSTER to devise a plan that would satisfy the South. California would be admitted to the Union as a free state. Other territories in the Southwest would be organized without mention of slavery. The slave trade in the District of Columbia would be abolished, but the federal government would pass a strong fugitive-slave law to prevent escaped slaves from being declared free. The final leg of the compromise, which among other things adjusted disputed borders in the Southwest between Texas and the New Mexico Territory, called for the federal government to assume debts that Texas had incurred before it was annexed to the United States.

The Compromise of 1850 was subjected to excruciatingly protracted negotiation and debate. The compromise pleased no one absolutely, but offered North and South sufficient concessions to preserve the union for another tense decade as extremists on both sides slid inexorably toward civil war. Ardent abolitionists saw the new Fugitive Slave Law as caving in to Southern pressures. With the admission of California as a free state, and the likely admission of New Mexico and Utah as free states in the future, Southern states' rights fanatics saw looming the certain end of any power they had in Congress. Once again, NATIONAL EXPANSION westward had threatened to sunder the body politic north and south; it would not be the last time.
—*Alan Axelrod and Charles Phillips*

SUGGESTED READING:
Craven, Avery O. *The Coming of the Civil War.* Rev. ed. Baton Rouge, La., 1957.

Hamilton, Holman. *Prologue to Conflict: Compromise of 1850.* Lexington, Ky., 1964.

COMPULSORY SCHOOL LAW, OREGON (1922)

Oregon's compulsory school law originated as an initiative measure backed by a wide range of nativist groups, including the KU KLUX KLAN. Adopted by voters in the November 1922 general election, the law effectively abolished private and PAROCHIAL SCHOOLS by requiring that all parents send their children to public schools. While Roman Catholic schools were the chief target, advocates of the law also attacked the elitism of other private schools. The United States Supreme Court unanimously struck down the law in *Pierce* v. *Society of Sisters* (1925) as a violation of the rights of parents and an infringement of the property rights of private school proprietors.

—*Carl Abbott*

SEE ALSO: Catholics

COMSTOCK LODE

The Comstock Lode, the most important mining site in the American West, produced $300 million in silver and gold between 1860 and 1880, while the technical innovations and corporate structures developed there shaped hard-rock mining down to the present. The Comstock stretches for two and a half miles across the eastern face of Mount Davidson, twenty-five miles south of Reno in northwestern Nevada. The sister towns of VIRGINIA CITY and Gold Hill lie directly on the deposit.

Discovery of the Comstock lode has been variously credited to the Grosch brothers or to two Irishmen, Peter O'Riley and Patrick McLaughlin; in any case, bombastic Henry Comstock rushed in and gave the find his name. The rush to the Comstock began in summer 1859, when the "blasted blue stuff" that placer miners had been discarding turned out to be extremely rich silver ore. From the beginning, experienced mine developers from California dominated the Comstock; much of the ore lay deep underground in a half-dozen major concentrations, so expertise and heavy infusions of capital available only west of the Sierra Nevada were needed to mine the ore. The first boom—from 1860 through 1863—was made possible largely by Philip Deides-heimers's square-set timbering, which allowed deep mining in the crumbly rock, and Almarin Paul's pan-amalgamation process, which separated silver and gold from the ore quickly and efficiently. Both techniques were widely adopted in other mining areas. A less positive innovation, perhaps, was the listing of Comstock mines—and accompanying wild speculation—on the San Francisco stock exchange.

As the original mines ran out of ore and stocks collapsed, WILLIAM CHAPMAN RALSTON's Bank of California bought controlling shares at extremely low prices. William Sharon, Ralston's Comstock agent, foreclosed mines indebted to the bank, while attempting to monopolize milling and shipping of ore. When new ore discoveries boosted production in the early 1870s, the "Bank Crowd" reaped much of the returns. But others broke the monopoly, most spectacularly the "Silver Kings"—JOHN W. MACKAY, JAMES GRAHAM FAIR, James Flood, and William O'Brien—who, by combining practical mining experience with insider trading, gained control of the "Big Bonanza" mines that produced $105 million between 1873 and 1882. The new strikes reached unprecedented depths—three thousand feet underground—that demanded innovations in ventilation and hoisting, plus massive capital outlays. But the bonanza was soon over; by 1880, the Comstock was clearly in decline.

—*Ralph Mann*

SEE ALSO: Mining; Silver Mining

SUGGESTED READING:
DeQuille, Dan (William Wright). *The Big Bonanza.* 1876. Reprint. New York, 1947.
Paul, Rodman. *Mining Frontiers of the Far West, 1848–1880.* New York, 1963.

CONCORD STAGE

SEE: Stagecoaches

CONDORS

The numbers and territory of the California condor *(Gymnogyps californianus),* which once fed on the dead fauna of the Ice Ages and ranged from Florida to California, have declined dramatically in the historic period. In the eighteenth century, condors were found along the Pacific Coast from Washington to California, but by the middle of the nineteenth century, they were found in California primarily below 38° north latitude. Members of the family of New World vultures, condors are carrion-eaters, who spot their food from great distances while soaring. With average wing-spans of up to nine feet and weights of twenty pounds, these orange, naked-headed birds are excellent foragers. They do not receive their mature plumage until they are six years old, and then their feathers are primarily black with a large white area of feathers on the under side of each wing. While they may live up to forty years, their rate of reproduction is low. Pairs breed only every other year and then lay only one egg. While soaring, they may fly up to ten miles in a straight line carefully maintaining their altitude. By extending their primary feathers, they create a high-aspect wing ratio, which lowers their stall speed and allows them to remain aloft in slowly developing thermals. Although quite graceful while in the air, they spend most of their time perched where they can preen, stretch, rest, and roost. Roosting usually occurred on cliffs or large conifers.

The spread of farming, ranching, and industrial and urban development in southern California progressively restricted the area where condors once foraged and subjected them to less traditional food sources and more hunting and other human pressures. Never existing in large numbers, condors declined steadily after Hispanic and Euro-American settlement along the Pacific Coast. By 1950, there were only some sixty condors left in the wild. The population continued to decline, and in 1986, all surviving wild condors were captured in order to initiate a captive breeding program. Although the program was successful and a few condors were released, at the close of the twentieth century, the future of North America's largest bird flying free once more in the West was still very much in doubt.

—*Phillip Drennon Thomas*

SUGGESTED READING:
Koford, Carl B. *The California Condor.* New York, 1953.
McClung, Robert M. *Lost Wild America: The Story of Our Extinct and Vanishing Wildlife.* Hamden, Conn., 1993.

Top: The Conestoga wagon carried the possessions of most settlers heading west. Once they arrived at their destinations, some settlers used the wagons as their first homes. *Courtesy Kansas State Historical Society.*

Bottom: Families on the overland trails crowded valued possessions from their lives back East into covered wagons. Frequently, as they journeyed westward, they had to discard the contents of their overloaded vehicles. *Courtesy National Archives.*

CONESTOGA WAGONS

Developed during the early eighteenth century to haul furs from a Lancaster County, Pennsylvania, trading post sixty miles to Philadelphia, Conestoga wagons took their name from the Conestoga River valley in which they were created. During the French and Indian War, General Edward Braddock adopted the Conestogas, used locally for transporting freight and produce to the frontier, as supply wagons in his disastrous march toward Fort Pitt in 1755. Pioneers pushing over the Appalachians into the Ohio Valley after 1763 used Conestogas to carry household goods and freight, as did settlers trekking south into the Shenandoah Valley and the western Carolinas.

Originally crafted by Pennsylvania Dutch from earlier wagon designs, the Conestogas were distinctive for their long, deep, forty-two-inch wagon beds that bowed downward in the middle like a boat. Both the front and back panels were slanted, as in a frigate. Fitted with somewhere between eight and sixteen bows of bent wood, over which freighters stretched canvas to keep out the rain, the conveyance featured tool boxes and a lazy board on the left side, feed boxes at the rear, and an iron hook to hold an axe. Drawn usually by six horses (probably of Flemish or German origins and called Conestoga horses), the Conestoga wagons were not designed for passenger travel. Teamsters or drivers walked alongside the wagon or sat on the left wheel horse to guide the contraption, which the pioneers, taking some pride, frequently painted blue with red trim on the running gear.

When wagon trains began heading west from Missouri in the 1840s, the wagons pioneers used to truck their worldly goods halfway across a continent varied from ordinary and hastily modified ten-by-four-foot farm wagons to specially built prairie schooners. These "covered wagons," traveling in trains of as many as 120 vehicles carrying 200 families and trailing 2,000 cattle, became an icon of Western migration. Although by then all covered wagons were being called Conestogas, those used by merchants on the Santa Fe Trail and the prairie schooners used by emigrants on the Oregon and California overland trails were not true Conestogas, but modifications differing somewhat in size, design, and purpose.

A prairie schooner could carry a three-thousand-pound load, but was light enough to be pulled efficiently by a yoke of oxen. Constructed of hardwoods with iron reinforcement and iron "tires" fitted to wooden wheels, the prairie schooner was hardly built for comfort; there were no springs, and the wagon bed, ten to twelve feet long, was a simple box without seats or other comforts. Hickory bows, over which a canvas or cotton cover was stretched, were fitted to the sides of the box, affording minimal protection for cargo and passengers. This "steamboat of the Plains" could cost as much as fifteen hundred dollars, a considerable investment for common folk who hoped to start over in the West.

—*Charles Phillips*

SUGGESTED READING:
Eggenhoffer, Nick. *Wagons, Mules, and Men.* New York, 1961.

CONGREGATIONALISTS

SEE: Protestants

CONJUNTO MUSIC

Conjunto music, an accordion-based folk style also known as *música norteña,* emerged among Mexicans along the Texas-Mexico border in the late nineteenth century. In the twentieth century, it became a culturally powerful style that spread over a broad area of Mexico and the American West. From its inception, *conjunto* music derived its unique identity from a combination of instruments—the diatonic, button accor-

dion and the Mexican twelve-string bass guitar, known as *bajo sexto;* the *tambora de rancho* (ranch drum), a native folk instrument, was also frequently used.

Exactly when and how the accordion appeared among Mexicans is uncertain, but research indicates that it may have been brought to northern Mexico in the 1860s by German immigrants who settled in Monterrey, Nuevo León. Another theory posits German or Czech groups who settled in Texas as the donor. Such an exchange between the Germans and Czechs and the northern Mexicans (*norteños*) and the Texas-Mexicans (TEJANOS) is possible, but the presence of the *bajo sexto* in the ensemble from early on makes the latter theory unlikely. Tense relations between Texas-Mexicans and European immigrants would seem to discourage cultural interchange as well.

Both the rural folk of northern Mexico and the Texas-Mexicans quickly adopted the accordion as a favored instrument. By the end of the nineteenth century, the incipient *conjunto* ensemble had become strongly associated with the celebrations of the poor country folk on both sides of the border. At the same time, the music acquired a negative value among more affluent Mexicans. The music's symbolic association with the lower classes lasted into the latter part of the twentieth century. Even when the music migrated to urban areas, it maintained strong ties to the working class.

Early *conjunto* performers and their audiences were quite familiar with the dance music imported from Europe into the Americas during the nineteenth century—the polka, redowa, schottishe, mazurka, waltz, and other genres. The polka, in particular, was subjected to a strong regional stylization early on, and it was this stylization that cemented the evolving ensemble's unique *tejano-norteño* identity. Even as the *conjunto* evolved, with the addition of the contrabass in the 1930s and modern trap drums in the late 1940s, the polka remained its trademark. In the 1940s, lyrics were grafted onto the basic polka, in the form of the *canción ranchera* (country song) recently popularized by the *mariachi* in Mexico. Similar to the American country-western song, the *canción ranchera* is dominated by the theme of unrequited love. With the addition of the *canción ranchera* and, shortly thereafter, the modern trap drums, the *conjunto* had reached maturity. By the 1950s, the standard ensemble consisted of three-row button accordion, *bajo sexto,* electric bass, and drums.

When *conjunto* music was first commercialized in the 1920s, the best-known performers were Texas-Mexicans. Narciso Martínez, known as the "father" of the *conjunto*, made innovations on the treble side of the accordion—innovations that broke with the older

Germanic style. Santiago Jiménez, Bruno Villarreal, and Lolo Vavazos were also among the early stylists. A new generation emerged after World War II and included Valerio Longoria, who introduced the drums and *canción rancher;* Tony de la Rosa, who standardized the style; and Paulino Bernal, whose *conjunto* of the 1960s represented the culmination of the Texas-Mexican tradition. Since the 1960s, the most important *conjunto* performer has been Flaco Jiménez, who popularized the music among a wider American audience.

In the 1940s, *conjunto-norteño* music migrated to urban areas, although even there, it retained a "country" flavor. At the same time, it was subjected to heavy commercialization—at first by local *tejano* and *norteño* recording companies and, since the 1980s, by major international recording companies. Despite commercialization, the music has maintained organic links to its folk, working-class roots, and at the end of the twentieth century, it stood as testimony to the power of an ethnic class-based music to retain a strong cultural identification. Thus positioned, *conjunto* music continued to speak for the cultural preferences of millions of Mexicans on both sides of the border.

—*Manuel Peña*

SUGGESTED READING:

Paredes, Américo. *A Texas-Mexican Cancionero.* Austin, Tex., 1995.

Peña, Manuel. *The Texas-Mexican Conjunto: History of a Working-Class Music.* Austin, Tex., 1985.

CONNOR, PATRICK E.

Indian fighter and mining entrepreneur Patrick E. Connor (1820–1891) was born in county Kerry in Ireland and christened Patrick Edward O'Connor. He immigrated with his family to New York in the 1830s. In 1839, O'Connor enlisted in the army and spent five years in the Kansas and Iowa territories. During the United States–Mexican War, he enlisted in the army under the name of P. Edward Connor. Promoted to captain, he was cited for bravery in the Battle of Buena Vista where he was wounded severely.

Connor moved to California after he received a medical discharge and engaged in various businesses. He married Johanna Connor, and the couple settled in Stockton.

By 1861, immigration had destroyed game and grass along the Overland Trail to California, and travelers were particularly vulnerable to attacks by starving Indians. The government called for volunteers, and Connor was appointed colonel of the Third California Volunteer Infantry. The volunteers arrived in Salt Lake City in October 1862.

After Indians killed several miners in January 1863, Connor marched to the Bear River in Idaho and defeated the Shoshones in the Battle of Bear River. The Indians lost more than 250 men, women, and children, while only twenty-four soldiers died.

Connor was promoted to brigadier general and in 1865 was assigned to command the Powder River expedition to halt Indian attacks along the Oregon Trail. He departed Fort Laramie, Wyoming, encountered an Arapaho village on the Tongue River, and captured it. The other columns reached the rendezvous after suffering severely from Indian attacks and weather. The failure of the campaign to end Indian depredations and charges of fiscal irregularities resulted in Connor's removal from command of the District of the Plains.

Mormon leader BRIGHAM YOUNG constantly feuded with Connor over Mormon polygamy (the practice whereby a man takes more than one wife at a time) and control of Utah. Connor felt that mineral discoveries would bring non-Mormons into Utah and end Mormon domination, and he authorized his soldiers to prospect in the region. In 1863, silver was discovered west of Salt Lake City, and Connor organized the first Utah mining district.

He was brevetted major general in 1866 and offered a regular commission as colonel but declined. In 1867, he moved his family to California where his wife remained, while he moved to Nevada to invest in mining.

Returning to Utah, he was active in politics. He backed the anti-Mormon Liberal party. Connor pursued mining ventures in Utah and Nevada, but due to financial reverses, he lost most of his investments in 1882.

—*Charles G. Hibbard*

SUGGESTED READING:

Hibbard, Charles G. "Fort Douglas 1862–1916: Pivotal Link on the Western Frontier." Ph.D. diss., University of Utah, 1980.

Madsen, Brigham D. *Glory Hunter: A Biography of Patrick Edward Connor.* Salt Lake City, 1990.

Rogers, Fred B. *Soldiers of the Overland.* San Francisco, 1938.

Varley, James F. *Brigham and the Brigadier: General Patrick Connor and His California Volunteers in Utah and along the Overland Trail.* Tucson, Ariz., 1989.

COOK, JAMES

British naval captain, navigator, and explorer James Cook (1728–1779) charted the seacoast and water-

James Cook, explorer of the Pacific. *Courtesy Library of Congress.*

ways of Canada and led three expeditions to the Pacific Ocean. His explorations, more than those of any other European navigator, changed the map of the world.

Cook was born in Yorkshire, England. His education was sponsored by the farmer who employed his father as a foreman. The young Cook's later apprenticeship in a general store located in the coastal village of Whitby whetted his appetite for a seafaring life. At the age of eighteen, Cook apprenticed to a Whitby ship owner and, after eight years at sea, took command of his own merchant vessel in the turbulent waters of the North Sea. At the same time, Cook studied mathematics. Seeking more excitement than that afforded by the North Sea trade, Cook joined the Royal Navy and advanced rapidly through the noncommissioned ranks. During the Seven Years' War between Great Britain and France, Cook saw action in North America (where the conflict was called the French and Indian War). His charts of the St. Lawrence River, Newfoundland, Nova Scotia, and Labrador were the most accurate of the century.

In 1766, Cook observed an eclipse of the sun, and his subsequent report made him a natural choice of the Royal Society to head an expedition to newly discovered Tahiti in order to observe the second phase of a rare celestial event, Venus's twin immersions in the sun, which occurred not more than once a century.

Cook's secret instructions for his voyage ordered him first to observe the transit of Venus from Tahiti and second to find the lost continent of Terra Australis Incognita, believed to have been sighted by Marco Polo, then by early Spanish and French voyagers, and more recently by the pirate Edward Davis. Aboard his ship *Endeavour,* Cook took astronomer Charles Green to help him observe Venus, young Joseph Banks, a protégé of Canadian explorer-artist Thomas Pennant, and a retinue, hired personally by Banks, of eight scientists, who formed a natural-history corps. When Cook landed on the southeast corner of Australia on April 19, 1770, after anchoring at both Tahiti and New Zealand, Banks and the scientists of his entourage—dazzled by the entirely new ecological system—dubbed the barren spot "Botany Bay." From there, Cook plied the east coast, surveying and mapping as he went, and successfully navigated the treacherous Great Barrier Reef, the Coral Sea, and the Torres Strait. Upon his return to England, he was promoted to commander and presented to King George III. Eager for more important discoveries, Cook was already planning a second voyage.

From 1772 to 1775, Cook successfully accomplished a west-east circumnavigation of the world, penetrated the Antarctic Circle, charted Tonga and Easter Island, and discovered New Caledonia in the Pacific and various islands in the Atlantic. After returning to London, he was promoted at last to captain, made a member of the Royal Society, and received its highest honor, the Copley Medal.

Back at sea in 1776, Cook explored the western coast of present-day Canada and Alaska in search of the elusive NORTHWEST PASSAGE. His travels took him to the Sandwich Islands (HAWAII) in 1778, where he received a cordial welcome from the native peoples. Continuing northward, he plied the western coast of North America without finding a sea route to Europe. In preparation for explorations into colder climes, Cook's crew purchased sea-otter pelts from the native tribes of the Alaska coast. They later discovered the furs brought astronomical prices in China. The publication of Cook's journals in 1784 encouraged large numbers of British and American traders to the Northwest in search of more furs.

Cook, however, did not live to see the publication of his writings or the beginnings of the Britain's FUR TRADE in the Northwest. Returning to the Sandwich Islands in November 1778, he and his men skirmished with natives over the theft of a British cutter. Cook was killed in the battle, and his crew departed a few days later.

—*Patricia Hogan*

SEE ALSO: Alaskan Exploration; Exploration: British Expeditions; Exploration and Science

SUGGESTED READING:

Beaglehole, J. C. *The Exploration of the Pacific.* 3d ed. Stanford, Calif., 1966.

———. *The Life of Captain James Cook.* Stanford, Calif., 1974.

Withey, Lynne. *Voyages of Discovery: Captain Cook and the Exploration of the Pacific.* New York, 1987.

COOK, JAMES HENRY

Cowboy and cattleman James Henry Cook (1857–1942) was born in Michigan. He went to Texas as a boy and became a cowboy. He later participated in five trail drives north to Kansas and beyond. He then managed the WS Ranch in southwestern New Mexico. In 1886, he married Kate Graham; a year later, he bought his father-in-law's northwestern Nebraska ranch and named it the Agate Springs Ranch. Important Miocene mammal fossils were later discovered on the ranch, which is now a national monument. Cook's autobiography is one of the better accounts of cowboy life and early trail driving.

—*David Dary*

SEE ALSO: Cattle Industry; Cowboys

SUGGESTED READING:

Cook, James H. *Fifty Years on the Old Frontier.* New Haven, Conn., 1923.

COOKE, JAY

Jay Cooke (1821–1905), banker, financier, railroad developer, and owner of a Utah silver mine, was born on a farm near Sandusky, Ohio. He began his career in Philadelphia where he clerked at the Washington Packet and Transportation Company. When the company collapsed, he entered the then unregulated, even chaotic, BANKING business, becoming a clerk in E. W. Clark and Company in 1839. Four years later, he became a partner in the firm and was partly responsible for opening branch houses as far west as St. Louis, Missouri, and Burlington, Iowa. During the United States–Mexican War, Clark and Company sold federal bonds at enormous profits. Nonetheless, the firm went bankrupt in the panic of 1857.

With William Moorhead, Cooke founded Jay Cooke and Company in 1861. Dealing in bank notes and stock, his company marketed federal bonds to banks after the beginning of the Civil War. Cooke then conceived of an idea whereby federal bonds could be marketed directly to the general public, and Secretary of the Treasury Salmon P. Chase appointed Jay Cooke

and Company agents for marketing federal bonds in October 1862. The stage was set for a revolution in the American financial system. Paying 6 percent interest and redeemable in as few as five years, but otherwise maturing in twenty, the bonds were called "five-twenties." Cooke hired twenty-five hundred agents to market as much of the half-billion dollar bond issue as he could. Although his firm earned less than 0.125 percent in profits, the belief was widespread that he had profited excessively from the sale of bonds.

Cooke supported establishing a national banking system. When the legislation passed, partly as a result of his support, he wrote a pamphlet entitled "How to Organize a National Bank under Secretary Chase's Bill" (1863). With Cooke as the second largest investor, the First National Bank of Philadelphia was the first bank to be chartered under the National Banking Act.

With the war over, Cooke's interests turned to RAILROADS, especially the Northern Pacific Railroad. Originally founded in 1864, the railroad was to cross the entire Northwest, connecting Lake Superior with the Pacific Ocean. The Northern Pacific received substantial federal aid in the form of land grants, but it received no money, nor were its bonds guaranteed. Cooke zealously undertook the task of raising the necessary one hundred million dollars. Troubles soon arose. Jay Cooke and Company was forced to supply the venture with its own capital; the company collapsed on September 18, 1873; and the Panic of 1873 was in full swing.

Five years later, the financially ruined Cooke became interested in a Utah silver mine. He incorporated the Horn Silver Mining Company and raised money for the construction of a railroad. Surprisingly, for a while, the mine was the richest silver mine in the world. After Cooke sold his mine stock in 1880, he was worth nearly $1 million.

—*Joseph F. Rishel*

SEE ALSO: Financial Panics

SUGGESTED READING:

Larson, Henrietta M. *Jay Cooke: Private Banker.* Cambridge, Mass., 1936. Reprint. New York, 1968.

Oberholtzer, Ellis Paxson. *Jay Cooke: Financier of the Civil War.* 2 vols. Philadelphia, 1907. Reprint. New York, 1968.

COOKE, PHILIP ST. GEORGE

Soldier and author Philip St. George Cooke (1809–1895) was born into a prosperous slave-owning family in Leesburg, Virginia. When Cooke's father died, he was forced to withdraw from Martinsburg Academy and immediately applied for admission to the United States Military Academy. Cooke received his

Philip St. George Cooke.
Courtesy National Archives.

appointment to West Point in 1823 and graduated in 1827. His first assignment was with the Sixth Infantry at Jefferson Barracks, Missouri.

In 1829, Cooke joined his commander, Major Bennet Riley, in escorting traders who were traveling from western Missouri into Mexico. In 1832, he volunteered to fight in BLACK HAWK'S WAR. At the end of the war, Cooke was promoted to first lieutenant and volunteered his services with the First Dragoons. Three years later, he was promoted to captain and began recruiting and training soldiers to provide safe passage to Americans traveling through Indian territory.

In 1843, President SAM HOUSTON of the Republic of Texas authorized JACOB SNIVELY and a band of volunteers to target merchants traveling from Santa Fe to Mexico and steal their horses, wagons, and goods. During a military run, Cooke came across the Snively band, disarmed its members, and sent them back to Texas.

During the United States–Mexican War, Cooke blazed a trail to California in 1846 with Colonel STEPHEN WATTS KEARNY and was then given command of some four hundred inexperienced soldiers to cut a trail to southern California. Traveling more than two thousand miles in ninety days, Cooke established a permanent route to the Pacific Ocean, a route later used by the railroads.

During the Civil War, Cooke remained loyal to the Union and fought under General George B. McClellan In 1865, he was promoted to major general. He retired in 1873.

—*Fred L. Koestler*

SUGGESTED READING:
Cooke, Philip St. George. *Scenes and Adventures in the Army.* Philadelphia, 1857.
Young, Otis E., Jr. *The West of Philip St. George Cooke.* Glendale, Calif., 1955.

COOLBRITH, INA

A poet and primary contributor to California's developing literary culture, Ina Coolbrith (Josephine D. Smith, 1841–1928) was the daughter of Agnes Coolbrith and Don Carlos Smith (brother of the Mormon prophet JOSEPH SMITH, JR.). She was born in Nauvoo, Illinois. When her father died, her mother remarried and moved the family to California, where Ina spent the rest of her life.

The pseudonym Ina Coolbrith was a combination of an early pen name (Ina) and her mother's maiden name. She adopted the pen name to hide both her Mormon background and her disastrous brief marriage to a pathologically jealous and violent husband.

Coolbrith's poems appeared in a wide variety of anthologies and magazines like the *Overland Monthly,* edited during the 1870s by BRET HARTE. Her poetry "piped but one silvery note, a wistful one in which unhappiness was temporarily submerged in pleasure over flowers, birds, and the wind," according to historian Franklin Walker. Heavy domestic responsibilities (she raised her sister's orphaned children and a daughter of the poet JOAQUIN MILLER) limited the development of her literary talents. Today, Coolbrith's work, like Harte's stories of California mining camps, seems old-fashioned and sentimental, but it formed an important bridge between the rough frontier and a more refined literary culture.

Perhaps one of Coolbrith's most important roles was as a literary companion to her better known contemporaries—including Charles Warren Stoddard, Bret Harte, Joaquin Miller, and MARK TWAIN—and as a mentor to a younger generation of California writers. During her thirty years as librarian at the Oakland Public Library and the Bohemian Club, she encouraged young writers including JOHN GRIFFITH (JACK) LONDON. In the monthly meetings of the California Literary Society, held in her home after 1915, she presided over readings and discussions of works in progress and contributed her own oral memories of the early San Francisco literary scene.

—*Gary Topping*

SEE ALSO: Literature; Magazines and Newspapers; Women Writers

SUGGESTED READING:
Walker, Franklin. *San Francisco's Literary Frontier.* New York, 1939.

COOPER, JAMES FENIMORE

Novelist and historian James Fenimore Cooper (1789–1851) created as the central figure of his Leather-Stocking Tales the archetypal frontier hero, a strong, moral loner who, understanding the ways of the wilderness and its Indian inhabitants, secures an untamed land for a westward moving civilization in which he no longer fits. According to many scholars, especially

Richard Slotkin, Cooper's chatacter Hawkeye became the model for the Western heroes who followed in dime novels, western genre fiction, and movie and television westerns.

The son of a federal judge, Cooper grew up in Cooperstown, New York, an area his father had personally "developed" from wilderness. After attending Yale for two years, he was expelled for a prank and joined the navy. Cooper resigned his commission to marry Susan De Lancey, a woman from an influential and wealthy New York family. It was she who challenged him to become a writer. The story goes that Cooper, who had just finished reading a popular English novel, turned to his wife and remarked, "I believe I could write a better story myself." She told him, in effect, to prove it, and in short order, Copper produced his first novel, *Precaution* (1820), a pale but moderately successful imitation of then-current British fiction. From this humble, almost accidental beginning, Cooper had suddenly found his vocation. Whereas his first story mimicked English writing, his next, *The Spy* (1821), used American subject matter exclusively. Set during the Revolutionary War, the book was an immediate success. In 1822, the Coopers moved to New York City, where he became a full-time professional writer and a leader among the city's intellectuals. From 1826 to 1833, Cooper lived abroad in England, France, Switzerland, and Italy. The experience gave him a sharp critical perspective on his own country. He wrote during his seven years away a fascinating assessment called *Notions of the Americans* (1829), and he developed its themes in some of his later nonfiction, including a bitter attack on American provincialism, *A Letter to His Countrymen* (1834), and especially a work of social analysis entitled *The American Democrat* (1838).

Cooper became a prolific and internationally popular writer whose novels were often ranked with those of Sir Walter Scott. While Cooper wrote in many genres—he is, for example, given credit for creating the sea story—by far his most important and best-known works were tales of the American wilderness. Of these, his finest novels are the Leather-Stocking stories: *The Pioneers* (1823); *The Last of the Mohicans* (1826); *The Prairie* (1827); *The Pathfinder* (1840); and *The Deerslayer* (1841). Taken together, the five novels present a vivid, epic picture of what Americans thought of as their vanishing wilderness. The books' focus is broad, sweeping and mythical in dimension, yet personal as Cooper develops the character of the novels' central figure, a back-woodsman named Natty Bumppo but better known as Leatherstocking, the Pathfinder, the Deerslayer, or Hawkeye. In Hawkeye, based loosely on Kentucky long hunter and trailblazer DANIEL BOONE,

James Fenimore Cooper. *Courtesy New York State Historical Association.*

Cooper presented his ideal American frontiersman: self-reliant, brave, and knowing but essentially innocent; at one with nature yet ill at ease in polite society. His closest comrades include two Indians, Chingachgook (also called John Mohican in *The Pioneers)* and Uncas, the last of the Mohicans. They are cast among a host of other characters who, in the general scheme of the novels, act either to exploit and despoil the American land or to help preserve it.

Cooper's weaknesses as a writer were manifest and infamous. He knew next to nothing about the Indian tribes who figure prominently in his wilderness fiction, and his treatment of individual Indians is both patronizing and racist. James Russell Lowell scolded Cooper for his snobbishness and his "flat" treatment of women; MARK TWAIN hilariously eviscerated the earlier novelist for his excessive romanticism in an essay from 1895 entitled "Fenimore Cooper's Literary Offenses." Cooper could be didactic, even schoolmarmish, and although he was fascinated by the possibilities of racial "mixtures," he fiercely rejected them, often to the detriment of the structures of his major works. Yet his characters were frequently more richly developed than his critics allowed; he composed a fascinating gallery of American types, and he bequeathed to American literature and culture, for better or worse, an enduring image of the vanishing frontier and frontiersman. Cooper created a drama of American evolution even as the momentous changes about which he wrote were taking place. His novels, at their best, constituted a record of American life and society unsurpassed before Nathaniel Hawthorne and Herman Melville. Taken together, they provide a frequently complex picture immensely influential in how Americans came to see themselves and on how they imagined they got that way.

—*Charles Phillips*

SEE ALSO: Literature; Violence: Myths about Violence

SUGGESTED READING:
Slotkin, Richard. *The Fatal Environment: The Myth of the Frontier in the Age of Industrialism, 1800–1890.* New York, 1985.
———. *Gunfighter Nation: The Myth of the Frontier in Twentieth-Century America.* New York, 1992.

———. *Regeneration through Violence: The Mythology of the American Frontier, 1600–1860.* Middleton, Conn., 1973.

Smith, Henry Nash. *Virgin Land: The American West as Myth and Symbol.* Cambridge, Mass., 1950.

COOPER, SARAH BROWN INGERSOLL

An educator, author, and cultural leader in San Francisco, Sarah Brown Ingersoll Cooper (1835–1896) was born Sarah Ingersoll in Cazenovia, New York. Educated at Cazenovia Seminary (from 1850 to 1853) and in 1854 at the Troy (New York) Female Seminary run by Emma Willard, Sarah Ingersoll had accepted a teaching post in a village school by 1852 and then moved on to become preceptress at the Fayetteville (New York) Academy. She moved south and worked as a governess for a year on a Georgia plantation before marrying Halsey Fenimore Cooper, editor of the *Chattanooga Advertiser* and a Cazenovia classmate, on September 4, 1855. With the start of the Civil War, the Coopers left Chattanooga to return to New York State. But, in 1863, Cooper's husband was named assessor of internal revenue in Memphis, and the family returned to Tennessee, where Sarah Cooper began teaching Bible classes for Union soldiers. A combination of overwork and grief following the death of her infant daughter Mollie made Cooper seriously ill, and, on the advice of physicians, she moved to St. Paul, Minnesota, in 1867. Her hope was that the bracing northern climate would restore her health. Two years later, in 1869, the entire family moved to California and settled in San Francisco.

It was in California that Cooper largely recovered her health. Encouraged by her husband, she became active in the literary, religious, and philanthropic life of San Francisco and soon emerged as one of the city's luminaries. Cooper composed a series of articles on the social role of women and published them in the *Overland Monthly,* the *San Francisco Bulletin,* and the popular religious press. At the behest of the United States commissioner of education, she issued a series of reports, from 1871 to 1885, on the educational systems of California.

In 1871, Cooper began teaching a Bible class in a San Francisco Presbyterian church. The classes quickly proved popular with a wide lay audience but were condemned as excessively liberal by church elders. When she refused to moderate her views, she was summoned to stand trial for heresy (1881). Cooper had specifically rejected the doctrines of infant damnation and everlasting punishment. The trial, closely followed by the public, backfired on the elders of the church. Cooper used the occasion as a platform from which she eloquently expressed and defended her liberal views. Not only was she acquitted, but by the end of the proceedings, she had emerged as a popular religious thinker of national renown. Although officially vindicated, Cooper voluntarily withdrew from the Presbyterian Church to join the more liberal Congregationalists.

While she was engaged in ecumenical matters, Cooper also pioneered the concept of kindergarten education. Her belief was that early childhood education would have a positive moral effect, and she intended to test this proposition in the slums of San Francisco's notorious Barbary Coast. By 1884, she had founded several kindergartens, which were incorporated as the Golden Gate Kindergarten Association. In 1891, she established a training school for kindergarten teachers, the Golden Gate Kindergarten Free Normal Training School. Her work received national and international notice and served as the model for kindergartens in the United States and elsewhere.

—*Alan Axelrod*

Suggested reading:

Roland, Carol. "The California Kindergarten Movement: A Study in Class and Social Seminism." Ph. D. diss., University of California, Riverside, 1981.

Stovall, Anna M. *Pioneers of the Kindergarten Movement.* San Francisco, 1924.

COPPER KINGS, WAR OF THE

In the last decade of the nineteenth century, politics in the new state of Montana were controlled and, indeed, crippled by the personal animosities and business rivalries of the state's leading copper magnates, William Andrews Clark and Marcus Daly.

The origins of the long-running feud between Clark and Daly probably lay in clashes over business dealings. Clark's bank in 1876 refused to accept Daly's draft when he purchased the Alice Mine in Butte; and Clark reportedly swindled Daly when he tried to secure water rights on Warm Springs Creek. Whatever the cause of the feud, it was fueled by name calling and petty jealousies. As vituperative as it was, however, Clark and Daly set aside their differences when common economic interests were at stake. Both Democrats, the two cooperated at Montana's 1884 constitutional convention. Clark, however, craved the power and prestige of political office and determined to become a United States Senator from Montana—regardless of the cost.

Clark first sought federal office in 1888 as the Montana Territory delegate to Congress. The Democratic nominee of a predominately Democratic region, Clark lost the election by five thousand votes to an obscure Republican candidate. Failing to carry the counties controlled by Daly's ANACONDA MINING COMPANY, the humiliated Clark charged Daly with manipulating the votes of his mining employees; Daly countered and the feud went public in the papers: Daly's *Anaconda Standard* against Clark's *Butte Miner*. The press in Montana became the tool of the warring copper kings.

When Montana became a state in 1889, Clark as a matter of course sought a U.S. Senate seat. The state legislature, mired in a battle over five contested seats that would disrupt the balance between Democrats and Republicans, sent four men to Washington, D.C., to fill the state's two Senate seats. The Senate, controlled by Republicans, sent Clark and the other Democrat packing and recognized the Republican representatives.

When the state legislature next prepared to elect a senator in 1893, Clark was rumored to have bought several legislators' votes. Daly and his friends also spent cash among the representatives, and Clark lost by three votes. The legislature failed to elect anyone before adjourning, and for two years, Montana had only one senator in Washington.

Clark and Daly clashed again the following year over the location of the state capital, to be determined by popular vote. By 1894, the choices remaining were Daly's Anaconda and Clark's Helena. Lavish parades, free liquor, heated newspaper editorials, and immense amounts of money colored the campaign. Clark reportedly spent $400,000; Daly sunk $2.5 million into the cause. As historian Michael P. Malone noted, each of the fifty-two thousand votes cast represented a $56 investment. Helena won; Clark basked in the victory; Daly never recovered from his defeat.

Clark's victory did not deter his quest for a Senate seat. When the legislature considered the choice of a senator in 1899, Clark was ready with his wallet. Despite accusations of bribery before a joint session of the state legislature, a grand-jury investigation into similar charges, and the condemnation of Daly's newspapers, Clark was finally elected. In the fray, a whistle blower in the legislature lost his seat but not before lecturing his colleagues: "Let us clink our glasses and drink to crime. The crime of bribery, as shown by the evidence here introduced, stands out in all its naked hideousness, and there are forty members seated here who, today, are ready to em-

brace it." Clark admitted to spending $272,000 on the campaign.

Clark went to Washington, D.C., but he immediately faced a Senate committee that spent three months investigating his election. When the committee voted to recommend the Senate deny Clark his seat, he resigned and thus avoided bribery charges.

With the Senate seat vacant, Montana's governor and Clark's foe, Robert B. Smith, had responsibility for naming Montana's new senator. While Smith was out of the state, Clark convinced the lieutenant-governor, A. E. Sprigg, to name Clark to the seat again. Smith revoked Clark's appointment and named PARIS GIBSON to the seat, but once more, Montana went without full representation in the Senate until 1901.

As the new century began, Clark's fortunes took a turn for the better. Daly's Anaconda Mining Company was taken over by the Amalgamated Copper Company, a holding company of Standard Oil, placing one of the largest mining companies in the hands of distant corporate bosses. During the November 1900 election, Clark joined forces with FREDERICK AUGUSTUS HEINZE, a young mining wizard and charismatic figure, in attacking Daly and his "copper trust." The collaboration succeeded, and Clark finally won a seat in the U.S. Senate; Heinze won friends in high places and allies in his feud with Amalgamated. Daly died a week after the election, ending the War of the Copper Kings.

Even in an age when colossal corporations and mining magnates routinely manipulated laws, bribed politicians, and juggled public opinion, the corruption of Montana politics at the hands of a few individuals with immense financial resources and unbridled political influence stands out in the blighted politics of the American West.

—Patricia Hogan

SEE ALSO: Butte, Montana

SUGGESTED READING:
Connolly, C. P. *The Devil Learns to Vote*. New York, 1935.
Glasscock, C. B. *The War of the Copper Kings*. New York, 1935.
Malone, Michael P. *The Battle for Butte: Mining and Politics in the Northern Frontier, 1864–1906*. Seattle, Wash., 1981.

COPPER MINING

Despite the romance of gold and silver, copper played a role far more essential to the development of extractive industries in the trans-Mississippi West, especially after the 1870s when—with the coming of electricity and its copper wiring—the profits from GOLD MINING found a fresh new field for investment. Before the Civil War, most of the country's copper was mined from small mass veins on Michigan's Keweenaw Peninsula or along Lake Superior's Calumet and Hecla conglomerate veins. After the Civil War, the tonnage of copper produced not only in Michigan but elsewhere in America increased dramatically, and by 1916, the United States was MINING two-thirds of all the copper produced in the world. Not a little of the metal came from the high-grade deposits at BUTTE, MONTANA, and farther south in Arizona. Some five thousand tons of the ore were wrested from the ground around Butte in 1882, the beginnings of what Colorado's MARCUS DALY, owner of the ANACONDA MINING COMPANY, would eventually call "the Richest Hill on Earth." Along with his rival WILLIAM ANDREWS CLARK, Daly quickly took advantage of the new RAILROADS in the region to exploit the rich veins of copper sulfides standing at steep angles thousands of feet thick and deep in the Rocky Mountains. In 1887, Montana replaced Michigan as the country's leading copper-mining region.

Daly and the other copper kings snapped up promising-looking claims from small operators in hard times, then—once they had established a mining district of sufficient size—sought outside investors and incorporated their mining company. Better capitalists than mine operators, they often hired men with the technical know-how actually to run the mines. Once the engineers had brough the mines into production, the Copper Kings quickly took advantage of the renewed opportunities for consolidation offered by their thriving enterprises. In fact they were in some ways driven to combination by the economics of copper mining, which required considerable capital for mills and smelters, refineries, sampling and assaying works, timber to prop up the underground shafts, coal to fire up all the machinery, waterworks for the mills, and railroads to transport the ore. By the mid-1890s, Daly's Anaconda, for example, not only held huge reserves of ore, coal, and lumber, it also housed the world's largest reduction works and a thoroughly modern refinery. Anaconda held title to nearby farmland and to Butte city lots; it ran railroads and hotels; it operated both waterworks and electrical plants.

By the turn of the century, huge combinations were dominating entire regions and whole sectors of the industry. American Smelting and Refining Company, Phelps Dodge, and the Amalgamated Copper Company not only dwarfed older operations, they themselves were sometimes controlled by larger organizations such as Standard Oil, which owned Amalgamated. Amalgamated swallowed Anaconda and consolidated the entire Butte cooper industry, only to dissolve and allow Anaconda to re-emerge as the leading corporation in Montana. By 1903, mining interests were so powerful in the state that they could intimidate the Montana legislature into passing any law they wanted simply by threatening to close mines, smelters, lumber camps, and mills and leave twenty thousand men out of work. When it reached peak production in 1916, the Anaconda was producing 176,000 tons annually.

At the end of the nineteenth century, Arizona's four high-grade deposits, though not nearly so rich as Montana's, had been brought into production. They had been discovered years before the railroad had made the copper's exploitation feasible. Veins of copper sulfides, shaped like lenses and embedded in Arizona limestone, were first mined in the eastern part of the state by the Lezinsky brothers before the Scottish Arizona Mining Company bought them out in 1880. Scottish Arizona built a more modern leaching plant, made a good deal of money, and then, in turn, sold out to Phelps Dodge in 1921. Phelps Dodge also took over the massive deposits at Globe, which others had been working since the 1890s, and the Copper Queen at Bisbee. Only in Jerome, site of the fourth Arizona deposit, where Phelps Dodge had decided back in 1880 to pass on the United Verde mine's offer to sell, did Arizona copper belong to somebody else: Montana's William Andrews Clark, who had bought the property in 1888 and, before he was finished, cleared some $60 million in profits.

Early in the twentieth century, the industry itself entered a truly revolutionary era. With new mass-production techniques, the working of low-grade porphyry—ore disseminated over relatively wide areas—became possible. A young engineer named Daniel C. Jackling had made the technological breakthrough around 1903. Armed now with new equipment, the steam shovel especially, a group of entrepreneurs from Cripple Creek, with Jackling's help, began to exploit vast, low-grade copper deposits in Bingham Canyon, south of the Great Salt Lake. Within thirty years, Jackling's Utah Copper Company had extracted some six billion pounds from what became the largest man-made hole in the world. The techniques developed in Utah spread to Arizona, Montana, and New Mexico. Anaconda, the Guggenheim's Kennecott Copper, and Phelps Dodge revitalized their holdings by using low-grade techniques. From that time forward, low-grade porphyries came to dominate American copper production, now centered firmly in the West, with Arizona taking the lead in 1907, and Utah assuming second place after 1926.

—*Charles Phillips*

SUGGESTED READING:
King, Joseph E. *A Mine to Make: Financing the Colorado Mining Industry, 1859–1902.* College Station, Tex., 1977.
Peterson, Richard. *The Bonanza Kings: The Social Origins and Business Behavior of Western Mining Entrepreneurs, 1870–1900.* Baltimore, 1961.

CORN GROWING

Native Americans in Meso-America (present-day Mexico and Central America) and South America developed hybrids of wild plants into domestic corn, or maize, in prehistoric times, and its cultivation spread northward. By the time Europeans arrived in the New World, corn was so much a staple of Indian life that the conquerors soon discovered one of the best ways to subject native peoples was to destroy their stores of maize. Columbus and early European explorers carried the grain to Europe, and from there, it grew to become a staple food of all the regions of the world with a climate suitable to its cultivation. Native Americans on the East Coast shared their knowledge of corn growing with early settlers in the compact seaboard colonies of the English, and the history of the Anglo-American westward migration is also a history of the expansion of corn growing from the Atlantic to the foothills of the Rocky Mountains. Laying in a few acres of corn was the preoccupation of homesteaders; as food for human consumption, as forage for livestock, and as a base for domestic liquor, corn was essential to the survival and well-being of each farm family.

Corn was grown in all states and most counties, but as the American economy developed under a rapid industrialization beginning around mid-century and exploded into growth after the Civil War, corn became a more problematic crop. Farmers grew more wheat, which was a better cash crop, and used it more frequently for human consumption, while they fed corn to their livestock, dairy animals, and poultry. As the market for beef boomed and the range CATTLE INDUSTRY spread, farmers began to think of better uses for their corn. High shipping rates set by the RAILROADS in the newly developed Western transportation network and volatile markets made corn growing a risky business, and farmers found that corn transmuted into whiskey, hogs, or cows was cheaper to produce and transport to market. The advent of rail shipments in KANSAS, NEBRASKA, and elsewhere put hog farmers and cattle raisers farther east in direct competition with cheaper Western range-fed livestock, and rising local real-estate values along with the consequent higher taxes made it less profitable to "waste" land by feeding cows in IOWA or Illinois on grass. The solution was

to feed corn to cattle on a large scale to fatten them quickly.

The result was the birth of the feed lot, where Midwestern livestock raisers fattened two-year-old steers (called "stockers") they bought from ranchers on the Great Plains with corn purchased from neighboring grain farmers or from the increasing number of operators that merely stored corn in huge grain elevators. The cattle raisers made sure that the corn consumed by their feeders went into meat and fat rather than the less edible bone and muscle that resulted from grass-fed cows driven long distances to market. Fenced in outdoor pens, steers feasted on shucked corn that farmers spread on the ground or poured into troughs. Hogs wandered the feed lots, scavenging whatever the cows found inedible and themselves growing fat. In the Midwestern feed-lot system, Midwestern farmers raised corn and hay together to fatten cattle from the West and locally raised pigs before their final trek to a CHICAGO slaughterhouse. Corn growing had become an intermediary stage in a vast new Western industry as well as a staple for homesteaders and a source of feed for domestic livestock and dairy cows. The American Corn Belt thrived, extending from Ohio across the Mississippi through Iowa to eastern Kansas and Nebraska.

Scientific advances in AGRICULTURE in the early twentieth century, many of them discovered in studies at the trans-Mississippi West's land-grant colleges, revealed the potential for greatly increased corn yields. By the 1920s, commercial seed men began to develop their own combinations, and in the 1930s, these high-yield hybrid corn seeds were on the market, soon replacing almost entirely open-pollinated seed corn. By

This eastern Oklahoma corn field reported a yield of fifty bushels per acre in about 1912. *Courtesy Western History Collections, University of Oklahoma Library.*

the late twentieth century, the United States grew half of the world's total corn crop, and two-thirds of the U.S. harvest was exported annually. Iowa remained the leading corn-growing state as it had been since the mid-nineteenth century, with Illinois, Nebraska, and Indiana running close behind in corn production. Corn was the most valuable of all U.S. crops, making up nearly a quarter of all crops harvested in the country, about twice the value of either cotton or hay, which were followed in order by wheat, soybeans, and tobacco. From the raising of an exotic native food, corn growing had developed into an agribusiness of extraordinary economic importance.

—*Patricia Hogan*

SEE ALSO: Colleges and Universities; Homesteading; Farming; Native American Cultures: Subsistence Patterns

SUGGESTED READING:

Cronon, William. *Nature's Metropolis: Chicago and the Great West*. New York, 1991.

Gates, Paul Wallace. *The Farmer's Age: Agriculture, 1915–1860*. New York, 1960.

Hardeman, Nicholas P. *Shucks, Shocks, and Hominy Blocks: Corn as a Way of Life in Pioneer America*. Baton Rouge, La., 1981.

CORN WOMAN

The Pueblo people ascribe the origin of their mainstay crop, corn or maize, to the Corn Mothers, one associated with blue corn (Blue Corn Woman) and one with white corn (White Corn Maiden). According to Pueblo beliefs, these beings brought corn with them from beneath the earth when they climbed through the surface of the kiva into our world. (The word *kiva,* which describes an underground or partly underground ritual chamber, means "the world below," the spiritual origin of life.)

Traditionally, at birth, each Pueblo child is given an ear of corn fashioned into a fetish (called a *latiku* by the people of Acoma), which embodies the heart and breath of the Corn Mothers. The Pueblo people keep their corn fetishes for life as a reminder of the origin of corn and, by extension, of life itself.

In Hopi practice, the Corn Mother fetish was placed beside the newborn, who was kept in darkness for twenty days. Before sunrise on the twentieth day, the child's mother picked the infant up in her arms. Holding the Corn Mother in her right hand, and accompanied by her mother—the infant's grandmother—they walked to the east, prayed, and cast pinches of cornmeal to the sun. When the sun rose above the horizon,

the mother held her child to the sun and said, "Father Sun, this is your child."

—*Alan Axelrod*

CORONADO, FRANCISCO VÁSQUEZ DE

Spanish explorer Francisco Vásquez de Coronado (1510–1554) was born in Salamanca, Spain, the second son of Juan Vásquez de Coronado and Isabel de Lujan. At the age of twenty-five, Coronado sailed for Mexico, where he married Dona Beatriz de Estrada, the daughter of a wealthy, socially prominent family. During his early years in Mexico, Coronado earned the respect of his contemporaries and was appointed councilman in Mexico City. In 1538, he was elevated to governor of Nueva Galicia.

In 1540, Coronado set out on an expedition in search of the Seven Cities of Cíbola. Leaving Mexico City with three hundred Spanish soldiers and an entourage of servants, Coronado traveled to the Pacific Coast through the Sinaloa and Sonora regions and crossed parts of Arizona and New Mexico. As winter set in, he settled next to the Rio Grande. With the arrival of spring, the explorers set out across the plains of Llano Estacado (the Staked Plains) of the Texas Panhandle, Palo Duro Canyon, Oklahoma, and Kansas until they reached the Arkansas River. The expedition was divided into several groups. The leader of one group, Hernando Alarcon, was the first European to reach California.

While the expedition failed to find treasures, it was successful in mapping the Southwest, and it set in motion the exploration and settlement of the Southwestern region of the United States. Coronado was the first European to travel through the lands of the Zuni, Pueblo, and Hopi Indians. Several sites in the West bear his name: the Coronado Mountains, Coronado Park, Coronado Trail, and Coronado Summit.

Coronado returned to Mexico City in 1542. Upon his arrival, his command of the expedition was questioned by the Spanish authorities, and he was charged with misconduct. Although he was fined for lack of judgment and discipline, the inquiry did not produce any evidence of dishonesty or improper actions. He resumed his political career, was reappointed councilman in Mexico City, and remained in the position until his death on September 22, 1554.

—*Fred L. Koestler*

SEE ALSO: Cíbola, Seven Cities of; Exploration: Spanish Expeditions

SUGGESTED READING:

Arciniegas, German. *The Knight of El Dorado*. New York, 1942.

Bolton, Herbert Eugene. *Coronado: Knight of Pueblos and Plain*. Albuquerque, N. Mex., 1949.

CORPS OF ENGINEERS

SEE: United States Army Corps of Engineers

CORPS OF TOPOGRAPHICAL ENGINEERS

The Corps of Topographical Engineers (1813–1863), a unit of the U.S. Army, was responsible for exploring and surveying the West. Awareness of a Western frontier that ended somewhere at the "South Sea" (as early geographers called the Pacific) spurred the founders of the United States government to include topographical engineers among the professional officers of the U.S. Army. Those topographers and their successors carried out explorations and surveys on a scale unknown in Europe. In 1777, General George Washington appointed a geographer and surveyor in the Continental Army, and the position was retained until the end of the Revolutionary War. Thomas Hutchins, the official geographer for the government under the Articles of Confederation, ran the first "Seven Ranges" in 1785 and 1786, thus beginning the system of land survey that continued throughout the nation's history. From that time until the War of 1812, however, topographical engineers were not a definable presence in the army. Early explorers, such as MERIWETHER LEWIS, WILLIAM CLARK, and ZEBULON MONTGOMERY PIKE, carried out duties as topographical engineers but were not described as such.

The U.S. Army gathered sixteen officers of captain or major rank into a branch known as the Topographical Bureau on March 3, 1813. The order creating the corps included instructions for defining the terrain wherein the enemy might be found and for describing changing land forms, rivers, ravines, hills, lakes, trails and roads, and villages. Of the two topographers remaining on active duty when the War of 1812 ended, one, Isaac Roberdeau, provided continuity to the corps. He became head of the Topographical Bureau when, in 1816, Secretary of War William H. Crawford recommended a military survey of the interior and exterior of the United States. The bureau's personnel consisted of ten topographical engineers, who made reconnaissances of overland routes to distant points in the West,

helped lay out canal routes, removed snags from the Red River, designed and cleared harbors, and ran geodetic surveys. The early work of Major STEPHEN HARRIMAN LONG, who later led an expedition across the Great Plains to the Rocky Mountains, is typical of the activities of the engineers in the bureau. Long's assignments even included supervising the building of marine hospitals in the lower Mississippi Valley.

In 1829, JOHN JAMES ABERT, a West Point graduate, became head of the Topographical Bureau. In addition to being an excellent engineer, he was also an astute politician. Due in great part to his lobbying, the army created the Corps of Topographical Engineers in 1838, an independent unit, equal to but separate from the UNITED STATES ARMY CORPS OF ENGINEERS. Abert headed the topographical corps with the rank of colonel. He established pride and loyalty among the small coterie of men in the unit, partly by rewarding good men with promotions.

Although just seventy-two officers (of whom sixty-four had been top cadets at West Point) made up the corps over its twenty-five year history, their contributions fill the annals of Western exploration; they were real pathfinders. Perhaps JOHN CHARLES FRÉMONT is the best known of these intrepid men, but many others did equally brilliant work. WILLIAM HEMSLEY EMORY accompanied STEPHEN WATTS KEARNY on an expedition to California from 1846 to 1847 and did liege service on the United States–Mexican Boundary Commission; later Emory was a commissioner for the survey that determined the Mexican-American boundary after the GADSDEN PURCHASE of 1853. John W. Gunnison worked on one of the Pacific Railroad Surveys and was killed by Indians. Howard Stansbury made a reconnaissance of Salt Lake, one of the most difficult achievements of the corps; at one time his men went forty hours without water, and many of their mules died of thirst. Joseph Christmas Ives explored the Colorado River and the Grand Canyon. Among other notable members of the corps were John N. Macomb, William Raynolds, Gouverneur K. Warren, and Colonel Abert's son, James W. Abert. Their official reports, still available in research libraries, are fascinating reading for the armchair explorer.

The corps was involved in major events of the westward movement. It conducted reconnaissances in the Southwest during the United States–Mexican War. It recommended routes for wagon roads in the Oregon Territory after 1846. It delved for artesian water on the Staked Plains of Texas. The corps was kept especially busy during the years of the Pacific Railroad Surveys.

In the corps' last few years, although its prestige had waned, a number of its officers distinguished themselves: Lieutenant Ives and Captain Macomb in the Southwest, Lieutenant Warren in the Great Plains, and Lieutenant John G. Parke along the forty-ninth parallel.

On March 3, 1863, the Corps of Topographical Engineers was merged with the army engineers.

—*Richard A. Bartlett*

SUGGESTED READING:

Goetzmann, William H. *Army Exploration in the American West, 1803–1863.* New Haven, Conn., 1959. Reprint. Austin, Tex., 1991.

———. *Exploration and Empire.* New York, 1966.

Wallace, Edward S. *The Great Reconnaissance.* Boston, 1955.

CORRIDOS

Almost all scholars agree that the *corrido* is a male narrative folk song of greater Mexico composed in eight-syllable lines that form four-line stanzas, or quatrains. The *corrido* is sung to a slow tempo in three-quarter or six-eighths time. The quatrains are structured in an *abcb* rhyme scheme with no fixed number of stanzas for any given song or performance. The opening stanza usually sets the scene, time, and central issue of the narrated events and may, on occasion, carry a request from the singer to the audience for permission to begin the song. Often the closing stanza offers an overall comment on the narrated events and may also announce that the ballad has ended and express a farewell from the singer to the audience. Finally, *corridos* in the words of John H. McDowell, "focus on events of particular consequence to the corrido community," on "events of immediate significance" that produce a "heightened awareness of mutual values and orientations."

Most scholars of the genre agree that *corrido*-like songs have been composed in Mexico since the conquest by the Spanish. There is also total agreement on the *corrido's* general indebtedness, in both form and theme, to the Spanish romance. Most scholars take their cue from Vincente T. Mendoza, Mexico's leading authority on the history of the *corrido,* and agree that "in its crystallized form, such as we know it today," the Mexican corrido is "relatively modern"; that is, it is a product of the late nineteenth and early twentieth centuries and especially of the intense social change caused by the Mexican Revolution. Merle Simmons also concludes that the *corrido* "finally evolved or solidified into its modern or definitive form during the last thirty years of the nineteenth century." Mendoza locates the geographical origins of the *corrido* in southern Michoacan, in deep southwestern Mexico. From

there, he believes, it traveled into the northern part of the country.

In 1958, Américo Paredes, an American scholar of Mexican descent, suggested a significantly different theory for the historical and geographical origins of the Mexican heroic ballad. Paredes located the *corrido's* temporal origins in the mid-nineteenth century and its geographical origins in southern Texas, an area he called the Lower Border.

The *corrido* focuses on events that are of particular significance to the author's community and that capture and articulate the community's values and orientations. Among such classes of events—natural disasters, the election of officials, the untimely death of a child—one theme seems to have struck a special resonance: confrontation, usually violent, between individual men. The characters sometimes represent larger social causes, but just as often they are concerned with their personal honor. In neither case, however, is the issue involved petty or small, and in some *corridos* both concerns are intertwined.

It is this image of the fearless man defending his rights with his pistol in hand that defines the male heroic world of the *corrido.* To the extent that his personal sense of honor and right is aligned with larger social values and conflicts, his heroic posture assumes an even more intense social significance. If this latter point is correct, we can begin to understand why the *corrido* flourished in the Lower Border region from the mid-nineteenth century and then declined after 1930.

Settled in the mid-eighteenth century by the Spanish as part of their northern expansion out of Central Mexico, the Lower Border was home to a relatively isolated folk society. Arid geography and nomadic Indians separated these people from the developing culture of central New Spain and, after independence, Central Mexico.

At the conclusion of the United States–Mexican War, the Lower Border people on the north bank were legally Americans, their homeland now part of Texas. They found themselves annexed into a new culture whose racism, religious prejudice, and linguistic xenophobia were directed toward them. Reinforced by the events at the Alamo and at Goliad, antipathy toward Mexicans continued as new Anglo settlers began to enter the Lower Border area from central Texas—the site of the initial Anglo core settlement—and the South. The political ineffectiveness, strict segregation, and racial violence that began at that time have not yet entirely disappeared. It was this sustained "conflict of cultures," as Paredes called it, that provided the prime ground for the heroic *corrido* to emerge along the Lower Border in the mid-nineteenth century.

According to Paredes, there is some fragmentary evidence of a heroic *corrido* from the early 1860s telling of an armed encounter between JUAN NEPOMUCENO CORTINA, a hero of the Lower Border, and the Anglo-American authorities after they mistreated a Mexican. Cortina kills a sheriff, organizes local Mexicans to fight the Anglos, and then, facing superior forces, escapes across the Rio Grande.

From the 1860s until the turn of the century, heroic *corridos* about such encounters began to appear in large numbers along the Lower Border. The concept of the local hero fighting for his right, his honor, and his status against external foes—usually Anglo authorities—became the central theme of the ballads, which reached their social and artistic zenith in the most popular *corrido*, that of GREGORIO CORTEZ. While focusing on the local hero and his right, the *corrido* consistently placed Cortez in relationship to broader social conflicts and emphasized the collective experience of Mexicanos versus Americanos.

Paredes also offered both an implied thesis to explain the relative absence of a heroic *corrido* tradition in Mexico's interior during most of the nineteenth century and an implied explanation for the heroic *corrido's* relative sudden emergence in Central Mexico during the period of the Mexican Revolution.

Certain enabling socio-cultural conditions for the corrido were absent from the Mexican interior before the revolution. Among the conditions needed for the emergence of a *corrido* tradition are a collective adversarial consciousness, a prolonged social conflict, a sense of a violated communal social order, an orally based culture, heroic actions by local heroes, a sense of a "lost cause" in the face of a fundamental cultural transformation, and finally, of course, the general if latent sense of a ballad tradition awaiting the appropriate social conditions to foster its emergence. While these conditions did not prevail in the Mexican interior throughout most of the nineteenth century, they did coalesce during the period of the revolution when they were set in motion by the same fundamental international political economy that had affected the Lower Border. The same essentially North American capitalist forces had been at work in Mexico since Porfirio Díaz came to power in 1876. The late nineteenth century was a period of intense political centralization and economic development in Mexico, but the development was of questionable benefit to the country as a whole.

This grossly uneven development led to the Mexican Revolution, revolutionary heroes, and new *corridos* about them and their battles, such as "El Corrido de Celaya." By 1910, however, the Mexican *corrido* was very likely a borrowing from across the border in Texas since so much of the revolutionary fighting took place in the northern Mexican states. Later, with the immigration of Mexicans into the United States after the revolution, these newer *corridos* joined those already created in the Southwest to become one repertoire of the greater Mexican community.

The *corrido* did not last, at least not at the full strength it acquired between 1848 and 1930. According to Paredes, by the 1930s "when Mexico's Tin Pan Alley took over the corrido, its decay was inevitable." Paredes explained: "At first radio and the movies employed folk singers and composers, and Mexican popular music had a brief golden age. But soon the demand for more and more new songs wore the folk material thin." It was as if the demand for *corridos* produced a new body of songs that were "thin" in their articulation of the traditional aesthetics and social vision.

Very few, if any, new *corridos* of epic heroic quality continued to be played after the 1930s. The earlier heroic *corridos*, like those of Celaya and Cortez, continued to be sung and were sometimes recorded and even played on the radio. But other kinds of *corridos* were played more often; they were concerned with more everyday themes and issues of interest to the community—natural disasters, betrayed love affairs, contraband, murders, and immigration. Despite their subject matter being rooted in the everyday experiences of the greater Mexican people, the new *corridos* tended to be the products of professional composers who, although closely related to the community, nonetheless had an ear out for the commercial demands of radio stations and recording companies. These demands tended to produce *corridos* more attuned to sensationalism (drug-dealing and murder, for example), and they were poetically constrained both by recording and radio play time and by a less-than-rigorous poetic aesthetic. Today, these kinds of *corridos* predominate, although the earlier epic heroic *corridos* may still be heard.

—*José E. Limón*

SUGGESTED READING:

Limón, José E. *Mexican Ballads, Chicano Poems: History and Influence in Mexican American Social Poetry.* Berkeley, Calif., 1992.

McDowell, John H. "The Corrido of Greater Mexico as Discourse, Music and Event." In *"And Other Neighborly Names": Social Process and Cultural Image in Texas Folklore.* Edited by Richard Bauman and Roger D. Abrahams. Austin, Tex., 1981.

Paredes, Américo. "The Ancestry of Mexico's Corridos: A Matter of Definitions." *Journal of American Folklore* 76 (1963): 231–235.

———. "The Mexican Corrido: Its Rise and Fall." In *Madstones and Twisters.* Edited by Mody C. Boatright, Wilson M. Hudson, and Allen Maxwell. Dallas, Tex., 1958.

———. *"With His Pistol in His Hand": A Border Ballad and Its Hero.* Austin, Tex., 1958.

Simmons, Merle. "The Ancestry of Mexico's Corridos." *Journal of American Folklore* 76 (1963): 1–15.

———. *The Mexican Corrido as a Source for the Interpretive Study of Modern Mexico (1870–1950).* Bloomington, Ind., 1957.

Savage, Lucida, C.S.J. *The Congregation of the Sisters of St. Joseph of Carondelet, St. Louis, Missouri (1650–1922).* St. Louis, Mo., 1923.

Smith, Anne Cecilia. *Educational Activities of the Sisters of Saint Joseph in the Western Province, 1870–1903.* Washington, D.C., 1953.

CORRIGAN, SISTER MONICA

Sister Monica Corrigan, C.S.J. (1843–1929), was a nun, educator, administrator, fundraiser, and archivist. She was born Anna Taggert in Hemmingford, Quebec, to Anglican parents. Details about her early life and education are minimal. While studying math at a college in Canada, she eloped with Catholic John Corrigan and moved to Kansas City, Missouri. After the death of her husband and children in 1866, the twenty-three-year-old widow began teaching at St. Teresa's Academy, established by the Sisters of St. Joseph of Carondelet (C.S.J.). After a year's deliberation and her conversion to Catholicism, she entered the C.S.J. community. She took her final vows in 1869 and was sent the following spring with six other sisters to open a school in Tucson, Arizona. Well educated and savvy, she kept a journal, *Trek of the Seven Sisters,* which detailed physical deprivations and described the humor and perseverance of the sisters who fought fear, fatigue, desert heat, dangerous terrain, and unwanted male attention.

For the next twenty-four years, Sister Monica helped establish schools, academies, and hospitals in Arizona, including St. Joseph's Academy in Tucson, Sacred Heart School in Yuma, and St. Joseph's Hospital in Prescott. Her determination and the sheer force of her personality combined with her math and business acumen to make her a formidable administrator, fundraiser, and important leader in the building of C.S.J. institutions in the Southwest. Her later life was spent working with children and orphans in Kansas City and collecting materials documenting C.S.J. activities in the trans-Mississippi West.

—*Carol K. Coburn*

SEE ALSO: Catholics; Missions: Nineteenth-Century Missions to the Indians

SUGGESTED READING:

Corrigan, Sister Monica. *Trek of the Seven Sisters.* Tucson, Ariz., 1991.

Coyne, St. Claire, C.S.J. "The Los Angeles Province." In *The Sisters of St. Joseph of Carondelet.* Edited by Dolorita Marie Dougherty. St. Louis, Mo., 1966.

CORTEZ, GREGORIO

Gregorio Cortez (1875–1916), a South Texas rancher, came to symbolize the struggle between Mexicans and Anglo-Americans in Texas. Born in northern Mexico, Cortez moved with his family to south Texas at the age of twelve. After he had worked as a vaquero or ranch hand for other ranchers, he and his brother farmed in the region. On June 12, 1901, the sheriff of Karnes County, Texas, arrested the Cortez brothers for horse stealing. Cortez denied the charges, and in an ensuing argument, in which neither side could understand the language of the other, the sheriff wounded Cortez's brother. Cortez then shot and killed the sheriff.

Pursued by a posse of three hundred men, Cortez quickly fled from the area. For ten days, he fought off posse after posse, rode more than 400 miles, and walked at least 120 miles in an attempt to reach the Mexican border. When Cortez learned that his family had been jailed, he relinquished his flight, and a posse finally captured him before he crossed the border, but another sheriff had fallen in the fight.

Mexicans, who saw Cortez's struggle as a fight against the injustice of the Anglos, contributed money for his defense. His legal struggles lasted almost four years. While he was acquitted of the charge of killing the sheriff of Karnes County, he was convicted of killing the second sheriff and was sentenced to life in prison. He was pardoned in 1913 and died three years later.

Cortez's struggle, immortalized in the "Corrido de Gregorio Cortez," a ballad Mexican Americans in Texas still sing, epitomized the inequality suffered by Mexican Americans (TEJANOS) in Texas throughout the period of Anglo-American settlement. Numbering about 160,000 people in 1900, Mexican Americans were dominated politically, socially, and culturally by the Anglo-Americans.

—*Candace Floyd*

SUGGESTED READING:

Paredes, Américo. *"With His Pistol in His Hand": A Border Ballad and Its Hero.* Austin Tex., 1958.

CORTEZ, CALIFORNIA

The third Japanese-Christian farming colony founded by KYUTARO ABIKO, Cortez, California, begun in 1919, was located in the San Joaquin Valley near the town of Livingston. The influential publisher of the Japanese-language newspaper, *Nichibei,* and successful entrepreneur, Abiko encouraged Japanese immigrants to establish roots in the United States and to take up farming as their best chance of success in their new homeland. Abiko purchased two thousand acres of land and settled about thirty families who worked farms varying in size from twenty to forty acres.

The first settlers faced an inhospitable land and even more inhospitable neighbors. Dust storms and voracious jackrabbits destroyed the first plantings of grapes the Cortez settlers cultivated. The farms required the labors of all family members: wives worked beside their husbands and children and then handled all of the housework as well. With the development of irrigation, the annual rabbit drives, and the coming of electricity in 1925, Cortez families finally established fruit-bearing vineyards, fruit orchards, and almond orchards.

Prior to the founding of Cortez, California passed its alien land law, prohibiting immigrants ineligible for citizenship from owning land. Cortez settlers circumvented the law by placing title to their lands in the names of their American-born children or in the names of corporations established specifically for this purpose. Anglo-Americans discouraged settlement at Cortez; the local Livingston *Chronicle* ran editorials condemning the arrival of Japanese families while it recruited members for a newly formed Anti-Japanese Association. In such a hostile environment during the harvest season of 1921, vigilantes attacked migrant Japanese laborers working the white-owned melon farms in the region.

In spite of these impediments to settlement, JAPANESE AMERICANS continued to settle in Cortez and to prosper steadily. It was the development of economic, religious, and educational institutions that fostered their financial independence and their cultural solidarity. With the establishment of the Cortez Growers Association in 1924, farmers banded together to buy supplies, fertilizers, and insecticides in bulk and at reduced prices. The collective sold the produce of all farmers, thereby enabling them to compete with larger farms. And the association eased the difficulties of dealing in a foreign language with unfamiliar business and legal practices. As the farmers of Cortez diversified their crops in response to market pressures, other associations—one for berry growers, another for vegetables—appeared in the late 1920s.

The settlers also founded a Presbyterian church, a Buddhist church, and an educational society. The Presbyterian church provided activities geared toward Japanese parents and special programs for their Nisei children. Cortez constructed an Educational Society Building, which housed the language school Nisei children attended after their public-school classes. A Young People's Club provided social activities for both Christian and Buddhist youths, including baseball teams.

Within two decades, the Cortez community was well established. On the eve of World War II and the forced internment of Cortez families at the Amache Relocation Center in Colorado, the Cortez community joined with other Abiko colonies and hired a white manager to run their farms for them. Unlike most Japanese Americans who lost their property during internment, the Cortez families returned to their farms after the war.

In the postwar years, Cortez underwent predictable changes. The Issei generation passed their farms onto their children, whose labor became more mechanized and encompassed larger tracts of land. Many of the Sansei generation, children of the Nisei, left the family farms for city life (although some returned to their family lands as mature adults), and the Cortez Growers Association included members not of Japanese descent. Cortez, a community of Japanese farm families for four generations, has become much like the Anglo-American communities that surround it, which its founder would have likely viewed as a success.

—*Patricia Hogan*

SEE ALSO: Alien Land Laws; Fruit and Vegetable Farming; Japanese Internment; Language Schools

SUGGESTED READING:
Matsumoto, Valerie J. *Farming the Home Place: A Japanese Community in California, 1919–1982.* Ithaca, N.Y., 1993.

CORTINA, JUAN NEPOMUCENO

Juan Nepomuceno Cortina (Cortinas) (1824–1894) was a Mexican general, governor of Tamaulipas, frontier *caudillo,* a celebrated folk hero, and charismatic revolutionary. Born at Camargo, Tamaulipas, Cortina served in the Mexican army at the battles of Palo Alto and Resaca de la Palma. After the UNITED STATES–MEXICAN WAR, he established a small ranch at San Jose, a short distance from Brownsville, Texas. He came to despise a clique of local attorneys and judges, whom he accused of expropriating land from Mexican Texans (TEJANOS) unfamiliar with the American judicial system. After wounding Marshal Robert Shears during a confrontation, Cortina, with seventy-five men, led a raid on Brownsville in September 1859 and left four townsmen dead. Two days later, he issued a proclamation asserting the rights of Mexican Texans. In what has been called the "Cortina War," he decisively defeated a force of Brownsville recruits and Matamoros militia and issued a second proclamation threatening to burn Brownsville if one of his lieutenants, Tómas Cabrera, were not released. When Cabrera was hanged by the Texas Rangers, Cortina retaliated by killing four rangers in an ambush north of Brownsville. It was not until 165 regulars of the U.S. Army under Major Samuel Peter Heintzelman arrived on the border that Cortina and five hundred followers were decisively defeated at Rio Grande City on December 27, 1859. He continued skirmishing with the rangers and the army and led an attack on the steamboat *Ranchero*. He eventually retreated into the Burgos Mountains in northern Tamaulipas and did not return to the border until May 22, 1861, when he raided Carrizo, the county seat of Zapata County. Defeated by Confederate Captain Santos Benavides, Cortina again retreated into Mexico. As a result of his activities on the border, he became a folk hero to many Tejanos and Mexicanos. *CORRIDOS* recalling his daring deeds became common in the years following the Cortina War.

Although Cortina rose twice to become governor of Tamaulipas and a general in the army of Benito Juárez, he briefly cooperated with the French imperialists. In 1875, he was accused by stockmen in the Nueces Strip of heading a large ring of cattle rustlers and was arrested by the government of President Sebastián Lerdo de Tejada, largely as the result of United States diplomatic pressure. After issuing a proclamation in support of General Porfirio Díaz and the Plan de Tuxtepec, Cortina fled Mexico City a year later. Back on the border in February 1877, he was again arrested, sent to Mexico City, and placed in the prison of Santiago Tlatelolco. Still under surveillance and in bad health, Cortina died at Azcapotzalco near Mexico City. His legacy would become an integral part of the history of the Texas-Mexico border.

—*Jerry Thompson*

SUGGESTED READING:

Goldfinch, Charles W. *Juan N. Cortina, 1824–1892: A Re-Appraisal*. Chicago, 1947.

Thompson Jerry, ed. *Juan Nepomuceno Cortina and the Texas-Mexico Frontier*. El Paso, Tex., 1994.

COSTIGAN, EDWARD PRENTISS

Edward Prentiss Costigan (1874–1939), lawyer, reformer, and politician, was born in King William County, Virginia. As a young lawyer in Denver, Colorado, Costigan battled for honest elections and municipal reform. Twice, in 1912 and in 1914, he unsuccessfully ran for governor of Colorado as a Progressive Republican. His defense of union members after the LUDLOW MASSACRE in 1914 secured acquittals and earned him the friendship of labor. His support of Woodrow Wilson in 1916 brought him an appointment to the U.S. Tariff Commission where he advocated lower tariffs during his tenure from 1917 to 1928.

At the outset of the Great Depression, Costigan promised Coloradans a "new deal" two years before Franklin Roosevelt popularized the term. Elected to the U.S. Senate in 1930, he favored federal grants to states to provide aid for the needy, and he damned HERBERT HOOVER's Reconstruction Finance Corporation as "billions for big business, but no mercy for mankind." By avidly supporting Roosevelt's relief programs and by advocating a federal antilynching law, Costigan put himself to the left of most Democrats. Coloradans thanked him for the 1934 Jones-Costigan Sugar Control Act that bolstered the state's sugar-beet industry, but in the 1934 Democratic primary, they rejected his candidate for governor, JOSEPHINE ASPINWALL ROCHE.

When ill-health prevented Costigan from seeking reelection to the Senate in 1936, he was succeeded by EDWIN CARL ("BIG ED") JOHNSON, an anti-New Deal Democrat. Costigan's wife, Mabel Cory Costigan, helped keep his memory and the causes they shared alive until her death in 1951. His legacy also persisted in several of his political protégés: Oscar L. Chapman (secretary of the interior), Charles F. Brannan (secretary of agriculture) and John A. Carroll (U.S. representative and senator).

—*Stephen J. Leonard*

SUGGESTED READING:

Greenbaum, Fred. *Fighting Progressive: A Biography of Edward P. Costigan*. Washington, D.C., 1971.

COTTON FARMING

First planted in North America during the colonial era, cotton emerged as the major cash crop in the Western United States in the early 1900s. Already important in the Southern states since 1800, cotton production spread from the coasts of Georgia and South Carolina

Harper's Weekly reports "The First Bale of the Cotton Crop," an illustration by Frenzeny and Tavernier, in the August 21, 1875 issue. *Courtesy Patrick H. Butler, III.*

westward to central Texas before the Civil War. This spread was made possible by Eli Whitney's invention of the gin, the growth of the mechanized textile industry, and the introduction of short-staple upland varieties that thrived in areas generally below 36° north latitude. In the early 1900s, even the arid regions of western Texas and southwestern Oklahoma, southern New Mexico and Arizona, and the Imperial and San Joaquin valleys of California became attractive to cotton farmers who sought to escape the devastation caused by the boll weevil. Once such types as Plains storm-proof and the long-staple Pima and Acala became available and irrigated agricultural systems were installed, these Western areas emerged as the premier center for raising the crop. After World War II, Texas and California consistently outranked all other states in annual cotton production.

Regardless of their location, cotton farmers have generally followed a pattern in crop production. At the end of harvest, the previous crop's stalks are shredded and then plowed under. Before the next season's planting, farmers prepare level, ridge, or furrow seedbeds. Once average soil temperatures exceed 60° F for at least ten days in the spring, normally between late March and late May depending on the region, farmers plant cotton seed at the rate of approximately six to eight seeds per foot. During a growing season that ordinarily ranges from 160 to 200 days, the plants are thinned and weeds removed. Finally, harvesting usually extends from September until January depending on climatic conditions.

During the harvest, cotton is dumped into wagons, trailers, or module builders and transported to the gin where the seeds are removed. The fiber is then cleaned and compressed into standardized bales of 480 pounds. The producer usually sells the cotton at the gin or through farmers' cooperatives, many of which are linked by telecommunications equipment to national market exchanges. From the gin, the bales are delivered to warehouses where shipper-merchants store, grade, and distribute the cotton to domestic mills or export outlets for use in making yarn or textiles. The seed not retained for planting is processed as edible oil products or animal feed. Plastics and paper are developed from the seed linters, and hulls are fed to livestock.

Scientific and technological breakthroughs during the forty years after World War II reduced the physical labor required to grow a crop while increasing pro-

In this photograph, taken about 1896 in Oklahoma, an overseer watches African American workers harvest cotton. *Courtesy National Archives.*

ductivity. Tractors capable of providing power for multirow planting and cultivation equipment replaced draft animals. Newly developed mechanical pickers and strippers eliminated most of the hand labor during harvest. With these innovations, the number of man-hours required to raise a bale of cotton dropped from 146 to 10. In addition, chemical fertilizers usually containing nitrogen and phosphorus to enhance growth, preemergence and postemergence PESTICIDES to control insects and HERBICIDES to destroy weeds, and continuing scientific research to develop improved varieties contributed to the increase of average yields from one-half bale to one bale per acre nationwide; California and Arizona farmers, however, frequently gathered as many as three bales of the Acala type per acre.

Although the capability of cotton farmers expanded dramatically, the restrictions of government programs and market demands limited annual production by the 1980s to approximately fifteen million bales, 60 percent of which were grown in the Southwestern states. With the crop's values reaching five billion dollars annually, cotton sales to foreign nations of approximately two billion dollars represented 6 percent of the total value of United States agricultural exports.

—*Garry L. Nall*

SEE ALSO: Agriculture; Farming

SUGGESTED READING:
Ebeling, Walter. *The Fruited Plain: The Story of American Agriculture.* Berkeley, Calif., 1979.
Fite, Gilbert C. *Cotton Fields No More: Southern Agriculture, 1865–1980.* Lexington, Ky., 1984.
Lichtenstein, Jack. *Field to Fabric: The Story of American Cotton Growers.* Lubbock, Tex., 1990.

Texas Agricultural Experiment Station. *Cotton Production in Texas.* Bulletin 938. College Station, Tex. 1959.

COUES, ELLIOTT

Ornithologist, naturalist, and U.S. Army surgeon Elliott Coues (1842–1899) was born in Portsmouth, New Hampshire. He studied natural history under Spencer F. Baird of the Smithsonian Institution in Washington, D.C. As a student at Columbian College and National Medical College, he began publishing articles on ornithology (the study of birds) and acquired field experience on a scientific expedition to Labrador.

From 1864 to 1881, Coues was an army surgeon. His first Western assignment was at Fort Whipple, Arizona, from 1864 to 1865. During Reconstruction, he served at various Southern posts and continued work on his monumental *Key to North American Birds,* which appeared in 1872.

Coues returned to the West as a surgeon and naturalist for the Northern Boundary Survey from 1873 to 1874. From 1876 to 1880, as secretary and naturalist for the U.S. Geological and Geographical Survey of the Territories, he published many major works on birds, mammals, and reptiles.

Infuriated at being ordered to return to Arizona for routine medical duty, he resigned his army commission. For the next several years, he taught at the National Medical College, embraced theosophy, and was natural-history editor for the *Century Dictionary.* He was president of the American Ornithologists' Union from 1892 to 1895.

In the 1890s, Coues turned his attention to the American West and edited the journals of MERIWETHER LEWIS and WILLIAM CLARK, ZEBULON MONTGOMERY PIKE, Alexander Henry, CHARLES LARPENTEUR, and Francisco Garcés. His extensive annotation of these journals gives ample evidence of his vast knowledge of the West.

Coues was married three times and had three children who lived to maturity. He died, of cancer, in Baltimore. Brilliant, energetic, and constantly embroiled in controversy, he was probably the best-known ornithologist of his time and was a notable contributor to the historical record of the West.

—*Michael J. Brodhead*

SUGGESTED READING:
Coues, Elliott. *Key to North American Birds.* Salem, Mass., 1872.
Cutright, Paul Russell, and Michael J. Brodhead. *Elliott Coues: Naturalist and Frontier Historian.* Urbana, Ill., 1981.
Hume, Edgar E. *Ornithologists of the U.S. Army Medical Corps.* Baltimore, 1942.

COUGARS

SEE: Mountain Lions

COURTRIGHT, JIM

Soldier, scout, rancher, lawman, and detective Jim (Timothy Isaiah) Courtright (1848–1887) was born in Iowa. During the Civil War, he served as a scout in the Union Army. In 1865, he moved to Texas and became a rancher. In 1876, he was elected marshal of Fort Worth.

Courtright, known as "Longhaired Jim," then moved to New Mexico, where he also served as marshal. In 1883, while working as a ranch foreman, he killed two squatters. He escaped to Latin America, returned three years later, and was acquitted of all charges.

Returning to Fort Worth, Courtright opened a detective agency that served as a front for his protection

Jim Courtright, soldier, scout, rancher, lawman, and badman. *Courtesy Western History Collections, University of Oklahoma Library.*

racket. After gambler LUKE SHORT said no to Courtright's demands, the stage was set for a confrontation. On February 8, 1887, the two men met in a Fort Worth saloon. Although Courtright drew first, it was Short who fired the deadly bullets into another lawman gone bad.

—*Richard A. Van Orman*

SUGGESTED READING:
Cox, William R. *Luke Short and His Era.* Garden City, N.Y., 1961.
Schoenberger, Dale T. *The Gunfighters.* Caldwell, Idaho, 1971.
Stanley, F. *Jim Courtright: Two Gun Marshal of Fort Worth.* Denver, 1957.

COWBOY OUTFITS

From head to toe, cowboy attire combined utility and individual taste into a distinctive style. Terrain, vegetation, climate, and working conditions exerted a profound influence on the apparel and accoutrements worn by Western cattle herders, as did cultural background and personal preference. While much of the typical cowboy's wardrobe represented adaptations of common work clothing, a few items, including boots, spurs, and hats, embodied distinctive modifications designed to meet specialized needs. The availability of manufactured goods in standard sizes, including ready-to-wear clothing, played an increasingly important role and eventually supplanted homemade and handmade varieties in all but footwear.

Wide-brimmed, tall-crowned hats, made of straw or felt derived from beaver, rabbit, and hare fur, shielded the heads and necks of herders from scorching sun and drenching rain. Cowboys also used their hats to fan cook fires, signal distant comrades, and as feedbags for their hungry mounts. The distinctive shape or crease of the hat crown often was a clue to the geographical origin of its owner. Mexican-style sombreros were sometimes embellished with elaborate silver and gold embroidery. Although mostly light gray or black in color, "conk covers" often sported decorative hatbands incorporating braided horsehair, tooled leather, and metal conchas. Some buckaroos also fitted their hats with a chin string designed to hold the hats in place in a strong wind.

After the Civil War, hatter JOHN BATTERSON STETSON's distinctive and sturdy creation, known as "the boss of the plains," became the most popular brand on the Western range and synonymous with cowboy headgear. During winters on the Northern Plains, however,

The cowboy's outfit combined the practical equipment needed for the job and a expression of individual taste. Note in this photograph the cowboy's hat, bandanna, boots, spurs, vest, chaps, and gloves. *Courtesy Bettmann Archives.*

some cowboys donned wool or fur caps with ear flaps. Otherwise, they simply tied their hat brims down over their ears with a bandanna or wool scarf.

Bandannas were usually worn knotted loosely at the throat; sometimes they were pulled over the face to screen out choking dust or winter wind. Produced in both patterns and in solid colors, these utilitarian squares of cloth, sometimes called "wipes" also saw duty as towels, tourniquets, slings, and bandages. Most were made of cotton, although some stylish cowboys possessed silk bandannas for special occasions. Cowpunchers in northern climates often replaced lightweight bandannas with woolen mufflers or flannel strips during the winter.

Shirts were nondescript, sometimes homespun but more often ill-fitting, mass-produced wool or flannel types. Most were pullovers, possessing neither collars nor pockets and closed at the chest and neck by buttons or lacing. On bib-front styles, buttons secured a cloth shield over the shirt face. Cowboys sometimes employed arm garters to adjust sleeve length. In the late nineteenth century, protective leather cuffs worn over shirt sleeves became popular among cowboys in some regions.

Dark, solid-colored shirts predominated, although stripes and other patterns were not unknown. White silk and sateen shirts were usually reserved for special occasions. Cowboys often added sweaters of various styles and hues with the onset of cold weather.

Like shirts, durable, dark wool trousers were the norm, although duck or twill varieties were also prominent, corduroy pants, less so. Some pants were homespun, but most, including those of military issue, were manufactured. The best were close fitting and comfortable for riding. One especially popular late nineteenth-century woolen style known as California or Oregon pants featured a plaid or striped pattern. Denim work trousers made by LEVI STRAUSS and other manufacturers did not become fashionable with cowboys until the 1890s.

Most "britches" possessed small front pockets, which angled downward toward the outer seam, and a cinch and buckle in the back to adjust the fit at the waist. Most cowboys wore suspenders rather than belts with their trousers but many wore neither. They often tucked their pant legs into the tops of their boots.

Evolved from European and American styles, cowboy boots possessed tall tops that reached almost to the knee, rounded or square toes, pegged soles, and tall, underslung heels that helped secure feet in saddle stirrups. Top hands favored the made-to-order creations of local craftsmen. Most boots were made of plain black leather, usually cowhide but sometimes kangaroo. Cotton stitching added strength as well as decoration to boot tops, which also sported heavy leather straps or pulls. Insulated, rubber-soled overshoes, called "ar'tics," also could be seen on ranches on the Northern Plains during the winter.

A variety of spur styles adorned cowboy boots. Many were the hand-wrought products of local blacksmiths; others, the mass-produced creations of Eastern manufacturers. By the late nineteenth century, definitive regional styles had emerged from a common Mexican ancestry in Texas and California and on the Northern Plains. Texas models featured simple, one-piece construction; small rowels; short shanks, either straight or raised; swinging buttons; and decorative metal overlays. California types boasted drooping shanks with chap guards and sizable rowels, welded to straight-line heel bands. Pacific Coast artisans often embellished their creations with engraving, bluing, and inlays of silver, nickel, copper, and brass. The Northern Plains–type borrowed from both the Texas and California styles. This amalgam was distinguished by one-piece construction, sculpted heel bands, engraved metal inlay or overlay, and large rowels.

During inclement weather, cowboys commonly donned Mexican-style cloth ponchos or waterproof pommel slickers originally designed for the seafarers. A slit in the rear of the slicker enabled a rider to wear the full-length, canvas or duck garment while on horseback. A few were black in color; the majority were yellow. Cowboys either stored their slickers or ponchos in their bedrolls or tied them behind the cantles of their saddles.

Cattle herders generally eschewed bulky coats and outerwear that did not lend itself to roping and riding. Few needed heavy clothing anyway, as most hands were laid off during the winter. Those kept on the payrolls made do with wool-blanket coats and mackinaws or lighter, flannel-lined garments, although seldom heavy buffalo coats.

Vaqueros in the brushy regions of the Southwest, however, depended on waist- or hip-length duck or leather jackets to shield their torsos from thorny plants. Many cowboys also kept a suit or sack coat in the bunkhouse or their bedroll for town wear, dances, and courting.

Leather chaps (short for the Spanish term *chaparejos*) protected a cowboy's legs in the mesquite-infested country of the Southwest. They were also popular in cool climates and timbered regions, where styles incorporating angora wool or animal fur provided warmth as well as protection. Some cowboys on the Great Plains embraced leggings too, although rarely for ground work like branding.

This cowboy, identified as a Native American working on the Montana range, likely dressed for a studio portrait, not for work. *Courtesy Library of Congress.*

Spurs were attached to boots by means of spur leathers attached to buttons on either side of the heel band and passing across the instep. Some spurs also sported tiny chains that extended under the soles in front of the heels.

Because most late nineteenth-century shirts lacked pockets, cowpunchers relied on snug, cloth and leather vests with many pockets in which to carry items such as tobacco, matches, herd tallies, and an occasional pocket watch. Available in both button and lace-up varieties, vests also provided warmth without hindering arm movements while a cowboy roped and rode.

In this image, the work gear of an unknown cowboy is displayed on a bunk. Photograph by Walker, Cheyenne, Wyoming. *Courtesy American Heritage Center, University of Wyoming.*

Seatless chaps were usually secured to the body by means of an attached waist belt and to the legs by heavy thongs and, later, metal clips. Shotgun-style chaps, worn tight around the full leg, predominated. After the close of the open range, the bat-wing form, with sculpted leather flaps on the outside of the legs, became popular. Fringe, brass tacks, silver conchas, and patch pockets adorned many styles.

Wrist-length buckskin gloves protected hands from cuts and rope burns, although cowboys usually avoided unwieldy gauntlets, whose extended tops tended to trap dust and debris and could easily hang up on a rope or saddle. Cowboys performing in the rodeo and in Wild West shows, however, embraced the fancy beaded types.

—*B. Byron Price*

SUGGESTED READING:

Beard, Tyler. *The Cowboy Boot Book*. Layton, Utah, 1992.
———. *100 Years of Western Wear*. Salt Lake City, 1993.
Rattenbury, Richard. "A Century of Western Fashion." *Persimmon Hill* 17 (Autumn 1989): 5–15.
Rickey, Don. *$10 Horse, $40 Saddle: Cowboy Clothing, Arms, Tools, and Horse Gear of the 1880s*. Fort Collins, Colo., 1976.
Vernam, Glenn R. *Man on Horseback*. New York, 1964.

COWBOYS

Mounted herdsmen associated with the range CATTLE INDUSTRY in the trans-Mississippi West after the Civil War, cowboys were wage laborers performing menial tasks. On the breeding grounds of the Southern Plains, they were employed to gather, sort, and brand cattle and drive them to market. Expansion of the rail system in the post–Civil War period made trailing cattle unnecessary, and cowboys on the Southern Plains became, as their counterparts on the Northern Plains had generally been, ranch hands. By 1890, the boom years of the cattle industry were over; and thereafter, cowboys passed from history to legend, lionized by writers

Frenzeny and Tavernier's cozy bunkhouse scene reveals nothing of the grinding, dirty, and decidedly unromantic work of the cowboy. *Courtesy Patrick H. Butler, III.*

who, if they had not known cowboys personally, were at least nostalgic for the era cowboys represented.

Decades of academic scrutiny have made cowboying among the more examined American occupations, and so it is perhaps surprising that more is not known about the men who did the job. In the matter of cowboy work, how it was done, and the equipment employed on ranch or range, the record is sufficient; but the demographics are less satisfying, because, in the context of their time and place, cowboys were considered unskilled laborers unworthy of the elaborate record keeping otherwise practiced by cattlemen. The conclusion that animals received more attention than men during the heyday of the range cattle industry is not unwarranted. Cattle were worth more and could be sold for money; cowboys could be hired almost anywhere for a dollar a day.

The historical record does not reveal how many cowboys went north with herds bound for market or how many rode the ranges of the West from 1865 to 1890. Whatever numbers one may encounter in the literature are merely estimates, usually based on the number of cattle assumed to have been sold. But these figures, too, are only estimates. To say that between four million and six million cattle went up the various trails from Texas after the Civil War is less than useful if the numbers are to be the basis for calculating the actual number of cowboys who must have accompanied them. No scholar can say with any degree of certainty how many cowboys there were, and no accurate determination can be made as to what percentage of the total were Anglo-American, Hispanic, African American, or Native American, although documentary and photographic evidence proves that each of these groups was represented among the cowboy population. And yet, while inconvenient, the historical anonymity of cowboys contributed directly to the eventual elevation of cowboy imagery to a position of prominence in American culture.

To artists and writers who saw them, cowboys held an undeniable appeal. Hired men they may have been, but they worked on horseback against a dramatic backdrop and thus were picturesque. On the trail, they were in a new place every day, and thus their lives suited a motif familiar to producers of fiction. But to many who knew them, including their employers, cowboys were an unsavory lot, distinguished only by their bad habits and rude behavior. WILLIAM F. ("BUFFALO BILL") CODY began to alter negative perceptions in 1884 when, as a matter of pure showmanship, he introduced a young ranch hand named William Levi Taylor to audiences attending Buffalo Bill's Wild West show as "Buck Taylor, King of the Cowboys." Cody and his publicists

A cow puncher poses beside the steer he has just lassoed. Graham, Country, Arizona Territory, about 1896. *Courtesy National Archives.*

fashioned a noble, patriotic biography to gain public acceptance for Buck Taylor, and parents were told that the tall Texan was gentle with children. Taylor's popularity grew each year, and by 1887, he was the putative hero of a series of dime novels written by long-time Cody associate Prentiss Ingraham. Acceptance of the new cowboy image was nearly complete by 1902 when former cowboy THEODORE ROOSEVELT was in the White House and OWEN WISTER published his novel, *The Virginian.* Thereafter, the plural cowboys of history became a singular, stereotypical cowboy of fiction and, later, film, radio, and television.

Cody and Wister, together with their imitators and successors, offered the public a cowboy unfettered by cows. The tactic permitted cowboy protagonists to become heroic because they were free of the responsibility to tend cattle. It also allowed them to avoid identification with menial labor—the grinding, dirty, and decidedly unromantic work of branding, castrating, de-horning, ear notching, and serving as surrogate mother to orphan calves. These activities and a great many others subsequently escaped public notice whenever the center of attention was a dashing fashion-plate, amply armed with shiny six-guns and astride a horse as wonderfully attired and nearly as smart as its rider. The process of distancing the cowboy from cattle continued in fiction, cinema, and electronic media until, by the 1950s, one found the label "working cowboy" applied by writers whenever they wished to discuss the real thing. The perception had even developed that rodeo cowboys, who were primarily entertainers, had more in common with athletes than with working cowboys from whose ranks many of them had come.

Owing to Hollywood's concentration on the stereotype in the 1910s and 1920s, cowboy imagery acquired some interesting dimensions. For example, it influenced country music, which later became

Top: A group of cowboys on the New Mexico range strike a pose for the photographer. *Courtesy National Cowboy Hall of Fame and Western Heritage Center.*

Bottom: Nearly all of the work of a cowboy was conducted on top of a moving horse. One of the few times a cowboy stood still long enough to have his picture taken was when he stopped at the chuck wagon for a meal. *Courtesy National Cowboy Hall of Fame and Western Heritage Center.*

country-and-western as a direct result. Performers at the Grand Ole Opry and other venues clearly preferred the hat and boots of the cowboy to the overalls and brogans of the hayseed. Musicians dressed as cowboys became the centerpieces, while musicians clad as bumpkins provided comedy—a relationship similar to that exhibited by Hollywood's singing cowboys and their sidekicks. There were indeed musicians with authentic cowboy backgrounds in the 1920s and 1930s—Otto Gray's Oklahoma Cowboys, for example, were stars of the RKO vaudeville circuit and helped demonstrate the feasibility of marketing commercial country music to urban audiences—but the preponderance of music offered to the public was either traditional music of the rural South or newer music with lyrics having nothing to do with cowboy themes.

By the mid-1950s, nearly every entertainment medium in America was to some extent involved with purveying cowboy imagery. The effect was striking, and, to some critics—fearful of the decline of American culture—alarming. News that a nationwide shortage of black dye had come about in 1950 because children were clamoring for clothes similar to those worn by their new television hero, Hopalong Cassidy, was taken to be indicative of more than a fad, but a fad is precisely what it was, and soon enough it had run its course. When television finally lost its fascination with nineteenth-century cowboy stereotypes, an "urban cowboy" image, supported by the songs of Willie Nelson, Waylon Jennings, and others, appeared late in the 1970s. It was the image of a contemporary loner altogether more antisocial than the cultural icon of the 1950s and riding in a pickup truck, not on a horse. The archetypal cowboy image for the 1980s and 1990s derived from Larry McMurtry's characters in *Lonesome Dove* (1985), a Pulitzer Prize-winning novel and successful television miniseries (1989), both of which had spawned sequels by 1993. McMurtry's cowboy seemed drawn from the pre-Cody era, when cowboys were popularly thought to possess few redeeming qualities.

Cowboys continued to work cattle on Western ranges through the twentieth century and went about their business regardless of popular attention or the lack of it. They had became part of an articulate subculture, expressing their views of the world and work in poetry and art and revealing the extent to which they differed from the uninitiated—ironically the same proposition advanced in a different, less believable way by purveyors of cowboy stereotypes fifty years earlier.
—*William W. Savage, Jr.*

SEE ALSO: Cowboy Outfits

A cowboy dance. *Courtesy Archives Division, Texas State Library.*

SUGGESTED READING:

Allmendinger, Blake. *The Cowboy: Representations of Labor in an American Work Culture.* New York, 1992.
Branch, E. Douglas. *The Cowboy and His Interpreters.* New York, 1926.
Erickson, John R. *The Modern Cowboy.* Lincoln, Nebr., 1981.

Cowboys branding a calf. *Courtesy Western History Collections, University of Oklahoma.*

Frantz, Joe B., and Julian Ernest Choate, Jr. *The American Cowboy: The Myth and the Reality.* Norman, Okla., 1955.

McCoy, Joseph G. *Historic Sketches of the Cattle Trade of the West and Southwest.* Kansas City, 1874.

Savage, William W., Jr. *The Cowboy Hero: His Image in American History and Culture.* Norman, Okla., 1979.

Siringo, Charles A. *A Texas Cowboy; or, Fifteen Years on the Hurricane Deck of a Spanish Pony.* Chicago, 1886.

Slatta, Richard W. *Cowboys of the Americas.* New Haven, Conn., 1990.

COWBOY SONGS

Cowboy songs began as traditional occupational folk songs of working cowboys of the mid- to late 1800s. Cowboys had to draw on their own resources for amusement and entertainment in the same way that loggers, sailors, miners, and men in other occupations that involved periods of relative isolation and hard, dangerous working conditions had done. Cowboys told tall tales and jokes, played pranks on one another, recited verse, and sang. These forms of folklore grew out of the work and everyday lives of the cowboys, and the songs and poems they made up reflected the content of their work and the conditions of their lives on the range. Songs such as "The Old Chisholm Trail" and "The Trail to Mexico" described the long trail drives. "When the Work's All Done This Fall" and "Little Joe, the Wrangler" tell of danger and fallen comrades. Even humorous songs, like "Punchin' the Dough" and "The Gol Durn Wheel" were often stark and realistic.

Not all the songs the working punchers knew were occupational cowboy songs. Many cowboys came West from homes in the South or the East, and they brought with them the familiar folk and popular songs they knew in their former homes. There were also Western songs that dealt with other aspects of the experience during the settlement period—such as emigration, hunting buffalo, fighting Indians, the exploits of outlaws, and romance. All these kinds of songs existed alongside the occupational songs in the cowboy repertoire, and it was not unusual to hear "The Streets of Laredo" followed by "Shenandoah" or "After the Ball."

Some cowboy songs were reworked versions of older tunes. "The Dying Cowboy," better known as "Oh, Bury Me Not on the Lone Prairie," is a parody of "The Ocean Burial (Oh, Bury Me Not in the Deep, Deep Sea)," written by a Universalist clergyman in 1839. "The Cowboy's Lament (The Streets of Laredo)" was derived from the much older British broadside ballad entitled "The Unfortunate Rake," in which a soldier dying of syphilis pleads for a military funeral.

Cowboys also made up poems and songs themselves. Contrary to conventional wisdom, many cowboys were literate and had some education before heading West, and they captured a great deal of the West and cowboy life in verse. It was a common practice for the verses to be set to familiar or popular tunes and eventually enter oral tradition as songs. For example, "The Sierry Petes (Tying the Knot in the Devil's Tail)," written by northern Arizona cowboy poet Gail Gardner in 1917, was put to the tune of "Polly Wolly Doodle" by another Arizona cowboy Billy Simon. "Polly Wolly Doodle" was such a simple and familiar tune that it became the melody for a number of cowboy songs, including "Windy Bill."

Most traditional cowboy songs came from the trail-drive era of the latter 1800s up through about 1920. By the end of the nineteenth century, the days of the long trail drive, when huge herds of cattle were moved up trails to Kansas and Montana, were coming to a close. The open range was fenced off and broken up into smaller ranches, and the old cowboy way of life was changing. It was during the early twentieth century that second-generation ranch poets, such as Gardner and Curly Fletcher, who wrote "Strawberry Roan," were active.

Despite the popular notion of the guitar-toting cowboy inspired by motion pictures, relatively few musical instruments were found on trail drives and in cow camps. Hauling around a guitar on a horse while trying to work cattle was not practical. The fiddle, however, was small and relatively portable—a cowboy could roll it up in his bedroll—and was thus the most common instrument. There were some good fiddlers among the cowboys from the South, who brought with them their basic repertoire of Southeastern dance tunes. An occasional harmonica or Jew's harp might also be found. Guitars, mandolins, and banjos did not become popular until after the turn of the century, when they were made available through mail order from Sears or Montgomery Ward. Most old-time cowboys would simply recite verses, or, if they could carry a tune, they would sing unaccompanied.

The first printed collections of cowboy songs appeared shortly after the turn of the century. N. Howard ("Jack") Thorp, a working cowboy who decided to collect the songs he heard in the cow camps, published *Songs of the Cowboys* in 1908; the book contained the words to 23 songs. Thorp also wrote several cowboy songs that entered tradition, including "Chop" and "Little Joe, the Wrangler." Two years later, folklorist John Lomax published *Cowboy Songs and Other Frontier Ballads,* which included 122 songs, 18 of them with melodies. These printed collections and later ones helped create a bridge between folk and popular cultures. It was now possible to learn cowboy songs from the printed page as well as from oral tradition.

By the 1920s, cowboy singers performed on radio and recorded for commercial record companies. In 1925, Texan Carl T. Sprague recorded "When the Work's All Done This Fall" for Victor. The recording was a tremendous best-seller and sparked the era of commercial cowboy music. Sprague was soon followed by other authentic cowboy singers, such as Jules Verne Allen, The Cartwright Brothers, Harry ("Haywire Mac") McClintock, and Billie Maxwell, the first woman to record cowboy songs. These performers did not perform unaccompanied but made recordings with very spare, basic guitar accompaniment (occasionally with fiddle or harmonica added) that suited the traditional, straightforward nature of the songs.

With the 1930s came western movies and, with them, the "singing cowboy." The cowboy as a larger-than-life American myth was nothing new, however. The heroic image had been nurtured since the days of NED BUNTLINE's dime novels and WILLIAM F. ("BUFFALO BILL") CODY's Wild West Show; actors such as TOM MIX and WILLIAM S. HART simply exploited the same image in a new medium. The first cowboy actor to sing in a movie was Ken Maynard in *The Wagon Master* (1929). Within a few years, Hollywood was full of singing cowboys. GENE AUTRY, Roy Rogers, Tex Ritter, and "The Sons of the Pioneers" all blazed their way across the silver screen and enjoyed success in both acting and recording careers.

While media cowboys still included a few traditional songs in their repertoire, most of the songs they performed were newly composed popular pieces by professional tunesmiths of Tin Pan Alley far removed from actual cowboy experiences. Unlike the harshly realistic older occupational songs, the new songs romanticized the cowboy's life and portrayed him as a gallant, carefree knight of the plains. Along with the change in lyrics came a change in vocal and musical styles. While the first cowboy recordings were made with very simple accompaniment, the new box-office buckaroos performed with bands and used not only fiddles and guitars but also bass, accordion, and other instruments common to popular and country music. They also incorporated influences from jazz and swing. For example, musicians such as Bob Wills and Milton Brown synthesized western swing by combining elements of old-time Southwestern fiddling with big band swing, and "The Sons of the Pioneers" introduced smooth, close-harmony singing to the genre. The singing cowboys were now almost always accompanied by polished, "hot" ensembles.

As western movies and music increased in popularity, performers of mainstream country music, essentially Southern in origin, adopted the cowboy image. Musical groups with no connection to Western culture used names like "The Prairie Ramblers" and "The Golden West Cowboys." Jimmie Rodgers, the "father of country music," did much to popularize the cowboy image in country music. Known as the "singing brakeman," he was usually associated with his railroad background, but he was also enamored of cowboys, was photographed in cowboy regalia, and recorded songs like "The Yodeling Cowboy" and "When the Cactus is in Bloom." The Western look eventually reached its most outrageous with the elaborate embroidered and rhinestone-studded stage costumes worn by Hank Williams and others during the 1940s and 1950s. Apparently, both country-music performers and their fans preferred the heroic cowboy image to the hillbilly-hayseed image fashionable in the early days of country music.

Traditional occupational cowboy folk songs had relatively little direct musical impact on the development of American popular and country music. The content and style of authentic cowboy songs were very different from later commercialized Western music, but there is no doubt that they did inspire Tin Pan Alley and Hollywood. The cowboy image and Western theme were borrowed from tradition and romanticized, becoming an integral part of our cowboy myth. Over the years, both myth and reality, the old and the new, have continued to coexist in American culture, ebbing and flowing in relative popularity. By the end of the twentieth century, even though the days of the trail drive and the open range were long gone, traditional cowboy songs, as well as contemporary songs that reflected the modern West, were still sung and were still important in the lives of many Westerners who were part of the ranching culture.

—*Charlie Seemann*

SEE ALSO: Rogers, Roy, and Dale Evans

SUGGESTED READING:

Cannon, Hall, ed. *Old-Time Cowboys Songs.* Layton, Utah, 1988.

Fife, Austin, and Alta Fife. *Cowboy and Western Songs.* New York, 1969.

Logsdon, Guy. *The Whorehouse Bells Were Ringing and Other Songs Cowboys Sing.* Urbana, Ill., 1989.

Lomax, John, and Alan Lomax. *Cowboy Songs and Other Frontier Ballads.* Reprint. New York, 1986.

Ohrlin, Glenn. *The Hell-Bound Train: A Cowboy Songbook.* Urbana, Ill., 1973.

Tinsley, Jim Bob. *For a Cowboy Has to Sing.* Orlando, Fla., 1991.

———. *He Wads Singin' This Song.* Orlando, Fla., 1981.

White, John I. *Git along Little Dogies: Songs and Songmakers of the American West.* Urbana, Ill., 1975.

COWBOY TOOLS AND EQUIPMENT

Cowboys depended on special saddles and ropes to handle livestock on the Western cattle range. Horned stock saddles, of Moorish and Spanish ancestry, developed in Mexico in the seventeenth century. The earliest models of the *silla de campo* consisted of simple, rawhide-covered trees rigged with stirrup leathers and secured by a single cinch extending below the pommel. Wood-block stirrups completed the outfit.

Many such saddles were covered with removable leather housings known as *mochilas,* fitted with slots to accommodate the horn and cantle. A *mochila* offered a horseman a more comfortable ride, while protecting his saddle rigging from inclement weather and the hide of his mount from thorny brush. Although most housings were plain, those of wealthy ranchers were often embellished with silver and gold mountings, fabric inlays and elaborate carving and embroidery featuring floral, bird, and animal motifs.

Until the mid-nineteenth century, most Western cattle herders depended on saddles imported from Eastern or Mexican sources or on homemade varieties dressed and rigged according to personal taste. By the 1850s, however, the influx of professional European and American saddlers into the West had produced distinct modifications of the basic Spanish-style stock saddle in both Texas and California. These adaptations were characterized by better workmanship and materials and variant structural elements.

California saddle-makers, for example, moved the cinch rigging from beneath the saddletree fork to a point midway on the sidebars. These centerfire models required neither cruppers nor rump housings to keep the rear of the saddle from riding up on a horse's back during roping. In Texas, a double-rigged saddle with twin cinches of angora wool, horsehair, or cotton webbing performed the same function and gave cowboys even more stability and leverage in the saddle.

Stirrup leathers on Western stock saddles were longer and set farther back on the tree than on Eastern and European models and allowed cowboys to stand in the saddle while roping. At first, saddle-makers suspended the narrow straps from rings tied to the sidebars of the tree or threaded through slots in the bars. With the demand for wider, sturdier stirrup leathers, however, saddlers began to drape them over broad notches cut in the bars.

Saddlers also began to attach *mochilas* permanently to saddletrees by means of tie strings, a style called the "Mother Hubbard." An increasing number of makers, however, discarded the bulky housings altogether and endowed their new creations with separate leather skirts, fenders, jockeys, and seats.

Sleek ox-bow-style stirrups, made by steaming and bending tough strips of hardwood, replaced crude, wood-block types. Many cowboys, however, still relied upon stirrups fitted with leather toe covers, known as *tapaderos,* which protected their feet from brush and cold and from fatal entanglements if unhorsed.

Lassoing heavy cattle strained even the best-made saddles. To minimize the stress, Mexican vaqueros developed a method of roping that became known in the West as the dolly welter or dally style, English corruptions of the Spanish term *dar la vuelta.* After catching his prey, a roper took several quick turns, or "dallies," around the saddle horn with the free end of his lariat and allowed it slip and avoided a solid jerk until the animal was successfully checked. This method was not without liabilities, however, as thumbs and fingers were sometimes severed when accidentally caught between the rope and the saddle horn.

Although the dally style of roping persisted among the buckaroos of the Pacific Coast, cowboys in the Southwest, where heavy brush restricted visibility, rope length, and loop size, usually tied their ropes hard-and-fast to the saddle horn.

Whereas dally ropers favored saddles with tall, slender horns and forks, the hard and fast style demanded shorter, thicker types. Experienced saddletree-makers favored the natural forks of hardwood trees, particularly elm. Persistent problems with splitting and warping, however, led in the early 1880s to experiments with metal horns and forks secured by long screws or bolts. Some saddlers and cowboys also fortified the necks of their horns with additional braided rawhide.

Amid the post–Civil War cattle boom, supply centers catering to ranchers and cowboys developed at railheads and livestock centers like San Antonio, Dodge City, Miles City, Denver, Pueblo, and Cheyenne. Buckaroos on the Pacific Coast depended on suppliers in San Francisco, Los Angeles, and Santa Barbara, California, and Pendleton, Oregon.

Custom-made saddlery, hand-crafted by individual artisans for a local clientele dominated the trade. A few sizable firms, however, developed substantial retail and wholesale operations, occupied spacious plants, and employed multiple hands, steam-powered machinery, and traveling salesmen. Some of the larger companies also advertised their wares and distributed trade catalogs. Most stamped their saddles with an identifying cartouche.

By the mid-1870s, Texas cowboys and drovers were discarding their "Mother Hubbard" rigs in favor of more sophisticated forms originating in Colorado, Wyoming, and Montana. Weighing thirty-five to forty pounds, these new models were heavier, sturdier, and better fitting than their predecessors. In the 1880s, a saddle style originating in Pueblo, Colorado, gained particular favor throughout the Great Plains.

Californians, meanwhile, continued to refine and embellish their distinctive centerfire rigs by incorporating smaller, rounded skirts, elaborate carving and mounting, and long *tapaderos*. The centerfire eventually spread into the Pacific Northwest and Great Basin before spilling onto the Northern Plains.

There it encountered competition from a hybrid three-quarter rig developed by Montana saddlers in the late 1880s or early 1890s. Discarding the rear cinch of the Texas-style saddle, saddlers located a single rigging point between the pommel and the California centerfire positions.

About the same time, sturdy but heavy iron stirrups began to supplant wooden types among many Western horsemen. Most were covered with leather as insulation against cold weather.

While advantageous to ropers, the tall and narrow saddletree forks of the nineteenth century offered riders little leverage on bucking horses. For extra support, horse-breakers often tied a slicker, coat, or blanket across the pommel of their saddles or padded bucking rolls that strapped or laced to the pommel. About 1904, however, Oregon saddle-makers addressed the problem with a swell fork, ranging from twelve to twenty-six inches in width. The widest varieties were known as freaks and bear traps.

The sport of rodeo produced still other changes in saddle design. By the 1920s, for example, a standardized "association saddle" had been adopted for bronc-riding competition. Competitive ropers, meanwhile, demanded double-rigged saddles with lower cantles and forks. Ornately carved and mounted saddles were often presented to rodeo champions. Fancy rigs also appealed to performers in Wild West shows and motion pictures but were too expensive for most working cowboys.

Western riders protected the backs of their mounts from the galling effects of saddletrees with fleece-lined skirts and coverings that ranged from soft wool or felt blankets to gunnysacks to woven Spanish moss. In the late nineteenth century, saddle blankets produced by Navajo weavers became favorites of cowboys throughout the Southwest.

Most cowpunchers kept a catch rope coiled on a thong on their saddle pommel. In open country, the length of the lariat varied from forty to more than one hundred feet, with fifty feet being about average. In brushy or timbered areas, twenty-five or thirty feet was adequate.

Durable but flexible plaited rawhide *reatas* predominated until the late nineteenth century, when lassos manufactured by Eastern cordage companies from cheap Philippine hemp became popular. Cowboys called the newcomers "whale lines."

Ropes fashioned from sisal and magauy fibers were also prevalent in some areas of the Southwest but were not generally strong enough for sustained heavy work. Nor were twisted or plaited horsehair types adequate, although they made serviceable and often artistic lead and tie ropes, reins and cinches.

—B. Byron Price

SEE ALSO: Cattle Brands and Branding

SUGGESTED READING:

Ahlborn, Richard E., ed. *Man Made Mobile: Early Saddles of Western North America*. Washington, D.C., 1980.

Rice, Lee, and Glen R. Vernam. *They Saddled the West*. Cambridge, Md., 1975.

Rickey, Don. *$10 Horse, $40 Saddle: Cowboy Clothing, Arms, Tools, and Horse Gear of the 1880s*. Fort Collins, Colo., 1976.

Severn, Bill. *Rope Roundup*. New York, 1960.

Vernam, Glen R. *Man on Horseback*. New York, 1964.

COWDERY, OLIVER

A cofounder of the CHURCH OF JESUS CHRIST OF LATTER-DAY SAINTS (Mormon Church), Oliver Cowdery (1806–1850) was born in Wells, Vermont, and moved to New York State in about 1825. In 1828, he began teaching school in Manchester, where he boarded with the family of Joseph Smith, Sr. There he became absorbed with the story of the "gold plates" from which JOSEPH SMITH, JR., was translating the BOOK OF MORMON. Mormons believe this book, translated under divine inspiration, contains the religious history of ancient inhabitants of the American continent who were visited by Jesus Christ.

Determined to find out more about this history, Cowdery went to Harmony, Pennsylvania, in April 1829, to meet young Joseph Smith, who had not proceeded very far with his work, partly because he did not have a permanent scribe to take dictation. Smith immediately put Cowdery to work. In less than two months, from April 7 to the end of June, he had recorded all the previously untranslated portions of the *Book of Mormon* as it was dictated by Smith.

Cowdery shared with Smith many of the profound spiritual experiences that provided the basis for the Mormon faith—personal visitations from ancient apostles and prophets as well as other visions and revelations through which various aspects of the ancient

Christian gospel were "restored." In June 1829, Cowdery was one of three special "witnesses" permitted actually to see and handle the gold plates. The testimony of the three witnesses is published in every edition of the *Book of Mormon*.

Cowdery's contributions to Mormonism were myriad. When the church was organized on April 6, 1830, he was named "second elder," making him second in importance only to Smith. A writer, church historian, and powerful preacher, Cowdery was also responsible for much of the church's publishing activities. Late in 1830, he led the first group of missionaries into Ohio and laid the foundation for Smith and most of his followers to move there. Cowdery's group, meanwhile, went to Jackson County, Missouri, which soon became another Mormon gathering place. Cowdery remained in Jackson County until the Mormons were expelled in 1833 and then returned to the church headquarters in Kirtland, Ohio. In 1836, in the newly completed Kirtland Temple, he and Smith received additional heavenly visions that became essential elements in the Mormon faith.

In 1837, Cowdery returned to Missouri, this time to the Mormon community of Far West in Caldwell County. Unfortunately, however, he found himself in serious disagreement with other church leaders over economic and religious practices. So serious was his dissent that he was excommunicated from the church in April 1838.

Deeply hurt, Cowdery returned to Ohio and took up the practice of law, first in Kirtland and then in Tiffin. Although his claim to have been a witness to the *Book of Mormon* made him the focus of ridicule and contributed to his defeat as a candidate for the state senate, he steadfastly refused to deny his testimony. He remained politically active, becoming a well-respected member of the community. While he joined the Methodist Protestant Church of Tiffin, he maintained ties with Mormon friends and tried to get his name cleared of the charges that had led to his excommunication.

In 1847, Cowdery moved to Elkhorn, Wisconsin, where he lost another election (though by a very narrow margin) because of published ridicule for his involvement with the *Book of Mormon*. Still, however, he refused to disavow his testimony.

Meanwhile, Smith was murdered in 1844, and the MORMONS were forced to leave Illinois, where they had gathered after being exiled from Missouri in the winter of 1838 to 1839. In 1847, they established a new gathering place in the Great Basin. Cowdery continued to make every effort to bring about a reconciliation. On October 21, 1847, he appeared before a conference of Mormons at Kanesville, Iowa, once more af-firmed his early spiritual experiences, and asked to be accepted back into the church. He was rebaptized on November 12, 1848, and planned to join the Mormons in the Great Basin. He died of a long-standing illness before he could begin his westward trek.

—*James B. Allen*

SUGGESTED READING:
Anderson, Richard Lloyd. *Investigating the Book of Mormon Witnesses*. Salt Lake City, 1979.
Gunn, Stanley R. *Oliver Cowdery: Second Elder and Scribe*. Salt Lake City, 1962.
Legg, Phillip R. *Oliver Cowdery: The Elusive Second Elder of Restoration*. Independence, Mo., 1989.

COWLITZ INDIANS

SEE: Native American Peoples: Peoples of the Pacific Northwest

COYOTES

Unique to North America and among the cleverest and most fabled animals of the American West, the coyote *(Canis laterans)* is now widely distributed through the United States. As its habitat was altered by settlement, and as it was forced to adapt to a new ecosystem, the coyote became the most destructive carnivore in America and the most consistently successful predator in the West. It may be found from the North Slope of Alaska to the jungles of Costa Rica and from the Pacific to the Atlantic oceans. Less territorial than its near relative the wolf and more flexible in the way it reacts to changes in its environment, the coyote continues to extend its range. It can be found not only on farm, ranch, and grasslands but also in the suburbs of cities. More than a century and a half of attempts to eliminate the animal by trapping, hunting, and poisoning have not been successful. From the spring of 1938 to the summer of 1945, 750,000 coyotes were taken by government hunters, but while their numbers have been reduced, their range has extended.

In spite of their fearsome reputations, coyotes are comparatively small predators. Although coyotes of more than seventy pounds have been taken, their average weight is between eighteen and thirty pounds. Their color is usually fulvous or light gray and red interspersed with black and white hairs. Their legs and feet are smaller than those of wolves and dogs of similar body size. While coyotes have a bark that sounds like that of a dog, it is their doleful howl that is recorded in the legends and literature of the West. Although litters of up to nineteen have been found, they normally give birth to five to seven pups. If they can avoid conflict with man, they may live on average from ten to eighteen years. Blessed with a strong sense of smell, sensitive hearing, and acute eyesight, they are very effective and opportunistic hunters and scavengers. In taking prey, coyotes often hunt in the evening, night, and early morning in pairs. They have diets that are quite varied: domestic and wild fruit, carrion, grasshoppers, beetles, other insects, rodents (such as prairie dogs, rabbits, ground squirrels, and gophers), lizards, toads, snakes, antelope, deer, elk, mountain sheep, beavers, turkeys, prairie chickens, meadowlarks, diverse songbirds, the eggs of almost any bird, domestic fowl, sheep, calves, and pigs. Reductions of their numbers always result in an increase in rodent populations. As settlement modified the ecosystems they had known for millennia and reduced and replaced their traditional native sources of food, coyotes began preying on less wary domestic animals that grazed on Western lands. There are no recorded incidents of coyotes in the wild attacking humans.

In the latter half of the nineteenth century as sheep began to be raised in greater numbers in the West and coyote predation increased, state bounties were placed on them. They were hunted, trapped, and poisoned. From 1860 to 1885, an extensive program of reducing coyote populations through the use of strychnine poisoning was practiced from the Missouri River to the Rocky Mountains and from Canada to Texas. From 1880 to 1890, Texas ranchers claimed that their annual loss of sheep and goats exceeded five hundred thousand dollars. Coyotes continued to be a problem for ranchers in the twentieth century. From 1940 to 1945, New Mexico's state game warden estimated that coyotes had killed 3,000 antelopes, 10,000 deer, 7,000 calves, and 60,000 sheep and lambs. In 1944, North Dakota calculated that coyotes had killed 5,800 calves, 12,500 sheep, 18,000 lambs, 92,000 turkeys, and 328,000 chickens for a value of over one million dollars. Private, state, and federal trappers met with only limited success in reducing coyote predation. Rabies often reduced populations of coyotes and wolves in the prehistoric period, and occasional rabies epidemics among them occurred in the nineteenth and twentieth centuries. There is always a concern that they will spread this disease to other wild and domestic animals.

With the decline in the use of the beaver pelt, coyote skins began to be taken. After 1860, wolfers, or "wolf poisoners," began to sell the hides for 75 cents to $1.50 a hide. In the twentieth century, the price fluctuated dramatically, ranging from $5 to $50 a pelt. While their long fur was used primarily for trim on collars, the coonskin jackets of the "roaring twenties" were usually made from coyote pelts. Hunting them for their furs has never seriously reduced their numbers, however.

The coyote remains the supreme opportunist, the master predator, and wily song dog of the West.

—*Phillip Drennon Thomas*

SUGGESTED READING:

Dobie, J. Frank. *The Voice of the Coyote*. Boston, 1949.

Leydet, François. *The Coyote: Defiant Songdog of the West*. Norman, Okla., 1977.

Van Wormer, Joe. *The World of the Coyote*. Philadelphia and New York, 1964.

Young, Stanley P., and Hartley H. T. Jackson. *The Clever Coyote*. Washington, D.C., 1951.

CRABTREE, LOTTA

A noted nineteenth-century entertainer, Lotta Crabtree (1847–1924) was born in New York City to English immigrant parents, John and Mary Ann (Livesey) Crabtree, and was christened Charlotte Mignon.

In 1852, Lotta and her mother joined John Crabtree in San Francisco and then settled in Grass Valley, where the internationally renowned entertainer LOLA MONTEZ encouraged the young girl's theatrical aspirations. In 1856, Lotta, accompanied by her mother, made her official debut in Petaluma, California. She also performed regularly at the rear of an auction house in San Francisco and presented a song and dance show at San Francisco's American Theatre.

By the early 1860s, "Miss Lotta, the San Francisco Favorite" starred in several benefits for local rifle brigades and fire companies. The banjo-strumming entertainer, who deftly improvised and mimed, sometimes in black-face, was cheered in California's melodeons and amusement parks, as well as in Tom Maguire's Opera House.

In April 1864, Crabtree and her ambitious mother sailed for New York and were soon joined by the rest of the family. After a disappointing critical reception in New York, she accepted alternative bookings in Chicago, where she performed successfully in "The Seven Daughters of Satan" through the end of the year. She enjoyed equal success in Boston and on the road in repertory presentations of "Uncle Tom's Cabin" and "Jenny Leatherlungs," a parody of the Swedish soprano Jenny Lind. In 1867, Crabtree enjoyed her greatest success in John Brougham's adaptation of Charles Dickens's *Old Curiosity Shop* and packed theaters in "The Pet of the Petticoats."

Noted for her high spirits, the petite red-head with the large brown eyes displayed at once an innocence and an eccentricity that delighted theater-goers. Throughout the 1870s and 1880s, Crabtree was the most highly paid actress in the United States. Her popularity in the music halls of the United States and Europe also grew from the fact that, instead of relying on local talent, she toured with her own company. She was particularly successful in commissioning plays by such notable playwrights as David Belasco and Edmund Falconer.

Crabtree never married but remained very close to her mother, who judiciously invested the actress's earnings in real estate, including theaters, a gold mine, a livery stable, and a cotton-brokerage firm.

In 1896, Crabtree gave San Francisco the landmark Lotta's Fountain on Market Street. She returned to the site on November 6, 1915, when throngs celebrated "Lotta Crabtree Day" at the Panama-Pacific International Exposition.

After having been injured in a fall on stage in May 1891, Crabtree divided her time between New York City and a country house in New Jersey. In 1909, she purchased the Hotel Brewster in Boston, where she resided until her death in 1924.

—*Gloria Ricci Lothrop*

SUGGESTED READING:

Bates, Helen Marie. *Lotta's Last Season*. Brattleboro, Vt., 1940.

Dempsey, David, and Raymond P. Baldwin. *The Triumphs and Trials of Lotta Crabtree*. New York, 1968.

Rourke, Constance. *Troupers of the Gold Coast, or The Rise of Lotta Crabtree*. New York, 1928.

CRADLEBAUGH, JOHN

Born in Circleville, Ohio, John Cradlebaugh (1819–1872) was educated at Kenyon College and Oxford University in Ohio. In 1858, he became United States associate justice for the district of Utah. He supervised the gathering of testimony in the MOUNTAIN MEADOWS MASSACRE, but because he was unable to provide military protection to witnesses, his success in prosecuting the guilty was limited. Cradlebaugh moved to the Nevada Territory and was elected U.S. congressman, serving from 1862 to 1863. He was an officer in the 114th Ohio Volunteer Infantry in the Civil War and was wounded at Vicksburg.

—*James A. Crutchfield*

SUGGESTED READING:

Brooks, Juanita. *The Mountain Meadows Massacre*. Norman, Okla., 1966.

CRAZY HORSE (SIOUX)

The Oglala Lakota war chief Crazy Horse (ca. 1840–1877) was born near Bear Butte, South Dakota. He defeated two of the army's best-known officers during the Great Sioux War of 1876. His father, also known as Crazy Horse, was a noted Oglala warrior and medicine man. His mother, Rattle Blanket Woman, was a Minneconjou Lakota.

By 1861, the young man had earned his adult name Crazy Horse. He was a skilled warrior and leader who earned the admiration of his own people and of his foes. During the Oglala leader RED CLOUD's war against white incursions on Lakota lands in Wyoming and Montana in the mid-1860s, Crazy Horse led warriors in the Fetterman fight at Fort Phil Kearny in 1866, the Hayfield fight in 1867, and the Wagon Box fight in 1867.

Crazy Horse earned a considerable following among nontreaty Lakotas, who increasingly looked to him as a chief. In 1868, Lakota Sioux gathered in northeastern Wyoming where, one witness recalled, the "old men or leaders" selected four young warriors, including Crazy Horse, as "head warriors [or 'shirt wearers'] of their people." The leaders told the four that they "represented in their commands and acts the entire power of the nation." Crazy Horse was a "shirt-wearer" until his participation in a violent controversy in 1870. A Lakota woman left her husband for Crazy Horse, and the husband shot Crazy Horse in the face with a pistol. His formal position as a "shirt-wearer" then ended.

By 1875, government officials and army officers acknowledged Crazy Horse as one of the conspicuous leaders of Lakota resistance. The issue before the Lakotas was the Black Hills of South Dakota and Lakota hunting grounds in the Yellowstone River basin, which were allocated to the Lakotas in an 1868 treaty. The government now desired the Black Hills because, in 1874, gold was discovered there. By 1875, Lakota leaders were furious about the increasing numbers of prospectors and miners in the Black Hills.

In December 1875, the government ordered the Lakotas and Cheyennes in the Yellowstone River and Powder River region to move to reservations in Nebraska or on the Missouri River within six weeks or face military action. The nontreaty Lakotas had no intention of moving their families and villages to the reservations during the harsh winter weather.

In March 1876, an army attack on a Northern Cheyenne village persuaded Crazy Horse and other Lakota and Northern Cheyenne chiefs to fight the army.

Crazy Horse and SITTING BULL, a Hunkpapa Lakota, emerged as two of the great leaders of the Lakota-Cheyenne alliance.

Crazy Horse was central to two of the most significant battles of the Sioux War of 1876. On June 17, he led approximately fifteen hundred warriors against Brigadier General GEORGE CROOK's thirteen-hundred-man military column. In the ensuing Battle of the Rosebud, Crazy Horse coordinated his warriors' attack and, in a strategic victory, stopped Crook's advance. Eight days later, Lieutenant Colonel GEORGE ARMSTRONG CUSTER and units of the Seventh Cavalry attacked the Lakotas and Northern Cheyennes in the Battle of Little Bighorn. Crazy Horse played an important role in the counterattack, which annihilated Custer and his immediate command.

The army continued to strike the Lakotas and Cheyennes in the Yellowstone River country during the winter of 1876 to 1877. Crazy Horse realized that further fighting was useless, and he and his followers surrendered at Camp Robinson in Nebraska on May 7, 1877.

Government officials and army officers were eager to meet the warrior who had so adroitly fought them. Because of the attention to Crazy Horse, jealous Oglala and Sicangu chiefs spread rumors about him. Inexperienced junior army officers believed the gossip and reported it to their superiors. By September 1877, the rumors induced army officers to arrest Crazy Horse. On September 5, during an attempt to incarcerate Crazy Horse at Camp Robinson, a soldier mortally bayoneted him, and he died a few hours later.

—*Joseph C. Porter*

SEE ALSO: Black Hills Gold Rush; Little Bighorn, Battle of; Sioux Wars

SUGGESTED READING:

Sandoz, Mari. *Crazy Horse: The Strange Man of the Oglalas.* New York, 1942.

Hardorff, Richard G. *The Oglala Lakota Crazy Horse: A Preliminary Genealogical Study and an Annotated Listing of Primary Sources.* Mattiuck, N.Y., and Bryan, Tex., 1985.

CRÉDIT MOBILIER OF AMERICA

Long before transcontinental-railroad fever gripped the United States in the middle of the nineteenth century, experience had taught veteran railroad organizers and Eastern financiers that they could make more money from construction contracts than from running a com-

pleted railroad. When Congress authorized the construction of the UNION PACIFIC RAILROAD during the Civil War, it placed in the railroad's charter financial restrictions that required the Union Pacific to sell its stock for cash at its par value per share. Wealthy investors, fully aware of the operating boondoggle many Eastern lines had been, doubted first that a continental line could actually be built and second that, if completed, such a line would ever turn a quick enough profit since it would span a vast region, unpopulated except by Indians, between Omaha and the Great Salt Lake, a territory whose immediate revenue potential seemed quite unpromising. Under these circumstances, Congress's restrictions proved impossible because nobody would buy the stock at par. But then THOMAS CLARK DURANT and other major shareholders in the Union Pacific, urged on by OAKES AMES, a U.S. congressman charged by President Abraham Lincoln to get the railroad moving, came up with a way they could make money by forming their own railroad construction company and, in effect, paying themselves to build the transcontinental line.

Called the Crédit Mobilier of America, the company was establish in 1864. As stockholders in the Union Pacific, Durant, Ames, and others used their influence to award lucrative construction contracts to Crédit Mobilier through dummy third parties. Crédit Mobilier inflated construction costs, sometimes by as much as twice the actual rate, and its bills were paid by checks from the Union Pacific that Crédit Mobilier in turn used as "cash" to buy the railroad's stocks and bonds at par. Having fulfilled the congressional requirement, Crédit Mobilier could resell these stocks and bonds to anyone at any price it wanted, which it did at figures below par but high enough to cover the actual construction costs it had already inflated. Crédit Mobilier owners, who also happened to be Union Pacific stockholders, simply pocketed the excess of what they charged the Union Pacific over what they brought in from the resale of stocks to cover construction costs. It was a complicated enough scheme, but in the long run, it ensured Crédit Mobilier a profit even if the Union Pacific operated at a loss, some $13 to $16 million in fact on an initial investment of around $4 million. To make sure that Congress continued to support their operation—some of the profits came from government loans—the promoters created a slush fund to bribe members of Congress and President Ulysses S. Grant's administration or made them stockholders in Crédit Mobilier.

Crédit Mobilier never made any truly serious attempt to hide what it was doing. For one thing, Crédit Mobilier's method of doing business was more or less typical of nineteenth-century railroad building, especially in the wide-open economic atmosphere out West; for another, many of the country's "best" people, and certainly a number of its most powerful, were involved in the company's financial machinations, which made its owners feel scandal-proof. Then came the 1872 presidential election, on the eve of which the New York *Sun* broke the "story" on Crédit Mobilier. Speaker of the House James G. Blaine, a Republican from Maine implicated by the *Sun,* hoped to put the scandal behind him and called for congressional hearings to investigate Crédit Mobilier. It was a major miscalculation, since the investigation kicked off an even wider scandal that remained an issue for four presidential elections and damaged the careers of several Gilded Age politicians, Blaine's among them. By the time it was over, Congress had censured two of its members, Oakes Ames of Massachusetts and another Union Pacific shareholder, James Brooks of New York. In its first year, the affair also tarnished the reputations of outgoing Vice-president Schuyler Colfax, incoming Vice-president Henry Wilson, and Representative James Garfield. Garfield steadfastly denied any involvement, and eventually he was elected president. Garfield fared much better than Blaine, whose entire career became blighted by the whiff of corruption, which most likely kept him from becoming president as well.

The Crédit Mobilier scandal passed into history as a leading example of Gilded Age corruption, an age of freewheeling finance sometimes called the "Great Barbecue," when robber barons went to any lengths to ensure immense profits and railroad corporations and their financiers wielded powerful influence over the national government, if they did not control it outright. Although many historians continue to subscribe to that view, others have pointed out that the Union Pacific had little choice but to do what it did, short of asking Congress for a new charter it was unlikely to grant. Some historians point out that other railroads, especially the SOUTHERN PACIFIC RAILROAD, used the same tactics to build transcontinental lines from the West without suffering the same consequences. Although this might be a result of the fire that "accidentally" destroyed all the Southern Pacific's financial records, it is a fact the Crédit Mobilier's methods were copied by railroads, large and small, across the West. Still, those methods only managed to corrupt state houses and city halls as well as the federal government. In the long run, a generation of Western taxpayers, who had mortgaged their futures to the coming of the railroad, were stuck with the bills for a shoddily constructed and ill-financed transportation network that virtually collapsed before being reorganized by a few large financial houses in the East late in the nineteenth century.

—*Charles Phillips*

SEE ALSO: Banking; Booms; Financial Panics

SUGGESTED READING:
Fogel, Robert W. *The Union Pacific Railroad: A Case in Premature Enterprise.* Baltimore, 1960.
Johnson, Arthur M., and Barry E. Supple. *Boston Capitalists and Western Railroads.* Cambridge, Mass., 1967.
Reigal, Robert. *The Story of the Western Railroads.* New York, 1926.

CREE INDIANS

SEE: Native American Peoples: Peoples of the Great Plains

CREEK INDIANS

SEE: Native American Peoples: Peoples Removed from the East

CRIMINAL SYNDICALISM LAWS

SEE: Industrial Workers of the World; Labor Movement

CRIPPLE CREEK, COLORADO

Cripple Creek, Colorado, the largest town in the Cripple Creek gold-mining district, is located west of Pikes Peak, some eighteen miles southwest of Colorado Springs. The Cripple Creek District, in fact, held eight towns and a number of unincorporated settlements and, as a whole, is significant in Western mining and labor history.

In October 1890, a local ranch hand, Robert Womack, discovered gold in Poverty Gulch near the site that later became the town of Cripple Creek. The district's odd volcanic formations did not provide common signs of hidden gold. There was no primary ore deposit, or "mother lode," common to other mining regions. In the Tertiary Period, a series of volcanic eruptions broke through the rock crust and created a cone and several minor craters. These land forms eroded to form rounded hills broken by a network of especially narrow fissures, into which salt solutions later carried minerals. Prospectors expected to find pure metals and then to follow them to the veins from which they had eroded. But there were few outcroppings of Cripple Creek's dull gray ores and virtually no free gold.

There was, consequently, no significant placer mining. Cripple Creek's mines were always deep shaft, industrial enterprises worked by wage laborers. Its wealth went to those who had the money or family contacts to invest in mines, railroads, and smelters. The area rapidly developed into an industrial mining center, financed by outside capital, much of it organized and funneled through nearby Colorado Springs.

Deservedly known as the "world's greatest gold camp," Cripple Creek mines produced more than $65 million in gold within a decade, thus saving Colorado's crashing economy when the Sherman Silver Purchase Act was repealed in 1893. Capital and labor flocked to the gold camp as silver mines closed throughout the Rockies. Cripple Creek's riches stabilized the gold-based national monetary system. The ore came from an area of only thirty-six square miles, with a central mineral belt of only six square miles. No other gold region has produced so much so rapidly from such a small area.

Like most industrial hard-rock mining centers, Cripple Creek developed quickly into an urban center. The first settlers lived in a motley collection of tents and cabins named Fremont, which soon combined with a second mill settlement, Hayden Placer, to become the town of Cripple Creek. Within a decade, the area held the towns of Cripple Creek, Victor, Anaconda, Cameron, Goldfield, Independence, Altman, and Gillet. Three railroads connected the towns and mines and carried the ore to refining facilities in Florence and Colorado City. In 1899, Teller County was created from portions of El Paso and Fremont counties, with the town of Cripple Creek as the county seat.

The district's population is a matter of some dispute. The 1900 U.S. Census enumerated 29,002 residents for the entire county, while district boosters claimed a population of some 50,000. The most reliable population estimates suggest that the district's peak population was approximately 32,000 in 1900. As in most Western hard-rock mining towns, the population was overwhelmingly working-class (about 80 percent in 1900). The relatively stable mining economy attracted family settlement, so that sex rations were less skewed than in more short-lived camps. The adult population was approximately 60 percent male in 1900, and 83 percent native-born. Most immigrants were Canadians or northern or western Europeans—Irish, English, Swedes, Germans, and Scots. Nevertheless, more than half of all adults were first- or second-generation immigrants. The proportion of foreign-born residents dropped in subsequent censuses, but the ethnic composition of the area remained similar, with no significant settlement by southern or eastern European, Finn, Hispano, or Asian immigrants.

The various towns were characterized by their places in the mining economy. The smaller settlements near the mines—Anaconda, Elkton, Altman, Independence, Lawrence, Cameron, and Goldfield—became residential centers for miners and their families. Overwhelmingly working class, they held single-family dwellings and rooming and boarding houses for single miners. The few churches and schools, the union halls, and bars served as local social centers. Victor, the "city of Mines," was the second largest town. Located in the heart of the mineral belt at the southern edge of the district, it held more schools, churches and union halls, more lodge halls and fraternal societies, more saloons and gambling houses, the Opera House (which offered everything from Shakespeare to vaudeville), and a sizable red-light district. Cripple Creek itself was the business and supply center and home to merchants and professionals. Victor and Cripple Creek had large business districts, and Cripple Creek's theaters, saloons, and vice district catered to the wealthy as well as to the majority working population.

The social stratification of the towns was magnified in the regional mining economy. Considerable capital was required to sink shafts, pay wages, construct railroads, and build milling and refining facilities. From 1890 to 1904, competing ownership coalitions raced to integrate their mines with transportation and reduction facilities. Many prominent owners lived in nearby Colorado Springs and Denver, where profits from Cripple Creek mines financed lavish homes and civic improvements.

Divisions among competing ownership groups were significant factors in two miners' strikes in 1893-1894 and 1903-1904 and during the intervening decade of union influence. After the strikes control of local labor relations shifted to antiunion owners, who blacklisted union members from working in the district's mines. Although the District continued to be a significant gold producer through the 1930s, the population steadily dropped. The census counted 13,117 people in the district in 1910; 5,682 in 1920; and 3,447 in 1930. The government closed the gold mines during World War II. Although some mining resumed after the war, the district's historical significance lies primarily in the extraordinary productivity and the labor relations of its first decades.

—*Elizabeth Jameson*

SUGGESTED READING:

Jameson, Elizabeth. *All That Glitters: Class, Culture, and Community in Cripple Creek, Colorado*. Urbana-Champaign, forthcoming.

Spell, Leslie Doyle, and Hazel M. Spell. *Forgotten Men of Cripple Creek*. Denver, 1959.

Sprague, Marshal. *Money Mountain: The Story of Cripple Creek Gold*. 1953. Reprint. Lincoln, Nebr., 1979.

Taylor, Robert Guilford. *Cripple Creek*. Bloomington, Ind., 1966

CRIPPLE CREEK STRIKES

From 1894 to 1904, the Cripple Creek, Colorado, Mining District was a stronghold of the Western Federation of Miners (WFM), known for its ties to the Socialist party and for its leadership in founding the Western Labor Union (WLU), American Labor Union (ALU), and the INDUSTRIAL WORKERS OF THE WORLD (IWW). The first strike, in 1893 and 1894, established for the district's mining laborers the right to belong to a union (but not a closed shop), an eight-hour workday, a three dollar minimum daily wage, and an organization base from which to extend these gains to other workers. The strike was called to resist some owners' attempts to lengthen the workday and cut wages. The fledgling Western Federation of Miners won its first major victory in Cripple Creek, in part because other owners accepted union wages and hours and operated with union labor throughout the strike, and in part because of atypical state support. Populist Governor Davis Waite sent the militia to Cripple Creek to preserve the peace, rather than to break the strike, and then helped negotiate the agreement that anchored union power until the major Cripple Creek strike of 1903 to 1904.

From 1894 to 1904, the district was a labor stronghold. Centered around nine WFM locals, some fifty-four local unions organized a majority of all workers by 1902, including everyone from waitresses and laundry workers to bartenders and newsboys in a working-class community. The unions were central social institutions in the social, economic and political life of the towns. They published a daily newspaper, the Victor and Cripple Creek *Daily Press* from 1899 to 1903, provided sick and death benefits, organized major holidays and recreation, and asserted considerable local political influence.

Relationships between labor and capital in the district affected Western labor as a whole. The unions exerted significant leadership within the WFM, the Colorado State Federation of Labor, the WLU, and the ALU. The disastrous second strike, one of many WFM strike losses in Colorado in 1903 and 1904, was one impetus to found the IWW, to achieve a stronger federation of industrial unions for future emergencies.

The 1903 to 1904 strike, called to withhold ore from Colorado City mills that fired and blacklisted WFM smelter workers, was part of a larger strike wave throughout the Colorado mining industry. Little linked the strikers, which had disparate causes, except for the willingness of Governor James Hamilton Peabody to deploy the militia to strike areas. Cripple Creek was under periodic martial law. The occupying troops were commanded by Adjutant General Sherman Bell, who was, in civilian life, the superintendent of major district mining properties.

As in the first strike, owners were divided. Mines that shipped to union smelters remained open. The WFM appeared to be winning until June 6, 1904, when an explosion ripped through the platform of the Independence Depot of the Florence and Cripple Creek Railroad. Thirteen nonunion miners were killed. The National Guard was reactivated, the Citizens' Alliance and Mine Owners Association "deposed" public officeholders, seized control of the local governments, and mobs wrecked the union halls, libraries, and cooperative stores. The military deported union leaders and civilian mobs "whitecapped" others. Troops occupied the Portland Mine, which had worked with a union work force through the strike, and forced it to reopen as a nonunion property.

Although each side accused the other of setting the explosion, the employers largely controlled both the outcome of the strike and its interpretation. The Independence Depot explosion achieved further significance following the 1905 murder of former Idaho Governor Frank Steunenberg. Harry Orchard confessed to the murder and accused an "inner circle" of the WFM of instigating the deed and other acts of violence, including the Independence Depot explosion. Orchard's allegations resulted in the kidnapping of WFM leaders Charles Moyer and William D. ("Big Bill") Haywood and former leader George Pettibone to stand trail in Idaho for the Steunenberg murder. Although Haywood, the first defendant, was acquitted, and charges against Moyer and Pettibone were dropped, Orchard's allegation that the "inner circle" hired him to bomb the depot was widely accepted. The facts of the case may never by proved, but there is some evidence to suggest that Orchard was hired by mine owners or their agents.

Many mines never reopened, and control was increasingly consolidated in a single company, the Golden Cycle Corporation. The deportations and blacklist ended the union era in the Cripple Creek District and destroyed the institutional base for working-class influence.

—*Elizabeth Jameson*

SUGGESTED READING:

Haywood, William D. *Bill Haywood's Book: The Autobiography of Big Bill Haywood.* 1929. Reprint. New York, 1974.

Jameson, Elizabeth. *All That Glitters: Class, Culture, and Community in Cripple Creek, Colorado.* Urbana-Champaign, forthcoming.

Langdon, Emma F. *Cripple Creek Strike: A History of Industrial Wars in Colorado. 1904-1905.* Reprint. New York, 1969.

Spell, Leslie Doyle, and Hazel M. Spell. *Forgotten Men of Cripple Creek.* Denver, 1959.

Sprague, Marshal. *Money Matters: The Story of Cripple Creek Gold.* 1953. Reprint. Lincoln, Nebr., 1979.

Suggs, George G., Jr. *Colorado's War on Militant Unionism: James H. Peabody and the Western Federation of Miners.* Detroit, 1972.

CROCKER, CHARLES

One of California's "Big Four" railroad tycoons, Charles Crocker (1822–1888) was born in Troy, New York, but moved as a boy with his family to a farm near Marshall, Iowa. During the CALIFORNIA GOLD RUSH, Crocker led a party including two of his younger brothers overland to the gold fields near Sacramento. There, after failing to strike it rich overnight, he set up as a retail merchant and later moved his operations to San Francisco where he became, in the course of a few years, one of the town's wealthier men. In partnership with COLLIS P. HUNTINGTON, AMASA LELAND STANFORD, and MARK HOPKINS, the hard-driving Crocker ran the construction for the CENTRAL PACIFIC RAILROAD. Using methods similar to those pioneered by the scandal-ridden CRÉDIT MOBILIER OF AMERICA, the Big Four enriched themselves by paying their stockholders' money to companies they owned for railroad construction at wildly inflated prices. It was Crocker who came up with the notion of hiring cheap Chinese labor to work on the railroad, and he drove the workers with a single-minded determination that set records unbroken for years afterward. Once the transcontinental line was completed, the Big Four turned their attention to the SOUTHERN PACIFIC RAILROAD. Crocker again oversaw the railroad's construction and helped create the monopoly on local transportation that allowed him and his cronies to run CALIFORNIA politics from behind the scenes for decades. Crocker turned to real estate, banking, and huge irrigation projects. Building mansions, buying ranches, moving to New York for a while, Crocker seemed never able to quench the thirsts created by his tremendous energies. After Crocker was badly injured during a carriage accident in New York, he returned to San Francisco. An overweight and stubborn diabetic, Crocker steadfastly refused to follow the diet his doctors had prescribed until he died.

—*Patricia Hogan*

SEE ALSO: Chinese Americans; Railroads

CROCKETT, DAVID (DAVEY)

Frontiersman, Congressman from Tennessee, defender of the ALAMO, and folk hero, David (Davey) Crockett (1786–1836) was born near present-day Rogersville in East Tennessee. He was raised in the backwoods of the Appalachian Mountains and received a limited education. As a young man, he joined the Tennessee militia and fought with ANDREW JACKSON against the Creek Indians in Alabama from 1813 to 1814. After military service, he lived in Jefferson, Lincoln, Franklin, Lawrence, Carroll, and Gibson counties in Tennessee. After serving as a justice of the peace, he was elected to the Tennessee legislature in 1821 and served for two terms. In 1826, he was elected to the U.S. House of Representatives as a Democrat.

Although he was an early supporter of the Jacksonian Democratic party, he later broke ties with Andrew Jackson. Crockett demonstrated a rare comprehension of and appreciation for governmental affairs and cared little for party views on issues. He voted instead on his own convictions. Unable to overcome President Jackson's immense political power, Crockett failed to win reelection in 1830, but two years later, he was returned to Congress on the Whig ticket.

Giving up politics after his defeat in 1835, Crockett moved to Texas. When he arrived at the Alamo, he was offered, but declined, command of the old mission. Although tradition holds that Crockett was killed within the walls of the Alamo, modern research has revealed that he may have been captured by the Mexican army and executed with several other defenders.

Even during his lifetime, Crockett established himself as a folk hero. Magazines and books of the period carried outlandish tales of his battles with wild beasts and human enemies. His death at the Alamo enlarged his bigger-than-life image. During the 1950s, several fanciful Hollywood movies about his exploits were released and starred Fess Parker. Coonskin caps, toy rifles, lunch boxes, and songs abounded during the revival and brought Crockett and his times once again to the forefront of the American imagination.

—*James A. Crutchfield*

Suggested reading:

Harper, Herbert L., ed. *Houston and Crockett: Heroes of Tennessee and Texas, An Anthology.* Nashville, Tenn., 1986.

Shackford, James A., ed. *David Crockett: The Man and the Myth.* Chapel Hill, N.C., 1956.

CROOK, GEORGE

An army officer whose career spanned from his graduation from the Military Academy at West Point in 1852 to his death, General George Crook (1828–1890) made

George Crook. *Courtesy Arizona Historical Society.*

his most noteworthy mark during the Indian wars in the West. Born in Taylorsville, Ohio, Crook graduated with a mediocre academic record but an excellent history of personal conduct. His lack of demerits may have been due to his quiet, even taciturn, personality. Yet he made some friends while at West Point, including classmate Philip H. Sheridan.

After graduation, Crook was stationed in the Pacific Northwest where he soon became involved in conflicts with the Rogue River and Pit River Indians. By 1856, Oregon Volunteers and Army Regulars exiled the Indians to reservations. It was in the Northwest that Crook first confronted the difficulties, including the moral dilemmas, posed by Indian warfare. He understood that American aggression and expansion played a key role in provoking Indian wars. At the same time, he believed peace could be achieved only through force. He also expected Indians would have to embrace Euro-American culture. Crook's reputation as an unusually humane officer stands up only if one assumes most army officers shared an antipathy toward Indians and an inclination to exterminate them. In fact, Indian-fighting officers proved more complicated than that. Crook's attitude toward Indian people and his ambivalence about their conquest was actually fairly typical.

After the Civil War, Crook returned to the Northwest where he inaugurated several tactics that characterized his efforts in the Indian wars: the use of Indian scouts (including speedy enlistment for those who had recently surrendered) and the use of pack mules. The latter tactic allowed his troops to move beyond their supply base. The use of Indian scouts allowed him to take advantage of Indian familiarity with terrain and to demoralize Indians still fighting the army. In addition, Crook was known for his reluctance to disclose his plans during campaigns, a characteristic that frustrated officers under his command. These novel tactics brought Crook great success in 1872 during the Tonto Basin campaign, which resulted in the confinement of more than six thousand Apaches and Yavapais on reservations. However, his approach brought only mixed results during the Sioux War of 1876. The Sioux turned his troops back at the Battle of the Rosebud in June of that year. Yet in November, Crook's soldiers destroyed a Cheyenne village in the Bighorn Mountains, which probably hastened some Indian surrenders.

Crook was not the only officer to hire Indian scouts, but his experiences with them garnered much publicity. In 1886, Sheridan concluded Indians were not trustworthy in that role. Meanwhile, during the Geronimo campaign, Crook secured the Apache leader's surrender with the aid of Indian scouts. Sheridan urged President Grover Cleveland to refuse anything short of un-

In 1886, General George Crook (seated, second from right) met with Geronimo (seated, fifth from left with a scarf on his head) to convince him to surrender. *Courtesy Library of Congress.*

conditional surrender, and when Geronimo, having second thoughts, slipped away, a disgusted and frustrated Crook resigned his command. Sheridan replaced him with rival NELSON APPLETON MILES. When Geronimo finally surrendered, all the Chiricahuas—including the loyal scouts—were shipped to Florida. His friendship with Sheridan forever severed, Crook complained about this outrageous treatment and, for his remaining years, lobbied unsuccessfully for the scouts' return to Arizona.

—*Sherry L. Smith*

SEE ALSO: Apache Wars; Sioux Wars; United States Army: Scouts

SUGGESTED READING:
Bourke, John G. *On the Border with Crook.* New York, 1891.
Crook, George. *General George Crook: His Autobiography.* Edited by Martin F. Schmitt. Norman, Okla., 1960.
Greene, Jerome A. "George Crook." In *Soldiers West: Biographies from the Military Frontier.* Edited by Paul Andrew Hutton. Lincoln, Nebr., 1987.

CROSS-DRESSING

SEE: Passing Women

"CROSS OF GOLD" SPEECH

WILLIAM JENNINGS BRYAN's "Cross of Gold" speech concluded a debate on silver coinage at the 1896 Democratic national convention, held in Chicago. Defending increased silver coinage, Bryan identified himself with the West. He presented one metaphor still central to his party's economic thinking when he claimed that his opponents wanted to increase the wealth of the well-to-do so that their prosperity might "leak through on those below," but that his party preferred to make "the masses" prosperous so their prosperity could "find its way up" to those better off. Bryan's dramatic conclusion gave the speech its name: "We will answer their demand for a gold standard by saying to them: You shall not press down upon the brow of labor this crown of thorns. You shall not crucify mankind upon a cross of gold."

Bryan's message—and his compelling and powerful voice—electrified the convention and prompted a frenzied demonstration that catapulted him from convention delegate to contender for the nomination. He won it on the fifth ballot but lost the election to Republican William McKinley.

In 1955, a poll of 277 professors of American history or government ranked the "Cross of Gold" speech among the fifty most significant documents in American history. It is still the standard example of capturing a convention through oratory.

—*Robert W. Cherny*

SEE ALSO: Currency and Silver as Western Political Issues

SUGGESTED READING:
Bryan, William Jennings. *The First Battle: A Story of the Campaign of 1896.* Chicago, 1896.
Cherny, Robert W. *A Righteous Cause: The Life of William Jennings Bryan.* Boston, 1985.

CROW DOG (SIOUX)

Crow Dog (Kangi Sunka, ca. 1835–1912), a Brulé Sioux, became the central figure in a controversy about Indian rights when he killed the prominent Brulé peace proponent SPOTTED TAIL in 1881 on the Rosebud Sioux Reservation. Crow Dog shot Spotted Tail in an argument over either a woman or tribal leadership, perhaps over both. Arrested by the Indian police and tried in the first district court in Deadwood, Crow Dog was sentenced to be hanged. On appeal, the U.S. Supreme Court in 1883 overturned his conviction, ruling in *Ex Parte Crow Dog* that federal courts had no jurisdiction over crimes committed on reservation lands. Crow Dog went free, but Congress then passed the Major Crimes Act of 1885, which made any Indian who committed a major crime against another Indian subject to the laws of the territory or state where the crime occurred.

In November 1890, Crow Dog led his band off the reservation into the South Dakota Badlands during the GHOST DANCE uprising. When the U.S. Army sent a party to negotiate with the Sioux, ensconced in an area they called the Stronghold, Crow Dog and other Brulé leaders agreed to return to Pine Ridge. Crow Dog died on the Rosebud Sioux Reservation in 1912.

—*Joseph C. Porter and Charles Phillips*

SUGGESTED READING:
Crow Dog, Leonard, and Richard Erdoes. *Crow Dog: Four Generations of Sioux Medicine Men.* New York, 1995.

CULT OF TRUE WOMANHOOD

In the late eighteenth and early nineteenth centuries, growing industrialization and the gradual shift toward urban life in the United States both shaped and reflected significant changes in gender roles for middle-class families. With husbands increasingly absent from the home during the day, wives took on unprecedented responsibility for—and indentification with—the domestic arena. Confusing culture with nature, American opinion-makers proclaimed that women were not the lustful and carnal gender they had once been assumed to be, but frail, retiring, creatures, far less passionate and more moral than men. Women's proper sphere was the home and the church, and their proper function was the moral instruction of their children and, by extension, the nation itself. Recent historians have come to call this infusion of household duties with high moral purpose the "ideology of domesticity," which by the mid-nineteenth century had given rise to the "cult of true womanhood." The narrowest version of the cult, offered in the ladies' magazines and moral advice books popular in Victorian America, held that women—whose cardinal virtues were piety, purity, domesticity, and submissiveness to male authority—were to shape national morality from the privacy of their hearths and leave public action to men. In a broader version, visible in reforms movements from abolition to TEMPERANCE AND PROHIBITION to the "good government" movement known as PROGRESSIVISM, women reached well beyond their own homes to make public life reflect domestic virtue.

Some Western historians have used the Victorian cult of true womanhood as reflected in the period's magazines, books, newspapers, and some private letters and diaries written by middle- and upper-class Western women to explain the role women played in the history of the trans-Mississippi West. According to this view, as middle-class women arrived in the West in greater numbers in the late nineteenth century, they determined to apply a healthy dose of domesticity to turn the wide-open Western camps and towns into respectable and sober communities with schools, cultural amenities, churches, and clubs.

Seen in this way, the cult of true womanhood might help explain such occurrences as the presence of a strong suffrage movement in the West (where a number of territories and states early on granted women the right to vote), the early and relatively strong prohibition laws in the West, and the alacrity with which the West took to Progressive reform. Seen from a more critical viewpoint equally indebted to the cult of true womanhood, middle-class Western women were reluctant pioneers who disliked leaving their family and social life behind in the East. Though they had plucked up bravely to serve as helpmates to their husbands, they ended up serving as exploited housewives whose loneliness and domestic isolation contrasted to the new opportunities their mates enjoyed in the West.

Other historians, Elizabeth Jameson among them, have cautioned that an overreliance on the Victorian cult of true womanhood to explain women in the West produces polarized images of genteel civilizers, helpmates, and oppressed drudges that continue to underscore passive roles and that, in any case, do not fit well with the way most Western women truly lived their lives. While some of the ideals expressed by some Western women match the cult of true womanhood as it was transfigured in the pages of *Godey's Lady's Book,* the roles the cult prescribed could be attained only by a few leisure-class women, who no longer performed productive labor and who were valued precisely because of their economic uselessness. The ideal of the Victorian true woman, says Jameson, was far from the reality not only for the traditional "bad" women of the West, prostitutes and dance-hall girls, but also for homesteaders, WORKING-CLASS WOMEN in mining camps and towns, Hispanic, Asian, and Native American domestics, or, for that matter, most urban mothers scratching to help their families make ends meet.

—*Charles Phillips and Patricia Hogan*

SEE ALSO: Divorce; Domestic Service; Homesteading

SUGGESTED READING:
Baker, Paula. "The Domesticization of Politics: Women and American Political Society, 1780-1920." *American Historical Review* 89 (June 1984): 620-647.
Jameson, Elizabeth. "Women as Workers, Women as Civilizers: True Womanhood in the American West." *The Women's West.* Edited by Susan Armitage and Elizabeth Jameson. Norman, Okla., 1987.
Jeffrey, Julie Roy. *Frontier Women: The Trans-Mississippi West, 1840-1880.* New York, 1979.
Welter, Barbara. "The Cult of True Womanhood: 1820–1860." *American Quarterly* 18: (Summer 1966): 151–174.

CULVER, HENRY

Southern California real-estate developer in the years of Los Angeles's phenomenal growth, Henry Culver (1880–1946) provided thousands of middle-class families with their first homes. Born in Nebraska, Culver spent his early career in a series of dissatisfying civil-service and sales positions. Heading to the LOS ANGELES area in 1910 at the age of thirty, he spent three years learning the real-estate business before founding his own Culver Investment Company through which he developed Culver City, a community of homes located between the cities of Los Angeles and Venice.

Culver mastered every step of land development. With only five thousand dollars of his own money, he secured capital for his city from Los Angeles land owners, bankers, and corporations. With a staff of 150 salesmen, he pitched home ownership to the legions of families pouring into the Los Angeles area in the 1920s. Ever sensitive that most of his customers were new to the area and first-time buyers, he pitched a new life, not just a new home. And he offered them easy terms: five hundred dollars down, eighty dollars a month at 7 percent interest, furnishings included.

Culver's success, however, lay in his promotions. His baby contests, raffles, road races, and booster parades attracted customers. Culver's sales soared when he convinced film producer Thomas H. Ince to locate his movie studios in Culver City in 1915, which became the Metro-Goldwyn-Mayer (MGM) studios of the 1920s.

Culver's fortunes grew along with his city throughout the 1920s; he sat on the boards of corporations and cultural organizations, maintained a private plane and pilot, spent his summers in Europe, enjoyed memberships in Los Angeles's best country clubs, and built a magnificent home for himself in 1928 on a four-acre lot near the California Country Club.

Culver City continued to prosper as well. RKO movie studios followed MGM to the community; the television studios of Desilu Productions moved there in the 1950s; and petroleum, aircraft, and electronics industries fueled the economy throughout the twentieth century.

—*Patricia Hogan*

SUGGESTED READING:
Starr, Kevin. *Material Dreams: Southern California through the 1920s.* New York, 1990.

CUNNINGHAM, TOM

Law officer in nineteenth-century northern California, Tom Cunningham (1838–1900) immigrated to Brooklyn, New York, from his native Ireland at the age of ten and worked as an apprentice to a harness-maker. Having acquired a skill and an education, Cunningham headed west six years later and settled in Stockton, California. At first he worked for a series of harness-makers, but by 1860, he had opened his own shop.

Shortly after settling in northern California, Cunningham stepped into public life. At first a Stockton volunteer fireman, he became the department's chief in 1865 and, at the same time, served as a city councilman. In 1871, he was elected to the position of sheriff, an office he held for twenty-seven years. Soft-spoken and mild-mannered, Cunningham seemed out of place in a tough-guy profession, but he was good at his job. He became known as the "Thief Taker of San Joaquin" and involved himself in manhunts of some of the most notorious outlaws of northern California: TIBURCIO VÁSQUEZ, BLACK BART, Bill Miner, and Sam Browning.

Cunningham was an early proponent of scientific criminology and detection. He developed systematic methods for the meticulous study of the habits, methods, and motives of outlaws and assembled, what was at the time, one of the United States's largest collections of photographs of known criminals. While sheriff, Cunningham also designed the San Joaquin County Jail, a model facility for its time, and organized a museum of crime, containing more than one thousand artifacts and curios. He died a year after retiring.

—*Patricia Hogan*

SEE ALSO: Law and Order

CURRENCY AND SILVER AS WESTERN POLITICAL ISSUES

During the last three decades of the nineteenth century, Western politics often focused on federal currency policy (*currency* refers to money actually in circulation). During those years, most prices went down (a situation called *deflation*) due partly to increased production and greater efficiency in agriculture and manufacturing and partly to federal monetary and tariff policies.

Deflation most damages individuals in debt. After the Civil War, much of the expansion of Western agriculture was accomplished on borrowed money. In the 1870s and 1880s, prices for corn, wheat, and other farm products fell sharply, but farmers' mortgage obligations remained the same. As a result, farmers had to produce more every year just to pay their debts and buy necessities.

The GREENBACK PARTY linked falling prices to the decline in the money supply per capita. Arguing that prices could be stabilized by issuing more currency, they urged the government to print more "greenbacks"—the paper money issued during the Civil War—which, unlike other currency, could not be exchanged for gold. The Greenbackers' call for inflation (that is, issuing more currency in order to raise prices) appealed most to debt-ridden farmers, especially in the Midwest and West. In the 1878 congressional elections, the Greenback party received nearly one million votes, and fourteen of its candidates for Congress were elected. In the 1880 presidential election, the Greenback party endorsed not only inflation but also many other reforms. Their presidential nominee, James B. Weaver, a Greenback congressman from Iowa, received only 3.3 percent of the popular vote.

Many Americans were suspicious of "fiat money"—paper money issued by the government without the backing of a precious metal. In the past, paper money had sometimes been issued in such large amounts that it became virtually worthless. That had happened, most recently, during the closing months of the Confederacy. Some inflationists, therefore, looked to silver as a better way of increasing the money supply. Before 1873, currency laws required the federal mint to accept both gold and silver bullion in unlimited quantities and to make it into coins. Thus, the FEDERAL GOVERNMENT did not buy gold and silver, but instead coined it at virtually no charge. Throughout the early nineteenth century, laws specified that a silver dollar had to weigh fifteen to sixteen times as much as a gold dollar. Hence, the nation practiced free and unlimited coinage of gold and silver at a ratio of about sixteen to one.

The official ratio undervalued silver compared to its price in commercial markets, so rather than taking silver to the mint, owners of silver bullion sold it. By the Civil War, silver dollars had disappeared. In 1873, during a recodification of coinage laws, Congress omitted the silver dollar from the list of approved coins. In part, the omission recognized the reality that no silver dollars had circulated for years; however, it also reflected the priorities of treasury officials who wanted the United States to be on the gold standard. Leading European nations had adopted the gold standard, and some economists and bankers argued that the United States had to do the same to compete effectively for capital and goods in international markets. Later condemned by inflationists as "the Crime of '73," this action soon became the center of conspiracy theories alleging that Congress had been duped by British banking interests.

At about the same time, discoveries of extensive silver deposits in the West caused silver prices to fall.

Inflationists now argued that remonetizing silver would draw large amounts of silver to the mint, inflate the currency, and stabilize prices. In silver-mining areas, silver coinage was popular because the metal would become more valuable if coined at the old ratio of sixteen to one. At the height of the Greenbackers' popularity, Congress passed the BLAND-ALLISON ACT OF 1878, which authorized coinage of a limited number of silver dollars. A compromise measure, it satisfied neither the proponents of the gold standard nor the inflationists, and the silver coined after 1878 did little to counteract deflation.

Battles over the currency intensified in the 1890s. In Congress, Western Republicans threatened to block legislation important to their party unless something were done to increase silver coinage. In response, Congress passed the SHERMAN SILVER PURCHASE ACT OF 1890, a compromise measure that increased the number of silver dollars but maintained limits.

Western Republicans had hoped that the Sherman Act might short-circuit the developing third-party movement in the West, but it did not. Throughout the West, state-level Populist parties appeared in 1890 and 1891; like the Farmers' Alliances from which they sprang, they supported greenbacks and "free silver" (the free and unlimited coinage of both silver and gold) among many other reforms. The national Populist party gave high priority to inflation and free silver, and its 1892 presidential candidate was Weaver, the former Greenbacker. In 1893, as the nation plunged into a major depression, President Grover Cleveland blamed the Sherman Act for the crisis and persuaded Congress to repeal it.

The 1896 presidential election has been called "the battle of the standards" because both the Democrats and the Republicans focused so much of their campaign on currency issues. When the Republican convention adopted a platform endorsing the gold standard, several prominent Western Republicans bolted. Led by Senator HENRY M. TELLER of Colorado, these Silver Republicans formed their own party and endorsed WILLIAM JENNINGS BRYAN, the Democrats' candidate for president, who centered his campaign on free silver and a bimetallic standard. The Populists, too, supported Bryan. With Bryan's defeat, Republicans passed the Gold Standard Act in 1900; then, during the late 1890s and early 1900s, several factors caused prices to stabilize and even to creep up, thereby removing much of the economic impetus for either greenbacks or silver.

A recurrence of deflation in the 1920s, which accelerated after the stock-market crash of 1929, combined with other factors to produce both acute economic distress in agriculture and renewed calls for inflation. Beginning in the early 1920s, a bloc of Western senators, mostly from silver-mining states, led a revival of the silver movement. Under strong pressure from congressional inflationists, President Franklin D. Roosevelt took the nation off the gold standard in 1933 and reluctantly agreed to the Silver Purchase Act of 1934, which was intended both to bring inflation and to subsidize the silver-mining industry.

—*Robert W. Cherny*

SEE ALSO: Agrarianism; Banking; Populism

SUGGESTED READING:
Brennan, John A. *Silver and the First New Deal*. Reno, Nev., 1969.
Friedman, Milton, and Anna Jacobson Schwartz. *A Monetary History of the United States, 1867–1960*. Princeton, N.J., 1963.
Nugent, Walter. *Money and American Society, 1865–1880*. New York, 1968.
Unger, Irwin. *The Greenback Era: A Social and Political History of American Finance, 1865–1879*. Princeton, N.J., 1964.
Weinstein, Allen. *Prelude to Populism: Origins of the Silver Issue, 1867–1878*. New Haven, Conn., 1970.

CURTIS, EDWARD SHERIFF

A photographer of Western American Indians, Edward Sheriff Curtis (1868–1952) was born near Whitewater, Wisconsin. He grew up in Minnesota and was fascinated by PHOTOGRAPHY at an early age. The family moved to Seattle, Washington, in 1888, and there he became a full-time photographer in 1891. By 1897, he was recognized as the premier portrait and landscape photographer in the Puget Sound area. During one of his frequent ascents of Mount Rainier, he came upon a lost climbing party that included C. Hart Merriam, GEORGE BIRD GRINNELL, and GIFFORD PINCHOT. The friendships he subsequently made with these men led to his appointment as photographer for the 1899 HARRIMAN EXPEDITION to Alaska. Funded by railroad tycoon EDWARD HENRY HARRIMAN, the 126-member research party studied the natural history of the southern Alaskan coast. Many of Curtis's photographs appeared in the resulting fourteen-volume report, edited by Merriam.

Curtis began taking photographs of Native Americans around Seattle in the 1890s. Contacts with Merriam and Grinnell, both acknowledged "Indian experts," quickened his interest. He formulated a long-range plan to make a unique photographic record of "all" North American Indian tribes before they "vanished," as he and many others thought they would. Beginning in 1903, he spent most of each year on various reservations in the West. Encouraged by President THEODORE ROOSEVELT and wealthy East Coast patrons, Curtis approached financier J. Pierpont Morgan in 1906 with a grandiose plan: the publication of twenty lavishly illustrated volumes and accompanying photogravure folios of ethnological materials on American Indians, printed in five hundred sets. Morgan agreed to provide seventy-five thousand dollars. Curtis raised additional monies through subscriptions and other sources. He and his assistants labored on *The North American Indian* project for twenty-three years. The coverage was a sampling of tribes in the Plains, the Southwest, California and the Great Basin, the Northwest, and Alaska. The ethnographic data are scattered and uneven, as Curtis later admitted, and the texts and photographs, while magnificent, present a highly romanticized view of the "vanishing" Indians. Except for horses, any hint of intrusive white culture was carefully removed from the photographs. The Native Americans are presented as primordial, noble savages fated to disappear before the onslaught of white civilization.

The final volumes of *The North American Indian* appeared in 1930. By then Curtis was ill, despondent, and broke. The Morgan family had spent about four hundred thousand dollars on the project; the total cost was estimated at two or three times that amount. Deposited in rare book rooms of libraries across the country, the twenty volumes and twenty folios, containing more than twenty-two hundred photographs and five thousand pages of text, were generally ignored by anthropologists and historians. In the 1960s, public interest in the photographs as artworks was heightened, and several studies appeared. By the 1990s, "original" Curtis Indian prints commanded thousands of dollars. His ethnographic data continue to be disregarded by anthropologists, however.

Curtis began making motion pictures of Indians as early as 1904. In 1914, he produced a full-length docudrama, *In the Land of the Headhunters,* an idealized portrayal of the Kwakiutl people of Vancouver Island. During the 1930s and 1940s, he was involved in mining and worked as a still photographer for various Hollywood studios. He died in Whittier, California.

—*Don D. Fowler*

SUGGESTED READING:
Curtis, Edward S. *The North American Indian*. 20 vols. Cambridge, Mass., and Norwood, Conn., 1907–1930.
Davis, Barbara A. *Edward S. Curtis: The Life and Times of a Shadow Catcher*. San Francisco, 1985.
Fowler, Don D., and Rachel J. Homer. *In a Sacred Manner We Live: Photographs of the North American Indian by Edward S. Curtis*. Barre, Mass., 1972.

CURTIS, SAMUEL RYAN

Samuel Ryan Curtis (1817–1866) was one of the most effective Union officers in the trans-Mississippi West; he turned back Confederate drives into Missouri including Price's Raid of 1864.

Curtis graduated from West Point in 1833. After service on the frontier, he resigned to become a civil engineer and, eventually, colonel of the Ohio militia. He served with Zachary Taylor in the UNITED STATES-MEXICAN WAR. In 1855, he left Ohio to settle in Iowa and practice law. He was elected to Congress as a Republican for three terms but resigned in 1861 to become colonel of the Second Iowa regiment. In May, he became brigadier general of volunteers.

In the spring of 1862, Curtis was given command of the Army of the Southwest and led a series of successful operations against the Confederates in the Missouri-Arkansas area—operations that culminated in victory at the Battle of Pea Ridge from March 6 to 8. That summer, he was sent to the West, and he occupied Helena and took control of the Western Indian tribes. That fall, he took a leave of absence to preside over the Pacific Railroad Convention in Chicago.

On his return to action, he commanded the Department of the Missouri until May 1863, then moved to the Department of Kansas until February 1865, and finally the Department of the Northwest until July 1865 when he left the service. After the CIVIL WAR, he was an Indian commissioner and examiner of the UNION PACIFIC RAILROAD.

—*Patrick H. Butler, III*

SUGGESTED READING:
Boatner, Mark D., III. *Civil War Dictionary*. New York, 1959.
Josephy, Alvin M. *The Civil War in the American West*. New York, 1991.

CUSHING, FRANK HAMILTON

An important early ethnographer of the Zuni Indians, Frank Hamilton Cushing (1857–1900) was born in North East, Pennsylvania. He received his training in natural science at Cornell University. A brilliant student, he was given an appointment at the age of eighteen to the Smithsonian Institution's Bureau of Ethnography, where he served until his death. His most important contribution to American ethnography was his study of the culture of the American Southwest. The anthropologist lived with the Zuni Indians for five years beginning in 1879. After a period of some distrust and even hostility, the Zunis warmly embraced him, and he was initiated into the Bow Priest Society.

Cushing mastered Zuni technology and crafts; he did not merely study them, but learned them by practicing the creation of everyday artifacts of Zuni culture until he himself had become an accomplished craftsman. He wrote voluminously on the Zuni. His findings are summarized in three seminal books: *Zuni Creation Myths* (1896), *Zuni Folk Tales* (1901), and *My Adventures in Zuni* (1941). His writings had a profound influence on the American artists who came to the Southwest on the eve of the artistic renaissance in Taos and Santa Fe.

—Alan Axelrod

CUSTER, ELIZABETH

Army wife, writer, and memorialist of George Armstrong Custer, Elizabeth ("Libbie") Custer (1842–1933) was the daughter of Judge Daniel Bacon and Eleanor Sophia (Page) Bacon. Born in Monroe, Michigan, she graduated as valedictorian from the Presbyterian Young Ladies' Seminary and Collegiate Institute. She married George Armstrong Custer on February 9, 1864, soon after his rise to brigadier general made him acceptable to the Bacon family.

Elizabeth Custer's charm and attractiveness proved assets to her husband's military career. She cemented ties with powerful Republicans during the Civil War, thereby helping Custer overcome suspicions regarding his strong attachment to his former commander—and Democratic presidential candidate—George B. McClellan.

In 1866, when Custer became lieutenant colonel of the Seventh Cavalry, Elizabeth Custer learned firsthand the privations and anxieties dependents of the Indian fighters endured at posts such as Forts Riley, Leavenworth, and Hays. In 1873, the Custers and the Seventh Cavalry moved to Fort Abraham Lincoln in the Dakota Territory. There in 1876, her husband and his battalion of 221 men suffered their famous defeat at the hands of the Sioux at the Battle of Little Bighorn.

After her husband's death, Elizabeth Custer learned that President Ulysses S. Grant had charged her spouse with disobedience and held him responsible for the loss. Throughout her fifty-seven years of widowhood, Elizabeth Custer worked untiringly to defend her husband's reputation and transform him into a hero. In her three books, *Boots and Saddles* (1885), *Tenting on the Plains*

(1887), and *Following the Guidon* (1890), she described her husband as the epitome of the chivalrous and Christian military hero, a loving spouse, a devoted family man, and a conscientious commanding officer.

Elizabeth Custer's tenacity influenced the writings of other Custer observers, such as Frederick Whittaker, E. S. Godfrey, NELSON APPLETON MILES, and Frederick Dellan-baugh. Army men and the public alike viewed her as a model wife and widow, and many Custer critics withheld public criticism of her husband during her lifetime. Since she survived until April 4, 1933, she outlasted most of her husband's detractors. It was not until 1934 that Frederic Van de Water's *Glory-Hunter*, the first critical biography of Custer, was published. The boy-general's reappraisal had begun, but Elizabeth Custer's steadfast loyalty and persuasive writings helped guarantee her husband a number of admirers to the present day.

—Shirley A. Leckie

SEE ALSO: Little Bighorn, Battle of

SUGGESTED READING:
Custer, Elizabeth B. *"Boots and Saddles"; or, Life in Dakota with General Custer.* New York, 1885. Reprint. Norman, Okla., 1961.
Leckie, Shirley. *Elizabeth Bacon Custer and the Making of a Myth.* Norman, Okla., 1993.
Merington, Marguerite, ed. *The Custer Story: The Life and Intimate Letters of General George A. Custer and His Wife Elizabeth.* New York, 1950. Reprint. Lincoln, Nebr., 1987.

CUSTER, GEORGE ARMSTRONG

Soldier, frontiersman, and Indian fighter who led the Seventh Cavalry at the Battle of Little Bighorn during the SIOUX WARS, George Armstrong Custer (1839–1876) was born in New Rumley, Ohio, but spent part of his childhood with a half-sister in Monroe, Michigan. He attended West Point Military Academy and graduated at the bottom of his class on the eve of the CIVIL WAR. Although a poor student, he excelled in the combat arts, and during the war, he proved himself a superb field soldier. As a staff officer for General George B. McClellan and later General Alfred Pleasonton, Captain Custer demonstrated such potential that he was promoted to brigadier general and was given command of the Michigan cavalry brigade. Twenty-three years old, with long yellow hair and a gaudy uniform, he won instant fame. From Gettysburg to Appomattox,

George Armstrong Custer. *Courtesy National Cowboy Hall of Fame and Western Heritage Center.*

he was known for slashing cavalry charges that often proved decisive and for a personal fearlessness that earned the devotion of his men. By the end of the war, he was a major general commanding a full division.

Custer returned to the postwar regular army as lieutenant colonel of the newly authorized Seventh Cavalry Regiment and made a new name for himself in the West. Garbed in fringed buckskin instead of black velvet and gold lace, he was the embodiment of the dashing Indian fighter, skilled plainsman, and hunter. In the frequent absence of the colonel, Custer usually commanded the Seventh, and in the popular perception, it was his regiment.

Custer's first experience with Indians, in Kansas in 1867, ended in embarrassing failure. Not only did he fail to defeat any Indians, but he was court-martialed and sentenced to a year's suspension of rank and pay.

In 1868, however, he surprised and attacked Chief BLACK KETTLE's Cheyenne village on the Washita River in present-day Oklahoma and laid the groundwork for his reputation as an Indian fighter. Guarding railroad surveyors on the Yellowstone River in 1873, he fought the Sioux in two battles that reinforced his Indian-fighting record.

Easterners viewed Custer as the army's foremost Indian fighter. In fact, he was no more successful than some of his peers. His regiment, moreover, was badly factionalized. Some of his troops worshiped him; others loathed him. But he wrote popular magazine articles and a book, *My Life on the Plains,* and always, he made good newspaper copy.

In 1874, Custer led the Seventh Cavalry out of his base at Fort Abraham Lincoln to explore the Black Hills of the Dakota Territory. Part of the Great Sioux Reservation, guaranteed to the Sioux by the Treaty of 1868, the Black Hills region had long been coveted by whites who thought its dark recesses held gold. Miners with the expedition found gold, and the news set off a gold rush.

Government attempts to buy the Black Hills and legalize the mining settlements failed. The aggression of the Sioux bands led by SITTING BULL and CRAZY HORSE against friendly Indians gave officials a pretext to wage a war that would solve the Black Hills problem by depriving the Sioux of their independence and their power to obstruct the sale.

The Great Sioux War of 1876 resulted. Custer and the Seventh rode with one of the armies that converged on the Indian country. On June 25, he attacked the village of Sitting Bull and Crazy Horse on Montana's Little Bighorn River. In a sequence of moves that will forever remain controversial, he and five companies were wiped out.

"Custer's Last Stand" stunned and angered white Americans and led to the conquest of the Sioux and the acquisition of the Black Hills. But it also awarded its namesake an immortality that fit his dashing persona. His adoring wife Elizabeth, or Libbie, devoted the rest of her long life to defending and glorifying his name. She wrote three books that stirred her contemporaries and are still minor classics today. The controversy over Custer's military moves keeps the battle alive in American consciousness, and the image of "Long Hair," erect on his hilltop with troopers falling around him and shouting Sioux closing in for the kill, remains a shining icon in American folklore.

In recent years, American Indians have made Custer the scapegoat for the ill treatment and injustice inflicted by white Americans and their government on the native population. "Custer died for your sins" was the slogan in the 1970s. Historically, Custer hardly mer-

"Scene of Gen. Custer's last stand, looking in the direction of the ford and the Indian village." Bones still litter the battlefield in this image taken in about 1877. *Courtesy National Archives.*

ited the distinction, but the legend was not difficult to bend to that purpose. Custer the villain, however, joins with Custer the hero to give George Armstrong Custer an even firmer grasp on the immortality he sought.

—*Robert M. Utley*

SEE ALSO: Black Hills Gold Rush; Custer, Elizabeth; Little Bighorn, Battle of; Sioux Wars

SUGGESTED READING:
Dippie, Brian W. *Custer's Last Stand: The Anatomy of an American Myth.* Missoula, Mont., 1976.
Hutton, Paul A., ed. *The Custer Reader.* Lincoln, Nebr., 1992.
Merington, Marguerite, ed. *The Custer Story: The Life and Intimate Letters of General Custer and His Wife Elizabeth.* New York, 1950. Reprint. Lincoln, Nebr., 1987.
Monaghan, Jay. *Custer: The Life of General George Armstrong Custer.* Boston and Toronto, 1959.
Utley, Robert M. *Cavalier in Buckskin: George Armstrong Custer and the Western Military Frontier.* Norman, Okla., 1988.

CUTTING, BRONSON

Born in Oakdale, New York, Bronson Cutting (1888–1935) moved to New Mexico in 1910 for health reasons. Settling in Santa Fe, he purchased both an English and a Spanish newspaper. In the newspapers he published and in his aspiring political career, Cutting championed Hispanics in New Mexico. He supported THEODORE ROOSEVELT's progressive Bull Moose party. In 1927, Cutting was appointed to fill the U.S. Senate vacancy for New Mexico. Although a Republican, Cutting frequently crossed the aisle on certain issues, opposed Herbert Hoover, and eventually campaigned for Franklin Roosevelt. He died in a plane crash on May 6, 1935.

—*Kurt Edward Kemper*

SUGGESTED READING:
Beck, Warren. *New Mexico: A History of Four Centuries.* Norman, Okla., 1962.